For my mother and daughter, who believe the world is wonderful and mysterious and share great hope for humankind. Like bookends, their optimism frames the content of this book.

Linda L. Price

Written in hopes of living up to the spirit of two great educators, my late uncle Robert S. Brumbaugh, professor of philosophy (and so much more) at Yale University, and the late Robert Netting of the University of Arizona, an inspiration to a generation of cultural anthropologists.

Eric J. Arnould

To my family and friends.

George M. Zinkhan

vi

Part Two

The Background of Consumption

Chapter Five
The Meaning and Nature of Culture

Chapter Six
Economic and Social Structures

Chapter Seven
The Self and Selves

Chapter Eight
Lifestyles: Consumption Subcultures

table of contents

Chapter Nineteen
Disposal, Recycling, and Reuse

674.

This book is an invitation to the diverse, intriguing, dynamic, global world of consumers. The world of consumers seems both smaller and larger than it did last year or even yesterday. Human societies have always mixed and changed, but people, ideas, and goods move farther and faster today than in previous decades. Cell phones, the Internet, mobile commerce, and global satellite communications bring us together quickly, frequently, and almost effortlessly. In the last decade, Internet communications have more than doubled every year. The global marketplace is a fact of life. The world seems smaller.

At the same time, the magnitude of our differences, our unique traditions, values, desires, and ways of living are salient and vibrant. Cultures are resourceful, resilient, and unpredictable. We meet Buddhist monks breakfasting at Denny's in L.A., order an orthodox Hindu menu at the McDonald's in Bombay, celebrate Chinese values and traditions with Sesame Street in Shanghai. In our own neighborhood, we find people, beliefs, and behaviors that seem strange, unfamiliar, and confusing. Rap music pervades the globe, but it sounds a lot different in Mongolia than it does in Canada, Turkey, or the United States. The world seems larger, more diverse. Local marketers can no longer assume that their local customers will share their particular views on the world.

Our intent with this book is to assist readers in making sense of consumers as cultures, social beings, families, and individuals. We are interested in behavior but also in what consumers think, feel, and say. We are interested in what consumers purchase but also in their consumption dreams and plans, their unfolding consumption experiences, and their consumption satisfaction and memories. We are interested in the meanings consumers attach to consumption and possessions. We are interested in how people dispose of things they no longer want and precious things they can no longer keep. We offer theories and tools borrowed from all the social sciences, including areas as diverse as neuroscience and evolutionary anthropology, to enable readers to thrive in a global marketplace.

Thriving in the global marketplace means looking closely at the cultures from which consumer desires emerge, the rituals and patterns associated with products, services, and experiences. Such an approach is especially important when cultures are in turmoil and technologies are disrupting established economic and social patterns of behavior. We believe that the best marketing courses teach students to be sensitive to cultural dynamics.

To research and write this book we brought together the multidisciplinary skills and viewpoints of three consumer researchers. All three of us have traveled extensively in recent years and been engaged in multicountry consumer research. We are committed deeply and resolutely to understanding and teaching consumer behavior. Each of us is blessed (or cursed) with an eclectic vision of consumers. However, we are grounded in different traditions. Eric Arnould brings to the project a cross-cultural approach to consumer behavior derived from anthropological training and many years of overseas work. Linda Price contributes perspectives from social psychology and more generally the intersections between cognition, society, and culture. George Zinkhan adds his many years of experience with issues in mediated communications, advertising, and marketing to his enduring interests in the literary arts. As authors, we are passionate and active teachers but also passionate and active researchers. The book offers a cutting-edge treatment of research and practice related to consumers with a wealth of contemporary, real-world examples and marketing applications.

Objectives

Consumers is intended to serve as a textbook for undergraduate and graduate courses in consumer behavior. The book could also be used as a supplementary text in courses desiring to offer a global perspective on marketing. The tone of the text is conversational, and we offer numerous examples and applications of consumer theory and research in various regions of the world.

The objectives of this book are:

- To highlight the importance and necessity of a global approach to understanding consumers. To offer a book that emphasizes and illustrates the relationships between individuals and the communities and cultures in which they live.
- To provide a comprehensive understanding of consumers adopting a culturally relative orientation. To illustrate how culture affects internal, individual variables such as perception, emotions, memory, and decision making as well as self-concept, lifestyle, values, and family structure.
- To illustrate the impact of the Internet and other technological advances on consumers' lives and actions. To illustrate the ways in which mediated communications such as television, the Internet, and e-mail influence consumers and consumer culture.
- To use simple language and examples to integrate complex contemporary discussions about consumers from a diverse number of disciplines.
- To provide a clear and wide-ranging treatment of the entire wheel of consumption from preconsumption thoughts, feelings, and actions, to consumption and postconsumption thoughts, feelings, and actions.
- To offer explicit treatment of topics often neglected or given cursory investigation in consumer behavior texts, including a chapter dedicated to consumer satisfaction and a chapter dedicated to consumer disposal behaviors.
- To highlight the connections between understanding consumers and good marketing practice.
- To create a book that conveys our own enthusiasm and wonderment about consumers and their cultures.

Supplements

We understand that new approaches can be foreboding; change is risky. So this package offers instructors comprehensive supplements and a full array of multimedia materials to use in the classroom. We blend the new and exciting features of global consumer behavior with the important features of other consumer behavior texts. Our approach incorporates the latest developments in instructional technology to facilitate efficient organization and delivery of concepts and information. We hope that the book will feel familiar but with a new and exciting flavor.

- An **Instructor's Manual,** written by Cathy Hartman of Utah State University and Pamela Kiecker of Virginia Commonwealth University in conjunction with the text's authors, goes beyond providing solutions to end-of-chapter questions and problems. It incorporates additional, new material and examples for professors to use with students. Sample course syllabi are also included.
- Our **PowerPoint Presentation,** also created by Pamela Kiecker in conjunction with the text's authors, is available on the book's website and on the Instructor's CD-ROM. It provides over 350 slides of text material and additional resources for use in class lectures and discussion.

- The **Test Bank,** written by Ronald Weir of East Tennessee State University, includes over 1,300 multiple choice, fill-in-the-blank, and essay questions. Many of the test questions have been class-tested by the text's authors over several semesters.

- The accompanying **Video Package** includes a collection of stories shared by consumer behavior teachers and researchers from around the world. These stories bring to life a variety of concepts from the textbook. Other video segments in the package emphasize the ritual aspects of consumption, illustrate consumption in different parts of the world, and provide examples of consumption within subcultures and communities.

- A set of **Four-Color Acetates** is available to adopters of this book. Seventy-five figures, examples, and advertisements from the text and other sources provide examples for class lectures.

- Our book-specific **website** at www.mhhe.com/Arnould offers complete classroom support for both students and professors. For students, the site provides student quizzing, an e-learning session, interactive activities, links to companies used as examples in the book, and Internet exercises. For professors, we provide downloadable supplements, a link to PageOut, and updated *Business Week* articles. Pamela Kiecker of Virginia Commonwealth University will provide updates to the website during the school semester.

- Our **Instructor's Presentation CD-ROM** provides professors with the Instructor's Manual, computerized test bank, images from the acetate package, video clips, links to company sites, and our PowerPoint slides.

Organization

The book is organized into four parts. The first part of the book is composed of four chapters. Chapter 1 introduces our perspective on the nature and scope of consumer behavior. We introduce the wheel of consumption that includes production, consumption, and disposal activities as a template that broadly structures the content of our book. Chapter 2 provides the crucial link between understanding consumer behavior and marketing strategy. Throughout the book we give additional examples and illustrations of the connection between understanding consumers and effective marketing strategy. Chapter 3 describes and illustrates a wide range of market research strategies and includes extensive discussion of the impact of new technologies (e.g., the Internet) and globalization on the effective and ethical conduct of market research. As compared to other textbooks, we provide more discussion of anthropological and sociological techniques and describe details on the Internet and multicountry market research. Chapter 4 overviews the changing world of consumption and illustrates consumption in different regions of the world with numerous examples. This chapter serves to contrast consumption patterns in less developed countries with those of the post-industrial world. In this chapter we also outline several important trends that shape global consumer behavior.

Part 2 provides a background to consumption. In Chapter 5, we outline the meaning and nature of culture and how it influences consumer behavior. This important chapter provides many basic ideas that are referred to throughout the text. Chapter 6 provides a thorough overview of how economic and social structures affect consumer behavior. This chapter is the longest chapter in the book, but other books frequently include multiple chapters on this topic. Rather than deal with these topics in a piecemeal fashion, we have integrated our discussion across the related topics of social class, ethnicity, gender, and age. Chapter 7 provides an overview of how consumers' self-concepts and personalities relate both to the environments in which they live and their consumption behavior. Chapter 8 follows up with a far-ranging discussion of consumer lifestyles that includes lifestyles in many parts of the world such as Japan and France; it discusses how consumer lifestyle is connected to cultural beliefs and values. Chapter 9 provides a basic and provocative overview of consumer perception. Again, our intent is to show how something as individual as perception is shaped by culture and environment. Appropriately, this chapter is rich with visual examples.

Part 3 focuses on consumer purchase and acquisition, the traditional heart of consumer research. In six action-packed chapters we cover traditional topics plus some new material. For example, Chapter 10 describes the many ways that consumers acquire products, services, and ideas. In contrast with conventional treatments, we emphasize gift giving and secondary markets (e.g., yard and boot sales) as important ways that consumers acquire things. In this chapter we also include many leading-edge ideas about how and why people shop and how we can understand and predict purchase behavior. Chapter 11 draws on our newest understandings of how humans develop in their cultural environments to cast in new light on the important topic of motivation. Although we cover the usual array of motivational techniques and research, we also emphasize cross-cultural differences. Chapter 12 follows on the heels of Chapter 11 by emphasizing how context and culture influence what consumers experience, learn, and remember. In contrast with other textbooks, we emphasize an understanding of consumer learning and how that relates to knowledge rather than focusing predominantly on consumer knowledge. We also consider how new technologies might affect what, when, and how consumers learn. Chapter 13 summarizes models, theories, and research about consumer decision making and attitude models. Again, we stress the power of situation and context for altering and framing how consumers decide what to believe, buy, or do. Although we cover conventional ideas about consumer decision making, we emphasize how consumers creatively construct choices to respond to a particular situation. In Chapter 14 we explore the role of households and formal buying groups in the acquisition and consumption process. We show how the structure of these groups affects acquisition. We summarize how internal resource pooling affects acquisition and consumption. Chapter 15 investigates the processes by which individuals and informal groups influence others' acquisition behaviors. We discuss the behavior of market mavens, celebrity endorsers, and reference groups, for example.

Part 4 provides an in-depth treatment of several of the most important topics in consumer theory and research. Some of these topics are given only cursory treatment, or no discussion, in other consumer behavior texts. This part is formulated around the consequences and outcomes of consumer acquisition. Chapter 16 provides a bridge between this and the previous part. It overviews how, why, and when consumers purchase new services and products and then discusses how and whether they integrate these innovations into their everyday lives. Chapter 17 describes what we know about consumer satisfaction. Although consumer satisfaction is considered a key to doing business, this is the first consumer behavior book with an entire chapter dedicated to examining the topic. In one chapter we compress the most recent research on how to deliver value and satisfaction to consumers. Chapter 18 focuses on what consumption means to consumers. We hope you find this chapter to be one of the richest in the book. Multinational firms are interested in predicting whether or not consumers will purchase, but they are also interested in what their products or services mean to consumers. We introduce many new ideas in this chapter and describe cutting-edge theories about consumer meaning. We employ numerous common-sense examples that help the reader understand the importance and nature of consumer meanings. The final chapter, 19, concludes with a discussion of consumer recycling, reuse, and disposal behaviors. In Chapter 4, we identify ecological concerns as a global trend; the final chapter addresses how consumers recycle, reuse, and dispose of things and discusses the micro and macro consequences of consumption. We argue that both marketers and consumers need to pay more attention to what happens after purchase and consumption, and we provide examples of how marketers can profit from understanding postacquisition attitudes and behaviors.

Chapter Structure

On the basis of extensive teaching and writing experience, we have included a number of features in each chapter that should help students learn about consumers. First and foremost, each chapter is global in theory and scope and up to date with reference to both contextual factors such as new technologies and topical theory and research. In addition, we offer a unique blend of old and new.

- **Introductory Vignette.** Each chapter opens with a consumer story that overviews many essential aspects of the chapter. The vignettes often draw from the authors' own experiences and are typically global in character. We refer back to these vignettes throughout the chapter to make subsequent theories more tangible for the reader.

- **Learning Objectives.** Each chapter begins by outlining a few essential learning objectives that readers can use to gauge their comprehension of the text.

- **Consumer Chronicles.** Each chapter includes several boxed and detailed consumer examples that help to illustrate a particular theory or idea with the real thoughts, feelings, and experiences of consumers around the world.

- **Good Practice.** Each chapter uses set-aside examples of marketing/management good practice related to consumers. Sometimes the Good Practice refers to what companies can, should, and are doing. Sometimes it provides a hands-on opportunity for readers to apply a good practice of their own. These sections are target opportunities for in-class discussion and exercises.

- **Industry Insights.** Each chapter includes examples from industry that help to highlight the application of consumer theory and research to the practice of marketing and management. As in the case of Consumer Chronicles, these set-aside illustrations help to texture readers' understandings.

- **You Make the Call.** In addition to a set of end-of-chapter questions and exercises, each chapter concludes with a short case that can help students grasp the big picture and elaborate on their own understandings of the chapter material. The cases are fun vehicles for class discussion, chapter review, and miniprojects. They may even generate some future research.

- **Abundant Use of Full-Color Material.** This book draws on a wide array of visual materials. We include author-developed charts, graphs, and exhibits but also cartoons, photos of billboards, packaging, advertisements, and consumers. More than simply eye-catching and aesthetic, this material is intended to convey the richness and complexity of global consumer behaviors. Numerous examples illustrate the Internet and emerging technologies, but other examples illustrate the many places that high technology has not yet penetrated.

Acknowledgments

Since this project has taken 10 years to bear fruit, a lot of people share the credit for coaxing us along. Mary Fisher and Bill Schopf of Austen Press, a short-lived experimental arm of Irwin Press, initially talked Linda and Eric into doing the book as part of a close-working team. Both have since gone on to pursue other dreams. Various editors at Irwin and later Irwin/McGraw-Hill have patiently nudged us forward, including Nina McGuffin and Barrett Koger. In fact, the whole team of people associated with McGraw-Hill/Irwin worked very patiently with us to bring the book and pedagogical package to fruition. We've had quite a bit of help from graduate students who collected materials and reviewed and edited drafts of this book. They include Stephanie Nelson (University of Nebraska–Lincoln) and Rich Gonzalez (University of South Florida). Austen Arnould provided excellent critical guidance from the perspective of a prospective undergraduate reader. Linda and Eric put up with and encouraged each other as part of their ongoing personal/professional experiment. Both want to thank co-author George Zinkhan, who was brought into the project when it already resembled a lumbering runaway train and has patiently helped guide it into the station by providing additional energy and insight. Michelle Morrison (University of Georgia) and George Zinkhan IV (Rice University) provided useful insights on later drafts of the manuscript.

    A number of reviewers, some of who appropriately read us the riot act at earlier stages of manuscript preparation, and others who gracefully offered constructive comments, all played a role in the development of the final product. In particular, we wish to thank:

Ellen Day, *University of Georgia*

Lon Camomile, *Colorado State University*

Paul Chao, *University of Northern Iowa*

Sylvia Clark, *CUNY, Queensborough*

Joel Cohen, *University of Florida*

Darren Dahl, *University of Manitoba*

Cathy Hartman, *Utah State University*

Jo Anne Hopper, *Western Carolina University*

Vaughan C. Judd, *Auburn University*

Dimitri Kapelianis, *University of Arizona*

Steven Kates, *Monash University, Australia*

Thomas I. Kindel, *The Citadel*

Jim Munch, *University of Texas*

Carmen Powers, *Monroe Community College*

Shelley M. Rinehart, *University of New Brunswick in Saint John*

Greg Rose, *University of Mississippi*

Amy Rummel, *Alfred University*

Jackie Snell, *San Jose State University*

T.N. Somasundaram, *University of San Diego*

Ajay Sukhdial, *Oklahoma State University*

Ottilia Voegtli, *University of Missouri–Saint Louis*

Terry Witkowski, *California State University*

Dr. Eric Arnould is Professor of Marketing at the University of Nebraska–Lincoln despite the fact that he holds a PhD degree in cultural anthropology from the University of Arizona (1982). He has also taught at Odense University, Denmark; the University of South Florida; California State University, Long Beach; and the University of Colorado at Denver. From 1975 to 1990, he worked on economic development in more than a dozen West African nations. Since 1990, he has been a full-time academic. Occasionally, he undertakes a consulting assignment. His research investigates consumer ritual (Thanksgiving, New Year's, football bowl games, Halloween, inheritance), service relationships, West African marketing channels, and the uses of qualitative data. His work has appeared in the three major U.S. marketing journals (*Journal of Consumer Research, Journal of Marketing,* and *Journal of Marketing Research*) as well as many other social science periodicals and books. Dr. Arnould is a frequent presenter at national and international conferences. He speaks French and Hausa and enjoys running, do-it-yourself work on his old house, and being a parent.

Eric Arnould
University of Nebraska, Lincoln

Dr. Linda L. Price is E.J. Faulkner Professor of Agribusiness and Marketing at the University of Nebraska–Lincoln. She received her PhD degree in marketing from the University of Texas–Austin in 1983. She has also been on the faculty at the University of South Florida; the University of Colorado, Boulder; the University of California, Irvine; Odense University, Denmark; and the University of Pittsburgh. Dr. Price has published over 50 research papers in areas of marketing and consumer behavior. Many of these papers appear in leading journals such as *Journal of Consumer Research, Journal of Marketing, Journal of Public Policy and Marketing,* and *Organization Science.* Linda is a frequent speaker at national and international conferences, universities, and community forums. She has consulted for several large multinationals but also for small enterprises, national and regional agencies, and not-for-profit organizations. Dr. Price's research focuses on consumers as emotional, imaginative, and creative agents and on the relational dimensions of consumers' behaviors. Her major areas of teaching include consumer behavior, market research, and marketing theory.

Linda Price
University of Nebraska, Lincoln

Dr. George Zinkhan is the Coca-Cola Company Chair of Marketing at the University of Georgia, Terry College of Business. He received his PhD degree in marketing from the University of Michigan in 1981. Besides the University of Michigan, he has also taught at the University of Houston, University of Pittsburgh, and the Madrid School of Business. Dr. Zinkhan has published more than 100 research papers in the areas of marketing, advertising, and electronic commerce. These papers appear in leading journals such as *Journal of Marketing, Journal of Marketing Research, Journal of Consumer Research, Strategic Management Journal, Journal of Applied Psychology, Decision Sciences,* and the *Journal of Advertising.* Among his recent co-authored books are *Electronic Commerce: The Strategic Perspective* (Harcourt, Inc., 2000) and *Advertising Research: The Internet, Consumer Behavior, and Strategy* (American Marketing Association, 2000). As indicated by the themes of these books, Dr. Zinkhan's research interests focus on consumer behavior, communication, electronic commerce, and knowledge development.

George Zinkhan
University of Georgia

Learning Objectives

Chapter 1

After completing this chapter, you should be able to:

- Define the domain of consumer behavior, including some areas of interest to consumer behavior researchers, policymakers, and marketers.

- Describe many examples of consumer behavior in people's daily lives.

- Explain why knowledge of consumer behavior is of value to you.

- Discuss the circle of consumption and how consumption relates to other technological and economic processes.

- Understand that consumer behavior is driven by general human motivations.

- Know the plan of the book.

Introduction
Production, Acquisition, Consumption, and Disposal

A Morning Ritual for Two Consumers

Denver, Colorado At 6:00 A.M. Monica's Timex Triathlon watch alarm buzzes, and she stumbles out of bed to make coffee and pour orange juice. She grinds her own coffee with a little Krups coffee grinder that was cheap and has lasted many years. She views it as one of her best buys. Monica notes that she's almost out of coffee filters. Sometimes she forgets to buy them and ends up using paper towels instead—luckily not this morning. After preparing the coffee, she heads for the orange juice carton in the refrigerator. Monica buys one of the several brands of "not from concentrate" orange juice available at the local grocery store. She buys the cheapest one, although the range in prices is never more than about 60 cents. Monica loves the smell of coffee brewing, but in the interest of efficiency she rushes to grab a shower, groom, and get dressed.

As background noise, she flips on a morning news show on the bedroom television on her way to the shower. Why does it always seem like one commercial after another? The shower feels great. She always enjoys the herbal smell of her shampoo and conditioner. Although it's a little pricey, it seems like it must be healthier and more natural, so she always buys it. Her after-shower grooming includes quite a few products (toothpaste, mouthwash, astringent, face cream, deodorant, hair gel, and a hair dryer). Then, it's that same old problem.

What to wear? Some mornings Monica feels like she's tired of everything in her closet. This is one of those mornings. Her work clothes are just no fun, and she doesn't feel quite like herself when she's in them. Monica settles on something easy

and conservative. She waxes a bit nostalgic as she slips into her cashmere sweater (a gift from a previous boyfriend).

After dressing, she heads for that long-awaited first cup of morning coffee. Finally, she's ready to put on makeup and head out the door. Monica doesn't ever spend more than 10 minutes putting on makeup. She puts it on the way the woman at the Clinique counter showed her two years ago. Occasionally, she tries a new brand of cosmetics or a new shade of something, but mostly she doesn't bother. As she heads out the door at 6:45 A.M., she pauses to dread the 45-minute commute through heavy traffic that has become a necessary evil in her current life.

Zinder, Niger In the dark at 5:00 A.M., Balla rises from the metal four-poster bed he shares with his wife, Aishatou. The bed was part of Aishatou's trousseau, provided by her family. Checked Chinese sheets, resembling an American country tablecloth, and a locally woven tapestry, also wedding gifts, serve as covers. He lights a small Chinese-made kerosene lantern with Boxer wooden matches and goes out of the sleeping alcove, through the front storeroom of the two-room adobe house into the courtyard. Balla retrieves a small plastic teapot with water remaining in it and goes to the entry of his compound.

Seated on a wooden seat locally made from cast-off packing crates, he carefully washes his hands, feet, head, and neck and rinses his mouth with water poured from the spout of the teapot. Then, as the muezzin at the nearby mosque begins to call for the first prayer at 5:30 A.M., Balla tosses his fluffy ram-skin prayer mat onto the ground and, facing to the east (toward the Khabah in Mecca), says his prayers. After prayer, he goes back into his house and slips into a pair of locally tailored, baggy drawstring cotton trousers, a long, faded blue, cotton gown, and a pair of plastic shower shoes, imported from neighboring Nigeria, and goes out through the entry way.

Pulling a short wooden stick from a pocket of his gown, Balla begins cleaning his teeth by chewing on one flayed end as he heads down the street. His first stop is the open-air meat market. Although the butchers aren't active at this hour, the place is bustling with men buying their breakfasts from a group of vendors. Balla finds a seat on a wooden bench with a group of fellow tanners, butchers, and other craftsmen preparing for the day's work. He goes to his regular vendor, Haro.

Without a word, Haro prepares Balla's preferred morning breakfast, having done so on many previous occasions. He dips a plastic mug into an old, steaming kerosene tin that now serves as a kettle and draws a mug full of *shai'i* (water in which herbs and spices have been steeped) from it. He pours the mug through a sieve into a Ducros glass imported from France. Then he takes a tiny spoon, pops the lid off a tin of Nescafé, and spoons in a half teaspoon of instant coffee. He stirs this vigorously. Next he takes a fat nail and, with the heel of his hand, jams it through the top of a tin of Bebe Hollandaise sweetened condensed milk. Then Haro overturns the tin on top of the glass and allows an inch of thick, creamy milk to flow to the bottom of the glass. Meanwhile he takes a knife, slices a French baguette in two, slits it down the edge, and slathers it with Bluebird margarine. Then Haro removes the condensed milk tin from the glass, stirs the mixture with a flourish, and hands it and the baguette to Balla.

When Balla is finished eating, he flips Haro a 100 CFA franc coin (US$0.50) and heads around the corner to the tannery to begin his day's work. En route, a boy pushing a handcart with two jute bags full of seedpods from the *bagaruwa* *(Acacia scorpiodes)* tree that the boy has gathered in the bush accosts him. Liking the price, Balla buys the pods that he will use in tanning and sends the boy on ahead into the tannery.

Overview

This book provides an introduction to the art and science of consumer behavior. We define **consumer behavior** as *individuals or groups acquiring, using, and disposing of products, services, ideas, or experiences.* Consumer behavior also includes the acquisition and use of information. Thus, communication with consumers and receiving feedback from them is a crucial part of consumer behavior of interest to marketers.

What Is Consumer Behavior?

Understanding and managing the production, acquisition, consumption, and disposal of products, services, ideas, and experiences is the focus of businesses, governments, and consumer organizations. Exhibit 1.1 provides a graphic illustration of the **domain of consumer behavior.** Consumers may consist of individuals or groups. Consuming groups include families, clubs and organizations, purchasing units within corporations, and governments, the latter varying from small rural communities to nation-states.

Acquiring includes a range of activities such as receiving, finding, inheriting, producing, and, of course, purchasing. Consuming also encompasses many different behaviors such as collecting, nurturing, cleaning, preparing, displaying, storing, wearing, sharing, evaluating, devouring, and serving. Finally, disposing spans a range of behaviors that includes giving, throwing away, recycling, and depleting.

As shown in Exhibit 1.1, each of these behaviors can involve products, services, ideas, and experiences. For example, many private homes include *products* such as furnishings and appliances that have been received as gifts, recycled, purchased, and inherited. Some travelers, scuba divers, and mountain climbers collect *experiences,* talking about places they have dived and mountains they have climbed. For instance, a recent ad for Yukon

Exhibit 1.1 The Domain of Consumer Behavior

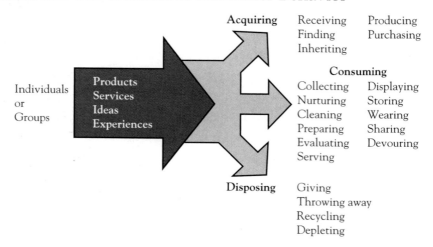

Acquiring
Receiving Producing
Finding   Purchasing
Inheriting

Individuals
or
Groups

Products
Services
Ideas
Experiences

Consuming
Collecting Displaying
Nurturing   Storing
Cleaning   Wearing
Preparing   Sharing
Evaluating Devouring
Serving

Disposing
Giving
Throwing away
Recycling
Depleting

Tourism tries to promote the magic and mystery of experiencing the Yukon. Prior to moving, many consumers visit their doctors, dentists, hairdressers, and restaurants to say good-bye and to acquire services that will tide them over until they establish new service relationships in a new community. We might say these consumers are trying to store *services.* Some corporations have disposed of the old functional specializations (e.g., research and development, engineering, marketing, customer service, materials handling) and have adopted new organizational forms such as parallel engineering and quality circles. These corporations are disposing of and acquiring *ideas.*[1]

Because the subject is so far ranging, topics that consumer behavior researchers study are limited only by their imaginations. For example, a consumer behavior researcher employed by a commercial firm may study how individuals differentiate among and choose brands of shampoo. Consumer behavior researchers may study how individuals and families acquire a pet or a preference for particular species of pet; plan, take, and remember a family vacation; celebrate the Chinese midsummer festival; prepare their morning coffee; or dispose of old telephone books. Consumer behavior researchers are also likely to study how firms choose and evaluate suppliers or even how a city chooses a landfill engineering company. Further, they are likely to study how these decisions are related to other psychological, demographic, sociological, cultural, and economic factors. For example, researchers have sought to relate changes in households' acquisition of consumer durables like microwave ovens or microcomputers to changes in gender and work roles.[2] Thus, many academic disciplines provide insights for understanding consumer behavior. Think about the principles you learned in course work in anthropology, sociology, economics, history, psychology, or political science. Principles from all of these fields can be useful in explaining consumer behavior.[3]

Why Study Consumer Behavior?

Studying consumer behavior is exciting and fun, but it is also important to you for a number of reasons. First, if you plan to go into business, understanding consumer behavior is critical. In market economies, businesses stay in business not by producing products, building accounting systems, generating dividends for their owners, or managing employees. Businesses stay in business by *attracting and retaining customers.* They do this by engaging in exchanges of resources—including information, money, goods, services, status,

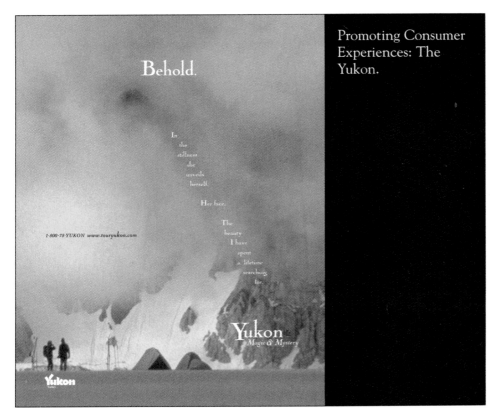

Promoting Consumer Experiences: The Yukon.

Source: Outside (magazine)

and emotions—with consumers, exchanges that both businesses and customers perceive to be beneficial.[4] When companies ask, Who are our customers? How do we reach them? What should we sell them? What will motivate them to buy? What makes them satisfied? they are asking questions that require a sophisticated understanding of consumer behavior. Let's take an everyday example. A knowledge of the principles of perception (Chapter 9) can help you design a restaurant menu to encourage people to notice and choose some items more than others. The placement on a page, vividness of presentation, and use of various kinds of perceptual surprises, as shown in the Ruby Tuesday menu below, can influence diners' choices. For example, items featured in the photos may be highly profitable for the restaurant, and merely by seeing them pictured on the menu, customers may be more likely to purchase them.

Marketers can benefit from both understanding what problems consumers have and understanding how consumers' themselves solve these problems. For example, about 15 years ago Rubbermaid introduced a product called Rough Totes that was intended for everyday storage. In fact, consumers are quite inventive in adapting this product for many kinds of uses. Rough Totes have been hugely successful because consumers have too much stuff; in the words of the CEO, "It's a classic example of how consumers' creativity drives solutions that you never even dream of and you just keep feeding the animal." In this same spirit, Microsoft uses the slogan "Where do you want to go today?" claiming, "We do a lot of our best work trying to keep up with your imagination." Many companies have learned that successful marketing often means keeping up with their customers' imaginations.

As the world grows smaller and the global reach of businesses expands, the job of at-

Practical Consumer Research: Ruby Tuesday menu design.

tracting and retaining customers grows ever more challenging. As in many other aspects of human behavior there are important universal elements but equally important local particularities governing consumer behaviors. For example, companies may have a hint that their customers are dissatisfied (e.g., sales may be declining), but they may not know the exact nature or content of this dissatisfaction. For instance, if managers at Ford Motor Company notice that sales of Ford Fiestas in the most recent quarter in Thailand are much lower than expected, they know that there is a problem in the marketplace. However, they may not know the specific cause of the problem. Do changing consumer tastes, preferences for new competitive products, changing economic conditions, inappropriate engineering, or something else cause it? (See Chapter 3 to find out.) Consumer behavior research is dedicated to deciphering, explaining, and predicting human needs and wants and measuring and understanding people's satisfaction (see Chapter 17) with various consumption activities—everything from buying a car, donating to a local charity, visiting church, or selecting a university to attend. By studying and understanding consumers, organizations can establish and maintain a competitive advantage in the marketplace.

An understanding of customer behavior can also be useful in business-to-business (B2B) marketing. In the B2B case, it is a business that is the customer. As customers, these businesses have experiences, perceptions, and preferences. Thus, some of the same tools that are used to understand behavior in consumer markets can also be applied to organizational markets.

Even if you don't plan to go into business, there's a good chance that understanding consumer behavior will be an important tool in your job. Many not-for-profit organizations (governments, arts organizations, and charities) define their mission in terms of satisfaction of human needs and wants of some sort. Knowledge of consumer behavior helps non-profit organizations understand donors' motivations, produce effective communication programs, and change behaviors (e.g., public service announcements that encourage the use of seat belts). As private individuals, we "market" ourselves to other members of society (e.g., to attract and solidify personal relationships, to get a job). Thus, it is good practice to imagine ourselves in another person's shoes—to think about other people's needs and motivations.

As implied above, understanding consumer behavior can be important from a personal perspective. We live in a marketing age where almost anything can be offered to someone as a possible object of consumption. Further, thousands of organizations and organizational groups work hard to persuade people to consume in ways beneficial to their goals. People need tools to help them understand the persuasive messages that bombard them and to devise strategies for sorting out what is meaningful to them and what is not. After completing this course, you will be better informed and prepared to exercise effective control over your own consumer behavior, because you will know more about the strategies and tactics marketers use to influence your behavior in the marketplace. You might also relate your ideas (e.g., through a website that solicits consumer comments) to companies so that they can improve their offerings and, in the long run, enhance overall life quality. You will also begin to understand more of the *why* behind some of your own consumption activities. Understanding the *why* can be useful. In this book, we invite you to think about how marketing activities relate to your own patterns of consumer behavior and consumption. In this vein, some consumer behavior specialists have even helped juvenile offenders reevaluate their criminal behavior and motives by discussing the ways in which marketing had influenced them.[5]

An Introduction to This Book

We offer several approaches for explaining the themes and organizational scheme of this book. In the next section we describe consumer activities in daily life. Following that discussion we identify some major themes and concepts in the field of consumer behavior; at the same time, we connect these concepts to the opening vignettes (short stories) and to other relevant examples.

Consumer Activities in Daily Life

If you stop and think for a moment, you'll realize that during a large part of your day you are involved in consumer activities. If you are anything like the two consumers we described in the introductory vignettes in this chapter, just the first hour of your day includes lots of consumer behaviors framed by your culture and lifestyle. Take a few moments right now and think about your first hour this morning. What are your morning routines and habits? What products or brands did you use? Do you regularly use or feel loyal to some of these brands? Do some of them have special meanings or remind you of certain people or events in your life?

The two consumers in the opening vignettes (Monica and Balla) live in different parts of the world and obviously lead very different lives. However, they probably share many patterns of consumption with you, including eating a routine morning meal, using branded consumer products, engaging in routine consumption behavior, consuming products imported from different countries, using and enjoying gifts, engaging in grooming rituals, making choices, purchasing products and services, and so forth.

To be successful, marketers need to understand the role of consumption activities in the daily lives of consumers like Monica, Balla, and you. And increasingly they need to have a more broad understanding of consumption. For example, Wolfgang Schmitt, chairman and CEO of Rubbermaid, Inc., stresses this very thing: the need to understand consumer trends in their broadest sense, including more than just demographics or lifestyle, but also fashion, color, technology, government, and law. He also emphasizes the necessity of firms to gain real insight into consumers' lives. Rubbermaid doesn't just use marketing communication tools to sell products; of equal importance to the firm is sharing experiences about how to use those products—how consumers might organize their kitchen or solve space problems in their child's room.[6] Visit their website featuring lots of stories about consumers' novel experiences with Rubbermaid products.

www.rubbermaid.com

As pointed out earlier, it is also important for marketers to understand customer needs and wants in a B2B setting. Some examples of business needs include low cost, high quality, prompt delivery time, inventory management, and profit maximization. If B2B marketers have a good understanding of their customers, they have a better chance to build a relationship that will last a long time and be mutually beneficial for buyer and seller.

Consumer Behavior as It Relates to the Organization of This Book

This section sketches in some topics in consumer behavior that the opening vignettes suggest to us. We use this sketch to give you an idea of the topics we discuss in the other 18 chapters of the book.

The study of consumer behavior includes focusing on relationships between what people think, feel, and do and the role of marketing strategies in molding these processes. For example, the introductory vignette describes Monica's beliefs and feelings about her shampoo. Monica thinks that the brand of shampoo she buys is healthy; she also feels good using it because of its herbal smell. Thus, Monica has a positive **attitude** toward her brand of shampoo. Her beliefs and feelings are compatible, and they are also consistent with her **purchase behavior.** As a consequence, we could describe Monica as brand loyal in her shampoo purchases.[7] **Brand loyalty** *is more than just repeat purchase behavior; it also includes a preference for a particular brand and a positive emotional response to the brand.* Chapter 2 expands on the relationship between marketing strategy and consumer behavior, and Chapter 13 describes how attitudes evolve and change. Chapter 17 expands on the relationship between consumer satisfaction and brand loyalty. Attitudes and behaviors are not formed in isolation. Very often other people influence our attitudes and behaviors (Chapter 15), such as in the case of Monica's purchase and use of Clinique cosmetics.

Learning about consumers is the key to successful marketing. We outline different ways to learn about consumers in Chapter 3. Consider a simple decision like the purchase and use of shampoo. Monica is loyal to her shampoo, but other consumers may be likely to experiment with different shampoos, choose the cheapest brand, or buy one they saw advertised on television. Companies such as Procter & Gamble, Unilever, or L'Oréal that produce a variety of shampoos and distribute them internationally are interested in research to establish how consumers around the world evaluate different brands and make shampoo decisions. Many of the chapters in this book will help untangle how these choices are made. For example, Chapter 9 describes how perceptions influence attention and processing of advertisements and product packaging, and Chapter 13 describes some different choice rules or heuristics that consumers employ in making purchase decisions. Monica is part of a **market segment** of consumers who value shampoo and other personal care products that are "healthy" and "natural." Companies in different parts of the world have found it profitable to target this segment with marketing appeals. For example, Herbaria is a leading player in the Hungarian herbal products market, targeting this segment in Hungary, Germany, Switzerland, Austria, and Italy.[8] Throughout this book, and especially in Chapters 2, 6, and 8, we will discuss how marketers identify, select, and target market segments.

To explain the consumer activities of Monica and Balla, we need to understand how their cultures and historical period inform their behaviors. For instance, Monica washes her hair every day. The frequency of this grooming ritual, a topic we discuss in Chapter 5, varies around the world.[9] In Hungary, Procter & Gamble is a market leader in the shampoo category with its shampoo Pantene. Procter & Gamble would like to grow the shampoo market by encouraging Hungarians to wash their hair more frequently than once or twice a week. However, many Hungarians believe it is unhealthy to wash hair more often.[10] In other countries, such as Mexico, water is a scarce resource, and daily hair washing would be a luxury that to many would appear wasteful. In Chapters 4 and 5, and throughout this book, we will talk about important cultural differences in virtually every aspect of consumer activity.

It's also important to observe that even a simple behavior like shampooing is tied to gender, social class, ethnicity, and age. For example, many hairstylists in Canada and the United States have loyal clienteles of middle-class and upper-middle-class senior citizen females who come each week to have their hair shampooed and styled. So, be careful not to assume that all American consumers buy shampoo. The impact of social and economic structures on consumer behavior is the topic of Chapter 6. Like culture, we often take for granted attitudes, feelings, and behaviors that reflect our own gender, social class, or ethnic background.

Both Monica and Balla also engage in morning grooming rituals, although the routines are somewhat different. Grooming rituals are important because they prepare people to enter the outside world and allow them to communicate specific messages about themselves. But Monica's and Balla's grooming rituals also reflect their self-concepts (Chapter 7), the way they live or their lifestyles (Chapter 8), their motivations (Chapter 11), as well as past experiences, learning, and knowledge (Chapter 12). Grooming rituals also reflect variations in household structures and stage in the family life cycle. Monica lives alone, like a growing segment of consumers in Europe and North America, whereas Balla is a family man, as are most people in his country. Household influences on consumption are described in Chapter 14. Do you think Balla's consumption routines would change if he had school children to get out the door in the morning?

Monica, Balla, and Haro use and reuse products in new ways to solve particular consumption problems. Monica sometimes uses paper towels as coffee filters. Balla uses a plastic kettle as a tool for washing, and Haro reuses an old kerosene tin as a big tea kettle. They engage in **use innovativeness.**[11] That is, *they are constantly on the lookout for novel ways* *to solve familiar problems or address familiar needs.* Many consumers and organizations are concerned with creating innovative solutions to consumption problems. The diffusion and adoption of innovative products in consumer and industrial contexts is an important field within consumer behavior. **Diffusion** refers to *the spread of a new product through a population.* Balla's breakfast of French bread, Dutch milk, Nigerian margarine, and Swiss (Nescafé) coffee drunk from a French glass are a good example of the effects of diffusion and are related to the fact that Niger was a French colony and borders Nigeria. Other diffusion research has revealed that over 90 percent of married couple homes in the United States by 1989 possessed microwave ovens, whereas virtually none did in 1970. In Japan, researchers explore the popularity of the Argentinean tango, a dance that has diffused to Japan via France. Innovation and resistance to innovation is the subject of Chapter 16. Notice too that Haro's kettle is recycled. In Chapter 19 we focus on consumers' and organizations' recycling, reusing, and disposal behaviors, and in Chapter 10 we describe alternatives to purchasing products, including the multibillion dollar "do it yourself" industry.[12]

An Expanded Overview of Consumer Behavior

In the previous section we offered a brief introduction to consumer behavior by focusing on the opening vignettes. In this part of this chapter we provide a broadened overview of consumer behavior. First, we briefly introduce the idea of consumer culture. Next, we discuss the global nature of this consumer culture. Finally, we describe the circle of consumer behavior. This provides a summary of the relationships between production, acquisition, consumption, and disposal activities. The model introduces the notion that product categories, products, and even particular acquisitions have a kind of biography or life history.[13]

Consumer Culture

Consumer culture reflects a general shift in the basic emphasis of economic and social systems from exchange or production to consumption. A consumer orientation is associated with a model of well-being that measures economic health in terms of consumer confidence and spending. At the individual level, it measures consumer well-being with self-expression, possessions, stylistic expertise, proficiency, and flair.[14] **Consumer culture** refers to *an organized social and economic arrangement in which markets govern the relationship between meaningful ways of life and the symbolic and material resources on which they depend.*[15] Even though there is a strong link between such a culture and materialism, this approach can also include the pursuit of nonmaterialistic goals such as happiness and quality of life.

At the dawn of the new millennium, the existence of a developed consumer culture dictates that organizations must adapt. Specifically, firms must be customer focused and customer oriented. They must determine the nature of consumer demand; then, they create products and services to satisfy demand. Such an approach is superior to the philosophy of mass producing an item and only then trying to figure out how to sell it to the general public.

A consumer culture perspective contrasts with past ways of thinking about economic affairs. For example, the economies of many premodern cultures were dominated by a concern with exchange, that is, with the circulation of goods and persons among social groups. Premodern communities measured wealth and well-being not by what one had but instead by who and how many persons one influenced or controlled through gift obligations.[16]

In Europe and North America, the production orientation was a precursor of our present consumer culture. The **production orientation** is *a model of wealth and well-being measured in stocks of productive assets and ownership of machinery and factories.* This model is enshrined in Adam Smith's eighteenth-century classic economic treatise, *The Wealth of Nations.* The philosophy that inspired Smith is called *mercantilism.* **Mercantilism** is concerned about improving the well-being of the nation-state not individual consumers; nonetheless, it led to the early development of the production of both industrial and consumer goods for national consumption. Indeed, Smith even held that "consumption is the sole end and purpose of all production."[17] Toys, stockings, pins and nails, starch, soap, knives, tobacco pipes, pots, ribbons and lace, and linen were among the early manufactures destined for consumer markets in the eighteenth century. The production orientation is also associated with the emergence of the **Protestant ethic,** as the great sociologist Max Weber termed it. This is *a worldview that emphasized individual initiative, hard work, and self-perfection.* This worldview spread through northern Europe and the United States from the seventeenth to the nineteenth centuries.

One of the dramatic events of the closing decades of the twentieth century is the sudden and recent **globalization** of markets and marketing. By globalization, we mean *that the constraints of geography on consumption and social and cultural arrangements are rapidly lessening.* As the definition implies, the world is becoming more interconnected and the variation among national markets is decreasing. Due to globalization, many companies are finding it necessary to design their marketing strategy across cultures. When developing a global marketing strategy, organizations should consider several factors, including market, cost, competitive, and environmental factors.

Consumer Behavior around the World

Geography is becoming much less important in where people shop and what they buy. Take one simple example. *Cosmopolitan* magazine claims to be more than a magazine; it's a lifestyle. The message is targeted at the young, career-oriented woman, and consumers can access *Cosmopolitan* from just about anywhere in the world. In 1998 there were 36 international editions of the magazine, making it the largest magazine franchise of its kind in the world. By the time this book comes to print, *Cosmopolitan* aims to expand to 50 different editions. Of course, if you can't find it at your local newsstand, you can check it out on the magazine's website.

 www.cosmomag. com

Although acquiring and consuming goods and services is restricted by access to money, consumption is, in principle, an activity open to everyone all over the world. Similarly there is no principle restricting what can be consumed. Marketing, design, public relations, and media professionals produce and distribute not just consumer goods but meaningful consumer goods. A number of these goods are beginning to acquire a global meaning. Thus, brands like Levi's, Sony, Benetton, Coke, Royal Dutch Shell, and McDonald's are recognized the world over.

The nature and dynamics of consumer behavior vary widely around the world because the factors that influence production, acquisition, consumption, and disposal vary widely from place to place. In addition, today's consumer cultures have evolved in different ways in different areas of the world. As we have said, modern consumer culture evolved first in Europe and North America. Nevertheless, the 150 years between 1850 and 2000, marked by steadily rising incomes and the advent of mass production and mass marketing, has led to a democratic shift in desire. More people than ever before have the right and opportunity to consume as they see fit.

The Internet represents one way that consumer culture becomes global. It is now quite possible to sit at a computer terminal and gather information about products for sale in six other countries, all within the space of a few minutes. At the same time, with the click of

Consumer culture in the less affluent world: Mali.

Source: The Material World

a mouse, products and services can be purchased via the Internet. These acquisitions can sometimes be delivered directly over the Internet (e.g., software, music, banking services). In other instances, the purchases arrive via the speed and convenience of overnight delivery services. In brief, the Internet and its multimedia component, the World Wide Web, serve to quicken the pace of consumer globalization.

Consumer culture is marked both by the commercialization of homegrown products, but especially by the adoption of a great many foreign product categories, products, and brands.[18] In the **newly industrialized countries (NICs)** of Japan and East Asia, so-called because they have *entered industrial manufacturing age in the last 50 years,* this desire for foreign goods is notable. **Adoption** refers to *the decision of consuming units to purchase new products and services regularly.* At the same time, these imported products are adapted to fit in with the local culture. In Japan, the impact of Western consumer culture is present in daily life. Westerners visiting Japan are struck by a combination of the exotic and the familiar. But even the familiar has been adapted and changed to fit Japanese culture. Consider the pizza parlor in Tokyo's fashionable Ginza district that features a squid topping. MosBurger (a Japanese imitator of the very successful McDonald's Japan) features a "riceburger" composed of *kimpira* (burdock root), bacon and seaweed served on *onigir* (grilled rice) pressed into the shape of a bun. These examples illustrate the important way in which products are changed to suit local desires as they cross cultural boundaries.

In the **less affluent world (LAW),** *including many of the countries of Asia, Africa, and Latin America,* the spread of Western-style consumer culture is encouraged by the extension of media access via satellite transmission, improvements in transportation, and an accelerated movement of migrants to the developed world and back again.[19] Indeed, the image of the "good life" in such countries is more and more one of being a successful participant in a consumption-oriented society. Nonetheless, the spread of consumer culture in the less affluent world tends to be limited by stagnant economic growth, unequal income distribution, and sometimes conflicts with traditional consumption values. In many of these countries, as the photo of a Malian family and their possessions suggests, consumption of basic necessities remains a challenge for many, while the few enjoy a luxurious consumption style on par with the most developed countries.[20]

Transitional economies *include the former socialist bloc countries of eastern Europe and other economies that were formerly dominated by the public sector.* Many of these were socialist economic systems where marketing concepts are being slowly introduced. In such economies, consumers sometimes express ambivalent (both positive and negative) attitudes towards consumerism and marketing. Over the past 10 years, eastern Europeans have experienced an absolute explosion of consumption alternatives. For eastern Europeans who grew up under communism, the availability of many different products and brands creates a fundamental tension between the individualism and self-expression offered by consumption and the communist ideological goals of equality and classlessness. They long to express their identity with the new clothes, perfumes, toys, and automobiles that surround them but still feel guilt and shame about these longings. In addition, the economic hardships faced by most eastern Europeans, like the Russian family pictured below,

Consumer culture in transitional economies: Russia.

Source: The Material World (book)

makes Western shopping malls more like museums than places to purchase products. Although satellite TV familiarizes eastern Europeans with Western brands and lifestyles, for many these consumer goods are frustratingly unattainable. We'll have more to say about consumer culture and the challenges that face global marketers in different regions of the world in Chapter 4.[21]

Just as consumer culture varies in different locales such as different countries and cities, **organizational cultures** can be unique. In different corporations, organizational culture *can differ with respect to dress, communication, learning, and decision-making styles; ethics; and so forth.* Just as consumer marketers strive to understand the cultural forces that influence the behavior of their customers in the developed world, transitional economies, and the less affluent world, so too do B2B marketers attempt to take account of the influence of corporate cultures on the organizational buying process.

The Circle of Consumption

The **circle of consumption** is illustrated in Exhibit 1.2. The circle of consumption refers to the fact that *the production and acquisition of goods and services, their consumption, and the disposal of used goods are part of a cycle of managerial and socioeconomic activities.* We will refer to this simple description of consumption throughout the text. Understanding each phase and the relationships between each phase is critical for marketers. Consumption is a thing that people do, along with productive work, exchange, and noneconomic activity. Consumption typically involves using things, and sometimes using them up, rather than making them or transferring them.

The processes of production, acquisition, consumption, and disposal are universal. (Please note that the terms disposal and disposition are used interchangeably in this text.) In every society, consumption is organized into behavioral systems involving varying constellations of goods and persons. As illustrated in Exhibit 1.2, the order in which the processes of production, acquisition, consumption, and disposal occur, and the participants in

Exhibit 1.2 Circle of Consumption

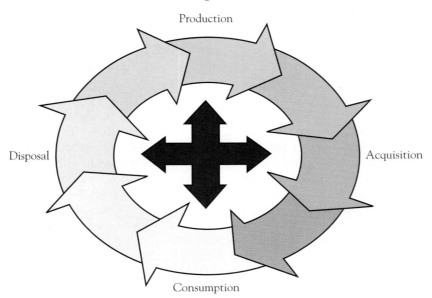

Exhibit 1.3 A Basic Model of Purchase Decisions

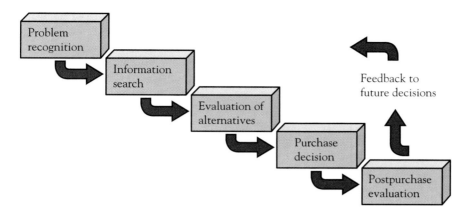

the processes, vary widely both within and between societies. Some are commercial processes and some are not. In marketing, we ordinarily think of the circle of consumption as moving from production by a manufacturer to acquisition by an industrial buyer or end consumer, who then consumes the product in industrial production or in final consumption. Both types of consumers then dispose of the waste generated by their consumption activities in some way. Indeed, we focus primarily on this type of consumption cycle in this book. However, the number of steps in the circle of consumption, as well as the order in which these steps occur, varies.

Much of the attention of marketers has focused on acquisition as the critical phase in the circle of consumption. In fact, marketers have focused mostly on one kind of acquisition—purchase decisions. They have studied how consumers and organizational buyers gather information, and evaluate and decide which products, services, and ideas to buy. A basic model of purchase decision making is provided in Exhibit 1.3.

This model suggests that consumers purchase products to solve identified consumption problems. Consumers engage in search and evaluation of alternatives and judge their purchase decisions in terms of how well the purchases solved their consumption problems. You can probably think of many of your own purchase decisions that fit this model. For example, perhaps you felt you needed easier access to a computer for schoolwork so you decided to purchase a personal computer. You may have engaged in a process very like the one described in Exhibit 1.3, including information search and alternative evaluation.

However, this model captures only one aspect of acquisition. For example, consider your first roller coaster ride. A manager wanting to understand how people decide to purchase a roller coaster ride would probably not get much help from Exhibit 1.3. To understand and market roller coaster rides, managers need to understand group dynamics (many people go on their first roller coaster ride because someone drags them on it) and the experience itself (the fantasy, feelings, and fun associated with consumption). As another example, consider expenditures on weddings. In many nations, families spend large percentages of their household resources on their children's weddings. Again, Exhibit 1.3 doesn't offer a very good explanation. To understand this pattern of spending, marketers need to understand culture, the role of the family in social life, and the importance of consumption memories. For example, a mother tells her daughter, "this is a day you will always remember," and it will "help you get through the hard times." In many countries a great number of pictures are taken to ensure that the event is remembered. In the United States, the more money spent on the wedding, the more money that is spent on photographing it. For many consumption experiences, value comes not only from acquisition or consumption experiences but also from the knowledge and memory of the consumption experience.[22] Kodak's "moments to remember" advertising campaign capitalizes on consumers' desire for vivid recording of important consumption events.

Exhibit 1.2 invites you to think about products—physical products, services, ideas, and celebrities, for example—as having biographies. Think of your collection of possessions. How were your possessions acquired? Consumption is not a simple outcome of a single purchase. For example, a consumer may purchase a koala bear doll on a holiday taken in Australia. She may then display the doll in her home. Perhaps following a move or a lifestyle change, the consumer may give the koala doll away to a young niece. It's conceivable that someday the doll could become what people call a collectible. At this point, the niece may decide that she would prefer to sell the doll rather than keep it. The biography of things can contribute value to objects beyond the value of consumer goods that are merely offered for sale. The American Girl Collection and Patek Philippe both use the idea that things may have a biography to promote different categories of consumer goods—a line of collectible dolls and high-end watches, respectively.

The idea that products have a biography may apply to industrial goods as well. Machinery such as printing equipment may be purchased new, resold as used equipment to a lower-tech producer, eventually donated to a charity, and finally lovingly restored and preserved in a museum of arts and industries. You have probably already realized that for both the consumer and industrial cases, each of the transfers present the current owners with entrepreneurial opportunities to manage the movement, use, and disposal of goods.

In the last few years, managerial focus has evolved to include the full circle of consumption. Understanding acquisition, which is very important to marketers, requires an understanding of the other steps because consumer beliefs, values, and attitudes are affected

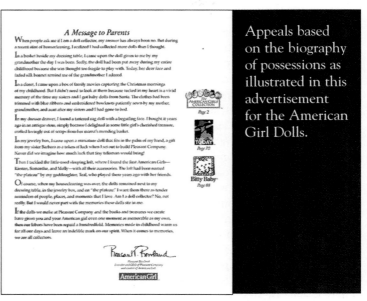

Source: American Girl Catalog

Source: American Girl Catalog

Source: New Yorker, 1998–1999

by these links. By understanding the links between these phases, managers can implement strategies to influence the timing and sequence of these phases, which in turn can affect demand for their product. For example, disposal refers to those processes by which consumers divest themselves of consumer goods. By looking at **disposal,** the circle of consumption highlights the importance of "thinking green" and the value to organizations of developing sustainable marketing practices (e.g., practices that are environmentally friendly and do not unnecessarily deplete the planet's resources).[23] The following examples are presented to help you understand the full implications of the circle of consumption.

From Disposal to Acquisition

At the urging of 11-year-old Austen, his family acquires a kitten unwanted by another family and advertised in the local newspaper as "free to good home." In the Netherlands, thousands of bales of used, unwanted clothing are collected from individual households through a public works program for the unemployed and shipped to less developed countries where they are refurbished and resold. Private dealers in the United States have been buying beat-up old British sports cars like MGs, Triumphs, and Austin Healeys and shipping them to Europe for restoration and resale at premium prices. In the United States, consumer durables such as washers, refrigerators, and air conditioners are almost all scavenged by parts dealers. Very few end up in landfills. Young married couples often put new households together from extra and leftover housewares retrieved from their parents' garages and basements.[24]

From Disposal to Production

An Arkansas firm called Advanced Environmental Recycling Technologies developed a process to recycle waste materials, including using ground-up plastic and wood chips to make termite- and weather-resistant window frames. A Tennessee company has found a way to recycle old newspaper to make pencil bodies. Consumers have long produced new products from old ones (e.g., women making use of fabric scraps to create beautiful quilts). Safety Kleen Corporation rinses the used industrial solvents it collects from garages so that the solvent can be reused; the solid waste products are incinerated and used in making concrete. Artificial vanilla flavoring is a by-product of the wood pulp industry and is used in a large number of confections. In West Africa, empty kerosene tins are used to deliver water from public pumps to home storage jars. In Senegal, craftsmen mold empty tuna fish and beer cans into attaché cases.

From Disposal to Consumption

In a worldwide advertising campaign, Patek Philippe suggests that consumers think of giving their watches as heirloom gifts: that is, one consumer's disposition is another's consumption. One of the authors owns a photograph showing a paper 7-Eleven Slurpee cup holding flowers placed on a grave on the Mexican Day of the Dead in Arizona. A nationwide organization of restaurant owners in the United States donates unused food to a nonprofit firm that provides it to shelters for the homeless. Cast-off rubber tires are used as planters and children's swings in the United States and as hoops in children's games in the less affluent world.

From Production to Consumption

Many firms make component parts that are consumed in the course of further industrial production, such as ball bearings used in the manufacture of conveyor systems. Mrs. Wood, a middle-class consumer, produces her family's evening meal from scratch, by baking a casserole in her gas convection oven. Rick, a mild-mannered professor, makes several trips to Home Depot and builds a deck for his family to enjoy on summer evenings. Farmers in the LAW produce and consume an important fraction of their own food, shelter, and clothing.

From Acquisition to Consumption

This category refers to items received for immediate consumption. Buying restaurant meals is a good example. On major life transition events such as weddings and on some calendrical rituals such as Mother's Day, Christmas, Hanukkah, or Id-l-Adha, consumers receive gifts of cards, flowers, food, and other things from relatives and friends. Hunter-gatherer groups in the Arctic, South America, Africa, Australia, and South Asia harvest natural products for immediate consumption, as do amateur game hunters and mushroom gatherers in the developed world.

From Acquisition to Disposal

The U.S. $6 billion gift industry involves the purchase of goods for immediate disposal through gift giving. Japanese tourists take the purchase of *omiyage,* souvenirs of foreign travel, for distribution as gifts to friends at home to a high art.[25] Some people frequent garage sales and flea markets to provision their own subsequent selling activities. Some impulse shoppers purchase expensive clothing for the thrill of the purchase and later return the goods unused to the retail store or even hide them away in drawers and closets unused.[26]

Motivational Dynamics in Consumer Culture

Consumer behavior is a dynamic aspect of our social life. Production, acquisition, consumption, and disposal of consumer products are driven in part by universal human motivations. We discuss motivation in more detail in Chapter 11. But we would like to

Exhibit 1.4 Motivational Dynamics

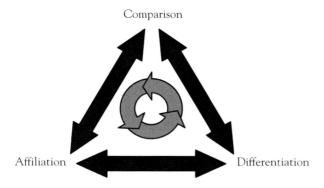

introduce a simple motivational model here since we relate a number of behaviors to it in the following chapters.

Within society two opposing motivational tendencies together drive many consumer behaviors. One we may call the motive toward integration or affiliation with other people, the other is the motive toward differentiation or distinction from other people. For example, sports fans communicate their affiliation with a team and fellow fans by sporting team colors and merchandise; at the same time, they communicate their differentiation from other teams and fan groups.

Consumers' taste preferences are expressed through recurring patterns of acquisition, consumption, disposal, and production. In consumer culture, marketers encourage people to go to the market to purchase goods and services that help them define with whom they are affiliated and from whom they are separated. These patterns of consumer preference are defined and refined through a third motivational process, a process of individual and social comparison. In other words, most of us are motivated to scan our social environment continuously for cues in the consumer behavior of others to help us define who we are and who we are not and the social groups to which we belong and the groups to which we do not.

These motivational drivers may not always be conscious, but they are reflected in the large number of consumption choices we make daily, choices that reflect and maintain the division of societies into distinct classes, ages, neighborhoods, ethnicities, lifestyles, occupations, personalities, nationalities, and so on. In other words, these motives and the consumer behaviors they stimulate integrate individuals with some groups and distinguish them from others. Thus, we are able to say that Germans differ from the French in their avid consumption of beer rather than wine. And within Germany we may distinguish groups of Germans by their preferences for brands of beer produced in particular regions.

Thus, the simple motivation model pictured in Exhibit 1.4 suggests that the needs for integration, differentiation, and comparison drive many decisions around the circle of consumption. We will refer to this simple model at a number of points in our text.

The Plan of the Book

This book is divided into four parts. The organization of the book is graphically displayed in Exhibit 1.5, where it is overlaid on the circle of consumption. In this chapter and Chapter 4, we provide an overview of the global marketplace context of consumption. Chapters

Exhibit 1.5 The Circle of Consumption and the Plan of the Book

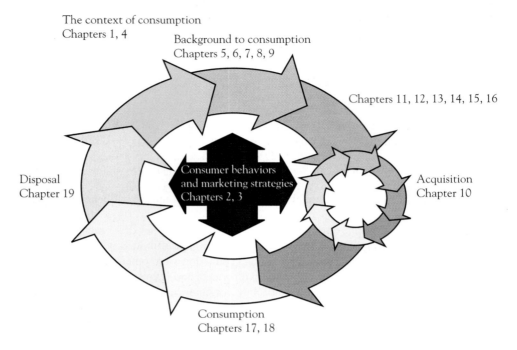

The context of consumption
Chapters 1, 4

Background to consumption
Chapters 5, 6, 7, 8, 9

Chapters 11, 12, 13, 14, 15, 16

Disposal
Chapter 19

Consumer behaviors and marketing strategies
Chapters 2, 3

Acquisition
Chapter 10

Consumption
Chapters 17, 18

2 and 3 define the role of consumer behavior in marketing and the ways in which knowledge of consumer behavior is obtained and linked to marketing strategy. In Exhibit 1.5 these two chapters are shown on the crossed arrows in the middle of the diagram to suggest that marketing strategies play a direct role in influencing production, acquisition, consumption, and disposal.

The second part of the book consists of five chapters and looks at what we call **preacquisition phenomena** that provide the background to consumption. In other words, we describe the various cultural, economic, social, and psychological influences that channel consumer behavior toward particular kinds of acquisition, use, and disposal behaviors. Important preacquisition phenomena include culture (Chapter 5), social class and ethnicity (Chapter 6), the self (Chapter 7), lifestyles (Chapter 8), and perception (Chapter 9). These phenomena both strongly influence and are strongly influenced by consumer behavior.

The third part of this book is concerned with purchase and acquisition behaviors. In Chapter 10 we discuss acquisition tactics themselves, focusing not only on purchase but also on alternatives such as barter and gift giving. In Chapters 11, 12, 13, 14, and 15 we examine the social, interpersonal, and individual processes and behaviors that steer groups and individuals toward particular acquisition behaviors and tactics. Needs, motivations, and involvements (Chapter 11) and experience, learning, and knowledge (Chapter 12) provide individuals with the drive and information they need to engage in acquisition behaviors. Placing the chapters that discuss them on a circle around Chapter 10 graphically portrays the fact that household organization, interpersonal influence, and individual consumer behaviors affect what and how consumers acquire goods.

The fourth and final part of the book discusses what happens after people acquire things. The four chapters in this section explore consumption and disposal. Our discussion includes both the processes that may accelerate demand for new products and those processes that lead consumers to resist and reject marketplace offerings (see Chapter 16). In Chapter 17 we investigate consumer satisfaction. This topic is crucial for marketers, since customer satisfaction is essential to marketing success and organizational survival. We inquire into the meaning of consumption in Chapter 18. Finally, in Chapter 19 we survey how consumers dispose of goods and services they no longer want when their value and meanings change.

Each chapter in this book has distinct sections. For instance, each chapter begins with a short list of learning objectives. These learning objectives focus on the key issues that you should understand once you have read the chapter. If you discover that you don't understand them, then turn back to the chapter to fill in the gaps in your understanding. Next, we introduce each chapter with one or more vignettes, short stories that we feel dramatize the key theories, concepts, and applications. The vignettes are followed by an overview that discusses the aims of the chapter. The body of the chapter follows, and we then provide a short chapter summary. Each chapter is followed by a short case example titled "You Make the Call" that includes some questions. These cases are designed to provide an applied example of theory and concepts discussed in the chapter. We aim to provide cases that are not unlike situations that you may encounter in your career. Finally, each chapter includes key terms and some review and discussion questions. If you read and think about these questions and write down the ideas that come to you, you should find yourself beginning to synthesize ideas from this chapter with other marketing and consumer behavior knowledge.

summary

Welcome to the world of consumer behavior. We define consumer behavior as individuals or groups acquiring, using, and disposing of products, services, ideas, or experiences. This definition includes the search for information and actual product purchase. The study of consumer behavior includes an understanding of consumers' thoughts, feelings, and actions and an understanding of relevant marketing strategies. Topics that consumer behavior researchers study are limited only by their imaginations.

Consumer behavior includes or is related to a wide variety of human activity. Consumers in different parts of the world lead very different lives. However, they share many patterns of consumption, including brand and service loyalties, using and enjoying gifts, partaking in rituals, making choices, and purchasing products, to name a few.

Consumer behavior is exciting and fun, but it is also important to you for a number of reasons. Organizations stay in business by attracting and retaining customers. However, even if you don't plan to go into business, there's a good chance that understanding consumer behavior will be an important tool in your job. Consumer behavior research is useful in any job for which the mission includes satisfaction of human needs and wants. Finally, understanding consumer behavior will make you a better-informed consumer.

Consumer culture reflects a general shift in the basic emphasis of economic systems from exchange or production to consumption. The nature and dynamics of consumer behavior vary widely from place to place depending on historical, macroeconomic, and cultural factors. The production and acquisition of goods and services, their consumption, and the disposal of used goods are part of a cycle of social and economic activities that we call the circle of consumption. The processes of production, acquisition, consumption, and disposal are universal, but the order in which the processes occur and the participants in the processes vary widely both within and across social systems. Much marketing attention has focused on one aspect of acquisition—purchase decisions. However, purchase decisions are just one aspect of consumption. In recent years, managerial interest has evolved to include the full circle of consumption. Several links are important for marketers to understand and manage, including disposal to acquisition, disposal to production, disposal to consumption, production to consumption, acquisition to consumption, and acquisition to disposal.

---

adoption   14
attitude   10
brand loyalty   10
circle of consumption   16
consumer behavior   5
consumer culture   12
diffusion   12
disposal   19
domain of consumer behavior   5
globalization   13
less affluent world (LAW)   14

market segment   11
mercantilism   13
newly industrialized countries (NICs)   14
organizational cultures   16
preacquisition phenomena   22
production orientation   13
Protestant ethic   13
purchase behavior   10
transitional economies   15
use innovativeness   11

---

1. Think of one of your important possessions. Write out its biography or life history from production to the present, paying special attention to its movement in and out of the marketplace.

2. Describe two purchase decisions that match the model shown in Exhibit 1.3 fairly well. Then describe two purchase decisions that don't seem to fit very well. Explain.

3. List three additional examples of products (including things, services, ideas, people, and places) that move from one stage of the circle of consumption to another with or without movement through the marketplace.

4. List several examples of products you have acquired both through various kinds of markets—retail outlets, flea markets, garage sales, wholesale warehouses—and through other acquisition processes mentioned in the text. Can you identify patterns of acquisition associated with particular product categories? Explain.

5. List several examples of products used in the ways described in Exhibit 1.1. Identify patterns of use associated with particular product categories.

6. List various ways in which you have disposed of particular products recently. Identify patterns of disposition associated with particular product categories.

7. Over the course of several days, set aside some time to make some diary entries about consumer behaviors you engage in that involve the basic motivational dynamics mentioned in the text. Pay attention to times that you consume something in order to be with or be like other people important to you. Pay attention to times that you consume

something in order to be unlike other people, to stand out, or to act on your own. Finally, pay attention to the comparative judgments you make in these consumption choices.

You Make the Call

Managing Conbini

Hidetoshi Nakatz is a Japanese soccer star who has been playing for Rome in a European football league. He is asked by the press to name the one thing he most misses about Japan. His answer? *"Conbini!"*

Conbini are Japanese neighborhood convenience stores. They are very popular with customers, and their popularity has been increasing in recent years. The 30,000 convenience stores have a special place in the Japanese economy, where frequent shopping is a necessity, since consumers often don't have much space to store things in their homes. Conbini are always open, and they are much smaller (average size only 100 meters) than the typical convenience store in the United States. An average Conbini receives 700 to 900 customers per day, and the average customer visits once every other day. Major corporations that operate chains of Conbini in Japan include Seven-Eleven, Family Mart, Circle K (UNY Corp), and Daiei Inc. (In Japan, the "Seven" is spelled out in the corporate name of the U.S. corporation 7-Eleven.)

Conbini are always looking for new products and services to add to the store selection. However, there is a problem because shelf space is so limited in the small stores. One recent solution is to add virtual products to the shelves through the introduction of an in-store Internet service called Loppi. In each store, Loppi appears as a terminal that connects to a portion of the Internet, thus forming a compact e-commerce system. Using Loppi, customers can order concert tickets, train/plane reservations, books (Yahoo!, Seven-Eleven, and a leading Japanese book distributor are part owners of the book-ordering system), hot meals, horoscope forecasts, and other offerings. Each of these services is delivered to the customer in a different way. For instance, customers pick up books at the same Conbini where they ordered them, a few days later. The hot meals, targeted at the children of older, homebound parents, are delivered to customers' homes. The concert tickets or the plane tickets can be printed out on the spot. At present, what do you think is the most popular service offered over Loppi? It turns out to be the horoscope forecasts.

What are the major challenges for a fledgling e-commerce firm? Among others, marketing expenses are high for start-up firms; and it is difficult and expensive to attract attention in an increasingly crowded market. Conbini are good partners for new e-commerce ventures, because in-store promotional expenses are low. In addition, as indicated by Hidetoshi Nakatz, customers flock to Conbini. The stores provide an excellent distribution system, both in terms of the existing warehouse system and the convenience of the stores as a final pick-up point for customers. For all of these reasons, Conbini make attractive e-commerce partners for start-up firms. Through Loppi, Conbini have a way to add product lines when shelf space is limited. Loppi also provides a way to overcome existing barriers to e-commerce in Japan, where the technology and infrastructure is not as developed as it is in the United States and where regulatory hurdles can sometimes be a problem for large stores. In the near future, customers will be able to surf the entire Web from the convenience of Loppi.

1. What is it that makes an American invention (i.e., the convenience store) so popular in Japan?

2. How has the original concept of the store evolved to fit the local culture and circumstances?

3. What do Japanese buyers like about Conbini?

4. What other kinds of new products or services could be introduced in the Conbini?

5. How should these new offerings be distributed (e.g., in store, delivered to the home, delivered over the local Internet)?

This case was adapted from Stephanie Strom, "E-Commerce the Japanese Way," New York Times, March 17, 2000, pp. A1, A4.

1. For a discussion of attempts to store services, see Robin A. Higie, Linda L. Price, and Julie Fitzmaurice, "Leaving It All Behind: Service Loyalties in Transition," in *Advances in Consumer Research,* vol. 20, Leigh McAlister and Michael L. Rothschild, eds. (Provo, UT: Association for Consumer Research, 1993), pp. 656–61.

2. R. S. Oropresa, "Female Labor Force Participation and Time-Saving Household Technology: A Case Study of the Microwave from 1978 to 1989," *Journal of Consumer Research* 4 (March 1993), pp. 567–679.

3. Daniel Miller, *Acknowledging Consumption* (London and New York: Routledge, 1995).

4. Richard Bagozzi, "Marketing as Exchange," *Journal of Marketing* 39 (October 1975), pp. 32–39; George Homans, *Social Behavior: Its Elementary Forms* (New York: Harcourt Brace and World, 1961); and John O'Shaughnessy, *Why People Buy* (New York: Oxford University Press, 1987).

5. Julie Ozanne and Ron Paul Hill, "Juvenile Delinquents' Use of Consumption as Cultural Resistance: Implications for Juvenile Reform Programs and Public Policy," *Journal of Public Policy and Marketing* 17, no. 2 (1998), pp. 185–96.

6. "Grand Masters of Marketing," *Marketing Management,* Summer 1998, pp. 22–28.

7. Jacob Jacoby and Robert W. Chestnut, *Brand Loyalty: Measurement and Management* (New York: John Wiley, 1978).

8. See the website www.itaiep.doc.gov/eebic/countryr/hungary/research/cos97.htm for a profile of the cosmetics industry in Hungary.

9. For a discussion of grooming rituals, see Dennis Rook, "The Ritual Dimension of Consumer Behavior," *Journal of Consumer Research* 12 (December 1985), pp. 251–64.

10. This is based on an interview with the Procter & Gamble marketing manager for shampoo in Hungary. As a note of comparison, the average French person bathes or showers 4.4 times a week, compared with 3.7 times in Britain and 3.8 times in Italy, according to the *Tampa Tribune,* October 23, 1998, p. 20A.

11. For a discussion of use innovativeness, see Elizabeth C. Hirschman, "Innovativeness, Novelty Seeking and Consumer Creativity," *Journal of Consumer Research* 7 (December 1980), pp. 283–95; Nancy M. Ridgway and Linda L. Price, "Development of a Scale to Measure Use Innovativeness," in *Advances in Consumer Research,* vol. 10, Alice Tybout and Richard Bagozzi, eds. (Provo, UT: Association for Consumer Research, 1983), pp. 679–84; and Nancy M. Ridgway and Linda L. Price, "Creativity under Pressure: The Importance of Consumption Situations on Consumer Product Use," *Proceedings of the American Marketing Association Summer Educator's Meetings,* 1991, pp. 361–68.

12. Marta E. Savigliano, "Tango in Japan and the World Economy of Passion," in *Re-made in Japan: Everyday Life and Consumer Taste in a Changing Society,* Joseph J. Tobin, ed. (New Haven, CT: Yale University Press, 1993), pp. 235–52.

13. Igor Kopytoff, "The Cultural Biography of Things: Commoditization as Process," in *The Social*

Life of Things, Arjun Appadurai, ed. (Cambridge: Cambridge University Press, 1986), pp. 64–94.

14. Colin Campbell, *The Romantic Ethic and the Spirit of Modern Consumerism* (Oxford: Basil Blackwell, 1987); Neil McKendrick, John Brewer, and J. H. Plumb, *The Birth of a Consumer Society: The Commercialization of Eighteenth Century England* (Bloomington: Indiana University Press, 1982); Chandra Mukerji, *From Graven Images: Patterns of Modern Materialism* (New York: Columbia University Press, 1983); and Rosalind H. Williams, *Dream Worlds: Mass Consumption in Late Nineteenth Century France* (Berkeley: University of California Press, 1982).

15. Don Slater, *Consumer Culture and Modernity* (Cambridge: Polity Press, 1997), p. 8.

16. Paul Bohannan and Laura Bohannan, *Tiv Economy* (Evanston, IL: Northwestern University Press, 1968); Frank Cancian, *Economics and Prestige in a Maya Community: The Religious Cargo System in Zinacantan* (Stanford: Stanford University Press, 1965); Jerry W. Leach and Edmund Leach, eds., *The Kula: New Perspectives on Massim Exchange* (Cambridge: Cambridge University Press, 1983); Claude Levi-Strauss, *The Elementary Structures of Relationship,* trans. by James Harle Bell, John Richard von Sturmen, and Rodney Needham (Boston: Beacon Press, 1969 [1947]); Claude Meillassoux, *Maidens, Meals, and Money* (Cambridge: Cambridge University Press, 1981); and Marshall Sahlins, *Stone Age Economics* (Chicago: Aldine, 1967).

17. Adam Smith, quoted in Slater, *Consumer Culture and Modernity,* p. 22.

18. Much of this section draws from Joseph J. Tobin, ed., *Re-Made in Japan: Everyday Life and Consumer Taste in a Changing Society* (New York: Yale University Press, 1993).

19. Mike Featherstone, ed., *Global Culture* (London: Sage Publications, 1990); Mike Featherstone, *Consumer Culture and Postmodernism* (London: Sage Publications, 1991); Güliz Ger and Russell W. Belk, " 'I'd Like to Buy the World a Coke': Consumptionscapes in the Less Affluent World," *Journal of Consumer Policy* 19, no. 3 (1996), pp. 271–304; and Deborah Sontag and Celia W. Dugger, "The New Immigrant Tide: A Shuttle between Worlds," *New York Times,* July 19, 1998, pp. A1, A12–14.

20. Eric J. Arnould, "Toward a Broadened Theory of Preference Formation and the Diffusion of Innovations: Cases from Zinder Province, Niger Republic," *Journal of Consumer Research* 16 (September 1989), pp. 239–67; and Güliz Ger, "Human Development and Humane Consumption: Well-Being and the 'Good Life,' " *Journal of Public Policy and Marketing* 16 (Spring 1997), pp. 110–25.

21. Clifford Schulz II, Russell W. Belk, and Güliz Ger, eds., *Consumption in Marketizing Economies* (Greenwich, CT: JAI Press, 1994); and Güliz Ger, Russell W. Belk, and Dana-Nicoleta Lascu, "The Development of Consumer Desire in Marketizing and Developing Economies: The Cases of Romania and Turkey," in *Advances in Consumer Research,* vol. 20, Leigh McAlister and Michael L. Rothschild, eds. (Provo, UT: Association for Consumer Research, 1993), pp. 102–7

22. Deborah J. MacInnis and Linda L. Price, "The Role of Imagery in Information Processing: Review and Extensions," *Journal of Consumer Research,* March 1987, pp. 473–91; and Eric J. Arnould and Linda L. Price, "River Magic: Extraordinary Experience and Hedonic Aspects of Service Encounters," *Journal of Consumer Research* 20 (June 1993), pp. 24–45.

23. Don Fuller, *Sustainable Marketing: Managerial-Ecological Issues* (Newbury, CA: Sage, 1999).

24. Some of the examples in this section can be found in William Rathje and Cullen Murphy, *Rubbish! The Archaeology of Garbage* (New York: HarperCollins, 1992).

25. Terrence H. Witkowski and Yoshito Yamamoto, "*Omiyage* Gift Purchasing by Japanese Travelers in the U.S.," in *Advances in Consumer Research,* Rebecca H. Holman and Michael R. Solomon, eds. (Provo, UT: Association for Consumer Research, 1991), pp. 123–28.

26. Thomas C. O'Guinn and Ronald J. Faber, "Compulsive Buying: A Phenomenological Exploration," *Journal of Consumer Research* 16 (September 1989), pp. 153–54.

Learning Objectives

After completing this chapter, you should be able to:

- Explain why effective marketing strategy depends on understanding consumer behavior.

- Identify the keys to adopting a market orientation and a customer focus.

- Understand the importance of marketing imagination to business success and know some keys to being an imaginative company.

- Describe market segmentation and identify a process for segmenting markets.

- Identify useful segmentation variables and criteria for effective market segmentation.

- Describe different kinds of market segmentation strategies and when they are appropriate.

- Understand the relationship between positioning and targeting.

- Describe different product positioning strategies.

Chapter 2

Consumer Behaviors and Marketing Strategies

Let's Go Shopping!

If you want to go shopping a good place to start might be the shopping channel at www.excite.com. Excite Shopping Search powered by the Jango search engine offers shoppers intelligent agent programs that will search the Web for a specified item, seeking the product or service at the best price according to specifications set by the user. Excite Shopping Search has won numerous awards since its first appearance in 1997. Excite, Inc., is part of a new world of commerce happening in marketspace instead of a marketplace. In this marketspace, the manufacturing, promotion, and delivery of products and services are becoming separate, open to independent manipulation and real innovation. Few companies are as successful in that game as Excite. The cartoon on page 30 humorously suggests how pervasive online shopping now is.

Six Stanford University graduates founded Excite, Inc., in 1994. They started the company in a garage with $15,000 borrowed from their families. Excite is now a global media company offering consumers a free online service with a simple front end to the Internet and extensive personalization capabilities; it offers advertisers the best one-to-one marketing services available online. Localized versions of Excite are available in France, Germany, the UK, the Netherlands, Sweden, Japan, and Australia. In 1998, Excite was named the fastest-growing public company in Silicon Valley for 1997 with revenues of $50.2 million and a calculated growth rate of 709 percent. Also in 1998, Excite had one of the most trafficked sites on the World Wide Web, with nearly 20 million unique individuals visiting its network each month.

"Can I call you back? I'm shopping."

Source: *New Yorker*

Overview

We aim primarily to provide you with a basic understanding of consumer behavior from the consumer's perspective. We also provide many examples throughout the text of how marketing managers use consumer behavior theory and research. This chapter focuses specifically on the intersection between managerial marketing strategy and the insights provided by consumer behavior research. **Strategy** can be defined simply as *the actions managers take to attain the goals of the firm.* **Marketing strategy** concerns *the actions managers take to improve the likelihood marketplace exchanges will occur between a firm and its target markets.* To this end, the opening vignette illustrates how important it is to anticipate the needs of consumers; it also illustrates how quickly the environment for marketplace exchange is changing. For example, in 1997–98 adult Internet access grew in the United States by 35 percent and approximately 16 million children were using the Internet.

Over the foreseeable future we can expect that more and more buyer-seller transactions will occur in *an information-defined arena* coined **marketspace.** Business-to-business online commerce or e-commerce is expected to grow from $43 billion in 1998 to $1 trillion in 2003. Online retail sales in Europe were worth $3.6 billion in 1999 and should nearly triple to $9 billion in 2000. There should also be $6 billion in sales in Asia, with Japan, Australia, and South Korea in the lead. From 1997 to 2002, Internet use in China is supposed to grow 571 percent to 9.4 million users. Internet use in Latin America should increase by 298 percent from 4.8 to 19.1 million users.[1]

The contents of marketspace transactions, the contexts in which they occur, and the support activities that enable them are all likely to be very different from exchanges in the physical marketplace. Consider one dramatic example. FreeMarkets, Inc., is a business-to-business Internet auction company that enables suppliers of components for manufactured goods to compete for manufacturers' orders in live, open, electronic auctions. FreeMarkets helps buyers standardize every item of their orders, finds and screens potential sellers, and runs the electronic auctions. The company's clients, like GE, Raytheon, Quaker Oats, and United Technologies, save more than 15 percent on parts, materials, and even services. During the online auctions, sellers can see exactly what the competition is bidding and how low they must go to pocket the order. FreeMarkets makes millions on its services. The cost savings represented by Internet auctions is so great that GM, Ford, DaimlerChrysler, and Toyota have rushed to set up their own versions, as have Sears Roebuck and Company and French retailer Carrefour. Like ATMs in consumer markets, business auctions have created a new marketspace interface between customers and companies that has dramatically changed the competitive dynamics of their respective industries.[2]

In this chapter we first discuss marketing strategy. We also discuss two essentials for developing effective strategy from insights from consumer research: a market orientation and a customer focus. We then talk about the idea of **marketing imagination.** Companies with marketing imagination *go beyond what consumers are able to tell researchers to find new ways to create value for them.* Excite focused on in the vignette, seems to have that kind of imagination. For example, beginning in fall 1998 Excite, offered all users the opportunity to create or join cyberspace communities. The rationale is to enable families and friends to create a gathering place online that stands in for the family living room or the friendly neighborhood—a familiar and comfortable place for people to visit time and again.

Although every successful marketing strategy is built on important skills and resources, none is more critical than the ability to sense the market. Effectively sensing the market produces knowledge, not just information. This kind of knowledge increases a firm's market orientation and results in improved service levels and more innovative products. Listening carefully to customers and remaining market focused leads to market offerings that are different from competitors' products and to improved profit margins. Excite and FreeMarkets are great examples of companies adept at market sensing.

In this chapter we also outline the segmentation, targeting, and positioning process and provide examples. Organizations need to understand consumer behavior in order to segment markets, choose market segments to serve, and develop and position products and services to attract current and potential customers. Developing and positioning products and services involves not just deciding on the form of the product or service but also determining what communications and promotions, distribution systems, and pricing techniques to use.

Marketing Strategies

As discussed in Chapter 3, consumer research can be used in numerous ways to assist managers in understanding their customers. One of the most important applications of consumer research is to improve marketing strategies. In general, customer-oriented marketing strategies improve the value customers derive from products or decrease the costs of products to customers.

One useful categorization of strategies identifies four strategy types: prospector, defender, analyzer, and reactor. **Defenders** are *firms with a narrow product market, a stable*

Defender Strategy: The McIlhenny Company uses market penetration strategy to increase sales and defend its brand's position.

www.church dwight.com/ company/ company_ information. htm

www.tabasco. com/cgi-bin/ historian.pl

customer group, and an established organization structure typically managed by older executives. Church & Dwight, maker of Arm & Hammer baking soda (founded 1846), and the McIlhenny Company, maker of Tabasco sauce (founded 1868), might be considered defenders. Nevertheless, Church & Dwight has successfully implemented both *product and market development strategies* by creating new products containing baking soda and new uses for those products. McIlhenny has implemented a *market penetration strategy* by extending its core brand and suggesting new uses for it to stimulate increased sales.[3]

Defender Strategy: Church & Dwight creates new uses for existing products through product line extensions.

Prospectors have a *changing product market, a focus on innovation and change, and a flexible organizational structure headed by younger managers.* A more specific example of a prospector strategy is a **differentiation strategy.** Such a strategy *emphasizes a product that is unique in the industry, provides a distinct advantage, or is otherwise set apart from competitors' brands in some way.* Entrepreneurial start-up firms like Excite, FreeMarkets, and other new Internet-based firms tend to be prospectors. Defenders and the prospectors lie on opposite ends of a continuum of competitive strategies. The **analyzer** strategy falls between defenders and prospectors on the continuum. Firms that *follow a price leadership strategy, also called a low-cost/low-price strategy,* are examples of analyzers. Korean electronics firms like Hyundai, Samsung, and Lucky Goldstar entered U.S. market using this approach. Finally, **reactors** do not really have a consistent strategy. They tend not to be very customer oriented and *adopt a "me-too" approach to marketing.*[4]

To deepen our understanding of the connection between consumer behavior and effective marketing strategy we can review the **marketing concept.** The marketing concept is a business philosophy, an ideal, and a policy statement. The essence of the marketing concept is a *market-focused, customer-oriented, coordinated marketing effort aimed at generating customer satisfaction as the key to satisfying organizational needs.* A study based on interviews with managers at almost 50 different U.S. companies summarized what managers mean by a market orientation and what organizational factors encourage or discourage this orientation. The answers were revealing.[5] First, managers agreed that a **customer focus** is the central element of a market orientation. Organizations with a customer focus *constantly look for ways to deliver greater value to current and prospective customers through mutually beneficial exchanges.*

Although every successful marketing strategy is built on important skills and resources, none is more critical than customer focus, or the ability to **sense the market.** Sensing the market refers to a *manager's ability to empathize with and gain insights from customers.* This is the single most important skill a manager can use to mobilize new technologies, develop product and service offerings, and design communications programs. In fact, all the elements of a company's strategic posture depend on this skill. We can think of many ventures that have been enormously successful because the founders brought this ability to their enterprises: Bill Gates (Microsoft), Mary Kay Ash (Mary Kay Cosmetics), Akio Morita (Sony), Sam Walton (Wal-Mart), Steve Case (AOL), Richard Branson (Virgin), and many others.[6]

Paying attention to the customer is certainly not a new idea, and yet many companies don't do it or don't do it well. For example, Encyclopedia Britannica's management disregarded the threat of CD-ROM technology and later bungled the company's entrée onto the Internet. The result has been a major decline in sales and profits. Ironically, Encyclopedia Britannica had CD-ROM technology in one of its other units, but the company failed to recognize its importance in the encyclopedia market. GE, which became one of FreeMarkets' biggest customers, initially rejected the idea when it was proposed in-house. By contrast with these bloopers, Toyota, which has a history of market sensitivity, is investing heavily in web technology, although it seems far from the company's core business, because it expects to build its web browser into its soon-to-be-computerized auto models.[7]

Managers sometimes confuse information about consumers with knowledge about consumers. Effectively sensing the market produces knowledge, not just information. We'll have more to say about this in the next chapter. General market data such as that provided by syndicated marketing research services show who is consuming what. But the data rarely show a company how customers relate to each other, the product, and the company.

Market Focused and Customer Oriented

Attending to this kind of knowledge produces many pay-offs. It increases a firm's market orientation, resulting in improved service levels and more innovative products. It leads to promoting products and services that are designed specially for different national markets. By listening carefully to customers and remaining market focused, a company can develop products that are fundamentally different from those of its competitors, which can result in increased profit margins. Finally, listening to the market favors differentiation over cost reduction even when the latter seems like the easier course of action.

Differentiation means *offering customers something they value and that competitors don't have*, like Excite's communities, FreeMarkets' vertical auctions, or Toyota's hybrid energy car.[8] Differentiation can occur at any point in the consumption chain—from how and when the product is acquired, to when consumers decide they no longer want it and decide to dispose of it. For example, Tesco Direct in the UK and Webvan in San Francisco are each working hard to solve the distribution problem in online supermarket shopping. Good Practice 2.1 identifies a series of questions managers can ask about their products and services to map the consumption chain and capture the consumer's total experience. The most important way to achieve differentiation is to completely analyze the consumer's experience with a company and its products: *What* are customers doing at each phase of the circle of consumption? *Where* are customers at each stage of the consumption chain? *When* are consumers engaged with an element of the consumption circle? *Who* else is with the customer points in the cycle of consumption? *How* are consumers' needs and desires being addressed at each stage of consumption? Yankelovich Partners' Brand Intelligence and Corporate Reputation Studies are examples of innovative research on customers' experience that answers these kinds of questions for firms.[9]

Next, many of the managers surveyed emphasized that a customer focus goes beyond conducting customer research. It involves taking actions based on market intelligence. **Market intelligence** includes *knowledge of environmental factors that affect both current and future*

needs and preferences of customers. The concern for future needs drives companies like Xerox, 3M, Toyota, and Procter & Gamble, for example, to invest heavily in new-product development and The Coca-Cola Company to invest heavily in trends research provided by companies like Yankelovich Partners. The idea that market intelligence includes anticipated customer needs is important because it often takes years for an organization to develop new product offerings.

Third, the managers emphasized the need for **coordinated marketing,** stressing that a market orientation is not just the responsibility of a marketing department. This means

that market intelligence must be distributed across the organization. Effectively sharing intelligence is important because it provides a basis for joint action by different departments. For example, the vice president of a manufacturing firm indicated that her organization spreads customer information by telling stories about customers, their needs, their personality characteristics, and even their families. The idea is to have the secretaries, engineers, and production personnel "get to know" customers. If they do, they are more likely to incorporate knowledge about customer needs into activities at every level of the firm.

Fourth, the managers emphasized that certain kinds of environmental conditions may make a market orientation more or less important to overall business performance. One example is a change in customer base. Two U.S. consumer food products companies included in the survey on which this section is based marketed their products in a specific region in the United States without doing much market research. The population in this region had remained unchanged and the preferences of customers were known and stable. Over the last few years, however, the region has received a new influx of population, forcing both companies to initiate research and develop new products. Similarly, the rapid transition to market-driven economies in countries such as Poland and Turkey has led to a rapid growth in customers and an increase in customer sophistication. Old state-run firms that cannot deliver value to meet changing consumer demand in these markets decline as market-oriented foreign firms rush in.[10]

Fifth, the managers also stressed that the degree of competition in an industry affects the importance of a market orientation. Increased competition makes it difficult for firms to develop distinctive product positioning strategies. A sales manager for an industrial product firm explained his firm's response to competitive pressure: "Historically, we were a technically driven company. In the early years it was a successful approach. If we had a better mousetrap, customers would search us out. However, as more companies came up with more solutions, we had to become more market oriented. Find out what solution the customer is looking for, and try to solve it."

Finally, the managers emphasized that profitability is not a part of a market orientation; it is a *consequence* of a market orientation. Findings from the interviews with managers can

1. **Recognize that "customer" means more than the next step in the distribution chain. An important corollary: Do not think of your marketplace offering as a commodity.**

   In many cases, businesses may have consumers (end users of products and services) as well as clients (organizations that may dictate or influence the choices or end users). Organizations must pay attention to both.

2. **Count on your customers for information not for insight.**

   Customers can describe their experiences and define their immediate needs. But only you can interpret their data and help them solve their problems. Being market focused is about your own creativity uncovering and solving your customers' problems.

3. **Don't expect brilliant insights each time you study a customer. Small operational shifts made from a market-focused perspective can also add up to significant improvements.**

   Through a succession of small moves it's possible to take critical steps toward delivering a new set of benefits to a market. It may be as simple as coming up with a more effective way to handle customer complaints or streamlining the sales organization on the basis of recent information about the distribution of customers.

4. **Involve all levels of the organization in the drive to become market focused.**

   Senior management's commitment and participation are vital for an organization to become market focused, but not sufficient for prolonged success. For maximum results, the market-focused mind-set must invade the entire organization.

Source: Francis J. Gouillart and Frederick D. Sturdivant (1994), "Spend a Day in the Life of Your Customers," Harvard Business Review (January–February), 116–27.

be summarized with a definition of **market orientation** as *the organizationwide generation of market intelligence, pertaining to current and future consumer needs, dissemination of the intelligence across departments, and organizationwide responsiveness to it.*

Simply engaging in market-oriented activities does not ensure the quality of those activities. For organizations to become more market oriented they often must acknowledge gaps between their current orientation and a market orientation. For example, a manager of a service organization (a hospital) noted that the company's employees felt they were very responsive to customer needs. However, when service interactions between these employees and customers were videotaped and played back to the employees, they were horrified at the callous ways they saw themselves treating customers. The videotape identified a gap between the hospital's current orientation and a preferred market orientation. Incorporating simple rules into interactions with customers—illustrated in Good Practice 2.2—can help managers improve their market orientation.[11]

The cornerstone of market orientation is a customer focus. Marketing and organizational strategies must be designed around an understanding of consumers' thoughts, feelings, and behaviors. Exhibit 2.1 summarizes the crucial relationship between marketing strategies and understanding consumers. Companies must avoid a narrow focus when trying to understand consumers. As discussed further in Chapters 4 and 5, these understandings must be formulated with due attention to the economic, social, and cultural environment of consumption. Consistent with the views of the managers discussed above, many global corporations from GM to GE to Nestlé to Mattel are organized into geographic units so that production and marketing are better coordinated and market offerings are more closely tailored to the demands of consumers in the United States, Europe, Asia, or Latin America. Global companies believe this will help them produce well-adapted products and will introduce economies of scale and scope. Mattel's Global Friends line of dolls is produced to appeal to consumers in each major global city. Gaining a global focus for Mattel is very important. Although Mattel is the world's largest toy company and currently holds about 16 percent of the market share for toys sold in the United States, its share in Europe is less than 8 percent. With 800 million children in Asia, 120 million in Latin America, and 70 million in Europe, toy makers are challenging each other to make an impact in international toy sales.[12]

Global consumer marketing usually requires firms to tailor their strategies in response to variations in their environment. Typical sources of pressure to respond to local conditions include (1) differences in consumer tastes and preferences, (2) differences in infrastructure and customary marketing practices, (3) differences in distribution channels, and (4) host government rules and regulations. We discuss differences in consumer tastes and preferences throughout this book so we need not dwell on them here.

Differences in infrastructure include variation in measurement units (metric versus English measures), electrical current (110 versus 220 v), and telephone service (land versus microwave systems), for example. Examples of differences in customary marketing practices include restrictions on advertising to children in Denmark and comparative

Exhibit 2.1 Marketing Strategy and Consumers

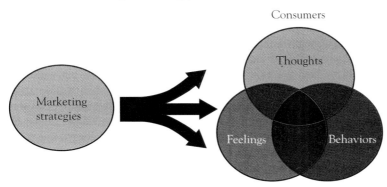

The Cultural Context of Consumption

tomers didn't like about the service. They identified a segment of people commuting to an industrial park area of a nearby city where there was no convenient direct access. The transport authority added a special bus two times a day that provides direct, convenient access. This made their current customers more satisfied and more regular users of the service, and it attracted a number of new users who now found public transportation more convenient. Similarly, in the Niger Republic in West Africa the National Transportation Company (NTC) introduced an air-conditioned, on-time express bus service linking major cities in this very poor country. Although the service was costly by local standards, NTC always filled the bus, and this service helped NTC become one of the few profitable state-run companies in Niger.

Finally, analyzing both consumer attitudes and behaviors can help managers pinpoint consumer segments that are not worth trying to develop. Anytime a company attracts new customers it is asking them to do something different from what they would have done in the absence of the marketing programs directed at them. They have to change their attitudes and their actions. Changing attitudes is difficult, as is changing behavior—changing both is expensive and sometimes impossible.

A growing consumer segment that dislikes a product and never buys bodes poorly for the company that makes it. Creative and future-oriented strategies are needed to respond. For example, some U.S. classical music orchestras have found that their audiences are aging and may not be replaced. Because of cutbacks in funding of public school music programs, many U.S. children reach adulthood with little exposure to classical music. In the short term, orchestra marketing directors can attempt to resolve the problem of shrinking audiences by offering them benefits other than classical music—meeting singles, firework displays, family picnics, and more popular musical fare. This, however, is an uphill battle because of other competitive options. In the longer term, orchestras like to play classical music and would like to develop audiences that enjoy their music. This suggests an active outreach program to replace cutbacks in school music programs and to attract future consumers by building positive consumer attitudes early. The Pacific Symphony Orchestra in Orange Country, California, has a very aggressive community outreach program. For example, they offer an "adopt a musician" education program serving 17,000 students in 20 schools. But one wonders whether and which school children could be targeted effectively with this outreach program. What do you think?[15]

| Marketing Imagination | The connection between understanding customers and designing effective marketing strategies requires creativity and imagination. Customers can often tell marketers what's important to them, and they can identify problems they face in their lives; but they usually can't identify what they'd like the company to do about it. Marketing intelligence attempts to find out what problems customers are trying to solve, and marketing imagination offers solutions.[16] Great consumer examples of marketing imagination include the following. Rollerblades invented not merely a product and a sport, street hockey, but an entire youth lifestyle tailored to urban living. Rollerblade has now attracted a global following. Benetton promotes its casual clothing along with the virtues of multiculturalism to a global market segment, allowing its brand to cross many political, social, and cultural borders. There are almost 30 Benetton outlets in Syria, for example, a country known neither for its promarket policies nor its fashion-forward orientation. In Bangladesh, GrameenPhone provided a solution to the notorious isolation of rural villages through small loans to village women that enable them to buy cellular phones. The women use the phones to sell airtime to their neighbors. The women entrepreneurs profit from the difference between retail and wholesale airtime costs, approximately $50 per month, twice Bangladesh's per capita income.[17] |

An Imaginative Company: Benetton promotes its casual clothing along with the virtues of multiculturalism through global marketing communications.

FreeMarkets' vertical auctions described earlier offer a business-to-business example of marketing imagination. Nalco Chemical and Betz Laboratories, two highly successful chemical companies, offer another. Originally, both of these companies thought of themselves as manufacturers and distributors of chemical products for use in water treatment. Over time, both companies concluded that everyone would benefit if they took over their

An Imaginative Company: Rollerblade, Inc. continues to grow through innovation. In 1995, *Business Week* magazine selected Rollerblades Bravoblades with automatic braking technology (ABT) as one of the best new products on the market.

© Photo courtesy of Rollerblade, Inc. The McGraw-Hill Companies © 1996.

customers' water-treatment processes themselves. For a monthly fee, Nalco and Betz guarantee the best available handling of all water-treatment issues. By having the imagination to connect a consumer problem with a marketing solution, both companies created new businesses that turned out to be immensely profitable. Industry Insights 2.1 provides another clever business-to-business example of the marketing imagination.[18]

Marketing imagination doesn't just involve finding solutions to consumer problems; sometimes it involves a different type of matching of consumer problems and solutions. Many companies develop new technologies and then attempt to determine what consumer problems these technologies can solve. When the goal is truly innovative products and markets, being customer-led is not enough.[19] Kodak offers an example. The company searched explicitly for markets that combined its traditional competence in chemicals (film) and electronic imagining (copying). What emerged was an idea for a new kind of film and camera system. The result was the Advantix system.

www.kodak.com /global/en/ consumer/aps/ index.shtml

A decade or two ago we weren't asking for portable computers, cellular telephones, CD players, digital video disks, automatic tellers, Palm Pilots, or the Internet. Nevertheless, each of these products has been successful and solves important customer problems. To realize opportunities, companies like FreeMarkets or Excite have the imagination to envision markets that do not exist and to stake them out ahead of the competition. Similarly, NEC is pursuing a telephone that can interpret between callers speaking in different languages, and Motorola envisions a world in which telephone numbers are attached to people rather than places. The marketing imagination requires deep insight into the needs, lifestyles, and aspirations of today's and tomorrow's customers. Companies with marketing imagination are able to lead customers where they want to go before customers know it themselves. A few important guidelines to nurturing the marketing imagination are described in Good Practice 2.3.

In this chapter we discuss tools for segmenting markets and positioning products; in

1. **Escapes the tyranny of the served market.** The imaginative company views itself as a portfolio of core competencies rather than as a portfolio of products. It avoids overly narrow business charters.

2. **Searches for innovative product concepts.** The imaginative company (1) adds important new functions to well-known products (Yamaha's digital recording piano); (2) develops novel forms to deliver an important function (automated teller machines and electronic pocket calendars); and (3) delivers new functions through entirely new product concepts (camcorders and home fax machines).

3. **Overturns traditional price/performance assumptions.** The imaginative company challenges existing price/performance trade-offs. To do this means envisioning the possibility that the function of a $50,000 technology can be delivered with a $500 price tag (this is what happened with VCRs) and so on. Often it means distinguishing functions from the traditional product form used to deliver those functions.

4. **Gets out in front of customers.** The imaginative company goes beyond traditional modes of market research. These companies observe up close the world's most sophisticated and demanding customers. They work to anticipate consumers future problems. These companies develop marketers with technological imagination and technologists with marketing imagination.

Source: Gary Hamel and C. K. Prahalad (1991), "Corporate Imagination and Expeditionary Marketing," Harvard Business Review (July–August), 81–92.

Chapter 3 we discuss tools for learning about consumers. We will not be able to give you a marketing imagination, however. Standing at the top of a ski slope, it helps to have good boots, appropriate skis and poles, and good instruction. However, only dedicated practice, many mistakes, and good luck make for a successful run. Although companies such as GE, Shell, Microsoft, Nestlé, Toyota, and Procter & Gamble are among the largest and most successful in the world, each has experienced many failures. But they learned from their mistakes and tried again. This book will help you develop deeper insight into the lives of consumers, but only diligent attention to consumer behaviors around you will give you a marketing imagination.

From a consumer behavior standpoint, the core of marketing strategy concerns market segmentation, targeting, and product positioning. We discuss each of these in detail in the next several sections of this chapter, but throughout the book we will give many examples of how consumer behavior theory and research enable and improve marketing strategies.

Market Segmentation and Mass Customization

Market segmentation is based on a simple idea: in general, not everyone wants the same things. From this idea comes **market segmentation,** which is the *process of dividing a market into identifiable groups of similar consumers.* By similar, we mean groups that are alike in their responses to marketing mix tactics that an organization can effectively and profitably develop. The **marketing mix** refers to *those basic building blocks of marketing strategy—a product, its price, promotional communications, and its place of purchase and delivery.* A potential segment, for example, might consist of people who share the attribute "red hair." But this attribute only becomes relevant to marketers if, as consumers, the people with red hair exhibit purchase behavior or have consumption needs that are similar and, at the same time, differ from those of other groups, such as people with black and brown hair. As it turns out, several shampoo manufacturers, including L'Oréal, Paul Mitchell, and Aveda, market shampoos especially for red-haired consumers.

www.mtfca.com

Until the 1980s, many consumer products firms were content to make a few products for large mass markets. One of the earliest examples was Henry Ford's Model T auto produced from 1909 to 1927. For much of the twentieth century, marketers spoke of marketing to the "average" consumer. However, in the **Triad regions** (*North America, Europe, and the Asian Pacific Rim*) by the 1980s the satisfaction of basic needs and the glut of competitive goods and services led to market saturation. As a result, the process of market segmentation has now become increasingly complex as marketers identify more specialized market segments, such as consumers interested in Ford's limited-production, retro Thunderbird. National markets have fragmented into smaller, more demanding, and more market-wise consumer segments. If they are to meet these markets needs, global companies face the additional complexity of responding to the cultural differences that exist between international markets (see Chapters 4 and 5).

Soon market segmentation may give way to **mass customization,** which a growing number of manufacturers are adopting. *Customization means manufacturing a product or delivering a service in response to a particular customer's needs, and mass customization means doing it in a cost-effective way.*[20] Saturn, Toyota, and even jeans maker Levi Strauss and Co. are moving in this direction. Hallmark Cards and American Greetings installed electronic kiosks in stores and other public places to enable people to create their own greeting cards. However, these systems have not fully exploited the potential of mass customization—they offer no opportunities to customize graphics and don't learn and remember customer preferences.

With the growth of the Internet, mass customization is likely to be a significant force in the next few decades, as more companies try to cultivate **learning relationships** with their customers. *By learning about the customer during each exchange,* companies can more precisely tailor products and services to the particular needs of that customer. Thus, Amazon.com provides suggestions to repeat customers on the basis of their previous orders. In the short-run, market segmentation will remain the tool of choice for most consumer marketing organizations. In this section we focus primarily on market segmentation, but many of the same principles apply when mass customization is the goal.

To develop a competitive advantage for a product or service with specific market segments, the organization needs to ask what consumer variables may affect the success of a particular marketing strategy. Many of the chapters that follow identify these kinds of consumer variables. A firm achieves a competitive advantage when it is able to deliver a bundle of benefits or values that consumers perceive to be unique to the product. If this

Exhibit 2.3 The Market Segmentation Process

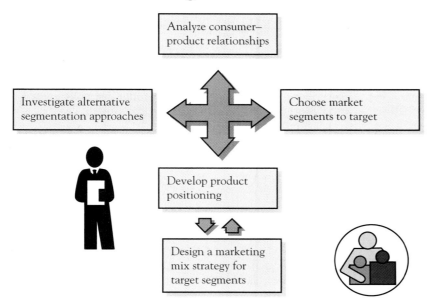

happens, the firm is in a position to benefit from repeated exchange relationships with product- or brand-loyal consumers, those who purchase the product repeatedly and feel positively about it. An approach to segmenting markets is illustrated in Exhibit 2.3. This process begins with a thorough investigation of consumer–product relationships.

Investigating Consumer–Product Relationships

From our perspective, the first step in developing a useful understanding of market segments is investigating consumer–product relationships. Throughout this chapter we have emphasized that marketing imagination, effective product differentiation, and market segmentation begin with a thorough understanding about consumer–product relationships for each phase of the circle of consumption. This involves answering a number of questions. Recall, Good Practice 2.1 identifies a series of questions managers can ask to capture the consumers' total experience and identify potentially unique ways to differentiate their products. In this section we discuss three questions about how consumers relate to particular products.

At the most general level, marketers need to ask, *What kind of environmental factors are involved in the purchase–consumption process for the product?* This question has many parts. What effect do macroeconomic factors have on product purchase and consumption? For example, in poorer countries with a low average income, companies may need to modify the product by selling in smaller quantities or reduce the price by developing more cost-effective production strategies. An economic downturn might inspire a firm to make its products more attractive by initiating creative credit policies for its products. Industry Insights 2.2 identifies an imaginative response to environmental factors in Germany.[21]

A second general sort of question marketers should ask is, *What does the product category mean to consumers and how involved are they in purchasing and consuming it?* This includes a wide range of questions such as, What sensory properties are associated with this product? What emotions are associated with the product? How does it relate to other consumption activities and products? How does it relate to the self and other people

Industry Insights 2.2

The automobile has long been revered as an emblem of freedom and prosperity in Germany; but the price of maintaining this cherished icon keeps rising. Germans pay some of the highest fuel prices in the world (more than $5 per gallon); they are also complaining about traffic congestion, accidents, and air pollution. In response, Bremen's public transportation system introduced a new approach to automobile use—car-sharing. A smart card provides access to 10 different car models available at 37 locations, and when the car is returned, a swipe of the card locks the car and records mileage for billing information. Rates are lower than for conventional car rentals: about $7 for a six-mile shopping trip and $85 for a two-day 120-mile excursion. There has been much interest in similar programs in other German cities and in other European countries sharing the Bremen context of high fuel prices, good public transit, and road congestion.

Source: Thomas T. Semon (2000), "Program Steers Germany in Right Direction," Marketing News, 8 May, 27.

important to the consumer? What images and memories are associated with the product? What risks are associated with the purchase and use of the product? and so on.

For example, if the product is children's favorite cartoon character, marketers need to understand how children relate to that character. What aspects of the child's imagination come into play? Does the character represent an important role model for children, and will they model their behavior after that of the cartoon character? To take another example, a program like the Bremen car-sharing system, described in Industry Insights 2.2, would be a difficult marketing challenge in the United States. Not having your own car is more inconvenient in the United States than in Europe; in addition, car use is much cheaper and the environmental movement, which supports the program in Europe, is far weaker in the United States. But most important, many U.S. citizens are emotionally involved with their cars.[22]

Frequently people use a product not because of its functional attributes but because of its meanings. Chapter 18 deals extensively with issues of product meaning. Snowboarding is an example of a sport that many youth take up and many adults avoid, in large part because of the lifestyle meanings associated with it, as Consumer Chronicles 2.1 illustrates. Procter & Gamble's introduction of disposable diapers in Japan, described in Consumer Chronicles 2.2, provides another example of the importance of product uses and meanings to purchase behaviors. Learning from its Japanese mistakes, P&G was more careful introducing disposable diapers in Korea, China, and elsewhere. It stuck to unisex white in these markets. In these countries sexism is very strong. Buying a pink diaper package like in the United States would make visible that the family has a less prestigious daughter instead of a more prestigious son.[23]

Another example concerns McDonald's in China. At the turn of the new century, McDonald's has become a favorite destination for children celebrating birthday parties. But birthday celebrations are themselves a recent innovation in China. Now many kids in China celebrate birthdays with McDonald's food and with "Auntie McDonald" playing hostess; it has become a preferred mode of consumption. Thus, the particular ways in which people consume McDonald's products are important to marketing strategy in Beijing. This example is useful since it also illustrates that marketers must often communicate not only with the end user of a product like a McDonald's Happy Meal but also with the purchaser, perhaps the child's grandparent, and possibly other decision makers, such as a child's parent or parents.[24]

It may sound strange to some readers to ask what kind of relationships consumers have with products and brands. After all we are talking about inanimate objects not people or pets. But people do develop complex relationships with some products and brands they use. Consumer Chronicles 2.3 summarizes some of the different types of relationships that people may form with products and brands.

At the extreme, some brands become the focus of **brand communities,** *groups of people who share a consciousness of a kind, share moral responsibility for other members, and perpetuate rituals and traditions associated with the brand.* Brand communities grow up around specific brands. They boost customer retention. For instance, Saturn owners are pretty loyal, even cultish. Thousands show up for the annual Saturn birthday party in Tennessee. And Saturn has been a leader in customer service and satisfaction, consistently ranked at the top of the J. D. Power and Associations sales satisfaction index. "Deadheads," followers of the rock group the Grateful Dead, and the 25,000 members of the Winnebago-Itasca (mobile homes or caravans) Travelers Group are other examples.[25]

A final question that marketers must ask about consumer–product relationships is, *What behaviors are involved in the purchase–consumption process for this product?* This includes questions such as, Where do they buy or use it? How do they buy or use it? How often and when do they buy or use it? The huge impact of Internet retailing on some categories of goods, especially those that can take digital form such as computer software, travel and event tickets, financial products, music, video, and books, illustrates the importance of these questions. Internet retailing may even kill off the traditional distribution channels for such products, although many Internet retailers have gotten hammered by failing to deliver on their advertising promises. On the other hand, websites are not much good for replicating the social function of shopping, nor for browsing around, nor for producing impulse purchases, all of which come from visiting a shopping center. Nor can e-commerce offer instant purchase gratification that many consumers expect. Traditional retailers will likely compete increasingly on these attributes.[26]

Consumer Chronicles 2.1

Snowboarding Is More than a Sport, It's a Lifestyle

Snowboarding, the in-your-face pastime of Generation Xers and their Gen Y younger siblings, is growing by 30 percent a year. One in 10 of those on ski slopes are shredders, slang for fans of the snowboard, essentially a skateboard for snow. The new sport has lots of lifestyle identification. That lifestyle is a blend of skateboarding, hip-hop fashion, and raucous youth, a combination that can be nerve-racking for typically older skiers, who often reluctantly share the slopes with snowboarders. Indeed, ski resort owner Alpine Meadow Inc. found that 87 percent of the Lake Tahoe–area and Utah skiers surveyed didn't want the daredevil shredders on their mountain.

Source: Irene Lacher (1994), "The Era of Fragments," Los Angeles Times (January 2nd), E4.

Investigation of Alternative Segmentation Approaches

An organization can segment a market in many ways. Although there is no best basis for segmenting a market, a firm must start somewhere. Usually segmentation of consumer markets is based on one or more of three basic criteria: consumer needs as related to (1) some geographic or demographic criteria, (2) psychographic variables, or (3) behavioral variables. The major segmentation variables for consumer markets are illustrated in

In the late 1970s, Procter & Gamble introduced Pampers diapers in Japan, the world's second-largest consumer market. At first, the efforts paid off, but at $50 a month they were expensive. More important, they were too bulky. Procter & Gamble had overlooked a critical culture difference. Japanese mothers change their babies' diapers about 14 times a day—more than twice as often as most Americans. They wanted a thin diaper that was easy to store and use. A Japanese manufacturer caught on, and its thinner disposable—the Moony—soon snared 23 percent of the market. A Procter & Gamble executive recalled, "It was clear that we were out of the ballgame."

Source: Alecia Swasy (1993), "Don't Sell Thick Diapers in Tokyo," The New York Times (October 3), F9.

Exhibit 2.4. Ultimately, the **segmentation bases** for a firm's customers are determined by continual refinement of market offerings as consumers respond to them through purchase and use.

Geographic segmentation *divides the market into different geographical units such as nations, states, regions, counties, cities, or neighborhoods.* Chapter 8 describes how lifestyle segments are often associated with geographic location. For example, the PRIZM system clusters U.S. consumers according to their zip code, socioeconomic status, and urbanization to derive 62 different kinds of neighborhoods.[27] Think about your own neighborhood. Are there certain products and services that could be targeted effectively to your entire neighborhood? In many parts of the world degree of urbanization is an important segmentation variable that influences what products are distributed, how they are distributed, and how they are priced and promoted—in other words, the full marketing mix. To see regional taste differences in action consider a simple food

Exhibit 2.4 Major Segmentation Bases

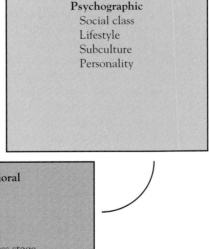

Geographic and Demographic		Psychographic
Region	Age	Social class
County size	Gender	Lifestyle
City or SMSA size	Family size	Subculture
Density	Family life cycle	Personality
Climate	Income	
	Occupation	
	Education	
	Religion	
	Ethnicity	

Behavioral
Occasions
Benefits
User status
Loyalty status
Buyer readiness stage
Attitude toward product

Relationship Form	Definition	Case Examples
Arranged marriages	Nonvoluntary union imposed by preferences of third party; intended for long-term exclusive commitment, although at low levels of affect	Adopting an ex-husband's preferred brands of cleansers or packaged foods
Casual friends, buddies	Friendship low in emotion and intimacy, characterized by infrequent engagement and few expectations for reward	Household cleaners
Best friendships	Voluntary union based on reciprocity principle; endures because of continued provision of voluntary rewards	Performance products like athletic equipment; personal products like soaps and moisturizers
Kinships	Nonvoluntary union with lineage ties	Brand preferences inherited from one's parents or grandparents
Flings	Short-term, time-bounded engagements of high emotional reward but devoid of commitment and reciprocity demands	Vacation of a "lifetime"; trial-size products; products bought on deal, e.g., a coupon
Enmities	Intensely involving relationship characterized by negative feelings and desire to avoid or inflict pain on the other	Partners' brands postdivorce or separation; recommended but rejected brands
Secret affairs	Highly emotive, privately held relationship considered risky if exposed to others	Treats of all kinds; racy lingerie

Source: Susan Fournier (1998), "Consumers and Their Brands: Developing Relationship Theory in Consumer Research," Journal of Consumer Research, 24 (March), 343–373.

such as soup. Industry Insights 2.3 illustrates differences in preferences for chicken noodle soup in different parts of the United States.[28]

Demographic segmentation consists of *dividing the market into groups on the basis of variables such as age, sex, income, occupation, education, religion, family size, family life cycle, and ethnicity.* Demographic variables are the most popular bases for distinguishing customer groups. Even when the target market is described in nondemographic terms (say, a lifestyle), a link to demographic variables is necessary in order to identify and reach the target segment. According to the U.S. government's 1990 census, America's demographic characteristics changed more rapidly in the 1980s than in any other decade of the twentieth century, and the rate of change was even greater than these statistics show

Industry Insights 2.3

Regional Preferences in Campbell's Chicken Noodle Soup Line

Detroit	Chicken Noodle with Mushrooms
Cincinnati	Red-and-white labeled Chicken Noodle
Seattle	Home Cookin' chicken with broad egg noodles
Milwaukee	Microwave Chicken Noodle
Baltimore	Healthy Request Chicken Noodle
Salt Lake City	Family Size Chicken Noodle
Denver	Chicken-flavor Ramen Noodle

Source: Ronald D. Michman and Edward M. Mazze (1998), The Food Industry Wars: Marketing Triumphs and Blunders, *Westport, Connecticut: Quorum Books.*

because of the undercounting of minorities.[29] A glance at the censuses of other countries, such as Australia, shows that learning to market to diverse population segments is crucial to the survival of firms around the world.

We can use the example of Campbell soup to illustrate the value of demographic segmentation.[30] Campbell Soup began making its first ready-to-serve soup in 1892, and today the company remains the U.S. market leader. Campbell has extended its reach worldwide, acquiring well-known brands in Great Britain, Japan, and other countries. Campbell's philosophy is to target markets locally. In the United States, Campbell has segmented on several demographic variables, including age (with products for the children's market and the aging baby boomer interested in low-fat, healthy alternatives); income (with upscale, premium brands marketed under the Pepperidge Farm name); and ethnicity (for example, selling spicy nacho-flavored cheese soup in California and Texas and using different promotional campaigns to reach Caribbean- and Mexican-Americans).

Psychographic segmentation divides buyers into *groups on the basis of differences in consumer lifestyle.* We can think of **lifestyle** broadly as *how people live; this includes their activities, interests, and opinions.* In some cases, researchers measure lifestyles in very broad terms by asking questions such as, Do you prefer to read a book or go to a party? For example, one market research group has segmented high-tech buyers into nine attitude categories, including cyber-snobs, media junkies, and sidelined citizens, the latter a technophobic group.[31] In other situations, lifestyles are measured in very specific terms. Kellogg's has been serving the health-conscious consumer market segment since the early 1900s and now has several distinct market subsegments, as illustrated in Industry Insights 2.4. Lifestyles are certainly related to demographics such as income, occupation, gender, family life cycle, ethnicity, and so on, but they also reflect a complex composite of a person's self and experiences. We talk more about psychographic segmentation in Chapter 8.

Increasingly, hybrid approaches that combine demographics, geographics, and psychographics are employed to segment markets more precisely. For example, using all three criteria, one recent study divided the Chinese market into four main segments, the nouveau riche (*baofahu*), yuppies (*dushi yapishi*), salary class (*gongxin jiceng*), and the working poor (*qiongiaogong*). Details about these groups can be found in Good Practice 2.4. Lifestyle orientations of these four segments hint at possible marketing opportunities. What ideas do you have?[32]

With **behavioral segmentation,** *buyers are divided into groups on the basis of differences in their knowledge, attitude, use, or response to a product.* Many marketers believe that behavioral variables offer the best starting point for identifying market segments. One powerful form of behavioral segmentation is benefit segmentation. **Benefit segmentation** divides buyers according to the *different benefits they seek from the product.* Behavioral segmentation is so important because segmentation only has value if it is related to consumer–product relationships. Perceived benefits of product consumption anchor such relationships.

Marketers have tried to explore what sorts of benefits are desired by different groups of consumers and which of these benefits leads to the greatest amount of consumer satisfaction (see Chapter 17). Benefits can take a variety of forms. For example, some derive benefits from the functions products perform. Others derive social benefits, for example, from anonymous disposition behaviors such as charitable giving to social service agencies. Still other consumers derive benefits from innovation, such as being the first to acquire a particular product or service. Some derive benefits from creative use of products that manufacturers did not intend, such as using carbonated water to remove wet spills from clothing or carpets. Others, as illustrated in the cartoon below, are like Calvin, the six-year-old comic strip hero

who won't eat any cereal that doesn't turn his milk purple. Not only do consumers derive different types of benefits from products in general, but also different consumers may derive different benefits from the same product. Suntan lotion, for example, may provide tanning, sun protection, moisturizing, or scenting benefits. Attention to benefit segmentation provides marketers with multiple positioning bases (see below) for their products.

Another kind of behavioral segmentation concerns how much of a product people use. Several different types of segmentation associated with product use are possible. Consider that for many products over three-quarters of the purchases are made by half of the customers. Often markets can be segmented into light, medium, and heavy user groups. This makes **usage rate segmentation,** *segmenting the market by amount of the product purchased or consumed,* valuable. For example, a recent study in Hong Kong segmented the green market into light and heavy green consumers. Heavy consumers enjoyed a higher education and a higher household income than light green consumers. Heavy green consumers reported that they liked to buy environmentally friendly products and that buying such products was considered good for their health and the environment and easy. Light users perceived that environmentally friendly products were difficult to obtain, were more

Segment/Attribute	Nouveau Riche	Yuppies	Salary Class	Working Poor
Size of segment	100,000	60 million	3,000 million	840 million
Geographics				
Residence place	Coastal urban areas	Major urban areas	Small cities	Small towns and rural areas, especially in the west of China
Demographics				
Household income	Above $5,000	$2,000–5,000	$1,000–1,999	Less than $1,000
Age	30–65	25–45	18–60	All age groups
Education	Various	College	High school	Elementary school
Occupation	Entrepreneurs, businesspeople, government officials, celebrities	Managerial, professional, technical	Office clerks, factory workers, teachers	Manual laborers, peasants, migrant workers
Psychographics				
Orientation	Optimistic	Hopeful	Status quo	Uncertain
Innovativeness	Innovators, trend setters	Early adopters, opinion leaders	Early majority, emulators	Late majority, laggards
Risk aversion	Low	Moderate	High	Very high
Readiness for foreign goods	High	Moderate	Low	Minimum
Lifesyles				
Mobility	Active	Mobile	Confined	Immobile
Activities	Wheel and deal, dine and wine in exclusive clubs; frequent shopping binges	Busy work schedule; frequent dining out and excursions	Trapped 8 to 5; limited disposable income; occasional outings; cameras and parks	Menial labor; hand-to-mouth; mass entertainment such as sports on TV

expensive, and did not have better quality. What strategies and marketing mix tactics would you use to reach these two groups of consumers?[33]

Another aspect of benefit segmentation relates to the occasions consumers associate with product use. Consumers reserve some purchases for particular occasions, wedding gifts, for example. They do not consider it appropriate to purchase them on other occasions. Americans like to purchase china and small appliances for weddings, whereas Nigeriens purchase beds and bedding, for example. And it is hard to imagine French consumers drinking the aperitif *pastis* at any time except the cocktail hour. In the United States the poultry industry has had a difficult time expanding sales of turkey because of its powerful symbolic associations with a particular occasion, Thanksgiving Day. Thus, **occasion segmentation** *divides buyers according to when they acquire or use a product.*

Occasion segmentation can help firms expand product usage. Frequently, an excellent way to increase demand is to get current consumers to use the product for more occasions. Numerous companies have promoted more usage occasions as a way to expand demand. In addition to the new uses promoted for Arm & Hammer baking soda and McIlhenny's Tabasco sauce discussed earlier in the chapter, a campaign by the Florida Orange Growers provides another example: "Orange Juice isn't just for breakfast anymore."

Another type of use segmentation focuses on **buyer readiness.** We discuss this in greater detail in Chapter 13. Buyer readiness refers to the fact that *at any time people are in different stages of willingness to buy a product.* For example, some people may be unaware of the product, others aware, some knowledgeable, some interested, and some intending to buy. The marketing program for new technological innovations, for example, will be dramatically affected by the relative numbers of people at different stages of readiness to buy. Notice that the Chinese market segments profiled in Good Practices 2.4 vary in their readiness to buy foreign goods.

Whichever segmentation criteria an organization chooses, four general rules of good segmentation can be identified. They are summarized in Good Practices 2.5. First, in selecting market segments, a firm should assess whether a segment is *measurable.* In other words, can the segment be clearly identified on the basis of measurable criteria? For example, we might like to know the number of Thai males ages 21–30, making between US$7,500 and US$15,000 annually, employed in the banking sector in Bangkok, the capital city of Thailand, to target for the sale of securities sold on the Hong Kong stock market. Good Practices 2.4 supplies measures of Chinese market segments.

A second important criterion is that of *substantiality.* Is the market segment large enough to warrant the expense of developing a market offering to meet its needs? In other words, does the segment exhibit adequate market potential? Revenues derived from exchanges with the segment must cover the costs of developing a differentiated market offering and provide the desired profits. Ideally a segment should be growing. For this reason, the over-55-year-old market in the Triad countries (North America, Europe, Japan) is becoming more significant to marketers than before. Likewise, the Chinese yuppie market profiled in Good Practice 2.4 is attractive because it is growing. Because of its growth, the Hispanic market has become attractive to mainstream marketers in North America. By contrast, niche marketers (see below) may be content with merely stable market segments with whom they can develop multiple, recurrent exchange relations. Above all, marketers should

Direct Mail in Japan

The avalanche of junk mail they receive on an almost daily basis has jaded U.S. consumers. As a result, many Americans don't even open this mail. By contrast, a Japanese is much more likely than an American to open the envelope and respond to the offer. A word for "junk mail" does not exist in the Japanese language. Although the number of Japanese consumers who shop by mail is currently quite small, these sales are growing at a rate of more than 20 percent per year. The Japanese are receptive to direct mail, making them accessible. However, Japanese are extremely resistant to having their names sold among list companies. This makes measurability of target segments more difficult. The sale of financial information about Japanese consumers is already restricted in Japan, and other legal restrictions on consumer listings are in the process of being formulated.

Source: Michael J. McDermott (1992), "Fishing for Customers" Profiles (November), 44–48.

avoid fickle segments. For this reason, while it might be perfectly feasible to develop a line of off-road in-line skates, or specialized surfboards for parachute surfing, there may not be adequate market potential to merit the costs of developing and marketing these items.

A third criterion for effective market segmentation is *accessibility*. Accessibility refers to the ability of an organization (1) to communicate with its customers and (2) to deliver products and services to its customers reliably. The ability to communicate relates to issues such as the existence of media that reach the market segment and the firm's skill at using that media.

Many factors affect accessibility. In the Triad countries, market and media fragmentation complicates accessibility. Some Hollywood studios, for example, are trying new strategies to communicate, such as showing prerelease screenings at conventions, providing sneak previews for online film critics, and even offering first-run films to college film studies courses, all to stimulate demand. Some groups are just hard to reach—college students, for example. Residential instability and constraints on media exposure due to studying are two of the factors that make them inaccessible. Media content significantly affects accessibility. Studies indicate that communication in the appropriate language and use of same language/same ethnicity spokespersons has a significant positive effect on attitudes toward commercial messages.[34] Media type also affects accessibility. Consumer Chronicles 2.4 reminds us that cultures vary in their responsiveness to particular media.[35] Until recently it has been difficult to communicate with the vast markets of east Asia due to the absence of television satellites. It is difficult to reach these markets because of high rates of illiteracy as well. Sound trucks remain popular advertising tools in such markets.[36]

The other component of accessibility is the ability to deliver goods and services reliably. Accessibility problems are sometimes self-inflicted. The 1999 holiday season was infamous for customer order fulfillment and distribution problems at new e-tailers like Toys "R" Us, Wal-Mart, and Etoys, for example. A variety of intrachannel barriers may keep firms away from potential markets. For example, many small firms cannot afford the slotting allowances charged by major retailers to place their products on the retailers' shelves. Sheer distances from point of production or geographic dispersal of the market are two geographic factors that may place some markets beyond an organization's reach. Limited production capacity may constrain a firm's ability to meet market demand, as happened in early 1990s to the manufacturers of Super Soakers water pistols. Finally, in international contexts, a variety of trade barriers erected by protectionist policies (currency controls, domestic content limits, size and labeling requirements, etc.) may make some markets inaccessible.[37]

The final criterion of effective market segmentation is *responsiveness.* A particular segment is likely to react differently than others to the elements of the marketing mix. For example, the Chinese nouveau riche profiled in Good Practice 2.4 are very responsive to Western market offerings. By contrast, the Chinese working poor—a large segment of 840 million—may not be very responsive to market offers because of low incomes. Similarly, in the Triad nations it is easy to identify working wives, and they can be accessed through specialized media and are a large percentage of the adult female population. However, working women's consumption behaviors do not differ dramatically from those of non-working women despite the problems of time constraints and overload they experience. Hence, they may not be as responsive to convenience-based appeals as some have thought. The mosquito-borne disease malaria provides a final, tragic example. Malaria kills millions of people each year in the tropics, but pharmaceutical companies have little incentive to develop a vaccine since most of the victims are poor and could not respond to a marketing campaign for it.[38]

Choosing Market Segments to Target

From a consumer behavior perspective, the next task in developing marketing strategy is selecting the most appropriate group or groups for the firm to serve. In choosing whom to serve, a firm may adopt three basic strategies. The first strategy is to *ignore differences between groups within a market and offer a single marketing mix to the entire market.* We refer to this strategic choice as mass or **undifferentiated marketing.**

"Who can afford *not* to moisturize?"

The cartoon of the elephant buying moisturizer suggests the logic of this approach; it applies when the product meets important needs of a large, responsive market. Classic examples include Ford's Model T automobile or the Hershey chocolate bar. Contemporary examples include the marketing of agricultural commodities such as soybeans or early versions of Internet portals like Yahoo and AOL. Until recently, most hospitals adopted undifferentiated marketing; each hospital tried to offer a full range of services to all the customers in a market area. Many state-owned consumer product firms in formerly socialist countries adopted such a strategy. Some firms offering new products and services find themselves adopting this approach if they do not precisely know the characteristics of their target market. Du Pont's Kevlar fiber was available for some years before it was adapted for specific uses such as in baseball bats, skis, and bulletproof vests.

Some benefits accrue to a firm using undifferentiated marketing, most notably cost economies in production and marketing. In the developed markets of the world, however, such an approach entails numerous disadvantages, including customer dissatisfaction and organizational vulnerability to competitors offering more differentiated products and services to market subsegments. Consumer dissatisfaction with the undifferentiated segmentation approach of state-owned firms in the former socialist countries was widespread.

A second strategic option available is to operate in several segments of the market and design separate marketing mixes for each segment. We refer to this as multisegment or **differentiated marketing.** A classic example is General Motors' old "price ladder." Younger, first-time buyers were directed to buy inexpensive Chevrolet models; older, repeat customers were urged to buy Oldsmobiles or Buicks; still older, wealthier repeat buyers could move up to a Cadillac. Contemporary examples include the strategies of Nike or Reebok, which seek to offer a perfect shoe for nearly every kind of active person participating in nearly every kind of activity and sport. The recent evolution of the diaper business has been in the direction of multisegment marketing, making differently sized and padded diapers available for children from newborns to age five and for boys and girls as well. Cisco Systems pursues a similar strategy in the business-to-business computer switching and networking market.

The multisegment option entails both benefits and costs for an organization. On the one hand, by creating special market mixes for each segment, the organization hopes to create more total sales, or in the case of nonprofits, to obtain more donations. On the other hand, multisegment marketing is likely to increase the research and development, production, and marketing costs incurred as a result of creating multiple marketing mixes. These costs make it crucial that firms carefully choose segments, using the criteria outlined above.

The final option available to an organization is to seek a large share of one or a few submarkets. We call this approach **concentrated** or **niche marketing.** The cartoon of Igor shopping for brains (p. 58) provides a humorous illustration of a peculiar niche-marketing strategy. There are many examples of successful niche-marketing strategies across a range of products and services. Celestial Seasonings offers a wide range of brewed, noncaffeinated beverages to the tea-drinking market; Bang & Olufsson offers a line of high-end stereo products to the audiophile; Goya foods in the northeast United States for many years has enjoyed more than 80 percent share of the Hispanic packaged foods market; Aston Martin targets its handmade automobiles toward the luxury car market; Orvis markets a line of specialty products to the advanced fly fisherman. Industry Insights 2.5 provides a dramatic business-to-business example in a transitional economy.[39]

Organizations that adopt a concentrated marketing strategy can enjoy a number of benefits. Among them are greater knowledge of their market segment's needs and wants, operating economies of scale, and increased loyalty from grateful customers. Some costs

With the collapse of the Soviet Union, the historic Polish shipyard Szczecin was plunged into financial crisis. Headed by a new management team installed in 1991, the shipyard embarked on a turnaround in three ways. First, to raise money, new management sold or gave away all but its core ship-building assets. Second, a new product strategy was chosen to more efficiently utilize the shipyard's capacity. Virtually all of the shipyard's capacity was moved to medium-sized container ships, resulting in a drastically shortened product-cycle time. Turnaround for a single ship was reduced from three years to 11 months. Finally, management began courting Western buyers. Two German firms placed a small order and received delivery six months earlier than they could have in Germany, and also realized 20 percent to 30 percent cost savings. Because these two firms were opinion leaders among German shippers (see Chapter 16), their order was quickly followed by a large number of other orders. By 1993, Szczecin had achieved a 40 percent world market share in its category.

Source: S. Johnson, D. Kotchev, and G. Loveman (1995), "How One Polish Shipyard Became a Market Competitor," Harvard Business Review, 73 (6), 53–72.

accompany this strategy too. The impact of product failure on the firm may be greater since risk is spread over fewer products; likewise, a loss of customer confidence might be difficult to mend. Perhaps more serious is the vulnerability to rapid and unpredicted changes in the segment's needs and wants. For example, Szczecin, featured in Industry Insights 2.5, was hardly prepared for the collapse of its assured Soviet ship market in 1990. Some firms in the Western aerospace defense business were likewise unprepared for the end of the Cold War and the abrupt decline in government arms procurement. Club Med struggled for a while when its "singles" vacation market changed to a family market. Further, a firm with a concentrated strategy may be vulnerable to competition from larger multisegment marketing firms that suddenly recognize opportunities in the niche market. In the United States, a number of cosmetics firms that operated in ethnic marketing niches now face competition from large firms such as Revlon.

In making the decision about what strategy to adopt, an organization's management needs to examine a number of questions. First, it must assess the skills and resources available to the organization. The more limited the skills and resources, the more likely undifferentiated strategies should be adopted. If only resources are lacking but the firm has good skills, as in the Szczecin case, concentrated strategies may be attractive. Second, the firm should assess market variability as suggested in the section on segmentation. If the market is not composed of identifiable, sizable, accessible, responsive segments, an undifferentiated strategy may be appropriate. Perhaps one size really does fit all. Alternatively, if many segments are identified, a differentiated or concentrated strategy is appropriate. A third, related issue is to ask, Just how variable is the product? For example, the market for bananas, mushrooms, or potatoes is relatively undifferentiated in the United States. Consumers perceive few differences between varieties. However, a firm marketing potatoes in Peru or Denmark, where numerous varieties of potato are grown, or mushrooms in France, where dozens of mushroom varieties are recognized, might be best advised to adopt a differentiated strategy. A fourth issue concerns the stage of the product life cycle. Typically, as in

Igor goes shopping.

the case of Internet portals like Yahoo, undifferentiated strategies may be used early in the product life cycle. Differentiated strategies become more common during the growth and maturity phases, and concentrated strategies may become fruitful during the maturity and decline phases. A nice example of this is the maintenance, repair, and operations supply company Richardson Electronics, whose motto is "on the trailing edge of [industrial] technology." Richardson specializes in providing outmoded electronic parts.

A final issue that a firm must evaluate in adopting a segmentation strategy is its competitors' strategies. Although we noted above that bananas are a relatively undifferentiated product in U.S. markets, Chiquita has sought to differentiate its product from other bananas on quality and image. In so doing it follows the lead of Sunkist, which successfully differentiated its brands of oranges from other nonbranded varieties. The costs of inattention to competitors' strategies can be great. In the United States, canvas shoe companies such as Keds and Converse that failed to adopt the multisegment strategies of Reebok and Nike experienced a drop in market share, and only recently have they fought back by adopting niche-marketing strategies.

Niche Marketer: Celestial Seasonings positions a wide variety of caffeine-free beverages to appeal to the tea-drinking market.

Product Positioning

Product positioning means *deciding how the organization wants the company and its brands to be perceived and evaluated by target markets.* In general, product positioning requires an organization to differentiate its market offerings from those of its competitors. However, it's not enough for the firm to distinguish its market offerings, it must do so in ways that are meaningful to its target market segments. For example, if the company has identified a profitable segment of skiers who are especially annoyed with the mechanics of skiing—getting their skis to and from the airport, from their car to the ski lift, picking up their lift tickets, and so forth—it might decide to offer a differentiated ski area. The key question is, What changes in what characteristics will clearly differentiate this ski area from competitors and communicate "ease of skiing" to the target skier segment? Deer Valley, located next to Park City, about half an hour from Salt Lake City, Utah, appeals to this segment of skiers with "valet ski service" and other amenities that make skiing more hassle free. Bear Hollow, another Utah ski area just north of Park City, caters to athletes in training and "weekend warriors" who want to experience the rush of ski jumping. Recreational ski jumping is a unique option not offered at most ski resorts.[40]

Firms seeking to enter their brands in another country's market may face large expenditures to build brand awareness and a positive brand image. Often, new market entrants use a particular kind of co-branding called a **brand alliance** to position brands. A brand alliance amounts to *renting a brand name known to target consumers from another*

Exhibit 2.5 Perceptual Map for Processed Meats

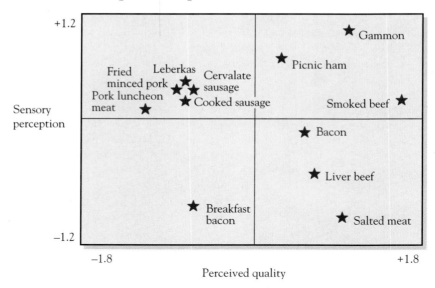

Source: Jan Benedict, E. M. Steenkamp, Hans C. M. Van Trijp, and Jos M. F. Ten Berge (1994), "Perceptual Mapping Based on Idiosyncratic Sets of Attributes," Journal of Market Research, 31 (February), 15–27. Photos supplied by the Dutch Commodity Board for Livestock and Meat.

firm. Fuji–Xerox, Northwest–KLM, and British Air–USAir are examples of international brand alliances. Montana-grown barley gets increased visibility through a brand alliance with Budweiser beer. Experiments with Japanese and U.S. consumers have shown that consumer evaluations of an unknown brand from another country become more positive when a brand alliance is used to position the product. Brand alliances also increase consumers' evaluations of the brand's parent firm.[41]

To effectively position products and services for a target segment, an organization often begins by identifying competitors. Competitors are identified as those companies that offer similar benefits to the target consumers. The organization then undertakes research to determine how consumers perceive and evaluate the competitors. This step provides the organization with information about how competitors are positioned in the market. By analyzing consumers' preferences, the company can determine a profitable, differentiated position for their product or service. For example, Lee brand jeans positioned its product as offering "best fit" for women. Competitor Levi Strauss offered "Levi's for Women," using an ad campaign featuring drawings of graceful female forms by women artists. Both firms seek to differentiate their product from traditional jeans made for men. Consumer research can then be used to monitor the organization's success in attaining or maintaining that position in the market. Levi's has sought to further differentiate itself from competitors by setting up in-store kiosks where customers order custom-fit jeans that are home delivered in 48 hours.

One technique often used to position products and services is **perceptual mapping.** A perceptual map is *a spatial picture of how consumers view products or brands within a market.* Exhibit 2.5 illustrates a perceptual map of 12 processed meats (ham, salami, etc.). A nationwide sample of female consumers in the Netherlands was polled to produce this map in a study that employed color photographs of 12 types of processed meat.[42] It is important to note that the set of competitive products is culturally based. The same study conducted in a different culture would include a different set of processed meats. In the study the two most important dimensions distinguishing perceptions of processed meat were those labeled *perceived quality* and *sensory perception.* The specific technique used to construct this map allowed consumers to describe and rate the different types of processed meat in their own terminology. The consumers then grouped together attributes, or descriptions, using statistical criteria. Characteristics of the meats that grouped together and represented perceived quality included not exclusive versus exclusive; cheap versus expensive; not pure meat versus pure meat; fat versus lean; bad for figure versus not bad for figure; and unwholesome versus wholesome. Characteristics that grouped together and represented sensory perception included bad taste versus good taste; tough versus tender; and fit for guests versus not fit for guests. The perceptual map shows that cooked sausage and fried minced pork are viewed as very similar on both perceived quality and sensory perception; thus, on these two important dimensions, they are substitutes for each other. Gammon rates highest on sensory perception and salted meat lowest, but both gammon and salted meat rate similarly on perceived quality. By combining the map with information about consumer preferences, a manufacturer could assess a desirable position for new processed meat products. For example, if enough consumers prefer high quality and high sensory ratings, a new processed meat could be positioned at the high end of the market using the usual tools of marketing communication.

Designing a Market Mix Strategy

Once management knows how it wants the company's product to be perceived and evaluated by consumers, it must then design a market mix strategy to accomplish that. This includes developing tactics for communicating the position of the product to target consumers. Many elements of the marketing mix associated with the product—its distribution, promotion, and price—communicate positioning to the customer. Consider, for example, two products marketed by the same company and based on the same chemical innovation.[43] L'Oréal markets both Niosome and Plenitude face cream to fight wrinkles. Niosome face cream is sold in exclusive, upscale beauty shops. Plenitude sells for one-sixth as much in supermarkets and discount stores. L'Oréal is one of the world's largest cosmetics companies because of its ability to span both the luxury market with brands such as Lancôme and Helena Rubinstein, and the mass market with Elsève and L'Oréal. L'Oréal first launches innovations as luxury products and then simplifies them and then relaunches the innovations under different brand names for the mass market. Niosome and Plenitude are distinguished by marketing mix tactics: their product formulation, packaging, advertising, media placement, distribution, and price.

Often a company will attempt to *change its image and position* in the market. This is accomplished by changing the marketing mix. Many bricks-and-mortar businesses, such as UK retailer Tesco and global retailer Wal-Mart, are currently trying to reengineer themselves as clicks-and-bricks businesses by developing a strong web presence. Fast-food retailer Burger King is following a more conventional repositioning strategy in an effort to regain its quality image. First it's remodeling its retail outlets. It also added a new spokesperson to its promotional effort, actress Kathleen Turner, to appeal to adults. It is reinforcing its movie-licensing program that gives it a boost with kids, through such items

Consumer Chronicles 2.5

In his guide, *Le Pieton a Paris,* Leon-Paul Fargue described the quintessential French café, with its long zinc bar and little round tables under gaily colored parasols spilling out over the pavement, as "the most solid of the institutions." That was 60 years ago. Now, if the experts are to be believed, the traditional corner café, the bistro (from the Russian word for quickly), the brasserie—call it what you will—is threatened with extinction.

In 1960, when France had 46 million people, there were reputed to be over 200,000 café-brasseries (defined as places with a license to sell alcohol on the premises as well as serving simple meals). Today, in a France of 58 million, only 50,000 remain, and even they are disappearing at a rate of around 3,000 a year. In Paris alone, more than 1,500 cafés closed last year, bringing the total down to half what it was in 1980.

There are several reasons for these closings. First, Parisians have no time to go to cafés. They are always in theirs cars. Cars and TV killed the café. Second, people can't find what they're looking for in a café. Surveys show that ambience is the first thing people look for when they go to a café. Third, we used to say cafés were *salon de pauvres,* the living room of poor people who had no heat. Today, everybody has central heat and air conditioning. A sharp rise in property prices in the 1980s put many struggling cafés into the hands of property developers. Alcohol consumption has fallen from an average of 18 liters of pure alcohol per person per year in 1960 to around 11 liters today (and the government, in an effort to discourage alcoholism, has introduced tax incentives to encourage cafés to give up their alcohol licenses). Desertification of the countryside has led to the closure of the traditional village café. And, finally, it costs a lot to go for lunch at the café in town. So people prefer to go to a fast-food restaurant like McDonald's, which arrived in France 25 years ago and has replaced the café for young people. With its 353 McDonald's fast-food restaurants, France ranks sixth among the 79 countries where the fast-food chain has outlets.

Source: Mark Seal, "Paris' Cafe Revolution," American Way, *July 15, 1993, pp. 40–43; Anonymous, "Mais Où Sont Les Cafés D'antan?"* The Economist, *June 10, 1995, http://www.economist.com/tfs/aarchive_tframeset.html.*

as Pokémon merchandise, and it has new menu items as well. In a different product category, retailer Ann Taylor went through a complete overhaul in the early 1990s.[44] In the 1980s the company was known for its tailored business suits and pants. Then workplaces grew less formal and women wanted more choice. Ann Taylor evolved to meet their needs. In 1992 a big-selling item became Ann Taylor jeans costing only $30. Similarly, Abercrombie and Fitch recently went from being a stuffy, conservative high-end clothing retailer to a lower-end fashion-forward youth marketer by changing its product line, pricing, retail formats, and so on.

It is difficult to *maintain a position in the market.* Constant monitoring and innovation are required simply to stay in the same place. Fast-food franchiser Burger King's repositioning effort comes because it lost its point of differentiation when McDonald's remodeled its kitchens to handle made-to-order food, long Burger King's single greatest advantage in the burger wars. A final example of how changing tastes and competitive conditions alter the position of products within a market is offered by the dramatic decline of the French café. Some 4,500 traditional cafés close each year, dwindling in France from 200,000 in 1960 to less than 70,000 today. Some of the reasons for this decline are described in Consumer Chronicles 2.5.

Marketing strategy concerns the actions managers take to improve the likelihood marketplace exchanges that meet firm and customer goals will occur. In general, customer-oriented marketing strategies improve the value customers derive from products or decrease the costs of products to customers. Firms may adopt any of four general strategic positions: prospector, analyzer, defender, and reactor. More specific strategies include differentiation, market penetration, and cost leadership.

One of the most critical skills for a successful business is to empathize with and gain insights from customers. A customer focus is the central element of this market orientation. A market orientation is not solely the responsibility of a marketing department, however; it requires the concerted action of everyone in the organization. Profitability is generally a consequence of a market orientation, but certain kinds of environmental conditions may make this orientation more or less important to overall business performance.

The connection between understanding consumers and designing effective marketing strategies requires creativity and imagination. Marketing intelligence attempts to find out what problems consumers are trying to solve, and marketing imagination offers solutions. But beyond the traditional modes of market research, marketing imagination requires deep insight into the needs, lifestyles, and aspirations of the customers of today and tomorrow.

Market segmentation, targeting, and positioning are central elements of marketing strategies. The process of market segmentation begins with a thorough investigation of consumer–product relationships. This investigation includes examining environmental factors involved in the purchase–consumption process for the product; what the product means to consumers and how involved they are in purchasing and consuming it; and the behaviors involved in the purchase–consumption process for the product. Then, an organization can investigate alternative market segmentation approaches. Geographic or demographic criteria, psychographic variables, and behavioral variables are bases for identifying market segments. Whichever segmentation approach an organization chooses, four general criteria of good segmentation are measurability, substantiality, accessibility, and responsiveness. After investigating alternative segmentation approaches, managers must select the most appropriate group or groups for the firm to serve. They can use undifferentiated marketing, differentiated marketing, or concentrated or niche marketing as the basis for choosing the segment or segments.

Next, the firm's managers must decide on product positioning: how they would like the company and its brands to be perceived and evaluated by target markets. One general technique that's often used to position products and services is perceptual mapping. Once they know how they want the company and its products to be perceived and evaluated by consumers, managers must design a market mix strategy to achieve or maintain the position. Everything associated with the product—its distribution, promotion, and price—communicates the position of the product to the customer. By managing the market mix, companies can establish, change, or maintain desired product positions.

1. Identify a firm in your community that you feel is highly customer oriented. Make a list of the firm's activities or behaviors that illustrate its market orientation. You might include tools the firm uses to sense the market.

2. Identify the marketing strategies adopted by some familiar consumer goods companies in terms of whether they resemble prospectors, analyzers, defenders, or reactors.

3. Suppose that the McIlhenny Company has discovered that its market can be segmented into light and heavy users of Tabasco sauce, with the smaller heavy-user group accounting for 75 percent of sales. What strategies and marketing mix tactics would you use to reach these two groups of consumers? (*Hint:* consider market penetration and market development strategies.)

4. Use the dimensions of perceived quality and sensory perception identified in the example perceptual map. Construct your own perceptual map using a selection of six processed meats that you know. If your perceptions were representative, what would be the managerial implications?

5. How could benefit segmentation be used to develop marketing strategy for the following?

      a. Health clubs   d. Ice cream
      b. Bath soaps   e. Education
      c. Cosmetics   f. Bicycles

6. Using cars as a product category, investigate different segmentation approaches (e.g., geographic and demographic; psychographic; and behavioral). Provide illustrations of different brands and models that segment the market using these different bases.

7. Review a popular commercial magazine and record the content of a series of print ads. Try to identify the positioning bases of the products featured in the ads.

8. Visit a local shopping district, such as a main street or mall. Go from store to store and observe the customers. Make a detailed composite portrait of the customers at each store using as many criteria as possible. Then, name the market segment you have described.

You Make the Call
Royal Caribbean Cruises

The cruise industry represents the most exciting growth category in the entire leisure market. The cruise industry is commonly divided into three segments: luxury, premium, and volume. The volume segment has per diem rates of less than $300 and last seven nights or less. Target customers for the volume segment are normally first-time cruise passengers.

Carnival targets the volume market with its Carnival Fun Ship line. These customers include mostly younger, less affluent passengers and families with children. These customers typically take land resort vacations. The Carnival line is the standard by which all lower-priced cruise lines are measured. Carnival is known to deliver all that it promises: Activities and entertainment are nonstop; the food is plentiful; and the cabins are comfortable. According to Bob Dickinson, CEO of Carnival, "If you tell people you are the Fun Ships you are going to attract people disposed to having fun." Everything about Carnival—the brand name, ship names like "Mardi Gras" and "Fantasy"—connotes fun. Many younger customers see the type of crowd Carnival attracts as a significant factor in their decision. While traditional cruise advertising has promoted ports of call, Carnival hypes the ships, where vacationers spend 80 percent of the time during a cruise. The product strategy has been centered on structuring fun ship tours into inexpensive, easy-to-book packages for the masses.

Royal Caribbean focuses on superior service to differentiate it from the other major competitors for first-time cruisers. However, consumers do not always perceive the higher quality and service to be worth Royal Caribbean's higher price, as evidenced by the lower number of first-time cruisers on the line relative to Carnival. (The actual difference in average price is quite small, $209 compared to $187 per night.) Consumers see Royal as being similar to Carnival but slightly more sophisticated and professional and less energetic. Royal appears to pursue an undifferentiated strategy targeting different markets with essentially one product. The strategy is to offer a quality product, with multiple activities and destinations at a reasonable price. Royal sees itself marketing to the lower-premium market and the upper-end of the volume market. The image one gets is that the service is likely to be very good, but the product a passenger gets in terms of atmosphere, types of people, and activities is somewhat unclear. Further, the company lacks a strong, consistent message such as Carnival's "Fun Ships" slogan.

Although both Carnival and Royal Caribbean continue to enjoy strong growth and profitability, Royal Caribbean seems to be losing ground to Carnival, especially in the volume market. Their appeal as a provider of high-quality cruise vacations seems to be losing out to Carnival's "fun" concept.

1. What should Royal Carribbean do?
2. Outline some steps Royal Caribbean can take to decide whether and how to target the volume segment of the cruise market.

This case was adapted from student reports and Eileen Ogintz, "Ignore Children's Needs and Risk Minor Mutiny," Los Angeles Times, September 13, 1992, Travel Section; Shirley Slater and Harry Basch, "The Right Ship For You," Los Angeles Times, September 8, 1991, Travel Section; Shirley Slater and Harry Basch, "Short Sailings Making a Big Impact," Los Angeles Times, September 27, 1992, Travel Section; Shirley Slater and Harry Basch, "Ship Builds Up for Caribbean Duty," Los Angeles Times, November 10, 1991, Travel Section.

1. "Shopping around the Web: A Survey of Ecommerce," *The Economist* 26 (February 2000); Charles W. L. Hill, *International Business* (Burr Ridge, IL: Irwin/McGraw-Hill, 2000), p. 380; Kathleen Schmidt, "Outlook 2000: Globalization," *Marketing News* 17 (January 2000), p. 9; Ellen Neuborne, "E-Tail: Gleaming Storefronts with Nothing Inside," *Business Week,* May 1, 2000, pp. 94, 98; and Mohanbir Sawhney and Steven Kaplan, "Let's Get Vertical," *Business 2.0,* September 1999, www.business2.com. The estimates on adult Internet access for 1997 and 1998 are from Mediamark Research Inc. and estimates on children use of the Internet are from the Federal Trade Commission.
2. Robert D. Hof, David Welch, Michael Arndt, Amy Barrett, and Stephen Baker, "E-Malls for Business," *Business Week,* March 13, 2000, pp. 32–34; Jeffrey F. Rayport and John J. Sviokla, "Managing in the Marketspace" *Harvard Business Review,* November–December 1994, pp. 141–50; Shawn Tully, "The *B2B* Tool That Really *Is* Changing the World," *Fortune,* March 20, 2000, pp. 132–45; and David Welch, "Oh, What a Feeling: *B2B,*" *Business Week,* May 15, 2000, p. 14.
3. R. Miles and C. Snow, *Organizational Strategy, Structure and Process* (New York: McGraw-Hill, 1978); and William G. Zikmund and Michael D'Amico, *Marketing,* 5th ed. (Minneapolis/St. Paul: West Publishing Co., 1993).
4. This section draws heavily from Ajay K. Kohli and Bernard J. Jaworski, "Market Orientation: The Construct, Research Propositions, and Managerial Implications," *Journal of Marketing* 54 (April 1990), pp. 1–18.
5. Francis J. Gouillart and Frederick D. Sturdivant, "Spend a Day in the Life of Your Customers," *Harvard Business Review,* January–February 1994, pp. 116–27.
6. David W. Cravens, Gordon Greenley, Nigel F. Piercy, and Stanley F. Slater, "Mapping the Path to Market Leadership," *Marketing Management* 7 (October 1998), pp. 29–39; and Emily Thornton, Larry Armstrong, and Kathleen Kerwin, "Toyota Unbound," *Business Week,* May 1, 2000, pp. 142–46.
7. Bryan A. Lukas and O. C. Ferrell, "The Effect of Market Orientation on Product Innovation," *Journal of the Academy of Marketing Science* 28 (Spring 2000), pp. 239–47.
8. This discussion and Good Practice 3.1 are adapted from Ian C. MacMillan and Rita Gunther McGrath, "Discovering New Points of Differentiation," *Harvard Business Review,* May–June 1997, pp. 133–45; and "Shopping around the Web," p. 33.
9. Michael W. Peng, *Business Strategies in Transition Economies* (Thousand Oaks, CA: Sage Publications, 2000); and C. K. Prahalad and K. Lieberthal, "The End of Corporate Imperialism," *Harvard Business Review* 76, no. 4 (1998), pp. 68–79.
10. Gouillart and Sturdivant, "Spend a Day in the Life of Your Customers."
11. Lisa Bannon, "Mattel Plans to Double Sales Abroad," *The Wall Street Journal,* February 11, 1998, pp. A1, A8.
12. Charles W. L. Hill, *International Business,* 3rd ed. (Burr Ridge, IL: Irwin/McGraw-Hill, 2000); Christian Homburg, John P. Workman, Jr., and Harley Krohmer, "Marketing's Influence within the

Firm," *Journal of Marketing* 63 (April 1999), pp. 1–18; Nathalie Laidler and John Quelch, "Gallo Rice," Case No. 9-593-018, Harvard Business School Publishing, Boston, 1993; Peng, *Business Strategies in Transition Economies;* and Prahalad and Lieberthal, "The End of Corporate Imperialism."

13. Peng, *Business Strategies in Transition Economies,* pp. 220–21.

14. A detailed list of education and community programs is offered on the Pacific Symphony Orchestra user-friendly website at www.ocartsnet.org.

15. Theodore Levitt, *The Marketing Imagination* (New York: Free Press, 1983).

16. Catherine Arnst, "Developments to Watch," *Business Week,* December 1, 1997, p. 119; "Up-Front," *Business Week,* December 15, 1997, p. 8; "The Road from Damascus," *The Economist,* August 15, 1998, p. 57; Michael Hoechsmann, *Benetton Culture: Marketing Difference to the New Global Consumer* (Thousand Oaks, CA: Sage Publications, 1997); and "Cell Phones Transform Bangladesh," *Lincoln Journal Star,* February 23, 2000, p. 7A.

17. Bennett Daviss, "The Subtle and Not-So-Subtle New Science of Advertising and Marketing," *Ambassador,* April 2000, pp. 18–20; and Gouillart and Sturdivant, "Spend a Day in the Life of Your Customers," pp. 123–24.

18. This section draws from Gary Hamel and C. K. Prahalad, "Corporate Imagination and Expeditionary Marketing," *Harvard Business Review,* July–August, 1991, pp. 81–92.

19. B. Joseph Pine II, Don Peppers, and Martha Rogers, "Do You Want to Keep Your Customers Forever?" *Harvard Business Review,* March–April, 1995, pp. 103–14.

20. Thomas T. Semon, "Program Steers Germany in Right Direction," *Marketing News,* May 8, 2000, p. 27.

21. Semon, "Program Steers Germany in Right Direction."

22. Irene Lacher, "The Era of Fragments," *Los Angeles Times,* January 2, 1994, p. E4; and Alecia Swasy, "Don't Sell Thick Diapers in Tokyo," *New York Times,* October 3, 1993, p. F9.

23. Ynuxiang Yan, "McDonald's in Beijing: The Localization of Americana," in *Golden Arches East,* James L. Watson, ed. (Stanford: Stanford University Press, 1997), pp. 77–109.

24. Rebecca G. Adams and Robert Sardiello, eds., *Deadhead Social Science* (Walnut Creek, CA: Altamira Press, 2000); Susan Fournier, "Consumers and Their Brands: Developing Relationship Theory in Consumer Research," *Journal of Consumer Research* 24 (March 1998), pp. 343–73; Albert Muniz, Jr., and Thomas O'Guinn, "Brand Community," working paper, University of Illinois, Department of Advertising, 1999; Kendra Parker, "Customer Retention: The Next Big Thing," *American Demographics,* January 2000, pp. 38–39; and John Schouten and James McAlexander, "Brandfests," in *Servicescapes,* John F. Sherry, Jr., ed. (Homewood, IL: NTC Publications, 1998), pp. 377–402.

25. "Shopping around the Web," pp. 11–12; and Ellen Neuborne, "Sites Not Worth Seeing," *Business Week e.biz,* May 15, 2000, p. EB16.

26. Michael J. Weiss, *The Clustering of America* (New York: Harper and Row, 1988).

27. Ronald D. Michman and Edward M. Mazze, *The Food Industry Wars: Marketing Triumphs and Blunders* (Westport, CT: Quorum Books, 1998).

28. Marlene L. Rossman, *Multicultural Marketing: Selling to a Diverse America* (New York: American Management Association, 1994).

29. Michman and Mazze, *The Food Industry Wars.*

30. Priscila A. LaBarbera and Zeynep Gurhan, "The Role of Materialism, Religiosity, and Demographics in Subjective Well-Being," *Psychology and Marketing* 14 (January 1997), pp. 71–97; Forrester Research, Inc., "Why Consumers Buy," *The Forrester Report,* December 1996; Paul C. Judge, "Are Tech Buyers Different?" *Business Week,* January 26, 1998, pp. 64–66.

31. Geng Cui, "Segmenting China's Consumer Market: A Hybrid Approach," *Journal of International Consumer Marketing* 11, no. 1 (1999), pp. 55–76; and Dexter Roberts, "China's Wealth Gap," *Business Week,* May 15, 2000, pp. 172–80.

32. Kara Chan, "Market Segmentation of Green Consumers in Hong Kong," *Journal of International Consumer Marketing* 12, no. 2 (1999), pp. 7–24.

33. Ronald Grover, "Come See My Movie—Please!" *Business Week,* May 8, 2000, pp. 153–54.

34. Michael J. McDermott, "Fishing for Customers," *Profiles,* November 1992, pp. 44–48.

35. Rohit Deshpandé and Douglas Stayman, "A Tale of Two Cities: Distinctiveness Theory and Advertising Effectiveness," *Journal of Marketing Research* 31 (February 1994), pp. 57–64

36. "Shopping around the Web," pp. 27–29; Hill, *International Business,* pp. 296–97; and Neuborne, "E-Tail."

37. Linda L. Price, Lawrence F. Feick, and Audrey Guskey-Federouch, "Couponing Behavior of the Market Maven: Profile of a Super Couponer," in *Advances in Consumer Research,* vol. 15, Michael J. Houston, ed. (Provo, UT: Association for Consumer Research, 1989), pp. 354–59; and Michael A. Reilly, "Working Wives and Convenience Consumption," *Journal of Consumer Research* 8 (March 1982), pp. 407–18.

38. S. Johnson, D. Kotchev, and G. Loveman, "How One Polish Shipyard Became a Market Competitor," *Harvard Business Review* 73, no. 6 (1995), pp. 53–72.

39. Kurt Repanshek, "White Gold: Utah's Invaluable Ski Industry," *Utah Business,* January–February 1994, p. 38.

40. Kevin E. Voss and Patriya Tansuhaj, "A Consumer Perspective on Foreign Market Entry: Building Brands through Brand Alliances," *Journal of International Consumer Marketing* 11, no. 2 (1999), pp. 39–58.

41. Jan Benedict, E. M. Steenkamp, Hans C. M. Van Trijp, and Jos M. F. Ten Berge, "Perceptual Mapping Based on Idiosyncratic Sets of Attributes," *Journal of Marketing Research* 31 (February 1994), pp. 15–27. Photos supplied by the Dutch Commodity Board for Livestock and Meat.

42. "L'Oréal Aiming at High and Low Markets," *Fortune,* March 22, 1993, p. 89.

43. "Ann Retaylored," *Business Week,* May 17, 1993, p. 70.

44. Aixa M. Pascual, "The Whopper Plays Catch-Up," *Business Week,* May 15, 2000, pp. 98, 100; and Mark Seal, "Paris' Cafe Revolution," *American Way,* July 15, 1993, pp. 40–43.

Learning Objectives

After completing this chapter, you should be able to:

- Describe the basics of consumer research and have an understanding of available consumer behavior research techniques.

- Explain the complexities in doing international consumer research.

- Outline the steps in the research process.

- Describe generally how to ask consumers questions.

- Identify some of the changes the Internet brings to consumer behavior research and some of the problems of evaluating secondary research.

- Appreciate the ethical issues raised by market research.

Chapter 3

Learning about Consumers

Adventure Travel

Check out www.gorptravel.gorp.com for adventure travel the world over, spanning Africa, Antarctica, Asia, and the Caribbean. A trip summary for Kahikatea, New Zealand, features a photo of white-water river rafting and promises eight days of adventure with upscale accommodations for the entire trip. And you can be back in your office on Monday morning. Or perhaps you'd prefer to sea kayak in Belize or take a white-water river expedition in Alaska with Adrift Adventures. To see what you are missing check out www.adrift.com. Adventure travel, including commercial white-water river rafting, is a fast-growing outdoor leisure services industry; commercial rafting trips are booked in many nations from Canada to Zimbabwe.

www.gorptravel.gorp.com

www.adrift.com

Our example focuses on Colorado and Utah, where many small firms operate on a half-dozen rivers and provide half-day to multiday trips to thousands of clients every year. The managers of a group of Colorado River Basin outfitters wanted to know how to increase consumer satisfaction and repeat business for their multiday river trips. They wanted to make their business more predictable. We conducted applied consumer research with several river-outfitting companies to help answer questions of interest to managers. Depth interviews with management and river-rafting guides suggested the hypothesis that customer satisfaction is related to concerns with the quality of food and amenities provided, safety, and lore about the natural and historical setting of the trips. We then collected written descriptions of river rafting from experienced rafters. Through content analysis of these descriptions, we found that rafters rarely mentioned food, safety, or information. Instead they spoke of exhilaration, personal growth, and growing closer to family and friends through their rafting experiences.

Next, we undertook participant observation research with rafters. That is, we accompanied participants on a number of multiday river trips to explore the experience of rafting and the meaning of rafting to customers. In addition, we conducted posttrip focus groups, and we sent mail surveys to customers both before and after their river trips. Our research revealed that participants had difficulty expressing what was really important to their satisfaction. It included experiencing personal growth, a sense of harmony with nature, and community with family, friends, and other participants. Management was only vaguely aware of these benefits to customers because their perception of what customers wanted was primarily based on pretrip inquiries rather than posttrip memories and reminiscences.

Our research showed that river guides are critical in orchestrating customer satisfaction, but customers hardly ever mention the guides' role. We, as researchers, didn't know why. We undertook surveys, focus groups, and further participant observation to describe more adequately the guides' role in orchestrating customer satisfaction. Because of the duration, intimacy, and purpose of the trips (fun, fantasy, and adventure), effective river guides became like friends to customers over the course of the trip. When things went well, customers were satisfied with the guides; but when things went badly they tended to blame the weather or other external factors rather than guides. The role of temporary friend is one that guides find stressful, management vaguely understands, and customers take for granted. These findings helped reorient some outfitters' training and promotional efforts.

Articles written about river rafting in specialized marketing journals contribute to basic consumer research. These articles increase marketers' general understanding of extended service encounters, through the long-term relationships between guides and customers. This research exposes the types of experiences that customers seek in leisure consumption contexts, and it also highlights the behaviors of frontline personnel in communicating expectations, values, and meanings to customers. In turn, our understanding of these concepts can be linked to a more general theory about relationships in social life.[1]

Overview

Learning about consumers is the key to implementing the marketing concept and exercising marketing imagination. The aim of this chapter is to introduce you to consumer research. Consumer research is not the only way we learn about consumers, but it is certainly one of the most important ways. **Consumer behavior research** is *the systematic and objective process of gathering, recording, and analyzing data for aid in understanding and predicting consumer thoughts, feelings, and behaviors.* With the globalization of markets, consumer research has assumed a truly international character, and this trend is likely to continue. At the simplest level, international consumer research involves studies in a single market outside the firm's domestic market. More elaborate and complex are international consumer research programs that are intended to help solve multicountry marketing problems. We will discuss examples of each type in this chapter.

The opening vignette mentions several kinds of research as well as several techniques for conducting it. We discuss these issues in more detail in this chapter. The value of consumer research can be measured by its contribution to solving practical problems or by advancing our general understanding of human behavior. The practical problems addressed by consumer behavior research range widely from those of organizations seeking to increase their customers' purchase frequency (see Chapter 12) to those of advocacy organizations seeking to enlist increased support from their constituents. It could even include research on disadvantaged consumers designed to promote changes in society or changes in the marketplace. Public policymakers also use consumer behavior research (e.g., to study how to enhance healthy or life-saving behaviors).

Consumer Research in the Twenty-First Century

This chapter illustrates the dramatically changing role of consumer behavior research in marketing. At no time has it been truer that there is nothing so useful as good theory, as marketing research professionals and marketers struggle to make sense of and use consumer behavior research effectively. Random sampling (introduced in the 1940s) and telephone interviewing (introduced in the 1970s) revolutionized consumer research during the twentieth century. The consumer researcher of the twenty-first century will be affected by four important factors: speed, the Internet, globalization, and data overload.[2] Compared to their predecessors, today's consumer researchers will need to be better trained, work smarter and faster, and have more varied skills.

Speed

Speed is becoming increasingly necessary to provide consumer insight more rapidly. Many technologies and services have speeded up delivery of information. Big companies such as Ford Motor Company used to spend several years researching and developing a new product. Now they attempt to shorten the length of time between the idea for a new product and the introduction of that product to the market. In addition, they attempt to better gauge not just what consumers say they want but how consumers actually use the product. The importance of observing use was brought home when Ford unsuccessfully introduced Fiesta into Thailand in the 1970s. Thai vehicles are regularly overloaded two to three times beyond their designed capacity, and so the Fiesta had frequent breakdowns. A sturdier model was introduced, but too late, and Ford incurred heavy losses.[3] Market research companies increasingly emphasize speed, combined with international research capabilities. The two ads shown on page 74 illustrate how the need for smarter, faster, more global marketing decisions is effecting market research promotion and practice.

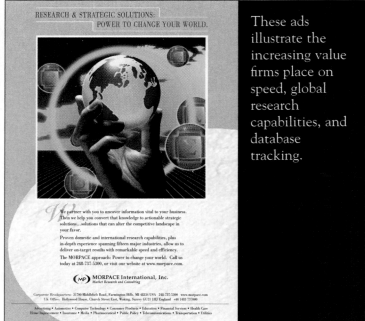

These ads illustrate the increasing value firms place on speed, global research capabilities, and database tracking.

The Internet

Consumers and professionals increasingly have access to the Internet. This represents a new data collection tool that consumer researchers must master to stay competitive. The unprecedented speed and low cost make greater use inevitable. Sotheby's site on the World Wide Web is typical. It posted a questionnaire to encourage visitors to give personal information and their tastes and opinions. Responses can help the art auction gallery modify its website to suit the needs of potential clients. In addition, the site provides a list of all the Sotheby's galleries around the world.

A 1999 study located and analyzed nearly 1,000 web surveys. Included were customer feedback questionnaires, various public opinion polls, university experiments, customer preference surveys, and other types of surveys. While we can't foresee the future of Internet survey technologies, experts see a lot of potential for use and for abuse. Prominent online marketing research firms predict that, based on current growth rates, the online research segment could account for 50 percent of all marketing research revenue. However, researchers' enthusiasm for the medium is lessened by their concerns for protecting respondent privacy and other potential misuses of the technology.[4] Experts fear oversurveying of users with quickly constructed and poorly implemented questionnaires targeted to whoever wants to answer; such data could be incorrectly interpreted as representing some broader population.[5]

Globalization

Globalization of business is so profound that it has been described as the second Industrial Revolution. Globalization demands that consumer researchers have experience and knowledge about individual countries and international conditions. Researchers must have the ability to synthesize data from different countries and interpret the factors on which they are based. Meaningful synthesis and comparison demands not just proficiency in statisti-

Exhibit 3.1 ESOMAR

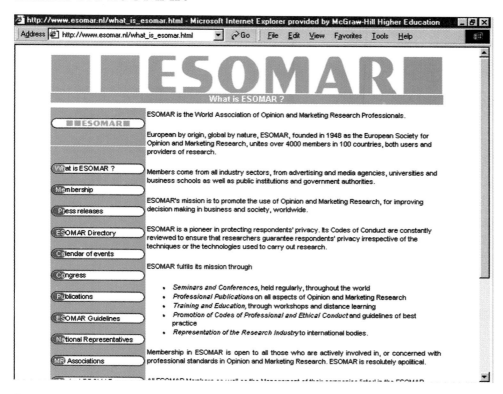

cal methods and languages but insights into cultural differences. Increasingly, international researchers understand that multicountry research requires comparability of meanings and not just comparable questions.[6]

Globalization and the Internet are dramatically changing the face of consumer research. Things move at lightening speed, and this in turn brings a sense of heightened vulnerability. Issues can spread rapidly across borders. A local mistake translates into a global blunder nearly instantly.[7] Globalization and the Internet have combined to create increased interest in standardizing both technical and ethical research procedures and reporting. For example, Canada, the United States, and Mexico are working to standardize how they report basic industry and demographic data. This is partially a response to NAFTA, but it also reflects marketers' needs to formulate strategy on a global basis. **ESOMAR** is the *World Association of Opinion and Marketing Research Professionals.* Exhibit 3.1 displays the screen produced by ESOMAR in the spring of 2000. This association unifies more than 4,000 members in 100 countries and provides information about global research practices. For example, it reports a 10 percent global increase in market research between 1997 and 1998, about US$13.4 billion. Expenditures on market research respond to economic crises. This relationship is evidenced in a 9 percent decline in market research in Japan, which faced a difficult economic situation in 1998. ESOMAR members comply with a code of ethics endorsed by major national professional bodies around the world. To examine some of its recent press releases, check out the organization's website. In 2000, ESOMAR was concerned with setting

www.esomar.nl

guidelines for conducting marketing and opinion research using the Internet. A version of the guidelines, shown in Good Practice 3.1, has been endorsed by the International Chamber of Commerce and the World Federation of Advertisers. But check the website for updates, because this is an area that is changing daily.

Data Overload

Data overload is a reality for both consumers and professionals. Historically, managers faced the problem of insufficient information. Much has changed with the information revolution that has been driven by dramatic developments in computer and telecommunications technology, including the Internet. Now, the managers' problem has shifted because huge amounts of information are readily available to organizations, even to small ones. While some may struggle with collecting information in transitional and developing economies, most organizations are more concerned with the dissemination and effective use of information within their organizations.

A **database** is a *collection of data and information describing items of interest.*[8] **Data mining,** which essentially involves *"fishing" in large data sets using statistical concepts to glean useful information,* is not new. However, the extremely large datasets too cumbersome for traditional analyses are new. Extracting useful information from large databases is quickly becoming the next wave for consumer researchers to ride. Organizations need people who can make sense of data results. In addition, with enormous records and potentially useful information, miniscule errors can involve millions of cases. Data integrity, storage, and cleaning become critical. Decision makers must consider the purpose and objective of a data-mining project, implementation and integration problems, the type of data-mining tools available, what form the output should take, and ease of use.

In addition, they must have a specific plan for integrating data mining into everyday business operations.

Learning about Consumers

Successful companies try to gauge consumers in many different ways. The Coca-Cola Company uses a three-pronged approach to gather information from customers and potential customers in all the countries in which it operates. Trend research seeks to understand broad societal and cultural factors that influence customer behavior. Traditional market research seeks to track real-time purchase and consumption behaviors. Under this approach researchers predict sales and utilize sophisticated mathematical modeling techniques. Finally, research is employed to predict customer responses to changes in the marketing mix for Coca-Cola products. All of the products of this research are available to marketing managers through the company's user-friendly intranet information system.

Some manufacturing companies go to great lengths to encourage information exchange between nonmarketing employees and customers. To cite one example, a manufacturer holds an annual open house for which manufacturing, not marketing, personnel hand delivers invitations to customers. Customers interact with shop floor personnel as well as white-collar employees. The president of this company notes that this impresses on manufacturing personnel that there are people who buy the product—"real, live-bodied, walking-around people."[9]

As another illustration of the range of ways to learn about consumers, consider Japanese companies. Many Japanese companies rely heavily on personal observation as a way of learning about customers. For example, when Canon Cameras was losing ground to Minolta, Canon sent three managers to the United States to look into the problem. The head of the team, Tatehiro Tsuruta, spent six weeks in the United States entering camera stores and acting like a customer. He noted how the cameras were displayed and how the clerks served customers. He realized that some dealers were not enthusiastic about Canon and drugstores and other discount outlets were not advantageous outlets. As a result of this research, Canon opened its own sales subsidiary.[10]

Finally, consider the strategy of a Weyerhaeuser sawmill for learning about customers. This sawmill was located far from company headquarters in the small community of Cottage Grove, Oregon. A cross section of employees, from the general manager to forklift drivers, began spending a week at a time as "employees" of their customers. For example, customer service representatives worked as sales assistants in Home Depot and other home centers. Buyers soon found that they were dealing with personnel who not only understood their problems but also frequently anticipated them because Weyerhaeuser employees were actively learning about them.[11]

Although there are many different ways of learning about consumers, the focus of our attention is on describing different types of consumer research. As we have noted, consumer research is increasingly an international enterprise. It is only natural that where marketing strategy is conceived on a multinational basis, consumer research would follow suit. Based on expenditures, about 40 percent of all marketing research is conducted in western Europe, 39 percent in the United States, 9 percent in Japan, and the rest in transitional economies or the developing world. There are more than 1,500 market research companies and consulting agencies in Europe. ACNielsen Corp. is ranked as the number one global research organization, based on revenues. Although ACNielsen is based in the United States, nearly 78 percent of its revenues come from other countries. We can expect the share of research conducted outside of Europe, Japan, and the United States to increase dramatically in the new millennium.

International consumer research includes two different kinds of research. First, it includes **single-country consumer research**—*research carried out in a country other than that of the research-commissioning organization.* For example, if a company is considering entering a new foreign market, it might conduct extensive research to understand foreign consumers as related to that product. In this case, the company is not necessarily trying to make comparisons between foreign consumers and other consumers of that product. Second, international consumer research includes **multicountry research**—*research conducted in more than one country with the intent of making comparisons.* For example, a company might be interested in contrasting health attitudes in Russia with those in the United States. International consumer research presents challenges that arise out of political, legal, economic, social, and cultural differences between nations. These national and cultural differences also contribute to problems of comparability of research results, especially in multicountry studies.

We distinguish two different types of consumer research. Both basic and applied consumer research can be conducted in domestic, foreign, or multicultural contexts. **Basic consumer research** attempts to *expand the limits of knowledge about consumers.* It is not concerned with the solution to any particular pragmatic problem. For example, an anthropologist may undertake research to try and understand the physical properties, symbolic meanings, and practical qualities of things, such as those that create a sense of homeyness for North Americans or *hyuggli* (coziness) for Danes.[12] Such research contributes to an understanding of broad issues of interest to many social sciences—issues of self, family, meaning, and material culture. This research reveals that homeyness is not a simple sum of material parts but an intangible, illusive quality. However, homeyness does have several physical properties. For example, homey colors are warm colors: orange, gold, green, and brown. Objects are homey when they have a personal significance for the owner. Arrangements are homey when they combine diverse styles of furnishing in a single room. A favorite characterization of a homey place is a description that emphasizes that it looks "as though someone lived there." Hyuggli environments share some of these qualities, but in addition they feature warm pools of light such as those provided by candles or low-powered spotlights.

Applied consumer research is conducted *when a decision must be made about a specific real-life problem.* Although the homeyness study was a basic research project, the results may have many useful applications. For example, some resort areas have found that people take better care of a homey condominium than a stark rental unit. By leaving pictures and personal touches around the rental unit and welcoming people to their "home," owners of these units are able to minimize theft and unnecessary wear. Suppose that managers of a small specialty retail store are interested in creating a homey or hyuggli feeling to reach a particular segment of North Americans or Danes. They may find many of the basic research results we described useful in beginning applied consumer research to develop a homey retail environment.

The Research Process

Whether consumer researchers are doing basic or applied research in domestic or foreign cultures, they engage in a research process to ensure that the consumer intelligence or understanding gained from the effort is relevant, timely, efficient, accurate, and ethical. The research is considered **relevant** if it *anticipates the kinds of information that will be required by decision makers, scientists, or policy advocates.* This is information that improves the quality of exchanges between organizations and their customers or stakeholders. **Timely** research is *completed in time to influence decisions.* Research is **efficient** when it is of *the best quality for the minimum expenditure and the study is appropriate to the research context.* Research is considered **accurate,** or valid, when *the interpretation can account for both consistencies and inconsistencies in the data.* An important way to improve accuracy is to incorporate multiple methods and perspectives in the research effort as both Colgate-Palmolive and The Coca-Cola Company do, for example. Finally, careful attention to the research process can ensure that it is **ethical,** that it *promotes trust, exercises care, observes standards, and protects the rights of all the participants in the research process.*[13] We discuss research ethics in greater detail later in this chapter.

A general outline of the research process is shown in Exhibit 3.2. The research process begins by defining the problem and scope of the project. Very often it will require numerous conversations with decision makers, experts, and consumers before the problem can be precisely defined. In the rafting research discussed in the vignette, for example, we would have misunderstood the nature of customer satisfaction, and indeed measured the wrong things, if we had relied solely on the impressions of the river outfitters. An especially important part of problem definition is clarifying the boundaries of the study. For example, we set out to study consumer behavior as it related to white-water river rafting in the United States; we quickly learned that such rafting in the eastern part of the country differs substantially from that in the west. After some preliminary research on both one-day trips and multiday rafting trips, we learned that these two types of trips have very different characteristics and attract different segments. We ended up focusing on multiday (mostly three- to five-day trips) white-water river-rafting trips in the Colorado River Basin.

Defining the Problem and Project Scope

Exhibit 3.2 Outline of the Research Process

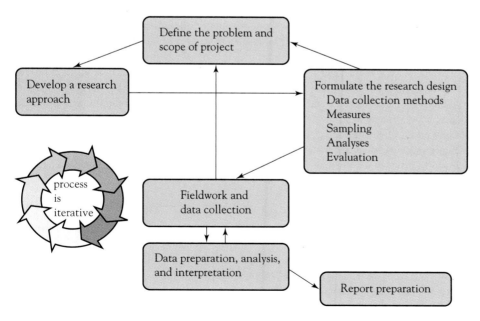

Subsequently, in discussing this research in Europe we discovered that there are important differences in the meanings of nature and wilderness between the North American and European contexts that further limit the generalizability of our results.[14]

The Research Approach

The second step of the process shown in Exhibit 3.2 involves development of a research approach to the problem. This involves deciding on what types of research are implied by the research objective. We can outline three basic types of research: exploratory (such as the basic research described above), descriptive, and causal. The three types of research have complementary roles; that is, each can contribute something to the overall research process.

Causal research *investigates a very specific relationship between two or more variables.* To take a very simple example of causal research, a firm might like to know if coupons mailed to prospective customers result in an increase in sales subsequent to the mailing. In other words, do coupons cause increased sales? Measuring retail sales before and after the mailing provides the answer. To take a more complex example of causal research, a researcher might be interested in whether female college students exposed to highly attractive models in ads will be less satisfied with their own physical attractiveness. To answer this question, the researcher might conduct an experiment that exposes female college students to different kinds of advertising models, some of whom are very attractive, and then measures the students' satisfaction with their own attractiveness.[15]

After finding that highly attractive models in ads do make women feel less satisfied with their own appearance, the researcher might be interested in finding out more about the thoughts and feelings that lead consumers to report less satisfaction with their own appearance. In this case, as in the participant observation rafting research described in the opening vignette, the research approach is exploratory. **Exploratory research** *seeks insights into the general nature of the problem, possible decision alternatives, or identification of relevant variables.* In this case, the research is attempting to identify the thoughts and feelings associated with exposure to attractive models in ads. The researcher does not know what variables or relationships between variables will be identified. The researcher conducts a focus group in which female college students first look at ads taken from fashion magazines featuring highly attractive models. Then, the students are asked to write their thoughts and reactions to the ads on a blank piece of paper. Finally, they discuss them as a focus group. The thoughts and feelings shared in this session offer a more textured understanding of the types of comparisons that occur. For example, this research suggests women tend to focus on that part of the model's body that they are most dissatisfied with. One woman noted, "I have wide hips. I always look at the hips. I guess I'm just jealous." This type of discussion can also give a richer understanding of the intensity of feelings associated with these comparisons. Consumer Chronicles 3.1 illustrates selected negative self-feelings from viewing ads that came out of the focus groups. Researchers could also undertake a study to profile the characteristics of women most likely to make negative self-assessments following exposure to highly attractive models. This type of study would be **descriptive research**—*research designed to profile some aspect of the consumer environment.*

The Research Design

The third step in the research process is to formulate the research design. A **research design** is *a framework or blueprint for conducting the marketing research project.* It includes deciding on the appropriate data collection method or methods. It also reports decisions about how to translate the research problem into specific measures (specific questions, observations, and stimuli), decisions about the sampling plan, decisions about how to analyze the data, and a critical evaluation of what the payoff from the research is likely to be. Many critical decisions are made in formulating the research design. Often the research design will be revised as data collection proceeds, according to changing needs and understandings. For example, in international consumer research the unit of analysis may shift from a country to a region as the researcher gains greater insight into consumers. Consider Belgium, which is divided in half between Wallonia in the south and Flanders in the north. Walloons use butter, but Flemish people use margarine. As preliminary investigation uncovers regional differences, additional research might be modified to better represent these regions.

Data collection methods can be divided into secondary and primary data collection approaches, and then each of these approaches can be further divided into several additional types. In this chapter we just provide an overview of some of the major approaches used to learn about consumers. Exhibit 3.3 outlines some secondary data collection approaches, including some examples, uses, and advantages and disadvantages. **Secondary data** are *data that have already been collected for purposes other than the problem at hand.* These data can be located quickly, easily, and inexpensively, and they should represent the starting point for any data collection effort. Because secondary data have been collected for purposes other than the problem at hand, they may lack accuracy, relevancy, or currency.

Secondary data are especially important in the case of international consumer research because primary international research projects can be very costly in terms of time and money. H.J. Heinz Company failed to successfully introduce Ketchup in Brazil. A more intensive look at the Brazilian food distribution system through secondary research might have helped avert this problem. Heinz concentrated on distributing through neighborhood shops, a strategy that worked well in Mexico. However, 75 percent of grocery shopping in São Paulo, Brazil, is done in supermarkets and not the smaller shops.[16] Many countries offer extensive data about their populations through departments of commerce. Much of this information can be obtained online, and because of the importance of foreign trade, many national commerce departments offer links to trade data relevant to other countries.

The United States Department of Commerce provides access to fast-breaking results related to trade and the economy. Five minutes after economic indicators are released by other federal agencies they can be accessed through the Department of Commerce. If you are trying to learn something about the United States a good place to start is www.fedstats.gov. This site has links to 70 federal agencies that issue statistical data, and the site's search engine covers reports from the 14 major statistical agencies.[17] Many standard market research texts offer in-depth descriptions on how to access and use U.S. Census data. A quick online search such as "census Australia" will turn up the Australian Bureau of Statistics and provide access to a wealth of information about Australians, much

 www.fedstats.gov

Selected Focus Group Comments: Negative Self-Feelings from Viewing Ads

Consumer Chronicles 3.1

"You look at these ads and you feel inadequate, like you can't measure up."

"It's frustrating when you start to realize you should look that way—I mean—I can't."

"I used to go through these magazines every day and look at [models in the ads] and wish I looked like them. I used to go running every day, and I really thought maybe I could look like them. I remember, I even picked one model in particular and cut out ads with her in them. I was pretty obsessed. And I finally realized this wasn't realistic. But I sometimes still look and think, 'Well, maybe.'"

"Sometimes [ads with models] can make you feel a little depressed."

"They make me feel self-critical" [participant viewing models in swimsuit ads].

Source: Marsha Richins, "Social Comparison and the Idealized Images of Advertising," *Journal of Consumer Research* 18 (June 1991), p. 75.

Exhibit 3.3 Secondary Data Collection Methods

Types	Examples	Uses	Pluses and Minuses
Scanner data	An "intelligent" terminal records the bar code on a product. Consumer panels are recruited to track purchase patterns and link to consumer profiles.	Scanners cover more and more product groups. Penetration is highest in the United States and Canada, but there is adequate scanner penetration in most European countries.	Large database that provides detailed information about consumer purchases; actual behavior. Often purchases can't be tied back to buyer, and in other cases buyers may not be very representative of general population. Links between retail outlets are not typically available.
Syndicated data sources	Global Scan provides detailed brand and category information on more than 1,000 products. Research International provides continuous panel data for 40 countries in the world. The ESOMAR website provides information on sources of syndicated data in various countries.	Syndicated data are collected for a set of information users with a common need. Scanner data, consumer panels, store audits, television viewer audits, and so on are examples of syndicated data.	The researcher must identify syndicated data sources for the country of interest. Subscription is expensive and data collection categories may not be relevant; quality is highly sensitive to sampling quality. Lots of information is available on a real-time basis.
Databases	National Trade Data Bank maintained by the U.S. Department of Commerce. World Atlas and World Development Report maintained by World Bank. Census of the Population from the U.S. Bureau of the Census.	There are thousands of sources of information that may be relevant to business decisions.	Many developing countries have data that are outdated or inaccurate. May be impossible to compare data collected from different countries. Very inexpensive and more accessible due to the Internet.
Internet	The PRIZM website provides extensive demographic and media use information organized by zip codes in the United States.	Information for research can be obtained at the company level, industry level, or macro level. Access to the information can be received directly by using the Internet address, but search engines and agents can also help obtain the information.	The Internet has only a limited number of search tools and does not provide extensive user support; information is not well structured; and quality of information is highly variable. The Internet is very low cost and offers information on a broad spectrum of topics.

of it in the form of reports to be purchased. The same is true for many other developed countries. Of course, secondary data are collected in different formats in different countries and are in some cases not comparable. Using secondary data for multicountry research can be challenging if not impossible.

Exhibit 3.4 outlines some primary data collection approaches, again including examples, uses, advantages, and disadvantages. **Primary data collection** is *research carried out for a specific purpose*. Management decisions may seem in many cases as if they rely on pure instinct. Primary data collection can help managers counterbalance these intuitions, monitor consequences, and review and refine a course of action. Of course, as compared

Exhibit 3.4 Primary Data Collection Methods: Qualitative Techniques

Types	Examples	Uses	Pluses and Minuses
Depth interviews	A consumer tells a trained interviewer how she feels about a trip to the dentist.	Detailed probing of the respondent. Discussion of confidential, sensitive, or embarrassing topics. Situations where strong social norms exist and the respondent may be easily swayed by group. Detailed understanding of complicated behavior. Situations in which the product consumption experience is sensory in nature, affecting mood states and emotions.	Excellent method for understanding consumer motivation and the **why** of behavior.
	Consumer stories reveal the meanings they assign to "homemade" food and holiday meals.		Time-consuming and costly, difficult to interpret. Should be used to identify the range of beliefs, attitudes, and behaviors on a particular topic, but not the frequency or prevalence of those beliefs. Requires interviewing and interpretation skills; opportunities of interviewer bias.
Focus groups	A group of French consumers describe their image and use of herbal teas for a Chinese tea manufacturer.	Understanding consumers' perceptions, preferences, and behavior concerning a product category; generating new ideas about products or impressions of new product concepts; developing creative ideas for marketing programs or preliminary consumer reaction to marketing programs.	Great opportunities for group synergies that result in unique insights.
	Focus groups with Japanese consumers reveal perceptions, preferences, and behavior regarding laundry detergent.		In international settings, the researcher must understand cultural traits and adapt process accordingly. Requires interviewing and interpretation skills; opportunities of interviewer bias.
Projective techniques	Word associations are used to help American marketers better understand Japanese consumers' perceptions of foreign countries.	Encourages respondents to project underlying motivations, beliefs, attitudes, or feelings through use of unstructured, indirect forms of questioning. Projective techniques should be used when the required information can't be accurately obtained through direct methods.	Requires highly trained interviewers and skilled interpreters. Tends to be expensive. Analysis and interpretation are difficult and subjective. There is risk of interpretation bias.
	Consumers, asked if their neighbor fears flying, are able to discuss more openly reasons for fearing flying than when asked if they themselves fear flying.		Establishing the equivalence of meaning across cultures is especially difficult in the case of projective techniques and their use in international research should be carefully considered. Can elicit responses that consumers would be unable or unwilling to give if they knew the true purpose of the study.
Ethnography	Intense observation combined with consumer interviews and consumer diaries are used to learn how U.S. consumers purchase beef.	Ethnographic research is especially useful for showing companies how consumers purchase and use products in their everyday lives. This technique was developed in anthropology, but it is becoming increasingly popular in market research. It can be used in new-product development, product promotion, and understanding competitive market structure from the consumers' perspective.	The diversity of the global marketplace and increasing demands for customization contribute to much greater interest in ethnographic studies. Such studies can offer rich insights into consumer meaning and use behavior.
	Interviews and participant observation are used to better understand an experience such as white-water river rafting.		Ethnographic research requires very special training, and typically requires apprenticing with someone well-trained in this methodology. The research is very time-consuming and intensive, and data interpretation is difficult.
	Mechanical observation (using video cameras) combined with consumer interviews is used to learn how consumers, especially children, use microwave ovens.		
	Observation and consumer interviews are used to learn how Mexican women purchase and use laundry cleaning products.		

to secondary data collection, primary data collection is difficult, expensive, and time-consuming. Exhibit 3.4 overviews some qualitative techniques: **depth interviews, focus groups, projective techniques,** and **ethnography. Qualitative techniques** *provide insights and understanding of a problem or topic* rather than trying to quantify the data and apply some form of statistical analysis. Most accomplished researchers treat qualitative and quantitative data as complementary input into understanding and predicting consumers. Qualitative research typically relies on a small sample and should not be used to infer a population distribution. Analysis and interpretation of qualitative data are particularly challenging, requiring skills of categorization, abstraction, comparison, integration, and so on.[18] Qualitative techniques are gaining in popularity as consumer researchers attempt to stay in touch with global diversity and the demand for customization.[19] Successful international consumer research is highly dependent on qualitative research.

Observation, survey research, and experiments are other very important primary data collection techniques. They are overviewed in Exhibit 3.5. **Observational techniques** *record actual behavior* (e.g., consumers eating spaghetti) *or traces of actual behavior* (e.g., an audit of spaghetti sauces, noodles, and so on in the consumer's pantry). Observation may yield either qualitative or quantitative data. For example, an observer may simply count the number of cars crossing an intersection as input on a decision about whether to locate a minimart at that location. This observation would yield quantitative data. Alternatively, an observer could record all relevant aspects of children playing with new toys, including their emotional responses, how long they played with the toys, what they did with them, and so on. For each child this could render a unique, detailed, qualitative account of his or her interaction with the toys.

Survey research is probably the most popular way of collecting primary data. Surveys are usually *conducted with the help of questionnaires, and question and responses are typically structured.* There are a number of ways surveys can be administered, including via face-to-face interviews, telephone, mail, fax, e-mail, and the Internet. The survey method has several advantages. Questionnaires are simple to administer, and coding, analysis, and statistical interpretation are relatively simple. However, wording questions properly is not easy, and respondents may be unable or unwilling to provide the desired information. It is very important for the survey instrument to be applicable in a given country and in a given situation. The researcher must be culturally sensitive. For example, respondents in many Asian countries provide responses they think will please the interviewer; Japanese people consider telephone surveys impolite; Middle Eastern respondents tend to exaggerate class, income, and position; Latin Americans are touchy about alcoholism; and Indians consider sex a taboo topic.[20]

Experiments are based on the principle of *manipulating one or more variables (termed independent variables) and observing changes in some other variable or variables (dependent variables).* So, for example, a company might test consumer preference toward two different packages, or three different promotional appeals, or a set of price and package size combinations. Experiments are especially useful for doing causal research, but they are extremely difficult to implement meaningfully in multicountry studies. All experiments must balance the need for precision with the need to make the experiment meaningful for the decision at hand.

Fieldwork and Data Collection

The fourth step in the research process is fieldwork or data collection employing some or all of the techniques outlined in Exhibits 3.4 and 3.5. Many researchers agree there is no substitute for doing a portion of the fieldwork or data collection themselves. This is particularly true of data collection techniques that require enormous skill and flexibility, such

Exhibit 3.5 Other Primary Data Collection Methods

Types	Examples	Uses	Pluses and Minuses
Observation	Ford Motor Company invites guests to test drive prototype models through a predetermined route. A trained observer rides along, making notes on the driver's reaction to the car. Content analysis is used to compare the information content in American and Japanese magazine advertising. A trained researcher participates with other consumers in a Harley-Davidson Brandfest to learn more about the behaviors and activities associated with these events.	Observational techniques can range from direct or even mechanical observation of particular consumption behaviors to observation of the natural "residue" of consumption behaviors (e.g., consumer's garbage). It is useful for learning what consumers do and can provide new ideas for product development, product complements, and substitutes.	Certain types of behavioral data can only be collected through observation. Observation, used alone, cannot determine underlying motives, beliefs, attitudes, and preferences. Observation can be difficult and time-consuming and in some cases may be unethical. The researcher's observations may be selective and biased.
Survey research	Interviewers are stationed at the entrance to a shopping mall in Toronto, Canada, to invite respondents to answer a questionnaire about snack-food preferences. Telephone interviews are conducted with members of a small art theater located in Lincoln, Nebraska, to profile members and learn more about their film and theater preferences. Busy German executives are first contacted by phone and then e-mailed a brief questionnaire to e-mail or fax back. The questionnaire is used to measure market potential for a U.S. software company's products.	Personal interviewing is the most flexible method of survey research and used most frequently in international consumer surveys. Telephone interviews are dependent on the quality of lines and also telephone etiquette, and these vary considerably between countries. Mail surveys depend on the availability of mailing list and literacy levels, which can also vary substantially between countries.	Conducting a survey is a complex task of gaining trust and building rapport with a respondent. The researcher needs to be familiar with important national and cultural traits of the countries where the research is being conducted and fluent in the local language. Designing good questions and good questionnaires requires considerable expertise laced with creativity. There are vast differences in the way different cultures react toward surveys. The respondent, the interviewer, and the topic can all bias the research results.
Experiments	How will a point-of-purchase promotion affect juice sales in the United States, the United Kingdom, and Japan?	Firms that sell on the Internet can create field experiments that test different prices, atmospheres, or service details.	Experiments by their very nature incorporate cultural differences. Transferring the same design across countries could result in erroneous conclusions. Experiments are probably the best way to do causal research. It is very difficult to ensure that all relevant variables have been measured or controlled. Laboratory experiments may be too contrived or artificial to provide much information about real consumer settings.

as depth interviews, participant observation, and certain projective techniques. However, this is also true of other data collection techniques. Even if the primary investigators intend to contract with a service to do a large-scale telephone interview, they may do a small number of calls themselves to get a firsthand feel for the survey process, response types, and potential problems. Proper selection, training, supervision, and evaluation of the field force helps to minimize data collection errors. Research experience can make a difference in the quality of the data attained. For example, research has found that inexperienced interviewers are more likely to commit coding errors, misrecord responses, and fail to probe; have a difficult time filling respondent quotas; and have larger refusal rates and more "don't know" responses or unanswered questions.[21]

Data Analysis and Interpretation

The fifth step involves data preparation and analysis or interpretation. This step will proceed very differently depending on the type of data collected and the general purposes of the research. For example, for some research projects, the data collected might include garbage, photos, videotapes, brain waves, eye movement traces, as well as or instead of written or recorded responses to probes and questions. In general, preparing data for interpretation includes editing, coding, transcribing, and verifying data. Data analysis includes all of the techniques used to interpret and give meaning to the collected data.

Analysis includes a broad range of techniques, both statistical and nonnumerical. In Chapter 2 we introduced the concept of perceptual maps, a product positioning tool based on a statistical technique called *multidimensional scaling*. In the river-rafting research, by contrast, interpretation was based on coding interview and observational data into thematic categories related both to progression through time and typical events that occurred on a given day.

As mentioned in the introduction, interpretation is one of the biggest problems that leading organizations face today. Their problem is that they are drowning in data compiled from secondary sources, **syndicated data,** and exploratory, descriptive, and causal consumer research. Managers are often too busy to examine all the data available to them. In many cases, they lack the training that would enable them to interpret one or more of the specialized studies they receive. One response to this problem is to standardize report formats. Thus, when managers are constructing reports from diverse data sources, they cannot reanalyze data or modify reporting formats. While this simplifies their task, it also robs them of opportunities to mine the data available to them.

Report of Findings

Generally, the final step of the project is a written or oral report describing the entire research process and presenting the results and major findings. Decision makers are likely to evaluate the report in terms of whether it addresses the problem, has a complete and understandable research design, uses appropriate research procedures and executes them correctly, provides a complete and objective interpretation, and clearly identifies the boundaries of the study and the generalizability of the findings. One of the most important and difficult aspects of market research is evaluation. A marketing manager needs to know what the research *means*. In a study of the Norwegian food marketing industry, one researcher found that managers felt deeply insecure about the meaning of research conducted by well-regarded advertising and marketing research firms. Since market success or failure often hangs on the meaning of research, their anxiety is understandable. In evaluating any explanation of data, readers will look for "symptoms of truth." These symptoms of truth are summarized in Good Practice 3.2.[22] These symptoms provide guidelines for evaluating the quality of a research project. Together these guidelines suggest that re-

1. The interpretation must be **exact,** so that no unnecessary ambiguity exists.
2. It must be **economical,** so that it forces us to make the minimum number of assumptions and still explains the data.
3. It must be mutually **consistent,** so that no assertion contradicts another.
4. It must be **externally consistent,** so that it conforms to what we independently know about the subject matter.
5. It must be **unified,** so that assertions are organized in a manner that subsumes the specific within the general, unifying where possible, discriminating when necessary.
6. It must be **powerful,** so that it explains as much of the data as possible without sacrificing accuracy.
7. The interpretation must be **fertile,** so that it suggests new ideas, opportunities for insight.

Source: Grant McCracken, *The Long Interview* (Newbury Park, CA: Sage Publications, 1988), pp. 50–52.

searchers must "tell a good story," a story that holds together internally and externally, grabs our attention, explains the data, and provides future direction.

In addition to the problem of data interpretation mentioned earlier, another major problem involves the dissemination and use of the results of consumer research, or *market intelligence* as it is sometimes called. Relevant decision makers don't necessarily use even good research that is well reported. Simplifying access, monitoring use of data sources by managers, and institutionalizing interfunctional teams of stakeholders to discuss how to use research results are just some of the ways organizations try and improve the dissemination and use of information.

Summary Features of the Research Process

Several general features characterize the research process we have just outlined. First, as suggested in Exhibit 3.2, *the research process is iterative.* The initial research problem may be completely reformulated as the researcher learns more about the consumer from initial data collection efforts. For example, Avon Products, Inc., which markets cosmetics to women, began a strategic initiative with the research question how to capture an increased share of the Hispanic market. At first, this seemed like the appropriate question since secondary data from the U.S. Census Bureau treats Hispanic females as one cultural group. However, depth interviews, pilot surveys, and observations of Hispanic communities revealed many segments of Hispanic females that differ in cultural and historic background as well as in attitudes and beliefs. On the basis of this early research, Avon redefined the research problem as one of how best to segment the Hispanic female market. Similarly, if Avon or any other firm were to conduct research in Australia, it would want to be sure to distinguish between the many national varieties of Asian-Australians such as Koreans, Vietnamese, and Chinese. A study of how women express assertiveness conducted by The Coca-Cola Company revealed that it needed to look at the issue in many national contexts.

Second, *the use of different methods and perspectives affects the research results.* It is impossible to be completely objective. That's why it is so important to incorporate multiple approaches and perspectives in research efforts. Very often researchers will find from observation that consumers behave in ways that are very different from how they report they behave in a questionnaire. For example, Ernest Dichter, the famous expert on consumer motivation, once conducted a study on the reasons people wear sunglasses. Sunglass-wearing people who were questioned on a cloudy day in New York City frequently maintained that sunglasses protected their eyes from the sun. Clearly their behavior contradicted their verbal responses, suggesting, as we all know, that there are other reasons for wearing sunglasses. The task of the researcher is to provide an interpretation that makes sense of the differences between the results of different kinds of data.[23] Similarly, by incorporating only one perspective on the research, findings may underrepresent or misrepresent other perspectives. For example, a study of consumer research showed that much of it makes inappropriate assumptions and presents misleading findings because researchers fail to take into account differences in the viewpoints and behaviors of men and women.[24]

Third, *no research is perfect.* Researchers must constantly make trade-offs between the costs and benefits of conducting different types and amounts of research as well as different types of error. For example, by asking several questions to measure a concept, researchers can feel more confident that they have actually measured the concept and not omitted important aspects of it. However, asking more questions can lead to respondent fatigue, resentment, and nonresponse, which can significantly bias the findings. Of course, the more researchers ask, the more it costs to collect, analyze, and interpret the data.

Asking Questions

One of the most important problems in data collection is how to ask research questions. Even if researchers collect data by observing behaviors, they generally want to be able to relate those behaviors to consumers' thoughts and feelings. To do this, they need to know how to ask questions. In this section we focus on a simple review of the basics for asking questions; but it's important to keep in mind that the type of questions asked in a focus group or depth interview will differ from those asked in telephone, mail, or mall-intercept surveys. Even mail and telephone formats cannot be used to ask the same type of questions. For example, mail questionnaires can generally ask people to make finer discriminations (using 7- or 10-point scales) than telephone surveys. Similarly, mall-intercept surveys or personal interviews can use visual and other sensory stimuli, whereas telephone interviews cannot.

| The Importance of How Researchers Ask Questions | You may be able to recall examples of promotions that feature responses to consumer surveys of one sort or another. For example, a car company may claim that it is number one in customer satisfaction, or a cough syrup manufacturer may claim to be the brand doctors recommended most, or a pharmaceutical company may claim a specific brand of aspirin is preferred by physicians if they are going to be stranded on a desert island. All of these claims imply valid research. In fact, the results are often based on biased questions. |

Similarly, polls conducted for particular political parties report voter preferences based on very specific questions that may bias the results. What happens if the companies that make these claims ask questions differently? Some years ago, fast-food company

Burger King ran a series of commercials in which it claimed that consumers preferred its method of cooking hamburgers over that of McDonald's by three to one. The question used to generate this data was Do you prefer your hamburgers flame-broiled or fried? An independent researcher asked the "same" question a different way: Do you prefer a hamburger that is grilled on a hot stainless-steel grill or cooked by passing the raw meat through an open gas flame? This version of the question resulted in 53 percent preferring McDonald's grilling process. When further description was added by noting that the gas-flame hamburgers are kept in a microwave oven before serving, the preference for grilled burgers was 85 percent. In this case, three technically correct descriptions of cooking methods produced preferences ranging from 3 to 1 for Burger King to 5.5 to 1 for McDonald's.[25] This example illustrates a critical principle of consumer research: How researchers ask questions is very important.

To build a quality questionnaire, the researcher should begin by asking three questions about each research question.[26] First, *can potential study participants understand the question?* The cartoon shown on this page illustrates the reaction of more than one consumer to what seems like gobbledygook from the researcher. Researchers bring their own perspectives and biases to questions, and these can be very different from those of the respondents.

Three Questions Researchers Should Ask about Research Questions

Next question: I believe that life is a constant striving for balance, requiring frequent trade-offs between morality and necessity, within a cyclic pattern of joy and sadness, forging a trail of bittersweet memories until one slips, inevitably, into the jaws of death. Agree or disagree?

Understanding the Question?

Four men—a Saudi, a Russian, a North Korean, and a New Yorker—are walking down the street. A marketing researcher says to them, "Excuse me, what is your opinion on the meat shortage?" The Saudi says, "What's a shortage?" The Russian says, "What's meat?" The Korean says, "What's an opinion?" The New Yorker says, " 'Excuse me?' What's excuse me?"

Source: V. Kumar, *International Marketing Research* (Englewood Cliffs, NJ: Prentice Hall, 2000), p. 202. Adapted from *India Herald,* May 22, 1998, p. 27.

An appealing illustration involves the pretest of a telephone survey to look at people's understanding of corporate profits. One of the first questions was, When I say profits, what comes to your mind? The first couple of interviews went fine, but in the third interview, an elderly woman responded, "Well, I know about Moses and Isaiah, but that is about all I know about prophets." This question was changed to ask about "corporate or business profits."[27] Obviously, the difficulty of ensuring that study participants understand the question is greatly increased when conducting international research. Consumer Chronicles 3.2 offers a short, humorous illustration.

Second, *can potential study participants answer the question?* Sometimes, the researcher will ask a question that study participants can understand but can't answer. For example, a researcher doing a telephone interview may call and ask, Exactly how much did your household spend on groceries last month? Participants may have an approximate idea about how much their household spent on groceries; but it's likely that the majority of respondents won't know exactly. To ensure that participants can answer the question also means making sure that response categories are mutually exclusive (nonoverlapping) and collectively exhaustive (everyone has something to mark). It's very easy to make mistakes in setting up response categories that make it impossible for study participants to answer the question accurately.

Third, *will potential study participants answer the question?* Even if you ask a simple, nonsensitive question, you might not get an answer. More than a third of all Americans contacted routinely shut the door or hang up the phone on interviewer questions. One Singaporean researcher conducting mall-intercept interviews in three Asian countries found that Chinese in the People's Republic were willing to answer his questions in part because he was a foreigner, whereas most of those in his own country refused to answer.[28] Sometimes it's possible to predict that at least a portion of potential study participants will find a particular question too personal and refuse to answer. For example, approximately 10 percent of U.S. survey respondents refuse to answer questions related to income. In Scandinavia, however, were salaries are more highly standardized, such questions are felt to be less personal. In countries with large informal economies, such as those of the transitional economies of eastern Europe, considerable resistance to such questions should be expected. Other times, the researcher needs a deep understanding of potential participants to predict what topics they will be sensitive about. Many years ago, while still in school, one of us did research for a Southwestern art magazine to profile their customers. The magazine was interested in establishing what type of advertising would appeal to its customers, with the hope of broadening its advertiser base. The mail survey was university sponsored, and care was taken to establish the legitimacy of the project and confidentiality of the respondents. However, questions about art types (not specific pieces or values) engendered a significant number of refusals. One respondent wrote that he was afraid that the chances of a break-in would increase if the type of art he owned were publicized (by his answering the questionnaire). As a poor graduate student hanging poster art on the walls, the researcher (one of us) was too distant from the experience of the potential respondent to have predicted this attitude.

To help answer the preceding three primary questions about questionnaire items, the researcher can apply what are known as the **BRONS guidelines.** The acronym BRONS serves to reinforce the important criteria—brevity, relevancy, objectivity, nonambiguity, and specificity—and to suggest a warning about poorly constructed questions: Be Right Or Necessarily Suffer.

Brevity is the first important criterion. A good rule of thumb is that questions should contain 20 words or less, excluding answer categories. Perhaps you've had the experience of a telephone interviewer asking a question that's so long you can't remember the beginning of the question by the time she gets to the end. Overly long questions can lead to confusion or misleading responses or nonresponses and should be avoided.

Relevancy is a second important criterion. Every question and every word in every question has a cost associated with it for all the participants. Relevancy in words and in questions is critical. Quite often, after the research problem and scope of the study have been defined, the client will begin to remark, "Wouldn't it be interesting to know . . ." This can be very dangerous. Sometimes, of course, this can lead to reconsidering the problem and scope and enrich the project, but very often this approach simply detracts attention from the intended purposes of the research. Before including the question, the researcher needs to be fairly sure that it's not just interesting, but it's interesting given the purposes and scope of the research.

Objectivity is a third important criterion. There are three common ways in which nonobjectivity arises. First, questions may suggest an answer. For example, if a focus group moderator exploring television show preferences in Egypt said, "You watch *Hilmiyya Nights,* don't you?" or if one in Brazil asked, "You watch *Torre de Babel* don't you?" she or he would be implying a socially desirable answer to focus group participants.[29] Asking leading questions like this could lead to very misleading results.

Second, questions may have answer categories that are biased (unbalanced response categories). For example, consider the following question: About how many soft drinks do you drink per week, with response categories 0–4, 5–8, 9–12, 12–15, over 15. Answers to this question could be very misleading because people who don't drink any soft drinks would be lumped with those who drink up to four per week. In general, a soft-drink manufacturer would be interested in separating out people who don't consume soft drinks. It's easy to imagine other, more sensitive topics where results reported without a "none" category would be very misleading (e.g., questions about alcohol consumption, drug use, sexual activity).

Finally, questions may be nonobjective because they don't contain sufficient information to allow respondents to make an informed choice. For example, a question such as, Do you favor abortion? does not contain enough information. Most people in the United States would agree that abortion is an unfortunate act. Many favor abortion only under particular circumstances. And most people in the United States do not favor abortion after the first trimester. Thus, the question lacks specificity. Very often researchers exploring consumer preferences are misled because the preference questions are not specific enough to allow informed choice.

Nonambiguity is the fourth important criterion to ensure good questions. Ambiguity can arise in two ways. Ambiguity arises when unfamiliar words are employed or when words have multiple meanings. Sometimes this is very difficult for researchers to judge themselves. After all, the researcher uses the word because he or she is familiar with it. Very frequently, we acquire specialized vocabularies that are widely shared by our circle of friends and co-workers. We are so familiar with these words and acronyms and use them so frequently that we may not realize that they are not used in other social circles.

Differences in familiarity and vocabulary are particularly relevant when study participants differ culturally from the researchers. Language creates highly sensitive issues in multicultural societies like those of North and South America, South Africa, Australia, and New Zealand. Language can also create problems when marketers whose countries of origin are culturally homogeneous (e.g., those of Scandinavia) find themselves working in multicultural or foreign environments.

Ambiguity also occurs in response categories. Perhaps you have filled out a questionnaire that asks about your consumption of some food or beverage using terms like "never," "rarely," "occasionally," "frequently," "all the time." Researchers ask questions this way because they are not sure how to be more specific. Unfortunately, what is "rarely" for one person may be "frequently" for someone else. Doctors and medical personnel commonly use this type of question in reference to alcohol consumption. A consumer whose social group drinks three or more portions of alcohol each day will see his or her own behavior differently than someone whose social group drinks only on holidays or not at all. A member of the first group who happens to drink one or two glasses of wine per week may report "rarely"; but someone from the second group who drinks one or two glasses per week may report "frequently." A Saudi Arabian will view the question differently than a German. In Saudi Arabia, all alcohol is taboo; in Germany beer is considered a food.

Avoiding ambiguous response categories is especially important for international consumer research. Qualitative research can help researchers understand what level and frequency of usage is normal. For example, from depth interviews with consumers and product managers in Budapest we learned that Hungarian consumers rarely wash their hair every day and commonly wash their hair about once per week, and many wash their hair less frequently. To compare Hungarian and American consumers in terms of shampoo usage requires specific response categories that include a wider range of likely responses, or response categories tailored to each country.

The fifth and final criterion is *specificity*. The researcher wants to try and balance the information requirements of the manager with the abilities of study participants to answer a question. Using an earlier illustration, the manager may want to know exactly how much the household spent on groceries last month, but the potential participant can at best give an estimate of what was spent. The goal is to provide the information needed without overtaxing the respondent. Sometimes no matter how specific the question, participants cannot answer accurately. When this is the case, it may be appropriate to use another form of data collection, such as observation, consumer diaries, or some unobtrusive measures, for example, a study of garbage to see how much alcohol is really consumed in a neighborhood.

We have outlined only the essentials of how to ask questions efficiently and effectively. The researcher would also need to evaluate the research instrument or questionnaire to ensure that it's appropriate in terms of sequencing, order, and other aspects of design.

Conducting International Consumer Research

We have already provided numerous examples in this chapter of the difficulty of conducting international consumer research. In this section we provide a more detailed description of some of the major problems. In developing theory, models, research questions, and hypotheses it is important to remember that differences in the sociocultural environment and other environmental factors may lead to differences in the formation of perceptions, attitudes, preferences, choices, and behaviors.

Cross-national consumer research is especially difficult because the researcher is attempting to produce comparable data in two different countries. That is, there is an interest in comparing what is discovered in one culture with what is found in another culture. Nevertheless, this type of research is extremely important to companies that market global brands like Mercedes automobiles, Nokia cell phones, Fuji film, Schweppes tonic water, Coca-Cola, Procter & Gamble's Tide detergent, or Nescafé instant coffee. To collect comparable information, the researcher may have to use nonidentical methods because of differences between the cultures. Good Practice 3.3 summarizes some important questions to ask when constructing a survey instrument for use in cross-cultural research.

The questions in Good Practice 3.3 are based on five specific problems that arise in trying to construct questions to compare two or more different cultures. One problem is that questions used in one cultural context may simply not be relevant in another cultural context. Research comparing valued consumer objects in Niger, West Africa, with valued consumer objects in the United States is illustrative of this problem.[30] One part of the study measured people's attachments to other people. The scale used in the United States included items asking the number of club memberships the respondent has and the frequency of talking on the phone with friends. These questions would not be relevant for the Nigerien sample. While telephone use is quite widespread in the United States, one half of the world's population has never placed a phone call. In this instance, comparable data were obtained from the Nigerien sample by including items that ask how frequently the respondent attends village association meetings and the frequency of visiting friends and participating in village gossip. Despite the fact that these items are not identical, they attempt to measure attachment to other persons through organized group activities and informal communications comparably.

A second problem is that the explicit meaning of a word, its denotation, may differ between cultures. For example, Nigeriens and Nepalese understand perfectly well the notion of markets as locations where things are sold. They will easily talk about "going to market," "buying things at the market," or "attending the market." However, a question like, Has the market for cosmetics/cloth/yogurt changed in recent years? may make little sense to them. (This problem may also still apply in many transitional economies.) In this question, *market* refers to an abstract notion of the market as an accumulation of exchanges between sellers and buyers taking place in many locations and at many times.

Questions to Ask in Constructing Cross-Cultural Research Instruments

Good Practice 3.3

- Is the word or concept relevant in both cultures?
- Is the explicit meaning of the word or concept the same in both cultures?
- Are the suggested, implied, or hinted-at meanings of the word or concept the same in both cultures? Is there congruence between cultural experiences with the word or concept?
- Are both cultures equally experienced and fluent with the research techniques employed?

Source: Adapted from the material contained in Eric J. Arnould and Melanie Wallendorf, "On Identical Methods in Cross-Cultural Research or the Non-comparability of Data Obtained with Seemingly-Comparable Measures," working paper, California State University, Long Beach, 1993.

Finding comparable words is essential in cross-cultural research, and it can be difficult. In Chapter 5 we discuss the List of Values as a way to measure consumer values. To conduct a comparative study in Germany, researchers used a standard process of translation and back translation. However, it was very difficult to translate the English concepts of "warm relationships with others" and "self-respect" into German. The results revealed that significantly fewer Germans than Americans hold these as their most important values. However, the researchers concluded that imprecise translation might be more responsible for these results than actual differences in value orientations.[31]

A third problem is that the suggested, implied, or hinted meanings of words (connotative meanings) may differ between cultures. This stems from a lack of overlap between dimensions of cultural experience. Anytime the cultural experience of an object or process varies between cultures, the issue of connotative meanings arises. For example, research might find that both Japanese and American consumers value courteous service providers in fast-food restaurants.[32] However, what does *courteous* mean in these two cultural contexts? In the United States, courtesy implies warmth and friendliness, whereas in Japan in implies formality and respect. For a company planning to open a service establishment in Japan, knowing that the customers like courteous service doesn't help very much. The company needs to know what *courteous* means and implies in that culture. Similarly, originality in product design carries different connotations with regard to innovativeness to the Dutch than it does to Americans.

Differences in the connotative meaning of words can cause confusion about how to interpret responses to questions as well. For example, in Japan, it is considered impolite to disagree. Japanese respondents are much more reluctant to disagree than their American counterparts when asked about their level of agreement with a set of statements. This might leave the researcher with the false impression that a new product will be well received, when in fact the respondent is simply trying to be agreeable. Some interesting cross-cultural research shows significant patterns of difference in reported customer satisfaction across cultures.[33]

A fourth problem is that respondents in various cultures may have different experiences with and fluency in research techniques. For example, respondents in Euro-American samples have little difficulty rating their degree of preference or agreement with statements on a seven-point scale like the following:

1   2   3   4   5   6   7

Strongly   Strongly

Agree   Disagree

Researchers have found that three- or four-point scales work best in Ghana and other developing countries because people there are not as used to making as fine a distinction in their opinions as those in highly developed consumer cultures are.[34]

A fifth, related, but even more profound problem is that most research techniques rely on collecting verbal information. Although this approach may work in cultures with high literacy rates, this method is much less appropriate in other cultures. The Diné people (Navajo) of northern Arizona, for example, are extremely close-mouthed, and Indonesian inhabitants of the island of Bali might not even interact with outsiders. The approach of most consumer research techniques makes very important assumptions about how people acquire, process, and retrieve information. Survey instruments are not very good at accurately retrieving data on certain kinds of sensory information such as smells and tastes, because people don't easily express this information using words. Nonetheless, survey research is still the norm in consumer research.

Of course, the problems we've talked about so far have to do with how to ask comparable questions in two different cultures. Anytime a company undertakes international research, it faces a host of other equally complex problems. Methods for collecting data and sampling techniques have to be carefully matched to the cultures. Again, we emphasize that to ensure comparability in cross-cultural research does not mean using identical methods. It means using data collection methods that have comparable levels of reliability. For example, in the United States and Canada, nearly every household has a telephone. As a consequence, telephone interviewing is the dominant mode of questionnaire administration in those countries. By contrast, in the transitional economies of central and eastern Europe, a telephone is still very much a luxury good. In India, less than 1 percent of households have telephones.[35] In one country, telephone interviews may be known to have a given level of reliability; in another country, in-home interviews, rather than telephone interviews, may have an equivalent level of reliability. Thus, telephone interviews should be used in the first country, and in-home interviews should be conducted in the second. In the same way, the penetration of Internet technology varies widely between countries. An Internet survey may provide representative data in the United States or Japan but be infeasible in India or eastern Europe.

Let's take another example. As we noted earlier, focus groups are a popular mode of data collection in the United States and are widely used in Europe and Australia. Focus groups tend to concentrate on particular activities, products, or problems; they are often used in the development of new products or services and to evaluate advertising copy and formats. Agree shampoo and conditioner, a familiar Australian brand, and Pantene shampoo and conditioner both employed focus group research in their development, for example.[36] However, sophisticated levels of cultural awareness become crucial when trying to conduct focus groups in a foreign culture. For example, in Japan, conformity is highly valued, as is deference to superiors, including anyone older. Conducting focus groups in Japan requires special attention to how group dynamics operate in that culture. In many countries in the Middle or Far East, people are hesitant to discuss their feelings in a group setting, and personal interviews should be used to ensure comparable reliability.[37] In the United States, a simple focus group may contain both males and females. Mixed-gender focus groups pose a challenge in the Middle East.

Conducting Research on the Internet

As we have already discussed, the Internet is a revolutionary tool that has the potential to change the nature of human interactions. Here, we provide a detailed framework for thinking about how the Internet can influence consumer behavior research, concentrating on three major ways: it can automate, inform, and transform (see Exhibit 3.6). We view all three of these functions from an organizational perspective: how an organization, such as Ford Motor Company, can use the Internet to communicate better with its stakeholders, such as research suppliers, customers, and dealers.

Automate means that paper-and-pencil methods are replaced with electronic transactions or communications. As suggested by the exhibit, Ford could collect and analyze consumer complaints online. Such an application would be classified as "automation." Of course, it is also possible for organizations to try to solve consumer problems online, either with a cleverly designed website or through e-mail communications.

Inform means that the organization finds new ways to communicate (e.g., with customers). As shown in the exhibit, a researcher could include a pop-up window in a web-

Exhibit 3.6 Internet Technology and Consumer Behavior Research

Network	Automate
Internet—Global	Develop interactive questionnaire design; the online questionnaire adapts to respondents as they supply answers
	Establish internet consumer panel
	Observe chat room behavior
	Collect data on viewing habits on websites and TV
	Use e-mail for purchase satisfaction surveys; customers reply via Internet to report consumption experiences
	Use incentives to increase response rates or identify committed customers
	Administer consumer questionnaire online (i.e., click-through data collection)
	Facilitate flow with online questionnaires (e.g., in terms of skip patterns, closure)
	Use chat rooms or newsgroups to reduce the number of concepts for new-product development and factor analysis
	Conduct follow-up verifications (e.g., to verify that a consumer has participated in a particular study) via e-mail instead of phone
	Recruit consumers online to participate in research studies; collect and analyze consumer complaints (e.g., customer satisfaction) online
	Create a website to explain the purpose of a study more fully to consumers
Intranet—Internal communications and processes	Provide repository of research information for internal access (library); for instance, online "book of scales" or tested measurements (e.g., to aid in questionnaire design); automate questionnaire design using online templates
	Automate the coding of open-end responses by key words
	Use search engine techniques to enhance qualitative analysis; create automated databases to summarize findings of previous studies
Extranet—Link between researcher and supplier (researcher) and research user (client)	Conduct interactive focus groups online (this could also be an Internet application)
	Use to send status reports to organizations that purchase consumer behavior research
	Send final results via extranet to organizations that purchase consumer behavior research
	Provide online access to presentations for clients
	Use to deliver a multimedia summary of results for (e.g., using audio, video, graphics)
	Share automated databases with clients and other business partners; simplifies selection of a research supplier (via online databases, prior bids, and histories of project satisfaction)

based survey to provide definitions and explanations for respondents who request such information. As a result of this information transfer, there should be less confusion, and consumers have a better chance of understanding the meaning of the words and concepts that appear on a data collection instrument.

Transform means that a new industry is created or that the organization finds a completely new way to transact business. As shown in the exhibit, virtual focus group interviews have the potential to revolutionize the research industry. A major problem with in-person focus groups is that researchers have to convince a group of respondents to show up at the

Network	Inform	Transform
Internet—Global	Communicate with consumers in a more cost-effective manner, via ongoing, online panels and interactive interviewing	Creates a new industry in the sense that online data collection replaces data collection by traditional means (telephone, mail, face-to-face interviews) if current problems (e.g., the sampling bias inherent in the Internet) can be overcome
	Use the Internet to tap into libraries of marketing research; undertakes customized searches	Provide syndicated Internet purchase data (i.e., Nielsen purchase data for e-commerce purchases, visits)
	Collect information about competitors more quickly and more effectively	Supplement or replace in-person focus groups with virtual focus groups, thus overcoming the inherent limits of geography
	Create pop-up windows to provide definitions and explanations for respondents who request additional information; thus, there is less confusion, and consumers understand a questionnaire better	Lessens importance of time of day in collecting data from consumers
		Test product concepts online
		Changes sampling methods: The use of self-selected samples increases (e.g., consumers are part of sample if they choose to participate by responding to e-mail solicitation and incentives)
Intranet—Internal communications and processes	Create a database of past research projects and best demonstrated practices	Data collection faster and less labor intensive; requires researchers who are highly technical and highly skilled
	Use to facilitate the flow of information between various participants in the research process (e.g., manager, questionnaire designers, coders, data analysts, report writers)	Transforms the offices of research providers (e.g., the triumph of the "paperless" office); less need for central offices as the "virtual" office becomes common
Extranet—Link between researcher and supplier (researcher) and research user (client)	Communicate with business partners more effectively; work more efficiently with business partners via extranet	Provides real-time syndicated data sites
	Communicate with research clients as the project unfolds, using a digital camera	Transmit information such as surveys, results, methods, and so forth to business partners online

same time and place. A major advantage of the virtual (online) focus group is that the limitations of geography can be overcome. Twelve people, all in different nations, could simultaneously participate in a focus group discussion, either using video cameras or e-mail. At the present time, most consumers do not have video cameras hooked up to the Web. So in the near future, this method would be more suitable for specialized audiences (e.g., managers who may be more likely to have access to such advanced technology).

Automation applications are usually the easiest changes to implement. Quite often, this type of application results in considerable cost savings, as paper-and-pencil methods are replaced by electronic data storage. Transforming applications are difficult to identify and difficult to implement successfully. Nonetheless, these transforming opportunities are what make the Internet such a potentially revolutionary force in society. If a transforming application is successful, then the entire industry changes for good.

In Exhibit 3.6, we also differentiate between three types of communication networks: Internet, intranet, and extranet. The **Internet** is *a global network of networks.* Any computer connected to the Internet can communicate with any server in the system. Thus, the Internet is well suited for communicating with a wide variety of stakeholders (e.g., customers, business partners, stockholders). Adobe, for example, uses its website to distribute software changes to customers and to provide financial and other reports to investors.[38]

An organization can establish an **intranet,** which is *an intraorganizational network that enables people within the organization to communicate and cooperate with each other.* Thus, an intranet is essentially a fenced-off, mini-Internet within an organization. A firewall is used to restrict access so that people outside the organization cannot access the intranet. Although an intranet may not directly facilitate cooperation with external stakeholders, its ultimate goal is to improve an organization's ability to serve those stakeholders by increasing the ability of employees to interact and communicate customer information with one another.[39]

Both the Internet and an intranet, as the names imply, are networks—arrays of computers that can connect to each other. In some situations, however, an organization may want to restrict connection capabilities. An **extranet** is designed to *link a buyer and supplier to facilitate greater coordination of common activities.* Thus, an extranet could link an organization with its alliance partners. It could link an organization with its suppliers or business customers. Communication is confined to the computers linking the two organizations. An extranet is specialized to support partnership coordination.

The examples shown in Exhibit 3.6 are related to the marketing research industry, which consists of research firms that collect a wide variety of consumer behavior data, along with other kinds of information. The exhibit is constructed from the point of view of a marketing research firm. For example, the entries in the exhibit show the kinds of automation changes a research firm could implement on an extranet. Thus, ACNielsen could use an extranet to send status reports to Ford Motor Company to describe the progress of a research project that has just gotten underway in California. Managers at Ford could examine an electronic database as it accumulates. Alternatively, they could look at a video of a focus group interview over the Web, or they could listen to an audio broadcast on the Web to hear customers' reactions to driving a new car model in Tokyo.

At this point it is somewhat difficult to predict all of the changes that the Internet will bring to business and society. However, Exhibit 3.6 provides a framework for thinking about the kinds of changes that might emerge. In the end, it is consumers themselves who will decide which technologies are successful and in what forms.

Ethics in Consumer Research

Globalization and technology have also contributed to increased attention to ethical issues. When companies operate abroad they run up against all sorts of new moral issues and ethical standards that differ among countries. Today, big businesses normally have a corporate ethics officer, although such a job description barely existed a decade ago. As many as one in five big firms has a full-time office devoted to ethics, and at United Technologies, for example, the business ethics department includes an international network of 16 business-ethics officers working in 24 different languages.[40]

1. Expect and prepare to encounter ethical dilemmas in consumer research.
2. Do not harm participants physically, emotionally, or psychologically.
3. Do not deceive participants.
4. Ensure that participation is willing and informed.
5. Employ proper research procedures.
6. Hold data in confidence.
7. Be guided by ethical maxims (e.g., the Golden Rule).
8. Where possible, debrief participants about the true purposes of disguised research.
9. Do not overpromise the benefits of research.
10. Do not distort research results to please clients.
11. Refuse to conduct research you consider unethical.
12. Be clear about your values, because no research is value-neutral.

Collecting, analyzing, and using the results of consumer research raises a number of ethical issues. Many people are concerned that marketing is essentially a manipulative profession that collects information in order to induce consumers to buy things they neither want nor need. Others are concerned about erosion of privacy and corporate control of huge quantities of information about the private lives of individuals. As a result, many people around the world increasingly refuse to respond to requests for information from polling organizations, market research firms, corporations, and individual researchers. In response, consumer researchers should resist pressures to construct even more intrusive data collection procedures and instead strive to construct and then adhere to professional standards for research practice. Some guidelines for professional research practice are shown in Good Practice 3.4. What are some examples of unprofessional research behavior? A number of unprofessional practices can be identified. For example, participants in research have a right to confidentiality unless they specifically waive that right. This principle seems straightforward, but with the profusion of catalog retailing and telemarketing (telephone marketing) and the advent of the Internet, much data are collected from and about consumers, sometimes almost incidentally. In some countries, these data are shared a little too liberally between firms, sometimes resulting in the invasion of consumers' privacy.

In addition, researchers are generally obligated to avoid deception. However, some deception is common in many types of research. For example, in experimental research, the true purpose of the study is often hidden from subjects so that their knowledge does not influence their responses to experimental stimuli. In participant observation research, continuous interaction between researchers and informants makes it impossible to ask for research consent every time data are recorded. Participant observation always involves some deceit, since researchers are trying to develop relationships with informants in order to collect data. Thus, limited deception is a part of most consumer research. As a result, researchers should strive to adhere to the research standards adopted by most professional research organizations.

Several types of unacceptable lapses in the obligation to avoid deception can be identified. Perhaps the least of these problems concerns deceiving participants about the length of a research task. If a personal interview is going to take 30 minutes, but the researcher does not specify this, it may be considered an unethical deception by omission. Reaction to this type of time deception varies a lot from culture to culture. For example, Germans are very conscientious about time and will cut off the interview if you go over. French and Italians are more flexible with their time, and many people living in Mediterranean countries like to converse.

More serious is misidentification of the researcher or research sponsor. Sponsor concealment is acceptable if it serves legitimate purposes of interviewer security or data integrity, not if disclosing the sponsor's identity will affect peoples' willingness to participate in the study. Worse still is sales prospecting and fund-raising under the guise of surveys. In one case, a major car company conducted a large phone survey. Participants were told the purpose of the survey was to measure their buying intentions and attitudes about cars. However, the data were turned over to local dealers who made sales calls to likely buyers. This example illustrates an unethical deception of respondents and leads to reduced cooperation in legitimate surveys.[41]

Emerging technology creates ethical dilemmas. For instance, the creators of websites may want to remember facts about a customer's visit to that site. Thus, many websites include "cookies," a mechanism for remembering details of a single visit or store facts between visits. A **cookie** is *a small file (not more than 4K) stored on the consumer's hard disk by a web application.* Thus, a cookie is a kind of instant, and automated, research tool that records details about consumer behavior.[42] A website like CNN uses cookies to customize its service. That is, CNN uses a cookie to remember that a site visitor is mainly interested in news about basketball or cooking. A cookie might also be used to determine what pages a person views on a particular website so as to improve site design. Similarly, a cookie can be used so that particular advertisements can be targeted to specific consumers. For example, if you frequently visit travel sites, you might get a banner ad from Delta popping up the next time that you do a search (e.g., on Yahoo).

Of course, some consumers do not like the fact that the creators of websites are secretly monitoring their behavior. Such an intrusion is viewed as an invasion of privacy. Both Internet Explorer and Netscape Navigator allow surfers to set options for various levels of warnings about the use of cookies. Concerned consumers can turn these features off altogether. Some marketers feel that service levels are diminished when cookies are turned off and the flow of information from consumer to website owner is disrupted. In this way, the advent of new technology creates ethical dilemmas. To what extent are firms allowed to collect information in an electronic way? Does such automated information collection provide better service, or does it invade consumer privacy?

The Exciting World of Consumer Research

We present hundreds of examples of different types of consumer research conducted in different parts of the world and for different purposes throughout this book. For example, in our discussion of motivation (Chapter 11) we describe the use of projective techniques to examine consumers' reasons for behaviors. In the chapter on consumption meanings (Chapter 18) we describe the use of in-depth interviews to examine the meanings that consumers attach to common consumption activities such as shopping and less common consumption activities such as plastic surgery. We also describe some new market research techniques that combine photographs and depth interviews with digital imaging technologies. In the chapters on purchase decisions (Chapters 10 and 13) we review some of the exciting developments with scanner technology. In the chapters on consumer satisfaction (Chapter 17), and recycling, reuse, and disposal (Chapter 19) we discuss a variety of observation techniques.

Learning about consumers is the key to implementing the marketing concept and exercising marketing imagination. Consumer behavior research is concerned with systematically collecting and analyzing information in order to improve the quality of exchanges between organizations and their customers or constituents. That is, organizations create value by improving the quality of exchanges. Consumer research may be basic or applied. Basic consumer research attempts to expand the limits of knowledge about consumers. It is not concerned with the solution to any particular pragmatic problem. Applied consumer research is conducted when a decision must be made about a specific real-life problem. There are five main steps in the research process, including: defining the problem and project scope, developing a research approach, formulating the research design, fieldwork and data collection, and data interpretation and communication of results.

The research process is iterative; different methods and perspectives lead to different research results, and no consumer research is perfect. Because collecting verbal and written information from consumers is so central to the research process and because it throws many important issues in the research process into relief, researchers must be particularly careful that they ask questions effectively. To build a quality questionnaire, the researcher should begin by asking three questions about each research question. First, can potential study participants understand the question? Second, can potential study participants answer the question? Third, will potential study participants answer the question? Brevity, relevancy, objectivity, nonambiguity, and specificity are also important criteria for evaluating questions.

Conducting international consumer research is even more complicated than conducting consumer research in a single, national context, so we also explore some of the problems encountered in cross-cultural consumer research. Here, we review special problems associated with conceptual equivalence, and sources of response bias.

The Internet is likely to have a dramatic impact on how consumer research is done over the next five years: by replacing paper and pencil methods with electronic transactions or communications, by enabling the organization to communicate in new ways, and by creating completely new ways to collect data. Collecting and analyzing information about consumer behavior raises a host of ethical questions. Consumer researchers should resist pressures to construct even more intrusive data collection procedures and instead strive to construct and then adhere to professional standards for research practice.

---

1. Go to the grocery store and observe four different consumers as they select a cereal brand to purchase. Write a diary to describe your experience. What process do the consumers go through? Do they look at packages and labels? Can you tell what specific aspect of the package they look at? Are prices important? How do consumers gather price information? Do some seem to purchase by habit? Do others (e.g., purchase pals, children) get involved in the decision?

2. Visit a local shopping district, such as a main street or mall. Go from store to store and observe the customers. Make a detailed composite portrait of the customers at each store using as many criteria as possible. Then, name the market segment you have described.

3. Outline a research design to determine the effects of attractive advertising models on males and females. Be specific. What is your design (e.g., experiment, survey, observation)? Who are your subjects? How are they selected? What do you measure? How can you be certain that your results are valid?

4. What are the strengths and weaknesses of secondary data? What questions should you ask when examining secondary data?

5. Conduct secondary research on the Internet to describe the auto industry in Brazil. How could a company such as Volkswagen use this information in understand their competitive marketplace in Brazil? (*Hint:* You might want to begin with a search on "Brazil automotive").

6. Write a questionnaire that you would use to carry out the research project introduced in question 3. Be certain to include the following measures: demographic data; perceived body image; media use (e.g., television programs watched, magazines read); estimated amount of time looking at ads on a typical day; overall attitude toward advertising in general. Also, include an introduction and an ending in your questionnaire. Include both open-ended and closed-end questions. Make certain that your questionnaire flows well. Pretest your questionnaire by having three friends fill it out. Ask them if they have any comments for improvement. Apply the criteria introduced in this chapter to evaluate the effectiveness and validity of your questionnaire.

7. British consumers are reluctant to talk about cockroaches in a focus group setting, but French consumers are happy to talk about them in a focus group. Describe at least five topics that people in your home country would be reluctant to discuss in a focus group.

8. Consider the focus group interview. Describe, in detail, a specific research question that could be well addressed by this method. Do the same for syndicated data.

9. What kinds of consumer behavior research do you consider unethical? Have you ever been asked to participate in a research study that you thought was unethical? If so, provide specific details.

You Make the Call

Blockbuster Brings Entertainment Home

Blockbuster Inc. is the global leader in rentable home entertainment with approximately 7,100 Blockbuster video stores in 27 countries, including Argentina, Australia, Canada, Italy, Mexico, Spain, Taiwan, the United Kingdom, and the United States. The company can be accessed internationally at *www.blockbuster.com*. In April 2000, Blockbuster launched a global advertising campaign with a "Bringing Home Entertainment" theme. The theme is intended to capitalize on the universal enjoyment of the home-viewing experience, and the campaign communicates that consumers in many international markets will enjoy the benefits of finding more copies of their most popular video releases at Blockbuster. It reinforces the emotional connection of watching a great movie at home and demonstrates the company's commitment to developing new ways to bring movies directly to people's homes through a range of alternatives from home delivery to digital streaming. A series of advertisements feature consumers anticipating the movie-viewing experience as they journey home with their evening movie rental. The campaign was launched in April in the United Kingdom, Australia, Mexico, Argentina, Chile, and Denmark. It subsequently aired in the United States, Canada, and Taiwan and was scheduled for release in Italy and Spain at the end of 2000.

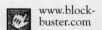 www.block-buster.com

Blockbuster is a successful global company, but it has made some big mistakes. For example, in 1995, Blockbuster opened seven stores in Munich and ten in Berlin. Preliminary consumer research showed it had good name recognition among young and middle-aged consumers. The stores failed for a variety of reasons, however, and were closed down only two years later. German consumers prefer to watch movies in theaters, and although the stores were located in downtown shopping areas, most existing video stores were in residential neighborhoods. In addition, pornography accounts for a third of all rentals in Germany and Blockbuster did not want to sacrifice its family-oriented principles. Moreover, because of the prevalence of pornographic videos, all video stores were seen as unfit places for children in Germany.

1. What are some of the cultural factors that will affect the success of Blockbuster's global campaign, "Bringing Entertainment Home"? What kind of consumer research could Blockbuster undertake to examine consumer response to the campaign? (Think global.)

2. What consumer research lessons can be learned from Blockbuster's failure in Germany? What types of consumer research might have helped Blockbuster avoid its failure in Germany? (Be as specific as possible.)

This case is adapted from press releases available on the Blockbuster website and from "Blockbuster Finds Success in Japan That Eluded the Chain in Germany," The Wall Street Journal, August 19, 1998, Khahn T. L. Tran, p. A14.

1. Eric J. Arnould and Linda L. Price, " 'River Magic': Hedonic Consumption and the Extended Service Encounter," *Journal of Consumer Research* 20 (June 1993), pp. 24–45; and Linda L. Price, Eric J. Arnould, and Patrick Tierney, "Going to Extremes: Managing Service Encounters and Assessing Provider Performance," *Journal of Marketing* 59 (April 1995), pp. 83–97.

2. James H. Fouss, "Faster and Smarter," *Marketing Research* 8, no. 4 (Winter 1996), pp. xx–xx.

3. For a discussion of Ford Motor Company's changing approach to new-product development, see Kirk Damon (1999) *Innovative Market Research for Breakthrough Product Design,* Report No. 99-113, Cambridge, Md: Marketing Science Institute. For more discussion of the Ford Fiesta case, see Vern Terpstra, *International Dimensions of Marketing,* 3rd ed. (Belmont, CA: Wadsworth Publishing, 1993), p. 91.

4. Dana James, "The Future of Online Research," *Marketing News,* January 3, 2000, pp. 1, 11.

5. For a discussion of Internet and web surveys, see Don A. Dillman, *Mail and Internet Surveys,* 2nd ed. (New York: John Wiley, 2000).

6. V. Kumar, *International Marketing Research* (Englewood Cliffs, NJ: Prentice Hall, 2000).

7. For a discussion relevant to several marketing industries, including market research, see Dana James and Kathleen V. Schmidt, "Getting Good Listing Attracts Volumes," *Marketing News,* January 3, 2000, pp. 8–9.

8. See Alvin C. Burns and Ronald F. Bush, *Marketing Research,* 3rd ed. (Upper Saddle River, NJ: Prentice Hall, 2000), for a discussion of databases. See also Raymond C. Pettit, "Data Mining: Race for Mission-Critical Info," *Marketing News,* January 3, 2000, p. 18.

9. This example is taken from interviews summarized in Ajay K. Kohli and Bernard J. Jaworski, "Market Orientation: The Construct, Research Propositions, and Managerial Implications," *Journal of Marketing,* 54 (April 1990), p. 5.

10. Johnny K. Johansson and Ikujiro Nonaka, "Market Research the Japanese Way," *Harvard Business Review,* May–June 1987, pp. 16–18.

11. This example is taken from F. Gouillart and F. Sturdivant, "Spend a Day in the Life of Your Customers," *Harvard Business Review,* January–February, p. 125.

12. Grant McCracken, " 'Homeyness': A Cultural Account of One Constellation of Consumer Goods and Meanings," in *Interpretive Consumer Research,* Elizabeth C. Hirschman, ed. (Provo, UT: Association for Consumer Research, 1989), pp. 168–83.

13. For a more complete description, see *The Code of Professional Ethics and Practices,* Marketing Research Association, Inc., Chicago, IL.

14. For a full description of this study, see Arnould and Price, "River Magic."

15. This example is based on the research reported in Marsha L. Richins, "Social Comparison and the Idealized Images of Advertising," *Journal of Consumer Research* 18 (June 1991), pp. 71–83. However, we've taken some license in ordering the studies reported in order to illustrate that research can iterate between the basic research types in many different ways

16. Dagnoli Judann, "Why Heinz Went Sour in Brazil," *Advertising Age,* December 5, 1988.

17. Daniel Melnick, "Federal Statistics at Your Fingertips," *American Demographics,* September 1998, pp. 25–30.

18. A good description of how to analyze and interpret qualitative data is provided in Susan Spiggle, "Analysis and Interpretation of Qualitative Data in Consumer Research," *Journal of Consumer Research* 21 (December 1994), pp. 491–503.

19. For an interesting discussion of the application of ethnography in applied consumer research, see Kendra Parker, "How Do You Like Your Beef?" *American Demographics,* January 2000, pp. 35–37.

20. For these and many other examples of the need for cultural sensitivity in survey research, see V. Kumar, *International Marketing Research (*Upper Saddle River, NJ: Prentice Hall, 2000).

21. Martin Collins and Bob Butcher, "Interviewer and Clustering Effects in an Attitude Survey," *Journal of the Market Research Society* 25 (January 1983), pp. 29–58; and R.F.Q. Johnson, "Pitfalls in Research: The Interview as an Illustrative Model," *Psychological Reports* 38 (1976), pp. 3–17.

22. M. Bunge, "The Weight of Simplicity in the Construction and Assaying of Scientific Theories," *Philosophy of Science* no. 28, 2 (1961), pp. 120–49. See also Grant McCracken, *The Long Interview* (Newbury Park, CA: Sage Publications, 1988), pp. 50–52; and Marianne Elisabeth Lien, *Marketing and Modernity* (Oxford: Berg, 1997).

23. For a discussion of how to build interpretations that consider different kinds of data collection, see Eric J. Arnould and Melanie Wallendorf, "Market-Oriented Ethnography: Interpretation Building and Marketing Strategy Formulation," *Journal of Marketing Research,* November 1994, pp. 484–504.

24. Julia M. Bristor and Eileen Fischer, "Feminist Thought: Implications for Consumer Research," *Journal of Consumer Research* 19 (March 1993), pp. 518–37.

25. *Advertising Age,* April 4, 1983, p. 18.

26. For this section on asking questions we are indebted to Robert Peterson, who taught one of us market research. This approach is also outlined in Robert A. Peterson, *Constructing Effective Questionnaires* (Thousand Oaks, CA: Sage Publications, 2000).

27. This example is provided in Petersen, *Constructing Effective Questionnaires,* p. 19.

28. Randall Rothenberg, "Surveys Proliferate, but Answers Dwindle," *New York Times,* October 5, 1990, pp. A1, A5; and Ian Phau, Internet query, July 1998.

29. *Hilmiyya Nights,* a soap opera, was a major media event in modern Egypt. See Lila Abu-Lughod, "The Objects of Soap Opera: Egyptian Television and the Cultural Politics of Modernity," in *Worlds Apart,* Daniel Miller, ed. (London: Routledge, 1995), pp. 190–210. According to *The Economist,* August 5, 1998, *Torre de Babel,* a soap opera, was the third most watched show in Brazil at the time.

30. Eric J. Arnould and Melanie Wallendorf, "On Identical Methods in Cross-Cultural Market Research or the Noncomparability of Data Obtained with Seemingly-Comparable Measures," working paper, California State University, Long Beach, 1993. Also see Melanie Wallendorf and Eric J. Arnould, " 'My Favorite Things': A Cross-Cultural Inquiry into Object Attachment, Possessiveness and Social Linkage," *Journal of Consumer Research* 14 (March 1988), pp. 531–47.

31. S. C. Grunert and G. Scherhorn, "Consumer Values in West Germany: Underlying Dimensions and Cross-Cultural Comparison with North America," *Journal of Business Research* 20 (1990), pp. 97–107.

32. Kathy Frazier Winsted, "Dimensions of Service Encounter Satisfaction: A Cross-Cultural Analysis," unpublished doctoral dissertation, University of Colorado, Boulder, 1993.

33. Kumar, *International Marketing Research.*

34. Wallendorf and Arnould, "My Favorite Things."

35. D. Sopariwala, "India: Election Polling in the World's Largest Democracy," *European Research,* August 1987, pp. 174–77.

36. Betty Holcomb, "The Focus Groupie," *Madison Avenue* 27 (September 1985), p. 47.

37. Naresh K. Malhotra, *Marketing Research: An Applied Orientation* (Englewood Cliffs, NJ: Prentice Hall, 1993), p. 780.

38. Richard T. Watson, Pierre Berthon, Leyland F. Pitt, and George M. Zinkhan, *Electronic Commerce: The Strategic Perspective* (Fort Worth, TX: Dryden, 1999).

39. Watson, Berthon, Pitt, and Zinkhan, *Electronic Commerce.*

40. "Business Ethics: Doing Well by Doing Good," *The Economist,* April 22, 2000, pp. 65–66, 67.

41. Eric J. Arnould "Ethical Concerns in Participant Observation/Ethnography," in *Advances in Consumer Research,* vol. 25, Joseph W. Alba and J. Wesley Hutchinson, eds. (Provo, UT: Association for Consumer Research, 1998), pp. 72–74; Seymour Sudman, "Survey Research and Ethics," in *Advances in Consumer Research,* vol. 25, Joseph W. Alba and J. Wesley Hutchinson, eds. (Provo, UT: Association for Consumer Research, 1998), pp. 69–71; and N. Craig Smith, "Ethics in Consumer Research," in *Advances in Consumer Research,* vol. 25, Joseph W. Alba and J. Wesley Hutchinson, eds. (Provo, UT: Association for Consumer Research, 1998), p. 68.

42. Watson, Berthon, Pitt, and Zinkhan, *Electronic Commerce.*

Learning Objectives

After completing this chapter, you should be able to:

- Discuss how economic indicators and global markets shape consumption.

- Outline some basic global trends influencing consumption.

- Define the major world consumption areas, including North America and western Europe; Japan and the newly industrialized countries; transitional markets in eastern and central Europe; and developing and Third World countries.

- Explain something about consumption patterns and preferences in major world areas.

- Describe some patterns in cultural values in major world areas.

- Identify trends and likely changes in consumer behavior for several different parts of the world.

The Changing World of Consumption

Nachos for Two

McDonald's Golden Arches, Sony Walkmans, LEGOs, and Guinness Beer show up on the streets of Pretoria, South Africa; Paris, France; London, England; and Tokyo, Japan. Corn-fed Nebraska beef can be purchased in Germany, Japan, and the Netherlands, and Argentine beef can be purchased in Nebraska. Globalization is affecting the lives of people who never leave the family farm, and it is an accelerating force. However, in each of these and many other cases, globalization combines with localization to determine the meaning, purchase, and use of consumption objects.

Probably any five-year-old world traveler (and there are quite a few) can attest to the nearly worldwide accessibility of the hot dog and can further distinguish the French hot dog, the American hot dog, the Danish hot dog, and so on. Moreover, there is a good chance that a five-year-old can distinguish the French hot dog served by street vendors in Paris from the French hot dog served up in Copenhagen, Denmark. She can probably also distinguish the New York City vendors' hot dog from the one served up as American in Paris, France. But this is not a story about hot dogs. It is a story about nachos.

Nachos are a highly variable snack food, typically consisting of corn tortilla chips, perhaps refried beans and spicy chicken, pork, or beef, certainly cheese (usually cheddar or jack) and spicy salsa, and topped off with guacamole, sour cream, and maybe hot jalapeño peppers. Even in the Tex-Mex region of the United States, typically thought of as home to at least the commercialization of nachos, there is considerable variation in

what consumers get when they order them. However, we were not prepared for the variations and omissions we experienced consuming nachos in Scandinavia. We never managed to acquire anything close to jalapeños or cilantro and experienced nachos with no cheese, odd cheese, mayonnaise, no salsa, odd salsa, no meat, great big hunks of odd meat, and so on. We had about decided that nothing resembling a Tex-Mex nacho could be had in the region. Then, late one night after a movie we stopped into an Irish pub for a late snack and were told by our server that he made the best nachos in town. By this time we were quite skeptical so we quizzed our server on how he had learned to make "the best" nachos in Odense, Denmark. He proudly claimed that he had learned in the United States. Well, after all, that did sound promising! Born and raised on the southwestern U.S. version of nachos, we asked where he learned to make them. He replied, "Connecticut." Now, if you are familiar with the geography of the United States, you know that Connecticut is a long way from Texas and Mexico, home of the nacho. However, despite not very spicy salsa and no jalapeños, these Irish pub nachos made from a Connecticut recipe and served to us in Odense, Denmark, were delicious. The consumer's world is increasingly made up, just like these nachos, of experiences and objects that combine the local and the global—combinations that will dismay, delight, and surprise.

Overview

The purpose of this chapter is to describe consumer behavior within a global context. The vignette above illustrates a consumption world that is molded by two important forces: globalization and localization. We talked about globalization and gave many examples in Chapters 1, 2, and 3. As defined in Chapter 1, globalization is a social process where geography's effect on social and cultural relations and actions is diminished.[1] For example, consumption ideas and trends (such as nachos) move easily across geographic space and national borders.

At the same time, however, localization is also an important force. We gave several examples in Chapters 1, 2, and 3 of ways in which consumer behavior, marketing strategy, and consumer research are customized to particular cultures and settings. **Localization** is about *preserving a sense of identity, home, and community.*[2] There is a revival of local culture. Consumers are expressing a return to their roots and adapting global consumer goods and meanings to fit their local cultures.

The development of taste and demand for such items as Vietnamese restaurants, Jamaican reggae music, Chinese films, and Afghan jewelry in the United States and Europe illustrate a dialogue between unique local identities and global flows of people, money, technology, media, and ideologies. The Swiss firm Nestlé offers a prominent example of the dialogue. Exhibit 4.1 illustrates the global production and consumption of this brand.

Exhibit 4.1 Global and Local Blends

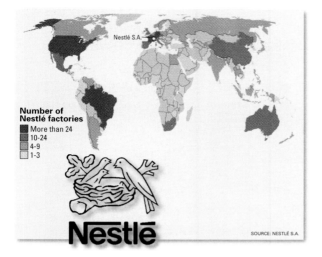

Source: Nestlé S.A.; from map insert in *National Geographic,* August 1999.

Notice that while Nestlé is a global company it also helps spread localization by, for example, making Asian noodles in Latin America. Similarly, Coca-Cola may taste pretty much the same in California and in Veracruz, Mexico, but the meanings and uses may vary dramatically between locales. The photo on page 110 illustrates the use of a Coca-Cola bottle to give a young Olmec boy jaguar spots for a ritual dance in Veracruz. To understand and predict consumer behavior in Peoria, Illinois, or Harare, Zimbabwe, requires knowing something about global trends and flows and also local tastes and preferences. We will discuss both in this chapter.

This chapter begins with an overview of the global economy and describes some important global trends. In previous chapters we have described globalization and the Internet and other technologies as being significant forces. This chapter outlines some other important global trends. The second portion of the chapter outlines some basic information about consumption patterns and preferences in different parts of the world. In Chapter 3 we described how secondary data can be used to learn some basics about different cultures. Here, we draw on secondary data along with other information to describe consumers in different parts of the world. We briefly describe consumption patterns and preferences in North America and western Europe, Japan and other countries in the Pacific Rim, the transitional economies of central and eastern Europe, and developing countries and the Third World. As you read through this information it is important to remember that these are oversimplified sketches of consumption around the world, but they are intended to give you a feel for the variety of consumer needs, wants, and abilities.

The Global Economy

Understanding consumers requires a basic understanding of the distribution of economic power and potential around the world. The nature of the economic system within a country affects nearly every facet of consumer behavior. As economies grow, markets become

The globalization of markets spreads products widely. Locally, consumers use them for their own purposes. An empty Coca-Cola bottle is re-appropriated to apply paint to this young Olmec boy.

National Geographic, August 1999, "Millennium Moments" front cover insert.

different, larger, and more demanding. With improved economies, the range of tastes, preferences, and variations of products sought by consumers increases.

Economic Indicators

Gross Domestic Product and Gross National Product

Gross domestic product (GDP) and **gross national product (GNP)** are two measures of a country's economic activity. GDP is *a measure of the market value of all goods and services produced within the boundaries of a nation.* GNP includes *the market value of goods and services produced by all that nation's business operations, including those in foreign countries.* Another useful indicator is the **average GNP per capita,** which can be represented as *the dollar value of a country's final output of goods and services in a year, divided by its population.*[3] The average GNP per capita in selected nations is shown in Exhibit 4.2. These figures indicate the purchasing power for each resident, that is, the amount of money an average person has to spend on consumer goods and services. While the United States ranks first in GNP, average purchasing power is greatest in the European Community. Average GNP per capita provides important information about consumer demand, but it can be misleading. It depends further on how GNP is distributed, how and what infrastructures support GNP, and what kind of growth in GNP is expected.

Consider first an example of the impact of GNP distribution. According to Exhibit 4.2, China has only about $3,300 per capita GNP. Yet, Levi is able to sell $75 pairs of jeans to

Exhibit 4.2 Average per Capita Income for Selected Countries

Country	GNP in $ per Capita	Country	GNP in $ per Capita
Argentina	$ 9,530	Hungary	$ 6,730
Armenia	2,160	Mexico	7,660
Australia	19,870	Nigeria	870
Austria	21,650	Russian Federation	4,190
Canada	21,380	South Africa	15,290
China	3,330	Sweden	18,770
Denmark	22,120	Turkey	6,060
El Salvador	2,790	United Arab Emirates	17,000
France	21,510	United Kingdom	19,960
Germany	21,110	United States	28,020
Guatemala	3,820	Vietnam	1,570

Source: The World Bank, *World Development Indicators* (Washington, DC: International Bank for Reconstruction and Development, 1998), pp. 12–15.

the youth culture of China because extended families there, as other places, are showering money on their children.[4] India has a massive middle class; but looking at average income alone in that country is misleading because there are wide differences in education, social mobility, exposure to media, and so on.

Two additional examples help illustrate the effects of GNP distribution on consumer culture. In Abidjan, Ivory Coast, hundreds of laundry workers toil at their own individual rocks cleaning thousands of garments each day. Almost no garments are lost, despite the apparent chaos. Clothes arrive at hotels and homes the next day, cleaned and pressed, for a small fee. In Abidjan, those who could afford to buy washing machines have little incentive to purchase them, since they can also easily afford to have someone else do their laundry. When eastern Europeans first began visiting the United States in large numbers after the fall of communism, they were dazzled by the huge department stores and the seemingly never-ending array of lovely things to buy. At the same time the poor and the homeless they saw on the streets shocked them. Under communism, everybody was equal in poverty.[5]

Infrastructure represents *capital goods that support the activities of many industries.* This would include paved road, seaports, energy supplies, and so on. If infrastructure does not develop with an expanding population and economy, then countries begin to lose economic ground. For example, shallow harbors and inadequate port equipment make it more expensive to ship computer equipment from Miami to San Antonio, Chile (less than 4,000 miles) than from Miami to Yokohama, Japan (about 9,000 miles). Only about 20 percent of the Chinese who live in the more affluent cities are accessible because of a poor distribution system for products in the interior of the country.

Growth in GDP and GNP is also an important factor. In 1960, east Asia accounted for just 4 percent of world economic output. The newly industrialized countries of east Asia accounted for 25 percent by 1998. While GNP in Europe and the United States has grown at about 3 percent or less per year over the past 25 years, many east Asian economies are growing at more than twice that rate, a trend that is expected to continue.[6] Transitional

Exhibit 4.3 World GDP Growth, 1995–2002

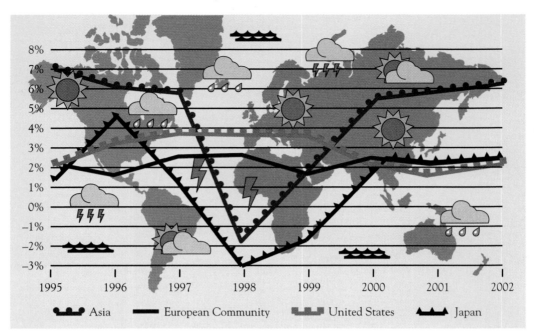

Source: *The World in 2000* (London: The Economist Publications, 1999), p. 13.

economies in central Europe such as Hungary, Poland, and the Czech Republic offer additional examples. Although average per capita GNP is still quite low, many sectors of these economies are growing rapidly and there is a lot of entrepreneurial activity. Exhibit 4.3 illustrates world growth in GDP for Asia, the European Community, the United States, and Japan. Note the enormous growth in GDP in Asia.

Another limitation of average GNP per capita is that it does not take into account government welfare programs that provide services to consumers. These are quite extensive in many European countries, for example. Such programs free up individual income for discretionary consumption expenditures. Nor do these figures take into account the extent to which consumers acquire goods and services through informal markets, as in the Russian Federation's barter economy (see Chapter 10), or through nonmarket means, such as gifts within or between extended family households, as in Nigeria. Researchers must take into account these factors and many others when determining consumer demand for any particular good or service.

Income Distribution

The distribution of income within countries is also important in determining demand. Income distribution gives us a better idea of the size and purchasing power of potential market segments than does per capita income. Consider the cases of the United States, the United Kingdom, and India. Most consumers in India make less than $5,000 per year, but only 18 percent in Britain and 8 percent in the United States make less than $5,000. However, 83 percent of British consumers make less than $15,000 per year, compared to only 33 percent of U.S. consumers. Fully 55 percent of American consumers make over

Exhibit 4.4 Gini Index for Selected Countries*

Country	Gini Index	Country	Gini Index
Argentina	—	Hungary	27.9
Armenia	—	Mexico	50.3
Australia	33.7	Nigeria	45.0
Austria	23.1	Russian Federation	31.0
Canada	31.5	Sweden	25.0
China	41.5	South Africa	58.4
Denmark	24.7	Turkey	—
El Salvador	32.0	United Arab Emirates	—
France	32.7	United Kingdom	32.6
Germany	28.1	United States	40.1
Guatemala	59.6	Vietnam	35.7

A dash indicates no data.

Source: The World Bank, *World Development Indicators* (Washington, DC: International Bank for Reconstruction and Development, 1998), pp. 68–71.

$20,000 per year, as compared to only 9 percent of British consumers and an insignificant number of Indian consumers. Thus there is a larger, wealthier consumer segment in the United States than in the UK, and a larger, wealthier segment in the UK than in India.

One way of comparing the distribution of income within countries is called the Gini index. Its measures the extent to which the distribution of income deviates from a perfectly equal distribution. A Gini index of zero represents perfect equality, whereas an index of 100 implies perfect inequality. Thus the higher the index, the more unequal is income distributed. Exhibit 4.4 provides Gini indexes for selected countries. The Gini index provides marketers guidance on the distribution of appropriate price points for consumer goods, for example.[7]

Variations in the Gini index imply different aspirations and possibilities for consumers in different nations. Exhibit 4.2 shows that the per capita income of Sweden is about $18,770 (in world purchasing equivalent terms), and we also know from the table that this income is fairly evenly distributed over the population of Sweden as a whole. The per capita income of El Salvador, by contrast, is only $2,790, but that income is more highly skewed with a smaller percentage of the population controlling a larger proportion of the national wealth. Sweden represents a large middle-class market, whereas El Salvador has a large low-end market and a small elite market.

Engel's Coefficient

Another useful measure of purchasing power is Engel's coefficient. This coefficient measures the percentage of an average household's income spent on food. For example, in the United States about 18 percent of expenditures go for food and beverages; comparable figures of just over 20 percent are reported in Japan and France. In China, India, and Turkey, three developing nations, the percentage is over 50 percent. As economies develop, Engel's coefficient goes down, indicating an increase in disposable income to spend on other things than food. For example, between 1992 and 1995, Engel's coefficient in South Korea declined from 30.4 to 28.5. In Japan, it declined from 24.8 percent in 1987 to 22.2 percent in 1996.[8]

Global Markets   The globalization of markets, restructuring of central and eastern European economies from command to market driven, trends toward economic cooperation such as the **North American Free Trade Agreement (NAFTA)** and the **European Community (EC),** and increased global competition make it important to view the global economy in the context of regions of the world. There have been economic links between almost all parts of the world since the sixteenth century. However, it is only in the latter half of the twentieth century that the world has truly become a global marketplace. The global movement of people, capital, information, materials, and products has gathered speed. The world of the twenty-first century is divided not into countries but into market areas. These market areas often share common characteristics that influence consumer behavior such as similar levels of income, culture, official languages, and rules concerning the conduct of business.

The three Triad regions introduced in Chapter 2—Europe, the Americas, and the Asian Pacific Rim—constitute a new economic order for trade and development. Global companies that are located in the Triad regions have *significant market power.*[9] At the economic center of each Triad region is an economic industrial power. In Europe it is the European Community; in North America it is the United States; and in Asia it is Japan. Each of these regions has strong single-country markets or multicountry markets that are bound together by economic cooperative agreements. We have already mentioned the EC and NAFTA partnerships. Two important multinational trading groups encompass the Asian Pacific Rim. **ASEAN** is the *Association of Southeast Asian Nations.* The group has a combined population of 480 million and a combined GDP of $560 billion. As of 1997, ASEAN countries included Brunei, Indonesia, Malaysia, the Philippines, Singapore, Thailand, Vietnam, Myanmar (Burma), and Laos. This is the primary cooperative agreement for that Asian Pacific Rim. **APEC** was formed in 1989 and is the *Asia-Pacific Economic Cooperation.* The APEC provides a formal structure for the major governments of the region, including the United States and Canada, to discuss mutual interests for trade and economic collaboration.

In addition to these **Triad powers,** there are emerging trading powers in the southern hemisphere such as the newly industrialized countries (NICs) of Southeast Asia (Singapore, South Korea, Thailand, Indonesia, Taiwan), South Africa, Brazil, Nigeria, and Saudi Arabia. These developing countries now also contain important consumer markets. These countries have rapidly industrialized in targeted industries and have per capita incomes that exceed other developing countries. NICs are impressive exporters of many products such as steel, machine tools, electronics, and clothing. They have instituted significant free-market reforms and are attracting trade and foreign direct investment. Brazil offers a great example of the growing importance of NICs in world trade.

Goods, services, and information are produced and consumed in every nation. The flow of goods, services, and information is global, but the distribution of production and consumption varies significantly. The developed countries consume more than twice the value of imported goods and services than do the developing countries ($33.6 versus $14.7 trillion dollars).[10] The economies of some countries are dependent on the production and export of one or a few commodities like oil, copper, or agricultural goods. Many Middle Eastern, African, and Central American countries are dependent in this way. The so-called banana republics get their name from this kind of product dependence. Thus, the economy of the island nation of Grenada is largely dependent on exports of the spices nutmeg and mace in addition to tourism. This concentration of production is often coupled with an uneven distribution of wealth and purchasing power. Those people who manage production and export are often elite consumers whose tastes and preferences resemble those of consumers in North America and Europe. The bulk of their fellow consumers, however, have a relatively small share of the nation's total purchasing power. Their consumption behavior may be molded by more local tastes and preferences and constrained by limited purchasing power.

Global Trends

Four trends influence consumption patterns around the world. Of course, these trends are more evident and accelerating more quickly in certain parts of the world. They represent areas of opportunity for consumer marketers.

The Service Economy

It is often said that countries in the Triad regions are moving toward a **service economy.** In fact, of the 1,000 largest corporations in the world today, almost 200 of them are service firms. North America, followed by Japan and the European Community, dominates the world market for the services that are consumed in the other nations of the world. They are likely to dominate the information boom as well. Nonetheless, developing countries' exports of services grew at an average annual rate of 12 percent in the 1990s, twice those of the Triad nations.

What does the shift to a service economy mean? It means that the share of the nation's productive output is shifting from the manufacture of tangible products to the management of the movement of services and information. Services include a wide range of activities, including accounting, management, and engineering services provided by firms such as Arthur Andersen, Deloitte and Touche, and Bechtel; insurance on an oil supertanker; logistics functions provided by firms like Mitsui Lines or Consolidated Freight; global information networks being designed by Time Warner or AT&T; and fax and photocopying services provided by manufacturers like Xerox and neighborhood copy centers like Kinkos or Alphagraphics. The shift to a service economy is also reflected in consumer behavior. Services typically account for between one-third and one-half of household consumption.[11]

Green Marketing

Increasingly, global concern for the environment extends beyond issues like industrial pollution, hazardous waste disposal, and deforestation to include issues that focus directly on consumer and industrial products. Historically, business has not given great thought to where its raw materials come from nor to where its products go after they have been purchased. Now all that is changing with the advent of **green marketing.** Nevertheless, by one estimate, only 20 percent of Triad nation companies can be described as proactive in their commitment to improve environmental performance.[12]

Industry is faced with the fact that raw materials are finite. For example, world reserves of a number of important minerals will last for less than a century at current rates of industrial consumption. Many companies have adopted the concept of eco-efficiency, including 3M, Procter & Gamble, and SC Johnson Wax. A program established at SC Johnson Wax has cut the company's manufacturing waste by half, reduced virgin packaging waste by 25 percent, and reduced the use of volatile organic compounds by 16 percent; at the same time, production has increased by more than 50 percent. One plant extracts methane from a nearby landfill for energy production, another continuously reuses

95 percent of its wastewater. The company has realized a more than $20 million annual cost savings.[13]

The recycling industry is another response to the recognition that resources are finite. Nearly 90 percent of the raw materials that go into an average automobile are recyclable, and firms are scrambling to do more. BMW is striving for the fully recyclable vehicle. Recently, one of the big three American automobile manufacturers found a way to recycle soft bumpers into taillight plastic.[14] In California, over 80 percent of all aluminum cans are recycled.

In some cases, environmental activists have moved aggressively against corporations with a poor green profile. For example, Mitsubishi has been targeted for its efforts to build salt plants in a Mexican bay where gray whales breed. Three major forest products producers, MacMillan Bloedel, Interfor, and Western Forest Products, all in British Columbia, were criticized for their clear-cutting of old-growth forests. They recently announced they intended to seek timber certification, indicating that they harvest in an environmentally sound way. Certification can provide competitive differentiation in the marketplace.[15]

More and more, companies must contend with green-marketing legislation that addresses the problem of what happens to goods after purchase. Germany has passed stringent green-marketing laws that regulate the management and recycling of packaging waste, called *take-back requirements*. Germany's packaging laws were introduced in three, increasingly stringent, phases between 1991 and 1993, the last phase requiring manufacturers to accept virtually all returned sales packaging. Some companies have responded proactively to impending legislation and changing values. Xerox has found that it is profitable to recycle its old copiers and toner cartridges. In 1994, the company saved some $2 million in raw material costs by reusing toner cartridges.[16]

Growing Gap between Rich and Poor

Another trend of significant concern is the growing gap between rich and poor nations of the world and between the rich and poor within nations of the world. The rapid economic growth in east Asia during the last decade has been accompanied by worsening inequality. In the United States, the income of the wealthiest one-fifth of the population has increased by 21 percent since 1980, while real wages of the bottom 60 percent of the population have stagnated. In Europe, immigration of poor foreign workers has fueled an anti-immigrant backlash in many countries. The poorest tenth in Britain are 13 percent worse off than they were in 1979 and the richest tenth are now 65 percent better off.[17] Although an increase in marketing activity has the general effect of delivering goods and services to consumers more effectively, market economies are not necessarily effective in providing for an equitable division of consumption possibilities. Thus, one response of marketers to the widening gap between rich and poor has been the development of two-tier marketing. That is, brands and retail formats are developed to cater to the top and the bottom of the market. Meanwhile, midpriced brands and stores may suffer.

A discussion of the growing gap between rich and poor must draw attention to the African continent.[18] Although in the mid-1990s there were signs of improvement, with some African countries showing growth rates of more than 6 percent, in 2000 the picture is very gloomy. African countries are at the bottom in World Bank compilations of GDP and GNP, and the gap between them and the rest of the world is widening. At least 45 percent of Africans live in poverty, and only 15 percent of Africans live in environments minimally adequate to sustain growth and development. The growth rate in sub-Saharan Africa as a whole was only 2 percent in 1999. The continent is plagued with floods, famine, diseases, and wars. Moreover, the next generation of Africans will be more numerous, poorer, less educated, and more desperate.

The final and perhaps most dramatic trend concerns **earthscaping,** *the accelerated movement of people, ideas, goods, capital, information, services, and popular culture around the world.* This accelerated movement has led to the uprooting of many consumption habits from their local context and their commercialization on a global scale. Consider the exchange of hamburgers for sushi and rock music for karaoke between Japan and the West; or the exchange of MTV for world music between North America and the rest of the world; or the appearance of Islamic consumption habits of dress and cuisine in northern Europe and North America to balance Western habits in Islamic North Africa and the Middle East.

Global earthscaping also results in the **creolization** of global consumer institutions, *a blending of local and global meanings.* Of course, creolization is what we are talking about in the story about nachos that we use to introduce this chapter. Fast-food restaurant franchises provide another example, one that has mutated into a myriad of forms in particular local markets. Also illustrative are theme parks, of which Disney World is merely the most dramatic example. Another example is the Christmas consumption holiday now celebrated around the world, including in non-Christian countries like Turkey and Japan.

Some global consumption, such as Christmas or the beauty pageant, become what some have called a **global structure of common difference,** *a consumer performance or ritual that enables people to play out different, yet related values through a shared collection of cultural practices.* This is easiest to understand in the context of an example. In all participating cultures, Christmas involves gift giving and families. But in Japan, Christmas is a gift-giving holiday that primarily concerns unmarried, dating couples. In Britain, Christmas cards are usually exchanged only within nuclear families. Among Anupiaq Inuit of Greenland, Christmas is used to link everyone in a wider gift-giving group that downplays the existence of nuclear families. In Trinidad, Christmas gift giving is employed to enhance the respectability of families vis-à-vis their neighbors. In all instances, these gift-giving patterns create opportunities for marketers, who can provide the goods and services that match this desire to give just the right gift.

Although customs and behaviors are moving very quickly from one culture to another, consumer behavior researchers must be careful not to fall into the trap of **self-referencing,** *using their own experiences or intuitions to try and understand the behaviors of others.* Sometimes, intuitions can be quite accurate. However, when the intuitions are about people in another culture, self-referencing can lead to erroneous conclusions. For instance, it would be very easy to assume that Christmas gift giving in Trinidad or Greenland is very similar to customs in the United States. However, as described in the preceding paragraph, there are important differences. As customs and rituals move from one culture to another, the importing culture frequently puts its own stamp on the new constellation of behaviors that surround the ritual.

Consumption in North America and Western Europe

The discussion of consumer behavior and consumption norms in North America and western Europe should probably also make reference to Australia, New Zealand, and other nations with substantial populations of European origin such as Argentina, Chile, or South Africa. However, we generally limit the following discussion to countries with average annual per capita incomes ranging from $5,000, as in Spain, to over $18,000, as in Sweden.

Consumption
Patterns and
Preferences

Four main topics highlight the consumption patterns in this group of nations: consumer skills, recreational shopping, leisure spending, and luxury fever. Countries in North America and Europe reflect a distinct consumption ideology.

Consumer Skills

Choice making, even for complex products such as pharmaceuticals, is a highly developed skill among consumers in North America and western Europe. As a result, many consumers are extremely price and value conscious. Highly developed choice-making skills fuel the growth of retail discount chains and do-it-yourself outlets. Consumers are accustomed to making fine distinctions between similar brands, and they are adept at detecting new uses for products offered by major manufacturers. Many consumers in these nations develop sophisticated relationships with favored brands that endure and change over their life span, a topic we address in more detail in Chapters 5 and 18.[19]

Recreational Shopping

The role of shopping and purchasing has taken on dramatic new meaning in these countries. Ever since the invention of the department store in nineteenth-century France, there has been a growing trend toward recreational shopping. The modern, self-enclosed shopping mall in all its variant forms has become a site to which consumers make frequent pilgrimages to satisfy a wide variety of needs, including those for aesthetic enjoyment, problem solving, and personal display. Consumers in Japan spent almost $8,000 per person in retail stores in 1990. Americans spent just over $8,000. By contrast, residents of Argentina spent only $662; residents of Malaysia spent $790; and residents of Iran spent $804 per person.

Perhaps these trends achieve their finest expression in malls like the West Edmonton Mall (Canada) and theme parks like Disney World, Universal Studios, and the like. These retail environments combine, in a seamless whole, both shopping and entertainment. In addition, we see the phenomenal persistence of a wide variety of occasional marketplaces such as arts and crafts shows, festivals, flea markets, swap meets, farmers' markets, street vending, and garage sales where people buy, sell, socialize, and are entertained.[20]

Leisure Spending

A distinctive feature of North American and European economies is the importance of leisure and tourist consumption. Organized gambling is commonplace in Europe and North America. It has quietly become one of U.S. consumers' favorite forms of entertainment, generating more revenue than movies, spectator sports, theme parks, cruise ships, and recorded music combined. Now, 37 states sponsor lotteries and 27 offer casino gambling. U.S. consumers wagered $550 billion in 1996. However, as suggested in Good Practice 4.1, gambling has a dark side.

The Japanese and elite consumers in other cultures have swelled the ranks of world tourism in recent years; but North America and Europe have traditionally had large tourist markets. The motives that inspire tourist consumption are diverse, ranging from nostalgic visits to historic towns and villages, to escapist entertainment at Mardi Gras, to romance at a Club Med or a cruise, to extraordinary adventures through African safaris, Himalayan trekking, or Outward Bound trips. The RV ad shown on page 120, clearly targeted for parents of preschoolers, suggests recapturing the experiences of childhood through a family trip in a recreational vehicle.

Luxury Fever

Some experts argue that luxury is experiencing an incredible boom.[21] In 1999, luxury spending in the United States was growing four times as rapidly as spending overall. The trend toward luxury auto purchases is accelerating, and the purchase of sport utility vehicles with sticker prices over $30,000 grew by 260 percent between January 1995 and October 1997. Luxury travel grew 130 percent between 1990 and 1995. There are long waiting lists for everything from premium wine to luxury jets. Suites costing from $750 to $1,800 a night at the Four Seasons Resort in Palm Beach are booked months ahead. The Four Seasons Hotel is one of many luxury service establishments benefiting from the luxury boom.

Family size has gone down, but house square footage has gone up. The average U.S. house at the end of the 1990s was nearly twice as large as its counterpart from the 1950s. U.S. consumers eat fewer meals at home, but they do so on more elaborate cooking equipment. One California executive admits that she cooks maybe seven times per year, but she has a $7,000 stove. Between 1995 and 1996, overall merchandise sales increased by only 5 percent, but U.S. spending on luxury goods—defined as goods in a category exceeding a given price threshold (such as $200 for a pair of shoes)—increased by 21 percent.

The United States is not the only economy suffering from luxury fever. For example, Japan, with fewer than half as many people as the United States, consumes over half the U.S. volume of luxury goods. Countries in Europe and Asia and even Russia and other transitional economies appear to have big and growing appetites for luxury goods. Luxury spending is a trend not just among the rich; it's found among middle and lower-income earners as well. There is considerable evidence that in the United States and other countries consumers are spending beyond their means.

Gambling: A Dark Side of Consumer Behavior?

Good Practice 4.1

Organized gambling has been a boon for the economies of a few Native American tribes who are free to organize gaming on their reservations. However, many tribes are concerned that the presence of gambling threatens their cultural values. States like the taxes generated by gambling. But some are concerned about the effect of gaming money on state legislators, with millions of dollars going into pro-gaming lobbying efforts. Finally, compulsive gambling is recognized as a disease, and one that is increasing. Do you think some forms of gambling should be more closely regulated or even prohibited?

Trends and Changes in Consumer Behavior

What trends will dominate as the twenty-first century unfolds?[22] Some experts predict that a move out of the industrial age and into the information age will alter culture and lifestyles in important ways. Some call it the era of fragmentation, or the culture of subcultures, where people can take a menu approach for their lifestyle, picking and choosing from day to day according to mood and current fashion. Because of advances in technology, marketers can cater to smaller and smaller niche segments, customizing products and services to individual tastes. In some ways, the information age connects people with each other; in other ways, it leads to isolation. In the developed countries, consumers can interact with the

May you wish upon a thousand stars.

May you catch a million fireflies.

May you return home with loads

of pearly shells, pressed flowers

and pink sand. And may you realize

just how much you learn when you

look at life through the eyes of a child.

Go RVing
Life's A Trip

For a free video and list of

RV dealers and campgrounds:

1-888-Go RVing

www.GoRVing.com

This ad for recreational vehicles reflects one of the important consumption trends in the Triad countries: strong growth in leisure spending. The ad suggests that RVing is a means to strengthen family ties and get in touch with what matters in life.

Sesame Street *Parents* magazine, June 2000, p. 64.

world via interactive TVs and computers. Tens of millions of people around the world are connected to electronic bulletin boards, and this number is growing at 10 percent monthly. Of course, these cyberspace lifestyles have the potential to make centralized offices obsolete. More and more people are beginning to work at home. This trend may make home and neighborhood much more important in developed countries than they have been for the last several decades. Incidentally, this trend also makes home shopping via the Internet and television a growth industry.

Consumption in Japan and the Newly Industrialized Countries of the Pacific Rim

The newly industrialized countries of the Pacific Rim usually refer to South Korea, Taiwan, Singapore, and Hong Kong. These four countries are also referred to as the Asian tigers. However, driven by aggressive investment from Japan and China among others,

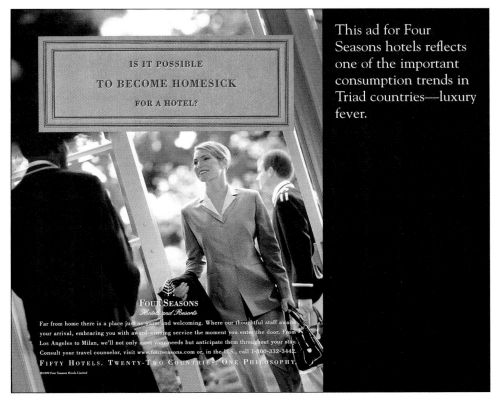

The Economist, May 13, 2000, back cover.

Malaysia, Thailand, Indonesia, and the Philippines (the "tiger cubs" or "little tigers") too are candidates for joining this group.

Consider Indonesia. Despite recent economic reversals and ethnic tensions, Indonesia has experienced substantial economic growth and is now the world's fourth most populous nation. One indication of Indonesia's remarkable progress is that in 1970 almost 60 percent of the population lived in poverty. By 1990 that figure declined to 15 percent, although a recent recession has reversed some gains. In the late 1980s Vietnam also adopted free markets. It is now flooded with Japanese comic books and karaoke, Hong Kong television dramas, French fashion, Chinese cultural goods, Hollywood movies, and Western-style billboards. The economic crisis that closed out the twentieth century (i.e., the Asian flu) may have interrupted the growth trend in the NICs but will not reverse it.[23]

Japan is one of the Triad nations, not a newly industrialized country. Economically it shares more with North America and western Europe than with countries of the Pacific Rim. For example, it is becoming a service economy in which younger people are increasingly embracing consumption rather than production and savings.[24] As one of the wealthiest nations in the world, Japan represents a huge market, changing quickly toward a culture of consumption.[25] Moreover, the direction of Japan's economic progress since World War II foreshadowed the changes we now see expanding in other countries of the Pacific Rim. Japan's direct investment and development aid to Southeast Asia have been instrumental in fueling the growth in this region. Japan shares many values with other countries of the Pacific Rim, where Confucianism forms the foundation for ethics and morality in business as well as in social and personal lives.

For international businesses attempting to penetrate the Pacific Rim it is tempting to lump the countries in the region together, as we have done. Nevertheless, culture and values and related opportunities differ across these nations. For example, cosmological belief systems vary greatly across the Pacific Rim, influencing both culture and consumption patterns. Although Buddhism and Confucianism are broad influences across the Pacific Rim, Indonesia has the largest Muslim population of any country in the world. These ideological differences have implications for market segmentation and product positioning strategies (see Chapter 6). Similarly, the geography, population, and resource base of the countries differ greatly. For example, Indonesia is a country of 184 million citizens. Malaysia, by contrast, has a population of just 19 million. In addition, some of these countries have relatively homogeneous populations with no significant minority groups such as those found in Japan and Korea. Others such as Indonesia and the Philippines experience significant conflict between religious, ethnic, and language groups within the nation. Such differences complicate segmentation, positioning, and marketing communications.

The annual per capita income in the NIC countries ranges from about $8,500 to about $24,000, lower in the "tiger cubs" and higher in Japan (more than $36,000). Most consumers in the NICs are rapidly becoming more educated and their household incomes are growing. More women are entering the workforce, especially in Japan, increasing the number of dual-income families. Many working-age Asian children live at home until marriage, so their disposable incomes have increased. With the acceleration of economic affluence, consumer interests are moving beyond basic necessities to include consumer appliances, electronic products, cars, and cosmetics.

Consumption Patterns and Preferences

As in North America and Europe, the general attitude in the Pacific Rim toward consumption is extremely diverse. Much of the development of markets in the NICs has resulted from the twin themes of modernization and rationalization. These nations have striven to replicate standards of living modeled on European and North American patterns. However, these two themes have also been, in part, responsible for the predominance of savings relative to consumer spending among consumers in the NICs.

In recent years, there has been a rapid adoption and localization of Western consumption styles, often in forms Westerners might consider highly artificial. Nonetheless, Japanese appreciate artificiality for its own sake and for its beauty. In a number of the NICs, the focus of consumer spending has, until quite recently, been on consumer durables. In China, for example, the six "big things" are VCRs, televisions, washing machines, cameras, refrigerators, and electric fans. Most consumers in NICs have had little experience with modern marketing, thus they depend on reputable brands and track records. In addition, consumers want information about products and brands rather than fancy packaging, displays, or promotional gimmicks. In markets like Japan and Hong Kong, a wide variety of image-based, luxury consumer goods also enjoy healthy growth, and the most up-to-date marketing methods are appropriate.

Consumers in the NIC countries are open to foreign goods, but as in Europe and North America, they are selective in their choices. For example, the European image is represented by traditional brands such as Mercedes Benz and Wedgewood china; the U.S. image is represented by brands and products such as Coca-Cola, jeans, cigarettes, and chain restaurants.[26] In China, Western imports have a very positive image among wealthier segments. Chinese consumers may even reject Western products manufactured in China if the packaging used does not resemble that used in international markets.

Dramatic changes are underway in the NICs of the Pacific Rim. Many of these nations are made up of youthful consumers; and the populations of these countries are growing rapidly. In almost all, we see a shift away from a savings orientation that has characterized the years since the end of World War II toward a new consumption orientation. As a result, personal bankruptcy has increased dramatically among young people. Nonetheless, financial services that provide savings opportunities, such as life insurance plans offered by the American International Group (AIG), remain popular.[27] In many of these countries, aggressive adoption of foreign goods, images, and products—everything from Coca-Cola to Levi's, and from KFC and McDonald's to Disneyland—by consumers is accompanied by aggressive marketing attempts to redefine these goods in ways that make them compatible with national cultural heritage and identity. In many countries, from Taiwan to Thailand, U.S.-style suburban shopping malls are mushrooming.[28] For example, Hong Kong consumers spent $5,524 and those in South Korea spent $3,118 in retail outlets per capita in 1990. Even Thai consumers spent $1,695 in retail stores that year.

Many leaders of Asian countries are concerned that the influx of Western culture will undermine traditional values. As a result, while Thailand, the Philippines, and Indonesia are moving to deregulate broadcasting, China, Malaysia, Singapore, and Vietnam continue to ban private ownership of satellite dishes. India is trying to impose restrictions on Western films and commercials deemed indecent.[29] Japan has launched an initiative to promote cultural exchanges among Asian nations.

Consumption in Transitional Economies: Eastern Europe

The term **transitional economies** refers primarily to the *countries formerly dominated by centralized command economies*. These include Albania, Bulgaria, the Czech Republic, Estonia, Hungary, Latvia, Lithuania, the Slovak Republic, Poland, Rumania, the former Yugoslavia and East Germany, Russia, and the 10 republics of the Commonwealth of Independent States. Some include Turkey in this group of countries. This sector represents a population of 430 million and about 15 percent of global GDP. However, there are parallels between these transitional economies and nations in other parts of the world that are shedding state-controlled economies and adopting free markets such as China.

The most advanced in the creation of market-led economies include Hungary, Poland, Turkey, and the Czech and Slovak Republics. Others such as Russia, Bulgaria, Romania, and Albania are well behind. The per capita income in these countries remains relatively low, ranging from lows of $700 in Albania, $1,124 in Romania, $1,390 in Bosnia, and $1,951 in Russia, to $2,503 in Poland and $4,072 in Hungary. Marketing executives in Hungary, Poland, and Bulgaria agree that consumers are becoming more demanding, which means that companies must refine their market segmentation and develop customized products. As competition increases, retailers are becoming more powerful and product life cycles are becoming shorter.

After the fall of communism in 1989, protected and subsidized economies began to liberalize. Industries were privatized, there was a dramatic influx of foreign goods and foreign investment, and national economies experienced a long period of inflation. At the same time, state-managed distribution systems declined in importance. In these transitional

Percentage Ranking 1 or 2	Total Sample (*n* = 2,309)
Competitive pricing	37.9%
Product quality	32.3
Company/brand reputation	15.2
Speed of reaction to customer requirements	14.6
Product performance	13.7
Close links with key customers	13.6
Product range offered	10.7
Prior market research	10.3
Product design	9.1
Finance and credit offered	9.0

Source: Graham J. Hooley, "Raising the Iron Curtain: Marketing in a Period of Transition," European Journal of Marketing 27 (November–December 1993), pp. 6–20.

economies, consumers' standards of living eroded under the impact of price inflation and the loss of guaranteed employment.[30]

Consumers have responded through a variety of strategies. For example, they get second jobs, spend more time producing their own food for consumption, and sell private products and produce directly to other consumers. Estimates from 1989 suggest that three-fourths of Hungarian households participate in secondary forms of employment.[31] Many consumers have also reduced consumption or learned to do more comparative shopping. But consumers have also changed their consumption patterns in unexpected ways. **Engel's law** states that *as real income goes down, so does the share devoted to luxury products.* However, in 1990 as real income decreased in Czechoslovakia, Hungary, and Poland, the demand for perceived luxury products increased. This may be explained by the nonavailability of luxury goods in the past or by the luxury boom gripping the United States, Japan, and other countries. This trend continues.

Industry Insights 4.1 lists what some marketing executives view as the key factors for success in reaching consumers in transitional economies in eastern Europe. Competitive pricing is most important in those countries where market transition is most advanced, such as Hungary. Product quality issues figure importantly in successful marketing as well. As competition between local and foreign products increases, product quality issues become more important.

Trends and Changes in Consumer Behavior

At this stage, multinational consumer products companies like Unilever, Nestlé, Procter & Gamble, and Colgate-Palmolive and numerous European firms like the German publishing giant Bertelsmann have experienced dramatic sales growth in eastern Europe. However, the buying binge of 1989–92 has settled.[32] Real household incomes in much of this region are stagnating, and penny-pinching is the norm. Moreover, shoppers in these transitional countries no longer view imported brands as necessarily superior. For example, perceptions of "made in Poland" are increasingly positive, and many shoppers in central and eastern Europe are looking for homegrown quality products. Some local firms have transformed themselves into successful marketing companies. Media are revolutionized; scores of consumer-oriented magazines are now available, as is commercial satellite television. Producers in almost all fast-moving consumer goods categories are offering smaller unit sizes to accommodate local budgets and little-and-often purchasing habits. For example, Unilever markets its upmarket OMO and Coral brands in single-use packets to lower the price barrier for trial purchases.

One clear trend is that the priorities of western Europe, which include the emergence of green segments and a voluntary simplicity movement, are not likely to characterize this part of the world in the short run. Consumers in transitional economies have been denied things for such a long time that there is a large demand for consumer products. As one eastern European woman remarked when she purchased a fur coat, "I do not think that you can apply First World ecological philosophy to Third World women." Simpler, more resource-conscious packaging may be a trend in western Europe; but in transitional economies, consumers first want to taste the privileges of a better standard of living before they work to save the planet.

The growth of Internet use is dramatic in eastern Europe. The Polish Public Opinion Research Center estimates that 2.5 million Poles (6 percent of the population) have access to the Internet, with approximately half of those considered active users. Internet use is predominantly by businesspeople, technical specialists, and students. The majority of access (approximately 38 percent) is at universities and schools. The popularity of the Internet in Croatia is fast approaching that of Western levels. The latest Croatian broadcaster to put its programs online is HRT, Croatian Radio and TV. The network makes live feeds of its three national radio networks, HR1, HR2, and HR3, plus its local station, Sljeme Radio, all available online in RealAudio stereo. Internet users can also tune into a live feed of HRT's channel three network, in RealVideo. These trends have provided growth markets for industrial computer suppliers like Unisys and personal computer makers like Compaq.[33]

 www.hrt.hr.

The advertising industry has grown dramatically in transitional economies in the past decade. In Poland, for example, advertising expenditures increased by 75 percent between 1993 and 1994 to $469 million, of which 60 percent was spent on television advertising. Nonetheless, consumers remain skeptical of heavy-impact, high-frequency advertising, as it reminds them of communist propaganda techniques. While western Europeans expect to be informed about brand differences, eastern Europeans expect advertising to provide information about products per se and expect variety in product range.

It is difficult to predict the future of consumer behavior in the transitional economies, and some will fare better than others. For example, the shallowness of Russia's democratic culture, primitive economic regulation, and hostility toward individual initiative constitute significant obstacles to the implementation of a market economy.[34] Furthermore, consumers in many of these economies have described a negative evolution in their experience of Western consumerism. It starts with an immense greed, a kind of fever, a wish to buy everything. Then, consumers discover powerlessness and relative poverty. Because of their poverty, many of these consumers view displays of Western consumer goods to be more like exhibits in a museum than the fruits of participation in a marketing economy.[35]

Privatization has taken hold in at least some of these countries, such as Hungary, Poland, and the Czech Republic. A distribution infrastructure is evolving in some major cities. If consumers can survive the inflation, recession, unemployment, and political turmoil surrounding them, they may soon begin to realize western European consumption lifestyles. Consumer Chronicles 4.1 is taken from an interview with a Hungarian grammar school teacher. She is divorced but would like to remarry and have a baby. She describes her consumer desires in simple terms.

At the moment I can say I am relatively happy these days. I am always trying to find goals in life that help me to get out of depression. My present goal is to get to Turin in Italy and next year to take a language exam—Italian. So these goals help me greatly to get beyond the deadlock which sometimes makes me feel unhappy. I sometimes feel unhappy for both private and social reasons. But they are correlated. Like so many people, my salary is very low. I will be 31 in a short time and have not achieved anything in my life. I could not and cannot produce anything. I have no child, and I do not belong to anyone but my parents.

My existence would be improved if I could have an apartment of my own and, of course, a car, which, in the twentieth century, is not an impossible dream. And I would like to travel a lot more. I do not have special dreams, just elementary things I need.

I have already told you about my income, and you have to know that a bedsitter, a one-room apartment, costs one and a half million forints [$18,750]. To rent an apartment is also very costly, or you can live in digs with a landlady or a whole family around. But it did not work in my case. I lived in digs for two years, but it cost a lot. The money that remained was enough for food only. I had to work in the summer so that I could buy clothes and things like that.

Whether the recent changes are positive or negative, no one can tell now. Historical events are being reinterpreted and all depends on the point of view from which they are examined. Ideologies always existed, but men in the street never determined politics.

Source: Leland R. Cooper and Andrea Kenesei, Hungarians in Transition: Interviews with Citizens of the Nineties *(Jefferson, NC: McFarland and Company, Inc., 1993), pp. 62–68.*

Consumption in Developing and Less Affluent Countries

We use the terms *developing world* and *less affluent world (LAW) countries* primarily to refer to nations in the Southern Hemisphere in Asia, Africa, and Latin America. We somewhat arbitrarily define the developing countries as those in which the annual per capita income is more than $1,500 and less than $5,000. These countries are primarily in Latin America and Asia. The LAW countries include those in which the annual per capita income is less than $1,500. These countries are primarily in Africa and Latin America.[36]

Some of these markets are attractive because of their large populations, 535 million in Africa alone. In many of these nations, access to basic necessities, adequate food, clean water, appropriate clothing, and sanitary housing are unavailable to a large part of the population, creating opportunities for sales of basic infrastructure to local companies and governments. However, the distribution of consumer incomes tends to be highly skewed, creating *small segments of very wealthy and large segments of very poor consumers,* or **dual income distribution.** For example, in Peru, 1 percent of the population accounts for nearly half of the national income. Marketers who cater to the middle class are likely to do less well in these countries than do those who cater to the wealthy and the poor. Still, the middle class is growing rapidly, even in developing countries such as India, where it numbers approximately 250 million people.[37] Consumer Chronicles 4.2 describes McDonald's in India.

The first McDonald's opened in India in 1997, with two outlets at Bombay and New Delhi. Since then, the company has added four in New Delhi and two more in Bombay and plan to open several outlets across India. The selling point for the Indian success is that McDonald's represents all things American. Despite the crowd that gathers around these outlets paying steep prices for a taste of the American icon, this represents the growing trend toward fast foods. This trend has seen entrants like Kentucky Fried Chicken and Domino's, which not only offer the product, but present the service so far unexplored in India.

The average price for a burger at McDon-ald's in India is 31 rupees, which is an equivalent of 80 cents in the United States. McDonald's doesn't serve up an all-beef patty, however. In order to appeal to the Hindus in India (who do not eat beef), McDonald's has centered marketing attention on the Maharaja Mac (comprised of two lamb patties, special sauce, lettuce, cheese, pickles, onions, and a sesame seed bun). In addition, McDonald's has introduced a vegetable burger and nuggets with chili and masala sauces to cater to the Indian palate.

Source: Adapted from L. S. Kadaba, "McDonald's Has No Beef in India," Houston Chronicle, Dining Guide, April 10, 1997.

Marketers seeking to do business in the less affluent world must be prepared to deal with less stable economic environments than in developed countries, the NICs, and even some countries with transitional economies. Sales tend to follow a boom and bust cycle. The payoff for investing in developing countries can be great, but so can the risks. For example, Whirlpool has invested hundreds of millions of dollars to modernize and cut costs in Brazil and solidify its position as the market leader in refrigerators, room air conditioners, washers, and other white goods. Many white goods, like microwaves, in the maturing or declining phase of the product life cycle in North America or Europe are in the growth phase in Brazil and other developing countries. Thus, only 15 percent of Brazilian households own a microwave oven, compared to 91 percent in the United States. Brazil is Whirlpool's biggest emerging market bet and, through much of the 1990s, its most profitable foreign operation. Sales at Brasmotor, Whirlpool's local subsidiary, soared 28 percent from 1994 to 1995 and 15 percent more in 1996. Forty years of operations in Brazil have earned strong brand loyalty. Whirlpool's refrigerators have 60 percent of the market. In 1998, Brazil skidded into a recession that shrank gross domestic product by 3 percent in 1999. Nevertheless, Whirlpool continues to make money while competitors like Sweden's Electrolux lost $14 million in Brazil in 1998. Once Brazil recovers, it should grow at 5 to 6 percent a year, as opposed to 1 to 2 percent growth rate in North America and Europe.[38]

Marketers must be prepared to meet the needs and respond to the particularities associated with traditional consumption sets, complexes of goods preferred in these countries. For example, many West African women like to decorate their sleeping huts or houses with

Consumption Patterns and Preferences

collections of matched enameled bowls basins and platters. In relatively wealthy homes, these may be stacked from floor to ceiling. Such goods exhibit the aesthetic attribute of "brilliance." Another dramatic example of the influence of local values on consumption processes comes from Indonesia. The consumption of clove-flavored cigarettes is a big business in Indonesia, so important that the central bank once intervened to maintain prices of cloves to benefit small producers.[39]

It may be useful to separate market strategies for different types of consumption behaviors involving subsistence necessities, social investments, and luxury expenditures. Many Third World people produce a larger share of their subsistence necessities for direct consumption than do those in the First World. As a result, there is a historical pattern of limited reliance on the marketplace for acquisition of basic goods and services. Associated with this is the tendency of many consumers to find sources of personal identity in productive roles. Nevertheless, marketing opportunities abound. For example, in the Ivory Coast, Nestlé introduced Bonfoutou, a product made entirely from local yams, at a cost of $4.6 million. Bonfoutou is very close to the original pounded yam dish, the traditional foutou. Its appeal is to urban working families.

In addition, limited means and a history of price inflation make many consumers in the developing world acutely price conscious. Thus, in Brazil, Argentina, Mexico, and China, the hypermarket concept—broad selections of inexpensively priced consumer necessities housed under one roof—has proven highly successful. Large, mixed retailers accounted for 12 percent of retail sales in Brazil in 1990 and 11 percent in Mexico, the latest year for which figures are available. The numbers have surely increased since then.[40] Industry Insights 4.2 shows a growing trend in Mexican retailing and describes how the successful strategy developed by PepsiCo in that country is being exported to other developing nations (e.g., India, China).

Wealthy consumers in developing countries often aspire to Euro-American consumption patterns. Using a global marketing strategy, targeting upper-income consumers, L'Oréal was able to introduce its Plénitude skin care line into the Ivory Coast. Nevertheless, L'Oréal emphasized products suited to the expectations of African women, such as a nongreasy skin care moisturizer suited to the climate.[41]

Among the more numerous poorer consumer segments, consumption choices are often faithful to patterns that are perceived to be highly traditional. These patterns do represent marketing opportunities. To illustrate, L'Oréal developed a line of inexpensive shampoos, soaps, and shower gels tailored to African tastes that emphasize skin softness, something to which West African women are sensitive. In a number of Middle East nations, the *chadour,* or veil, has increasingly become required dress for women. In Algeria, beautiful lace veils become one of the few permissible outlets for fashion expression among middle-class women. Indian women continue to wear the traditional *sari.* The sari symbolizes cultural continuity and "correct" female attitudes. Minor modifications in blouse and *pullu* (the loose end that hangs over the shoulder or is pulled over the head) are considered daring fashion statements.[42]

Another distinctive type of consumption behavior in many developing or Third World nations is the tendency to devote considerable amounts of disposable income to social investments designed to contribute to social status and prestige. The Hindu social order and in turn the cosmic order, or dharma, is even predicated on an interdependence between and circulation of gifts and commodities among the various social castes in India. Diverse examples of social consumption expenditures include pig feasts of highland New Guinea, the exchange of *kula* valuables (shell necklaces and armbands) throughout the southeastern New Guinea archipelago (islands), the Saints' day fiestas of Central America, and the char-

Industry Insights 4.2

Late last year, PepsiCo, Inc., CEO Roger Enrico entered a *changarro* in Mexico City that is smaller than his bedroom at home. Inside the crowded store, he congratulated the bemused shop owner on becoming the 8,000th retailer in Mexico to adopt the company's "Power of One" strategy, the large colorful displays that unite snacks and soft drinks that has led to average sales increase of 36 percent for PepsiCo products. Enrico's trip also underscored the snack-food supremacy of FritoLay Co. in Mexico, where its Sabritas brand boasts an 81 percent share of the salty-snack market. That's why PepsiCo is exporting its business model for Mexico to other emerging nations, from India to China, where it now has three snack-food plants. Much is at stake because the company's greatest growth prospects for its all-important snack-food business are outside the United States. In this arena, it's not merely a game of capturing market share but of increasing consumption of snacks by keeping prices as low as 1.5 pesos or 16 cents. This is a key part of the success formula in Mexico. "Our focus is being the lowest-cost producer because our success is based on making our product more affordable to consumers," says Roger Rebolledo, who leads Frito-Lay's operations in Latin America and Asia Pacific.

Source: Adapted from Johan A. Byne, "Today, Mexico, Tomorrow . . . ," Business Week, April 10, 2000, p. 184.

itable donation of mosques and public buildings in Islamic communities in Africa. Throughout the less affluent world, expenditures on dowry and bride wealth are an important form of social investment that involves constellations of consumer goods. The nature and value of goods and services purchased and consumed as social investments are the object of group evaluation, decision making, and, of course, gossip.[43]

Finally, consumers in developing countries make important purchases of luxury goods of foreign origin, especially consumer electronics and motorbikes, that may symbolize a cosmopolitan orientation to them. For example, Coca-Cola's phenomenal distribution and advertising system has made it a common feature of the consumption landscape in many developing and LAW countries. Many can occasionally afford this luxury. Provincial Argentineans exhibit considerable loyalty to Western brands and may travel long distances to Bolivia's duty-free markets to obtain designer goods more inexpensively than in Argentinean shops.

Luxury consumption patterns continue to be influenced by the colonial experience in Third World nations. French-speaking Africans consume a high proportion of French luxuries, and English-speaking Africans consume more English luxury goods. English-speaking Caribbean islanders enjoy the British game of cricket and its attendant consumption rituals; whereas French-speaking Caribbean islanders prefer soccer.[44] Quite often, consumers in these nations adopt different patterns of purchase and consumption, depending on the context. This is consistent with patterns of creolization that we discuss further in Chapter 5. Consumer Chronicles 4.3 provides an example of consumer creolization from the personal experience of one of the authors of this book.

Some years ago, I found myself waiting in the Algiers airport for an Air Algérie flight from Algiers, Algeria, to Paris, France. I waited for many hours; there was no posted flight schedule, and the only information given were occasional announcements in Arabic on an absolutely unintelligible public address system. When I asked some employees for information I was brusquely advised to return to my seat. Hence, I had ample time to observe my fellow travelers.

One group in particular drew my attention. This was a large family of Algerians waiting for the same flight as I. The group included two men. They wore tan jellaba, or ankle-length, long-sleeved, open-necked, embroidery-trimmed gowns. Pointed yellow leather, backless slippers protruded from under one gown; dark Western business shoes from under the other. There were also four women. The

women were covered from head to toe. Their faces were veiled. Their gowns too were in neutral colors. Their veils were distinctive in that they were made of exquisite white lace. I was intrigued by the presence of a pair of bright red, stiletto-heeled shoes under the hem of the gown of one of these otherwise shapeless forms.

Finally, our flight was called and I proceeded to my seat on the plane. I was just settling back for a long-postponed nap when out of the corner of my eye, I caught a flash of the red stiletto heels moving briskly up the aisle. I looked up and instead of a shapeless form, I now saw a beautiful young Algerian woman, hair freshly coifed, and wearing a short, stylish Parisian dress. She had a lovely smile. She had lost no time in switching outfits as consumption contexts changed.

Trends and Changes in Consumer Behavior

The developing countries are in the throes of a dramatic mutation. Changes in macroeconomic and demographic factors (e.g., economic liberalization, the growth of a monetary economy) have transformed customary modes of acquisition. Populations are growing rapidly, and there is a visible gap between basic needs and ability to meet them. For example, liberalization has brought a flood of foreign consumer goods to Argentina after decades of protectionist economic policies. In Mongolia, half of the population is younger than 21. After a decade of liberalization, the United States has become the strongest influence on consumer culture. Expansion of commercial radio and satellite TV results in new desires for novel consumption goods. In many LAW nations, marketers must proceed with care in promoting exotic consumer goods in order to avoid becoming the target of antiforeign sentiments. Some consumers in Latin America and Asia see the recent miraculous explosions of Euro-American consumer goods as evidence of **cultural imperialism,** *the imposition of foreign values and practices through the power of advertising hype.* Thus, Kentucky Fried

Chicken has been picketed in India because of concerns about health and violations of Hindu vegetarian values.

One interesting Third World trend is the creative recycling and reconsumption of goods produced in the First World (see Chapter 16). Often, these are instances of the movement of goods on the wheel of consumption from disposal to consumption. For example, kerosene lamps made of cast-off Pepsi cans are common in rural Malaysia. Moroccan sardine cans serve the same function in West Africa. Recycled Western clothing provides some young African men with the means to make a rebellious fashion statement, not unlike their teenage counterparts in the Triad nations. In Senegal, some enterprising craftsmen do a bustling trade in briefcases and lunch pails fabricated of Dutch-made Heineken beer and Senegalese tomato paste cans and lined with French, colored, comic papers. In many countries in the Southern Hemisphere, 20-foot steel shipping containers are recycled into retail shops, warehouses, and even housing.[45]

In many parts of the less affluent world, civil servants and other new elites act as a relay for the diffusion of Western styles of consumption (see Chapter 16). In Brazil, soap opera stars are so influential that product placement in the soap operas, or *novelas,* is an important market communications strategy for products such as Kellogg's Corn Flakes, Johnson's Wax, Tang, or Atari computer games. In San Salvador, El Salvador, the evening hangout of choice for many more affluent people are full-service gas stations run by Esso, Shell, and Texaco. Open air, security guards, lots of foreign imports, and an opportunity "to copy the gringos" provide the draw. Social comparison possibilities and the motive to integrate with perceived elite consumer patterns fuel the fad.[46]

Elite consumers in the less affluent world often adopt "modern," or Euro-American, consumption orientations. But they do not simply mimic idealized Euro-American styles of consumption. Because **nationalism,** *the idea of the nation-state as the sovereign authority,* often developed at the same time as former colonies achieved their independence, consumption preferences often take on blended or creolized styles. Such consumption patterns combine elements of local, traditional consumer behavior with cosmopolitan or imported consumer behaviors. Consumers may wear both foreign designer sunglasses and traditional dress; they may preserve traditional tastes in food but drive Peugeot and Mercedes Benz automobiles. In Argentina, the traditional idea of shopping—*hacer compras*—conveys an image of tedious, functional buying. The English word *shopping,* however, conjures up images of the American good life. Thus, the creolized name of one shopping center in provincial Argentina is *Paseo Shopping.* The name combines the image of North American lifestyle shopping with the traditional idea of the *paseo,* a leisure stroll or tour of the sights.[47] Creolization is an outcome of the acculturation of people to different cultural settings, discussed more fully in Chapter 5.

This chapter outlines the basic contours of the global market economy and identifies opportunities and constraints created by the global economy. Average GNP per capita is a useful indicator of aggregate purchasing power, but it has many limitations as a tool in estimating consumption (e.g., does not take government welfare programs into account). Important trends in global consumption include the move toward a service economy, global concern for the environment, a growing gap between rich and poor, and a number of earthscaping processes.

A global perspective of consumer behavior is important because both marketers and

summary

consumers face a global marketplace. In North America and western Europe, consumers thrive in an information-rich environment. Consumption patterns and preference are defined by the enormous consumption possibilities that exist in these countries, and consumers are accustomed to making fine distinctions between similar brands. Experts predict important trends and changes in consumer behavior as we move into the twenty-first century. Perhaps most important is the fragmentation into smaller subcultures and customized consumer segments.

Consumption patterns in Japan and the newly industrialized countries of the Pacific Rim differ somewhat from those in the western world. Japan is not a newly industrialized country, but it is such a dominant influence in the Pacific Rim that the success of this region is closely tied to Japan. Cultural values and economic problems and opportunities differ greatly across these nations, but it is still possible to characterize some of the commonalities in this region of the world. Access to market information is expanding dramatically with the introduction of new telecommunications satellites and the Internet. Consumption patterns and preferences are extremely diverse. In a number of the NICs, the focus of consumer spending has, until quite recently, been on consumer durables. In other markets, especially Japan and Hong Kong, a wide variety of luxury goods and services enjoy healthy growth.

One of the most dramatic changes in the late twentieth century was the shift of the centralized command economies in former communist states to market economies. Each of these countries has its own special economic problems and differs in its evolution to a market-driven economy. The transformation has been dramatic, but the future remains unpredictable. Consumers are definitely learning to discriminate quality and now have access to the same explosion of media options as North America and western Europe.

Many developing countries and Third World nations have ancient and well-developed market institutions but lack modern marketing infrastructures. The recent spread of global satellite communications has had a dramatic effect on access to marketing communications. Third World consumers are remarkably loyal to local values. In these countries, the future is likely to be mapped by the continued clash between foreign goods and values and local traditions and beliefs. An especially interesting aspect of consumption in these countries is creolization—adapting foreign products and services to local needs and tastes.

You will learn more about global consumption throughout this book. The purpose of this chapter is to set the tone for thinking about marketers and consumers interacting in a very fast-paced, creolized, global world.

---

1. Discuss likely advantages and disadvantages of introducing strong U.S. brands in developing country markets.

2. Collect three or four examples of green marketing. What messages are being communicated by the manufacturer? What claims support those messages?

3. Outline five or six ways in which the information age is likely to change aspects of consumer behavior.

4. Outline some consumption behaviors characteristic of a trend toward green consumerism.

5. There seems to be a growing preference among many women in Budapest, Hungary, for Avon cosmetics. Avon is a U.S. company that offers a full line of moderately priced women's cosmetics products. An unusual feature of the company is that the product line is distributed through Avon representatives who are most often women who sell the product to friends, relatives, and acquaintances as a part-time job. Considering the information you have about consumer behavior in eastern and central Europe, analyze Avon's success.

6. What recommendations would you offer to a U.S. company planning on introducing computer games in China?

7. What recommendations could you offer to a U.S. company planning to introduce its brand of toothpaste in central and eastern Europe? (Assume that the toothpaste is commonly available in U.S. markets.)

8. What recommendations could you offer to a U.S. company planning to introduce its brand of toothpaste in the Third World? (Assume that the toothpaste is commonly available in U.S. markets.)

You Make the Call

U.S. Hospitals Seek Opportunity with Mexican Patients

Faced with mounting cost-cutting pressures at home and lured by the prospect of an improved Mexican economy, more and more U.S. hospitals are trying to drum up business in Mexico. Despite substantial risks, they have gone south of the border in search of consulting contracts, investment opportunities, and, most important, patients.

So far, the Mexican government and most Mexican physicians have welcomed the attention, despite the potential loss of business to U.S. health care providers. But the economic road south is not without potential potholes. Buying spare parts for high-tech equipment and dealing with labor laws are just some of the problems. In the 1980s, Humana Inc. gave up on its Mexico City hospital after the Mexican economy went into a tailspin. Moreover, in a nation where the average minimum wage is less than $4.50 a day, the size of the potential market remains uncertain. While some analysts estimate that more than 10 percent of Mexico's 90 million citizens can afford private hospital care, few have examined the Mexican health care market in great detail; and government figures on both sides of the border are sparse.

With the passage of the North American Free Trade Agreement, most hospital executives expect interest and investment in the Mexican market to grow.

1. Assume that you are the business development director at a major hospital in Houston, Texas. What steps would you recommend for exploring and developing opportunities in Mexico?

2. Would you recommend marketing services directly to Mexican consumers or going through other channels? Explain.

This case is adapted from Robert Tomsho, "U.S. Hospitals See Opportunity in Mexico," The Wall Street Journal, August 13, 1993, pp. B1, B4.

1. Malcolm Waters, *Globalization* (London and New York: Routledge, 1955), p. 3.
2. See Daniel Miller, *Worlds Apart: Modernity through the Prism of the Local* (London and New York: Routledge, 1995); and Thomas L. Friedman, *The Lexus and the Olive Tree: Understanding Globalization* (New York: Farrar, Straus, Giroux, 1999). A good discussion of globalization and localization as related to marketing strategy is included in Güliz Ger, "Localizing in the Global Village: Local Firms Competing in Global Markets," *California Management Review* 41 (Summer 1999), pp. 64–83.
3. The World Bank Group, May 4, 2000, www.worldbank.org/depweb/english/modules/economic/-gnp/map1.htm.
4. Philip R. Cateora and John Graham, *International Marketing,* 10th ed. (New York: Irwin/McGraw-Hill, 1999). See also, Sheila Tefft, "Xu's Have Western Taste," *Advertising Age,* April 18, 1994, pp. 1–10.
5. Slavenka Drakuli, *How We Survived Communism and Even Laughed* (New York: Harper Perennial, 1993).
6. Anthony Pecotich and Clifford J. Shultz II, *Marketing and Consumer Behavior in East and South-East Asia* (New York: McGraw-Hill, 1998).
7. The World Bank, *World Development Indicators* (Washington, DC: International Bank for Reconstruction and Development, 1998), pp. 68–71.
8. "Major Economic Statistics," *Kotra Trade and Investment* 16 (March–April 1998); and *Report on the Family Income and Expenditure Survey* (Tokyo: Statistics Bureau, Management and Coordination Agency, October 1997).
9. Kenichi Ohmae, *Triad Power* (New York: Free Press, 1985).
10. United Nations, *International Trade Statistics Yearbook,* vol. II (New York: Department for Economic and Social Information and Policy Analysis Statistics Division, United Nations, 1996), p. S2.
11. The World Bank, *World Development Indicators,* pp. 27, 170.
12. World Resources Institute, *World Resources, 1998–99* (New York: Oxford University Press, 1998), p. 166.
13. World Resources Institute, *World Resources, 1998–99,* p. 167.
14. This story was broadcast on "Marketplace," *American Public Radio,* April 15, 1993.
15. Marguerite Holloway, "Will It Be Timber for Green Logs?" *Business Week,* October 19, 1998, pp. 81, 84.
16. World Resources Institute, *World Resources, 1998–99,* p. 167; and Marco Thyssen, "Europe Turns Different Shades of Green," *Progressive Grocer,* September 1991, pp. 20–22.
17. *The Guardian,* November 25, 1996, p. 12.
18. "Africa, the Heart of the Matter," *The Economist,* May 13, 2000, pp. 22–24.
19. Patricia Braus, "Selling Drugs," *American Demographics,* January 1998, pp. 26–29; Susan Fournier, "Consumers and Their Brands," *Journal of Consumer Behavior,* 1997, pp. 31–39; Albert Muniz and Thomas O'Guinn (2001), "Brand Community," *Journal of Consumer Research* 27 (March); and Barbara Olsen, "Brand Loyalty and Consumption Patterns: The Lineage Factor," in *Contemporary Marketing and Consumer Behavior,* John F. Sherry, Jr., ed. (Beverly Hills: Sage Publications, 1995), pp. 245–81.

20. George M. Zinkhan, Suzana de M. Fontenelle, and Anne L. Balazs, "The Structure of São Paulo Street Markets: Evolving Patterns of Retail Institutions," *Journal of Consumer Affairs* 33, no. 1 (1999), pp. 3–26.

21. Robert H. Frank, *Luxury Fever* (New York: Free Press, 1999).

22. For a summary, see Irene Lacher, "The Era of Fragments," *Los Angeles Times,* January 2, 1994, pp. E3–E4.

23. "Indonesia: The Long March," *The Economist,* April 17, 1993, pp. 3–18.

24. For information on Japan's move to a service economy, see D. Kilburn, "In Japan, Voice of Authority, or Flattery, a Call Away," *Advertising Age,* February 1, 1988, p. 46. For a discussion of Japan's move to a culture of consumption, see Laurel Anderson and Marsha Wadkins, "Japan—A Culture of Consumption?" in *Advances in Consumer Research,* vol. 18, Rebecca H. Holman and Michael R. Solomon, eds. (Provo, UT: Association for Consumer Research, 1991), pp. 129–34.

25. C. Smith, A. Rowley, D. Givson, L. doRosario, C. Perry, and S. Anwanohara, "Japan 1990," *Far Eastern Economic Review* 148 (June 21, 1990), pp. 37–66.

26. *The Economist,* "Asia's New Consumers: Pamper Them," February 16, 1992, pp. 56–57; Tom Eglinton (1992), "Asia Lifestyles Special Report," *Far Eastern Economic Review,* July 30, 1992, pp. 37–52; August 27, 1992, pp. 29–40; September 10, 1992, pp. 37–51.

27. Salah S. Hassan and Roger D. Blackwell, *Global Marketing: Perspectives and Cases* (Fort Worth: Dryden Press, 1994), pp. 359–80.

28. Mary Yoko Brannen, " 'Bwana Michey': Constructing Cultural Consumption at Tokyo Disneyland," in *Re-Made in Japan,* Joseph J. Tobin, ed. (New Haven, CT: Yale University Press, 1992), pp. 216–34; and Alison Jahncke, "Thailand's Super Shoppers Get U.S.-Style Superstores," *Christian Science Monitor,* July 16, 1997, p. 8.

29. Sheila Tefft, "Contest over Asia: Satellite Broadcasts Create Stir among Asian Regimes," *Christian Science Monitor,* December 8, 1993, pp. 12–13.

30. Graham J. Hooley, "Raising the Iron Curtain: Marketing in a Period of Transition," *European Journal of Marketing* 27, November/December (1993), pp. 6–20.

31. Istvan R. Gabor, "Second Economy in State Socialism: Past Experience and Future Prospects," *European Economic Review* 33 (1989), pp. 597–604.

32. David McQuaid, "Poland: After the Gold Rush," *Business Eastern Europe,* October 24, 1994, p. 7.

33. Bureau of Economic and Business Affairs (1997), *Country Commercial Guides,* Washington, DC: U.S. Department of State, www.state.gov/www/issues/economic/html.

34. Andrew Kopkind, "From Russia with Love and Squalor," *Utne Reader,* May–June 1993, pp. 80–89.

35. See Slavenka Drakulic, *How We Survived Communism* (1993), op. cit., p. 121.

36. Peter Menzel and Charles C. Mann, *Material World* (San Francisco: Sierra Club Books, 1994), p. 248.

37. G. Koretz, "Why Asian Countries Blossomed while Latin America Wilted," *Business Week,* August 28, 1989, p. 16; Robert C. Schmults, "The African Market: A Lion Awakes," *Insight,* August 9, 1993, pp. 18–21; and Amy Kaslow, "World Bank Says to Poor Nations: Be More Efficient," *Christian Science Monitor,* June 22, 1994, p. 8.

38. Ian Katz, "Whirlpool: In the Wringer," *Business Week,* December 14, 1998, pp. 83–84.

39. Eric J. Arnould, "Toward a Broadened Theory of Preference Formation and the Diffusion of Innovations: Cases from Zinder Province, Niger Republic," *Journal of Consumer Research* 16 (September 1989), pp. 239–67.

40. *International Marketing Data and Statistics* (London: Euromonitor, 1997), p. 356.

41. Nathalie Boschat, "Catering to Africa's Consumers," *World Press Review,* June 1993, p. 40.

42. Naseem Khan, "Asian Women's Dress from Burqah to Bloggs—Changing Clothes for Changing Times," in *Chic Thrills: A Fashion Reader,* Juliet Ash and Elizabeth Wilson, eds. (Berkeley: University of California Press, 1992), pp. 61–74.

43. Eric J. Arnould, "Toward a Broadened Theory of Preference Formation and the Diffusion of Innovations: Cases from Zinder Province, Niger Republic," *Journal of Consumer Research* 16 (September 1989), pp. 239–67.

44. Constance Classen, "Sugar Cane, Coca-Cola and Hypermarkets: Consumption and Surrealism in the Argentine Northwest," in *Cross-Cultural Consumer Behavior,* David Howes, ed. (London and New York: Routledge, 1996), pp. 39–54.

45. Anna Husarka, "The First Casualty," *The New Yorker,* April 19, 1993, pp. 57–65.

46. "Salvadorans Find Fun, Fuel at Gas Stations," *Long Beach Press-Telegram,* January 3, 1993, p. A3; and Philip Cateora, *International Marketing* (Homewood, IL: Irwin, 1993), p. 526.

47. Clayton Jones, "From Carpet Bombing to Capitalism in Laos," *Christian Science Monitor,* November 19, 1993, pp. 10–11.

Learning Objectives

After completing this chapter, you should be able to:

- Understand the meaning and nature of culture.

- Discuss the ideas of cultural blueprints, categories, and principles.

- Explain why the fact that culture is learned is significant to marketers.

- Describe the importance of cultural values to consumer behavior and some ways of measuring cultural values.

- Give some examples of cultural myths and symbols and marketing's role in reproducing them.

- Explain and identify some examples of consumer rituals.

- Explain cultural creolization and the role of marketing in this process.

Chapter 5

The Meaning and Nature of Culture

The Baby Jogger

While living in Denmark, we purchased a California-style jogging stroller (shown on page 140) so that we could be together with our three-year-old daughter while we ran in the city of Odense's lovely river park. We wondered how likely the Danes we encountered were to adopt jogging strollers. To us it seemed to be a product in harmony with our understanding of Danish culture, although we rarely saw one in Denmark. We wondered what people were saying about the jogger as we ran past them in the park. And we wondered why it attracted attention. So the question became, Would Danish culture favor the spread of the baby jogger among consumers, or not?

Consider some findings. The Danes we encountered on the island of Fyn love to do things outside. They treasure their rustic summer beach houses. They like to bicycle, run, ride, and swim. Fyn and the city of Odense are crisscrossed with paved bicycle paths. In the winter, we often saw elderly people walking in the park using walking aids. Year-round, babies nap in snug cribs that are kept in unheated porches in Danish day care centers. In addition, Rollerblades™ became quite popular while we were in Denmark. Doing things in family groups, such as eating breakfast, exercising, drinking in pubs, or summering at a beach house, is important in Fyn. Strange as it may sound to North Americans, Danes tend to express individualism primarily through membership in particular groups, for example, as members of the freshman class, jogging or football clubs, and so on. That is, U.S.-style individualism is not well regarded in Denmark. And it doesn't pay to stand out from the crowd too much. Finally, Danes on Fyn currently favor big fancy baby buggies with springs and chrome

Contrasting consumer reactions to the baby jogger in the United States and Denmark emphasize the subtle impact of culture on consumers' preferences.

See www.babyjogger.com.

wheels. They say this is for comfort and durability, but we detected a certain amount of subtle showing off in a family's choice of baby carriage. Families like to stroll with baby carriages through the downtown shopping streets on Saturday mornings, as they take advantage of the morning shopping hours, and through the parks in the afternoons. Rows of babies in big buggies often sleep contentedly in front of stores while their parents shop inside.

So what is your prediction? Would baby joggers become popular items among Danish consumers?

As it turned out, our jogging stroller scandalized many Danes. A Danish friend confided to us that people we gaily passed commented that our daughter was probably handicapped and that we were probably not very good parents for confining her to such an uncomfortable stroller. Indeed, they felt it was egotistical on our part to do so. Apparently, walking with your child in a snug, cozy buggy in the middle of winter is a good thing, but running with your child in a light, airy jogging stroller is not. Things do not look good for the baby jogger in Denmark.

Overview

The chapter will provide you with an introduction to the nature of culture. We pay particular attention to consumer culture. As the opening vignette illustrates, when we visit another culture, we are often surprised by the experience. Things we take for granted—that babies might enjoy an outing in a jogging stroller, for example—do not necessarily hold true in a different cultural context. Our discoveries help to show us the limits of our own cultural assumptions—that, for example, some Danes believe that a jogging stroller is a bad thing for babies. In the case of the jogging stroller, a difference in cultural values results in a difference in preferred consumption patterns. In this chapter, in order to help you understand and manage the interaction of culture and consumer behavior, we discuss the meaning of culture and its expression in cultural values, myths, symbols, and rituals. We also introduce you to some ideas about the evolving relationship between marketing and culture.

The Meaning and Nature of Culture

Social sciences such as sociology, anthropology, and psychology offer varying definitions of culture. Marketers also hold varying conceptions of culture. A traditional marketing view is shown on the left in Exhibit 5.1. In this perspective, culture is viewed as a relatively

Exhibit 5.1 Two Views of Culture and Consumer Behavior

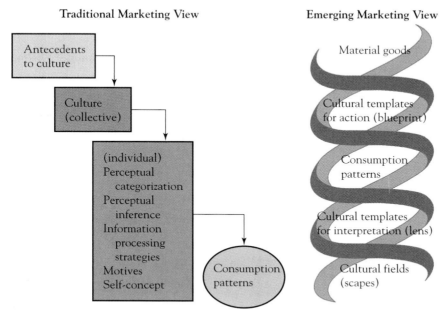

Sources: Daniel John McCort and Naresh K. Malhotra, "Culture and Consumer Behavior: Toward an Understanding of Cross-Cultural Consumer Behavior in International Marketing," *Journal of International Consumer Marketing* 6, no. 2 (1993), pp. 91–127; Douglas B. Holt, "Consumers' Cultural Differences as Local Systems of Tastes: A Critique of the Personality/Values Approach and an Alternative Framework," *Asia Pacific Advances in Consumer Research 1* (1994), pp. 178–84; and Mary Douglas and Baron Isherwood, *The World of Goods: Toward an Anthropology of Consumption* (New York: Basic Books, 1979).

unchanging background for behavior, consisting primarily of values and norms. **Values** are *enduring beliefs about desirable outcomes that transcend specific situations and shape one's behavior.* If asked, people can usually state important values: honesty, dependability, and so forth, for example. Cultures vary in the strength of members' beliefs in a limited number of universal values. **Norms** are *informal, usually unspoken rules that govern behavior.* Waiting one's turn in an orderly line for a cashier is an example of a normative behavior in a retail context. People may not be able to articulate norms, and cultures vary widely on the norms that people obey.

The diagram on the left provides a linear view of culture. Causality flows from top to bottom. Values and norms help to determine perceptual and cognitive principles that, in turn, influence people's attitudes to marketing offerings and consumption practice. In this perspective, the key questions for marketers are to what extent should they adapt market offerings to other cultural contexts, and how should they do it.[1]

Our view of culture and consumer behavior differs from the traditional view and is shown on the right in Exhibit 5.1. Following some anthropologists (scientists who study human culture), we define a society's **culture** as *frameworks for action and understanding that enable one to operate in a manner acceptable to other members.* The frameworks vary between cultures, but they always incorporate language, norms, values, and objects, as well as the myths, symbols, and rituals that we discuss later in the chapter. Both individuals and firms that wish to operate successfully in a culture require these kinds of knowledge. In this view, values, norms, and other cultural elements differ in kind, not merely in strength, between different cultures.

To complicate matters, culture cannot be reduced to a list of language, things, people, behaviors, or values, although all of these are important in a culture. Our list of facts about the Danes did not lead us to correctly predict the popularity of baby joggers, for example. Instead, as the double helix on the right side of Exhibit 5.1 indicates, culture can be thought of *as a set of dynamic models.* Members of a culture use these models to perceive, relate to, and interpret their world. Thus, *culture consists of shared frameworks or blueprints both for action and for understanding.*[2]

Blueprints for action and interpretation are constructed by culture from two basic elements. First is through **cultural categories,** which *organize time, space, nature, and the human community.* For example, class, occupation, ethnicity, gender, and age (discussed in Chapter 6) are examples of cultural categories. These categories help organize a system of social distinctions that arranges the world of consumption. Before the development of consumer culture, cultural categories like these were more rigid than they are today. As an example of quickly changing cultural categories, consider that many of today's information technology jobs did not exist even in the recent past. Other jobs like the once-prestigious category of "textbook author," for example, have changed because the information revolution has shifted what "authors" do to the less prestigious category of "content provider." Especially in the Triad countries, cultural categories are subject to frequent change. The globalization of markets has increased the pace of change of the nature and meaning of cultural categories.

In addition to cultural categories, blueprints for action and interpretation are also shaped by **cultural principles,** *the values, norms, and beliefs that allow things to be grouped into cultural categories, ranked, and interrelated.* For example, cultural principles enable us to classify products into categories and identify new brands as belonging to particular categories. Some cultural principles are expressed in sayings and folk wisdom such as "hard work pays," "there is virtue in loyalty to the state," "you get what you pay for," "seeing is believing," "possession is nine-tenths of the law," or "the nail that sticks up gets hammered down." Some cultural principles operate at very basic levels. For example, in a sequence of advertising images, Western viewers will tend to see those at the right as coming later in time than those at the left. The same would not necessarily be true for members of Arabic cultures for whom text may wrap around the page, or of Chinese cultures where text may flow in columns down the page. Thus, cultural principles structure the perception of time and many other things.

The issue of language comes up in a number of the examples we use in this chapter. Language has a significant influence on our blueprints for action and interpretation. The view of the world that people have depends very much on the character and structure of the language they speak. Users of different languages (a set of cultural principles and categories) are led toward different types of observations and different evaluations of similar observations (interpretations). Language is not only an instrument for describing events, it also shapes events. Observers using different languages will present different facts in the "same" situations, or they will arrange similar facts in different ways.

For example, Dutch and Scandinavian languages have words for "togetherness" that express much more than "being together" and that do not exist in the Anglo-American world. The words are *gezellig* (Dutch), *hyggelig* (Danish), *mysigt* (Swedish), and *kodikas* (Finnish). The Danes use it even in combinations like *hyggetime* (together time) and *hyggemad* (together food). These terms imply sharing one's feelings and philosophies in a very personal way while being together in a small group. Members of other cultures will not understand the concept. Asked about *gezellig,* an Englishman living in the Netherlands might say, "It's so intrusive." As a template for action, the concept means Dutch people prefer a small dinner party to a larger group, for example. A small group is not even considered a "dinner party" by the British, who tend to apologize if there are not more than two couples for dinner. These shared cultural principles of togetherness help to account for the greater collective orientation of the Dutch and the Scandinavians when compared to the more individualistic Anglo-Americans, for example (see the discussion of cultural values).

For the Dutch and Scandinavians, the togetherness concept can be effective in advertising for the type of product used during get-togethers, such as coffee, candies, pastries, and drinks. During the past century, Sara Lee/Douwe Egberts has used it successfully for advertising the company's brand of coffee in Holland and has earned a substantial market share through its use.

Language is much more important than many international marketers realize. It is common knowledge among those who are bi- or trilingual that advertising copy carrying cultural values is difficult to translate. People who speak a single language do not understand this. If translations are needed, particularly for research purposes, the best system is translating and back-translating the questions (translating the foreign language version back into the original language version) to be sure that at least the questions have the same meaning. Yet, the values included in the words cannot be translated easily, and sometimes, equivalent words and meanings are not found.[3]

The diagram on the right side of Exhibit 5.1 suggests that one of the ways that cultural categories are established is through material objects. Objects, especially consumer goods, contribute to the construction of the culturally constituted world because they are a visible record of blueprints for action and interpretation. Products provide tangible markers and symbols of meaning. Consumer goods give cultural meanings concrete forms. People's ways of acquiring, using, and disposing of goods and services enable them to act out cultural blueprints. The baby stroller vignette illustrates how consumer goods, like material objects in general, make blueprints for action and interpretation tangible. In other words, Danish baby carriages symbolize certain cultural values and impose certain cultural ways of behaving (norms). At the same time, they exclude other ways of believing and behaving. Thus, a big baby buggy imposes a certain pace on how one walks, keeps a baby cozy, and encourages sleep. Consumer goods also provide symbols of membership in, and boundaries around, consumption communities. Goods provide others with symbols of these identities as well. To oversimplify a bit, we could say that big, fancy baby buggies symbolize coziness and status to Danes, whereas lightweight baby joggers symbolize health and fitness to Californians. And in the Danish mind, Californian jogging strollers may symbolize poor parenting as well.

As the vignette suggests, cultural categories and cultural principles are expressed simultaneously in consumer goods. You cannot have one without the other. When consumer goods show a distinction between two cultural categories, they express the cultural principles that distinguish the categories. For example, in the United States horses are not food. This categorization expresses the principle that animals may be divided into at least two groups: domestic animals and livestock. It would violate the cultural principles that define the categories to eat horses or other domestic animals like dogs, cats, canaries, and gerbils. Hence, most North Americans do not. Dogs are not classified as domestic animals in some parts of the Philippines, nor are cats among the Gourmantché people of Burkina Faso, Africa. Hence, the flesh of these animals is appropriate for consumption. Many examples of differences in categories and principles could be provided.

Clothing, like other publicly consumed products, is valuable in separating cultural categories of time, space, gender, ethnicity, and class. Clothes represent cultural principles—we agree on some of their meanings. For example, formal attire and cocktail dress imply time and action categories as well as categories of appropriate settings; evening wear is not worn to work for instance and may involve an atmosphere that encourages chitchat and alcohol consumption, for example. In many developing countries, the category of Western dress contrasts with traditional dress. The former represents categories such as cosmopolitan, elite, educated, and foreign; traditional dress represents categories such as local and authentic.

Clothing represents many other cultural categories and principles. Trousers and dresses represent not only gender differences but also cultural principles that distinguish the behavior of these categories of persons. When Western women began wearing business suits, it was a way for them to express the blueprints for action and interpretation associated with the business world—seriousness, authority, efficiency, and the like—and asserted their position in a category from which they had been excluded before. Consumer Chronicles 5.1 adds some details to how the symbolic system of business dress codes is developing.[4]

Acting in conformity with cultural blueprints, members of a community or market segment constantly reinforce the distinctions between cultural categories through their purchase choices and consumption decisions. Members of consumer culture are constantly engaged in making the cultural categories and principles by which they live. Through our consumer behavior, we define and redefine the meanings of self, community, and products and services themselves. When we encounter devoted members of a Harley-Davidson owner's group, a Winnebago-Itasca traveler's group, a fan club (e.g., a Trekkie or Deadhead), a new religious sect, or a political party, we can often see these behaviors pretty clearly.

Consumers' expressions of likes and dislikes (cultural principles) distinguish both goods and consumers from one another. In this way, consumers are also divided into cultural categories. Thus, in the Central American nation of Belize a distaste for eating traditional country dishes (cultural principle) like cowfoot soup categorizes someone as a member of the urban middle class. In the same way, a dislike for eating imported foods like pizza or tuna fish sandwiches (cultural principle), coupled with a preference for cowfoot soup categorizes someone as a Belizean neotraditionalist. As these examples suggest, consumer likes and dislikes and the market segments they define have important implications for marketers.[5]

Fashion trends are fast changing and often difficult to predict. Nonetheless, the Western business suit communicates that the wearer is a serious person who is ready to conduct business. The appropriate style for men remains fairly constant over time. In contrast, there is not a consistent "uniform" for women. When male executives were asked to rate the ability of ensembles to create an "executive look" for women, they came up with the following ranking, from most favorable impression to least favorable impression:

Skirted suit

Dress or skirt with blazer

Dress with matching jacket

Man-tailored pants suit

Simple dress

Skirt and blouse

Slacks and blouse

Skirt and sweater

Slacks and sweater

Women who rely on mass-media images for ideas about work clothing perceive a wider range of acceptable outfits. Women who rely on work associates' and superiors' ideas about appropriate clothing for work have a narrower range of acceptable outfits. As mentioned at the outset, fashion trends evolve over time. As more and more firms introduce the idea of casual Friday (or everyday casual, as in Silicon Valley), standards of acceptable business attire continue to change. Nonetheless, manner of dress remains as an important tool for impression management in all cultures.

Source: Carol S. Saunders and Bette A. Stead (1986), "Women's Adoption of a Business Uniform: A Content Analysis of Magazine Advertisements," Sex Roles 15 (3/4), pp. 197–205.

Consumer Chronicles 5.1

Our vignette provides an example of cultural blueprints in action with regard to rules for choosing and using baby strollers in Denmark. In our view of culture, a key question for marketers becomes how to align their products with cultural blueprints, categories, and principles. To successfully communicate how to use products, who should use them, and what benefits their use provides, marketing communications should build on cultural blueprints. A challenging question for marketers concerns whether and how the introduction of new products and services may contribute to the development of blueprints, categories, and principles.

As the discussion of cowfoot soup illustrates, while we talk of culture as widely shared blueprints for action and understanding, culture is really a systematic collection of values, norms, behaviors, and so on that also reflects *substantial variability*. Thus, we did see one or two Danish couples using baby joggers, but not many. The diversity that may exist in a particular culture is fostered by many factors, including ethnic and class differences (Chapter 6), individuals' lifestyles (Chapter 8), family and household traditions (Chapter 13), and personal experience.[6] For example, some research suggests that the values of managers working in global business environments may reflect professional values that contrast somewhat with the values most characteristic of their national cultures.[7] You may also recall from Chapter 4 that as a result of the globalization of marketing practices, consumers in many developing countries and those in transitional economies confront clashes between Euro-American and traditional cultural beliefs and behaviors. Cultural variability often leads to the development of differences in consumer lifestyles within and across national borders, a topic we discuss in Chapter 8.

Having given you a basic introduction to culture, we now turn to a more specific discussion of several aspects of culture and their relationship to marketing and consumer behavior. These topics include cultural values, myths and symbols, and rituals.

Cultural Values

Consumer researchers interested in culture have devoted most of their attention to understanding cultural values. And cultural values are a good example of what we have called a template or cultural blueprint for action. Values include **instrumental values,** *shared beliefs about how people should behave,* and **terminal values,** or *desirable life goals.* Examples of instrumental values include competence, compassion, sociality, and integrity. Ambition is an instrumental value that might help one attain a comfortable life, which is a terminal value.[8] An example of an instrumental value widely held in Western consumer cultures is a belief that people have choices and that free choice is good. Terminal values include social harmony, personal gratification, self-actualization, security, love and affection, and personal contentedness. The desire for security is used to promote many products ranging from insurance to breath mints and deodorant; many products and services are positioned to appeal to other terminal values.[9]

Cultural values are shared broadly across a society. They are learned, reinforced, and modified within subcultures, ethnic groups, social classes, and families. Values are organized into systems that differ in their importance to consumers. They transcend particular situations. Some believe that behaviors develop from attitudes, which in turn derive from more general or abstract cultural values. This is referred to as the **value-attitude-behavior hierarchy.** According to this model, within any given consumption choice situation, *abstract values affect midrange attitudes that lead to specific consumer behaviors.* Therefore, some researchers believe that values could influence and explain a variety of individual and collective consumer behaviors. For example, the abstract values of security and self-confidence may be linked to attitudes about preventing cavities and providing clean, white teeth, respectively. Consumers with these attitudes may seek these benefits in the toothpaste they buy.[10]

Consistent with the traditional view of culture shown on the left side of the diagram in Exhibit 5.1, attempts have been made to identify and measure a universal set of values. This would allow researchers to compare consumers in one country with those in another. Results of these comparisons, in turn, would enable marketers to adjust the marketing mix to suit the value preferences of different markets.

Among the frequently used value measures are the Rokeach Value Survey, the List of Values, and Hofstede's worker values. Researchers have found considerable cross-cultural differences in levels of these general sets of values. In addition, researchers have sought to correlate these values with consumer behaviors such as how they rank product features, or attributes, and the way they respond to advertising claims.[11]

The **Rokeach Value Survey (RVS)** identifies a set of 18 terminal values, or desired end states, and instrumental values, or desirable actions. A comparison between Brazil and the United States on a few of Rokeach's terminal values shows substantial differences. The most important values in the United States—family security, a world at peace, freedom (independence), and self-respect—are ranked substantially lower in Brazil (seventh, fifth, sixth, and ninth, respectively). The highest-ranking Brazilian values—true friendship, mature love, happiness, and inner harmony—were ranked lower in the United States (tenth, fourteenth, fifth, and thirteenth, respectively).[12] The U.S. terminal value rankings on the RVS have remained remarkably stable over time.[13]

A comparison of Rokeach's instrumental values between China and the United States reveals some differences as well. The top values in China included cheerfulness, politeness, independence, honesty, and ambition. The first two values may be related to Confucian traditions (discussed in Chapter 4). The top values in the United States included honesty, ambition, responsibility, forgiveness, and broad-mindedness.[14]

The RVS has not been widely applied to consumer behavior issues. However, one study found a connection between higher television viewing and lower scores on some Rokeach values such as independence. Another found consumers of a primarily individualist orientation less likely to prefer television comedies than those who value security. One problem with the Rokeach Value Survey, like other measures of cultural values, is that the values are not closely related to consumers' daily lives. For example, world peace ranks as very important, but the link between this value and consumer behavior is not easy to establish.[15]

As a response to criticisms of RVS, researchers at the University of Michigan Survey Research Center developed an alternative **List of Values (LOV)** measure.[16] The LOV includes eight values: sense of belonging, fun and enjoyment, warm relationships with others, self-fulfillment, being well respected, a sense of accomplishment, security, and self-respect. Differences in the strength of these values between regions of the U.S. and between the United States, Norway, and Germany have been detected.[17] In the United States, the LOV has been related to a number of important measures of mental health, well-being, and adaptation to society.

The LOV has been related to some U.S. consumer behaviors, including shopping, spending, nutrition attitudes, natural food choice, fashion items, and gift giving. For example, people who value warm relationships with others give gifts for "no occasion." In an international study, Israeli thrill and adventure seekers scored higher on three values—warm relations with others, fun and enjoyment, and self-respect—than thrill-avoiders. However, a study that attempted to test the degree to which consumers from two different cultures, the United States and Germany, would identity LOV values in TV advertisements ran into trouble when the value-based terms were translated into German. German subjects viewed the terms differently than did the Americans and consequently interpreted the meanings of advertisements differently. Some terms were difficult to translate from English to German, and some that could be translated did not really share the same set of meanings in the two cultural settings. Not surprisingly, therefore, measures linking the LOV and particular patterns of consumer preferences are often weak or inconsistent across cultures and contexts. This problem of translation limits the usefulness of the List of Values and lends support to the view that cultural blueprints differ in kind between cultures.[18]

Another general value dimension of considerable interest to marketers involves individualism versus collectivism. This dimension derives from **Hofstede's worker values.** His study of people from 40 countries revealed that the United States and the English-speaking countries have high levels of individualism (competition is high, independence and separateness are valued, and people believe individual status and position are earned and changeable). By contrast, Latin American and east Asian countries like Japan and China have lower levels of this social value. We have already mentioned that Danes are more collectivist in their value orientation than are U.S. citizens.[19]

Confusing and inconclusive results are unfortunately typical of studies that have sought to link consumer behaviors and Hofstede's abstract cultural values. Part of the problem is that values do not translate well. The blueprints for action and interpretation that would express values such as individualism or collectivism vary between cultures. In addition, specific behaviors linked to these values also differ between cultures. These limitations complicate the use of schemes of abstract values by international marketers.[20]

One intriguing study conducted with a student sample in Hong Kong may help explain the effect of interdependent value orientation on the processing of advertising messages.[21] (You will learn more details about processing strategies in Chapter 13.) In one experiment, researchers found that only consensus information (others' evaluations of the product) influenced Hong Kong consumers' evaluations. Interestingly, only product characteristics guide evaluations in similar experiments conducted in the U.S. The pattern of findings could be interpreted in two ways. First, consumers with different cultural backgrounds may differ in their preference for advertising processing strategies. For example, heuristic-based processing (simplifying rules to make judgments) using consensus cues, for example, may be more preferred in interdependent cultures like that of Hong Kong. Or systematic (extensive use of product cues) and heuristic processing may occur across different cultural contexts, but the information that is perceived as most important may vary across cultures.

The results from a second experiment that manipulated the accessibility of cues provided support for the second hypothesis. This pattern of results suggests fundamental similarities in the ways in which both Hong Kong and North American consumers process advertising content. However, cross-cultural differences found in importance of cues—specifically elaborate consensus information—may lead to the differences in attitudes. Information of this type is useful to marketers in helping them tailor advertising messages to different cultural contexts.

Researchers have identified less universal values than those found in the RVS, the LOV, and Hofstede's study. Culture-specific sets of core values help define a particular culture's blueprints for action and interpretation. Understanding core cultural values may be useful even if cross-cultural comparisons of values are not always useful. The reason is that consumers' purchases are indirectly connected to fulfilling core values. Core values are like goals that can motivate action (see Chapter 10). For example, results of a recent study of advertising effects using Japanese and American samples confirmed that when advertising cues are processed at a low level, cultural-value-based differences in consumer preferences exist. Therefore, understanding these values may be useful for product positioning purposes, including marketing communications.[22]

Exhibit 5.2 compares a constellation of U.S. values with one of Japanese values. As illustrated in the exhibit, these core values are closely connected with each other. For example, for many U.S. citizens the quantity and quality of their material possessions measures achievement and success. Achievement and success are obtained in turn through applying the instrumental values of individual competitive effort. A terminal value for many U.S. citizens is that all people should have equal opportunities for achievement; they believe that through effort, entrepreneurship, and courage (instrumental values), anyone can succeed. Not surprisingly, then, one common motive for purchasing in the United States is rewarding oneself for personal achievement. Similarly, *wa* (harmony) is a Japanese terminal value that strongly affects product design and packaging. Face-saving is a related important terminal value in many Asian NICs, including Japan. The values of harmony and face-saving lead Japanese, and Koreans, to give gifts on set occasions that are chosen from established brand names and that reflect standard status differences in their societies.[23]

Researchers have identified other terminal value clusters in other countries. For example, a study in Bangladesh found five important values: gratification, love and tranquility, harmony, hedonism, and spiritual orientation. In contemporary mainland China, dili-

Exhibit 5.2 Core Japanese and American Values

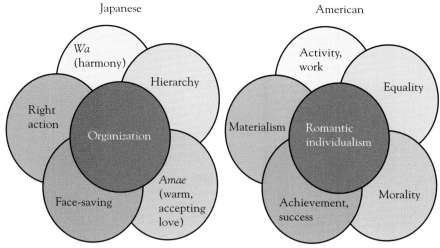

gence, face-saving, frugality, tolerance, pride in Chinese history, tradition, modernity, technological sophistication, and above all, a warm and loving family are important values. Because of their persuasive force, the latter four are frequently used in Chinese television ads to position products.[24]

Another value concept that interests marketers is **consumer ethnocentrism.** Ethnocentrism may be thought of as an instrumental value that helps provide a template for action. It is *a belief that one's own system of tastes and preferences is better than that of another cultural group.* This value influences consumers to purchase goods produced in their home country, regardless of actual product quality. Thus, consumers' views of foreign countries influence their perception of the quality of products designed or produced in those countries. In a recent study, highly ethnocentric U.S. consumers rated both the status and quality of a car designed, engineered, and manufactured in America more highly than one produced in Japan. They also expressed positive attitudes toward buying U.S.-made cars. By contrast, low-ethnocentric consumers appeared to favor foreign cars.[25] Marketers may wish to diminish the foreign associations with their products when marketing to ethnocentric consumer segments.

Good Practice 5.1 provides a scale to measure consumer ethnocentrism. Each of the 17 items is scored on a 7-point scale, with 1 meaning strongly disagree and 7, strongly agree. Highly ethnocentric consumers have high average scores. To measure ethnocentrism in other countries, researchers can substitute different country references for the U.S. references in the scale items, as some have done for France, Japan, Germany, and Russia.[26]

Consistent with our dynamic perspective on culture outlined in Exhibit 5.1, we do not want to leave you with the impression that cultural values, however important they may be, are unchanging. In fact, cultural values are subject to influence by marketing practices. For example, by manipulating the level of ease of recall of value-based associations embedded in marketing communications, some research provides evidence that cultural preferences may be relatively pliable. For example, when value-based associations were subtle and not easy to recall, an experiment demonstrated that Japanese preferred peacefulness associations (e.g., peaceful, mild, shy) with a brand. By contrast, U.S. participants preferred a ruggedness appeal. However, when the value-based associations were made more vivid and easier to recall, a different pattern of results occurred. Culture-based differences were eliminated. Further, members of the nontarget culture participating in the experiment elaborated more on the novel, yet vivid, and positively phrased value-based associations. Elaboration yielded increasingly positive thoughts, which subsequently affected their attitudes.

From a manager's perspective, these findings suggest that global brands based on culturally distinct associations (e.g., BasuKurin bath salt in Japan, Marlboro cigarettes in the United States) still may use global advertising campaigns. But such campaigns should aim to increase the accessibility of the associations (e.g., ruggedness in Japan) rather than shift the meaning of the brand (imbuing Marlboro with less rugged but more exciting associations in Japan). Or a campaign could aim to increase the value of the associations (attempting to make ruggedness more important in Japan). The implication is that such campaigns may eventually alter the structure of cultural values across cultures.[27]

Finally, a value of interest to marketers is **materialism.** Materialism is a terminal value defined as *the importance a consumer attaches to worldly possessions* or as *a consumption-based orientation to happiness seeking.* Further, materialism is a combination of other value orientations, including nongenerosity, possessiveness, envy, and preservation (a tendency to hang on to things).

Materialism has generally been seen as a Western trait that achieved an elevated place with the development of industrial and postindustrial life. Most researchers see the spread of materialism and consumer culture as going hand in hand. Some cross-cultural research has found higher levels of materialism in Western cultures and in urban samples in non-Western cultures where consumers are more exposed to marketing. High levels of materialism comparable to those in the United States and New Zealand, for example, can be found in places experiencing an explosion of new consumer goods and culture such as Romania, the Ukraine, and Turkey. But this research has also found that materialism is not identical across cultures. Consumers in countries that have experienced dramatic increases in the supply of consumer goods, such as formerly communist countries like Romania or the Ukraine, focus more on tangible evidence of consumer wealth such as consumer electronics and cars. The materialism of western Europeans who enjoy greater social stability relates more on the consumption of experiences, art, and aesthetics.[28]

Value-based approaches to culture have been criticized. Faced with problems such as those encountered in the study of German and American interpretations of the values in ads (see page 147), some argue that values differ qualitatively between cultures. Hence, they cannot meaningfully be compared across cultures where different languages are spoken. Others maintain that even if you can get consumers to provide rankings of values, those values are not necessarily the values that matter in a particular culture. Critics also argue that values such as in the RVS, the LOV, or Hofstede's survey are too abstract to provide much help in understanding particular consumption patterns. Can they really help managers account for the Danish distaste of California-style jogging strollers discussed in the vignette, the peculiar popularity of the Argentine tango in Japan, or other preferences we discuss below? Finally, critics argue that the procedures used to develop scientifically valid, cross-cultural measures of values remove the cultural aspects from the instruments, rendering them practically useless.[29]

More work is needed to understand how cultural values relate to consumer behavior and how they vary cross-culturally. Better understanding of the relationships between culture, value preferences, consumers' evaluation of product or service offerings, and purchase and consumption behavior would be useful for more effective cross-national marketing. Without understanding basic values, it is unlikely that marketers can influence specific behaviors within a culture. Of course, marketers need to understand how an individual's values stem not only from shared cultural values but also from regional, social (ethnic and religious), and family values and personal life experiences. And as our introductory vignette makes clear, marketers need to understand how values interact to produce consumption preferences. In future chapters we will discuss these influences and how they vary with consumption lifestyles.

Cultural Myths and Symbols

In addition to values, societies also possess sets of myths and symbols. Myths and symbols are an example of what we have called a template or cultural blueprint for interpretation because they help us understand what we observe in social life. **Myths** are *stories containing symbolic elements that express shared emotions and cultural values.* In

La-Z-Boy furniture ads often link the popular recliner with "snapshots" of a mythical ideal family.

traditional cultures, people conveyed cultural knowledge to their children through myths, legends, and fairy tales. The Chinese moon cake tradition, discussed later (see "Cultural Rituals") is based on the myth of Chang E, a beautiful woman who lives on the moon with her pet rabbit. Today, many popular culture media like television programs, advertisements, movies, comics, cartoons, and novels build on mythic themes and convey cultural knowledge to consumers. Knowledge of myths and how they work is useful to marketers.[30]

Myths serve several important functions in culture. First, they emphasize *how things are interconnected.* The recent U.S. movie *You've Got Mail* is built on a myth that emphasizes interconnections. Much as in Shakespeare's 500-year-old comedic plays *A Midsummer's Night's Dream* and *As You Like It,* people in the movie who are "meant to be together" overcome enormous odds and numerous comic obstacles to come together. A movie like *Medicine Man,* starring Sean Connery, reinforces the mythic value of nature and the interconnectedness of life. Some brand appeals also use the idea of interconnectedness, for example, a La-Z-Boy furniture ad that links its furniture to "snapshots" of a mythical family's life.

Second, myths *maintain social order by authorizing a social code.* Richard Wagner's operas, such as *The Ring Cycle,* draw on ancient Norse myths and reinforce ideas of heroism and national destiny for many Germans. French comic books about the mythical Asterix the Gaulois who lives in Roman times use hilarious caricatures to reinforce French social values and poke fun at the behavior of other Europeans. The European Cinderella myth teaches us how a miserable but deserving person can be blessed with wealth and happiness. This rags-to-riches story resonates with the U.S. immigrant experience. Therefore, variants of the Cinderella myth reappear in many media products, including recent films like *Pretty Woman* and *Working Girl.* The Cinderella rags-to-riches story also has special meaning for the Japanese, who see this story as relating to the post–World War II Japanese experience. Indeed, Tokyo Disneyland chose to feature Cinderella's castle instead of Sleeping Beauty's castle as at the original Disneyland. In the Middle East, several fanciful Egyptian soap operas of recent years have provided a mythical vehicle to work out conflicting models of behavior related to women's roles in society and the place of Islam in a modern nation.[31]

Consumer Chronicles 5.2 illustrates a modern form of mythmaking, an urban legend that authorizes a social code. **Urban legends** are *stories passed by word of mouth that purport to be nearly firsthand accounts of real events but are fictitious. They contain a moral lesson.* We know the story about the cookie recipe is a myth: A world-class retailer would not behave this way, and internal contradictions like the price of the salads (too low) detract from the truth claim. Reality is not the point however. This is a moral story about the rules of market exchange and how customers may reasonably resist retailers' violations of these taken-for-granted rules. In short, it is a story about the rules of fair place. Other common examples of urban myths with implications for marketers include product tampering and adulteration scares. When poorly handled, such as the 1999 Belgian Coke scare, urban myths like these can lead to panic and costly product recalls. Myths are powerful![32]

Third, myths provide *psychological models for individual behavior and identity.* Many myths teach models of heroic or right action. Disney films such as *The Lion King, Mulan,* and *Tarzan* are examples of films whose heroes act out models where individualism and personal integrity are promoted. The actor Harrison Ford has starred in a string of Hollywood movies that promote the value of male heroism and the protection of the nuclear family. The late Toshiro Mifune starred in scores of Japanese movies that dealt with cultural themes of duty and honor. Similarly, the late film actor Marcello Mastroionni became an icon of sophisticated European male values of the 1950s and 1960s.

What constitutes heroic or right action varies between cultures. A Japanese movie, *Masseur Ichi and a Chest of Gold,* illustrates a Japanese version of heroic behavior that differs from U.S. myths. In this movie, the hero, a blind samurai, is motivated to save face and protect the honor of a superior. These motivations lead him to help struggling farmers, who have been disloyal to their superiors, retrieve a chest of gold from some thieves. In this case, the unassuming hero's inner strength of character allows him to overcome great odds.

Understanding myths is important for creating successful media products, and they play a role in building the image of a company and products. McDonald's ran a series of advertising campaigns that replayed U.S. myths. In one, an elderly couple enjoys a romantic meeting at McDonald's. In another, a man demonstrates his commitment to fatherhood by taking his son to breakfast at McDonald's. In a third, an elderly man (with a Protestant work ethic) gets a job after retirement at McDonald's. In a fourth, a young boy stops in at McDonald's for (his now deserved) breakfast after finishing his paper route. Each of these stories features primary U.S. values such as work and activity, the value of individual effort, and equality.

Industry Insights 5.1 provides an example of global mythmaking. It suggests that *Star Wars* not only drew on Western mythology for its plot elements and heroes but that the film has actually contributed a kind of secular mythology to world consumer culture. Today, marketing and merchandising have become deeply involved in building culture.[33]

Important behaviors in any society can be better understood by reference to shared **cultural symbols,** *objects that represent beliefs and values.* Culture is well reflected in **core symbols,** symbols that are *emotionally powerful and that contain multiple meanings.* In the United States, core symbols include George Washington and the Wild West. In France, core symbols include the Louvre museum (and former royal palace), the tricolor French flag, and Marianne, a mythical figure whose face adorns French coins, money, and

This is a true story, this is not a joke . . .

My daughter and I had just finished a salad at Neiman-Marcus Cafe in Dallas and decided to have a small dessert. Because both of us are such cookie lovers, we decided to try the Neiman-Marcus cookie. It was sooo excellent that I asked if they would give me the recipe and the waitress said with a small frown, "I'm afraid not but, you can buy the recipe." Well, I asked how much, and she responded, "Only two-fifty, it's a great deal!" I agreed, just add it to my tab I told her.

Thirty days later, I received my Visa statement from Neiman-Marcus and it was $285. I looked again and I remembered I had only spent $9.95 for two salads and about $20 for a scarf. As I glanced at the bottom of the statement, it said, "Cookie Recipe—$250." That's outrageous! I called Neiman's accounting department and told them the waitress said it was "two-fifty," which clearly does not mean two hundred and fifty dollars by any possible interpretation of the phrase.

Neiman-Marcus refused to budge. They would not refund my money, because according to them, "What the waitress told you is not our problem. You have already seen the recipe. We absolutely will not refund your money at this point." I explained to her the criminal statutes that govern fraud in Texas. I threatened to refer them to the Better Business Bureau and the state attorney general for engaging in fraud. I was basically told, "Do what you want, it doesn't matter, and we're not refunding your money."

I waited, thinking of how I could get even or even trying to get any of my money back. I just said, "Okay, you folks got my $250, and now I'm going to have $250 worth of fun." I told her that I was going to see to it that every cookie lover in the United States with an e-mail account has a $250 cookie recipe from Neiman-Marcus . . . for free. She replied, "I wish you wouldn't do this." I said, "Well, you should have thought of that before you ripped me off," and slammed down the phone on her. So here it is!!!

Please, please, please pass it on to everyone you can possibly think of. I paid $250 for this. I don't want Neiman-Marcus to ever get another penny off of this recipe.

Neiman-Marcus Cookies

Recipe may be halved

2 cups butter

4 cups flour

2 tsp. soda

2 cups sugar

5 cups blended oatmeal (measure oatmeal and blend in a blender a fine powder).

24 oz. chocolate chips

2 cups brown sugar

1 tsp. salt

1 8 oz. Hershey Bar (grated)

4 eggs

2 tsp. baking powder

2 tsp. vanilla

3 cups chopped nuts (your choice, but we liked pecans best)

Cream the butter and both sugars. Add eggs and vanilla; mix together with flour, oatmeal, salt, baking powder, and soda. Add chocolate chips, Hershey Bar, and nuts. Roll into balls and place two inches apart on a cookie sheet. Bake for 10 minutes at 375 degrees. Makes 112 cookies.

Have fun! This is not a joke; this is a true story. Ride free, citizens!
Please pass this to every one you know!

Industry Insights 5.1

To make *Star Wars,* [George] Lucas began by studying the mythology of other cultures, noting recurring plot twists and cruxes and moments-of-no-return that reappeared in the stories humans told themselves. He took elements from myths found in *The Golden Bough,* Sufi legends, *Beowulf,* and the Bible and tried to combine them into one epic story. He ransacked Joseph Campbell's books on mythology, among other sources. It was a kind of get'em-by-the archtypes-and-their hearts-and-minds-will-follow-approach to screenwriting. One could go through *Star Wars* and almost pick out the chapter headings from Campbell's *The Hero with a Thousand Faces:* the hero's call to adventure, the refusal of the call, the arrival of supernatural aid, the crossing of the first threshold, the belly of the whale, and the series of ordeals culminating in a showdown with the angry father, when at last, as Campbell writes, "the hero . . . beholds the face of the father, understands—and the two are atoned"—which is precisely what happens at the end of *Jedi.*

I asked Jack Sorensen [the president of LucasArts] if he could explain the appeal of *Star Wars* as culture, and he said, "I'm as perplexed by this as anyone, and I'm right in the midst of it. I travel all the time for this job, and I meet people abroad, in Italy or in France, who are totally obsessed with *Star Wars.* I met this Frenchman recently who told me he watches it every week. I don't really think this is caused by some evil master plan of merchandisers and marketers. The demand is already out there, and we're just meeting it—it would exist without us. . . . I feel like *Star Wars* is the mythology of a nonsectarian world. It describes how people want to live. People all view politics as corrupt, much more so in Europe than here, and yet people are not cynical underneath—they want to believe in something pure, noble. That's *Star Wars.*"

The marketing is the culture and the culture the marketing. The space that the marketing of *Star Wars* takes up in the culture . . . is validation for the fans of the movies—a kind of return on their investment—just as, in a smaller way, the marketing of the WASP lifestyle by Ralph Lauren is a validation of . . . preppy culture. *Star Wars* is both something to buy (marketing) and something to be (culture), through the buying: becoming a *Star Wars* fan.

Source: John Seabrook (2000), Nob®ow: The Culture of Marketing—the Marketing of Culture, *Alfred A. Knopf, pp. 143, 145.*

buildings. In Japan, core symbols include Mount Fuji. The Danish flag, Danbø, is a core symbol, commemorating a miraculous, long-ago victory over the Poles.

People use core symbols in different ways. The U.S. flag is a public symbol, typically used to mark official places and events. Danes use their flag as an intimate, domestic symbol. A Danish traveler returning from abroad might expect to be met at the airport by his friends waving small Danish flags. And no birthday is complete without Danish flags as part of the celebration.

Marketers can use cultural symbols to help position products and services. Because of positive symbolic associations, French wine and cheese is often stamped with the French flag, for example. The Taj Mahal, a famous Indian building, is a popular name for Indian restaurants all over the world. An animated George Washington (who resembles the image on the paper dollar) has been used in a U.S. government television ad campaign to reassure consumers that the "golden dollar" coin is OK with him. Mayflower uses an image of the pilgrims' ship to symbolize the positive benefits of moving with this company. The examples are endless.

Not only can products and services be positioned using key cultural symbols, but consumer goods can also become cultural symbols. For example, the blue and white BMW logo and the Mercedes circle emblem have become global high-status symbols of distinctive German engineering. Harley-Davidson motorcycles too enjoy a special symbolic status globally.

Consumer goods may become national symbols. French symbols include the old DS (pronounced déese, the French word for goddess) luxury-model Citroën, the favorite car of the war hero and president General de Gaulle, as well as the famous 2CV Citroën. 2CV fan clubs have formed everywhere in France. McDonald's Golden Arches redesigned with a traditional Serbian cap, a *sajkaca,* jauntily perched over one of the arches has become a symbol of national pride in Serbia (former Yugoslavia). This symbol reinforces the identification of McDonald's as a Serbian company. In Egypt, religious commodities provide symbolic protection to believers, such as a copy of the Qur'an (Koran) encased in a velvet box, covered in shrink-wrap, and set in the back window of a taxi. Singha Beer provides a good example of a brand to which many Thai beer drinkers are highly loyal. It has strong associations with Thai national identity due to a long promotional campaign on the slogan "our beer, our nation." You may notice that "authentic" Thai restaurants abroad serve Singha Beer.

www.members. tripod.co.uk/~ BARRS_IRN_ BRU/main.htm

Consumer goods may also become regional symbols. Friele coffee, made by a company based in Bergen, Norway, is an example. Older women can be very attached to this regional brand. Another example is a soft drink called Irn Bru, made in Glasgow, Scotland, for the past half century. Glaswegians "know" it to have remarkable curative qualities for illnesses induced by hard drinking. It has a special, well-guarded formula. It sells incredibly well locally and is the preferred soft drink of many young people. Irn Bru has been the subject of songs, stories, jokes, films, and more. It became famous because of its ads that poked fun at those of Pepsi and Coke, positioning it as an alternative to these U.S. brands. There is even a Church of Irn Bru website.[34]

Some categories of consumer goods are apt to convey important symbolic meanings, and certain types of symbolic meanings are apt to be conveyed by consumer goods. As suggested in Chapter 1, social distinction is one meaning that is commonly invested in consumer goods. We have already discussed how publicly consumed products like clothing, housing, and transportation products serve as symbols of social and economic categories such as class, gender, ethnicity, age, and profession. Adopting a veil, or chador, is a contentious religious symbol of difference among Muslim women in France, for example, because of its implied rejection of core French values. Adopting Indian dress in Guatemala or Peru affirms integration with Indian ethnicity and rejects identification with mixed, or creole, identity. Obviously, people may adopt different costumes to symbolize leisure or work, home or workplace, day and night, and so on.

Food is a flexible symbol of identity, capable of symbolizing fine distinctions. What an individual eats may tell others that the person is young or old; male or female; high status or low status; or sick or well. For example, an old joke from the 1970s stated, "real men don't eat quiche." At the same time, food may also reference wider cultural identities, for example, implying that the person is a Jew, Muslim, or Hindu, or French, British, or Brazilian. On some occasions the food a person chooses to eat might tell something about his or her self-image and how that person wishes to be perceived by others. These meanings are evoked in different social contexts and at different times through particular food items. One study found people chose more ethnic foods when dining with members of the same ethnic group than when dining with consumers of mixed ethnicity. For example, a person of Italian heritage living in New York City may be more likely to eat Italian with other Italians than when dining with non-Italians.[35] On Robert Burns night (commemorating the Scottish poet), a citizen of the United Kingdom might eat haggis (stuffed sheep stomach) and mashed neeps (potatoes) to symbolize a regional Scottish, rather than British, identity.[36]

Some places become symbols of quality, with value linked to products from particular areas. The districts of Champagne and Cognac in France have been successful at protecting their specific regional product names. This enables producers of champagne and cognac to charge higher prices because of the attached symbolic value of these regions. In Beijing, McDonald's is an attraction because it offers a fulfilling experience symbolic of U.S.–fast-food culture. From the tourist industry we know souvenirs often symbolize place. Japanese tourists desire *omiyage* (souvenir) gifts that capture *meibutsu,* or the essence of place. Other goods become symbols of domestic places, such as home-cooked meals.[37]

Consumers use goods in many transitional or developing societies to symbolize modernity or their ability to participate in global consumer society. Consumers' **conspicuous consumption** of status symbols is a frequent by-product of economic development. Conspicuous consumption is the *acquisition and visible display of luxury goods and services to demonstrate one's ability to afford them.*[38] In Thailand and other parts of Asia, in part through the promotion activities of part-Thai player Tiger Woods, playing golf has become an aspirational symbol of modernity and internationalism. In China, in successive waves of conspicuous consumption, the *san dajian,* "three big items," that convey the most status on their owner have changed. During the 1960s and 1970s, they were wristwatches, bicycles, and sewing machines. In the 1980s, these gave way to color TVs, refrigerators, and washing machines. In the 1990s, the three big items were telephones, air conditioners, and VCRs. Of course, conspicuous consumption of symbols of wealth and power is not limited to consumers in developing economies; it is also common among newly rich consumers in developed economies.[39] We will have more to say about how symbols (shared blueprints for interpretation) work in Chapter 9 and about the symbolic meanings of goods in Chapter 18.

Cultural Rituals

In Chapter 1, using the example of grooming, we introduced the concept of rituals and briefly described their importance in consumer behavior. **Cultural rituals** are a good example of activities that combine blueprints for action and understanding. They consist of *behaviors that occur in a relatively fixed sequence and that tend to be repeated periodically.* Knowledge of rituals simplifies behavioral choices such as how to behave at a wedding, for example. In addition, a ritual makes symbolic statements about the social order, often by dramatizing cultural myths and often linking the present with the past. U.S. Thanksgiving Day and the Mexican Day of the Dead (see the vignette for Chapter 18), for example, dramatize cultural myths and link the present with the past.

Rituals organize people's feelings and facilitate and simplify group communications. That is, rituals organize life experience and give it meaning. They are particularly useful in handling situations involving risk, whether the risk is social, emotional, or physical. One outcome of holidays like U.S. Thanksgiving or the Chinese Moon Festival, for example, is family togetherness. Family unity is often threatened by members' migrations and life-cycle changes. Shared family consumption rituals reinforce or repair the social fabric.

Exhibit 5.3 Kinds of Rituals

Primary Behavior Source	Kinds of Rituals	Examples
Cosmology	Religious Magical Aesthetic	Baptism, meditation, mass, Feast of the Sacrifice, Passover, Christmas Healing, channeling, gambling Performing arts
Cultural values	Rites of passage Calendrical	Graduation, marriage, school entrance exams Festivals, holidays (Christmas, New Year, World Cup, Super Bowl, May Day, U.S. Thanksgiving
Group learning	Civic Small group Family	Parades, elections, trials Fraternity initiation, business negotiations, office parties, gift giving, integration rituals Mealtime, bedtime, birthday and holiday celebrations, moving, gift giving, disposition
Individual aims and emotions	Personal	Grooming rituals, possession rituals, household rituals
Biology	Ethological	Greeting, mating

Source: Dennis Rook, "The Ritual Dimension of Consumer Behavior," Journal of Consumer Research *12 (December 1985), pp. 251–64.*

Cultural rituals propose principles and blueprints for consumer behavior that provide marketers with many opportunities for product positioning. Thanksgiving and the Moon Festival reinforce cultural values for people in the United States and China, respectively. Both are widely celebrated. Both celebrate consumption values of abundance and fullness; in both, fat—butter in the United States, lard in China—are consumed in unusual amounts. Christmas is another widely celebrated consumption ritual. It celebrates a principle of family generosity in the United States and Britain and serves as a blueprint for group generosity among the Inuit peoples of Greenland, courtship among Japanese couples, and family generosity to the community in Trinidad.[40]

In Chapter 1 we presented a vignette that focused on ritual behavior that is the product of individual motives and emotions—morning grooming rituals that move participants from the private domestic space of leisure to the public space of work and activity. At the other extreme, rituals can be stimulated by a culture's cosmological belief system, by cultural values, or as a source of group learning. One possible typology of ritual experience is provided in Exhibit 5.3.[41]

In rituals, consumers manipulate objects and symbols. In taking ritual action, people in consumer societies naturally have recourse to consumer goods, the ready-to-hand material of consumer culture. Rituals, like goods, help to establish and stabilize culture categories and principles. Rituals activate the pertinent social meanings of consumer goods. Without ritual, categories and principles remain latent and consumer goods rest inert. Marketers may use marketing communications to initate ritual use of goods, but consumers develop their own household and community rituals as well. The objects and symbols that people manipulate allow them to give form to ritual experience and to associate a shared emotion with these experiences. Subsequently, this shared emotion can develop motivational force (see Chapter 11) that may shape purchase and consumption decisions and behaviors.[42]

Four important types of *consumer rituals* are those relating to possession, grooming, divestment, and exchange (we discuss these at further length in Chapter 18). People undertake **possession rituals** when products move from the marketplace to the home or workplace where they are consumed. Possession rituals also occur when people move into a new home or take possession of preowned goods, which may involve cleansing, customization, or making offerings such as the Jewish custom of tacking a *mezuzah* to the door frame. Removing tags and packaging, customizing, placing, arranging, monogramming, relabeling, framing, storytelling about special possessions, and so on are some of the ritualized activities people engage in to symbolize ownership.

Grooming rituals tend to be private behaviors that aid in the transition from private to public self and back again (see Chapter 7). Clean/dirty, public/private, work/leisure are three of the symbolic transformations that are often involved in grooming rituals. Numerous beauty products (shampoos, cosmetics, perfumes) and personal services (salons, spas, health clubs, fat farms, resorts, etc.) are marketed on their contribution to making grooming rituals successful. Grooming rituals may also be related to possession rituals, as when people clean, polish, restore, or renovate things they own. Hence the marketing success of Pledge furniture polish, for example.

Divestment rituals occur when consumers relinquish possession of objects. These rituals are discussed in Chapter 19, where we explore the topic of disposition.

Exchange rituals, like holiday gift giving, are an extremely important ritual type that we discuss in Chapter 12. An important class of exchange rituals involve **rites of passage.** In rites of passage, like college graduation, participants mark events that symbolize changes in their social status. Rites of passage symbolize the permanence of a change in social status and the behaviors associated with that change. We classify them with exchange rituals because participants often exchange gifts. Debutante balls provide an example of a Western high-society rite of passage that is experiencing renewed popularity. It formalizes coming of age for young women and their entrance into the matrimonial market. Through the ball, the women are "given" to high society.[43]

Many rituals involve the consumption or exchange of goods that have symbolic value: food and drink, jewelry, stationery, diplomas, candles, household furnishings, or ceremonial clothing, such as gowns worn by brides or first communion celebrants. Moon cakes, exchanged as gifts in huge numbers during the Chinese Midsummer Festival, are a good example. Haagen Dazs has come out with an ice cream version to capitalize on the tradition. Ritual goods are indispensable to the meaning of the ritual experience and are used to communicate symbolic messages.[44]

For marketers, providing ritual goods has pluses and minuses. For example, vendors at some Shinto temples in Japan that specialize in childbirth blessings do a thriving business in protective charms and support garments. Stationery and party supply stores provide all sorts of goods for calendrical rituals such as birthdays, Carnival, or Halloween. Other retailers provide symbolic goods that allow fans to express their affiliation with sports teams and contests. Sometimes, a consumer product becomes almost identical with a ritual or even triggers the ritual. For example, Mother's Day was created in order to sell more flowers. And it works. For florists, Mother's Day is the biggest revenue-producing day of the year. Consider a less positive example of the relationship between ritual and consumer demand. Demand for cranberry sauce increases dramatically during the U.S. Thanksgiving holiday. However, for a long time its ritual use affected the marketability of cranberry products for nonholiday meals.[45]

Rituals have life cycles; they decline and gain in popularity, and new cultural rituals emerge as others fade. One by-product of the globalization of marketing is the emergence of global consumption rituals. Christmas and the World Cup soccer championship provide examples of the few ritualized celebrations that are widely celebrated around the world. The Christmas exchange ritual is even celebrated in countries without a Christian tradition, such as Japan and Turkey, and among Greenland's Inuit peoples. And of course, both Christmas and the World Cup induce a flood of consumer spending.

Guidelines for Cultural Awareness

For marketing managers, our model of culture presented on the right in Exhibit 5.1 offers many advantages over the traditional marketing model. To help you become more culturally aware, we present some additional guidelines here. It is important to note that although culture is shared, people hardly ever notice their own culture. This is because culture is an all-encompassing phenomenon like gravity. People don't notice gravity. Nor do they notice a host of behavioral norms of significance in consumer behavior until they are confronted with the different norms or beliefs of members of another culture. For example, consider the cultural blueprints for action concerning verbal communication as reflected in television commercials. In the UK, the United States, and Germany, one of the preferred formats is the "personalized lecture" style in which a celebrity endorses a product. The focus is on the celebrity's persona and its rub-off on the product (see Chapter 17). This format is consistent with a cultural emphasis on personal identity and individualism. By contrast, much of the advertising in Japan is entertainment oriented, with nonverbal rather than verbal communications emphasized. If celebrities are involved, they rarely address the audience explicitly. They play a more symbolic role, associating with the product rather than directly endorsing it. Such a style is compatible with a collectivist culture, where maintaining face is important.[46]

Failure to appreciate such differences because of the all-encompassing quality of culture causes global marketing blunders. For example, U.S. airlines with routes between Japan and Hawaii initially experienced erratic success. Some days the flights were full; others, the planes flew nearly empty. Eventually the airlines figured out the problem. Japanese consider certain days especially lucky for weddings. Honeymoons naturally follow these lucky days, and Hawaii is a favored destination. To even out loads, airlines began offering discounts when honeymooners were not flying.[47]

Different norms governing the use of time, interpersonal interaction, personal space, and body language, among other things, are also primary reasons consumers from one culture often misunderstand service experiences in other cultures. In Africa, most people don't treat time as a resource to be saved or wasted. The idea of buying time—the theme of a North American commercial campaign for a major telecommunications company a few years ago—would not have popular appeal in most of Africa. Western tourists may encounter this important difference in templates for action and interpretation the first time they wait half a day in line for service at an African bank or post office! Similarly, the European expectation that meals will take a long time to serve and to eat drives time-conscious Britons and Americans to distraction and makes them believe (incorrectly) that European waiters are inattentive. Europeans generally dislike American waiters' professional smiles and phony intimacy ("Hi, my name is George and I'll be your waiter today"). Similarly, Asian waiters' unwillingness to smile makes Americans think they are unfriendly. All these examples reflect differences in taken-for-granted cultural templates for action or norms about service interaction. These differences become significant for marketers when firms operate internationally or when they serve customers of different cultural backgrounds. Adaptation of marketing mix elements is then required.

Even though people don't notice their own culture very often, and generally don't remember learning about it, culture is learned. *Learning a culture by growing up in it as a native* is called **enculturation.** Like enculturation in general, consumer enculturation begins early. Marketing communications and marketing mixes can provide sources of enculturation. Thus, many North American three- to four-year-olds recognize and express a preference for McDonald's french fries. Danish children of that age enjoy liver paté as a snack. The Disney kids' movies mentioned in the section on cultural myths enculturate U.S. values of individual initiative.

A major source of multinational marketing blunders is a lack of appreciation for the learned nature of culture and the tenacity of learned preferences. Many food products have required taste modifications to appeal to local consumers. For example, Nestlé makes dozens of versions of its popular instant coffee to suit national tastes. Failure to adapt is costly. The French hypermarket chain Carrefour recently suffered losses in Southeast Asia because it failed to tailor product assortments to local tastes.[48]

Marketing is playing an increasingly active role in the enculturation process. For example, marketers in the UK have used cultural meanings associated with women's changing roles and increased economic activity in attempts to position products in the so-called women's market. Marketers target women by symbolically associating products with lifestyles and images that reflect, reinforce, and propagate these cultural meanings. For example, PPP Health Care's 1997 "Women's Plan" and The Prudential's recent "Wanna Be" campaign are built on the cultural assumption that women of the 1990s are independent. This value of independence draws on liberal feminist thinking in British and North American culture that promotes women's freedom from male domination. This independence is symbolized in the insurance companies' promotional literature as the outcome of the contemporary trend toward high divorce rates and single-parent households. The insurance companies then position their financial products on the risks (lack of male financial support) and benefits (freedom of choice) associated with women's financial independence. As a result, marketing practices are involved in creating behaviors (purchasing financial services products) that reinforce and propagate cultural values and norms associated with one kind of woman's consumer identity.[49]

 www.ppphealth-care.co.uk

Learning a new or foreign culture through direct or indirect experience of others is known as **acculturation.** Through changes in consumption, immigrants learn new cultural templates for action and interpretation. One study found that some U.S. retailers play a role in acculturation among Mexican immigrants and earn the loyalty of these new customers in the process. Sometimes immigrants overshoot some aspect of the new consumption behavior, which then becomes an exaggerated version of that of natives. One study found Mexican Americans overspending on choice meats compared to the native U.S. population. Complete acculturation is impossible, and natives often detect cultural differences in the consumer behaviors of acculturating immigrants. When foreign corporations or media promote foreign templates for action and interpretation, they are encouraging acculturation. For example, MTV, which has affiliates in Brazil, India, China, Europe, and North America, has helped to create a global youth culture.[50]

As you can tell from many of the examples, culture supplies boundaries on our behavior, often with implications for consumer behavior. For example, culture conditions basic biological functions and body image, tells us who and how to marry, sets norms for family relationships, and guides how we believe power and resources should be distributed. Some are concerned that fashion advertising plays too strong a role in establishing

Individualistic heroes: Bill Gates, James Bond and the Energizer Bunny™

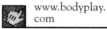
www.bodyplay.
com

blueprints for acceptable body images. Fads in body manipulation test some body image boundaries; see the *Body Play* magazine website to learn a lot about such fads. The Japanese are frank about bodily functions; Japanese commercials provide graphic and humorous ads for products like hemorrhoid remedies. North Americans might be embarrassed by the frankness in the ads. In Ghana, funerals are an important event for elaborate display and consumption of consumer goods; funerals in many other cultural contexts are not.[51]

Cultural boundaries are formalized through social institutions that levy sanctions, or punishments, and provide rewards to encourage us to conform to expected cultural behaviors. In Scandinavia, for example, government taxation and income subsidies level and equalize citizens' consumption possibilities. In the United States, retailers, schools, and the police often limit youth culture fashions and behaviors with negative sanctions. Some commonly seen signs in the United States read "No shirt, no shoes, no service," or "No skateboarding or in-line skating in mall." In such ways, consumption and consumer goods figure in the policing of cultural borders.

Another point is that culture is patterned. Cultural blueprints for action and interpretation are patterned in at least three slightly different ways. First, *they are repeated and reinforced throughout the society,* contributing to a pattern of culture. This is done, in part, through stories, myths, and symbols, including those used in commercial media. Thus, the American value of rugged individualism is repeated in the mythical lives of action heroes like James Bond, industry tycoons like Bill Gates, and even cartoon characters like the Energizer Bunny!

Second, blueprints for action and interpretation are *reaffirmed and renewed through ritual consumption experiences.* The typical Dutch or Swedish *kafferep,* a get-together over coffee, is a widespread ritual that reinforces values of equality, ironic humor, and community.

Third, culture blueprints *tell people what things connect with what other things.* Chil-

Oriental carpets.

Danish design furniture.

Japanese boxed lunch.

1950s American appliances.

dren learn early what consumption objects go with different occupational roles in their culture; the stethoscope goes with the nurse and doctor, the hardhat goes with the construction worker, and the microphone goes with the pop star, for instance. They learn what boys do and what girls do, who wears what kinds of uniforms, and what kinds of people drive particular types of cars or live in particular types of houses.

People also learn the aesthetics typical of their culture, what consumer goods it is tasteful to pair together. Preferred colors, smells, tastes, and sounds differ between cultures. We mentioned in Chapter 1 the aesthetic patterns that create a homey decor in Canadian homes. The patterning of sensory elements gives Bakhtiari carpets (Iran) their distinctive look, differentiates Chinese from Italian opera, and provides Danish furniture, Japanese lunch boxes, and American appliances of the 1950s their distinctive flair. In Chapter 18 we illustrate how Danes and Britons have different but strong ideas about what kinds of furnishings should go together in a tasteful living room. Consumer Chronicles 5.3 provides an illustration of the learning, patterning, and the taken-for-granted, all-encompassing qualities of consumer culture.[52]

Assuming for the moment that bread or toast is an acceptable part of your breakfast, what do you like to put on it? In Italy and parts of France and the UK, Nutella is one popular product. Nutella is a creamy spread made from chocolate and hazelnuts. In Australia, Vegemite could be the spread of choice. Vegemite is a yeast-based product with a pungent, sour flavor. In Denmark, liver paté manufactured by a number of firms is commonly spread on a slab of fine dark bread as a morning treat. And North Americans are infamous the world over for their inexplicable taste for peanut butter. So perhaps Jif is your spread of choice.

The answer to the question of what you like on your morning bread (and by the way, do you like your toast warm as in North America or cold as in the UK?) nicely illustrates a number of points about culture made in the text. Our tastes are cultural patterns that we learn through enculturation. We often take our tastes for granted unless or until we are exposed to alternatives (did any of our choices cause you to make a face?). Culture supplies boundaries on our behavior that in some respects are arbitrary. That is to say, there's nothing inherently proper about paté, Vegemite, Nutella, or peanut butter as a breakfast spread. And our tastes are embedded in broader patterns of behavior that are likewise learned through enculturation. If you'd like to learn more about the products we've mentioned, or even join a product fan club, check the Internet. You'll be surprised by what you find.

Jif Peanut Butter

Nutella

Patterns of consumption aesthetics impose normative pressure on consumers. This is called the **Diderot effect.** The Diderot effect is *the "force that encourages an individual to maintain a cultural consistency in his/her complement of consumer goods."*[53] The Diderot effect is quite common. For example, a woman may buy a new outfit on sale and then reflect that she doesn't have anything to go with it. She may then search for shoes and other accessories to go with the piece of clothing. By the time she is through shopping, she has a complement of consumer goods that "go together," but perhaps she has spent more than she expected.

In addition to the marketing of clothing (outfits) and home furnishings (matched sets), the Diderot effect comes into play in lifestyle marketing and sports merchandising. Scuba-diving hobbyists are encouraged to buy matched fins, masks, snorkels, wetsuits, and tanks, for example. And team regalia sold in team colors and carrying sports team logos fuels demand for a virtually endless array of merchandise. The Manchester United Football Club (UK), founded in 1878 and renowned the world over, offers an array of gear for fans such as the merchandise shown on page 166, for example.

A final contrast to draw between our model of culture presented in Exhibit 5.1 and the traditional marketing model is that we emphasize that culture is adaptive and dynamic. This point is illustrated in the discussions of evolution in the women's market and the pliability of values in advertising. A society's culture does evolve in a given environment combining people, materials and objects, resources, and ideas and beliefs. But cultures are **open systems,** meaning that *they influence and are influenced by changes in their environment.* Culture changes, although it usually doesn't change quickly. For example, American culture has been described as materialistic since the early 1800s. Consumer Chronicles 5.4 suggests that American culture may become less materialistic and the cultures of developing nations more materialistic as they are exposed to more marketing communications and consumer goods.[54]

Some now argue that marketing is changing cultures very dramatically. The global spread of branded consumer goods like Nike, Benetton, and The Gap; retail formats like Wal-Mart or Carrefour; fast-food franchises like McDonald's or Jolibee; consumer holidays like Christmas; popular culture forms like hip-hop, reggae, and world music; and institutions such as beauty pageants are changing cultures the world over. Some argue that the very nature of culture is changing. New global cultural forms provide consumers with common templates for action and interpretation through which to express national and local cultural diversity. Thus, in the era of consumer culture, cultures are no longer separate from one another and relatively unchanging. Instead, they are overlapping dynamic

---

Comparing Turks and Americans on Materialism

Consumer Chronicles 5.4

Materialism has been defined as the importance a consumer attaches to worldly possessions. Materialism has generally been seen as a Western trait that achieved an elevated place in industrial and postindustrial life. A surprising new study, however, shows that Turks are more materialistic than Europeans or Americans. One way of explaining this surprising result is by looking at cross-cultural research on the Protestant work ethic. These studies find that the Protestant work ethic is now strongest in Third World countries, regardless of dominant religion, and weakest in highly developed, postindustrial nations. Once wealth is achieved by devotion to the Protestant work ethic, the motivation to commit to that ethic dissolves. Similarly, some argue, high-level materialism also contains the seeds of its own destruction, because such consumption is ultimately unfulfilling.

Source: Güliz Ger and Russell W. Belk (1990), "Measuring and Comparing Materialism Cross-Culturally," in Advances in Consumer Research, *Vol. 17, in Marvin E. Goldberg, Gerald Gorn and Richard W. Pollay, eds., pp. 186–192.*

The Manchester United Football Club website offers fans the opportunity to purchase a wide range of merchandise.

systems that conform to social boundaries that are heavily influenced by the spread of consumer goods and global marketing communications.[55]

Globalization, Consumer Culture, and Cultural Creolization

The concentration, expansion, and internationalization of the consumer goods industries, the growth of affluent consumer segments in every nation, democratization, loosening of class boundaries, and a quickened flow of information through the commercial media all contribute to global market expansion. These developments have led to the development of global consumer culture.

As stated in Chapter 1, *consumer culture* refers to an organized social and economic arrangement in which markets govern the relationship between meaningful ways of life and the symbolic and material resources on which they depend.[56] Consumer culture may be characterized first by *the global marketing of virtually every good, service, image, idea, and experience.* In other words, in consumer culture everything from beanie babies to politicians is evaluated in terms of its market value. A second defining characteristic is *the increasing importance of materialism among new consumers.* A third element *is a parallel change in personal identity.* A number of authors argue that in advanced consumer cultures personal roles and identities assume an apparently elective quality, and are subject to frequent and significant changes. The elective quality of personal identity means that consumers may declare or claim the cultural categories or lifestyles (see Chapter 8) they inhabit. Given the fluidity of personal identity, individuals satisfy the freedom and responsibility of self-definition through the meanings of consumer goods they acquire and consume.[57]

A fourth element that spreads consumer culture is the *rapid movement of economic migrants, religious pilgrims, and guest workers between even remote villages in the developing world and cosmopolitan centers* in the Triad nations. Not only do these migrants purchase airline tickets, but also they return from their travels with suitcases stuffed with novel consumer goods and often with a positive change in attitudes toward those goods.[58]

A final defining characteristic of consumer culture is the exceptional influence of the fashion industry and *the rapid pace of turnover in fashions* of every kind. In fact, an important source of consumer culture is the fashion industry, an industry that now includes movies, music, food, advertising, and interior design as well as clothing. High fashion "is challenging to our time," says Japanese designer Issey Miyake. This means that high-fashion designers borrow from around the world to create new cultural meanings and to associate new products with available meanings. In summer 2000, Victoria's Secret promoted silk sarong skirts, for example, a cloth and style borrowed from Southeast Asia. Shared taste in particular national markets then becomes an active force in a process of selection, setting limits on and guiding the development of consumer culture locally. Simultaneously, cultural values, norms, and beliefs undergo refinement and organization through attachment both to novel goods and specific social groups. We'll say more about the fashion industry in Chapter 18.[59]

One significant trend in consumer culture is the global spread of brands and consumption practices (see Chapter 16 for more discussion of diffusion and adoption). Pepsi has the goal of developing one global image that is powerful for everybody. Fast-food outlets, especially McDonald's, provide consumers everywhere one route to express some shared consumption values and preferences. Global brands like Nivea, Nescafé, Coca-Cola, or Sony are marketed globally with few local market adjustments and have a wide appeal. However, while there are global brands, there really are not global people. The success of the Sony Walkman, for example, is based on distinct templates for action in the Eastern and Western worlds. Western consumers purchase Walkmans to enjoy music without being disturbed by others; the Japanese inventor of the Walkman, however, wanted a way of listening to music without disturbing others.[60]

A second important trend in global consumer culture is the creolization of consumption patterns. As discussed in the previous chapter, this refers to *consumption patterns that combine elements of local and foreign consumption traditions.* Creolization concerns consumers in all nations. Thus, Jolibee enjoys a 59 percent market share in the Philippine fast-food market thanks to local modifications of the McDonald's formula. Similarly, traditional Turkish fast food called *kepab,* or shish kebab, has experienced a revival as Western-style fast-food outlets have penetrated the Turkish market. As the motivational model presented in Chapter 1 suggests, these choices allow Philippine and Turkish consumers to express varying degrees of cultural conformity and cultural difference through their fast-food choices.

Similarly, the beauty pageant has become a popular consumer celebration in Belize in Central America. Some pageants judge contestants according to Euro-American ideals of beauty; others use local ideals of feminine accomplishment. Both also celebrate Caribbean values of respectability and reputation and express tensions between different ethnic groups in Belizean society that hold different value orientations. The Belizean beauty pageant is a good example of a creolized consumption event.[61]

Creolization is also evident in some areas of consumer behavior in Europe and North America. Examples include the blended musical forms common in world music and creolized cuisines. We provided one example of creolized Japanese cuisine, the MosBurger,

1. Naresh Malholtra, James Agarwal, and Mark Peterson, "Methodological Issues in Cross-Cultural Marketing Research," *International Marketing Review* 13, no. 5 (1996), pp. 7–43; Daniel John McCort and Naresh K. Malhotra, "Culture and Consumer Behavior: Toward an Understanding of Cross-Cultural Consumer Behavior in International Marketing," *Journal of International Consumer Marketing* 6, no. 2 (1993), pp. 91–127; and Shalom H. Schwartz and Warren Bilsky, "Towards a Universal Psychological Structure of Human Values," *Journal of Personality and Social Psychology* 53 (1987), pp. 550–662.

2. Ward H. Goodenough, "Cultural Anthropology and Linguistics," in *Report of the Seventh Annual Round Table Meeting on Linguistics and Language Study,* P. Garvin, ed. (Washington, DC: Georgetown University, 1957), pp. 167–73; Douglas B. Holt, "Consumers' Cultural Differences as Local Systems of Tastes: A Critique of the Personality/Values Approach and an Alternative Framework," *Asia Pacific Advances in Consumer Research* 1 (1994), pp. 178–84; and Douglas B. Holt, "Post-Structuralist Lifestyle Analysis: Conceptualizing the Social Patterning of Consumption in Post-Modernity," *Journal of Consumer Research* 23 (March 1997), pp. 326–50.

3. Marieke de Mooij, *Global Marketing and Advertising: Understanding Cultural Paradoxes* (Thousand Oaks, CA: Sage Publications, 1998), pp. 53–55.

4. Carol S. Saunders and Bette A. Stead, "Women's Adoption of a Business Uniform: A Content Analysis of Magazine Advertisements," *Sex Roles* 15, no. 3–4 (1986), pp. 197–205; and Craig J. Thompson and Diana L. Haytko, "Speaking of Fashion: Consumers' Uses of Fashion Discourses and the Appropriation of Countervailing Cultural Meanings," *Journal of Consumer Research* 24 (June 1997), pp. 15–43.

5. Dorinne Kondo, "The Aesthetics and Politics of Japanese Identity in the Fashion Industry," in *Re-Made in Japan,* Joseph J. Tobin, ed. (New Haven: Yale University Press, 1993), pp. 176–203; and Richard R. Wilk, "'I Hate Pizza': Distaste and Dislike in the Consuming Lives of Belizeans," working paper, Indiana University, Department of Anthropology, Bloomington, IN, 1994.

6. James Clifford, *The Predicament of Culture: Twentieth Century Ethnography, Literature, and Art* (Cambridge: Harvard University Press, 1988).

7. Geert Hofstede, "The Quality of Life Concept," *Academy of Management Review* 9 (1984), pp. 389–98.

8. Milton Rokeach, *Understanding Human Values* (New York: Free Press, 1979). See also Wagner A. Kamakura and Jose Afonso Mazzon, "Value Segmentation: A Model for the Measurement of Values and Value Systems," *Journal of Consumer Research* 18 (September 1991), pp. 208–18.

9. Milton Rokeach, *The Nature of Human Values* (New York: Free Press, 1973).

10. Pamela Homer and Lynn A. Kahle, "A Structural Equation Test of the Value-Attitude-Behavior Hierarchy," *Journal of Personality and Social Psychology* 54, no. 4 (1988), pp. 638–46; and de Mooij, *Global Marketing and Advertising,* pp. 117–18. See also Madhav N. Segal, Uma A. Segal, and Mary Ann Palmer Niermezycki, "Value Network for Cross-National Marketing Management: A Framework for Analysis and Application," *Journal of Business Administration* 27 (May 1993), pp. 65–83.

11. Zhengyuan Wang, C. P. Rao, and Angela D'Auria, "A Comparison of the Rokeach Value Survey (RVS) in China and the United States," in *Asia-Pacific Advances in Consumer Research,* vol. 1, Joseph A. Cote and Siew Meng Leong, eds. (Provo, UT: Association for Consumer Research, 1994), pp. 158–90.

12. Data are from Kamakura and Mazzon, "Value Segmentation," p. 211.

13. Milton Rokeach and Sandra J. Ball-Rokeach, "Stability and Change in American Value Priorities, 1968–1981," *American Psychologist* 44 (May 1989), pp. 775–84.

14. Wang, Rao, and D'Auria, "A Comparison of the Rokeach Value Survey."

15. B. Becker and P. Conner, "Personal Values of Heavy Users of Mass Media," *Journal of Advertising Research* 21 (1981), pp. 2, 37–43; and Sharon E. Beatty, Lynn R. Kahle, Pamela Homer, and Shehkar Misra, "Alternative Measurement Approaches to Consumer Values: The List of Values and the Rokeach Value Survey," *Psychology and Marketing* 2, no. 3 (1985), pp. 181–200.

16. Lynn R. Kahle, *Social Values and Social Change: Adaptation to Life in America* (New York: Praeger, 1983). See also Lynn R. Kahle, Sharon E. Beatty, and Pamela Homer, "Alternative Measurement Approaches to Consumer Values: The List of Values (LOV) and Values and Life Style (VALS)," *Journal of Consumer Research* 13 (December 1986), pp. 405–9.

17. Beatty, Kahle, Homer, and Misra, "Alternative Measurement Approaches to Consumer Values: The List of Values and the Rokeach Value Survey"; Pamela M. Homer and Lynn R. Kahle, "A Structural Equation Test of the Value-Attitude-Behavior Hierarchy," *Journal of Personality and Social Psychology* 38 (1988), pp. 50–56; and Lynn R. Kahle, Ruiming Liu, and Harry Watkins, "Psychographic Variation across United States Geographic Regions," in *Advances in Consumer Research,* vol. 19, John F. Sherry, Jr., and Brian Sternthal, eds. (Provo, UT: Association for Consumer Research, 1992), pp. 346–52.

18. Frauke Hachtmann, "German and American Students' Perception of Social Values as Depicted in Magazine Advertisements," doctoral thesis, University of Nebraska, Lincoln, 1997; Ronald E. Goldsmith, Jon B. Freiden, and Jacqueline C. Kilsheimer, "Social Values and Female Fashion Leadership," *Psychology and Marketing* (1993), pp. 399–413; Aviv Shoham, Bella Florenthal, Frederic Kropp, and Gregory M. Rose, "The Relationship between Values and Thrill- and Adventure-Seeking in Israel," in *European Advances in Consumer Research,* vol. 3, Anna Olofsson and Basil Englis, eds. (Provo, UT: Association for Consumer Research, 1997), pp. 333–38.

19. Geert Hofstede, *Cultures and Organizations: Software of the Mind* (London: McGraw-Hill, 1990).

20. A. Wolfe Kapoor and J. Blue, "Universal Value Structure and Individualism-Collectivism: A U.S. Test," *Communication Research Reports* 12, no. 1 (1995), pp. 1112–13; de Mooij, *Global Marketing and Advertising;* S. Schwartz, "Universals in the Content and Structure of Values: Theoretical Advances and Empirical Tests in Twenty Countries," *Advances in Experimental Psychology* 25 (1992), pp. 25, 1–165; Sarah Todd, Rob Lawson, and Hadyn Northover, "Value Orientation and Media Consumption Behavior," in *European Advances in Consumer Research,* vol. 3, Anna Olofsson and Basil Englis, eds. (Provo, UT: Association for Consumer Research, 1997), pp. 328–32; and Harry Triandis, C. McCusker, and C. Hui, "Multimethod Probes of Individualism and Collectivism," *Journal of Personality and Social Psychology* 59, no. 5 (1990), pp. 1006–20.

21. Jennifer L. Aaker, "The Influence of Culture on Persuasion Processes and Attitudes: Diagnosticity or Accessibility?" *Journal of Consumer Research* 26 (March 2000), pp. 340–57.

22. Jennifer L. Aaker and Durairaj Maheswaran, "The Effect of Cultural Orientation on Persuasion," *Journal of Consumer Research* 24 (December 1997), pp. 315–28; Russell W. Belk and Richard W. Pollay, "Images of Ourselves: The Good Life in Twentieth Century Advertising," *Journal of Consumer Research* 11 (March 1985), pp. 887–98; and Sang-Pil Han and Sharon Shavitt, "Persuasion and Culture: Advertising Appeals in Individualistic and Collectivistic Societies," *Journal of Experimental Social Psychology* 30 (1994), pp. 326–50.

23. Geert Hofstede, *Culture's Consequences* (Beverly Hills: Sage, 1980).

24. Hong Chen and John C. Schweitzer, "Cultural Values Reflected in Chinese and U.S. Television Commercials," *Journal of Advertising Research* 36 (May–June 1996), pp. 27–46; James W. Gentry, Sunkyu Jun, Gyungtai Ko, and Heesuk Kang, "Korea," in *Marketing and Consumer Behavior in East and South-East Asia,* Anthony Pecotich and Clifford Schultz II, eds. (Sydney: McGraw-Hill, 1998), pp. 371–412; de Mooij, *Global Marketing and Advertising;* and Mohammed Abdur Razzaque, "Demographics, Psychographics and Consumer Value Dimensions: A Study of Consumers in a Traditional Asian Society," in *Advances in Consumer Research,* vol. 2, Flemming Hansen, ed. (Provo, UT: Association for Consumer Research, 1995), pp. 183–92.

25. Glen H. Brodowsky, "The Effects of Country of Design and Country of Assembly on Evaluative Beliefs about Automobiles and Attitudes toward Buying Them: A Comparison between Low and High Ethnocentric Consumers," *Journal of Consumer Marketing* 10, no. 3 (1998), pp. 85–113.

26. Srinivas Durvasula, J. Craig Andrews, and Richard G. Netemeyer, "A Cross-Cultural Comparison of Consumer Ethnocentrism in the United States and Russia," *Journal of International Consumer Marketing* 9, no. 4 (1997), pp. 73–93; Richard G. Netemeyer, Srinivas Durvasula, and Donald R. Lichtenstein, "A Cross-National Assessment of the Reliability and Validity of the CETSCALE," *Journal of Marketing Research* 12 (January 1991), pp. 5–21; and Terry A. Shimp and S. Sharma, "Consumer Ethnocentrism: Construction and Validation of the CETSCALE," *Journal of Marketing Research* 24 (August 1987), pp. 280–89.

27. Aaker, "The Influence of Culture on Persuasion Processes and Attitudes."

28. "Ready to Shop until They Drop," *Business Week,* June 22, 1998, pp. 104–16; Güliz Ger and Russell W. Belk, "Measuring and Comparing Materialism Cross-Culturally," in *Advances in Consumer*

Research, vol. 17, Marvin Goldberg, Gerald Gorn, and Richard Pollay, eds. (Provo, UT: Association for Consumer Research, 1990), pp. 186–92; and Güliz Ger and Russell W. Belk, "Cross-Cultural Differences in Materialism," *Journal of Economic Psychology* 17 (1996), pp. 55–77.

29. Holt, "Consumers' Cultural Differences as Local Systems of Tastes"; and Holt, "Post-Structuralist Lifestyle Analysis."

30. Craig S. Smith (1998), "Moon Cake Madness Hits Again," *The Globe and Mail* 10/31/98, p. A21.

31. See Mary Yoko Brannen, "'Bwana Mickey': Constructing Cultural Consumption at Tokyo Disneyland," in *Re-Made in Japan,* Joseph J. Tobin, ed. (New Haven: Yale University Press, 1992), pp. 216–34; and Lila Abu-Lughod, "The Objects of Soap Opera: Egyptian Television and the Cultural Politics of Modernity," in *Worlds Apart,* Daniel Miller, ed. (London and New York: Routledge, 1995), pp. 190–210.

32. "Belgians Close Coke Probe," *Lincoln Journal Star,* April 23, 2000, p. 5G.

33. John Seabrook, *Nob®ow: The Culture of Marketing—the Marketing of Culture* (New York: Alfred A. Knopf, 2000), pp. 143–45.

34. Robert Block, "How Big Mac Kept from Becoming a Serb Archenemy," *The Wall Street Journal,* September 3, 1999, pp. B1, B3; Gregory Starrett, "The Political Economy of Religious Commodities in Cairo," *American Anthropologist* 97 (March 1995), pp. 41–50; and Douglas Brownlie, Philippe Jourdan, Kritsadarat Wattanasuwan, and Einar Brevik, personal communications.

35. Douglas Stayman and Rohit Deshpandé, "Situational Ethnicity and Consumer Behavior," *Journal of Consumer Research* 16 (December, 1989), pp. 361–71.

36. Alison James, "Cooking the Books: Global or Local Identities in Contemporary British Food Cultures," in *Cross-Cultural Consumption,* David Howes, ed. (London and New York: Routledge, 1996), pp. 77–92.

37. Søren Askegaard and Güliz Ger, "Product-Country Images: Towards a Contextualized Approach," in *European Advances in Consumer Research,* vol. 3, Anna Olofsson and Basil Englis, eds. (Provo, UT: Association for Consumer Research, 1997), pp. 50–58; Güliz Ger and Per Østergaard, "Constructing Immigrant Identities in Consumption: Appearance among Turko-Danes," in *Advances in Consumer Research,* vol. 25, Joseph W. Alba and J. Wesley, eds. (Provo, UT: Association for Consumer Research, 1998), pp. 1–4; Raj Mehta and Russell W. Belk, "Artifacts, Identity, and Transition: Favorite Possessions of Indians and Indian Immigrants to the United States," *Journal of Consumer Research* 17 (March 1991), pp. 398–411; and Yunxiang Yan, "McDonald's in Beijing: The Localization of Americana," in *Golden Arches East,* James L. Watson, ed. (Stanford: Stanford University Press, 1997), pp. 77–109.

38. John Brooks, *Showing Off in America* (Boston: Little, Brown, 1981); and Thorstein Veblen, *The Theory of the Leisure Class* (New York: Macmillan, 1899).

39. Russell W. Belk and Janeen Arnold Costa, "The Mountain Man Myth: A Contemporary Consuming Fantasy," *Journal of Consumer Research* 25 (December 1998), pp. 218–40; Andrew Tanzer, "Tiger Woods Played Here," *Forbes,* March 10, 1997, pp. 96–97; and Yan, "McDonald's in Beijing."

40. Daniel Miller, ed., *Unwrapping Christmas* (Oxford: Clarendon Press, 1993); Victor Turner, *The Ritual Process* (Chicago: Aldine, 1969); Judith Waldrop, "Same Stuffing Next Year," *American Demographics* 13 (November 1991), p. 4; Melanie Wallendorf and Eric J. Arnould, "'We Gather Together': The Consumption Rituals of Thanksgiving Day," *Journal of Consumer Research* 18 (June 1991), pp. 13–31; and William D. Wells and Qimei Chen, "Melodies and Counterpoints: American Thanksgiving and the Chinese Moon Festival," in *Advances in Consumer Research,* vol. 26, Eric J. Arnould and Linda Scott, eds. (Provo, UT: Association for Consumer Research, 1999), pp. 555–61.

41. Dennis W. Rook, "The Ritual Dimension of Consumer Behavior," *Journal of Consumer Research* 12 (December 1985), pp. 251–64.

42. Mary Douglas (1971), *Purity and Danger,* New York: Praeger; Mary Douglas and Baron Isherwood (1979), *The World of Goods,* New York: W. W. Norton; Tom F. Driver (1998), *Liberating Rites,* Boulder, CO: Westview Press; Ronald L. Grimes, ed. (1996) *Readings in Ritual Studies,* Upper Saddle River, NJ: Prentice Hall; Douglas B. Holt (1992), "Examining the Descriptive Value of 'Ritual' in Consumer Behavior: A View from the Field," *Advances in Consumer Research,* vol. 19, John F. Sherry, Jr. and Brian Sternthal, eds., Provo, UT: Association for Consumer Research, pp. 213–218; Victor Turner (1969), *The Ritual Process: Structure and Anti-Structure,* Baltimore, MD: Penguin Books.

43. Jennifer Edson Escales, "The Consumption of Insignificant Rituals: A Look at Debutante Balls," in *Advances in Consumer Research,* vol. 20, Leigh McAlister and Michael L. Rothschild, eds. (Provo, UT: Association for Consumer Research, 1993), pp. 709–16; and Clifford J. Schultz II and Gary Bamossy, "Vicarious Fanatic Consumption: The Consumption Experience and Consummations of Soccer Fans and Hooligans," presented at the Annual Conference of the Association for Consumer Research, October 1–4, 1998, Montreal, Canada.

44. Rook, "The Ritual Dimension of Consumer Behavior," p. 253; Mary Douglas and Baron Isherwood, *The World of Goods: Toward an Anthropology of Consumption* (New York: Basic Books, 1979); and Smith, "Moon Cakes: Gifts That Keep on Giving."

45. Rika Houston, "Through Pain and Perseverance: Liminality, Ritual Consumption, and the Social Construction of Gender in Contemporary Japan," in *Advances in Consumer Research,* vol. 26, Linda Scott and Eric J. Arnould, eds. (Provo, UT: Association for Consumer Research, 1998), pp. 542–48.

46. de Mooij, *Global Marketing and Advertising,* pp. 162–63.

47. David A. Ricks, *Blunders in International Business* (Cambridge, MA: Blackwell Business, 1993), p. 30.

48. Ricks, *Blunders in International Business,* p. 25; and Salah S. Hassan and Roger D. Blackwell, *Global Marketing: Perspectives and Cases* (Fort Worth: Dryden Press, 1994), pp. 359–80.

49. Pamela Odih, "The Women's Market: Marketing Fact or Apparition?" *Consumption, Markets, Culture* 3, no. 2 (1999), pp. 165–93.

50. Güliz Ger and Per Østergaard, "Constructing Immigrant Identities in Consumption: Appearance among the Turko-Danes," in *Advances in Consumer Research,* vol. 25, Joseph W. Alba and J. Wesley Hutchinson, eds. (Provo, UT: Association for Consumer Research, 1998), pp. 48–52; Thomas C. O'Guinn, Wei-Na Le, and Ronald J. Faber, "Acculturation: The Impact of Divergent Paths on Buyer Behavior," in *Advances in Consumer Research,* vol. 13, Richard Lutz, ed. (Provo, UT: Association for Consumer Research, 1986), pp. 579–83; Lisa Peñaloza, "*Atravesando Fronteras*/Border Crossings: A Critical Ethnographic Exploration of the Consumer Acculturation of Mexican Immigrants," *Journal of Consumer Research* 21 (June 1994), pp. 32–54; Harry Triandis, Vasso Vassilou, George Vassilou, Yasumas Tanka, and A. Shanmugan, *The Analysis of Subjective Culture* (New York: John Wiley, 1972); and Melanie Wallendorf and Michael D. Reilly, "Distinguishing Culture of Origin from Culture of Residence," in *Advances in Consumer Research,* vol. 10, Richard Bagozzi and Alice Tybout, eds. (Provo, UT: Association for Consumer Research, 1983), pp. 699–701.

51. Sammy Bonsu and Russell W. Belk, "Death Becomes Us: Funerary Rituals and Products for Negotiating Consumer Identities in Ghana," working paper (Greensboro: University of North Carolina); and Jean Kilbourne, *Deadly Persuasion: Why Women and Girls Must Fight the Addictive Power of Advertising* (New York: Free Press, 1999).

52. Russell W. Belk, Kenneth D. Bahn, and Robert N. Mayer, "Developmental Recognition of Consumption Symbolism," *Journal of Consumer Research* 9 (June 1982), pp. 4–17.

53. An excellent discussion of the Diderot effect can be found in Grant McCracken, *Culture and Consumption* (Bloomington, IN: Indiana University Press, 1988), p. 123.

54. Ger and Belk, "Measuring and Comparing Materialism Cross-Culturally." See also Albert O. Hirschmann, *Shifting Involvements: Private Interest and Public* (Princeton: Princeton University Press, 1982); and *Utne Reader,* no. 90 (November–December, 1998).

55. Arjun Appadurai, "Disjuncture and Difference in the Global Cultural Economy," in *Global Culture: Nationalism, Globalization and Modernity,* Mike Featherstone, ed. (London: Sage Publications, 1990), pp. 295–311; Mike Featherstone, *Undoing Culture: Globalization, Postmodernism and Identity* (London: Sage Publications, 1995); Daniel Miller, ed., *Worlds Apart* (London and New York: Routledge, 1995); Daniel Miller, ed., *Unwrapping Christmas* (Oxford: Clarendon Press, 1993); James L. Watson, *Golden Arches East: McDonald's in East Asia* (Stanford: Stanford University Press, 1997); and Richard Wilk, "Rituals of Difference and Identity: Connecting the Global and the Local," presented to the Ph.D. course "Modern Times, Modern Rituals," Department of Ethnography and Social Anthropology, University of Aarhus, Aarhus, Denmark, 1997.

56. Don Slater, *Consumer Culture and Modernity* (Cambridge: Polity Press, 1997), p. 8.

57. Dominique Bouchet, "Marketing and the Redefinition of Ethnicity," in *Marketing in a Multicultural World,* Janeen Arnold Costa and Gary J. Bamossy, eds. (Thousand Oaks, CA: Sage Publica-

tions, 1995), pp. 68–104; Mary Douglas and Baron Isherwood, *The World of Goods* (New York and London: Routledge, 1996); Kenneth J. Gergen, *The Saturated Self* (New York: Basic Books, 1991).

58. Anna Husarka, "The First Casualty," *The New Yorker,* April 19, 1993, pp. 57–65.

59. This paragraph paraphrases Herbert Blumer, "Fashion," *International Encyclopedia of the Social Sciences* (New York: Macmillan, 1968), pp. 341–45.

60. Akita Morita with Edwin M. Reingold, *Made in Japan* (New York: Dutton, 1986); and Leon E. Wynter, "Minorities Play the Hero in More TV Ads as Clients Discover Multicultural Sells," *The Wall Street Journal,* November 24, 1993, pp. B1, B7.

61. Richard Wilk, "Learning to Be Local in Belize: Global Structures of Common Difference," in *Worlds Apart,* Daniel Miller, ed. (London and New York: Routledge, 1995), pp. 110–33.

62. Carol Hendrickson, "Selling Guatemala: Maya Export Products in U.S. Mail Order Catalogues," in *Cross-Cultural Consumption,* David Howes, ed. (London and New York: Routledge, 1996), pp. 106–24.

63. Fuat Firat, "Consumer Culture or Culture Consumed?" in *Marketing in a Multicultural World,* Janeen Arnold Costa and Gary Bamossy, eds. (Thousand Oaks, CA: Sage, 1995), pp. 105–23.

Learning Objectives

After completing this chapter, you should be able to:

- Explain the impact of social class, ethnicity, age, gender, and religion on consumption choices.

- Understand the bases for ethnic segmentation and targeting.

- Appreciate the difference between acculturation and assimilation and their relevance to consumer behavior.

- Understand the idea of age cohorts and recognize the different kinds of cohorts relevant to marketing.

- Recognize some of the key differences in consumer desires between class, ethnicity, gender, and age segments.

- Understand the difference between sex and gender and its relevance for marketing.

- See how the concept of cultural capital can be used to position products and services.

Chapter 6

Economic and Social Structures

Just Another Day in a Venture Capitalist's Life[1]

A wispy early morning fog still hugs the gnarled oaks on Menlo Park's Sand Hill Road as venture capitalist Kevin Fong pulls his Ferrari 355 F1 into the parking lot of the Mayfield Fund. The relaxed foothill setting here is ironic: It masks some of the new economy's most ferociously competitive action. Sand Hill Road is the apex of the Valley's highlife—work obsessed, wealth spewing, and fast paced. The Mayfield Fund, 31 years old this year, is among the most venerable of the blue-ribbon venture firms on this hill.

Years ago Mayfield backed such "Old Valley" winners as Silicon Graphics, 3Com, and Genetech. But today Fong is leading a new charge for building the backbones of the new economy. Broad Vision and Redback Networks, two of Fong's recent investments, may be less familiar to consumers, but they are laying the wire and systems and infrastructure of the new digital universe.

Fong arrives at his bright airy corner office and slips his personal digital assistant in the cradle by his PC. As on most days, he's dressed business casual, in an open-necked shirt and slacks. He is articulate and tightly wound, but with an easy and friendly smile. Fong's father was one of the legendary Hewlett-Packard Co.'s very first engineers and the first of his Chinese immigrant family to leave San Francisco's Chinatown.

Fong's typical day is a whirl of new opportunities, board meetings, and interviews with job candidates; a tsunami of new business plans arrive bidden, unbidden, and sometimes even

violently. Recently, he was rear-ended in San Francisco, and as soon as the other driver realized who Fong was, he not only vowed to fix and detail Fong's car but pleaded with him to review his business plan for a broadband start-up. In the Valley, venture capitalists are as famous as sports stars—and every bit as competitive.

Today the Mayfield Fund's Kevin Fong is one of the Valley's many high-flying venture capitalists—literally. During the week he drives his red Ferrari 355 F1 to his Sand Hill Road office, but on the weekends, in the few waking hours when he isn't doing deals, he pilots his Cessna Citation II jet up to Tahoe for skiing and snowboarding at Squaw Valley. For Fong, life and work in Silicon Valley "is all about change and being comfortable with change."

Overview

The opening vignette illustrates a popular American story of social and economic mobility. Fong, grandson of immigrants to San Francisco's Chinatown, lives in a hub of new wealth and multibillion dollar risks and opportunities. Consumers participate in a number of economic and social structures, and that participation integrates and differentiates them from other consumers. Fong now belongs to the Silicon Valley and Internet lifestyle, and the people and traditions of nearby Chinatown are remote. The structures discussed in this chapter—class, ethnicity, caste, religion, gender, and age—are major organizational categories in societies around the world. Membership in these categories is often expressed through the purchase and use of products and services. Clusters of goods and services purchased and consumed are often connected to social status and personal identity, which these economic and social structures help define. Individual structures vary in how they affect purchase and consumption options in particular contexts. For example, religion may have a significant effect on whether a person eats certain types of food (pork, beef), wears particular clothes (veils for women), purchases products at particular times (Saturday, Sunday), and so on. However, many consumption choices may have nothing to do with religion.

Economic and social structures are dynamic. Like our Silicon Valley entrepreneur, groups and individuals may experience social mobility, which may in turn change consumer behavior. In other cases, as with overseas ethnic communities, such as the Chinese business **diaspora**—a term that comes from *a Greek word meaning a scattering*—membership may tend to orient consumer behavior in international rather than local consumption patterns. The preferences and consumption behavior of members of age-based groups may be relatively consistent over time. For example, young boys yearn for the freedom afforded by independent transportation in many parts of the world—whether car, scooter, motorcycle, or bicycle. However, individual members' preferences shift over time as they undergo life transitions from youth through old age.[2] Regardless of culture, old age creates certain consumption problems: medical, mobility, and mortality, for example.

Economic and social structures anchor and mold consumer preferences and consumption patterns or lifestyles. Not only do they predict the resources controlled by consumers, but consumer skills and values are learned by individuals as members of these groups. Basic consumption tastes and preferences, such as for sweetness, saltiness, and tartness in food, are molded not just by culture but also by social class. Members of social and economic groups tend to create and defend certain consumption niches, such as the "work hard, play hard" orientation of our Silicon Valley entrepreneur. **Sumptuary laws** that attempt to *restrict certain types of consumption based on social class* date back to the Roman Empire at least four centuries before Christ. Centuries later, in the Ottoman Empire, merchants were not permitted to wear furs, a restriction that did not apply to government officials.[3] Although sumptuary laws are less common today, less formal social norms and consumer skills still defend social boundaries. As part of their management programs major U.S. universities such as Northwestern, Harvard, and the University of Pennsylvania (Wharton) regularly include extracurriculum courses such as wine tasting in efforts to equip their graduates to cross social class boundaries. Managers find economic and socially defined groups to be useful targets because they possess unifying characteristics that distinguish their desires, choices, and decision-making styles from other groups. Every element of the marketing mix may require adjustments to match the distinctive characteristics of economic and social segments we discuss in this chapter.

Economic and Social Structures

Social class, ethnicity, tribe, and caste influence consumers' behaviors, often indirectly rather than directly. For example, economic and social structures affect a person's identity (Chapter 7) and lifestyle (Chapter 8), and these in turn influence many consumption behaviors. As with culture, the influence of economic and social structures is easiest to discern in people whose class, ethnicity, tribe, or caste differ from our own. In addition, consumers may embrace and switch between social structures, up and down the social ladder, depending on contexts in their daily lives. For example, a study showed that middle-class Haitian immigrants to the United States in one context distanced themselves from Creole (as the language of lower-class Haitians) and in another context embraced it as the language of Haitians.[4] What part of a person's identity relates to social class and what part to ethnicity? Many American middle-class blacks struggle with this issue, sometimes embracing their ethnicity and on other occasions feeling their social class alienates them from their ethnic roots.[5]

As detailed in Chapter 2, many firms and organizations focus their efforts on fine-tuned marketing strategies targeted to different segments of consumers. Some of these consumer segments are based on social class differences. To understand the effect of cultural differences and similarities on consumer values, we must consider social class.[6] Most authors agree that class distinctions are based on some combination of factors, including inherited wealth, income, occupation, residential location, and educational attainment.[7] We might say **social classes** are *groupings across society, broadly recognized by members of that society, involving inequalities, or certainly, differences in such areas as power, authority, wealth, income, prestige, working conditions, lifestyles, and culture.* People of any one class tend to associate much more with one another than they do with members of other classes.[8]

The existence of different groups of workers is a technical necessity in a complex economy. How these divisions are reflected in income, education, and occupational differences is what is important for marketers. These class variables influence consumption

Class Variation in Consumer Behavior

patterns, customer privileges, and lifestyle distinctions.[9] However, class relates differently to consumption depending on cultural context. For example, the life of a middle-class Latin American household is different from middle-class life in the United States or much of Europe, making it hard to say for sure what middle-class Latin Americans may or may not be interested in buying. The head of household for a middle-class Latin American household probably has less education (primary school only) and a larger household size than one from the United States or Europe. These as well as other differences translate into different consumer needs.[10]

The way in which elements of income, education, occupation, and residential location combine to form a specific **social class hierarchy,** *whereby some individuals have higher status than others,* differs according to a society's history.[11] Social class is deeply significant in a number of Latin American nations, where ownership of property remains an important resource and stark class differences exist.[12] The French and the British, who share a tradition of a landed aristocracy, are more aware of class differences than are Americans or Australians, who lack this tradition. Similarly, without this legacy of noble ownership of the land, the Norwegian upper class differs more from its counterparts in the rest of Europe than it does from the Norwegian working class. Postwar Japan is hierarchical in structure. However, the Japanese express socioeconomic differences in numerous fine gradations of consumption practices rather than in a small number of distinct social classes. In the transitional economies of eastern Europe, new economic elites have emerged by staking out controlling interests in resources formerly owned by the state. Many of these people were part of the political elite under old Communist Party regimes.[13] In much of Africa, classes are differentiated by a combination of older ethnic distinctions and newer differences in occupation, education, and access to government jobs and subsidies. While the traditions differ, class differences themselves are not soft and temporary. Instead, they are tough and persistent patterns of customary social relationships that include consumption behaviors.[14]

| How Social Class Is Determined | A key criterion of social class is income. For example, in countries as diverse as the United States and Zimbabwe, people often draw socioeconomic boundaries on the basis of income differences. And differences of income are especially significant for marketers as these resources are related to purchasing power. Also, absolute income and differences in income levels indicate the size of potential markets.[15] Despite the importance of income as an indicator of social class and of consumption patterns, it can also be inaccurate, unavailable, or misleading. Reasonable estimates of income are frequently unavailable in the developing world and inaccurate or unavailable in transitional economies. Moreover, money goes further in some places than in others. For this reason, the World Bank lists all countries by **purchasing power parity** in its annual World Bank Atlas. The index allows researchers to compare the *relative purchasing power of goods in a particular country to what those same things cost in the United States.*[16] In the United States, income level plays an unclear role in class identification. In 1994, 74 percent of the working class and 63 percent of the middle class reported household incomes between $15,000 and $74,999. But 10 percent of the upper class also reported making less than $15,000, and 4 percent of the lower class reported making over $50,000 a year.[17] |

In the Triad countries, people typically perceive of their own class position on the basis of **relative income,** that is, *how one's purchasing power seems to compare to that of others of similar occupation or lifestyle.* In many countries, this aspect of socioeconomic status is growing in importance as a result of the globalization of the consumer economy. Income-based status is readily signaled and easily communicated through some consumption activ-

ities that are not strongly related to other aspects of social class but require money, such as the purchase of designer brands and foreign travel to expensive destinations. In some contexts, furniture, clothing, automobiles, cuisine, and housing have been found to convey relatively consistent messages about socioeconomic status. In Britain today, for example, you are what you drive. Automobile models sold in Britain come in more variations than anywhere else in Europe because of Britons' desire to precisely convey their socioeconomic status. And, as American marketers and consumers already know, by adding and subtracting gadgets and options, consumers can create a hierarchical system of great complexity. Similarly, in Sydney, Australia, citizens define themselves in terms of residential location. Evaluating social position according to residence is based on consumers' widespread knowledge of relative real estate values and implied socioeconomic status.[18]

Throughout the First World, education, occupation, and social background are mutually reinforcing criteria that more precisely define social class than income alone. A landmark study asked Americans what class they belonged to and then went on to analyze why they classified themselves the way they did. According to this study, 8 percent identified with the poor, 37 percent with the working class, 43 percent with the middle class, 8 percent with the upper-middle class, and 1 percent with the upper class. Topping the list of reasons they belonged to a particular social class was occupation, followed by education and then lifestyles values and attitudes.[19] Occupation is a pretty reliable indicator of social class, and occupations tend to be ranked in terms of prestige. However, rankings vary cross-culturally. In many less affluent nations, government positions are relatively prestigious; engineers are highly regarded in south Asia; university professors are more highly regarded in France than in the United States; and so on.

Education is a determinant of occupation, and it increases social and cultural capital (concepts we discuss later in this chapter), hence it is a critical element of social class and social mobility. Advertisements for executive education programs at the Kellogg Graduate School of Management, Northwestern University play on the connection between education and social mobility, as shown above.

Vietnam's success at reducing poverty through growth in the past decade is in large part attributable to the equitable distribution of education across the population. Even in the poorest households, the educational attainment is similar to that of the wealthiest households. Many other countries tend to have highly inequitable distributions of education assets, which makes it difficult to replicate the Vietnam success story.[20] Sweden, Denmark, and Norway show the highest levels of population literacy.[21] Consistent with this equitable distribution of education, these Nordic countries also have less pronounced social class distinctions (see Exhibit 6.1).

In many countries, higher-education choices are determined by standardized examinations that tend to favor those with higher-class backgrounds. In the UK, as elsewhere, educational choices affect language use and accent, both of which people treat as indicators of social class. Despite moves to democratize educational opportunities in many First World nations, the best public universities (e.g., the French *grands écoles,* Oxford and Cambridge in the UK, Tokyo University, Stanford and Harvard) enroll a disproportionate number of students with higher socioeconomic profiles. Meanwhile, the UK's "red brick" universities, like second-tier state schools and community colleges in the United States, enroll students of lower socioeconomic profiles.

Consumption of higher education is often biased by social class. In Brazil, the state supports the free public universities, but only the socioeconomic elite can afford the expensive private schools that provide students with the tools to pass the entrance exams. In Sudan, a huge Islamic nation in northeastern Africa, the urban, commercial classes have far greater access to education than do rural farmers and herders.[22] Only 10 percent of applicants win places at Turkish universities. The rich can have their children coached for exams or send them abroad, but the poor have to rely on underfunded state schools. Some worry that the education system is creating two Turkeys: one of them wealthy and dynamic, the other, poor, resentful, and vulnerable to political extremism. As in many other places, in Turkey the gap is widening between the rich and the poor.[23] More than 54 percent of New Zealanders are categorized as middle class, and New Zealand has a strong tradition of accessible education. However, in New Zealand, as in many other parts of the world, the quality of education is partially determined by the social status of parents.[24]

The Geography of Social Class

On a global level, most of the world's poor live in the less affluent world, where some 4.4 billion have been mostly left out of the consumption explosion of the last two decades. Although per capita gross domestic product (see Chapter 4) is growing at a brisk rate in China, less than 15 percent of households have income sufficient to buy a refrigerator. Only about 5 percent of Columbians have the purchasing power to afford a car.[25]

The richest one-fifth of the world's population live in the Triad nations, where they consume the bulk of goods and services produced in the world. On a national level, wealthy, middle, and working class residential areas are reasonably stable.[26] Therefore, it is possible to target groups, site retail outlets, and deliver effective market communications to them. For example, in Europe and Latin America wealthy people tend to inhabit inner cities and enjoy second homes in rural areas. Although only three in ten Mexican households are middle class, 58 percent of Mexico City households are classified as middle class. Cities such as São Paulo, Brazil, and Mexico City also have significant numbers of upper-class households with the economic power to buy high-end and luxury goods. Income per capita in Buenos Aires province is roughly double that of poorer Argentina provinces.[27] Lower-socioeconomic profile consumers live in the near suburbs either in high-rise apartment blocks or shantytowns. In North American, by contrast, the poor are concentrated in the inner cities, and wealthier consumers inhabit the suburbs. Japanese "salarymen" also inhabit the suburbs, while remnants of the old nobility are clustered in the oldest urban neighborhoods. However, demographic shifts made possible by development of the information economy have resulted in the emergence of new pockets of affluence in America and Europe.[28]

The globalization of a market economy and of consumer society has resulted in changes in class structure and the relationship between class and consumption. Changes in class structure are most dramatic in many NICs and the LAW nations. Upper-income groups of the "new rich" have emerged in these markets. Three decades of economic growth produced a huge Korean middle class of 36 million people. India and Indonesia likewise have a middle class of more than 20 million each. Recent financial stability and economic growth in Latin America has meant that 10 million people a year are moving into the middle consumer classes. New middle and elite classes have emerged in the transitional economies of eastern Europe as well. Many Triad countries have also seen their class structures change to reflect more pronounced gaps between the haves and have-nots.

Symbolic Capital

Changes in class structure have accompanied the globalization of consumer culture. Global marketing has led to the proliferation of consumer goods, services, and experiences. Technological advance has led to great communication across class boundaries and wider accessibility of goods, travel, and media by all but the poor. Innovative styles and designs now diffuse more rapidly between elite and mass markets and between developed and developing countries. Simple models linking social classes with a stable set of class-related products and brands are no longer very useful to marketers. Lower-class consumers now consume many of the same goods and participate in many of the same activities as higher-class consumers. What really differentiates consumers in different social classes is *how* they consume.[29]

It is useful to segment social class consumption on the basis of how people *compete for higher status,* or what some call **symbolic capital.**[30] To obtain symbolic capital, people draw on three types of resources: economic, social, and cultural capital. **Economic capital** means *financial resources, including income.* **Social capital** includes *relationships, organizational memberships, and social networks that are often nurtured in schools, jobs, or neighborhoods.* **Cultural capital** is a more complicated construct, a product of a person's class heritage. One aspect of cultural capital is *implicit practical knowledge and skills* such as how to use chopsticks, tie a bow tie, or set a formal dining table. A second aspect consists of *access to consumer goods and objects such as fine arts and heirlooms.* And a third is *degrees, diplomas, and memberships in clubs and associations that certify certain qualities to others.* Consumer researchers might find it useful to think of cultural capital as knowledge of high-status consumption activities, including culinary, literary, artistic, and travel. Knowledge of these consumption domains comes about in part through informal learning and socialization. Shared consumption experiences, such as attending a particular class at a particular school or working under a particularly visionary leader, can help equip a person with cultural capital. Cultural capital, in the form of codes of proper consumption behavior among the old elites of New York, the French aristocracy, or feudal Japan, for example, was very elaborate. While we might see these behaviors depicted in popular movies, an ordinary person could not become fluent in these codes of behavior unless socialized into the upper class from childhood.

In general, across classes we see a heightened emphasis on **status-oriented consumption,** that is, *behavior involving competition for symbolic capital often associated with status symbols.* **Status symbols** are *consumer products, activities, or services that indicate a person's position in the class hierarchy.* The domains of competition for status

Traditional sailor-suited teddy bear portrayed in an original sculpture by Lenox

symbols vary across classes, from unique sports cars like a Lamborghini Diablo among the wealthy to "Precious Moments" porcelain dolls and ceramic plates among the working class. The ads shown above were targeted to lower-middle and working classes in the United States. The same magazine issue included several other such ads for collections. Notice how each ad makes it easy to buy with multiple small payments, guarantees authenticity, and ensures a "limited edition."

Status symbols vary internationally as well: knowledge and appreciation of classic Kampuchean dance or Chinese opera are elite tastes, but mainly among Cambodians and Chinese. Taking an expensive cruise may be an indicator of cultural capital among upwardly mobile Thais, while knowledge of fast-food restaurants may serve this role among lower-middle class Brazilians. The point is that even when what is consumed overlaps, lower social class groups consume differently than upper social class groups. A member of the old French bourgeoisie buys a piece of fine china to add to a family heirloom set, whereas a new economy entrepreneur buys a whole new set to demonstrate social mobility, for example. Marketers must position products for different social class groups in different ways to accommodate this fact.[31]

Effects of Social Class on Consumption

Social class influences a variety of consumer behaviors. Social class is a variable for segmenting product markets that satisfy needs related to such lifestyle expressions as housing, clothing, furniture, travel, sports, cuisine, and entertainment. It is also a variable with positioning implications. Consumption experience with a variety of products and services increases in higher social classes, leading to more developed consumer decision-making skills. In part, this is due to the direct effects of income on consumption, but is also due to the cultivation of cultural capital that comes with educational and occupational attainment.

Store patronage is related to social class. Research shows that Americans produce consistent rankings of retail outlets in terms of perceived status, and these rankings become more consistent with higher social class of respondents.[32] Hence, upwardly mobile, high-income African Americans are less likely than the average American to shop at Sears, once the nation's largest mass-market retailer, which has a working-class image.[33] Brand loyalty also is related to class, tending to decrease with higher social class, but this depends on degree of purchase and consumption experience. Purchase and consumption experience may outweigh the effects of social class on brand loyalty.[34] For example, in Latin America brand menus are less developed than in the United States; buyers tend to go for what looks good at the moment rather than drawing from a standard list of favorites.[35]

Consumption Patterns and Class-Based Segments

It can be misleading to look for neat social class divisions segmented on the basis of income, education, occupation, and residence. Nevertheless, it is valuable to develop measures of the rough size of such groups for targeting purposes. Three main class-based segments are upper class (including both old, established elites and the upper echelons of technical and managerial groups), middle class, and lower class (including the underclass). Exhibit 6.1 shows various models of class structure found around the world. The Japanese and Nordic (Denmark, Finland, Norway, and Sweden) models contain the three segments noted above, with smaller upper and lower classes bracketing a large middle class. Often finer class distinctions can be made, as suggested by the other models in the exhibit.

We can make a number of points about identifying social class hierarchies for marketing purposes. One is that globalization reproduces a similar sort of class hierarchy around the world. This has led to **upward mobility,** *a move to a higher social class, usually associated with educational or occupational achievement,* in many transitional, NIC, and LAW countries. It has also led to **downward mobility,** *a move to a lower social class,* for millions of people in some of the Triad countries and in many transitional and LAW countries as well.[36] Downward mobility has been associated with a loss of agricultural and low-level manufacturing and managerial jobs in the Triad countries due to the move to an information economy, the collapse of state enterprises in the transitional economies, and a failure of many enterprises to produce for competitive global markets in LAW countries.

Exhibit 6.1 Class Structure by World Areas

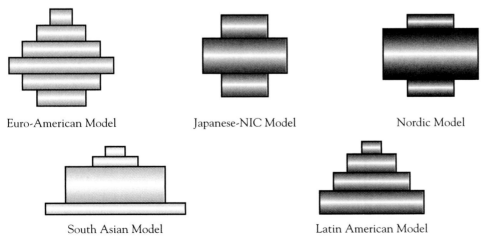

Euro-American Model   Japanese-NIC Model   Nordic Model

South Asian Model   Latin American Model

Source: Adapted from Wayne D. Hoyer and Deborah J. MacInnis (2001), *Consumer Behavior,* 2nd ed., Houghton Mifflin Corp. Exhibit 14.3, p. 334.

www.walmart.
com

A second point of significance is that global class segments may be over- or underrepresented in different countries. Thus, upper-class segments are now overrepresented in the Triad countries while the traditional industrial working class is now overrepresented in the developing world. Companies as diverse as Louis Vuitton Moet Hennessey (LVMH), the luxury-brand conglomerate, and Wal-Mart have globalized their retail operations to take advantage of the world of class-based segments. At this time, Wal-Mart is the largest retailer in the world and operates stores in Argentina (10), Brazil (16), Canada (166), China (8), Germany (95), Korea (5), Mexico (460), Puerto Rico (15), and the United Kingdom (236), in addition to all 50 United States. In the United States, Wal-Mart promotes a working-class image, but at home and abroad the store appeals to a wide spectrum of social class.

A third point is that the upper-middle and middle classes are now increasingly drawn from the ranks of service and information businesses, many of which create distinctive corporate cultures. This group also includes the many information entrepreneurs that have contributed so much dynamism to the marketing economies at the millennium.

Finally, members of the very lowest classes, ranging from native peoples in the developing world to ghetto gangbangers in the Triad nations, now play an important role as sources of images and styles. Successful companies incorporate these trends in their global marketing plans, capitalizing on the **status float** that occurs when *fashion trends start in the lower class and spread upward.* Products as diverse as sneakers, tattoos, and some musical styles like rap and world beat have benefited.[37] Chapter 8 includes more discussion of these global consumption lifestyles.

Upper-Class Segments

Because of its wealth, marketers have targeted upper class consumers around the world with distinctive media and product offerings. In addition, marketers have tended to segment this group into old money, nouveau riche, and the Get Set.

Old money corresponds to the capitalist class or *the upper-upper class.* Old money individuals distinguish themselves through organized philanthropy and other activities that have more to do with the way in which money is spent and less with what is purchased. This is the world of America's old WASP elite, the British and Japanese nobility, and the old French bourgeoisie, for example. First-generation computer billionaires have begun to mimic this pattern of philanthropic concern usually associated with the old money elite. Old money tends to value products that they view as simple, comfortable, and refined and engages in heavy consumption of custom-made products.

The old money bourgeois lifestyle remains strong in many European and Latin American national cultures. It is a segment that prizes quality, prestige brands, and spending with good taste, as well as being distinctively recognized for doing so.[38] In France, for example, money is a means of maintaining a distinctive social identity rather than signaling one's progress on the consumption ladder. In French bourgeois circles, "earned" money is deemphasized in favor of inherited wealth, the *patrimoine.* These bourgeois rarely talk about prices and purchases; they play down commercial relationships; hence, marketing to such groups must focus on other factors such as aesthetic appreciation.[39]

In Mexico and other Latin American nations such as Argentina and Guatemala, regular participation is expected of members of elite families in elaborate, extended family ritual consumption occasions such as births, christenings, girls' fifteenth birthday celebrations, engagement parties, marriages, hospital visits, funerals, and weekend dinners. This round of rituals involves considerable expenditures on reciprocal gifts and provides a context in which to conduct business.[40] As Consumer Chronicles 6.1 shows, these networks also have interesting implications for product and brand loyalty.

Nouveau riche means *new money*. Nouveau riche consumers *combine qualities of the middle class with those of the upper classes.* Like our new economy entrepreneur introduced in the opening vignette, they tend to consider hard work to be the source of their new-found wealth; but besides working hard, they spend or play hard as well. This is the group people associate with conspicuous consumption, discussed in Chapter 5. Conspicuous consumption refers to people's desire to provide prominent visible evidence of **social mobility,** *the passage of individuals from one social class to another.* Social mobility has enabled them to afford luxury goods. Conspicuous consumption often involves purchase and display of status symbols, conventional indicators of wealth and power. Thus, members of southern China's new rich spend enormous amounts of money on first-growth French Bordeaux wines, restaurants, and karaoke entertainment.

Conspicuous consumption tends to be highly conventional, because the nouveau riche want to convey meanings that are conventional indications of success. Being rich enables these consumers to buy beauty through such services as personal trainers, prestigious health spas, and plastic surgery. Like the Silicon Valley entrepreneur in the opening vignette, nouveau riche tend to have expensive hobbies like auto racing or yachting. Often, imagined European aristocratic consumption norms provide inspiration to this group. Thus, exports to Asia's nouveau riche account for more than 50 percent of total turnover for LVMH, the French conglomerate of luxury labels. Cognac producer Remy Martin ships 58 percent of its foreign sales to Asian markets. Spurred by globalization, the nouveau riche in other countries, such as Russia, also tend to consume the same types of luxury products. Their consumption may even be influenced by the syndicated TV series "Lifestyles of the Rich and Famous," which has broadcast nouveau riche lifestyles around the globe. Because of their unfamiliarity with the goods and services appropriate to their new station, the nouveau riche are a valuable target for fashion and design professionals.[41]

Finally, as a result of changing attitudes toward consumption brought about by the globalization of marketing and consumer culture, the *upper-middle class* is reemerging as what marketers call the **Get Set.** Some limitations on income may cause this group to be more selective in their purchase behavior than the other two upper-class groups. However, firms such as Mercedes or Waterford Crystal find that the quality appeal of their brands can be used to encourage members of the Get Set to trade up. It is possible that the increasing ability of middle-class consumers to purchase the goods and services normally reserved for upper-class groups is reviving status competition through symbolic culture. Thus, theme weddings are apparently popular with the Indian Get Set. The U.S. Get Set is buying aggressively functional or very expensive practical things (e.g., big SUVs, or Thermador gas ranges; see ad on page 190). Such goods continue to enjoy the prestige of authenticity and high quality that mass-produced, mass-marketed consumer goods do not provide.[42]

Lower-upper and upper-middle segments in the United States purchase in distinctly frugal ways. This is probably related to North America's unique Calvinist religious heritage.[43] One study found that ordinary Fords were the typical automobiles purchased by

create.

The Jet Set buys very
expensive practical
things like
Thermador® ranges.

*Every so often something comes along that has a way
of bringing about to life. And makes you more relaxed.*
Even a small room daring. Something that says go ahead, improvise a little. You've got all the help
in the world. Thermador. Let it spark your imagination. 1-800-656-9226 www.thermador.com

Thermador®

these groups. Recent research suggests upper- and upper-middle-class consumers in the
United States are frequent customers of discount warehouse stores. Upper-class frugality
is unlikely to be found among elite consumers in countries without Protestant religious traditions. In Muslim Africa or the NICs, for example, demonstrations of wealth and generosity toward members of the family, ethnic group, or neighborhood are expected of elite
consumers.

The emergence of affluent market segments in the NICs—with many people still
learning how to be affluent—represents a new market opportunity. The growth of affluence
in Asia includes China, whose standard of living is likely to double by the year 2000.[44] It
is also likely that the First World nations of North America and Europe will retain their affluent segments; in those countries, a significant share of national wealth, at least 25 percent, is controlled by less than 5 percent of the population.[45]

Targeting the affluent is not always easy. One reason is that the numbers are small.
Second, the truly affluent may own multiple residences. And finally, wealth may be used
to purchase some degree of anonymity. Nevertheless, from social registers, real estate
maps, listings of boards of directors of major companies and charitable organizations, and
other census data, it is often possible to pinpoint the wealthy. For example, Exhibit 6.2 lists
the 10 most affluent areas in the United States in 1990. Looking at Exhibit 6.2, several distinct areas of New York and Washington, D.C., make this list.

Finally, lifestyle variations (i.e., bourgeois, post-yuppie, countercultural, intellectual,
political, risk-taking, New Age, etc.) that have emerged over the past generation exist ver-
tically within upper-middle-class groups, often combining people from several classes (see
Chapter 8). These lifestyle subdivisions are probably more important for positioning goods
and messages than are the named classes in many Triad nations.

Middle-Class Segments

Sizable middle classes can be found in at least half of the more than 200 nations of the
world. Most Americans think of themselves as middle class. In 1978, 75 percent of Americans enjoyed middle-class status, although this number has since decreased somewhat.

Exhibit 6.2 Top 10 U.S. Areas with Household Incomes of $100,000 or More in 1990

Rank	Metro Area	Total Households	Percent Most Affluent
1	New York	319,657	17.8%
2	Newark, NJ	148,627	17.4
3	Bridgeport, Stamford, Norwalk, Danbury, CT	305,167	17.3
4	New York	431,167	17.0
5	San Francisco	95,233	17.0
6	Washington, DC	282,903	16.2
7	Washington, DC	304,486	16.2
8	Middlesex, Somerset, Hunterdon, NJ	88,819	16.1
9	Middlesex, Somerset, Hunterdon, NJ	38,152	15.2
10	New York	84,891	15.1

Source: Rebecca Fetto and John Fetto, "Off the Map," *American Demographics,* June 2000, p.72.

In the United States, middle-class status would generally include incomes between $37,000 and $100,000. Possessing a college education and marriage are also important to this status. Specialized managerial or professional skills are also found among members of this class.

The American middle class is increasingly multiethnic. For example, by 1988 about 51 percent of African-American families were middle class with a median income of $27,000. Since 1970, the numbers of African-American–owned businesses has more than doubled. The number of African-American managers has nearly tripled and the number of African-American lawyers has increased more than sixfold.[46]

Middle-income segments now predominate in European societies as gross domestic product (an economic measure of output) doubled and quadrupled between 1980 and 1995. The economic boom of the early 80s led to the emergence of an upwardly mobile middle-class group named the yuppies, found both in the United States and Germany; their newfound economic well-being fueled a huge demand for goods to express their new selfhood.[47] Over half of New Zealanders consider themselves middle class as well. And when asked, 90 percent of Japanese reply they are middle class.[48]

New middle classes represent growth opportunities for international marketers. In India, for example, only 2.8 percent of the population were middle class at independence in 1947, but today it accounts for 15 percent of a population of 800 million and is growing fast. In Asia, the middle class is expanding dramatically. The number of South Korean households making more than US$2,000 a month is expected to triple by the turn of the century. In Indonesia, this group numbers some 17.4 million, or 10 percent of the population. Up to 20 percent of Thailand's and Malaysia's populations (11 and 3 million people, respectively) may be considered middle class, and even in China 120 million people, or 10 percent of the population, already own their own homes and TVs. Overall, the number of non-Japanese Asian households earning $18,000 annually was expected to quadruple, or reach 75 million, in the year 2000.[49]

In many countries, middle classes adopt values familiar to many Americans, such as education, upward mobility, a future orientation, and material self-improvement. These values lead to heightened expenditures on education and culture (e.g., theater attendance and taking foreign vacations), household furnishings, and popular leisure activities like sports, and they increase brand loyalty. The Mexican middle class spends much of its disposable income on cars, clothing, vacations, and household goods. The trend of a slowly shrinking education gap in the United States is leading to changes in class position and lifestyle choices of African Americans. Indeed, many minorities in the United States perceive access to education to be a key to class advancement and attaining related lifestyle and consumption prerogatives.[50]

Marketing to middle-class segments in Asia, the Middle East, and Africa requires appeals that meld traditional and innovative values with great consideration of local norms and values. For example, the Indonesian middle class is relatively passive and conformist. Part of the explanation lies with the internalization of traditional Confucian-style values—submission to authority, suppression of initiative, and an unquestioning approach to established norms.[51]

Although the middle class is expanding in some developing nations, relatively rapid growth of per capita GDP is often accompanied by extreme income inequality. The problem of rapid growth without redistribution to a middle class afflicts many developing countries. For example, in spite of improvements in quality of life that have accompanied the transition to popular democracy in South Africa, in 1994 the poorest 20 percent of South Africans earned a GDP per capita of only $516, compared to the richest 20 percent, who earned $9,897.[52]

An increase in **discretionary income** characterizes the gains in income of these middle-class households. Discretionary income is *the income over and above that required to meet basic consumer needs.* Discretionary income increases as overall income goes up. Consumers often desire to translate improvements in earning power into evidence of social mobility.[53] People moving from lower- to higher-income groups often signal their new social class pretensions through changes in consumer goods. Thus, in the NICs these income trends are fueling increasing demand not only for consumer durables but for higher-quality food products and luxuries like recreation and private transportation as well. Volkswagen, GM, and other automakers were quick to establish plants in China in anticipation of the emergence of a middle class with increased discretionary income.

Working-Class and Under-Class Segments

Working- and under-class segments constitute a majority of the population of the world. Half of the nations of the world have per capita incomes of less than $2,000; in two-thirds of the world, per capita income is less than $5,000. In China, 285 million people, mostly in the western half of the country, earn incomes of $150 to $750 annually. In the United

States, ranking tenth in per capita income in the world ($22,000), more than 30 million Americans live in poverty and 40 million U.S. households have annual incomes of less than $25,000. In the UK, almost 20 percent of households have incomes below half the average national income.[54] Poor First World households tend to be associated with single mothers, low education levels, and a disproportionate number of minorities, young people, and the aged.

Studies of the working poor and working class in the United States and in developing countries show that official income figures conceal numerous sources of informal income. In addition, intense networks of exchange of goods and services among kin and neighbors effectively increase demand for many goods and services among poorer consumers. In the First World, these groups also receive a disproportionate amount of public assistance.[55] Networks of reciprocal exchange act to improve standards of living. Such networks also redistribute consumer goods as suggested in Consumer Chronicles 6.2.

One extremely widespread institution among the poorer classes in many developing societies is the rotating credit association. Found throughout Asia, Africa, and Latin America, and among Korean immigrants to the United States, the consumers in these voluntary associations pool a portion of their income on a weekly or monthly basis. Each week or month, one member receives the total amount collected. Members use these sums to fund important purchases of durable and consumer goods.[56] The fact that many working-class consumers may spread the cost of acquiring desired goods among kin and neighbors (see Consumer Chronicles 6.3) by charging user fees or pooling income suggests marketers need to develop strategies to target these supraindividual, suprafamilial consumer groups among the lower classes. Self-reliance and widespread using of pooling mechanisms means that many working-class consumers avoid dealings with banks. In the United States, such consumers tend to use expensive check-cashing services for their limited banking needs. As Industry Insights 6.1 shows, some banks have seen an opportunity here.

Studies in Triad nations as well as in some developing nations have found that working-class consumers are resistant to changes in the basic characteristics of their lifestyles. Brand loyalty and cost consciousness are examples. These characteristics have been little altered by broader patterns of global change, even in the technological environment. Other characteristics include limited social and geographic horizons, centrality of family and clan influences on behavior, and devotion to nation and neighborhood.[57] Loyalty to local sports teams is also common.[58] Working-class consumers tend to be externally oriented and emulative. They take status goods and other markers of the good life to heart. Fatalism and magical beliefs in luck, astrology, psychic powers, and miracles are not uncommon. Downmarket tabloids often contain advertisements for products and services promising magical diagnoses or cures.

Productive Consumption in Lima

Consumer Chronicles 6.3

Those families in Ciudadela Chalaca, Lima, Peru, that own television sets may also choose to allow neighbors to pay two soles, Peruvian currency, to watch special shows. The most popular are the daily afternoon soap operas, or *novelas*, which are watched by women, and the sports shows, particularly the soccer matches, watched by men on the weekends. The *novelas* are most commonly produced in Peru, Mexico, or Venezuela and reflect an idealized version of middle- and upper-class values; they not only function as entertainment but also provide knowledge of middle- and upper-class behavior patterns, much of which is of use to migrants in dealing with urban situations.

Source: Susan Lobo, A House of My Own: Social Organization in the Squatter Settlements of Lima, Peru *(Tucson, AZ: University of Arizona Press, 1982).*

Bank to Cater to Low Income Consumers

With an eye to winning the loyalty of a largely untapped group of potential customers, the working-class immigrants of Los Angeles, Union Bank launched full-scale competition with the high-cost check-cashing services that substitute for banks in many lower income neighborhoods. In a shopping district of heavily Latino Huntington Park, the bank opened what may be the state's first stand-alone center combining check-cashing and basic banking services.

Union Bank hopes to eventually convert many of its check-cashing customers into regular banking clients with checking accounts and unsecured credit. "In part this will be an educational process," Huntington Park mayor Richard Loya said. "A lot of Latinos don't like banks—maybe because they were cheated by the banks in Mexico."

Source: Michael A. Hiltzik, "Union Bank Outlet to Cater to Low-Income Customers," Los Angeles Times, June 7, 1994, pp. D1; D2.

Working-class consumers seek to participate in the consumer economy not through the contribution of innovative ideas but through consumption of familiar goods and services that strengthen existing social relationships. They use consumption to claim status in a straightforward way. Lower- or working-class cultures value group conformity, localism, and authority. A characteristic behavior is keeping up with the Joneses, so to speak, but not getting ahead of them, which often means favoring regional and mass-merchandise brands. The home and family is a focus for working-class consumption, with home repair being a typical activity in countries as diverse as the United States, France, and Norway.[59] In working-class homes in many industrial nations, products exemplifying values such as orderliness and prosperity are often favored.

Working-class demographics and value orientations might suggest that these consumers represent unattractive markets. However, even in the United States almost 40 percent of consumers fall into working-class groups. Hence, mass merchandisers and discount retailers that offer quality basics at fair prices may expect to cultivate loyalty with such groups. Recognition of this has led to the emergence of what is sometimes called **two-tiered marketing.** In two-tiered marketing, *firms differentiate their retail outlets or product or service offerings into two groups, targeted at upper- or lower-class consumers, respectively.* In addition, these firms minimize offerings to middle income segments. Banana Republic, The Gap, and Old Navy stores provide an example of multitier marketing. All are owned by the same company, but price points and image for each type of outlet varies from exclusive boutique to a warehouse style. Another example is the success that the Grameem group has had in marketing cellular telephone services to the poor in Bangladesh.

In distinction to the working class, a behavioral underclass composed of poor, chronically unemployed, and ill-educated people who are deprived of most consumer options has emerged. This group is increasingly socially isolated from mainstream society as the deindustrialization of First World and devaluation of unskilled labor in the transitional and LAW nations cut off the bottom rungs of the employment ladder. Members of this underclass allegedly engage in antisocial behaviors, especially crimes against property and persons. Shoplifting, burglary, and looting linked to urban disturbances and ethnic or caste-based (see below) warfare are also associated with this group. Overconsumption of alcohol, tobacco, and illegal drugs are also an affliction for them. Across urban America, some authors estimate that this group numbers between 1.5 and 2.5 million people. A similar class may be found in some of the UK's worst housing estates, among the "lost generation" of former East Germany, and in places like Haiti or Sierra Leone. Even countries with significant consumer welfare policies are facing challenges from the problems of alienation and economic marginalization experienced by the underclass.[60]

Quick, what do the United States, Canada, Israel, Indonesia, Australia, and Germany have in common? Ethnic diversity is the answer. Twenty-nine percent of Americans and 25 percent of Australians are of non-Anglo origin. Twenty percent of Israelis are Arabs, while the Ashkenazi (European)/Sephardic (Middle East/North African) ethnic distinction divides the majority Jewish population. Germany is home to over two million Turks and five million other ethnic minorities. Eleven percent of the Canadian population is of non-Anglo origin; the largest group is Chinese. Indonesia is a mosaic of hundreds of ethnic groups. Many other countries, including the UK and Russia, have significant ethnic minority populations. As a result of stagnant growth in mainstream market segments, relatively strong rates of demographic growth among ethnic communities and recognition of their purchasing power—15 percent of the U.S. total, for example—marketing consultants from the United States to Australia and South Africa extol the virtues of **multicultural marketing,** or *special targeting of ethnic minorities.*[61]

Ethnicity

Targeting and positioning products to appeal to ethnic groups is at the heart of multicultural marketing. So, what is ethnicity? **Ethnicity** is defined in terms of *frequent patterns of association and identification with common national or cultural origins of a subgroup found within the larger society.* In addition to a sense of common origin, four elements often define ethnicity. These elements are (1) a self-perpetuating population; (2) shared cultural values; (3) a field of communication and interaction, facilitated by a common language; and (4) membership that defines itself and is identified by others as a distinguishable category. As mentioned earlier in this chapter, social class is based on economic capital, then elaborated through social and cultural capital. By contrast, ethnicity is based more on social capital (relationships, networks, and personal connections) and then elaborated through economic and cultural capital and expressed in consumption.[62]

At the individual level, ethnicity also involves self-identity, or **felt ethnicity,** *an individual's perceptions of him- or herself as a member of an ethnic group.* Worldwide felt ethnicity has increased in the last two decades. In the United States, as Consumer Chronicles 6.4 shows, consumers who feel drawn to their ethnic African roots mark felt ethnicity by celebrating Kwanzaa. In addition to consumption of symbolic products like those associated with Kwanzaa, felt ethnicity affects reactions to advertising. When felt ethnicity is aroused by an ethnic context such as a television show or favorable magazine article, for example, consumers may feel more positively toward ads using ethnic models as well as the products they promote.[63]

When *expressions of ethnicity vary with social context,* this is termed **situational ethnicity.** In other words, while shared cultural values remain stable, the expression of ethnic values varies with social situation. Individuals attending an ethnic festival on the basis of their felt ethnicity may consume foods and entertainment associated with their ethnic background, whereas in mixed-ethnic company their consumption choices might not reflect their ethnic background. During an African-American football weekend in Tampa, Florida, consumers actively build social capital, renewing networks and reestablishing school ties. As important, they consume the "black experience" through an intense round of dinners, parties, tailgating, sports events, and dressing up. Among the multitude of ethnic festivals celebrated in the United States, Czech, Swedish, and Polish festivals are common in the Midwest. But consumer assertions of ethnic identity occur in many countries. West Indian Carnival, for example, is celebrated in London, England, and Brooklyn, New York. Ethnic festivals offer lucrative marketing and sponsorship opportunities to marketers; by providing products or services that help consumers express ethnicity, marketers can build loyalty in ethnic communities.[64]

To understand the role of ethnicity in consumer behavior it is necessary to clarify two

Chapter 6   Economic and Social Structures   **195**

Kwanzaa is based on ancient east African harvest celebrations. Kwanzaa is celebrated seven days from December 26 to January 1, a period that represents the end of an old year. East African harvest celebrations have five basic aspects that Kwanzaa also shares:

- Gathering of the people.
- Special reverence for the Creator and creation.
- Commemoration of the past, especially paying homage to ancestors.
- Recommitment to the highest ethical and cultural values, especially the Nguzo Saba, the Seven Principles.
- Celebration of the good of life, especially family, community, and culture.

The estimates predict that more than 18 million people worldwide participate in the seven-day celebration of family, community, and culture. But even in southern California, where Kwanzaa was created about 30 years ago by Dr. Maulana Karenga—chairman of the Black Studies Department at California State University, Long Beach—many people are unaware of its existence and uninformed about its specifics. However, that's changing. Kwanzaa, a holiday founded amid the activism of 1960s America and spread globally by word-of-mouth and the nurturing of spirits, is about being embraced by capitalism and modern mass media. Several years ago, Hallmark introduced a line of Kwanzaa greeting cards. American Greetings has also added its line of Kwanzaa cards to gift shop shelves from coast to coast. Bookstores offer the story of Kwanzaa in the children's section along with stories of Hanukkah and Christmas. Even the U.S. post office is in on the act with a special issue of Kwanzaa holiday stamps each year.

Source: Dave Wielenga, "Kwanzaa Goes Mainstream," Press-Telegram, December 19, 1993, pp. J1; J10.

related concepts: acculturation and assimilation. Acculturation, discussed in Chapter 5, produces changes in knowledge, beliefs, values, and behaviors when an individual member of an ethnic group comes into prolonged contact with a dominant culture. Thus, Greenlandic immigrants to Denmark noticed changes in their concepts of time, space, and nature during their years in Denmark. Acculturation produces identification with the dominant culture, including a preference for its language. It also means adopting consumption patterns of the dominant culture. Again, like acculturating ethnic groups everywhere, Greenlanders in Denmark mention changes in their consumption of food, fashions, and leisure triggered by their move to mainland Denmark.[65]

At one time, it was thought that acculturation leads inevitably to a second state called **assimilation,** *a process of interpenetration and fusion in which persons and groups acquire memories, sentiments, and attitudes of other persons or groups and, by sharing their experience and history, are incorporated with them in a common cultural life.*[66] The idea of a country as a melting pot reflects this process, with immigrants assimilating into the dominant culture. The gradual loss of Cajun French language and culture in Louisiana was due to assimilation brought about by the stigma attached to Cajun identity historically. Likewise, many immigrants to the United States—be they from Asia, Europe, or elsewhere—demonstrate the idea of progressive assimilation to mainstream values in their evaluation of cars, stereos, coffee, laundry detergent, and so on.

Amid a worldwide renewal of ethnic identities, the recent mosaic metaphor recognizes that assimilation is a far from certain outcome.[67] Ethnic and regional ethnicities have reemerged throughout the world. Ethnic identities today are more voluntary than in the past, and they represent a creative mix of values, beliefs, and consumption styles. Consistent with our argument in Chapter 5 that culture is now marketed, ethnic identity has become a marketed commodity. Thus, Cajun identity has been revived in part through the popularity among consumers of Cajun cuisine and zydeco music.

A study of Mexican immigrants to the United States showed that the outcome of the acculturation process varies. The researcher identified four reactions to the host consumer culture. Some immigrants had *assimilated* to some consumption patterns associated with U.S. consumer culture, yet they also *maintained* aspects of the consumption patterns they had acquired in Mexico. They tended to buy Mexican brands and products, for instance. Informants also expressed concerns about getting caught up in U.S. consumer culture and actively *resisted* its pull. So, they dislike frozen and prepackaged foods and banks, for example. The majority of the informants inhabited sites in the United States that were physically and socially *segregated* from members of the dominant culture. Voluntary segregation not only inhibits assimilation, it limits the ability of mainstream marketing organizations to establish trust with potential ethnic clients. Consumer Chronicles 6.5 describes a man's experience as an immigrant from Hong Kong to Canada. He continues to *operate on the margin* of both Chinese and Canadian society, referred to as a **deculturation** mode.[68]

Others studies have shown that some Mexican Americans, Chinese, and Koreans *over-acculturate*. Some Mexican Americans show exaggerated consumption of some presumably mainstream Anglo products, whereas some assimilated Koreans show exaggerated reliance on advertising and word-of-mouth relative to mainstream U.S. citizens. Chinese Canadians too abandon their Chinese identity in preference to their Canadian citizenship. We find similarly diverse and creative consumption behaviors among ethnic consumers in other contexts. This complicates the tasks of targeting ethnic consumers and positioning products and services to appeal to them.[69]

Ethnic Group Segments

The following section will make special reference to ethnic diversity in the United States, but the marketing implications will be similar for countries experiencing increased immigration or a renewed sense of ethnic identity among certain population segments, a trend noted in many parts of Europe, North, and South America.[70]

Consumer Chronicles 6.5

Neither Chinese Nor Canadian

Colin is 30 years old and arrived in Canada three years ago as an immigrant from Hong Kong. Colin has had trouble coming up with an ethnic group to which he belongs, but he has decided it really shouldn't be Chinese; perhaps it is Hong Kongese. Although he is a Canadian citizen, he doesn't consider himself Canadian. He does not socialize much with non-Chinese. All his friends are Chinese, and he only socializes with *gwailo* (foreign devils) in the workplace. He subscribes to Chinese cable television and Chinese newspapers and shops for groceries in Chinatown. However, he doesn't speak Chinese unless he is asked to; he prefers English. Many Chinese traditions are not to his liking, and he feels lucky to have escaped them by living in Canada. Colin lives on the margin of both Chinese and Canadian society.

Source: Adapted from Ed Chung, "Navigating the Primordial Soup: Charting the Lived Worlds of the Migrant Consumer," Journal of Consumer Marketing *17, no. 1 (2000), pp. 36–54.*

African Americans are the largest ethnic minority, numbering nearly 34 million. They represent over $500 billion in spending power. More than 13 percent of black households may be considered affluent. Of course, African Americans are not homogeneous in their ethnic identity. For example, middle-class Haitian immigrants are lumped with African Americans in the United States, but they distance themselves from this group. They also distinguish themselves from other Caribbean immigrant groups, such as Jamaicans, although they shop in the same markets.[71]

Recognition and respect are two key value orientations that are more meaningful to African Americans than the general population. Style and trend-setting, concern with self-image and elegance, and concern for cultural heritage are also significant orientations among African-American consumers. For example, cosmetics niche marketer African Pride combines an appeal to heritage with an appeal to style. Middle-class, affluent African Americans are also cautious and conservative and respond to mainstream middle-class value-based appeals.

Hispanic Americans are the next largest ethnic U.S. segment. There will be 40 million U.S. Hispanics in 2010. This is a youthful population. Hispanics contributed 47 percent of the U.S. population growth in the 1990s and doubled their purchasing power from what it was in 1980. The Hispanic-American market is currently estimated to represent almost $400 billion in purchasing power.

Hispanic Americans are not a homogeneous group, and marketers should tailor their campaigns to capture these differences. National origin—Mexico, Cuba, and Puerto Rico, for example—is the single most important segmentation variable among Hispanic Americans. Cuban Americans report lower levels of assimilation than most other Hispanic groups, except Puerto Ricans. Hence, Spanish language media and appeals to traditional values will be appropriate for them. Mexican Americans report feeling most assimilated. But even highly assimilated Hispanics appreciate marketing efforts that acknowledge their characteristics and purchasing power.

Hispanics exhibit some distinctive value orientations that affect product and advertising evaluation. To them, age means acquired experience and knowledge. Responsibility and a strong work ethic is characteristic, as is a religious orientation. Gender roles tend to be more conservative and divorce less common than among the majority population. Hispanics are family centered; their primary loyalties are to the family. Consequently, consumption activities are generally to do with the family. Hispanics are often concerned with aesthetics and emotions and place considerable emphasis on quality of life and enjoyment.[72]

Asian Americans are the fastest growing and most affluent minority market in the United States, their numbers tripling between 1980 and 2000 to 10.9 million, or 3.9 percent of the population. Four out of 10 live in California; they are youthful (mean age of 30), affluent (one-third live in households with incomes over $75,000 per year), and well educated (39 percent having attend four years of college versus 17 percent of all Americans). Asian-American purchasing power is estimated at US$229 billion per year. Asian Americans are diverse. Chinese Americans and Filipino Americans now surpass Japanese Americans in number, and Korean and Indian Americans almost equal their numbers. Koreans and Chinese living in Chinatowns tend to be relatively unacculturated and are difficult to reach through mainstream marketing. Second- and third-generation Asians tend to be highly assimilated.[73] Like Hispanic Americans, Asian Americans should be segmented into national groups. Family, tradition, cooperation, and a strong work ethic are among the distinctive values that affect product evaluation among Asian Americans, but each national group displays distinctive cultural characteristics. The advertisement for Webmiles appeals to beliefs about and feelings toward the extended Chinese family.[74]

This ad appeals to beliefs and feelings about the extended Chinese family.

Targeting and Positioning Issues in Multicultural Marketing

In developing targeting and positioning strategies to reach ethnic markets, marketers should consider a number of issues. One is intensity of ethnic identification. Consumers who strongly identify with their ethnic group will exhibit a preference for specialized ethnic media, marketing communications that use national languages, ethnic products and services, and an ethnic consumer lifestyle. These preferences tend to vary inversely with language use and acculturation. Highly targeted media, native language advertising, and niche products and services are appropriate to less assimilated groups and can reap big rewards for marketers. Native language media tend to be much less expensive than mainstream media, exert more effective reach, and translate into higher levels of brand awareness and eventually loyalty among ethnic consumers.

Marketers must determine empirically whether identifiable ethnic groups constitute market segments for ethnic media and ethnically targeted products and services. This will be based in part on whether their cultural values translate into distinctive preferences. Take a simple example. Everyone recognizes that rice varies in stickiness. However, for Koreans this is a very positive attribute, for most Americans it is a negative one. The rice market may be segmented ethnically on the basis of the stickiness of the rice that is offered. As another example, Goya foods thrived for years by marketing packaged tropical foods to Hispanic markets in the northeastern United States.

A preference for Spanish language book titles led big U.S. book chains to double-digit sales growth in this category in the early 1990s. Similarly, African-American media are thriving because of their distinctive value orientation. A handful of magazine titles like *Essence, Black Enterprise,* and *Vibe* have an aggregate circulation of 4.5 million and have been enjoying record advertising sales. Companies such as Cadillac have used minority ad agencies to produce ads that are sensitive to distinctive African-American values.[75]

As Consumer Chronicles 6.4 on Kwanzaa suggests, African Americans' ethnic self-identification expressed through consumption may be increasing. African Americans display some distinctive product preferences, such as a taste for cognac and mealtime desserts, and they may use products somewhat differently than other consumers. For example, the Carnation Company found black consumers using its Instant Breakfast drinks as a compliment to, not a substitute for, a regular breakfast.[76]

Successful ethnic marketing often depends on appealing to the basic motivational drive to express integration, in this case ethnic affiliation, through benefit- and values-based segmentation.[77] Colgate-Palmolive, Metropolitan Life, and other firms target Asian Americans with messages that subtly emphasize family, tradition, and cooperation. Asian-American families are portrayed as the locus of daily life, in contrast to the individualism and separatism portrayed in Anglo families. Ads for Tsingtao beer developed by New York agency Lee Liu & Tong feature young and old enjoying the brew at a friendly family party.[78] Since family values are also important to Hispanic Americans, Metropolitan Life increased sales of insurance to Hispanics by 150 percent by using a nationwide ad campaign that referred to the importance of protecting the family's future. Grocery chains in Florida, Texas, and California have found it profitable to develop groceries targeted to Hispanics. The South Dekalb Mall in suburban Atlanta is famous for rejuvenating its profit picture by adopting an Afrocentric style. Afrocentric retailing has proven successful for JCPenney and KFC as well. These retail venues provide an outlet for expressions of situational ethnicity discussed earlier.[79]

Successful marketing firms sometimes must adapt to distinctive evaluative criteria employed by ethnic consumers in decision making. Many Hispanic consumers, for example, favor advertisements that indicate product purpose, benefits, or use over image-based ads. In the Bay Area of California, Macy's was named by 36 percent of Asian Americans as their favorite department store because of its long tradition of selling high-quality clothing in small sizes, suitable to Asian-American frames. Macy's successfully traded on Asians preferences for established brands, quality, and companies that show respect for their customers.[80]

Understanding acculturation affects language choice in marketing communications. Advertising is more effective when it taps motivations in the language in which those drives are spontaneously expressed. More than 25 million Americans speak a language other than English at home. For example, only one-third of Hispanics speak English almost exclusively. Many Hispanics are brand-conscious and become loyal to companies that advertise in Spanish. Sparkletts Water Systems of Los Angeles increased loyalty and market share by effectively using Spanish-language television to leverage an observed preference for their Aquavend brand into brand differentiation. The ad agency Mosaica, which specializes in marketing to Asian Americans, also emphasizes the value of culturally pertinent advertising in national languages for these groups.

Targeting ethnic minorities through special language media may sometimes cause problems. Acculturated target groups may identify with the values and goals of the dominant culture instead of the ethnic values emphasized in the ad. Or the target may perceive the ads as condescending. The ad may use the wrong dialectical variation. For example, an insecticide company's posters guaranteed the company would kill all *bichos,* which means bugs to Mexican Americans. Unfortunately, it means a man's genitals to Puerto Ricans. Oops![81]

Style is often important to ethnic consumers. Since style is a shared set of preferences, it is a way for ethnic groups whose social status is primarily based on social capital (networks, relationships, and connections) to transform it into symbolic capital. Ethnic groups may be recognized for a particular style or for stylishness in general. Marketers facilitate this process when, in their search for new product ideas, they mass market fashion or events like Cinco de Mayo developed by ethnic minorities. A recent example of this ongoing process of converting social into symbolic capital is shown in Consumer Chronicles 6.6.[82]

A final note of warning: There is no generic ethnic market segment, such as the Hispanic, Turkish, or Chinese market; instead there are multiple subsegments. Further, ethnicity is not a static demographic characteristic like income that can be used in a simple way to segment or target a market. Instead, ethnicity varies with individual felt ethnicity, situation, and stage of life cycle. Ethnic marketing campaigns must attend to these issues on a case basis.

Tribe and Caste

The term **tribe** is derived from the Latin word *tribus,* which referred to the threefold division of the people of ancient Rome. A more recent definition of *tribe* is *a group of people forming a community and descending from a common ancestor.*[83] Tribes are often associated with the peoples of Oceania, Amazonia, and Africa who lived in stateless societies for centuries. Tribal loyalties persist in many of these countries. The borders of most African states reflect the administrative boundaries drawn by the old European colonial powers rather than tribal realities. Consequently, the typical African country contains a number of different tribes. Tribal loyalties also assert themselves in other places such as the Balkans, a historical mélange of different tribes and civilizations.[84] Many current political conflicts can be traced to intertribal disputes. The millennium is also marked by the emergence of **global tribes** that *combine the sense of common origin and shared values with geographic dispersion.* Notably successful examples of global tribes include south Asians, Chinese, Lebanese, Palestinians, Greeks, Gitanos (gypsies), and Jews. Such groups may be important not only as market segments but also as conduits for the spread of patterns of preference, purchase, and use of goods and services to their home communities.[85]

Caste is a social category almost unique to south Asia, primarily India, secondarily Indonesia and Bali. It cannot be compared to either ethnicity or class insofar as it *combines* *both hierarchical (vertical) and lateral (horizontal) systems of inequality.* The four major Indian castes from highest to lowest are (1) *Brahmins* (priests, scholars), (2) *Kshatriyas* (warriors and princes), (3) *Vaisyas* (merchants and artisans), and (4) *Sudras* (laborers and servants). These four groups are divided into over 3,000 subcastes. In addition, there are hundreds of millions of "untouchables," uncasted persons relegated to the lowest levels of society and now becoming part of the global underclass. Caste membership is associated with occupations, rights, and duties toward other castes, and castes have an explicit moral dimension. Higher-caste groups are considered morally superior to lower groups. Thus, like class in the United States, it is not terribly fashionable to discuss caste and its implications in public debate. Caste differences are very distinct and enter into many lifestyle differences; hence, marketing communications need to be sensitive to caste differences both in positioning products and presenting models and spokespersons.[86]

Other Structural Segments

Age, gender, and religion are three additional social structures that affect consumer behavior and thus marketing strategy. It is important to keep in mind that there are many interactions between each of these social structures. For example, gender roles and acceptable patterns of consumption are influenced by religion and age. And, of course, these social structures are also influenced by social class, tribe, and caste. For example, women in lower-class households often have more stereotypical gender roles than women in middle- or upper-class households. Children from upper-class households receive different allowances and spend their money differently than children from poorer households. An exhaustive discussion of age, gender, and religion segments is beyond the scope of this chapter; however, we'll further discuss some of these segmentation bases in Chapter 8 (on lifestyles) and Chapter 14 (on households).

Age

Like ethnicity, age is a subcultural system marketers use to segment and target markets. People's wants change with physical aging over the course of the **life cycle,** *the movement from birth to death.* Consumers' preferences, and their access to resources, vary with age. In general, young adults focus on the accumulation of functional items needed for independent living, such as a motor scooter or car, a cassette player, or a stereo system. Mature adults place greater value on altruism and emotional satisfaction than possession, whereas older adults are interested in products and experiences that encode and express family and social history.[87]

Age-related **life transitions**—*socially recognized changes in status*—engender demand for specialized products and services. Examples of age-related life transitions include entering school, becoming a teenager, entering military service, pledging a fraternity or sorority, entering adulthood, graduating school or college, celebrating a twenty-fifth wedding anniversary, and retiring from the workforce. Finally, the collective experiences of certain **age cohorts,** that is, *groups of people who have grown up during specific time periods and share experiences, memories, and symbols translate into similar preference patterns.* Thus, people who were young during the turbulent 1960s differ in outlook from the youth who experienced the growing economy and horizon-expanding technological changes of the 1990s. As shown in Exhibit 6.3, U.S. marketers have distinguished millennials, baby boomers, generation X, and generation Y, among other age cohorts.

Exhibit 6.3 Vital Statistics on U.S. Generations

Generation	Year Born	Age in 2000	U.S. Population (millions)	Percent of U.S. Population
GI generation	Pre–30	71+	25.3	9.1%
Depression era	1930–39	61–70	17.8	6.5
War babies	1940–45	55–60	15.6	5.7
Baby boomers	1946–64	36–54	77.4	28.2
Generation X	1965–76	24–35	44.9	16.4
Generation Y	1977–94	6–23	70.7	25.8
Millennials	1995+	0–5	22.9	8.3

Source: Rebecca Gardyn and John Fetto, "Off the Map," *American Demographics* (June 2000), p. 72.

Children (Millennials and Generation Y)

Children's consumer demands represent considerable market opportunities for those who can meet their distinct needs and cognitive competencies. There are more than 800 million children aged 4–12 years in the industrialized world, and they are not being ignored. Nickelodeon and the Cartoon Network compete for the worldwide kids' business. PepsiCo, through its Sabritas subsidiary, has a major share of the candy and bubble gum business in Mexico and is expanding into Spain and Brazil. Mattel has made Barbie a worldwide brand of doll, and Denmark's Lego has had similar success in construction toys. The Pokémon craze swept across the industrialized world in 1999 and will not soon be forgotten. Children between the ages of 6 and 14 spend approximately US$77 billion a year. The ads "Stevies shoes" and "My America" books from *Girl's Life* shown below and on page 204 are indicative of the lifestyle and media products increasingly now targeted at preteens.

Stevies shoes targets the increasingly market savvy pre-teen segment.

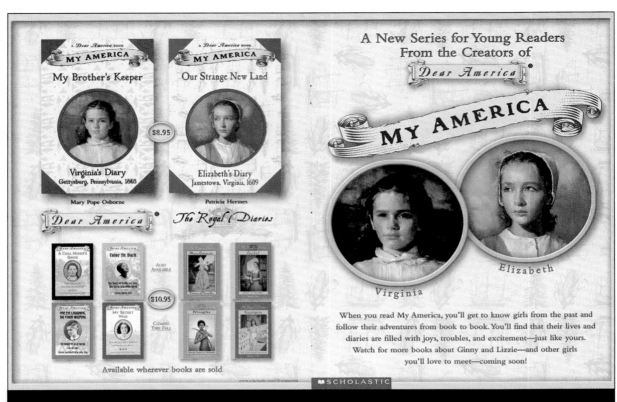

My America books appeal to the pre-teen market and their parents.

In Western consumer society, we now recognize the cognitive sophistication of consumers as young as five to seven years old, as well as children's role in influencing adult consumption. Kids encourage up to $120 billion in family spending in the United States alone, for example (see Chapter 14). Businesses in the NICs are also waking up to kids' buying power, or at least their influence on parents' spending habits. There are about 85 million kids aged 10–19 in the region, and their economic clout is considerable. In Japan, toy sales total $3.1 billion a year and children's shoes and clothing come to about $8.8 billion. And two out of three Japanese elementary students play games on their families' computers.[88]

Children assume the role of consumer decision makers at a young age.[89] Children as young as two years old rely on symbolic brand attributes when forming preferences and making choices among consumer goods. Visual cues such as television advertising and vivid packaging influence their learning and attitudes toward brands. Children as young as three recognize heavily advertised cartoon characters; this recognition produces positive attitudes toward products associated with these characters. Young children's letters to Santa Claus reveal something surprising. About 50 percent of their gift requests are for specific branded items, and about 85 percent of the children mention at least one brand name in their letters to Santa.[90] Sometime between preschool and second grade, children begin to make inferences about people, such as occupation and age, based on things like their cars and houses.[91] By sixth grade, U.S. children have a keen sense of the social meaning and prestige associated with certain types of products and brand names.

Children play an important role in influencing parental shopping and spending habits. A study reveals that urban Chinese children directly or indirectly influence up to two-thirds of parents' purchase decisions. In part because of China's one-child policy, children have significant income from and influence on both parents and grandparents beginning as early as age four. Another study reports that urban Chinese middle school students spent 66.3 percent of their parents' combined incomes.[92] The China case is unique in some respects, but many children globally are exerting significant influence on consumption behavior. In Thailand, for example, the liquid milk market grew by 21 percent from 1995 to 1996 alone as more and more young Thais consumed milk purchased by their parents with the intent of improving dietary quality. One author reports Turkish parents selling milk in order to buy candy bars for their children. Another reports the tensions that arise between Ecuadoran parents and children over the children's preference for manufactured bread over traditional barley cereal. Ignoring kids can keep shoppers away from stores. Making retail outlets kid-friendly can bring in shoppers and increase purchases initiated by children.[93]

The proliferation and globalization of marketing has both pluses and minuses. For many urban, lower-class children in the United States, watching commercial TV at home or congregating in the shopping malls are some of the only relatively safe leisure venues available to them, making consumer activities a pervasive part of their lives. In addition, children's demands may fuel deep conflicts over family, class relations, and tradition, both in First World and developing societies. In the NICs like Korea, the recent rapid economic growth, industrialization, and the introduction of Western consumer culture has often fueled a tremendous generation gap in values. This gap is expressed in striking differences in consumer preferences. In the developing world, children's power in introducing consumerism into more traditional communities cannot be underestimated.

One important controversy in consumer research concerns the ability of children to defend themselves against the claims advertisers direct to them. Some contend that children develop considerable abilities to counterargue against commercial messages. Others posit that children, particularly young children, with less developed problem-solving abilities have ineffective defenses against commercial claims. Most research supports that television advertising has a powerful influence on children's product preferences and choices and at least a moderate role in perception and usage of products such as cigarettes, alcohol, and heavily sugared, non-nutritious foods.[94] Recent legislative and judicial decisions concerning tobacco marketing reflect the view that children's cognitive defenses against advertising are not adequate. Hence, government-financed programs to demarket tobacco products are enjoying popularity.[95] Online privacy has also begun to attract attention, particularly with regard to marketing tactics directed at children.

Teens (Generation Y)

Teens are a popular target for marketers for many reasons.[96] First, they are numerous. There are almost 31 million teenagers in the United States, and by 2010 there will be 35 million. The young are an even more significant factor in many markets. One-third of China's population is younger than 20 years old. In Cambodia, over half the population is currently younger than 15. In Hong Kong, South Korea, Thailand, and Singapore, consumers younger than 30 years of age represent between 50 and 70 percent of the population. In Turkey, the young represent 67 percent of the population, and in Mexico, the young represent 71 percent of the population.

Second, young people in the Triad and newly industrialized nations (generation Yers) enjoy enormous discretionary purchasing power. U.S. teenagers aged 12 to 18 get an

average $50 a week in cash from parents, and not surprisingly, as household income increases so do allowances for teens. At the same time, over 80 percent of teenagers indicate that they save at least half of the money they get. Millions of youngsters are regularly putting money into mutual funds and the stock market. Two websites illustrate appeals to savvy, young consumers—allowanceNET and doughnet.com. The latter is an online one-stop shopping, education, and banking enterprise launched in June 1999. It also enables kids to donate to nonprofits and favorite causes.

A third reason teenagers are an attractive segment is that they are increasingly market savvy and involved with consumer culture. Many people make their initial purchases as teenagers, so this age group offers an ideal target market for promoting brand loyalties. A number of studies of teens in the UK have shown that they use advertisements and brands in creative ways to craft and comment on their lives and communities. Japanese generation Yers are innovative consumers of the latest electronic gear. One U.S. study found that 88 percent of teenage girls go to shopping malls 40 percent more often than other demographic groups. And one in nine American teenagers has a credit card. Teenagers in many of the transitional economies (e.g., Czech Republic, Poland, and Hungary) have grown up with a market economy and are much more comfortable shopping and making consumer decisions than their parents or grandparents.

Teenagers make purchase decisions for an everwidening variety of their own products, from books to clothes, making them attractive targets for marketing communications. In addition, teenagers appear to be extremely brand aware and often fiercely brand loyal. One study found that 50 percent of female generation Yers had already developed cosmetics brand loyalties. Of course, at the same time, their loyalties tend to be quite volatile, perhaps due to their rapid personal development.[97] "Coolness" goes a long way toward determining which brands are most popular. Nike, Adidas, and Tommy Hilfiger dominate the cool chart among teenagers, with Abercrombie and Fitch and Old Navy on the rise. Entertainment in Abercrombie and Fitch and Old Navy is important—everything is hip and contemporary.

From Singapore to Greenland, teenagers globally are increasingly wired into the Internet. This facilitates the spread of images, ideas, values, and trends among teenagers around the world. The Internet drives both increased similarity and fragmentation in generation Y or Net generation (N-geners) consumer tastes. For example, basketball has emerged as a global teen sport of preference. And Coca-Cola is conducting a multiyear study called the Global Teenager that it hopes will define a global teen market for its products. That N-geners are so accustomed to computers makes them a distinctive market segment in a number of ways. First, due to zapping and surfing, N-geners' wants, fashions, and brand loyalties may be transient. Second, because the Internet makes it easy to search and compare, N-geners demand customization to meet their personal preferences. More and more niche products will be required to meet their needs. And mass-market products may lose share to niche products. Third, in a mind-set developed by clicking on a computer mouse or remote control, choices do not necessarily stick. N-geners thus like to change their minds. Fourth, since interactivity is the hallmark of the Internet, N-geners prefer to try things out themselves rather than rely on promises. Giving away core products and services and charging for additional services and augmented products will probably become more common. N-geners are therefore important candidates for more relational approaches to marketing. Finally, unlike the baby boomer generation, N-geners are not dazzled by technology; they care about function.[98]

This connectedness to and familiarity with the Internet has gained the attention of marketers because of children's distinct influence on their parents. Today's children and teens are more techno-savvy and more knowledgeable about Internet- and computer-related products than their parents. For example, a majority of parents in the U.S.-based Roper survey consider children as an important reason for purchasing home computers. Thus, marketers have to appeal to several different audiences in designing communications for such products. Some researchers have begun to look at how N-geners are teaching parents about products and services. If children are instrumental in a parent's learning about the Internet and computers, it stands to reason that they might also be instrumental in shaping a parent's techno-consumer behavior, whether it be online shopping or purchasing home computer products or services. So marketers have begun to think of creative ways to use this alliance to their advantage.

As the number of single- and working-parent families increases in Triad countries and many transitional economies, many teenagers are also becoming the primary shoppers for their families. Teens are thrifty shoppers and tend to look for deals. Like adults, teens rely on personal sources of information, friends, and family for high-risk purchases.[99]

A final reason that young people are attractive to marketers is that everywhere they go through rapid periods of physical, mental, social, and emotional change. This generates rapidly evolving physical, self-expression, and self-realization needs. Teenagers and young adults often vacillate between consuming to fit in and consuming to differentiate themselves from their peers. One study found that 13–17-year-old American girls tend to be conformists in their orientation to fashion trends. These characteristics make wired global teenagers attractive markets for global and regional brands like Guess, The Gap, Mennen, XOXO, Kookai, Van's, Nintendo, and Sega; print magazines like *Sassy, YM, Details;* and comic books, MTV, and online 'zines.[100]

Generation Y is a difficult and elusive group to target effectively. They are market-wise, highly suspicious of advertising, pros at TV zapping, zipping, and channel surfing, and subject to rapid shifts in fad and fashion. Generation Yers readily reject traditional advertising they see as too hard-sell or manipulative. Marketers will be forced to develop more concept-rich communications as kids will see through fluff and eye candy. Generation Yers place greater faith in authenticity than in big brands; they are more willing to buy from small firms run by pure enthusiasts. Further, a side effect of teenagers' Internet experience has been an increasing fragmentation of the teen and young adult market into smaller groups that are less easy to target on national, regional, ethnic, or gender lines.[101]

Common to affluent nations with large, youthful populations is the phenomenon of the **youth subcultures.** First identified in the United States in the 1950s, youth subcultures are common today in Europe, Japan, and even China. In the LAW nations, universities often provide the setting for the timid emergence of youth subcultures. In Japan, they often take the form of parodies of familiar U.S. subcultures such as bikers, punks, and rock 'n' rollers. Youth subcultures typically combine behaviors simultaneously expressive of values characteristic of the dominant culture and values deviant from them. Today, marketers quickly convert youth street styles into marketed commodities, even antistyles such as grunge or gangsta rap. This fuels the rapid rise and fall of youth fads and fashions as young people seek to differentiate themselves by developing consumption styles that are different from mass-market offerings.[102]

Boomers, Depression Era, and War Babies

The population is aging in many of the most developed nations (see Exhibit 6.4). Elderly segments will grow dramatically in the next 20 years in the Triad nations, especially the oldest segment. For example, the 80+ segment is currently the fastest-growing one in the United States. In the year 2000, there will be 35 million Americans older than 65, and by the year 2010, 18 percent of the population, or 55 million people, will be aged 60 and older. The 77-million member baby boom generation will be the aging market of the late

Exhibit 6.4 Aging of the Triad Nation's Populations

Country	Total Population 2010 (millions)	Percent of the Total Population 60 and above
Australia	20	19.3%
Canada	33	20.4
France	60	22.5
Germany	81	25.1
Italy	55	26.1
Japan	127	29.8
Sweden	9	26.0
United Kingdom	59	23.3
United States	294	18.8
High-income countries	964	21.8

Source: The World Bank, *World Development Indicators* (Washington, DC: International Bank for Reconstruction and Development, 1998).

1990s. In many other Triad nations, the aging will comprise a larger percentage of the population than in the United States, particularly so in Japan, where about 30 percent of the population, or 38 million people, will be older than 60 in the year 2010. This segment represents opportunities and challenges for marketers.

To reach the new senior segments of the world's markets, marketers must start from two bases: (1) abandon stereotypes concerning aging consumers; and (2) understand that the aging consumers of tomorrow are going to be very different from those of today. Although baby boomers are probably the least homogeneous of any cohort, common among them is the idea that they aren't getting older no matter what the calendar says—they intend to stay young forever.[103] In contrast to the stereotypical view of the elderly as retiring, solitary, and relatively poor, in the United States consumers older than 60 control 50 percent of the discretionary income and 75 percent of the nation's assets. There will continue to be more female elderly people than male; but the elderly will also be less traditional than those of the past. Some of the elderly may be more socially isolated because of current reproduction and divorce patterns throughout the Triad countries. On the other hand, many of the new elderly will be used to living singly and may be more adventuresome than ever before.

Older adults should be divided into subsegments on the basis of not just chronological or physical age but mental or **cognitive age** as well. Cognitive age *represents how people see themselves and their actual levels of cognitive processing.* Cognitive age tends to be about 10 years younger than the chronological age. In any case, cognitive age and chronological age do not overlap very well, segmenting on chronological age alone is not very effective. For example, those in a segment labeled the "young again" (50 to 65 years of age) tend to think of themselves as about 15 years younger than their chronological age. They lead active lifestyles more like those of the baby boomers.[104]

The elderly of the future will be more affluent, better educated, and more active than those of today. Hence, marketers should position goods and services to take advantage of these trends. One indication of these changes is the growth of participation in cyberculture of older people. The minutes-per-month of computer use among Americans aged 50 and

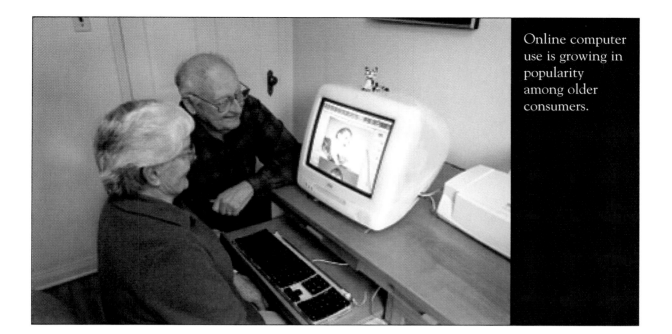

Online computer use is growing in popularity among older consumers.

older who have computers was 47 percent higher than the average for all age groups in one recent poll. For example, Thirdage.com, a clearinghouse for information of interest to the elderly, has drawn over 250,000 visitors a month. This trend is obviously good news for makers and retailers of devices that facilitate Internet access and for Internet service providers. Computers could be targeted to the young again segment, for example, as in the photo shown above.

thirdage.com

Other businesses enjoying the boom in the aging population are the leisure and educational industries. The recreational vehicle industry is an example. Many seniors are taking to the road in their Winnebago RVs, as you can see at Winnebago-Itasca Traveler's Club website. Consumer Chronicles 6.7, on Elderhostel, illustrates another industry that is likely to benefit dramatically from the aging of the Triad nations. The young again segment is a prime target for recreational and vacation activities such as those provided by Winnebago or Elderhostel.[105]

winnebagoind. com/club.htm

The growing economic significance of the elderly segment has generated increasing interest in the unique responsiveness of the elderly to common marketing variables. For example, recent research has found similarity between elderly U.S. consumers' brand sets and those of younger consumers. A study of elderly shopping behavior in the United Kingdom indicated some general preference among the elderly group for locally operated (familiar) rather than nationally operated store options.

Price discounts for senior citizens have interesting effects. Some older consumers reject such discounts because they wish to avoid thinking of themselves as actually being senior citizens. Others reject such discounts because they wish to avoid the negative connotations of being perceived as senior citizens by others. Finally, some elderly consumers assign positive meanings to stores that promote the use of senior citizen discounts. Older consumers do patronize discount stores, perhaps because of a tendency toward frugality among war babies and depression era seniors. In the United States, younger elderly consumers seem to exhibit negative responses to age segmentation; older elderly consumers

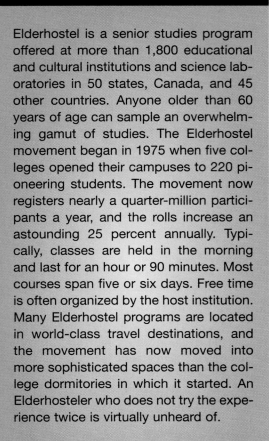

are more apt to accept it. In other words, people get used to it. Moreover, responses to age segmentation cues should vary with the perception of the elderly within particular cultures.[106]

Age differences in information search behavior have been examined. In some cases, older consumers consider fewer product characteristics and alternative brands than younger consumers because of greater experience and brand familiarity. With unfamiliar products and brands, however, older consumers may search less because they cannot hold and manipulate numerous alternatives in memory, because of diminished working memory capacity. The elderly show poorer recognition memory for advertising claims; thus, they are more likely to miscomprehend advertising assertions, sometimes misconstruing new claims as old and believing them as a result. This may lead to lower levels of satisfaction with purchase choices. In addition, memory deficits may make it difficult for elderly consumers to take advantage of new information sources, such as nutritional and medical labeling, or advertising designed to improve their decision making.

Research on the effects of different advertising strategies on the memory, attitudes, and product choice of the elderly has found that information-rich ads are more favorably received than music-based, emotional appeals. Imagery-based advertising—that is, the use of visual information, such as symbols and pictures, and concrete language in print and television ads—can improve elderly recall of ad claims.[107]

Other studies have examined the use of elderly figures in advertising. Many elderly people perceive middle-aged and older models to be more credible than younger models. Hence, we may expect to see older models in ads as the population ages.[108]

Gender

Gender is a significant segmentation and targeting criterion in marketing. It is defined as the *sex-based divisions of humanity and the norms, values, and beliefs associated with gender roles*. People often use a shorthand in describing gender roles, referring to values, behaviors, and products as masculine or feminine. Gender is a significant segmentation and targeting variable for at least three reasons.

First, every culture distinguishes at least two genders. Homosexual, bisexual, and other gender identities are recognized in some cultures, denied in others. Evident physiological differences between men and women lead to specialized product needs in nutrition, health, and personal care, for example. Marketers often use stereotypical appeals that combine biology with gender. For example, the ad for Tampax shown on page 211 associates

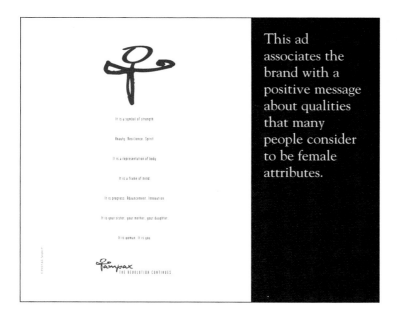

This ad associates the brand with a positive message about qualities that many people consider to be female attributes.

It is a symbol of strength

Beauty. Resilience. Spirit

It is a representation of body

It is a frame of mind

It is progress. Advancement. Innovation

It is your sister, your mother, your daughter

It is woman. It is you.

Tampax
THE REVOLUTION CONTINUES

the brand with the universal biological symbol for female and with a positive message about feminine qualities.

What constitutes stereotypically masculine or feminine behavior varies across cultures. For example, French men seem to have a more egalitarian view of men and women than do U.S. men; however, a closer inspection reveals that French men still hold gender stereotypes of women. For instance, French men, like their American counterparts, seem to view consumption as being a feminine concern. But many stereotypes in the two cultures are different. For U.S. men, sports is a masculine trait; not so for French men. And although they hold different stereotypes, both French and U.S. men feel conflicting demands and changes in gender roles that make it more difficult to be a man today.[109] Contemporary advertisements reflect consumers' changing conceptions of gender roles and gender boundaries.[110] Gender role stereotypes may be found along with suggestions of gender blending, bending, and boundary crossing. The photo on page 212 is typical of high-fashion images that employ stereotypical images of women.

Gender Roles

A second reason that gender is significant to marketers is because gender roles are learned early and play a formative part in personality development and self-identity (see Chapters 7 and 11). For example, U.S. research on young consumers consistently finds that males report more materialistic values than females.[111] Patterns of wants and responses to market appeals vary with gender. Obviously, many products are designed to appeal to or even accentuate gender-specific wants. Males and females are portrayed differently in U.S. advertising to children, and the majority of gender portrayals follow gender-stereotyped norms. Almost twice as many males as females are shown. Generally, men are portrayed as working and women as mothers or other relatives.[112]

Research in developing and transitional economies suggests how marketers have successfully positioned products to appeal to men and women differently. Not surprisingly, certain products appear to be more appropriate for one gender than the other. Nevertheless, products may become less gender-typed as gender roles change. Team sports increasingly

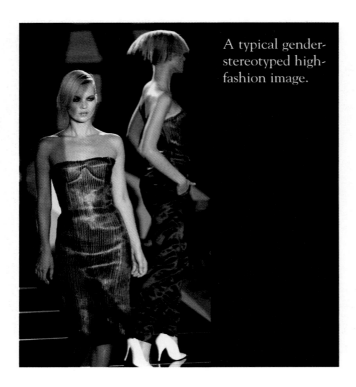

A typical gender-stereotyped high-fashion image.

target women with specialized leagues and products. High-fashion brands like Chanel are targeting men with cosmetics ads. Cigar smoking, a traditional male activity, has become popular among women as shown in the ad on page 213. And the U.S. firearms industry has targeted women with campaigns that appeal to their security concerns (see Chapter 11).[113]

Traditional gender-related differences in information processing and response to marketing appeals have been identified. When forming judgments, a masculine orientation involves the use of a single cue or small set of highly salient cues that converge to imply a single inference or course of action. The cues that men use tend to be meaningful to the masculine self. In contrast, a feminine approach to judgment makes use of multiple cues and attempts to assimilate both highly salient and subtler cues. In addition, a masculine orientation to goal seeking tends to be more impersonal and individualistic than a feminine orientation. A feminine orientation is more oriented toward social integration than is a masculine one.

Masculinity is associated with an instrumental orientation, that is, a concern with goals external to social relations. Femininity is associated with an expressive orientation and places a priority on dealing with others, on being actively interdependent and relational. Brand names with numbers in them appear to have a more masculine appeal perhaps because of an association with instrumentality. Men emphasize the functional (self-oriented) benefits of clothing, and women emphasize social (other-oriented) concerns. In a Canadian study of Christmas shopping, men were found to be more object focused and women more interested in the relational meanings conveyed by the gifts chosen for purchase. Similarly, the huge international romance novel market is driven by the relationship-oriented values conveyed by the books.[114]

Gender roles definitely persist and influence consumer behavior, but the behaviors of male and female consumers often defy these stereotypes. For example, 80 percent of all

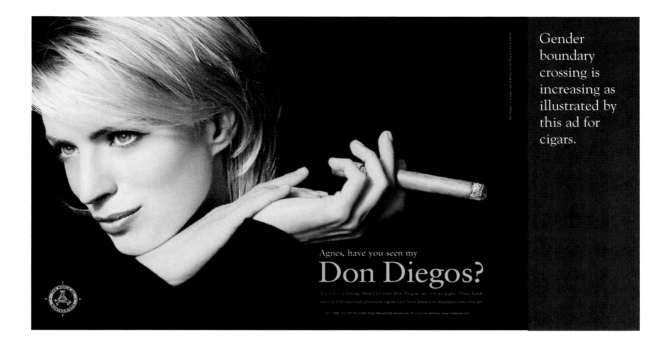

Gender boundary crossing is increasing as illustrated by this ad for cigars.

Agnes, have you seen my

Don Diegos?

households in the United States are made up of dual-career couples, and women are the chief wage earners in about a quarter of all U.S. households. Even in China, a very traditional male-oriented society, gender roles are changing. In urban China, where the one-child policy is strictly enforced, parents have strikingly similar aspirations for their female or male children and both boys and girls are receiving the same parental investments in their education and future career goals. However, rural areas of China continue to show a bias against female offspring, resulting in selective abortions and abandoned girl babies.[115]

Gender-Based Needs, Segmentation, and Targeting

A third reason gender is a significant segmentation and targeting variable is that it is associated with relatively distinct endowments of cultural and social capital. That is, one gender often specializes in certain purchase and consumption behaviors for consuming units such as families, households, and organizations. For example, in countries as diverse as Japan, the UK, and the United States, shopping is primarily viewed as women's work. In a number of Triad countries, gift giving, sending greeting cards and letters, and staging consumption celebrations that reinforce social and family ties is also primarily women's work.[116]

Some research suggests that in positioning of products marketers need to be sensitive to gender-based differences in product meaning and symbolism. Gender-based meanings are conveyed by products, persons, words, and even sounds. Angularity, sharpness, and simple designs are stereotypically masculine characteristics of products. Roundness, softness, and refined design are considered more feminine product features. Cross-cultural evidence indicates these associations are quite widespread. Another study found that fresh fruits and vegetables as well as prepared food have pronounced gender symbolism. Consumption of feminine foods decreased with lower social class, and women in working-class, heterosexual couples tended to consume more masculine foods. A study of celebrity endorsers also found gender-based differences in attractiveness of both male and female endorsers.[117]

Life with her husband, singer Arpaporn Nakornsawan tells her audiences, was a drag. He had little time for her, and in the end she said good-bye and good riddance. "I have already left," Arpaporn's hit song of the same name begins. And she isn't in a rush to find a new man, the overnight sensation tells her fans. That never would have happened a generation ago. Thirty years earlier, girls shed tears over the wildly popular song "Wang Bua Baan" ("The River of Lotus Blossoms"), which told the story of a young woman who drowns herself in a river after waiting for a lover who never returns.

The contrast between the two popular songs speaks volumes about changing attitudes toward marriage among Thai women. They are, at least when it comes to men, not their mothers' daughters: Nowadays, Thai women are saying "so long" to rotten relationships instead of suffering through them. In some cases, it's not even bad relationships that women are avoiding. A growing sisterhood of women in Thailand is choosing to stay single—and loving it.

Better educational and financial opportunities have given women a new perspective on life and boosted their expectations of marriage. Such trends have appeared in more economically advanced Asian societies—notably Singapore. But because Thai culture is traditionally more accommodating than that of other Asian countries, Thai women are finding the freedom to make choices about how to live their lives at an earlier stage in the nation's economic development.

Sociologists say women's financial independence is the most important factor in the new attitude toward marriage. Greater access to education for women in recent decades has been crucial in fostering that independence. In 1993, female students at public universities outnumbered males for the first time. Over half of those graduating from public universities were women, with the proportion increasing to 57 percent in 1996. Many women feel it's difficult to find a man who suits them intellectually. This is the result of a paucity of men of the same social level in the same age group as these women. Their male counterparts tend either to have married earlier or prefer wives who are younger.

In the past, a woman's social status was defined through her husband's station in life. But as a result of Thai culture's relative flexibility—witness the country's live-and-let-live attitude toward prostitutes, transvestites, and homosexuals—it is acceptable for a woman to express her identity through her own education and work. This cultural liberalism shouldn't be overlooked in explaining why Thai women—compared to those in other Asian countries—are eschewing marriage.

Source: Prangtip Daorueng, "Sole Sisters: Greater Financial Opportunities and a Flexible Culture Are Enabling a Growing Legion of Independent-Minded Thai Women to Choose the Single Life in Bangkok," Far Eastern Economic Review, September 3, 1998, p. 36.

As women enter the wage labor force and gain access to economic resources, a blurring of gender role differences with higher income and educational and professional attainment occurs.[118] Research suggests changes in gender roles in countries as diverse as Hungary and India.[119] And as Consumer Chronicles 6.8 shows, even in a developing country like Thailand gender roles are changing, presenting marketers with new opportunities.

Proactive marketers should follow changing women's needs closely. Some industries, such as the big automobile makers, have responded slowly to women's increasing share of economic resources. Finally, driven by the estimated $65 billion spent by women who purchase 49 percent of new cars sold in the United States, the automotive industry learned to be more responsive to their needs. Lowered trunk lifts, easier-to-lift hoods, adjustable seat belts, deeper door handles, and shorter distances between steering wheels and controls are just a few of the changes made. Manufacturers have also redesigned cars with more safety features; and the Saturn division of GM introduced fixed pricing and low-pressure sales tactics in response to women's consumption values.[120]

Changes in gender roles sometimes suggest a trend toward global standards of behavior. As suggested in Chapter 5, there is evidence that the globalization of beauty pageants is leading to the emergence of norms of beauty for women that provide multinational firms like L'Oréal, Revlon, and Clarins with lucrative markets for cosmetics, fitness, and fashion in LAW nations like India. However, changes in gender roles do not necessarily mean Westernization. Among Islamic women in Turkey, who accept Islam, both fashion and gender-segregated resorts are growth industries.[121]

In much of the developing world, gender roles and interests are fairly compartmentalized or separate. Such differences can be reflected in preference for a wide variety of products and services, including entertainment products. In Peru, television soap operas, or *novelas,* are viewed primarily by women, soccer matches by men. But gender segregation can lead to lucrative marketing opportunities. In India, the cassette market for traditional music is at least a $60 million industry and remains gender specific in terms of performers and audiences. To take another example, Avon has done well marketing door to door to secluded Muslim women in the Middle East. Another example of a gender-segregated marketing opportunity is provided by the First Women's Bank of Pakistan, discussed in Industry Insights 6.2.[122]

One additional important change in the role of gender in marketing efforts concerns the recognition of gays as a distinctive market segment. Several books have profiled the economic clout and distinctive value orientations of gay consumers. Marketing communications firms have emerged that specialize in the gay market. And major advertisers across an array of product categories are devoting increasing resources to target the gay market. In the United States, for example, brewer Anheuser-Busch is among a dozen or so major companies that have taken the step of targeting gay and lesbian customers directly. Others include Camel cigarettes, American Express, Virgin Atlantic airline, Absolut vodka, and The Gap. Swedish furniture maker IKEA is thought to have produced the first television commercial to make use of explicitly gay spokespersons.[123]

Religion is a cultural subsystem that refers to *a unified system of beliefs and practices relative to a sacred ultimate reality or deity.* Consumer research has not extensively studied the impact of religion on consumer behavior or the purchase and consumption of religious goods and services. This is remarkable given the global resurgence of organized **religiosity,** *the degree to which beliefs in specific religious values and ideals are held and practiced by consumers.* The spread of Christian, Islamic, and Hindu fundamentalism, the reemergence of the Russian Orthodox Church after the collapse of the Soviet Union, and religious conflict in Northern Ireland and the Balkans are just a few of the indications that religion remains a powerful influence over human behavior, including consumer behavior. The United States exhibits a high degree of religiosity. Forty-five percent of American adults claim to worship at a church, synagogue, or other religious meeting place at least once a week. The only European country to exceed the United States in religiosity is Ireland, where Sunday church attendance reaches 82 percent. As with ethnicity, the predictive power of

Religion

Gender-Based Banking in Pakistan

Pakistan's smallest bank in the public sector is a four-year-old institution run for women, by women. According to Akram Khatoon, the president, First Women's Bank (FWB) far outpaces any other public sector bank. Initially set up with reserves of 100 million rupees (US$3.34 million), FWB was meant to work as a development-oriented bank to provide credit to poor and middle-class women who often failed to get support from traditional banks. From its initial five branches, the FWB has expanded to 23 branches across the country. There are plans to set up two more this year. With that expansion, profits have soared as well. Last year, the bank earned almost 29 million rupees (US$985,000) in profits. Earnings this year are expected to jump to 50 million rupees (US$1.67 million), almost a 68 percent increase. Unlike other public sector banks, however, where clients have defaulted on a staggering 80 billion rupees (US$2.66 billion), the FWB claims that only 3 percent of its loans have gone sour. Ms. Khatoon argues that cooperation with clients and a more responsible attitude on the part of women borrowers holds the key to the bank's success. "Basically, women feel more responsible and honest in paying back their loans," she says.

Source: Farhan Bokhari (1993), "Pakistan's Profitable First Women's Bank Carves New Niche," Christian Science Monitor, Oct 25, p. 6.

religion probably varies with perceived religiosity, that is, self-identification with a religion and its values, the strength of this identification, and situational factors. For example, Denmark has a state religion, but most Danes appear to exhibit low religiosity.[124]

Religion-based segments and consumer behavior certainly merit more investigation; in the United States alone, religion is a multibillion dollar industry employing thousands of people in which there is intense competition between competing products. This competition is most obvious with regard to proselytizing (the act of conversion) denominations like the Seventh Day Adventists and the Church of Latter Day Saints; other denominations also advertise for converts and engage in active lobbying, as displayed by televangelists. So-called mega churches have perfected marketing techniques to lure members of the baby boomer generation back to church. The Catholic Church has launched marketing programs in many cities to attract customers to its parochial schools, using high-quality academic performance, traditional values, and discipline as some of the positioning variables. Low-income and single-parent families are considered prime target markets. The sisters of St. Benedict has even spurred something of a marketing revolution among religious orders in the United States, Ireland, and Canada by successfully pioneering aggressive, humor- and relationship-based marketing campaigns to recruit new nuns to its convents.[125]

Religious segmentation may be salient where religion becomes one of the main tools in the construction of a distinctive ethnic identity. In the United States, for example, the Jewish community is notable for a high degree of congruence between culture and religion. Perhaps this is true of other historically socially isolated groups and religious minorities in other nations, such as Jains in India, Copts in Egypt, American Black Muslims, and so on. Research conducted on the American Jewish community suggests specific reasons that marketers might value religious segmentation; the high value placed on information seeking, information exposure, and educational attainment within this community suggest that Jewish consumers may be relatively more innovative and more prone to diffuse information about new products at least within the community. These consumers may be opinion leaders, but they may also exhibit less brand loyalty.[126]

In addition, religion may be a useful segmentation variable because it influences value systems. Value systems in turn influence preferences of all kinds.

In the United States, the Protestant working-class segment associated with the revivalist and born-again movements has significant marketing implications. This segment contains both African-American and white subsegments. Important values include literal belief in biblical texts, respect for authority, passionate expression of belief (e.g., through testimonial and gospel singing), and personal success achieved through faith in and obedience to revealed divine will. Products targeted at this market sell well. A *Women's Devotional Bible* has sold more than two million copies, for example. Televangelists target this segment, as do schools and leisure services, positioned on values of importance to this segment. Overall, this segment may be of broad interest for marketers in that its conservatism, traditionalism, and relatively lower tolerance of diversity may lead to greater male dominance in major purchase decisions and higher brand and store loyalty.[127]

The economic and social structures discussed in this chapter are the major organizational categories in societies around the world. Membership in these categories is often expressed through the purchase and use of products and services. They anchor and mold consumer preferences and consumption patterns or lifestyles, but they are dynamic. When these categories change consumer tastes and preferences will change as well. Managers find economic and socially defined groups useful, because they possess unifying characteristics that distinguish desires, choices, and decision-making styles from other groups. Often the influence of these structures on consumption choices is indirect rather than direct. As with culture, their influence is easiest to discern when we meet people whose class, ethnicity, tribe, or caste differ from our own.

Social classes are groupings involving differences in such areas as power, authority, wealth, income, prestige, working conditions, lifestyles, and culture. People of any one class tend to associate much more with one another than they do with members of other classes. A key criterion of social class is income differences. For example, in countries as diverse as the United States and Zimbabwe, people often draw socioeconomic boundaries on the basis of income differences. Throughout the first world, education, occupation, and social background are mutually reinforcing criteria that more precisely define social class than income alone. Social class has a residential dimension both at the global level and within nations and states. However, global marketing has led to the proliferation of consumer goods, services, and experiences. Technological advance has led to great communication across class boundaries and wider accessibility of goods, travel, and media by all but the poor. What really differentiates consumers in different social classes is not *what* but *how* they consume. People compete for status through economic, social, and cultural capital. Economic capital means financial resources, including income. Social capital includes relationships and social activity. Cultural capital includes practical knowledge and skills, access to consumer goods and objects, and degrees and memberships. Targeting the very affluent is not easy. Their numbers are small, they may own multiple residences, and wealth may be used to purchase some degree of anonymity. Sizable middle classes can be found in at least half of the over 200 nations of the world. Most Americans think of themselves as middle class. New middle classes represent growth opportunities for international marketers. The middle-class segment is expanding rapidly in many parts of the world including India, East Asia, Korea, Indonesia, and China. In many countries, middle classes adopt values that include education, self-improvement, upward mobility, a future orientation, and interest in material self-improvement. Working- and under-class segments constitute a majority of the population of the world. Studies both in Triad nations, as well as in some developing nations, have found that working-class lifestyles are resistant to changes in their basic characteristics. Brand loyalty, tempered by cost consciousness, is characteristic.

Frequent patterns of association and identification with common national origins of a subgroup define ethnicity. Ethnicity involves self-identity or felt ethnicity, an individual's perceptions of him- or herself as a member of an ethnic group. Ethnic and regional ethnicities have reemerged throughout the world. Ethnic identities today are more voluntary than in the past, and represent a creative mix of values, beliefs, and consumption styles. In developing targeting and positioning strategies to reach ethnic markets, marketers should consider a number of issues. One issue of interest for marketers is intensity of ethnic identification. Marketers must also determine whether ethnicity translates into distinct consumer tastes. Successful ethnic marketing often depends upon appealing to the desire for ethnic affiliation. Ethnicity is not a static demographic characteristic, but varies with individual felt ethnicity, situation, and stage of life cycle.

Age, gender, and religion are three additional social structures that impact consumer behavior and affect marketing strategy. Consumers' preferences vary with age as does their access to resources. Age-related life transitions stimulate demand for specialized products and services, and age cohorts often share similar values and consumer preferences. Children's consumer demands represent considerable market opportunities. Children play an important role in influencing parental shopping and spending habits, and television advertising has a powerful influence on children's product preferences and choices. Teens are a popular target for marketers because they make up a large part of the population and they often enjoy substantial discretionary income. Teens are market savvy and involved with consumer culture, and are undergoing many physical and emotional changes. Many initial purchases are made as a teenager and so this age group offers an ideal target market for promoting brand loyalties. Teenagers globally are increasingly wired into the Internet. This facilitates the spread of images, ideas, values, and trends among teenagers around the world. The population is aging in many of the most developed nations. The elderly of the future will be more affluent, better educated, and more active. Hence, it makes sense to position goods and services to take advantage of these facts.

Gender is a significant segmentation and targeting criteria in marketing. Evident physiological differences between men and women lead to specialized product needs in nutrition, health, and personal care, for example. Gender roles are learned early and play a formative role in personality development and self-identity. Patterns of wants and responses to market appeals vary with gender. Traditional gender-related differences in information processing and response to marketing appeals have also been identified. Obviously many products are designed to appeal to or even accentuate gender-specific wants. Gender roles definitely persist and influence consumer behavior, but the behavior of male and female consumers often defies these stereotypes. Even in very traditional male-oriented societies, we see important changes in gender roles. When women enter the wage labor force in developed and developing nations and gain access to economic resources, a blurring of gender role differences occurs.

Religion refers to beliefs and practices relative to the sacred. Surprisingly, consumer research has not extensively studied the impact of religion on consumer behavior or the purchase and consumption of religious goods and services. As with ethnicity, religion's influence varies with the consumer's identification with a religion and its values, the strength of identification, and situational factors. Religion may be a useful segmentation variable because religion influences value systems. Value systems in turn influence preferences of all kinds. Religion-based segments and consumer behavior certainly merit more investigation, because in the United States alone religion is a multibillion dollar industry, employing thousands of people, in which there is intense competition between competing products.

1. Give an example of a form of symbolic capital consumption that provides social mobility for members of lower social classes.

2. Do social conditions in your town foster the emergence of distinctive patterns of ethnic identity and consumption behavior? Explain.

3. Identify an ethnic festival that you have attended. What products and services enabled consumers to express the defining features of ethnicity mentioned in the chapter?

4. How would you identify your own social class? Give reasons for your answer. Ask your parents about their social class and their reasons for identifying themselves in that class. How do you and your parents compare? Can you think of consumption behaviors that relate to your social class? Explain.

5. Select and compare an advertisement that you feel portrays gender stereotypes with one that breaks those stereotypes. Do you think the target audiences for these two ads would be different or similar?

6. Interview a female friend and a male friend about their perceptions of masculine roles and products and feminine roles and products. Compare and contrast their answers. Be sure to include some questions that relate to roles and products you personally see as more feminine and more masculine.

7. Rent a video movie set in a contemporary time and analyze the economic and social structures depicted in the movie. How would you describe the social class, age cohort, gender roles, religion, ethnicity, and so on illustrated in the movie? How did various consumption objects included as movie props help you decide about these economic and social structures? Explain.

8. Check out the websites for Banana Republic, The Gap, and Old Navy. If possible, check out the brick-and-mortar retail outlets as well. In what ways are the images of these brands the same and in what ways are they different? Describe the characteristics that you think might best distinguish the target markets for these brands.

You Make the Call

Translating "Got Milk" for Latinos

It was late February when Jeff Manning began to focus on a phenomenon he had never had occasion to think about before: slathering peanut butter and jelly on a tortilla. The executive director of the California Milk Processor Board, Manning was poring over a report on the Latino community, searching for a way to reverse an industry sales slump in the heavily Hispanic southern portion of the state. And there on page 12, the answer seemed to jump out at him: The ranks of Hispanic teenagers, it noted, are projected to swell to 18 percent of the U.S. teen population over the next decade, up from 12 percent now.

But appealing to these youngsters, he learned, is not as simple as cutting an ad in Spanish with tried-and-true Hispanic themes. The kids often live in two world: one rich in traditional Latino values such as a strong commitment to family and religion, the other in which they eagerly take part in mainstream teen America. The report described how they bounce between hip-hop and rock en Español; watch "Buffy the Vampire Slayer" with their friends and Spanish telenovelas (nighttime soap operas) with their parents; blend Mexican rice with spaghetti sauce—and spread peanut butter and jelly on tortillas.

When it comes to "young biculturals," the "conventional model" of straight Spanish-language advertising "is irrelevant," Roxana Lissa, a Beverly Hills public relations consultant who had prepared the report, told Manning.

To Manning, who spent 25 years at major ad agencies before joining the milk board in 1993, Lissa's advice made perfect sense. Soon, he was talking up the possibility of a "cutting-edge" milk ad shot in "Spanglish." He foresaw combining distinctive Latino imagery with sights and sounds that are seductive to teenagers of all backgrounds. "I want to capture both worlds," Manning declared.

Four months later, a milk spot aimed at Hispanic teens is now ready. It will be aired across California starting next week on the Spanish-language network Telemundo. But the end result is radically different from what Manning and his team first envisioned—a turn of events that stirred passions and raised a question with broad implications: What is the smartest way to peddle products to one of the fastest-growing demographic groups in the country?

Focus groups with Hispanic teenage boys and girls produced some surprising findings. A mainstream ad for Kellogg's Corn Pops was their favorite. A Spanish-language ad for Mountain Dew with the Chilean techno-rock band La Ley didn't resonate much. And they found a bilingual ad for Levi's confusing. By contrast, their response to existing Got Milk? ads was highly positive. They found them funny and compelling. They did not say a word about the English language format nor the lack of a bicultural perspective. These results led Manning to a decision to take the existing Got Milk? spots and air them without any change on Spanish-language television.

Consultations with Lissa and Anita Santiago, head of a Santa Monica, California, ad agency specializing in Hispanic consumers, turned up significant discomfort with the idea on their part. Manning says in order to justify a brand-new campaign for Latino teens "you've got to start with problems. . . . Where were the big problems with Got Milk?" Santiago felt the campaign was somehow just "too Anglo." She voiced concern that its appearance on Spanish television could conflict with her agency's milk commercials target at Hispanic moms. Being deprived of milk—the basis for the humor throughout the Got Milk? ads—is not funny to "an older Hispanic audience," she says. Lissa raises concerns too. Unlike previous immigrant groups, she says, many Latinos embrace their language and heritage more strongly as they get older and become more established in America; advertising in English, therefore, may be a lousy way to foster long-term product loyalty. Beyond that, she worries that sticking the Got Milk? on Spanish-language television could well be perceived as an insult, especially among Latino community leaders. Mostly she and Santiago argue that they're letting a tremendous opportunity slip away and that, at a minimum, a lot more research into bicultural teens is needed. "You can say these teens are the same as everybody else, but they're not," Santiago says later. "They don't look the same. They don't talk the same."

But Manning would not budge. He says that he'll certainly look to place more Latino actors in the regular Got Milk? campaign. And he may further explore a bicultural ad at some point. But any urgency he had to develop a whole new campaign has waned. "I don't want to look like we're backing off this group of people," he says. "But as a marketer, I can't find a rationale" for launching a bunch of new ads. He is confident that this alternate scheme will "extend the reach" of Got Milk?—without having to shell out hundreds of thousands of dollars for new creative work.

1. Is Manning drawing the correct conclusion from the focus group results? Why or why not?

2. What alternative conclusions might you draw from these results?

3. What are some reasons the focus group results might not apply to the actual television viewing situation?

4. How would you do more research into bicultural teens to probe the appropriateness of the Got Milk? campaign for Hispanic television?

5. What are some aspects of Hispanic ethnicity that Manning may be neglecting in devising his campaign?

This case is adapted from Rick Wartzman, "When You Translate 'Got Milk?' for Latinos What Do You Get?" The Wall Street Journal, June 3, 1999, pp. A1, A8.

1. Adapted from Joan O. C. Hamilton, "Valley of the Dollars," *Town and Country,* June 2000, pp. 190–91, 231–34.
2. James C. Ward and Peter H. Reingen, "Sociocognitive Analysis of Group Decision Making among Consumers," *Journal of Consumer Research* 17 (December 1990), pp. 245–62.
3. Alan Hunt, *Governance of the Consuming Passions* (New York: St. Martin's Press, 1996).
4. Laura Oswald, "Culture Swapping: Consumption and the Ethnogenesis of Middle-Class Haitian Immigrants," *Journal of Consumer Research* 25 (March 1999), pp. 303–18.
5. Miriam B. Stamps and Eric J. Arnould, "The Florida Classic: Performing African American Community," in *Advances in Consumer Research,* vol. 25, Joseph W. Alba and Wes Hutchinson, eds. (Provo, UT: Association for Consumer Research, 1998), pp. 578–84.
6. C. Kagitcibasi and J. W. Berry, "Cross-Cultural Psychology: Current Research and Trends," *Annual Review of Psychology* 40, (1989), pp. 493–531; and J. L. Spates, "The Sociology of Values," *Annual Review of Sociology* 9 (1983), pp. 27–49.
7. Richard P. Coleman, Lee P. Rainwater, and Kent A. McClelland, *Social Standing in America: New Dimensions of Class* (New York: Basic Books, 1978); and Richard P. Coleman, "The Continuing Significance of Social Class to Marketing," *Journal of Consumer Research* 10 (December 1983), pp. 265–80.
8. Arthur Marwick, *Class: Image and Reality in Britain, France and the USA since 1930* (New York: Oxford University Press, 1980), p. 19.
9. James E. Fisher, "Social Class and Consumer Behavior: The Relevance of Class and Status," in *Advances in Consumer Research,* vol. 14, Melanie Wallendorf and Paul Anderson, eds. (Provo, UT: Association for Consumer Research, 1987), pp. 492–96.

10. Chip Walker, "The Global Middle Class," *American Demographics,* September 1995, pp. 40–46; and Ignacio Galceran and Jon Berry, "A New World of Consumers," *American Demographics,* March 1995, pp. 26–32.

11. Anthony Giddens, *The Class Structure of the Advanced Societies* (New York: Harper & Row, 1973), p. 110.

12. Diana Balmori, Stuart F. Voss, and Miles Wortman, *Notable Family Networks in Latin America* (Chicago: University of Chicago Press, 1984); Marianne Gullestad, "The Transformation of the Norwegian Notion of Everyday Life," *American Ethnologist* 18 (August 1991), p. 483; Larissa Adler Lomnitz and Marisol Perez-Lizaur, *A Mexican Elite Family, 1820–1980: Kinship, Class, and Culture* (Princeton: Princeton University Press, 1987); Marwick, *Class: Image and Reality.*

13. Out There News, "Who Runs Russia?" www.megastories.com/russia/power/cover.htm (May, 1998).

14. R. W. Connell, *Ruling Class Ruling Culture* (Cambridge: Cambridge University Press, 1977), p. 217.

15. Russell W. Belk, *Elite Consumer Behavior in Zimbabwe* (Salt Lake City: Odyssey Film Productions, 1999); Connell, *Ruling Class Ruling Culture; Money, Morals, and Manners* (Chicago: University of Chicago Press, 1992); Michele Lamont, p. 70; and Scott Dawson, Bruce Stern, and Tom Gillpatrick, "An Empirical Update of Patronage Behaviors across the Social Class Hierarchy," in *Advances in Consumer Research,* vol. 17, Marvin E. Goldberg, Gerald Gorn, and Richard W. Pollay, eds. (Provo, UT: Association for Consumer Research, 1990), p. 836.

16. Walker, "The Global Middle Class."

17. Rebecca Piirto Heath, "The New Working Class," *American Demographics,* January 1998, pp. 51–55.

18. Lamont, *Money, Morals, and Manners,* pp. 85–86; and Scott Dawson and Jill Cavell, "Status Recognition in the 1980s: Invidious Distinction Revisited," *Advances in Consumer Research,* v. 14, Melanie Wallendorf and Paul Anderson, eds. (Provo, UT: Association for Consumer Research, 1987), p. 487.

19. Mary Jackman and Robert Jackman, *Class Awareness in the United States* (Berkeley: University of California Press, 1986).

20. "Vietnam in Transition: New Evidence on Growth and Poverty," *Poverty Lines,* June 1998.

21. "The Uses of Literacy," *The Economist,* June 17, 2000, pp. 56–57.

22. Fatma Babiker Mahmoud, *The Sudanese Bourgeoisie: Vanguard of Development* (London: Zed Books, 1984), pp. 104, 106.

23. "Multiple Choice," *The Economist,* June 10, 2000, p. 18.

24. Roger Marshall, Christina Kwai-Choi Lee, and Kim Marshall, "New Zealand: Consumers in Their Market Environment—Profiles and Predictions," in *Marketing and Consumer Behavior in East and South-East Asia,* Anthony Pecotich and Clifford J. Shultz II, eds. (New York: McGraw-Hill, 1998), pp. 523–48.

25. Walker, "The Global Middle Class."

26. Marwick, *Class: Image and Reality,* pp. 347–50.

27. Walker, "The Global Middle Class"; and "It's an Unfair World," *The Economist,* May 6, 2000, p. 15.

28. Japan Travel Bureau, *"Salaryman" in Japan,* 1997; Takie Sugiyama Lebra, *Above the Clouds: Culture of the Modern Japanese Nobility* (Berkeley: University of California Press, 1993); Sharon O'Malley, "Country Gold," *American Demographics,* July 1992, pp. 26–33; Jenny Tabkoff, "Suburb Snobs," *Sydney Morning Herald,* December 26, 1998, Spectrum, pp. 1ff; and UN Development Program, *Human Development Report* (New York: United Nations, 1998).

29. Doug Holt, "Does Cultural Capital Structure American Consumption?" *Journal of Consumer Research* 25 (June 1998), pp. 1–25; Geri Smith, Elisabeth Malkin, Ian Katz, and Gail DeGeorge, "Marketing in Latin America," *Business Week International Edition,* February 9, 1998, pp. 50ff; and Jennifer Veale, "Economic Crisis Robs Koreans of Money, Pride," *The Globe and Mail,* July 28, 1998, Metro, p. A11.

30. See Pierre Bourdieu, *Distinction: A Social Critique of the Judgment of Taste* (Cambridge: Harvard University Press, 1984).

31. J. R. Whittaker Penteado, "Fast Food Franchises Fight for Brazilian Aficionados," *Brandweek,* June 7, 1993, pp. 20–24.

32. Dawson and Cavell, "Status Recognition in the 1980s: Invidious Distinction Revisited," p. 490; Elizabeth C. Hirschman, "A Descriptive Theory of Retail Market Structure," *Journal of Retailing* 54 (Winter 1978), pp. 29–48; and Arun Jain and Michael Etgar, "Measuring Store Image through Multidimensional Scaling of Free Response Data," *Journal of Retailing* 52 (Winter 1976), pp. 61–70.

33. Brad Edmondson, "Where They Live," *American Demographics,* November 1989, p. 27.

34. Dawson, Stern, and Gillpatrick, "An Empirical Update of Patronage Behaviors," p. 833; Rajesh Kanwar and Nolis Pagiavlas, "When Are Higher Social Class Consumers More and Less Brand Loyal than Lower Social Class Consumers? The Role of Mediating Variables," in *Advances in Consumer Research,* vol. 19, John F. Sherry, Jr., and Brian Sternthal, eds. (Provo, UT: Association for Consumer Research, 1993), pp. 593–94; and Sidney J. Levy, "Social Class and Consumer Behavior," in *On Knowing the Consumer,* Joseph W. Newman, ed. (New York: John W. Wiley and Sons), pp. 146–60.

35. Galceran and Berry, "A New World of Consumers."

36. Katherine S. Newman, *Falling from Grace* (New York: Free Press, 1988).

37. Michael R. Solomon, "Deep-Seated Materialism: The Case of Levi's 501 Jeans," in *Advances in Consumer Research,* vol. 13, Richard J. Lutz, ed. (Provo, UT: Association for Consumer Research, 1986), pp. 619–22.

38. Jim Gullo, "Great Scott!" *Town and Country,* June 2000, pp. 166–71, 220–24; Pierre Bourdieu, *Distinction* (Cambridge: Harvard University Press, 1984); Richard P. Coleman, "The Continuing Significance of Social Class to Marketing," *Journal of Consumer Research* 10 (December 1983), p. 271; Bonnie H. Erickson, "What Is Good Taste For?" *Canadian Review of Sociology and Anthropology* 28, no. 2 (1991), pp. 255–78; and Lamont, *Money, Morals, and Manners,* p. 90.

39. Lamont, *Money, Morals, and Manners,* pp. 67–68; and Beatrix Le Wita, *French Bourgeois Culture* (Cambridge: Cambridge University Press, 1994).

40. Balmori, Voss, and Wortman, *Notable Family Networks in Latin America;* and Lomnitz and Perez-Lizaur, *A Mexican Elite Family, 1820–1980.*

41. Nancy Y. Wong and Aaron C. Ahuvia, "Personal Taste and Family Face: Luxury Consumption in Confucian and Western Societies," *Psychology and Marketing* 15 (August 1998), pp. 423–41.

42. "Wedding Bliss," *The Economist,* May 27, 2000, 64; Janeen Arnold Costa and Russell W. Belk, "Nouveaux Riche as Quintessential Americans: Case Studies of Consumption in an Extended Family," in *Advances in Nonprofit Marketing,* vol. 3, Russell W. Belk, ed. (Greenwich, CT: JAI Press, 1990), pp. 83–140; Dean MacCannell and Juliet Flower MacCannell, "Social Class in Postmodernity," in *Forget Baudrillard?* Chris Rojek and B. S. Turner, eds. (London and New York: Routledge, 1995), pp. 124–45; and Pia Polsa and Bai Change Hong, "China, Part II," in *Marketing and Consumer Behavior in East and South-East Asia,* Anthony Pecotich and Clifford J. Schultz II, eds. (Sydney: McGraw-Hill, 1998), pp. 161–212.

43. Colin Campbell, *The Romantic Ethic and the Spirit of Modern Consumerism* (Oxford: Basil Blackwell, 1987).

44. *Far Eastern Economic Review,* "Lifestyles: A Special Report," June 10, 1992, pp. 37–51; July 30, 1992, pp. 29–43; and August 27, 1992, pp. 27–40; see also Joseph C. H. Chai (1992), "Consumption and Living Standards in China," *The China Quarterly* 131 (September 1992), pp. 121–49.

45. Marwick, *Class: Image and Reality,* p. 340.

46. "A Virtuous Circle," *The Economist,* July 18, 1992, p. 27; Greg J. Duncan, Timothy M. Smeeding, and Willard Rodgers, "The Incredible Shrinking Middle Class," *American Demographics,* May 1992, p. 36; and Judith Waldrop, "Shades of Black," *American Demographics,* September 1990, p. 33.

47. Dawson and Cavell, "Status Recognition in the 1980s: Invidious Distinction Revisited," p. 488.

48. Japan Travel Bureau, *"Salaryman" in Japan;* Peter S. H. Leeflang and W. Fred van Raaij, "The Changing Consumer in the European Union: A Meta-Analysis," *International Journal of Research in Marketing* 12 (1995), pp. 373–87; and Marshall, Lee, and Marshall, "New Zealand."

49. Pete Engardio, Joyce Barnathan, and William Glasgall, "Asia's Wealth," *Business Week,* November 29, 1994, p. 102; Mark Clifford, "Hair-Shirt Harmony," *Far Eastern Economic Review,* May 17, 1990, pp. 40–42; and Editorial, *Business Week,* October 25 1993, p. 125.

50. Matthew Grimm, "Live Large, at Home," *American Demographics,* June 2000, pp. 66–67; and "Middle Class on $10,000 a Year," *American Demographics,* September 1994, pp. 15–17.

51. Philippe Le Corré, "Raz-de-marée télévisuel sur le continent asiatique," *Le Monde Diplomatique,* January 1994, pp. 26–27; Michael Vatikiotis, "Discreet Charms," *Far Eastern Economic Review,* March 21, 1991, pp. 30–32; Clifford, "Hair-Shirt Harmony"; Eric J. Arnould, "Toward a Broadened Theory of Preference Formation and the Diffusion of Innovations: Cases from Zinder Province, Niger Republic," *Journal of Consumer Research* 16 (September 1989), pp. 239–67; and Paul M. Lubeck, "Islamic Protest under Semi-Industrial Capitalism: Yan Tatsine Explained," *Africa* 55, no. 4 (1985), pp. 369–89.

52. Africa News Service, "Positive Spin-Offs from Democracy," November 9, 1998.

53. Jonathan H. Turner, *Sociology: Concepts and Uses* (New York: McGraw-Hill, 1994).

54. Dexter Roberts, "China's Wealth Gap," *Business Week,* May 15, 2000, pp. 170–80; Jan Larson, "Reaching Downscale Markets," *American Demographics,* November 1991, p. 38; "A Virtuous Circle," *The Economist,* July 18, 1992, p. 27; and P.P.L. McGregor and V. K. Borooah, "Is Low Spending or Low Income a Better Indicator of Whether or Not a Household Is Poor? Some Results from the 1985 Family Expenditure Survey," *Journal of Social Policy* 21, no. 1 (1992), p. 54.

55. Larson, "Reaching Downscale Markets," p. 39.

56. See for example, Clifford Geertz, "The Rotating Credit Association: A 'Middle Range' in Development," *Economic Development and Cultural Change* 10, no. 3 (1962), pp. 241–63.

57. Fisher, "Social Class and Consumer Behavior," p. 494.

58. Coleman, "The Continuing Significance of Social Class to Marketing," pp. 265–79; and Peter Manuel, *Cassette Culture* (Chicago: University of Chicago Press, 1993), p. 192.

59. Lamont, *Money, Morals, and Manners,* p. 120; and Gullestad, "The Transformation of the Norwegian Notion of Everyday Life," pp. 489–90.

60. "How the Other Tenth Lives," *The Economist,* September 12, 1992, pp. 63–64; William Kornblum, "Who Is the Underclass?" *Dissent,* Spring 1991, pp. 202–11; Carole Marks, "The Urban Underclass," *American Journal of Sociology* 17 (1991), pp. 445–66; William Julius Wilson, *The Truly Disadvantaged* (Chicago: University of Chicago Press, 1987); and William Julius Wilson, "Another Look at the Truly Disadvantaged," *Political Science Quarterly* 106, no. 4 (1991–92), pp. 639–56.

61. Rebecca Gardyn and John Fetto, "Off the Map," *American Demographics,* June 2000, p. 72; Andrew Hornery, "Ethnic Expert Says Keep Eye on Bottom Line," *Sydney Morning Herald,* Business, Marketing, and Advertising, March 12, 1998, p. 28; Tony Koenderman, "Marketing in a Multicultural Society," *Financial Mail,* April 4, 1998; and Marlene L. Rossman, *Multicultural Marketing: Selling to a Diverse America* (New York: American Management Association, 1994).

62. Michel Laroche, Annamma Joy, Michael Hui, and Chankom Kim, "An Examination of Ethnicity Measures: Convergent Validity and Cross-Cultural Equivalence," in *Advances in Consumer Research,* vol. 18, Rebecca H. Holman and Michael R. Solomon, eds. (Provo, UT: Association for Consumer Research, 1991), p. 150; William L. Yancey, Eugene P. Ericksen, and Richard N. Juliani, "Emergent Ethnicity: A Review and Reformulation," *American Sociological Review* 41 (June 1976), pp. 391–99; and Mark H. Haller, "Recurring Themes," in *The Peoples of Philadelphia,* Allen F. Davis and Mark Haller, eds. (Philadelphia: Temple University Press, 1993), pp. 277–91.

63. David B. Wooten and Tiffany Galvin, "A Preliminary Examination of the Effects of Context Induced Felt Ethnicity on Advertising Effectiveness," in *Advances in Consumer Research,* vol. 20, Leigh McAlister and Michael L. Rothschild, eds. (Provo, UT: Association for Consumer Research, 1993), pp. 253–56.

64. Stamps and Arnould, "The Florida Classic"; Douglas M. Stayman and Rohit Deshpande, "Situational Ethnicity and Consumer Behavior," *Journal of Consumer Research* 16 (December 1989), pp. 361–71; May Waters, *Ethnic Options: Choosing Identities in America* (Berkeley: University of California Press, 1990); Johanna Zmud and Carlos Arce, "The Ethnicity and Consumption Relationship," in *Advances in Consumer Research,* vol. 19, John F. Sherry, Jr., and Brian Sternthal, eds. (Provo, UT: Association for Consumer Research, 1992), pp. 443–49; and Judith Waldrop, "The Mexican May," *American Demographics,* May 1992, p. 4.

65. Søren Askegaard and Eric J. Arnould, "Acculturation of Greenlandic Peoples to Danish Consumer Culture," presented at European Association for Consumer Research Conference, HEC, Jouy-es-Josas, France, June 22–26, 1999; and Thomas O'Guinn and Ronald Faber, "New Perspectives on Acculturation: The Relationship of General and Role-Specific Acculturation with Hispan-

ics' Consumer Attitudes," in *Advances in Consumer Research,* vol. 12, Elizabeth C. Hirschman and Morris Holbrook, eds. (Provo, UT: Association for Consumer Research, 1985), pp. 113–17.

66. Robert Ezra Park and E. W. Burgess, *Introduction to the Science of Sociology* (Chicago: University of Chicago Press, 1924).

67. S. P. Douglas and C. S. Craig, "Advances in International Marketing," *International Journal of Research in Marketing* 9 (1992), pp. 291–318; and L. J. Vaughan, "Cosmopolitanism, Ethnicity, and American Identity: Randolph Bourne's 'Trans-national America,' " *Journal of American Studies* 25, no. 3 (1991), pp. 443–59.

68. A. Weisberger, "Marginality and Its Direction," *Sociological Forum* 7, no. 3 (1992), pp. 425–44. Lisa Peñaloza, "Atravesando Fronteras/Border Crossings: A Critical Ethnographic Exploration of the Consumer Acculturation of Mexican Immigrants," *Journal of Consumer Research* 21 (June 1994), pp. 32–54.

69. Dominique Bouchet, "Marketing and the Redefinition of Ethnicity," in *Marketing in a Multicultural World,* Janeen Arnold Costa and Gary J. Bamossy, eds. (Thousand Oaks, CA: Sage Publications, 1995), pp. 68–104; Gary Boulard, "Louisiana Cajuns Celebrate Bid to Promote Their Culture," *Christian Science Monitor,* December 28, 1993, p. 7; Wei-Na Lee and Koog-Hyang Ro Um, "Ethnicity and Consumer Product Evaluation: A Cross-Cultural Comparison of Korean Immigrants and Americans," in *Advances in Consumer Research,* vol. 19, John F. Sherry, Jr., and Brian Sternthal, eds. (Provo, UT: Association for Consumer Research, 1992), pp. 429–36; Melanie Wallendorf and Michal D. Reilly, "Ethnic Migration, Assimilation, and Consumption," *Journal of Consumer Research* 10 (1983), pp. 292–302; and William L. Yancy, Eurgene P. Ericksen, and Richard N. Juliani, "Emergent Ethnicity: A Review and Reformulation," *American Sociological Review* 41 (June 1976), pp. 391–403.

70. Ignacio Redondo-Bellon, "The Effects of Bilingualism on the Consumer: The Case of Spain," *European Journal of Marketing* 33, no. 11–12 (1999).

71. Laura Oswald, "Culture Swapping: Consumption and the Ethnogenesis of Middle-Class Haitian Immigrants," *Journal of Consumer Research* 25 (March 1999), pp. 303–18.

72. Rebecca Gardyn and John Fetto, "Off the Map," *American Demographics,* June 2000, p. 72; Marlene L. Rossman, *Multicultural Marketing* (New York: American Management Association, 1994); and Geraldine Fennell, Koel Saegert, Francis Piron, and Rosemary Jimenez, "Do Hispanics Constitute a Market Segment?" in *Advances in Consumer Research,* vol. 19, John F. Sherry, Jr., and Brian Sternthal, eds. (Provo, UT: Association for Consumer Research, 1992), pp. 32–33.

73. Thomas O'Guinn and Timothy P. Meyer, "Segmenting the Hispanic Market: The Use of Spanish Language Radio," *Journal of Advertising Research* 22 (December 1984), pp. 9–16; and Rossman, *Multicultural Marketing.*

74. Gardyn and Fetto, "Off the Map," p. 72; William O'Hare, "A New Look at Asian Americans," *American Demographics,* October 1990, pp. 26–31; Rossman, *Multicultural Marketing;* and "Japanese Language Ranked 11th among Foreign Languages," *Rafu Shimpo,* April 24, 1993, p. 1.

75. Patricia Horn, "U.S. Book Industry Learns a New Language," *Christian Science Monitor,* March 8, 1994, p. 8.

76. Rossman, *Multicultural Marketing;* Waldrop, "Shades of Black," p. 30; and Dave Wielenga, "Kwanzaa Goes Mainstream," *Press-Telegram,* December 19, 1993, pp. J1, J10.

77. John P. Cortez, "KFC Stores Boast Flavor of Neighborhood," *Advertising Age,* May 31, 1993, pp. 3, 46; Eric Hollreiser, "Caddy Tweaks Ad Mix to Woo Blacks," *Brand Week,* November 21, 1994, p. 10; and Maria Mallory and Stephanie Anderson Forest, "Waking Up to a Major Market," *Business Week,* March 23, 1992, pp. 70–73.

78. Jonathan Burton, "Targeting Asians," *Far Eastern Economic Review,* January 21, 1993, pp. 40–41.

79. Leon D. Wynter, "Business and Race," *The Wall Street Journal,* June 2, 1999, p. B1.

80. Dan Fost, "California's Asian Market," *American Demographics,* October 1990, p. 36; Bradley Johnson, "Supermarkets Take 'Position,' " *Advertising Age,* May 10, 1993, p. S1; Lee and Um, "Ethnicity and Consumer Product Evaluation," p. 430; and Robert E. Wilkes and Humberto Valencia, "Hispanics and Blacks in Television Commercials," *Journal of Advertising,* March 1989, pp. 19–25.

81. Hornery, "Ethnic Expert Says Keep Eye on Bottom Line," p. 28; Carol J. Kaufman, "Coupon

Use in Ethnic Markets: Implications from a Retail Perspective," *Journal of Consumer Marketing* 8 (Winter 1991), p. 44; Rossman, *Multicultural Marketing;* Joyce Oliver, "To Reach Minorities, Try Busting Myths," *American Demographics,* April 1992, pp. 14–15; and Bickley Townsend, "Quenching Hispanic Thirst," *American Demographics,* December 1989, p. 15.

82. Ayse S. Caglar, *"McDöner: Döner Kepab* and the Social Positioning Struggle of German Turks," in *Marketing in a Multicultural World,* Janeen Arnold Costa and Gary J. Bamossy, eds. (Thousand Oaks: Sage Publications, 1995), pp. 209–30; and Eugene Roosens, "Interest Groups with a Noble Face," in *Marketing in a Multicultural World,* Janeen Arnold Costa and Gary J. Bamossy, eds. (Thousand Oaks: Sage Publications, 1995), pp. 126–44.

83. *Oxford English Dictionary,* 1933.

84. Veljko Vujai, "Nations, Regions, Mentalities: The Many Faces of Yugoslavia," in *Identities in Transition,* Victoria E. Bonnell, ed. (Berkeley: University of California Press, 1996), pp. 103–16.

85. "Africa: The Heart of the Matter," *The Economist,* May 13, 2000, pp. 22–24; Morton H. Fried, *The Notion of Tribe* (Menlo Park, CA: Cummings Publishing, 1975); Harold Issacs, *Idols of the Tribe* (New York: Harper and Row, 1975); Joel Kotkin, *Tribes* (New York: Random House, 1993); and Mike Featherstone, ed., *Global Culture* (London: Sage Publications, 1994).

86. "Massacres Promised," *Lincoln Journal Star,* June 20, 2000, p. 2A; and Andre Beteille, "Race, Caste and Gender," in *Society and Politics in India: Essays in a Comparative Perspective,* Andre Beteille, ed. (London: Athlone Press, 1991), pp. 15–37.

87. Mihaly Csikszentmihalyi and Eugene Rochberg-Halton, *The Meaning of Things: Domestic Symbols and the Self* (Cambridge: Cambridge University Press, 1981); Vicky Goodhead, "Marketing to Mature Adults Requires a State of Being," *Marketing News,* December 9, 1991, p. 10; and Howard Schlossberg, "Expert on Aging Warns Against 'Stupid Marketing,'" *Marketing News,* September 28, 1992, pp. 2–3.

88. Special Report on Asia, CNBC, June 18, 2000; and Zoher Abdoolcarim, "Consumer Kids Get Star Billing," *Asian Business* 30 (October 10, 1994), pp. 22–25.

89. For an excellent review of research on children as consumers, see Deborah Roedder John, "Consumer Socialization of Children: A Retrospective Look at Twenty-Five Years of Research," *Journal of Consumer Research* 26 (December 1999), pp. 183–213.

90. Cele Otnes, Chan Kim Young, and Kyungseung Kim, "All I Want for Christmas: An Analysis of Children's Brand Requests to Santa Claus," *Journal of Popular Culture* 27 (Spring 1994), pp. 183–94.

91. Russell W. Belk, Kenneth D. Bahn, and Robert N. Mayer, "Developmental Recognition of Consumption Symbolism," *Journal of Consumer Research* 9 (June 1982), pp. 4–17; and Robert N. Mayer and Russell Belk, "Acquisition of Consumption Stereotypes by Children," *Journal of Consumer Affairs* 16 (Winter 1982), pp. 307–21.

92. James U. McNeal and Chyon-Hwa Yeh, "Development of Consumer Behavior Patterns among Chinese Children," *Journal of Consumer Marketing* 14, no. 1 (1997), pp. 45–59; James U. McNeal and Mindy F. Ji (1999), "Chinese Children as Consumers: An Analysis of Their New Product Information Sources," *Journal of Consumer Marketing,* 16, 4, pp. 345–64.

93. Christian Derbaix and Joel Bree, "The Impact of Children's Affective Reactions Elicited by Commercials on Attitudes toward the Advertisement and the Brand," *International Journal of Research in Marketing* 14 (July 1997), pp. 207–29; Cynthia Frazier Hite and Robert E. Hit, "Reliance on Brand by Young Children," *Journal of the Market Research Society* 37 (April 1995), pp. 185–93; M. Carole Macklin, "Preschoolers' Learning of Brand Names from Visual Cues," *Journal of Consumer Research* 23 (December 1996), pp. 251–61; Richard Mizerski, "The Relationship between Cartoon Trade Character Recognition and Attitude toward Product Category in Young Children," *Journal of Marketing* 59 (October 1995), pp. 58–70; Rodney Tasker, "Potential for Milking," *Far Eastern Economic Review,* April 3, 1997, p. 46; and Paco Underhill, "Kids in Stores," *American Demographics* 16, no. 6 (1994), pp. 22–27.

94. John, "Consumer Socialization of Children."

95. Merrie Brucks, Gary M. Armstrong, and Marvin E. Goldberg, "Children's Use of Cognitive Defenses against Television Advertising: A Cognitive Response Approach," *Journal of Consumer Research* 14 (March 1988), pp. 471–82.

96. Jeff Brazil, "Play Dough," *American Demographics* (December 1999), pp. 56–61; and Anthony Pecotich and Clifford J. Shultz II, eds., *Marketing and Consumer Behavior in East and South-East Asia* (New York: McGraw-Hill, 1998).

97. "Those Precocious 13-Year Olds," *Brandweek,* January 25, 1993, p. 13; Roshan D. Ahuja, Louis M. Capella, and Ronald D. Taylor, "Child Influences, Attitudinal and Behavior Comparisons between Single-Parent and Dual-Parent Households in Grocery Shopping Decisions," *Journal of Marketing Theory and Practice* 6 (Winter 1998), pp. 48–62; Jill Brooke, "Girl Power," *ADWEEK,* Eastern Ed., February 2, 1998, pp. 18–20; Robert Gray, "Keeping Up with the Kids," *Marketing,* February 24, 1997, pp. 26–29; Ellen Newborne and Kathleen Kerwin, "Generation Y," *Business Week,* February 15, 1999, pp. 80–88; and Mark Ritson and Richard Elliott, "The Social Uses of Advertising: An Ethnographic Study of Adolescent Advertising Audiences," *Journal of Consumer Research* 26 (December 1999), pp. 260–77.

98. Special Report on the Internet in Asia, CNBC, June 18, 2000; George Carey, Xiaoyan Zhao, Joan Chiaramone, and David Eden, "Is There One Global Village for Our Future Generation? Talking to 7–12 Year Olds around the World," *Marketing and Research Today* 25 (February 1997), pp. 12–16; Don Tapscott, *Growing Up Digital: The Rise of the Net Generation* (New York: McGraw-Hill, 1998); and Shawn Tully, "The Universal Teenager," *Fortune,* February 4, 1994, pp. 14–16.

99. George P. Moschis and Roy L. Moore, "Decision Making among the Young," *Journal of Consumer Research,* September 1979, pp. 101–12; Lisa Marie Petersen, "I Bought What Was on Sale," *Brandweek,* February 22, 1993, pp. 12–13; Dennis H. Tootelian and Ralph M. Gaedeclke, "The Teen Market: An Exploratory Analysis of Income, Spending, and Shopping Patterns," *Journal of Consumer Marketing,* Fall 1994, pp. 35–44; and Laura Zinn, "Teens: Here Comes the Biggest Wave Yet," *Business Week,* April 11, 1994, pp. 76–86.

100. Jane L. Levere, "A New Survey Charts the Habits of Teen-Agers around the World," *New York Times,* June 11, 1996, p. D8; Jaime Troiano, "Brazilian Teenagers Go Global—Sharing Values and Brands," *Marketing & Research Today* 25 (August 1997), pp. 149–62; and "Brand Crazy," *Women's Wear Daily,* February 19, 1998, pp. S22–24.

101. Emily DeNitto, "Brands Take a Berating at Cash Register," *Advertising Age,* August 23, 1993, pp. S4, S11; Adrienne Ward Fawcett, "When Using Slang in Advertising: BVC," *Advertising Age,* August 23, 1993, p. S6; Bruce Horowitz, "Lucrative Side of Teenage Anxieties," *Los Angeles Times,* October 4, 1992, pp. D1, D3; Jeff Jensen, "A New Read on How to Reach Boys," *Advertising Age,* August 23, 1993, pp. S10, S11; Junu Bryan Kim, "For Savvy Teens: Real Life, Real Solutions," *Advertising Age,* August 23, 1993, pp. S1, S4; Janine Lopiano-Misdom and Jopanne De Luca, *Street Trends* (New York: Harper Perennial, 1997); Cyndee Miller, "Marketers Find Alternative Way to Appeal to Young Music Lovers," *Marketing News,* October 12, 1992, p. 18; Cyndee Miller, " The Way Xers Watch TV Has Advertisers Watching Them," *Marketing News,* December 6, 1993, p. 5; Ernie Mosteller, "In Search of Cool," *Shoot,* October 24, 1997, pp. 4–6; Fumiteru Nitta, "Shopping for Souvenirs in Hawaii," in *Re-Made in Japan,* Joseph J. Tobin, ed. (New Haven: Yale University Press, 1992), pp. 204–15; Howard Schlossberg, "What Teenagers Find Hot Today Will Be Old News Tomorrow," *Marketing News,* December 6, 1993, p. 7; and Carolyn E. Setlow, "Kids Are Savvy, Affluent Consumers Who Retailers Should Court," *Discount Store News* no. 36, 18 (September 15, 1997), pp. 20–21.

102. Dick Hebidge, *Subculture: The Behavioral Basis of Style (*London: Methuen, 1979); Ikuya Sato, *Kamikaze Biker* (Chicago: University of Chicago Press, 1991); and Julie Tilsner, "From Trash Can Straight to Seventh Avenue," *Business Week,* March 22, 1993, p. 39.

103. Joan Raymond, "The Joy of Empty Nesting," *American Demographics,* May 2000, pp. 49–54.

104. Raymond, "The Joy of Empty Nesting"; Carol M. Morgan, "The Psychographic Landscape of the 50-Plus," *Brandweek,* July 19, 1993, pp. 28–32; and Robert E. Wilkes, "A Structural Modeling Approach to the Measurement and Meaning of Cognitive Age," *Journal of Consumer Research,* September 1992, pp. 292–301.

105. Bern Keating, "Elderhostel: The Mature Traveler's Ticket to Intriguing Adventures," *Hemispheres,* October 1992, pp. 52–54; Richard C. Leventhal, "The Aging Consumer: What's All the Fuss about Anyway?" *Journal of Consumer Marketing* 8 (Winter 1991), pp. 29–34; and Jim Carlton, "Web Sites, Other PC Wonders Draw Crowds of Retirees," *The Wall Street Journal,* January 29, 1998, p. B1.

106. "America's Aging Consumers," *Discount Merchandiser,* September 1993, pp. 16–28; and Kelly A. Tepper, "The Role of Labeling Processes in Elderly Consumers' Responses to Age Segmentation Cues," *Journal of Consumer Research* 20 (March 1994), pp. 503–19.

107. Sharmistha Law, Scott A. Hawkins, and Fergus I. M. Craik, (1998), "Repetition-Induced Belief in the Elderly: Rehabilitating Age-Related Memory Deficits," *Journal of Consumer Research* 25 (September 1998), pp. 91–107.

108. Steve Burt and Mark Gabbott, "The Elderly Consumer and Non-Food Purchase Behaviour," *European Journal of Marketing* 29, no. 2 (1995), pp. 43–57; Catherine A. Cole and Siva K. Balasubramanian, "Age Difference in Consumers' Search for Information: Public Policy Implications," *Journal of Consumer Research* 20 (June 1993), pp. 157–69; and A. J. Greco, "Representation of the Elderly in Advertising: Crisis or Inconsequence?" *Journal of Consumer Marketing* 6, no. 1 (1989), pp. 37–44.

109. Allan J. Kimmel and Elisabeth Tissier-Desbordes, "Masculinity and Consumption: A Qualitative Investigation of French and American Men," in *Gender, Marketing and Consumer Behavior,* vol. 5, Jonathan Schroeder and Cele C. Otnes, eds. (Urbana, IL: University of Illinois Publication Service, 2000), pp. 1–18.

110. Lisa Peñaloza, "Crossing Boundaries/Crossing Lines: A Look at the Nature of Gender Boundaries and Their Impact on Marketing Research," *International Journal of Research in Marketing* 11, no. 4 (1994), pp. 359–79.

111. John, "Consumer Socialization of Children."

112. Judy Cohen, "Gender Portrayal in Children's Advertising," in *Gender Marketing and Consumer Behavior,* vol. 5, Jonathan Schroeder and Cele C. Otnes, eds. (Urbana, IL: University of Illinois Publication Service, 2000), pp. 47–68.

113. Carrie Goerne, "Gun Companies Target Women: Foes Call It Marketing to Fear," *Marketing News,* 1, 2; Timothy Burke, *Lifebuoy Men and Lux Women* (Durham: Duke University Press, 1996); Margaret Littman, "Women Fans Have Gridiron Pros Grinning," *Marketing News,* February 2, 1997, pp. 1, 14; and Lorraine A. Woellert, "For the WNBA, It's No Easy Lay-up," *Business Week,* May 1, 2000, pp. 102, 106.

114. Janice Radway, "Interpretive Communities and Variable Literacies: The Functions of Romance Reading," in *Rethinking Popular Culture,* Chandra Mukerji and Michael Schudson, eds. (Berkeley: University of California Press, 1991), pp. 465–86; Barbara Stern, "Two Pornographies: A Feminist View of Sex in Advertising," in *Advances in Consumer Research,* Rebecca H. Holman and Michael R. Solomon, eds. (Provo, UT: Association for Consumer Research, 1991), pp. 384–91; Eileen Fischer and Steven J. Arnold, "More than a Labor of Love: Gender Roles and Christmas Gift Shopping," *Journal of Consumer Research* 17 (1990), pp. 333–45; Pamela Kiecker, Kay M. Palan, and Charles S. Areni, "Different Ways of 'Seeing': How Gender Differences in Information Processing Influence the Content Analysis of Narrative Texts," *Marketing Letters* 11, no. 1 (2000), pp. 49–65; and Cele Otnes, Tina M. Lowrey, and Y. C. Kim, "Gift Selection for Easy and Difficult Recipients, a Social Roles Interpretation," *Journal of Consumer Research* 20 (1993), pp. 229–44.

115. Ann Veeck, Laura Williams, and Naihua Jiang, "Sons and Daughters: The One-Child Policy, Education and Gender Stratification in Urban China," pp. 78–79; Cele Otnes and Mary Ann McGrath, "Beyond the Stereotype of Male Shopping Behavior," p. 101; and Suraj Commuri, "Husbands Play 'Men': Feminist Interpretation of Women's Participation in Preserving Male Stereotypes," p. 101; in *Gender Marketing and Consumer Behavior,* vol. 5, Jonathan Schroeder and Cele C. Otnes, eds. (Urbana, IL: University of Illinois Publication Service, 2000).

116. Theodore Caplow, "Christmas Gifts and Kin Networks," *American Sociological Review* 48, no. 6 (1982), pp. 383–92; David Cheal, *The Gift Economy* (New York: Routledge Press, 1988); Micaela Di Leonardo, "The Female World of Cards and Holidays: Women, Families, and the Work of Kinship," *Signs: Journal of Women, Culture and Society* 12 (Spring 1987), pp. 440–53; Fischer and Arnold, "More than a Labor of Love"; Margaret L. Rucker, L. Leckliter, S. Kivel, M. Dinkel, T. Freitas, M. Waynes, and H. Prato, "When the Thought Counts: Friendship, Love, Gift Exchanges and Gift Returns," in *Advances in Consumer Research,* vol. 18, Rebecca H. Holman and Michael R. Solomon, eds. (Provo, UT: Association for Consumer Research, 1991), pp. 528–31; John F. Sherry, Jr., and Mary Ann McGrath, "Unpacking the Holiday Presence: A Comparative Ethnography of Two Gift Stores," in *Interpretive Consumer Research,* Elizabeth Hirschman, ed. (Provo, UT: Association

for Consumer Research, 1989), pp. 148–67; Melanie Wallendorf and Eric J. Arnould, " 'We Gather Together': The Consumer Rituals of Thanksgiving Day," *Journal of Consumer Research* 18 (June 1991), pp. 13–31; Eric J. Arnould, "Marketing and Social Reproduction in Zinder, Niger Republic," in *Households: Changing Form and Function,* Robert Netting, Richard Wilk, and Eric Arnould, eds. (Berkeley: University of California Press, 1984), pp. 130–62; and Daniel Miller, *A Theory of Shopping* (Ithaca: Cornell University Press, 1998).

117. Deborah Heisley, "Gender Symbolism and Usage Expectations in Food," p. 104; Lynn Langmeyer, "Exploring Gender Influences on Meanings in Celebrity Endorsers," pp. 158–67; and Teresa M. Pavia and Janeen A. Costa, "Gender Dimensions of the Alphabetic Characters with Implications for Branding," pp. 173–85; all in *Gender and Consumer Behavior,* Janeen Costa, ed. (Salt Lake City: University of Utah Printing Service, 1991); see also Michael J. Baker and Gilbert A. Churchill, "The Impact of Physically Attractive Models on Advertising Evaluations," *Journal of Marketing Research* 14 (November 1997), pp. 538–55.

118. William O. Adcock, Elizabeth C. Hirschman, and Jac L. Goldstucker, "Bank Card Users: An Updated Profile," in *Advances in Consumer Research,* vol. 4, William D. Perrault, Jr., ed. (Atlanta, GA: Association for Consumer Research, 1977), pp. 236–41; Amardeep Assar and George S. Bobinski, Jr., "Financial Decision Making by Baby Boomer Couples," in *Advances in Consumer Research,* vol. 18, Rebecca H. Holman and Michael R. Solomon, eds. (Provo, UT: Association for Consumer Research, 1991), pp. 659–60; and Elizabeth C. Hirschman, "Differences in Consumer Purchase Behavior by Credit Card Payment System," *Journal of Consumer Research* 6 (June 1979), pp. 58–66.

119. Alladi Venkatesh, "Gender Identities in the Indian Context: A Sociocultural Construction of the Female Consumer," in *Gender and Consumer Behavior,* Janeen Costa, ed. (Salt Lake City: University of Utah Printing Service, 1993), pp. 119–29.

120. "Automakers Learn Better Roads to Women's Market," *Marketing News,* October 12, 1992, p. 2.

121. Manjeet Kripalani, "From the Runway to Runaway Sales," *Business Week,* June 19, 2000, p. 68; and Güliz Ger, personal communication, 2000.

122. Susan Lobo, *A House of My Own: Social Organization in the Squatter Settlements of Lima, Peru* (Tucson, AZ: University of Arizona Press, 1982), p. 53; Peter Manuel, *Cassette Culture: Popular Music and Technology in North India* (Chicago: University of Chicago Press, 1993), pp. 66, 159–60; and Farhan Bokhari, "Pakistan's Profitable First Women's Bank Carves New Niche," *Christian Science Monitor,* October 25, 1993, p. 6.

123. Jerry Berger and Al Stamborski, "Anheuser-Busch Print Ads Begin Featuring Gay People," *St. Louis Post-Dispatch,* April 21, 1999, p. C1; Steven M. Kates, *Twenty Million New Customers! Understanding Gay Men's Consumer Behavior* (Binghamton, NY: Harrington Park Press, 1998); Daniel L. Wardlow, *Gays, Lesbians, and Consumer Behavior: Theory, Practice, and Research Issues in Marketing* (New York: Haworth Press, 1996); and Lisa N. Peñaloza, "Crossing Boundaries/Drawing Lines: Gender Trouble in Consumer Research," in *Gender and Consumer Behavior,* Janeen Costa, ed. (Salt Lake City, UT: University of Utah Printing Service, 1991), p. 89.

124. Nejdet Delener, "The Effects of Religious Factors on Perceived Risk in Durable Goods Purchase Decisions," *Journal of Consumer Marketing* 7 (Summer 1990), p. 27; Lawrence J. Goodrich, "Religion Is Alive and Diverse in U.S.," *Christian Science Monitor,* January 10, 1994, pp. 11–13; and Elizabeth C. Hirschman, "Effects of American Jewish Ethnicity upon Consumer Behavior," *Journal of Marketing* 45 (Summer 1985), p. 108.

125. Meera Louis, "Modern Marketing Helps Sell Life as a Nun," *The Wall Street Journal,* May 11, 1999, pp. B1, B12; Malise Ruthven, *The Divine Supermarket: Shopping for God in America* (New York: William Morrow and Co., 1989); and "Public Relations Firm to Present Anti-Abortion Effort to Bishops," *New York Times,* August 14, 1990, p. A12.

126. C. Eric Lincoln, *The Black Church since Frazier* (New York: Schocken Books, 1974); and Hirschman, "Effects of American Jewish Ethnicity upon Consumer Behavior," p. 108.

127. Delener, "The Effects of Religious Factors on Perceived Risk in Durable Goods Purchase Decisions," pp. 27–38; E. Franklin Frazier, *The Negro Church in America* (New York: Shocken Books, 1974 [1963]); Ruthven, *The Divine Supermarket,* pp. 255–76; and Deborah Hale Shelton, "Niche Book Publishing Affects How Even the Bible Is Marketed," *Marketing News,* October 12, 1998, p. 2.

Learning Objectives

After completing this chapter, you should be able to:

- Know the characteristics of self-concept and understand more about how you characterize yourself and how others are likely to describe you.

- Recognize the I-self, the me-self, and the looking-glass self.

- Explain how self-concept affects intrapersonal processes such as self-narrative, information processing of self-relevant information, and the regulation of affect.

- Describe how self-concept affects interpersonal processes such as lifestyle, interaction strategy, and interpersonal influence.

- Discuss the relationship between people's self-concepts and their consumption behavior, including relating self-concept to the circle of consumption.

- Recognize how the self-concept varies cross-culturally.

- Explain the relationship between personality traits and self-concept and discuss applications of personality theory to consumer behavior.

The Self and Selves

Harry's Cowboy Boots

I lived in Texas most of my life. My mother's family grew up on a farm. As a child I used to love to go to the ranch and enjoy the country. As I grew up through secondary school, I lived in the city and in the part of town that valued Polo and Jordache jeans, not cowboy boots. I stayed in Texas for college, but I went to a Republican, yuppie university that didn't value the simpler life. Since I graduated three years ago, I've lived in Boston, Sacramento, and now Colorado. While being away from home, I've begun to long for things that remind me of simpler things, not careers, graduate school, or other materialistic possessions associated with becoming a professional and an up-and-coming individual. On my visit home to Texas around Christmas time I went into a western store. I saw these blue-gray Justin Roper boots. Immediately I got this feeling that I should buy them. However, I thought the cost was too high, and I left without making the purchase. During my visit, we had a large family get-together. It was there that I saw most of my cousins who are about the same age wearing Justin Ropers. I knew then that I would go back to the store and buy those blue Ropers regardless of the cost. I like to think that these boots show my down-home nature. I sometimes feel that I get too caught up in becoming this ambitious professional. I love knowing that they are in my closet. I have worn them a few times on snow days. Also, I have started going western dancing so that I can use them. The boots reinforce my idea that I'm a true Texan at heart and that no matter what I do or become, I will always love the country and the good down-home life.

Overview

Understanding perceptions of the self, the social world, and relationships between the self and others are among the most central concerns in consumer behavior. Self-concept organizes the wants and goals of individuals. As the opening vignette suggests, individuals use possessions such as cowboy boots and consumption activities such as western dancing to define who they are, to say things about themselves, and to make conjectures about how, when, and what kinds of other people buy, use, and discard products. Consumption and ideas like self-concept, self-image, and self-presentation are closely intertwined. Topics such as motivation, perception, information processing, and interpersonal influence, which are the subjects of other chapters, rely on understanding the self.

Self-concept is a complex topic because of competing definitions and cross-cultural and historical variations in concepts of the self. In addition to marketers, philosophers, social scientists, and literary critics are interested in self-concept and identity issues. The definition of **self-concept** we will use is in this chapter is *an organized configuration of perceptions of the self, which are available to awareness.* In other words, self-concepts are perceptions people have about themselves. Self-concept is an active configuration that influences many *intrapersonal,* or inner, processes, including motivation (Chapter 11) and information processing (Chapter 13). Self-concept also affects a variety of *interpersonal* processes, including perception (Chapter 9), interpersonal influence (Chapter 15), and reaction to others' feedback.[2]

Perhaps the most important thing to be said about self-concept is that it is *not* distinct from society and culture. The sense of self grows out of interactions with three aspects of one's environment. First, as suggested by Harry's interaction with his Justin-boot-wearing cousins, individuals with whom people interact in various roles are crucial to forming the self. Consumers vary in the importance they place on others in determining self-definition. Second, materials and objects (including the physical environment) that support and intervene in people's social relations, like the cowboy boots, affect the development of the self. Consumers also vary in the importance they place on products in determining self-definition.[3] Third, ideas, beliefs, and values—such as those associated with the Republican university mentioned in the vignette, but also including spiritual ideas—influence the way people perceive and respond to their environment. Individuals develop a concept of self though interaction with all three elements, which are themselves related to each other.

A basic relational approach to how self-concepts develop is depicted in Exhibit 7.1.[4] This four-part framework gives us a way of thinking about the changing concepts of self and a way to compare self-concepts between cultures. When there is a major change in any of the three elements—in significant others, the material environment, or the ideas and beliefs surrounding an individual—we can expect change to take place in the self and in consumer behavior.

Virtually any **role transition,** such as Harry "becoming a professional and an up-and-coming individual," creates changes in one or more of the three entities in the environment of the self. A role transition is *a major change in the rights, duties, and responsibilities expected of an individual by a social group.* Consequently, role transitions are likely to influence self-image and purchase and consumption behavior.[5] Of course, many other factors beyond the self influence consumption behavior, including culture, social class, peer groups, and lifestyles. In this chapter, we emphasize the self and its relationship to some of these other factors. We introduce some ways of understanding self and the relationship of self to consumer behavior. We also compare Western concepts of the self with those of

Exhibit 7.1 The Relational Self

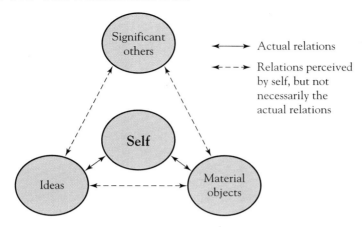

other parts of the world. Finally, we discuss the challenge of measuring dimensions of the self and relating these dimensions to consumption behaviors. In this discussion, we introduce the idea of personality and some methods for measuring self.

Self-Concept

One way to begin thinking about self-concept is to answer this question: Tell me about yourself. Take a few minutes right now and think about how you would respond. Surely you have been asked to talk about yourself many times, in very different situations by different people. A normal and important aspect of social exchanges is a sharing of information about selves. You may have noticed several things about your own responses to this question.

You might observe that your own *self-concept is multifaceted*. It includes a collection of images, activities, goals, feelings, roles, traits, and values. If you ask a small child to tell you about herself, she might respond by describing that she has a big brother who teases her all the time and a kitten that she loves very much. She might tell you how old she is and that she will go to school next year, but today she is staying home to play with her dolls. She might also tell you that her favorite color is pink and she's seen the movie *Beauty and the Beast* three times. She answers the question of who she is with a catalog of characteristics and relationships, including consumption behaviors. Social scientists now refer to the *multiplicity* of identity, indicating that selfhood is a collection of diverse but related self-perceptions. In fact, *the self includes a multiplicity of things that people are to themselves and to one another.* Consumer researchers want to know which aspects of the self are most relevant in marketing communications and how these aspects are linked to products and product images.

Self-Concept Is Multifaceted

The multiple nature of the self has long been recognized in psychology.[6] Psychologists recognize the **I-self,** *the active observer, the knower, or the information processor.* The I-self attends to matters of importance to the individual and helps that person

This Balnéo Grandform ad plays on the concept of the extended self in referring to your body ("votre corps") as your most precious possession.

maintain self-esteem (as we discuss below). The I-self may come into play when consumers choose inconspicuous products such as the many shopping goods that do not have a well-developed image.

Psychologists also recognize the **me-self,** that is *the known, observed, and constructed self-image.* One influential formulation of the idea of the me-self concept is the **looking-glass self.** In this view, the me-self concept is formed as an individual gathers the reflected opinions of significant other people toward him or her. These others' opinions are gradually incorporated into the me-self concept. The looking-glass self may come more into play when consumers are choosing status goods, conspicuous products, or heavily advertised products with a well-developed product image that incorporates the opinions of others.

Psychologist William James, who formulated the I-self idea, thought it produced self-concept. Charles Horton Cooley, who formulated the concept of looking-glass self, thought the opinions of others matter most in producing self-concept. Both elements mold self-concept, in Euro-American cultures at least, and from these ideas, we get two elements of the contemporary four-element model of the self, shown in Exhibit 7.1.

The third element of Exhibit 7.1 is material things and goods. Things also help to form a person's sense of self, even though they are outside the actual self. Considerable research has established the idea that purchase, display, and use of consumer goods communicates meaning to the individual and to others. *Individual consumer behavior is often directed toward enhancing self-concept through the consumption of goods as symbols.* (Symbolic consumption is discussed in Chapter 5 and at further length in Chapter 18.) *Self-concept is enhanced through the transfer of socially accepted meanings of the product or brand to*

The *tuku* head scarf worn by Herero women in Botswana is central to their social selves.

oneself. This then enhances the value of the self. Interaction with others, as well as the products and brands, is also required since social recognition provides meaning to products and brands. In short, individual consumers use products and brands to express something about themselves, and self-concept is reinforced as positive responses from others support their consumption behaviors. This is called the **image congruence hypothesis.** Thus, since consumers evaluate brands partly in terms of how those products might enhance their self-image, marketers should build self-enhancement meanings into marketing communications.[7]

Russell Belk says that *external objects to which we are emotionally attached and that we consider a part of ourselves* comprise the **extended self.**[8] Belk found that things consumers incorporated into the extended self symbolize key elements of the self; in other words, they are highly congruent with or match a person's sense of self. U.S. women, for example, generally see their bodies as more central to their identities than U.S. men do.[9] The text of an ad for Balnéo Grandform, French maker of bathtubs, plays on this idea of the body as part of the extended self. It reads, "Balnéo Grandform . . . because your body is your most precious possession." Dwellings, automobiles, and favorite clothes are among the material possessions Belk found most closely related to the self. Subsequent research has led to a measure to determine the extent of possession incorporation into the extended self; some people's extended selves include collections, pets, mountain bikes, and tattoos.[10]

Most work on the extended self has been conducted with people in the United States. However, findings from some other parts of the world show that the relation between possessions and an extended social self assumes some importance. To Maya farmers of Central America, for example, *milpa* cornfields represent a collaboration between man and the gods that is the basis for life. Even Maya who don't need corn still make a *milpa*. Keeping a *milpa* is considered very close to the Maya conception of self. Similarly, the elaborate dress and *tuku* (headscarf) worn by Herero women in Botswana and the reggae music

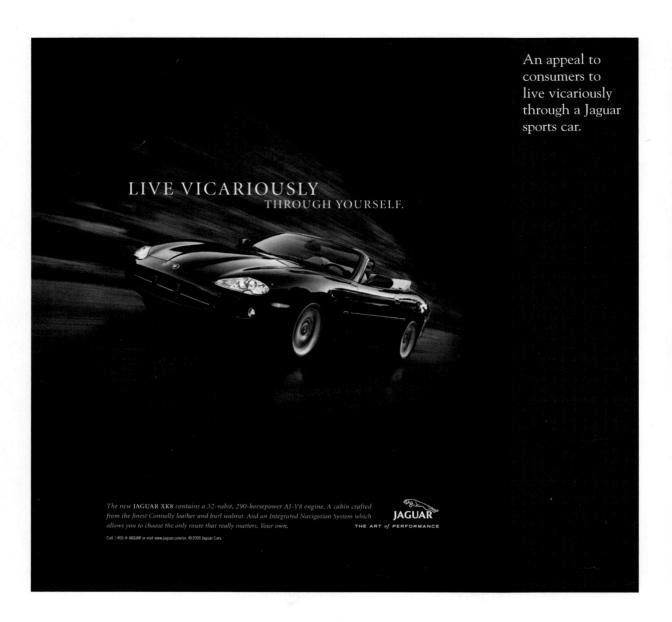

LIVE VICARIOUSLY
THROUGH YOURSELF.

The new JAGUAR XK8 *contains a 32-valve, 290-horsepower AJ-V8 engine. A cabin crafted from the finest Connolly leather and burl walnut. And an Integrated Navigation System which allows you to choose the only route that really matters. Your own.*

Call 1-800-4-JAGUAR or visit www.jaguar.com/us. © 2000 Jaguar Cars.

JAGUAR
THE ART *of* PERFORMANCE

and material goods associated with Rastafarianism (a Jamaican folk religion) are important sources of personal and social (ethnic) selfhood simultaneously.[11]

The concept of extended self has numerous implications for consumer behavior. For example, people may live vicariously through things incorporated into the extended self. Pets are a good example. North Americans spend $23 billion a year on pet food and supplies and more than $2 billion on pet goodies. The worldwide market is very large indeed. As another example, the accompanying advertisement for the Jaguar XK8 invites consumers to live vicariously through this automobile. The tendency to care for something within the extended self will lead the individual to purchase accessories for the particular object and devote resources to its care and improvement. This has considerable relevance for marketers of lifestyle products like mountain bikes, collections, and heirlooms, for example, not to mention pets, cars, and scooters.[12]

You might observe that your response to the invitation to tell others about yourself *depends on situations and motives*. Some research suggests that individuals focus on whatever *aspects of themselves that are most relevant in a particular social setting or situation*. Consumer researchers term this idea the **working, or activated, self-concept.**[13] Culture, gender, ethnic, and other characteristics of identity become significant to consumers in particular circumstances, for example, when marketers invite consumers to attend to them as in the ads on pages 237 and 239 that focus on African-American pride or when consumers find themselves in a consumption context that brings such characteristics into view. Consumer Chronicles 7.1 illustrates how the ethnic identity of Greenlandic immigrants to mainland Denmark is activated by Danes reactions to some traditional Greenlandic possessions.[14]

Marketers and policymakers should be sensitive to how different self-concepts get activated in social situations. In some university communities, *not* drinking alcohol is a distinctive consumer behavior and thus becomes a relevant dimension of self-concept. In a sample of undergraduate students at a small U.S. college (61 percent under legal drinking age), only 20 percent were nondrinkers. More than half said they typically drink five or more servings of alcohol one day per week. Their reasons for drinking included "Because people I know drink," "So I won't feel left out," and "Because of pressure from others." In this case, reducing alcohol-related problems on campus might require changes in social relationships to change drinkers' activated self-concept.[15]

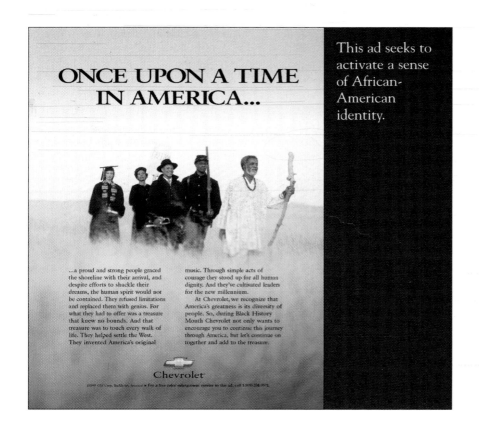

ONCE UPON A TIME
IN AMERICA...

...a proud and strong people graced the shoreline with their arrival, and despite efforts to shackle their dreams, the human spirit would not be contained. They refused limitations and replaced them with genius. For what they had to offer was a treasure that knew no bounds. And that treasure was to touch every walk of life. They helped settle the West. They invented America's original

music. Through simple acts of courage they stood up for all human dignity. And they've cultivated leaders for the new millennium.
At Chevrolet, we recognize that America's greatness is its diversity of people. So, during Black History Month Chevrolet not only wants to encourage you to continue this journey through America, but let's continue on together and add to the treasure.

Chevrolet

This ad seeks to activate a sense of African-American identity.

The Activated Immigrant Greenlandic Self

When I came from Greenland, I brought my jewelry, I can't live without them. I don't wear it here, but I have to bring them. They are various amulets and the like, made from bone or stone. . . . I take them out occasionally and look at them, but, uh-oh, I don't wear them because I think it is a bit . . . In Qaportoq [Greenland] I often wear them but here in Denmark people look at me and think: "What is it made from? Oh, it's made of bone! Poor animal!" So maybe it is mostly to spare people for that, that I don't wear it. A bear claw I have or something like that would scare them to death. "Are you into voodoo or something like that?" So you are a little afraid of what people might think. You don't want them to believe you're some kind of cannibal.

Occupation: student; gender: female; age: 25; residence: from the Disco Bay, living temporarily in Vanløse.

Source: Søren Askegaard, Dannie Kjeldgaard, and Eric J. Arnould (1999), "Identity and Acculturation: The Case of Food Consumption by Greenlanders in Denmark," Paper presented at the 1st International Conference on Consumption and Representation, Plymouth, UK, 1st–3rd September.

People selectively retrieve different aspects of their self-concept depending on goals and motives. Think about how your answer to "tell me about yourself" might vary as a function of who is asking the question: your teacher, your date, or a potential employer. Your answer might be quite accurate in each case, but the part of your self-concept that comes to mind—what we call the working self-concept—would be likely to be quite different because you are motivated to communicate different things about yourself in each situation.

Even during a single day, as situations change a consumer may desire to represent self either publicly or privately in a variety of different ways through consumption. Fashion offers a way to express different aspects of the self and helps people create and represent different identities.[16] As illustrated in the opening vignette, a manager in a small high-technology company wears his cowboy boots to let people know that he likes country and western music. As another example, a successful woman executive may go into board meetings with an audacious Vivienne Westwood leggings outfit underneath her conservative attire.

Depending on the situation, consumption may activate different aspects of the self. For example, acquiring a new pair of athletic shoes may trigger a child's self-concept in such a way as to play basketball more aggressively. Setting out crystal wine glasses for a dinner party may activate self-schemas of pride and competence, creating both memories and expectations. A study in the UK found that drink choice in pubs might activate different aspects of the self. Sometimes consumers may contrive to use products to trigger aspects of the self. For example, you may have noticed that the clothes you wear subtly change your body language. More formal attire triggers, almost unconsciously, more formal aspects of your self. Try staging a candlelight dinner on a weeknight. Does it trigger different aspects of your self-concept? Marketers position products to take advantage of the power of products to activate aspects of the self, such as in the nostalgic advertisement for Lands' End, shown on page 241.[17]

Behavioral Constraints on Possible Selves

When you think about your answer to the question, Tell me about yourself, you might observe that your own *behavior is constrained by factors other than your self-concept*. For example, you may describe yourself as fun loving and carefree but have trouble, especially during exams, remembering the last time those self qualities were reflected in your behavior. In a recent study of self-concept, one man in his late 20s said, "I am torn between two ideas of the real me. There is the day-to-day real me, how I usually function, and the rare occasion of the real me I want to be. These times are a total reversal of everyday life."[18] As

a consequence of restrictions on behavior, self-concept will not always be directly revealed in behavior. Its impact may be revealed more indirectly in mood changes, in what aspects of self-concept are dominant and accessible, in the nature of self-presentation, and in the choice of social setting.

Thus, one way of thinking about self-concept is that it is composed of self-representations, or **self-schemas**, each *consisting of a system of knowledge structures organized in memory and self-relevant information*, including ideas and information about others and things.[19] Some self-representations are more important and more elaborated than others. Some are positive, some negative. Consumers are aware of some self-representations, but they are unaware of others because they are either fairly automatic or repressed in daily life. For marketers, these constraints on self-expression may modify the relationships between expressions of self and consumption behaviors. By identifying barriers to self-expression marketers can develop or position products and services to alleviate them. Bread- and pasta-making machines, for example, are products that allow consumers to express a nurturing, "home-baked" self when other time commitments frustrate the expression of this aspect of self.

Self-representations may refer to actual I-selves and also to **possible selves**—selves we could be, would like to be, or are afraid of becoming.[20] Possible selves consist of *self-schemas created for domains of activity that give personal meaning to the past and the future*. People are likely to attribute certain consumption behaviors to these possible selves, both negative and positive.[21] For example, one of the attractions of Las Vegas for consumers willing to take risks is the opportunity to take on a possible self. This is the

The Self Is Dynamic

In response to research about experiences that make one feel like "this is really me," one young woman said:

> Last summer, I took a course called "Copy and Layout" in which I learned how to design advertisements for the first time. On the first day of class, we were given an assignment which entailed coming up with a newspaper advertisement for any product we wanted as long as we sold the product in the ad. Immediately, I came up with several ideas, and within an hour after class my advertisement was finished. I found out right then that creative work in advertising was truly me—my senses seemed to come alive as I started thinking about different products and how I could advertise them.

composed, self-confident "player" like the Tom Cruise character Charlie Babbitt in the movie *Rain Man.*[22]

Possible selves may refer to past, present, or future views of the self. Advertising for perfume, cosmetics, fitness, and self-help products often makes an appeal to a possible future self. One study found that established brands served some women consumers as a link to an imaged past era where things had enduring meaning and value. For these women, shopping became a personal quest for products that would provide a personal sense of stability, security, and quality.[23] Our discussion of Japanese *enka* music later in the chapter suggests that its appeal too is to a past-oriented self. Some self-schemas refer to the "ought" self—the self we think that we should be. Diet, self-help, and exercise products and services often appeal to this ought self.

Because of the existence of possible selves and different working selves, consumers may have conflicted self-conceptions. Some research suggests that conflicted self-representations can cause emotional disorders, anxiety, and depression. However, other research suggests that complex self-conceptions and multiple identities can lead to better mental health. Part of the key seems to be whether or not the identities can be successfully integrated with each other.[24] Often purchases and possessions can help facilitate an integration of different aspects of the self. Harry's boots described in the opening vignette are a good example. Although he's fighting his way to the top of the corporate ladder, his boots remind him of his down-home nature and symbolically represent that aspect of his self-concept. The specialty catalog retailer The J. Peterman Company sought to build this idea into its corporate mission, noting that "people want things that make their lives the way they wish they were."[25] Marketers can develop new product positioning by identifying key problems of self-integration and designing products that help consumers do this, for example, high-quality packaged convenience foods that integrate a woman's self as nurturing mother and self as high-achieving corporate executive.

multiple self-concept · *Imp·*

Self-Concept Is Changeable

When you think about your answer to the question, Tell me about yourself, you might recognize that your *self-concept is flexible and changeable,* not only between situations but in a more enduring way. New self-conceptions are added periodically, self-conceptions change in meaning, and the relationship among self-conceptions changes. For example, you may contrast your self-concept in secondary school with your self-concept at university. You may have added new roles (perhaps joined new clubs and organizations), new relationships (friends, classmates, co-workers), new activities, new traits (hardworking, studious), or new goals (career success). In Consumer Chronicles 7.2, one young woman describes the discovery of new self-aspects.

ex role transition

Consumers' self-concepts are particularly dynamic during certain role transitions, such as between secondary school and university, when changing jobs, or after a divorce. Role transitions are often accompanied by changing consumption patterns that reflect

you don't just want clothes. you want clothes that make you feel completely at ease with yourself. like when you were six.

1-800-881-8899 landsend.com

Life is in the details.

Nostalgic ad for Lands' End activates consumer self-expression.

changing conceptions of the self.[26] For example, before heading for college, a young woman who has worn her hair long all through high school may decide it's time for a new look to go with the new self that she intends to be. She may associate her new haircut with being more outgoing, athletic, or a variety of other desired selves. Consumer Chronicles 7.3 illustrates a Japanese role transition and the important relationships between identity, material goods, and the influence of society that together work to transform the identity of Japanese young adults.[27]

Some very interesting research has been conducted with consumers who have undergone plastic surgery. Patients seem to seek plastic surgery during role transitions. Plastic surgery allows these consumers to take greater control of their bodies and their appearance. As a result of the surgery, their self-esteem—or degree to which they have a positive attitude toward themselves—improves substantially. Plastic surgery has many elements of a rite of passage, discussed in Chapter 5, including separation from old roles, considerable physical and mental pain, and a period of isolation (convalescence) before the new self emerges.[28]

Many products are designed to facilitate role transitions, and role transitions are often marked by changes in consumption patterns. Weddings and baby showers typically incorporate products that mark role transitions. The traditional baby shower serves the economic purpose of equipping the new mother with the clothes, toys, and furnishings she will need. Such an event also serves the social function of reinforcing the mother's dependence on a network of kin and friends. "Insider knowledge" about the usefulness of products is communicated to the new mother, as each gift is opened. Similarly, on April 1 of every year a million new employees at Japanese businesses receive business cards and corporate lapel

Of the countless ceremonies held regularly in Japan, my favorite was Seijin-shiki, the coming-of-age ceremony held annually on January 15. On that date, each year all the Japanese who will turn 20 during the year are toasted and honored in official ceremonies during which they are officially recognized as adult citizens of Japan, with all the associated rights and many responsibilities. This is considered so important that January 15 is a national holiday. Every city, town, and rural hamlet in the country—3,200 jurisdictions in all—gathers its newly minted adults into the town hall or school auditorium for a combination reunion/party/lecture.

New clothes are a key part of coming of age. The Seijin-shiki is generally the first occasion in a young woman's life when she can wear a formal adult kimono. Most girls jump at the chance. After all, a halfway decent kimono, together with the necessary obi, sandals, hair ornaments, handbag, handkerchiefs, pins, and other assorted accoutrements, runs about $6,500 nowadays. The men's business suits, in contrast, were probably priced under $500, even for those who chose the seven-point *setto* (or set). These prices, well beyond the reach of most 20-year-olds, constitute one reason why so many kids show up for a formal ceremony on their day off. There's an implicit deal at work: Parents want their kids to attend Seijin-shiki, so they pay for the expensive outfits. The kids want the formal kimono or business suit, so they agree to attend.

Source: T. R. Reid (1999), Confucius Lives Next Door, *New York: Vintage Books, pp. 161–166.*

badges and learn their corporate songs during annual entering-the-company ceremonies held throughout Japan. Consumer behaviors such as these that mark role transitions are a nearly universal feature of human cultures, and marketers may position products to take advantage of this fact. Thus, participants in Japanese coming-of-age ceremonies receive gifts of promotional consumer goods provided by marketers interested in cashing in on their changing consumer needs, in addition to receiving their kimonos and business suits.[29]

The Dynamic Self-Concept

Exhibit 7.2 illustrates a dynamic model of self-concept that summarizes a lot of what we have described above. The currently active set of dynamic self-representations is the working self-concept, which regulates both intrapersonal and interpersonal processes.

Intrapersonal Processes

The working self-concept regulates intrapersonal processes in several important ways. First, the self-concept integrates and organizes an individual's self-relevant experiences into a self-narrative. **Self-narratives** consist of *stories that are coherent, context-sensitive accounts of experiences that provide a sense of personal continuity in time and space.* These stories often refer to events past, present, and future; they contain a judgmental or evaluative component and are woven together to appear coherent to the storyteller.[30]

Often people use consumption to give coherence to their stories about the self. For example, cherished possessions are cherished in part because they become a repository for stories about the self. Some research has shown that consumers try to build preferred elements of self-narratives into custom-made homes.[31]

Consumers also may use consumption to create new self-narratives and change self-concept. A tattoo artist describing his clients' motivations for getting tattoos in Consumer Chronicles 7.4 provides one example of the relationship between using consumption and self-narrative to change self-concept during a role transition.[32] The contribution of commercial high-risk adventures to self-narrative and identity construction is illustrated in Consumer Chronicles 7.5. In this example, skydiving affords a young woman skydiver a way to organize a new and possibly central self-concept. White-water river rafting also contributes to the development of self-narrative. As the rafter's story indicates, consuming high-risk experiences may provide psychological resources to guide behavior in other contexts.[33]

Second, self-concept influences the processing of **self-relevant information,**[34] the *internalized self-*

Tattooing and a New Sense of Self

I do see that many people get tattooed to find out again . . . to say, "Who was I before I got into this lost position?" It's almost like a tattoo pulls you back to a certain kind of reality about who you are as an individual. Either that or it transfers you to the next step in your life, the next plateau. A woman will come in and say, "Well I just went through a really ugly divorce. My husband had control of my _____ body and now I have it again. I want a tattoo. I want a tattoo that says that I have the courage to get this, that I have the courage to take on the rest of my life. I'm going to do what I want to do and do what I have to do to survive as a person." That's a motivation that comes through the door a lot.

Source: Clinton R. Sanders, Customizing the Body: The Art and Culture of Tattooing (Philadelphia: Temple University, 1989), p. 43.

Consumer Chronicles 7.4

Exhibit 7.2 A Dynamic Model of Self-Concept

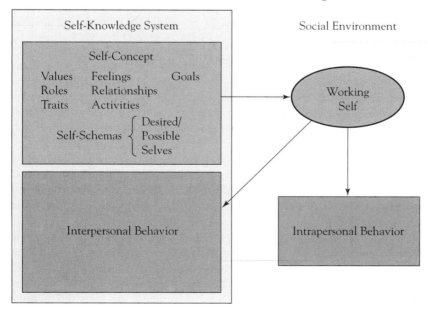

Consumer Chronicles 7.5

High-Risk Leisure Consumption and Self-Narrative

A young woman, interviewed after 325 jumps, said about skydiving,

I work for the weekend. I work to make a living and to make jump money. The DZ (drop zone) is the enjoyable part of my life.

In recollections of a river-rafting experience, one participant noted:

[You] develop a personal enrichment especially if you encounter a situation in which you become frightened and overcome the obstacle of the situation. And finally, long after it's done, even years later, you'll find your mind escaping/returning back to the journey and reliving the thrill and when you encounter a situation in life where you're afraid or unsure the river experience often enables you to overcome it because you are inevitably more self-assured.

Source: Richard L. Celsi, Randall L. Rose, and Thomas W. Leigh, "An Exploration of High-Risk Leisure Consumption through Skydiving," Journal of Consumer Research 20 *(June 1993), p. 9.*

schemas *that represent a reference value or standard of comparison for new information from the environment.* Consumers' attention to self-relevant information is guided by the need for self-consistency, or the need to maintain a balance between self-image and behaviors ascribed to the self. In other words, people pay attention to information, including marketing communications, that reinforces self-concept. Individuals are more sensitive to information that is self-relevant. Self-relevant information is more efficiently processed; and people remember and recognize self-relevant information better. Finally, consumers are resistant to information that is incongruent with their self-representations. For example, a recent study presented individuals with a pair of letters, each pair containing a letter from their name. Asked to quickly choose which letter they preferred, individuals reliably chose the letter from their own name. When given a chance to study the letter pairs carefully, they had no awareness that a letter from their name was embedded among the pairs of letters. Similarly, researchers have observed that individuals can hear their name mentioned from across a room filled with conversations, even when involved in a conversation with someone else.[35]

It is important for marketers to understand the effect of product self-relevance on self-concept and processing of information. Regular acquisition and consumption of a particular brand, say Prada fashions, or a product category, say designer clothing, may lead to the formation of a self-schema or reference point in self-concept that one is an affluent, fashionable person. If the consumer of the Prada fashion then receives compliments about being fashionable from significant others or receives promotions from other designer-clothing retailers, and these messages match her self-schema, this will tend to reinforce and consolidate this aspect of self-concept. In this way, being fashionable in general, and being a Prada consumer in particular, may also become more central to self-concept. If fashionability becomes more central to self-concept, the consumer is then more likely to be open to other fashion-based appeals. At the same time, brands like Prada may become self-relevant product symbols, and repeat purchase is more likely. By the same token, any kind of brand or product category that becomes a widely recognized symbol of particular kinds of people, say Tommy Hilfiger fashions and hip-hop stars or Hickey Freeman suits and business executives, leads people to adopt such product symbols as a vehicle to create their own possible selves.[36]

Self-relevance is likely to be an important determinant of consumer involvement with and processing of marketing communications. Recent advertising in *PC Globe* magazine shows a full-page ad for a laser printer with the name of the subscriber custom printed in bold, black letters in the middle of the ad. Because people attend to self-relevant information, many studies suggest that this personalized advertising approach should attract sub-

Closing the gap between desired and actual selves: This ad invites consumers to compose their own lives.

Comfort is the underpinning of real style. The kind of comfort that allows us to move through the world with confidence and ease. To compose our own lives—in clothing that inspires us, **simply, to be ourselves**.

EILEEN FISHER

scribers' attention. At a more subtle level, of course, advertisers employ images they hope will be congruent with consumers' self-concepts and associate those images with their product.[37]

Third, self-concept influences the *regulation of affect.* Individuals defend their self-concepts against negative emotional states and interact with others and interpret events in ways that enhance and promote their self-concept. Many studies have documented self-serving biases in how individuals interpret events. One way that people regulate negative affect is by reducing self-awareness. For example, as discussed in Chapter 9, people may not pay attention to marketing communications that conflict with preferred self-image.[38]

Some related recent research has focused on **self-gifts** (see Chapter 10). Many Euro-Americans give themselves presents, that is, they think of certain purchases or consumption activities as gifts for themselves. Often, these presents help people regulate their emotional balance. For example, a person may treat himself to an ice cream cone because he had a hard day at work; another may buy herself flowers as a way to maintain an especially good mood. As messages from and to the self, self-gifts can be elevating, protective, or soothing.[39] Self-gifts frequently carry messages about identity and self-distinctiveness, which contributes to self-esteem.

Finally, self-concept has important effects on motivation, discussed in Chapter 11. In considering the effect of self-concept on motivation, recall that the self-concept includes many images of possible selves, feared and desired. **Desired selves** comprise a particularly important subset of people's possible selves, that is, *what they would like to be and think they really can be.* Depending on the importance and commitment to these self-definitions, desired selves can define goals and move individuals to action. As suggested by the Eileen Fisher ad shown above that invites consumers to "compose our own lives," marketing

Category	Product or Service	Target Audience	Main Appeal	Relevance to Self-Concept
Products	Frozen food	Single working people	Romantic appeal	Desired self-concept
Convenience	Domestic beer		Adventure and macho appeal	Desired self-concept
Shopping	Instant rice	Blue-collar men		Product attribute
Specialty	Athletic wear	Working women	Quick dinner	Desired self-concept
	Distinct tequila	Ages 16–49 years	Healthy, sexy image	Desired self-concept
	Luxury car	Upscale educated women	Cosmopolitan and party image	Desired self-concept
		Wealthy men	Display of wealth	
Services				
Tangible	Retail grocery chain	Upper income women aged 25–49 years	Ideal family image	Desired self-concept
	Major airline	Frequent business traveler	Need for praise from the boss	Desired self-concept
	Real estate company	Families	Portray believable lifestyles	Mix of actual and desired self-concept
	Department store	Wide target	Models are average	Mix of actual and desired self-concept
	Hospital	Nurse recruitment	Actual nurses enjoying hobbies	Mix of actual and desired self-concept
	Auto parts store	Men 16–49 years	Products and prices	Product attribute
	Fast-food restaurant	Wide target	Fun place to go	Product attribute
	Mass-transit system	Wide target	Actual bus riders	Actual self-concept
	Craft and home warehouse	Wide target	Actual customers having fun in store	Actual self-concept
Intangible	Staff leasing company	Small business	Relieve time pressure	Actual leading to desired self-concept
	Long-distance 800 service	Individuals	Hope for broken marriage	Actual leading to desired self-concept
	ATM card	Anti–high-status person	Product information	Product attribute

communication often appeals to consumer behavior directed at closing the gap between actual and desired selves.[40]

Often, advertising appeals to a consumer's desired self-concept; thus, an ad for a Piaget gold watch might appeal to a consumer's desire to appear wealthy or chic. Exhibit 7.3 shows a decision process that advertisers might use to create effective advertising. First, the diagram shows that ads that are congruent with a consumer's self-concept will be more

Category	Product or Service	Main Appeal	Relevance to Self-Concept
Products	Beef	Benefits of eating steak	Product attribute
	Carlton cigarettes	Lowest tar and nicotine	Product attribute
	Arid deodorant	Nonwhitening features	Product attribute
	Nonalcoholic beer	Tastes as good as regular beer with fewer calories	Product attribute
	Rémy Martin	Relaxed and comfortable feeling	Desired self-concept
	Mazda sports car	Owner will stand out in a crowd	Desired self-concept
	Calphalon cookware	Quality cookware	Product attribute
	Nike	Self-image of conquering any obstacle	Desired self-concept
	Piaget gold watch	Wealthy image	Desired self-concept
	First Colony coffee	Buyer has expensive and good taste	Desired self-concept
Services	Intercoiffure salons	Glamorous and beautiful look	Desired self-concept
	Ritz Carlton hotels	Relaxation and luxury	Desired self-concept
	United Airlines	First-class amenities	Product benefit and desired self-concept
	NationsBank	Many different services offered	Product attribute
	American Express	Owner is self-sufficient	Product attribute
	Communication in schools: Nonprofit	Invest in our children	Product benefit and desired self-concept

Sources: *http://www3.itu.ch/virtexh/botswana/botdoll4.htm; Hazel Rose Markus and Shinobu Kitayama, "Culture and Self: Implications for Cognition, Emotion, and Motivation,"* Psychological Review 98 (1991), pp. 224–53; Harold H. Kassarjian, *"Social Character and Differential Preference for Mass Communication,"* Journal of Marketing Research 2 (May 1965), pp. 146–53; and George M. Zinkhan, Diana Haytko, and Allison Ward (1996), *"Self Concept Theory: Applications in Advertising,"* Journal of Marketing Communications 2, pp. 1–19.

effective than one that is not. Second, it shows that an appeal to actual self-concept is more effective in evoking associations in memory than is an ad that appeals to desired self-concept. If advertisers want to change consumer attitudes, just the reverse is true. Appeals should be made to the desired self-concept.[41]

A group of 24 ad agency personnel were interviewed about self-concept and its potential application to advertising strategy. The results of these interviews are shown in Industry Insights 7.1. Here, advertised products are separated into three groups: convenience (e.g., frozen food), shopping (athletic wear), and speciality (a luxury automobile). Services are separated into two groups: tangible (a retail grocery chain) and intangible (a leasing company). For each entry, the agency personnel identified (1) the target audience, (2) the main appeal of the ad, and (3) the relevance of that appeal to self-concept, or product attribute. For instance, athletic wear that is targeted to young consumers may project a main appeal of health and sex. In turn, this "health and sex" message can be viewed as an appeal to desired self-concept. As shown in the table, self-concept can have value for advertisers and their agencies as they create promotional strategies and advertising copy.[42]

Exhibit 7.3 Self-Concept and Advertising Effectiveness

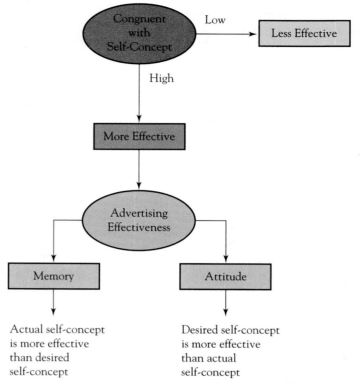

Source: Adapted from George M. Zinkhan, Diana Haytko, and Allison Ward, "Self-Concept Theory: Applications in Advertising," *Journal of Marketing Communications* 2 (1996), pp. 1–19.

Interpersonal Processes

The working self-concept provides a guide for interpreting social experiences. People use self as a reference point for evaluating other people, selecting friends, and directing interactions with others. People tend to judge others on characteristics that are personally important, tend to choose friends and partners who reinforce beliefs about their desired selves, and use a variety of strategies and tactics to present preferred identities to others.

Just as individuals use products as symbols of various aspects of the self or as vehicles to create a self, simultaneously those same products present identity externally to others. In Western societies, for example, consumers expect a home to be decorated in a fashion that meaningfully represents the character of its inhabitants. Consequently, consumers expend considerable resources on personalized home decoration. Consumer goods used to convey meaning to others vary cross-culturally. In earlier chapters we discussed how in China successive groups of consumer durables were used over time to convey their owners' conventional middle-class status to others.

Because of the link between self-concept and consumption, audiences infer characteristics of self by using consumption as a reference point. Consumer goods thus help create elaborate communication systems of socially shared meanings about identity. As suggested in Chapter 5, consumption expresses and defines the self through group membership and values conveyed by the shared symbolic meaning of consumer goods. Researchers have examined whether and how consumers attribute characteristics to others on the basis of their clothing choices, preferred possession, and lifestyle choices.[43]

Adopting shared consumption patterns enable people to construct and maintain a sense of personal and group identities simultaneously. Thus, people derive significant psychological benefits from shared consumption. In Western cultural contexts, shared consumption also often creates some conflicts because of the exaggerated value Westerners place on individual identity. Research has examined how the individual identities of members of a few well-defined market segments vary.[44]

Some research on interpersonal self-processes has studied self-presentation, or impression management. The tendency to manage self-presentation to fit the social situation through consumption differs between people. Some people are **high self-monitors;** *they are concerned that their behavior is consistent with their conception of how people behave in a particular situation.* Other people are **low self-monitors;** *they are more concerned with being themselves in various situations* and less with whether their behavior matches how other people look and act.[45] Degree of self-monitoring varies over the life cycle, between cultures and individuals, and between situations.

How is self-monitoring relevant to consumer behavior? Many teenagers in consumer society tend to be both high self-monitors and concerned with defining their self-concept. As a result, marketing communications that invite members of this market segment to be themselves while at the same time promoting brands that symbolize simple group identities tend to be highly effective. In a British study of consumption of alcoholic soft drinks, it was found that high self-monitors selected drinks that helped them to support the image they wished to project within different consumption situations. Low self-monitors reported a more pragmatic range of influences on their drink choices.[46] Cross-cultural variance in the tendency to self-monitor is evident. For example, the novel and film *Rising Sun* portrays Japanese as adapting their presentation of self to the social situation. As suggested by our earlier description of the annual ceremonies that Japanese businesses hold for new employees, Japanese consumers are in fact sensitive to the particulars of situation and their role in that situation, and they adapt their self-presentation accordingly.

Regardless of whether they are high or low self-monitors, all people present various identities to different audiences.[47] Sometimes the audiences are internalized others; other times the audiences are external. Advertising commonly appeals to consumers' internalized audiences. An advertisement might show a woman looking at shoes or makeup and picturing herself wearing them, deciding whether she approves of how she will look. Such

You Are Where You Live

- Psychologist Edward Sadalla of ASU and his colleagues selected 12 upper-middle-class homeowners, questioned them on 36 aspects of their personality, and took slides of the living room and front exterior of their homes. The homeowners themselves all believed their homes expressed their identity "fairly well" or "very well."

- The researchers showed 99 students slides of the insides or outsides and asked them to try to infer the personalities of the owners using the same 36-item questionnaire.

- Students made especially accurate judgments about personalities after only a glance at the living room. They also formed relatively accurate impressions by viewing the outside of the house.

- The inside and outside reveal different aspects of personality. For example, interior areas communicate accurate information about intellectualism, venturesomeness, and family orientation. Exterior areas communicated about privacy and artistic proclivities.

Source: Vincent Bozzi, "You Are Where You Live," Psychology Today *22 (May 1988), p. 12.*

Exhibit 7.4 Consumer Goods and Consumption Behavior

Consumption Behavior

- Integrate incompatible self-conceptions
- Close gap between actual and desired self
- Try on a possible self

- Contribute to self-narrative
- Illustrate aspect of self
- Symbolize or mark self-change

---

an ad appeals to a tendency for a person's I-self to stand outside the self and evaluate the self-image, the me-self.

In Japan, *enka* music and musicians provide a looking-glass image that appeals to the external audience of older, blue-collar Japanese listeners. According to one critic, *enka* music encodes Confucian values of rank and hierarchy, traditional gender roles, striving and hardship, and nostalgia for old village times (*furasato*), all values close to the selves of the *enka* consumer. In listening to or singing *enka,* consumers uphold and personify these values to an audience of which they are a part. Recall that researchers have referred to this process of trying to look at self-identity through the eyes of others as the looking-glass self.[48]

People infer characteristics of the self from the sets or patterns of consumer goods others consume. But do internal and external audiences agree on what is being communicated? Often they do. Even at very young ages, U.S. children make connections between consumption objects, such as houses and cars, and characteristics of their owners. Moreover, subtle consumption patterns such as food preferences (e.g., salty or sweet), drink preferences, and location of television set communicate social class and cultural influences. By observing consumption constellations believed to express identity, strangers are able to accurately match the owner's own reported personality profile. Consumer Chronicles 7.6 describes a study reported in *Psychology Today* relating pictures of the interiors and exteriors of homes to the owners' selves.[49]

Exhibit 7.4 summarizes some of the ways that consumer behaviors are linked to self-concept. People use consumption to illustrate or symbolize aspects of their self-concept. They acquire and consume goods that contribute to their self-narrative. Consumers may also use goods to close the gap between actual and possible selves or to experiment with desired selves. Finally, consumption behaviors often make evident a change in self-concept during role transitions.

Self-Concept and the Circle of Consumption

Self-concept affects consumption patterns during each phase of the circle of consumption (introduced in Chapter 1). In this section, we offer a few related examples of how self-concept influences the phases of consumption, but we encourage you to think of your own examples.[50]

Production An important segment for marketers of high-end kitchen products are people who are into cooking (e.g., the production of gourmet meals). For these customers, the production of elegant meals is used to make a statement about who they are. Men and women have different notions of what types of meal production are consistent with their self-image. For example, men grill and make cappuccino. An example of how cooking can feature prominently in self-narratives is provided in a recent movie entitled *Household Saints.* In this movie, an old Italian mother tells a self-narrative of how in the early years she and her husband were so poor they dug clam shells out of the garbage can outside a local seafood restaurant, but she still managed "to make a very good soup" from them. The retail and catalog store, Williams Sonoma, makers of high-end barbecue equipment like Weber, and department stores in Japan like Mitsukoshi and in the UK like Fortnum and Mason cater to market segments that imagine gourmet cooking as part of self-concept.

 www.mitsukoshi.
co.jp

www.fortnum
andmason.com

Acquisition Consider how self-image enters into decisions about how to redesign a kitchen. At a time when household size was declining, consumers in the United States spent $88 billion in 1991 alone to remodel their kitchens. Research suggests that these decisions had more to do with self-image than with food. For example, men want a high-tech look where everything is flush and sleek, so as to convey the feeling that there is a professional in charge, although that is rarely the case. By contrast, women see the kitchen as the heart of the home, the nerve center of the household. For them, the kitchen is about nurturing, and it is likely to be a more significant element of their extended self—a reflection of their care and nurturing of the family. Empty-nest couples whose children have left the home (see Chapter 14) often have powerful emotional attachments to their kitchens. It is frequently a central aspect of their self-concept. Consequently, they are good prospects for kitchen remodeling jobs.

Often, the desired self enters into kitchen remodeling decisions. For example, working women have a dream of having husbands who help them prepare meals. Consequently, their dream kitchens are being designed so two people can cook at once.

Consumption In the United States we think of kitchens as a place for consuming food, but many more important things get consumed in the kitchen. Thus, a recent advertisement for General Electric appliances reads, "You may call it a kitchen, but we know it's your living room." People use their kitchen for family socializing, entertaining, study, or work and as a place for solitude and relaxation. Family socializing in the kitchen is tied to self-concepts of warmth and nurturing. Of course, the multipurpose consumption occurring in the kitchen makes certain features more important. Quiet appliances become a priority, because families want to be able to have household conversations in the kitchen. Thus, if you go to the GE website you can find out all about the Triton dishwasher, advertised as "The Cleanest Wash You Never Heard."

 www.ge
appliances.com/
triton

Disposal Concern with caring for the environment is a much more important self-aspect than it was in the past. Fifteen years ago, few families recycled or needed storage areas for recyclable materials. Now more than half of all U.S. households recycle cans, bottles, or newspapers, and recycling rates are much higher in some European countries. Self-concepts have changed to include the belief "I care about the environment," and that change is reflected in recycling behaviors. Consequently, kitchens must change to include storage areas for recycled materials. So if you go to the Real Goods website you can find out about countertop composting crocks, aluminum can crushers, and compost bins, all products designed to make recycling in the kitchen easier.

 www.realgoods.
com/products

Self-Concept around the World

In 1938, anthropologist Marcel Mauss wrote that the self is primarily a product of social factors and remains an imprecise, delicate, and fragile category. His essay and much subsequent work shows that the self varies substantially across cultures.[51] How then do different cultures define the self? What is universal and what is culturally variable in people's thinking about the self? How can these variations be explained? How do an individual's notions of the self inform that person's ability to comprehend alternative formulations? And what is the significance of cultural differences in the self for consumer behavior?

These questions are of compelling interest and importance. However, we don't know all the answers. What we do know is that the self is configured differently in different cultures. We can refer back to Exhibit 7.1 to help us understand some of the variability. For instance, role relations may be primarily oriented toward the individual (self) or toward significant others. Or cultural ideas or materials and objects may be the primary basis for defining self-other relations. As different aspects of the relational self are emphasized in different cultural contexts, the self and associated consumer wants are likely to vary.[52]

Individualism, autonomy, and self-assertion—doing your own thing—rather than accommodation of others characterize the Euro-American self. The Euro-American self strives for a high degree of self-reliance and independence. Materials and objects play an important role in self-realization and in defining relationships with others. Consequently, in successful Euro-American advertising, consumer goods are often depicted as ways of realizing personal aspirations, expressing the real self or possible selves, and creating family togetherness or other social relationships.

The traditional Chinese self, by contrast, is more oriented toward significant others rather than toward the individual. Even among the most rapidly modernizing segments of the Chinese population, *people tend to act primarily in accordance with the anticipated expectations of others and social norms rather than with internal wishes or personal attributes.* A traditional male Chinese would consider himself a son, a brother, a husband, a father, but more rarely *himself.* In contrast to Euro-Americans, for Chinese people, cultural ideas and values rather than materials and objects are also dominant in defining self-other relations. Thus, the traditional Chinese self, like the self in other Asian societies and those in the less affluent world, is a **relational self** built on enduring social relations and cultural ideas.[53] Differences in the traditional Chinese and Euro-American self have broad implications for consumer behavior. For example, the relational self enjoys a high degree of security, but at the same time relations and ideas may be so rigidly defined that there is a higher degree of resistance to innovation and change than among Western consumers. On the other hand, when change occurs, it tends to move quickly through the group.[54]

The principal, overarching concept of an Asian society imbued with Confucian teaching is that of harmony and order. This ordering principle is reflected in Chinese society and is also fundamental to the Japanese perception of self. The Japanese word for self, *jibun,* refers to one's share of the shared life space; thus, belonging, or a sense of identification with others, is central to the Japanese sense of self. *Proper role behavior and behaviors that convey identification with the needs of others and contribute* to **relationship harmony,** rather than a constant sense of self, are dominant components of the Japanese self.[55] In Japanese companies, morning rituals symbolize the collectivity and the sense of belonging. Employees do gymnastics together or sing company songs. In Japan, "belonging" is often cemented with material objects. For example, lapel pins and company shirts and

Exhibit 7.5 Key Differences between an Independent and Interdependent Self-Concept

Characteristics	Independent Western self-concept	Interdependent east Asian self-concept
Definition	Separate from social context	Connected to social context
Structure	Bounded, unique, separate, stable	Fluid, flexible, variable
Tasks, often realized through consumption	Be unique, separate from others	Belong; connect and fit in with others
	Express self	Occupy one's proper place
	Realize internal qualities	Engage in appropriate action
	Promote own goals	Promote other's goals
	Be direct—say what's on your mind	Be indirect—read others' minds
Role of others	Self-evaluation: others are important for social comparison and reflected appraisal	Self-definition: relations with others in specific contexts comprise the self

Source: Hazel Rose Markus and Shinobu Kitayama, "Culture and Self: Implications for Cognition, Emotion, and Motivation," *Psychological Review* 98 (1991), pp. 224–53.

baseball caps are popular ways of signaling belonging and membership. Japanese youth subcultures also like to use brands and logos to symbolize their group memberships.[56]

Japan offers an interesting example of how a change in the individual's relationship with material objects can begin to alter self-definitions. Being satisfied with one's lot in life has been an old-fashioned Japanese virtue. However, the Japanese are not as satisfied with their lives as Americans. One explanation is that learning to be content was a necessity in post–World War II Japan. However, today's economic success makes self-denial more difficult. As more Japanese travel abroad, they learn that their material possessions do not measure up to those of people in many Western countries. Perhaps this explanation accounts in part for the popularity in today's Japan of designer products, which provide a globally recognized standard of quality.[57]

We summarize some contrasts between self-concepts in the Triad nations of the West with those in Japan, China, and the NICs of east Asia in Exhibit 7.5. Particularly noteworthy is the conception of tasks for the self that may well be expressed in consumer behavior. Thus, Exhibit 7.5 suggests that hard selling is inappropriate in east Asian cultures because the seller should try to feel and think what customers are feeling and thinking without being told and should try to help customers satisfy their wishes and realize their goals rather than those of the seller. Note how Harry's behavior with regard to his cowboy boots reflects an independent self, whereas the consumer behaviors of the Japanese undergoing role transitions to adulthood or employment mentioned earlier reflect the interdependent self. We'll say more about the contrasts between Western and Eastern concepts of the self in our discussion of motives in Chapter 11.[58]

Next, consider the self proposed by Hinduism, an important religious tradition among the 1.5 billion people of India, Sri Lanka, and Indonesia. The Hindu self-concept is part of religious doctrine dating to at least 700 B.C. (the ideas and beliefs component of the relational self). The Hindu conception of self is that there is one and only one being in existence, the absolute. This absolute (Brahman) is without form. The multitude of other beings, souls, selves, beasts, stars, and planets is a mistaken imposition on the One. The goal of individual human life is to break through this delusion of multiplicity and achieve identity with the One. Also, the apparent self (which is part of the delusion of multiplicity) is not sovereign and infinitely varied; rather, it is ill defined and weak in the Hindu conception. The person is not viewed as individual but as "dividual," or divisible—made up of varied substances, which may reproduce in others something of persons from whom they have originated. Thus, as for people in east Asian cultures, for Hindu people family and lineage is a more prominent aspect of self than it is for an American or European.

The ways in which this self-concept resonates across south Asian societies are complex and well beyond the scope of this book, but they have profound implications for how south Asians think about what is self and not self. In simple terms, whatever the body is, it is not the self. Thus, if Belk did his study of the extended self in India we might expect that body parts would not be viewed as central aspects of self. Concepts of self and nonself in south Asian thought influence intrapersonal and interpersonal information processing as well. Indian movies produced by a successful studio system based in Bombay, India, always depict stereotyped personages. Everyone is either good or bad. There are no shades of gray. Woody Allen's or Ingmar Bergman's films, built around individuals' murky existential struggles, would have little appeal to most south Asians.[59]

Africa provides examples of other conceptions of self. Africa is characterized by great cultural diversity, but some common characteristics can be identified. First, while practical, the African self is simultaneously spiritual. Second is the idea that persons are part of an all-encompassing, vital life force. Third, the self is not a bounded entity as in Western notions but a permeable one subject to the influence of many forces. Fourth, the African self is an interdependent self linked to the individual's kin group and often to ancestral spirits. As a result, there seems to be a **socially oriented achievement motivation** among many Africans. A socially oriented achievement motivation means *an individual's striving for success is bound up with the success of others,* as, for example, in a tendency for small-scale marketers to prefer to accumulate together rather than through purely individual initiative.[60]

The consumer consequences of such conceptions are many, although little research has been conducted on the relationship between the self and consumption on the African continent. For example, in some contexts, conspicuous consumption is regarded as evidence of an individual's or family's control of the vital life force. The permeability and interdependence of the self may be seen in the tendency for groups of people to dress in identical clothing, based on a variety of social bonds, on public occasions. In other contexts, people's desire to ensure ancestorhood for themselves leads to significant consumption expenditures associated with death and mortuary rites. In still other contexts, consumption may be inspired by the desire to fulfill one's role as a family member rather than personal desires.[61]

Personality

Up to this point in the chapter we have talked about self and selves rather than about personality. Personality is best understood as a different idea about the person than the self. We define **personality** as *the distinctive and enduring patterns of thoughts, emotions, and behaviors that characterize each individual's adaptation to the situations of his or her life.* An individual's consistent self-representations form the basis for what we understand as personality. For example, an individual may have a self-schema of herself as hardworking and honest. This self-schema may be activated in a variety of situations, initiating behavior consistent with these traits.[62]

The study of personality addresses a question critical to all of us: How can we best judge other people's characters and know what to expect of them? Early Egyptian, Chinese, and Greek efforts to understand personality relied on astrology. About 2,500 years ago, early Western philosophers, such as Hippocrates and Aristotle, compiled lists of connections between facial characteristics and character traits. Contemporary interest in personality dates from the twentieth century founder of modern psychology, Sigmund Freud, and his popularizers in marketing, the so-called motivation researchers who were prominent in marketing research after World War II. Over the years, a number of psychologists (e.g., Freud, Carl Jung, Henry Murray, and S. H. Schwartz) have created theories of personality, some of which are discussed in more detail in Chapter 11. The long-standing desire to predict behavior on the basis of character traits endures in personality theory and its consumer behavior applications.[63]

Personality **traits** are *characteristics in which one person differs from another in a relatively permanent and consistent way;* that is, personality traits are supposed to endure over time and over situations. Tests of personality based on measuring so-called personality traits were initiated during World War I (1914–18). Today many psychologists regard personality psychology as synonymous with the study of traits, and psychologists have developed many trait inventories. Good Practice 7.1 shows some examples of personality traits that are of interest to psychologists and consumer behavior researchers.[64] As illustrated, some traits are negative (e.g., powerlessness), and some are positive (e.g., interpersonal trust). Relative stability is a key aspect of personality traits. Marketing researchers frequently measure personality with respect to specific traits, using a tool such as the Social Character Scale shown in Good Practice 7.2, which comes from a study relating the traits of introversion and extroversion to mass media preferences.[65]

Traits

Recently, a book of consumer behavior scales has been compiled that includes numerous individual differences shown to affect consumer behavior.[66] Among the scales represented in this book are social character (i.e., inner- and other-directedness), self-concepts, need for cognition, consumer ethnocentrism, and the sexual identity scale. Good Practice 7.2 shows some of the items used to measure inner- and other-directedness.[67] For instance, a respondent who prefers partying with a smaller group is likely to be inner-directed. A respondent who likes larger parties ("the more the merrier") is more likely to be other-directed (see item 1 in Good Practice 7.2). In the second item, the respondent chooses between an evening at home (inner-directed) and going out with friends (other-directed). As illustrated in the measurement instrument, inner-directed consumers look to their own inner values and standards for guiding their behavior. In contrast, other-directed consumers depend on the people around them to provide direction for their actions. Thus, inner-directedness is similar to the trait of introversion (looking internally for motivation), whereas other-directedness is similar to extroversion (looking externally for sources of inspiration).

Marketers' interest in traits is practical. Do personality traits predict consumer behavior? One review across numerous studies found that personality traits only explain about 10 percent of the variation in consumers' purchase, product preference, and innovation behaviors. This suggests trait-based approaches should be combined with other variables to improve predictions.[68]

The development of the Five Factor Personality Structure, consisting of five clusters of traits, has recently reinvigorated the trait literature. Research over several decades indicates that the dimensions of emotional stability (or neuroticism), extroversion (or

Label	Definition	Consumer Behavior Application
Dogmatism	An individual's tendency to be more or less resistant to new ideas and change	Dogmatic consumers will be more resistant to new marketing practices
Interpersonal trust	An individual's expectation that the behavior, promises, or statements of others can be relied upon	Those high in individual trust may find salespeople and product endorsers more believable
Introversion/ extroversion	Introverts are shy, prefer to be alone, and are anxious socially; extroverts are outgoing, sociable, and often conventional	Introverts may be less likely to find out about new products from others because they avoid social channels
Locus of control	Degree to which individuals attribute responsibility for events to themselves or to external forces	Externally oriented persons place responsibility of product or service failure on manufacturers or service providers; internally oriented consumers may blame themselves for product or service failures
Need for cognition	Degree of pleasure individuals derive from effortful thinking	Consumers with a high need for cognition enjoy products with a heavy learning component, enjoy product search, and react positively to technical product information
Powerlessness	Low expectations for control of events	Powerlessness favors conforming behaviors
Self-esteem	An individual's overall feelings of self-worth or self-acceptance	Low self-esteem is related to a number of dark-side consumer behaviors
Self-monitoring	The degree to which individuals look to others for cues about how to behave	High self-monitors are more responsive to image-oriented ads; low self-monitors are more responsive to quality claims in ads

Source: Lawrence A. Pervin, ed., Handbook of Personality: Theory and Research (New York: Guilford, 1990).

outgoingness), openness to experience, agreeableness, and conscientiousness provide a good catalog of personality traits. Research in China, Germany, Holland, Japan, Korea, Norway, the United States, and the United Kingdom lend support for the generality of the "big five" traits. These traits have demonstrated a bit more explanatory power than other personality traits, but relating these traits to buying behavior has just begun. In a Korean study, these traits were shown to differentiate shopping styles and product preferences.[69] Overall across dozens of studies, the results of trying to relate personality traits to consumer behaviors have been mixed at best. These difficulties have led some researchers to other methods for learning about the self.[70]

Some approaches for measuring personality traits allow individuals more leeway to describe themselves in their own ways on dimensions of their own choosing. For example, participants might be presented with open-ended probes such as, Tell us about yourself, Tell us what you are not, and so on. One innovative tool for studying personality is the personal project. A personal project is a set of interrelated acts extending over time that is intended to maintain or attain a state of affairs foreseen by the individual. A wide range of

1. With regard to partying, I feel
   a. The more the merrier (25 or more people present).
   b. It is nicest to be in a small group of intimate friends (6 or 8 people at most). ✓

2. If I had more time,
   a. I would spend more evenings at home doing the things I'd like to do. ✓
   b. I would more often go out with my friends.

3. I believe that
   a. It is difficult to draw the line between work and play and therefore one should not even try it.
   b. One is better off keeping work and social activities separated. ✓

4. I would rather join
   a. A political or social club or organization. ✓
   b. An organization dedicated to literary, scientific, or other academic subject matter.

5. I would be more eager to accept a person as a group leader who
   a. Is outstanding in those activities which are important to the group. ✓
   b. Is about average in the performance of the group activities but has an especially pleasing personality.

6. I like to read books about
   a. People like you and me. ✓
   b. Great people or adventurers.

7. For physical exercise or as a sport, I would prefer
   a. Softball, basketball, volleyball, or similar team sport. ✓
   b. Skiing, hiking, horseback riding, bicycling, or similar individual sport.

8. I believe
   a. Being able to make friends is a great accomplishment in and of itself. ✓
   b. One should be concerned more about one's achievements rather than making friends.

9. It is more desirable
   a. To be popular and well liked by everybody.
   b. To become famous in the field of one's choice or for a particular deed. ✓

10. With regard to clothing,
    a. I would feel conspicuous if I were not dressed the way most of my friends are dressed.
    b. I like to wear clothes which stress my individuality and which not everybody else is wearing. ✓

11. On the subject of social living,
    a. A person should set up his own standards and then live up to them. ✓
    b. One should be careful to live up to the prevailing standards of the culture.

12. I would consider it more embarrassing
    a. To be caught loafing on the job for which I get paid. ✓
    b. Losing my temper when a number of people are around of whom I think a lot.

Source: Lawrence A. Pervin, ed., Handbook of Personality: Theory and Research (New York: Guilford, 1990).

Good Practice 7.3

List of Projects	1 Importance	2 Enjoyment	3 Difficulty	4 Visibility	5 Control	6 Irritation	7 Stress	8 Time adequacy	9 Outcome	10 Self-identity	11 Others' view	12 Value congruency	13 Positive impact	14 Negative impact	15 Progress	16 Challenge	17 Absorption	18 With whom?	19 Where?
1																			
2																			
3																			
4																			
Etc.																			

Source: Brian R. Little, "Personal Projects: A Rationale and Method for Investigation," Environment and Behavior 15 (May 1983), pp. 273–309.

related, goal-driven activities might constitute a personal project. Learning to ski, graduating from university, achieving a career goal, or building a house are examples of personal projects. The method for investigation of personal projects is not outlined in detail here, but an example of a matrix of personal projects that can be used for data collection is reproduced in Good Practice 7.3. Take a few minutes and think about your personal projects. Think about how these projects do or do not reflect your self. Do some of your personal projects involve consumption? Many personal projects constitute core aspects of a person's life and have a great deal of consumption content.[71]

Self-Esteem and Self-Efficacy

Self-evaluation, how a person feels about him- or herself, is an important aspect of personality. Self-evaluations affect the goals people set; their motives; the anxiety, stress, and depression they experience in various situations; and their selection of preferred environments. Self-esteem is one way of talking about self-evaluation. **Self-esteem** is *the positivity of a person's attitude toward him- or herself.* It has been linked to consumer behavior in a number of important ways.

Low self-esteem is related to exaggerated concern with the looking-glass self, the self as viewed through the opinions of others. Quite a bit of research suggests that consumer culture, with its exaggerated emphasis on the beauty of the physical self, may lead to low self-esteem among consumers. Low self-esteem in turn is related to compulsive and addictive behaviors, such as eating disorders, compulsive gambling, television addiction, shoplifting, and compulsive buying. In one series of focus group interviews about skin care, conducted with groups of women with similar demographic profiles, it was found that low-esteem women avoid buying certain products because they don't feel that it is worth spending money on themselves. Therefore, low self-esteem may sometimes lead to overconsumption and sometimes to underconsumption, depending on other individual characteristics.[72]

In contrast to the large number of social science research on compulsive gambling or eating disorders, the investigation of **compulsive buying** behavior is relatively new.[73] We can define compulsive buying as the *inability to restrain the impulse to buy*. Most of us make impulse purchases at one time or another, but when the impulse results in repetitive and excessive buying we term it compulsive buying. Reports estimate that 10 percent of the U.S. population and up to 7 percent of the Mexican population may be considered compulsive shoppers. Compulsive buying is relatively new in Mexico and may be related to the globalization of consumer culture. Recent studies in the United States, Mexico, and Germany show that compulsive spenders have relatively lower self-esteem than other consumers, and they believe in the power of money to enhance self-esteem or to influence and impress others.[74]

By contrast, other research shows that high self-esteem is related to certain types of spending, not compulsive, however. One series of studies found that people who feel good about themselves, particularly those who perceive themselves to be competent in domains that they feel are important, are more likely than others to spend more on a variety of products and services that make them feel good. This affects the marketing of a whole host of products, including entertainment, alcoholic beverages, and especially beauty-enhancers.[75]

Another way of talking about self-evaluation is self-efficacy. **Self-efficacy** is defined as *people's beliefs about their capabilities to exercise control over events that affect their lives.* Within the context of a set of tasks, some people will believe that they can succeed (take effective action), whereas other individuals will believe that they will fail. Perceived self-efficacy has been linked to numerous cognitive, affective, and motivational processes. For example, individuals who have a high sense of efficacy visualize success scenarios that provide positive guides for performance. When faced with failures, adversities, and inequities, individuals with high self-efficacy quickly recover their self-assurance. That is, a resilient sense of personal efficacy enables individuals to override rejection. Self-efficacy is also related to affect. Individuals who do not believe they can exercise control over potential threats experience high levels of stress and anxiety arousal. Dwelling on these negative and anxiety-arousing images, people low in self-efficacy avoid activities and social relationships that can then lead to bouts of depression.[76]

Some research has related self-efficacy to consumer behavior. Studies in Denmark and the United States have found that perceived consumer effectiveness (PCE) influences environmental concerns and some behaviors like recycling. Greater PCE was related to greater concern. Several researchers have suggested that self-efficacy influences decisions involving technological innovations. One study sought to relate perceptions of self-efficacy to the use of new technologies, finding that consumers' perceptions of their ability to use a technology reduce their resistance to accepting that technology.[77]

Self-efficacy should vary cross-culturally. Euro-Americans tend to score relatively high on measures of self-efficacy and sometimes believe that buying power can be used to solve social problems. By contrast, a study conducted in Thailand found that Thais scored low on perceived efficacy to preserve the environment.[78]

Consumer behavior research is filled with examples of personality trait measures, or what are also called individual difference measures. Motivation research conducted in the 1950s and 1960s examined the relationship between consumers' perceptions of products and actual or ideal personality traits using self-administered questionnaires. In general, it proved difficult to predict consumer brand choices using personality traits alone. For example, knowing that a particular consumer was a risk taker did not help predict whether that person would purchase

Applications to Consumer Behavior Research

a Ford or a Chevrolet. Nonetheless, even in recent years it has become quite common to see an ad for a sports car targeted toward consumers who like to take risks.

Going beyond the realm of brand choice, personality variables are related to consumption behaviors. For instance, materialism (a personality trait discussed in Chapter 5) is related both to impulsive and compulsive buying behavior. Similarly, self-esteem, need for cognition, and locus of control are related to the likelihood that a buyer might consult a friend or expert prior to making a purchase. Self-efficacy, as noted above, is related to belief in the influence of buying power on social change. Advertisers often use such personality traits to segment markets.[79]

Although it may be difficult to predict single instances of behavior with very much accuracy from personality measures, it may be possible to predict behavior averaged over a sample of situations or occasions. For example, we cannot predict whether the novelty-seeking trait will lead an individual consumer to seek out information about a particular new product, but we might predict that a high level of novelty seeking would lead to higher levels of new-product awareness when averaged over a sample of new products.[80] Following this approach, advertisers can use personality traits to segment markets and target their market offerings.

Self-concept is a dynamic interpretive structure that influences both intrapersonal and interpersonal processes. Self-concept varies both cross-culturally and historically. The self develops out of interactions with significant others; materials and objects; and ideals, beliefs, and values. Whenever any of these entities changes, we can expect some change to take place in self-concept. Several observations are helpful in understanding self-concept. First, the self includes the multiplicity of things people are to one another and to themselves. A person's body, objects, places, time periods, other people, and pets may be considered central to the self and are part of what is called the extended self. The self includes many self-schemas or self-representations, both positive and negative, actual and possible, compatible and incompatible. Second, a person's working self-concept depends on situations and motives. People selectively retrieve different aspects of themselves depending on the situation and our goals. Third, because of restrictions on behavior, self-concept is not always directly revealed in people's actions. Finally, self-concept is malleable or dynamic both between social settings and over time. Self-concept is especially dynamic during role transitions.

Self-concept regulates intrapersonal processes in several important ways. Self-narratives are important in helping to integrate and organize self-relevant experiences. Also, self-relevance is important to every aspect of information processing, the regulation of affect or mood, and as a motivator of behavior. Self-concept is also important in interpersonal processes, offering a guide for evaluating people, selecting friends, and directing interactions.

Self-concept is closely linked to many consumption behaviors. People use consumption to symbolize, change, integrate, or experiment with aspects of their selves. Studying the communication properties of consumption provides many insights about the activated, working self-concept. We suggest that consumption can accurately communicate aspects of self to others, the meaning of consumption objects changes between different times and social settings, and even young children can make connections between consumption objects and characteristics of their owners.

The self is configured differently in different cultures. By looking at how people relate to significant others, materials and objects, and ideas and values, we can form comparisons between the concepts of self in different cultures. We can ask whether role relations are oriented toward the individual or toward significant others and whether cultural ideas or materials and objects are the primary basis for defining self.

The focus of this chapter is on self-schemas and self-representations rather than on personality. Trait measures (e.g., risk taking, materialistic) can be used to gain insights about consumer behaviors (e.g., compulsive buying) and to segment markets. Newer approaches for measuring traits give consumers more leeway to describe themselves in their own ways on dimensions of their own choosing. Many trait measures have been developed in consumer behavior. In general, they are not very effective in predicting specific brand choices. However, they may predict behavior averaged over a sample of consumption situations or occasions.

As you read about perception, learning, information processing, lifestyle, the diffusion of innovations, and many other consumer behavior topics, your own thinking about self-concept will be valuable. The interpretive structure that constitutes self-concept is central to the way that you will process this learning experience. For example, if you can make consumer behavior self-relevant by relating it to aspects of your own life, you will find it easier to learn and remember and more fun to think about and discuss.

compulsive buying 259	relationship harmony 252
desired selves 245	role transition 232
extended self 235	self-concept 232
high self-monitors 249	self-efficacy 259
image congruence hypothesis 235	self-esteem 258
I-self 233	self-gifts 245
looking-glass self 234	self-narratives 242
low self-monitors 249	self-relevant information 243
me-self 234	self-schemas 239
personality 254	socially oriented achievement motivation 254
possible selves 239	traits 255
relational self 252	working, or activated, self-concept 237

1. Draw a picture of your extended self. Draw your perception of the extended self of a close friend or family member. How are they different? How are they similar?

2. Lori has just graduated from a state university in the southern United States, where she shared an apartment with some friends she's known since high school. She has taken a job with a medium-sized manufacturing company in the Midwest and has rented a small, one-bedroom apartment about two miles from her new office. Would you expect Lori's self-concept to change? Explain.

3. How could the concept of desired selves be used to develop marketing strategy for:
   - a. Health clubs
   - b. Bath soaps
   - c. Sports cars
   - d. Cosmetics
   - e. Cruises
   - f. Towels

4. Some research suggests that individuals focus on whatever aspects of themselves are most distinctive in a particular social setting or situation. How could this finding be used by an advertiser? Describe the target market and the nature of an appeal for swimming suits.

5. Think about features of your own home or your parent's home. Can you relate these features to your personality or the personalities of your parents? Explain.

6. Build your own set of examples to illustrate the relationship between self-concept and the circle of consumption. (*Hint:* In the book we used examples related to the kitchen.)

7. Add more entries to Industry Insights 7.2. For instance, identify a specialty product other than a luxury car. Find an ad for that product, and identify the target audience for that ad. What is the main appeal in the ad? Is that appeal related to a product attribute or to a desired self-concept? In the same way, find an ad for an intangible service and repeat the assignment.

8. Think of a brand that you frequently purchase and list the characteristics and image of that brand. If that brand were a person, what kind of person would that brand be? What is the brand's personality? Now, make a list of personality traits that describes who you are. Compare the two personality lists (your personality and your favorite brand's personality). How are these lists alike? How are they different? Why do you like this brand?

You Make the Call

A New Target for Maybelline

Maybelline, a mass-market cosmetics maker, has just introduced a new line of cosmetics, Maybelline Revitalizing. The line is geared to women 35 and older. Company representatives believe that the new cosmetic line will help this target market to look younger. The new foundations, concealers, blushes, and powders contain moisturizers, sunscreens, Vitamin A, and light diffusers that the company says counteract or hide signs of aging. The company is making an unusually direct pitch in television and print ads that feature age-appropriate models—crow's feet and all—and the slogan "The Age-Denying Makeup." The company's president, Bob Hiatt, claims, "We'll have models the consumer can identify with, to help them deal with the effects of being a little older." Several concerns are being voiced: (*a*) women may be reluctant to admit they're getting old; (*b*) customers will quickly ditch the line if they don't make realistic claims; (*c*) by climbing the age scale, Maybelline may lose its younger customer base. Drawing on some of the things you've learned about self-concept,

1. Address these concerns, for example, how might the campaign be influenced by or influence customers' possible selves?

2. Draw on ideas about both inter- and intrapersonal processes to indicate how successful you think Maybelline's strategy will be.

This case is adapted from Gabriella Stern, "Aging Boomers Are New Target for Maybelline," The Wall Street Journal, April 13, 1993, p. B1.

1. For theory and research consistent with this definition, see Valerie S. Folkes and Tina Kiesler, "Social Cognition: Consumers' Inferences about the Self and Others," in *Handbook of Consumer Behavior,* Thomas S. Robertson and Harold H. Kassarjian, eds. (Englewood Cliffs, NJ: Prentice Hall, Inc., 1991), pp. 281–315; Hazel Markus, "Self-Schemata and Processing Information about the Self," *Journal of Personality and Social Psychology* 35 (February 1977), pp. 63–78; and Beth A. Walker and Jerry C. Olson, "The Activated Self and Consumer Behavior: A Cognitive Structure Perspective," working paper, Arizona State University, 1993.

2. This section draws on the work of Hazel Markus, who is arguably the most influential contemporary psychologist doing research on the self. See, for example, Hazel Markus and Elissa Wurf, "The Dynamic Self-Concept: A Social Psychological Perspective," *Annual Review of Psychology* 38 (1987), pp. 299–337. An excellent review of how cognitive processes influence ways in which consumers think about the self and the relationship of self-concept to consumer behavior is provided in Folkes and Kiesler, "Social Cognition."

3. Eugene Sivadas and Karen A. Machleit, "A Scale to Determine the Extent of Object Incorporation in the Extended Self," in *Marketing Theory and Applications,* vol. 5, C. Whan Park and Daniel C. Smith, eds. (Chicago: American Marketing Association, 1994), pp. 143–49.

4. This conception of the self largely follows ideas presented in George Herbert Mead, *Mind, Self, and Society* (Chicago: University of Chicago Press, 1934); Godwin C. Chu, "The Changing Concept of Self in Contemporary China," in *Culture and Self: Asian and Western Perspectives,* Anthony J. Marsella, George Devos, and Francis L.K. Hsu, eds. (New York: Tavistock Publications, 1985), pp. 252–77; and Brian Morris, *Anthropology of the Self: The Individual in Cultural Perspective* (London and Boulder, CO: Pluto Press, 1994).

5. For a general theory and some empirical support, see Alan R. Andreasen, "Life Status Changes and Changes in Consumer Preferences and Satisfaction," *Journal of Consumer Research* 11 (December 1984), pp. 784–94. Several recent treatments examine this topic in specific contexts. For example, see Melissa Martin Young, "Disposition of Possessions during Role Transitions," in *Advances in Consumer Research,* vol. 18, Michael Solomon and Rebecca Holman, eds. (Provo, UT: Association for Consumer Research, 1990), pp. 33–39. Teresa Pavia, "Dispossession and Perceptions of Self in Late Stage HIV Infection," in *Advances in Consumer Research,* vol. 20, Leigh McAlister and Michael L. Rothschild, eds. (Provo, UT: Association for Consumer Research, 1993), pp. 425–28, balances out perspective by showing how much more important loss of control of self-defining activities and behaviors (such as jobs) is than loss of possessions.

6. J. Michael Munson and W. Austin Spivey, "Assessing Self Concept," in *Advances in Consumer Research,* vol. 7, Jerry C. Olson, ed. (Ann Arbor, MI: Association for Consumer Research, 1980), pp. 598–603.

7. Richard Elliott, "Existential Consumption and Irrational Desire," *European Journal of Marketing* 31, nos. 3–4 (1997), pp. 256–89; E. Grubb and H. Grathwohl, "Consumer Self-Concept, Symbolism and Market Behavior: A Theoretical Approach," *Journal of Marketing* 31 (October 1967), pp. 22–27; Margaret K. Hogg, Alastair J. Cox, and Kathy Keeling, "The Impact of Self-Monitoring on Image Congruence and Product/Brand Evaluation," *European Journal of Marketing* 34, nos. 5–6 (2000), pp. 641–67; Rebecca H. Holman, "Clothing as Communication: An Empirical Investigation," in *Advances in Consumer Research,* vol. 7, Jerry C. Olson, ed. (Ann Arbor, MI: Association for Consumer Research, 1980), pp. 372–77; and M. Joseph Sirgy, "Self-Concept in Consumer Behavior: A Critical Review," *Journal of Consumer Research* 9 (December 1982), pp. 287–99.

8. Russell B. Belk, "Possessions and the Extended Self," *Journal of Consumer Research* 15 (September 1988), pp. 139–68; and Russell B. Belk, "My Possessions Myself," *Psychology Today,* July–August 1988, pp. 50–52.

9. A touching portrayal of how self-concept is related to body parts is provided in Marilynn J. Phillips, "Damaged Goods: Oral Narratives of the Experience of Disability in American Culture," *Social Science Medicine* 30, no. 8 (1990), pp. 849–57. She talked with 33 people with visible, physical disabilities. These conversations revealed how disability frames social interactions between disabled and nondisabled individuals and how such interactions affect the self-images of disabled persons. The narratives reveal that society perceived disabled persons to be damaged goods, and the popular media of language and images perpetuate the notion of the wrongness of their bodies. Not

surprisingly, the self-concept of disabled individuals is dramatically influenced by these cultural themes.

10. Russell W. Belk, *Collecting in a Consumer Society (Collecting Cultures)* (London and New York: Routledge, 1995); Kimberly J. Dodson, "Peak Experiences and Mountain Biking: Incorporating the Bike into the Extended Self," in *Advances in Consumer Research,* vol. 23, Kim Corfman and John Lynch, eds. (Provo, UT: Association for Consumer Research, 1996), pp. 317–22; Elizabeth C. Hirschman, "Consumers and Their Animal Companions," *Journal of Consumer Research* 20 (March 1994), pp. 616–32; Eugene Sivadas and Ravi Venkatesh, "An Examination of Individual and Object-Specific Influences on the Extended Self and Its Relation to Attachment and Satisfaction," in *Advances in Consumer Research,* vol. 22, Frank Kardes and Mita Sujan, eds. (Provo, UT: Association for Consumer Research, 1995), pp. 406–12; and Anne M. Velliquette, Jeff B. Murray, and Elizabeth H. Creyer, "The Tattoo Renaissance: An Ethnographic Account of Symbolic Consumer Behavior," in *Advances in Consumer Research,* vol. 25, Joseph W. Alba and J. Wesley Hutchinson, eds. (Provo, UT: Association for Consumer Research, 1998), pp. 461–67.

11. Peter Canby, *The Heart of the Sky: Travels among the Maya* (New York: HarperCollins, 1992), pp. 23–24; Deborah Durham, "The Predicament of Dress: Polyvalency and the Ironies of Cultural Identity," *American Ethnologist* 26 (May 1999), pp. 389–411; Barbara Olsen, "Consuming Rastafari: Ethnographic Research in Context and Meaning," in *Advances in Consumer Research,* vol. 22, Frank Kardos and Mita Sujan, eds. (Provo, UT: Association for Consumer Research, 1995), pp. 481–85; and http://www3.itu.ch/virtexh/botswana/botdoll4.htm.

12. Dodson, "Peak Experiences and Mountain Biking"; and Arlene Weintraub, "For Online Pet Stores, It's Dog-Eat-Dog," *Business Week,* March 6, 2000, pp. 78, 80.

13. McGuire and his colleagues have done quite a bit of work on how individuals selectively represent the self. Their research suggests how many aspects of the situation affect the self that's represented. See, for example, William J. McGuire and Claire V. McGuire, "Content and Process in the Experience of Self," *Advances in Experimental Social Psychology* 21 (1988), pp. 97–144. A nice paper that draws the connection between the activated self and consumer behavior in various situations is Walker and Olson, "The Activated Self and Consumer Behavior."

14. Søren Askegaard, Dannie Kjeldgaard, and Eric J. Arnould, "Identity and Acculturation: The Case of Food Consumption by Greenlanders in Denmark," paper presented at the first International Conference on Consumption and Representation, Plymouth, UK, September 1–3, 1999.

15. Jean C. Darian, "Social Marketing and Consumer Behavior: Influencing the Decision to Reduce Alcohol Consumption," in *Advances in Consumer Research,* vol. 20, Leigh McAlister and Michael L. Rothschild, eds. (Provo, UT: Association for Consumer Research, 1993), pp. 413–18. See also John L. Lastovicka, John P. Murray, Jr., Erich A. Joachimsthaler, Gaurav Bhalla, and Jim Scheurich, "A Lifestyle Typology to Model Young Male Drinking and Driving," *Journal of Consumer Research* 14 (September 1987), pp. 257–63.

16. Craig J. Thompson and Diana L. Haytko, "Speaking of Fashion: Consumers Use of Fashion Discourse and the Appropriation of Countervailing Cultural Meanings," *Journal of Consumer Research* 24 (June 1997), pp. 15–42; and Fred Davis, *Fashion, Culture, and Identity* (Chicago: University of Chicago Press, 1994). For a collection of readings on how the clothing we buy and wear reflects our identities, see Juliet Ash and Elizabeth Wilson, eds., *Chic Thrills: A Fashion Reader* (Berkeley: University of California Press, 1993).

17. Munson and Spivey, "Assessing Self-Concept." This discussion is adapted from Walker and Olson, "The Activated Self and Consumer Behavior," which provide a richer discussion of the role of products in triggering the working self or activated self.

18. This quote comes from the same source as the stories in the introductory vignette. The research was based on the authors' investigation of "really me" experiences, purchases, and possessions of graduate and undergraduate business students at two different state universities.

19. Hazel Markus, "Self-Schemata and Processing Information about the Self," *Journal of Personality and Social Psychology* 35 (February 1977), pp. 63–78; and Hazel Markus and Keith Sentis, "The Self in Social Information Processing," in *Psychological Perspectives on the Self,* Jerry Suls, ed. (Hillsdale, NJ: Erlbaum, 1982), pp. 41–70.

20. Hazel Marcus and Paula Narius, "Possible Selves," *American Psychologist* 41 (September 1986), pp. 954–69, discuss the motivating power of "possible selves." They note that possible selves func-

tion as incentives for behavior and provide an evaluative and interpretive context for the current view of self.

21. Amy J. Morgan, "The Evolving Self in Consumer Behavior: Exploring Possible Selves," in *Advances in Consumer Research,* vol. 20, Leigh McAlister and Michael L. Rothschild, eds. (Provo, UT: Association for Consumer Research, 1993), pp. 429–32.

22. Norman K. Denzin, "Rain Man in Las Vegas," *Symbolic Interaction* 16, no. 1 (1993), pp. 65–77.

23. Craig J. Thompson, Howard R. Pollio, and William B. Locander, "The Spoken and the Unspoken: A Hermeneutic Approach to Understanding the Cultural Viewpoints That Underlie Consumers' Expressed Meanings," *Journal of Consumer Research* 21 (December 1994), pp. 432–33.

24. For some of the research on this topic see Edward T. Higgins, "Self-Discrepancy: A Theory Relating Self and Affect," *Psychological Review* 94 (July 1987), pp. 319–40; Patricia Linville, "Self Complexity as a Cognitive Buffer against Stress-Related Illness and Depression," *Journal of Personality and Social Psychology* 52 (April 1997), pp. 663–76, on self-concept complexity; Paula R. Pietromonaco, Jean Manis, Katherine Frohart-Lane (1986), and "Self-Complexity as a Cognitive Buffer Against Stress-Related Illness and Depression," *Psychology of Women Quarterly,* 10 (4, December), pp. 373–81, on integrating identities with each other.

25. The J. Peterman Company, *Owner's Manual,* no. 14, 1991, cited in Amy J. Morgan, "The Evolving Self in Consumer Behavior: Exploring Possible Selves," in *Advances in Consumer Research,* vol. 20, Leigh McAlister and Michael L. Rothschild, eds. (Provo, UT: Association for Consumer Research, 1993), p. 431.

26. Andreasen, "Life Status Changes and Changes in Consumer Preferences and Satisfaction."

27. T. R. Reid, *Confucius Lives Next Door* (New York: Vintage Books, 1999), pp. 161–66.

28. Shay Sayre, *Consumption, Markets, and Culture* 3, no. 2 (1999), pp. 99–128; and John Schouten, "Selves in Transition: Symbolic Consumption in Personal Rites of Passage and Identity Reconstruction," *Journal of Consumer Research,* March 17, 1991, pp. 412–25.

29. Eileen Fischer and Brenda Gainer, "Baby Showers: A Rite of Passage in Transition," in *Advances in Consumer Research,* vol. 20, Leigh McAlister and Michael L. Rothschild, eds. (Provo, UT: Association for Consumer Research, 1993), pp. 320–24; Cele Otnes and Tina M. Lowry, "'Til Debt Do Us Part: The Selection and Meaning of Artifacts in the American Wedding," in *Advances in Consumer Research,* vol. 20, Leigh McAlister and Michael L. Rothschild, eds. (Provo, UT: Association for Consumer Research, 1993), pp. 325–29; and Reid, *Confucius Lives Next Door,* pp. 153–55.

30. Jennifer Edson Escalas, "Advertising Narratives: What Are They and How Do They Work?" in *Dimensions of Consumers Motives, Goals, and Desires: Emerging Perspectives and Applications for a New Century,* S. Ratneshwar, David Glen Mick, and Cynthia Huffman, eds. (New York and London: Routledge, 2000); Clifford Geertz, "Making Experiences, Authoring Selves," in *The Anthropology of Experience,* Victor W. Turner and Edward M. Bruner, eds. (Urbana: University of Illinois Press, 1986), pp. 373–80; Kenneth J. Gergen and Mary M. Gergen, "Narrative and the Self as Relationship," in *Advances in Experimental Social Psychology,* vol. 21, Leonard Berkowitz, ed. (San Diego: Academic Press, 1988), pp. 17–56; Kristin M. Langellier, "Personal Narratives: Perspectives on Theory and Research," *Text and Performance Quarterly* 9 (October 1989), pp. 243–76; and Theodore R. Sarbin, ed., *Narrative Psychology* (New York: Praeger, 1986).

31. C. B. Claiborne and Julie L. Ozanne, "The Meaning of Custom-Made Homes: Home as a Metaphor for Living," in *Advances in Consumer Research,* vol. 17, Marvin E. Goldberg, Gerald Gorn, and Richard W. Pollay, eds. (Provo, UT: Association for Consumer Research, 1990), pp. 367–74; and Linda L. Price, Eric J. Arnould, and Carolyn Curasi, "Older Consumer's Disposition of Cherished Possessions," *Journal of Consumer Research* 27 (September 2000), pp. 179–201.

32. Clinton R. Sanders, *Customizing the Body: The Art and Culture of Tattooing* (Philadelphia: Temple University Press, 1989), p. 43. See also Kathleen A. O'Donnell, "Good Girls Gone Bad: The Consumption of Fetish Fashion and the Sexual Empowerment of Women," in *Advances in Consumer Research,* vol. 26, Eric J. Arnould and Linda Scott, eds. (Provo, UT: Association for Consumer Research, 1999), pp. 184–89. Similar examples of the use of consumption to give agency and coherence to life narratives is provided in Eric J. Arnould and Linda L. Price, "Questing for Self and Community in Post Modernity," in *Dimensions of Consumer Motives, Goals, and Desires: Emerging Perspectives and Applications for a New Century,* S. Ratneshwar, David Glen Mick, and Cynthia Huffman, eds. (New York and London: Routledge, in press).

33. Richard L. Celsi, Randall L. Rose, and Thomas W. Leigh, "An Exploration of High-Risk Leisure Consumption through Skydiving," *Journal of Consumer Research* 20 (June 1993), pp. 1–23; Eric J. Arnould and Linda L. Price, "River Magic: Extraordinary Experience and the Extended Service Encounter," *Journal of Consumer Research* 20 (June 1993), pp. 24–45; and Jerry Adler, Daniel Glick, Patricia King, Jeanne Gordon, and Alden Cohen, "Been There, Done That," *Newsweek,* July 19, 1993, pp. 42–49.

34. Folkes and Kiesler, "Social Cognition"; and Anthony G. Greenwald and Anthony R. Pratkanis, "The Self," in *Handbook of Social Cognition,* vol. 3, Robert S. Wyer, Jr., and Thomas K. Srull, eds. (Hillsdale, NJ: Erlbaum, 1984), pp. 129–78.

35. The name-letter effect is documented in Joseph R. Nuttin, *Motivation Planning and Action: A Relational Theory of Behavioral Dynamics* (Hillsdale, NJ: Lawrence Erlbaum, 1984). Markus and Wurf, "The Dynamic Self-Concept" provide a review of this literature. Herbert A. Simon, *Reason in Human Affairs* (Stanford: Stanford University Press, 1991), and Richard E. Nisbett and Lee Ross, *Human Inference: Strategies and Shortcomings of Social Judgment* (Englewood Cliffs, NJ: Prentice Hall, 1980) are also good references for these kinds of self-relevant stimuli effects.

36. Newell D. Wright, D. B. Claiborne, and M. Joseph Sirgy (1992), "The Effects of Product Symbolism on Consumer Self-Concept," *Advances in Consumer Research,* vol. 19, John Sherry and Brian Sernthal, eds. (Provo, UT: Association for Consumer Research, 1992), pp. 311–18.

37. Anthony G. Greenwald and Clark Leavitt, "Audience Involvement in Advertising: Four Levels," *Journal of Consumer Research* 11 (June 1984), pp. 581–92; Michael L. Rothschild, "Perspectives in Involvement: Current Problems and Future Directions," in *Advances in Consumer Research,* vol. 11, Tom Kinnear, ed. (Ann Arbor, MI: Association for Consumer Research, 1984), pp. 216–17.

38. For a discussion of how drugs and alcohol are used to protect self-representations see Jay G. Hull, Ronald R. Van Treuran, Susan J. Ashford, Pamela Propsom, and Bruce W. Andrus, "Self Consciousness and the Processing of Self-Relevant Information," *Journal of Personality and Social Psychology* 54 (March 1988), pp. 452–65. For a more general discussion of self-serving biases and how they affect information processing see Anthony G. Greenwald (1980), "The Totalitarian Ego: Fabrication and Revision of Personal History," *American Psychologist,* 35:603–18.

39. David Glen Mick and Michelle DeMoss, "Self-Gifts: Phenomenological Insights from Four Contexts," *Journal of Consumer Research* 17 (December 1990), p. 325.

40. Barry R. Schlenker, *Impression Management: The Self-Concept, Social Identity, and Interpersonal Relations* (Melbourne, FL: Krieger, 1980), introduces the concept of desired selves. Robert A. Wickund and Peter M. Gollwitzer, *Symbolic Self-Completion* (Hillsdale, NJ: Lawrence Erlbaum, 1982), stress the importance of commitment to these self-definitions in motivating behavior. For a review of literature on the relationship between self-concept and product preference, see Sirgy, "Self-Concept in Consumer Behavior."

41. George M. Zinkhan, Diana Haytko, and Allison Ward, "Self-Concept Theory: Applications in Advertising," *Journal of Marketing Communications* 2 (1996), pp. 1–19.

42. Zinkhan, Haytko, and Ward, "Self-Concept Theory."

43. Marsha Richins, "Valuing Things: The Public and Private Meanings of Possession," *Journal of Consumer Research* 21 (December 1994), pp. 504–21. For research on the relationship between self-concept and social perception, see G. G. Sherwood, "Self-Serving Biases in Person Perception: A Reexamination of Projection as a Mechanism of Defense," *Psychological Bulletin* 90 (1981), pp. 445–59, B. R. Schlenker provides a discussion of the relationship between self-concept and relationships in Barry R. Schlenker, ed., *The Self and Social Life* (New York: McGraw-Hill, 1985).

44. Mark Ritson, Richard Elliot, and Sue Eccles, "Reframing IKEA: Commodity-Signs, Consumer Creativity, and the Social/Self Dialectic," in *Advances in Consumer Research,* vol. 23, Kim Corfman and John Lynch, eds. (Provo, UT: Association for Consumer Research, 1996), pp. 127–31; and Ajay K Sirsi, James C. Ward, and Peter H. Reingen, "Microcultural Analysis of Variation in Sharing of Causal Reasoning about Behavior," *Journal of Consumer Research* 22 (March 1996), pp. 345–72.

45. The psychology of self-monitoring is developed extensively by Mark Snyder in numerous articles and books. A fairly comprehensive treatment of the topic is provided in Mark Snyder, *Public Appearances Private Realities: The Psychology of Self-Monitoring* (New York: W. H. Freeman and Company, 1987).

46. Margaret K. Hogg, Alastair J. Cox, and Kathy Keeling, "The Impact of Self-Monitoring on Image Congruence and Product/Brand Evaluation," *European Journal of Marketing* 34, no. 5–6 (2000), pp. 641–67.

47. One of the most influential books on the subject of the self is Erving Goffman's *The Presentation of Self in Everyday Life* (New York: Doubleday, 1959). For a discussion of internal and external audiences for the self, see Barry R. Schlenker, ed., *The Self and Social Life* (New York: McGraw-Hill, 1985). For a general discussion of impression management strategies, see Schlenker, *Impression Management;* and Michael R. Solomon, "The Role of Products as Social Stimuli: A Symbolic Interactionism Perspective," *Journal of Consumer Research* 10 (December 1983), pp. 319–29. See also Raj Mehta and Russell W. Belk, "Artifacts, Identity, and Transition: Favorite Possessions of Indians and Indian Immigrants to the United States," *Journal of Consumer Research* 17 (March 1991), pp. 398–411.

48. Diane Barthel talks about advertising that appeals to self-presentation by representing the voices of internal audiences in her book *Putting on Appearances: Gender and Advertising* (Philadelphia: Temple University Press, 1988). She argues that advertising constantly reinforces males as the audience for women's consumption behaviors. A classic example is the long-running advertising campaign that asserts "Gentlemen prefer Hanes" and shows a model in a short skirt getting all the attention. See also John V. Canfield, *The Looking-Glass Self* (New York: Praeger, 1990); and Christine Yano, "Inventing Selves: Images and Image-Making in a Japanese Popular Music Genre," *Journal of Popular Culture* 31, no. 2 (1997), pp. 115–29.

49. There is a lot of novel and interesting research on this topic. A good review is offered by David Mick, "Consumer Research and Semiotics: Exploring the Morphology of Signs, Symbols, and Significance," *Journal of Consumer Research* 13 (September 1986), pp. 196–213. See also Rebecca H. Holman, "Apparel as Communication," in *Symbolic Consumer Behavior,* Elizabeth C. Hirschman and Morris B. Holbrook, eds. (Ann Arbor, MI: Association for Consumer Research, 1981), pp. 7–15. A fun study using Halloween costumes as the consumption context is reported in Trudy Kehret-Ward and Richard Yalch, "To Take or Not to Take the Only One: Effects of Changing the Meaning of a Product Attribute on Choice Behavior," *Journal of Consumer Research,* March 1984, pp. 410–16. Russell Belk, Kenneth Bahn, and Robert Mayer, "Developmental Recognition of Consumption Symbolism," *Journal of Consumer Research* 9 (June 1982), p. 417, study children's consumption symbolism. Of course, we shouldn't neglect the classic work of Sidney J. Levy, "Symbols for Sale," *Harvard Business Review,* July–August 1959, pp. 117–24.

50. These examples are adapted from Susan Kraft, "The Heart of the Home," *American Demographics,* June 1992, pp. 46–50.

51. Marcel Mauss, "A Category of the Human Mind: The Notion of Person; the Notion of Self," in M. Carrithers, S. Collins, and S. Lukes, eds., *The Category of the Person* (Cambridge: Cambridge University Press, 1985), pp. 1–25.

52. Michael Carrithers, Steven Collins, and Steven Lukes, eds., *The Category of the Person: Anthropology, Philosophy, History* (Cambridge: Cambridge University Press, 1985); and Brian Morris, *Anthropology of the Self: The Individual in Cultural Perspective* (London and Boulder: Pluto Press, 1994).

53. C. Kagitcibasi, "The Autonomous-Relational Self: A New Synthesis," *European Psychologist* 1 (1996), pp. 180–86; and Hazel Rose Markus and Shinobu Kitayama, "Culture and Self: Implications for Cognition, Emotion, and Motivation," *Psychological Review* 98 (1991), pp. 224–53.

54. M. H. Bond, *The Psychology of the Chinese People* (New York: Oxford University Press, 1986); and Chu, "The Changing Concept of Self in Contemporary China."

55. V.S.Y Kwan, M. H. Bond, and T. M. Singelis, "Pancultural Explanations for Life Satisfaction: Adding Relationship Harmony to Self-Esteem," *Journal of Personality and Social Psychology* 73 (1997), pp. 1038–51.

56. E. Hamaguchi, "A Contextual Model of the Japanese: Toward a Methodological Innovation in Japan Studies," *Journal of Japanese Studies* 11 (1985), pp. 289–321; George DeVos, "Dimensions of the Self in Japanese Culture," in *Culture and Self: Asian and Western Perspectives,* Anthony J. Marsella, George DeVos, and Francis L. K. Hsu, eds. (New York: Tavistock Publications, 1985), pp. 141–84. See also Yumiko Ono, "Designers Cater to Japan's Love of Logos," *The Wall Street Journal,* May 29, 1990, pp. B1.

57. Robert Levine, "Why Isn't Japan Happy?" *American Demographics,* June 1992, pp. 58–60.

58. Markus and Kitayama, "Culture and Self."

59. For a more complete discussion of Hindu views of the self, see Agehananda Bharati, "The Self in Hindu Thought and Action," in *Culture and Self: Asian and Western Perspectives,* Anthony J. Marsella, George DeVos, and Francis L. K. Hsu, eds. (New York: Tavistock Publications, 1985), pp. 185–230.

60. R. Agarwal and G. Misra, "A Factor Analytic Study of Achievement Goals and Means: An Indian View," *International Journal of Psychology* 21 (1986), pp. 717–31; Gracia Clark, *Onions Are My Husband* (Chicago: University of Chicago Press, 1994); Paul Clough, "The Social Relations of Grain Marketing in Northern Nigeria," *Review of African Political Economy* 34 (December 1985), pp. 16–34; and A-B. Yu and K-S. Yang, "The Nature of Achievement Motivation in Collectivistic Societies," in *Individualism and Collectivism: Theory, Method, and Applications,* U. Kim, H. C. Triandis, C. Kagitcibasi, S.-C. Choi, and G. Yoon, eds. (Thousand Oaks, CA: Sage Publications, 1994), pp. 239–50.

61. Morris, *Anthropology of the Self,* pp. 118–47.

62. For an insightful review of the relationship between personality, the core self, and the self-schema that gets activated in a particular purchase or consumption situation, see Walker and Olson, "The Activated Self and Consumer Behavior."

63. Harold H. Kassarjian and Mary Jane Sheffet, "Personality and Consumer Behavior: An Update," in *Perspectives in Consumer Behavior,* 4th ed., Harold H. Kassarjian and Thomas S. Robertson, eds. (Englewood Cliffs, NJ: Prentice Hall, 1991), pp. 281–303.

64. Curtis R. Haugtvedt, Richard E. Petty, and John T. Cacioppo, "Need for Cognition and Advertising: Understanding the Role of Personality Variables in Consumer Behavior," *Journal of Consumer Psychology* 1, no. 3 (1992), pp. 239–60; Carl G. Jung, *Man and His Symbols* (Garden City, NY: Doubleday, 1964); David Glen Mick and Claus Buhl, "A Meaning-Based Model of Advertising Experiences," *Journal of Consumer Research* 19 (December 1992), pp. 317–38; John P. Robinson, Phillip R. Shaver, and Lawrence S. Wrightsman, eds., *Measures of Personality and Social Psychological Attitudes* (San Diego: Academic Press, 1991); Leon G. Schiffman, William R. Dillon, and Festus E. Nkrumah, "The Influence of Subcultural and Personality Factors on Consumer Acculturation," *Journal of International Business Studies,* Fall 1981, pp. 137–43; Mark Snyder and Kenneth G. DeBono, "Appeals to Image and Claims about Quality: Understanding the Psychology of Advertising," *Journal of Personality and Social Psychology,* September 1985, pp. 586–97; and Bernard Weiner, "Attribution in Personality Psychology," in *Handbook of Personality: Theory and Research,* Lawrence A. Pervin, ed. (New York: Guilford, 1990), pp. 465–84.

65. Harold H. Kassarjian, "Social Character and Differential Preference for Mass Communication," *Journal of Marketing Research* 2 (May 1965), pp. 146–53; J. W. Hong and George M. Zinkhan, "Self-Concept and Advertising Effectiveness: The Influence of Congruency and Response Mode," *Psychology & Marketing* 12, no. 1 (1995), pp. 53–77.

66. William O. Bearden, Richard G. Netemeyer, and Mary F. Mobley, *Handbook of Marketing Scales: Multi-Item Measures for Marketing and Consumer Behavior Research* (London: Sage Publications, 1993).

67. David Riesman, *The Lonely Crowd* (New Haven: Yale University Press, 1950).

68. Kassarjian and Sheffet, "Personality and Consumer Behavior: An Update."

69. R. R. McCrae, P. T. Costs, Jr., G. H Del Pilar, J.-P. Rolland, and W. D. Parker, "Cross-Cultural Assessment of the Five Factor Model: The Revised NEO Personality Inventory," *Journal of Cross-Cultural Psychology* 29 (1998), pp. 171–88; Woonbong Na and Roger Marshall, "Validation of the 'Big Five' Personality Traits in Korea: A Comparative Approach," *Journal of International Consumer Marketing* 12, no. 1 (1999), pp. 5–19; and Samp V. Paunonen, Moshe Zeidner, Harald A. Engvik, Paul Oosterveld, and Rodney Maliphant, "The Nonverbal Assessment of Personality in Five Cultures," *Journal of Cross-Cultural Psychology* 31 (March 2000), pp. 220–39.

70. Kassarjian and Sheffet, "Personality and Consumer Behavior: An Update."

71. The work of William J. McGuire and his colleagues is especially important in breaking free of reactive measures of self. See for example, W. J. McGuire, "Search for the Self: Going beyond Self-Esteem and the Reactive Self," in *Personality and the Prediction of Behavior,* R. A. Zucker,

J. Aronoff, and A. I. Rabin, eds. (New York: Academic Press, 1984), pp. 73–120. Work on personal projects is reviewed in Brian R. Little, "Personal Projects: A Rationale and Method for Investigation," *Environment and Behavior* 15 (May 1983), pp. 273–309. A fun novel built around an important personal project is Tracy Kidder, *House* (Boston: Houghton Mifflin, 1985).

72. Susan Harter, "Vision of Self: Beyond the Me in the Mirror," in *Developmental Perspectives on Motivation,* J. E. Jacobs, ed. (Proceedings of the Nebraska Symposium on Motivations, Lincoln: University of Nebraska Press, 1993), pp. 99–144.

73. For a general discussion of the relationship between self-esteem and addictive and compulsive behaviors, see D. Krueger, "On Compulsive Shopping and Spending: A Psychodynamic Inquiry," *American Journal of Psychotherapy* 42 (1988), p. 454. On compulsive buying, see Thomas O'Guinn and Ronald Faber, "Compulsive Buying: A Phenomenological Exploration," *Journal of Consumer Research* 16 (1989), pp. 147–57.

74. See Alice Hanley and Mari S. Wilhelm, "Compulsive Buying: An Exploration into Self-Esteem and Money Attitudes," *Journal of Economic Psychology* 13 (1992), pp. 5–18; James A. Roberts and Carlos Ruy Martinez, "The Emerging Consumer Culture in Mexico: An Exploratory Investigation of Compulsive Buying in Mexican Young Adults," *Journal of International Consumer Marketing* 10, no. 1–2 (1997), pp. 7–32; James A. Roberts and Cesar J. Sepulveda M., "Money Attitudes and Compulsive Buying: An Exploratory Investigation of the Emerging Consumer Culture," *Journal of International Consumer Marketing* 11, no. 4 (1999), pp. 53–74; Gerhard Scherhord, Lucia A. Reisch, and Gerard Raab, "Addictive Buying in West Germany: An Empirical Study," *Journal of Consumer Policy* 13, no. 4 (1990), pp. 355–87; and J. Trachtenberg, "Shop Until You Drop?" *Forbes,* January 11, 1988, p. 40.

75. This example is taken from Nancy Giges, "Buying Linked to Self-Esteem," *Advertising Age,* April 13, 1987, p. 68.

76. Bandura and his colleagues have published extensively on the topic of self-efficacy. A good overview article is Albert Bandura (1989), "Human Agency in Social Cognitive Theory," *American Psychologist* 44, no. 9 (1989), pp. 1175–84. An article that relates self-efficacy to the use of new technologies is Pam Scholder Ellen, William O. Bearden, and Subhash Sharma, "Resistance to Technological Innovations: An Examination of the Role of Self Efficacy and Performance Satisfaction," *Journal of the Academy of Marketing Science* 19, no. 4 (1991), p. 297.

77. S. Grunert and R. Rohme, "Consumers' Environmental Concern: Are We Really Tapping True Concern That Relates to Environmentally Ethic Behavior?" presented at the *ESOMAR Conference on Marketing Research and a New World Order* (Amsterdam: ESOMAR, 1992); Pam Scholder Ellen, Joshua L. Weiner, and C. Cobb-Algren, "The Role of Perceived Consumer Effectiveness in Motivating Environmentally Conscious Behaviors," *Journal of Public Policy and Marketing* 10 (Fall 1991), pp. 102–17; and Scholder Ellen, Bearden, and Sharma, "Resistance to Technological Innovations," pp. 297–307.

78. Gillian Rice, Nittaya Wongtada, and Orose Leelakulthanit, "An Investigation of Self-Efficacy and Environmentally Concerned Behavior of Thai Consumers," *Journal of International Consumer Marketing* 9, no. 2 (1996), pp. 1–21.

79. George M. Zinkhan and Ali Shermohamed, "Is Other-Directedness on the Increase? An Empirical Test of Riesman's Theory of Social Character," *Journal of Consumer Research* 13, no. 1 (1986), pp. 127–30.

80. For a summary of individual difference measures used in studying consumer behavior, see William Bearden and Richard Netemeyer, eds., *Handbook of Marketing Scales* (Walnut Creek, CA: AltaMira Press, 1998). For excellent reviews of predicting behavior with personality, see Seymour Epstein, "The Stability of Behavior: I. On Predicting Most of the People Much of the Time," *Journal of Personality and Social Psychology* 37 (July 1979), pp. 1097–126; and Seymour Epstein, "The Stability of Behavior: II. Implications for Psychological Research," *American Psychologist* 35 (September 1980), pp. 790–806.

Learning Objectives

After completing this chapter, you should be able to:

- Identify role-related product constellations.

- Describe psychographics and lifestyle research.

- Understand the use of lifestyles data to profile lifestyle segments, identify related lifestyle interests, and locate lifestyle segments geographically.

- Recognize lifestyle typologies such as VALS, LOV, Japan VALS, and Global Scan.

- Understand how lifestyle may be used at various levels of aggregation.

- Identify the value and limitations of lifestyle research.

Lifestyles: Consumption Subcultures

Keepin' It Real: The Hip-Hop Engine[1]

The hip-hop lifestyle emerged in the Bronx, New York, out of broader African-American cultural roots. The hip-hop lifestyle incorporates four prominent elements: breaking (dancing), tagging or bombing (marking the walls of buildings and subways with graffiti); DJ-ing (collaging the best record fragments using multiple turntables); and MC-ing (making and performing rap songs). Fashion is also a prominent part of the hip-hop style. Rappers made heavy gold chains and pendants fashionable, for example.

Hip-hop is in many respects a classic youth subculture, rejecting the norms and values of the mainstream, measuring success in terms of peer approval, and equating power with the ability to influence the subculture's constantly changing insider cues, language, tastes, and values. Its strengths are its energy and creativity. An estimated 97 percent of urban African-American teens like and listen to rap music. It is the universal element in their experience. Rap music embodies and reaffirms traditional African-American modes of oral expression. It demands adherence to its orthodoxies as a condition of acceptance, a quality rendered hazardous by the culture's macho encouragement of risk taking—substance abuse, promiscuity, being a "street player." For many U.S. hip-hoppers, "keepin' it real" means emphasizing ties to the harsh realities of the African-American inner city.

This is also a media-oriented audience, but one that perceives media messages as a kind of living experience rather than cognitive themes. The film *Wild Style* is seen as "the dopest," capturing the essence of the lifestyle. Urban Box Office, a successful start-up planning a series of music, art, and

e-commerce websites targeted at different segments of the millions who love hip-hop culture and media, hopes to launch as many as nine more sites in 2000.

Hip-hop has become a global lifestyle. Greenlandic rappers rap in the Inuit language and Danish about the challenges faced by these multicultural youth. An Arab women rap trio, Les Messagères, rap about Algeria's bloody civil war. The group is so popular that it is a household name throughout Algeria. Older people are scandalized, but the members of the trio claim that rap is their best means of expression. So too with Intik, a group of male rappers who sing about the "crazy violence" of the war as well. Rap mixed with traditional raï music has become so popular it can now even occasionally be heard on Algerian state radio. Algerian rap and the rap made by young North African artists in France's immigrant districts are vigorously cross-fertilizing. For example, another young Algerian group, MBS, explores the discomforts of growing up both in Algeria and in France.

South Africa's biggest musical craze sounds rather like American gangsta rap, and this is no coincidence. Kwaito stars admire and emulate transatlantic rappers. But their music is more than imitation. The songs are about life in the townships and about the experiences of the postapartheid generation. Kwaito's popularity in South Africa depends a lot on the incorporation of local rhythms and bass lines, and it reflects young black South African culture in a way that no imported dance track could.

"Keepin' it real," or authenticity, is the key to reaching the hip-hop audience. But it is a moving, mutating target whose most powerful evolutionary engine is the hip-hop culture, fashion, hairstyles, and worldview of a generation alienated not only from Eurocentric culture but to a surprising degree from its own African-American heritage. The universal teenage rejection of authority extends in the street culture even to an admired celebrity speaking outside the celebrity's area of expertise. A disbelief in the future also undercuts efforts to address this audience. The strong identification with street culture renders any depiction of "the street" not scrupulously accurate and current suspect. "That's not the way it happens around here," is not just a criticism, it's a rejection. Adherence to reality is judged in terms of the portrayed attitude and behaviors, not specifics of locale. "Keepin' it real" is one way of defending the hip-hop lifestyle against assimilation into the mainstream, a concern common to many alternate lifestyle groups.

Although the charge of going "commercial" is often the kiss of death to rap musicians, hip-hop has become a marketing phenomenon. The first hip-hop record was released in 1980—"back in the day"; 20 years later annual revenues from rap music exceed $1 billion and hip-hop music has outsold the previous top-selling format, country. Hip-hop music has driven independent recording labels like Cash Money Records and Def Jam Records to major positions within the pop music industry. Hip-hop street culture has become a positioning device for all sorts of companies, including Nautica jeans and Bizo shoes and skateboards. Music company executive and hip-hop performer Master P rapped out an unusual TV marketing strategy for a new Converse athletic shoe. In the deal between Master P's No Limit Entertainment and Converse, the new basketball shoe called All Star MP is supported with TV spots featuring Master P, aka Percy Miller, playing basketball in different urban venues. Artists like Chuck D of Public Enemy are now quoted in *Inc.* magazine, and some prominent rappers like Snoop Doggy Dog have moved to upscale gated communities. You can visit Chuck D's website.

 www.defjam.com

 www.nautica jeans.com

 www.bizo.com

 www.Rapstation. com

For marketers, the task of imbuing a message with "street life" is twofold—to make it shareable and to give it sufficient longevity for the sharing to take place. It must be entertaining, engaging, and couched in terms that conceal any origins of mainstream values. Furthermore, the message must remain valid long enough to win street acceptance. This is no easy task in a culture characterized by constant change, a dynamism captured in the term "flav."

Overview

The focus of this chapter is on consumers' lifestyles—that is, how consumers live. Lifestyle includes consumers' activities, interests, likes and dislikes, attitudes, consumption patterns, and expectations. The term *lifestyle* suggests a patterned way of life into which consumers fit various products, activities, and resources.[2] We can trace the origins of the interest in lifestyle to the work of Thorstein Veblen's turn-of-the-century classic *The Theory of the Leisure Class,* in which the conspicuous consumption of the nouveau riche (Chapter 6) was first identified and ridiculed. In making use of the lifestyle concept, marketers often rely on the idea that consumer lifestyles are a reflection of individuals' attempts to realize a desired or ideal self-concept, a notion discussed in Chapter 7.[3]

Marketing's conception of lifestyle emerged from four main developments: (1) the desire to develop an easily measurable, more objective variant of motivational research that was popular in the 1950s and 1960s; (2) the emergence of more sophisticated statistical techniques and the computer power to run them; (3) the desire to give traditional personality research a narrower consumer focus; and (4) the inability to describe increasingly diverse consumption patterns with then-existing tools (for example, demographic or social class analysis). The concept that resulted combines the attitudinal clustering typically associated with personality research with a wider domain of person measures.[4]

Consumers' lifestyles influence many of their production, acquisition, consumption,

Caterpillar clothing uses a lifestyle positioning in this global ad campaign.

and disposition activities. In many cases we might think of marketers as selling pieces of a style of life, not isolated products.[5] A series of ads for Caterpillar clothing provides a good illustration of how a product is depicted as a part of a style of life. Two examples from this international ad campaign are provided here. Notice the gritty urban settings and the "ordinary" look of the models. What style of life do you think these ads are trying to convey?

Decisions that consumers make about purchase, consumption, and disposal can alter or reinforce their lifestyles. Hence, lifestyles are dynamic and constantly changing. For example, a consumer may decide to start jogging in order to get into better shape. This decision may reinforce her already health-oriented lifestyle. However, as she integrates this behavior into her life, she may find that this change also alters her lifestyle—when she gets up in the morning, her meals, her bedtime, her reading, and her other leisure or vacation activities. Jogging may even influence her social groups, her wardrobe, her hairstyle, and other seemingly unrelated aspects of the way she lives. Hence, deciding to jog doesn't just influence the purchase of a pair of shorts, a running bra, and a pair of running shoes; it also has the potential to alter many other facets of a consumer's daily life.

Lifestyles are influenced by many factors, including demographics, social class, reference groups, and family. As illustrated in the vignette about hip-hop, many aspects of the cultural environment can influence lifestyle. An individual's self-concept, as discussed in Chapter 7, serves as the basis for one's lifestyle. In fact, we might think of lifestyle as an outward manifestation of aspects of the self. This means that, in some ways, each person, family, and household has a unique lifestyle. It also means that individuals, families, and households may practice multiple lifestyles, depending on how situations and participants shift to alter important lifestyle dynamics. For example, many households with school-age children have a different lifestyle during the summer months than during the school year.[6]

Of course, many products and marketing strategies focus on an explicit recognition of a particular lifestyle that is shared by a market segment. We show two ads for PowerBar. One appeared in *Sierra* (the magazine of the Sierra Club); the other appeared in *Runner's World*. The ads are each tailored to appeal to consumers who share a particular lifestyle, in this case backpacking and running. Such advertising is very common. In fact, lifestyle

PowerBar tailors its lifestyle message to two slightly different segments.

differences or lifestyle patterns constitute one of the most important bases for segmenting markets.

Lifestyle differences might be recognized and targeted by marketers at various levels of aggregation. The hip-hop lifestyle describes a form we might consider a global structure of common differences as discussed in Chapter 5. It has mutated into a variety of national and transnational forms that nonetheless always incorporate values connected with youth, authenticity, opposition to the mainstream, poetry, and rhythm into the local variations. Similarly, some authors have described a cosmopolitan lifestyle, which expatriates from several national cultures organize around concepts of self, personal goals, consumption of "exotic" foreign products, and adventuresome travel. We might define the lifestyle characteristics of a whole generation, such as generation Xers. Alternatively, we could talk about the lifestyle of a particular segment within a generation, such as the "privileged poor." This is a subset of generation Xers who cobble together a lifestyle combining some lavish consumer spending on fashion with handouts from parents and odd jobs. Or we might identify migrating seniors, a group of older consumers who retire to take up new lifestyles in retirement communities in subtropical climates.[7]

Marketers often define a lifestyle segment around a single activity such as cycling, soccer, bowling, or hiking. For example, the Football Collector ad on page 276 invites soccer enthusiasts to buy merchandise reflective of their favorite teams and heroes. Marketers may also create an ad campaign to appeal to consumers reacting against a lifestyle rather like the disclaimant reference groups discussed in Chapter 15. For example, with so many restaurants promising low-fat, healthy, and even vegetarian food, Wienerschnitzel appeals to consumers who want, at least occasionally, to rebel against that healthy lifestyle in the cheeky ad shown on page 276.

This lifestyle ad appeals to enthusiasts of a particular leisure activity.

This tongue-in-cheek ad disclaims a particular lifestyle.

Lifestyle research can be applied to solve a variety of marketing problems, including identifying the target market, positioning a brand, locating where the target group lives, identifying how to communicate with the target group, and gaining insight into why the target group acts the way it does.[8] For instance, if a medical center wanted to offer a new line of service (for example, treating and preventing sports-related injuries), then a lifestyle segmentation might be completed to determine who would want such a service and who would be willing to pay for such a service. In addition, a lifestyle segmentation would be useful to help choose a media vehicle (for example, a specific magazine such as *Women's Soccer World*) for promoting the new hospital service.

The key for lifestyle marketers is really to figure out what goes with what and, in many cases, to help define product and service assortments for particular lifestyles. This often involves figuring out what attitudes and values go with what activities and products. An example of a creative application of lifestyle marketing is the highly successful marketing behind the No Fear Apparel company. Sales for the company rose to $200 million in less than five years. Jim Hancock, the marketing director, sought to convey a particular feeling with the marketing strategy and the logo. The apparel is designed to speak to a myriad of subcultures (for example, auto racing, rock climbing) that have as a common emotional link the "No Fear" attitude. According to Jim Hancock, the No Fear attitude is about taking on the challenge and fear that's in every and any kind of task and overcoming it.[9]

This chapter will introduce you to some of the most important tools marketers use to figure out what goes with what. We begin with a brief discussion of product clusters, or constellations. This will help you to understand and identify different behavioral lifestyles. Then, we introduce some important tools for implementing lifestyle marketing, including psychographic segmentation schemes such as VALS, LOV, PRIZM, and Global Scan. We also discuss the use of psychographic methods to chart social and cultural trends. We conclude the chapter with a discussion of emerging criticisms of lifestyles research.

Product Constellations

Products are important for communicating social information. For example, what image do you have of a minivan driver versus a sports car driver? The term *lifestyle* implies a pattern of behavior that is reflected in and reflects the consumption not merely of single products but of interrelated product clusters, or **product constellations.** Product constellations are *clusters of complementary products, specific brands, or consumption activities.* Product constellations are socially meaningful sets of consumption stimuli that are used by consumers both for self-definition and for the categorization of others. Some early analyses of supermarket purchases demonstrated that purchases do fall into meaningful bundles and that groups of consumers with shared consumption patterns also shared demographics, tastes, and values such that consumption lifestyle groups could be meaningfully identified. In the mid-1980s, Levi Strauss and Company divided the U.S. men's clothing market into five product-based segments, including the utilitarian jeans wearer, who wears jeans for work and leisure, and the classic independent, a tailored, pinstripe suit professional, who shops alone.[10]

In the late 1960s, two U.S. researchers employed product usage data concerning 80 products in an attempt to identify behavioral lifestyles. They identified 10 groups of men who used multiple products, such as the car-conscious man, who bought aftermarket products and accessories; the cosmopolitan traveler, who engaged in air travel and car rental;

Professional	Salesman	Suit Salesman	Businessman
Seiko watch	Farrah slacks	Zenith TV	Tiffany jewels
Burberry raincoat	Budweiser beer	Oldsmobile 98	Steuben glass
Lacoste shirt	Buick Skylark	Whirlpool freezer	Italian leather
Atlantic magazine	Coca-Cola	Gillette shaver	briefcase
Brooks Bros. suit	McDonald's	Old Spice cologne	Cross pen
Bass loafers	M & M's candy	Miller beer	Cuff links
Silk tie	Puritan golf shirts	JVC stereo	Ralph Lauren shirt
French wine	Fayva shoes		VCR
BMW	Samsonite luggage		Lincoln Continental
	Timex watch		*Wall Street Journal*

Attorney	Blue-Collar Worker	Public Defender	Unskilled Worker
Prince tennis racket	Schaefer beer	Levi's cords	Chevrolet
Leather briefcase	AMF bowling ball	Wallaby shoes	Goldstar TV
American Express gold	Ford pickup truck	Calvin Klein glasses	*NY Daily News*
card	Levi's jeans	Molson beer	Hanes T-shirts
Cadillac Eldorado	Marlboro cigarettes	L.L. Bean shirts	Levi's jeans
Michelob beer	RCA TV	RCA VCR	Coca-Cola
Vantage cigarettes	*Field and Stream*	Volkswagen Rabbit	Miller beer
Cigars	Black & Decker tools	*Esquire*	McDonald's
Johnston & Murphy	McDonald's		Camel cigarettes
shoes			
L.L. Bean catalog			

Source: Michael R. Solomon and Henry Assael, "The Forest or the Trees?: A Gestalt Approach to Symbolic Consumption," in Marketing and Semiotics: New Directions in the Study of Signs for Sale, *Jean Umiker-Sebeok, ed. (New York: Mouton de Gruyter, 1987), p. 206.*

the cigar and pipe smoker, who purchased many smoking articles; and so forth. These authors also reported some evidence of distinctions between these segments and consumption of particular brands of beer. Industry Insights 8.1 shows the contents of product constellations elicited for some male social roles in the United States.[11]

Lifestyle profiles can be organized around a single product category. Such profiles are the bread and butter of many marketing research firms and offer valuable insights on specific appeals and vehicles to use in targeting product category users. Consumer Chronicles 8.1 profiles the *Otaku,* a youth-oriented hacker lifestyle associated with *anime* (Japanese animation) and an antisocial orientation. The Otaku even inhabit a weird novel by famed sci-fi author William Gibson called *Idoru.*[12] On a more mainstream note, Industry Insights 8.2 describes an activity-based lifestyle profile designed to get a handle on the characteristics and golf-related spending of 24 million U.S. golfers.

Some particularly strong product-to-role relationships have led researchers to speak of **brand tribes** for *people who are devoted to a particular brand,* such as clothes by No Fear in the United States or by Naf Naf or Clark's in Europe. The ad for Clark's shown on page 281 was featured in an issue of the UK pop magazine *The Face* devoted to Great Britain's

The blurring of man and machine, of reality and what comes in over the video display terminal, is spawning a generation of Japanese kids who are opting out of the conformity of Japan, Inc., in favor of logging onto computer networks. They have been dubbed the *Otaku* by the Japanese media, from the most formal way of saying *you* in Japanese, the implication being that there is always some kind of technological barrier between people. The Otaku came of age in the 1980s with "prehistoric" 186 computers and Atari Pac-Men as playmates. They were brought up on junk food and educated to memorize reams of context-less information in preparation for multiple-choice high school and college entrance exams. They unwind with ultraviolent slasher comic books or equally violent computer games. They discovered that, by interacting with computers instead of people, they could avoid Japanese society's dauntingly complex web of social obligations and loyalties. The result: a generation of Japanese youth too uptight to talk to a bank teller but who can go hell-for-leather on the deck of a personal computer or workstation. First identified by the Japanese lifestyle magazine *SPA!*, 200,000 hardcore Otaku are Japan's newest information age product. "These kids are unlike any who preceded them in Japan," *Lap Top* magazine editor Abiko Seigo says of the subculture of 16- to 25-year-olds. "Where they are coming from is a world where all the usual perspectives—like whether something is good or bad, smart or stupid—are irrelevant, because all of those things are judgments based on social relations. If you don't socialize, you don't have much sense of morality. The only thing that matters to them is data. How much do you have, and how much can you memorize?"

An alternative version of what Otaku means is as follows: Otaku is a Japanese expression for an obsessive fan or hobbyist, taken from *otaku-zoku,* which translates as "home tribe." Otaku mythology roughly corresponds to America's antisocial computer hacker, but the passion for obscure trivia (often traded as databases over computer networks) also attaches to a wide variety of pop enthusiasms from video games, Ultraman, and manga to teen-idol singers, American hip-hop, and Hong Kong action movies. Though still something of an insult in Japan, along the lines of "homebody" or "fanboy," the term has gained currency, in part via the Internet, as a badge of honor among American anime (Japanese video animation) devotees. A large number of websites, such as http://www.otakuworld.com, are devoted to each of the consumer "obsessions" mentioned above.

Source: Karl Taro Greenfeld, "The Obsession of the Otaku," Los Angeles Times Magazine, September 12, 1993, pp. 40–43; and www.altculture.com/aentries/o/otaku.html.

garage band scene. When product-to-role relationships are especially strong, the brands become a defining symbol of a communal identity, hence the term *brand tribe.*

Lifestyle profiles such as those shown in Industry Insights 8.2 have both strengths and weaknesses from a marketing perspective. Such profiles aid in identifying consumer segments. Each role can be associated with a specific constellation, or collection, of products and services. Marketers may offer new products to reinforce role identities or reinforce product and brand loyalty by emphasizing product-to-role relationships. Product constellations

Seven golfing consumer segments were identified in a new study by the Professional Golfers' Association of America:

- **Dilettante Duffers:** Male, comprise 27 percent of American golfers, average age of 41, annual household income of $64,200. They play only 16 rounds of golf per year, mostly on weekends. When they do golf, they want to look good, and they spend a larger than average share of their annual vacation time golfing.

- **Tank Tops 'n Tennis Shoes:** These male golfers make up 17 percent of U.S. golfers and are the youngest segment, average age of 35 with annual incomes of $36,700. They do much of their golfing on weekends, only golf 13 rounds a year, and spend less on golfing than any other segment.

- **Pull-Carts:** These male golfers make up 15 percent of U.S. golfers, with an average age of 52 and annual income of $32,200. Six out of 10 are retired or unemployed. They play 32 rounds of golf annually and spend $1,400 per year on the sport.

- **Public Pundits:** These zealous middle-aged male golfers are 13 percent of U.S. golfers. They play almost 52 rounds a year, but almost entirely on public golf courses despite an average income of $50,600. They do spend $2,000 per year on the sport, well above average.

- **Junior Leaguers:** These female golfers are about 15 percent of U.S. golfers, play around 24 rounds of golf a year, and spend close to the average for the sport ($1,600 annually). Their annual household income is $57,800.

- **Country Club Traditionals:** These men are only about 9 percent of U.S. golfers, but with annual household incomes of $77,300, they fork out an average of $4,400 on golf. They play an average of 60 of their 69 rounds a year on private courses.

- **Swingin' Seniors:** These women make up 6 percent of U.S. golfers. Although they report a lower than average household income they may be enjoying retirement on tidy nest eggs. They play over half their 42 annual golf rounds on private courses, and almost half belong to a golf club.

Source: Deborah Bosanko, "Seven Ways to Swing a Club," American Demographics, July 1995, pp. 16–18.

can be matched with demographic profiles and media preferences to improve targeting. Advertisers can use product constellations to engineer the context of ads (e.g., to indicate what other products should appear alongside the advertised brand). Product constellations also have implications for store layouts. For example, merchandisers may place complementary items together rather than organize the store by product categories.[13]

Lifestyle profiles constructed from product constellations also have some weaknesses. Troublesome problems with the statistical procedures used to profile consumers of particular product bundles exist. In addition, the same person may enact multiple social roles,

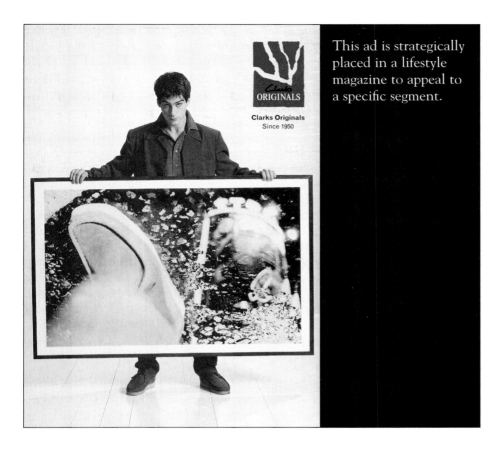

This ad is strategically placed in a lifestyle magazine to appeal to a specific segment.

Clarks Originals
Since 1950

such as manager, mother, wife, daughter, runner, and Red Cross volunteer. If a product is too closely associated with one role that conflicts with other roles, it may not suit the consumer's needs. Further, lifestyle profiles are also insensitive to effects of potential innovations, environmental influences, and changes in corporate strategy. For example, two products in Industry Insights 8.1 would no longer be included in their product constellations. Lacoste shirts disappeared from the American marketplace during a recession in the 1980s in part because of their association with a yuppie lifestyle. Camel cigarettes were repositioned with a juvenile image for a more youthful market. Marketers using such lifestyle profiles need to be especially sensitive to changing trends that may alter the product constellation in either subtle or dramatic ways. Marketers must also avoid allowing the product constellation to become a cliche (à la Lacoste shirts) so that potential customers begin to shun it.[14]

Psychographics and Lifestyle

Psychographics is *an operational technique to measure lifestyles.* Psychographics is more comprehensive than demographic, behavioral, and socioeconomic measures. Using a psychographic technique involves systematically linking individual psychological factors to characteristic patterns of overt consumer behavior to determine who the market segment is. The basic idea is that cognitive processes or properties, including values, aptitudes, beliefs, and opinions, affect the likelihood of groups within the market to make a particular decision about a product, person, or ideology, to hold an attitude, or to use a communication medium like TV or the Internet.

Psychographic techniques were developed in marketing to overcome the idiosyncratic and overly Freudian results of the motivational research that was developed in the 1950s and 1960s. Lifestyle research data are also employed to give flesh and blood to sample demographic surveys that provide little information about the *why* of consumer behavior.

Psychographic techniques divide the total market into segments on the bases of activities, interests, values, opinions, personality characteristics, and attitudes using various statistical procedures. The term *psychographic* is often used interchangeably with **AIO measures,** or *statements to describe the activities, interests, and opinions of consumers.* AIO statements may be general activities and motivations, or they may focus on statements that are product or brand specific. Psychographic methods might be termed *backward segmentation* because they group people by behavioral characteristics before seeking purchase and consumption correlates.[15]

To execute a psychographic analysis, researchers poll prospective or actual members of a market segment using standardized survey instruments. Researchers can administer these forms in person, by phone, by mail, or electronically (for example, on the Web), or they might send such surveys in the form of warranty cards, sweepstakes entries, or customer profiles. These data are then analyzed in a statistical sense to tease out various consumption typologies.

Profiles may be very general, as in a study by the Newspaper Advertising Bureau that produced eight male psychographic segments, including the quiet family man (8 percent of the total) and the ethical highbrow (14 percent of the total). At the other extreme, they may be product specific, as in a segmentation of stomach-remedy users that produced four segments, including severe sufferers, active medicators, hypochondriacs, and practicalists. Good Practice 8.1, entitled "The Average American Consumer Quiz," provides a few examples of the many statements that have been used in psychographic surveys of American consumers.[16]

Most of you are probably familiar with psychographic research since many products now include lifestyles surveys with their warranty cards. Consumers are asked to mail in these cards to ensure their warranty (Good Practice 8.2). The data contained on the card are then added to computer databases to help marketers pinpoint buyer characteristics. That is, marketers can combine the information from the warranty card with other kinds of consumer information to create a lifestyle inventory. Such an inventory could include demographic, purchase, and psychographic information.

Many products, including household soap, stomach remedies, and automobiles, have been successfully positioned or repositioned using lifestyle segmentation. In the early 1970s, the Ford Pinto was advertised as a friendly, romantic little car not unlike today's updated VW Beetle. The Pinto was subsequently repositioned as economical, basic transportation when typical buyers' lifestyles were identified more carefully. An unsuccessful example of lifestyle repositioning was Oldsmobile's "It's Not Your Father's Oldsmobile" campaign, which alienated its traditional, conservative male buyers without attracting a new generation. At the retail level, the restructuring of many department stores in the Triad nations into lifestyle boutiques and the success of Nike Town or Virgin megastores, which are divided into lifestyle meccas, are notable examples of the successful application of lifestyle segmentation.[17]

How well do *you* know the average American consumer? Try guessing the answers to these AIO inventory items. If your intuition is not too good, you have demonstrated the value of careful psychographic research to marketers. Find the answers in the footnote.

Statements	Percentage of Consumers Agreeing	
	% Men	% Women
1. A nationally advertised brand is usually a better buy than a generic brand.	_____	_____
2. I went fishing at least once in the past year.	_____	_____
3. I am a homebody.	_____	_____
4. Communism is the greatest peril in the world today.	_____	_____
5. The government should exercise more control over what is shown on television.	_____	_____
6. Information from advertising helps me to make better buying decisions.	_____	_____
7. I like to pay cash for everything I buy.	_____	_____
8. The working world is no place for a woman.	_____	_____
9. I am interested in spices and seasonings.	_____	_____
10. The father should be the boss in the house.	_____	_____
11. You have to use disinfectants to get things really clean.	_____	_____

Source: Steven J. Hoch, "Who Do We Know: Predicting the Interests and Opinions of the American Consumer," Journal of Consumer Research 15 (December 1988), pp. 315–24. Answers to the quiz are (1) M = 36, W = 35; (2) M = 52, W = 34; (3) M = 75, W = 71; (4) M = 63, W = 61; (5) M = 29, W = 33; (6) M = 66, W = 74; (7) M = 72, W = 70; (8) M = 17, W = 11; (9) M = 57, W = 79; (10) M = 68, W = 50; (11) M = 48, W = 54.

VALS, LOV, and Other Psychographic Segmentation Schemes

In this section we describe some widely used approaches to lifestyle marketing. Although each of these has gained rapid acceptance and widespread use, each has certain limitations. For example, marketers must be careful about the cultural assumptions they make in their

1 1. ☐ **Mr.**   2. ☐ **Mrs.**   3. ☐ **Ms.**   4. ☐ **Miss**   **244C**

First Name: Initial: Last Name:

Address: (Number and Street)   Apt #:

City: State: Zip Code:

2 E-Mail Address:

(Example: kaimathi@aol.com)

3 Phone #:   **4** Date of Purchase:

Month   Day   Year

5 Model Purchased: (Example: CSD-EX110)

6 Serial #:   **7** Purchase Price:

8 Store Name: $ .00

(EXCLUDING TAX)

9 Is this: (Check **all** that apply)
1. ☐ A first time purchase of this product type?
2. ☐ A replacement purchase of this product type?
3. ☐ An additional purchase of this product type?
4. ☐ A gift for you or someone else?

10 What three (3) factors **most** influenced your purchase of this Aiwa product?
1. ☐ Size
2. ☐ Special Features
3. ☐ Price/Value
4. ☐ Quality
5. ☐ Aiwa Reputation
6. ☐ Magazine/Newspaper Article
7. ☐ Previous Aiwa Experience
8. ☐ Friend/Relative Recommendation
9. ☐ Salesperson Recommendation
10. ☐ Other_____

11 What other brand(s) did you consider?
1. ☐ RCA   5. ☐ Sanyo   9. ☐ Magnavox
2. ☐ Koss   6. ☐ Fisher   10. ☐ Kenwood
3. ☐ Sony   7. ☐ JVC   11. ☐ Other
4. ☐ Panasonic 8. ☐ GPX   _____

12 Which of the following products do you own or plan to purchase?

	Own	Plan to Buy
1. Head Phones	1. ☐	2. ☐
2. Portable CD Player	1. ☐	2. ☐
3. Portable Cassette Player	1. ☐	2. ☐
4. Mini Audio System	1. ☐	2. ☐
5. Multi Media Computer Speakers	1. ☐	2. ☐
6. VCR	1. ☐	2. ☐
7. Mini Disc	1. ☐	2. ☐

13 If you purchased a clock radio, what 3 features would you like most?
1. ☐ Dual Alarm   5. ☐ Cassette Player
2. ☐ Red LED Display   6. ☐ Digital Tuner
3. ☐ Green LED Display 7. ☐ Color_____
4. ☐ CD Player   8. ☐ Other_____

14 If you purchased a portable CD player, how much buffer memory would you want?
1. ☐ 3 seconds   3. ☐ 20 seconds
2. ☐ 10 seconds 4. ☐ 20+ seconds

15 What type of radio do you prefer to have in your headphone stereo, portable stereo or radio?
1. ☐ Digital   3. ☐ No preference
2. ☐ Analog

16 Do you own a personal computer?
1. ☐ Yes   2. ☐ No

17 Date of Your Birth:
Month   Day   Year

18 Marital Status: 1. ☐ Married 2. ☐ Single

19 Education (Check which category applies):
1. ☐ High School   3. ☐ Completed College
2. ☐ Some College   4. ☐ Graduate School

20 Which best describes your family income?
1. ☐ Under $15,000   5. ☐ $50,000-$74,999
2. ☐ $15,000-$24,999   6. ☐ $75,000-$99,999
3. ☐ $25,000-$34,999   7. ☐ $100,000-$149,999
4. ☐ $35,000-$49,999   8. ☐ Over $150,000

21 Including yourself, what is the total number of people living in your household?

22 NOT including yourself, what are the AGES of any other people living in your household?

Age (in years)

Male:

Female:

23 In the last six (6) months have you or your spouse:
1. ☐ Purchased clothes through the mail?
2. ☐ Purchased gifts through the mail?
3. ☐ Worked in your garden?
4. ☐ Traveled on vacation?
5. ☐ Purchased a PC or PC software?
6. ☐ Purchased two or more books?
7. ☐ Purchased cassettes/CDs?
8. ☐ Donated to wildlife/environmental causes?
9. ☐ Donated to charities?

Thank you for filling out this questionnaire. Please check here [ ] if you would prefer not to participate in additional market research for Aiwa or obtain information on new and interesting opportunities from other companies.

use of these psychographic segmentation schemes. Sometimes these approaches can be used to identify lifestyle segments across country borders, but this requires considerable managerial judgment and expertise.[18]

A team of researchers at the Stanford Research Institute (SRI) developed several influential values-based lifestyle segmentation schemes widely used by firms in North America. **VALS 1** was based on the work of two psychologists: Abraham Maslow's hierarchy of human needs and David Reisman's concept of social character. The researchers sent questions concerning both general and specific attitude statements and demographic items to a national probability sample of Americans in a 1980 mail survey. Using the data gathered, they partitioned the market into nine groups, or VALS 1 segments, based on Maslow's hierarchical model of human needs (from most basic physiological needs to most abstract self-actualization needs) and Reisman's model of external or internal basic goal orientations. Exhibit 8.1 compares a profile of North American and European VALS 1 segments and shows the approximate percentage of U.S. residents in each group. The size of some segments is extremely small; others are extremely large.

VALS 1 enjoyed massive early success for clients as diverse as Merrill Lynch, Dr. Pepper, Clairol, and Folonari wine. Some versions of Merrill Lynch's long-running advertising campaign featuring a lone bull were targeted to achievers. By the late 1980s VALS 1 had outlived its usefulness. Among the criticisms were that the classifications were too abstract and general. In addition, its origins in developmental psychology does not seem especially applicable to consumer markets. As a result, there are too many similarities and too few differences between groups. Also, given the imbalance in size between segments, the system was not useful for identifying markets.

In response to criticisms of VALS 1, the team at SRI developed the **VALS 2** scheme that classifies people into segments on the bases whether they control abundant or minimal resources and three aspects of their basic motivational self-orientations: principles, status, or action. Using the dimensions of self-orientation and resources, VALS 2 has defined eight consumer segments with differing attitudes and behavior patterns. The groups are fairly balanced, proportionately ranging from 8 percent to 16 percent of the population, so that each represents a viable consumer target. The VALS 2 framework is shown in the Exhibit 8.2, along with brief descriptions for each of the eight segments. Marketers are advised to take different approaches when dealing with principle-oriented consumers versus status- or action-oriented ones. **Principle-oriented people** are *guided by intellectual matters*. The principle-oriented segments are labeled as fulfilleds and believers. **Status-oriented people** *alter their behavior to fit their surroundings to win the approval of important reference groups and individuals*. The two status-oriented segments are labeled as achievers and strivers. One difference between these two segments is the amount of resources available, indicated by the vertical axis in Exhibit 8.2. Achievers have access to more resources than strivers, as defined by the VALS 2 framework.

Action-oriented people *thrive on new social or physical activities*. Experiencers and makers are two such segments. The resource measure (the vertical axis in Exhibit 8.2) indicates the ability of a particular group to respond to an appeal to buy. VALS 2 recognizes that a wide range of constraints, from financial to psychological, can prevent a person's values from having free expression in the way they live. As shown in the exhibit, increasing resources are associated with increased ability to indulge their self-orientation through consumption.

The VALS 2 survey can be found at the SRI websites. The survey itself is relatively short, and some example questions are shown in Exhibit 8.3. By studying the actual questions in the exhibit, you may get a better idea of what the various VALS 2 segments mean.

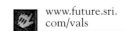
www.future.sri.
com/vals

Exhibit 8.1 Comparison of VALS 1 Segments in North America and Europe

	The Needy		Outer-Directed Goal Orientation		
Country	Survivors	Sustainers	Belongers	Emulators	Achievers
United States	Elderly, extremely poor, deprived, marginalized, lost. Highly price conscious, focused on basic, immediate needs. (4%)	Embittered, insecure persons. Streetwise. Near poverty, live off part-time, casual jobs. Price wise and cautious buyers. (7%)	Elderly, conservative patriots, sentimental, stable, traditional, middle class. Middle and lower mass markets; family and home-centered buying behavior. (35%)	Young, ambitious machos, dandies; upwardly mobile; demanding of themselves and others; dream of a future of self-fulfillment. Conspicuous consumers; purchase trends; imitative. (9%)	Middle-aged, prosperous leaders, sure of themselves, materialist; satisfied defenders of the status quo. Want products showing success; luxury and gift markets; new and improved products, top of the line. (22%)
France	Few in number but similar to the American segment. Share traits with sustainers and belongers.	Retirees and elderly persons often living in the country, poorly educated, creatures of habit, unwilling or unable to change.	Elderly; attached to the family, financial security, appearances, health, and others' opinions of oneself.	Young, but older and more reserved than in the U.S. Better educated, suspicious of ideologies, preoccupied with health.	Two groups: the first more mature and similar to Americans, the second is young and more intuitive, concerned with ecology and the environment.
Italy	Similar to North American survivors; often live in the slums around northern industrial cities.	The elderly. Poorly educated, originally from the country. Welfare recipients, fugitives.	Aging, authoritarian, fatalists, savers; reflective of their society and its problems.	Young, male, well educated; independent of their families. Materialists, avid readers.	Between two ages: tied to their family and religion (especially women), preoccupied with success.
Sweden	This group can be subdivided into two categories: an elderly group similar to that in the United States and a group of young school dropouts.	Typically better off than in the other countries. Anxious for their children, suspicious of public institutions, concerned about their security and their retirement.	Similar to the U.S., but more critical of social institutions and business.	A bit older, more preoccupied with their status. Desire a comfortable house and a calm lifestyle.	As interested by social standing as by money. Buy things that their children can inherit. Middle-class values.
Great Britain	Similar to Sweden. The school dropouts tend to be more aggressive and often organized into marginal subcultures: soccer hooligans, skinheads, and punks.	Traditional bearers of working-class values. Focused on their families. Critical or suspicious of public institutions; women are overrepresented.	Two groups: one similar to the U.S., the other more active and demanding.	Older, often female. Concerned with fashion and their social status.	Not very numerous; rich; older and fairly traditional.
Germany	More psychologically than materially disadvantaged. Fearful, alienated, envious, antibusiness. Women are overrepresented.	Negative and pessimistic, resigned and apathetic. More psychologically than materially disadvantaged; hypochondriac.	Similar to those in the U.S., but richer and better educated. Preoccupied with social status and prestige.	Very young, knowledgeable, masculine; preoccupied with social status and prestige.	Similar to those in the U.S., although more politically active and more concerned with the "green" movement.

Inner-Directed Goal Orientation

I Am Me	Experiential	Societally Conscious	Integrated
Exhibitionistic and narcissistic; young, impulsive, creative, active. Display their taste; clique buying; source of far-out fads. (5%)	Young, educated, artistic types eager for direct experience; person centered. Outdoor adventure; makers and doers. (7%)	Societally responsible; well educated; interested in inner growth; small is beautiful, simplicity. Conservation emphasis in consumption. (9%)	Psychological maturity; tolerant; self-actualizing; global perspective; sense of fittingness. Esthetically oriented; one-of-a kind buying. (2%)
Older, informed, contemplative; high job satisfaction; little concern with financial success.	Young, male, dissatisfied with their jobs; invest more in their leisure activities; hedonists and bon vivants.	Few in number; more occupied with societal responsibilities than those in the U.S.	Similar to the U.S. group; arbiters of cultural taste.
Knowledgeable; 25–35 years old; reject traditional values; extreme political views; live for the moment; easily bored.	Few in number; similar characteristics to the I am me's.	Well informed; very young; born after the 1960s; activists; strong cultural appetites.	Similar to the U.S. group; arbiters of cultural taste.
Older; entrepreneurial; reject alcohol and drug use. Favor an intense and highly emotional lifestyle.	Hedonists; like high risk and dangerous activities. Ready for anything.	In search of an authentic life; active members of the community. Preoccupied with the environment and society in general.	Similar to the U.S. group; arbiters of cultural taste.
Few in number; exhibitionistic but also societally conscious.	Knowledgeable, adventurous, creative; want jobs that allow them to demonstrate these qualities.	Young, well-educated, creative, family-oriented; want jobs that allow them to achieve. Critical of authority and technology.	Similar to the U.S. group; arbiters of cultural taste.
Older; invest in their work. Would like to influence society. Anxious, searching for ideals.	Few in number.	Few in number.	Similar to the U.S. group; arbiters of cultural taste.

Exhibit 8.2 VALS 2 Segment Profiles

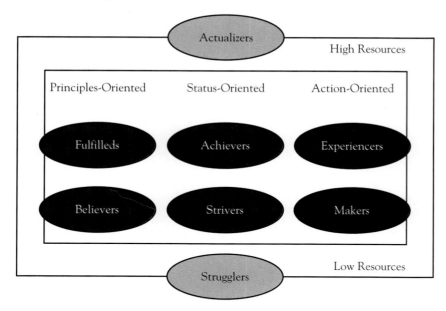

Actualizers are successful, sophisticated, active, take-charge people with high self-esteem and abundant resources. They are interested in growth and seek to develop, explore, and express themselves in a variety of ways—sometimes guided by principle, and sometimes by a desire to have an effect, to make a change.

Fulfilleds are mature, satisfied, comfortable, reflective people who value order, knowledge, and responsibility. Most are well educated and in (or recently retired from) professional occupations. They are well informed about world and national events and are alert to opportunities to broaden their knowledge. Content with their career, families, and station in life, their leisure activities tend to center around the home.

Achievers are successful career and work-oriented people who like to, and generally do, feel in control of their lives. They value consensus, predictability, and stability over risk, intimacy, and self-discovery. They are deeply committed to work and family. Work provides them with a sense of duty, material rewards, and prestige. Their social lives reflect this focus and are structured around family, church, and career.

Experiencers are young, vital, enthusiastic, impulsive, and rebellious. They seek variety and excitement, savoring the new, the offbeat, and the risky. Still in the process of formulating life values and patterns of behavior, they quickly become enthusiastic about new possibilities but are equally quick to cool. At this stage in their lives, they are politically uncommitted, uninformed, and highly ambivalent about what they believe.

Believers are conservative, conventional people with concrete beliefs based on traditional, established codes: family, church, community, and the nation. Many believers express moral codes that are deeply rooted and literally interpreted. They follow established routines, organized in large part around home, family, and social or religious organizations to which they belong.

Strivers seek motivation, self-definition, and approval from the world around them. They are striving to find a secure place in life. Unsure of themselves and low on economic social and psychological resources, strivers are concerned about the opinions and approval of others.

Makers are practical people who have constructive skills and value self-sufficiency. They live within a traditional context of family, practical work, and physical recreation and have little interest in what lies outside that context. Makers experience the world by working on it—building a house, raising children, fixing a car, or canning vegetables—and have enough skill, income, and energy to carry out their projects successfully.

Strugglers live constricted lifes. Chronically poor, ill educated, low skilled, without strong social bonds, elderly, and concerned about their health, they are often resigned and passive. Because they are limited by the need to meet the urgent needs of the present moment, they do not show a strong self-orientation. Their chief concerns are for security and safety.

Source: www.future.sri.com/vals.

Exhibit 8.3 Example Questions from the VALS 2 Survey

Question	Related VALS 2 Dimension
I love to make things I can use everyday.	Makers
I follow the latest trends and fashions.	Strivers
Just as the Bible says, the world literally was created in six days.	Believers
I like to learn about art, culture, and history.	Resource/skills question
I often crave excitement.	Experiencers
I would rather make something than buy it.	Makers
I dress more fashionably than most people.	Strivers
The federal government should encourage prayers in public schools.	Believers
I like trying new things.	Experiencers
I like to lead others.	Actualizers
I like doing things that are new and different.	Experiencers

Response format: mostly disagree; somewhat disagree; somewhat agree; mostly agree.

Demographic information is also collected: gender; age; level of formal education (a resource question); income (a resource question).

If you go to the website and take the survey yourself, you will find that you will be segmented into one of the following VALS types: actualizers, fulfilleds, achievers, experiencers, believers, strivers, makers, and strugglers. Actualizers are the highest in terms of resources. Strugglers are the lowest. Also on the website, you have the option of reading about each individual segment and the activities that are popular with each.

Some problems with the survey may include the wording of the questions and the lack of a neutral response. Most questions are worded in such a way that respondents may choose an answer that is socially desirable rather than one that is strictly honest. Questions are repeated several times with hardly any word changes. Thus, the survey might seem to be rather repetitive to some respondents. Finally, respondents are forced to agree or disagree with each statement. There is no option to be neutral about any of the questions, and level of agreement is either "somewhat" or "mostly," which may not be appropriate for extremely worded questions.

Other problems with the survey have been identified by Douglas Holt. According to Holt, segmenting people according to their values and lifestyle will give researchers some idea of what they consume, but how they consume will still be missing. Thus, it is important to take into account the context of consumption in order to understand the segments. Ethnographic research provides a way to understand various contexts, including in-depth interviews about how people use the products and services that they buy.[19] In contrast, psychographic research relies on a personality or values-based approach, where consumption patterns are identified for categories of goods owned and activities pursued. For instance, by administering a survey, it is discovered that achievers tend to own patio furniture at a higher than average rate.[20] Patio furniture is assumed to express the achiever lifestyle

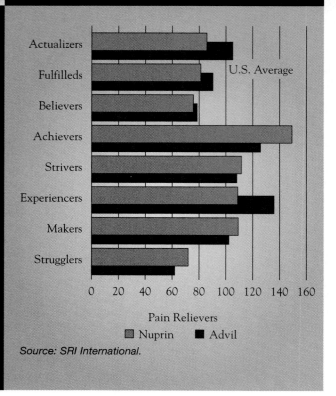

Pain Reliever Use by VALS 2 Type

Actualizers
Fulfilleds — U.S. Average
Believers
Achievers
Strivers
Experiencers
Makers
Strugglers

0 20 40 60 80 100 120 140 160

Pain Relievers

■ Nuprin   ■ Advil

Source: SRI International.

regardless of how it is understood and used by the actual consumers. Holt argues that an ethnographic approach (as an improvement on the survey method shown in Exhibit 8.3) allows for a deeper understanding of how people interact with consumption objects. He also points out that it is important to understand the full constellation of objects that people consume.

Like VALS 1, VALS 2 clarifies understanding of consumer segments for targeted marketing. As a first step, marketers might identify the light, heavy, and nonusing segments of the product category in question. For example, Industry Insights 8.3 compares pain reliever users by VALS 2 segments. The graphs show that experiencers, achievers, and strivers are most likely to use Advil, whereas achievers, strivers, experiencers, and makers are likely users of Nuprin. The graph also shows that Nuprin has a lower usage index among actualizers and experiencers than does Advil. The manufacturer might wish to target these groups. Alternatively, the marketer could investigate further to determine which groups are the heaviest users of pain relievers. It turns out that 43 percent of actualizers are heavy users of pain relievers but seem to prefer Advil.

Nuprin might wish to try to alter its approach to attract more actualizers, perhaps using words—such as variety, personal freedom, and excellence—and symbols—such as people who are involved and happy, active people—identified by SRI as attractive to actualizers.

The VALS systems have been used to segment markets and to target new product introductions. For each group one may define key product constellations as well as appropriate communication styles, media of communication, and particular elements of the marketing mix to emphasize.

Japan VALS

SRI has recently extended the VALS system to Japan. Like VALS 2, its typologies are based on product usage and behavior as well as attitudes. The **Japan VALS** identifies leaders of change and their relationship to emerging social trends. Japan VALS identifies five important dimensions:

Exploration—an individual's active involvement and motivation to master new challenges.

Self-expression—sociable, enjoys sports, and impulsive shoppers.

Achievement—career, status, leadership, and culture.

Tradition—stability, order, community, and traditional beliefs.

Realists—follow a reactive orientation to life; relatively unconcerned with self-improvement or fashion.

The exploration and achievement dimensions are statistically designed to predict activity with regard to innovation, consumption, production, and social control or mediation. Four main groups—change leaders, adapters, followers, and change resisters—divided into 10 standard segments emerge from the Japan VALS analysis. The Japan VALS analysis and characteristics of the groups are shown in Exhibit 8.4. In addition to the standard segmentation, Japan VALS defines three other levels of analysis that allow subscribers to focus on specific industry markets, niche segments for specific products and market opportunities, and international comparisons.

Understanding pressures experienced in different cultures can translate into market opportunities. For example, U.S. strivers want fun, stylish, fast, good-value cars. Japanese strivers consider their car like an extra room and will spend to add lace curtains or expensive stereos to them. A value appeal that might work well with a U.S. striver would be lost on a Japanese striver.[21]

List of Values (LOV) Approach

An alternative to the VALS scheme is the List of Values (LOV) approach developed at the University of Michigan. This approach was introduced in Chapter 5 in our discussion of cultural values. The LOV approach aims to assess adaptation to various roles through value fulfillment. People's dominant values are identified from a list of nine, including self-respect, security, warm relationships with others, sense of accomplishment, self-fulfillment, sense of belonging, being well respected, fun and enjoyment in life, and excitement. Research has found a significant number of predicted relationships between LOV dimensions and various criterion variables such as participation in certain commercially available activities like skiing, backpacking, camping, and so forth, and consumption of certain products.

Certain LOV values are associated with the values identified in VALS, such as an inner- or outward orientation, self-fulfillment, and accomplishment. Unlike VALS, there is no implicit evaluative dimension in the LOV such as the developmental contrast between marginal survivors and wealthy, healthy integrateds.

Cohort Analysis

Another useful way of anticipating lifestyle trends is to understand the power of cohorts. We provided some discussion of age cohorts in Chapter 6. In lifestyle terms, an age cohort is the group of people born over a relatively short and contiguous time period who are deeply influenced and bound together by the events of their formative years. In twentieth-century America, the passage to adulthood occurs roughly between the ages of 17 and 21. Events that happen when people first come of age create habits and attitudes that often last a lifetime and influence future attitudes and behaviors toward savings, sex, a good meal, musical preferences, and products and service preferences. Exhibit 8.5 outlines four of the six age cohorts that define the U.S. consumer market.[22]

Understanding cohort effects can improve predictions about changing lifestyles by sensitizing marketers to how generations will age differently than they have in the past. For example, consider coffee consumption. Over the past 40 years, coffee consumption has risen with age, while cola consumption has declined with age. Also, the number of 18- to 34-year-olds declined by 4 million in the 1990s, while the number of older adults grew by 24 million. This might on the surface suggest that demand for coffee will increase while demand for cola declines. However, this is based on a crucial premise that historic consumption rates by a particular age group will prevail in the future. A **cohort analysis** might instead suggest that younger, cola-intensive cohorts will continue to consume soft drinks even as they age. Meanwhile, older, coffee-intensive groups will age and move out of the marketplace. Baby boomers and other lower-consuming cohorts will replace them. This

Exhibit 8.4 Japan VALS Segments

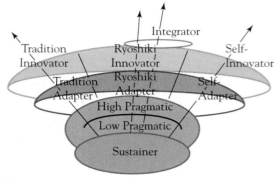

Change leader segments show high levels of consumer activity, a clear distinct self-concept, and high interests in many areas of life.

Adapter segments tend to follow the trends of change leaders near them, but at moderate levels of activity.

Follower segments tend to show no distinct pattern except risk avoidance.

Change resister segments show low consumer activity, generally reserved attitudes, and few strong interests.

Source: SRI International

Exploration

Integrators are well educated, very affluent, sociable adventurous, and stylish. Their values are modern and include Western values and some traditional ideas. They enjoy the new and risky and rank highest on a variety of consumer indicators. Integrators travel and read widely and are attracted to high-quality, prestigious products.

Sustainers are at the low end of the exploration dimension. They are resistant to change and lead lives of calm simplicity and traditional routine.

Self-Expression

Self-innovators are young, active, sociable, and very interested in fashion and leisure sports. They spend more on themselves in proportion to their income and are able to do so because many live with parents or friends. Some "office ladies" would be found in this group.

Self-adapters pattern their activities and product choices after the self-innovator group but are somewhat older and less active. They have below-average incomes and are less educated. They are shy, unassertive, and sensitive to others' opinions. They enjoy sports, tend to be impulsive shoppers, and read comics (which are huge in Japan) and fashion and lifestyle magazines.

Achievement

Ryoshiki innovators are committed to career and the social status quo. They have high education but average income, and many are middle-aged specialists or teachers. Their tastes tend toward cultural pursuits, fashion, exercise, socializing with spouses, and continuing education for self-betterment.

Ryoshiki adapters have higher incomes than Ryoshiki innovators. They are less assertive, less stressed, and more down to earth, well adjusted, and active. They have a moderate, modern outlook on life. Many own European furniture, expensive artwork, and home computers, and many play golf. They read the business newspaper *Nikkei* and business magazines.

Tradition

Tradition innovators are mostly middle-aged homeowners with jobs in middle management and primary industries who are active in community affairs. They are successful but avoid risk. They are highest in use of organic foods, health magazines, home repair, carpentry, local newspapers, and large luxury cars.

Tradition adapters are high but not extreme in the traditional orientation and have adapted the traditional innovator lifestyle. They are younger and better educated than traditional innovators and are the second most affluent of all the groups. Many are managers, entrepreneurs, farmers, or work in primary industries. They travel frequently on business, read health magazines, and enjoy doing home repair, fishing, and playing golf. They put their money into real estate and postal insurance funds.

Realists

High pragmatists are middle-aged, above average in income and education, but average in consumption. The group least likely to agree with any attitude statement, they seem withdrawn and suspicious. They are unconcerned about self-improvement, fashion, leading others, or preserving traditional customs. They appear to follow a flexible, even reactive, orientation to life with few fixed beliefs.

Low pragmatics are attitudinally negative and show a strong psychological tendency, except a slightly more positive stance, toward traditional customs. This group includes married women who take care of children at home and men who work as laborers, farmers, and fishermen. Their housing is modest, and many commute by bicycle. They are below-average consumers and prefer inexpensive goods and established brands.

Exhibit 8.5 Cohort Cartography: Some Age Cohorts That Define the U.S. Consumer Market

The World War II Cohort—born: 1922 to 1927; coming of age: 1940 to 1945; age in 1994: 67 to 72; current population: 11 million; share of adult population: 6 percent.

People who came of age in the early 1940s were unified by a common enemy and shared experiences. A sense of deferment was especially strong among the 16 million Americans in the military and their loved ones at home. Consequently, the World War II cohort became intensely romantic. Although it was not a boom time, unemployment was no longer a problem.

The Boomers I Cohort—born: 1946 to 1954; coming of age: 1963 to 1972; age in 1994: 40 to 48; current population: 33 million; share of adult population: 17 percent.

The two boomer cohorts are separated by the end of the Vietnam conflict. The Kennedy assassination, followed by those of Martin Luther King and Robert Kennedy, signaled an end to the status quo and galvanized the large boomer cohort. Still, the boomers I cohort continued to experience economic good times and wants a lifestyle at least as good as the one experienced as children in the 1950s.

The Boomers II Cohort—born: 1955 to 1965; coming of age: 1973 to 1983; age in 1994: 29 to 39; current population: 49 million; share of adult population: 25 percent.

After Watergate, something changed people coming of age in America. The idealistic fervor of youth disappeared. Instead, the boomers II cohort exhibited a narcissistic preoccupation with themselves, which manifested itself in everything from the self-help movement to self-deprecation in the media. Changes in the economy had a profound effect on this group. Debt as a means of maintaining a lifestyle made sense.

The Generation X Cohort—born: 1966 to 1976; coming of age: 1984 to 1994; age in 1994: 18 to 28; current population: 41 million; share of adult population: 21 percent.

Generation X has nothing to hang on to. These are children of divorce and day care, the latch-key kids of the 1980s. They are searching for anchors with their seemingly contradictory retro behavior: the resurgence of proms, coming-out parties, and fraternities. Their political conservatism is motivated by a what's-in-it-for-me? cynicism. Their alienation is reflected in the violence and brutal sex of their popular culture.

J. Walker Smith and Ann Clurman, Rocking the Ages: The Yankelovich Report on Generational Marketing *(New York: Harper Business, 1997); and Geoffrey Meredith and Charles Schewe ("The Power of Cohorts,"* American Demographics, *December 1994, pp. 22–31. See also Joseph O. Rentz and Fred D. Reynolds, "Forecasting the Effects of an Aging Population on Product Consumption: An Age-Period-Cohort Framework,"* Journal of Marketing Research *28 (1991), pp. 355–60; and Norman B. Ryder, "The Cohort as a Concept in the Study of Social Change,"* American Sociological Review *30 (December 1965), pp. 843–61.*

trend indicates that despite an aging population, demand for cola will not decline (e.g., the reverse effect). As other examples, consider food and music preferences. Certainly some eating habits are affected by aging. However, baby boomers aren't going to start baking lots of tuna casseroles and listening to Lawrence Welk when they turn 50. Because the enduring taste preferences of cohorts are often formed during the teenage years, they probably will still eat pizza and listen to rock 'n' roll. For example, the popularity of the Rock 'n' Roll Hall of Fame in Cleveland and the opening of Microsoft billionaire Paul Allen's rock 'n' roll museum outside of Seattle both speak to the enduring involvement of North American baby boomers with this music.[23]

Regional Lifestyles

For a variety of reasons, consumer culture varies geographically, or by region. These reasons include climate and topography, ethnic history, and the distribution of jobs and industries, among others. For example, in Latin America economic resources are often concentrated in a few large cities. Mexico City alone represents 60 percent of the purchasing power of Mexico. Southern Germans with their Catholic heritage differ in outlook from people in northern and eastern Germany with their Protestant and Prussian heritage. And those from southern and northern Germany differ from eastern Germans who experienced 50 years of Soviet domination. French-speaking, Catholic Quebecois differ in outlook from Anglican and Protestant English-speaking Canadians. Inclusive civic institutions and parenting styles in east Asian countries like Singapore and Japan moderate the rebelliousness and permissiveness associated with teenage lifestyles. By now we are all familiar with the regional differences that divide many countries politically as well. The point here is that lifestyle marketing needs to take regional variations into account.[24]

Regional differences affect consumption. In northern Europe, for example, butter is a prime ingredient in traditional cooking, whereas southern Europeans favor olive oil. In northern India, the staple food and drink is wheat (bread) and tea; in the south it is rice and coffee. In the United States, light vegetable, pasta, and fruit-laden California cuisine contrasts with the meat, potatoes, and gravy traditions of the Midwest, the Mexican-influenced cuisine of the Southwest, and the Caribbean-influenced cuisine of south Florida, for example.

A number of lifestyle segmentation systems have been developed to take **regional lifestyles** into account. Take, for example, the **nine nations of North America.** North America, excluding Quebec, has been divided into "nations" according to differences in cultural value orientations and lifestyles. Exhibit 8.6 summarizes these differences. Fun, enjoyment, and excitement is valued most by inhabitants of The Islands, comprising the

Exhibit 8.6 Psychographic Differences between the Regional Nations of North America[a]

Values	New England	The Foundry	Dixie	The Islands	Breadbasket	Mex-America	Empty Quarter	Ecotopia
Self-respect	22.5%	20.5%	22.5%	25.0%	17.9%	22.7%	35.3%	18.0%
Security	21.7	19.6	23.3	15.6	20.2	17.3	17.6	19.6
Warm relationships with others	14.2	16.7	13.8	9.4	20.5	18.0	5.9	18.5
Sense of accomplishment	14.2	11.7	10.0	9.4	12.4	11.3	8.8	12.2
Self-fulfillment	9.2	9.9	8.4	3.1	7.5	16.0	5.9	12.7
Being well respected	8.3	8.7	11.0	15.6	10.1	2.7	2.9	4.2
Sense of belonging	5.0	8.4	7.5	12.5	7.8	6.7	17.6	7.9
Fun, enjoyment, excitement	5.0	4.5	3.5	9.4	3.6	5.3	5.9	6.9

[a] The French-speaking region of Canada is excluded in this table.

Exhibit 8.7 Psychographic and Lifestyle Differences in the Seven Nations of China

	South	East	North	Central	Southwest	Northeast	Northwest
Household income	$27,481	$24,659	$12,993	$13,831	$14,008	$8,683	$7,770
Psychographics							
Satisfaction with life	66.6%	67.5%	81.3%	80.2%	66.8%	81.3%	67.6%
Work hard and get rich	33.3	31.6	30.7	34.6	42.3	44.2	67.1
Favor foreign brands	36.4	27.5	22.2	24.1	19.6	28.1	35.7
Lifestyle activities							
Going to movies	33.3	41.0	40.4	37.2	41.4	2.4	10.0
Listening to music	75.0	62.5	42.4	50.0	43.6	35.6	36.6
Traveling	25.0	23.1	17.7	27.9	22.3	32.9	4.3
Media usage							
Cable TV	83.3	69.2	68.3	68.9	68.8	28.3	14.3
Magazine	25.0	30.8	40.1	44.7	36.7	32.9	9.9
Consumer durables							
Refrigerator	91.7	94.9	74.7	69.6	64.2	39.6	24.7
Color TV	100.0	97.5	90.8	85.4	79.0	87.3	44.3
PC	18.2	7.7	4.5	3.2	4.5	2.7	2.9

Source: Geng Cui and Qiming Liu, "Regional Market Segments of China: Opportunities and Barriers in a Big Emerging Market," Journal of Consumer Marketing *17, no. 1 (2000), pp. 55–70.*

southern tip of Florida, for example. A sense of belonging is most highly prized by residents of the Empty Quarter, comprising Idaho, Montana, Wyoming, Utah, Nevada, and parts of some other states. Like other values-based schemes, the nine nations model has some intuitive appeal, but it has limited power to predict the values of any given consumer or his or her consumer behavior. Because of intracultural variation, other factors must be taken into account in explaining individual consumer behaviors.[25]

China too has been divided into regional lifestyle segments, seven in this case. Regional markets in the south and east represent China's growth markets. They are more economically developed and contain more affluent consumers. South China represents the Min-Yue culture, with plenty of contact with the outside world and great emphasis on mercantile entrepreneurship. South Chinese speak Cantonese and Fukienese. East China, located around the Yangtze River Delta, is densely populated, urbanized, and prosperous. Shanghai, the financial and industrial capital of China, is located here. East China represents the Hai-pai culture, well known for producing products that enhance quality of life. Consumers here are highly innovative and fashion trendsetters.

China's emerging markets are to be found in the north, central, and southwest. Each has its own distinctive culture and language differences. For example, in the north China city of Beijing, the capital of the country, the Jing-pai culture is strong, which attaches great value to Confucian doctrines. Consumers here are relatively more conservative than in the south. Finally, China's untapped markets are to be found in the northeast and northwest. Northwest China contains a large number of ethnic minorities. A few of the many intriguing psychographic and lifestyle differences between these complex regions are summarized in Exhibit 8.7.[26]

PRIZM cluster	Upward Bound	New Ecotopia	River City, USA
Description	Young, upscale, white-collar families	Rural, white/blue-collar, farm families	Middle-class, rural families
Demographics			
Age group	Under 18, 35–54	45+	Under 18, 45–54
Work status	Professional	White-collar, blue-collar, farming	Blue-collar, farming
Household income	$62,000	$39,000	$39,000
Percent of U.S. households	1.83%	0.9%	1.78%
Most likely to . . .	Be brand loyal Buy a new station wagon Have a 401(k) plan Watch "The Tonight Show" Read *Vogue*	Go cross-country skiing Own a dog Have a Keogh account Watch "Jeopardy!" Read *Prevention*	Go target shooting Travel by train Own a cat Watch TNN Read *Country Living*
Live in neighborhoods like . . .	Simi Valley, CA Herndon, VA Nashua, NH	Sutter Creek, CA East Chatham, NY Grafton, VT	Silver Creek, MN Springville, IA Coopers Mill, ME

Source: Adapted from yawyl.claritas.com/clusterlookup.asp?cluster.

PRIZM

PRIZM is *a lifestyle segmentation system that deals with regional lifestyles at a micro level.* It is based on the principle that people with similar lifestyles tend to live near one another. As the familiar saying predicts, birds of a feather flock together. Claritas, Inc.—a market research firm in Arlington, Virginia—originally created PRIZM over 20 years ago. It describes every U.S. neighborhood in terms of 62 distinct clusters, based on census data, consumer surveys, and other methods.[27] Industry Insights 8.4 shows some examples of the PRIZM clusters. In brief, the clusters are defined in terms of buying habits and media patterns. For instance, members of the Upward Bound cluster are more likely than the average household to read *Vogue* magazine and watch "The Tonight Show." At the same time, this cluster is brand loyal and more likely to purchase a new station wagon. As the name implies, the Upward Bound cluster consists of professional workers with relatively high incomes. People in this cluster live in towns such as Simi Valley, California, and Herndon, Virginia.

PRIZM is useful for marketers because it can identify groups of consumers who perform at or above average levels for product purchases. PRIZM identifies neighborhoods where existing customers live, and it can be used to predict where prospective customers are likely to be found. The reports generated by PRIZM can be used to answer such questions as: Who are my targets? What are they like (e.g., in terms of demographics)? Where can I find them? For instance, PRIZM software can be used to create prospect lists for direct-mail campaigns, or it could be used to suggest media vehicles (e.g., magazines) for an ad campaign.

PRIZM ... ode: Athens, GA 30605

Industry Insights 8.5

PRIZM cluster	Towns and Gowns			God's Country	Middleburg Managers
Description	College singles			Executive exurban families	Midlevel, white-collar couples
Demographics					
Age group	18–3...			35–64	35–44, 65+
Work status	White-collar, se...			White-collar	Professional, white-collar
Household income	$19,...			$65,300	$42,000
Percent of U.S. households	1.39...			2.63%	1.72%
Most likely to . . .	Be c... ba... Own... co... Have... lo... Watch "Friends" Read *Glamour*	...ect ...ave ...rs Watch BET Read *GQ*	Watch country music TV Read *Southern Living*	Shop online each month Own a garden tiller/tractor Have tax-sheltered annuities Watch "This Old House" Read *Colonial Homes*	Jog or run Own a laptop computer Have a home equity loan Watch the QVC channel Read *PC* magazine
Live in neighborhoods like . . .	Madison, WI Bowling Green, OH Gainesville, FL	Saginaw, MI Shreveport, LA Mobile, AL	McQueeney, TX Opolis, KS West Rockport, ME	South Austin, TX Forsyth, IL Watertown, CT	East Olympia, WA Charleston, WV Panama City, FL

Source: Adapted from yawyl.claritas.com/clusterlookup.asp?cluster.

PRIZM data can be accessed via postal zip codes. Each zip code may contain many clusters. Industry Insights 8.5 shows the top five clusters for the zip code 30605, which is part of a college town, Athens, Georgia. Important clusters in this zip code include the Towns and Gowns, college-town singles who are likely to own a computer and have a school loan. Another key cluster in 30605 is the New Homesteaders (young, middle-class families). This group is likely to shop by direct mail, buy microwave cookware, and read *Southern Living*. Go to the Claritas website and look up your own zip code to learn more about the PRIZM system of lifestyle segmentation. Do the PRIZM clusters that appear for your zip code make sense? Why or why not? It is important to realize that a single zip code can contain more than 15 significant clusters, so the five that appear on the website may not always seem complete to you.

 yawyl.claritas.com

Shifting Lifestyles

In this chapter we have talked mostly about psychographic segmentation schemes designed to identify and profile similar groups in the current marketplace. However, another very important focus for lifestyle and psychographic research is to provide general insights into emerging social trends and evolving lifestyles. Identifying lifestyle trends is one of the most difficult applications of psychographic research, and yet it is perhaps one of the most vital. Lifestyle trends are triggered by major demographic shifts, such as Japanese women entering the workforce, U.S. women having babies later in life and returning to work sooner, or U.S. baby boomers aging. But lifestyle trends are also triggered by important attitudinal shifts, such as European consumers' growing commitment to organic food or the casual dress trend in corporate America. Lifestyle trends such as these affect the lives and welfare of numerous industries and can be decisive for many products and services. Successful strategic planning relies on identifying these trends early and separating out trends from fads (see Chapter 16 for a discussion of trends versus fads). Let's look at just a couple of specific lifestyle trends and consider their implications for products and services.

Consider the dramatic increase in the number of Japanese working women. Although Japanese women haven't become as liberated as Western women, they are at least as busy. More than half of Japan's married women now hold full- or part-time jobs, and women account for 40.5 percent of the Japanese workforce. Although many Japanese advertisers still use images of the stereotypical housewife, others are addressing the new breed of working women in products as diverse as frozen vegetables, cigarettes, and nonsmear lipstick.[28] Nonsmear lipstick didn't even exist ten years ago, but now it's a $45 million a month business in Japan. The popularity is attributed to the working Japanese woman who prefers brands that eliminate time-consuming reapplications. As an aside, it solves a common problem for Japanese men as well. A survey by a Japanese cosmetics manufacturer (Shiseido) found that 40 percent of all male commuters have been smeared by lipstick in Tokyo's jam-packed trains and subways. "This can cause a riot at home," a Shiseido spokesman said, and in a culture that abhors a loss of face, the nonsmear lipstick helps avoid this problem.

Another subtle lifestyle shift that has important implications for clothes makers is the trend toward dressing down in corporate America as suggested by the photo on page 299. A recent study revealed that almost 90 percent of U.S. workers are dressing down at least some of the time. The casual Friday trend has created an important growth in corporate casual clothing. Companies like Levi Strauss are aggressively attempting to capitalize on the trend. Levi Strauss is targeting businesses with newsletters to human resources managers about why casual dress codes should be adopted and following up with how-to kits, videos on the fine art of dressing down, and casual dress fashion shows. Its competitor, Haggar, long known for custom-fit suits and sports suits, is moving toward casual wear with a line called City Casuals.

Sometimes, a single person can personify a lifestyle. One example in the United States of such a person is Martha Stewart, a woman who has created an empire to promote her ideas about a style of elegant living. She is viewed as the "ultimate homemaker," and she strives to teach the masses how to create "the good life." She provides an example of a marketer who teaches cultural capital—knowledge of specialized consumption genres—to the upwardly mobile nouveau riche as discussed in Chapter 6.

The Martha Stewart lifestyle did not exist in the early 1960s, but it is a conspicuous force in the early twenty-first century. In fact, Martha Stewart, Inc., is a public corporation with the following components: magazines (*Martha Stewart Weddings, Martha Stewart Entertaining*), books (*Martha Stewart Cookbook*), cable TV ("From Martha's Kitchen"),

Levi Strauss and Haggar are just two of the companies capitalizing on the lifestyle trend toward casual business dress.

Internet sites (chat groups, *askMartha*), catalogs (Martha by Mail), specialty products (a garden equipment line for Kmart), and others. Martha Stewart sees herself as a purveyor of information. She got her start by catering elaborate parties in the 1970s. Subsequently, she published her landmark book, *Martha Stewart Entertaining,* which has sold more than 500,000 copies. In brief, the Martha Stewart lifestyle represents investing a large amount of time in adding ornamentation to life, especially in the areas of cooking, home decor, design, gift giving, celebrations (e.g., weddings), and parties. It involves a search for casual elegance and sometimes is seen as embodying the "perfect housewife" image. As with any trend, however, there is a countertrend. For instance, detractors say her name has become synonymous with an unobtainable and slightly ridiculous standard in the domestic arts. Many of Martha Stewart's recommended household projects seem as if they require hours, if not days, to complete. Some U.S. consumers put out welcome mats that say, "Martha Stewart doesn't live here."[29]

International Lifestyle Segments

Lifestyle segmentation schemes are popular worldwide. National and international schemes have been developed in all the major European countries and for European consumers as a whole. In France, the COFRECMA Sociostyles scheme is widely used, and in Denmark a popular scheme called Minerva identifies lifestyle segments by color.

Backer Spielvogel & Bates Worldwide (BSB) has created **Global Scan,** *an evolving psychographic segmentation scheme including at least 18 countries* (mostly Triad and Pacific Rim countries). Global Scan measures a wide variety of attitude and consumer values,

Global Scan

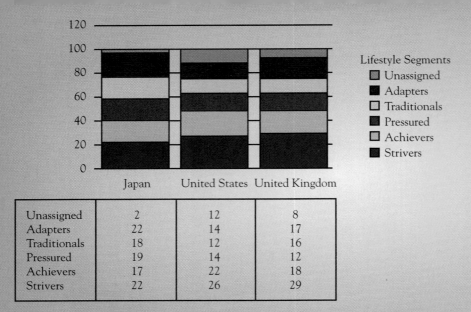

	Japan	United States	United Kingdom
Unassigned	2	12	8
Adapters	22	14	17
Traditionals	18	12	16
Pressured	19	14	12
Achievers	17	22	18
Strivers	22	26	29

Source: Rebecca Piirto, Beyond Mind Games, Ithaca, NY: American Demographics Books, 1991.

media use, and buying patterns. Repeat surveys are conducted annually in each country to ensure the model remains reflective of the population. Both higher-order values like self-sufficiency and self-esteem and personality characteristics are included in the survey, as are political opinions and attitudes about social issues. To improve applicability, consumers are questioned directly on their use of more than 1,000 brands and products.

BSB claims 95 percent of the combined population of all the countries surveyed can be assigned to five segments. These segments are **adapters** (18 percent), **traditionals** (16 percent), **pressureds** (13 percent), **achievers** (22 percent), and **strivers** (26 percent). A three-country comparison is shown in Industry Insights 8.6. As can be seen from the diagram, the five general groups are found in varying proportions in the countries studied. For example, there are fewer traditionals in the United States than in Japan or the UK, while the UK has proportionately more strivers and Japan has more adapters.

Global Scan allows marketers to identify cross-cultural and local differences. Canadian strivers are more open-minded and liberal than their U.S. counterparts, but they are also more materialistic, ambitious, optimistic, and risk taking. Canadian achievers, the affluent opinion leader segment, enjoy one of the highest-quality lifestyles of any country surveyed. The pressured segment, those with familial and financial worries, are found in greater proportion in Quebec than in any other Canadian province.

In the next section, we briefly present examples of lifestyle segments that exist in three countries: Turkey, New Zealand, and China. It is interesting to note how these lifestyle segments differ across the three nations and how they differ from lifestyle segments that have been identified in the United States (for example, VALS 2). These three countries are discussed because recent lifestyle research has been completed there and because they represent regions where lifestyles are likely to be quite different from those discussed in traditional schemes (for example, VALS).[30]

Exhibit 8.8 Lifestyle Segments in New Zealand

Segment Name	Population	Description
Active family values people	15.5%	Family and community focus Traditional principles Positive outlook
Conservative quiet lifers	13.5	Homebodies Conservative views Reflective and nostalgic
Educated liberals	9.0	Socially concerned Progressive and egalitarian Enjoy variety and diversity
Accepting mid-lifers	17.1	Observe rather than partake Accepting of status quo Content
Success-driven extroverts	16.4	Self-oriented Value free enterprise Actively ambitious
Pragmatic strugglers	14.7	Family survival focus Politically conservative Determined
Social strivers	13.0	Outer directed Conformist Feel life is a struggle

Source: Sarah Todd, Rob Lawson, and Fiona Faris, "A Lifestyle Analysis of New Zealand Consumers," Asia Pacific Journal of Management and Logistics 10, no. 3 (1998), pp. 30–47.

Turkish Lifestyles

In a recent study, three lifestyle segments were identified for Turkish consumers. The first segment is labeled liberals/trendsetters. These consumers are somewhat similar to those in Western nations. They are mostly college educated and high-income earners. Important characteristics for these consumers include quality, workmanship, prestigious brand name, and style. Price is not especially important to this group.[31]

The second and third clusters are labeled moderates/survivors and traditionalists/conservatives. A major difference between clusters two and three is that the former contains mostly males. Group three contains many females, but key purchase decisions (for example, automobiles) are made by male family members. Prestige and style are not so important. Price is very important. As a whole, the traditionalist segment does not have a favorable attitude toward imported Western products, in contrast to the relatively positive attitudes of the liberals/trendsetters.

New Zealand Lifestyles

In a 1998 study of 3,773 New Zealanders, six major segments were identified (see Exhibit 8.8). These include active family values people, conservative quiet lifers, educated liberals, accepting mid-lifers, success-driven extroverts, pragmatic strugglers, and social strivers. Some of the segments have parallels in VALS 2. For instance, the pragmatic strugglers are somewhat like the strugglers in VALS 2, but this group also shares something in common with the VALS's makers. As the name implies, the strivers and the social strivers are similar. The VALS's achievers and the New Zealand extroverts share common characteristics.[32]

The accepting mid-lifers is one group that doesn't have a clear counterpart in the VALS 2 classification system. The mid-lifers are generally accepting of their lives and of society. They lack a strong feeling regarding political and social issues. They like things as they are and are not so willing to try new things (for example, new brands or products). With regard to food products, their most important criterion is taste. They are not so concerned with sugar or cholesterol intake. Mid-lifers don't received much enjoyment from shopping. At the same time, they are not very brand loyal. They are likely to use credit cards and purchase items such as videocassette recorders, compact disc players, and more than one television. The New Zealand study illustrates the value of combining psychological variables (for example, novelty seeking) with marketing information (for example, data about the purchase of specific brands or products).

Segments for Chinese Females

A segmentation study for females living in greater China was completed in 1998.[33] Greater China is defined as residents of three different countries: People's Republic of China, Taiwan, and Hong Kong. A total of four segments was identified for females between the ages of 18 and 35: conventional women (40.7 percent of the population), contemporary women (21.9 percent), searching singles (19.4 percent), and followers (18.1 percent).

It is interesting to note that the conventional segment corresponds somewhat to the traditionalist/conservative segment identified in Turkey. Conventional women are proud of having a close-knit family, and they consider family to be the most important aspect of their life. In terms of recreation, they are indoor types and prefer reading newspapers and books or watching television.

Contemporary women share some characteristics in common with conventional women, especially with regard to the importance of family. However, this group believes that work is also important, and they try to combine family and work into their lifestyle. Unlike the conventional women, contemporary women are likely to voice a complaint when they are dissatisfied with a product or service. They are very concerned about their appearance and prefer imported and branded products.

Searching singles have more progressive ideas about the role of women in society. For instance, they are more career oriented, and they postpone marriage longer. Females in this group like to go shopping and are concerned with the image of the store where they shop. They are especially influenced by sales announcements and the image of the brand. Also, they are heavy users of fast food and entertainment services.

Women in the fourth and final segment, followers, are not very active in social, cultural, or other physical activities. They don't make as many shopping trips as those in some of the other groups. More than half of them are single, and they have achieved relatively low levels in both education and income. Followers lack confidence and are somewhat uncertain about the future. Consequently, they like to seek advice from salespeople about the products they buy.

In general, the Chinese segments do not share much in common with the segments identified in New Zealand. The New Zealand segments are more like those that might be found in a European or North American country. The Chinese segments are more similar to those found in Turkey. This makes sense in that China and Turkey are both developing nations, and both have a culture that sometimes clashes with consumption values as they are represented in the Triad nations.

Criticisms of Lifestyles Research

It is important to note the major criticisms of lifestyles research. These criticisms warn of overenthusiastic use of psychographic data and point out challenges for future marketing research. First, there is a general conceptual problem. The central concepts (i.e., lifestyles, psychographics, AIO research) tend to be ill-defined. Also, it is not always clear *why* particular segments express particular consumer preferences. Predictions of emerging patterns are especially difficult. Are psychographic profiles predictive of consumer behaviors (e.g., purchase behaviors)?

Second, there is a problem associated with the secret, often ad hoc, nature of the methods used to develop lifestyle schemes. To what extent are lifestyle segments stable over time? Current lifestyle measures are not very good at capturing the fluidity of lifestyle segment membership. That is, people are likely to change lifestyle segments over time. Finally, there tends to be a fairly low correlation between lifestyle segments and particular behaviors such as brand choice that are of great interest to many companies. The consumption of many low-involvement products may not be closely related to lifestyle variables.[34]

summary

In this chapter, we describe the concept of consumer lifestyle. We then introduce the notion of role-related product constellations and the idea that consumers can perceive sets of products as belonging together to help them express personal and group identity. We next discuss psychographics and AIO as ways of implementing lifestyle research. We show how lifestyles segmentation studies have been used by firms to link segments and products, to position products, and to target media vehicles effectively. Several highly influential commercial lifestyles segmentation schemes (VALS, LOV, PRIZM, Global Scan, and cohort analysis) are explored. The chapter also shows that lifestyles may be profiled at different levels of aggregation depending on marketers' purposes. We discuss regional, national, and international lifestyles schemes such as one used in China, PRIZM, and Global Scan in some detail. Brief portraits of lifestyles in Turkey, New Zealand, and China are introduced. We conclude with a discussion of some limitations associated with lifestyle research.

key terms

achievement   290
achievers   300
action-oriented people   285
adapters   300
AIO measures   282
brand tribes   278
cohort analysis   291
exploration   290
Global Scan   299
Japan VALS   290
nine nations of North America   294
pressureds   300
principle-oriented people   285

PRIZM   296
product constellations   277
psychographics   281
realists   290
regional lifestyles   294
self-expression   290
status-oriented people   285
strivers   300
tradition   290
traditionals   300
VALS 1   285
VALS 2   285

1. Assume you have recently been employed by Starbuck's coffee to prepare an analysis of the market for iced coffee. The marketing director is interested in doing a psychographic study and has asked you to prepare a questionnaire. Be sure to indicate the specific content of the questionnaire and some sample questions.

2. Governmental sources show that, between 1983 and 1992, the number of U.S. births rose 11.7 percent. This abundance of babies is causing major lifestyle changes. Not only are women having more babies, they are giving birth later and returning to work more quickly afterward. Develop a list of products and services that are affected by this trend. For one product or service, develop a promotional appeal incorporating the lifestyle of a new mother, over 30 years old, who returned to a professional job eight weeks after her baby boy was born.

3. Develop a short description of your own lifestyle and the lifestyle of a close friend or relative. How are they similar? How are they different? Now consider all of the psychographic measures presented in this chapter. Which scheme fits best with your lifestyle and that of your friend? Try to label yourself and your friend using one of the breakdowns given.

4. Assume that you are in charge of targeting a new no-fat, premium-priced cookie that tastes sinful. What lifestyle segments can you identify for this type of product?

5. Assume that you are in the hosiery industry and are attempting to forecast future demand for pantyhose. What lifestyle trends can you identify that might affect the growth of pantyhose sales over the next five years? Explain your answer.

7. You are in charge of marketing, attendance, and membership for a new independent film theater that has just opened in your city. Using the VALS 2 framework, develop different appeals to reach principle-oriented, status-oriented, and action-oriented consumers.

8. Your company markets a fashionable, expensive, and high-performance line of ski clothing. You are finalizing partnering arrangements to distribute your line in Japan. Which Japanese VALS segments would you target with your ski clothing? Outline some promotional appeals that you might use.

9. Suppose you have been asked to design a social marketing campaign to encourage a drug-free lifestyle to run on Planet Hip-Hop Radio DJ-ed by Ice T, found at www. mediatrip.com/per/Radio/Planet_Hip-Hop_Radio.html. Describe some key elements of source and message that you would use.

You Make the Call

Earth's Best Baby Food

Have you heard of Earth's Best Baby Food? Maybe not. But in the 15 years since Earth's Best Baby Food was born it has moved into a solid number four position behind category powerhouses Gerber, Beech Nut, and Heinz—despite the fact Earth's Best's retail price is at least 50 percent higher. Earth's Best Baby Food is a tiny Colorado company with only a few dozen employees. Unable to afford big-budget ad campaigns, Earth's Best opts for folksy direct mail, co-marketing with other green marketers, and development of a user-friendly website.

www.earthsbest.com

This strategy is in keeping with its wholesome image as a purveyor of pure, healthy baby foods. The website provides information on organic foods and links to related websites. Earth's Best communicates that it is a little company that really cares and is out to do something right for babies and the world. According to Mike Mondello, vice president of marketing, "The idea moves beyond organic." A important part of the company's promotion is a periodic newsletter *Earth's Best Family Times.* The newsletter promotes brand loyalty with the sale of items such as Earth's Best place mats, T-shirts, and bibs as well as rebate and coupon offers. The newsletter also includes an invitation to send the company the name of a new mother who might like receiving the newsletter. The website includes a Q&A section where a physician will answer health care questions related to pregnancy and baby care. The newsletter and website serve to nurture the caring image of the company by including advice from pediatricians and answers to parents' questions.

The whole company is built around relationship marketing, but a key question is, Who buys Earth's Best Baby Food and what is their lifestyle? By answering this question, Earth's Best hopes it can be more effective in developing a relationship with their customers and growing in a way consistent with their customers' lifestyle needs. Management believes that positioning the product as a cut above other baby foods is a surefire hook with working mothers who feel a bit guilty about spending less time with their children.

1. Take a look at the website. Then, see if you can profile the Earth's Best Baby Food buyer.

2. Assume the vice president of marketing is interested in doing a psychographic study and has asked you to prepare a questionnaire. Describe the specific content you would put in and give some sample questions.

3. Describe the lifestyle segments that Earth's Best appeals to.

4. Discuss the strengths of Earth's Best's system for research and strategy.

5. Describe some alternative strategic/promotional directions for Earth's Best.

This case is adapted from public corporate communications.

1. Sources for this vignette are "From Raï to Rap," *The Economist,* June 10, 2000. p. 91; "Moreover: One Way to Get Rich in Soweto," *The Economist,* March 4, 2000, pp. 85–86; Ayse S. Caglar, "Popular Culture, Marginality and Institutional Incorporation: German-Turkish Rap and Turkish Pop in Berlin," *Cultural Dynamics* 10 (November 1998); Wayne Friedman, "Converse Hopes Master P Can Dunk Shoe Sales Trend," *Advertising Age,* Midwest region edition, June 7, 1999, p. 50; Scot Johnson and Amanda Bernard, "The New Arab Woman," *Newsweek International,* June 12, 2000, pp. 22–23; Devin Leonard, "Living without a Leader," *Fortune,* March 20, 2000, p. 218; Kembrew McLeod, "Authenticity within Hip-Hop and Other Cultures Threatened with Assimilation," *Journal of Communication* 49, no. 4 (Autumn 1999), pp. 134–50; Allison Samuels, "Rap's Ultimate Outsiders," *Newsweek,* February 28, 2000, p. 67; Scott Stossel, "Gate Crashers," *The New Republic,* August 30, 2000, pp. 16–18; and Juliana Verdone, "Music to the People," *Inc.,* May 16, 2000, p. 98.

2. See David G. Moore, "Life Style in Mobile Suburbia," in *Toward Scientific Marketing,* Stephen A. Greyser, ed. (Chicago: American Marketing Association, 1963), pp. 140–49; and W. Thomas Anderson, Jr. and Linda L. Golden, "Lifestyle and Psychographics: A Critical Review and Recommendation," in *Advances in Consumer Research,* vol. 11, Thomas C. Kinnear, ed. (Provo, UT: Association for Consumer Research, 1984), pp. 405–11.

3. Anderson and Golden, "Lifestyle and Psychographics."

4. Anderson and Golden, "Lifestyle and Psychographics."

5. See Eugene J. Kelley, "Discussion," in *Toward Scientific Marketing,* Stephen A. Greyser, ed. (Chicago: American Marketing Association, 1963), pp. 164–71.

6. Douglas B. Holt, "How Consumers Consume: A Typology of Consumption Practices," *Journal of Consumer Research* 22 (June 1995), pp. 1–16; and William Wells, *Lifestyle and Psychographics* (Chicago: American Marketing Association, 1974).

7. Julie Caniglia, "Lifestyles of the Privileged Poor," *Utne Reader,* July–August 1993, pp. 21–22; and Craig J. Thompson and Siok Kuan Tambyah, "Trying to Be Cosmopolitan," *Journal of Consumer Research* 26 (December 1999), pp. 214–41.

8. future.sri.com/vals, May 25, 2000.

9. Jim Hancock and No Fear Apparel are profiled in "The Marketing 100," *Advertising Age,* June 26, 1995, p. S28.

10. Susan Fournier, David Antes, and Glenn Beaumier, "Nine Consumption Lifestyles," in *Advances in Consumer Research,* vol. 19, John Sherry and Brian Sternthal, eds. (Provo, UT: Association for Consumer Research, 1991), pp. 329–37.

11. Michael R. Solomon and Henry Assael, "The Forest or the Trees?: A Gestalt Approach to Symbolic Consumption," in *Marketing and Semiotics: New Directions in the Study of Signs for Sale,* Jean Umiker-Sebeok, ed. (New York: Mouton de Gruyter, 1987), p. 206.

12. Karl Taro Greenfeld, "The Obsession of the Otaku," *Los Angeles Times Magazine,* September 12, 1993, pp. 40–43; and www.altculture.com/aentries/o/otaku.html.

13. J. N. Kapferer, "Publicité: Une révolution des méthodes de travail," *Revue Française de gestion,* September–December 1985, pp. 102–11.

14. Lewis Alpert and Ronald Gatty, "Product Positioning by Behavioral Lifestyles," *Journal of Marketing* 33 (April 1969), pp. 65–69; Brenda Gainer and Eileen Fischer, "Community and Consumer Behavior," working paper, Queen's University, Ontario, Canada, 1995; Jeff Kaye, "The Raves of Europe," *Los Angeles Times,* 1993, pp. F1, F7, E1, E3; Michael R. Solomon, "Mapping Product Constellations: A Social Categorization Approach to Consumption Symbolism," *Psychology and Marketing* 5 (Fall 1988), pp. 233–57; Michael R. Solomon and Punam Anand, "Ritual Costumes and Status Transitions: The Female Business Suit as Totemic Emblem," in *Advances in Consumer Research,* vol. 11, Thomas Kinnear, ed. (Provo, UT: Association for Consumer Research, 1984), pp. 315–18; Solomon and Assael, "The Forest or the Trees?" pp. 189–218; and Pierre Valette-Florence, *Les styles de vie: Bilan critique et perspectives* (Paris: Nathan, 1994).

15. Harold H. Kassarjian and Mary Jane Sheffert, "Personality and Consumer Behavior: An Update," in *Perspectives in Consumer Behavior,* 4th ed., Harold H. Kassarjian and Thomas S. Robertson, eds. (Englewood Cliffs, NJ: Prentice Hall, 1991), pp. 281–303.

16. Steven J. Hoch, "Who Do We Know: Predicting the Interests and Opinions of the American Consumer," *Journal of Consumer Research* 15 (December 1988), pp. 315–24; and William D. Wells, "Psychographics: A Critical Review," *Journal of Marketing Research* 12 (May 1975), pp. 196–213.

17. Kassarjian and Sheffert, "Personality and Consumer Behavior"; Wells, "Psychographics: A Critical Review"; "Consuming Images," video, Corporation for Public Broadcasting; and Shirley Young, "Research Both for Strategic Planning and for Tactical Testing," *Proceedings,* 19th Annual Conference, Advertising Research Foundation, New York, 1971, pp. 13–16.

18. Arnold Mitchell, "Nine American Lifestyles: Values and Societal Change," *The Futurist* 18 (August 1984), pp. 4–13; and Wagner A. Kamakura and Jose Alfonso Masson, "Value Segmentation: A Model for the Measurement of Values and Value Systems," *Journal of Consumer Research* 18 (September 1991), pp. 208–18.

19. Douglas B. Holt, "Poststructuralist Lifestyle Analysis: Conceptualizing the Social Patterning of Consumption in Postmodernity," *Journal of Consumer Research* 23 (March 1997), pp. 326–50; and Douglas B. Holt, "Does Cultural Capital Structure American Consumption?" *Journal of Consumer Research* 25 (June 1998), pp. 1–25.

20. Arnold Mitchell, *The Nine American Lifestyles* (New York: Warner, 1983).

21. Rebecca Piirto, *Beyond Mind Games: The Marketing Power of Psychographics* (Ithaca: American Demographics Books, 1991).

22. J. Walker Smith and Ann Clurman, *Rocking the Ages: The Yankelovich Report on Generational Marketing* (New York: Harper Business, 1997); and Geoffrey Meredith and Charles Schewe, "The

Power of Cohorts," *American Demographics,* December 1994, pp. 22–31; see also Joseph O. Rentz and Fred D. Reynolds, "Forecasting the Effects of an Aging Population on Product Consumption: An Age-Period-Cohort Framework," *Journal of Marketing Research* (1991), pp. 355–60; and Norman B. Ryder, "The Cohort as a Concept in the Study of Social Change," *American Sociological Review* 30 (December 1965), pp. 843–61.

23. Meredith and Schewe, "The Power of Cohorts," p. 31.

24. Ronald A. Fullerton, "Marketing and the Economic Redevelopment in East Germany: Field Observations and Theoretical Analysis," in *Marketing and Economic Restructuring in the Developing World,* Luis V. Dominguez, ed. (San Jose, Costa Rica: INCAF, 1993), pp. 145–51; T. R. Reid, *Confucius Lives Next Door* (New York: Vintage Books, 1999); and Thomas Tan Tsu Wee, "An Exploration of a Global Teenage Lifestyle in Asian Societies," *Journal of Consumer Marketing* 16, no. 4 (1999), pp. 365–75.

25. Joel Garreau, *The Nine Nations of North America* (Boston: Houghton Mifflin, 1981); and Lynn R. Kahle, "The Nine Nations of North America and the Value Basis of Geographic Segmentation," *Journal of Marketing,* April 1986, pp. 37–47.

26. Geng Cui and Qiming Liu, "Regional Market Segments of China: Opportunities and Barriers in a Big Emerging Market," *Journal of Consumer Marketing* 17, no. 1 (2000), pp. 55–70.

27. yawyl.claritas.com, May 2000.

28. Jack Russell, "Working Women Give Japan Culture Shock," *Advertising Age,* January 16, 1995, p. 124; and Jack Russell, "At Last, a Product That Makes Japan's Subways Safe for Men," *Advertising Age,* January 16, 1995, p. 124.

29. Diane Brady, "Inside the Growing Empire of America's Lifestyle Queen," *Business Week,* January 17, 2000, pp. 63–72.

30. Bernard Cathelat, *Styles de vie: Courants & scénarios,* vol. 2, Collection CCA (Paris: Les Editions D' Organisation, 1985); Bernard Dubois, *Comprendre le consommateur* (Paris: Duboz, 1994), pp. 195–97; and Valette-Florence, *Les styles de vie: Bilan critique et perspectives.*

31. Orsay Kucukemiroglu, "Market Segmentation by Using Consumer Lifestyle Dimensions and Ethnocentrism: An Empirical Study," *European Journal of Marketing* 33, no. 5–6 (1999), pp. 1–9.

32. Sarah Todd, Rob Lawson, and Fionna Faris, "A Lifestyle Analysis of New Zealand Consumers," *Asia Pacific Journal of Marketing and Logistics* 10, no. 3 (1998), pp. 30–47.

33. Jackie L. M. Tam and Susan H. C. Tai, "Research Note: The Psychographic Segmentation of the Female Market in Greater China," *International Marketing Review* 15, no. 1 (1998), pp. 25–41.

34. Bernard Dubois, *Comprendre le consommateur* (Paris: Duboz, 1994), pp. 195–97; Wells, "Psychographics: A Critical Review"; and William D. Wells, "Discussion," in *Advances in Consumer Research,* vol. 7, Jerry C. Olson, ed. (Ann Arbor: Association for Consumer Research, 1980), p. 473.

Chapter 9

Learning Objectives

After completing this chapter, you should be able to:

- Explain the meaning of and relationship between perceptions and sensations and discuss some basic facts about the classic five sensory receptors: vision, smell, hearing, touch, and taste.

- Describe how sensory thresholds are used by marketers, including marketing applications of Weber's law.

- Outline the process through which our sensory systems select, organize, and interpret stimuli, including preattentive processing, perceptual selection, organization and categorization, interpretation, and elaboration.

- Describe some basic tools consumers use in primitive categorization, including grouping, figure, and ground, and develop marketing applications using these three tools.

- Explain how elaboration of marketing stimuli influences consumer perceptions and preferences.

- Define some basic features of perceptual preferences and consumer tastes.

Perception: Worlds of Sensations

Herb Tea, Madeleine Cookies, and the Remembrance of the Past[1]

Many years had elapsed during which nothing of [my childhood in] Combray . . . had any existence for me, when one day in winter, as I came home, my mother, seeing that I was cold, offered me some tea, a thing I did not ordinarily take. I declined at first, and then, for no particular reason, changed my mind. She sent out for one of those short, plump little cakes called "petites madeleines," which look as though they had been molded in the fluted scallop of a pilgrim's shell. And soon, mechanically, weary after a dull day with the prospect of a depressing morrow, I raised to my lips a spoonful of the tea in which I had soaked a morsel of the cake. No sooner had the warm liquid, and the crumbs with it touched my palate than a shudder ran through my whole body, and I stopped, intent upon the extraordinary changes that were taking place. An exquisite pleasure had invaded my senses, but individual, detached, with no suggestion of its origin. And at once the vicissitudes of life had become indifferent to me, its disasters innocuous, its brevity illusory—this new sensation having had on me the effect which love has of filling me with a precious essence; or rather this essence was not in me, it was myself. I had ceased now to feel mediocre, accidental, mortal. Whence could it have come to me, this all-powerful joy? I was conscious that it was connected with the taste of tea and cake, but that it infinitely transcended those savours, could not, indeed, be of the same nature as theirs. Whence did it come? What did it signify? How could I seize upon and define it?

I drink a second mouthful, in which I find nothing more than in the first, a third, which gives me rather less than the second. It is time to stop, the potion is losing its magic. It is plain that the object of my quest, the truth, lies not in the cup but in myself. The tea has called up in me, but does not itself understand, and can only repeat indefinitely, with a gradual loss of strength, the same testimony; which I, too, cannot interpret, though I hope at least to be able to call upon the tea for it again and to find it there presently, intact and at my disposal, for my final enlightenment.

Overview

Perception is a process of giving meaning to sensory stimuli. People act and react on the basis of their **perceptions,** *the way they sense and interpret the world around them.* Consumers' perceptions are fundamental to understanding acquisition, consumption, and disposal of goods and services. The symbols used in language and writing, in marketing communication in all its forms, gain concrete meaning by reference to perceptions. Hence, in a very basic way, perceptions underlie preferences. When consumers order curry chicken for dinner or buy silk lingerie or listen to Nine Inch Nails or select Magie Noire as their evening fragrance or refuse to buy plaids even when plaids are the fashion statement for the year, they reflect their **sensory preferences**—*sights, sounds, tastes, smells, and feelings that they like over other sensations.* Of course, culture, family, friends, motivations, experience, and a myriad of other factors influence these sensory preferences. Sophisticated understanding and management of sensations and perceptions are necessary if marketing communication, packaging, design of consumer food products, and creation of "servicescapes" and retail environments are to be effective. As we examine perceptions, we are beginning to move from a consideration of background factors in the wheel of consumption toward those factors that influence acquisition and consumption.

The study of perceptions is a basic way to try and understand consumers. Nonetheless, there is something elusive and fleeting about perceptions, and they have many aspects. Consider the vignette that opens this chapter. For Marcel Proust, the smell and taste of a madeleine cookie is associated, at first unconsciously and later consciously, with many rich experiences from his past. Perhaps you've had similar sensory perceptions. Perhaps you've had the sensation of walking into a building and having the smell evoke many emotions of warmth and caring. At the time, you may not even be able to describe the smell. Later, you may consciously realize that it smells like your grandmother's house—a place that evokes many special and loving memories. This sort of perception is the act of sensing something and knowing its meaning and value. Perception, in this sense, does not use the symbols or rules of language or logic. Clearly, cognitive or symbolic knowledge comes *after* these perceptions, although experiences, learning, and memories may be bound up with them. In contrast, when we speak of the perceived quality, perceived risk, or perceived value, we are clearly talking about something that refers to perception, although the actual sensations at the root of these judgments may seem far away, transformed by judgment, thought, and logic. Nevertheless, sensation is an important ingredient of consumer learning and decision making (see Chapters 12 and 13).

Underlying both meanings of perception (i.e., the immediate sense of delight in the taste of something sweet versus the judgment that the colors in a gown do or do not go together) is **sensation,** *the immediate and direct response of sensory systems to stimuli.* Sensations vary between persons, social groups, and cultures.

In this chapter we examine the cultural, social, psychological, and physiological bases of perception. You will learn first about sensation and the sensory systems. Then, we introduce the four phases of perception. Next, we discuss some inference processes of particular importance in consumer behavior. Finally, we discuss the perceptual and sensory preferences that constitute what people call matters of taste. As you read about perception, you will understand that it is closely related to topics we will take up in more depth in later chapters. For example, perception is closely related to needs, motivation, and involvement (Chapter 11); experience, learning, and knowledge (Chapter 12); and decision making and attitude formation (Chapter 13).

The Subjective Nature of Perception

Many aspects of the perception process remain mysterious to science. While we know considerably more about the way neurons work when exposed to light, sound, taste, smell, and touch than was known even 30 years ago, we still do not understand much about our subjective awareness of perceptual phenomena. Consciousness is the experience of knowing our sensations as though they were displayed before us, but how this display works is enigmatic. There is little about neural activity that helps us understand the subjective judgments we make about sensations.[2] We often do not recognize that our perception of the world is created through indirect inference. Psychologists call this bias **phenomenal absolutism** and point out that we often assume that all other observers perceive the situation as we do. If others respond differently than we do, we assume it is because of error or bad intention rather than, as is often the case, because they are acting on different perceptual inferences. An important conclusion is that perceptions are learned as part of the enculturation process; as a result, they may be manipulated and altered.[3]

The subjective nature of perception presents challenges for global marketers, as illustrated in Consumer Chronicles 9.1. Of course, culture and the social world can play an important role in influencing consumers' subjective perceptions and interpretations. As the P&G experience in Poland illustrates, the media can also play an important role in influencing perceptions.

Sensation and Sensory Thresholds

Sensory stimuli are inputs to the senses. People detect stimuli through a variety of **sensory receptors.** These are the organs of perception. Although we may think of them in terms of the classic five—vision, smell, hearing, touch, and taste—it turns out that the organs of perception are more numerous and specialized than this. Indeed, some researchers suggest there are as many as 32 different sensory systems! There are, for example, separate sensory pathways in the eye for color, motion, form, and depth; separate pathways in skin to detect pressure, pain, and temperature; and multiple pathways connecting the olfactory organs of the nose to the multiple limbic structures in the brain (e.g., prepiriform cortex, amygdala, hypocampus).[4] While recognizing the diversity of the perceptual apparatus, we nonetheless organize our discussion of sensation around the five traditional systems.

Sensory Systems and Marketing Effects

There is debate about whether sensations are **autonomic responses** (i.e., automatic neural responses) or **learned responses** (the product of enculturation). This issue is important for marketers because they may rely on simple physical stimuli to produce certain responses in consumers.

Vision

Human eyes have separate mechanisms that gather the light, pick out an important or novel image, focus it precisely, pinpoint it in space, and follow it. They work like top-flight stereoscopic binoculars. Vision can rush through fields and travel across time, country, and outer space. Seventy percent of the body's sense receptors cluster in the eyes. People often vividly remember scenes from days or even years earlier, viewing them in their mind's eye. Of course, humans can even picture completely imaginary events, if they wish.

Because vision is a dominant sense in humans, it has been studied in great detail and more is known of it than the other senses. Studies find that exposure to warm hues (red-orange-yellow) raises blood pressure, heart rate, and perspiration, whereas exposure to cool hues (green-blue) has opposite effects. Applying these findings to commercial environments, studies show that yellow booths speed up phone calls; yellow walls and fixtures move people through stores faster; orange fixtures in fast-food joints stimulate hunger; and blue and pink hues reduce patient anxiety in doctors' waiting rooms and hospitals. See Consumer Chronicles 9.2 for an example related to the workplace.

Color can play an important role in the success of marketing stimuli, such as the colors used in advertising or package design. In a study of a print ad for a fictitious paint company, the researchers found that the colors used in the ad influenced consumers' feelings of excitement and relaxation.[5] Colors that stimulate excitement appear whitish, as if the color white had been mixed in to create a pastel effect. Colors that evoke relaxation are fully saturated. That is, they have a high level of pigment in them. Much of the research on the role of color in marketing is anecdotal. Generally, red is an effective color to use in restaurants because it leads people to eat more.[6] Red also makes people lose track of time, making it a good color for use in casinos.[7] In brief, marketers frequently find that they don't have firm foundations for making decisions about color, even though they realize that such decisions are quite important.

Smell

The sense of smell is less important for humans than many other animals. Yet, odors have a persistent and enveloping quality that may be difficult to escape. Smells can be extraordinarily precise, but in many cultures it's almost impossible to describe how something smells to someone who hasn't smelled it. Smells tend to be described in terms of how they feel emotionally (e.g., disgusting, delightful). Try it yourself. Can you describe the smell of your favorite pastry, flower, sauce, chair, or room?

Smell is the most direct of the senses. Nothing is more memorable than a smell (see again the description in the opening vignette). Exposure to odors remembered from childhood can induce mood effects like those experienced in childhood. Marketers are attuned to this and have found ways to build mood effects into products through their odors. For example, three of the best-selling perfumes in the U.S. market are scented with baby powder. The appeal of the perfumes may be more basic than the flashy promotional campaigns with which they are associated—rooted in the warm feelings associated with the fragrance of baby powder.

The relationship between odors, thoughts, and behaviors is not a simple one. Odor greatly affects an individual's evaluation of things and other people. For example, if consumers are handed two cans of identical furniture polish, one with a pleasant odor and one with no odor, they will swear the scented one works better. Odor also affects consumer responses in a multitude of other ways. For example, people are more alert in a room with a light, pleasant smell. Similarly, environmental fragrancing can reduce errors in computer key punch operators. Psychologists have found that the odor of spiced apple has a calming effect and that various food odors, including spiced apple, can lower blood pressure in some people by inducing a relaxation of respiratory patterns. As marketers seek to tap consumers' feelings and memories directly, aromachology and the home fragrance industry has become a growing aspect of the economy.[8]

Sometimes odors are used as a way of communicating product attribute information, such as with perfume or household cleaners. Sometimes they are directly related to the product being sold, such as the scent of fresh-baked bread in a grocery store or the aroma of ground coffee in specialty shops. However, marketers have become interested in the notion that pleasant scents that are not necessarily related to the products being sold can also affect consumer feelings, thoughts, and behaviors. For example, research has found that pleasant odors increase lingering and the amount of time spent in a store.[9]

Manipulating Sensations in the Workplace

Consumer Chronicles 9.2

The ideal workplace, says Robert A. Baron, should have lights with a pink glow. The sound level should be low, the air clean and mildly fragrant, perhaps with the scent of peppermint or lemon. It should be cool in the summer and warm in the winter. There should be plenty of space for each person. Baron, a psychologist at Rensselaer Polytechnic Institute, and industrial designer Fred Haber recently received a U.S. patent for an "Apparatus for Enhancing the Environmental Quality of Work Space." Baron's invention is aimed at improving three factors: noise, air quality, and fragrance. The Invomatic 120 combines a powerful air filter, a white-noise generator, and a fragrance release system in a triangular box about the size of a toaster.

Source: R. A. Baron, S. G. Daniels, and M. S. Rea, (1992). "Lighting as a Source of Environmentally-Generated Positive Affect in Work Settings: Impact on Cognitive Tasks and Interpersonal Behaviors," Motivation and Emotion 14, pp. 1–34; R. A. Baron, and M. I. Bronfen (1994), "A Whiff of Reality: Empirical Evidence Concerning the Effects of Pleasant Fragrances on Work-Related Behavior," Journal of Applied Social Psychology 13, pp. 1179–1203; R. A. Baron and J. Thomley (1994), "A Whiff of Reality: Positive Affects as a Potential Mediator of the Effects of Pleasant Fragrances on Task Performance and Helping," Environment and Behavior 26, pp. 766–784.

Hearing

Sound is an onrushing, cresting, and withdrawing wave of air molecules that roll to the ears, where they make the eardrum vibrate and move the three tiniest bones in the body. These three bones press fluid in the inner ear against membranes, which brush tiny hairs that trigger nearby nerve cells, which telegraph messages to the brain. As a result, people hear.

What people hear occupies a large range of intensities. People have a surprising ability

The Taste of Olive Oil

"Artisan-made olive oil is like silk or velvet in your mouth. It has the beautiful aroma of olives, but is more earthy. What I like is as you swallow it, there's a long finish of black pepper in the back of your throat," says Michelle Anna Jordan, author of *The Good Cook's Book of Oil and Vinegar.* In the United States, consumption of olive oil increased 50 percent from 1987 to 1992, according to the USDA. Forecasted consumption for 1993 is 278 million pounds, putting per capita consumption at about one pound per person. So how do you judge olive oil? Taste it.

Source: Kristen A. Conover, "Olive Oil Branching Out," Christian Science Monitor, *March 3, 1994.*

to move some sounds to the almost unnoticeable rear and drag others right up front. For example, a mother wakes quickly to the sound of her colicky baby at the other end of the house, but she may sleep through the louder and more abrasive sound of a garbage truck. At a busy cocktail party, people can slice straight through all the noise when they hear their name mentioned across the room.

Sound patterns can create a mood of relaxation or stimulation. Religions and cults have long made use of music to induce trances or other mood states. The Muzak Corporation, among others, offers functional music to relax, stimulate, or liven up shoppers. Other piped-in music is designed to reduce absenteeism among workers.

Touch

Our skin stands between the world and us, and it serves many functions. It protects us and imprisons us. It gives us individual shape, cools us down, and heats us up. Most of all, it harbors the sense of touch. There are many complex sensations that constitute touch, and various parts of the body are much more sensitive than others. In language, there are many metaphors for touch. We call our emotions "feelings," and we care most deeply when something "touches" us. The importance of touch is not just represented in language and poetry, it is evident in many other ways. Touch affects the whole organism.

Numerous studies detail the vital affects of touch. For example, massaged babies gain weight as much as 50 percent faster than unmassaged babies. Touch is critical in the psychological and physical development of children. Sustained touching reduces heart rate and has a calming effect. Stroking of pets has a similar effect; in one study of longevity following heart attack, the single most important factor was the presence of pets in the patients' environment. The capacity of fabrics such as wool, silk, and fur to evoke associations directly has apparently fueled the development of synthetic fabrics with the tactile associations of the natural ones. Given a recent increase in concern with animal rights, interest is especially high in developing false fur with the feel of the original.

Taste

What people eat suggests the powerful role of culture in determining taste. Thus, the Masai drink cow's blood; some Asians eat stir-fried canine; Germans eat rancid cabbage (sauerkraut); North Americans eat decaying cucumbers (pickles); Italians eat whole deep-fried songbirds; Vietnamese eat fermented fish dosed with chili peppers; Japanese and others eat fungus (mushroom); French eat garlic-soaked snails. People eat rodents, grasshoppers, snakes, flightless birds, kangaroos, lobsters, and bats. When the explorer Dr. Livingston died in Africa, his organs were apparently eaten by two of his native followers as a way to absorb his strength and courage.

Taste is also an intimate sense. As Consumer Chronicles 9.3 illustrates, how people taste things may be as individual as fingerprints. Every culture uses food as a sign of approval or commemoration. Some foods are eaten symbolically, ritualistically, or for their supernatural powers. Food gods have ruled the hearts and lives of many peoples. Food is a big source of physiological and emotional pleasure in most people's lives.

So, how do people taste? Taste buds are exceedingly small, and adults have about 10,000, grouped by theme (salt, sour, sweet, bitter), at various sites in the mouth. Inside each one, about 50 taste cells busily relay information to a neuron, which will alert the brain. People use the tip of the tongue to taste sweet things, the back to taste bitter, and the side to taste sour. Up front and along the surface, they taste salty things. Smell is also important to taste, and it hits us faster. It takes 25,000 times more molecules of cherry pie to taste it than to smell it. In fact, a food's flavor includes its texture, smell, temperature, color, and painfulness (as in spices), among many other features. Food engineers create products to assault as many of the taste sensors as possible. There has been considerable interest in creating substances that fool taste buds, such as artificial sweeteners and fats that mimic the taste of sugar and the saturated fats that give many meat and dairy products their flavor. At any one time, there are multiple and conflicting trends related to culinary fashions. In the United States there is a growing segment of health-conscious consumers who are concerned about the cholesterol and the fat contents of the foods they eat. At the same time, there is a segment of consumers who indulge and prefer foods that are high in fat, those as rich and savory as possible (see Consumer Chronicles 9.4).

A Sensory Preference for Fatty Foods

Consumer Chronicles 9.4

North American fast-food restaurants have gone off their diet. Their menus are increasingly filled with grease-laden sandwiches: Wendy's International, Big Bacon Classic; McDonald's MegaMac; KFC's Popcorn Chicken; Little Caesar's Enterprises Big! Big Cheese pizza, and so on. The fast-food industry hasn't had much luck with skimpy dietetic products. The reason for these flops: People crave large quantities of fatty fast foods. Experts on food trends say North Americans are sick and tired of the stern dietary warnings issued by physicians and dietitians. Rebellious consumers want their food indulgences to be as rich and savory as possible. Fast-food chains have been inspired by the popularity and higher margins of specialty sandwiches, which tend to be larger and more expensive than regular burgers.

Source: Gabriella Stern, "In a Turn About Fast-Food Fare Becomes Fattier," The Wall Street Journal, August 8, 1993, pp. B1; B6.

Sensory Thresholds

Sensation is provoked, not by some unit of sensation but by changes in sensory input. It's these differences in input that people perceive. Several differences in input, or **sensory thresholds,** are important in marketing; these include the absolute threshold and the differential threshold, or the just noticeable difference.

Absolute Threshold

The **absolute threshold** is *the lowest level of input to be detected by the various sensory receptors in the human body.* Some examples are given in Consumer Chronicles 9.5. The absolute threshold should not be confused with the threshold of consciousness. Perceptual scientists recognize that there are sensations to which people attend and those to which they do not attend. Some of the latter may nonetheless affect behavior, if they exceed the absolute threshold of perception.

Marketers sometimes make use of sensations that are not obvious to customers. Although customers may not notice the background music in a grocery store (i.e., it does not receive conscious attention), the music nevertheless affects buyer behavior. The Magic Kingdom and Epcot Center at Walt Disney World in Orlando, Florida use a machine called a "smellitzer" that dissipates scents on their rides, including the odors of oranges, bubble gum, and volcanoes.[10]

Marketing stimuli must reach the absolute threshold if they are to affect consumers. Receptors adapt quickly to environments. Hence, any continuous low-level sensation quickly becomes mere background, and the sensory receptors stop responding. The absolute threshold may increase for physiological reasons, such as increasing age. Physiological factors may reduce the likelihood of some persons receiving sensory input. Thus, younger people tend to be more sensitive to olfactory sensations than elderly people. Research has found that olfactory sensitivity (smell) decreases more with age than taste sensitivity, a fact related to loss of appetite and undernourishment among the elderly.

The absolute threshold also varies with demographic factors. Women seem to be more sensitive than males. For instance, women seem to exhibit superior performance in a variety of tasks involving odor information than men.[11]

Thanks in part to commercial media (the saturation of the media with marketing messages), consumers in the Triad countries live in a stimulus-rich environment. Consumers adapt to this sensory environment in part by "disattending," by applying **perceptual filters** to screen out unwanted stimuli. As an illustration of perceptual filters, consider the experience of Northwestern Mutual Life Insurance Company when it placed coupons worth $10 in an informational mailing. To redeem it, all one had to do was find the coupon in the mailer. Virtually no one redeemed the coupon. People simply tuned this input out.

Marketers frequently attempt to provoke consumers into re-attending by crossing the absolute threshold in novel ways. One technique that radio or TV advertisers may use to increase attention is to alter the volume of certain frequencies. Another technique is to remove sounds that tend to drown others out—just as low-frequency wind and road noise tend to cancel out the highs on a car radio, making the music harder to hear. To avoid this effect, advertisers may try to filter out as much masking noise as possible, which could make a sound track seem quieter than it is. In addition, some frequencies are more piercing than other frequencies. Acoustic researchers have found that the human voice has the most impact in the frequency range between two and six kilohertz. Thus, by electronically manipulating a voice sound so that it always stays within that band, audio engineers can enhance its effect on a listener. Even the way a commercial is written can make a difference because the ear is more sensitive to consonants than vowel sounds.[12]

Weber's Law and the JND

Another important sensory threshold is the **just noticeable difference (JND)**, or **differential threshold.** This conveys the idea of the *minimum change in sensation necessary for a person to detect it.* Note that the JND differs from absolute threshold in that the former focuses on *changes* in sensations not *minimum* sensation.

Any first-time touch or change in touch (from gentle to stinging, say) sends the brain into a flurry of activity. However, an additional dose of stimulus at the same level results in a much lower level of excitation of sensory preceptors. To explain this phenomenon, a theorem known as **Weber's law** states that *the stronger the initial sensory stimulus, the greater the additional intensity needed for the second stimulus to be perceived as different*. A corollary of this theorem is that an additional level of stimulus equivalent to the JND must be added for the majority of people to perceive a difference between the resulting stimulus and the initial stimulus.

The most important implication of Weber's law for marketers is the necessity of determining the JND to optimize any changes in the marketing mix. Sometimes it will be optimal to introduce stimuli or changes in the marketing mix that are equal to the JND. In this case, the challenge for marketers is to determine the amount of change necessary in a given component of the marketing mix, in particular marketing environments for particular market segments. Change less than the JND is wasted because it is not perceived. More than the JND is wasted because it may stimulate no additional response—no more repeat business, no further sales. For example, a household cleaner might distinguish itself with "more lemon scent." In this case, the lemon scent should be noticeably stronger than it was in the original version.

According to Weber's law, the level of a just noticeable difference will depend on the strength of the initial stimulus. Hence, the JND is in contrast to economic principles that would contend that a $5 savings is a savings, whether the savings is on $10 or $10,000. In contrast, Weber's law suggests that a $5 savings on $10 is likely to be noticeable, but on a larger amount, say $10,000, a $5 savings is likely to go unnoticed. On a related note, a study was done of U.S. consumers' response to retailers' price promotions. This study found that consumers *discount* the price discounts; that is, consumers are so used to discounts that small discounts fail to stimulate a reaction. Consumers do not change their intentions to buy unless the promotional discount is above a threshold level. Moreover, this threshold point differs for name brands and store brands. The threshold for name brands is lower than for store brands. In other words, stores can attract consumers by offering a smaller discount on name brands than they would have to offer on store brands.[13] Weber's law applies to many stimuli. If a product is generally unsalted, just a little salt will be readily discernible. However, that same amount of salt added to potato chips is likely to go unnoticed.

A familiar example of how differential thresholds work in practice is found in the engineering of commercial sound tracks. Many radio listeners and TV viewers assume that stations turn up the volume for advertisements. The practice is prohibited in the United States by federal statutes, and for reasons of efficiency, stations always operate at the highest audio signal allowed. In fact, there is no difference between the peak decibels of a broadcast program and an advertisement. The key word here is *peak*. Advertisers do tend to aim for an average level of sound as close to the maximum as possible. Thus, during a program, the needle on a decibel meter will fluctuate, but during a commercial it will stay near the high end. The overall effect is to make the ad sound track seem louder to listeners. The difference in percentage of sounds broadcast near the peak in an advertisement is indeed noticeable to listeners.[14]

Sometimes a marketer's objective is to change the product *without* the consumer noticing. The key is to stay just below a noticeable difference. For example, a marketer might advertise "all the same good taste with only half the sodium." In this case, the marketer would continue to cut salt until the consumer noticed that the product didn't taste as good—that is, just below the JND for reduced salt. This may be easy to do with very salty products but much more difficult with products already low in sodium.

Often, firms want to introduce changes in products and services that are not readily discernible to customers in order to save money or else reposition the brand (e.g., reductions in product size, changes in package design). Thus, they may try shrinking candy bars slightly while retaining the same size package. The strategy of downsizing the package or decreasing contents is a popular way of implementing price increases. Often consumers more readily notice a price change, especially on relatively inexpensive products, than a change in the quantity. During periods of rising coffee prices, a slight increase in the percentage of inferior coffee beans may be introduced into ground coffees.[15] Packaged-goods marketers frequently change the package design but usually do so in small stages. As a result, consumers often do not notice these subtle changes in package design, color, or wording.

The Perceptual Process

People think of the senses as windows on the world, but a primary function of sensory systems is to discard irrelevant or useless information. As such, the sensory systems serve as selection systems. Humans may agree on certain events only because we share a common biology and thus are similarly limited by our sensory selection systems. Perhaps the most striking trend in the psychology and physiology of perception in the past two decades is the increasing understanding of the interactive and constructive nature of ordinary awareness.

Our experience of the world involves a wide range of unconscious inferences about perceptual categories that we create from personal experience. For example, we cannot immediately know whether a given chair is physically closer than others because we do not possess a direct monocular sense of distance. Instead, if we assume that two objects we are looking at are the same size, then we infer the one that looks larger would be closer to us. That is, we make a prediction about the proximity of the chair based on our personal constructs or categories.[16] In this section we look in more detail at how sensory systems make predictions, that is to say, how they select, organize, and interpret stimuli. For the sake of discussion, we divide the process of perception into four parts.

1. Preattentive processing
2. Selection
3. Organization
4. Interpretation and elaboration

Preattentive
Processing

Perception begins with an **exposure** to a stimulus. By exposure we mean that *the stimulus is in sufficient proximity to the sensory receptors that the opportunity exists for sensory activation.* When you flip through a magazine, you are exposed to the advertisements, but do you attend to them?

Preattentive processing refers to *the simultaneous preconscious monitoring of all sensory channels for events that will require a shift in attention.*[17] This kind of preattentive processing is what makes it possible for us to suddenly hear our name spoken across a crowded, noisy room or wake at the cry of a baby but not a garbage truck. Considerable research suggests that preconscious processes operate in the selection of stimuli for further processing. However, some recent research has demonstrated that preattentive processing *may* also have an effect on preference formation. The possibility that consumer attitudes can be influenced without consumers being able to identify the factors responsible for that influence has many implications for marketers.[18]

There's an extraordinary amount of competition for people's attention in the marketplace. Media environments everywhere are becoming increasingly rich, led, of course, by the commercial media based in the Triad countries. As explained by the principle of sensory thresholds, as the background becomes more saturated with sensation, peoples' filters become stronger and more immune to each individual sensory input. In effect, the perceptual system is a nonconscious, parallel information-generation device that selects and creates the small array of information that the higher-order system will process.[19] **Perceptual selection** refers to the fact that *consumers select only a small portion of the stimuli to which they are exposed for conscious processing,* or what we might term *focal attention.* To get the consumer's focal attention, an escalation of sensory impulses is required. Evidence is easy to find in a comparison of the staid, single-shot TV commercials of television's first decades with today's rapid-fire explosions of sounds and images pioneered in many cases by MTV and entertainment advertisers.

Merely escalating the intensity of stimuli is likely to be an ineffective way of cutting through perceptual filters and provoking potential customers to pay attention. Consumers will concentrate on some stimuli, be unaware of others, and avoid some commercial messages. Many poorly targeted direct-mail pieces, for example, are discarded, unopened and unread. A variety of factors will lead to increased selection, as we outline in the next several paragraphs.

Motives

One of the most important factors influencing selection of stimuli for further processing is consumers' motives and goals. Consumers are more likely to attend to stimuli that relate to themselves or their current needs. In addition, consumers' goals serve to direct their attention to information that is relevant or important to those goals.[20] Perhaps you've noticed how once you get interested in purchasing a particular product, all of a sudden there seems to be lots of information available on that product. Or perhaps, right after purchasing a new car it seems like you suddenly see that model of car everywhere you look. Both of these common examples illustrate information selectivity. This type of need-specific attention is called **perceptual vigilance.**

The idea of perceptual vigilance has important implications for marketers. For example, producers of radio commercials are advised to include personal references in their spots. The use of a question format in advertisements appears to have the capacity to draw attention to a message and thus engage listeners. Incidentally, the philosopher Protagoras introduced the question format as a rhetorical technique in the fourth century, B.C.[21]

An important application of perceptual vigilance for marketers is to target consumers whose needs have changed. During transitional periods, consumers may be especially attentive to relevant information that addresses their changing needs. For example, when consumers make a long-distance move, they must establish relationships with many new services (everything from schools and insurance to laundries and barbers) and buy many new and replacement goods (tools, furnishings). Some marketers keep careful track of new home purchases, a matter of public record in the United States, and target new buyers with promotional materials. Other marketers keep track of birth, marriage, and divorce records for similar purposes, secure in the knowledge that consumers faced with these life-changing events will be more attentive to campaigns focused on meeting their needs.[22]

Nature of the Stimulus

Some of the time, the perceptual stimulus attracts the consumer's attention. **Involuntary attention** can occur via the **orientation reflex,** when *surprise, threat, or violation of expectations elicits attention automatically.* A variety of mechanisms increase attention to messages. For example, **atypicality** of execution format can provoke perceptual selection. Thus, black and white commercials on color television and clear advertising pages in opaque magazine pages will elicit attention. These particular examples also illustrate that **contrast effects** elicit attention. More generally, perceptual surprises may increase the likelihood of selection. Increased size of advertisements or life-size images of products are surprising, as in the Salvatore Ferragamo shoes ad shown above. Especially vivid images such as those employed in a series of Benetton ads during the late 1980s and early 1990s can also evoke the orientation reflex. Benetton drew both attention and controversy with ads depicting actors dressed as a priest and nun kissing, a young man dying of AIDS in his parents arms, and a shipping disaster.

Organization

The third part in the perceptual process is **perceptual organization.** Consumers classify perceptions into categories (categorization) and apply prior knowledge about the categories to organize them. Basically, **categorization** involves *comparison between a perceived target and categorical knowledge.*[23] Categorization is a fundamental sense-making activity that encompasses all forms of stimulus situations. When we identify a moving object in a tree as a bird, we are categorizing. Whenever we reason about *kinds* of things, we employ categories. Whenever we intentionally perform any *kind* of action, say something as ordinary as drinking a soda, attending a class, or exercising, we are using categories. Whenever we talk for a reasonable length of time we employ dozens, if not hundreds, of categories. Categorization schemes allow people to give coherence to their general knowledge about other people, objects, and situations. By putting stimuli into categories, consumers are able to decide how they should behave in certain situations and also what they can expect. For example, some recent research looks at how the outside facade and the inside seating arrangement of an eating establishment lead consumers to categorize the establishment as a fast-food, family, or fancy restaurant. This classification, in turn, affects how consumers believe they should behave and should be treated by service staff. Simple aspects of restaurant appearance (e.g., the intimacy of the lighting, the flexibility of seating arrangements) lead to different categorizations of the stimuli.[24]

A key feature of categories is that they are functional and, as such, are shaped by personal goals, values, or the need to respond. Whereas early research presented categories as relatively stable structures, recent research emphasizes that categories are influenced by context and by goals or judgment purposes.[25] By altering context, systematic differences in category judgments occur. In fact, a different context invites people to organize their knowledge structures differently and create categories appropriate to the context. The formation of a particular goal also leads people to create categories to fit that specific goal. Such categories are referred to as **ad hoc categories.** For example, a student residing in a university town may construct a category of "places to go with friends for FAC (Friday afternoon club) on Friday afternoon." This particular category reflects the context and consumer goals of the student.[26]

Another key feature of categories is that they are socially and culturally constructed and learned.[27] For example, the Australian aboriginal language Dyirbal has a category, *balan,* that includes women, fire, and dangerous things. Native speakers of Dyirbal use the category *balan* automatically and effortlessly, but speakers of English try to comprehend it and ponder it in terms of their normal categories of thought and are rarely able to employ it.

Categorization operates at different levels of abstraction. In this section, on organizing perceptions, we are interested in some principles that affect the initial, often automatic, and unconscious categorization of stimuli. We refer to this *initial classification of an object into a category* as **primitive categorization.** To appreciate the problem of primitive categorization, we need to understand that people derive meaning from the totality of the perceptual information they receive at a given moment. They frequently derive meaning from partial perceptual data, inferring the rest from previous learning. So, for example, it is no problem to infer the weather outside is very cold, if from inside we view falling snowflakes. Marketers often make use of our human tendency to make sense of perceptual data through primitive categorization on the basis of partial information. Three especially common illustrations of this tendency are grouping, figure-and-ground discriminations, and the closure principle. Each of these shows how, when presented with ambiguous stimuli, people try to impose familiar categories on their perceptions.

Grouping

In the first case of primitive categorization, **grouping,** people tend to *assume that options found in proximity to one another go together.* The Dada movement in art of the early part of this century had great fun with this concept, such as Marcel Duchamp's urinal, which he hung upside-down on a wall and called "Fountain." The joke lies in the context in which the urinal was placed; if hung with other art objects, it must be art! Advertisers and retailers, through grouping, try to create an ambient perceptual environment for their goods and services that creates a particular image for them. Architects, designers, and landscapers use perceptual cues to suggest an overall landscape. Ralph Lauren has gone to considerable lengths to create an overall perception of his Polo line that conveys a classic, old money, country-club image. In the 1980s, the American wine producer Gallo sought to upgrade its down-market image among wine consumers by picturing upgraded products with gourmet foods, a linen napkin, and a napkin ring, images that some consumers would associate with

Gallo Wine: Upscale Dining. This ad employs the principle of grouping.

a more formal, upscale dining situation. All these examples use the principle of grouping to suggest to consumers that the objects are all members of a single category.

Figure and Ground

In the second case of primitive categorization, referred to as **figure and ground,** people try to *determine what aspects of stimuli they should focus on.* People tend to place "important" stimuli in the foreground and move less important stimuli to the background. Classic figure-and-ground tricks developed by psychologists illustrate how we may perceive something as foreground, until an alternative perception is pointed out to us. Exhibit 9.1 illustrates the vase/face trick. The figure and ground will shift back and forth as we attempt to see one element, such as the faces, and then the other, the vase, as foreground. An interesting aspect of figure-and-ground problems is that people cannot perceive both objects as figure simultaneously.

There are many instances of the use of figure-and-ground principles in marketing. For example, people often say that contrast attracts attention. But what they are really saying is that a stimulus has forced something into the foreground that would otherwise have been treated as background. Thus, in a U.S. campaign, Toyota, using a sports figure as a celebrity spokesperson, brought an otherwise ordinary figure into the foreground of our attention with the line, "I'm Eric Karras, the *lowest paid* player in baseball!"

Subway, the successful U.S. sandwich franchiser, used a print ad that could be read in two ways, depending on whether the reader brought red or black text into focus as foreground. A recent craze for computer-generated color images that when stared at resolve themselves into a "hidden" picture relies on a figure-and-ground effect. An example produced for the Beverly Connection shopping mall in Los Angeles is shown on page 323.

The literature on the effects of background and foreground music in retail settings is mixed. Foreground music differs from background music in that it includes original artists and lyrics, unlike background music that uses primarily instrumental treatments played by anonymous musicians. A number of studies have reported that playing slow-paced background music results in increased sales in grocery settings. A study in a restaurant found

Exhibit 9.1 A Classic Figure-and-Ground Problem

What Do You See?

"Don't Blend In"
Beverly Center.
An application of the
figure-and-ground
principle.

ingle ells,
ingle ells.

The holidays aren't the same without J&B

Applications of the
principle of closure.

Schhh...!

Schhh...!

Schweppes
INDIAN TONIC

that more alcohol, but not food, was consumed when slow music was played. Soft, soothing music may be an appropriate background in retail settings requiring extensive sales interaction and in those where customers make infrequent, big-ticket, high-risk purchases.[28]

Closure

The third principle of perceptual organization that illustrates the consumer's use of partial cues to complete an image is **closure.** In radio or television ads, it is not uncommon to repeat a jingle or slogan several times and then to leave it incomplete as the advertisement ends. Advertisers know that the listener will imagine the final bars of the tune. Through this heightened level of involvement with the ad, the listener is then more likely to remember the message itself. Print and outdoor advertising examples are also common. Justerini & Brooks' clever Christmas time ad for J & B Scotch relies on the audience's tacit knowledge of a popular seasonal song "Jingle Bells" to get them to fill in the missing letters in the ad shown above. Similar techniques are employed by Vin & Spirit to promote their Absolut brand of vodka in the United States and by Schweppes to promote their tonic water. On bus kiosks in Europe, there are two versions of the Schweppes ad, one that includes the brand name and one that does not. Consumers are supposed to fill in the brand name for themselves, after having viewed the first ad.

Gestalt Psychology

Gestalt psychologists are responsible for much of the work on perceptual organization.[29] These researchers attempt to identify the rules that govern how people perceive patterns in the world. In German, *gestalt* means "pattern" or "configuration." The gestalt perspective is the study of how individuals make sense of the stimuli to which they are exposed. Many of the rules pertain to the ways in which people decide what things go together. Some of the rules are grouping, figure and ground, and closure.

The fourth part in the perceptual process is interpretation. Obviously, organization and interpretation are intertwined. Both have to do with comprehension and sense making. Whereas the principles of perceptual organization are most often applied unconsciously, at least part of the time, interpretation is a conscious process. The interpretation of perceptual stimuli involves the application of learned associations between perceptual cues, or signs, and meanings to novel stimuli. These associations are, in turn, based on individual expectations, motivations, and experiences grounded in cultural convention. Hence, interpretation depends on consumers' knowledge structures.

At least two different sorts of knowledge structures are important to interpretation. One type, called **schemas,** includes *organized collections of beliefs and feelings that a person has about objects, ideas, people, or situations.* As illustrated earlier, many consumers have a schema for a "fancy restaurant" that includes beliefs, feelings, and likely attributes of such an eating establishment. The second type of knowledge structure, called **scripts,** includes *sequences of actions associated with objects, ideas, people, or situations.* For example, when going to a "fancy restaurant" in the United States, the consumer probably expects to be seated or told to wait, expects to give an order to a waiter, expects to have a sequence of ordering steps, expects to receive the bill at the end of the meal, and may expect to have the waiter handle the payment transfer. Even schemas and scripts for something as basic as going to a restaurant are quite complicated and typically allow for many different contingencies and context effects.[30] Whether we are aware of it or not, knowledge about cultural roles, settings, goals, and event sequences are basic to interpretation. We will talk more about knowledge structures and how they influence consumer choices and behaviors in Chapters 12 and 13.

Semiotic Process of Interpretation

Interpretation comes about through a fundamental **semiotic process** that links three components of every stimulus. The semiotic process is *how people obtain meaning from signs.* Every stimulus, including marketing communications, is constructed of three components. To illustrate the linking of these components, consider a print ad for Prescriptives Comfort Cream, a skin cream, which ran a few years ago. The first component of the semiotic system is the product or service that is the *object* of the communication. In this advertisement, the object was the Prescriptives Comfort Cream. The object was identified in the copy of the ad and in the label of a photograph of an open jar. The object is also represented by a second element, at least one sensory image, called a *sign.* This ad showed at least two significant signs: a glass jar and a teddy bear. The third element is called the *interpretant,* which is the meaning derived from the image.

The Prescriptives ad depicted is a convenient one for our purposes since it also illustrates that signs may be of several types or bear (pun intended!) several kinds of relationships with the product or service it represents. In this case, the teddy bear is presumed to be an **index** of the product. An indexical sign *shares presumed properties with the product or service.* Thus, teddy bears are thought to be soft, youthful, ageless, comforting, cuddly, a source of security, and like our skin, bare (bear)! A lemon scent added to a number of household cleaning products in North America is another example of an indexical sign. The scent suggests the product shares the clean, fresh properties North American consumers associate with the lemon odor. The small glass jar with the silver top is also a sign. It, however, is just a **symbol.** A symbol is related to the product through *a purely conventional association.* Size, shape, and color of packaging are commonly employed to make symbolic suggestions about products. The clear Prescriptives jar might suggest value, simplicity, and costliness to Western consumers. The final type of sign is what is called an **icon,** *a sign that resembles the product in some way.* A plastic lemon or lime used for packaging lemon or lime juice would be an iconic sign. Commercial Japanese boxed lunches, called *Ekiben,* often employ iconic signs as containers: one containing crab meat resembles a crab; one containing chestnuts is shaped like a nut; one containing scallops is shaped like a scallop shell.[31]

Trademarks, product symbols, and even packages can be tremendously effective product symbols, and ones of great value to firms. The Pillsbury Doughboy, the Playboy bunny, the Marlboro cowboy, Harley Davidson's wings, and Royal Dutch Shell's shell are just a few examples of the shorthand perceptual units linking symbol, product, and meaning for millions of consumers.

Perceptual Inferences

An important aspect of interpretation is **perceptual inferences.** Inferences are *interpretations that go beyond the information given.* Our understanding of how and when consumers make inferences is still limited. Yet, we do know that consumers rarely have complete information. They have to make judgments and purchase decisions about products on the basis of limited or incomplete information. Frequently, consumers use a small number of cues to make inferences. For example, Westerners associate a dark-brown color with rich flavor for both coffee and chocolate. Merely darkening the color of the product will lead people to insist the product is indeed richer in flavor. As you can see from this example, some inferences are made more or less automatically, and we are largely unconscious of the cues we use in making them.

Elaboration

Sometimes consumer interpretation of perceptual stimuli also includes high levels of **elaboration.** Elaboration reflects *the extent to which perceptual stimuli are integrated with prior knowledge structures.* Interpretation always involves some elaboration, that is, some accessing of prior knowledge structures; but this can be at low levels such as simple recognition. At high levels of elaboration, people engage in processes such as counterarguing, problem solving, daydreaming, and fantasizing. Elaboration produces freedom of memory and attitude from the specific details of the original message or its setting. It can even result in a **boomerang effect** where *the attitude change is opposite to that advocated in the persuasive message.*[32]

Of course, stimuli that encourage elaboration can also be enormously effective. Such stimuli are likely to be remembered longer, and attitudes formed are likely to be much stronger than those associated with stimuli processed at a lower level of elaboration. For example, one form of high elaboration would be **role taking.** In the context of advertising, role taking involves placing the self into the ad or product experience. Through this vicarious transformation into the person or situation depicted in the ad, the potential consequences of product use or nonuse become more vivid and concrete for the viewer. **Transformational advertising** encourages this kind of empathic identification, because it figuratively transforms the viewer watching the ad. Such transformations are likely only when the viewer is highly motivated to process the ad and when the ad contains sufficient cues to allow for such a transformation. For example, a strictly informational ad that contains no cues about feelings or emotional consequences is unlikely to elicit role taking.[33] A transformational ad can also serve to transform the product-use experience. For instance, drinking a soft drink may be perceived as more than just quenching a thirst. Through the influence of advertising imagery, consumers may feel that sipping the soft drink is now akin to playing volleyball on the beach with a group of friends on a beautiful summer day.

Perceptual Judgments and Marketing Strategies

Most consumer perception research deals with perceptual interpretation. This is fundamental to issues of perceived product and service quality, for example. In the global marketplace, the issue of product-country image comes to the fore. Although we are dealing with perceptual judgments, sensations at the root of these judgments seem far away, transformed by knowledge and beliefs (see Chapters 12 and 13).

Perceptual judgments begin with selective attention to perceptual stimuli in the marketing landscape. Through selective exposure and attention, consumers form basic images of brands, products, and marketing communications, for instance. They draw basic perceptual inferences about the attributes of these marketing stimuli. Through learning and experience, consumers eventually form summary perceptual judgments that link the sensory stimuli to outcomes they consider probable. These judgments may be thought of as schemas, as discussed earlier. Depending on the judgment in question, quality, or product-country image, for example, both the perceptual stimuli to which people attend and the importance of those stimuli in forming judgments vary. Because consumers use information selectively, marketers must examine such issues as perceived quality and PCI in developing an understanding of particular consumers' perceptual judgments of particular market offerings.[34]

Perceived Quality

Perceived quality has been a central preoccupation in consumer and organization marketing. **Perceived quality,** whether in reference to a product or service, has been defined as *the consumer's evaluative judgment about an entity's overall excellence or superiority in providing desired benefits.* Quality is a key determinant of national competitiveness, responsible in part for the economic ascendancy of Japan and Germany. Perceived quality can reduce costs, extend market share, increase profitability, and create a differential advantage by erecting barriers to entry and lessening price elasticity. Research suggests that customers may care more about quality than economy; hence, marketers believe that providing evidence of incremental quality is a key to competitive advantage. While something is known of the way in which some consumers evaluate quality in the West, very little research has been conducted on quality judgment cross-culturally. Even in the West, however, the study of perceived quality is incomplete. For example, research on product and service quality tends to be conducted separately.[35]

Perceived quality is a judgment derived by a comparison of performance perceptions against expectations or evaluative standards. According to one theory, consumers use an array of sensory cues as indicators of quality. Cues are used according to their **predictive value,** *the degree to which consumers associate a given cue with product quality, the confidence value of a cue, and the degree to which consumers have confidence in their ability to use and judge that cue accurately.* The value of cues varies across product categories. Consumers in developed markets find it relatively easy to interpret cues for shopping goods like personal care items; consumers in transitional markets do not always find this so easy. Cues must be learned of course. Even in the West, consumers find it less easy to interpret cues for credence goods such as auto repair or medical care.

Consumers rely on both **extrinsic cues,** such as price, brand name, packaging, store name, country of origin, and even color, and **intrinsic cues,** such as taste, texture, and aroma, when assessing product quality. In developed markets, consumers frequently use brand name as a gestalt cue. That is, the brand name represents a composite of information about product attributes. A brand's perceived quality may exert a positive influence on the perceived value of a retail firm, for example. Depending on the product category, intrinsic cues also have high predictive and confidence value for consumers. Consider, for example, shopping for fruit and vegetables. Color, texture, firmness, and aroma all help cue whether the fruits and vegetables are fresh and ripe.[36]

Belief in price-quality relationships has been found to differentiate groups of U.S. consumers and affect marketplace behavior. This means that consumers who believe in a positive price-quality correspondence rely on price as a cue to quality, often preferring high-priced products, and demonstrate higher price-acceptability levels. Younger, lower-income, and less experienced consumers tend to use belief more strongly in this perceptual schema. Recent research in urban China has found two groups of consumers: those who believe in a price-quality relationship and are likely to pay more for products, and those who are less trusting of a price-quality relationship and are likely to pay lower prices for products. This suggests that in some transitional markets price does not yet have the same cuing value as in Western market economies.[37]

In the West, studies comparing private labels (retailers) to national brands (manufacturers) show that consumers often use both intrinsic product attributes and extrinsic attributes to discriminate against private-label brands. In one study, extrinsic cues such as a national brand name are more predictive of consumers' quality judgments than intrinsic cues, such as ingredients. Nonetheless, many large retailers, including Lobo's, a Canadian firm, and Carrefour, a French firm, have successfully leveraged private-label brands for competitive advantage.

Perceived service quality has often been measured using the **SERVQUAL scale,** which contains *five generic dimensions of perceived quality: tangibles, reliability, responsiveness, assurance, and empathy.* The tangibles dimension refers to characteristics of the service provider and the service delivery environment, also called the *servicescape.* Perceived service quality also varies with the participative role of the service provider, including the length of contact with the service provider, spatial intimacy, and affective content of the service delivered. Little research has been conducted on combined product/service-quality perceptions despite that it has long been recognized that much of what is purchased in the marketplace combines features of products and services.[38] However, one study combining automobile product quality and automobile dealership service quality suggested both were better predictors of perceived quality than either alone.[39]

Product-Country Image Effects	Research on product-country image (PCI) has mainly studied **country of origin,** or country of manufacture, as a cue used by consumers to infer beliefs about product attributes. Country of origin is conveyed through packaging, promotional materials, ingredients (e.g., Kobé or Nebraska corn-fed beef), and conventional symbols such as national flags. Country-of-origin cues are like other extrinsic cues such as price, brand name, and retailer reputation in that they can be manipulated without changing the physical product. Consumers often use extrinsic cues as signals of product quality. Product-country image also plays a role in judgments about industrial products. Sometimes, however, product-country image is clouded by confusion between country of origin and country of manufacture. Nike, for example, has a positive image as a U.S. origin brand, but it suffers from negative connotations as a company that uses low-paid labor in Southeast Asian manufacturing facilities.[40]

Provided that the basic criteria for perceptual selection like vividness, clarity, and intensity are met, consumers' use of country-of-origin cues is determined by their power to predict positive consumption outcomes. This predictive relationship is shaped by **product-country image,** which is a *schematic mental representation of a country's people, prod-*

ucts, culture, and national symbols. A particular PCI may contain information about place of design (e.g., Italy), origin, manufacture (e.g., Germany or Japan), raw materials (e.g., cashmere from Kasmir), and so forth. It also contains information about the competitive market context, that is to say, the value of a product made in the United States compared to a product made in Japan, in the Japanese market, for example. Thus, Starbucks has become very successful in Japan, not known as a coffee-drinking country, because Starbucks conveys an "authentic" American coffee house image. Finally, PCI contains meanings pertaining to the usage scripts (see section on interpretation and elaboration above) it evokes. Each of the elements of the PCI may be used in targeting and positioning the product in a particular market context.[41]

Product-country images contain widely shared cultural stereotypes, or simplifying categories. For example, French-sounding brand names have a positive effect on consumers' evaluations of hedonic products like perfume and wine but a negative effect on the evaluations of utilitarian products like cars and computers. For this reason, the Champagne and Cognac regions of France have zealously guarded the use of these regional names as product cues. These effects persist even when consumers actually experience products. Product-country images contain general impressions of countries and idiosyncratic beliefs about a country's products formed through direct or indirect experiences.

Consumers' evaluations of country of origin are based in part on a match between product and country. Consumers prefer country X as an origin for a specific product when they believe that there is a match between the perceived strengths of country X and those needed to produce a particular product. Thus, high-tech products from Japan and Germany enjoy a kind of halo effect, or positive perceptual gestalt, because of a perceived match between their national strengths and what is required to make high-tech products. McDonald's has enjoyed a positive reception in some Asian markets because of its association with the United States and the idea of "modern" consumption. Similarly, some NICs and LAW nations like India face market resistance based on less positive country stereotypes.[42]

Product-country image is not merely another cognitive cue, however. It has symbolic and ritual meaning to consumers. Country of origin may associate a product with status, authenticity, and exoticness. It links a product to a rich product-country imagery, with sensory, emotional, and ritual connotations. Country of origin may relate a product to national identity, which can result in a strong emotional attachment to certain brands and products, such as a second-generation immigrant strongly attached to home-country products. Some authors report that consumers link country of origin not only to product quality but also to feelings of national pride and memories of past vacations. Such emotional and symbolic connotations transform country of origin into an expressive or image attribute and are part of the reason country of origin has been reformulated as the broader concept of PCI, or product-country image.

Symbolic aspects of PCI may influence consumer preferences and contribute to brand loyalty. For example, some authors found that in India a Western origin had a substantial positive effect on brand attitudes, even holding quality constant. This effect was most powerful for consumers with a high admiration for Western lifestyles and for publicly consumed products. Similar findings have been reported in Romania and Turkey, whereas consumers in Niger in West Africa attach symbolic value to products coming from Mecca in Saudi Arabia.[43]

The term **consumer voting** captures *the normative dimension of product-country images.* In other words, by deciding to purchase or avoid a country's products, consumers "vote" for or against the policies of its government. There are numerous global examples, including Jewish consumers boycotting German products because of the Holocaust, Australians boycotting French products because of French nuclear tests in the Pacific, and

African-Americans boycotting products made in South Africa during the apartheid (racial separation) regime. Some Chinese consumers' willingness to buy Japanese products is negatively affected by the rivalry between these two countries. There are also instances where consumers reward sympathetic countries through selective purchase of their products.

PCI may also trigger the norm to buy domestically. Some consumers consider it morally appropriate to buy products that are manufactured or grown domestically. Trends in Poland suggest a resurgent preference for venerable Polish brands, although a number of these have been taken over and brought up to Western quality standards by Western firms. A study in South Africa showed that groups with an African national identity were more likely to use brands with South African or ambiguous product-country images, whereas groups with a European national identity were more likely to use brands with British or American product-country images. The United States, Canada, and the UK have sponsored buy-domestic campaigns, although there is limited evidence for the effectiveness of these. Consumer ethnocentrism, discussed in Chapter 5, serves as an important motivation of the decision to purchase domestically.[44]

Not all products evoke strong product-country images, and not all consumers use product-country images in developing product preferences. For example, a study of Israeli consumers found they were indifferent to country of origin for shoes but attended to country of origin for consumer durables. And a study comparing U.S. and Canadian consumers found low rates of country-of-origin knowledge.

In short, PCI plays a role in judgments of product and brand quality. The influence of product-country image on behavior varies, but there is no doubt that it plays a role and that its relative importance may in fact equal or exceed that of other extrinsic cues depending on situational and other factors.

Matters of Taste: Aesthetic Bridges between Goods

The idea of taste is fundamental to the success of many industries, including architecture, interior design, packaging, and fashion. A variety of specialized institutions, including fashion, food, wine, architecture, magazines, department stores and shopping malls, fashion shows, museums, and even television, have become important sources for the dissemination of perceptual judgments that we call fashion, style, and taste.

The department stores that emerged in Paris and London at the end of the nineteenth century were intended as taste-making instruments, designed to teach and market good taste. American department stores offered for public consumption both elite consumer lifestyles and democratic consumer lifestyles promoted by the decorative arts movement. Interestingly, Crate and Barrel and Renovation Hardware have revived the decorative arts look. In 1926, Wanamaker's department store in Philadelphia offered interior design consulting to its patrons. Contemporary Japanese department stores, or *depato*, not only feature elaborate displays of Western goods and classes in their appreciation, they also offer classes in kimono wearing, pottery making, calligraphy, flower arranging, the preparation of Japanese delicacies, and the tea ceremony. In Sweden, the annual IKEA catalog distributed in August is an anxiously awaited repository of taste; a corporate effort to limit distribution only to consumers above a certain income threshold was hotly debated in the national press. The catalog is now translated into 17 languages for 28 different countries. In each case, the stores display a commitment to exploring and conveying conventional symbols of shared cultural identity, or taste.[45]

In this chapter we have explained how consumers' perceptions underlie preferences.

www.ikea.com

Just about every consumer decision reflects sensory preferences and perceptual judgments. Often, we refer to differences between consumers in their sensory preferences as a "matter of taste." Take a moment and imagine what you think we mean by the term **taste.** You've probably heard it used in a variety of ways, for example, in ways that simply imply a difference in taste (That's more to his taste than mine) or in ways that imply evaluation (That was in bad taste). Modern use of the term obviously extends beyond sensory preferences and perceptual judgments to include combinations of sensory stimuli (e.g., home decor) and even behaviors and activities (table manners or jokes). However, discussions of taste are closely linked to perception. We will use the term to refer to *the making of judgments based on ideas of beauty, order, and arrangement.*

There are a few important general points to make about taste. First, taste is a culturally and historically specific preference for certain things. A quick look at your parents' photo album is likely to reveal clothes and looks that to you seem absolutely ridiculous. But don't laugh too hard because you may be wearing those same styles in a few months or years. Second, taste is not only about raw sensory stimuli; it's also about the interpretation of those stimuli. It's possible to like short skirts in one fashion cycle and find them distasteful in a different cycle. Third, tastes as a form of cultural capital (see Chapters 5 and 6) give us membership in some groups and exclude us from others. They are used to signal and distinguish who we are. Sometimes these tastes are very subtle, and people are hardly aware of how they cue social class or cultural heritage. For example, our taste for predominantly salty or sweet foods signals our social class. Sometimes tastes are adopted or acquired in order to signal membership in a group (e.g., a taste for tattoos, body piercing).[46] Fourth, each culture has arbitrators of taste, like Martha Stewart, discussed in Chapter 8, or the late Princess Diana, who function to define and change what's tasteful and what's not. This is what fashion and home-decorating consultants do.

Specialized taste-making institutions have been around a long time. Royal courts in both Europe and Asia were important taste-making centers in the past. Prevalent in Tudor England (fifteenth century) was a concern for the aesthetic value of "patina," or the perceived age of durable consumer goods. An elaborate, highly prescriptive eleventh century guide to the court fashion of imperial Japan survives. This guide focuses on the creation of subtle color effects geared to the season of the year, to occasions, and to the age and social status of the wearer. Fashion broadside sheets from England and several different types of block-print fashion publications from eighteenth-century Japan also survive. Of the latter, one type resembles the global fashion magazine *Cosmopolitan.*

We do not want to leave you with the impression that consumers are passive recipients of perceptual meanings. Consumers often develop their own tastes from elements provided by the taste-making institutions and perceive consumer goods in terms of them. That is, taste is a matter of individual perception and judgment. But at the same time, taste is part of the social world and helps consumers find their place in that world.

summary

In examining perception, we are beginning to move from a consideration of background factors in the wheel of consumption toward those factors that more directly influence acquisition and consumption. Perception is a process of giving meaning to sensory stimuli.

Underlying perception is sensation. By sensation we mean the immediate response of the sensory systems to stimuli. Sensations vary between persons, social groups, and cultures. People detect stimuli through a variety of sensory receptions. These are the organs of perception. Sensation is provoked in large part by changes in sensory input. Two different sensory thresholds are important in marketing. One is the absolute threshold and the other is the just noticeable difference or differential threshold. A related idea, Weber's law, states that the stronger the initial sensory stimulus, the greater the additional intensity needed for the second stimulus to be perceived as different.

A primary function of sensory systems is to discard irrelevant or useless information. That is, sensory systems serve as selection systems. Perception begins with an exposure to a stimulus. Preattentive processing refers to the simultaneous preconscious monitoring of all sensory channels for events that will require a shift in attention. Perceptual selection refers to the fact that consumers select only a small portion of the stimuli to which they are exposed for conscious processing.

Perceptual organization is the third part in the perceptual process. Categorization schemes allow people to give coherence to their general knowledge about other people, objects, and situations. Three illustrations of this tendency—grouping, figure-and-ground discriminations, and the closure principle—are especially common. In all cases, when presented with ambiguous stimuli, people try to clarify their perceptions.

The fourth part in the perceptual process is interpretation. While the principles of perceptual organization are often applied unconsciously, interpretation is usually a conscious process. At least two different sorts of knowledge structures are important to interpretation: schemas and scripts.

Interpretation comes about through a fundamental semiotic process that links three components of every stimulus: object, sign, and interpretant. Another important aspect of interpretation are perceptual inferences. Inferences are interpretations that go beyond the information given. Perceptions of quality and country-product images are examples. Sometimes consumer interpretation of perceptual stimuli also includes high levels of elaboration. Marketing stimuli that encourage elaboration can be enormously effective.

Finally, sensory preferences, or taste, are primary influences on the decisions consumers make. The idea of taste is important to the success of design and business practice (e.g., creating effective advertisements).

1. Discuss how cereal manufacturers can apply their knowledge of differential threshold during periods of (a) increasing competition, (b) rising ingredient prices, and (c) changing consumer attitudes regarding nutrition.

2. Find two or three ads that use the grouping technique to influence consumers' interpretation of the ad. Explain how grouping is being used in the advertisement.

3. Select an ad or a package and describe how the semiotic process of interpretation could be applied. Identify the object(s), the sign(s), and the interpretant(s). See if you can identify the types of sign as well.

4. Midas International Corporation wants to be known for more than mufflers. It wants to reposition itself as an auto systems expert. Although the company has been offering services such as computerized alignment and suspension work for years, consumers still view Midas as a muffler shop. How would you recommend that Midas goes about changing its image?

5. Develop a description of your own schema for (a) a cruise, (b) a movie theater, and (c) a birthday party. Talk about the different sensory systems that are engaged in your schemas. Do your schemas involve sights, sounds, smell, tastes, and tactile sensations? Now, take just one of your descriptions and indicate the potential importance to marketing managers if your description represents a significant segment of consumers.

6. For each of the following product categories, develop a basic example of how role taking might be used in advertising to encourage high elaboration of the message:

   a. Mountain bikes
   b. Portable phones
   c. Airline travel

7. As the owner of a small bed and breakfast in the Colorado Rockies, you rely on favorable word-of-mouth messages and repeat patronage to attract guests each year. What sensory and perceptual tactics could you use to help people remember their experience with you so that they pass the word on and also come back again?

8. Zapping is a common problem for marketers. Consumers use remote controls to switch between channels during commercials or mute out commercial messages. What perceptual tactics can advertisers use to get the prime-time television audience to pay attention to their ads and brands?

9. Try to imagine cellular phones, cars, lamps, bottled water, and chocolate made in Sweden, Mexico, and Japan. For each of these three countries, write down a list of the words you might associate with each product (e.g., Swedish chocolate), including beliefs, feelings, and any moral ideas you might attach to them. Try to explain whether and why your product-country images are positive or not.

You Make the Call

Odorama!

The use of fragrance to sell products is an area of high growth and great controversy. Because smell is believed to be the most closely linked of all the senses to memory and emotions, stores are trying to use it to put people in the mood to shop. Odors may have an impact on spending behavior for a variety of products, including tennis shoes, clothing, and gambling. This has led one auto manufacturer to look for a fragrance—sort of an eau de honesty—that can be pumped into showrooms to increase the likelihood of consummating a deal. Consumer groups have blasted the use of scents in the retail environment and label the practice everything from sleazy to disgusting. Fragrance marketers defend the practice, arguing that the retail environment is under their control.

As the manager of a national chain of men's clothing stores, you are currently considering whether or not to add a scent to your retail environment. Your stores currently offer an inventory of predominantly Italian suits and European-styled dress and casual wear. Aromysys, a distributor of fragrance machines, has devised a way to dispense a fragrance electromagnetically. The scent is distributed in a consistent fashion. For less than $2,000 and with one machine, retailers can scent 3,000 square feet with an aroma.

1. How would you determine what scent to use in your chain of stores?

2. Discuss the pros and cons of adding scent to your retail environment.

3. What would you recommend?

This case is adapted from Cyndee Miller, "Scent as a Marketing Tool," Marketing News, *January 18, 1993, pp. 1–2.*

1. This opening vignette is from Marcel Proust, *Remembrance of Things Past,* 1934.
2. Edmund Blair Bolles, *A Second Way of Knowing* (Englewood Cliffs, NJ: Prentice Hall, 1991).
3. Marshall H. Segall, Donald T. Campbell, and Melville J. Herskovits, *The Influence of Culture on Visual Perception* (New York: Bobbs-Merrill, 1996); and Linda M. Scott, "Images in Advertising: The Need for a Theory of Visual Rhetoric," *Journal of Consumer Research* 21 (September 1994), pp. 252–73.
4. Bolles, *A Second Way of Knowing;* Alan R. Hirsch, "Effect of Ambient Odor on Slot Machine Usage in a Las Vegas Casino," working paper, Smell and Taste Treatment and Research Foundation, Chicago, 1994; and Michael E. Long, *National Geographic* 182 (November 5, 1992), pp. 3–41.
5. Gerald J. Gorn, Amitava Chattopaduyay, Tracey Yi, and Darren W. Dahl, "Effects of Color as an Executional Cue in Advertising: They're in the Shade," *Management Science* 43, no. 10 (1997), pp. 1387–400.
6. Gorn, Chattopaduyay, Yi, and Dahl, "Effects of Color."
7. J. Argue, "Color Counts," *Vancouver Sun,* June 10, 1991, p. B7.
8. Wayne Weiten, *Psychology: Themes and Variations* (Pacific Grove, CA: Brooks/Cole Publishing Company, 1998); and Deborah J. Mitchell, Barbara E. Kahn, and Susan C. Knasko, "There's Something in the Air: Effects of Congruent and Incongruent Ambient Odor on Consumer Decision Making," *Journal of Consumer Research* 22 (September 1995), pp. 229–38.
9. See Mitchell, Kahn, and Knasko, "There's Something in the Air"; and Susan C. Knasko, "Lingering Time in a Museum in the Presence of Congruent and Incongruent Odors," *Chemical Senses* 18 (October 1993), p. 581.

10. The idea of using scents in Disney World and the Epcot Center came from Disney Imagineering, which designs and develops all of the company attractions. Disney purchases its scents from Selton International.

11. William S. Cain, "Physical and Cognitive Limitations on Olfactory Processing in Human Beings," in *Chemical Signals in Vertebrates,* D. Muller-Schwarz and M. M. Mozell, eds. (New York: Plenum, 1977), pp. 287–301; William S. Cain, "Odor Identification by Males and Females: Predication vs. Performance," *Chemical Senses* 7, no. 2 (1982), pp. 129–42; B. J. Cowart, "Development of Taste Perception in Humans: Sensitivity and Preference throughout the Lifespan," *Psychological Bulletin* 90 (1981), pp. 43–73; Joseph C. Stevens, Linda M. Bartoshuk, and William S. Cain, "Chemical Senses and Aging: Taste versus Smell," *Chemical Senses* 9, no. 2 (1984), pp. 167–79; and M. Schleidt, B. Hold, and G. Attili, "A Cross-Cultural Study on Attitude toward Personal Odors," *Journal of Chemical Ecology* 7 (1981), pp. 19–31.

12. John Koten, "To Grab Viewer's Attention, TV Ads Aim for Eardrum," *The Wall Street Journal,* January 26, 1984, Eastern Edition, p. B1.

13. Sunil Gupta and Lee G. Cooper, "The Discounting of Discounts and Promotion Strategies," *Journal of Consumer Research* 19 (December 1992), pp. 401–11.

14. Koten, "To Grab Viewers' Attention, TV Ads Aim for the Eardrum."

15. John B. Hinge, "Critics Call Cuts in Package Size Deceptive Move," *The Wall Street Journal,* February 5, 1991, p. B1.

16. Robert E. Ornstein, *The Psychology of Consciousness* (New York: Pelican Books, 1972). See also Jerome Bruner, "On Perceptual Readiness," *Psychological Review* 64 (1957), pp. 123–52; and George Kelly, *The Psychology of Personal Constructs,* vols. 1 and 2 (New York: Norton, 1955).

17. Anthony G. Greenwald and Clark Leavitt, "Audience Involvement in Advertising: Four Levels," *Journal of Consumer Research* 11 (June 1984), pp. 581–92; and Chris Janiszewski, "Preconscious Processing Effects: The Independence of Attitude Formation and Conscious Thought," *Journal of Consumer Research* 15 (September 1988), pp. 199–209.

18. Janiszewski, "Preconscious Processing Effects"; Philip M. Merikle and Jim Sheesman, "Current Status of Research on Subliminal Perception," in *Advances in Consumer Research,* vol. 14, Melanie Wallendorf and Paul Anderson, eds. (Provo, UT: Association for Consumer Research, 1987), pp. 298–302; and William R. Wilson, "Feeling More Than We Can Know: Exposure Effects without Learning," *Journal of Personality and Social Psychology* 37, no. 6 (1979), pp. 811–21. A related area of research also speaks to the question of whether consumers' preferences and behavior can be influenced by factors independent of cognition. This stream of research regards what has been termed the "mere-exposure" effect. Because much of this research relies on *remembered* exposure or attention, we reserve this important discussion for Chapter 13 where we explicitly discuss attitude formation.

19. Geoffrey Hall, *Perceptual and Associative Learning* (Oxford: Clarendon, 1991); Keith J. Holyoak, Koh Kyunghee, and Richard E. Nisbett, "A Theory of Conditioning: Inductive Learning within Rule-Based Default Hierarchies," *Psychological Review* 96 (April 1989), pp. 315–40; and Chris Janiszewski and Luk Warlop, "The Influence of Classical Conditioning Procedures on Subsequent Attention to the Conditioned Brand," *Journal of Consumer Research* 20 (September 1993), pp. 171–89.

20. Greenwald and Leavitt, "Audience Involvement in Advertising"; and Richard L. Celsi and Jerry C. Olson, "The Role of Involvement in Attention and Comprehension Processes," *Journal of Consumer Research* 15 (September 1988), pp. 210–24. The topic of involvement and attention is also discussed in Chapter 11. See also Cynthia Huffman and Michael J. Houston, "Goal-Oriented Experiences and the Development of Knowledge," *Journal of Consumer Research* 20 (September 1993), pp. 190–207.

21. Rhonda Gibson, Huiuk Yi, and Dolf Zillmann, 1994, "Incidental Learning from Radio Advertisements with and without Curiosity-Arousing Questions," in *Advances in Consumer Research,* vol. 21, Leigh McAlister and Michael Rothschild, eds. (Provo, UT: Association for Consumer Research, 1993), pp. 282–85; Robin Coulter Higie, 1994, "A Test of Prescriptive Advice from the Rossiter-Percy Advertising Planning Grid Using Radio Commercials," in *Advances in Consumer Research,* vol. 21, Chris Allen and Deborah Roedder John, eds. (Provo, UT: Association for Consumer

Research, 1993), pp. 276–81; Romain Laufer and Catherine Paradeise, *Marketing Democracy* (New Brunswick, NJ: Transaction Books, 1990), p. 8; Richard E. Petty, John T. Cacioppo, and Rachel Goldman, "Personal Involvement as a Determinant of Argument-Based Persuasion," *Journal of Personality and Social Psychology* 41, no. 5 (1981), pp. 847–55; and Richard E. Petty, John T. Cacioppo, and Martin Heesacker, "Effects of Rhetorical Questions on Persuasion: A Cognitive Responses Analysis," *Journal of Personality and Social Psychology* 40, no. 3 (1981), pp. 432–40.

22. James Heckman, "Say 'Buy-Buy': Baby Product Makers School Marketers in Reaching Elusive Targets," *Marketing News* 11 (October 1999), pp. 1, 19.

23. Joel B. Cohen and Kunal Basu, "Alternative Models of Categorization: Toward a Contingent Processing Framework," *Journal of Consumer Research* 13 (March 1987), pp. 455–72; and Carolyn B. Mervis and Eleanor Rosch, "Categorization of Natural Objects," in *Annual Review of Psychology,* vol. 32, Mark R. Rosenzweig and Lyman W. Porter, eds. (Palo Alto, CA: Annual Reviews, Inc., 1981), pp. 89–115.

24. Anat Rafaeli, "When Appearance Matters: Visible Aspects of Organizations as Precursors of Service Expectations," in *Proceedings of the Fourth International Research Seminar in Service Management,* Pierre Eiglier and Eric Langeard, eds. (Aix-en-Provence, France: I.A.E., 1996), pp. 83–86.

25. Lawrence W. Barsalou, "Ad Hoc Categories," *Memory and Cognition* 11 (1983), pp. 211–27; William D. Wattenmaker, Gerald I. Dewey, Timothy D. Murphy, and Douglas Medin, "Linear Separability and Concept Learning: Context, Relational Properties, and Concept Naturalness," *Cognitive Psychology* 18 (1986), pp. 158–94; Craig J. Thompson, "The Role of Context in Consumers' Category Judgments: A Preliminary Investigation," in *Advances in Consumer Research,* vol. 16, Thomas Srull, ed. (Provo, UT: Association for Consumer Research, 1989), pp. 542–47; and Emilie M. Roth and Edward J. Shoben, "The Effect of Context on the Structure of Categories," *Cognitive Psychology* 15 (1983), pp. 346–78.

26. Recent research suggests that *frames* rather than independent feature lists provide the fundamental representation of knowledge. Frames include both abstract attributes and specific values for those attributes; and also connect attributes into a pattern of relationships. For a more complete discussion, see Lawrence W. Barsalou, "Frames, Concepts and Conceptual Fields," in *Frames, Fields, and Contrasts: New Essays in Semantic and Lexical Organization,* Eva Kittay and Adrienne Lehrer, eds. (Hillsdale, NJ: Erlbaum, 1992), pp. 11–35.

27. For an entertaining discussion and many examples of how categories vary cross-culturally, see George Lakoff, *Women, Fire and Dangerous Things* (Chicago: University of Chicago Press, 1987); Roy G. D'Andrade, "Cultural Meaning Systems," in *Culture Theory: Essays on Mind, Self, and Emotion,* Richard A. Shweder and Robert A. LeVine, eds. (Cambridge: Cambridge University Press, 1984), pp. 88–119; and Ajay K. Sirsi, James C. Ward, and Peter H. Reingen, "Microcultural Analysis of Variation in Sharing of Causal Reasoning about Behavior," *Journal of Consumer Research* 22 (March 1996), pp. 345–72.

28. Ronald E. Milliman, "Using Background Music to Affect the Behavior of Supermarket Shoppers," *Journal of Marketing* 46 (Summer 1982), pp. 86–91; Ronald E. Milliman, "The Influence of Background Music on the Behavior of Restaurant Patrons," *Journal of Consumer Research* 13 (September 1986), pp. 286–89; Lee Rath, "Store Music Directly Affects Buying Trends: Expert Advises Tailoring It to Suit Clients," *Merchandising,* August 1984; Jeff Ware and Gerald L. Patrick, "Gelson's Supermarkets: Effects of MUZAK Music on the Purchasing Behavior of Supermarket Shoppers," *MUZAK Research Report,* 1984; and Richard F. Yalch and Eric Spangenberg, "Effects of Store Music on Shopping Behavior," *Journal of Consumer Marketing* 7 (Spring 1990), pp. 55–60.

29. Gestalt psychology was founded by Max Wertheimer (1880–1943). Other influential pioneers in this area include Kurt Koffka and Wolfgang Kohler.

30. For examples directly relevant to restaurant scripts, see Roger Schank and Robert Abelson, *Scripts, Plans, Goals and Understanding* (Hillsdale, NJ: Erlbaum, 1977).

31. Junichi Kamekura, Gideon Bosker, Mamoru Watanabe, *Ekiben: The Art of the Japanese Box Lunch* (San Francisco: Chronicle Books, 1989).

32. Deborah J. MacInnis and Linda L. Price, "The Role of Imagery in Information Processing: Review and Extensions," *Journal of Consumer Research* 13 (March 1987), pp. 473–91; and Greenwald and Leavitt, "Audience Involvement in Advertising."

33. Deborah J. MacInnis and Bernard J. Jaworski, "Information Processing from Advertisements:

Toward an Integrative Framework," *Journal of Marketing* 53 (October 1989), pp. 1–23; and Chris Puto and William D. Wells, "Informational and Transformational Advertising: The Differential Effects of Time," in *Advances in Consumer Research,* vol. 11, Thomas Kinnear, ed. (Ann Arbor, MI: Association for Consumer Research, 1984), pp. 638–43.

34. Güliz Ger, "Country Image: Perceptions, Attitudes, Associations, and Their Relationships to Context," in *Proceedings of the Third International Conference on Marketing and Development,* R. R. Dholaki and K. C. Bothra, eds. (New Delhi, Academy of Marketing Science, 1991), pp. 390–98; D. Maheshwaran, "Country of Origin as a Stereotype: Effects of Consumer Expertise and Attribute Strength on Product Evaluation," *Journal of Consumer Research* 21, no. 2 (1994), pp. 354–65; and David Mazursky, "Forming Impressions of Merchandise and Service Quality," in *Perceived Quality: How Consumers View Stores and Merchandise,* Jacob Jacoby and Jerry C. Olson, eds. (Lexington, MA: Lexington Books, 1985), pp. 139–53.

35. Robert Jacobson and David A. Aaker, "The Strategic Role of Product Quality," *Journal of Marketing* 51 (October 1987), pp. 31–44; Leonard A. Morgan, "The Importance of Quality," in *Perceived Quality: How Consumers View Stores and Merchandise,* Jacob Jacoby and Jerry C. Olson, eds. (Lexington, MA: Lexington Books, 1985), pp. 61–64; Joseph A. Limprecht and Robert H. Hayes, "The Incline of Quality," *Harvard Business Review* 60 (September–October 1982), pp. 137–45; Michael E. Porter, *Competitive Strategy* (New York: Free Press, 1980); and Michael E. Porter, "The Competitive Advantage of Nations," *Harvard Business Review* 69 (March–April 1991), pp. 73–93.

36. Dhruv Grewal, R. Krishnan, Julie Baker, and Norm Borin, "The Effect of Store Name, Brand Name and Price Discounts on Consumers' Evaluations and Purchase Intentions," *Journal of Retailing* 74, no. 3 (1998), pp. 331–52; Jacob Jacoby, Jerry Olson, and Rafael Haddock, "Price, Brand Name and Product Composition Characteristics as Determinants of Perceived Quality," *Journal of Applied Psychology* 55 (December 1971), pp. 570–79; Jerry Olson and Jacob Jacoby, "Cue Utilization in the Quality Perception Process," *Proceedings, 3rd Annual Conference,* M. Venkatesan, ed. (Urbana, IL: Association for Consumer Research, 1973), pp. 167–79; Jacob Jacoby and Jerry C. Olson, eds., *Perceived Quality: How Consumers View Stores and Merchandise* (Lexington, MA: Lexington Books, 1985); Ashkay R. Rao and Kent B. Monroe, "The Effect of Price, Brand Name, and Store Name on Buyers' Perceptions of Product, Quality: An Integrative Review," *Journal of Marketing Research* 26 (August 1989), pp. 351–57; Valarie A. Zeithaml, "Consumer Perceptions of Price, Quality, and Value: A Means-End Model and Synthesis of Evidence," *Journal of Marketing* 52 (July 1988), pp. 2–22; and Jan-Benedict E. M. Steenkamp, "Conceptual Model of the Quality Perception Process," *Journal of Business Research* 21 (December 1990), pp. 309–33.

37. Ann Veeck and Alvin C. Burns, "An Investigation of the Use of Price-Quality Schema by Urban Chinese," in *Advances in Consumer Research,* vol. 22, Frank Kardes and Mita Sujan, eds. (Provo, UT: Association for Consumer Research, 1995), pp. 297–302; and Rose L. Johnson and James J. Kellaris, "An Exploratory Study of Price/Perceived-Quality Relationships among Customer Services," in *Advances in Consumer Research,* vol. 15, Michael Houston, ed. (Provo, UT: Association for Consumer Research, 1988), pp. 316–22.

38. Mary Jo Bitner, "Servicescapes: The Impact of Physical Surroundings on Customers and Employees," *Journal of Marketing* 56 (April 1992), pp. 57–71; Mary Jo Bitner, "Evaluating Service Encounters: The Effects of Physical Surroundings and Employee Responses," *Journal of Marketing* 54 (April 1990), pp. 69–82; Linda L. Price, Eric J. Arnould, and Patrick Tierney, "Going to Extremes: Rethinking Service Encounter Management and Provider Performance," *Journal of Marketing* 59 (April 1995), pp. 83–97; and Valarie Zeithaml, A. Parasuraman, and Leonard L. Berry, *Delivering Quality Service: Balancing Customer Perceptions and Expectations* (New York: Free Press, 1990).

39. Joseph A. Bellizzi, Harry F. Krueckeberg, John R. Hamilton, and Warren S. Martin, "Consumer Perceptions of National, Private, and Generic Brands," *Journal of Retailing* 57 (1998), pp. 56–70; Ronald P. Brensinger, *An Empirical Investigation into Consumer Perceptions of Combined Product and Service Quality: The Automobile,* doctoral dissertation, Department of Marketing, University of South Florida, Tampa, 1993; Isabella C. M. Cunningham, Andrew P. Hardy, and Giovanna Imperia, "Generic Brands versus National Brands and Store Brands," *Journal of Advertising Research* 22 (October–November 1982), pp. 25–32; Christine T. Ennew and Martin R. Binks, "Impact of Participative Service Relationships on Quality, Satisfaction and Retention: An Exploratory Study," *Journal of Business Research* 46 (October 1999), pp. 121–32; Paul S. Richardson, Alan S. Dick, and

Arun K. Jain, "Extrinsic and Intrinsic Cue Effects on Perceptions of Store Brand Quality," *Journal of Marketing* 58 (October 1994), pp. 28–36; and Steenkamp, "Conceptual Model of the Quality Perception Process."

40. Peter W. J. Verlegh and Jan-Benedict E. M. Steenkamp, "A Review and Meta-Analysis of Country-of-Origin Research," *Journal of Economic Psychology* 20, no. 5 (1999), pp. 521–46.

41. Søren Askegaard and Güliz Ger, "Product-Country Images: Toward a Contextualized Approach," in *European Advances in Consumer Research,* vol. 8, B. Englis and A. Olofsson, eds. (Provo, UT: Association for Consumer Research, 1997), pp. 50–58; and N. Papadopoulos, "What Product-Country Images Are and Are Not," in *Product-Country Images: Impact and Role in International Marketing,* N. Papadopoulos and L. Heslop, eds. (New York: International Business Press, 1993), pp. 3–35.

42. M. C. Han, "Country Image: Halo or Summary Construct?" *Journal of Marketing Research* 26 (May 1989), pp. 222–29; Irwin P. Levin, J. D. Jasper, John D. Mittelstadt, and Gary J. Gaeth, "Attitudes toward 'Buy America First' and Preference for American and Japanese Cars: A Different Role for Country-of-Origin Information," in *Advances in Consumer Research,* vol. 20, Leigh McAlister and Michael L. Rothschild, eds. (Provo, UT: Association for Consumer Research, 1993), pp. 625–29; Aysegul Ozsomer and S. Tamer Cavusgil, "Country-of-Origin Effects on Product Evaluations: A Sequel to Bilkey and Nes Review," in AMA *Educators' Proceedings,* vol. 2, Mary C. Gilly et al., eds. (Chicago: American Marketing Association, 1991), pp. 269–77; Nader T. Tavassoli, Lauren Goldberg Block, Bernd H. Schmitt, and Morris B. Holbrook, "Perceptions of Western Products in Transforming Socialist Countries," in *European Advances in Consumer Research,* vol. 1, Gary J. Bamossy and W. Fred van Raaij, eds. (Provo, UT: Association for Consumer Research, 1993), pp. 226–31; James L. Watson, ed., *Golden Arches East* (Stanford: Stanford University Press, 1997).

43. Eric J. Arnould, "Toward a Broadened Theory of Preference Formation and the Diffusion of Innovations: Cases from Zinder Province, Niger Republic," *Journal of Consumer Research* 16 (September 1989), pp. 239–67; Güliz Ger, Russell W. Belk, and Dana N. Lascu, "The Development of Consumer Desire in Marketing and Developing Economies: The Cases of Romania and Turkey," in *Advances in Consumer Research,* vol. 20, Leigh McAlister and Michael Rothschild, eds. (Provo, UT: Association for Consumer Research, 1993), pp. 102–7; Rajeev Batra, Dana L. Alden, Jan-Benedict E. M. Steenkamp, and S. Ramachander, "Effects of Brand Local/Non-Local Origin on Consumer Attitudes in Developing Countries," *Journal of Consumer Psychology* 9 (2, 1999), pp. 113–18; David McQuaid, "Poland: After the Gold Rush," *Business Eastern Europe,* October 24, 1994, p. 7; and Tavassoli, Block, Schmitt, and Holbrook, "Perceptions of Western Products in Transforming Socialist Countries."

44. Steven M. Burgess and Mari Harris, "Social Identity in an Emerging Consumer Market," in *Advances in Consumer Research,* vol. 26, Eric J. Arnould and Linda M. Scott, eds. (Provo, UT: Association for Consumer Research, 1999), pp. 170–75; K. G. Dickerson, "Imported versus U.S.-Produced Apparel: Consumer Views and Buying Patterns," *Home Economies Research Journal* 10 (March 1982), pp. 241–52; Susan B. Hester and Mary Yuen, "The Influence of Origin on Consumer Attitude and Buying Behavior in the United States and Canada," in *Advances in Consumer Research,* vol. 14, M. Wallendorf and P. Anderson, eds. (Provo, UT: Association for Consumer Research, 1987), pp. 538–42; and M. Wall and L. A. Heslop, "Consumer Attitudes toward Canadian-Made versus Imported Products," *Journal of the Academy of Marketing Science* 14 (Summer 1986), pp. 27–36.

45. Stephen Bayley, *Taste: The Secret Meaning of Things* (New York, Pantheon Books, 1991), p. 125; Millie R. Creighton, "The *Depato:* Merchandising the West while Selling Japaneseness," *Re-Made in Japan: Everyday Life and Consumer Taste in a Changing Society,* ed. Joseph J. Tobin (New Haven: Yale University Press, 1992), pp. 42–57; Liza C. Dalby, *Kimono: Fashioning Culture* (New Haven: Yale University Press, 1993); Grant McCracken, "The Making of Modern Consumption," *Culture and Consumption* (Bloomington: Indiana University Press, 1988), pp. 1–30; and Rosalind H. Williams, *Dream Worlds: Mass Consumption in Late Nineteenth Century France* (Berkeley: University of California Press, 1982), p. 71.

46. Dorothy George and George M. Zinkhan, "Why People Get Tattoos," *Skin & Ink,* July 2000, pp. 25–34.

Learning Objectives

After completing this chapter, you should be able to:

- Describe consumer acquisition strategies, behaviors, and major models of exchange.

- Be familiar with some basic approaches to consumer purchase decision making.

- Recognize some links between purchase timing, frequency, and marketing tactics.

- Explain the relationships between brand switching and marketing tactics.

- Discuss the nature of barter behavior and its implications in marketing.

- Identify the uses of countertrade in interorganizational purchase behavior.

- Recognize the importance of gift exchange in consumer behavior.

- Describe the differences between interpersonal and self-gifts.

Acquiring Things

Bartering in Russia[1]

Wrapped tightly against chilling winds, Valentina Novikova, a pensioner, stands expectantly at a lonely crossroads outside the old glass- and crystal-making town of Gus-Khrustalny, her champagne flutes tucked neatly into cardboard boxes, stacked on makeshift birch tables.

"Don't have money for champagne," she says sheepishly, displaying the glasses to passersby under gray skies, hoping to earn a few dollars a week to feed her grandchildren. In felt boots and a padded coat, she often walks miles to the crossroads with a tote bag of crystal. "I don't have much," she sighs.

The above description provides a poignant tableau from a little understood yet pervasive phenomenon in Russia's disorderly transition to free markets. The glass and crystal sold on the roadside here are the lifeblood of the local economy. Workers are paid in glass, receive their social benefits in glass and must sell the glass to stay alive. The glass has become a kind of substitute money. The workers and their glass factory are part of a vast transactional web of barter, trading, and debt—all using surrogates for the ruble.

In Volgograd, workers at the Armina factory decided to go on strike, according to the newspaper *Izvestia*. The reason: Their monthly wage of approximately $50 is paid in brassieres. "All our relatives and friends have got them already, and we do not know what to do with the rest," a worker laments. "See for yourself. We are paid in bras at 18,000 rubles each. That makes seven to nine bras a month. That is too many for one woman."

Movie theaters in the Siberian city of Altai started charging two eggs for admission because people had no cash to spare. However, the theaters ran into a problem in the winter when hens lay fewer eggs and audiences began to dwindle. As a remedy, the movie houses are now taking empty bottles as payment, returning them to the bottlers for cash. This flood of surrogate money has touched virtually every sector, every factory, and every worker in Russia. Thus, a trend that began a few years ago at a time of runaway inflation has persisted and become even more widespread as inflation has cooled. Nonetheless, the Russia economy still suffers from a variety of problems such as corruption, money laundering, and the effects of the recent Asian currency crisis, so industry continues to languish.

Overview

Acquisition is at the heart of consumer behavior research. Consequently, it is that part of the wheel of consumption that marketers know the most about. Some may think of impersonal marketplace transactions as the culmination of the wheel of consumption. There is a sense in which all persuasive marketing efforts are directed at facilitating commercial exchanges that lead to consumption behaviors. We might assume that such transactions are the universal vehicle through which customers obtain necessary goods and services in exchange for money. Marketers do tend to focus their attention on this kind of purchase behavior. Also, purchase behavior is a good label for impersonal marketplace transactions and exchanges of money for goods or services. But as anyone who has haggled in a Turkish bazaar, lingered in a hair-styling shop, participated in a Tupperware or Mary Kay cosmetics party, bought at auction, or even hung around in a small town café knows, much of the behavior associated with purchasing is far from impersonal. It often includes considerable amounts of emotion and interpersonal give and take. Purchase behaviors as diverse as haggling in a Turkish bazaar or buying Tupperware at a home-party sale are *embedded* in interpersonal relationships. Interpersonal ties may cause customers to buy when they have reasons for avoiding or postponing such a purchase. It may cause sellers to extend favors to good customers or cause buyers to exhibit loyalty to a particular retail outlet or service provider. Thus, purchase behaviors often include more than just impersonal acquisitions of need-fulfilling goods and services.[2] For example, **embedded purchases** are an integral part of the surrounding social world.

Acquisition is a more general consumer behavior concept than purchase behavior. Acquisition may involve goods and services; but it may not involve money. This is the case in **barter transactions,** also called **countertrade.** Countertrade is quite common in international marketing and in transfers of assets within large diversified holding companies or corporate conglomerates. Barter is also common in unofficial, informal economic transactions such as those illustrated in the opening vignette about Russian workers. In many developed nations, some consumers organize local bartering networks where goods and services are exchanged.

Other types of acquisition behaviors may involve money, but the tangible goods or services obtained are deemphasized in favor of the meanings or feelings evoked by the goods and services. This is the case with **gift-giving behaviors.** Gift giving is at the heart of a enormous amount of consumer behavior, and the retail industry often lives or dies by its sales of gifts during Christmas and other important international holidays. In the United States, for example, consumers spend $4 billion per day or $2.8 million per minute during the Christmas season. In Denmark, a nation of five million people, consumers spent 6 billion Crowns (about $1.07 billion) in the 1996 Christmas season.[3]

In this chapter we provide an introduction to each of these acquisition behaviors. In Chapters 11 through 13 we develop the theme of individual purchase behavior in greater detail. In Chapters 14 and 15 we expand on the interpersonal aspects of acquisition behaviors.

Note that other kinds of acquisition behaviors exist. For example, one may find objects by accident or may have stolen them. Found objects have played an interesting role in some modern art movements, such as Dada and pop art, but are not central to the study of consumer behavior. Thefts, including what retailers refer to as "inventory shrinkage," or shoplifting, is an important "darkside" consumer behavior, but we will not deal with it extensively here. Inheritance, another form of acquisition, is discussed in Chapter 19. Finally, consumers may produce homemade possessions for themselves or for subsequent giving. While not discussed in this chapter, it is worth noting that handicrafts received as gifts are frequently highly valued by some consumers.[4]

Discretionary purchase behavior, purchases devoted to satisfying wants rather than needs (see Chapter 11), is a relatively recent phenomenon even in the Triad countries, although it has a history in ancient China. So-called **lifestyle shopping,** *shopping as a form of leisure devoted to cultivating a consumer self-image,* is a phenomenon that emerged only in the late nineteenth century with the growth of the department store in Europe. Consumers in the transitional economies of the former Soviet bloc and emergent economies such as Turkey and India are often still learning to purchase and consume branded goods. They are still learning to understand price competition, promotions, and other marketing tools that many Euro-American marketers take for granted. Steeped in socialist values and habits, eastern Europeans often respond in surprising ways to these tactics. Shopping is still an occasional activity in developing parts of the world, especially where discretionary spending is quite limited. In these regions, acquisition behaviors are characterized by the values and habits of older, gift-based economies. In such economies, the value of possessions is realized primarily through acts of generosity, literally giving things away. Hence, the marketplace behavior in these societies often works in ways that Westerners might find peculiar.[5] Though not discussed extensively, we make some references to such economies in this chapter.

Acquisition Models

Consumer researchers and marketers examine acquisition behavior from five perspectives: (1) utility maximizing, (2) decision making, (3) experiential or hedonic, (4) behavioral influence, and (5) meaning transfer. The utility-maximizing view is derived from classic microeconomic theory. Marketers explore how consumers deliberately collect information, weigh alternatives, and make acquisition decisions that lead to the largest net benefit to them in terms of the exchange resources at issue. From the decision-making perspective, consumers engage in problem-solving tasks, in which they move through a series of stages (see Chapter 13).

The experiential or hedonic perspective holds that, in some cases, consumers acquire things to create feelings and experiences rather than to solve problems. The behavioral influence approach argues that consumers often act in response to situational, environmental

Excerpts from an interview with a 57-year-old female U.S. homemaker.

Consumer: I would definitely have to say The Gap is where my loyalty in clothing can be found. . . . The first time I bought an item at The Gap was around four years ago. I bought a pair of jeans on sale. . . . I have always been a shopper for clothes. It was almost a sickness of some sort. Some of my most shopped stores have been T. J. Maxx and Marshall's. I never bought things in small lots, everything I purchased was almost in what seemed to be bulk. And none of it was full-priced. I always bought on sale. The better the sale the more I bought. I also like to buy everything that matches. I do not mean by color but by label. If I bought a pair of slacks that were made by Ralph Lauren, I had to have a shirt from Ralph Lauren. When I bought the jeans at The Gap four years ago, I also had to buy a matching shirt. Nowadays, I have lost the appetite to buy in bulk (and my closet has gotten smaller). And I have stopped shopping at T. J. Maxx and Marshall's. I buy everything at The Gap. I still like to find a bargain, but now I will buy some things at regular price. Everything in The Gap matches each other, from belts, to socks, to slacks, and shirts. I have also made friends with the management team here in Brandon. They let me know when they are going to mark items down and when the new shipments will be in. I just love it. I feel like I am their friend and they are mine. On top of buying their clothes I also buy stock in the company. So, I actually own a piece of where I spend all my money. . . . The Gap makes quality clothing in my eyes. I still own that pair of jeans I first bought from them. They have stood the test of time and hiking in Colorado. The Gap has just all-around good clothing. I have never had problem with any of their clothes. And if something did go wrong I know that they will take the clothes back and give me a full return. Having a good return policy is important.

Interviewer: How would you feel if this product/company was no longer around?

Consumer: Devastated. I love their clothes and everything in my closet matches and is made by The Gap. On top of that I own a piece of the company so I would be losing money.

Interviewer: Do you feel like you have a relationship between you and the product/company?

Consumer: I have a buying relationship for their clothes and I have a friendship relationship with their workers. I feel special when I walk to The Gap and all the girls working say hello to me by my name. And these young girls don't treat me like an old lady.

Interviewer: If you could use one word to describe their product what would it be?

Consumer: Unique.

pressures, such as perceptual cues in retail environments (see Chapter 12). The newest view, the meaning-transfer view, argues that acquisition and consumption behaviors are often motivated by the desire to obtain meanings that are valuable within consumers' life stories (see Chapter 18). Each approach has merit. None alone is adequate to account for the full range of acquisition behaviors.

The five perspectives are complementary because they focus on different aspects of the acquisition process. More than one type of behavior may occur simultaneously, as illustrated in The Gap interview presented in Consumer Chronicles 10.1. In this description the consumer is influenced by (1) utility-maximizing factors ("I always bought on sale. The better the sale the more I bought"; "On top of buying their clothes I also buy stock in the company"); (2) decision-making factors ("Everything in The Gap *matches* each other from belts, to socks, to slacks, and shirts"); (3) hedonic factors ("It was almost a sickness of some sort"; "I just love it. I feel like I am their friend and they are mine"); and (4) meaning-transfer factors ("They have stood the test of time and hiking in Colorado").

Similarly, automobile buyers may be influenced by utility-maximizing factors ("The dealer is offering low interest rates"); that is, they may collect comparative interest-rate information to see how to minimize the financial burden incurred through the purchase. Consumers may also evaluate automobile purchase alternatives through a consideration of attributes and benefits (e.g., seating, horsepower) in order to develop their choices. Such behavior may be understood through the decision-making perspective ("The car I buy must have room for six passengers"). In addition, they may imagine the feelings associated with riding in a convertible or impressing their friends with a sporty, luxury, or specialty vehicle ("Imagine driving along the beach with the top down"). Such behaviors can be understood through an experiential or hedonic perspective. Finally, they may think of themselves as the type whose lifestyle is realized through possession of a certain type of vehicle or whose self-image is completed by the possession of such a vehicle ("I'm a sports car kind of person"). Behaviors of this kind can be understood best through a meaning-transfer perspective.[6]

Social Exchange

The sociologist George Homans proposed a model of exchange that is shown in Exhibit 10.1. One key idea presented in **Homans's model of exchange** is that buyers and sellers exchange resources (i.e., money, goods, services, social status, information, love) in varying proportions to meet their needs and in conformity with generally understood standards of fairness and propriety, subject to constraints of time, knowledge, and experience. For example, the consumer in Consumer Chronicles 10.1 states "I buy everything at The Gap,"

Exhibit 10.1 Homans's Model of Exchange: Resource Flows and Outcomes

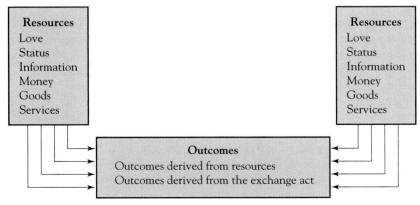

Source: George C. Homans, "Social Behavior and Exchange," *American Journal of Sociology* 63 (May 1958), pp. 597–606.

Exhibit 10.2 A Continuum of Acquisition Mechanisms and Motives

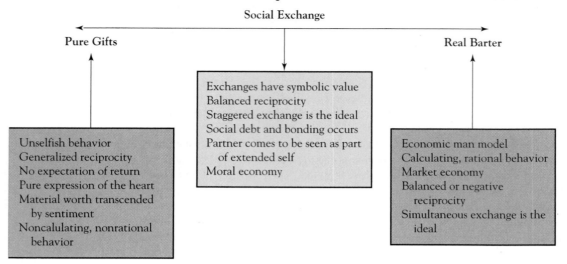

Source: Jonathan K. Frenzen and Harry L. Davis, "Purchasing Behavior in Embedded Markets," *Journal of Consumer Research* 17 (June 1990), pp. 1–12; Alvin W. Gouldner, "The Norm of Reciprocity: A Preliminary Statement," *American Sociological Review* 25 (April 1960), pp. 161–178; George C. Homans, "Social Behavior as Exchange," *American Journal of Sociology* 63 (May 1958), pp. 597–606; John C. Mowen, "Beyond Consumer Decision Making," *Journal of Consumer Marketing* 5 (Winter 1988), pp. 15–25.

in part because "The Gap makes quality clothing in my eyes." She also states, "the management team . . . lets me know when they are going to mark items down and when the new shipments will be in." Here, her focus is on outcomes. But Homans's exchange model also includes the idea that consumers derive value both from the things acquired and from the processes of acquisition, such as shopping, bartering, or gift giving. Thus, our consumer also states, "I have a friendship relationship with their workers." Here, her focus is on the process of exchange, from which she derives value. We discuss the outcome and process dimensions of exchange further in Chapter 17.

Exhibit 10.1 helps us to understand acquisition behavior. Successful marketers blend resources in novel ways to create distinctive market positionings and strive to ensure that both parties of an exchange derive benefit from it. In a simple purchase of a packaged good, the consumer derives the benefits of the good while the marketer derives the benefits of the money exchanged for it. But if a consumer shops for a diamond necklace at the exclusive Fred's or Bulgari jewelers, she also would expect to receive status and other benefits in exchange for her money. All acquisition behaviors can be represented on an exchange continuum between real barter and pure gifts (see Exhibit 10.2). Social exchange also appears on this continuum, as a midpoint between real barter and pure gifts.

Real barter conforms to the economic man acquisition model, in which exchange partners are calculating and highly rational in their exchange behaviors. At this end of the continuum transactions are a onetime phenomenon. Partners place no value on future exchanges, so they try to maximize current value of exchange resources. In such transactions the overriding norm is caveat emptor, let the buyer beware. Real barter is associated with the ideal markets of microeconomic theory. Commodities markets, used-car sales, utilitarian shopping, and flea market haggling all provide examples of such utilitarian acquisitions.

Purchases may also fall more toward the **social exchange** part of the continuum shown in Exhibit 10.2. In social exchange, utility-maximizing motives are present, but other factors moderate these motives. For instance, cultural norms of fairness may come into play. Exchange partners also may consider the long-term value of ongoing exchanges and hence be willing to sacrifice current utility for the sake of the long-term relationship. Sometimes, an emotional, personal relationship develops with the exchange partner; mutual favors are exchanged; and social debt is incurred.

Markets such as those created by in-home purchase parties can be explained as a form of social exchange in which social outcomes are equal to, or larger than, material ones. For example, many home shopping parties (where Tupperware or cosmetics might be sold) exhibit traits associated with social exchange rather than pure barter. The relationship marketing strategy in a business-to-business setting recognizes that embedding acquisition in social ties can increase customer loyalty and enhance organizational performance. Relationship marketing recognizes that firms should manage their customer interactions with a long-term view, as repeat purchase behavior is a key to creating a sustainable competitive advantage.[7]

At the other extreme from pure barter are **pure gifts.** Here, acquisition processes are embedded in relationships of **generalized reciprocity.** In such cases, exchange partners who assume things will work out in mutually beneficial ways worry little about short-term costs and benefits. Some behaviors resemble the gift-like characteristics of the Japanese *keiretsu,* the immense interlocking holding companies that dominate much of Japanese business. In these companies, member firms occasionally forgo profit or forgive the debt of another member firm that is suffering from a downturn in the business cycle. Such behavior is also characteristic of channel partners in some developing countries, such as wholesalers and retailers who may prefer to accumulate together rather than seek to maximize individual gain in their volatile marketing environments. Generalized reciprocity may also characterize gift-giving behaviors, such as those between loved ones, and may provide a motive for participants in local, self-organized barter economies and garage sales.[8]

Good marketing managers recognize that buying and selling involves multiple motives (see Chapter 11) and exchange orientations. No single orientation will drive every participant in a market transaction. Good salespeople also take a multiorientation approach knowing that customers are driven by different exchange motives. As shown simply in Exhibit 10.1, buyers are motivated both by extrinsic rewards, such as product or service performance, and intrinsic rewards, such as their enjoyment of the purchase or deal-making process.[9]

Purchases

Types of Purchase Decisions

Purchase Decisions

Consumers make many kinds of purchase decisions. We can distinguish a number of them, each of which has different managerial implications. First, a consumer may make a basic **purchase decision** in response to need recognition (see Chapter 11), as when communication needs trigger the decision to purchase a telephone. Second, the consumer may opt to make a particular **product category decision,** such as buying a cellular phone rather than a conventional phone or a shortwave radio. A cellular phone purchase decision is likely if conventional phone services are poorly developed, as in many transitional or

Swap meets, garage, boot, and rummage sales are popular alternative marketing channels.

developing countries. Of course, this decision is also affected by lifestyle (see Chapter 8) and many other factors.

Third, the consumer may make a **brand purchase decision** as when consideration of alternatives leads to the choice of a Nokia, Ericsson, Philips, or Motorola cell phone. Much marketing communication in the Triad countries, especially manufacturers' advertising campaigns, aims to influence this kind of decision. For instance, a Nokia campaign associates its digital communications products with the movie *The Saint*.

Fourth, the consumer may make a **channel purchase decision,** that is, deciding whether to purchase from a retail outlet, directly from a manufacturer, through a catalog, in a duty-free airport shop, or perhaps online. In addition to television or radio advertising, newspaper circulars and direct mail often are employed to influence this type of decision. Of course, consumers are not limited to these formal channels. Our opening vignette provides an example of a direct channel between a producer and a consumer. Farmers' markets are similar. North American consumers also will be familiar with the weekend garage sale where buyers circulate between sellers; whereas UK consumers prefer the weekend car boot sale, where sellers collect in a given spot.

Fifth, a **payment decision** is made to determine the payment method and terms of payment. Both retailers and credit card companies seek to influence these types of decisions. Both institutions benefit from the interest charge on credit purchases, but the former must choose between the benefits of immediate cash flow and the potential costs of unpaid debts. Sixth, there is a distinction between an **initial purchase decision** and a **repeat purchase decision.** This is especially important in organizational buying decisions (see Chapter 14). Many utility companies and consumer marketers have become interested in trying to automate repeat purchase decisions through such devices as automatic payroll deduction plans. As suggested, marketers may seek to influence one or more of the phases of the purchase decision process just outlined.

Purchase decisions need not be made in the order indicated above. For example, a payment decision may precede and even determine a brand decision or channel purchase decision. An international business traveler may seek out a restaurant that accepts American Express cards, because she lacks local currency.

Exhibit 10.3 portrays a simple model of the brand (or product category) purchase decision model widely used in consumer behavior research. It is based on the decision-making perspective of consumer purchase behavior. Of course, many purchase decisions may not match this model very well, especially those motivated by affective or meaning-

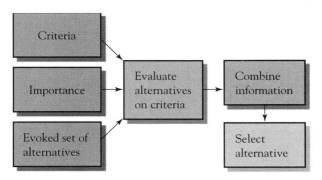

transfer desires. A good example are impulse purchases, which we will discuss in the following section.

The model presented in Exhibit 10.3 suggests that, in anticipation of making a purchase, consumers develop lists of criteria that are of significance to them because of the perceived benefits (e.g., needs, feelings, meanings) they provide. The consumers then rate these criteria in terms of importance. When making a product category decision, buyers might rate communication effectiveness highly, thus evaluating conventional versus cellular phones differently. In deciding where to shop, buyers might rate discount stores differently than specialty stores, depending on whether price or selection and service were more important criteria. Consumers also develop a set of alternative products, brands, or stores that they think will provide these benefits from memory, through external information search, or some combination of the two (see Chapters 12 and 13). They then combine all three types of information to reach a decision.

Marketers seek to understand the criteria that consumers use to select and rank stores or products or brands. Such knowledge can be used to position market offerings effectively by highlighting these criteria and rankings in promotional messages or other communications targeted to consumers.

A good example of a common purchase decision *not* explained well by the decision-making model of acquisition is the impulse purchase. Although early work on the topic tried to divide products into impulse and nonimpulse goods, it is now clear that almost anything can be subject to an impulse purchase. Although impulse purchases are typically unplanned, not all unplanned purchases are impulse purchases. **Impulse purchases** *occur when consumers experience a sudden, often powerful, and persistent emotional urge to buy immediately.* Impulse purchases also entail a sudden mental match between the meaning of a product and a consumer's self-concept. Consumer Chronicles 10.2 provides a good example of the experience of an impulse purchase.[10]

Impulse purchases do not conform to economic man or decision-making man perspectives in consumer behavior. Instead, the impulse to buy is a hedonically (pleasure-seeking) complex one. High emotional activation, low cognitive control, and largely reactive behavior characterize impulse buying. In one study, more than 75 percent of impulse buyers reported that they felt better after making such a purchase. Those with positive feelings believed that they got something they needed or accomplished a necessary task. In contrast, 16 percent reported that they felt no different and only 8 percent reported that they feel

Impulse Purchases

An Impulse Purchase Decision

I was excited to get a chance to mountain bike in this mecca for mountain bike riding (Moab, Utah). The first day the winds howled all day. . . . I felt so alive to be out there by myself, me and my bike against nature. After my ride, we stopped at the visitors center so I could change. There I saw this poster of these arches that I had just experienced on my ride. I felt that this picture would always capture my adventure. I walked right up to the cashier and bought it. . . . I immediately felt like this picture was my personal adventure. The price didn't matter. I just bought it. It is a picture of an adventure that I alone experienced.

worse after such a purchase. Those with negative reactions reported feelings of guilt or ambivalence.[11]

Impulse purchases have the potential to disrupt the consumer's ordinary behavioral stream. Because of the urge toward immediate action, impulse buying is prone to occur with diminished regard for the consequences of making the purchase. It may stimulate emotional conflict. Respondents often describe how the impulse arouses both pleasure and guilt. Many consumers report negative consequences from impulse buying, such as financial problems, disappointment with the product, or the disapproval of significant others. Sound familiar? Most consumers engage in impulse purchases at some time or another.[12]

Some impulse buying is related to various aspects of general acquisitiveness and materialism associated with the overall development of consumer culture. Thus, some impulse purchases are driven by the desire to fulfill imagined future needs.[13] An increase in recreational shopping is probably linked to impulse purchases too, since the positive mood generated in recreation may decrease self-control. It may also be that various marketing factors support impulsive purchase behavior, such as the availability of consumer credit, credit cards, ATM machines, television and on-line shopping, and long retail hours. Anonymous shopping or consumption contexts like telemarketing or online shopping may encourage impulse buying because the threat of social sanctions that dampen the buying impulse is diminished. Finally, impulse purchase behavior varies with individual personality traits such as variety seeking and risk aversion. Variety seekers may be more prone to impulse purchases, whereas risk-averse persons may be less prone.

On the surface, impulse purchases seem harmless enough. However, in some cases, impulse purchase behavior is transformed into compulsive purchase behavior. This is a darkside of consumer behavior—a clinical condition similar to eating disorders and compulsive gambling that may require medical treatment. Good Practice 10.1 shows questions researchers have used to screen for consumers' tendencies toward compulsive purchase behaviors. Care to take the test?[14]

Managing and Controlling Purchases

One goal of marketing is to predict and manage consumers' purchasing behavior. A great deal of the work in this area has been spurred by the growth of purchase behavior databases. Begun by the hotel and airline industries, database marketing has been adopted by many retailers and financial services companies. To implement the technique, marketers combine sophisticated marketing mix tools with equally sophisticated statistical methods to manage purchase frequency and timing, repeat purchase behavior and market share, and other indicators of marketing success.[15]

Work focused on managing purchase timing and quantity traditionally adopts an economic or decision-making perspective on consumer purchase behavior, more rarely a behavioral influence perspective. In this section we discuss findings that adopt these more traditional perspectives on consumer behavior.

Instructions for Q1: Indicate whether you agree or disagree with the following statements.

	Strongly agree	Somewhat agree	Neither agree nor disagree	Somewhat disagree	Strongly disagree
Q1. If I have any money left at the end of a pay period, I just have to spend it.	1	2	3	4	5

Instructions for Q2 through Q7: Indicate how often you have done each of the following.

	Very Often	Often	Sometimes	Rarely	Never
Q2. Felt others would be horrified if they knew of my spending habits.	1	2	3	4	5
Q3. Bought things even though I couldn't afford them.	___	___	___	___	___
Q4. Wrote a check when I knew I didn't have enough money in the bank to cover it.	___	___	___	___	___
Q5. Bought myself something in order to make myself feel better.	___	___	___	___	___
Q6. Felt anxious or nervous on days I didn't go shopping.	___	___	___	___	___
Q7. Made only the minimum payments on my credit cards.	___	___	___	•___	___

Scoring equation = $-9.69 + (Q1 \times .33) + (Q2 \times .34) + (Q3 \times .50) + (Q4 \times .47) + (Q5 \times .33) + (Q6 \times .38) + (Q7 \times .31)$

If score is ≤ -1.34, you are classified as a compulsive buyer.

Source: Ronald J. Faber and Thomas C. O'Guinn, "A Clinical Screener for Compulsive Buying," Journal of Consumer Research 19 (December 1992), pp. 459–69.

Timing and Frequency

Marketers are very interested in the timing of consumer purchases. **Purchase timing** refers to sequences of repetitive purchase events that occur over time. Consumers dispose of many goods (see Chapter 19) and therefore must replace them at regular intervals. Since a current purchase is worth more to a firm than a future purchase, marketers stimulate consumers to purchase frequently, and they attempt to shorten the interval between purchase occasions. Some tactics used to stimulate purchases include coupons, price cuts, point-of-purchase displays, and feature advertisements. Retail atmosphere and design can also influence purchase timing.

The notion of **purchase frequency,** especially repeat purchase behavior, is closely related to timing. A knowledge of purchase frequency helps marketers time promotional mailings, encourage greater purchase frequency, or estimate sales for particular product or service categories. Generally, it is more profitable for a firm to stimulate repeat purchases among loyal customers than to attract new ones. Through databases that identify frequent shoppers, firms can target customers for promotional mailings that they hope, based on past purchase behavior, will stimulate increased purchase frequency.[16]

Predicting Timing and Frequency Marketers are interested in predicting and influencing purchase timing and frequency. Predicting timing and frequency makes it possible to plan production, delivery, and estimate revenues and profits. By effectively managing timing and frequency, marketers can improve their knowledge of how modifications of the marketing mix will affect buying behavior.

We could assume that purchase timing is totally random. At the other extreme, we could assume *purchase behavior to be totally regular like clockwork.* We call this **deterministic timing.** Researchers have found that for consumer goods like crackers, coffee, yogurt, toothpaste, and the like, purchase timing and frequency are neither purely random nor totally deterministic but somewhere in between. To simplify, the chance of a repeat purchase occurring varies over time. Most researchers agree that there is a kind of dead period after a given purchase. Then the probability of a purchase reoccurring increases for a while. After a certain interval, the probability of the purchase reoccurring begins to decrease. In other words, for a segment of consumers, marketers can predict the likelihood a purchase will occur, but they can never be certain when a particular household or individual will make a purchase. This means that purchase timing and frequency can be predicted using the laws of probability. The mathematical details of the models used are not important here. Probabilistic models of purchase timing do a reasonably good job of predicting timing in stable markets over short periods, and increasingly researchers are able to incorporate more marketing variables into their predictive models. As suggested by Industry Insights 10.1, models show there is significant regularity in purchase timing for some consumer goods in stable markets.[17]

In addition to product purchases, probabilistic models have also been extended to describe frequency of household trips to grocery stores over time. These models furnish good descriptions of the frequency of store trip behavior. Models that provide a standard against which repeat purchase behavior can be compared are quite useful in stable markets. They can be used to compare the purchase frequency behaviors of different consumer segments or repeat purchase patterns among products, brands, or stores. Knowledge of purchase frequency enables marketers to time promotions effectively. Probabilistic models are less useful for predicting the purchase frequency of innovative products or in dynamic, rapidly changing markets where purchase patterns are unstable. Hence, applying them to transitional or developing country markets may not be possible.[18]

Managing Purchase Timing and Frequency Promotions are often designed to increase purchase frequency and are a powerful tool for managing purchase timing. The three top promotion-using industries in the United States are all markets crowded with many similar brands: food products, toiletries and cosmetics, and beer, ale, and soft drinks. In the late 1980s, U.S. manufacturers spent over $20 billion on trade incentives and distributed over 215 billion manufacturer coupons per year. Similarly, mass merchandisers like Marks and Spencer produce reams of coupons in the UK. In the UK, "instant win" promotions have blossomed across a wide range of products.[19] Behind the promotions are fulfillment houses that process coupon redemptions and consumer mailings (e.g., sweep-

Industry Insights 10.1

To understand the use of probabilistic models, consider an analysis of instant and ground coffee consumption data collected from scanner panel data. Researchers found common interpurchase times of 7, 14, and 21 days. The study found that price cuts increased purchase rates of instant coffee (by over 15 percent), that each additional ounce of coffee purchased increased the time to next purchase (by 24 percent), and that a household with two adults has a higher purchase rate than a household with one adult (12 percent higher). Among marketing mix variables, the researchers found that newspaper ads affected ground coffee purchases timing the most, while price cuts affected instant coffee purchase timing the most. They also discovered interpurchase periods in the timing of saltine crackers purchases in one U.S. market area of 7, 14, 21, and 28 days. In spite of these intriguing results, the researchers showed the difficulty of estimating interpurchase times using simple statistical predictive models, because unobserved factors have a big impact on purchase timing. This study concluded that more complex statistical procedures are required to get reasonable estimates of purchase timing.

Source: Rita D. Wheat and Donald G. Morrison, "Regularity, Recency and Rates," European Journal of Operational Research 76 (July 1992), pp. 283–89.

stakes entries, rebates), mail out checks or merchandise, and judge sweepstakes or contests. The global market research firm ACNielsen is the largest coupon redemption firm in the United States, handling coupon offers from over 180,000 U.S. retailers.[20]

Direct marketers use computerized databases to identify customers who are most likely to provide repeat business. Cooperating clients are asked to answer questionnaires and surveys in return for a coupon or premium. Results are entered into a database, and the information is used to determine the best promotional tactics for communicating with these buyers in the future. By observing the purchase patterns from their customer lists, early direct marketers developed a theory of purchase frequency known as the **RFM rule** (recency, frequency, monetary value). That is, *the likelihood of a response to a particular promotional mailing was influenced by the recency of the last purchase, the frequency of purchases over the past year, and the monetary value of a given customer's purchase history.* Segmenting markets in terms of deal proneness on the basis of criteria such as these three variables—recency, frequency, and value—helps marketers to predict the impact of promotional programs on purchase timing.[21]

Promotions are used to influence timing especially in product categories where there is little reason for consumers to choose between competitive brands. Examples of such product categories in the United States include ground coffee, instant coffee, toothpaste, laundry detergent, aluminum foil, and bathroom and facial tissue. Purchase timing is also found to accelerate with advertised price cuts.[22]

Limitations on Trying to Control Timing and Frequency The goal of managing purchase timing and frequency is likely to remain elusive in spite of improvements in predictive models. One reason is that consumers are not passive but active agents. Marketing tactics designed to influence purchase timing and frequency can and do backfire. For

example, marketing tactics may backfire in catalog sales. Common industry wisdom dictates that the more catalogs an organization sends to consumers, the more likely they are to purchase from a cataloger. In other words, purchase frequency is directly related to regular receipt of catalogs. However, consumers reach a catalog saturation point and tune out offers that exceed this threshold. Catalog purchase frequency increases at low levels as more catalogs are received within a year—until the mailbox hits tilt at some saturation point. After that point, consumers become less likely to purchase if they receive more catalogs.[23]

Promotions and other incentives designed to increase frequency can prove to be counterproductive in the long run. This occurs when consumers buy because of the promotion, not because of the product itself. In some Triad countries there is concern that consumers buy many packaged goods only when they are on some special deal or sale. Brand loyalty is thus sacrificed for purchase frequency. Consumers switch brands in favor of promoted brands. This behavior is not seen in some European countries where such deals are heavily restricted or illegal. Similarly, in Japan, discount selling remains in its infancy.[24]

Purchase Quantity and Brand Switching

Many marketing efforts are designed to create and maintain brand loyalty (see Chapter 17). Thus, marketers are concerned with **brand switching.** Brand switching is *the tendency for consumers to purchase competitors' brands within a product class.* Many factors stimulate brand-switching behavior. Environmental causes include stock-outs, price changes, deals, and advertising. Consumer-related factors include curiosity, boredom, and the need to balance among different needs and attributes possessed by competing brands and products. Consumers may also engage in switching when motivated by the desire for identification with an admired valued reference group (see Chapter 15).

Through switching, consumers sometimes seek to achieve a desired combination of attributes or benefits that do not exist in any one brand. That is, consumers may have a sense of an ideal product. If they find it in one brand, they may then stick with it, exhibiting brand loyalty. If not, they may combine switches between different brands in order to approach their ideal.

In a study of the French automobile market, it was found that brand switching patterns are nonrandom and structured. That is, managers can study these patterns and discover underlying patterns that can help them understand and predict market behavior. For instance, in the study of the French market, it was found that Citröen was not successfully implementing a targeted marketing plan. As a result, former Citröen owners were switching to other brands when it came time to make a new car purchase.[25]

Managing and Controlling Brand Switching Determination of the brand-switching cycle length can help managers develop a product line and create competitive strategies. For example, a company may wish to develop a full cycle of brands, that is, the limited set of brands among which consumers choose over time. Or a firm could specialize in one brand, which is one part of a purchase cycle that is complemented by the company's other brands. This one brand may be a large part of the cycle of a few or many consumers or a small component of the majority of the consumers. It may be that firms should not waste efforts trying to take over a full cycle with any one brand, but introduce brands that will substitute for others in a cycle.[26]

Deals and promotions affect switching behavior; that is, price differences between brands can influence brand-switching behavior. For example, retailers and manufacturers have an interest in determining the cross-price elasticities (or price sensitivity) and switching behavior associated with the complete set of ground and instant coffee brands. Such a determination enables managers to evaluate the impact of a price change, by their company or by a competitor, on the sales of all brands in a product class. Managers can also develop indicators of the clout or vulnerability of individual brands. **Clout** can be *measured by evaluating the effect of a price cut on one brand on sales of the other brands.* **Vulnerability** is *measured by summing the effects of price cuts of the other brands on sales of the brand of interest.* A study of the ground decaffeinated coffee category, for example, found that the Brim brand loses a larger percentage of its volume when two competing brands discount their prices than it gains when its price is discounted. Conversely, price increases on the other brands add substantially to Brim's sales. The net result is that demand for Brim is more sensitive to competitors' pricing actions than is either Maxwell House or Sanka, two other brands with larger market shares.[27]

Advertising affects switching behavior, as does consumers' need for novelty. Often, consumers' desires for the perceived benefits of competing brands fluctuate while perceptions of the brands remain stable, which leads to brand switching. One of the marketing implications of this idea is that advertising for an established brand, particularly a well-differentiated one, will be much more effective if it exploits the brand's positioning. Specifically, advertising should exploit the important elements of positioning that differentiate the brand from competing brands in a cluster in order to stimulate desire for the particular pattern of benefits it provides relative to other, similar brands. This kind of advertising can stimulate switching to the differentiated brand.[28]

Countertrade and Barter

We now discuss a different approach to acquisition. *Countertrade* is an inclusive term used to describe transactions where all or partial payment is made in kind (goods and services) rather than in cash. The basic countertrade where goods are traded for other goods is an age-old feature of foreign trade. Countertrade moves us away from Homans's model of pure barter and toward the social exchange part of his continuum.

Countertrade is a popular means of acquisition. Estimates of the extent of countertrade in international trade range between 20 and 30 percent. Countertrade in North America alone amounted to $8.4 billion in 1997. Forty percent of industrial sales in Russia were conducted through barter in 1996.

Why is countertrade a popular means of acquisition? It is a good way for firms to open new markets and establish long-term relationships with new customers, while reducing costs. Countertrade is also a good way of disposing of unwanted products and services. Policymakers have recently encouraged a number of African countries to expand countertrade. Shortages of hard currency (convertible, stable money) plus the massive foreign debt that burdens many of these countries makes countertrade an attractive alternative to purchase. In Russia, some companies use countertrade to hide income and thus evade the country's confusing tax policies. It is also a way to get around protectionist policies that limit foreign imports in some countries. The countries where countertrade is popular are also those most likely to experience rapid economic growth in the coming decades.[29]

Firms engage in four types of countertrade. **Barter** is the *direct exchange of goods between two parties in a transaction.* A simple example of corporate barter involves Sharp Electronics. Sharp arranged for 50 staterooms for 100 passengers on a major Mediterranean cruise line for its dealers, in exchange for surplus inventory traded to the cruise line. In the 1970s, the Swedish pop group Abba undertook a successful tour of Poland. They received payment for their musical services in potatoes! Subsequently, Abba organized deals for Russian heavy machinery and Czechoslovakian glass among other goods in exchange for its live concerts in these countries.

Barter can get complicated. In the early 1990s, SGD International, an American-based bartering company, supplied latex rubber to a Czech firm in exchange for 10,000 yards of finished carpeting. SGD then traded the carpeting to a hotel for room credits. The rooms were then traded to a Japanese company for electronic equipment, which was then bartered away for convention space. The cycle of exchanges ended when SGD traded the convention space for advertising space. Corporate barter is attractive because firms can usually recover their cost of goods and ultimately make a profit. It also allows them to do business in regions of the world where traditional economic transactions are somewhat difficult to secure.

Consumers also engage in barter trade. The opening vignette suggests some examples from a Russian context. In this case, barter is a response to the breakdown of the formal economy. In every developed economy some people trade goods and services informally through garage sales, swap meets, or car boot sales to earn extra income, to get around the market economy, for fun, or to avoid paying income taxes.[30] A most interesting example of a consumer barter system is provided by the rapid growth of the LETS systems discussed in Consumer Chronicles 10.3. Barter systems like LETS represent a small-scale challenge to traditional business practices.[31]

Compensation deals are *barter transactions that involve payment both in goods and in cash.* The former Soviet Union made frequent requests to Western suppliers for deals of this type. In one deal, General Motors sold $12 million worth of locomotives and diesel engines to Yugoslavia and took cash and $4 million in Yugoslavian cutting tools as payment.

Counterpurchase is the most common type of countertrade. In counterpurchase, *the seller agrees to sell a product at a set price to a buyer and receives payment in cash; however, the deal is contingent on a second agreement in which the original seller buys goods from the original buyer for the total monetary amount involved in the first sale or for an agreed-on percentage of that amount.* There is often a delay between completion of the first and second transaction so that the buyer of the goods in the second transaction has the time to find markets for them.

One example of a counterpurchase comes from Russia. The Sverdlosk region around Ekaterinburg in Russia exports certain products to the UK. Proceeds from these sales are deposited in an account at the Moscow Narodny Bank in London. In exchange, the UK Health Care Consortium provides health care products and services to an integrated health care program in the region.

Another interesting case comes from two developing countries in West Africa. Merchants in Ghana sometimes send salt north to Niger for sale. A Nigerien onion merchant travels with the Ghanaian truck until it reaches the capital of Niger, Niamey. There, the Ghanaian trucker hands over the money obtained for the sale of the salt to the Nigerien merchant in the form of a loan, with a one-month payback period. With the loan, the Nigerien merchant buys onions produced in Niger, loads them onto the Ghanaian truck, and returns to Ghana, where he sells the onions and repays the loan. In this way, the Ghanaian merchant secures a loan, and the Nigerien merchant risks less capital on the trade. In addition, the Ghanaian trucker is assured of a return load, a very important asset in this region where uncertain market conditions make commerce quite risky.[32]

Product buyback agreement is the final type of countertrade. This type of agreement usually *involves an initial sale of plant, equipment, or technology.* In one kind of buyback agreement, the seller of the plant or equipment accepts as partial payment a portion of the output of the new facility. In the other, the seller receives full price initially but agrees to

LETS stands for local employment and trading system. LETS systems represent a rebellious trend in consumer acquisition strategies motivated by four principles: (1) consume less; (2) consume local products; (3) avoid mass-merchandised, mass-manufactured goods; and (4) avoid cash and use alternative acquisition mechanisms.

The first LETS system was initiated in 1983 on Vancouver Island, Canada, by a business student who observed that many local people had skills and products to offer but lacked money to permit them to trade with one another. The objectives of LETS include both stimulating trade and building community relationships. LETS organizations are local. In the UK, the average membership of the 400 or so local LETS organizations is about 250.

The way it works is that a computerized system allows people to get in touch with each other and negotiate a trade at a price in the LETS currency. LETS members exchange everything from home decorating to baby sitting, time at vacation cottages to acupuncture. No money is exchanged, but individuals' accounts are credited and debited to the amount they agree on for the goods and services exchanged. Sometimes, they haggle over equivalents; other times rates of exchange are fixed. No interest is ever charged, and members are committed to the idea that accounts will balance in the long run, in conformity with the idea of generalized reciprocity. The face-to-face nature of these systems makes it easier to establish the necessary level of trust. By regularly publishing the balance position of members' accounts, members are discouraged from freeloading or running up big debts.

LETS systems can be found in North America, Europe, and Australia. Ithaca, New York, has a thriving LETS system that has even begun to develop a health insurance savings program. In Australia, it is now possible in some areas to pay local taxes in the special LETS currencies.

Source: Gabriel Yiannis and Tim Lang, The Unmanageable Consumer *(London: Sage, 1995), www.btwebworld.communities/lets; www.newciv.org./worldtrans/GIB/BOV-.*

buy back a certain portion of the output. In an example of the first type, Polish factories producing Fiat cars and International Harvester tractors discharged their obligations by sending back part of their production to the original licensors. Levi Strauss once had this same kind of agreement with Hungary. There, Levi Strauss took part of the Hungarian output of jeans for subsequent sale in Western Europe. In such a deal, the licensor gets new market access; the buyer gets new technology and know how, in addition to the plant and equipment.

Countertrade arrangements enjoy both advantages and disadvantages. Obviously, they involve a higher level of trust and relationship management than a simple cash-for-goods purchase. Hence, countertrade gives rise to specialized firms and corporate departments (Ford Motor Company has one, for example) that act as go-betweens and guarantors of a partner's trustworthiness. Industry Insights 10.2 summarizes some of the objectives buyers and sellers have in such transactions.

Sellers' Objectives

Gain access to marketing networks and
  expertise
Dispose of surplus, obsolete, or perishable
  products
Signal a high-quality product
Generate customer goodwill
Establish long-term relationships with new
  trading partners
Gain entry into new or difficult markets
Capitalize on strong bargaining power
Increase sales volume, market share, and profits
Help countertrade partner conceal a price cut

Buyers' Objectives

Generate goodwill
Acquire badly needed products and technology
Secure low-cost sources of production or raw
  materials
Establish long-term relationships with new
  trading partners
Conserve hard currencies
Help conceal a price cut
Reduce heavy debt burdens
Bypass trade restrictions
Free blocked funds
Circumvent an overvalued currency

Critics of business-to-business countertrade point out that it increases administrative costs; undercuts prices of competitive goods since goods are often sold at a discount; can lead to charges of dumping in the country receiving the goods; and can be used to conceal bribes or evade taxes. These criticisms have merit, but there is no doubt that countertrade is an effective means of clearing imperfect markets in a dynamic global economy.[33]

Gift Giving and Receiving

Gift giving and receiving is the final acquisition strategy we will discuss. As distinct from other acquisition strategies, **gifts** are *ritualized offerings that frequently represent connections to other people.* Gift exchanges have the potential to affect social relations in a way that purchases often do not. By "ritualized," we are referring to occasions when items or resources are given according to convention and occasions where the giving/receiving partners conform to cultural norms. In an increasing number of countries, if an unmarried woman accepts the ritual gift of a diamond ring, she is symbolically stating her commitment to marry the giver, for example. Similarly, in some traditional herding societies, gifts of livestock pass from the groom's family to the bride's family to solemnize the wedding commitment. In Japan, noted for the formality of its gift-giving procedures, bottles of scotch whiskey graded by the relative status of the exchange partners are often exchanged between business suppliers and customers at the New Year.[34]

The economic significance of gifts attracts marketers' attention. Consider that at least 10 percent of retail purchases in North America are given as gifts. North Americans buy 8 million greeting cards a day at more than one dollar per card. The commercial value of the Christmas cards exchanged in the UK in 1991 reached 250 million pounds (about $400 million). Over 1.3 million Japanese tourists visit Hawaii (their most popular destination) each year, spending on average about $100 per day on obligatory souvenir gifts, called

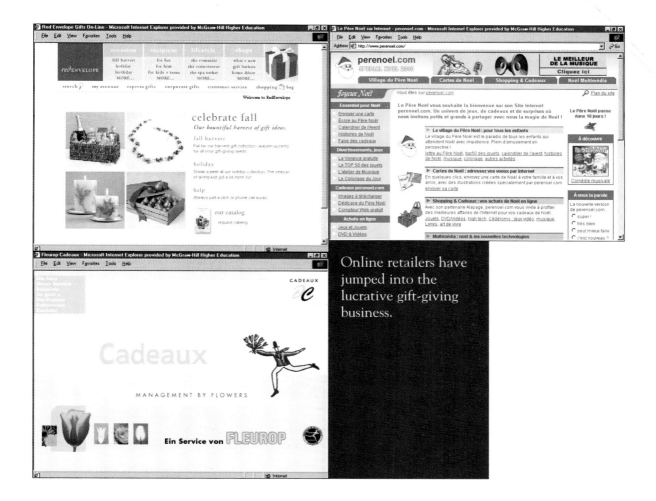

Online retailers have jumped into the lucrative gift-giving business.

omiyage. Recognizing the social importance of gift giving, online retailers have jumped into the gift business, as shown by the array of international websites pictured above.[35]

The importance that consumers attach to gift giving provides many opportunities for marketers. Although gifts often convey meanings that are difficult to put into words, many find the language of gift giving hard to master. Mistakes, disappointment, and gift-giving failures are not uncommon. These difficulties provide gift stores, online gift sites, executive gift-buying services, greeting card companies, and luxury good marketers with opportunities to facilitate consumer gift-giving exchanges.

Marketers may try to position objects to reinforce their suitability as gifts. The cut-flower market in the United States provides an example of a product category where promotional campaigns are used to strengthen the positioning of the product as a gift. Global marketers of luxury goods may try to interest new segments in luxury gifts as you can see at the FTD website. Another good example is the success the DeBeers cartel has enjoyed in marketing diamonds in Japan and other countries where they were not given traditionally. Finally, marketers may try to provide gifts to match occasions or even create occasions for gift giving, such as Secretaries' Day in the United States, Mother's and Father's Day in China, or Christmas in non-Christian countries.

 www.ftd.com

Although gift giving is universal, the language and rituals associated with gift giving are culturally specific. Guide books on doing international business sometimes feature useful discussions of the dos and don'ts associated with gift giving. In business-to-business contexts, marketers often must distinguish gifts from bribes and learn a new etiquette for appropriate gift giving to avoid embarrassment. Hence, analysis of gift giving as a mode of acquisition and consumption requires culture-specific analysis of consumer behaviors.[36]

Gift Exchange in Cross-Cultural Perspective

Gift exchange predates marketing; it is as old as human culture. The **norm of reciprocity** (also discussed in Chapter 15) describes the fact that *receiving a gift often creates a strong sense of obligation to make a return gift.* Such reciprocity may take the form of a tangible object, but it also can involve such intangible resources as deference (status) and gratitude. As the Homans model (Exhibit 10.1) suggests, such exchanges tend to strengthen social bonds. Because of the norm of reciprocity, gift giving encourages return giving, which in turn stimulates further giving. When such acts are multiplied across individuals and groups, societal stability is enhanced. Thus, the norm of reciprocity is a kind of glue that holds traditional societies together, prior to the development of written law, the marketplace, and specialized policing institutions.[37]

In premarket societies, gift exchanges organized numerous economic, social, and religious activities. Consider the **potlatch** of Native Americans in the coastal northwest. Gifts of blankets, seal oil, cedar chests, and native copper plates are given away at great feasts. Chiefs of one segment of the tribe host these feasts for other segments of the tribe in order to compete for titles and prestige. The photo on page 361 shows a native copper valuable of the type given away at a potlatch feast.[38]

Types of Gift Exchange

Modern gift giving is different from that practiced in traditional societies. To examine modern practices we'll focus on gift relations between persons and groups, specifically, interpersonal gifts and self-gifts.

Interpersonal Gifts

Exchanges of **interpersonal gifts** are provoked by specific conditions. These conditions can be either structural or emergent. Among the **structural occasions,** gift giving marks territorial passages, such as housewarmings, reunions, bon voyage parties, visiting, and farewell parties. Second, gift-giving occasions establish social placement, such as weddings, showers, baptisms, and christenings. Structural gift-giving occasions include those associated with rites of passage, such as debutante balls for society girls, initiation into a motorcycle gang, French wedding showers, bar or bas mitzvahs, graduations, and retirements. Third, there are those structural occasions associated with rites of progression, such as anniversaries, birthdays, and all the **calendric holidays,** for example, Christmas, Mothers Day, Halloween, and New Year. In part due to marketing activities, many countries have imported these gift-giving holidays.[39]

There are also **emergent occasions** for interpersonal gift giving. These include occasions designed to initiate a relationship, for example, an exchange of business cards between newly introduced business acquaintances. Gifts are also used to repair relationships, such as a "peace offering" in a domestic dispute. Finally, gifts may be given to deepen or intensify a relationship, as when a young man gives a school jacket to a young woman to symbolize that they are going steady. Similarly, an organization gives an employee a bonus to reward exceptional selling, service, or performance. The significance for marketers lies

Ceremonial copper ingot given in Native American potlatch ceremony.

www.peabody.harvard.edu/potlatch/default.html.

in identifying products that help consumers mark both structural and emergent occasions and, in some cases, identifying and inventing occasions for gift giving such as Secretaries' Day.[40]

Exhibit 10.4 presents a two-by-two table of interpersonal gift giving. The table contrasts altruistic with self-serving gift giving and voluntary with obligatory gift giving and provides some examples. These contrasts exist cross-culturally.

Gift giving differs from other modes of acquisition discussed here and in later chapters. This is because gift giving, especially voluntary, altruistic giving resists explanation in terms of the economic man model of acquisition. In terms of Homans's social exchange paradigm introduced in Exhibit 10.1, pure gifts are *noncalculating and nonrational. They are altruistic and voluntary; may express unselfish love; and are given with no expectation of return.* We sometimes refer to this form of giving as *generalized reciprocity.* Donating time at a soup kitchen, cooking a casserole for a bereaved neighbor, making a sacrifice in order to present a lover with a special gift, or even sending a greeting card to a distant relative provide additional examples of pure gifts. Notice the material worth of the gift is often less important than the sentiment it conveys.

Voluntary, altruistic gifts are associated with devotion for a beloved person or even an

Exhibit 10.4 Interpersonal Gift Giving

	Altruistic	**Self-Serving**
Voluntary	Charitable giving Giving a stranger change for a parking meter Surprising a friend with her favorite chocolates	Inviting the boss for dinner A Christmas gift for a service provider Competitive giving
Obligatory	Family members deciding how much to spend on Christmas gifts Bequests	Wedding gifts *Omiyage* Contributing to a charitable office pool

institution, such as a university or historic building. Voluntary giving is also associated with the behavior of market mavens and opinion leaders, who are driven to share market knowledge with others (see Chapter 15).

People are often willing to make low-value charitable donations, such as a bag of old clothes or can of food, voluntarily. Such gifts are relatively easy to elicit, but contribution-driven organizations often have difficulties eliciting donations above a certain threshold. To elicit higher-value donations, contribution-driven organizations employ tactics to increase consumer involvement, discussed in Chapter 12. Some may use the tactic of personal sponsorship for a poor child or a threatened ecosystem. Fund-raisers often employ the tactic of providing opportunities for personalizing contributions in this context to stimulate greater giving, such as the commemorative lists of donors seen in museums or the naming of university buildings or classrooms. The Heifer Project International (HPI) catalog page pictured on page 363 offers donors the opportunity to send a letter to the person to whom they donate money to buy livestock. HPI also offers testimonials about the dramatic impact of livestock on the quality of life of recipients.

Unlike altruistic giving, self-serving gift giving is *undertaken with some instrumental purpose; it is a means to an end.* Of course, altruistic giving may make givers feel better about themselves, but this does not make it less altruistic. Similarly, instrumental giving to enhance personal relationships is not necessarily antisocial. Thus, dating often involves a sequence of gift exchanges intended initially to establish sincerity or express thanks, later to express confidence in or commitment to a partner or to express apology for a disagreement. Gift giving may help partners evaluate compatibility by communicating taste and lifestyle preferences or symbolize preferred images of a romantic partner. A gift to a romantic partner of housewares conveys something different than jewelry, for example.

Self-serving or instrumental giving often expresses power dynamics. This was one aspect of the traditional Native American potlatch mentioned above. In the potlatch great chiefs demonstrated their wealth and power to others. Similarly, in modern Japan the norm is that more powerful business partners should receive more valuable presents than less powerful ones. In many countries men express power over women by paying for dating expenses, giving valuable gifts, or underestimating the value of gifts women give to them. A guide to doing business in Korea warns that Korean hosts may shower visiting business partners with gifts and gestures of hospitality. The book points out that the Koreans' cal-

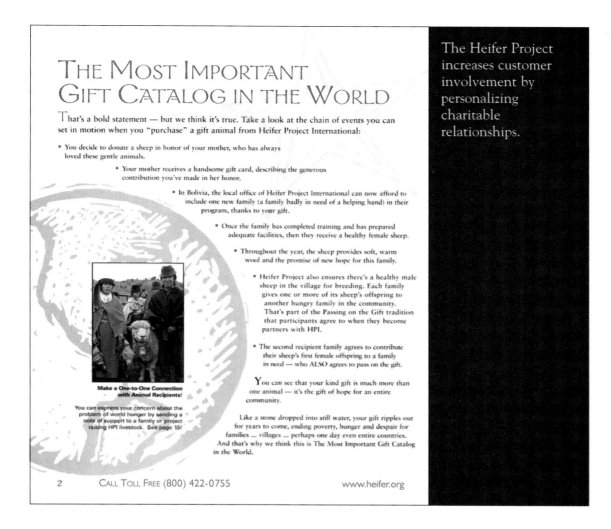

THE MOST IMPORTANT GIFT CATALOG IN THE WORLD

That's a bold statement — but we think it's true. Take a look at the chain of events you can set in motion when you "purchase" a gift animal from Heifer Project International:

- You decide to donate a sheep in honor of your mother, who has always loved these gentle animals.

- Your mother receives a handsome gift card, describing the generous contribution you've made in her honor.

- In Bolivia, the local office of Heifer Project International can now afford to include one new family (a family badly in need of a helping hand) in their program, thanks to your gift.

- Once the family has completed training and has prepared adequate facilities, then they receive a healthy female sheep.

- Throughout the year, the sheep provides soft, warm wool and the promise of new hope for this family.

- Heifer Project also ensures there's a healthy male sheep in the village for breeding. Each family gives one or more of its sheep's offspring to another hungry family in the community. That's part of the Passing on the Gift tradition that participants agree to when they become partners with HPI.

- The second recipient family agrees to contribute their sheep's first female offspring to a family in need — who ALSO agrees to pass on the gift.

You can see that your kind gift is much more than one animal — it's the gift of hope for an entire community.

Like a stone dropped into still water, your gift ripples out for years to come, ending poverty, hunger and despair for families ... villages ... perhaps one day even entire countries. And that's why we think this is The Most Important Gift Catalog in the World.

Make a One-to-One Connection with Animal Recipients!

You can express your concern about the problem of world hunger by sending a note of support to a family or project raising HPI livestock. See page 15!

2   CALL TOLL FREE (800) 422-0755   www.heifer.org

The Heifer Project increases customer involvement by personalizing charitable relationships.

culated generosity might inhibit the foreign business partner from making objective business decisions. A sense of obligation to reciprocate leads to being less critical and more cooperative in negotiations. You may recognize that this as an apt illustration of the power of the gift to command a countergift.[41]

Self-serving gifts are also employed to communicate identity. A number of studies show that gifts chosen in North America usually represent something about the giver's self-concept. Unique gifts help givers express their feelings about the uniqueness of the recipient as well. Gifts to children may have a socializing function, indicating desired role identities, as when boys are given toy soldiers or girls are given tea sets or baby dolls. Elderly persons often give heirloom gifts that express aspects of self-identity they wish to pass on to their descendants.[42]

Voluntary giving is motivated by personal, idiosyncratic reasons, but *social norms or pressures drive obligatory giving.* As in the potlatch, obligatory gifts are situated more toward the social exchange part of the Homans model. Some structural gift-giving occasions such as an exchange of Christmas cards or wedding gifts have an obligatory dimension to them. People also may feel obliged to reciprocate a gift in order to avoid the feelings of dependence the initial gift creates. Contemporary North American consumers both accept and are sometimes troubled by the obligatory dimensions of structural gift giving. Few such problematic connotations seem to be associated with obligatory giving in countries with well-formulated gift-giving rules such as Japan.[43]

Obligatory gift giving is associated with many structural gift-giving occasions and lends itself to stereotypical giving. This is the type of gift giving to which marketers may most easily respond. For example, Christmas cards, birthday party kits, and retail wedding lists provide consumers with simplified gift giving that communicates standardized meanings and emotions. In general, marketing communications can be employed to create or reinforce associations between conventional items and conventional gift-giving occasions. In cases such as the purchase of an engagement ring, buyers often seek help from retail personnel and specialized gift consultants, thus providing marketers with opportunities to influence gift purchase decisions.[44]

Self-Gifts

Self-gift behavior is not documented in premarket societies and does not seem to be recognized in China, but it is common in Western consumer societies. In **self-gifts,** *consumers give to themselves.* Self-gifts are differentiated from other personal acquisitions by their situational and motivational contexts. One study detailed two types of self-gift experiences: reward and therapeutic self-gifts. Self-gifting often occurs in a context of personal accomplishment, distress, or holiday occasion. The findings suggest that self-gifts are a form of personal, symbolic self-communication. In terms of outcomes, self-gifting can positively enhance self-concept, consistency, or esteem (see Chapter 7). Self-gifts can be products, services, or experiences, such as the Hawaiian holidays popular among single Japanese women.[45]

Self-gifts include ritualistic dimensions. For instance, self-gifts can involve sacrifices, such as abstaining from personal acquisitions in preparation for self-gifting. Because people consider self-gifts to be special, they may gift themselves infrequently to maintain the special qualities associated with a self-gift. Certain products are conventionally used as self-gifts. Clothing and travel are more frequently used as reward gifts than as therapy gifts, while fast food, grocery food, and personal care services are more often used as therapy gifts than reward gifts.[46]

Self-gift behavior correlates with socioeconomic traits such as age, financial condition, and gender. Older Americans self-gift less than younger ones do, for example. Wealthier consumers self-gift more than poorer ones. Similar to their use of interpersonal gifting behaviors for relationship building and maintenance, women self-gift therapeutically or to be nice to themselves. It appears men self-gift to create goal-related incentives for themselves.[47]

Self-gift purchasing may be linked to both cultural and personal values. A study showed that materialists are more likely to give self-gifts than nonmaterialists. This is especially true for occasions relating to mood management. Self-gift behavior may be particularly linked to cultural beliefs that purchasing and consumption are appropriate to the pursuit of individual happiness. In cultural contexts where purchase and consumption is not viewed in this way, self-gifting may be less common.[48]

Factors in the retail setting that affect self-gift behavior include the novelty or preselection of the brand, the brand's price, and the salesperson's empathy for the buyer's personal situation. Some managerial implications of these results are that retail advertising and point-of-purchase displays should employ themes to emphasize the increasing professional and personal independence of women. Marketing communications like these may heighten the self-gift purchase behavior of some market segments.[49]

Marketers will be most interested in gifts that take tangible form, although understanding the intangible resources they convey (investments of love, status, and time) is critical to the successful gift marketing. Tangible gifts include items consumers have made themselves or those held in their possession for a long time, such as heirlooms, and gifts purchased with the intention to give them to others. While research indicates that handcrafted gifts often convey strong emotional and relational cues to recipients, purchased gifts are obviously of special concern to marketers. However, as shown in the Heirloom Pocket Watch ad, marketers sometimes position purchased gifts as future heirlooms because of the value of heirlooms to consumers.

Some categories of goods are only given as gifts, such as greeting cards. Other categories of goods may be treasured by particular market segments as especially appropriate to give as gifts. Flowers, perfume, expensive liquors, or diamonds often serve this function in the West. Status brands are preferred by new elite consumers in the NIC countries and many Japanese tourists who shop for *omiyage* while abroad. Tourism provides endless opportunities to create souvenirs for giving. For example, devout persons may treasure items associated with holy places such as Jerusalem, Mecca, or Lourdes in France, while Disney World seeks to provide souvenirs for every taste and pocketbook. Hence all sorts of objects may convey important meanings.[50]

Is money an appropriate interpersonal gift? There is an enormous cultural variation in the symbolism of money that influences its suitability. Not surprisingly, therefore, money is sometimes appropriate and sometimes inappropriate as a gift, depending on cultural and situational context. For example, in many gift exchanges in Japan, exact monetary repayment is the norm. Money is often given on Hanukkah and Chinese New Years. Wedding guests may pin money to a bride's wedding dress in some Mediterranean cultural contexts. Sino-Vietnamese mothers associate money with savings and future utility and so like to give it to their children as gifts. One poll conducted in the United States found that for nearly every age, education, and income group, money is the most popular gift. In North America, cash gifts are often presented in situations where the level of knowledge of the specific wants and needs of the recipient are not well known. Cash gifts can lessen the uncertainty felt by givers, but they can also increase anxieties associated with potential violations of social norms.

Heirloom Pocket Watch And Glass Dome
Start a new family tradition by presenting him with our exquisite Heirloom Pocket Watch. Just like one his Grandfather might have had, with high-quality quartz movement and champagne dial with arabic indicators. Resting in a full-size, shimmering brass-plated case, handsomely etched with elegant vertical lines and his three initials. Comes to you complete with a 12" Waldemar Station Chain and reusable, wooden valet gift box. Quality craftsmanship by Colibri®.

For a distinctive display, rest your watch in our handsome Glass Dome. Removable top hook with polished brass base. A beautiful way to showcase collectibles. Measures 6"H.

#1038A Watch...$79.95
#2516A Dome...$26.95

Call Free On Board •759

Positioning a gift as a potential heirloom can increase its worth.

Restoration Hardware Encourages Self-Gifts

Up until this minute, I didn't even know that it was possible to have good taste in dustpans. But I am standing in front of one of the world's finest dustpans—admiring its capacious, open-mouth design, its sturdy metal construction, the elegant horsehair of the accompanying brush—and I can't tell you how much I yearn for it. If I owned this dustpan, I would be the sort of person I want to be. I'd take time to appreciate the beauty of everyday objects. I'd inhabit a world of simple craftsmanship, not of mass-produced clutter. I'd be one of those rare souls who have so much cultivation to spare that they can be thoughtful even about their cleaning equipment.

I've come across this admirable dustpan in a store called Restoration Hardware. And on my way to the sales desk I look around and find there's so much else I want. I want the ribbed steel flashlights I remember from summer camp . . . I want the old-fashioned kazoo, the mission-style magazine rack, the Moon Pies that I didn't even know were still made . . . the glass-and-steel Pyrex beakers just like the ones my doctor used to keep the tongue depressors in.

Source: David Brooks, "Annals of Consumption: Acquired Taste," The New Yorker, January 25, 1999, pp. 36–41.

www.restoration hardware.com

Some studies have revealed the existence of constraints on the use of money as a gift. For example, an investigation conducted in the UK used an extended-diary method to study aspects of the Christmas gifts given and received by 92 undergraduate students. The researchers found that cash money often lacks the attributes necessary for conveying information about intimacy and can possess attributes that may transmit inappropriate messages about the relative status of giver and receiver. Hence, in market economies the need for tangible gifts other than money persists. Marketers can provide alternative forms of giving money as gifts, such as American Express Gift Cheques, investment accounts, cash contributions to charities, and gift certificates that provide more symbolically suitable means of giving money than cash.[51]

Gift shopping affects product category purchase selections. Sales may be affected when a product is classed as appropriate for gift giving or as product classification changes. Because sales of U.S. housewares figure in the tens of billions of dollars, U.S. manufacturers were concerned by a slump in the purchase of housewares as gifts. This slump has been attributed in part to the trend toward later marriages. As age of marriage increases in other Triad countries, do you think a similar slump will occur? Recently, some retailers have found a way to reposition novelty housewares as suitable gifts. Restoration Hardware provides an example. Consumer Chronicles 10.4 indicates that by positioning its goods on nostalgia and promising tantalizing symbols of self-completion (see Chapter 7), Restoration Hardware tempts baby boom consumers to self-gift.[52]

As Consumer Chronicles 10.4 illustrates, marketing communications can create or sustain the associations between goods and their suitability as gifts. For example, marketers may encourage gift givers to reduce the risks of their purchase decisions by buying status brands as gifts that may impress receivers and increase the symbolic meaning of the presents.

The behavior associated with the search for gifts tends to differ from shopping for personal use. For instance, consumers respond differently to pricing tactics when shopping for gifts than for personal use. As the success of Restoration Hardware indicates, high-status retailers can effectively merchandise highly profitable, high-status brands that are purchased as gifts.[53]

Perhaps the most dramatic influence of gift giving on retailing concerns specialty gift stores. This type of store is found throughout the Triad countries and is also common in tourist destinations that serve Triad consumers. Ethnographies of specialty gift retailers lead to several managerial propositions. First, shoppers experience the store itself as a gift. By creating delightfully fantastic environments, gift stores can impart an added significance to the merchandise that consumers in turn imbue with meanings. Second, because gift giving is the work of women in North American culture, gift stores play an important role in the giving that helps them to maintain a gift economy. Using gifts purchased at gift stores, women consumers construct intimate relationships and "networks of love" between family members and close friends. Third, personnel, browsers, and purchasers alike appreciate the objects in the store. Meanings imputed to and through these objects by all of these stakeholders create and reinforce particular values associated with the items selected as gifts. Hence, encouraging interaction in gift stores is valuable to management. Fourth, purchasers recount that gift choice often is imprecise or indescribable. Shoppers know the gift is concealed somewhere within the store and assume it will reveal itself to them eventually. Search behavior for gifts appears to be motivated by hedonic processes, involving longing, imagination, romance, and desire. This finding suggests designing stores to facilitate a kind of treasure hunt and training service personnel to aid consumers in the hunt. Fifth, successful owners are highly involved with their businesses. Merchandise selection often reflects owners' identity and values. Hence, target markets and merchandise should be allowed to evolve with the owners' interests over time.[54]

Gifts Shape and Influence Behavior

Gift giving can shape and influence consumer behavior. Often marketers use gifts in an effort to command a countergift. Experimental research provides support for use of this tactic. For example, in some brand-choice experiments executed on personal computers, researchers found giving a small gift led consumers to reciprocate with greater belief in product claims and increased their willingness to try unusual or less familiar products.[55]

Gift giving can be used to improve customers' evaluations of services. Providing extras or unexpected touches can lead to an increase in customer satisfaction. Recall that the exchange model from Exhibit 10.1 stresses that both exchange outcomes and exchange processes affect consumers' evaluations and that the model proposes that every transaction involves the exchange of multiple types of resources. Analysis of service breakdowns shows that consumers' perceptions of interactional fairness (a process) influence their evaluation of breakdowns (an outcome; see Chapter 17).

Gifts are often used in direct-mail campaigns. Here they can be used as a foot-in-the-door tactic (see Chapter 15) to induce a purchase or charitable contribution or to encourage participation in marketing research. In devising direct-mail campaigns, many marketers include free gift offers to get better responses from customers. Do you or any of your family members receive gifts of calendars, cards, or return address labels from charitable organizations you support? These gifts are offered as tokens of the organizations' gratitude for your generosity. Of course, requests for more contributions usually accompany these gifts.

Tangible gifts are just one element of a successful direct-marketing campaign. Such campaigns may also stress the intangible benefits of the offer. There is value in providing a money-back guarantee, which customers may interpret as a kind of (intangible) gift that lends credibility to the offer and confidence to the buyer. Encouraging the consumer to interact with the company may also increase sales, by offering the (intangible) gift of information. One study showed that a coupon offer coupled with a requirement that the customer complete a questionnaire generated significantly more sales than the coupon alone. From a social exchange perspective, customers may view the questionnaire as a request for the gift of information in exchange for the coupon that they have received as a prior gift.[56]

The propriety of using gifts as a marketing tactic varies globally. Given its universality, exchanges of token gifts among business partners are a widespread practice. The website Management by Flowers shown earlier is a good example of a business gift service, for example. Among cosmopolitan business segments, giving premiums is a widespread and effective practice to reward customer loyalty. Business gifts travel well, and business customers everywhere insist on similar (high) standards of quality. However, one must always be sensitive to the boundaries between relatively altruistic gifts and relatively self-serving bribes. With this in mind, many countries restrict the use of premiums, coupons, rebates, and other "gifts" to consumers. Germany is quite strict in this regard. Nonetheless, in most developing countries, the practice of occasionally gifting regular customers with extras is widespread.[57]

This chapter explores a number of behaviors related to the acquisition of goods and services. Acquisition is a general consumer behavior concept. Marketers tend to focus their attention on the important, but relatively impersonal marketplace exchanges that we call purchase behavior. Purchase is the outcome of an array of other consumer behaviors and is often only an incidental part of these behaviors. Acquisition may involve goods and services; but it may not involve money. This is the case in barter transactions or countertrade. In gift-giving behavior goods or services may be obtained, but often the physical products are deemphasized relative to the relational significance or feelings gifts evoke.

Homans's exchange model provides a framework for understanding diverse consumer acquisition behaviors. Homans showed that both outcomes and processes are important to people in exchange, and identified some of the resources people bring to exchange. A continuum of exchange transactions may also be identified with utilitarian pure barter at one extreme, pure gifts characterized by generalized reciprocity at the other, and social exchanges in the middle.

Five complementary models of purchase behavior employed in consumer research include (1) utility-maximizing, (2) decision-making, (3) behavioral influence, (4) hedonic, and (5) meaning transfer perspectives. Often purchase behavior is best explained by a combination of perspectives. Impulse purchases are another kind of emotionally-driven purchase behavior that conforms poorly to the standard decision-making models. Compulsive purchase behavior is an extreme form of impulse behavior that occurs when normal behavioral inhibitors are somehow suppressed.

Purchase behavior management is one goal of marketing. Two main issues of concern are purchase frequency and timing, and brand switching behavior. Purchase timing refers to sequences of repetitive purchase events that occur over time. Purchase frequency refers to patterns of repeat purchases over time. Brand switching refers to consumers' tendency to alternate purchases between different brands. Mathematical tools of purchase behavior prediction make use of large scanner panel databases that provide use models in stable markets for basic products. Marketers tend to assume consumers adopt the utilitarian norms of pure barter in their purchase behavior. Marketers face a number of limitations in managing purchase behavior including consumers' evolving marketing savvy and the disruptive role of innovations.

Four main types of countertrade can be identified: barter, compensation deals, counter-purchase, and product buy-backs. Each is significant for business-to-business acquisition behaviors and helps to overcome market inefficiencies in some contexts. Consumer-to-consumer barter emerges in some economies when formal markets fail. Formal, consumer-initiated barter systems can be found in a number of countries around the world in which the exchange of resources other than money is central to the acquisition process. These systems fall toward the social exchange part of the exchange continuum.

Gift-giving is close to the pure gift on Homans's exchange continuum. Gift-giving motivates a very large volume of purchase behavior in all societies. In consumer culture, gift-giving animates a moral economy of sentiment that parallels the formal economy. The cultural roots of gift-giving may be found in pre-market economies. Two major types of gifts are interpersonal gifts and self-gifts. Both structural and emergent occasions may provoke interpersonal gift-giving. Interpersonal gifts may be voluntary or opportunistic. Managers may identify gift-giving occasions, influence gift-giving purchases, and design retail environments to encourage gift purchases.

1. Ask a friend to keep a log of some purchases for a particular nondurable consumer product category over a few weeks. Keep a log yourself of the same product category. After a few weeks, compare your purchase histories. Discuss purchase timing and frequency with your friend, and look for evidence of brand loyalty and brand switching. What are the implications of your behavior for marketing managers?

2. Does acquisition and self-gifting lead to happiness? Check out the World Data Base of Happiness at www.eur.nl/fsw/research/happiness/index.htm, maintained by Erasmus University in the Netherlands. Look at some of the national happiness scores. Compare scores between Triad, transitional, NIC, and developing nations. What do these scores suggest about the relationship between consumer culture and happiness?

3. Identify a consumer barter network in your community. Are you part of such a network? How does it work? What exchange model describes participants' motivations and acquisition strategies?

4. Describe some features that impulse purchases and self-gifts have in common. How does acquisition behavior involving gifts differ from other acquisition behaviors?

5. Not all feelings involved with gift giving are positive. What are some ways in which gift giving can evoke negative feelings?

6. What are some motivations for the purchase of self-gifts? What sorts of occasions may motivate self-gifting? Describe a recent occasion when you gifted yourself.

7. Discuss a recent gift-giving purchase with a friend. Find out how the item was chosen and what occasion stimulated the purchase. Did your friend take into account the recipient's personality? Does the gift reflect your friend's self-image? What message was your friend trying to convey? Was the gift successful? Why or why not?

8. Visit a gift store. Analyze the image created by the store in terms of the five managerial propositions discussed in the text.

You Make the Call

How to Sell More to Those Who Think It's Cool to Be Frugal

When the ultimate status symbols become acquiring scarce intangibles like a happy marriage, well-adjusted children, a balanced life, and interesting vacations, marketers may need to reassess their strategies. The Yankelovitch Monitor finds that today's yardsticks of success include satisfaction with self, getting control of your life, and having a great family. The challenge for marketers then becomes, How do organizations sell more goods to segments whose shopping strategy is less is more? One approach for responding to this challenge is to reposition products so as to align them with these shifts in values. For ex-

www.patagonia. com

ample, Patagonia, Inc., a sportswear manufacturer, has reduced the number of items in its catalogs, offers to repair used goods, highlights its fleece-wear made from recycled soda bottles, and promotes its garments as rugged enough to be passed along to the next generation. Industries affected by this change in values include clothing (e.g., the trend toward casual clothes), home builders (the price of log cabin logs has tripled, check out Norse

www.norse-log-homes.com

log homes at website), fragrances, hotels and other vacation-related businesses (stress-relieving vacations are in), and high-tech gear such as computers (fewer gadgets, please). Check out a few websites, and consider what you know about acquisition strategies, purchase timing and frequency, gift giving, and retail design and image.

1. Making use of this knowledge, give specific advice to corporate clients in one of the industries affected by the belief that less is more.

2. How should they modify their marketing strategies?

3. How can this business take advantage of the evolving values of the frugal consumer?

This case is adapted from Ellen Graham, "How to Sell More to Those Who Think It's Cool to Be Frugal," The Wall Street Journal, September 30, 1996, pp. B1, B2; and Kathleen Hughes, "Kids, Cabins, and Free Time Say Status in Understated 90s," The Wall Street Journal, September 30, 1996, pp. B1, B2.

1. David Hoffman, "Barter Now Replacing the Ruble," *International Herald Tribune,* February 1–2, 1997, pp. 1, 7.

2. Linda Price and Eric J. Arnould, "Commercial Friendships: Service Provider–Client Relationships in Social Context," *Journal of Marketing* 63 (October 1999), pp. 38–56; Clifford Geertz, "The Bazaar Economy: Information and Search in Peasant Marketing," *Supplement to the American Economic Review* 68 (May 1978), pp. 28–32; and Jonathan K. Frenzen and Harry L. Davis, "Purchasing Behavior in Embedded Markets," *Journal of Consumer Research* 17 (June 1990), pp. 1–12.

3. Lars Andersen, "Julegaver for 6 milliarder," *Jyllandsposten,* December 9, 1996; and Pat Bean, "Shopping Madness Is Here!" *Ogden Standard/Examiner,* www.standard.net:80/snweb/special_report/CHRISTMAS/Stories2.html.

4. Melanie Wallendorf and Eric J. Arnould, "My Favorite Things: A Cross-Cultural Inquiry into Object Attachment, Possessiveness, and Social Linkage," *Journal of Consumer Research* 14 (March 1988), pp. 531–47.

5. John Brewer and Roy Porter, eds., *Consumption and the World of Goods* (London: Routledge, 1994); James Carrier, *Gifts and Commodities: Exchange and Western Capitalism since 1700* (London: Routledge, 1995); Colin Campbell, *The Romantic Ethic and the Spirit of Modern Consumerism* (Oxford: Blackwell, 1987); Güliz Ger, "The Positive and Negative Effects of Marketing on Socioeconomic Development," *Journal of Consumer Policy* 15 (3, 1992), pp. 229–52; Rosalind H. Williams, *Dream Worlds: Mass Consumption in Nineteenth Century France,* Berkeley: University of California Press, 1982); and Terrence H. Witkowski, "Painting the Domestication of Consumption in 19th-Century America," in *Advances in Consumer Research,* vol. 26, Eric Arnould and Linda Scott, eds. (Provo, UT: Association for Consumer Research, 1999), pp. 644–51.

6. Craig J. Thompson, Barbara B. Stern, and Eric J. Arnould, "Narrative Analysis of a Marketing Relationship: The Consumer's Perspective," *Psychology and Marketing* 15 (May 1997), pp. 195–214; and John C. Mowen, "Beyond Consumer Decision Making," *Journal of Consumer Marketing* 5 (Winter 1998), pp. 15–25.

7. Susan Fournier, Susan Dobscha, and David Glen Mick, "Preventing the Premature Death of Relationship Marketing," *Harvard Business Review,* January–February 1998, pp. 42–51; Jonathan K. Frenzen and Harry L. Davis, "Purchasing Behavior in Embedded Markets," *Journal of Consumer Research* 17 (June 1990), pp. 1–12; and Charles W. Smith, "Auctions: From Walras to the Real World," in *Explorations in Economic Sociology,* Richard Swedberg, ed. (New York: Russell Sage Foundation, 1993), pp. 176–92.

8. Russell W. Belk and Gregory S. Coon, "Gift Giving as Agapic Love: An Alternative to the Exchange Paradigm Based on Dating Experiences," *Journal of Consumer Research* 20 (December 1993), pp. 393–417; Stewart Clough, "The Social Relations of Grain Marketing in Northern Nigeria," *Review of African Political Economy* 34 (1985), pp. 16–34; and Stewart Macaulay, "Non-Contractual Relations in Business: A Preliminary Study," in *The Sociology of Economic Life,* Mark Granovetter and Richard Swedberg, eds. (Boulder, CO: Westview Press, 1992), pp. 265–85.

9. Paul F. Anderson and Terry M. Chambers, "A Reward/Measurement Model of Organizational Buying Behavior," *Journal of Marketing* 49 (Spring 1985), pp. 7–23; and Richard L. Wessler, "Premiums: The Psychology of Motivation," *Marketing Communications* 9 (May 5, 1984), pp. 29–32.

10. James E. Burroughs, "Product Symbolism, Self Meaning and Holistic Matching: The Role of Information Processing in Impulsive Buying," in *Advances in Consumer Research,* vol. 23, Kim Corfman and John Lynch, eds. (Provo, UT: Association for Consumer Research, 1996), pp. 463–69.

11. Meryl Paula Gardner and Dennis W. Rook, "Effects of Impulse Purchases on Consumers' Affective States," in *Advances in Consumer Research,* vol. 15, Michael Houston, ed. (Provo, UT: Association for Consumer Research, 1988), pp. 127–30.

12. Dennis W. Rook, "The Buying Impulse," *Journal of Consumer Research* 12 (December 1987), pp. 251–64; Dennis W. Rook and Robert J. Fisher, "Normative Influences on Impulsive Buying Behavior," *Journal of Consumer Research,* 22 (December 1995), pp. 305–26; Peter Weinberg and Wolfgang Gottwald, "Impulsive Consumer Buying as a Result of Emotions," *Journal of Business Research* 10 (March 1, 1982), pp. 43–57; and Stephen J. Hoch and George F. Lowenstein, "Time-Inconsistent Preference and Consumer Self-Control," *Journal of Consumer Behavior* 17 (March 1991), pp. 492–507.

13. Geoff Bayley and Clive Nancarrow, "Impulse Buying: A Qualitative Exploration of the Phenomenon," *Qualitative Market Research* 1, no. 2 (1998).

14. Thomas C. O'Guinn and Ronald J. Faber, "Compulsive Buying: A Phenomenological Exploration," *Journal of Consumer Research* 16 (September 1989), pp. 147–57.

15. Kevin Lane Keller, "Conceptualizing, Measuring, and Managing Customer-Based Brand Equity," *Journal of Marketing* 57 (January 1993), pp. 1–22.

16. "The Future of Bank Card Authorization: Providing Incentives with Frequency Programs," *Chain Store Age Executive* 69, no. 10 (October 1993), pp. 86–87; and Simon Knox and Leslie de Chernatony, "A Buyer Behaviour Approach to Merchandising and Product Policy," *International Journal of Retail & Distribution Management* 18, no. 6 (November–December 1990), pp. 21–30.

17. Sunil Gupta, "Stochastic Models of Interpurchase Time with Time-Dependent Co-Variates," *Journal of Marketing Research* 28 (February 1991), pp. 1–15; Dipak C. Jain and Naufel J. Vilcassim, "Investigating Household Purchase Timing Decisions: A Conditional Hazard Function Approach," *Marketing Science* 10, no. 1 (Winter 1991), pp. 1–23; and Fred S. Zuyfryden, "The WNBD: A Stochastic Model Approach for Relating Explanatory Variables to Consumer Purchase Dynamics," *International Journal of Research in Marketing* 8 (September 1991), pp. 251–58.

18. Gil A. Frisbie, "Ehrenberg's Negative Binomial Model Applied to Grocery Store Trips," *Journal of Marketing Research* 17, no. 3 (August 1980), pp. 385–90.

19. Robin Cobb, "Marketing Services—Sales Promotion and Premiums: Lucky Dip Promo Ploys Soar," *Marketing,* July 8, 1993, pp. 22, 24.

20. Bob Gatty, "Incentives Move Products—and People," *Nation's Business* 69, no. 9 (September 1981), pp. 66–68, 70.

21. Paul Berger and Thomas Magliozzi, "The Effect of Sample Size and Proportion of Buyers in the Sample on the Performance of List Segmentation Equations Generated by Regression Analysis," *Journal of Direct Marketing* 6, no. 1 (Winter 1992), pp. 13–22; and Eileen Norris, "Direct Marketing: Databased Marketing Sets Enticing Bait," *Advertising Age* 59, no. 3 (January 18, 1988), pp. S10–S12, S15.

22. L. G. Schneider and I. S. Currim, "Consumer Purchase Behaviors Associated with Active and Passive Deal-Proneness," *International Journal of Research in Marketing* 8 (September 1991), pp. 205–22.

23. Melissa Dowling, "Mailbox Overload," *Catalog Age* 11, no. 12 (December 1994), pp. 1, 37; and Vicki G. Morwitz, Eric Johnson, and David Schmittlein, "Does Measuring Intent Change Behavior?" *Journal of Consumer Research* 20, no. 1 (June 1993), pp. 46–61.

24. "Facts Survey: Consumer Incentives," *Incentive* 165, no. 5 (May 1991), pp. 50–55.

25. Dawn Iacobucci and Geraldine Henderson, "Log Linear Models for Consumer Brand Switching Behavior: What a Manager Can Learn from Studying Standardized Residuals," in *Advances in Consumer Research,* vol. 24, Merrie Brucks and Debbie MacInnis, eds. (Provo, UT: Association for Consumer Research, 1997), pp. 375–80.

26. Moshe Givon and Eitan Muller, "Cyclical Patterns in Brand Switching Behavior: An Issue of Pattern Recognition," *European Journal of Operational Research* 76, no. 2 (July 28, 1994), pp. 290–97.

27. Randolph E. Bucklin and V. Srinivasan, "Determining Interbrand Substitutability through Survey Measurement of Consumer Preference Structures," *Journal of Marketing Research* 28, no. 1 (February 1991), pp. 58–71.

28. S. Kent Stephan and Barry L. Tannenholz, "The Real Reason for Brand-Switching," *Advertising Age* 65, no. 25 (June 13, 1994), p. 31.

29. "The Cashless Society," *The Economist,* March 15, 1997, www.economist.com/issue/15-03-97/fn6634.html; Beatrice B. Lund, "Corporate Barters as a Marketing Strategy," *Marketing News* 31, no. 5 (March 3, 1997), p. 8; and Dorothy A. Paun and Aviv Sholam, "Marketing Motives in International Countertrade: An Empirical Examination," *Journal of International Marketing* 4, no. 3 (1996), pp. 29–48.

30. Russell W. Belk, John F. Sherry, Jr., and Mealnie Wallendorf, "A Naturalistic Inquiry into Buyer and Seller Behavior at a Swap Meet," *Journal of Consumer Research* 14 (March 1988), pp. 449–70; Gretchen M. Herrmann, "His and Hers: Gender and Garage Sales," *Journal of Popular Culture* 29 (Summer 1995), pp. 127–45; Gretchen Hermann and Stephen M. Soiffer, "For Fun and Profit: An

Analysis of the American Garage Sale," *Urban Life* 12, no. 4 (1984), pp. 397–421; Myriam Hivon, "'Payer en liquide,' l'utilisation de la vodka dans les échanges en Russie rurale," *Ethnologie Française,* October 1998, pp. 515–24; and John F. Sherry, Jr., "A Sociocultural Analysis of a Midwestern American Flea Market," *Journal of Consumer Research* 17 (June 1990), pp. 13–30.

31. Gabriel Yiannis and Tim Lang, *The Unmanageable Consumer* (London: Sage Publications, 1995); www.btwebworld.communities/lets; and www.newciv.org/worldtrans/GIB/BOV-.

32. Eric J. Arnould, "West African Marketing Channels: Environmental Duress, Relationship Management, and Implications for Western Marketing," in *Contemporary Marketing and Consumer Behavior: An Anthropological Sourcebook,* John F. Sherry, Jr., ed. (Thousand Oaks, CA: Sage Publications, 1995), p. 168.

33. Gerald Albaum, Jesper Strandskov, Edwin Duerr, and Laurence Down, *International Marketing and Export Management,* 2nd ed. (Reading, MA.: Addison-Wesley, 1994); ALM Consulting, Frere Cholmeley Bischoff, and KPMG Peat Marwick, *Doing Business in Russia* (Lincolnwood, IL: NTC Publishing, 1993); Arnould, "West African Marketing Channels"; Philip R. Cateora, *International Marketing,* 8th ed. (Homewood, IL: Irwin, 1993); Stanley Paliwoda, *International Marketing,* 2nd ed. (Oxford: Butterworth-Heinemann, 1993); and Roger C. Riddell, ed., *Manufacturing Africa* (Portsmouth, NH: Honeymoon Educational Books, 1990).

34. David Cheal, "Showing Them You Love Them: Gift Giving and the Dialectic of Intimacy," *Sociological Review* 35, no. 1 (1987), pp. 150–69; and Cele Otnes and Richard F. Beltramini, eds., *Gift Giving: A Research Anthology* (Bowling Green, OH: Bowling Green State University Press, 1996).

35. Fumeritu Nitta, "Shopping for Souvenirs in Hawaii," in *Re-Made in Japan,* Joseph J. Tobin, ed. (New Haven: Yale University Press, 1992), pp. 204–15; and Mary Searle-Chatterjee, "Christmas Cards and the Construction of Social Relations in Britain Today," in *Unwrapping Christmas,* Daniel Miller, ed. (Oxford: Clarendon Press, 1993), pp. 176–92.

36. Belk and Coon, "Gift Giving as Agapic Love"; Russell W. Belk, "Special Session Summary: The Meaning of Gifts and Greetings," in *Advances in Consumer Research,* vol. 23, Kim P. Corfman and John G. Lynch, Jr., eds. (Provo, UT: Association for Consumer Research, 1996), p. 13; Kimberly J. Dodson and Russell W. Belk, "The Birthday Card Minefield," in *Advances in Consumer Research,* vol. 23, Kim P. Corfman and John G. Lynch, Jr. eds. (Provo, UT: Association for Consumer Research, 1996), pp. 14–20; Joy Hendry, *Wrapping Culture* (Oxford: Oxford University Press, 1995); Nitta, "Shopping for Souvenirs in Hawaii"; and Deborah Scammon, Roy T. Shaw, and Gary Bamossy, "Is a Gift Always a Gift? An Investigation of Flower Purchasing," in *Advances in Consumer Research,* vol. 9, A. Mitchell, ed. (Ann Arbor, MI: Association for Consumer Research, 1982), pp. 531–36.

37. Alvin Gouldner, "The Norm of Reciprocity: A Preliminary Statement," *American Sociological Review* 25 (1960), pp. 161–78; and Claude Levi-Strauss, "The Principle of Reciprocity," in *Sociological Theory: A Book of Readings,* Lewis A. Coser and Bernard Rosenberg, eds. (New York: Macmillan, 1964).

38. Macel Mauss, *The Gift: The Form and Reason for Exchange in Archaic Societies,* W. D. Halls, trans. (New York: W. W. Norton, 1990/1924); and Marshall Sahlins, *Stone-Age Economics* (Chicago: Aldine, 1972).

39. Dodson and Belk, "The Birthday Card Minefield"; Denise Girard, "Le shower: Enterrer sa vie de jeune fille," *Ethnologie Française,* October 1998, pp. 472–79; and Regine Sirota, "Les copains d'abord: Les anniversaires de l'enfance, donner et recevoir," *Ethnologie Française,* October 1998, pp. 457–71.

40. David Cheal, *The Gift Economy* (London: Routledge, 1988); I. Chukwuere, "A Coffin for the 'Loved One': The Structure of Fante Death Rituals," *Current Anthropology* 22, no. 1 (1981), pp. 61–68; Miller, *Unwrapping Christmas;* Constance Classen, "Sugar Cane, Coca-Cola and Hypermarkets: Consumption and Surrealism in the Argentine Northwest," in *Cross-Cultural Consumption,* David Howes, ed. (London: Routledge, 1996), pp. 39–54; John F. Sherry, Jr., "Gift Giving in Anthropological Perspective," *Journal of Consumer Research* 10 (September 1983), pp. 157–68; Sherri Athay, "Giving and Getting," *American Demographics* 15, no. 12 (December 1993), pp. 46–52; Carole B. Burgoyne and David A. Routh, "Constraints on the Use of Money as a Gift at Christmas: The Role of Status and Intimacy," *Journal of Economic Psychology* 12 (March 1991), pp. 47–69;

Constance Hill and Celia T. Romm, "The Role of Mothers as Gift Givers: A Comparison across Three Cultures," in *Advances in Consumer Research,* vol. 23, Kim P. Corfman and John P. Lynch, eds. (Provo, UT: Association for Consumer Research, 1996), pp. 21–27; Daniel R. Horne, Shay Sayre, and David A. Horne, "Gifts: What Do You Buy the Person Who Has ~~Everything~~ Nothing," in *Advances in Consumer Research,* vol. 23, Kim P. Corfman and John P. Lynch, eds. (Provo, UT: Association for Consumer Research, 1996), pp. 30–34; Jonathan Parry and Maurice Bloch, "Introduction: Money and the Morality of Exchange," *Money and the Morality of Exchange* (Cambridge: Cambridge University Press, 1989), pp. 1–33; and Margaret Rucker, Anthony Freitas, and Jamie Dolstra, "A Toast for the Host: The Male Perspective on Gifts That Say Thank You," in *Advances in Consumer Research,* vol. 21, Chris T. Allen and Deborah Roedder John, eds. (Provo, UT: Association for Consumer Research, 1994), pp. 165–68.

41. Russell W. Belk and Gregory S. Coon, "Can't Buy Me Love: Dating, Money, and Gifts," in *Advances in Consumer Research,* vol. 18, Rebecca H. Holman and Michael Solomon, eds. (Provo, UT: Association for Consumer Research, 1991), pp. 521–27; and Margaret Rucker et al., "When the Thought Counts: Friendship, Love, Gift Exchanges and Gift Returns," in *Advances in Consumer Research,* vol. 18, Rebecca H. Holman and Michael Solomon, eds. (Provo, UT: Association for Consumer Research, 1991), pp. 529–31.

42. Carolyn Folkman Curasi, Linda L. Price, and Eric J. Arnould, "You Can't Take It with You: An Examination of the Disposition Decision of Older Consumers," working paper, University of South Florida, 1996; and Mary Finley Wolfinbarger, "Motivations and Symbolism in Gift-Giving Behavior," in *Advances in Consumer Research,* vol. 17, Marvin E. Goldberg, Gerald Gorn, and Richard W. Pollay, eds. (Provo, UT: Association for Consumer Research, 1990), pp. 699–706.

43. Boye De Mente, *Korean Etiquette and Ethics in Business* (Lincolnwood, IL: NTC Publishing, 1988); Cele Otnes, Julie A. Ruth, and Constance C. Milbourne, "The Pleasure and Pain of Being Close: Men's Mixed Feelings about Participation in Valentine's Day Gift Exchange," in *Advances in Consumer Research,* vol. 21, Chris T. Allen and Deborah Roedder John, eds. (Provo, UT: Association for Consumer Research, 1994), pp. 159–64; and John F. Sherry, Jr., Mary Ann McGrath, and Sidney J. Levy, "The Dark Side of the Gift," *Journal of Business Research* 28 (1983), pp. 225–44.

44. Cathy Goodwin, Kelly L. Smith, and Susan Spiggle, "Gift Giving: Consumer Motivation and the Gift Purchase Process," in *Advances in Consumer Research,* vol. 17, Marvin E. Goldberg, Gerald Gorn, and Richard W. Pollay, eds. (Provo, UT: Association for Consumer Research, 1990), pp. 690–98; Martine Ségalen, "Où est déposé la liste? Une enquête sur les cadeaux de mariage," *Ethnologie Française,* October 1998, pp. 480–93; Belk and Coon, "Gift Giving as Agapic Love"; Sherry, McGrath, and Levy, "The Dark Side of the Gift"; and Sharon E. Beatty, Lynn R. Kahle, and Pamela Homer, "Personal Values and Gift-Giving Behaviors: A Study across Cultures," *Journal of Business Research* 22 (March 1991), pp. 149–57.

45. Annamma Joy, "When a Gift Is Not a Gift," working paper, Concordia University, Montreal, 2000; David Glen Mick and Michelle DeMoss, "Self-Gifts: Phenomenological Insights from Four Contexts," *Journal of Consumer Research* 17 (December 1990), pp. 322–32; David Glen Mick and Michelle DeMoss, "To Me from Me: A Descriptive Phenomenology of Self-Gifts," in *Advances in Consumer Research,* vol. 17, Marvin E. Goldberg, Gerald Gorn, and Richard W. Pollay, eds. (Provo, UT: Association for Consumer Research, 1990), pp. 677–82; and Nitta, "Shopping for Souvenirs in Hawaii."

46. David Glen Mick, Michelle DeMoss, and Ronald J. Faber, "A Projective Study of Motivations and Meanings of Self-Gifts: Implications for Retail Management," *Journal of Retailing* 68 (Summer 1992), pp. 122–44.

47. David Glen Mick and Michelle DeMoss, "Further Findings on Self-Gifts: Products, Qualities, and Socioeconomic Correlates," in *Advances in Consumer Research,* vol. 20, Leigh McAlister and Michael L. Rothschild, eds. (Provo, UT: Association for Consumer Research, 1994), pp. 140–46.

48. Kim K. R. McKeage, Marsha L. Richins, and Kathleen Debevec, "Self-Gifts and the Manifestation of Material Values," in *Advances in Consumer Research,* vol. 20, Leigh McAlister and Michael L. Rothschild, eds. (Provo, UT: Association for Consumer Research, 1993), pp. 359–64.

49. Mick, DeMoss, and Faber, "A Projective Study of Motivations and Meanings of Self-Gifts."

50. Sherry, "Gift Giving in Anthropological Perspective"; and Terence H. Witkowski and Yoshito Yamamoto, "Omiyage Gift Purchasing by Japanese Travelers in the U.S.," in *Advances in Consumer*

Research, vol. 18, Rebecca H. Holman and Michael Solomon, eds. (Provo, UT: Association for Consumer Research, 1991), pp. 123–28.

51. Athay, "Giving and Getting"; Burgoyne and Routh, "Constraints on the Use of Money as a Gift at Christmas"; Hill and Romm, "The Role of Mothers as Gift Givers"; Horne, Sayre, and Horne, "Gifts: What Do You Buy the Person Who Has Everything Nothing?"; Parry and Bloch, "Introduction: Money and the Morality of Exchange"; and Rucker, Freitas, and Dolstra, "A Toast for the Host."

52. "Study Tracks Housewares Buying, Information Sources," *Marketing News* 17 (October 14, 1983), p. 16; and David Brooks, "Annals of Consumption: Acquired Taste," *The New Yorker* (January 25, 1999), pp. 36–41.

53. Iris D. Rosendahl, "The Search for Profits: Selling General Merchandise," *Drug Topics* 126 (March 15, 1982), pp. 52–61; Bruce E. Mattson, "Situational Influences on Store Choice," *Journal of Retailing* 58 (Fall 1982), pp. 46–58; Richard Thaler, "Mental Accounting and Consumer Choice," *Marketing Science* 4 (Summer 1985), pp. 199–214; and David M. Andrus, Edward Silver, and Dallas E. Johnson, "Status Brand Management and Gift Purchase: A Discriminant Analysis," *Journal of Consumer Marketing* 3 (Winter 1986), pp. 5–13.

54. John F. Sherry, Jr., and Mary Ann McGrath, "Unpacking the Holiday Presence: A Comparative Ethnography of Two Gift Stores," in *Interpretive Consumer Research,* Elizabeth C. Hirschman, ed. (Provo, UT: Association for Consumer Research, 1989), pp. 148–67; and Melanie Wallendorf, Joan Linsday-Mulliken, and Ron Pimentel, "Gorilla Marketing: Customer Animation and Regional Embeddedness in a Toy Store Servicescape," in *Servicescapes,* John F. Sherry, Jr., ed. (Lincolnwood, IL: NTC Business Books, 1998), pp. 151–98.

55. Barbara E. Kahn and Alice M. Isen, "The Influence of Positive Affect on Variety Seeking among Safe, Enjoyable Products," *Journal of Consumer Research* 20 (September 1993), pp. 257–70.

56. Luther Brock, "The 10 Most Fatal Mistakes in Selling by Mail," *Marketing Times* 30 (November–December 1983), pp. 41–44; and Arthur L. Porter, "Strengthening Coupon Offers by Requiring More from the Customer," *Journal of Consumer Marketing* 10, no. 2 (1993), pp. 13–18.

57. "Barbarians at the Check-Out," *The Economist,* October 26, 1996, p. 84; and Margaret Bennett, "Premiums and Incentives: Bearing Gifts," *Marketing,* April 6, 1989, p. 47.

Learning Objectives

After completing this chapter, you should be able to:

- Explain why people buy and consume the things that they do and discuss the meaning of and relationship between consumer needs, wants, and motivations.

- Appreciate the diversity of human motivations and understand the relationship between motives and culture.

- Identify four classic approaches for accounting for human motivation and derive managerial applications from these theoretical approaches to motivation.

- Describe some research methods for identifying motives.

- Discuss the concept of involvement and how it is applied in consumer behavior and explain the difference between low-involvement and high-involvement situations.

- Describe some measurement approaches for assessing consumer involvement.

Why Do People Buy? Motivation, Needs, and Involvement

Magaji's Gold

I have known Magaji for 20 years. He worked for me as a research assistant when he was a young secondary school dropout, when I conducted research in Niger. Magaji was a tireless and able assistant who compiled large amounts of data for me in one village while I worked on data collection elsewhere. After our collaboration ended and I left Niger, Magaji found work as a rural health worker, giving vaccinations to children. He earns a pittance when he is paid, and because of Niger's economic difficulties, his salary is paid irregularly. He has married, fathered five children, and helped his father and younger brothers who work as farmers when he could. We have kept in regular correspondence, and I occasionally send him money to ease his hand-to-mouth existence as best I can.

Magaji recently wrote me a letter in which he explained that I should send him three gold necklaces with matching earrings and a gold ring. I knew that he meant jewelry that was at least 18-carat gold. He further explained that he needed to give these gifts to his wife, Mariama, and his teenage daughters.

Given Magaji's poverty, how can we account for his desire to buy expensive gold jewelry, presumably a luxury product, for his wife and daughters? To understand we need to know that gold jewelry is not just an economic resource, it is part of a gift economy and is connected to ideas of selfhood and social status. In rural Niger, a young woman's fate is tied to her marriage prospects; marrying well or marrying ill determines much of her subsequent life course. Marrying well depends in part on the amount of dowry the bride's family can contribute to

the marriage. One form that dowry takes is in the jewelry worn by the bride. Bringing gifts of gold to the marriage lifts the bride's prospects and increases her social status. Hence, as a loving and responsible father Magaji wants to do the best he can for his daughter. Giving a gift of gold is an excellent way to do this. This gold is a status symbol that the bride may use to attract young girls who may then help her in her chores in expectation that she may be able to help them in the future. It also becomes a small but important economic resource for the bride. If necessary, she may use some of it to invest in livestock or, should her husband's crops fail, to buy food for her children.

But what about the gift of gold to Magaji's wife? In Niger, buying gold jewelry is generally restricted to women in the commercial and governmental elites. Men may acquire prestige indirectly through their wives' display of gold jewelry. A gift of gold jewelry is a way for Magaji to signal his social status. At the same time, wearing gold provides Mariama with a token of midlife success and makes a statement about her husband's respect for her and his esteem, which are in turn positive aspects of self-worth.

Overview

Why do people do the things they do? More specifically, why do they buy and consume the products, services, experiences, and brands they do? This question is at the core of consumer behavior, and this chapter provides some answers. Although human motives have been studied for a long time, there are many ways of thinking about motives. We define **motivation** as *an inner drive that reflects goal-directed arousal.* In a consumer behavior context, the result of this internal drive is a desire for a product, service, or experience.[2] The motivated consumer is aroused, ready, and willing to engage in an activity. Here, we concentrate on applying motivational concepts to the realm of consumer behavior. From a marketing management perspective, it is crucial to bring marketing strategy in line with consumers' motivations and needs.

In this chapter we will discuss both drives and goals as aspects of motivation. A **drive** is *an internal stimulus.* For example, hunger, thirst, pain, and other physically experienced states are described as drives. Other emotionally experienced states such as the desire for affiliation or self-esteem can also be described as drives. **Goals** are *ends or aspirations that direct action.* To be considered a motive the goal should have independent power to bring about action. For example, in the opening vignette Magaji is motivated to be a good husband and father—gold jewelry is a way of achieving that goal. Gold jewelry could be used to attain other goals. For example, in Chapter 1 we described the important dual motivations of integration and differentiation. When Magaji's daughter displays her gold jewelry she will be integrated in her culture and at the same time distinguished as the daughter of a loving father. For Magaji's daughter the gold jewelry serves different goals than it does for Magaji. Having gold is not a goal but may be the means to fulfilling many different goals. Understanding the goals consumers are pursuing can provide important insights into many aspects of their behavior, including how they perceive and interpret the world around them (see Chapters 7 and 9). Human goal striving is very complex and varied. Many psychologists have constructed extensive lists of basic goals or needs. We will describe some of the most famous of these need typologies in this chapter. We will also describe how needs and motivations are influenced by a variety of marketing activities.

Human motivation is the product of interaction between events and things in the social world and interpretations of those events and things in people's minds. As described in the opening vignette, Magaji's drive to acquire gold jewelry for his wife and daughter reflects his love of his family and his understanding of the meaning of gold jewelry in his social world. In his social world, the gold his daughter wears will be read as a statement of his relationship to her. The gold jewelry will also influence her opportunities to marry and do well in the world.[3] Magaji makes his request very matter-of-factly, not recognizing that in other cultures gold jewelry might be viewed as a luxury rather than in the same category with providing basic clothing for the children. The authors of this text also want to be good parents, but we *may* view many different ways to accomplish that goal. Compared to Magaji's traditional and homogenous culture, our cultures provide less direction about how the goal of good parenting should be achieved, and the question of how to be a good parent is constantly revised on the basis of new incoming information.[4] An advertisement for Nabisco provides an illustration of how extensive that information can be. The ad advises parents to buy sport-shaped snack crackers to motivate their daughters to succeed in sports. Leafing through any parenting magazine provides numerous product appeals targeted to consumers who want to be good parents. In this chapter we emphasize how consumers' perceptions of social and cultural situations shape their desires and goals for action.

Motivational psychologists typically distinguish needs and wants. They describe **needs** as *broad, fundamental biological and psychological requirements that propel behavior,* including the need for food, water, and shelter. **Wants** are described as *the particular form of consumption that is capable of satisfying an underlying need,* for example, what food is consumed to relieve hunger.[5] However, consumers don't always experience distinctions between wants and needs; in fact, in many such cases the distinction is trivial. For example, in the vignette Magaji experiences this drive not as a want or desire but as a need—a need to provide for the welfare of his family. Although all human cultures probably share some common bases of motivation (because of their common biology), motivation researchers have been unable to identify a single set of universal motives, spot them in behavior, and explain situational variation in their expression.[6] In this chapter we will discuss some new insights into consumers' minds that can help us understand the relationship between culture and motivation.

In addition to discussing motivations, drives, and needs, we also introduce the companion concepts of effort and involvement. **Effort** reflects *the time and energy consumers are willing to commit to a goal.* When motivation to achieve a goal is high, consumers are likely to commit substantial effort. When motivation to achieve the goal is lower, they commit less time and energy to accomplishing the goal, although they may still engage in activities relevant to that goal. Involvement is closely related to both effort and motivation. Felt **involvement** is the *psychological outcome of motivation.* Pursuing goals, motivated consumers may feel *interest, excitement, anxiety, passion, engagement, and flow.* These are feelings of involvement with the goal objects. In this chapter we will describe and discuss different types of involvement motivated consumers may experience.

Marketers have a renewed interest in understanding why consumers do what they do. They want to get inside the behaviors and understand the reasons for those behaviors. In Chapter 3, we talked briefly about some consumer research methods such as projective techniques that can be used to understand motivations. In this chapter we describe in more detail some techniques for uncovering consumer motivations and measuring consumer involvement.

Classic Theories of Motivation

We begin with a discussion of some classic theories of motivation and needs. Each of these theories presents a psychological perspective and adopts an internal and universal view of motivation. That is, these perspectives assume that basic motives are shared. Several new insights into the evolution of the human mind and the role of culture in the mind's development challenge this premise. Nevertheless, these theories form a background for any discussion of motivation. To some extent, it may seem confusing that there are so many (sometimes conflicting) accounts and lists of human needs. One reason for this is that needs are not directly observable. They are psychological constructs. We hypothesize that needs exists, but it is hard to prove. We cannot see or touch a need or a motivation or want. We can only infer the existence of such concepts. Four motivational frameworks are considered:

- Sigmund Freud's concept of drives (e.g., as mediated by the id, ego, superego).
- Carl Jung's concept of archetypes (e.g., the self, the great mother, the hero).
- Abraham Maslow's concept of need hierarchy (e.g., physiological needs, safety needs).
- Henry Murray's list of human needs (e.g., abasement, acquisition, affiliation).

Freud's Psychoanalytic Theory

Sigmund Freud, an Austrian physician and pioneer psychoanalyst, was born in 1856. His insights about the existence of the unconscious mind profoundly changed people's notions about human motivations and needs and are now part of everyday thinking. Some argue that Freud's methods and conclusions were in error. Nonetheless, his work continues to exert a strong influence on many current beliefs about human motivation.

Overview of Freud's Theory

In brief, Freud described how many observed (abnormal) behaviors were easily explained if we would but consider the powerful unconscious forces at play.[7] In contemplating human motivation, Freud believed that the human psyche is broadly divided into the conscious and the unconscious. The **ego** represents the **conscious mind.** It is *composed of perceptions, thoughts, memories, and feelings.* The ego gives the personality a sense of identity and continuity. In many respects, Freud's notion of ego is a precursor to modern theories about self-concept (see Chapter 7).

The **unconscious mind** is called the **id.** It includes all *the instincts and psychic energies that exist at birth.* In this sense, the id (to a large extent) is biologically determined. The motivations that derive from the unconscious mind are both innate and unique to the individual. These strong motivations must be satisfied. From this perspective, human life can be understood as a constant struggle to find a way to control the surrounding environment so as to achieve goals and drives that emanate from the id. The power of the unconscious is so strong that ignoring its impulses can cause the rational processes of the ego to become distorted and result in neuroses, phobias, delusions, and other irrationalities. In this sense, Freud concentrated his attention on abnormal behaviors. His account of human motivation is very much an account of abnormal individuals—people who, for one reason or another, had trouble fitting into society.

Some kinds of consumer behaviors are driven by unconscious motives. Consumers often have difficulty articulating exactly why they like something or why they have purchased something. For this reason, marketing researchers often make use of techniques (e.g., the depth interview) that facilitate an understanding of unconscious motives. In a depth interview, a consumer is asked to explain in great detail the impressions that he or she has about a product or brand. Sometimes, the services of a trained psychoanalyst are employed to help elicit and decipher a consumer's hidden motives. Depth interviews were quite popular in the 1950s, and they are becoming more popular again. For example, Ernest and Julio Gallo is experimenting with the depth interview to learn more about how people perceive wines and how they buy them. John Bowen, director of the Center of Global Brand Management at Columbia University, consults with a psychoanalyst to understand how consumers react to brand names and how they interpret their experiences in the marketplace.[8]

The **superego** is the third structure hypothesized by Freud. It *represents the traditional ideas and values of society.* These values are learned at childhood and are transmitted largely through identification with parents. The superego serves as a conscience and attempts to curb the passions that emanate from the id. The id is wild and untamed. It represents primal, animal instincts. The superego attempts to exert a civilizing force. At the same time, the superego comes into conflict with the ego. The superego attempts to compel the ego to pursue goals that match the morality dictated by society and culture.[9]

The superego is like a filter or a conscience. Humans do not act on every impulse. People do not turn every thought into an action. Some thoughts are suppressed. Some ideas people have do not lead to action (such as purchase or consumption behavior). Freud's notion of the superego is applied in modern marketing theories, such as the **quick-choice model** (see Exhibit 11.1). Under this model, consumers respond to the constant flow of ideas (one of which is the father of another) by making use of a mechanism like Freud's concept of the superego. That is, *the flow of ideas is filtered by a consumer's notion of right or wrong.* Small children enticed by candy in end displays at the checkout counter of supermarkets are taught to interrupt their impulse to "grab it" by a filter that tells them not to steal. The quick-choice model is discussed in more detail in Chapter 13, under the topic of consumer decision-making models.

The main contribution of Freud's thought to motivational theory is the following. Freud's simple framework provides a way to think about the interplay between biological forces (represented by the id), societal forces (the superego), and human consciousness (the ego). These three forces are the foundations for explaining human motivations and

Exhibit 11.1 Quick-Choice Model

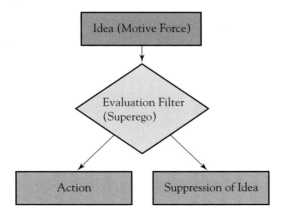

needs as they influence behavior. Whatever model we create to explain human motivation has to include a role for each of these major influences: biology, society, and the self. Freud believed that these psychological concepts were useful aids for understanding the mind's dynamics. It is important to recognize that Freud's three psychological structures do not necessarily have biological counterparts in the human brain. Nonetheless, these are interesting concepts for thinking about human motivation and how consumers balance conflicting desires.

Implications of Freud's Theory for Marketing

From a marketing perspective, new-product managers may try to create brands that fulfill needs of the id, ego, or superego. Similarly, advertising managers can use Freud's concepts to inspire creative copy. For instance, advertisers often use sexual symbols in ads; and the effectiveness of these ads is easily explained through Freudian theory. Many observers declared that the cartoon character Joe Camel looked like a phallus. Thus, many promotional themes appeal to consumers' unconscious motivations; and Freudian theory provides an interesting framework for thinking about these unconscious urges.

Another way to tap into the unconscious mind is by exposing respondents to specific images. For instance, a Freudian-trained psychotherapist might make use of a Rorschach test, the so-called inkblot test. A trained therapist can interpret a respondent's reactions to these seemingly random blots on a page. Marketing researchers have adapted this technique and are quite interested in studying consumers' reactions to visual images, again as an alternative to gathering information in a strictly verbal fashion. In the final section of this chapter we discuss the Zaltman Metaphor Elicitation Technique, or ZMET, as an example of a current image-based elicitation technique for understanding consumers' basic motivations.

Jung's Psychoanalytic Theory

Carl Jung agreed with Freud's core position about the importance of unconscious motivations. If anything, Jung believed that the unconscious mind was a stronger force in determining human action than did Freud. Jung maintained that the conscious life we experience is only one small part of the human mind. To understand human motivation, he felt that it was necessary to delve beneath the surface to understand vast unconscious forces at work.

Overview of Jung's Theory

In some sense, Jung's account of human motivation is more sophisticated than that provided by his mentor, Sigmund Freud. In particular, Jung specified that there were forces beyond the individual (the collective unconscious) that played an important role in directing human behavior. He conceived of the unconscious as being subdivided into the personal unconscious and the collective unconscious, which together hold all the hidden contents of the mind. The **personal unconscious** holds *previously conscious experiences that have been repressed, forgotten, suppressed, or ignored.* When these unconscious thoughts or feelings cluster, or constellate, in an organized group, they are termed *complexes.* Jung believed that complexes are held together by a nucleus that gathers related experiences around it. Although stored in the unconscious, the nucleus and its associated experiences can become conscious in the form of intuitions or similar inexplicable urges.

The concept of the collective unconscious is the most difficult of Jung's ideas about human motivation. Jung saw archetypes as an important bridge between the ways humans consciously express their thoughts and a more instinctive, visual form of expression. **Archetypes** are *a common reservoir of images that represent the collective unconscious.* In

Exhibit 11.2 Six Archetypes

Archetype	Common Symbolic Representations
Persona: The social mask a person dons to interact with others according to social convention and tradition as well as in response to the individual's own inner archetypal needs. The purpose of the public personality is to impress others, and it may conceal the individual's true nature. This facade develops out of an archetype, which reinforces as useful the assumption of a social role and set of related behaviors. Some individuals may lose touch with where the persona ends and the real self begins.	Masks; houses; actors; hats and other articles of clothing; shells
Anima/animus: The means by which one apprehends the opposite sex. Jung asserts that humans are essentially bisexual due to the presence of both masculine and feminine hormones in every individual's body. Living with the opposite sex throughout the millennia has conditioned humans to adopt some of the manifestations of the other sex. The threshold where the opposite can be understood is in the anima (within the male) and the animus (within the female).	Twins; the yin/yang sign; gods who have male/female avatars; oppositions such as dark/light, sun/moon; cloaks or caps
Shadow: The locus of animal instincts that humans have inherited during the process of evolution from lower life forms. This is where the concept of human sin lodges. When projected outward, it becomes the enemy or the devil. It is responsible for the appearance in the consciousness and behavior of unpleasant or socially reprehensible thoughts, feelings, and actions. It is hidden from view by the persona, but it still permeates the ego and personal unconscious.	Monsters; the left (side) animals such as the monkey or the dog; things that are hidden, especially in caves or cellars; the devil, hell
Self: The midpoint between the ego and the unconscious around which all other systems of the personality are constellated. This archetype represents human striving toward total unity of the personality—an ideal many strive for but few attain. It functions as a stabilizer by holding together the various systems of the personality while providing unity and equilibrium. Many people follow a religious path in search of the self. This archetype does not become evident until people reach middle-age because it requires all components of the personality to be fully developed and individuated.	Stones, mandala, crystals; spheres; a circle encompassing a square; the child (representing the original wholeness or totality of the unspoiled personality)
Great mother/earth mother: Represents life force on a sensing, feeling basis; the cycles of nature that serve as a reminder of the irrational and ungovernable primordial powers to which humans must submit; all that which is mysterious and not yet under the control of man, including birth, magic, and witchcraft; mortality.	The moon; landscapes; vessels of containment; eggs and rabbits; spring and summer; cattle; fruits and vegetables with seeds inside, such as corn or peas; rain and bodies of water; goddesses
Hero/rescuer: The familiar worldwide theme of hero and rescuer of his people who, although devoured by a monster or otherwise sacrificed, appears again in a miraculous manner, having overcome that which had seemed to have swallowed him. This symbolizes youth giving way to maturity by experiencing and, ultimately, overcoming the vices and impulses of the youngster. The need for such a fable to arise was to reaffirm and strengthen the ego. The universal pattern of the myth seems to have four phases:	Trees; rites of initiation or passage; quaternity (the element of "fourness"); male religious figures and their symbols, such as the cross
The trickster: Characterized by instinctual, infantile behavior and lacking in any purpose beyond gratification of the self; often cruel, cynical, and unfeeling.	Usually an animal figure such as the monkey
The socialized being: More mature stature, the transformer of human culture.	The hare, the coyote, and the spider; gifts
The he-man: Passes tests of strength and exhibits superhuman powers of intellect or strength; often has powerful companion who compensates for any of his weaknesses and who eventually departs leaving him and his offspring on earth.	Weapons; the square or rectangle (earthbound matter); the eagle often serves in the companion role

(continued on next page)

Exhibit 11.2 Six Archetypes—Continued

Archetype	Common Symbolic Representations
The union of duality: Often represented as human twins, each exhibiting contrasting attitudes (introversion/extroversion), functions (thinking, feeling, sensing, intuiting) and compensating for each other's deficiencies; they make an invincible team until they become too dangerous, at which point, they are made into a human sacrifice to save the world; resurrected, they become one in the process of transcending their differences; immortality.	Any identical pairs with differences under the surface; two-sided masks; creatures that move between two worlds, such as birds, snakes, or machines such as rockets (many phallic symbols are considered to be in this category); figure-eight symbol of infinity

Sources: Calvin S. Hall and Gardner Lindzey, *Theories of Personality* (New York: Wiley, 1978); and Carl G. Jung, M. L. von Vranz, Joseph L. Henderson, Jolande Jacobi, and Aniela Jaffe, *Man and His Symbols* (Garden City, NY: Doubleday, 1964).

his quest to better understand and describe human behavior, Jung studied the rituals and customs of primitive cultures, symbols, dreams, myths, religion, and works of art, as well as the symptoms of neurotics and the delusions of psychotics. The synthesis of his investigations led him to assert that the similarity of the brain's structure in all humans is due, in part, to a common evolution; he believed that the **collective unconscious** was *a storehouse of latent memory traces, or archetypes, inherited from the human ancestral past,* including prehuman or animal ancestry.[10]

Jung's archetypes are illustrated in Exhibit 11.2. This exhibit provides six examples of archetypes described by Jung, as well as symbols that are thought to be identified with them. The persona, the anima/animus, the shadow, and the self are considered so highly evolved and so important that they are often treated as separate symbolic systems. The hero/rescuer and the great mother/earth mother archetypes provide examples of global archetypes found in myths throughout the world. In this sense, Jung's research method follows a similar approach to that used by many contemporary social scientists who base their theories on a careful study of simple stories passed on from generation to generation.

Jung proposed that archetypes predispose humans to react to the world in a selective fashion. As the foundation of human motivation, the collective unconscious shapes a person's perceptions of the world and serves as a guiding influence by identifying itself with objects in the world that correspond to the image of its archetypes. For Jung, the collective unconscious explains why spiritual concerns are so deeply rooted in human life across cultures and why people in different cultures share certain myths and images, such as "mother" as a symbol of nurturing.[11] Jung was careful to point out that the archetypes, while shared universally, are also universally individualized. In this sense, Jung's notion about human goals is very similar to other theories of motivation.

Implications of Jung's Theory for Marketing

Jung's approach is important for marketers because it provides a way to explore myths, images, and symbols. In turn, myths and symbols are the building blocks for creating marketing phenomena, such as advertisements and promotions. To make use of Jung's archetypes, advertisers need to isolate the positive characteristics associated with myths or symbols (discussed in Chapters 5 and 18). According to Jung's theory, humans do share deep-seated, eternal similarities. Since this is the case, Jung's theory provides a path for describing one way that marketers' messages can be globalized. By selecting universal symbols to enhance communication, marketers have an opportunity to use similar promotional campaigns in many different cultures.

Because many of the visual arts are considered a rich source of knowledge about the archetypes of the collective unconscious, two graphic examples of their use in well-known promotional campaigns are briefly discussed here: the Calvin Klein jeans promotion and the Land O'Lakes dairy products logo.

The Calvin Klein jeans promotion is one of the most controversial and memorable ad campaigns in the last decade. From teen actress Brooke Shields purring "Nothing comes between me and my Calvins" to a fantasy spread featuring couples attired in the product and little else, Calvin Klein jeans promotions are heavily imbued with the sensuality and suggestiveness of **the shadow.** One of Jung's archetypes, the shadow is where *hide all the inadvertent aspects of the personality that may be unfavorable, nefarious, or suppressed, in addition to the instinctive and creative impulses.* When the ego attempts to see what is hidden in the shadow, it becomes aware of those forbidden qualities and impulses that are denied in the self but seen in other people. The erotic promotions, often featuring very young models, invite the consumer to experience the urges of the shadow by wearing Calvin Klein jeans.

The Millennium Center ran an ad that provides an interesting example of an appeal to "the forbidden." This advertisement for the grand opening of a Budapest shopping center appeared in a Hungarian-language magazine. Anyone buying this magazine speaks Hungarian. This was the only English-language advertisement appearing in the magazine. Both shopping and speaking English used to be forbidden fruit. Now, the Millennium Center draws on the Judeo-Christian story of Eve and encourages consumers to not resist temptation. The advertisement appeals to the power of the shadow—hidden longings.

The Land O'Lakes brand of dairy products uses promotions that are heavily loaded with symbolic references to the **great mother/earth mother** archetype. In Western culture this archetype is expressed in such mythical characters as the Greek goddess Gaea, the daughter of Chaos and both mother and wife to Uranus (the sky) and Pontus (the sea). As such, Gaea is the mother and nourisher of all things. Kneeling on the earth, the Native American maiden who adorns all of the Land O'Lakes promotions reinforces the natural linkages between milk products, nourishment, and females. Both Native American and female, she is doubly charged with the stereotypic associations assigned those groups in Western culture: beings who are highly attuned to their nonrational, instinctual drives and who commune with the primordial forces of nature. The summer landscape with gentle hills and a lake, often featured in the background of the Land O'Lakes ads and packaging, resonates with symbols relating the product to the great mother/earth mother archetype.

In order to avoid any harmful consequences vis-à-vis the consumer, it is important for advertisers to exercise restraint and delicacy when using powerful archetype material. Recent controversies over ad appeals to the shadow archetype, such as the Calvin Klein jeans promotion, highlight the ethical concerns involved in promotional campaigns. In general, there is a concern that advertising messages have the potential to exert extraordinary influence on consumers. Following Jung's analysis, advertising can operate on the unconscious mind and create strong impressions by appealing to universal archetypes.

Maslow's Hierarchy of Needs

There are a variety of systems for classifying human needs. By far, the most popular and well known is based on the research of psychologist Abraham Maslow.

Overview of Maslow's Theory

Maslow's **hierarchy of needs** is illustrated in Exhibit 11.3. The hierarchy appears as a pyramid, with the broad base (i.e., physiological needs) of the pyramid representing the most dominant needs. Self-actualization is shown at the top of the pyramid. Maslow's approach specifies that *needs are arranged in a sequence from lower-level needs to higher-level needs.* Altogether, five needs are identified:

1. **Physiological**—the biological needs for food and water and sleep.
2. **Safety and security**—shelter, protection, and security.
3. **Social**—affection, friendship, and acceptance.
4. **Ego**—prestige, success, accomplishment, self-esteem.
5. **Self-actualization**—self-fulfillment and enriching experiences.

The lower-level needs (starting with the physiological, at the bottom of Exhibit 11.3) are considered to dominate the higher-level needs. That is, consumers must satisfy lower-level needs before they begin to pursue higher-order needs. For example, once a consumer feels satisfied in terms of biological and safety needs, then that person is capable of relating to other people (i.e., pursuing social needs). The highest level of need, according to Maslow, is related to self-actualization. Consumers desire to live up to their full potential. They want to maximize the use of their skills and abilities. This need for self-actualization only becomes activated if all four of the lower-level needs have already been satisfied.

Although Maslow's hierarchy provides a useful organization for thinking about needs and motives, it is overly simplistic. The hierarchy ignores the intensity of the needs. For example, how hungry does a person need to be before that need dominates the need for friendship, self-esteem, or self-fulfillment? The avid consumption of luxuries in poor transitional economies illustrates this oversimplification. Some researchers have documented contradictions in Maslow's model.[12] For example, they tell of Romanian families foregoing needed food in order to afford refrigerators that then remain empty and of Turkish fam-

Exhibit 11.3 Maslow's Hierarchy of Needs

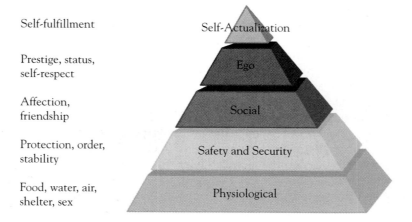

Self-fulfillment — Self-Actualization

Prestige, status, self-respect — Ego

Affection, friendship — Social

Protection, order, stability — Safety and Security

Food, water, air, shelter, sex — Physiological

ilies selling nutritious cow's milk in order to buy candy for their children who have seen it advertised on TV. These examples may seem extreme, but each of us can probably think of instances where it seems as if higher-level needs won out over basic needs. Even in ancient cultures, in which people often struggled to meet basic needs, we see evidence of human tendencies to make art and assemble collections. For example, cave paintings can be traced back at least 30,000 years. Some researchers argue that the desire for the beautiful is a basic need.[13]

In addition, Maslow's ordering of needs may not be consistent across cultures. In fact, research supports that a somewhat different hierarchy applies in the East.[14] Some cultures certainly put more value on social needs and belonging and less on ego needs and self-actualization. As we discussed in Chapter 7, different cultures have varying conceptions of the self that are likely to influence whether they value self-fulfillment or collective fulfillment.

Implications of Maslow's Theory for Marketing

From a consumer behavior perspective, the optimal use for Maslow's system is to classify needs. Maslow's need hierarchy provides a useful summary or inventory of human needs that may guide consumer behavior. Such a list is quite useful for marketing managers who are interested in understanding their customers' needs. However, marketing managers should be cautious in assuming that a hierarchy of needs holds.[15] Maslow's list of needs can serve as key input for product design. For example, the core product can be designed to represent a basic physiological need, reliability and ontime product delivery or warranties can be equated with safety, and customer interaction can be related to belongingness.[16] Many ad campaigns are designed to appeal to one or more of the needs represented in Maslow's hierarchy. The Blazer ad below illustrates an appeal to safety.

This ad uses a safety appeal.

Murray's Theory of Motivation

Henry Murray was a pioneer in shifting attention away from motives as internal states or drives, to thinking about motives in terms of goal-striving.[17] His research preceded Maslow's work by almost 20 years, but in many ways it was much more sophisticated. His work influenced and continues to influence many students of motivation.[18]

An Overview of Murray's Theory

The three previous motivation researchers we have described set out to summarize human motives in as simple a structure as possible. By contrast, Murray set out to list an inventory of every possible need he could distinguish. Just his basic list of major human needs includes 22 different ones. Murray believed that people differ in their priority ranking of these needs. Modern interpretations of his list suggest that some of these needs are never salient while others assume great importance, depending on social and cultural circumstances.

Like Freud, Jung, and Maslow, Murray had a view of the self and motives that derived from Western psychology, and his theory is **culture-bound,** that is, *it doesn't necessarily apply outside the society where the theory was developed.*[19] However, because his inventory of motives is so comprehensive it is more adaptable to different cultural traditions. One of the major criticisms of Murray's work is that it is just a lengthy inventory of needs, which makes it difficult and impractical for marketers to use. We later describe how Murray's work can be used to provide a more cross-cultural perspective on motives, but first we outline a couple of unique contributions of Murray's theory for marketers.

Implications of Murray's Theory for Marketing

Murray's detailed list identifies several needs specifically associated with objects. He identified **acquisition needs** (*to gain possessions and property*), **order needs** (*to put things in*

order, achieve cleanliness, arrangement, organization, balance), and **retention needs** (*to retain possession of things; to hoard; to be frugal, economical, and miserly*) as among the most basic human needs. Marketers often appeal to these needs for acquiring and retaining possessions. For example, an advertisement for insurance for valuable possessions (see facing page) ties together the joy of having with the fear of losing. We mention each of Murray's motives in terms of consumption behavior. For example, in Chapter 5 we talk about materialism, which is related to the need for acquisition, and the Diderot effect, which can be related to the need for order. We talk about older people's desire to retain their precious possessions and pass them forward through kinship networks in Chapter 19. This behavior can be related to the need for retention.

Acquisition may be a basic human need, but major religions discourage excess in acquisition and encourage restraint. Judeo-Christian, Buddhist, Taoist, Hindu, and Native American traditions all encourage restraint in materialist desires. Acquisition can be tied to four of the seven deadly sins in the Judeo-Christian tradition: greed, pride, gluttony, and envy.[20] Nevertheless, we give examples throughout this book from many different cultures about the desire to acquire, order, and retain possessions. Although the meaning and importance of possessions varies substantially among different peoples both within a given culture and between cultures, most people seem to need to acquire and retain certain special objects. We will have more to say about this theme when we discuss consumption meanings in Chapter 18.

A Cross-Cultural Examination of Motives

We have already described that the study of motivation centers on why people begin, stop, and persist in specific actions in particular circumstances.[21] Marketers are interested in this at different levels. For example, they are interested in the basic need for acquisition of possessions or the particular desire for a type of product, but they are also interested in understanding and predicting why a particular consumer in a specific social, cultural setting buys a special brand. These turn out to be enormously complicated questions.

The question of motivation is intertwined with several topics we have already discussed and some others to come. For example, motivation varies with people's perceptions (Chapter 9), self-concept (Chapter 7), and experiences and knowledge (Chapter 12). As you know from our earlier discussion of Freud and Jung, motivation also relates to basic problems of consciousness—for example, how much does our unconscious influence our specific actions in particular circumstances. Even more basic, motivation depends on people's biology, including and perhaps especially their brains. It's not too difficult to understand how motivations derive from basic physiological needs such as the needs for food, water, air, sex, and shelter, but the role of the brain in driving higher-level needs is more complicated.

The most recent research on how brains develop involves highly technical details about anatomy and organic chemistry. For example, the primary cell type in the brain is the neuron, or nerve cell, and the connections between neurons are called synapses. The brain has about 10 billion neurons and a million billion connections. Consciousness emerges from complex interactions of these billions of neurons.

One of the leading experts in the evolving debate about consciousness and the mind is Nobel Prize–winner Gerald Edelman. Edelman's theory draws very directly from

How the Brain, Mind, and Motivation Are Linked

Foraging theory has established a secure place in archeological analyses of economic decisions in prehistoric societies. Much of the use of these foraging models has focused on the survival behavior of hunter-gatherers or pastoralists. One can imagine applications in urbanized, industrial economies. For instance, taxi drivers act as predators seeking to optimize the benefit-to-cost ratio of encountering and "harvesting" their prey. Routinely, they must decide whether to actively search or to use a sit-and-wait, ambush tactic. Political scientists have also applied foraging theory to lobbying in state legislatures.

One of the more interesting recent applications of foraging theory is to analyze and optimize patterns of "information foraging" on the Internet. Computer scientists are applying these models to design effective information gathering mechanisms from the World Wide Web and other large-scale databases. It turns out that a theory that was designed to understand prehistoric hunter-gatherers is now proving useful in understanding information-seeking readers on the Internet.

Source: Adapted from Bruce Winterhalder and Eric Alden Smith, "Analyzing Adaptive Strategies: Human Behavioral Ecology at Twenty-Five," Evolutionary Anthropology 9 (2, 2000), pp. 51–72.

Darwin; in fact, he refers to his theory as **neural Darwinism.** He argues that *each individual brain, even before birth, uses a process that resembles natural selection to develop during its own lifetime.* This means that every person's individual mind is shaped by Darwinian rules of selection to provide a structure (networks of connections between neurons) that will enable that person to cope with the world. Genetics predisposes certain connections, for example, those related to reaching for and grasping objects (which most babies seem to do instinctively). However, the actual pattern of connections in a brain is unpredictable. Those connections that prove most helpful in the outside world become stronger; those that prove unhelpful weaken and disappear. This and other emerging theories have profound implications for the study of motivation.[22]

These theories lead us to a central conclusion: Consumers are uniquely shaped by cultural and social settings, and they are constantly adapting based on what works and what doesn't. Our brains are not like computers; they are more like the ecology of a jungle. Each of us is a product of our environment—our minds are dynamic entities defined by our relationship to the world around us, and each of us has at least a somewhat unique set of experiences that shape our particular mind. Motivations are likely to be both unique to an individual and variable across social and cultural environments more than we previously thought. Consumers' interpretation of culture messages will depend on the specific connections and strength of those connections in their minds.[23] Moreover, motivations are more likely to change as the world around us changes. Consumers will adapt their motivations and actions to fit with what works in that new environment. Industry Insights 11.1 discusses how the basic and primitive human skill of foraging is shifted to foraging on the Internet in contemporary society.

Following from our discussion of the mind, there is not a direct relationship between culture and motivation. Not everyone in a particular culture behaves the same because each has an individual set of experiences that shapes how they interpret and respond to their world. Nevertheless, our discussion of the mind does suggest that motivations vary between cultures. Particular motivations would be supported in some cultures and not in others. In this section we describe just one of the ways in which culture can affect motivation: through the relationship between culture and self-concept.[24]

In Chapter 7 we described how some cultures stress an **independent self.** This idea of *a unique, self-contained, autonomous entity* is clearly illustrated in American culture and many western European cultures. The cultural imperative centers on maintaining independence and separateness. No wonder Maslow's highest goal is self-actualization. Researchers coming from Maslow's tradition assume that motives related to the need to express one's agency or competency (e.g., the achievement motivation) are common to everyone. However, many cultures have an interdependent view of the self. The **interdependent self** is characteristic of Japanese, other Asian cultures, African cultures, Latin-American cultures, and some southern European cultures. In this view, the *self is part of an encompassing social relation, and behavior is dependent on and organized by perceptions of the thoughts, feelings, and actions of others in the relationship.* The self is not separate from the social context and the social unit. The cultural imperative in this case is to seek connectedness, social integration, and interpersonal harmony. Magaji (from the opening vignette) has an interdependent self that is anchored in his role as a father, husband, and son. Consumer Chronicles 11.1 illustrates how an independent versus interdependent view of self influences perceptions and motivations. Research has demonstrated that these differences translate very directly into what types of advertising strategies work. For example, ad messages featuring "older people" and "experts" are more persuasive to consumers from the People's Republic of China than to Australians. This appeals to the interdependent need to admire and defer to a superior. The Chinese from the PRC are less likely to lodge a complaint for a faulty product, consistent with the need to comply, behave well, and not stand out. They are less likely to purchase new products when compared with Australians. Being different and standing out are not valued; staying with tradition is.[25] As illustrated in Exhibit 11.4, Murray described many needs that have particular salience for those with interdependent selves. In the next few pages, we outline some needs that marketers often use in promotions that are sensitive to a particular self-concept.

How Motivation and Culture Are Linked

If you leaf through just about any U.S. or western European magazine, you will see a high proportion of ads are targeted toward one of five consumer needs. Two of these—the needs for power and uniqueness—are likely to be much higher in independent than interdependent cultures. Three of these—the needs for achievement, affiliation, and self-esteem—are likely to be important in both but have different meanings and actions associated with them. Advertisements often emphasize more than one of these needs.

Five Consumer Needs in Cultural Perspective

The Achievement Motive

One of the most studied and talked about motivations is the need for achievement. The **achievement need** is defined as *the need to experience emotion in connection with evaluated performance.*[26] This definition allows for variety in the type of performance involved. Consumer Chronicles 11.2 contains a vignette about Marilyn's passion for soccer. Marilyn started playing soccer as a young child. She excelled. She continued to advance through

Consumer Chronicles 11.1

Contrasting Independent and Interdependent Selves

In America, "the squeaky wheel gets the grease." In Japan, "the nail that stands out gets pounded down." American parents who are trying to induce their children to eat their suppers are fond of saying "think of the starving kids in Ethiopia and appreciate how lucky you are to be different from them." Japanese parents are likely to say "Think about the farmer who worked so hard to produce this rice for you: if you don't eat it, he will feel bad for his efforts will have been in vain." A small Texas corporation seeking to elevate productivity told its employees to look in the mirror and say "I am beautiful" 100 times before coming to work each day. Employees of a Japanese supermarket recently opened in New Jersey were instructed to begin the day by holding hands and telling each other that "he" or "she is beautiful."

Source: Hazel Markus and Shinobu Kitayama, "Culture and the Self: Implications for Cognition, Emotion, and Motivation," Psychological Review *98 (April 1991), p. 224.*

the different levels of competition, finally becoming a successful collegiate player. Viewed in this way, Marilyn's association with the sport provides her with an outlet for achievement. She wants to be the best player that she can be.

Whereas the individually oriented achievement motive implies striving for its own sake, the socially oriented achievement motive has the goal of meeting expectations of significant others. Several studies have distinguished between these two types of achievement motivation, showing that the motive to achieve goals can be for social and collective reasons. For example, Chinese children strive to achieve the goals of others, such as family and teachers.[27] Some research compares Anglo-Irish and Chinese-Vietnamese mothers' gifts to their children. It shows that Anglo-Irish mothers, representing extreme individualism, prefer not to give gifts to reward their children's academic endeavors; they feel achievement should have an internal/intrinsic basis. Chinese-Vietnamese mothers, representing extreme collectivism, give gifts to reward their children's academic progress. These mothers also registered different gift-giving motivations. Anglo-Irish mothers give gifts to gain short-term benefits for their children such as enhanced self-concept, and for themselves (their children's love). Chinese-Vietnamese mothers give gifts to attain long-term benefits for their children and mention no personal benefits.[28]

Exhibit 11.4 Interdependent Needs

Abasement—the need to comply and accept punishment or self-depreciation.
Affiliation—the need to form friendships and associations.
Avoidance of blame—the need to avoid punishment, be well-behaved, and obey the law.
Deference—the need to admire and willingly follow a superior.
Nurturance—the need to nourish, aid, or protect another.
Similance—the need to imitate or emulate others.
Succorance—the need to seek aid, projection, or sympathy; to be dependent.

Source: Adapted from Henry A. Murray, *Explorations in Personality* (New York: Oxford University Press, 1938).

My name is Marilyn Jones. My identity is soccer. Almost everyone knows how much I enjoy playing, coaching, and watching soccer. Soccer has been a big part of my life for many years. I began playing soccer when I was seven years old. At the time, seven years old seemed like a young age, but now children usually begin at age four and in some cases age three. I played youth soccer within my town for years but never made a traveling team until I was 12 years old. I gave up other sports and activities in order to play youth soccer within my town in the fall, indoor soccer in the winter, and travel soccer for my town in the spring. Sacrificing my other interests paid off when I reached high school because I was chosen for the varsity soccer team my freshman year. I accomplished a great deal in my high school soccer career. I am still the only female athlete to receive All-New England honors in my high school.

A lot of changes took place when I began preseason soccer at Providence College (PC). I was no longer the big fish in the little pond, I was the little fish in the big sea. We had a freshman phrase, "high school hero turned PC zero." I worked extremely hard during preseason and earned a starting position. I maintained my starting position at PC for the entire four years, but I never achieved the "star" status I was striving for. During my collegiate career, I also had the opportunity to play for a club team, the Boston Bolts, and travel to Arizona for the national tournament.

Just prior to graduation I was hired for the assistant coach position at PC. Once again I was confronted with many changes and faced with an entirely different challenge. I took the challenge and it proved to be extremely profitable (not in a monetary sense, of course). I was exposed to the coaching side of soccer and I loved it. Now, one year later, I am attending the master's program at the University of Georgia. At first I felt like a stranger in a strange world, but then I met a group of soccer players. Immediately there was a connection between us, a common bond. Because of this bond, I have become good friends with many of my new teammates. I look forward to coaching this spring for Cedar Shoals High School in Athens. I believe I am less homesick now that I have found and been inducted into the Athens, Georgia, soccer community.

The Power Motive

The **power need** is defined as the *need to have control or influence over another person, group, or the world at large.*[29] One specific (appropriate or inappropriate) manifestation of the need—to "make a splash" or create excitement—is particularly situation dependent.[30] Researchers have reached the general conclusion that people who have a high need for power strive to be assertive.[31] Again, many of the needs associated with an interdependent self and described in Exhibit 11.4 are almost the opposite of the need to assert oneself, including deference and abasement. Although everyone may have some desire for agency and control, assertiveness may not be the control strategy of choice. For example, people in many Asian cultures appear to use what is termed **secondary control.** This involves *accommodating existing circumstances* and may mean limiting individualism in order to fit with present circumstances. In Chapter 14 we talk about the art of feng shui. Feng shui is practiced to *control* the

1. **Ego-enhancement.** Some consumers are motivated to create web pages by the feeling of importance that a home page on the Web provides. They use it as an opportunity to show off, impress others, or to look cool. They enjoy the awareness that many people will be looking at their home page.

2. **Social status/prestige.** Individuals who are motivated by social status feel that a home page on the Web provides prestige and establishes a place for them in society.

3. **Gain attention of others.** The creation of a web page provides an opportunity to attract attention to the page owner on two levels. First, it is a topic of conversation. It can attract attention and admiration related to the achievement of being at the cutting edge of the new technology. Second, the author gains attention through having others visit the home page.

4. **Control/mastery over the environment.** Some consumers gain a feeling of having conquered technology by creating a personal home page. They feel that understanding now will create leverage in the future, allowing them to take advantage of the benefits the Internet has to offer. Other consumers feel they impact the environment by sharing what they know with the world.

Source: Adapted from George M. Zinkhan, Margy Conchar, Ajay Gupta, and Gary Geissler, "Motivations Underlying the Creation of Personal Web Pages: An Exploratory Study," in Advances in Consumer Research, *vol. 26, Eric J. Arnould and Linda M. Scott, eds. (Provo, UT: Association for Consumer Research, 1999), pp. 69–74.*

environment through *harmony* with the environment. Feng shui is sometimes referred to in advertisements for products ranging from real estate and cars to home and personal care, playing on the idea of control through harmony with the environment.

One socially acceptable way for people to fulfill their power need is by collecting prestige possessions, or symbols of power. These possessions may include credit cards, watches, computers, cars, cellular phones, and so on.[32] If a man has an important interview coming up, he may purchase a "power" tie. Similarly, a woman may wear a power suit to such an interview. With the growth in popularity of the World Wide Web, new opportunities exist for image projection. For example, as Consumer Chronicles 11.3 illustrates, creating a personal web page can be a source of power. In this study, technologically sensitized college students wrote a brief story or commentary about the likely motives of an imaginary web page creator (i.e., a projective technique). Nevertheless, there are many opportunities for creating unique images using existing signals (e.g., related to clothing). To promote her book, author Jane Gallop wears a skirt that is made of men's silk ties. This skirt turns the traditional dress code on its head while at the same time creating a unique image for the author.[33] Advertisers often try to position products as symbols of power or as means to achieve power and control as suggested by the Globalstar advertisement shown on page 395. This ad shows how satellite phone technology can provide power and freedom to the owner.

The Uniqueness/Novelty Motive

We introduced the basic motives of integration and differentiation in Chapter 1. Blending
in and not standing out (e.g., integration or affiliation) is very important in interdependent-
self cultures. However, individuals in independent-self cultures express the desire to be independent and unique (e.g., differentiation or distinction). The Yamaha motorcycle ad
shown below appeals to independence. Notice that although the promotion promises independence, it also promises social approval—"you'll be turning heads from here to eter-
nity." The **uniqueness need,** that is, *the need to perceive oneself as different from others,*
has been called the "pursuit of difference."[34] Apple Computer's famous slogan "Think Different" typifies appeals to the need for uniqueness. Many Western cultures and Americans
in particular put a premium on standing out and being unique. Americans struggle to enhance self-perceptions of uniqueness.[35] The need for uniqueness is closely related to self-
esteem motives. Individuals with an independent view of the self seek to maintain self-
esteem by distinguishing and differentiating themselves from others.

In much of the modern world, the majority of products are mass marketed. In this climate, many people feel that it is difficult to create and project uniqueness. Just as the mass
market exerts strong pressure to conform, so too the modern workplace exerts strong pressures to conform. For instance, in most organizations, a corporate culture prescribes how employees should act and dress. These prescriptions apply even to so-called casual Fridays, on

Yamaha appeals to uniqueness and independence motives.

which, theoretically, employees are free to wear anything that they like. In reality, in many organizations, every single employee will dress the same on casual Friday. At Coca-Cola, for example, most employees will wear khaki slacks and a sports shirt to signal casual dress.

One way consumers can differentiate themselves is through attitudes and beliefs. Another way a person can be different is through **uniqueness attributes,** for example, *physical qualities, information or experiences.* For example, consumers with a high need to express uniqueness are especially attracted to scarce products.[36] These consumers search for new and special products to maintain a sense of specialness relative to others.[37] As discussed in Chapter 7, clothes, cars, computers, and other commodities may signal a person's uniqueness as part of one's *extended self.*[38] Western advertisers often try to position products as symbols of uniqueness or novelty, as suggested by the advertisement for Yamaha (above).

Youths in many Triad cultures focus on irreverence, nonconformity, noncommitment, detachment, difference, and fragmentation in their consumer behaviors.[39] Increasingly fragmented life experiences offer the potential for many choices of self-images. Again, computer technology can be used to create a unique image or to express individuality. Communicating in cyberspace can provide thrills, excitement, and a feeling of uniqueness. Consumers' interactions on the Web can be exciting to the senses.[40] In some instances, buyers on Internet auction sites are willing to pay more for products they purchase elsewhere online because of the spectacle and excitement provided by the purchase environment.[41]

The Affiliation Motive

In Chapter 1 we described the motivation to be integrated with others. One of people's most basic social behaviors is the urge for contact.[42] Our ancestors evolved in small, cohesive groups. The universality of the need to belong is revealed by the use of ostracism as a punishment in many societies. Brain research reveals that feelings of belonging are strongly motivating. In fact, neuroscientists now support a social view of the brain, believing that a kind of sociality that does not distinguish self from other is woven deeply into the primate brain. Many research studies have shown the importance of mutual imitation and shared action for both infants and mothers. Despite the importance of belonging, in some cases the urge for contact and shared action can take primitive and even destructive forms such as mob behavior or mob hysteria. Feelings, ideas, and perceptions become contagious under mob conditions.

The **affiliation need** is defined as *the need to be with people.*[43] We might expect that the need for affiliation would be higher in interdependent than independent cultures. Surprisingly, however, studies have not found this. But researchers have discovered that the meaning of affiliation and the behaviors that accompany affiliation do differ. For example, a person's concern with adjusting his or her self to occupy a proper place with respect to others is more important in interdependent cultures.

One recent trend in industrialized society is that consumers feel more and more detached as the twentieth century unfolds.[44] Large institutions and mass media have the effect of insulating and detaching consumers from their fellows. As a result, consumers sometimes experience a strong motivation to reconnect and associate with groups of kindred spirits. Many consumers are eager to find a way to overcome feelings of detachment, depersonalization, and isolation. Advertisers often try to position products and services as symbols of affiliation or as means that will enable consumers to achieve connection with people.

The Self-Esteem Motive

Another motive that has received a lot of attention is *the need to maintain a positive view of the self,* or the **self-esteem need,** as discussed in Chapter 7. Studies of Americans show that even at a very early age they *take credit for successes, explain away failures, and see themselves as better than most others in most ways.*[45] This is referred to as a **self-enhancing bias.** Studies of Japanese college students show a strong bias in the reverse direction—that is, self-effacing.

The self-esteem goal is seen as fundamental in Western cultures. Themes such as "express yourself" and "be yourself" are common appeals to self-esteem used in American advertising. However, these appeals are perceived quite negatively in Japanese culture. In Japan, expressing the inner self is not valued. What is important is to control the expression of the inner self in order to fit in with others and maintain harmony. Research has demonstrated that Japanese put much less emphasis on consistency between feelings and actions than Americans.[46] In fact, self-esteem among those with interdependent selves may heavily depend on self-control and self-restraint that enable belonging and fitting in.

Needs Related to the Shopping Process

In this section we discuss and illustrate two consumer needs related to the shopping process: deal proneness and self-sacrifice. This is not intended to comprise a comprehensive list of shopping motives but only to suggest how shopping environments can relate to consumer needs.

Deal Proneness: Winning at the Game of Shopping

For some consumers, shopping is like a contest or game. They like to do well at the game, and they like to succeed. Of course, there are different ways of measuring success. One measure might be "getting a good deal." So, a consumer may shop for hours and make many comparisons so as to make just the right purchase. This purchase may be evaluated in terms of the amount of money saved. In other instances time may be the objective function. That is, consumers may be delighted to discover that they have saved time through a purchase or that they have completed a transaction in record time. In this sense, the deals that marketers offer can be viewed as a key motivator of behavior.

The Trouble with Sales

It is a compulsive act for me, I have to look to avoid the feeling that perhaps I'm missing a good opportunity. Of course, I end up buying 10 T-shirts (they will always come in handy), three pairs of espadrilles (I need them), and a dozen pairs of panties I can't resist, just because they are cheap. All at the cost, as I explain to myself as soon as I am back at home, of "no money at all." What is more important is that buying so much for so little gives me a sense of satisfaction.

This is an art, I think, proud of myself for a moment. But no, it is not, and deep down I know it. Buying junk is not an art, it is only a sad necessity. Or, in my case, a bad habit that you can't get rid of, like smoking. For Christ's sake, times have changed, everything has changed, says my husband. You make some money now. You don't live in communist Yugoslavia any longer. You can buy what you want. I try to explain to him that I can't, but I am afraid he does not quite understand me. After all, he is a Western European.

Source: Slavenka Drakulić, Café Europa: Life after Communism *(Penguin Books, 1996), pp. 72–73.*

Marketers offer deals to consumers for many reasons. Examples of deals include everything from coupons to rebates to free samples. From one perspective, a deal (such as a special coupon) serves to draw attention to the brand. Such a deal may stimulate or trigger purchase behavior. At the same time, a deal (such as a two-for-one offer) may appeal to a consumer's desire to be an efficient shopper. A deal may appeal to a shopper's urge to win the shopping competition (i.e., to get a good bargain). As described here, **deal proneness** can be viewed as a kind of consumer need. When combined with other needs, it has the potential to explain the "why" of consumer behavior. Consumers' responses to deals can also be viewed as a personality variable. For instance, we may say that some consumers are particularly deal prone. These consumers seek out deals for a wide variety of reasons, including saving money, having fun, or being efficient shoppers. Of course, as with other motives we have discussed, the specific type of deal can influence whether deal proneness is activated.[47]

Consumers often haggle over prices. **Price haggling** involves *give and take by buyer and seller in order to establish a price acceptable to both.* The prevalence of price haggling varies considerably between cultures. As described in Chapter 10, many economies operate on a barter system and rely heavily on haggling to set prices. When consumers price haggle we might assume that they are motivated to obtain a better dollar value for their purchases—that is, economic motives. However, noneconomic benefits are very important. One U.S.-based study used an analysis of depth interviews to illustrate that consumers can fulfill three primary needs, including achievement, affiliation, and dominance, by haggling over price.[48] For example, some of these depth interviews described consumers flaunting the superior deals they got on their cars. Other interviews talked about seizing control of negotiations. Finally, some price hagglers use their skill for friends' benefit. They work to negotiate effective deals that cement bonds of friendship. We will talk more about some of these behaviors in Chapter 15 when we discuss purchase pals and interpersonal influence in more detail.

Deal proneness and price haggling, like other needs, are shaped by the shopping culture or environment the consumer experiences. Consumers in transitional economies may be particularly motivated by sales because of the previous lack of goods and lack of price differentiation among goods. Slavenka Drakulić devotes a whole chapter in her book *Café Europa* to explaining why she is particularly susceptible to sales because she grew up in eastern Europe in a nonmarket economy. Consumer Chronicles 11.4 describes some of her thinking.

An invitation to express love through purchase for others.

Tastes Like Somebody Loves You.

Often we interpret shopping as a pleasure or a self-gift. People report that when they are feeling low or want to reward themselves they go shopping. Bumper stickers that support this view of shopping are commonplace in the United States—for example, "When life gets tough, the tough go shopping." A perspective that may be the source of rich insights for marketers interprets shopping as **self-sacrifice**.[49] The findings are based on an ethnography of lower- and lower-middle-class women in the United Kingdom, although an ethnographic study of lower- and lower-middle-class Chicago women reports similar findings.

Daniel Miller, an anthropologist, argues that women shop out of devotional love for their families. Their shopping is an investment in their families and relationships with family members. Purchases are rationalized not in terms of what was spent but in terms of savings and thrift. The savings and thrift generated through shopping then constitute funds that can be given to dependents and descendants. In this perspective, provisioning of the family through shopping is an important way of constituting and preserving the family. Interestingly, many shopping centers in the United Kingdom emphasize an ideology of family shopping that is consistent with this theory. The advertisement for Hunt's Snack Pack pudding shown above is consistent with this theory. The advertisement appeared in a women's magazine. It doesn't encourage women to make something, such as pudding, to show family love; instead, it suggests they buy something. The idea that women can use purchases to show their family they love them is common in many U.S. magazines. If shopping is viewed as provisioning the family rather than a pleasurable, self-indulgent activity, then marketers would use different appeals to encourage the purchase of their products.

Shopping as Self-Sacrifice

Consumer Involvement

Motives need to be understood in terms of the effort that consumers are willing to commit. When motivation to achieve a goal is high, consumers are likely to invest substantial effort. Pursuing goals, the motivated consumer may feel involved—interest, excitement, anxiety, passion, engagement, and flow.[50] Magaji, introduced in the opening vignette, is very involved in acquiring gold for his wife and daughters. Because of the substantial importance of this goal to the future well-being of his family, he commits effort over time to achieving this goal. We can think of Magaji as mobilizing his physical, mental, and energy resources to achieve a personally relevant goal.[51] Other men in Magaji's social position may also wish to acquire gold but feel less able to do so. They may feel they have fewer opportunities or fewer resources to draw on. We will discuss how resources and ability influence goal striving in Chapter 12.

Types and Characteristics of Consumer Involvement

Involvement can include *heightened thinking and processing information about the goal object,* referred to as **cognitive involvement.** Involvement can also or instead include *heightened feelings and emotional energy,* referred to as **affective involvement.** Marketing can stimulate one or the other or both types of involvement. Ads that encourage people to experience the feelings and sensations associated with a product are stimulating affective involvement. Ads that provide a detailed enumeration of information about a product or web-

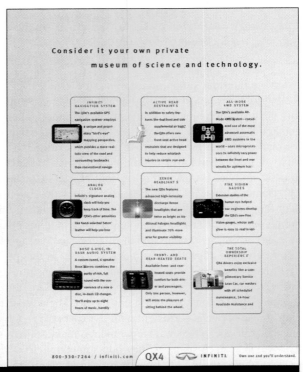

The Infiniti ad encourages cognitive involvement, while the Jaguar ad encourages affective involvement.

sites that include comprehensive brand comparisons appeal to cognitive involvement. Two car advertisements taken from the same issue of *Motor Trend* magazine illustrate these different appeals. People who purchase this magazine are probably involved with cars, perhaps because they love cars or because they are trying to decide what car to buy. Shown on page 400 are two pages of a six-page ad for Infiniti QX4. The promotion includes lots of detailed information about the specific features of the car. This ad appeals to cognitive involvement. By contrast, a two-page spread for Jaguar promotes the sensation of driving the car, especially the first 5.4 seconds. This ad appeals to affective involvement.

When involvement peaks it is referred to as **flow.** A flow experience is when *a person's attention is completely absorbed by the activity or the goal object.* This kind of experience creates a merging of action and awareness. Achieving flow requires a clear goal, a strong sense of whether progress is being made, and skilled performance—accomplishing the goal requires effort and demands the individual's capabilities. Many people report flow as an outcome of engaging in extreme activities such as skydiving or mountaineering.[52] An advertisement for Outward Bound, shown below, reflects the potentially transcendent experience of an absorbing, extreme activity. Although extreme activities are often associated with flow, any activity that fully engages an individual can be a source of a flow experience.

Consumer involvement is a function of the goal object, the individual, and the decision situation. Involvement is the perceived level of personal importance or interest evoked by a stimulus within a specific situation.[53] Therefore, a consumer's involvement level varies with that person's interpretation of a given stimulus and according to his or her personal values or interest. From this perspective, involvement is equivalent to a person's activation level at a particular moment of time.[54] Involvement becomes activated when personal needs, values, or self-concept are stimulated within a given situation. For that reason, any particular product category's corresponding level of involvement can fluctuate depending on the variability of the consumer's interaction with the stimulus over time. For example, bathing suits may not evoke a consumer's interest when she is shopping for a gift for her mother-in-law, but they may evoke considerable interest when she is shopping two weeks before her beach vacation.

Some products and brands may generate many feelings and thoughts; others may stimulate almost no feelings or thoughts. As an example, for some people luxury sports cars stimulate high involvement. They find it fun to look at pictures of fast cars, to drive them,

Many extreme outdoor sports provide a sense of flow to participants.

I am not sure exactly when it happened, but sometime within the last two years I became intrigued with scents. Rather than splashing on traditional perfumes, I prefer scented shower creams and lotions. My morning ritual includes showering with a scented cream and then applying the corresponding lotion. Throughout the course of the day when I wash my hands or no longer smell "good," I carry a travel-size lotion in my purse for easy reapplication. My boyfriend quickly noticed the difference between traditional perfumes and my newfound scents because they typically smell fruity; he constantly tells me how good I smell. I am particularly fond of sun-ripened raspberry, enchanted apple, and peach hyacinth. He even calls me "Peaches" since that's his favorite scent and the one I wear most frequently.

How did I acquire this desire? It wasn't through advertising, since Victoria's Secret doesn't advertise. Perhaps I am drawn by a need for uniqueness, which is why I crave lotions as opposed to splash-on perfumes. Or perhaps I am motivated by products that I believe exude femininity, such as lotions and shower gels. Or perhaps I view Victoria's Secret as a sensuous store and am hoping to be perceived as a sensuous woman. Or perhaps I am a victim of operant conditioning and have learned to smell "fruity" by the positive reinforcement of attention rewarded to me by my boyfriend. Or perhaps I am just a consumer with too much time and dry skin on my hands!

and to talk about them with friends or even strangers. Of course, sports cars are not interesting to every consumer. Some people don't drive at all or don't want to drive a sports car.

The same product can have different involvement levels across people.[55] One reason for this difference across people is that all consumers do not share the same motivations and needs at the same time. Consumer researchers distinguish between enduring product involvement and situational product involvement. **Enduring involvement** represents *the long-term interest that a consumer has in a product class.* Products that consumers continue to be involved with over time are central to a consumer's values, needs, or self-concept.[56] In Consumer Chronicles 11.5 Misty talks about her motivations for buying scents. She has enduring involvement with her scents, although she can't pinpoint exactly why. Most consumers only experience enduring involvement in a few products or activities. A consumer might express enduring involvement in anything, including a sports team, cosmetics, clothes, cars, Beanie Babies, or Mickey Mouse. That is, consumers can be involved with products, brands, or even very specific variants of a brand, such as Levi's 101 jeans or Progresso Mushroom Spaghetti Sauce. Enduring involvement may decline with length of use. As time passes, personal relevance and interest levels may weaken. For example, Misty may lose interest with scents, especially if she changes her boyfriend or some other aspect of her life (recall our discussion in Chapter 7). If a consumer has used a product for a long time, strong preferences and brand loyalty may develop. Thus, search behavior may be attenuated, and consumers may not spend so much time making decisions as they did previously.

Characteristics of the decision situation can influence consumer involvement. The term **situational involvement** is used to describe *temporary interest in a purchase or con-*

sumption process. For example, consumers may be interested in reading and learning about cars when they are in the market for a car but not after they have made a purchase decision and feel satisfied with their decision. Many aspects of the decision situation can influence situational involvement. The more important the reason for purchase, the greater consumer involvement. The greater the social pressure for purchase, the greater the involvement. The faster that a decision has to be made, the greater the involvement. The more irrevocable, or final, a decision is, the greater the involvement. Situational purchase or consumption involvement levels increase when financial risk and social risk are high. If consumers are required to invest a lot of money to buy a product or service, then this financial risk catches their attention. They are highly motivated to make the right choice and find this choice to be personally relevant. In the same way, if the potential social costs are high this decision situation becomes both interesting and relevant.

In almost all cases, the purchase of a house to live in is highly involving. A lot of money is at stake. The decision will have implications for years to come. That one, single purchase will have innumerable implications for future decisions (e.g., what furniture to buy, how to decorate, what lawn care products to purchase). There is a lot of risk involved. A house purchase is an ego-involving decision—as discussed in Chapter 7, people's homes reflect their selves. As such, consumers spend a lot of time and invest a lot of resources to ensure that they make the best decision possible.

Marketing Implications of Different Levels of Involvement

High involvement and low involvement affect attention, information search, purchase, and consumption satisfaction differently. Thus, the marketing strategies used vary with level of involvement, and marketers use involvement to identify segments in the market. Because involvement affects decision making and attitudes, we will revisit the marketing implications of involvement in Chapter 13.

High-Involvement Purchase and Consumption

When consumers are highly involved with a purchase, they are willing to expend greater levels of shopping effort. They are concerned with the purchase and feel that it is important to their life.[57] In other words, the higher the level of involvement, the greater the amount of time and money that consumers are willing to spend and the greater number of stores they will visit.[58] With **high involvement,** attention is increased and more importance is attached to the stimulus object. Memory is enhanced. The purchase process is more complex for highly involved consumers,[59] and they are motivated to make a careful purchase decision.[60] They search extensively for relevant information about products or brands that are personally relevant. They consciously evaluate alternatives and make detailed comparisons before making a final selection. High-involvement consumers have strongly held beliefs about brands and perceive great differences between brands in a product class. They often have a favorite or preferred brand and are brand loyal. For example, when a highly involved consumer shops for clothing, she is more likely to be influenced by a desire to find something new rather than focusing on the potential poor performance of the clothing.[61]

Purchase involvement is positively related to search activities. That is, consumers with high involvement place greater importance on major information sources and engage in an active search process, and they are heavy users of newspapers and advertising.[62] However, they are more likely to generate negative cognitive responses to product-related messages.[63] Highly involved consumers find shopping more interesting and enjoyable. They are more likely to value purchasing and shopping activities than consumers of low involvement.[64] Involved consumers like to get the best value for their money and are much more concerned with attributes that assure value in purchasing, such as favorable return policies.[65]

Highly involved consumers often show more satisfaction with products.[66] Since high involvement motivates consumers to spend time and effort to avoid postpurchase dissatisfaction, these consumers generally report higher satisfaction and less negative disconfirmation with the product they purchase. However, there is some question about how satisfaction levels change over time. For example, two months after purchase, highly involved automobile owners showed a decline in their satisfaction. In contrast, low-involvement consumers' satisfaction increased after the two month period.[67] As in many areas of consumer behavior, we don't know much about how involvement levels ebb and flow over time and how the relationship between involvement and other variables, such as satisfaction, may vary over time.

Low-Involvement Purchase and Consumption

It is important to keep in mind that in many purchase situations the consumer couldn't care less; that is, there is **low involvement.** For paper towels, consumers may make the purchase, switch brands, and ignore commercials. Consumers are thinking about the important decisions in their lives; they don't have time to worry about what paper towels to buy.[68] The average supermarket has more than 10,000 brands on display. By way of comparison, the average U.S. college graduate has a vocabulary of 7,000 words. Given these numbers, there is great risk of information overload. The only way to survive is to take many decision shortcuts. Decision making is minimal for low-involvement products.

Low-involvement consumers are not active information seekers. Because the decision is of little importance, such consumers are not active information processors.[69] They tend to make little comparison among brands or among product attributes.[70] Often, low-involvement consumers are indifferent among a group of brands. They don't see a lot of differences between these brands and view them as reasonable substitutes for one another. That is, they don't have special preferences for a particular brand, and brand loyalty is not very strong. The purchase decision may result from simple recognition of the product on the shelf. Since low-involvement purchasers are not paying much attention, they may get easily confused, or they may make mistakes. In many instances, however, the low-involvement purchaser may not really care too much about the mistakes. If a purchase error is made, the consumer might not even notice.

Consumption experiences may also not involve much arousal or involvement. For instance, if an employee is late for work and rushing, she may not really notice which breakfast cereal she is eating. Later in the day, if a co-worker asks what she had for breakfast, she may not be able to say with certainty. There definitely was eating and chewing involved. But attention levels may be so low that the behavior is barely noticed and quickly forgotten.

Low-Involvement Marketing Strategies

Marketers of a product that evokes low involvement may consider strategies that will increase consumers' involvement with a product or brand over a short period or for longer periods. For example, special promotions such as sweepstakes or seasonal clearance sales may temporarily raise consumers' involvement levels. The level of involvement consumers have with a certain product can be influenced over longer periods of time by creative marketing strategies, such as effective advertising or product usage campaigns. For instance, a humorous advertising campaign about facial tissue can generate some interest, even though the product category is generally considered boring.

Also, marketers may link low-involvement products with high-involvement issues, such as health. For example, marketers may link low-involvement food products with a high-involvement health attribute such as cancer prevention. Similarly, a low-involvement tobacco product could be linked with a high-involvement health attribute such as low tar.

Another way to raise involvement levels is to adapt the advertising medium to the product category. For instance, information presented in a print medium, such as a magazine ad, is more highly involving than the same information presented in a broadcast environment (e.g., a television ad).[71] In Chapters 7 and 9 we talked about how making an advertisement, product, or service experience personally relevant can increase a consumer's involvement in that stimulus. The Web is also a highly involving medium, as it is interactive and requires constant consumer input. That is, consumers have to search actively on the Web; messages do not come automatically as they do on radio or TV. Thus, marketers can raise the involvement level of the situation by promoting their product in a high-involvement medium (e.g., the Web) instead of a low-involvement medium (e.g., radio). Of course, the product advertised must be interesting enough to motivate consumers to respond. It is less likely that consumers would pursue a complicated click stream to receive detailed information about bubble bath. However, they may be more likely to search the Web to find the best deal on a CD purchase. Thus, marketers must tailor the complexity of their message to suit the inherent involvement level of their product or service.

On the one hand, brand managers of low-involvement products may not be thrilled with the idea that consumers don't really care about their product. On the other hand, consumers in a low-involvement situation are willing to try unfamiliar brands without a full search for information and without forming a strong preference first. Complete evaluation of the brand comes after the brand has been purchased and used. Thus, marketers can appeal to low-involvement consumers through extensive distribution networks or through clever in-store displays.

Involvement as a Segmentation Variable

Involvement can be a useful segmentation variable. For instance, consumers can be segmented into the following four groups based around their involvement with a product category and with particular brands:

1. **Brand loyalists**—those who are highly involved both with the product category and with particular brands.

2. **Information seekers**—those who are highly involved with a product category but who do not have a preferred brand.

3. **Routine brand buyers**—those who are not highly involved with the product category but are involved with a particular brand in that category.

4. **Brand switchers**—those who are not involved with the product category or with particular brands.

For each of the above descriptions, try to list a product category or brand for which you would fall into that segment.

Researching Motives

Motivational research can provide insights into the whys of consumer behavior and can reveal unsuspected motivations concerning product and brand usage. It can be used to develop new ideas for promotional campaigns and also to explore consumer reaction to new product ideas. There are many different motivational research techniques, some of which

Find two consumers who you can talk to for about 5–10 minutes each. Try to find a quiet place where you won't be interrupted.

- Begin the interview by stating:
  Assume that you were in the market for [insert product name]. What factors [or benefits] do you consider when you are deciding what brand of [product name] to buy for yourself?
- Then ask:
  What two factors [or benefits] are most important to you in making your decision?
- Then do the laddering:
  Why is [factor one] important to you?

Why is [factor two] important? What does [factor one or two] give you?

- Continue this process until the consumer cannot go on, and then end the interview.
- Draw out the two means-ends chains you measured for each person. Discuss what you have learned about these consumers' product knowledge and what implications this analysis could have for developing marketing strategies. Finally, discuss problems that you had with the measurement procedures. Was this process easy or hard for the consumers? Why do you think so?

were discussed in Chapter 3. Some motivational techniques have proved useful in new-product development and the development of new ideas of promotional campaigns. The means-ends chain and laddering provide a basic way of moving from product attributes to underlying motives; the Zaltman Metaphor Elicitation Technique (ZMET) combines consumer images and stories to help researchers understand motives.

The Means-Ends Chain and Laddering

As discussed in Chapter 2, consumers don't buy products or services; they buy benefits.[72] A chief goal of the marketing department is to understand the underlying consumer motivations for purchasing and then to communicate these motivations to the rest of the organization. The **means-ends chain** provides a way to dig beneath the surface and to discover layers of consumer meaning. The name is derived from the assumption that *a brand is a consumer's means of achieving a desired end or goal.*[73] Thus, the means-ends chain suggests a clear method for discovering a consumer's pattern of motivations. Instructions for administering a means-ends chain are shown in Good Practice 11.1. Sample outputs from the measurement process are shown in Consumer Chronicles 11.6, where the responses from one consumer, Karen, are summarized.

At the first step, the respondent narrows down the list of important factors, or benefits, to the two that are seen as most important. In this instance, when Karen thinks of candy bars, she perceives two important product benefits: (1) they give her a burst of energy, and (2) they are good for the "growlies." Presumably, the growlies refer to hunger pangs or hunger sounds. At the second step of measurement, the respondent is asked to say why that particular benefit is important. This is the start of the **laddering** process. Karen responds that a burst is important because it gets her through the next class—"stretchable and sneakable in class." The interviewer keeps asking Why? until the informant responds with a value (e.g., achievement, affiliation) or until the informant becomes fatigued and can no longer answer. In this sense, the interviewer is a bit like a two-year-old, interminably asking Why? Why? Why? This *succession of "why" questions* is referred to as the laddering process.

Karen's means-ends chain terminates with a statement that reflects the achievement motive—"I can get more things done." Presumably, the majority of consumer means-ends chains will culminate with a basic motive or value. As the consumer proceeds through the laddering process, he or she can respond with concrete product attributes (e.g., "Crest toothpaste has fluoride") or with product attributes that are more abstract (e.g., "Crest protects my teeth"). Note that the laddering technique requires an in-depth interview that is potentially time-consuming and possibly frustrating for the respondent (e.g., being continually confronted with why questions). Thus, the means-ends chain method is usually applied to small samples. It is not particularly feasible for large-scale applications.

The Zaltman Metaphor Elicitation Technique

With the Zaltman Metaphor Elicitation Technique, or **ZMET,** researchers use pictures and nonvisual images generated by consumers to elicit and probe the metaphors that represent consumers' thoughts and feelings about a topic.[74] The *use of one form of expression to describe or represent feelings about another* is called a **metaphor;** for example, earlier in this chapter we said the brain is like the ecology of a jungle. By having people select their own images, the ZMET process gives participants control of the research stimuli and a sense of involvement with the topic. Participants are able to represent their thoughts and feelings more fully and personally than when responding to stimuli created and presented by the researcher. The technique is especially effective at helping consumers uncover hidden or tacit knowledge—understanding they didn't know they had. It has been used to help many companies develop promotional campaigns or identify new product ideas. For example, the technique was useful at early stages in helping Procter & Gamble develop ideas for their Swiffer product, a new style "dust mop" that uses disposable cloths to pick up air and dirt.

Each ZMET interview is a one-on-one discussion, approximately two hours long. In preparation for the interview, participants spend considerable time thinking about the topic and locating appropriate visual images. As a result, participants arrive for their in-depth interview at an advanced stage of thinking, ready to discuss their thoughts and feelings.

The ZMET interview employs several steps to identify consumers' key thoughts and feelings. The technique is based, in part, on the fact that most human communication is nonverbal and that much of nonverbal communication is visual. Each step in the ZMET

1. **Storytelling about pictures.** Participants describe how each picture they brought to the interview represents thoughts and feelings about a particular topic of interest. Stories are excellent sources of metaphors and important sources of insight about participants. Participants spontaneously state the theme (overall meaning) of each picture during storytelling for that picture.

2. **Laddering.** During the storytelling step, the interviewer often uses laddering. The interviewer asks the participant to describe why something is important or relevant.

3. **Missing pictures.** Participants are asked if there were important ideas they wanted to express but for which they could not find relevant images. If this happens a record is made of the idea and kind of image that might represent those thoughts and feelings.

4. **Kelly grid and laddering.** The Kelly repertory grid seeks to identify concepts and distinctions and concepts at a higher level. The interviewer asks the participant to examine three pictures and to indicate how any two pictures are similar, but different from the third, with regard to the topic.

5. **Metaphor probe/expand the frame.** ZMET employs several other probing techniques to encourage participants to elaborate their thoughts and feelings (meanings) more deeply and completely. For example, participants are asked to widen the frame of one or more selected pictures and describe what else might enter the picture that reinforces the original idea. Participants imagine themselves in the picture and discuss what might take place and what they are thinking and feeling. Participants invite someone or something into the picture that will help them with their problem and describe who or what it would be.

6. **Sensory (nonvisual) metaphors.** Each participant is asked about other sensory images that are related to the topic of interest. For instance, the interviewer might ask participants what is (and what is not) the color, taste, smell, touch, sound, and emotion of "a product to refresh the spirit." The interviewer probes each answer to explicate its meaning and relevance for the participant.

7. **Vignette.** Participants may be asked to create a short story or movie that expresses important ideas about the topic. If necessary, participants are prompted to describe the location, time of day, and season; who, if anyone, was present; what else was happening; and so on.

8. **Digital imaging.** Finally, at the end of the interview, each participant creates a summary digital image with the skilled assistance of a computer graphics imager. When the image is finished, the participant gives a verbal description, which serves as an interpretative tour through the summary image. Thus, the digital image provides a visual and verbal summary of the participant's thoughts and feelings about the topic of interest.

process provides a different window for identifying and understanding metaphors, thereby gaining a deep understanding of consumers' thoughts and feelings. The use of multiple steps also increases the likelihood of uncovering an important idea that might be missed by more narrowly focused techniques. At the same time, each step provides validation of ideas from other steps. ZMET capitalizes on consumers' ideas about stories and movies to get at deeper meanings. Storytelling is a technique that focuses on individuals rather than on arguments or averages.[75] A story shows, rather than tells. Consumers use stories to give feelings and experiences personal relevance and meaning.[76] They develop the context and relevant relationships instead of merely positing raw data. They are open-ended and metaphorical. Stories unfold in time, and a specific place, instead of being presented as timeless, and they are emotionally evocative.[77] The central steps of the ZMET interview procedure are described in Good Practice 11.2.

ZMET offers researchers a way to tap into the unconscious mind. It provides a way to understand consumer motivations that are not necessarily tied to verbal expressions. One advantage of the technique is that it can provide unique input to advertising copywriters. Much of marketing research is summarized by statistics or by a written report. ZMET provides consumer-based images that can become part of the visual portion of an ad campaign.[78]

Measuring Involvement

Both means-ends chains and ZMET can be used to understand involvement because they show how product attributes are related to important aspects of the self and basic consumer problems and goals. Because we lack a clear definition about the essential components of involvement, there is a lot of variation in the measurement of involvement. Some measures focus on cognitive involvement, others on behaviors or outcomes of involvement, and

Exhibit 11.5 The Revised Personal Involvement Inventory (RPII)

Five cognitive items:

Important	___ ___ ___ ___ ___ ___ ___	Unimportant
Relevant	___ ___ ___ ___ ___ ___ ___	Irrelevant*
Means a lot to me	___ ___ ___ ___ ___ ___ ___	Means nothing to me
Valuable	___ ___ ___ ___ ___ ___ ___	Worthless
Needed	___ ___ ___ ___ ___ ___ ___	Not needed

Five emotional items:

Interesting	___ ___ ___ ___ ___ ___ ___	Uninteresting
Exciting	___ ___ ___ ___ ___ ___ ___	Unexciting*
Appealing	___ ___ ___ ___ ___ ___ ___	Unappealing*
Fascinating	___ ___ ___ ___ ___ ___ ___	Mundane*
Involving	___ ___ ___ ___ ___ ___ ___	Not involving

Indicates item is reverse scored.

others on measuring the enduring involvement the product has for the consumer. In short, there are many different quantitative measures to assess the degree of involvement people have with products, promotions, purchases, consumption experiences, and so on.[79] Most agree that involvement should be measured on a continuum rather than as a dichotomy of high and low involvement, and many use multiitem scales.

One measure of involvement is called the Revised Personal Involvement Inventory, the **RPII,** shown in Exhibit 11.5.[80] The scales displayed in the exhibit make use of the semantic differential method.[81] The semantic differential consists of a series of bipolar items, each measured on a seven-point scale.[82] There are three main advantages of the RPII. First, it contains only 10 items. This makes it easy to include in a survey or experiment. Second, the RPII is divided into two overall factors—cognitive and affective, consistent with involvement theory. A third major advantage of the RPII is that it can be used to measure involvement with a wide variety of stimulus objects, including products, ads, or purchase decisions.

Motivation is an inner drive that reflects goal-directed arousal. The motivated consumer is aroused, ready, and willing to engage in an activity. Understanding the goals consumers are pursuing can provide insights into many aspects of their behavior, including how they perceive and interpret the world around them.

Many psychologists have constructed extensive lists of basic goals or needs. To some extent, it may seem confusing that there are so many, sometimes conflicting, accounts and lists of human needs. One reason for this is that needs are not directly observable. We cannot see or touch a need or a motivation or want. Although all human cultures probably share some common bases of motivation, because of their common biology, motivation researchers have been unable to identify a single set of universal motives, spot them in behavior, and explain situational variation in their expression.

Four classic theories of motivation are: Sigmund Freud's concept of drives (e.g., as mediated by the id, ego, superego); Carl Jung's concept of archetypes (e.g., the self, the great mother, the hero); Abraham Maslow's concept of need hierarchy (e.g., physiological needs, safety needs); and Henry Murray's list of human needs (e.g., abasement, acquisition, affiliation). Each can be used by marketers, but each has limitations. Freud, Jung, Maslow, and Murray had views of the self and motives that derived from Western psychology. Their theories are culture-bound. They can still be very useful, but marketers must be wary of assuming they apply to everyone regardless of culture.

Consumers' perceptions of social and cultural situations shape their desires and goals for action. Research on the brain and mind support that consumers are uniquely shaped by cultural and social settings and they are constantly adapting based on what works and what doesn't. Our brains are not like computers; they are more like the ecology of a jungle. Each of us is a product of our environment—each of us has a unique set of motivations. Moreover, particular motivations are supported in some cultures and not in others.

Many cultures have an interdependent rather than an independent view of the self. The interdependent self is not separate from the social context and the social unit. Different self-concepts associated with different cultures affect motivation. There are five needs important in Western advertising appeals. Two of these—the needs for power and uniqueness—are likely to be much higher in independent than interdependent cultures. Three of these—the needs for achievement, affiliation, and self-esteem—are likely to be important in both, but they have very different meanings and actions associated with them. Marketers appeal to all of these five needs. Two other important consumer needs related to the shopping process are deal proneness and self-sacrifice.

Motives need to be understood in terms of consumer effort and involvement. Pursuing goals, the motivated consumer may feel involved, exhibiting interest, excitement, anxiety, passion, engagement, and flow. A flow experience is when a person's attention is completely absorbed by the activity or the goal object—peak involvement. Involvement can include cognitive or affective involvement. Marketers can stimulate one or the other or both types of involvement. Consumer involvement is a function of the goal object, the individual, and the decision situation. Consumer researchers distinguish between enduring product involvement and situational product involvement. Most consumers experience enduring involvement only in a few products or activities. Situational involvement describes temporary interest in a purchase or consumption process. Many aspects of the decision situation can influence situational involvement.

It is important to keep in mind that in many purchase situations the consumer couldn't care less. Low-involvement consumers are not active information seekers or active information processors. Often, low-involvement consumers are indifferent among a group of brands. Several strategies can be used by marketers for products that evoke low involvement.

Some research methodologies can be useful in analyzing motives and measuring involvement. The means-ends chain provides a way to dig beneath the surface and to discover layers of consumer meaning. At the first step, the respondent narrows down the list of important product benefits to the two that are seen as most important. The interviewer continues to ask why to get at the most basic reasons or motives for valuing these benefits. The Zaltman Metaphor Elicitation Technique, or ZMET, uses pictures and nonvisual images gathered or generated by consumers to elicit and probe the metaphors that represent consumers' thoughts and feelings about a topic. The technique offers a way to tap into the unconscious mind. It provides a way to understand consumer motivations that are not necessarily tied to verbal expressions. One measure of involvement is called the Revised Personal Involvement Inventory, or the RPII. The measure is short, easy to use, and can be used to measure involvement with ads, products, or purchase decisions.

---

1. Distinguish between needs and wants. Can you think of examples where this distinction can be useful to marketers? Can you think of examples where the distinction might not be useful?

2. Select an advertisement that seems to be based on an independent view of the self and appeals to the achievement need. How might this advertisement be adapted for an interdependent view of the self?

3. Select one of the needs described in Exhibit 11.4 as salient in cultures with an interdependent view of the self. Design an ad that would appeal to one of these needs.

4. Develop a set of appeals for a shopping center or for a product category that would appeal to women who view shopping as self-sacrifice and an expression of love for their families. Can you find instances of advertisements that use this appeal?

5. Survey three friends that use a particular brand of a product. Use the means-ends chain technique to find out why they use that product. Compare and contrast their chains as well as their termination points. Do they all have the same basic reason for using that particular brand?

6. Evaluate the following statement: Advertisers manipulate consumers and create wants and desires that wouldn't exist otherwise. Do you agree or disagree? Identify an example from the marketplace where this statement seems to be true. Identify another example where the statement appears to be false.

7. Write a vignette to describe a consumption situation that involves only one need. After your vignette is complete, write an analysis of that vignette so as to highlight the issues related to consumer behavior.

8. Write a vignette to describe a consumption situation that involves more than one need. After your vignette is complete, write an analysis of that vignette so as to highlight the issues related to consumer behavior.

9. Find a print ad designed to appeal to each of the five needs discussed in depth in this chapter. Describe in detail how the need is represented in the ad, emphasizing both visual and verbal cues.

You Make the Call

"Why Haggle?"

"Name your own price . . . and save!" That may be the slogan of Priceline.com. But name your own price is a misnomer. You might not realize this from news reports, but almost without exception, the analyses of these so-called name-your-price businesses have missed the most basic point: Priceline has never run a name-your-own price business. It is a propose-your-own-price business—something altogether different.

The so-called name-your-price approach to business may well harness the power of the Internet, data-mining, and other software secrets patented by Jay Walker, the founder of Priceline. But in the end, the business is not about naming prices, but haggling.

Haggling is a venerable and preferred price-making mechanism for certain goods in the Arab world, in sub-Saharan Africa, and even in Latin America. Haggling can even be found in exchange economies lacking money such as historic societies in the South Pacific. But generally haggling is most developed for high-value goods and luxuries. Over the past century or so, consumers in Western capitalist societies have agreed, via social contract, that for everyday commerce it is more efficient not to haggle over everyday goods.

Indeed for many consumers, one true breakthrough of the Web has been to reduce the haggling and bickering involved in buying a car and other big-ticket items. Do your research online and you can get a pretty good idea of the dealer's invoice price for any given automobile or home theater, for example.

Brian Elk, chief spokesman for Priceline, says that seven million customers have used the company's service and that nearly 40 percent have come back again. "In our view," Mr. Elk said, "name your price means make a reasonable offer, and we'll see what we can do for you." Generally, he said, Priceline's consumers of air tickets, hotel room, and car rentals are college students, retired people, or parents of large families—"People who have time they are willing to trade, if they can get deep discounts." Some think the model can be extended to items like airline seats, theater seats, and other goods for which the seller bears a fairly low marginal cost for each additional item, particularly, if the items have no value at all if they go unsold by takeoff or curtain time.

So maybe it's worth saving $300 on an airline ticket to Barcelona, Spain, next Wednesday at 0200 h via Istanbul even if a direct flight at noon was what you originally had in mind. But isn't life too short to go online and dicker over a jar of JIF peanut butter—particularly if there is no certainty that the price you "name" bears any relationship to what somebody's willing to sell it for? At a time when the Web is dangling the promise of ending car-dealer dickering in our lifetimes, would anyone think the public is eager to bring haggling to the meat case at Safeway or any other grocery store?

Not surprisingly perhaps, WebHouse is unwinding its operation after its founder, Mr. Walker, pulled the plug. He and other WebHouse executives blamed the current investment climate, not their business model, for failing to give the grocery-haggling service enough time to prove itself. A WebHouse spokesman said the company's typical customer was "a woman, shopping for her family, who would be flexible on the brands she wanted and who wanted to save money." He conceded that the system—make an offer for Ragu and wait for a response, bid on Cream of Wheat and see if it takes—demanded more time and patience than many people might tolerate. "One of the complaints we hear overwhelmingly from consumers and manufacturers was, 'Look this takes too long; it's too hard,'" the spokesman said.

1. How might Maslow's hierarchy help to position Priceline and other similar services more effectively?

2. How might Murray's theory be used to improve marketing communications for Priceline and other similar services?

3. How might some shopping-related motives be used to segment the market for Priceline and other similar services?

4. In what ways will a knowledge of consumer involvement be relevant to the success of offerings like Priceline and other similar services?

Source: Adapted from Tim Race, "There's Just One Thing Wrong with Name-Your-Own-Price Businesses: You're Not Naming Your Own Price," The New York Times, *October 23, 2000, C4.*

1. Deborah J. MacInnis, Christine Moorman, and Bernard J. Jaworski, "Enhancing and Measuring Consumers' Motivation, Opportunity, and Ability to Process Brand Information from Ads," *Journal of Marketing,* October 1991, pp. 32–53; Roy G. D'Andrade, "Schemas and Motivation," in *Human Motives and Cultural Models,* Roy D'Andrade and Claudia Strauss, eds. (Cambridge: Cambridge University Press, 1992), pp. 23–44; and Douglas G. Mook, *Motivation: The Organization of Action* (New York: W. W. Norton, 1987).
2. Brian Mullen and Craig Johnson, *The Psychology of Consumer Behavior* (Hillsdale, NJ: Lawrence Erlbaum, 1990), p. 3.
3. Annelies Moors, "Wearing Gold," in *Border Fetishisms: Material Objects in Unstable Spaces,* Patricia Spyer, ed. (New York: Routledge Press, 1998), pp. 208–23.
4. Anthony Gidden, *The Consequences of Modernity* (Stanford, CA: Stanford University Press, 1990).
5. Gerald Zaltman and Melanie Wallendorf, *Consumer Behavior* (New York: Wiley, 1979), p. 318.
6. Claudia Strauss, "Models and Motives," in *Human Motives and Cultural Models,* Roy D'Andrade and Claudia Strauss, eds. (Cambridge: Cambridge University Press, 1992), p. 3.
7. Zaltman and Wallendorf, *Consumer Behavior,* p. 365.
8. Bernd Schmitt, "Experiential Marketing: The New Edge in Branding," *Branded Environments,* Orlando, FL, December 3–4, 1998.
9. Zaltman and Wallendorf, *Consumer Behavior,* p. 365.
10. Carl G. Jung, M. L. von Vranz, Joseph L. Henderson, Jolande Jacobi, and Aniela Jaffe, *Man and His Symbols* (Garden City, NY: Doubleday, 1964).
11. David G. Meyers, *Psychology* (New York: Worth Publishers, 1998).
12. Russell W. Belk, "Third World Consumer Culture," in *Marketing and Development: Toward Broader Dimensions,* Erodoan Kumcu and A. Fuat Firat, eds. (Greenwich, CT: JAI Press, 1988), pp. 103–27; Güliz Ger, "The Positive and Negative Effects of Marketing on Socioeconomic Development: The Turkish Case," *Journal of Consumer Policy* 15, no. 3 (1992), pp. 229–54; and Güliz Ger and Russell W. Belk, "I'd Like to Buy the World a Coke: Consumptionscapes of the 'Less Affluent World,'" *Journal of Public Policy* 19, no. 3 (1996), pp. 271–304.
13. Güliz Ger, "Human Development and Humane Consumption: Well-Being beyond the Good Life," *Journal of Public Policy and Marketing* 16 (Spring 1997), pp. 110–25. Recent research on the brain, discussed later, also lends support to the primacy of beauty/aesthetics as a need.
14. Edwin C. Nevis, "Cultural Assumptions and Productivity: The United States and China," *Sloan Management Review* 24, no. 3 (Spring 1983), pp. 17–29.
15. For some examples of research related to this see Lynn Kahle, David Bousch, and Pamela Homer, "Broken Rungs in Abraham's Ladder: Is Maslow's Hierarchy Hierarchical?" in *Proceedings*

of the Society for Consumer Psychology, David Schumann, ed. (Nashville, TN: The Society for Consumer Psychology, 1988), pp. 11–16; and Richard Yalch and Frederic Brunel, "Need Hierarchies in Consumer Judgments of Product Designs: Is It Time to Reconsider Maslow's Theory?" in *Advances in Consumer Research,* vol. 23, Kim Corfman and John Lynch, eds. (Provo, UT: Association for Consumer Research, 1996), pp. 405–10.

16. Mike Herrington, "What Does the Customer Want?" *Across the Board* 30 (April 1993), p. 33.

17. Henry A. Murray, *Explorations in Personality* (New York: Oxford University Press, 1938); see also E. R. Hilgard, *Psychology in America: A Historical Survey* (New York: Harcourt Brace Jovanovich, 1987).

18. For example, see Hazel Rose Markus and Shinobu Kitayama, "Culture and the Self: Implications for Cognition, Emotion, and Motivation," *Psychological Review* 98 (April, 1991), pp. 224–53.

19. M. M. Suarez-Orozco, "Psychological Aspects of Achievement Motivation among Recent Hispanic Immigrants," in *Anthropological Perspectives on Dropping Out,* H. Trueba, G. Spindler, and L. Spindler, eds. (London: Falmer Press, 1989), pp. 99–116.

20. John L. Lastovicka, Lance A. Bettencourt, Renée Shaw Hughner, and Ronald J. Kuntze, "Lifestyle of the Tight and Frugal: Theory and Measurement," *Journal of Consumer Research* 26 (June 1999), pp. 85–98; and Russell W. Belk, "Worldly Possessions: Issues and Criticisms," in *Advances in Consumer Research,* vol. 10, Richard P. Bagozzi and Alice M. Tybout, eds. (Ann Arbor, MI: Association for Consumer Research, 1983), pp. 514–19.

21. Mook, *Motivation: The Organization of Action.*

22. There are many books and articles on evolving ideas of the mind. Two good articles are Steven Levy, "Dr. Edelman's Brain," *The New Yorker,* May 2, 1994, pp. 62–73; and Gerald Zaltman, "Consumer Researchers: Take a Hike!" *Journal of Consumer Research* 26 (March 2000), pp. 423–28. See also, Leslie Brothers, *Friday's Footprint: How Society Shapes the Human Mind* (New York: Oxford University Press, 1997); Gerald M. Edelman, *Bright Air, Brilliant Fire: On the Matter of the Mind* (New York: Basic Books, 1994); and J. Allan Hobson, *Consciousness* (New York: Scientific American Library, 1999).

23. Naomi Quinn and Claudia Strauss, "Cognition and Culture," in *Cultural Models in Language and Thought,* D. Holland and N. Quinn, eds. (Cambridge: Cambridge University Press, 1993), pp. 3–40; and Michelle Z. Rosaldo, "Toward an Anthropology of Self and Feeling," in *Culture Theory: Essays on Mind, Self, and Emotion,* R. Shweder and R. A. LaVine, eds. (Cambridge: Cambridge University Press, 1984), pp. 137–57.

24. A good basic source for this discussion is Markus and Kitayama, "Culture and the Self."

25. Anthony Chun-Tung Lowe and David R. Corkindale, "Differences in 'Cultural Values' and their Effects on Responses to Marketing Stimuli," *European Journal of Marketing* 32, no. 910 (1998), pp. 843–67.

26. David C. McClelland, *The Achievement Motive* (New York: Appleton-Century-Crofts, Inc., 1953), p. 79.

27. See Markus and Kitayama, "Culture and the Self," for a discussion and bibliography.

28. Constance Hill and Celia T. Romm, "The Role of Mothers as Gift Givers: A Comparison across Three Cultures," in *Advances in Consumer Research,* vol. 23, Kim Corfman and John Lynch, eds. (Provo, UT: Association for Consumer Research, 1996), pp. 21–29.

29. D. G. Winter, *The Power Motive* (New York: Free Press, 1973).

30. J. Veroff, "Assertive Motivations: Achievement versus Power," in *Motivation and Society,* D. G. Winter and A. J. Stewart, eds. (San Francisco: Jossey-Bass, 1982).

31. David C. McClelland, *Human Motivation* (New York: Cambridge University Press, 1987).

32. Winter, *The Power Motive.*

33. Courtney Leatherman, "A Prominent Feminist Theorist Recounts How She Faced Charges of Sex Harassment," *Chronicle of Higher Education,* March 7, 1997, p. A45.

34. C. R. Snyder and Howard L. Fromkin, *Uniqueness: The Human Pursuit of Difference* (New York: Plenum Press, 1980), p. 198.

35. Snyder and Fromkin, *Uniqueness.*

36. M. Lynn, "Scarcity Effects on Value: A Quantitative Review of Commodity Theory Literature," *Psychology and Marketing* 8 (1991), pp. 43–57.

37. C. R. Snyder, "Product Scarcity by Need for Uniqueness Interaction," *Basic and Applied Social Psychology* 13, no. 1 (1992), pp. 9–24.

38. Russell W. Belk, "Possessions and the Extended Self," *Journal of Consumer Research* 15, no. 3 (1988), pp. 139–68; and M. Csikszentmihalyi and Eugene Rochbert-Halton, *The Meaning of Things: Domestic Symbols and the Self* (Cambridge, MA: Cambridge University Press, 1982).

39. Alladi Venkatesh, "Modernity and Postmodernity: A Synthesis or Antithesis?" in *Proceedings of the 1989 AMA Winter Educators' Conference,* T. Childers, ed. (Chicago: American Marketing Association, 1989), pp. 99–104.

40. A. Fuat Firat and Alladi Venkatesh, "Postmodernity: The Age of Marketing," *International Journal of Research in Marketing* 10 (1993), pp. 227–50.

41. Richard Watson, Patrick McGowen, and George Zinkhan, "Pricing on the Web," working paper, University of Georgia, 1998.

42. An excellent discussion of the social dimension of brain activity and the social mind is provided in Leslie Brothers, *Friday's Footprint: How Society Shapes the Human Mind* (New York: Oxford University Press, 1997).

43. McClelland, *Human Motivation,* p. 347.

44. Firat and Venkatesh, "Postmodernity."

45. Susan Harter, "Causes, Correlates and the Functional Role of Global Self-Worth: A Life Span Perspective." In *Competence Considered,* Robert J. Sternberg and John Kolligian, Jr., eds. (New Haven, CT: Yale University Press, 1987), pp. 67–97; and B. E. Whitley, Jr., and Irene Frieze, "Children's Causal Attributions for Success and Failure in Achievement Settings: A Meta-Analysis," *Journal of Educational Psychology* 77 (1985), pp. 608–16.

46. L. T. Doi, *The Anatomy of Conformity: The Individual versus Society* (Tokyo: Kodansha, 1986).

47. Donald R. Lichtenstein, Richard G. Netemeyer, and Scot Burton, "Assessing the Domain Specificity of Deal Proneness: A Field Study," *Journal of Consumer Research* 22 (December 1995), pp. 314–26.

48. Michael Jones, Philip Trocchia, and David Mothersbaugh, "Noneconomic Motivations for Price Haggling: An Exploratory Study," in *Advances in Consumer Research,* vol. 24, Merrie Brucks and Debbie MacInnis, eds. (Provo, UT: Association for Consumer Research, 1997), pp. 388–91.

49. Daniel Miller, *A Theory of Shopping* (Ithaca, NY: Cornell University Press, 1998). This book is reviewed in Eric J. Arnould, *American Ethnologist* 26 (November 1999), pp. 999–1000. See also Marjorie L. DeVault, *Feeding the Family: The Social Organization of Caring as Gendered Work* (Chicago: University of Chicago Press, 1991).

50. Judy L. Zaichkowsky, "Measuring the Involvement Construct," *Journal of Consumer Research* 12 (December 1985), pp. 341–52.

51. Theo B. C. Poiesz and J.P.M. DeBont, "Do We Need Involvement to Understand Consumer Behavior," in *Advances in Consumer Research,* vol. 22, Frank Kardes and Mita Sujan, eds. (Provo, UT: Association for Consumer Research, 1995), pp. 448–52.

52. Richard L. Celsi, Randall L. Rose, and Thomas W. Leigh, "An Exploration of High-Risk Leisure Consumption through Skydiving," *Journal of Consumer Research* 20 (June 1993), pp. 1–23.

53. J. H. Antil, "Conceptualization and Operationalization of Involvement," in *Advances in Consumer Research,* T. C. Kinnear, ed. (Provo, UT: Association for Consumer Research, 1984), pp. 203–9.

54. Joel B. Cohen, "Involvement and You: 1,000 Great Ideas," in *Advances in Consumer Research,* R. Bagozzi and A. Tybout, eds. (Ann Arbor, MI: Association for Consumer Research, 1983), pp. 325–28.

55. John L. Lastovicka, "Components of Involvement," in *Attitude Research Play for High Stakes,* John C. Maloney and Bernard Silverman, eds. (Chicago: American Marketing Association, 1978), pp. 53–73.

56. Peter H. Bloch, "An Exploration into the Scaling of Consumers' Involvement in a Product Class," in *Advances in Consumer Research,* Kent B. Monroe, ed. (Ann Arbor, MI: Association for Consumer Research, 1981), pp. 61–65.

57. R. Ohanian and A. Tashchian, "Consumers' Shopping Effort and Evaluation of Store Image Attributes: The Roles of Purchasing Involvement and Recreational Shopping Interest," *Journal of Applied Business Research* 8, no. 4 (1992), pp. 40–49.

58. M. E. Salma and A. Tashchian, "Selected Socio-Economic and Demographic Characteristics Associated with Purchase Involvement," *Journal of Advertising* 18, no. 30 (1985), pp. 9–20.

59. G. Laurent and J. N. Kapferer, "Measuring Consumer Involvement Profiles," *Journal of Marketing Research* 22 (1985), pp. 41–53; and Salma and Tashchian, "Selected Socio-Economic and Demographic Characteristics Associated with Purchase Involvement."

60. Zaichkowsky, "Measuring the Involvement Construct."

61. Jerome Bruner, *Actual Minds, Possible Worlds* (Boston: Harvard University Press, 1986).

62. Ohanian and Tashchian, "Consumers' Shopping Effort and Evaluation of Store Image Attributes."

63. Bloch, "An Exploration into the Scaling of Consumers' Involvement in a Product Class."

64. Laurent and Kapferer, "Measuring Consumer Involvement Profiles."

65. Ohanian and Tashchian, "Consumers' Shopping Effort and Evaluation of Store Image Attributes."

66. Sharon E. Beatty, Lynn R. Kahle, and Pamela Homer, "Theory and Implications," *Journal of Business Research* 16, no. 2 (1988), pp. 149–67.

67. Bloch, "An Exploration into the Scaling of Consumers' Involvement in a Product Class."

68. Judy L. Zaichkowsky, *Defending Your Brand against Imitation* (London: Quorum Books, 1995).

69. Harold H. Kassarjian, "Low Involvement: A Second Look," in *Advances in Consumer Research,* vol. 8, Kent B. Monroe, ed. (Ann Arbor, MI: Association for Consumer Research, 1981), pp. 31–34.

70. Beatty, Kahle, and Homer, "Theory and Implications."

71. Herbert E. Krugman, "The Impact of Television Advertising: Learning without Involvement," *Public Opinion Quarterly* 29 (Fall 1965), pp. 349–56.

72. Jagdish N. Sheth, Banwari Mittal, and Bruce Newman, *Customer Behavior: Consumer Behavior and Beyond* (Fort Worth, TX: Dryden Press, 1999).

73. William D. Wells and David Prensky, *Consumer Behavior* (New York: John Wiley, 1996).

74. ZMET is a patented process. Any use of the process or its constituent elements is prohibited unless under license or by other written permission of the patent holder. This includes indirect, unauthorized third-party use of any aspect of ZMET. Also included under this prohibition is inadvertent use where any party unknowingly uses or accepts use of the process or its elements. Gerald Zaltman, "Rethinking Market Research: Putting People Back In," *Journal of Marketing Research* 34 (November 1997), pp. 424–37.

75. John Allen Paulos, *Once Upon a Number: The Hidden Mathematical Logic of Stories* (New York: Basic Books, 1998).

76. Catherine Kohler Riessman, *Narrative Analysis* (Newbury Park, CA: Sage Publications, 1993).

77. Paulos, *Once Upon a Number.*

78. Jerry Zaltman and Robin Higie Coulter, "Seeing the Voice of the Customer: Metaphor-Based Advertising Research," *Journal of Advertising Research* 35, no. 4 (1995), pp. 35–51.

79. For a review of involvement measures in advertising and consumer research, see J. Craig Andrews, Srinivas Durvasula, and Syed H. Akhter, "A Framework for Conceptualizing and Measuring the Involvement Construct in Advertising Research," *Journal of Advertising* 19 (1990), pp. 27–40.

80. Judy L. Zaichkowsky, "The Personal Involvement Inventory: Reduction, Revision, and Application to Advertising," *Journal of Advertising* 23, no. 4 (1994), pp. 59–70.

81. Zaichkowsky, "Measuring the Involvement Construct," p. 342.

82. Charles Osgood, George J. Suci, and Percy H. Tannenbaum, *The Measurement of Meaning* (Urbana, IL: University of Illinois Press, 1957).

Learning Objectives

After completing this chapter, you should be able to:

- Describe the relationships among consumer experience, learning, memory, and knowledge and the distinctions between these concepts.

- Discuss the different kinds of consumer experiences, their relationship to other kinds of consumer behavior, and marketing implications.

- Explain the role of anticipated consumption and provide examples and details.

- Describe the different ways that consumers learn and understand the marketing implications.

- Distinguish between the two types of behavioral theories—classical conditioning and operant conditioning—and apply these concepts to consumer behavior settings.

- Appreciate the intricacy and diversity of human memory and relate memory concepts to marketing actions.

- Appreciate the role of context in shaping consumer memory and knowledge and describe the ways that context influences consumer behavior.

Experience, Learning, and Knowledge

Making Up Time in Hungary[1]

We met Éva over coffee in our Western-style hotel, where she began the conversation by apologizing for her English. She explained that now every younger woman speaks English, but when she was in school, she had to learn Russian and was not permitted to study English. Éva is well educated and cosmopolitan. She lives in Budapest, Hungary, with her husband and eight-year-old son. She is 37 years old, tall, slender, with a beautiful complexion and an air of elegance and refinement. We talked with Éva about a range of topics from cosmetics to cars to children, went shopping with her, and learned something about her hopes and dreams. She is proud of her country, suspicious of its political leadership, but hopeful for the future. She notes with pride that although in 1990 even basic baby cosmetics were not available, now everything she sees or hears about in Western media she can buy in Hungary within a month. In the last decade, Éva like other central European women has experienced and learned many new things.

Éva relies for fashion advice on *Walla* and *Cosmopolitan*. After seeing an ad in *Walla* for Clinique's perfume (new at the time), she went by the Clinique shop and got a sample. She can't remember the name of the perfume, but thinks it smells nice. Éva likes Clinique cosmetics because, with their light-green packaging and clean looks, they appear fresh and natural, important product characteristics to Éva. She buys some Clinique products, but for others she's reluctant to ask the price, afraid she can't afford them. Later, we visit a Clinique shop and the salesperson gives us free samples of Happy. Éva confirms

that such a behavior—free samples to try—was unheard of in 1991; yes, "everything and everyone has changed."

She laments that because cosmetics were not available when she was young she never really learned to use them, the way young women do today. Even now, she doesn't feel confident about using certain cosmetics, but she's trying to learn. Éva takes us to visit one of her friends, about the same age, who she considers very daring because this friend wears eye shadow and experiments with different looks and shades—very unusual for this age group. Éva sticks to the basics and takes her lead from fashion articles.

Over the past decade, Éva has identified preferred brands, but like many other central European women she is not exactly brand loyal. For example, as we shopped with her she would describe a pattern of trying new products and returning to favorites. Sometimes she feels overwhelmed with the choices and confused by the type of information provided. The situation is much worse for her 70-year-old mother, who has never used any cosmetics. Éva buys cosmetics for her mother and encourages her to use them, telling her "now is the time you have to use cosmetics because you have to stay young, to care, you have to look young." She observes that in 6 years Hungary has changed like other countries change in 20 years. "This is like a bomb."

Overview

People experience everyday life, and most try to learn from those experiences. Often, knowledge is one outcome of that learning, and this knowledge in turn influences future perceptions and experiences. Experience, learning, and knowledge are the focus of this chapter; and it makes sense to think of the three as progressing in an order—from experience to learning to knowledge. There is a dynamic interplay among them, and of course some experiences people don't learn from and some knowledge doesn't come from experience. Like Éva, people learn things in different ways, sometimes through their own experiences, other times vicariously, through the reported or observed experience of others. As we discuss in Chapter 15, sometimes people trust experts or others similar to them; other times they see something and decide to try it themselves.

People's environment influences what they experience and what is important to know, and these things are constantly changing. In this sense, consumer knowledge is a moving target. Some adapt better to changing patterns of information than others, but everyone tries to fit new experiences with prior knowledge. Categorization helps people understand what something is by relating it to prior knowledge. As discussed in several earlier chapters, categories reflect a unique composite of a person's cultural environment and individual experiences. In this chapter we will talk more about how people construct and work with concepts, sets of associations and categories, and how cultural categories help people learn and make decisions.

Sometimes people find it easy to put things in familiar categories; in other cases the experience is so unique or the product so different that it doesn't really fit in an existing category. Minivans offer a great example. The minivan category is now a taken-for-granted one, but in the mid-1980s there was little knowledge of or agreement about what a minivan is or how it relates to station wagons, sedans, and full-size vans. Over time the minivan category stabilized and producers began to introduce models into this category, and consumers began to search within this category.[2]

People also *create unique groupings of things (people, objects, places, etc.) that serve a particular goal*—**goal-based categories.** For example, a mother might have a category called "things for children to do on a rainy day," and a college student might have a category called "good places to eat close to campus." Conflicting goals and ambiguous (uncertain or unknown) goals change how people group objects and make choices.[3] For instance, consumers sometimes use unusual, creative categories to help them resolve goal conflicts or clarify goals.

Learning requires both forward and backward thinking. Sometimes people engage in backward reasoning to understand their actions; in other situations they look forward and anticipate likes and dislikes based on previous experiences. Thus, actions are partly a response to **preferences**—*feelings and beliefs about what a person likes and dislikes.* But actions also help consumers identify and predict new preferences.[4] For example, through product trial Éva learns that she likes Clinique's new perfume Happy. Sometimes consumers have firm and stable preferences; but more often they (like Éva) compare new alternatives with old favorites or find that, because of their own changing circumstances, they need or require different things. People use context and other cues to help them guess what they will like and dislike. For example, Éva uses packaging as a cue to the quality and characteristics of cosmetic products. In Chapter 9 we discussed many different perceptual cues consumers use in forming evaluations and making decisions.

Many times situations arise that make consumers, like Éva, reflect on the past, comparing and contrasting it with the present. Here again, categories, concepts, and the stories they build around them are important in how and what they describe about the past. In this sense, remembering is constructive. The past is filtered through recent understandings to create and rework social worlds. Telling stories helps consumers make sense of events and actions in their lives.[5] Sometimes, however, consumers feel they are "reliving" an experience when they remember. In fact, brain research confirms that when people remember a particular episode, the neurons that were active together during the episode are reactivated, recreating a representation of the event. This is why, with especially significant events, people may feel the emotions and physical sensations they experienced at that time.[6] This has many implications for marketers, which we will discuss in this chapter.

Feelings and emotions are an important part of experience, learning, and knowledge. To disavow them as somehow irrational is a big mistake. Emotion and reason can't be separated. In fact, we can define **emotion** as *the combination of a mental evaluative process* (which can be simple or complex) *with dispositional responses to that process, resulting in an emotional body state and additional mental changes.* Let's take a simple example. Think of a time you were very frightened. Replay the event in your mind. Do you feel some of the same emotions you felt then? Your mind and body are working together—the content of your thoughts is changing your body state, and your thoughts are again reflecting on those changes. In this chapter we will talk about how feelings and emotions relate to experience, learning, and knowledge.

As we have observed in previous chapters, experience, learning, and knowledge are related to self-concept, perceptions, motivations, and involvements and, of course, to the cultures, social groups, and families in which people live their lives. What people experience, learn, and know *influences* their attitudes and decisions and also *reflects* those attitudes and decisions. We will talk more about attitudes and decisions in Chapter 13.

Consumer Experiences

Consumer experiences are at the heart of consumer behavior. Often, the best way to sell the product is by associating it with a more fundamental life experience. Marketers need to remember that consumers buy products and services hoping that those purchases will contribute to how they, and others they care about, experience life. Examples abound of retailers and manufacturers (click and brick) that offer more than an array of goods and services for sale—they offer a shopping experience. You can adventure on the climbing wall at REI, enjoy the playground at McDonald's, be enveloped in a sensory exploration at Victoria's Secret, and enter into an interactive sports museum at Niketown USA. A short walk down Michigan Avenue in Chicago offers an array of themed retailing that combines experience and shopping. The Polus Center, a shopping mall in Budapest, Hungary, that opened in 1998, illustrates a Western theme (below).

Whether extraordinary or mundane, experience has an important impact on what consumers learn and remember. Positive experiences may lead to repeated behaviors. Negative experiences may lead to avoidance behaviors. Some peak experiences (e.g., climbing a mountain while on vacation) may come to dominate wake-time thoughts. Other experiences (e.g., TV shows watched two months ago) are quickly forgotten.

Polus Shopping Center: Themed Retailing in Hungary.

The New
Experience
Economy

omic value now turns on more than a high-quality
s on engaging consumers in a memorable way—of-
er, transforming them by guiding them through ex-
iomic value increases as offerings move from com-
3 we talked about how adventure tourism such as
ewed and valued as a **transformational experience,**
k and feel about themselves and the world around
ed economic pyramid.[7] Notice that when marketers
odities toward experiences and transformations they
Many aspects of the offering change along with this
i offering experiences marketers are concerned with
norable and personal. When the offering is transfor-
duct. The marketer only succeeds if the individual is
omotions are organized around promising a transfor-
n advertisement in a fashion magazine that portrays
g that the reader too can be transformed.
deal of effort goes into designing the best store lay-
iences will be positive and rewarding. Likewise, de-
signers attempt to construct websites so that consumers' search experiences will be efficient and fun. Nonetheless, consumers' shopping experiences are more than just those
behaviors that can be directly observed.[8] Shopping experiences also include the mental
events and emotional states surrounding purchase events.

For some product categories (e.g., a snack food) the consumption experience is over
quickly. For example, a consumer may buy a candy bar on the way out of the grocery store
and eat it entirely before the groceries are packed in the car. Other consumption experiences stretch out long after the time of actual purchase. For instance, when consumers purchase some entertainment services such as a concert or a sporting event, the allocation (and
expenditure) of time is perhaps more important than the allocation of money. Many service experiences (e.g., taking a vacation, attending a concert) stretch out over time. Consumers invest their time in these activities, just as they invest their money. Transformational

Exhibit 12.1 The Economic Pyramid

Exhibit 12.2 A Classification of Consumer Experie

Anticipated Consumption	Purchase Experiences	Consumption Experiences	Remembered Consumption and Nostalgia
Searching (in person; using traditional media; via the Web; talking to friends)	Choice Payment Bundling product (for transport)	Sense experiences (taste, touch, feel, sight, sound) Satiation	Reliving past experiences; looking at photographs Telling stories
Planning for future purchases	Service encounter	Satisfaction/dissatisfaction	Comparing (old times to new)
Daydreaming	Atmospherics (in-store environment)	Arousal/flow (other experiences shown in Exhibit 12.2)	Talking with friends from days gone by
Budgeting		Transformation	Playing "what if"; remembered consumption
Fantasizing			Daydreaming
			Sorting through memorabilia and other mementos

experiences typically unfold over time and must be sustained through time. Losing weight, stopping smoking, or changing personal patterns through therapy are all potentially transforming but also arduous, effortful investments.

As shown in Exhibit 12.2, experiences related to consumer behavior can be classified into four groups: (1) anticipated consumption (including search behavior); (2) the actual purchase of the good or service; (3) consumption experiences; and (4) remembered consumption (experiences that are relived over a period of days or weeks or months, perhaps retold to others). Over the next several chapters we will be discussing these aspects of experience in more detail. In this chapter we will focus primarily on anticipated consumption and how it relates to learning and knowledge and on remembered consumption as one dimension of memory.

Anticipated Consumption

Anticipated consumption experiences include **prepurchase search** that *occurs in response to the activation of a consumption problem or desire.* For instance, Sam is a typical college student in the southeastern United States. He has several CDs recorded by the rap artist Coolio. He is interested in attending a Coolio concert, so he checks appropriate websites for information about upcoming performances near his hometown. He talks with some of his friends about dates that best suit their schedules. He finds out the costs of attending the concert, including ticket prices and travel expenses. He sets aside money in his budget to cover these expenses; and he checks his exam schedule to make certain that there are not critical conflicts.

Anticipated consumption can also include thoughts, feelings, and sensory images that surround the upcoming event. Imagined consumption is an important element. Prior to attending the Coolio concert, Sam finds that it is difficult to concentrate on his studies. His mind wanders to the concert arena. After class, he rushes to find his friends so that they can further discuss their upcoming plans for attending the concert. He completes more web searches to find the best places to stay and eat near the concert venue. All of these activities come under the rubric of anticipated consumption.

Anticipated consumption may begin a long time before actual purchase. For example, many parents begin college funds for their children even before those children are born, and young boys in the United States start anticipating car purchases well in advance of when they are old enough to drive or rich enough to sustain car payments. Their attention to information about cars has an ongoing quality—they are building a bank of information for future use.[9] Of course, much anticipated consumption never results in a purchase. Colette, a first grader, is saving earnings and windfall profits for a pony, but her parents are hoping that her intentions waver before she has amassed sufficient capital to go pony shopping. In Chapter 13 we will discuss in more detail why purchase intentions often don't translate into purchase behavior.

Anticipated consumption is related to consumers' aspirations, which in turn are based on their environment, knowledge, and experiences. Colette believes it is reasonable to save for and acquire a horse because her friend Willie is saving for one, her father had one when he was growing up, and her uncle and grandfather have horses. The relationship between anticipated consumption and consumer knowledge is important to pay attention to. Consider as an example the transitional economies of eastern and central Europe. Many consumers in these environments are experiencing an increasing **aspiration gap,** *a disparity between the consumption level they earnestly desire and strive for and the level actually attainable.* The explosion of media and consumer goods that promote a new consumption standard create disillusionment and frustration for many consumers who view these things as unattainable. Seeing ads with nice houses, cars, and clothes, they are frustrated and disillusioned because they can't see how they will ever attain these things.[10] Marketers can influence consumers by changing their aspirations or the perceived aspiration gap. For example, attractive auto loan programs available in the late 1990s in Hungary reduced the aspiration gap—Hungarian consumers were able to buy the cars they dreamed of for years, and they did.

As implied in the previous section, there are many kinds of consumer experiences. In his best-selling book *Finding Flow,* Csikzentmihalyi provides a typology for understanding different types of human experiences.[11] This typology, which is particularly applicable for understanding consumer experiences, is shown in Exhibit 12.3. We briefly discussed flow in Chapter 11 but did not distinguish other types of experiences. Two key dimensions distinguish experiences—level of skill and level of challenge. For instance, when skills and challenges are low, experiences are boring. When skill levels are high and challenges are low, people have relaxing experiences.

Consumer experiences are effective appeals to use in an ad campaign. From this perspective, Exhibit 12.3 provides a useful framework for listing the kinds of experiences that advertisers might want to use in their campaigns. For example, some ads show consumers how to escape boredom and apathy (the lower-left quadrant). Relaxation can be an effective appeal. The prospect of flying long distances on an aircraft may evoke hassles for some, or it may evoke boredom for others. The Korean Air ad shows how customers can relax on this airline. In this way, the advertised service moves the consumer from a negative part of the experience grid to a positive point (relaxation).

When challenges are high and skill levels are moderate, consumers have arousing experiences. Learning is one example of such arousal. Learning is discussed in the next major section of this chapter. People's favorite activities are classified as flow experiences, described in more detail in Chapter 11. As shown in Exhibit 12.3, flow results when both skills and challenges are at their maximum. This is what makes flow experiences favorite activities. Some examples of flow experience include a pilot flying a test aircraft, a doctor

A Typology of Consumer Experiences

Exhibit 12.3 Flow: A Combination of Challenge and Skill

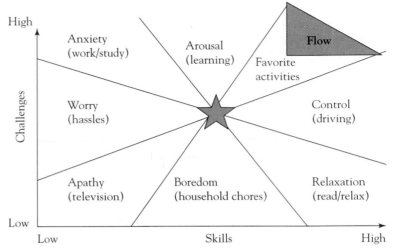

Source: Mihaly Csikzentmihalyi, *Finding Flow* (New York: Perseus Books, 1997).

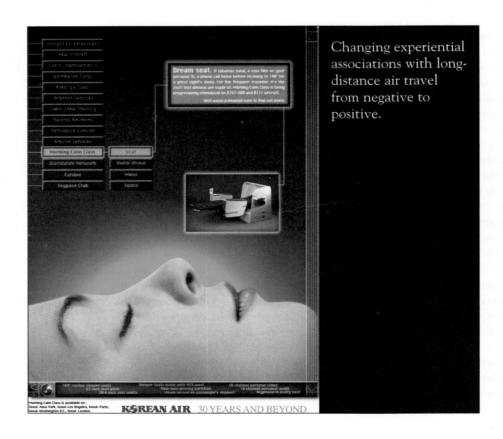

Changing experiential associations with long-distance air travel from negative to positive.

performing surgery, a professor teaching a class, the process involved in making social contacts and forging intimate relationships, playing a video game, climbing a mountain, and participating in a professional conference. Remember, a flow experience for one consumer may be boring or irritating to another consumer—it depends on their skills and challenges. When challenges and skills required are low, then negative human emotions result. For instance, apathy comes when challenges and skills are at their lowest levels. Worry comes when skills are low and challenges are moderate. Boredom comes when skills are moderate and challenges are low (see Exhibit 12.3).

The activities and emotional states shown in Exhibit 12.3 could be used as appeals in advertising. For example, flow would make an effective advertising appeal for some kinds of brands. Look at the ad for Nike shown above. Tiger Woods's flowing figure, as he strikes the ball, evokes the flow concept. Golf, as a product category, is appropriate for this kind of promotional appeal. Many golfers seek flow in the sport. They search for the moment when everything comes together and they too strike the ball like Tiger Woods, prowling the course.

Only a small fraction of consumer experiences can be classified as flow activities. Nonetheless, flow activities are pivotal because they represent peak experiences. They may come at work or in leisure time. To a large extent flow experiences may come to dominate leisure time. A large portion of nonwork time is spent on rest or relaxation. But through anticipating future flow experiences or by looking back nostalgically at such past experiences, consumers may devote quite a bit of their active leisure time to pursuing or remembering these flow periods.

From a marketing perspective, it is difficult to underestimate the importance of the experiences that consumers have with products and services. Now that we have introduced a classification scheme (Exhibit 12.3) for thinking about and understanding the kinds of experiences that consumers have, we'll highlight one specific kind of consumer experience: learning.

Consumer Learning

In the opening vignette Éva talks about learning to speak English, apply makeup, shop for cosmetics, and use various cues such as packaging to assist in making brand choices. She believes that Clinique's packaging cues clean and natural products; and she revealed in the interview on which the vignette was based that she believes products sold in the "China market" (open-air market) are not trustworthy and might be counterfeit. Consumers hold many everyday beliefs about the world and how it works. But how do consumers learn the rules about buying and consuming?

What Is Learning?

(People know learning when they see it) but a precise definition is more difficult.[12] It's actually a mysterious and challenging concept even for neuroscientists. Imagine this. Consumers (not to mention pigeons, dogs, and monkeys) encounter a small number of events or objects and after this exposure adaptively categorize or recognize an indefinite number of novel objects (even in a variety of contexts) as being similar or identical to the small set that they first encountered. This is an amazing process and nobody understands exactly how it happens. Learning is complicated because it involves object definition and generalization in a world that is not prelabeled by any a priori scheme. Moreover, consumers can learn, retain, and act on information via unconscious and implicit learning processes that are hard to identify and poorly understood.[13]

We define (**consumer learning** as *connecting categories to behaviors that have adaptive value in terms of consumer goals.*)[14] Fundamental to this definition is that (learning is adaptive and determined by the value systems, desires, and needs of the learner) Also, of course, it depends on what the learner already knows) That is, new information is assessed in terms of existing beliefs and past experiences. An example makes this definition easier to understand. In the opening vignette, Éva learns about Happy perfume from a magazine advertisement. She connects this perfume with her already existing beliefs about Clinique, which include good quality, expensive, natural, good service, and so on. Other cosmetics also belong to the category of good quality; for example, (Éva believes in the quality of Nivea products, and although she continues to experiment with other brands, she always comes back to Nivea face cream.) Both Nivea and Clinique products are associated with numerous unique experiences that might be triggered when Éva thinks about or is exposed to these products. For example, as she talked with us about Nivea face cream she recalled using the baby sun protection lotion on her son when he was quite small. This in turn triggered a flood of memories about his childhood, vacationing at the beach, and so on.

Although learning plays a fundamental role in many consumer theories and models, it is seldom investigated directly. Only a few studies have looked at the basic ways in which consumers learn. That research suggests that we can think of consumers as generating guesses or hypotheses about the way the world works, in order to make adaptive choices that move them toward their goals. Sometimes these guesses may be unconscious or implicit, sometimes so much a part of consumers' cultural background that the guesses are completely taken for granted. Visiting Denmark for the first time and not speaking the language, we went grocery shopping and selected something that we guessed from the picture would be chocolate-covered ice cream bars. To our surprise, they were licorice-covered ice cream bars, a product concept our young daughter found totally disgusting. Coming from the United States, we never considered this possibility. Similar to other consumers in these types of situations, we didn't generate very many hypotheses (only one)

Exhibit 12.4 A Simplified Model of Consumer Learning

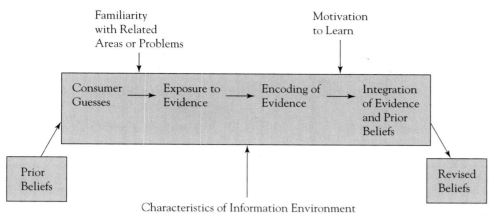

Source: Adapted from Stephen J. Hoch and John Deighton, "Managing What Consumers Learn from Experience," *Journal of Marketing* 53 (April 1989), pp. 1–20.

and we clearly underestimated the likelihood of unspecified alternative hypotheses.[15] Exhibit 12.4 provides a simplified model of consumer learning based on consumer guesses and exposure to evidence.

The model provided in Exhibit 12.4 suggests that as consumers are exposed to events that seem to require explanation they trigger a search from prior experiences and among existing beliefs to develop a hunch about what might be going on. Their exposure to evidence, encoding of evidence, and integration of evidence with prior beliefs depends on their familiarity with other things that they believe relate, their motivation to learn, and characteristics of the information environment. **Encoding** evidence is the process by which *consumers select a word or visual image to represent a perceived object.* For example, for Éva the distinctive light-green packaging of Clinique products is coded as "fresh, clean, and natural." **Integration** is how *they relate that evidence to other information and beliefs.* Both encoding and integration rely on learned cultural categories as well as individual experiences. For example, past experience has led Éva to believe that packaging provides information about product quality, and many cultural beliefs (Hungarians traditional emphasis on natural herbal treatments) and individual experiences (her son's sensitive skin and allergic reactions) focus her attention on finding clean and natural cosmetics. How people encode and integrate information also depends on other factors such as gender and age.[16] A few comments are appropriate. First, consumers only generate guesses when objects or events are unexpected, novel, or block goals. Much of the time consumers just apply already "good enough" learned rules to make decisions and take action.[17] Second, as in the example of licorice ice cream bars, previous experience can interfere with generating new guesses or recognizing new diagnostic evidence. For example, had we looked closely at the package picture the coating on the ice cream bar would have appeared more black than brown (new diagnostic evidence). Third, when consumers scan through what they know to decide what to do in a new situation, they often make guesses by drawing on their familiarity with unexpected domains. Marketers can't always determine inferences consumers will make to formulate guesses and achieve goals. For example, in trying to decide about the safety of food that has been genetically modified, some

U.S. consumers apply inappropriate rules they have learned about food safety, such as the need to cook meat thoroughly or wash vegetables properly.[18] These rules in turn derive from deeply embedded, culturally learned ideas about food and the ability to transform nature.[19] Finally, the information environment can have a dramatic impact on consumers' exposure, encoding, and integration of evidence to accomplish goals. For example, one of the most important reasons that Éva now experiments with and learns about new products is that she is able to. In 1991, women did not have women's fashion magazines available unless they visited select Western-style hotels. Cosmetics retail clerks protectively hovered over glassed-in counter spaces. They only reluctantly allowed consumers to touch or hold the packaged product, much less actually try the product as is common in Western-style department stores and cosmetics retail shops.[20]

Types of Learning	Consumers can learn from description.[21] This is a very efficient way to learn and includes listening to, observing, and remembering what other people tell us. Parents, teachers, books, friends, TV, billboards, magazines, sales representatives, Internet sites, package labels, and instruction manuals are just a few of the ways that people learn by description. Consumers may imitate or model a fashion look they see on MTV, carefully follow a recipe on the back of a soup can, or check out a critic's movie recommendations on the Internet. *Through repetition, people learn lots of things almost by accident.* This type of learning is referred to as **incidental learning.** In fact, advertising information may be most likely to influence consumers when they are not aware of its influence.[22] **Learning by description** includes *acquiring information from vicarious or indirect encounters.* For marketers, advertising is a primary tool for teaching consumers, and it relies on learning by description. For example, advertisers use celebrity spokespersons in their campaigns to provide consumers with opportunities for **vicarious learning.** A cartoon character can also serve this purpose, as can an appealing advertising model who is not necessarily a well-known entity but with whom the consumer can identify. Even though consumers do not have their own direct experience, they can learn by observing the experience described in advertising. In the United States, kindergarten children can recall brand names within several different categories, and even preschoolers can associate brand names with picture and color cues for several different types of products.[23]

Consumers also learn from firsthand, **direct experience.** Learning from experience differs from indirect or vicarious learning because of its *interactive character* and because consumers tend to privilege conclusions drawn from experience. Experiences are easier to remember because they are more vivid and concrete; they are also more credible than someone else's reported experiences and are likely to be more involving and motivating. Consumers may also gain feelings of competence, or flow (as we discussed earlier), from their experiences. A paradox of experiential information is that while it is learned fast, it is also the most fragile, context-dependent, and subject to distortion.[24]

It would be a mistake to think that experience provides a perfect match between action and consequence, making it easy to learn what to do next time. Much experience is ambiguous. For example, often consumers don't know what went wrong when a product or service fails and may feel confused about how to avoid future failures. Whether they actively search for explanations and how they explain what happened depends on their cultural knowledge and experience. For example, many people in non-Western cultures are content to leave the mystery of what happened unquestioned and unresolved, often attributing the outcome to fate or magic.[25] Some research has shown that consumers rely on the consumption experience when evaluating brands *if* the experience is unambiguous, but they rely on prior opinions or advertising claims when the experience is ambiguous. For example, coffee prepared to taste bitter (an ambiguous and relative experience) tastes less bitter to individuals who have been exposed to advertising claiming the coffee has no bitterness. Moreover, exposure to advertising *after* an ambiguous experience can affect how consumers report on and evaluate that experience.[26]

In addition, it would be a mistake to think that experiences are recalled just the way they happened. For example, research has shown consumers' recollections of product or service experiences can be influenced and shaped by marketing communications following the experiences. Consumers' memories often include interpretation and details that help the experience make sense within the broader scope of their lives and in terms of the outcomes that transpired and the audience for whom the story is told. The mental procedures used in putting together a memory rely as much on constructive processes as on retrieval.[27]

Much of how people make sense of things happens after the fact, sometimes a long time after. How consumers describe their first car purchase will differ depending on when they are asked and what has happened since then. For example, an accident, a birth, a marriage, or anything that makes certain attributes more or less salient may change how consumers describe the factors they considered when they bought the car. Consumers are very vulnerable to **hindsight bias,** the *"I knew it all along" effect.* After experiencing a product or service, consumers tend to *falsely believe that they knew the outcomes in advance of their experience.*[28]

Up to this point in our discussion we have described learning as a mental process that is adaptive and directed toward advancing consumer goals. Based on the most recent understandings of how the brain works, our perspective has emphasized the mysterious and contextual quality of learning. Nevertheless, by just looking at behavior researchers have discovered a lot about learning, both in humans and in animals. Two **behavioral learning theories,** typically reviewed at length in several other academic courses but briefly discussed here, are classical conditioning and operant conditioning. Both take a behaviorist approach to learning. They treat human memory processes as a black box—processes that are not really necessary to understand. Under the behaviorist approach, consumers operate on the environment (e.g., people do things). In turn, consumers experience consequences from the environment (e.g., rewards, punishments, pairings of stimuli). These consequences determine the probabilities of future behavioral responses.

Behavioral Learning Theories

Classical Conditioning Theory

Classical conditioning is a specific procedure that creates a learning environment, but other learning processes may operate simultaneously with this procedure.[29] Classical conditioning became well known from the Russian psychologist Ivan Pavlov. Pavlov is most famous for his experiments with dogs. When he administered meat powder to dogs, they would naturally salivate. Every time that he administered the powder, he would sound a bell. Through repetition, the dogs learned to associate the sound of the bell with the coming of food. Eventually, the dogs would salivate upon hearing the sound of the bell, even when the meat powder was not present. In this way, Pavlov took a neutral object (the bell) and over time associated it with a meaningful object (the meat powder). An important part of this procedure is that the bell and the meat powder occur close together in time as opposed to far apart in time. The **temporal contiguity principle** states that *stronger associations are learned when events occur close together in time as opposed to far apart in time.* This principle has been used to explain why people spend more freely using credit cards than cash. Credit cards separate the joy of consuming from the pain of paying by at least 30 days, whereas with cash the costs and benefits occur close together.[30]

Exhibit 12.5 An Example of Classical Conditioning: Steven Spielberg's *JAWS*

Unconditioned Stimulus

Shark ->

Unconditioned Response

Emotion (fear, anxiety, panic)

Paired with

Music (neutral stimulus) - - - - - - - - - - - - ->

No response

Conditioned Stimulus

Music ->

Conditioned Response

Emotion (fear, anxiety, panic)

The classical conditioning procedure can be applied in a media or an advertising environment. An important feature of classical conditioning is that it does not require conscious attention or involvement of the audience. Consider the popular Steven Spielberg movie *JAWS*. In this film, the man-eating shark (presumably hungry for beachgoers) is paired with a signature piece of music. This pairing takes place repeatedly throughout the film. By the movie's end, the music itself elicits fear and anxiety. This happens even though the audience wasn't really paying attention to the music.[39] This example is shown pictorially in Exhibit 12.5. Advertisers today try to accomplish the same purpose. They start with a neutral object (a new brand name) and make it a symbol of something else by repeatedly associating it with stimuli that naturally evoke positive emotions or physical responses. For example, cuddly puppies, cute kittens, and pets in general frolic in ads for many products unrelated or only tangentially related to pets (see below). Why? Many viewers have natural positive emotional (affective) responses to these animals.

Classical learning research helped generate early understanding of stimulus generalization. **Stimulus generalization** refers to the tendency of *stimuli that are similar to evoke similar responses.* That is, consumers make a leap of sorts. They make a judgment that one stimulus is similar enough to another that it warrants a similar response. This is exactly what happened in the case of the licorice ice cream bars we described earlier. Categorizing new stimuli in order to guide action is a basic learning principle and doesn't just apply in the case of classical conditioning. Nevertheless, Pavlov's research drew attention to the power of stimuli generalization. He was able to get his dogs to salivate based on a variety of sounds that were similar to the original bell.

Marketers use stimulus generalization to devise branding and product strategies. These strategies include family branding, brand extensions, licensing, and look-alike packaging. **Family branding** is the practice of *using a company name (or umbrella name) on a set of brands.* For instance, Heinz puts its name on catsup, canned tomatoes, mustard, pickles, and many other food products. Similarly, Kellogg's is a family brand name for cereals. However, within this family brand there are recognized individual brand names, such as Rice Krispies and Apple Jacks. **Brand extension** refers to the practice of *using an existing brand name to promote a new product.* The new product may be in the same category as the original brand, or it may be in a very different category. For instance, Kellogg's could introduce a new kind of cereal (e.g., a Korean rice porridge), or it could use the Kellogg's name to promote a noncereal brand (e.g., by introducing a Kellogg's energy

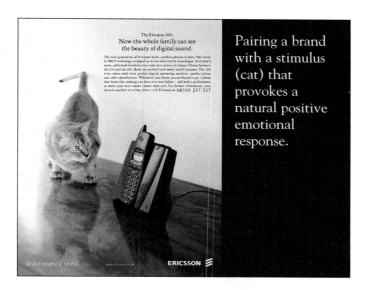

Pairing a brand with a stimulus (cat) that provokes a natural positive emotional response.

bar). **Licensing** means *lending an established brand name to a new venture.* For example, Kellogg's could license its name to a toy manufacturer, which could then include small facsimiles of Kellogg's cereals as part of a child's cooking set. As the name implies, **look-alike packaging** means *introducing a package that appears to be very similar to existing packages.* The hope is that consumers will make an inference that the brand with the similar package will have all of the traits of the original brand, whose package was imitated. For all four of these strategies—family branding, brand extensions, licensing, and look-alike packaging—the perceptual process of stimulus generalization is crucial. All four strategies depend on the consumer perceiving a new stimulus to be similar to an existing stimulus that evokes positive response. Because of this perception, consumers will respond favorably to the new brand (the new stimulus).

Operant Conditioning

Operant conditioning, also called *instrumental conditioning,* occurs as *consumers shape their behaviors to respond to rewards and punishments in the marketplace.* Under operant conditioning, the frequency of occurrence of a behavior is modified by the consequences of the behavior. That is, the frequency of behavior is conditioned by the extent of reinforcement associated with that behavior.[32] *Responses are made deliberately,* as opposed to the involuntary responses illustrated by classical conditioning. Under operant conditioning, consumers' satisfaction with purchases serves to reinforce future behavioral responses, specifically, repeat purchases. The stream of associations that occur during consumption (e.g., imagery, daydreams, emotions) may also serve as important reward mechanisms.[33]

The American psychologist B. F. Skinner is the social scientist who did a lot of the early work to discover and support the operant conditioning model of learning. His original work used pigeons as subjects. He placed them in a "Skinner box," where, among other things, the pigeons could peck appropriate objects to receive rewards. In some experiments, pigeons learned to peck a lever multiple times to receive a reward (food). In other experiments, pigeons were rewarded for pecking other objects. Of course, the pigeons may not have been conscious of their learning. In contrast, the same kind of mental processes in humans are often available to conscious thought.

Marie, a U.S. college freshman, tells the following story about her mother's shopping behavior.

As my mother walks into the cosmetics section of Rich's Department Store, her eyes dart hungrily from side to side, hot in pursuit of a good deal. Any customer, entering any cosmetics department, at any time of year, is certain to observe my mother's so-called good deal. Out of the 20-odd cosmetics houses that are usually represented, at least 3 or 4 will be offering a "free-with-purchase gift." Clinique may require a $20 purchase, upon which the proud customer will receive a free mirror and two lipsticks, whose colors seem especially designed for circus folk. Lancôme will have an offer for customers who buy a fragrance. Upon purchase, they receive a free beach bag.

"Marie, look at that special offer from Estée Lauder!"

"Incredible," I think. A sample perfume, lipstick, and a comb—all free for customers who spend $20!

Inevitably, on display, will be a revolutionary new product for combating the aging process. Given half a chance, the sales clerk can easily convince my mother to scoop up $60 worth of cream, guaranteed to enhance a youthful appearance. And don't forget that "fabulous" free gift!

"What a deal!" exclaims my mother.

I, of course, remain perfectly silent. I don't want to spoil her fun.

It doesn't really matter that my mother is not a regular user of Estée Lauder. If mother gets something for free, then it was a successful shopping trip.

Operant conditioning involves several important concepts for our understanding of consumer behavior, including shaping, reinforcement, and punishment schedules.

Shaping Under **shaping,** *the desired behavior is learned over time, as intermediate actions are rewarded.* For example, a new retail store may offer several activities during opening week, encouraging visitors to enter the store. Next, the retail store may offer discounts, encouraging visitors to buy. The retail store may also offer a gift just for getting a store charge card, thus encouraging commitment. Strategies such as these help shape consumer responses.

Reinforcement Both **positive reinforcement** (*the presence of reward*) and **negative reinforcement** (*the absence of punishment*) strengthen or increase the probability of a target response. Marketers make use of many different rewards such as coupons, trading stamps, loyalty programs, rebates, and prizes. In some countries, however, some or all of these tactics are considered unfair marketing practice and prohibited. An example of both shaping and positive reinforcement that is common in the United States and parts of Europe (where it is legal) is the use of gifts offered in some cosmetic departments and described in Consumer Chronicle 12.1. Learning occurs faster through **continuous reinforcement;** when *a reward is given each and every time the response occurs;* but **partial reinforcement,** when *the reward is given only some of the time the response occurs,* causes learning to persist for longer after the reinforcement is discontinued.

Punishment Punishment weakens the probability of a target response. When consumers have a bad product or service experience they may feel punished for their product choice; they may explain this punishment in terms of the choice rule they used, saying "that's what happens when you buy the cheapest brand." Some advertisements advise that you will be "punished" if you do not use a product or brand. In a Korean ad for milk, the headline promises that "your bones will be full of holes" if you don't drink milk. The image of a chair that is full of holes like a piece of Swiss cheese reinforces this claim, making an analogy between the support that a piece of furniture supplies and the support provided by the human spine. The sponsor is an agricultural association (dairy farmers).

Memory and Knowledge

Few consumer decisions are based just on the information in the environment.[34] Almost all consumer decisions include some memory component. For example, seeing some brands may remind consumers of other brands or products for which they then search. As consumers go through a grocery store, they commonly buy some vegetable or meat that looks especially attractive—because of price, freshness, uniqueness, or other attributes—and then search through memory and the store for things that would go with that product. With regard to brand selection, although the package may contain lots of relevant information, consumers rarely examine this information, again, perhaps relying more on memory to make their decision.

What Is Memory?

A crucial piece in the puzzle of how and what people learn is **memory.**[35] Memory begins as an internal experience: an image, a fragment of recalled conversation, a vivid scene. It travels outward and then returns to the privacy of one's own mind. People build up neural pathways for memories, and the more often a particular memory is invoked, the stronger that neural pathway becomes. Memory depends on a variety of neural activities that converge to create recollections. How and what someone remembers depends on a host of factors: the person's brain, the specific clue that triggers a particular search for memory, age, how the person took in the information in the first place, how much time has elapsed since the original experience, frequency of recall of the memory, and what the person is doing and feeling at the moment of recall. These are just some of the factors that influence the quality and precision of a particular act of recollection.

Recent years have brought great advances in what we know about memory. For example, we know that the neural mechanisms that lead to memory are similar to those used for imagining things. Research now shows that each time people say or imagine something from their past they are putting it together from bits and pieces that may have, until now, been stored separately. No wonder people change, add, and delete things from a remembered event. Research on cultural differences in how people organize information implies that how people think about what they are doing may influence the process of remembering.[36] In addition, cultural differences affect whether and how people recall the past. For instance, compared to people in Western cultures, Korean mothers and their children refer to the past less frequently and focus less on personal experience of a past event. One study compared **autobiographical narratives**—*stories about the self*—of four- to six-year-old Korean, Chinese, and U.S. youngsters. The research suggested that although all the children were equivalent in their overall memory capacity, they differed in what they recalled.

American children were more likely to include descriptive terms, references to internal states, and evaluations. Compared to Korean and Chinese children, they also mentioned themselves as opposed to others more often.[37] This finding, of course, is consistent with our discussion of self (Chapter 7) and motivation (Chapter 11).

| The Social Nature of Memory | The more we know about the physiological and social bases for memory, the more we are left in awe and bewilderment when trying to explain people's lives, shifting, and vivid recollections. Memory must be understood as a kind of dynamic interplay between inner and outer settings. Memories are shaped by the complex and potent settings that involve other people. Moreover, memories are both private and public. The moment that an internal image, sound, smell, or scene is told to another person, it becomes something else, something that depends as much on motivation and social context as neural network. For example, the moment a person tells another about his or her most recent purchase decision, what may have been fleeting takes on substance, what may have been disorganized or irrational |

Exhibit 12.6

The Doonesbury cartoon illustrates the concept of vicarious memories. Here, Zonker Harris describes a series of student high jinks, including an incident with the dean's Volvo. Finally, Doonesbury interrupts him to say, "Uh . . . Zonker? We never did any of those things." Zonker replies, "I know, but one day we'll think we did."

Source: Reprinted by permission of Universal Press Syndicate, Copyright © 1975–2001 by Garry Trudeau.

takes on sequence and reason, what may not have even been clearly marked as a memory is now embedded as something remembered, something from the past.

Remember Colette, the girl saving for a pony? Like many American children, she likes to "recall" for anyone who will listen the story of the day she was born. She tells the story in vivid and imaginative detail from the moment mom left for the hospital to the time daddy cut the umbilical cord and laid her washed, clean, and hungry on mommy's breast, and she will go on from there. Of course, one of the unique qualities of this recollection, however vivid and autobiographical the story appears, is that her parents *created the memory.* She has internalized their shared and verbalized memories of the event in which she was clearly an important participant. By telling her this story, they signaled the drama and significance of this past moment and, like other parents, helped establish and sustain a sense of unique and ongoing intimacy.[38]

There are three interesting aspects of Colette's "recollection." First, people talk about collective or shared memories. Many times people feel *vividly familiar with events they never actually experienced.* They are able to construct an image, scene, or constellation of information that serves as a kind of **vicarious memory.** These vicarious memories are an important source of individual meaning as well as cultural life. The cartoon shown in Exhibit 12.6 illustrates vicarious memory of activities common to a time. Moreover, even when people share the common experience of an event, they do so from their own particular reference point. Consumer Chronicles 12.2 illustrates that these accounts of what happened may be at odds with a formal record of what happened. As people tell and trade stories around an event or a time in history, they communicate what is idiosyncratic and private, but they also exchange and build on shared versions of what happened.[39] Consumers' idiosyncratic reference points can provide a richer and more complex picture of an event. For example, one study asked husbands and wives to remember long lists of information. In each list, some of the information drew on the women's expertise and some drew on the men's expertise. Each couple acted as a team, with the man and woman in each spontaneously taking responsibility for the terms they would most easily remember. This type of *collaborative remembering* is referred to as **transactional memory.**[40] In trying to accomplish household consumption tasks (preparing meals, grocery shopping, getting the children to soccer practice) it is quite likely that collaborative remembering plays a significant role.

Second, with her birth story Colette reflects a society that values and uses autobiographical memories as an important source of information about the self. By telling the story she is projecting a cultural point of view about life stories and about what is worth talking about. This viewpoint is reinforced in many conversations she has with other children and adults. For example, a small American child reporting to first grade with her arm in a cast is immediately bombarded by peers' questions about what happened, how it happened, what the doctor did, and how it felt. The story is told and retold, each retelling responding in detail to the parts the audience likes best. These questions communicate that in this social setting it is appropriate to tell a story about the self that includes an ordered

British Psychologists Try to Remember

Two British psychologists secretly recorded a discussion that took place after a meeting of the Cambridge Psychological Society. Two weeks later, the psychologists contacted all the participants and asked them to write down everything they could remember about the discussion. When these accounts were checked against the original recording, it turned out that respondents typically omitted more than 90 percent of the specific points that had been discussed. Moreover, of the points that were recalled, nearly half were substantially incorrect. Respondents recalled comments that were never made, they transformed casual remarks into lengthy orations, and they converted implicit meanings into explicit comments.

Source: Ian M. L. Hunter, Memory *(Harmondsworth, UK; Penguin, 1968).*

Consumer Chronicles 12.2

Industry Insights 12.1

Orangina Wants You to "Shake It"

An important quality Orangina wants to associate with its drinks is naturalness. According to Orangina, the orange pulp proves its naturalness. That means that before you drink it you should "shake it." Orangina has enlisted big names in entertainment to do just that. In 1972, the concept "Shake the bottle to wake the taste" was featured in "Barman" films produced by Jean Jacques Annaud and Pierre Etaix. In 1994–95, a series of films produced by Alain Chabat introduced the new signature "Shake it." The shaking action included new heights of humor and daring. They are now broadcast worldwide.

Source: Adapted from the Orangina website, www.orangina.fr.

sequence of events and emotions. In many other cultures such a story would be inappropriate. In focus groups with Hungarian women in the early 1990s, several reflected hesitation at talking about cosmetics, stressing the many more pressing social problems. Raised in a culture that abhorred the use of makeup, these women had been trained to believe that recalling stories about personal use of cosmetics was not appropriate for conversation.

Finally, and most important, the birth story reflects that there is no meaningful representation of the past outside of the one constructed in exchanges with others. Remembering is a culturally constructed, social activity. The influence of others on memory is startlingly powerful. In fact, there are now a number of studies suggesting people can be led by others to remember what they have not really experienced.[41] In everyday consumer life, beyond the courtroom or therapy session, remembering and reminiscing are consequential, influencing how others see us, our relationship with others, others' behaviors (including the memories they share); and the stories others share with yet others.

Is Memory Like a Computer?

Many people use a computer metaphor to describe the sequence involved in remembering. Obviously, the dynamic, interactive, social quality of memory just described suggests the limits of this metaphor. Nevertheless, some useful ideas can be gained from using the computer metaphor.[42] Using this metaphor, memory is viewed as occurring in three stages: input, storage, and output.

Input

www.orangina.fr

The form and organization of the input of an experience has a strong impact on how, how long, and how well a person recalls something. Experiences can be input as words, sensations, images, or stories. A person might code Orangina as a sparkling orange juice drink; alternatively, the person might represent it in terms of its familiar brand logo, its flask-like bottle, or its look, taste, and smell. The person might also code Orangina connected to images of France or top-level sporting events such as the Tour de France. Industry Insights 12.1 illustrates one way Orangina would like consumers to think about the drink.[43] Experiences can be organized into groups or as a random list. For example, one of the most primary and natural ways to organize and retain an experience is in the form of sequences or scripts. Consumers learn many scripts at an early age, such as a script for grocery shopping, going to a fast-food restaurant, eating dinner at home, and so on.[44] These scripts affect their expectations and the way they make choices and behave. A script is a special form of schema; it's a schema about how to do things. Consumers have a variety of other schemas, stored networks of associations about objects or topics. (See Chapter 9 for a discussion about scripts and schemas.) Experiences can be tagged in terms of their relationship to other similar experiences or tagged as unique. If incoming information can be associated with knowledge that is already in memory, then the new information has a better chance of being retained. To cite a marketing example, it is beneficial if the brand name is linked to the physical characteristics of the product category. For instance, the name of the communications company Bell South may remind many consumers about the bell that rings to signal that someone should answer. If the consumer answers the bell, communications will be forthcoming. Similarly, the plumber's helper Drain-O reminds the consumer where to put the product—that is, down the drain.

Storage and Output

After input comes storage. Scientists still don't know exactly what it means to say that a memory stays in the brain. This remains a black box in memory research. Most of what we know about storage is inferred from what we have learned about output or retrieval. However, we also know that what is *available* in memory is different from what is *accessible* from memory.[45] As we noted earlier, retrieval doesn't work at all like a computer. Memories are *not* like copies of experiences on deposit in some sort of memory bank.[46] A computer may have a memory bank, but the mind does not seem to work in the same way. Rather, memories are constructed at the time of withdrawal.[47] That is, memories are reconstructed, in a split second. At the time of recall, people use logical inferences to fill in missing details and use associated memories to add detail to the original memory. People put past experiences together from bits and pieces of memories stored separately. For example, schemas and scripts are not stored whole; instead, they represent patterns of activation across a network of units. The human mind reconstructs schemas and scripts when the individual needs them and in ways that respond to the particular context.

Memory can be differentiated in terms of short-term and long-term memories. **Short-term memory** is very short indeed, a few minutes at most; and storage capacity for short-term memory is very small. Short-term memory can be viewed as conscious thought and is also sometimes described as working memory. A significant amount of research suggests consumers can only hold an average of seven units or chunks of information, plus or minus two, in short-term memory.[48] In fact, that's why U.S. telephone numbers are seven digits long. Marketers can further facilitate consumers' memory for telephone numbers, or e-mail addresses, by providing words rather than individual numbers or digits. For example, 1-800-4-A-Yukon is a number to call to learn about GMC's Yukon XL sports utility vehicle. Similarly, advertisements might summarize or chunk a variety of different pieces of information to facilitate retrieval. Commercials are most effective when visual and verbal cues work together.[49] See the logo presented in Good Practice 12.1. Here, the visual and verbal parts of the logo send the same message: crane. Consumers recall this kind of logo better than one that is either visual or verbal. The combination of crane in the company name and cranes in the picture enhances consumer learning and memory. If the name or the image were used alone, then the ad would not be so effective. The mental pathways for visual and verbal stimuli are thought to be separate and distinct. But when advertisers send the same message via two channels (e.g., visual and verbal), the resulting ads are more effective.

Memory researchers distinguish a particular category of short-term memory called **sensory memory.** This information is stored *only a few seconds* and doesn't require the individual to pay attention to it or try to store it. For example, you might be listening to the radio while you do homework. Your roommate walks into the room and indicates she loves that group. You haven't really been paying attention but you realize that you have been listening to Stone Temple Pilots and you say, "Yeah, I like that too!" Information in sensory memory is stored in its actual sensory form. If it is not processed it is lost.

Anything that is retained for more than a few minutes becomes long-term memory. Researchers have identified two different types of long-term memories: semantic and episodic.[50] **Semantic memory** refers to *things people recall without any sense of when*

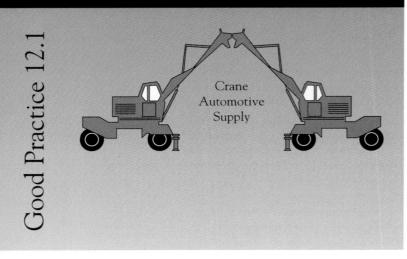

Crane
Automotive
Supply

www.kookai.fr

they learned them. Semantic memory is often thought of as **knowledge.** Consumer knowledge is one type of semantic memory that includes the structure and content of information related to aspects of purchase and consumption.[51] Consumers have vast amounts of information about brands, market environments, consumption experiences, and so on that have been acquired over time, often without knowing when or how. For example, most consumers would be stumped with a question such as "when did you first learn about the brand Coca-Cola?" Many people, even in rather remote parts of the world, have grown up with Coca-Cola. Similarly, many purchase and consumption scripts are not attached to a particular event or experience but acquired through repetition over time.[52] Consumer knowledge includes many different types of information, including (1) knowledge about terminology (e.g., the consumer knows what "partially hydrogenated vegetable shortening" means on a package); (2) knowledge about specific brands and products ("Pert shampoo is for bouncin' and behavin' hair"); and (3) knowledge about the rules to use when evaluating a brand ("never buy pastries that contain partially hydrogenated vegetable shortening"). One important aspect of the knowledge structure is that the various types of information enable a consumer to perceive differences in the features of a stimulus object and to make fine distinctions between that object and others. This *ability to make distinctions* is called **cognitive differentiation.**

Consumers also have **episodic memory,** *memories that come tagged with information about when and where they happened.* Because episodic memory focuses on things that have happened to the individual, it is sometimes termed *autobiographical memory.* You may distinctly remember the first time you went on a roller-coaster ride, your first trip alone, the first time you bought a new car, a recent trip to the dentist, or a variety of other purchase and consumption events. In real life, many of consumers' memories are a blend of semantic and episodic memory. For example, many people eat and enjoy Chinese food. They have general knowledge about going to a Chinese restaurant, ordering food, what food goes together, and how to eat Chinese food. Depending on a variety of circumstances, they may also recall particular salient episodes of eating Chinese food.

One type of knowledge that marketers are especially interested in is consumer thoughts about brands. **Brand image** is *the perceptions about a brand as reflected by the associations held in consumer memory.* Consumers have a variety of different associations with brands. To take a specific example of the application of brand image, consider the French brand Kookaï, a very popular ready-to-wear clothing brand for European women. Kookaï's target market is composed of young women between 15 and 25. The prices are quite low and the advertisements show attractive and sassy young women as illustrated on the website. When women between 19 and 39 were interviewed about the brand, many had a very clear image of the typical user, called a "kookaïette." Associations for Kookaï ranged between 17 and 176 and included all the types shown in Exhibit 12.7.[53]

For both semantic and episodic memories, the question arises of what is remembered

Exhibit 12.7 An Associative Network of Memory for Kookaï

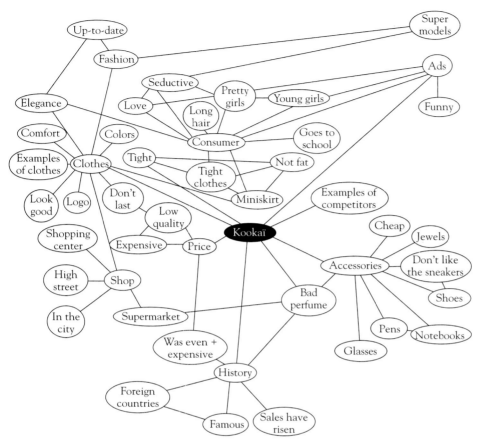

Source: Michaël Korchia, "Brand Image and Brand Associations," working paper. Paris, France: ESSEC.

and what is not. People may remember certain things and not others for a variety of reasons, including the mood they're in when they recall them, the uniqueness of the memory, or because they have rehearsed them a number of times. Several characteristics of consumers influence what they recall. For example, being in a positive mood can enhance recall both by encouraging elaboration and by affecting rehearsal of information.[54] However, mood congruency is also important, so someone in a negative mood may be more likely to recall negative information. Expertise also affects what people recall. Even the existence of categories makes it easier to encode new information. Compared to novices, experts have more complex categories in memory, with a greater number of higher- and lower-level categories and more detail within each category. Because of involvement and interest, experts have also rehearsed the associations among and between related categories, making the paths between them stronger.[55] Exhibit 12.8 compares the types of thoughts generated by an expert and a novice in response to memory probes about motorcycles. Can you guess which thoughts represent those of the expert and those of the novice? The novice has never owned a motorcycle and does not read motorcycle magazines, but she does have friends who own motorcycles. The expert has owned eight motorcycles, is an

Exhibit 12.8 Motorcycle Associations

Can You Name the Expert?

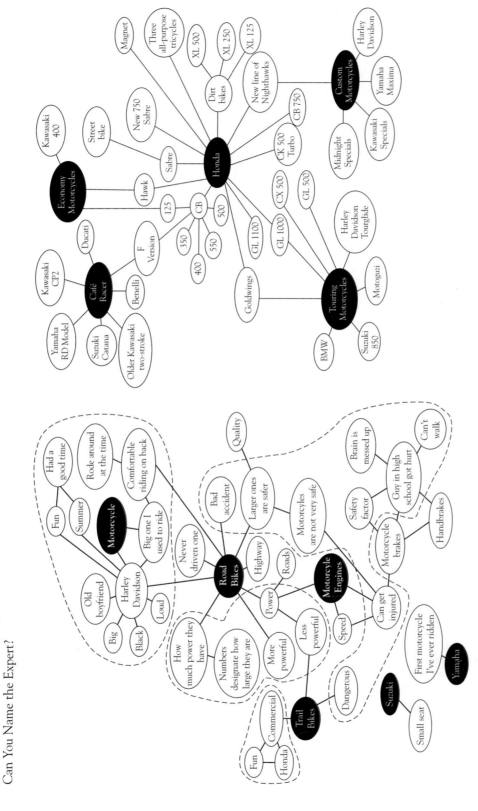

Source: Andrew A. Mitchell and Peter A. Dacin, "The Assessment of Alternative Measures of Consumer Expertise," *Journal of Consumer Research* 23 (December 1996), pp. 219–39.

avid reader of motorcycle magazines, and has five friends who own motorcycles. Looking at these two sets of thoughts about motorcycles, it is easy to see that the expert has much greater awareness and knowledge about alternative models and organizes information around product types. Experts also have information about the characteristics of different alternatives, making it easier to compare models and infer the performance of new models or performance in different usage situations.

Of course, marketers are interested in enhancing consumer memory for their own products and services and may be interested in interfering with consumer memory for competitive products and services. Good Practice 12.2 summarizes research on how marketers can influence consumer memory. Of course, this list is overly simple and does not include how these factors might interact in making a choice.[56] Marketers are also interested in learning and measuring what consumers remember. Consumer researchers must decide carefully about what type of retrieval cues, if any, to provide to consumers. Industry Insights 12.2 illustrates the procedure for looking at what consumers recall using **aided recall.** In this example *consumers are given cues to recall slogans and brand names.* **Free recall** exists when *consumers can recall something from memory without any cues or help.*

There is information overload in many consumer environments. There is so much that people have to know to live their daily lives effectively. Consumers are continually asked to make choices—choices about important life events (e.g., what college to attend), about what products and brands to buy, about when to stop one activity and start another. In brief, consumers are overwhelmed with information and choices. But there are coping strategies that consumers can use to help them access relevant information. Some of these are related to memory constraints that can sometimes lead consumers to make less than optimal decisions (see discussion of satisficing in Chapter 13). However, these decision shortcuts are also adaptive in many situations. Another important coping strategy for dealing with information overload involves the use of technology to sort and categorize information. We will also touch on this topic in a slightly different way in Chapter 15 when we talk about interpersonal influence.

Memory Constraints

Memory-related constraints have a strong impact on judgment and decision making. In this section we outline a few of the ways that memory influences consumer decision making. In the next chapter we will discuss consumer choice models.[57] Much of the research on memory constraints has emphasized how consumers are led astray in their beliefs and behaviors. Nevertheless, many of these memory effects are also highly adaptive. For example, research shows that most people overestimate their ability to achieve a goal, but that overestimation helps motivate them and increases their chances of succeeding. In many cases, memory distortions are regulating mechanisms that help people get through the day.[58]

Context Effects Consumers making evaluations and decisions *use pieces of information, objects, and other issues that happen to be present at the time even when they are irrelevant to the judgment task.* This is termed a **context effect.** Context effects relate to what information is gathered. The most common context effects are contrast, assimilation, and framing. A **contrast effect** occurs when *consumer judgment is changed because of a contextual reference point.* Real estate agents have learned that by first showing a not-so-nice house at the lower end of a consumer's price range and then a house at the high end of a consumer's price range they can get the consumer to shift his or her reference point toward the high end of a price range. The **assimilation effect** is almost the opposite. In this case, *when two very similar objects or issues are compared perceived similarity tends to be*

Chunking Helping consumers put a group of relevant information about a brand into a single chunk will make it easier to hold in short-term memory and increase the chance that it will move to long-term memory.

Rehearsal The use of catchy jingles and slogans can encourage consumers to repeat and think about the information.

Recirculation Consumers should be repeatedly exposed to marketing communication. This effect can be enhanced if varied executions are employed.

Elaboration Stronger memory traces are established when consumers think about the information and consciously relate it to existing information. Advertising that encourages consumers to relate to important past experiences may be an effective way of encouraging elaboration.

Primacy Consumers seem to remember best what they learn first. Marketers can try to control the order of consumer exposure to information. However, be advised, less knowledgeable consumers are more susceptible to this effect than more knowledgeable consumers. And a competitor advertising right after another can sometimes cause interference.

Emotion Overall evaluations or feelings tend to be more accessible than specific brand information. Marketers can encourage consumers to generate positive feelings about their product or service.

Salience Information that stands out as unique or important will be more accessible than other information. Marketers can work to make their product-relevant information salient to the consumer.

Prototypicality Brands that are considered typical of a product class also tend to be more accessible. Marketers that are first to market have an advantage over later entrants because they define the product class. Category leaders may also have this type of advantage.

Congruence When multiple associations for a product are congruent or consistent with one another the information tends to be more accessible. Marketers can work to ensure that information about a product is consistent, thereby strengthening the associative links that connect a set of ideas to the product.

Priming When items are commonly recalled together, activating one item may prime other items that consumers commonly link with it. If marketers understand these links they can effectively promote their product through links to other associations. An effective example of this would be the "Got Milk" campaign that primed consumers' appetite for milk by promoting products that go with milk such as cereal, cookies, cupcakes, and so on.

Procedure

Consumers are told that a new magazine is coming out, and the publisher wants to test the concept and the appeal of the articles. This cover story is called an experimental "guise."

Consumers enter a reading room and are given the magazine to read through. Most consumers read the magazine for about one hour, front to back. The magazine contains a mixture of news articles, features, and advertisements. Altogether there are approximately 20 ads in the magazine for a wide range of products and services. In this particular instance, the researchers are interested in the 5 ads for hair care products that are placed throughout the publication. The ads are for five different brands and are quite distinct from one another in terms of creativity, copy points, and layout.

Questionnaire

The following day, respondents are contacted again and asked some questions about the ads and the articles. For instance, respondents answer some of the following questions about the shampoo ads:

14. Which of the following brands do you remember seeing advertised in the magazine (check all that apply)?
    a. Pert Shampoo
    b. Prell Shampoo
    c. Givens Shampoo
    d. Crest Shampoo
    e. Head and Shoulders Shampoo

15. Which of the advertised shampoos uses the slogan, "Shower and go!" (fill in the brand name)?

    Check here if you don't know ___

---

greater than actual similarity. The example we gave earlier of imitative packaging to take advantage of stimulus generalization is consistent with this type of effect. A **framing effect** is *a shift in judgment that occurs when a consumer focuses on different possible reference points.* Many charities and not-for-profit organizations attempt to take advantage of setting different reference points. For example, National Public Radio might shift the reference point on an annual donation to the price per day the listener pays for a cup of coffee. Research has shown that *choices differ dramatically when the problem is framed in terms of losses instead of framed as gains, even if the net value is the same.* We will talk more about this particular framing effect, the **prospect theory,** in Chapter 13.

Consumers' judgments are biased not only by what information is gathered and used as relevant but also by simplifying strategies they use to reduce the effort required to make an evaluation or decision. These *simplifying strategies* are referred to as **cognitive heuristics.** Four common ones are representativeness, availability, simulation, and anchor-and-adjust.

The **representativeness heuristic** has to do with *assigning characteristics to an object based on similarity to another object.* Our earlier example of accidentally purchasing licorice-covered ice cream bars is an example of this type of simplifying strategy. In many situations, consumers guess about the performance or characteristics of objects, people, and ideas based on their similarity to what the consumers already know. Of course, this is one of the reasons that brand extensions can be so successful. In addition to occasionally leading consumers astray, this kind of learning by analogy is also an important tool for understanding and dealing with unfamiliar things. We can think of **analogical learning** as

using a familiar domain to understand a novel domain. Let's take an example. Suppose you are interested in the offline web readers used to download web pages to your computer's disk drive. You could learn more about this by relating it to something you understand better, such as a VCR. Using this knowledge, you might note that both allow you to retrieve and store media content, that both use a storage device (tape, disk); and you might surmise, on the basis of your VCR experience, that both will be difficult to program.[59] E-commerce companies rely heavily on analogical learning—just flip through any e-company or e-shopping magazine. The Bowstreet ad shown above encourages viewers to make an analogy between roads and business webs.

The **availability heuristic** has to do with *making predictions by using what comes easily to mind from memory.* For example, a person might guess at the likelihood of a delayed flight on an airline according to his or her ability to retrieve examples of such an event from memory. Unfortunately, memories are influenced by a lot more than absolute frequency of particular events. For example, events that have occurred more recently are more memorable than those that occurred long ago. Vivid and publicized events also come readily to mind. All of these memory influences, and more, can lead consumers to erroneous predictions.

The **simulation heuristic** relates to the fact that *simply imagining an event or sequence of events increases the perception that it will occur.* Good stories or convincing imagery can be powerful in leading consumers to believe in the possibility of an event or a sequence of events. However, the actual possibility of such an event or sequence of events may be relatively remote. Recall what you learned in statistics about **conjunctive probabilities:** even *if two events are relatively likely (.5), the likelihood of their joint occurrence* *is much lower (.25).* Consumers often play out consumption events in their mind, rehearsing how things will be; and they are quite likely to be disappointed, because it relies on a sequence of events unfolding exactly as planned. For example, young people and their families in many cultures work hard envisioning weddings and trying to make them happen just that way. But they hardly ever do. Of course, sometimes the things that went wrong are the very things that make the event vivid and special, and in turn these things become the source of future stories.[60]

The **anchor-and-adjust heuristic** has to do with *using an initial estimate and then modifying it to account for a different, unknown event.* Again, it is easy to see how this strategy is related to fundamental memory processes of searching through memory for something similar to the target problem and then adjusting to try to take into account the differences. For example, imagine how you might go about guessing how a friend of yours would like a movie that you recently saw. You might begin by thinking about how much you liked the movie, how similar you are to your friend in terms of movie tastes, and then guessing whether your friend would like the movie too. Now imagine that you are guessing how an average person in your community would like this movie? You might take exactly the same approach, but in this situation, you know less about how similar or different the average person is to you and how much you should adjust your guess accordingly.[61]

Partnering with Technology

As the information age accelerates, life doesn't seem to get any simpler. Often, it seems, technology makes life more complicated rather than making it simpler. As in many areas of modern life, people may turn to technology to solve the problem. A pressing need is to provide consumers with useful tools to help them navigate through the morass of information that has become available through satellite, cable, and the World Wide Web. Ideas that a short number of years ago were just possibilities are rapidly becoming realities.[62] One alternative for information-weary consumers is a "knowbot," a type of robot. A knowbot may serve to screen out and organize the flood of information that bombards people every day. It thus has the potential to reduce information overload.

A knowbot may be designed to attach itself to a combination TV/VCR. A consumer might program the knowbot to tape his favorite program. Then, he may ask the knowbot to screen out all of the commercials. The next day, he may decide that he's in the market for some new athletic shoes. He asks the knowbot to tape all of the athletic shoe commercials and put them together into a block. Then, because of prior experiences, he asks the knowbot to delete all of the Keds commercials. In this way, the knowbot serves as a buffer between the consumer and the commercial world. Advertisers will have to design commercials to appeal to mechanical intermediaries. It may not be enough to create a commercial message that is eye-catching and attention-getting for humans. In addition, advertisers may have to create commercials that can get past mechanical screens (such as knowbots).

Of course, such screening already takes place on the World Wide Web when consumers use search engines. Web page designers try to include key words that will be popular when consumers conduct a guided search. In addition, web designers have methods to ensure that their page will appear at the top of any search list that is generated. As knowbots become more sophisticated, advertisers in turn find clever ways to subvert the system. In the next generation, the knowbots are more sophisticated again. This is true technological warfare. Of course, one dilemma is how to design intelligent agents that can learn and respond to the needs of consumers.[63] Researchers argue that consumers need help on at least three fronts: formulating preferences, finding and organizing relevant information, and evaluating attractive alternatives and choosing among them. Good Practice 12.3 summarizes the goals of electronic agents.

Goal	Features
Improve decision quality	➤ Assist consumers in learning about the product and preferences
	Reduce decision complexity
	Be a warehouse for good information
	Provide an appropriate consideration set for evaluation
	Adapt over time in response to new information and feedback
Increase satisfaction	➤ Be flexible and responsive to users' requests
	Increase the match between consumers' taste and products
	Be simple to operate and use
	Allow consumers to have good experiences
	Set realistic expectations
Develop trust	➤ Satisfy and protect users' best interests
	Reassure users that they are getting a good value

Source: Adapted from Pat West et al., "Agents to the Rescue?" HEC Symposium on Advances in Choice Theory, Marketing Science Institute, report no. 99-121, 1999, pp. 5–7.

summary

This chapter has outlined some of the major aspects of how and what consumers experience, learn, and know. There is much yet to discover, and many mysteries about the interplay between experience, learning, and knowledge are yet to be imagined. Emotions, culture, and context are fundamental to their nature and the interplay among them. Consumer experiences, learning, and knowledge also contribute to meanings in ways this chapter has only touched on. In Chapter 18 we will delve in depth into the construction of meaning from experiences and memories of experiences.

Consumer experiences are at the heart of consumer behavior, and many industry experts argue that economic value turns on offering memorable experiences or better, transformational experiences. A typology of consumer experiences includes anticipated consumption, purchase, consumption, and remembered consumption. Marketers need to understand how anticipated consumption relates to consumers aspirations and goals. In Chapter 17 we will describe postconsumption experiences, and in Chapter 18 we will discuss further how consumption experiences create consumer meaning.

Learning, memory, and knowledge are closely linked. Consumer learning is adaptive and determined by value systems, desires, needs, and what the learner already knows. Consumers generate guesses or hypotheses about the way the world works, in order to make adaptive choices that move them toward their goals. There are lots of different ways to learn, including learning from experience and learning by description. Two important behavioral learning theories are classical conditioning and operant conditioning. These two approaches have helped researchers discover useful techniques for stimulating learning.

Almost all consumer decisions include a memory component. Each time consumers say or remember something they put it together from bits and pieces stored separately in their brain. Memory is constructive, and it is a culturally constructed, social activity. Memory is not like a computer, but we can think of it as occurring in three stages: input, storage, and output. Consumers have a variety of schemas and scripts that help them organize experiences. Memories can be distinguished as short term and long term, and long-term memories can be further categorized as semantic or episodic. Semantic memories are what we generally think of as knowledge. One type of knowledge marketers are especially interested in is brand knowledge. Consumers have many types of associations about brands, and marketers can use several different techniques to influence memory.

Consumers are overwhelmed by information and choices. Memory-related constraints have a strong impact on judgment and decision making. Although these constraints may lead consumers to make less than optimal choices, they are also adaptive and many times help consumers feel good and attain their goals. Some common context effects are contrast, assimilation, and framing. Some cognitive heuristics that consumers use to collect and use information and knowledge include representativeness, availability, simulation, and anchor and adjust. On the horizon we see the development of a variety of electronic agents, or knowbots, that will help consumers gather, store, and output relevant information.

summary

key terms

aided recall   443
analogical learning   446
anchor-and-adjust heuristic   447
aspiration gap   425
assimilation effect   443
autobiographical narratives   435
availability heuristic   446
behavioral learning theories   431
brand extension   432
brand image   440
classical conditioning   431
cognitive differentiation   440
cognitive heuristics   445
conjunctive probabilities   446
consumer learning   428
context effect   443
continuous reinforcement   434
contrast effect   443
direct experience   430

emotion   421
encoding   429
episodic memory   440
family branding   432
framing effect   445
free recall   443
goal-based categories   421
hindsight bias   431
incidental learning   430
integration   429
knowledge   440
learning by description   430
licensing   433
look-alike packaging   433
memory   435
negative reinforcement   434
operant conditioning   433
partial reinforcement   434
positive reinforcement   434

preferences   421
prepurchase search   424
prospect theory   445
representativeness heuristic   445
semantic memory   439
sensory memory   439
shaping   434
short-term memory   439

simulation heuristic   446
stimulus generalization   432
temporal contiguity principle   431
transactional memory   437
transformational experience   423
vicarious learning   430
vicarious memory   437

1. Select a product category that you know a lot about and make a picture of your network of product associations. Now ask a less knowledgeable friend to do the same. How is his or her picture similar and different from your picture?

2. How is memory like a computer? How is it different from a computer? Use an example of a personal memory to trace input, storage, and output.

3. Think of your own examples of the different levels of the economic pyramid shown in Exhibit 12.1. How do you think the role of the marketer changes? How do you think the role of the buyer changes?

4. Consider the context effects such as contrast, assimilation, and framing outlined in the chapter. Can you think of examples of how these are used by marketers?

5. Operant conditioning is said to occur through positive reinforcement, negative reinforcement, or punishment. Name some products that promise that "good things will happen" if you buy or use them. What are some products that tell you that you will be "punished" if you don't buy them? Try to name products or behaviors for which you are told that you will be "punished" if you do buy or use them. Discuss and expand.

6. Can you think of some products that have similar packaging? Similar shapes? Similar names? Do you think that these look-alikes are effective at taking sales away from existing, popular brands? Explain and relate to principles of how learning and memory work.

7. What can marketing managers do to encourage consumer learning and knowledge development? Identify some advertisements that seem to be following your suggestions.

8. Give some examples of anticipated consumption. Is there a consumption experience that you are anticipating now? Describe the elements and details of that anticipation.

You Make the Call

Affinity.com

Affinity Internet, Inc., is a web-hosting and applications services provider (ASP) that guides small and medium-sized businesses seeking to build a successful e-business. The Los Angeles–based company offers a wide range of turnkey Internet solutions, including web hosting, e-commerce, dedicated servers, and advanced hosting services to business customers in more than 100 countries.

Examine the advertisement for Affinity above. This company promotes that it will help your business harness the strength of the Internet.

1. How is memory important in this advertisement?

2. Do you think analogical learning plays a role in this advertisement? Explain.

3. Can you identify cultural models or schemas that are important in the meaning of this advertisement?

4. Who is the target audience for this advertisement?

5. What are the strengths and weaknesses of Affinity's approach?

6. Affinity provides services in 100 countries. How global is this advertisement? Explain.

This case is adapted from material found on the Affinity website, www.affinity.com.

1. This vignette is based on an interview with Éva conducted by Robin Higie Coulter and Linda L. Price in fall 1998. See also, Robin Higie Coulter, Lawrence F. Feick, and Linda L. Price, "Making Up Time in Hungary: Are the Changes Purely Cosmetic?" working paper, University of Connecticut, 2000.
2. José Antonio Rosa, Joseph F. Porac, Jelena Runser-Spanjol, and Michael S. Saxon, "Sociocognitive Dynamics in a Product Market," *Journal of Marketing* 63 (special issue 1999), pp. 64–77. See also Paul Thagard, *Conceptual Revolutions* (Princeton: Princeton University Press, 1992).

3. Lawrence W. Barsalou, "Deriving Categories to Achieve Goals," in *The Psychology of Learning and Motivation,* vol. 27, Gordon H. Bower, ed. (New York: Academic Press, 1991), pp. 1–64; and S. Ratneshwar, Cornelia Pechmann, and Allan D. Shocker, "Goal-Derived Categories and the Antecedents of Across-Category Consideration," *Journal of Consumer Research* 23 (December 1996), pp. 240–50.

4. Hillel J. Einhorn and Robin M. Hogarth, "Decision Making: Going Forward in Reverse," *Harvard Business Review* 65 (January–February 1987), pp. 66–70; James R. Bettman, Mary Frances Luce, and John W. Payne, "Constructive Consumer Choice Processes," *Journal of Consumer Research* 25 (December 1998), pp. 187–217; and Patricia M. West, Christina L. Brown, and Stephen J. Hoch, "Consumption Vocabulary and Preference Formation," *Journal of Consumer Research* 23 (September 1996), pp. 120–35.

5. Catherine Kohler Riessman, *Narrative Analysis* (Newbury Park, CA: Sage Publications, 1993); Leslie Brothers, *Friday's Footprint: How Society Shapes the Human Mind* (New York: Oxford University Press, 1997); and James R. Bettman, "The Decision Maker Who Came in from the Cold," in *Advances in Consumer Research,* vol. 20, Leigh McAlister and Michael L. Rothschild, eds. (Provo, UT: Association for Consumer Research, 1993), pp. 7–11.

6. Brothers, *Friday's Footprint;* and Antonio R. Damasio, *Descartes' Error: Emotion, Reason and the Human Brain* (New York: Avon Books, 1994).

7. B. Joseph Pine II and James H. Gilmore, *The Experience Economy* (Boston: Harvard Business School Press, 1999).

8. Morris B. Holbrook and Elizabeth C. Hirschman, "The Experiential Aspects of Consumption: Consumer Fantasies, Feeling, and Fun," *Journal of Consumer Research* 9 (September 1982), pp. 132–40.

9. Peter H. Bloch, Daniel L. Sherrell, and Nancy M. Ridgway, "Consumer Search: An Extended Framework," *Journal of Consumer Research,* June 1986, p. 120.

10. Russell W. Belk and Güliz Ger, "Problems of Marketization in Romania and Turkey," in *Research in Consumer Behavior: Consumption in Marketizing Economies,* vol. 7, Clifford J. Shultz II, Russell W. Belk, and Güliz Ger, eds. (Greenwich, CT: JAI Press, 1994), pp. 123–55; Brian Lofman, "Polish Society in Transformation: The Impact of Marketization on Business, Consumption, and Education," in *Research in Consumer Behavior: Consumption in Marketizing Economies,* vol. 7, Clifford J. Shultz II, Russell W. Belk, and Güliz Ger, eds. (Greenwich, CT: JAI Press, 1994), pp. 29–55; and Lawrence F. Feick, Robin A. Higie, and Linda L. Price, "Consumer Search and Decision Problems in a Transitional Economy: Hungary, 1989–1992," *Marketing Science Institute,* report no. 93-113, August 1993.

11. Mihaly Csikzentmihalyi, *Finding Flow* (New York: Perseus Books, 1997).

12. This section draws primarily from these sources: Gerald M. Edelman, *Bright Air, Brilliant Fire: On the Matter of the Mind* (New York: Basic Books, 1992); Stephen J. Hoch, "Hypothesis Testing and Consumer Behavior: 'If It Works, Don't Mess with It,'" in *Advances in Consumer Research,* vol. 11, Thomas Kinnear, ed. (Provo, UT: Association for Consumer Research, 1984), pp. 478–81; Stephen J. Hoch and John Deighton, "Managing What Consumers Learn from Experience," *Journal of Marketing* 52 (April 1989), pp. 1–20; and J. Wesley Hutchinson and Joseph W. Alba, "Ignoring Irrelevant Information: Situational Determinants of Consumer Learning," *Journal of Consumer Research* 18 (December 1991), pp. 325–45.

13. Gilles Laurent, "Introduction—HEC Symposium on Advances in Choice Theory: Conference Summary," *Marketing Science Institute,* report no. 99-121, 1999.

14. A more common definition of learning is to gain knowledge, understanding, or skill by study, instruction, or experience, but this definition tells us little about how it happens. Our definition derives from Edelman, *Bright Air, Brilliant Fire.*

15. Charles G. Gettys, Thomas Mehle, and Stanley Fisher, "Plausibility Assessments in Hypothesis Generation," *Organizational Behavior and Human Performance* 24 (1986), pp. 93–110.

16. For a discussion of male and female differences based on Joan Meyer-Levy's and others' work, see Malcolm Gladwell, "Listening to Khakis," *The New Yorker,* July 28, 1997, pp. 54–57.

17. Barsalou, "Deriving Categories to Achieve Goals"; and C. Whan Park and Daniel C. Smith, "Product-Level Choice: A Top-Down or Bottom-Up Process?" *Journal of Consumer Research* 16 (December 1989), pp. 289–99.

18. Ahmet Ekici and Linda L. Price, "Exploratory Study of American Consumers' Knowledge and Responses to Genetically Modified Food Products," *Proceedings,* American Marketing Association Winter Educators' Meetings (Chicago: AMA, forthcoming 2001).

19. Claude Lévi Strauss, *The Raw and the Cooked* (London: Cape, 1964).

20. Coulter, Feick and Price, "Making Up Time in Hungary." For related descriptions from Moscow, see Caroline Humphrey, "Creating a Culture of Disillusionment: Consumption in Moscow, a Chronicle of Changing Times," in *Worlds Apart,* Daniel Miller, ed. (London and New York: Routledge, 1995), pp. 43–68.

21. Hoch, "Hypothesis Testing and Consumer Behavior," and Hoch and Deighton, "Managing What Consumers Learn from Experience."

22. Elizabeth F. Loftus and Jacqueline E. Pickrell, "The Formulation of False Memories," *Psychiatric Annals* 25 (December 1995), pp. 720–25.

23. Scott Ward, Daniel Wackman, and Ellen Wartella, *How Children Learn to Buy: The Development of Consumer Information Processing Skills* (Beverly Hills: Sage, 1977); and M. Carole Macklin, "Preschoolers' Learning of Brand Names from Visual Cues," *Journal of Consumer Research* 23 (December 1996), pp. 251–61.

24. Kathryn A. Braun, "Postexperience Advertising Effects on Consumer Memory," *Journal of Consumer Research* 25 (March 1999), pp. 319–34. See also Alice A. Wright and John G. Lynch, "Communication Effects of Advertising versus Direct Experience When Both Search and Experience Attributes Are Present," *Journal of Consumer Research* 21 (March 1995), pp. 708–18; and Gay Snodgrass, "The Memory Trainers," in *Mind and Brain Sciences in the Twenty-First Century,* Robert L. Solso, ed. (Cambridge: MIT Press, 1997).

25. Lee Ross and Richard Nisbett, *The Person and the Situation: Perspectives of Social Psychology* (New York: McGraw-Hill, 1991).

26. John Deighton and Robert Schindler, "Can Advertising Influence Experience?" *Psychology and Marketing* 5 (1988), pp. 103–15; Stephen Hoch and Yi Ha, "Consumer Learning: Advertising and the Ambiguity of Product Experience," *Journal of Consumer Research* 13 (1986), pp. 221–33; Jerry Olson and Phillip Dover, "Disconfirmation of Consumer Expectations through Product Trial," *Journal of Applied Psychology* 64 (1979), pp. 179–89; and Braun, "Postexperience Advertising Effects on Consumer Memory."

27. A delightful book that summarizes much recent memory research is Susan Engel, *Context Is Everything: The Nature of Memory* (New York: W. H. Freeman and Company, 1999).

28. Rik Pieters and Rami Zwick, "Hindsight Bias in the Context of a Consumption Experience," in *European Advances in Consumer Research,* vol. 1, Gary Banossy and Fred van Raaij, eds. (Provo, UT: Association for Consumer Research, 1993), pp. 307–11.

29. Chris Janiszewski and Luk Warlop, "The Influence of Classical Conditioning Procedures on Subsequent Attention to the Conditioned Brand," *Journal of Consumer Research* 20 (September 1993), pp. 171–89; and John Kim, Chris T. Allen, and Frank R. Kardes, "An Investigation of the Mediational Mechanisms Underlying Attitudinal Conditioning," *Journal of Marketing Research* 33 (August 1996), pp. 318–28.

30. R. A. Feinberg, "Credit Cards as Spending Facilitating Stimuli," *Journal of Consumer Research* 13 (1986), pp. 348–56.

31. A study that used pleasant background music to evoke higher brand evaluations is Gerald J. Gorn, "The Effects of Music in Advertising on Choice Behavior: A Classical Conditioning Approach," *Journal of Marketing* 46 (Winter 1982), pp. 94–101. See also Terence A. Shimp, Eva M. Hyatt, and David J. Snyder, "A Critical Appraisal of Demand Artifacts in Consumer Research," *Journal of Consumer Research* 18 (December 1991), pp. 273–83.

32. Harold W. Berkman, Jay D. Lindquist, and M. Joseph Sirgy, *Consumer Behavior* (Lincolnwood, IL: NTC Business Books, 1997).

33. Holbrook and Hirschman, "The Experiential Aspects of Consumption."

34. Joseph W. Alba, J. Wesley Hutchinson, and John G. Lynch, Jr., "Memory and Decision Making," in *Handbook of Consumer Behavior,* Thomas S. Robertson and Harold H. Kassarjian, eds. (Englewood Cliffs, NJ: Prentice Hall, 1991), pp. 1–49; Wayne D. Hoyer, "An Examination of Consumer Decision Making for a Common Repeat Purchase Product," *Journal of Consumer Research* 11 (December 1984), pp. 822–29; and Stephen J. S. Holden and Richard J. Lutz, "Ask Not What the Brand

Can Evoke: Ask What Can Evoke the Brand," in *Advances in Consumer Research, v*ol. 19, John Sherry and Brian Sternthal, eds. (Provo, UT: Association for Consumer Research, 1992), pp. 101–7.

35. This section draws heavily from Engel, *Context Is Everything.* See also Daniel Schacter, *Searching for Memory* (New York: Basic Books, 1996).

36. M. Cole, J. Gay, J. Glick, and D. Sharp, *The Cultural Context of Learning and Thinking* (New York: Basic Books, 1971); and Michael Cole and Sylvia Scribner, "Cross-Cultural Studies of Memory and Cognition," in *Perspectives on the Development of Memory and Cognition,* R. V. Kail, Jr. and J. W. Hagen, ed. (Hillsdale, NJ: Lawrence Erlbaum, 1977), pp. 239–72.

37. M. Mullen and S. Yi, "The Cultural Context of Talk about the Past: Implications for the Development of Autobiographical Memory," *Cognitive Development* 10 (1995), pp. 407–19. See also Shinobu Kitayama and Hazel Rose Markus, *Emotion and Culture: Empirical Studies of Mutual Influence* (Washington, DC: American Psychological Association, 1994).

38. Susan Engel, *The Stories Children Tell* (New York: W. H. Freeman, 1995); and R. V. Kail, *The Development of Memory in Children* (New York: W. H. Freeman, 1990).

39. An excellent discussion of this intersection of the internal and external aspects of human experience can be found in Bradd Shore, *Culture in Mind: Cognition, Culture, and the Problem of Meaning* (New York: Oxford University Press, 1996).

40. Daniel Wegner, "Transactive Memory: A Contemporary Analysis of the Group Mind," in *Theories of Group Behavior,* Brian Mullen and George R. Goethals, eds. (New York: Springer-Verlag, 1987), pp. 185–208.

41. Saul M. Kassin and Katherine L. Kiechel, "The Social Psychology of False Confessions: Compliance, Internalization and Confabulation," *Psychological Science* 7 (May 1996), pp. 125–28.

42. Most theory and research in consumer behavior has conceptualized human memory as an information processing system. For classic references with this perspective, see James R. Bettman, *An Information Processing Theory of Consumer Choice* (Reading, MA: Addison-Wesley, 1979); R. C. Atkinson and R. M. Shiffrin, "Human Memory: A Proposed System and Its Control Processes," in *Advances in the Psychology of Learning and Motivation Research and Theory,* vol. 2, K. W. Spence & J. T. Spence, eds. (New York: Academic Press, 1968); John R. Anderson, *The Architecture of Cognition* (Cambridge: Harvard University Press, 1983); and R. S. Wyer and Thomas K. Shrull, *Memory and Cognition in Its Social Context* (Hillsdale, NJ: Lawrence Erlbaum, 1989).

43. Deborah J. MacInnis and Linda L. Price, "The Role of Imagery in Information Processing: Review and Extensions," *Journal of Consumer Research,* March 1987, pp. 473–91.

44. For some examples of how scripts are used in consumers' behavior, see Thomas W. Leigh and Arno J. Rethans, "Experiences in Script Elicitation within Consumer Decision-Making Contexts," in *Advances in Consumer Research,* vol. 10, Richard Bagozzi and Alice Tybout, eds. (Provo, UT: Association for Consumer Research, 1983), pp. 667–72; and Ruth Ann Smith and Michael J. Houston, "A Psychometric Assessment of Measures of Scripts in Consumer Memory," *Journal of Consumer Research,* September 1985, pp. 214–24.

45. Gabriel Biehal and Dipankar Chakravarti, "Consumers' Use of Memory and External Information in Choice: Macro and Micro Perspectives," *Journal of Consumer Research,* March 1986, pp. 382–405; John G. Lynch, Howard Marmorstein, and Michael F. Weigold, "Choices from Sets Including Remembered Brands: Use of Recalled Attributes and Prior Overall Evaluations," *Journal of Consumer Research,* September 1988, pp. 225–33.

46. Scott Plous, *The Psychology of Judgment and Decision Making* (Philadelphia: Temple University Press, 1993).

47. E. F. Loftus, *Eyewitness Testimony* (Cambridge: Harvard University Press, 1979).

48. The first one to develop this idea was G. A. Miller, "The Magical Number Seven, Plus or Minus Two: Some Limits on Our Capacity for Processing Information," *Psychological Review* 63 (1956), pp. 81–97. This research has subsequently been replicated many times. See, for example, A. Newell and Herbert Simon, *Human Problem Solving* (Englewood Cliffs, NJ: Prentice Hall, 1972).

49. Kathy A. Lutz and Richard J. Lutz, "Effects of Interactive Imagery on Learning: Applications to Advertising," *Journal of Applied Psychology* 62 (August, 1977), pp. 493–98.

50. Endel Tulving, *Elements of Episodic Memory* (New York: Oxford University Press, 1983).

51. Merrie Brucks and Andrew A. Mitchell, "Knowledge Structures, Production Systems and Deci-

sion Strategies," in *Advances in Consumer Research,* vol. 8, Kent B. Monroe, ed. (Ann Arbor: Association for Consumer Research, 1981), pp. 750–57; A. Mitchell and P. F. Dacin, "The Assessment of Alternative Measures of Consumer Expertise," *Journal of Consumer Research* 23 (December 1996), pp. 219–39.

52. Joseph W. Alba and J. Wesley Hutchinson, "Knowledge Calibration: What Consumers Know and What They Think They Know," *Journal of Consumer Research* 27 (September 2000), pp. 123–56.

53. Michaël Korchia, "A New Typology of Brand Image," in *European Advances in Consumer Research,* vol. 4, Bernard Dubois, Tina M. Lowry, L. J. Shrum, and Marc Vanhuele, eds. (Provo, UT: Association for Consumer Research, 1999), pp. 147–54. For a detailed review of brand image from a consumer memory perspective, see Kevin Keller, *Strategic Brand Management* (Upper Saddle River, NJ: Prentice Hall, 1998).

54. Angela Y. Lee and Brian Sternthal, "The Effects of Positive Mood on Memory," *Journal of Consumer Research* 26 (September 1999), pp. 115–27.

55. Gordon H. Bower, "Mood and Memory," *American Psychologist,* February 1981, pp. 129–48; and Joseph Alba and J. Wesley Hutchinson, "Dimensions of Consumer Expertise," *Journal of Consumer Research* (13 March 1987), pp. 411–454.

56. This list draws from a number of references already listed. A more in-depth discussion of many of these factors is provided in Plous, *The Psychology of Judgment and Decision Making;* and Wayne Hoyer and Debbie MacInnis, *Consumer Behavior* (New York: Houghton-Mifflin, 1997), pp. 171–85. See also Elizabeth Cowley, "Primacy Effects: When First Learned Is Best Recalled," in *European Advances in Consumer Research,* vol. 4, Bernard Dubois, Tina M. Lowry, L. J. Shrum, and Marc Vanhuele, eds. (Provo, UT: Association for Consumer Research, 1999), pp. 155–60.

57. Numerous references are available on each of these topics. A couple favorites include Daniel Kahneman, Paul Slovic, and Amos Tversky, *Judgment under Uncertainty: Heuristics and Biases* (Cambridge, UK: Cambridge University Press, 1982); and John W. Payne, James R. Bettman, and Eric J. Johnson, 'The Adaptive Decision-Maker," in *Judgment and Decision Making Theory and Applications: A Tribute to Hillel Einhorn,* Robin M. Hogarth, ed. (Chicago: University of Chicago Press, 1997).

58. Shelley Taylor, *Positive Illusions* (New York: Basic Books, 1989).

59. This example and discussion comes from Jennifer Gagen-Paxton and Deborah Roedder John, "Consumer Learning by Analogy: A Model of Internal Knowledge Transfer," *Journal of Consumer Research* 24 (December 1997), pp. 266–84.

60. MacInnis and Price, "The Role of Imagery in Information Processing."

61. A couple of terrific studies that illustrate these types of anchor-and-adjust effects are Stephen J. Hoch, "Who Do We Know: Predicting the Interests and Opinions of the American Consumer," *Journal of Consumer Research* 15 (December 1988), pp. 315–24; and Harry L. Davis, Stephen J. Hoch, and E. K. Easton Ragsdale, "An Anchoring and Adjustment Model of Spousal Predictions," *Journal of Consumer Research* 13 (June 1986), pp. 25–37.

62. Roland T. Rust and Richard W. Oliver, "Notes and Comments: The Death of Advertising," *Journal of Advertising* 23, no. 4 (December 1994), pp. 71–78; and Mark Pesce, "Toy Stories," *The Sciences,* September–October 2000, pp. 25–31.

63. Pat West et al., "Agents to the Rescue?" *HEC Symposium on Advances in Choice Theory,* Marketing Science Institute, report no. 99-121, 1999, pp. 5–7.

Learning Objectives

After completing this chapter, you should be able to:

- Explain the difference between consumer cognitions, affect, and behavior and describe their role in decision making.

- Discuss theories that are applied to attitudes and attitude formation, and describe the role of attitudes in consumer behavior.

- Talk about competing hierarchy of effects models, as they relate to attitude formation.

- Distinguish between awareness, knowledge, liking, preference, behavioral intentions, and behavior in consumer decision making.

- Describe the influence of involvement in consumer choice.

- Explain the concept of quick choices and the difference between the central and the peripheral routes to persuasion.

- Discuss the multiattribute model of consumer choice and the elaboration likelihood model of persuasion.

- Outline the strengths and weaknesses of the Fishbein models of attitudes.

- Describe other choice models, including expected utility theory, satisficing decisions, consumer heuristics, and prospect theory.

Attitude Models and Consumer Decision Maki...

Tom Buys a Digital Camera:
An Inference-Making Process

Tom is 35 years old. He sells stocks and bonds at a small brokerage house. He specializes in trading high-technology financial instruments. Tom lives in a small town and likes to participate in individual sports, such as golf. In the last two years he has tried downhill skiing a few times; but he doesn't ski that often because he lives a long way from the mountains. Tom is a sports car buff, and he especially likes old British Triumphs and MGBs.

Even though Tom is fairly affluent, he likes to save money, and he likes to get a good deal. He surfs the Internet for bargains, and he keeps track of his own personal stock portfolio through the use of online financial software.

Tom wants to purchase a new digital camera to take photographs at his younger sister's wedding. The wedding is one week away, so Tom doesn't have a lot of time to make this purchase. He looks at a few catalogs and talks with his friend Terrell, who is a camera buff. Tom is aware of several camera shops in the surrounding area, but he decides that the one closest to his work (Wolf Camera) is the most convenient.

As the wedding approaches, Tom uses his lunch hour to visit Wolf Camera. As he looks at the selection, he notices that some brands that he saw in the catalogs don't seem to be on display. In addition, some of the prices seem higher than what he remembered seeing in the catalogs.

As Tom talks to the saleswoman, he has a little trouble

Two roads diverged in a yellow wood,
And sorry I could not travel both
And be one traveler, long I stood
And looked down one as far as I could
To where it bent in the undergrowth;

Then took the other, as just as fair,
And having perhaps the better claim,
Because it was grassy and wanted wear;
Though as for that the passing there
Had worn them really about the same,

And both that morning equally lay
In leaves no step had trodden black.
Oh, I kept the first for another day!
Yet knowing how way leads on to way,
I doubted if I should ever come back.

I shall be telling this with a sigh
Somewhere ages and ages hence:
Two roads diverged in a wood, and I—
I took the one less traveled by,
And that has made all the difference.

Robert Frost, 1916

judging the quality of the cameras that she shows him. How is he to know which camera is best? Finally, he narrows his choice set down to two digital cameras—a Kodak and a Minolta. He remembers seeing ads for cameras that these companies make. However, while at the store, Tom can't recall exactly if these ads were for digital cameras or for 35 mm cameras. Nonetheless, he believes that these two companies have strong reputations. Tom decides that these two brands can do all of the things a typical digital camera can do.

Tom holds the two cameras in his hands—the Kodak in his left hand and the Minolta in his right. The Kodak seems a little lighter than the Minolta, so he decides to buy the Minolta. He takes a lot of photographs at his sister's wedding, and he's generally pleased with the results.

Overview

Consumers make many choices every day. They choose when to wake up and when to get out of bed. They decide how to travel to work (e.g., by train or bus). They decide how to spend their leisure time (e.g., playing golf versus watching TV). They decide how to complete the maintenance tasks necessary to live life (e.g., to put the clothes in the washing machine or to drop them off at the laundry). They decide "which roads to travel," as illustrated in the Robert Frost poem in Consumer Chronicles 13.1. Sometimes, the decision trade-off made at such forks in the road is relatively trivial. Other times, as price versus nutrition in food or environmental protection versus convenience in a variety of goods, the trade-off makes "all the difference."

Similarly, some brand choices consumers make are relatively simple (pushing the button for Diet Coke or Sprite on the vending machine on the fourth floor of an office building). In other situations, consumers make brand choices that require extensive information search and difficult choices. In the opening vignette, Tom searches for a camera. He makes a series of choices. He decides where to look for information (in catalogs). He chooses whom to talk to about his upcoming purchase (his friend Terrell and the salesclerk at the camera shop). He chooses which store to visit (Wolf Camera). Finally, he chooses which brand to buy. In this way, as indicated in Chapter 10, consumer purchase behavior can be divided into a series of choices.

How do consumers cope with the decisions they must make? In this chapter we discuss two broad approaches for thinking about the choices that individual consumers make: consumer attitudes and attitude models, and models of consumer choice. Throughout the chapter we emphasize understanding how individual consumers make decisions. How do individual consumers make choices in the marketplace? What are the internal and external factors that influence these choices? Attitudes are key internal factors that shape individual consumer choices, and these are discussed at length in the following section.

Consumer Attitudes and Attitude Models

In the sections below we introduce the concept of *attitude* as a way to summarize consumers' thoughts, feelings, and actions. These three elements can be combined into a hierarchy of effects model, where one element (e.g., cognition) precedes the others. To date, several hierarchies have been proposed, depending on situational factors such as the kind of purchase and consumer involvement levels. Alternative theories are introduced to explain how consumers learn attitudes and to explain how attitudes are formed.

Attitude models provide *a description of how consumer information processing, including cognitions and emotions, influence consumer choice processes.* Some of the attitude models discussed include the standard hierarchy, the low-involvement hierarchy, the experiential hierarchy, the Fishbein multiattribute model, and the elaboration likelihood model. A theory is a kind of model, as both theories and models attempt to provide a coherent account of how the world works. The attitude theories that are discussed in this chapter include the functional theory of attitudes, self-perception theory, social judgment theory, balance theory, and the theory of cognitive dissonance. Throughout this section consumer examples are introduced and implications for marketing management are discussed.

Attitudes: A Summary of Consumer Thoughts, Feelings, and Actions

Attitudes are important because they reflect what consumers think and feel. They also can be used to explain what consumers intend to do. That is, attitude models help to describe how consumers make choices.[1] The thinking portion of an attitude is called a *cognition*. The feeling or hedonic portion relates to emotion.

The term **attitude** is widely used in common speech (see Consumer Chronicles 13.2). Here, we limit the definition of attitude to *a consumer's overall, enduring evaluation of a concept or object, such as a person, a brand, a service.* An attitude is not fleeing; it is an orientation that lasts over time. An attitude is general in that it summarizes consumers' evaluations over a wide range of situations. For example, Tom has an attitude toward winter sports; he likes them. His attitude covers many different circumstances, products, and people. If Tom meets Ben, a cross-country skier, for the first time, he may infer something about Ben's personality and how compatible Ben's interests and experiences might be with his own. Anything toward which one has an attitude is called an attitude object (A_o). Thus, Tom can have an attitude toward Ben, an attitude toward skiing, an attitude toward the Veniton line of skis, or an attitude toward extreme skiing in Colorado.

Attitudes are a product of information acquisition. That is, attitudes are learned

Attitude in Common Speech

The term *attitude* is frequently used in everyday conversations. Here are some examples:

- When Marika was young, her mother used to tell her, "Don't take that attitude with me, young lady!"
- When Marika's mother returns from a shopping trip, she tells Piet, "I didn't mean to project an attitude, but the salesclerk told me I did."
- As soon as Marika's mother leaves, Piet says, "I'm heading down to Locos for some attitude adjustment."
- Dirk's teacher tells him, "I don't like your attitude in class."
- In 1931, the psychologist L. L. Thurstone described attitude as the amount of *affect* that a person has for or against an object.

beliefs, feelings, and reaction tendencies. **Beliefs** are *thoughts linking an object to some feature or characteristic.*[2] For instance, Tom holds the belief that $11.99 is a good price to pay for the latest Belle & Sebastian CD, "Fold Your Hands Child." Feelings refer to the emotional reaction associated with using some object.[3] Listening to "Fold Your Hands Child" makes Tom feel happy and relaxed. Reaction tendencies are a disposition towards action. A reaction tendency is equivalent to a behavioral intention. After listening to "Fold Your Hands Child," Tom promises himself that he will shop at the same music store, and he intends to listen to some of the earlier Belle & Sebastian CDs.

Attitudes help consumers to make many kinds of choices. Some of these choices are relatively minor (e.g., what to have for lunch); others are quite important (e.g., what college to attend). Thus, a consumer could have an attitude toward a restaurant and an attitude toward a college. Also, as mentioned at the outset, a consumer can have an attitude toward a friend or an attitude toward a marketing message (e.g., an ad). Consumers can also have attitudes about themselves (e.g., a self-concept), as discussed at length in Chapter 7.

Why Are Attitudes Formed?

The **functional theory of attitudes** explains the role of attitudes in guiding and shaping social behavior.[4] In other words, this theory attempts to explain *why* attitudes form. It explains the role that attitudes play in helping us deal with everyday life. The functional theory *describes where attitudes come from by understanding the human motivation for forming attitudes.* Four major functions of attitudes are discussed here: utilitarian, value expressive, ego defensive, and knowledge. The significance of each of these functions in a given context will depend on individual and cultural factors outlined in Chapter 11. Each of these functions can be viewed as a kind of appeal that marketers can make to consumers via advertising and promotional messages.

The **utilitarian function** is *based on rewards and punishments.* This concept is similar to operant conditioning, where consumers learn through repetition and the consequences that follow stimuli. Following this process, there is a tendency for consumers to develop attitudes that lead toward perceived rewards and avoid any perceived punishments. An example of a utilitarian appeal is shown in an advertisement for Andersen Windows. In it, the sponsor reminds the reader that rewards (i.e., protection from the elements) will result for those who purchase the advertised brand. On the other hand, if the consumer fails to buy Andersen Windows, then inclement weather is shown on the horizon. Small panels

A value-expressive appeal.

also show the aesthetic beauty of the windows. This is an emotional appeal. According to operant conditioning (see Chapter 12), such an ad may be especially effective if it is repeated several times.

The **value-expressive function** refers to *a consumer's central values or self-concept.* As discussed above, self-concept includes the attitudes that consumers have about themselves. In many cultures including the United States and western Europe, consumers attempt to project their self-concept to the external world. They also form value-expressive attitudes so as to express their values to the external world through product consumption. The Renault Twingo ad shown above projects the image of being optimistic. This is a value-expressive appeal. "Roll with optimism" the slogan advises.

In a Western cultural context, the **ego-defensive function** of attitude *serves to protect the person from threats or internal feelings of threat.* Through ego-defensive attitudes, consumers strive to realize personal goals and images. See the Canadian Clorets ad on page 462. The text of the ad promises protection from offensive mouth odors. Many personal hygiene ads appeal to the ego-defensive function and promise protection both from embarrassing conditions (e.g., body odor) and from the internal states that might follow from these threats (e.g., feelings of social rejection and unpopularity). Notice that this ad could also fit with a more Asian idea of fitting in and not offending others as discussed in Chapter 11, a similar but different type of ego-defensive function.

The **knowledge function** refers to *the need for order, meaning, and structure.* This concept is similar to the notion of knowledge structures, as discussed in Chapter 12. The HelloBrain.com ad uses this appeal. HelloBrain.com is promoted as a way to "source solutions to any problem." The ad suggests that this service will enable the buyer to solve cognitive problems as tough as landing a spaceship on Mars. This appeal promises to bring order and meaning to the consumer's life. At the same time, the ad provides information about the brand (e.g., "just post your project and let the best minds from around the world find you") that add to the consumer's knowledge about the brand.

An attitude can serve more than one function; but typically one function will dominate. If marketers can understand the dominant function that a product serves, they can create

An ego-defensive appeal.

Source: Wei Yew, *Gottcha Twice: The Art of the Billboard 2,* Edmonton, Canada: Quon Editions, 1996, p. 49.

brands that better satisfy consumers and design promotional campaigns that communicate these functions to consumers.

Cognition, Affect, and Behavior

Attitudes have three components: cognition, affect, and behavior. Rearranging the first letters of these terms, researchers identify the ABC model of attitudes. In this model, **cognition** refers to *the beliefs a consumer has about an attitude object.* **Affect** refers to *the way a consumer feels about an attitude object.* **Behavior** involves *the person's intentions to do something with regard to an attitude object.*[5] The actual purchase is not included as a component of attitude because behavior is something quite distinct from attitudes. Attitudes are thought to influence behavior; but the terms *attitude* and *behavior* are not synonymous. In fact, they are distinct processes.

The relative importance of the three components of an attitude varies. What matters to consumers depends in part on their level of motivation. It also depends on the stimulus object, like a product, service, or experience. If a stimulus object is inherently interesting, consumers will likely pay more attention to it, compared to other information in the environment. The importance of the attitude components also varies with the consumer's culture. Cognitive elements may be more salient to some, emotional elements to other consumers.

What is the relationship between affect, behavior, and cognition? As we discussed in

A knowledge appeal.

WITH OUR HELP,
THE MARS LANDER MIGHT HAVE ACTUALLY
LANDED ON MARS.

HelloBrain.com

Chapter 11, thoughts and feelings are always intertwined. However, a hierarchy of effects model provides a way to explain the relative impact of these three components. Three competing hierarchy of effects models are discussed here: (1) the **standard hierarchy of effects,** which *emphasizes a problem-solving process;* (2) the **low-involvement hierarchy of effects,** which is *based on consumer experiences, good or bad;* and (3) the **experiential hierarchy of effects,** which *emphasizes emotional responses.*

The Standard Hierarchy

The standard hierarchy is shown in Exhibit 13.1. According to this model, consumer responses come in the following order—cognition, affect, then behavior, or learn–feel–do, as the sequence is sometimes phrased. In the marketplace, inputs to the consumer include elements of the marketing mix (e.g., promotions, price information), along with environmental factors (e.g., communications from competitors, economic trends). In the standard hierarchy, cognition is the first kind of consumer reaction to an external stimulus. For this example, assume that the stimulus object is an advertisement for Pantene shampoo, "For Hair So Healthy It Shines." (Pantene is the largest beauty care brand in the world. Annual international sales top $1.4 billion. Pantene is the third most profitable Procter & Gamble brand in the world.) Cognitions are divided into two components—awareness and knowledge. Thus, awareness is the first kind of reaction that a consumer has when she is exposed to the Pantene ad. The customer—call her Melanie—becomes aware of the ad. It is difficult to imagine how a commercial message can be effective if consumers do not notice it. Recall that in Chapter 9 we discussed how to get consumers' attention and awareness.

The second kind of cognitive response is knowledge. Through the ad exposure, and exposure to other stimuli in the environment, a consumer learns that Pantene shampoo comes in a blue bottle. Melanie *knows* that the usual price is about $3.00, for 500 ml (15 fluid ounces). She *knows* that the usual slogan is, "For hair so healthy it shines."

Following the cognitive evaluation of the stimulus object, consumers experience affective reactions. Again, these come in two varieties—liking and preference—with preference indicating a greater degree of consumer commitment than liking. For instance, our

Exhibit 13.1 Three Hierarchy of Effects Models

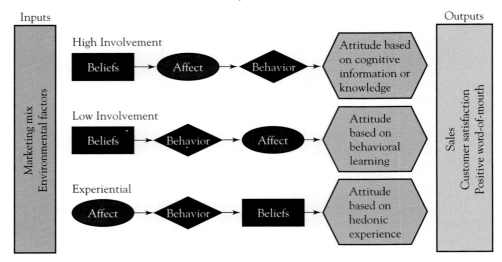

Source: George H. Zinkhan and Claes Fornell (1989), "A test of the Learning Hierarchy in High & Low Involvement Situations," in *Advances in Consumer Research, XVI*, T. Srull, ed., Provo, UT: Association for Consumer Research, pp. 152–59.

consumer may like the color of Pantene shampoo, and she may like the way the model's hair looks in the ad. Preference comes when Melanie includes Pantene shampoo in her **evoked set**—*the set of brands a consumer would consider purchasing*—and when she ranks Pantene higher than some of the other brands in her set of evoked brands.

According to the standard hierarchy, behavior follows affect. In other words, behaviors are formed by attitudes. First, consumers decide what they like and prefer, using cognition as input into this decision. Then, the affective judgments (attitudes) shape intentions and behaviors. Two kinds of behaviors are represented in Exhibit 13.1. Intention to buy is a kind of probability, and this consumer intention is considered to be a kind of attitude since it exists only in the consumer's mind and not in the observable world. For example, after being exposed to the Pantene ad campaign, Melanie may estimate that there is a 20 percent chance that she will buy Pantene the next time she goes shopping. In this case, actual behavior means the outcome of the shopping trip (e.g., does she buy Pantene shampoo or not?).

Just as Exhibit 13.1 depicts a role for inputs, it also depicts a role for outputs. Several kinds of outputs are relevant. Marketing managers are interested in purchases, which accumulate to create sales levels and market shares. From a consumer perspective, outputs could include satisfaction levels and word of mouth. For instance, Melanie may try Pantene shampoo and decide that she is satisfied with the way it makes her hair feel. She then tells her friend, Barb, about the experience.

As described above, the standard hierarchy assumes that consumers are rational processors of information. They form beliefs, attitudes, and intentions that causally determine behavior. In this sense, the arrows shown in Exhibit 13.1 show cause and effect relationships. For instance, consumer knowledge (which could include beliefs about product attributes) causes consumer affect (including attitudes about specific brands). In turn, these attitudes or preferences cause behavioral intentions, and these cause consumer choices (e.g., brand selections).

Marketing communications in some cultural environments relies more heavily on the standard hierarchy than in others. Marketers in the United States, Great Britain, and especially Germany make use of demonstration, lecture, and testimonial advertising formats (see Chapter 18) consistent with the cultural emphasis on individualism, rationalism, logic, and reason in these environments.[6]

The Low-Involvement Hierarchy

The low-involvement hierarchy shares some elements in common with the standard hierarchy, but it specifies that consumer responses occur in a different order. See Exhibit 13.1 for a visual display of the low-involvement hierarchy. As shown there, cognition comes first in the persuasion process; but behavior comes next. Affect comes last in the chain and is influenced by behavior. Affect and emotion emerge in response to consumption experiences. The low-involvement hierarchy is sometimes called the learn–do–feel sequence.

As the name suggests, this model applies to low-involvement purchase situations where both motivation and perceived risk are low. Suppose that Tom is standing in the checkout line of the local supermarket. He sees a pack of triple-A batteries that seem to be on sale. He is not familiar with the brand, but the promotional display has caught his eye. Since the price seems reasonable, Tom buys the batteries. Here is an example of the low-involvement hierarchy at work. Tom notices the batteries and looks at the price (cognition). Then, he buys the batteries (action), without really evaluating them in any detailed way (buying without affect). Sometime after Tom makes the purchase, he will evaluate the batteries. That is, he will form an opinion (positive or negative) about the batteries after he has had some experience with using them.

This kind of low-involvement choice process makes sense when the product is inexpensive. Tom is not risking much in terms of search time and financial resources when he makes the battery purchase. It saves him time to buy now and evaluate later. In this way, his attitudes are based more on consumption experiences than on information or affect that is communicated in the marketplace. Thus, in low-involvement situations, a main objective of promotional campaigns is to capture consumer attention. Once attention is captured, crucial information can be communicated in order to induce trial. In Tom's case, the battery distributor accomplishes this goal with two promotional techniques—the in-store display and the sale price for the product.

Exhibit 13.2 shows a model of quick choices that explains low-involvement purchase

Exhibit 13.2 Quick-Choice Model

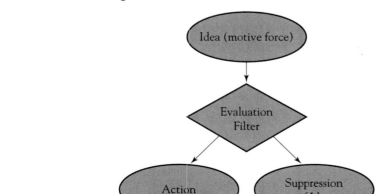

je ne peux pas y résister J'M

A quick-choice appeal. I just couldn't resist.

Source: Wei Yew, *Gottcha Twice: The Art of the Billboard 2,* Edmonton, Canada: Quon Editions, p. 125.

behavior. Recall we first introduced this model in Chapter 11. Under this model, a consumer's flow of ideas serves as a motive force. In a sense, this is the way that people experience life—as a flow of ideas, one after another. One set of ideas is the father and mother of subsequent idea, and so forth. Each idea that enters the conscious mind is then evaluated or filtered. Tom notices the battery display and the price. He then asks himself, Should I buy this pack of batteries? Perhaps his (Freudian) superego tells him, No, you already have too many unopened battery packs in the kitchen drawer! In that case, his idea is rejected; it does not become the basis of action. Tom's attention turns to something else.

In another circumstance, his superego may return the opposite answer, Yes, buy the batteries. The remote control for the TV isn't working quite right. New batteries might solve the problem. In this case, Tom's original idea has survived the filtering effect of the superego, and the idea becomes the basis for action (i.e., making the purchase).

Notice that there is no role for emotion or affect in the quick-choice model. Ideas (cognition) are followed almost immediately by behaviors. Certainly, this kind of model is useful for explaining the kinds of impulse purchases that take place in checkout lines or in response to behaviorally oriented ads such as the Canadian one shown above, in which the impulsive behavior (I just couldn't resist) is eating at McDonald's. For these kinds of low-involvement or impulse purchases, a thorough evaluation of the brand and purchase come later in the process, following the consumption experience. Affect comes last in the hierarchy of consumer responses.

The Experiential Hierarchy

The experiential hierarchy that is illustrated in Exhibit 13.1 stresses the importance of consumers' emotions. Sometimes, consumers buy things just because they like them. Tom likes to order pizza with his friends. He doesn't even care so much what kind of pizza is ordered. With his friends, he's even willing to eat anchovies, a topping he usually avoids if he orders a pizza with Melanie.

In contrast to the low-involvement hierarchy, the experiential hierarchy describes a situation in which consumers are often highly involved in decision making. However, consumers don't seem to follow the step-by-step process that is implied by the standard hierarchy. Instead, they evaluate the overall stimulus and make a decision. Although the experiential hierarchy is sometimes referred to as the do–feel–learn sequence, these kinds of consumer choices prove more difficult to decompose into individual stages than is the case with products that are purchased following the standard hierarchy. Good examples of this kind of decision making occur in the areas of art or music appreciation.

Consider the day that Melanie purchased an oil painting of three pillows for her bedroom. She was browsing at an art show, and the painting caught her eye. When Tom asks, Melanie has trouble explaining exactly why she bought the painting. Whatever her motivation, the standard hierarchy doesn't seem to apply. What knowledge did she gain about the painting? How did she come to prefer it to other paintings that she saw that day, and other days? Melanie evaluates this particular painting as a totality, as a *gestalt*. Her subjective reactions are more important than any cognition that she is aware of. Even after the painting hangs in her bedroom for a long time, Melanie has some difficulty in describing exactly why it appeals to her so much. "Somehow, these pillows touch me," she says.

Some authors argue that another hierarchy of effects sequence works in the Asian context, specifically, Japan. Here the sequence is feel–do–learn. The purpose of Japanese marketing communication is to please the consumer and to build dependency (*amae*) on the firm. This is done through indirect approaches. Japanese commercials often use serene, mood-creating nature symbols, for example, and aim to entertain rather than persuade. As a result, feel is the initial response of the Japanese consumer, after which action is taken: a visit to a retail shop to purchase the product. Only after this comes cognitive knowledge.[7]

Attitude toward the Ad and Attitude toward the Store

When consumers make decisions, they form attitudes about brands and attitudes about products. For instance, Tom likes old British sports cars. He has a positive affect toward this product category. Also, Tom particularly likes the MGB brand. It is important to realize that in a decision-making situation consumers form attitudes toward objects other than the product itself; and these attitudes can influence their ultimate selections. For instance, consumers form attitudes toward the advertisements that they see. These are called **attitudes toward the ad** (A_{ad}) and are defined as *a predisposition to respond in a favorable or unfavorable manner to a particular advertising stimulus during a particular exposure occasion*. What this means is that ads have entertainment value. Positive feelings are generated by an ad, and consumers experience a variety of emotional responses when they are exposed to ads.

Determinants of A_{ad} include attitude toward the advertiser, evaluation of the ad execution itself, the mood evoked by the ad, and the degree to which the ad affects viewers' arousal levels. It is generally agreed that commercials have the potential to stimulate at least two kinds of positive emotions: pleasure and arousal. Negative emotions, such as intimidation, are also possible. Mood-management theory assumes that consumers strive to eliminate or at least diminish bad moods and perpetuate good ones by selecting appropriate media. For example, when given a choice, bored subjects select exciting TV programs to watch, whereas stressed subjects opt for relaxing shows. Through a process of classical conditioning, the moods created by commercials can be transferred to the advertised brands, as was discussed in Chapter 12.

Consumers can also have attitudes toward the stores that they visit. For example, in the opening vignette, Tom may form an attitude about Wolf Camera. If he doesn't like the digital camera that he buys, he may decide that Wolf Camera is a good place to get film developed but not a good place to buy a new camera.

How Attitudes Are Formed and Learned

Attitudes can form through a variety of processes. In particular, attitudes can be formed following the learning patterns described in Chapter 11, including classical conditioning and operant conditioning. As discussed below, there are important links between the learning theories and the **attitude formation** processes. In addition, attitudes are formed through one of three related processes: (1) compliance, (2) identification, and (3) internalization.

As an example of classical conditioning, Melanie might develop a positive attitude toward a perfume because of the romantic, classical music that is played in the background every time the perfume is displayed in a TV ad. Through a process of repetition, the positive affect is transferred from the music in the advertising to the advertised brand. This kind of affect can be conceived of as an attitude toward the brand.

Alternatively, attitude formation can follow a path specified by operant conditioning. Here, Melanie's attitude toward the perfume is reinforced by her consumption experiences. Tom seems to behave in a more romantic way when Melanie is wearing the perfume. In this instance, Tom's romantic behavior acts as the reinforcer to shape Melanie's attitude toward the perfume.

Some attitudes are formed following a process of **compliance** that is related to operant conditioning. In this case, *attitudes are formed to gain reward or avoid punishment.* For example, Tom's nephew, Brian, doesn't smoke cigarettes because his parents don't approve of the habit and don't allow it in their house. However, when Brian goes away to college he starts smoking occasionally, since the punishment has been removed. To some extent, the compliance explanation for attitude formation is consistent with operant conditioning. Consumers shape their behavior so as to respond to rewards and punishments in the marketplace.

Attitudes also form through a process of **identification,** which is related to operant conditioning. Here, *attitudes are formed so as to allow the person to fit in, or to be similar to others.* For example, Brian found that he tended to smoke cigarettes at night when he was hanging around with his fraternity brothers. However, in the summer time, when he was working as a life guard in Atlantic City, he found that he didn't care for smoking so much, and he resolved to quit.

Attitudes can also be learned through a complex cognitive process. For instance, after several visits to an après-ski bar in Steamboat Springs, Colorado, Tom finds the experience to be somewhat boring. No one says very much. However, after a few visits, Tom learns that a good way to stimulate conversation is by starting a good rousing argument. If he adopts the attitudes of a conservative politician and advocates conservative policies, he finds that many people will join in and argue with him until closing time. When Tom returns to that bar, after a 10-month absence, the bar keeper welcomes him with, "Hey Tom, we haven't had such a good argument since you were here the last time!"

When attitudes are **internalized,** typically through a more complex process than mere conditioning, *they become part of a person's value system.* In these instances, attitudes are strongly held and difficult to change. This notion of attitude strength (and weakness) is discussed in more detail in the following section.

The Relative Strength of Attitudes	As outlined above, attitudes can be formed and learned in different ways. Attitudes are not all of equal strength. Some attitudes are backed up by strongly held beliefs and are not easily changed. For instance, Melanie hates to go to the movies. She believes that if you've seen one, you've seen them all. No amount of coaxing, including the marketing efforts of film distributors, will convince her to attend the showing of a first-run film.

Other attitudes are not so strong. When Tom sees an ad for a new kind of toothpaste, Morning Calm, his interest is piqued. It is based on an ancient Chinese formula, and Tom is impressed. He remembers the name and laughs at the joke contained in the commercial. Nonetheless, the next time that Tom is in the grocery store, he doesn't even look for Morning Calm. Instead, he buys his regular brand, Colgate. He has a positive attitude toward both the new brand and the amusing toothpaste ad. But this attitude is relatively weak. It is easily swamped by existing habits and other stimuli in the environment.

The strength of an attitude is also influenced by a consumer's level of commitment to

Melanie recently purchased a new refrigerator. At first, she was quite pleased with her choice. She felt as if she got a good deal, and she enjoyed many of the features. The new appliance certainly looked better in the kitchen than her old one had. Nonetheless, soon after Melanie purchased the refrigerator, she noticed that it seemed to make a lot of noise when the motor was running. She thought that other refrigerators that she looked at also made a lot of noise, but she wasn't certain. Melanie found herself paying attention to appliance ads, and she poured through issues of *Consumer Reports* to compare refrigerator brands and to search for information about operating noises. She listened to the sounds that were made by her neighbors' appliances. Finally, she convinced herself that her refrigerator was no louder than most others.

In this instance, Melanie originally has a positive attitude toward her new purchase. However, the noise of the new appliance bothers her. Thus, there is a conflict between what Melanie expected and what she got. She is confronted with an inconsistency. On the one hand, she likes the look of her new appliance. But on the other hand, the noise level makes her wonder if she made the right purchase. She gathers more information and eventually decides that her new refrigerator isn't really that noisy after all. She changes her attitude (about noise levels) that had been causing her to experience dissonance.

an attitude. In general, the degree of commitment is related to level of involvement with the attitude object. For example, Melanie's niece is highly involved with the product category of perfume. She is also quite committed to her particular brand, Shalimar, because it is the same brand that her mother wears.

The desire for consistency is a strong human motivation. Consumers strive to attain consistency between their attitudes. According to the principle of **cognitive consistency,** consumers strive to *maintain harmony between their thoughts and behaviors.* That is, people will adjust beliefs or attitudes in order to maintain consistency. Alternatively, they will adjust their behaviors to maintain balance with their attitudes.

An internal state of **cognitive dissonance** results when there is a *discrepancy between behavior and attitude.* According to the theory of cognitive dissonance, consumers will actively seek to resolve or reduce this discrepancy.[8] In other words, people seek to reduce dissonant behavior or feelings. An example of dissonance and its resulting effect on attitude formation is shown in Consumer Chronicles 13.3. Here, Melanie is faced with an inconsistency between two attitudes—her initial, positive reaction to her new refrigerator and her perception that the refrigerator's motor is very loud. She searches for information and eventually revises her negative impressions associated with the motor noise of the refrigerator. In the end, she regains her cognitive balance.

As illustrated in Consumer Chronicles 13.3, cognitive dissonance is a state of psychological discomfort that is caused by a disequilibrium between cognitive elements. In

The Importance of Consistency and Cognitive Dissonance

this sense, cognitive elements are defined as "any knowledge, opinion, or belief about the environment" or about one's behavior.[9] When a consumer experiences dissonance, there is a strong motivation to reestablish balance. That is, consumers change their attitudes so that they are consistent with their public behavior, or vice versa. This motive is especially strong when the consumer's current cognitive structure does not provide sufficient justification for the seemingly incongruent behavior.[10] Of course, in some cultures consistency between attitudes and behavior is not very important and having consistent attitudes and behaviors is also not important.

Self-Perception

Self-perception theory provides another way to explain dissonance effects.[11] This theory describes how *people observe their own behavior and use these observations to shape their own attitudes*. This theory seems especially relevant to the low-involvement hierarchy, where consumers derive an attitude, or affect, after they have engaged in some behavior. For example, Tom eventually buys the Chinese toothpaste, Morning Calm. After using it, in order to retain psychological balance he begins to think of himself as an adventurous user of Asian products. He also likes the toothpaste.

Self-perception theory explains the effectiveness of some sales techniques.[12] One such method is the *foot-in-the-door technique,* which advises that a salesperson should first ask a prospect for a small favor. Once that favor is granted, the salesperson can then proceed to ask for something larger (i.e., the sale). This technique is discussed in more detail in Chapter 15.

Social Judgment

Social judgment theory stipulates that *people understand the world by matching up new stimuli with information that is already stored in memory.*[13] In this sense, social judgment theory is similar to self-perception theory. That is, both theories specify that people adjust their attitudes and beliefs so as to respond to new information. Under social judgment theory, a consumer's initial attitude acts as a frame or reference. New information is categorized in terms of this existing standard. We discussed framing effects in Chapter 12.

By following this existing standard, consumers can judge the new information to be acceptable or unacceptable. Marketing communications that are judged to be reasonably similar to preexisting information are readily accepted. Marketing communications that are perceived to contrast with preexisting information are rejected. This latter phenomenon is known as the contrast effect, discussed in Chapter 12. Here, the contrast is between two bits of information, one that is in the environment and one in memory. The contrast effect explains one way that new information is processed and eventually influences attitude structure.

The Importance of Balance

Balance theory describes how *consumers evaluate elements that belong together.* In balance theory, *consumer perceptions are classified as either positive or negative. Perceptions are altered to make them consistent.*[14] This theory describes elements in the environment as appearing in groups of three. Each triad contains (1) a consumer and her perceptions, (2) an attitude object (such as a brand), and (3) some other person. An example of balance theory is shown in Exhibit 13.3. Here, Tom originally has a negative attitude toward Evening Star mouthwash, a brand that is imported by the same organization that distributes Morning Calm. Tom originally learned about Evening Star in some promotional literature that accompanied a tube of Morning Calm. Nonetheless, Tom is quite familiar with other mouthwash brands, and he wonders why he has never heard of this brand before. Thus, his original reaction is somewhat negative.

Exhibit 13.3 Balance Theory and Attitude Change

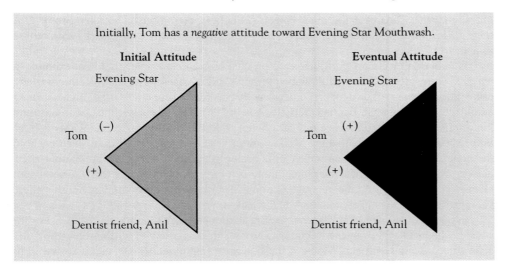

Initially, Tom has a *negative* attitude toward Evening Star Mouthwash.

Initial Attitude   **Eventual Attitude**

One of Tom's best friends is Anil, a dentist who currently lives in Seattle. In a recent e-mail message, Anil told Tom that he is recommending Evening Star as an especially effective preventative of gum disease. Now, Tom is faced with a dilemma. He can either change his attitude toward Evening Star or change his attitude toward Anil. As implied in the section on attitude strength, it can be predicted that Tom's attitude toward Anil (a friend) is going to be much stronger than his attitude toward Evening Calm (a mouthwash that he has seen promoted only once). Thus, Tom changes the weaker attitude. He now has a much more positive attitude toward Evening Star.

Celebrity endorsers are prominently featured in advertising. For instance, it is estimated that advertisers pay more than 550 million dollars a year to famous athletes to endorse their products.[15] What do advertisers received in return for this investment? Balance theory provides one kind of explanation (another is found in Chapter 18). Celebrities enjoy considerable popularity among some segment of the public. Advertisers are hoping that, by using celebrities in their ads, they can convince target consumers to change their attitudes about advertised brands, in much the same way that Tom changes his attitude about Evening Star mouthwash in Exhibit 13.3. An example of a celebrity ad shows popular business writer, John Naisbitt, wearing a Hathaway shirt. From a balance theory perspective, this ad may work as follows. Initially, consumers will have a positive attitude toward John Naisbitt. He has written many best-selling business books, including *Megatrends.* Because Naisbitt is shown endorsing the shirt, consumers may increase their positive evaluation of the shirt, in order to maintain balance. As the ad concludes, there is a Hathaway shirt for "every . . . successful . . . management style."

MultiAttribute Attitude Models

Attitude models have been developed to specify and explore the different elements that affect attitudes. For example, an object's attributes influence consumers' attitudes. **Multiattribute attitude models** explore the many attributes that might influence a consumer's decision-making process. In a marketing context, these models specify that *consumers' attitudes about brands depend on the beliefs they have about a group of brand attributes.*

That is, consumers evaluate brands by considering the many attributes that make up a brand. In general, multiattribute models consist of three important elements: (1) attributes, characteristics of the attitude object; (2) beliefs, cognitions about the specific attitude object; and (3) importance weights, reflecting the priority consumers place on the object.

In a marketing context, attributes are product or brand characteristics. For example, a Miele vacuum cleaner has the following attributes: price, ease of use, suction effectiveness, color, attractiveness of design, and others. As discussed above, beliefs are thoughts linking an object to some feature or characteristic. A belief is a state of knowledge. Awareness and unawareness represent the extremes of a belief.[16] At the positive extreme of this continuum, Melanie may believe that the Miele vacuum cleaner is easy to use; and she may hold the belief that the Miele vacuum cleaner is easier to use than any of the competing alternatives. In other words, Melanie thinks there is a high probability that the Miele vacuum cleaner is easy to use. At the negative extreme, Tom may not even know about the Miele vacuum cleaner. He is unaware this brand exists.

Importance weights describe the priority that consumers give to an attribute. For instance, when Melanie evaluates vacuums, she considers a variety of attributes: suction, design, price, and ease of use. Which of these is most important? If Melanie were asked to rank order these attributes, she would say that suction is most important and ease of use is the second most important. She considers price and design, but she believes these attributes are not as important as suction or ease of use.

Multiattribute models are important because they explicitly recognize that consumers face trade-offs. One kind of trade-off involves time use. Should Tom and Melanie go to Cancun, where Melanie likes to relax in the sun, on their vacation, or should they go to Steamboat Springs, Colorado, where Tom could learn to ski? Of course, each of these destination spots has many attributes. Cancun is attractive because of the sun, the swimming, the natural beauty of the place, the Latin bands (which Melanie likes to dance to), and the nearby historical sites. Steamboat Springs is attractive because of the skiing (which Tom enjoys), the sun, the natural beauty, and the nightlife at the lodge. How will Melanie and Tom decide where to spend their vacation time? They have to make trade-offs. One vacation spot may be superior on one attribute, but it may be inferior on another. Multiattribute models try to take into account these trade-offs that consumers face when they make choices in the marketplace.

The Basic Fishbein Model of Consumer Choice

The **Fishbein model** is an example of a popular multiattribute model that is frequently applied in marketing research. This model measures: *(1) salient beliefs, (2) object-attitude linkages, and (3) evaluations of each of the important attributes.* Martin Fishbein's first, basic formulation of an attitude was:

$$A_o = \sum_{i=1}^{n} B_i a_i$$

where:

A_o is the attitude toward an object.

B_i represents the strength of the belief that attribute I is related to the object (e.g., that the toothpaste has a decay-fighting ingredient).

a_i is the value, or importance, of this attribute to the consumer.

n is the number of salient attributes.

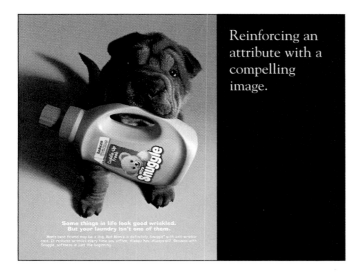

Reinforcing an attribute with a compelling image.

In a marketing context, the beliefs are usually measured with respect to product attributes. For example, consumers might be asked to indicate their beliefs about how effective Pantene shampoo is at fighting tangles (a product attribute). Continuing in a marketing context, value is frequently measured as attribute importance. For instance, consumers would be asked to indicate how important it is that their shampoo fight tangles (attribute importance).

In plain words, the Fishbein model says that attitudes are a sum of beliefs and their evaluations. In a marketing context, the beliefs are about attributes (e.g., Tom believes that Morning Star toothpaste brightens his teeth). The evaluations are importance ratings. For instance, Tom rates brightness as a very important attribute for toothpaste. At the same time, he rates price as a relatively unimportant attribute. That is, he is prepared to pay a premium for a toothpaste that simultaneously cleans his teeth and brightens his smile.

There are several strategic applications of the Fishbein model. For instance, organizations can attempt to capitalize on relative advantages that they have in the marketplace. Promotions can be used to strengthen belief in the linkage between an attribute and a brand. An example of this is shown in a Snuggle fabric softener ad. Here, the sponsor strengthens the association between the brand, Snuggle, and a key attribute, anti-wrinkling, while the image of the floppy Sharpei dog reinforces its anti-wrinkling attribute.

Communications can also be used to add a new attribute to consumers' consciousness. The Tampax ad provides an example. Here, the sponsor emphasizes the fact that a different amount of absorbency is needed on different days. Thus, Tampax introduces the multipack, an advantage that competitors may not have. In this way, a new attribute is introduced to the product class. If this attribute catches on with consumers, then competitors have to imitate and make this attribute available in their brands.

Influencing competitors' belief ratings is another advertising or positioning tactic that is related to the Fishbein model. Comparative ads serve to accomplish this objective. Consider a Royal Doulton ad. The ad emphasizes that Royal Doulton is an imported product, from Stoke on Trent, England. At the same time, the headline emphasizes that Lenox china, a main competitor, comes from Pomona, New Jersey. The ad repositions Lenox china, a product that many U.S. buyers thought was imported. Apparently, many U.S. consumers share the perception that imported china is better than domestic china. Royal

All in one box.

Doulton credits a 6 percent gain in market share to this one advertisement. In terms of the Fishbein model, the purpose of the Royal Doulton ad is to lower consumers' attribute ratings for Lenox's country of origin. At the same time, this kind of comparative ad has the potential to increase the attribute rating for the sponsor. That is, consumers may give a higher rating to the country-of-origin dimension. However, comparative ads are rarely used in Europe or Asia. In Asia, comparative advertising is confrontational and is perceived to denigrate the competitor, which may entail a loss of face or a threat to harmony.[17]

The Extended Fishbein Model

The **extended Fishbein model** is called the *theory of reasoned action*.[18] Recognizing that social pressure can have a strong influence on behavior expands the initial Fishbein model. The model can be represented as:

$$BI = f(A, NB_s \times MC, NB_p)$$
$$B = f(BI, EE)$$

where,

B = Behavior
A = Attitude
NBs = Social normative beliefs
MC = Motivation to comply
NBp = Personal normative beliefs
BI = Behavioral intention
EE = Judged influence of extraneous events

The model implies that behavioral intention can be predicted from knowledge of consumers' attitudes, social beliefs, and personal beliefs. In turn, behavior is predicted from knowledge of behavioral intentions and the judged influence of extraneous events.[19] In this model, social normative beliefs attempt to capture expectations of peer groups, friends, and family. For instance, Tom has promised his father that he will not go skydiving. Even though this promise was made more than 15 years ago, Tom still sticks by it. Motivation to comply reflects how strongly a person feels that he must comply with the wishes of other people he knows. Thus, Tom is more likely to comply with social pressure applied by his father than social pressure applied by a friend he has known for a relatively short time.

The extended Fishbein model attempts to take into account the strong influence that other people can have on a person's behavior. People don't always make choices just to please themselves. They also try to please other people they know and cherish. In some instances, these social influences can be as strong or stronger than the personal reasons people have for making choices.

The model also tries to take into account the influence of extraneous events on individual choice. Extraneous events could include such things as time pressures, technological constraints, competitive promotions, or economic constraints. For instance, Tom may be shopping for a CD to buy Brian for his birthday. On his way to Brian's birthday dinner, he stops by the music store. At first, Tom intends to by an early CD by Widespread Panic. When he can't locate that CD, Tom doesn't spend a lot of time looking through the rack before selecting an alternative gift. Time pressure and product availability are two important extraneous events that shape Tom's gift choice.

Limitations of the Fishbein Model

There are certain obstacles to predicting behavior via the extended Fishbein model. For example, the model was designed to deal with actual purchase behavior, not outcomes of behavior, such as consumption or word of mouth. In addition, some outcomes are beyond the consumer's control. That is, behavior is not always intentional. Impulse action is not explained in a convincing way by the Fishbein approach. Many times, consumers' direct, personal experience has a stronger influence than any other elements (e.g., attitudes that result from exposure to company-sponsored communications).

Consumer attitudes are always evolving. When market researchers attempt to track attitudes over time, they must try to take many snapshots, not just a few. Attitudes change to reflect new realities in the marketplace. They change to reflect new consumer experiences and beliefs. And they vary situationally. As implied by the three hierarchy models discussed above, variations in involvement levels may result in the activation of different cognitive processes with different behavioral results.

The Elaboration Likelihood Model of Persuasion

Persuasion refers to *an active attempt to change individual attitudes.* The **elaboration likelihood model** (ELM) has been proposed to explain how persuasion works. The model is diagrammed in Exhibit 13.4. The ELM describes how individual consumers process new information.[20] It proposes that consumers process new information via different routes, depending on the personal relevance of this information (see Chapter 11 for a complete discussion of involvement). When consumers are highly involved, the central route to persuasion is dominant. In processing through the central route to persuasion, the consumer determines if the message is relevant. The person will actively think about the arguments presented and generate either positive (cognitive reactions) or negative (counterarguments) responses. This route usually involves processing information via the traditional hierarchy

The Elaboration Likelihood Model: High-Involvement Persuasion

Consider a situation where Piet is surfing the Internet looking for a new piece of financial software. He is looking for "freeware," but he is also willing to pay a small fee for software that has some superior features. This choice situation is high involvement for several reasons. First, the Internet is a relatively high-involvement medium. It is interactive, so consumers have to pay attention. They have to click their mouse to move the search forward, and they have to keep responding to receive new information. Second, Piet is motivated to find just the right software package for him.

In this situation, Piet probably will not be influenced so much by peripheral cues. He may notice that a certain website has great graphics and interesting music, but these weak arguments will not convince him to download some software that does not meet his major criteria. Instead, Piet will be persuaded by strong arguments. He pays close attention to the price of the software (free versus otherwise). Also, he pays close attention to the arguments that the software companies present about their product features.

of effects. That is, the rational, cognitive arguments presented in the message are quite important; and the consumer evaluates these arguments carefully. For example, a recent Roche Pharmaceuticals ad contains a number of main arguments that are potentially quite persuasive. The ad evokes the problems faced by adolescents who suffer from severe acne and is directed to Hispanic parents who tend to be very concerned about their children's well-being. It points out that the teenager feels that he has lost out in many ways and that his peers do not understand how badly the acne makes him feel. The ad addresses parents directly, stating that acne causes more problems than they might imagine; it urges parents to find a solution via a visit to a dermatologist. The ELM argues that this ad will be effective, *if* a consumer evaluates it under a high-involvement situation (e.g., when the consumer is motivated to process potentially complex persuasive arguments).

When consumers are exposed to new information under conditions of low involvement, the peripheral route to persuasion dominates. In the peripheral route, consumers are not so motivated to think about the main arguments. Instead, they rely on other cues to evaluate the message. One example of a peripheral cue is looking at the package. For instance, Melanie may look at a box of ice cream just as she is leaving the frozen foods

Exhibit 13.4 Elaboration Likelihood Model of Persuasion

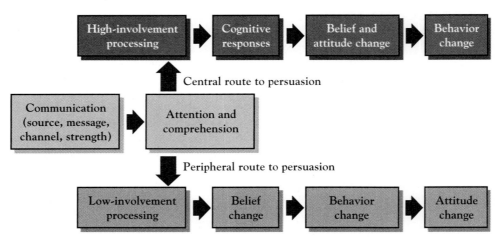

section of the supermarket. The green color of the package cues a healthy image (as researchers have found), so she may put it in her grocery cart to try it out. This particular choice of ice cream describes a low-involvement purchase. Melanie doesn't read the detailed information on the back of the package. Instead, she looks at the colors on the box.

Crucial variables in the ELM include (1) message-processing involvement (high or low) and (2) argument strength (strong or weak). The model predicts which kind of arguments (strong or weak) will be more persuasive under different involvement situations. Under high involvement, consumers are highly motivated to process the main message and to pay attention to strong arguments. Under low involvement, consumers are not involved with the decision situation, so they are not motivated to process the main message and are not influenced as much by strong messages. Instead, weak messages (i.e., peripheral cues) are more persuasive than strong message arguments.

Two examples are presented here to illustrate the ELM. The first, presented in Consumer Chronicles 13.4, shows a high-involvement situation in which the main message and strong arguments are the main persuasive elements in the choice situation. The second example, in Consumer Chronicles 13.5, describes a low-involvement situation in which peripheral cues are more influential in guiding consumer choice.

The Elaboration Likelihood Model: Low-Involvement Persuasion

Consider a situation where Marika is tired from a long day of work, and she is watching TV. A commercial comes on for hand soap. The commercial uses a slice-of-life approach and includes appealing background music. For a variety of reasons, this is a low-involvement situation for Marika. Under most circumstances, television is a low-involvement medium. Consumers don't necessarily have to pay a lot of attention to watch it. When the commercial for a low-involvement product comes on, Marika is paying even less attention. She is not really motivated to process a complex message about the soap.

Under these low-involvement circumstances, peripheral cues will have more influence than strong arguments about the advertised brand. The background music in the ad is one type of peripheral cue that may serve as an important persuasive element. Thus, Marika may purchase this brand of soap on her next shopping trip even though she has not actively processed much information from the ad.

Consumer Chronicles 13.5

The elaboration likelihood model and the multiattribute models of attitudes on which it is based represent a psychological approach to analyzing how consumers acquire, organize, and use information to assist in choice behavior. An underlying assumption is that consumers want to solve problems and choose rationally. Under this assumption, choice models do not take symbolic, hedonic, and aesthetic motives into account. Further, they are biased toward verbal information and linguistic performance and tend to disregard pictorial, music, and other nonlanguage aspects of marketing communications. These models thus display a Western bias and omit information that may be important in non-Western cultures.

How people acquire, organize, and use information is related to the type of information they are used to processing. People in interdependent, relatively homogeneous cultures are used to processing indirect communication, symbols, and signs. People in individualistic, heterogeneous cultures, like the United States, for example, are used to words and explanations. Cultures that favor associative thinking, like Italy, Spain, and France, for example, prefer oral, face-to-face communication that is rich in nonverbal elements, whereas cultures in which people prefer deductive thinking, like the United States, Germany, or Austria, will tend to prefer verbal and written information.

Differences in how people are used to processing information should affect marketing communications. For example, 90 percent of French advertising is visual, whereas 80 percent of German magazine ads are copy. In a typical Japanese ad, visuals and music are used first to develop trust and understanding, and only then is the brand, company, or product name shown. These differences suggest that the so-called central and peripheral routes to persuasion may be reversed in some way in cultures that rely more on indirection, symbols, and nonverbal information. The ELM model and the hierarchy of effects models described earlier deal poorly with these cultural differences in information processing.

Another problem with the ELM and hierarchy of effects models is their emphasis on the individual as an information processor. The problem becomes clear in highly interdependent cultural contexts. If we were to ask how the individual processes persuasive information in Japan, the answer would be that there is neither a persuasive process nor is it useful to look at it at the individual level. Marketing communications in this cultural context cannot persuade individuals directly. Instead, products and marketing communications must adapt to group influence, defining groups rather than the self. In their decision making, Japanese tend to depend at least in part on members of their in-group or on people who in other ways merit their trust. As a result, Japanese marketing is based more on building trust than persuasion. In sum, more different models of information processing are needed to understand persuasive processes and decision making in a global marketplace.

| How Consumers Respond to Persuasion Attempts | Marketers are very interested in persuading consumers; but how do consumers respond to persuasion attempts? A broadened view of persuasion takes into account consumers' persuasion knowledge. The **persuasion knowledge model** posits that *consumers develop knowledge about persuasion and use this knowledge to respond to persuasion experiences.* Persuasion knowledge includes consumers' theories about persuasion and beliefs about marketers' motives, strategies, and tactics. It also includes information about ways to respond to or counteract persuasion attempts and the effectiveness and appropriateness of persuasion tactics. Persuasion knowledge is not a schema but a loose set of beliefs about persuasion that may be accurate or inaccurate. People's persuasion knowledge is constantly changing and of course depends on the kinds of persuasion they encounter in their social environment and on their developmental stage (children have different knowledge than adults). For example, years of Soviet propaganda campaigns have made many consumers in the former Soviet states suspicious of all advertising claims. Moreover, consumers who have a more interdependent view of the self may be more likely to consider the motives of others and thus be more likely to draw on persuasion knowledge in interpreting persuasion attempts. |

While viewing advertisements, interacting with retail salespeople, and browsing the aisles of the local grocery store, consumers draw on their persuasion knowledge to interpret information and make decisions. For example, a consumer may wonder about a salesperson's motives for recommending a product. Research suggests that in the case of clothing retailers, consumers often interpret salespeople's comments as "trying to sell something." An advertisement that employs an attractive spokesperson or a celebrity endorser may arouse suspicion or even anger if the consumers interpret this as a marketing tactic to get them to buy.

The persuasion knowledge model can supplement the elaboration likelihood model by explaining when and why such things as celebrity endorsers, lengthy claims, or claims accompanied by statistics will be interpreted as tactics and what types of inferences and evaluations these tactics call to mind. More work is needed, but we know that consumers' use of persuasion knowledge depends on many of the framing and context effects discussed in

Chapter 12. For example, if suspicion is cued, consumers are more likely to look for ulterior motives behind salespeople's messages and behaviors. Marketers need to keep in mind consumers' persuasion knowledge and how it effects the interpretation of persuasion attempts.[21]

Marketing managers are interested in attitudes because attitudes are predictive of **behavioral intentions.** That is, if a consumer has a favorable attitude toward a brand, then that consumer will have a higher probability of purchasing that brand. Unfortunately, behavioral intentions are not the same as behaviors. There is often a gap. For instance, Tom may intend to purchase Ben & Jerry's Cherry Garcia ice cream on his next grocery shopping trip. That is, there is a high probability that Tom will choose the Cherry Garcia flavor the next time that he purchases ice cream. However, when he visits the store, he finds that store brand ice cream is on a special two-for-one sale, so he buys that instead. The next time that Tom goes shopping, he stops in a convenience store. He looks for Cherry Garcia, but finds that the convenience store doesn't carry it. Once again, he buys another kind of ice cream. In brief, knowledge of consumer attitudes doesn't always help us to understand or predict consumer behavior. There are many environmental variables (e.g., competitors' promotions, distribution breakdowns, situational factors) that can influence consumer choice at the point of purchase, even when consumers' prior probabilities for purchasing a particular brand are high. In addition, some kinds of attitudes are linked only indirectly to consumer choice. Consider the variable "attitude toward the ad," discussed earlier. A consumer may love a particular commercial and think about it frequently. However, if this same consumer never encounters the product directly or never has the opportunity to try it, he may never purchase the advertised brand.[22]

Culture affects behavioral intentions. Cultures vary in the extent to which people make definite concrete plans. They also differ in the extent to which they believe their own actions will produce definite results. Americans believe strongly in their ability to exert control over their environments. People of Muslim and Confucian heritage do not. Cultural differences such as these can lead to wrong expectations with respect to buying intentions. For example, research suggests that if 55 percent of people who try a new product in Italy say they will definitely buy it, the product is likely to fail (because their behavior will not match their predictions); but if 5 percent of those trying the product in Japan say they will definitely buy it, the product is likely to succeed. The difference is explained by cultural difference in the strength of intentions. Consumers with a Catholic heritage and who speak Latinate languages (French, Italian, Spanish, etc.), tend to overclaim their purchase intentions. Consumers from a Protestant background may be less likely to overclaim their intentions. Consumers in Asian cultures influenced by their Confucian or Buddhist heritages follow a more middle way and avoid declarative statements like "I definitely will buy." In Asian and African cultures with an interdependent or more collective orientation or with an Islamic heritage, consumers assume that fate or other people may intervene in intentions and deflect certainty about behavior.[23]

Choice Models

How do consumers make choices? How do they decide which services or brands to purchase or what retail outlets to patronize? To some extent, there may be as many **choice models** or strategies as there are consumers. But answering our question will depend on identifying consumers' goals (some mix of utilities, emotions, situational factors, and social motives), the alternatives and criteria they consider meaningful, and how they combine information to make decisions.[24] Here, we attempt to identify patterns and to group consumers into overall patterns. The attitude models discussed above provide one way to describe the process of consumer information search and choices. In the following sections we discuss other choice models: expected utility theory; consumer heuristics, including satisficing decisions; and prospect theory.

Expected Utility Theory

As discussed in Chapter 10, economics provides a model of consumer decision making. This model is called **expected utility theory.** It assumes that decision makers are rational and that they have complete information; that is, consumers are assumed to have complete information about the probabilities and consequences attached to each alternative course of action. They are expected to understand this information and be able to calculate the advantages and disadvantages of each alternative. Finally, consumers are supposed to compare these calculations and select the course of action that maximizes expected utility.[25] Thus, *consumers make choices in a manner that maximizes a utility function, subject to the constraints of time, money income, information, and technology.*

People are most likely to have well-articulated preferences when they are familiar and experienced with the choice problem, and rational choice theory may be applicable in such situations. Industrial purchasing processes may sometimes correspond to the model. But individual consumers and households rarely act in the ways that are assumed by expected utility theory. Information about alternatives is often missing or uncertain. Perception is selective. Memory is imperfect and biased.[26] Consumers do not have unlimited time and energy to make choices. They don't want to spend all of their waking hours making consumer purchases. Thus, bounded rather than complete rationality characterizes most of us (at best!) when we make decisions. And situational factors may intrude. Thus, expected utility theory is more an idealized model than a description of how consumers actually make market choices. Nonetheless, utility theory has been adapted in marketing to provide descriptions of consumer utility for specific attribute levels. These descriptions take the form of utility functions.

Exhibit 13.5 Utility Curve for Almonds in Candy Bar

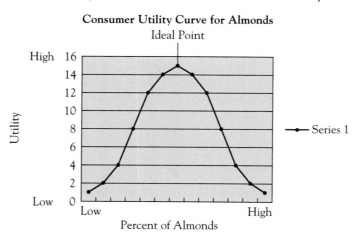

Rank order the following four candy bars from 1 to 4, with 1 being your most preferred brand and 4 being your least preferred brand. All percentages are measured in terms of weight.

Percentages do not add to 100 percent, because all ingredients are not included in the profiles.

Profile A:	**Rank** ____	**Profile B:**	**Rank** ____
Almonds:	15%	Almonds:	0%
Chocolate:	20%	Chocolate:	40%
Sugar:	5%	Sugar:	10%
Calories:	260	Calories:	310
Price:	80 cents	Price:	60 cents

Profile C:	**Rank** ____	**Profile D:**	**Rank** ____
Almonds:	30%	Almonds:	15%
Chocolate:	0%	Chocolate:	20%
Sugar:	5%	Sugar:	0%
Calories:	260	Calories:	210
Price:	$1.00	Price:	80 cents

Utility Functions

An example of a **utility function** is shown in Exhibit 13.5. Here, *utility* refers to the amount of happiness that a consumer derives from a product or from a product attribute. The amount of utility is plotted on the y-axis in Exhibit 13.5. The amount of an attribute present is plotted on the x-axis. The resulting shape of most utility functions is an inverted U, which implies that consumer utility increases through the low range of an attribute but then comes to a peak at some moderate range. Exhibit 13.5 shows Melanie's utility function for the amount of almonds in a candy bar. She is generally unhappy with a small amount of nuts. For her there is also such a thing as too many almonds, which interferes with the chocolaty taste. The ideal level of almonds is shown in the exhibit.

Utility functions are useful in consumer behavior research because they can be estimated with a method called **conjoint analysis.** There are many ways of administering this method. One way is to ask consumers to rank order a series of brands, all in the same product category. As shown in Good Practice 13.1, each candy bar in the conjoint study can be represented by a profile. Good Practice 13.1 shows four different profiles with five candy bar attributes: amount of almonds, amount of chocolate, amount of sugar, number of calories, and price. To construct Exhibit 13.5, Melanie would be asked to make trade-offs between the group of four candy bars, each represented by a profile. As part of the data collection task, she would rank order the four candy bar profiles. From the rank ordering,

Exhibit 13.5 can be drawn. Such a figure can be constructed for an individual consumer, for a market segment, or for an entire market.

Imagining the consumer as an individual utility maximizer is a weak strategy to adopt in marketing to members of interdependent cultures in the Asian NICs or in most developing countries. Buyers in these cultures will seek out more social information and are more likely to be interested in outcomes that produce or reinforce trust and relationships between buyers and sellers. In highly egalitarian cultural environments (e.g., Scandinavia), decisions may also emerge through a consensus-building process in which the differing preferences of several people in a household or business buying group are worked out.[27]

Constructive Choice Processes

Two human characteristics—bounded rationality and limiting processing capacity—have led many researchers to believe that consumers construct the most reasonably complex or novel choices as situations demand. People often lack well-defined preferences; instead, they construct them as needed. Consumers use **constructive choice processes** because they bring multiple goals to their consumer decisions. Furthermore, rather than adopting one invariant approach to solving choice problems, consumers use a variety of approaches, again often developed on the spot. Consumers may also develop representations of the decisions they face on the spot by structuring or restructuring the information they consider. Moreover, consumers' decision-making processes may change as they learn more about their options; moreover, the decision processes will be sensitive to the way problems are conceived in local terms. Thus, preferences will often be context dependent. Nevertheless, we can describe some of the ways consumers make decisions and some of circumstances in which these choice processes apply.[28]

Two traditional ways to describe how consumers make choices is to divide them into compensatory and noncompensatory models. In **compensatory models,** *consumers assess the importance of each brand or product attribute and assign a subjective value to each attribute level. Then, consumers consider the alternatives multiplying each attribute's subjective value times its importance weight and adding across these sums to obtain an overall value for each brand or product option.* A brand may be low on attribute; but it may be chosen anyway as long as it is very satisfying on another important attribute. The second attribute compensates for the low rating on the first attribute. This model of choice closely resembles the multiattribute attitude model.

Not all attributes are treated equally. For example, consumers seem to be more resistant to trading off some quality to get a better price than accepting a higher price to get better quality. People may resist trading off attributes that encode core values like freedom, health, or family against other less important attributes. Some consumers may also distinguish between goals like pleasure and resources like time or money when they make trade-offs. Unfortunately we do not know too much about the limits on attribute trade-offs and certainly less about this cross-culturally.[29]

Product-rating schemes offered in magazines like *Consumer Reports* in the United States or *Products* in Japan, by prestigious testing services like *Stiftung Warentest* in Germany, and by some electronic agents on websites invite and assist consumers to engage in compensatory decision making. Compensatory models are relatively effortful to use; hence, consumers are more likely to use them as the desire for making good choices increases. Also, consumers may use compensatory models for highly involving, highly risky, or emotionally important choices. Similarly, they are less likely to use them as the number of alternatives increases. Product-rating guides help to simplify the process for consumers.[30]

Consumer Heuristics

A **heuristic** is a *general rule of thumb that consumers use to simplify a decision task.* It is a sort of short cut. We discussed some memory-related heuristics in Chapter 12. A variety of noncompensatory decision models illustrate the idea of consumer heuristics. In one variety of heuristics, the **noncompensatory model,** *a low rating on a single attribute can eliminate a brand from consideration.* In this case, high ratings on other attributes do not compensate for low ratings on the first attribute. Robert Frost describes this process of human decision making in his poem "The Road Not Taken" (see Consumer Chronicles 13.1). When two roads diverge in a yellow wood, the narrator is "sorry I could not travel both." Both alternatives are tempting, and he has a feeling that he will never have a chance to experience the road that he does not select today. In the end he chooses the road that "was grassy and wanted wear." He takes the "one less traveled" and finds that this one, simple decision changes his life: "That has made all the difference." This poem illustrates a noncompensatory strategy. The narrator believes that amount of wear on the path is the most important attribute. He wants to take a path that few have taken. Perhaps it is this path that leads the narrator to become an artist, a poet. The bittersweet tone of the poem captures the idea that consumers often use noncompensatory strategies to make choices that are laden with negative emotions. In this case, by focusing on the "less traveled" attribute, the poet avoids considering the possibility that sacrificing the other path forfeits other valued attributes, since he does not consider them in his decision.[31]

Noncompensatory models are likely to be used in many simple and low-involvement consumer decisions because they offer shortcuts and reduce cognitive effort. However, they are likely to be used in very important choices as well, but for a different set of reasons. When choosing homes, spouses, jobs, careers, and what road to take, people construct choices as they go along, and information is often ambiguous and untidy. Moreover, these choices are apt to operate at the gut-feeling or gestalt level and do not translate neatly into attributes and attribute weights.

Satisficing Decisions

Consumers often make purchase decisions in situations in which information about some alternatives is not available. The opening vignette offers one example. In some circumstances consumers may have information about an attribute, but they don't know what it means. For instance, Tom believes that oat bran is healthy to eat because it lowers cholesterol levels. However, he is not certain exactly how much oat bran he has to eat each day to lower his cholesterol.

To provide a description of this kind of real-life decision making, Nobel Prize–winning economist Herbert Simon proposed the idea that people satisfice rather than optimize when they are making decisions.[32] In **satisficing decisions,** *consumers choose an alternative that satisfies their most important goals. Other goals might be sacrificed.*[33] As an example, consider the time that Tom rented his first apartment, after finishing university. He considered price and location to be the most important attributes. Space and safety were also key choice criteria, but he didn't consider them to be as important as the first two attributes. Tom looked at four or five apartments, but he certainly didn't make an exhaustive search of every available apartment complex. In the end he rented an apartment that passed his cutoff point on price and location. Stated another way, Tom considered options that passed a predetermined cutoff point; those that did not received no further consideration. Satisficing is the choice process that Tom used to find and rent that first apartment. Such abbreviated search behavior is adaptive, because it saves time, an important consumer resource. However, this adaptiveness is different from the maximization described under expected utility theory. In most circumstances, expected utility theory represents an ideal model of consumer decision making, whereas satisficing theory is more descriptive of how consumers actually make choices.

Elimination by Aspects

Another kind of noncompensatory consumer heuristic is to *eliminate some options on the basis of a single attribute.* Tom is shopping for a soccer ball in a large sporting goods store. First, he eliminates all balls that are not black and white. Second, he eliminates all balls that cost more than $50. Third, he eliminates all balls that are not manufactured in the United States. He continues with this process until all balls, save one, are eliminated. Under this **elimination by aspects** strategy, a consumer could reject alternatives by starting with the most important attribute first, but this does not have to be the case. A consumer could also start with any random attribute rather than with the most important. Elimination is a consumer choice strategy that is adopted to deal with the information overload that exists in many markets.

The cartoon below shows an example of elimination by aspects. Here, the man in the foreground decides to halt his journey where he stands. If he proceeds any further, his cell phone will be out of range. The traveler believes that the attribute—keeping within range of his cell phone—is the most important factor to consider when choosing the path and extent of his journey. When his cell phone limit is reached, he does not continue. That is, the

"I can't go any farther. My cell phone will be out of range."

traveler does not appear to make trade-offs between a set of attributes. The traveler is not willing to sacrifice on the cell phone attribute to receive some benefit that may accrue from some other attribute (e.g., reaching the summit that beckons in the background).

When decision makers apply the **conjunctive rule,** they *eliminate any alternatives that fall outside of certain predefined boundaries* (as in the cell phone example). Consider another example: When a college selects its incoming student body, it may decide to reject all those applicants whose combined SAT scores fall below 950. The admissions officers don't even examine other attributes (e.g., grade point average, letters of recommendation) if this one criterion is not met. In other words, no trade-offs are made. This conjunctive rule is also an example of satisficing rather than optimizing.[34]

Inference Making

Inference making is another kind of consumer short cut. It enables consumers to make *a choice without complete information by generalizing from the information they know.* We described several examples and types of consumer inferences in Chapter 12. Consider the example in the opening vignette of this chapter. Tom infers missing attribute values from the information he does have. For example, he assumes that a Minolta brand camera can do all of the things that digital cameras usually do. That is, he uses his intuition, assuming something like the average value of the attributes for other brands in the category probably apply to the Minolta camera as well. He also uses the Minolta brand name as an indicator of quality, and he uses the brand name as a cue to infer missing information. In the end, he is fairly pleased with his purchase, even though he took some shortcuts. Notice how inference making illustrates how a consumer constructs preferences as needed rather than applying a stable set of well-defined ones.[35]

List Making

List making is another simplification strategy that consumers use. Before going grocery shopping, Melanie always makes out a list. That way, she won't forget anything, and she won't buy something that she doesn't really need. Even when Melanie shops on the Internet she uses lists. When following this method, consumers have already made detailed selections, even before arriving at the store. A list becomes a kind of script. It tells the consumer what to do, what paths to take at the store or at the website.

A list can contain products or brand names, but it can also contain attributes. For example, when Brian is deciding what college to attend, he might make an elaborate list. One college offers small classes. Another is near the beach, but not so near a large urban area. A third college has the reputation for placing its graduates with prestigious engineering firms, and so forth. After sorting through all of the information on the list, he makes a final decision. Such list making implies that a compensatory strategy, rather than a noncompensatory strategy, is being employed. That is, list making helps consumers to make difficult trade-offs between a relatively large set of attributes. If one of Brian's colleges is low on one attribute (e.g., not near beach), that doesn't necessarily eliminate that college from consideration. Other attributes possessed by the college (e.g., good placement record) may compensate for the relatively weak performance on the first attribute. Under this kind of list-making strategy, consumers make explicit trade-offs, just as they do in the conjoint example above (related to almonds versus chocolate content of candy bars).

Relational Heuristics

Others to whom one is accountable may evaluate consumer decisions. This is often true in households and businesses (see Chapter 14) but also in interdependent cultures in the NICs or the less affluent world that devalue individualism. Accountability and the need to justify decisions effect how consumers make them. In some situations people cope with accountability by deferring to the preferences of those to whom they are accountable (elders, spouse, co-workers). Or they may simply choose the status quo option. If the preferences of others are not known or powerful justifications for decisions are required, we might expect consumers to use more elaborate compensatory decision-making strategies. They may search for good reasons to use as justifications for decisions. In this situation the decision maker might *compare the relative advantages and disadvantages of an option to those of other options in a particular background context.* Thus the consumer applies a **relational heuristic** to the choice process. The weightings for relative advantages of different attributes of the options considered will reflect the background context, including perhaps notions about others' preferences.[36]

Prospect Theory

Prospect theory, introduced in Chapter 12, builds on the notion that consumers have to give up something in order to get something back in the marketplace. Prospect theory proposes that people's decisions are based on how they value the potential gains and losses that result from making choices.[37] This theory is based on an individual's value function (see Exhibit 13.6). This function reflects consumers' anticipation of the pleasure or pain associated with a specific decision outcome.[38] The gains or losses are calculated with respect to some reference point. A crucial aspect of prospect theory is that the value function for gains is quite different than that for losses. As shown in Exhibit 13.6, the value function for gains appears above the horizontal axis. This gain function is concave and not so steep. In contrast, the loss function lies below the horizontal axis. It is convex and steeper than the corresponding loss function.[39]

Because the value function for losses is steeper than the function for gains, losses loom larger than gains. What this means in practical terms is that *consumers resist giving up things that they already own.* This phenomenon is called the **endowment effect.** When consumers are asked to name a selling price for something they already own, they often

Exhibit 13.6 A Value Function: Gains and Losses

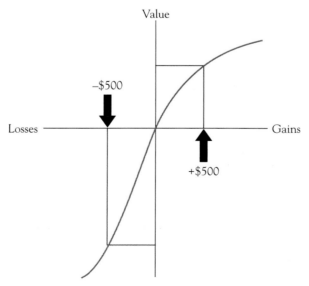

Source: Figure adapted from D. Kahneman and Amos Tversky, "Prospect Theory: An Analysis of Decision under Risk," *Econometrica* 47 (1979), pp. 263–91.

require much more money than they would pay to own the very same item. For example, when a stranger approaches Tom on the street and offers him $45 for tickets to a Belle & Sebastian concert that he has just paid $35 for, Tom rejects the offer. Due to the endowment effect, Tom values the tickets more after he owns them. To give up the tickets is viewed as a loss, and losses are felt more strongly than equivalent gains.[40]

Prospect theory predicts that preferences will depend on how a problem is framed (see Chapter 12). If the reference point is defined in a way that the outcome appears to be a gain, decision makers will be risk averse. In contrast, if the same outcome appears to be a loss, decision makers will be risk seekers. Marketers sometimes make use of consumers' differing perceptions about gains and losses. For instance, a dry cleaner has two ways of presenting a sales promotion. First, the cleaner could advertise a 25 percent price reduction. A second alternative is to offer to clean one shirt free with each order of three shirts. These two promotions offer the same gain to consumers—four shirts cleaned for the price of three. As described by prospect theory, consumers will value the free service more than the discounted service, even though the two promotions involve the same price savings.[41]

Another application of prospect theory is revealed in retail pricing. In general, it is more effective for retailers to promote cash discounts than to implement a policy of surcharges for customers who choose to use credit cards. Consumers perceive cash discounts to be gains (money retained). In contrast, surcharges are perceived as out-of-pocket losses. Even though the pricing structure may be the same, consumers will strive to avoid the surcharges, which are viewed as losses. Prospect theory also explains the retailing tactic of including "suggested retail prices" on all merchandise. Consumers use suggested retail prices to form a reference point (see Exhibit 13.6). Given this reference point, sale prices will seem like savings.[42]

There are limits associated with prospect theory. First, many positive consumer experiences do not involve receiving anything. When Tom takes his nephew, Brian, for a whitewater rafting trip, there is no monetary gain with respect to a reference point (as specified by prospect theory). In situations like this, where no monetary gains are received, it is not clear how to apply or even draw the curves shown in Exhibit 13.6.

A second problem with prospect theory is that it assumes that outcomes can be scaled along a single metric, such as monetary rewards or the risk of a disease (a potential loss). For situations when consumers are forced to make trade-offs between two or more attributes, multiattribute models are more appropriate than prospect theory. When such trade-offs are made among attributes, there is not necessarily an optimal solution.[43] That is, there may be more than one type of value that a consumer derives from a positive outcome. For instance, when Tom and Brian go rafting, they derive at least three kinds of positive outcomes: (1) a close bond between two family members; (2) the aesthetic beauty of the river; and (3) skill-building in rafting. Against these positive outcomes are the costs of the trip, both monetary costs and investments of time. Prospect theory doesn't offer a coherent way to account for this kind of consumer experience, and it doesn't provide a way to explain how consumers make trade-offs when more than one attribute is involved.

This chapter examines how individual consumers make choices. Some choices involve a lot of thought, deliberation, and effort. Other choices are almost automatic and don't require much effort (e.g., low-involvement decisions, quick choices). Consumer attitudes and attitude models and models of consumer choice are two broad ways of understanding

summary

consumer choices. An important point to emphasize is that consumers use a variety of approaches in solving choice problems and select and even construct their approach based on the situation. Constructive choice processes are especially common when consumers face complex or novel choice situations. Decision processes and preferences are typically context dependent.

Attitudes are a product of information acquisition, and they reflect how consumers think and feel. In a sense, attitudes are learned. As such, learning theories (e.g., operant conditioning, classical conditioning) can be used to understand the process of attitude formation. People form attitudes for four reasons: utilitarian function, value-expressive function, ego-defensive function, and knowledge function. In addition, people can form attitudes toward a number of objects, including other people, brands, products, themselves, advertisements, and stores. Important attitude concepts include cognitions, affect, and behavior. These concepts can be combined into three competing hierarchy of effects models, including the standard hierarchy, the low-involvement hierarchy, and the experiential hierarchy. Each is appropriate for understanding a different kind of consumer decision making. Hierarchy of effects models display a Western cultural bias, and other models may be needed to explain attitude formation in non-Western cultural environments.

A number of attitude models and theories exist to describe how consumers make choices. Four important theories are the theory of cognitive dissonance, self-perception theory, social judgment theory, and balance theory. The two main attitude models are the multiattribute model and the elaboration likelihood model. Two widely applied multiattribute models are the Fishbein model and the extended Fishbein model. The main components of the former are beliefs and their evaluations. The latter model is called the theory of reasoned action and adds in components of the social world, including motivation to comply and personal normative beliefs.

A main managerial implication of attitudes is the process of persuasion, as marketers and advertisers are interested in convincing consumers to try their brands. The elaboration likelihood model describes two routes to persuasion: the central route to persuasion and the peripheral route. Under the central route, consumers pay attention to main message arguments. Under the peripheral route, consumers attend to secondary cues like music, or weaker arguments. In different cultural contexts what counts as central and peripheral cues for consumers may vary.

Among the choice models consumers use in decision making are the expected utility theory; consumer heuristics, including satisficing decisions; and prospect theory. Expected utility theory provides an idealized description of how consumers choose. Consumers are hypothesized to select the alternative that maximizes utility, subject to certain constraints. In marketing research, we use conjoint analysis to understand how consumers make trade-offs between two or more relevant attributes.

Two contrasting descriptions of consumer decision making are compensatory and noncompensatory models. In the former, a high score on one can compensate a low score on another attribute. In noncompensatory models there is no compensation. Consumer heuristics describe shortcuts that consumers make to save time and effort. Examples of consumer heuristics include noncompensatory models, inference making, and list making. Satisficing too presents a shortcut alternative to utility maximization. It describes how consumers are often satisfied with choices that are good enough.

Prospect theory, through the concept of value function, describes the different ways that consumers perceive gains and losses. In general, losses loom larger than gains. What this means in practical terms is consumers resist giving up things that they already own, and this gives rise to the endowment effect.

1. Describe a choice that you have made in each of the following categories:
    a. A career choice
    b. A low-involvement consumer choice
    c. A high-involvement consumer choice
    d. A quick choice
    e. A choice relating to your friends
    f. An academic choice

    How are these choices alike? How are they different? For each choice, describe a model or theory that explains this choice.

2. Look at some ads in a magazine that you usually read. Try to identify ads that make utilitarian appeals, value-expressive appeals, ego-defensive appeals, and knowledge appeals. Also, try to identify ads that have a primary goal to influence:
    a. Consumer cognitions
    b. Consumer emotions
    c. Consumer actions

3. Think of ways your attitude is affected by advertising. As an example, what is your attitude toward the Bud frogs commercials? Do you buy Budweiser beer? Why or why not? What do you think of the Budweiser frogs and lizards? What benefits does Budweiser achieve from this kind of advertising? What kinds of liabilities are there? Why

does Budweiser use a different ad agency for the lizard commercials than it uses for the frog commercials?

4. Distinguish between the standard hierarchy, low-involvement hierarchy, and experiential hierarchy. In what sense are these models competitors, and in what sense are they complementary? Think of purchases that you have made to construct elaborate examples of each hierarchy in action. Are other hierarchies needed to account for consumer responses to stimuli in the marketplace? Explain.

5. Why are marketing managers interested in consumer attitudes? What evidence do we have that attitudes exist?

6. As far as you are concerned, which element of the hierarchy of effects model (affect, behavior, or cognition) do you believe has the strongest influence over you when you want to buy a CD or DVD player? When you take a special friend out to lunch? When you take this same friend out to dinner? When you buy a soft drink? When you turn on the radio and a political commentator's voice comes out? In each case, explain your reasoning.

7. Think of a time when someone used the foot-in-the-door approach on you. Did you buy the product? Why or why not?

8. Name some celebrity endorsers who are very popular with the public. Why are they popular? Name some celebrity endorsers who have fallen into disfavor with the public. How do you suppose this has affected the sales of the product they endorsed? Did any of the companies stop using these endorsers? Do you believe celebrity endorsement works? If so, under which circumstances?

9. Describe different kinds of consumer heuristics (i.e., shortcuts). Under what examples are these heuristics used to make consumer decisions? Give examples from your own life. Describe a decision situation where you used some shortcuts. Why did you take these shortcuts? Was your resulting decision optimal or satisfying? Why or why not?

10. In plain words describe the Fishbein model and the extended Fishbein model. Contrast these two models. What are the limitations of these models?

You Make the Call
Nebraska Corn-Fed Beef

The Nebraska Cattlemen's Association (NCA) is exploring several international markets for entry under its Nebraska corn-fed beef (NCFB) campaign. The cattle are fed on a ration of corn and corn-products for at least 90 days prior to slaughter, which produces a juicier, better-flavored meat. The association hopes to market its end cuts (e.g., roasts) for which it feels it has a price advantage. To produce NCFB-certified meat, certain breeds of cattle with a reputation for producing tough meat are excluded from the program. The cattle are tracked from the cow and calf operations, through the feedlots, and on to the processing facilities to guarantee quality. The NCA believes that the breeding and feeding characteristics of the meat, as well as its USDA "Choice" certification, may attract Polish, Japanese, and Korean consumers. NCFB is attractively packaged and comes with advertising circulars promoting the cowboy image of rural Nebraska. American beef has a positive image in many markets. Japanese grocers sometimes display videos of U.S. cattle ranches at their beef counters. Other products with a Western and American image, such as Levi's jeans and Marlboro cigarettes, have done well in international markets, as have some food products like McDonald's.

Currently, Koreans often import grass-fed Australian beef, and Poles eat the meat of dairy cattle that have passed their milk-producing prime. Neither type of meat can compete in quality with Nebraska corn-fed beef. The NCA proposes a product trial program to demonstrate the improved flavor of corn-fed beef. Funds will be provided to train Polish chefs and meat cutters in the best ways to process NCFB beef, for example. And the association expects that attitudes about Nebraska will work in favor of the product. Images of the American West and the American cowboy figure in its marketing communications.

The beef does contain hormones and is the product of artificial insemination. It is also true that NCFB does not guarantee that the corn is free from genetically modified organisms (GMOs). The association believes that consumer education, government lobbying efforts, and consumer trial may change consumer attitudes about hormones and GMOs that are relatively negative in Europe and Asia.

1. What positive associations do consumers have with Nebraska corn-fed beef that should be reinforced? How should they be reinforced?

2. How should the NCFB program attempt to modify consumer beliefs about competing products?

3. How might balance theory be used to develop marketing communications for NCFB?

4. How might ELM models be employed in the NCFB program's marketing communications to affect behavioral intentions?

For more information about NCFB visit their website at: necornfedbeef.com.

---

1. Gerald Zaltman and Melanie Wallendorf, *Consumer Behavior: Basic Findings and Management Implications* (New York: John Wiley & Sons, 1979).
2. Brian Sternthal and C. Samuel Craig, *Consumer Behavior: An Information Processing Perspective* (Englewood Cliffs, NJ: Prentice-Hall, 1982).
3. Sternthal and Craig, *Consumer Behavior*.
4. Daniel Katz, "The Functional Approach to the Study of Attitudes, *Public Opinion Quarterly* 24 (1960), pp. 315–20.
5. Michael R. Solomon, *Consumer Behavior: Buying, Having, and Being* (Upper Saddle River, NJ: Prentice Hall, 1999).
6. Marieke de Mooij, *Global Marketing and Advertising: Understanding Cultural Paradoxes* (Thousand Oaks, CA: Sage Publications, 1998), pp. 271–75.
7. de Mooij, *Global Marketing and Advertising*, pp. 166–72.
8. L. Festinger, *A Theory of Cognitive Dissonance* (New York: Row, Peterson, 1957), p. 3.
9. Festinger, *A Theory of Cognitive Dissonance*.
10. Zaltman and Wallendorf, *Consumer Behavior*.
11. D. Bem, "Self-Perception Theory," in *Advances in Experimental Social Psychology*, L. Berkowitz, ed. (New York: Academic Press, 1972), Vol. 6, pp. 1–62.
12. Solomon, *Consumer Behavior*.
13. Muzafer Sherif and Carl I. Hovland, *Social Judgment: Assimilation and Contrast Effects in Communication and Attitude Change* (New Haven, CT: Yale University Press, 1961).

14. Fritz Heider, *The Psychology of Interpersonal Relations* (New York: Wiley, 1958).

15. Sam Walker, "Home-Run Heroes Bring in Few Endorsements," *The Wall Street Journal,* October 21, 1998, pp. B1, B4.

16. Zaltman and Wallendorf, *Consumer Behavior.*

17. de Mooij, *Global Marketing and Advertising,* pp. 267–68, 281.

18. Martin Fishbein, "A Theory of Reasoned Action: Some Applications and Implications," in *Nebraska Symposium on Motivation,* Vol. 27, H. Howe and M. Page, eds. (Lincoln, NE: University of Nebraska Press, 1980), pp. 65–116.

19. Sternthal and Craig, *Consumer Behavior.*

20. Richard E. Petty, John T. Cacioppo, and David Schumann, "Central and Peripheral Routes to Advertising Effectiveness: The Moderating Role of Involvement," *Journal of Consumer Research* 10 (1984), pp. 135–47.

21. Margaret C. Campbell and Amna Kirmani, "Consumers' Use of Persuasion Knowledge: The Effects of Accessibility and Cognitive Capacity on Perceptions of an Influence Agent," *Journal of Consumer Research* 27 (June 2000), pp. 69–83; Marian Friestad and Peter Wright, "The Persuasion Knowledge Model: How People Cope with Persuasion Attempts," *Journal of Consumer Research* 21 (June 1994), pp. 1–31; and Hazel R. Marcus and Shinobu Kitayama, "Culture and the Self: Implications for Cognition, Emotion, and Motivation," *Psychological Review* 98 (April 1991), pp. 224–53.

22. Russell H. Fazio, Martha C. Powell, and Carol J. Williams, "The Role of Attitude Accessibility in the Attitude-to-Behavior Process," *Journal of Consumer Research* 16 (December 1989), pp. 280–88.

23. de Mooij, *Global Marketing and Advertising,* pp. 130–32, 172.

24. James R. Bettman, Mary Frances Luce, and John W. Payne, "Constructive Consumer Choice Processes," *Journal of Consumer Research* 25 (December 1998), pp. 187–217.

25. Scott Plous, *The Psychology of Judgment and Decision Making* (Philadelphia: Temple University Press, 1993).

26. Plous, *The Psychology of Judgment and Decision Making.*

27. de Mooij, *Global Marketing and Advertising,* pp. 130–33.

28. Bettman, Luce, and Payne, "Constructive Consumer Choice Processes."

29. Jonathan Baron and Mark D. Spranca, "Protected Values," *Organizational Behavior and Human Decision Processes* 70 (April 1997), pp. 1–16; Ravi Dhar and Itamar Simonson, "Consumption Context Effects on Choice: Matching versus Balancing," working paper, School of Management, Yale University, New Haven, CT, (1997); Stephen M. Nowlis and Itamar Simonson, "Attribute-Task Compatibility as a Determinant of Consumer Preference Reversals," *Journal of Marketing Research* 34 (May 1997), pp. 205–18; and Philip E. Tetlock, "The Impact of Accountability in Judgment and Choice: Toward a Social Contingency Mode," in *Advances in Experimental Social Psychology,* vol. 25, Mark P. Zanna, ed. (San Diego, CA: Academic Press, 1992), pp. 331–76.

30. Bettman, Luce, and Payne, "Constructive Consumer Choice Processes"; John Clammer, "Aesthetics of the Self: Shopping and Social Being in Contemporary Urban Japan," in *Lifestyle Shopping: The Subject of Consumption,* Ron Shields, ed. (London: Routledge, 1995), pp. 195–215; and de Mooij, *Global Marketing and Advertising,* p. 274.

31. Mary Frances Luce, "Choosing to Avoid: Coping with Negatively Emotion-Laden Consumer Decisions," *Journal of Consumer Research* 24 (March 1998), pp. 409–33; and Mary Frances Luce, James R. Bettman, and John W. Payne, "Choice Processing in Emotionally Difficult Decisions," *Journal of Experimental Psychology: Learning, Memory and Cognition* 23 (March 1997), pp. 384–405.

32. Simon, "Rational Choice and the Structure of the Environment."

33. Plous, *The Psychology of Judgment and Decision Making.*

34. Plous, *The Psychology of Judgment and Decision Making.*

35. Susan M. Broniarczyk and Joseph W. Alba, "The Role of Consumers' Intuitions in Inference Making," *Journal of Consumer Research* 21 (December 1994), pp. 393–407; Gary T. Ford and Ruth Ann Smith, "Inferential Beliefs in Consumer Evaluations: An Assessment of Alternative Processing Strategies," *Journal of Consumer Research* 14 (December 1987), pp. 363–71; Joel Huber and John M. McCann, "The Impact of Inferential Beliefs on Product Evaluations," *Journal of Marketing Re-*

search 19 (August 1982), pp. 324–33; and William T. Ross and Elizabeth H. Creyer, "Making Inferences about Missing Information," *Journal of Consumer Research* 19 (June 1992), pp. 14–25.

36. Luce, "Choosing to Avoid"; Itamar Simonson and Amos Tversky, "Choice in Context: Trade-Off Contrast and Extremeness Aversion," *Journal of Marketing Research* 29 (August 1992), pp. 281–95; and Amos Tversky and Itamar Simonson, "Context-Dependent Preferences," *Management Science* 39 (October 1993), pp. 1179–89.

37. D. Kahneman and Amos Tversky, "Prospect Theory: An Analysis of Decision under Risk," *Econometrica* 47 (1979), pp. 263–91.

38. Michal Ann Strahilevitz and George M. Zinkhan, "The Utility Consumers Derive from Giving: A Model of Donation Behavior," working paper 7, University of Georgia, Athens, 1998.

39. Plous, *The Psychology of Judgment and Decision Making.*

40. Plous, *The Psychology of Judgment and Decision Making.*

41. Plous, *The Psychology of Judgment and Decision Making.*

42. Robert Thaler, "Mental Accounting and Consumer Choice, *Marketing Science* 4 (1985), pp. 199–214; and Plous, *The Psychology of Judgment and Decision Making.*

43. Plous, *The Psychology of Judgment and Decision Making.*

end notes

Chapter 14

Learning Objectives

After completing this chapter, you should be able to:

- Characterize organizations using six main dimensions: membership structure, organization, resources, motives and goals, roles, and culture.

- Understand how organizational structure and characteristics relate to consumption activities.

- Identify the major segments of organizational buyers and the basic types of purchases.

- Explain how household structure and characteristics relate to consumption activities.

- Recognize the important role of the family life cycle in consumption activities.

- Distinguish decision roles and decision-making styles in households and organizations.

- Describe a variety of consuming collectives besides households and business organizations.

Organization and Household Consumer Behaviors

A Navajo Family Buys a Pickup Truck

Ruby had been sitting in her mother's *hoogan* (the traditional octagonal Navajo house) for several hours now, helping her mother comb raw wool. They had not spoken in over an hour. Baby Ben played on the floor with a twist of wool. Without looking up, Ruby said to her mother, Agnes, "Kids wouldn't have to walk so far to the school bus stop if we had a truck." Her mother nodded her head in agreement. They went on combing the wool in silence.

Several days later Ruby was visiting her sister Edna to help dip sheep. After several hours of herding sheep through the murky water of the sheep-dip tank (to remove parasites), Ruby remarked to Edna, "Saw a used red truck over at the Begay spread." Edna said she'd seen it too. Ruby noted it sure would be good to help those kids get back and forth to the bus stop. Edna did not reply. Bertha, their grandmother, nodded.

A few weeks later at the Laundromat in Chinle, Arizona, Agnes and her sister Betty were taking clothes from the dryer. Agnes mentioned the secondhand truck for sale over at the Begay spread and how it was sometimes hard to get those kids to walk to the bus stop.

Several weeks later when Betty sold a rug to the trader at Tec Nos Pos, Arizona, she passed Agnes some money with the suggestion that she "get something for those kids." About this time, Agnes received a money order from her son Hosteen, working construction in Los Angeles. Grandmother Bertha and Edna returned from a trip to Windowrock, Arizona, with some money that Edna had received for pawning some old jewelry she had inherited from her mother. When Edna learned that Bertha

and Agnes had received some money, she sold some lambs to the cooperative down in Chinle. Some days later, Agnes urged Ruby and Edna to stop by the Begay's spread. She advised them to check in on old Abigail Begay. To no one's surprise, Ruby and Edna returned to Agnes' *hoogan* with the red 1995 pickup purchased from the Begays.

Overview

The opening vignette helps us start thinking about groups and their purchase and consumption activities. A **group** simply refers to *two or more individuals who have certain implicitly or explicitly defined relationships to one another such that their behavior is interdependent.* In this chapter we will talk about two categories of groups: organizational consumers and families and households. In Chapter 15 we will talk about reference groups, a special category of groups.

Understanding groups is crucial in understanding consumer behavior because, as the vignette illustrates, many consumption activities involve groups rather than individuals. In fact, almost all consumer behavior involves groups at one or more of the stages in the circle of consumer behavior. For example, an individual acquisition decision may be followed by group consumption (e.g., individual purchase of the ingredients of a meal for a dinner party), or group acquisition by individual consumption (Mom decides to purchase a pet for Junior), and so on. Even decisions that appear on the surface to be individual decisions often are not. For example, you may not be surprised to learn that North American students often report that their parents actively participated in their first automobile purchase.

The opening vignette illustrates things many of us already know from experience with groups. First, groups vary in terms of their **membership structure.** There are many different kinds of consuming entities, including business organizations, households, buying clubs, and even gangs. As the vignette suggests, households made up of family members are significant consumption groups cross-culturally. Second, groups vary in terms of their decision-making style or organization. Family participants in the group decision may vary. Thus, the Navajo Indian family mobilizes and pools resources from a network of people related through women. In the case of the Navajo family the mobilization of resources to buy a truck is egalitarian and takes time and patience. The decision-making style for your household's purchase of an automobile might be quite different. Third, groups mobilize resources in order to realize their consumption choices. The Navajo family pools wages and income from selling wool, rugs, and pawned jewelry, for example. The group's resources and mechanisms for mobilizing resources both facilitate and constrain consumption. Fourth, group consumption choices often involve a mix of motives or goals. Group consumption choices include practical and purposeful behaviors, symbolic and status concerns, and habits of which consumers are often unaware. Fifth, group members, like Ruby, Edna, and Agnes in the vignette, play different roles in the purchase process. Sixth, groups have a culture that influences their purchase and consumption behaviors. In seeking to understand, predict, and manage group purchase behaviors, these six elements need to be understood regardless of whether we are dealing with households and families or purchasing groups within business organizations. Marketers and consumer advocates should be aware of these factors and anticipate their influence on group consumption decisions, as illustrated in Industry Insights 14.1, for example.

In the first section of this chapter we will overview some of the general characteristics of organizational and domestic groups that are significant in analyzing their consumer behaviors. We will discuss organizational consumers, beginning with a discussion of group culture and identity. Next we will describe some characteristics of organizational buyers and types of organizational purchases and discuss the three major segments of organizational consumers.

The next major section of the chapter focuses on families and households. The first part focuses on different compositions and structures for households, trends in household structure, patterns of coresidence, and the concept of the family life cycle. The next part focuses on the range of domestic group activities that have implications for marketers. The final part of the discussion of domestic groups is dedicated to distinguishing both roles and decision-making styles in the household decision processes. The chapter concludes with a brief description of consuming collectives other than organizational consumers and domestic groups.

Group Structure and Characteristics

One way to think about groups is in terms of their membership structure and characteristics. Important structural considerations include size; formality; voluntary or involuntary membership; primary or secondary interpersonal contact; and affect.

Group Size

Group size is a structural dimension that may vary over the phases of the circle of consumption. One family member may be the sole decision maker for routine purchases. In a large organization, a small purchasing group or even a single individual may also have decision authority for a variety of purchases, even though they constitute a significant outlay of funds. A kin group may share durable goods purchased by a single family, such as the Navajo family's truck. Married siblings and their families may purchase and share a vacation home.[1]

For marketers, another aspect of size is the **purchasing power** of the group. For example, firms are often interested in identifying large groups that make large aggregate purchases. The Center for the Persuasive Arts in San Antonio, Texas, competes for all of the marketing communications needs of corporate and government clients. Airbus Industrie and Boeing compete for national airline orders. Ford Motor uses fleet sales to corporate buyers to increase Ford Taurus sales relative to rival Honda Accord. Maine Iron Works sells one product, naval destroyers, to one large customer, the U.S. government, although it is totally dependent on government contracts.

Group Formality

Another way in which we can classify the structure of consuming groups is in terms of formality; groups may be more or less formal or informal. **Formal groups** are *bound together by a contractual relationship*. For example, marriage, birth and baptismal certificates, wills, and titles to property provide formal bases for the existence of families and households. Employees of business organizations are often bound by contracts specifying their duties. Other documents stipulate compensation, health benefits, pensions, and other items of value they may receive from the organization.

Informal groups are not bound by such formal ties, but may be *identified by regular interaction, common lifestyle, or interests*. Market segments constitute informal groups. Informal groups may be significant to consumers or as consuming entities. Being a devotee of hip-hop or world beat music entails significant purchase behaviors and consumption styles, although no one formally signs up to participate in these communities and there is little joint purchase behavior. We discuss the influence of some informal groups in Chapters 6 and 15.

Voluntary or Involuntary Membership

Membership in consuming groups may be **voluntary** or **involuntary.** All people are involuntary members of at least some groups. No one chose his or her culture, race, social class, or family; yet membership in involuntary groups, which might also include a church or school, may influence the person's consumption patterns and preferences. The impact of involuntary group membership on consumption patterns is extreme in the case of military personnel, prison inmates, nursing home patients, and other members of **total institutions.** Total institutions *make their members' most basic as well as discretionary consumption choices.* Such groups have often attracted the interests of marketers hoping to cater to their aggregate needs or social policy advocates eager to change their consumption regimes. A recent U.S. court case ruling in favor of inmates seeking redress from the effects of secondary cigarette smoke in jail is an example.

Exhibit 14.1 indicates that voluntary and involuntary groups can be either formal or informal. Examples in each category are provided. Corporate employees belong to formal organizations where membership is voluntary. Public school students belong to a formal organization and sometimes participate involuntarily in consumption behaviors, such as wearing school uniforms. Members of families and market segments are informal groups in which membership is involuntary. Fans are voluntary members of an informal group, unless of course they join a fan club, which is a formal group.

Exhibit 14.1 Kinds of Groups

	Formality	
Membership	Formal	Informal
Voluntary	Corporation Religious congregation Social service organization Youth organization	Fan culture Brand tribe Brand-loyal shopper Disability group
Involuntary	Nursing home Public school Prison Doomsday cult	Family, ethnic group Culture, nation Social class Market segment

Primary and Secondary Groups

The structure of consumption groups may be distinguished by whether they are primary or secondary. *Groups characterized by frequent interpersonal contact* are referred to as **primary groups.** *Groups characterized by limited interpersonal contact* are called **secondary groups.** Primary consumption groups include the household and family. Primary groups play an important role in consumer socialization, discussed in depth later in the chapter; they instill core values that guide a person's consumer behaviors throughout his or her life. Secondary groups like corporations, social clubs, professional organizations, or groups like supporters of a summer arts program influence values and consumption behaviors but not so fundamentally as primary groups.

Affect

One additional aspect of groups that should not be neglected is the important cement provided by **affect** between group members. Affect softens the role of personal self-interest in purchase consumption decisions; group members compromise self-interest to maintain long-term relationships. *Love, attraction, commitment, and emotional support* are characteristics that motivate considerable consumer behavior in households. Affect plays a role even in relationships between industrial buyers and sellers.[2]

Organizational Culture, Identity, and Consumption Activities

Organizational Culture

Organizational culture refers to the meanings organizational members share about the organization—how individuals make sense of the organization. We can define group or **organizational culture** as *the pattern of shared values and beliefs that help individuals understand organizational functioning and thus provide norms for behavior in the organization.*[3] Organizations are not simply economic groups, they vary in their expressive and

MARKETING

Source: Scott Adams, *Build a Better Life by Stealing Office Supplies: Dogbert's Big Book of Business,* New York: Harper, 1994.

symbolic aspects as well. Understanding organizational culture, like the culture of other consumer groups, is useful in developing strategies to target organizational buyers.

An organization's culture often manifests itself to outsiders in terms of its reputation or image. For example, the corporate images of the largest automobile manufacturers—General Motors, Ford, DaimlerChrysler, Toyota, and Volkswagen—are distinct and diverse. The different images reflect different organizational philosophy and culture with regard to product, quality, styling, and marketing.[4]

Organizational culture often reflects more general cultural values. For example, the organizational philosophy of Amway Corporation is rooted in the American Dream. This very successful company, based on personal sales of home-cleaning products, promotes the idea that every individual can be successful through hard work and competition. How might these values affect marketing strategy to this firm?

Any given organization is likely to comprise multiple cultures, such as professional, management, or technical subcultures. A study of technical professional company employees in the Silicon Valley of California illustrates that multiple cultures cut across an organization.[5] Cartoonists often poke fun at marketing subculture, for example, as shown on page 500. Looking for multiple cultures within organizations can be useful for ensuring effective targeting and positioning.

Organizations socialize new members into the culture to achieve a sense of organizational identity and commitment and to enable coordinated action. This socialization occurs through mechanisms that create and convey organizational culture. Mission statements, organizational stories, slogans, rituals, and other symbolic processes help create the organization's culture. For example, there may be an unwritten corporate ethos: "If you've got anything that is controversial, you just don't bring it up."[6] Sometimes the symbolic processes that help create the culture are very subtle and difficult to uncover. Other times, as with dress codes, they are so much a part of the environment that they are inescapable. Three tools for creating and conveying culture are worth some special attention: (1) corporate mission statements, (2) organizational stories, and (3) performances and rituals.

Mission Statements

Corporate **mission statements** help *create and convey organizational culture.* Contrast the mission statements of two familiar apparel companies that offer casual and well-styled clothing, The Gap and Esprit. The business mission of The Gap is to offer well-styled clothes at affordable prices in a friendly environment. The culture at The Gap encourages responsibility to society through a companywide commitment to an in-house community program, but the focus of the culture is on consistent quality, low price, and helpful service. The business mission of Esprit is quite different. Susie Tompkins, founder of the company, was quoted as saying, "Profits are a means for Esprit to stay socially responsible; my aim is that Esprit inspires good values." When asked what the aim of Esprit was, Tompkins stated, "To have a solid business with a strong emphasis on humanistic values." The commitment reflected in Esprit's mission statement both to employees and customers is "Be informed. Be involved. Make a difference."[7] This mission statement is displayed in all employee staff rooms in the retail stores, and all employees are aware of Esprit's socially conscious philosophy. How might these differences in mission affect marketing to these two organizations?

Organizational Stories

Organizational stories are another important way of conveying a firm's culture.[8] Stories, like the myths discussed in Chapter 5, explain and give meaning to the everyday world. An example of how stories are used in one organization is provided in Industry Insights 14.2. Stories help maintain cohesion and provide guidelines by sharing legends of the company to new employees in a powerful way. Stories often portray the organization in heroic terms to members and outsiders. Stories don't typically tell about values and feelings directly; instead, their meaning is couched in symbolic terms.[9]

Both households and companies with strong cultures are adept at recognizing and creating situational heroes. **Heroes** are those *individuals who do extraordinary things under the circumstances and who embody the culture's ethic of success.* An example of a story that features a situational hero and also embodies household values and beliefs is provided in Consumer Chronicles 14.1.[10]

The business press often portrays successful CEOs in heroic terms. For a U.S. company, the situational hero may be the sales manager who through an extraordinary feat of

Belief in the Importance of Experience in the Field

The Agency for International Development (AID) is a highly professional, relatively high-status agency. In-depth interviews with 19 officials of this agency revealed numerous stories conveying agency mission and ideals. The most prominent theme was that working in the field is important for understanding the development process and realizing the agency's mission. What's interesting about this is that the bulk of the work of the permanent staff is done in Washington, DC. Work in the field is more a symbol of professional identity than a description of activities.

Source: Juliane Mahler, "The Quest for Organizational Meaning: Identifying and Interpreting the Symbolism in Organizational Stories," Administration and Society *20 (November 1988), pp. 344–68.*

Yankee ingenuity, timing, and finesse manages to win a big account away from the foreign competition. The story is told and retold again and again, with embellishment. The story and the hero remind members of the organization that it can triumph over strong competitors by holding onto the values of that organizational culture.

Performances and Rituals

Groups need a sense of identity, in addition to other kinds of resources, for their survival. Like individuals, they require tangible symbols of their status and well-being. To this end, groups typically engage in expressive consumption activities through which members communicate to one another and to others information about their status and well-being. Thus, groups engage in performances and rituals, especially life transition rituals. **Performances** help to *express values, beliefs, status, and well-being* at different times during the year and in different ways. **Life transition rituals** *acknowledge changes in status and reassure members of the organization's continued well-being.*[11]

Among U.S. business organizations, a good example of a performance that reflects organizational culture is casual dress on Fridays. Research in an insurance company showed that employees felt casual dress revealed management's trust in employees and projected a progressive image to customers, although some felt it was an imposition and others that women's preferences were not taken into account. At a more general level, the casual dress policy displays an organizational culture more tolerant of individual differences than one imposing a rigid policy.

Annual performances include corporate retreats, dinners, and parties. Among selling organizations, such as Avon or Amway, award celebrations for top sellers are not uncommon. The presentation involves a ceremony where all work comes to a halt. Although the ceremony involves some humor, it is a very serious event that makes corporate values clear to everyone and provides signs of belonging to the culture.[12] Roasts, retirement parties, Outward Bound excursions, and the like provide examples of life transition rituals undertaken by organizations. By paying attention to organizational performances and rituals, marketers can gain insight into values that may influence purchase behavior.

Organizational Consumers

Organizational consumers constitute enormous, diverse, and complex markets. They may be categorized in a variety of ways as we discuss below.[13] Organizational consumers also share a number of characteristics. Typically, organizations rely on a small number of buyers to fill their needs. Recent moves by big organizational buyers to consolidate suppliers through online auctions are the latest example of this characteristic. Within organizations, buyers are often organized into temporary or permanent **buying centers,** or buying task groups.[14] A buying center includes all those persons involved in the buying decision process, such as the

1. Initiator—the member who identifies a need.
2. Gatekeeper—the member who collects and controls information about the purchase.
3. Decider—the member who determines what product or service to purchase.
4. Buyer or purchasing agent—the member who physically acquires the product or service.
5. Users—the members who consume the product or service.

To market successfully to organizations, salespeople must identify and communicate with the participants in the organizational buying process.[15]

Organizational buyers display other characteristics. Organizational buyers are sometimes geographically concentrated in a region of a country. Good examples include Silicon Valley in northern California, home to many computer and information processing companies; Rotterdam in the Netherlands, home to many important shipping and transport companies; and, Milan, Italy, home to a number of fashion and design firms.

Another characteristic of organizational buyers is professionalism. Industrial goods are purchased by professional purchasing agents; in the United States many belong to the National Association of Purchasing Managers (NAPM), and there are similar organizations in other nations. Specialized organizations like National Association of Buyers Agents in Canada, ORCAB (Organisation des Coopératives d'Achats pour les Artisans du Bâtiment), the National Association of Building Trades Buyers in France, or the international Institute of Chartered Shipbrokers also exist. Associated with professionalism is heightened formality in organizational purchasing and the use of a variety of buying instruments, such as quotations, proposals, purchase contracts, bids, and so forth.

Organizational consumers are often relatively price inelastic. But why should they be relatively insensitive to minor price changes? First, they often buy customized products that are inherently more expensive. Second, many buyers are more concerned with long-term service and supply relationships with their sellers. These relationships help ensure a minimum of costly production downtime and reduce the costs of finding supplies. Third, organizational customers often require certain raw materials regardless of price fluctuations; no matter what, makers of aluminum cans require aluminum and governments require military uniforms, for example. Fourth, organizational demand is derived from the demand for finished consumer goods; petroleum refiners must buy oil to meet consumer demand for gasoline and heating oil.

A final characteristic of organizational buyers that is taking on increasing importance in the global marketplace is close customer-supplier relationships. In business-to-business marketing buyers and sellers seek to extract advantage in the purchase process. However,

Household Heroes

A female head of household of one family describes a story about wedding preparation during World War II. She wanted to sew a wedding gown from an expensive fabric such as silk but could only afford cotton material. An airman engaged in parachute training near her family's farm landed off course in the pasture of the farm. Because he ripped his parachute on landing, he left it behind. She recovered it, was delighted to discover that it was made of silk and constructed an elegant, "expensive looking" wedding gown from the salvaged material. This story is used to communicate the tenacity and ingenuity of the family and is told again and again to convey that the family can "make do" during adversity in creative ways.

Source: Nancy M. Ridgeway and Linda L. Price, "Creativity Under Pressure: The Importance of Consumption Situations on Consumer Product Use," American Marketing Association Proceedings (Summer 1991), pp. 361–68.

Consumer Chronicles 14.1

many firms are finding that to compete effectively internationally, they must build interorganizational alliances to confront similar organizations. Because of the changing marketing environment, ongoing buyer-seller relationships, referred to as *relational exchanges,* have become more common.[16]

Close supplier-customer cooperation is the norm in many nations and provides the industries and governments of such nations with competitive advantages. Newly industrialized countries in the Pacific Rim provide good examples of strong interorganizational alliances. Sometimes these groups are informally organized through the traditional Chinese idea of *guanxi,* loosely translated as "personal connections." And sometimes they are formally organized through interlocking firms like the Korean *chaebol* or Japanese *keiretsu.* Intraindustry alliances are also the norm in traditional businesses in Africa. Firms in a number of European Community countries also prefer intraindustry alliances to the pronounced competition more characteristic of the U.S.[17]

Interorganizational relationships may become critical to company success in different ways. For example, many buying organizations want greater certainty in their relationships with suppliers. In addition, the need for increasingly rapid response to shifting patterns of demand and rising consumer concern with quality mean that industrial consumers must work more closely with suppliers to ensure built-in quality.

If organizations are to develop lasting exchange relationships they must adapt to each other's needs. Organizations adapt to each other because of power or trust.[18] The role of power in interorganizational relationships is very important. **Power** refers to *the ability of one partner in an exchange relationship to impose its preferences on the other party.* Power does not have to be used to be possessed; it is the potential that is important.[19] Power derives from having critical resources and from controlling alternative sources of those resources. Organizations respond to the demands of other organizations that control resources critical to them. We can refer to this as a **power-dependence** situation. Thus, big global retailers like Wal-Mart and Carrefour have the power to impose requirements on their suppliers because of their financial and logistical resources.

Firms also adapt to each other to show their trust and commitment to the relationship. **Trust** refers to *one party's belief in the reliability and integrity of an exchange partner.* **Commitment** refers to *an enduring desire to maintain a valued relationship.* Commitment by industrial buyers to sellers is maintained by the costs of leaving, a perceived lack of alternatives to replace the relationship, and relational and social norms that build trust between buyers and sellers.[20]

Trust- and commitment-based adaptations are often reciprocal: Buyers and sellers adapt to each other. One organization may adapt a product to satisfy a customer. Another organization will adapt production processes to show commitment. These adaptations are also called *asset-specific investments.* They help to maintain buyer-seller relationships because it becomes costly to switch suppliers when such investments have been made. Reciprocal commitments to shared problem solving and information sharing, for example, are not based on power-dependence; instead, they are investments that strengthen relationships between organizations in expectation of positive future outcomes. Informal interorganizational relationships supplement and reinforce formal contracts.[21]

Types of Organizational Purchases

Organizational purchases can be distinguished by what is called their **buy class.**[22] We discuss three basic buy classes: new task buys, modified rebuys, and straight rebuys.

New task buys are relatively rare, but the sale can be very large in dollar terms. The

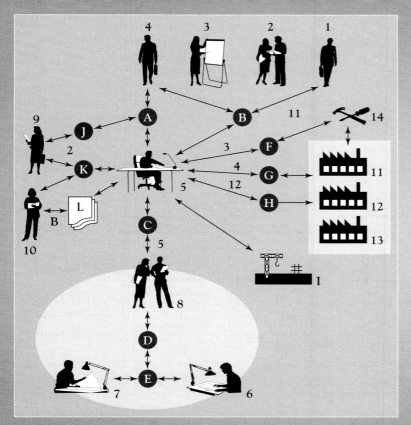

1. President	A. Decision
2. Finance department	B. Discussion of production and sales plans
3. Sales headquarters	C. Production of packing process plan
4. Production chief	D. Request for consultation
5. Production department	E. Production of new product marketing plan
6. Product development department	F. Discussion on design of prototype machine
7. Marketing department	G. Prototype machine order
8. New products development committee	H. Order placement
9. Research staff	I. Overseas machine exhibitions
10. Foreman	J. Request for testing of prototype machine
11. Supplier A	K. Production of basic design
12. Supplier B	L. Production of draft plans
13. Supplier C	
14. Makers design and technical staff	

Source: Adapted from Anonymous, Japan Economic Journal, *23 December 1980, p. 29.*

buying center for these buys tends to be large, solution of the problem is of paramount concern, and economic considerations are secondary. New buys are considered risky, and buyers are willing to consider many alternatives. Engineers often play a key role in these decisions.

A Japanese illustration of an industrial buying center and buying process for a new task buy is shown in Industry Insights 14.3. Note that three key individuals—the president, production chief, and foreman—as well as seven departments—financial department, sales headquarters, production department, new products development committee (NPDC), research staff, product development department, and marketing department—play roles in the process. The roles played by individuals and departments in the buying process differ. The NPDC engages in problem recognition, that is, the existence of an unmet need, and initiates the buying process. The research staff provides a general need description and, in so doing, plays an influencer role in the process. The production department coordinates the supplier's search and solicits proposals, in this case prototype machines, from potential suppliers. The NPDC includes marketing and the product development department, which influence the process through the NPDC. The production department plays a gatekeeping role by soliciting proposals from only a certain number of companies, perhaps including those from which the firm has purchased in the past. Research staff and the production chief play influential roles first in defining product specifications and then in testing the prototypes. Supplier selection and a purchase decision are made only after consultation, and perhaps negotiation, between the production chief, finance department, sales headquarters, and, of course, the president. Once a buy decision has been reached, the production department specifies the order routine for delivery with the supplier. Not shown in Industry Insights 14.3 is the final stage in the buying process, performance review, which determines whether the firm continues to buy from its chosen supplier, thus simplifying subsequent rebuying. If the firm is dissatisfied, a new buy procedure is initiated.[23]

The **straight rebuy** is the most common purchase situation. The purchasing agent is the primary influence and the buying center is very small and quick to decide. To minimize purchase costs (information search, proposal solicitation and evaluation, and so forth), buying organizations may also seek to engage in straight rebuys by identifying reliable sellers that deliver goods of consistent quality on time and for an agreed-upon price, thus minimizing their uncertainty. Loyalty plays a role in the process as well. Selling firms will work to convince their organizational customers of the virtue of engaging in straight rebuys for routine replacement of standardized items on a stable schedule at a stable price. Computerized automated order systems have enabled firms to automate the straight rebuy process in many cases.[24]

The **modified rebuy** has a mix of new task and straight rebuy features. The buying center is somewhat larger and the purchasing agents somewhat less influential than for the straight rebuy. In modified rebuy situations, buyers sometimes revert to straight rebuy behavior, choosing known suppliers and thereby closing off opportunities for outside suppliers.

The extent to which organizations engage in each type of buy class depends on various factors, including environmental (e.g., the rate of technological change in an industry), organizational (e.g., the degree of hierarchy and centralization), and interpersonal (e.g., quality and character of interaction between organizations' selling and buying representatives).[25] Features of the purchase situation, including the newness of the problem to the buyer and the need for information, are the most important determinants of the buy-class decision. Recent research suggests that the size, formality, and membership of the buying center will vary depending on purchase risk, how frequently the organization encounters new tasks, and high information needs.[26]

Major Segments of Organizational Buyers

Organizational buyers can be divided into three main parts, two in the private sector—industrial markets and reseller markets—and one in the public sector, governmental markets. More detailed classification systems exist, such as the Standard Industrial Classification (SIC) system which are of value in segmenting business markets, but we will not discuss these finer distinctions here.

Private Sector: Industrial

The **industrial market** consists of *all the individuals and organizations that acquire goods and services to use in the production of other products or services that are sold, rented, or supplied to others.* Industrial markets, also called *business markets,* include firms involved in agriculture, forestry, fisheries, mining, manufacturing, construction, communications, utilities, banking, finance, insurance, and other services. These customers spend more dollars and consume more different kinds of things than do households and individual consumers.

The individuals who make up industrial buying centers are concerned with a number of factors when making purchase decisions. Like households and other organized consuming groups, they are influenced by environmental, organizational, interpersonal, and individual factors when making buying decisions. For example, a downturn in an index of economic indicators can lead purchase managers to delay purchases of capital equipment, whereas regulatory tightening in the waste disposal industry can lead firms that manage landfills to invest in liners, monitoring equipment, and high-tech separators and chemical cleanup products.

Interpersonal factors such as authority, status, empathy, and persuasiveness influence the purchase process in industrial firms. Information about these processes within the buying center is difficult for salespeople to discover except through long-term relationships with buyers. Finally, individual differences among members of a buying center play a role in the buying process. Buyers can be old-time industry insiders who have heard it all, cost-conscious penny-pinching deal seekers, loyal buyers, cautious quality buyers, information-seeking comparison buyers, and so on. In short, personal factors vary widely; industrial sellers need to know their customers and adapt to their personal styles.

The **reseller market** consists of hundreds of thousands of wholesale firms and millions of retail firms in the United States alone, with many US\$ trillions purchased annually. Much of what was said above about industrial buying centers applies to resellers as well. They too are affected by environmental, organizational, interpersonal and personal factors.

One difference between the two types of markets is the importance of **assortment** to resellers. Resellers handle a variety of products for sale, and do so in part to satisfy consumer expectations of what particular resellers handle. Resellers may compete for customers by opting to carry exclusive assortments, carrying only Gucci or Joan & David shoes or Komatsu or Caterpillar heavy equipment, for example. Resellers may compete for customers by opting to carry a deep assortment, such as specialized boutiques that carry entire product families produced by several suppliers. Office supply stores, beauty products outlets, and kitchenware boutiques are good First World examples. In Africa, many marketplaces feature specialty cloth sellers retailing wax print cloth produced locally and in Dutch, British, and French mills. Resellers may compete for customers by opting to carry a broad assortment—several product lines—consistent with their particular niche. Convenience stores do this. The corner *tienda* in Latin America or *boutiques* in French-speaking Africa often restock their own broad, shallow assortments (*pacotille*). Firms in the First World that supply resellers compete on their ability to deliver assortments appropriate to the resellers' clientele.

Resellers use roughly the same buying process as industrial buyers. For standard items, resellers simply reorder when inventory gets low. If margins or market share erode, buyers may shop around to renegotiate prices with sellers, initiating a modified rebuy process. One organizational difference between industrial buyers and resellers is the important roles played by buyers, such as those who buy apparel for major department store chains, and store managers, such as those in the grocery business. These individuals are key decision makers who make numerous modified rebuys and who can make or break new products in new-buy situations.

ACNielsen reports that for new buys resellers are influenced by evidence of customer demand, well-designed advertising and sales-promotion plans (cooperative advertising,

Private Sector: Reseller Market

advertising aids, sponsorship of in-store demonstrations), and generous financial incentives (return and exchange privileges for the reseller, stockless/just-in-time purchasing that reduces reseller inventory costs, cash discounts, lengthy payment periods, and allowances for merchandise markdowns by the reseller). For example, in the Côte d'Ivoire, local onion wholesalers prefer to purchase from more expensive regional suppliers than less expensive Dutch suppliers, in part because regional suppliers offer more generous credit terms than do the Dutch.[27]

Public Sector

Governmental markets include units at the national (federal or national), regional (state, province, département, canton, autonomous region, tribe), and local (county, parish, city, commune, town, arrondissement, and so on). In many, if not most, countries governments are the largest organizational customers.[28]

Government buying practices are complex and are often frustrating to suppliers. The buying process and bidding practices are often highly formalized. Considerable paperwork is required. The buying center includes multiple layers of bureaucracy, potentially diluting influence. Procurement personnel (buyers) often change. Government buyers' decisions are subject to public review in some nations, especially those of the First World, and sensitive to policy shifts brought about by changing administrations. Since many government branches do not operate in competitive markets, they may initiate purchases because regulatory or watchdog groups approve of them, for example, when purchases from national or minority-owned firms are mandated or because funds are available in the budget and may be withdrawn if not expended.[29] Low-price bids, subject to considerable postcontract revision, are sometimes prioritized at the expense of quality. Delays in government buying decisions are common, but once made, rapid fulfillment is expected.

Families and Households

Description

Domestic groups are perhaps the most widely distributed social unit. They comprise *a primary, involuntary unit of social life between the individual and the community.* Domestic groups vary in formality and the role of affect. Domestic groups are the most important unit of analysis for consumer behavior because they make most acquisition, consumption, and disposition decisions. Consumers in domestic groups decide how to choose household products and services and the amount of time to spend on different tasks and leisure activities. Because so many decisions are made in domestic groups, consumer market segmentation and targeting schemes should take domestic group structure and activities into account.

Domestic groups, families, and households differ. **Families** comprise *individuals related by blood, marriage, adoption, and emotional commitment.* However, we know from our own experience that family includes a broader range of people than the domestic group with whom we regularly reside, interact, and make consumption decisions. **Households** are another group, defined as *coresident, activity groups.* Although the terms *domestic group* and *household* are closely related, they are not necessarily the same. Some domestic groups may not share a home yet share consumption decisions. And households are often made up of family members but may also include **fictive kin,** *individuals informally adopted into a household as family members* and nonkin. One research team found that 70 percent of African-American mothers surveyed in the United States had fictive kin as children.[30] And the mother of one of the authors of this book grew up in a household comprising her mother, grandmother, sister, and a fictive kinsperson, known as M'amselle, to reflect her Belgian heritage. Does your household include any fictive kin? In the rest of the chapter we will use the term *household* rather than *family* or *domestic group*.

Membership in households varies depending on culture, class, ethnicity, and environmental influences. For example, the **nuclear family** composed of *a married couple and their children* is a common household form in many First World contexts, and it is becoming more so in many developing countries. However, the nuclear family was only briefly, if ever, the dominant form of domestic unit, even in the United States. The percentage of nuclear families in Triad nations varies substantially. About 27 percent of U.S. families, 33 percent of Kiwi families (residents of New Zealand), and 62 percent of Japanese families could be described as nuclear families.[31]

In many places in the world, households are often composed of multiple generations of family members, and in some contexts joint households are composed of the families of married adult brothers. These are termed the **extended family** households. The three-generation family was the norm until after WWII in much of east Asia, and the joint household persists in parts of south Asia.

In many parts of the less affluent world, poor households do best by engaging in extending strategies to increase their members. Nieces, nephews, brothers, sisters, and cousins are brought into the household around a married couple or a woman and her children. While extending is difficult and requires strict budgeting to meet expenses on food, the incremental productive labor of family members makes extended family household survival possible.

Membership in Households

As indicated earlier, coresidence or cohabitation is one common way of defining households. In many U.S. states, lengthy coresidence is legally used to bind individuals together as family and define financial and other obligations. However, it is by no means uncommon for members of households to go on extended migrations. For example, long-distance, long-term male labor migration to obtain resources for household use is a fact of life for many poorer families in the LAW nations. Hence, coresidence alone cannot be used to define the household.[32]

Coresidence is significant for marketers because it implies acquisition and maintenance of a dwelling—a home. The home is an increasingly important focus of consumer spending around the world. From a national sample of households in the Netherlands, researchers learned that households spent about 75 hours and over 2,000 guilders (US$862) a year on do-it-yourself maintenance activities. Home furnishing companies and specialized media devoted to the home may be found throughout the Triad countries and in many transitional and developing nations. As average household sizes shrink in the developed world, consumers furnish and maintain more dwellings. An example of a typical ad for home remodeling product that appeals to domestic life as lived is shown on page 510.

Households vary in the focus of their spending. For example, Japanese, Europeans, and middle Easterners tend to focus on interiors; North Americans often focus on exterior appearance as well. A room where guests are received may be the focus of spending in some cultures, such as among Greeks; private rooms may be the focus of spending by others. Some, like the British, neglect bathrooms; others make them splendid. Lower-middle-class North Americans prefer a homey looking dwelling. As suggested in Consumer Chronicles 14.2, expenditures on dwellings sometimes involve conspicuous consumption. And as Consumer Chronicles 14.3 suggests, for some people the home must reflect

Coresidence and Dwellings

By the early 70s around 35 percent of all fishing houses in Ambakandawila [on the isolated north coast of Sri Lanka] were built of brick and tile. By the mid-70s this number had risen to over 50 percent. What was striking about these houses was their very gaudy and loud style and decoration and that their owners always compared them to other houses in Ambakandawila or other near-by villages. Thus A's house would have one more room than B's, and the reason it had one extra room would be simply to have one more room. Or C's house would have a carport not because they had a car or were likely to have a car— nor was a car likely to come to a house on top of a sand dune half a mile from the road—but because no one else in the village had a car-

port. One of the best examples of this sort of behavior was a house with an overhead water tank when the nearest pipe water was three miles away and the owner had no intention of installing a pump. The point about all these objects was simply to own them and for them to be displayed. The aim was to arouse jealousy in others. The prestige of these objects derived from their association with the Sinhalese middle class, yet these objects were never used in the way the middle class used them.

Source: R. L. Stirrat, "Money, Men and Women," in Money and the Morality of Exchange, *Jonathan Parry and Maurice Bloch, eds. (Cambridge: Cambridge University Press, 1989), pp. 94–116.*

«Les idées foisonnaient, mais quand on n'est pas bricoleur...»

Faites équipe avec Lapeyre

The dwelling is an important focus of consumer spending.

Escrow officer Catherine Chiou was working with a Chinese couple who were getting a great buy on a house they loved. But just two weeks into escrow (i.e., property is held in trust by a third party only to be turned over upon fulfillment of a condition), the couple abruptly backed out of the purchase. Chiou was not surprised. The couple's feng shui master had nixed the deal.

The ancient Chinese art of feng shui (pronounced "fung sui") takes the real estate maxim "location is everything" to a whole new plane. Feng shui links the placement of objects to fate. According to its tenets, each direction of the compass controls certain aspects of life. If you pay attention to the orientation of your house or office, and the arrangement of your belongings and furnishings, you may have good feng shui. Luck, wealth and health will follow. If you have bad feng shui, watch out. Bad luck, poor health, poverty, even death may overtake you. Literally, feng shui means wind and water. But to real estate agents and home builders it means dollars and cents. "It happens about four times a year," said Chiou, who has been with Century Escrow in Monterey Park since 1983. "People make an offer, get as far as escrow instruction and then they have a feng shui master check it out." Chiou said she wishes people would check the feng shui before they get to escrow. But she never blames anyone who drops a deal because of bad feng shui.

Source: Kirsten M. Lagatree, "The Power of Place," Los Angeles Times, 18 July 1993; K1; K6.

mystical associations as well. Household members' investments in the dwelling help build loyalty to the household and also avoid conflict over alternative individual resource uses.[33]

Family Life Cycle

A useful conceptual tool for marketers and consumer policy activists is that of the developmental cycle of domestic groups, or as marketers term it, the **family life cycle** (FLC). This is the idea that *domestic groups typically undergo a cyclical process of birth, growth, decay, and dissolution over time.* The important point of the concept for marketers is that domestic groups at each stage of this life cycle can be grouped into market segments with distinct needs, attitudes, and desires.

Exhibit 14.2 illustrates a developmental cycle for North American households. A person begins as a dependent and then moves through a sequence of household arrangements over their life span. Household types vary with the age of their members and the presence or absence of children. The frequency and sequence of stages varies across various North American subcultures. This model includes life-cycle stages that are appropriate for many upper-income domestic groups in Europe, Latin America, and Asia as well. It is probably not appropriate for many poorer urban domestic groups and certainly not for many developing nations where many people make their livelihoods partly from farming. In both of these other contexts, extended, multiple-generation domestic units based on a variety of family ties are the norm.[34]

Exhibit 14.2 The Family Life Cycle

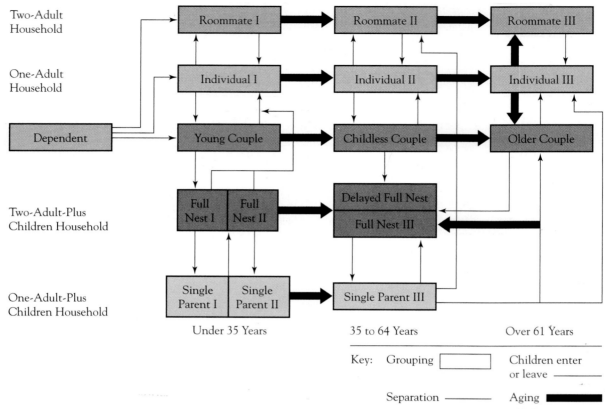

Source: Mary C. Gilly and Ben M. Ennis "Recycling the Family Life Cycle," *Advances in Consumer Research,* vol. 9, Andrew M. Mitchell, ed. (Ann Arbor, MI: Association for Consumer Research, 1982), pp. 271–76.

Changing Household Segments and Demographic Trends

A number of demographic trends have emerged in the last decade in North America and other Triad nations. These trends have important implications for domestic unit structure and consumer behavior. One is a trend toward smaller households, including young people, the old, and the very old. This trend is observed in Great Britain, where 27.4 percent of households are composed of single persons, and in Japan, where 20 percent are singles. It can be observed in New Zealand and Australia as well as many European countries. Larger households are still the norm in many LAW countries, although a shift toward smaller households may be discerned in the NICs like Taiwan. This trend increases demand for basic household goods and services.

Another demographic trend for First World countries is toward increasing numbers of single-parent households. Single-parent households now account for at least 8.1 percent of all households in North America, 6.4 percent in Great Britain, and 9 percent in Australia. About 16.5 million never-married American women are now mothers, accounting for part of the growth in woman-headed households. They make up almost one-fourth of all unmarried women ages 18 to 44. Although poorer, less educated, minority women constitute

Exhibit 14.3 U.S. Household Lifestyle Shifts in the Early 1990s

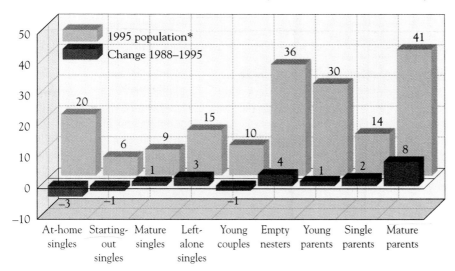

Life Cycle Stages

* 1995 population expressed in millions.

Source: J. Walter Thompson and The U.S. Bureau of the Census.

the greatest numbers of unwed mothers, the largest rates of increase are among white women, college-educated women, and professional managerial women who choose unwed motherhood. Demand for child care, other services, and convenience goods is linked to this trend toward single parenting.[36]

A third trend in First World countries is an overall aging of households. In many parts of the First World, declining birthrates, growing life expectancies, and youthful desires for independence have led to the emergence of a market segment that is likely to grow in importance throughout the 90s. Aging households may be found both in Triad and transitional countries; they comprised over 13 percent of Japanese households in 1994, for example. In the Triad these households are relatively well off; in transitional countries they tend to be poor. Indeed, in the United States, spending by older households has risen faster than for any other group. Older households need new forms of housing and are likely to spend more on various kinds of health-related products and services.[37]

Finally, later age at marriage and high rates of divorce (50 percent of first marriages) are also resulting in a diversification of household forms. A big increase in the category of "other households," including all sorts of blended and nonfamily arrangements, will challenge marketers who wish to target them. For example, recently in the United States, there has been some interest in **boomerang kids,** *adult children who have returned to their parents' homes for reasons of financial insecurity or divorce.* Forty percent of young adults have experienced this boomerang.[38]

U.S. households can be divided into nine main segments. Exhibit 14.3 shows the nine main household segments and how these have changed in the 10 years between 1980 and 1990. These changes are consistent with changes elsewhere in the Triad nations.

How Marketers Use the Family Life Cycle

For marketers, households differentiated by the family life cycle represent different potential market segments. Households' needs across FLC stages vary. Typically, households representing a small proportion of all households spend disproportionately on certain categories of goods and services. We provide a few examples below.[39]

Married with Children

In the United States, married couples with children accounted for 41.4 percent of grocery store sales in 1990, although they represented only 27 percent of the households.[40] Married couples with children 6 to 17 years old account for 49 percent of total spending children's clothing and furnishings. Meanwhile couples with school-age children, 14.3 percent of U.S. households, account for 21 percent of new-vehicle purchases. A third spending category, children's clothing, has a relatively obvious relationship to household segments. Households composed of married couples with children accounted for 65 percent of these expenditures. Having children in the family makes a difference to a household having a computer or not. In 1997, 51 percent of the households with children owned computers, compared to 30 percent of households without children.[41] The ad for baby carriages illustrates an example of a need specific to this segment; the detail suggests this is a highly involving purchase for a segment of Italian households.

Empty Nesters

Segments whose importance will grow throughout the remainder of the century are the category of empty nesters and mature couples who tend to have a disproportionate share of disposable income. In the United States, 12.5 percent of households are composed of *empty nesters*—middle-aged adults, ages 55–64, mostly married (63.7 percent), living in households of three or less (71.2 percent), and without dependent children and the financial obligations they bring. Moreover, empty nesters had the highest net worth of all U.S. households, since many are homeowners. By comparison, 6 percent of Australian households fall into this category, and this is a growing segment in Japan. This segment is grow-

Fulfilling a need specific to an FLC segment.

ing fast and is attractive because of high disposable incomes. These households spend proportionately less on clothing, services, food, and transportation and more on retirement programs, life insurance, medical care products and services, and leisure entertainment, including travel. Childless couples are a significant target market for the automobile industry. In the United States in the early 1990s they purchased 25 percent of new vehicles.[42]

Single-Parent Families

Single-parent households have increased dramatically in numbers. Single-parent households face stretched budgets and severe time constraints; convenience goods appeal to them. Sole parents tend not to be brand loyal, and they are more experimental, impulsive, and style-conscious in their purchases than the average consumer. Single-parent households rely heavily on time-saving, microwaveable, and convenience food products. Single parents head only 5.8 percent of households in the United States but account for 13 percent of expenditures on children's clothes. Research has shown that children exert significant influence in single-female-headed households. However, their influence is product specific, varying with convenience foods, household maintenance products, and snack foods. Children's influence for maintenance products is somewhat elevated, perhaps given their increased role in household management.[43]

Dynamic Households

We can expect to see more diverse household forms and consumption patterns. For example, co-housing, which first emerged in Denmark in the 1970s, is a form of cluster living in which residents have their own homes but share meals, durable goods, labor, and other activities. Already there are 50 co-housing communities in the United States and hundreds more in the planning stages. How would you target a household in such a community?[44]

The family life cycle is useful for market segmentation in many cultural contexts, since some needs and some patterns of decision making vary systematically between life-cycle stages. At the same time, the characteristics associated with various FLC stages vary from nation to nation and within nations as well.

Household Consumption Activities

Households organize themselves to carry out a range of activities, many of which have implications for marketers. These activities include socialization, production, resource pooling, acquisition, consumption, and disposition. We provide examples of household consumption activities throughout this book. In Chapter 19 we discuss disposition. Here we will discuss consumer socialization, production, pooling, and acquisition.

Households are the primary site for the socialization of young people. Products and services are often positioned to appeal to this household activity, as in the ad for music schools from an Australian weekly magazine, shown on page 516.

In addition, much consumer socialization occurs within domestic groups. **Consumer socialization** refers to *imparting the values, norms, beliefs, and procedures associated with behaving as competent consumers in a given cultural setting*. Typically we speak of parents or adults as the agents of socialization and children as the recipients of socialization.[45] Of course, it's more complicated than that. For example, young adults may often feel that they are imparting to their parents behaviors and beliefs associated with the

Consumer Socialization

This Australian ad recognizes that household consumption behavior is directed toward children.

changed consumer marketplace (with which their parents have lost touch). This is especially true with regard to the Internet and other aspects of the information economy. Children's influence increases as they age, a finding consistent with research showing U.S. children's consumer decision-making skills are quite highly developed by adolescence. Children's influence is lessened in households with highly educated mothers with greater gender-role autonomy. The Pokémon vitamin ad shown below pokes a little fun at the knowledgeable and influential child.[46]

In developing countries and NICs, and even in Europe, which is more wedded to tradition than the newer nations of North America and the Pacific, young people are often more innovative than their parents and lead the way in the adoption of new goods and services. For example, MTV Europe caters to a pan-European youth market with a single set of music and programs. In highland Ecuador, intergeneration conflict over the consumption of store-bought bread versus homemade barley gruel is symptomatic of a more gen-

This ad recognizes children's influence in household consumption.

U.S. research demonstrates that parental style helps explain whether socialization is direct or indirect and the amount of influence the household has in consumer socialization as compared to external sources of influence such as peers, teachers, and media. Five different parental styles are described that vary on warmth, restrictiveness, anxiety, and emotional involvement. The five styles are Authoritarian, Permissive, Rigid Controlling, Authoritative, and Neglecting.

Authoritarian parents, for example, believe in parental omnipotence. They show little nurturance and encouragement of interaction, expect relatively little mature behavior, enforce rules in a strict and limiting manner, and value conformity. Authoritarian parents believe their children have few rights. They have very defined expectations for their children's development and they are very concerned with setting consumer goals and refereeing the information children receive from television and other media. They grant very limited consumption autonomy.

Authoritatives, like Permissives, are warmer than other parents. Authoritative parents encourage children to verbalize feelings more than Authoritarian and Neglecting parents. They foster responsibility less than Rigid Controlling and Neglecting parents. They favor placing early maturity demands on children more than other groups with the exception of the Rigid Controlling parents. They are the most restrictive group and strongest proponents of strict discipline. They attempt to enrich the child's environment with cultural and educational activities. They interact with children through co-shopping and asking children's opinions.

Permissive parents encourage communication but regard themselves as resources and want their children to experience the world, including the consumer world, with minimal interference. They interact with children through co-shopping and asking children's opinions. They grant greater consumption autonomy than other groups.

As you might infer, Neglecting parents do not encourage verbalization and tend to avoid communication. They don't engage in much direct socialization and don't referee or restrict information received from other media.

Source: Les Carlson and Sanford Grossbart, "Parental Style and Consumer Socialization of Children," Journal of Consumer Research 15 (June 1988), pp. 77–94.

Consumer Chronicles 14.4

eral trend toward intergenerational conflicts associated with economic development and modernization in the less affluent world.[47]

Consumer socialization takes two forms: **direct socialization** in which *parents purposively train children in consumer knowledge;* and **indirect socialization** which *involves more passive learning through modeling of children's behaviors based on parental models.* Although parents are not the only influence on children, they do determine the degree to which their children will be exposed to other socialization sources such as television, salespeople, and peers. Consumer Chronicles 14.4 indicates that U.S. households vary in their use of direct and indirect consumer socialization efforts.[48] Research in a First World context suggests that direct consumer socialization may be characteristic of upper-class households, whereas lower-class households may focus on discussions about brand names. Middle-class households may focus on attributes of products such as price.[49] Experience in East Asian and African contexts suggests that indirect socialization is characteristic of the majority of consumers. Given these differences in socialization style, marketers may wish to direct different kinds of communication at different household segments. For example, preserving brand quality by associating it with stable brand names may be consistent with lower-class household socialization style.

Many studies have explored advertising and other types of mass media as socialization agents. Another way in which consumer socialization occurs is through **co-shopping.** Co-shopping involves *children accompanying their parents on shopping trips.* It is a good example of indirect socialization. Visiting market places, boutiques, and malls provides children with enormous opportunities to absorb the taken-for-granted understandings of products, prices, negotiating behaviors, market settings, times, and locations for consumption so necessary to effective consumer behavior. Despite the difficulties they encounter, a majority of U.S. parents (58.4 percent) of children between the ages of 6 and 11 report that their children accompany them on major grocery shopping trips with some regularity. U.S. parents who engage in more frequent co-shopping with their children also place more value on their children's input in family consumer decision making and take a more direct role in guiding their children's consumer development.[50]

Production Activities

Most households engage in **direct** or **indirect production** activities to acquire goods for their own sustenance. In the LAW nations, direct production of goods for household survival might involve building a shelter, growing food, or, as in the Navajo vignette, raising sheep for meat and wool. We return to direct production in "You Make the Call" at the end of the chapter. Many households, especially in more developed economies, engage in production activities that indirectly produce sustenance for the household. That is, the production activities are used to acquire resources that are then exchanged for needed goods.

Not all direct production activities have disappeared in First World households, and some are actually moving back in. For example, as in the Mrs. Smith's advertisement shown on page 519, family meal preparation is an important production activity to many households. Kitchen appliances and gadgets constitute a significant share of all U.S. household spending even though many households spend almost as much on meals taken outside the home as inside the home.[51] Restoring old cars and machinery, sewing quilts, and doing needlepoint are production activities that have inspired specialized retailing and marketing media.

Resource Pooling

Consumer researchers have focused on two aspects of household acquisition: pooling (resource mobilization and allocation) and decision roles in the purchase process. In this section we will discuss resource pooling. Understanding the mobilization and allocation of resources within domestic units is useful in targeting goods and services and marketing communications to households.

There are big differences both between and within cultures about how households allocate resources. Below we describe several different household resource allocation models that are typical for some different cultures. We show these resource models using a technique called **household resource mapping.** All households face the problem of allocating scarce resources to competing consumption projects that benefit members of the household differentially. Mapping can help marketers distinguish between various kinds of pooling models that households often take for granted. A combination of mapping household funds and flows could help in tailoring marketing programs to the needs and decision-making styles of particular types of households. The following descriptions of resource

models will give you an idea of how much variety there is in how households manage funds. As you review these models, consider how your household pools resources.

Anglo-American Household Resource Model

Exhibit 14.4 illustrates what we might call the Anglo-American model of household resource allocation. In this model all cash and labor resources flow into a general fund. A portion of this fund is drawn on for necessities, determined by Engel's Law (introduced in Chapter 4). The household head apportions the leftover to other uses. Investments, for example, include the purchase of a home, securities, education expenses, or even exchanges that link household resources between households. This model covers different kinds of household types, including patriarchal households, lower-income extended African-American households that may be headed by matriarchs, and entrepreneurial overseas Chinese households. If positioning products for market segments characterized by this model, marketers should target the household head.[52]

Ashanti Household Resource Model

We can call another common model the Ashanti resource allocation model, after the Ashanti people of Ghana. Ashanti spouses maintain a high degree of autonomy and do not necessarily share a dwelling. Husbands earn income from farming, women from trading. Each decides on some proportion of their funds that will be committed to the household's operating expenses. Wives usually contribute more to household maintenance, whereas husbands contribute to the household's capital equipment and durable goods. In addition,

Exhibit 14.4 Anglo-American Household Resource Management Model

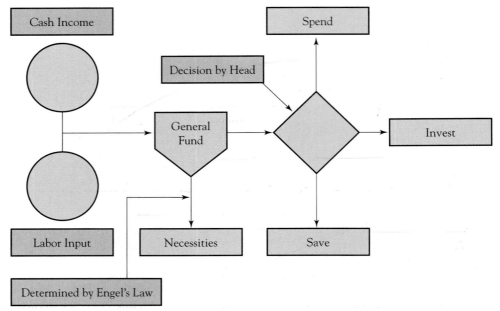

Source: Adapted from Richard R. Wilk, "Decision Making and Resource Flows Within the Household: Beyond the Black Box," in *The Household Economy: Reconsidering the Domestic Mode of Production,* Richard R. Wilk, ed. (Boulder, CO: Westview Press, 1989), p. 32.

both husbands and wives should "invest" in their children, but wives and their lineages have much greater responsibility in this regard than do husbands. Spouses' commitments to the household vary with the emotional bonds between the two.[53] Something like this Ashanti model of pooling might apply to some dual income, no children (DINK) households, nonfamily households shared by roommates, or gay households. If positioning products for market segments characterized by this model, marketers should target adults in the households separately.

Working-Class English Household Resource Model

Exhibit 14.5 shows what we can call the working-class English household resource model. Here the husband splits his income, keeping part but giving most to his wife as a housekeeping fund. A small part of his discretionary income goes to personal expenditures and some for occasional purchases of durable goods and investments. The husband's contribution and the wife's wages go to housekeeping, with an overflow returning for the wife's personal expenses. Children's earnings are turned to their mother, who allocates some back to the children as their allowance and the rest is used for housekeeping expenses. This model of resource flows and decision points suggests targeting the female household manager for many products; but there is scope for the exercise of interpersonal influence over decisions based on contributions to household resource pools. This model is not so different from the traditional Japanese household model, in which "salarymen" turn over their earnings to their wives for management, and there are surely other examples.[54]

Most of the world's households probably lie somewhere between a resource model

Exhibit 14.5 Working-Class English Household Resource Management Model

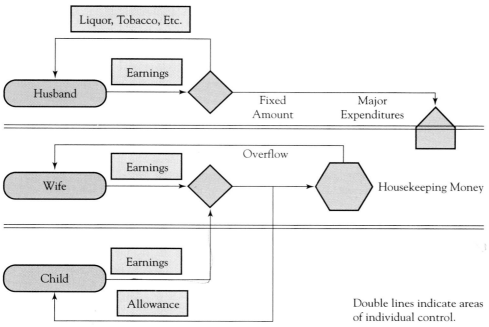

Source: Adapted from Richard R. Wilk, "Decision Making and Resource Flows Within the Household: Beyond the Black Box," in *The Household Economy: Reconsidering the Domestic Mode of Production,* Richard R. Wilk, ed. (Boulder, CO: Westview Press, 1989), p. 39.

with one fund managed by the household head and one with no household fund. These models neglect the fact that resources are sometimes pooled across households, as in the Navajo family's truck purchase in the opening vignette. This is also true of the poor, of single-parent households and of old and young family members who live in different households. Little consumer research has examined the impact of interhousehold pooling on purchase and consumption behaviors.[55]

Marketers and consumer policy activists alike have a compelling interest in understanding the how, what, when, and where of the acquisition of goods and services among domestic groups. Unfortunately, research on household acquisition strategies is fragmentary. Most of the academic marketing research has focused on purchase of household durables and services and expenditure patterns, especially related to convenience foods. Industry studies of purchase decisions include a range of products and have recently been advanced by the availability of scanner data based on universal product codes (UPC). However, these studies are primarily limited to package-goods purchases in the most developed economies. From household budget studies conducted in many countries there is quite a bit of aggregate data on expenditures. Unfortunately, very few studies from any source allow us to get inside the household to see how acquisition decisions are actually made and to see the roles members play in acquisition. Research is really just beginning on household shopping behavior.[56]

Acquisition Strategies

Household Decision Making

Moral Framework for Decisions

In contrast with other organizations, household resource allocation and consumption decisions are often based on altruism and kinship—that is, they are moral rather than economic decisions.[57] Institutionalized kinship ties modify market-based constructs of individualism in the direction of a **moral economy** of *resource sharing, altruism, and mutual accommodation in purchase and consumption.* For example, Tommy's new bicycle is not purchased to increase the efficiency of the household but to make Tommy happy.[58]

One moral criterion for resource allocation that is particularly important in many households is fairness, or equity. Of course, what is fair is likely to be defined quite differently between different cultures. Nevertheless, individual consumption decisions are evaluated in terms of household members' estimations of the overall fairness or equity of consumption decisions taken. Thus, perceptions of members' relative preference intensities play an important role in household decision making.[59]

Decision Roles and Decision-Making Styles

Each household member is influenced by background conditions, including culture, social class, ethnicity, and so on. These conditions tend to determine individual's attitudes concerning both lifestyle norms, such as valued ends and acceptable means of achieving them, as well as sex and age-role norms. These norms interact with specific situational factors at given points of time to determine appropriate behavior for each person. In every cultural and economic setting, households negotiate purchase and consumption decisions in different ways using different rules.

More household members are likely to be involved with significant household consumption decisions in more developed societies. In these societies the number of market-based consumption choices is greater, and household income is higher. Consumer knowledge is also more widely distributed. Recognizing that households operate as consuming units, many firms target entire families with promotional materials, including Kmart, Hilton Hotels, and DaimlerChrysler, maker of minivans; even the resort town Las Vegas, Nevada, does so.[60]

In general, households act as **cooperative groups.** They are cooperative groups because the members' primary goals are compatible. In a family these shared primary goals are likely to concern affiliation, security, and trust. Studies of family decision making emphasize couples' cooperative concern for each other's preferences and for fairness. Families compromise either overtly or subtly to maintain long-term relationships. One sort of solution is the second-choice solution. If household members cannot agree on a first choice, they may settle for each other's second choice. The underlying logic is that the group chooses the product alternative that perturbs individual preferences the least.[61]

In looking at household members' **decision roles** in the acquisition process, we can distinguish both roles and decision-making styles. The roles include the five roles identified for organizational buying centers (see page 503) as well as the caretaker role, the household member who services, cleans, and maintains products or services, sometimes across generations.[62]

Household decisions are well captured in the Calvin cartoons shown on page 523. In the first, Calvin is playing the role of initiator, hoping that his "goo-goo" eyes will persuade his mother, the decision maker, of the legitimacy of his desire for a flame thrower. In the second, Calvin's mother plays initiator and gatekeeper, persuading Calvin's father

of the wisdom of a joint purchase decision, a VCR. The intended VCR consumer, Calvin, is seemingly unaware of the decision making going on around him.

Household members' decision roles vary by authority structure, product category, and stage of the decision-making process. Distinguishing these roles helps marketers more effectively tailor marketing communications to the preferences and values of particular role players within the household. Thus, one study found English wives more concerned with the stylistic aspects of a new-home purchase, husbands with the financial dimensions, although shared decision making was reported. In Kenya, recruiting women to the nation's family planning staff is an effective strategy for reaching wives and daughters who are likely to be initiator, gatekeeper, buyer, and prime user of family planning aids.[63]

Consumer researchers ask what kinds of decisions are made by a group or coalition in the household, called **syncretic,** or joint, **decisions;** what kinds are made by a single household member, usually the husband or wife alone, called **autonomic decisions;** and what kinds are made with one spouse dominant in the process.[64]

Past research has shown that whether a decision is syncretic or autonomic depends on two types of variables. The first type consists of variables such as family life cycle, socioeconomic status, and lifestyles. The second type consists of situational factors such as perceived risk, importance of purchase, and time pressure. Members of households mention that the greater competence of one partner, preference for dividing responsibilities in household management, greater importance of the decision to one of the spouses, being too busy to decide together, and peer group norms are primarily responsible for autonomic decisions. Decisions tend to be autonomic for households with either no or grown-up children, in low or middle socioeconomic classes, and with the wife in some blue-collar occupation. Social class, education, income, family size, and the wife's employment status are all factors that influence whether a family makes syncretic or autonomic decisions. Attitudinal variables such as gender-role orientation and locus of control (whether or not members believe that events are dependent on their own behavior or not) also influence decision making. One study showed that women with modern gender-role attitudes were more likely to have their own checking accounts and individual credit card accounts, examples of autonomic behavior. Joint checking and savings accounts were related to lower incomes, whereas higher incomes were related to joint investments.

Within different product categories, role structures vary by the nature of the decision to be undertaken or the phase of the decision process. Products in the decision-making domain of men and women partners tend to be quite stable over time, but as gender roles become more flexible decision making becomes more complex across households.[65]

Decision-making styles will vary with the quality of household interactions between parents and children. Children play influencing roles in democratic and permissive households, for example. Decision-making styles also vary with communication styles within the household: socio-oriented or concept oriented, for example. **Socio-oriented communication** styles favor *adherence to conventional norms of authority and preservation of the domestic status quo.* Socio-oriented communication may be found in authoritarian households. **Concept-oriented communication** is *more egalitarian and favors a flow of information between all household members.* Democratic and permissive households favor concept-oriented communications. Household decision making and communication styles also vary with culture, class, situational factors, gender-role orientation, and product category.[66]

When household members' perceptions and attitudes differ, conflict arises. The household then employs **conflict management strategies.** These strategies may include conflict-avoidance or conflict-resolution techniques that may affect decision making, purchase decisions, and satisfaction.[67] Some contentious household decisions are not made jointly; instead, individuals pursue their own decisions while attempting to minimize conflict. Although husband and wife may end up thinking they made a decision together, they actually pursued a "disjointed, unstructured, and incremental strategy," the main goal of which was to "muddle through" and keep the marriage going, whatever the actual decision reached.[68]

| Role Specialization | One way households cope simultaneously with individual interest and potential disagreements in purchase and consumption decisions is through **role specialization.** That is, in certain product or service domains, household members agree that they may make autonomic decisions without consulting other household members. For example, one member of the household may shop for groceries with only special requests as input from other family members. Special occasions may lead to autonomic decision making as well.[69] |

Household members' role specialization in consumption choices is likely to be more highly developed in First World contexts where there are more consumption choices to be made in the marketplace. However, there is ample evidence of specialization of tasks between husbands and wives in most national contexts.

Role specialization may be differentially distributed over roles in the buying process. In U.S. households, children between the ages of 6 and 11 are considered experts in the categories for which they are the primary consumers. In approximately one out of four such households, the child is credited with an expert role in purchasing snacks, ice cream, macaroni and cheese, corn and tortilla chips, soft drinks, and frozen pizza. Thus, as suggested by the Pokémon vitamin ad shown earlier, although children are neither purchasers nor decision makers, as initiators, information seekers, and ultimate consumers of many products they influence the use of household resources. In Islamic countries in West Africa, unmarried girls also have important household purchasing roles. In these contexts it is often because of negative public attitudes toward married women appearing in public places such as the marketplace. Marketers need to tailor their targeting and promotional activities to match household role specializations.[70]

Perceived **role overload** is a situation in which competing demands on the consumer's time and energy become overwhelming. Role overload may influence participation in particular purchase decisions and may lead to handing over some purchase decisions to another family member.[71] The increased role burden of professional women spills over onto teenage girls especially. In the United States, one-third of teen females and one in five teen males do some of the family's major food and grocery shopping.[72] The point in this is that marketers must acquire a clear understanding of which household members are involved in an acquisition decision and tailor marketing communications to appeal to all concerned household members.

Gender-role orientation, *the behavioral standards and cultural norms that define appropriate behavior for men and women in their society,* influences the household decision-making process. Where inegalitarian gender-role orientation prevails we find a higher incidence of autonomic, or one-spouse-dominant, decisions, typically male dominance. This reflects a higher level of gender-role specialization in the household. Adherence to culturally prescribed gender-role orientations may increase an individual's influence over decisions considered to be within his or her domain. In the First World, it is possible to identify a trend: Women's influence in household decision making is increasing. Still there are differences; one study found roles more highly structured by gender in a Dutch sample, irrespective of the employment status of the wife, than in an American sample. As gender-role orientations become more egalitarian, a higher incidence of joint and one-spouse-dominant (male or female) purchase decisions occur.[73]

Some generalizations may be drawn with respect to household decision making cross-culturally. In every cultural context, some decision situations are believed to conform to either masculine or feminine roles. In more developed consumer societies, the resources that a spouse brings to a marriage affect his or her relative decision-making power. Variations in a nation's economic and social development can also explain some variations in household decision making. That is, LAW nations tend to exhibit greater male bias in household decision making, whereas Triad nations tend to exhibit more egalitarian household decision making. Joint decision making is more common in more developed consumer societies. Of course, this generalization does not hold in contexts with significant number of female-headed households, such as Jamaica or Ghana, for example. In attempting to define household purchasing decisions cross-culturally, researchers need to investigate a number of product categories, since decision-making behavior varies across categories.[74]

Gender-Role Orientation

Other Consuming Collectives

Examples of consuming collectives other than business organizations, households, and families are endless. In the United States, a Pop Warner football league raises money by selling Fourth of July fireworks to purchase uniforms and equipment for their team. Or a family reunion group rents a large block of hotel rooms at a rural conference center. In Sierra Leone, West Africa, a women's saving association takes up a collection so that each woman in turn can purchase cloth to make matching dresses for a public celebration. In Indonesia, male members of a neighborhood congregation give 10 percent of their earnings to support a popular cleric and build a modest mosque. In highland Mexico, members of the village saint's cult purchase new clothing for the images of saints in their local church and buy food and beverages to host their annual village festival.

One interesting and prevalent buying collective is the home shopping party, typically organized among women but sometimes including both genders. They originated in the United States in the 1950s by companies like Tupperware and Avon; however, these firms have found new success in LAW markets such as Mexico, Asia, and the Middle East. At the same time, these collectives are declining in First World markets, although home lingerie parties have given the form a boost. Examples of buying collectives like these could be repeated almost indefinitely. We could never describe buying collectives exhaustively.

Nonetheless, there are several important points to be made about buying collectives. First, all of them can probably be described in terms of the six main dimensions we mentioned at the outset of this chapter. For example, some of these groups may be formal organizations with a written charter, such as a Boy Scout or Girl Guide troop; others may be purely informal networks, such as the home shopping group or alumnae of a particular school or graduating class. Groups are likely to exhibit an internal division of labor in regard to roles in the purchasing process. Volunteers who organize a reunion of some particular affinity group may, for instance, exert special control over the choice of mementos or gifts purchased by the groups as a whole. Next, marketers may wish to target such collectives explicitly since their aggregate demand for particular goods and services may be significant. Further, home shopping clubs have been effective because of the bandwagon effects they produce. Aggregate sales are pushed higher than they might otherwise be by competition and status motives within the groups. Finally, policymakers and consumer activists might be interested in such groups for the uniqueness of their expertise and collective vulnerability to persuasive appeals.[75]

summary

In this chapter we talked about two important categories of groups: organizational consumers and households. Almost all consumer behavior involves groups at one or more of the stages in the circle of consumer behavior. Groups vary in terms of their membership and structure and their decision-making style and organization. They mobilize resources in order to realize consumption choices. Their consumption choices involve a mix of motives or reasons. Group members play different roles in the purchase process. Each group has a cultural history that influences purchase decisions.

Organizational consumers constitute an enormous market. Successfully marketing to organizations involves identification of and communication with participants in buying centers. Because of changing environmental demands, an area of increasing importance to marketers is an understanding of ongoing buyer-seller relationships. Three basic buy classes can distinguish organizational purchases: new task buys, modified rebuys, and straight rebuys.

Because so many decisions are made in domestic groups, their structure and shifts in their structure have significant implications for marketing. Four trends in household structure have emerged in the Triad nations: smaller households, increasing numbers of single-parent households, aging of households, and diversification of household forms. Coresidence or cohabitation is one common way of defining households. Coresidence is important to marketers because it requires acquisition and maintenance of a dwelling. An important tool for marketers and social policy activists is the family life cycle. Domestic groups at each stage of this cycle can be grouped into market segment with distinct needs, attitudes, and desires.

Domestic groups carry out a range of activities, including socialization, production, resource pooling, and acquisition. Much, but not all, consumer socialization occurs within domestic groups. Consumer socialization takes two forms, direct and indirect socialization. Direct production of goods is most often associated with less developed economies. Greater indirect production activities characterize many First World and newly industrialized countries' households. There are big differences both between and within cultures in how households allocate resources.

We also discuss how households acquire goods and services. However, research on household acquisition strategies is fragmentary. Households generally act as cooperative groups. Studies on family decision making emphasize that conflict resolution is dominated by couples' cooperative concern for each other's preferences and for fairness. Changes in household structure and organization may lead to role conflicts, especially conflicts between work, family, and individual interests.

In addition to organizational consumers and households, there are various other kinds of consuming collectives. Most of them can be described in terms of the dimensions used to describe organizational and household consumer behaviors.

1. Select an organization and characterize it in terms of membership structure, organization, resources, motives and goals, roles, and culture.

2. Using yourself as an example, characterize the groups you belong to in terms of whether they are formal or informal, membership is voluntary or involuntary, and interpersonal contact is primary or secondary. Now consider your decision role in any two of those groups. Is your decision role influenced by these factors? Explain.

3. Mission statements can help create and convey organizational culture. Below is the mission statement for The Nature Conservancy, a nonprofit U.S. corporation, formed for scientific and educational purposes.

   The mission of The Nature Conservancy is to preserve plants, animals, and natural communities that represent the diversity of life on Earth by protecting the lands and waters they need to survive.

   What cultural values does this mission statement reflect? In what ways do you feel it might impact the culture at The Nature Conservancy? Be as specific as you can. For example, how might it impact purchase orders for raw materials to print their magazine?

4. Stories and heroes are often used to convey an organization's values and beliefs. Use an often-told story from your family or from an organization you now belong to (i.e., sorority or fraternity, student AMA chapter, etc.), and illustrate the connection between the story and the organization's culture.

5. How do the following buying situations affect the organization's buying-decision process?
   a. Purchase of a custom-designed machine to manufacture a key component part for a new toy the company is introducing later in the year
   b. Purchase of a dedicated copier for the fifth floor office staff who have been going to the fourth floor to complete their copying
   c. This month's purchase of particle board used in construction of inexpensive home office furniture

6. How might the buying decision for a computer system differ between a large electronics firm and a family?

7. Provide one example each of resellers that you think compete by providing
   a. An exclusive assortment
   b. A deep assortment
   c. A broad assortment

   Explain your choices.

8. How would you use the family life-cycle phases depicted for North America in marketing the following?
   a. Cars
   b. Vacations
   c. Major appliances
   d. Pianos

9. Develop a resource map for your household. How could this map help marketers trying to target your household with products and services?

10. Describe in detail a recent purchase decision made by your family or household. Be sure to include decision roles, decision-making and communication styles, conflict management strategies (if any), and household satisfaction with the purchase.

You Make the Call

Buying Genetically Modified Seed

The dusty, sleepy seed market on the North China plain in Baoding seems worlds away from any technological revolution. But here, when cotton farmers plant they favor cutting-edge science. All but a fraction of the cotton fields in Baoding and surrounding Hebei province are sown with seed genetically implanted with a bacterium that is toxic to cotton boll worms. "The farmers really welcome these seeds," says seed-seller Meng Xinghe, standing amid sacks of corn and soybean seed in his small market stall. "Without them, they'd be wiped out." With memories of famine fresh and dwindling arable land to feed its 1.26 billion people, China has enthusiastically pursued genetically modified foods and seen little of the debate that has raged in Europe and elsewhere over their safety.

But in other Asia-Pacific nations, the controversy over biotechnology has far exceeded its actual use. In India, Japan, New Zealand, Thailand, and the Philippines, consumer movements are demanding controls on the use of genetically modified crops.

Proponents contend that genetically altering crops to resist pests, drought, or other adverse conditions may be the only way to ensure food security in the developing world, particularly in densely populated Asia, home to more than half of humanity. Such crops, they argue, can drastically reduce the need for harmful pesticides, restore ravaged ecosystems, and promote public health with foods genetically enhanced with essential nutrients or vaccines. But the technique for splicing genes from one organism into another has also provoked fears of freak, unforeseen hazards to health and the environment.

In Southeast Asia, only Singapore has come out strongly in favor of biotechnology, viewing it as a promising new industry. "If it is safe for the Americans, it is safe for us," says Lee Sing Kong, a member of Singapore government's Genetic Modification Advisory Committee, brushing aside growing debate in the United States (see www.psb.gov.sg/news/food/v1i3v1i4v2i1/V1I3Article3.htm).

The source of the technology—mainly the research labs of governments and corporations in industrialized countries—raises political hackles too. Farmers in southern India torched cotton test fields operated by St. Louis–based biotech giant Monsanto (www.monsanto.com/monsanto/default.htm) last year, complaining the seeds were too expensive.

In the Philippines, 7 of 10 farmers are landless, renting fields from landlords or working for large corporations like Dole Foods (www.dole.com). Leftist groups (see Philippine Peasant Institute at www.ppi.org, for example) argue that genetically modified crops will give the companies that sell seeds and farm chemicals even greater power. "Big landlords and transnational corporations will call all the shots," said Wim De Ceukelaire, a consultant for the Peasant Movement of the Philippines (jsa-44.hum.uts.edu.au/signposts/contacts/Philippines/NGO/197.html). "In the case of small farmers, it means going deeper and deeper into debt." The Peasant Movement plans demonstrations against genetically modified foods later this year, joined by counterparts in Thailand, India, and elsewhere.

Genetic engineering has potentially explosive ramifications for ethnically divided countries like Malaysia and Indonesia. "If people were aware that animal genes might be used in plants, maybe from cows or pigs, there would be a lot of religious objections from Hindus and Muslim," said Haji Muhammad Haji Abdul Majid, a professor of biotechnology at the University of Malaya in Kuala Lumpur, Malaysia.

Such concerns are largely absent in China. Provincial and central governments have backed research into genetic engineering. Debate over biotechnology in the state-controlled media has been muted.

1. Identify the different kinds of groups in terms of basic group characteristics (size, formality, membership, primary versus secondary, and affect) involved in the consumption of genetically modified seeds.

2. How does decision making differ between these groups?

3. Identify potential buying centers and roles for genetically modified seeds in the Chinese case.

4. Supposing you worked for a global seed company like Monsanto, how would you propose developing marketing strategy for each of these groups? In each case, what would be your product, and what would your marketing communication strategy be like?

5. Check out Watching Monsanto at www.monsanto.vigil.net. If you were Monsanto, how would you respond to this form of consumer activism?

This case is adapted from "Asians Ponder Biotech Foods Promise," Lincoln Journal Star, *July 4, 2000, p. 7A.*

1. W. E. Patton III, Christopher P. Puto, and Ronald H. King, "Which Buying Decisions Are Made by Individuals and Not by Groups?" *Industrial Marketing Management* 15 (1986), pp. 129–38.

2. Linda L. Price and Eric J. Arnould, "Commercial Friendships: Service Provider Client Relationships in Context," *Journal of Marketing* 63 (October 1999), pp. 38–56.

3. Rohit Deshpande and Frederick E. Webster, Jr., "Organizational Culture and Marketing: Defining the Research Agenda," *Journal of Marketing* 53 (January 1993), pp. 3–15. Our discussion of organizational culture draws heavily from this article.

4. Roy J. Lewicki, "Organizational Seduction: Building Commitment to Organizations," *Organizational Dynamics* (Autumn 1981), pp. 5–21.

5. Kathleen L. Gregory, "Native-View Paradigms: Multiple Cultures and Conflicts in Organizations," *Administrative Science Quarterly* 28 (September 1983), pp. 359–76.

6. Linda Smircich, "Concepts of Culture and Organizational Analysis," *Administrative Science Quarterly* 28 (September 1983), pp. 339–58.

7. For an overview of The Gap, see Alice Kahn, "Filling Every Gap," *New York Times,* August 23, 1992, section 9, p. 1. The first quote on Esprit's corporate mission comes from Laura Zinn, "Will Politically Correct Sell Sweaters?" *Business Week,* March 16, 1992, pp. 60–61. The second quote is from Elsa Klensch, "Susie Tompkins: The Spirit in Esprit," *Vogue* (August 1987), p. 376.

8. Terrence E. Deal and Allan A. Kennedy, *Corporate Cultures: The Rites and Rituals of Corporate Life* (Reading, MA: Addison-Wesley, 1982).

9. Julianne Mahler, "The Quest for Organizational Meaning: Identifying and Interpreting the Symbolism in Organizational Stories," *Administration and Society* 20 (November 1988), pp. 344–68.

10. Nancy M. Ridgway and Linda L. Price, "Creativity under Pressure: The Importance of Consumption Situations on Consumer Product Use," *American Marketing Association Proceedings,* Summer 1991, pp. 361–68.

11. Deal and Kennedy, *Corporate Cultures;* and Lewicki, "Organizational Seduction."

12. Deal and Kennedy, *Corporate Cultures;* and Mark E. Hill and Karen James, "Casual Dress Is More Than Clothing in the Workplace," *Consumption, Markets, Culture* 3, no. 3 (2000), pp. 239–82.

13. Michele D. Bunn, "Understanding Organizational Buying Behavior: The Challenges of the 1990s," *Annual Review of Marketing,* 1992, pp. 227–59.

14. F. E. Webster, Jr., and Yoram Wind, *Organizational Buying Behavior* (Englewood Cliffs, NJ: Prentice Hall, 1972); and Robert Spekman and Louis W. Stern, "Environmental Uncertainty and

Buying Group Structure: An Empirical Investigation," *Journal of Marketing* 43 (Spring 1977), pp. 54–64.

15. See Yoram Wind, "Preference of Relevant Others and Individual Choice Models," *Journal of Consumer Research* 3 (June 1976), pp. 50–57; and Yoram Wind, "On the Interface between Organizational and Consumer Buying Behavior," in *Advances in Consumer Research,* vol. 5, H. Keith Hunt, ed. (Ann Arbor: Association for Consumer Research, 1978), pp. 657–62.

16. F. Robert Dwyer, Paul H. Schurr, and Sejo Oh, "Developing Buyer-Seller Relationships," *Journal of Marketing* 51 (April 1987), pp. 11–27.

17. Jose Tomas Gomez Arias, "A Relationship Marketing Approach to Guanxi," *European Journal of Marketing* 32, nos. 1–2 (1998), pp. 145–56.

18. Classic references on power and trust include Peter Blau, *Exchange and Power in Social Life* (New York: John Wiley, 1964); and Richard Emerson, "Power Dependence Relations," *American Sociological Review* 27 (February 1962), pp. 31–41. For applications of these concepts to organization relationships, see Jeffrey Pfeffer and Gerald R. Salancik, *The External Control of Organizations: A Resource Dependence Perspective* (New York: Harper and Row, 1978); and Lars Hallen, Jan Johanson, and Nazeem Seyed-Mohamed, "Interfirm Adaptation in Business Relationships," *Journal of Marketing* 55 (April 1991), pp. 29–37.

19. Kim P. Corfman and Donald Lehmann, "Models of Cooperative Group Decision-Making and Relative Influence: An Experimental Investigation of Family Purchase Decisions," *Journal of Consumer Research* 14 (June 1987), p. 2.

20. Robert M. Morgan and Shelby D. Hunt, "The Commitment-Trust Theory of Relationship Marketing," *Journal of Marketing* 58 (July 1994), pp. 20–28.

21. Christine Moorman, Gerald Zaltman, and Rohit Despandé, "Relationships between Providers and Users of Marketing Research: The Dynamics of Trust within and between Organizations," *Journal of Marketing Research* 29 (August 1992), pp. 314–29; Charles C. Nielson, "An Empirical Examination of the Role of Closeness in Industrial Buyer-Seller Relationships," *European Journal of Marketing* 32, nos. 5–6 (1998), pp. 441–63; and Sang Hyeon Kim and Ji Hea Kim, "The Relationship between Interfirm Commitment and Opportunism in Marketing Channels," in *Marketing Theory and Applications,* vol. 9, Dhruv Grewal and Connie Pechman, eds. (Chicago: American Marketing Association, 1998), pp. 272–82.

22. The buy-class theory of purchasing was introduced by Patrick J. Robinson, Charles W. Faris, and Yoram Wind, *Industrial Buying and Creative Marketing* (Boston: Allyn and Bacon, 1967). A review and test of those authors' buy-class theory is provided by Erin Anderson, Wujin Chu, and Barton Weitz, "Industrial Purchasing: An Empirical Exploration of the Buyclass Framework," *Journal of Marketing* 51 (July 1987), pp. 71–86.

23. Adapted from *Japan Economic Journal* 23 (December 1980), p. 29; see also Philip Kotler, *Marketing Management,* 7th ed. (Englewood Cliffs, NJ: Prentice Hall, 1991), p. 209.

24. Ju-Young Park, Ravipreet S. Sohi, and Ray Marquardt, "The Role of Motivated Reasoning in Vendor Consideration," *Psychology and Marketing* 14 (September 1997), pp. 585–600.

25. Thomas V. Bonoma, Richard P. Bagozzi, and Gerald Zaltman, "Industrial Buying Behavior," working paper, no. 77-117, Marketing Science Institute, Cambridge, MA, 1977.

26. Robinson, Faris, and Wind, *Industrial Buying and Creative Marketing;* and Anderson, Chu, and Weitz, "Industrial Purchasing."

27. Eric J. Arnould, *Niger: Export Marketing of Nigerien Onions* (Agricultural Marketing Improvement Strategies Project, Washington, DC: USAID, Post-Harvest Institute for Perishables, University of Idaho and Abt & Associates, 1992); Philip Kotler, *Marketing Management,* 7th ed. (Englewood Cliffs, NJ: Prentice Hall, Inc., 1991), p. 212.

28. These figures are from the Statistical Abstract of the United States (Washington, DC: United States Bureau of the Census, 1999).

29. Kjell Gronhaug, "Exploring Environmental Influences in Organizational Buying," *Journal of Marketing Research* 13 (August 1976), pp. 225–29.

30. Judy Cohen and Carol Kaufman, " Consumption Choice within the Black Extended Family Network," in *Advances in Consumer Research,* vol. 19, John F. Sherry, Jr., and Brian Sternthal, eds. (Provo, UT: Association for Consumer Research, 1991), pp. 338–45; and Judy Cohen and

Carol Kaufman, "The Cultural Variant Perspective in Black Family Research: Consumption Choice within the Extended Family Network," *Proceedings of the Households Conference,* University of California–Irvine, Irvine, CA, 1991.

31. Roger Marshall, Christina Kawi-Choi Lee, and Kim Marshall, "New Zealand," in *Marketing and Consumer Behavior in East and South-East Asia,* Anthony Pecotich and Clifford J. Shultz II, eds. (Sydney: McGraw-Hill, 1998), pp. 523–48; and Tsutomu Okahashi, N. Clay Gary, and Steven Cornish-Ward, "Japan," in *Marketing and Consumer Behavior in East and South-East Asia,* Anthony Pecotich and Clifford J. Shultz II, eds. (Sydney: McGraw-Hill, 1998), pp. 315–70.

32. Simon Appleton, "Women-Headed Household and Household Welfare: An Empirical Deconstruction for Uganda," *World Development* 24 (December 1996), pp. 1811–27; H. Razoun, "The Sociofamilial Impact of Labor Migration by Jordanian Family Heads," *Dirasat: Human and Social Sciences* 24 (February 1997); and Richard R. Wilk, ed., *The Household Economy: Rethinking the Domestic Mode of Production* (Boulder, CO: Westview Press, 1989).

33. Kirsten M. Lagatree, "The Power of Place," *Los Angeles Times,* July 18, 1993, pp. K1, K6; and Richard R. Wilk, "House, Home and Consumer Decision Making in Two Cultures," in *Advances in Consumer Research,* vol. 14, Melanie Wallendorf and Paul Anderson, eds. (Provo, UT: Association for Consumer Research, 1986), pp. 303–7.

34. Mary C. Gilly and Ben M. Ennis, "Recycling the Family Life Cycle," in *Advances in Consumer Research,* vol. 9, Andrew M. Mitchell, ed. (Ann Arbor: Association for Consumer Research, 1982), pp. 271–76; and William D. Danko and Charles M. Schaninger, "An Empirical Evaluation of the Gilly-Ennis Updated Household Life Cycle Model," *Journal of Business Research,* August 1990, pp. 39–57.

35. Anthony Pecotich and Clifford J. Shultz II, eds., *Marketing and Consumer Behavior in East and South-East Asia* (Sydney: McGraw-Hill, 1998); and UK Department of the Environment, Transport and the Regions, *English House Condition Survey of 1996,* www.housing.detr.gov.uk/research/ehcs96/summary/2.htm.

36. UK Department of the Environment, Transport and the Regions, *English House Condition Survey of 1996;* and Roshan "Bob" D. Ahuja and Kandi M. Stinson, "Female-Headed Single Parent Families: An Exploratory Study of Children's Influence in Family Decision Making," in *Advances in Consumer Research,* vol. 20, Leigh McAlister and Michael Rothschild, eds. (Provo, UT: Association for Consumer Research, 1993), pp. 469–74.

37. Thesia I. Garner, "Changing Welfare in a Changing World? Income and Expenditure Inequalities in the Czech and Slovak Republics," in *The Distribution of Welfare and Household Production,* Stephen P. Jenkins, Arie Kapteyn, and Bernard van Prang, eds. (Cambridge: Cambridge University Press, 1996); Okahashi, Gary, and Cornish-Ward, "Japan"; Joan Raymond, "The Joy of Empty Nesting," *American Demographics,* May 2000, pp. 49–54; and Cheryl Russell, "The New Consumer Paradigm," *American Demographics,* April 1999, pp. 50–58.

38. Laurie Lofland and H. Razzouk, "The Changing American Household: Impact on Consumptive Behavior," *Proceedings of the Households Conference,* University of California at Irvine, Irvine, CA, 1991.

39. Alan R. Andreasen, "Life Status Changes and Changes in Consumer Preferences and Satisfaction," *Journal of Consumer Research,* December 1984, pp. 784–94; and "The Future of Households," *American Demographics,* December 1993, pp. 27–40.

40. See U.S. Bureau of Labor Statistics, *Consumer Expenditure Survey,* stats.bls.gov/csxhome.htm.

41. Alladi Venkatesh, Eric Chuan-Fong Shih, and Norman C. Stolzoff, "A Longitudinal Analysis of Computing in the Home Based on Census Data 1984–1997," paper presented at the Home Informatics Conference, Wolverhampton, UK, June 28–30, 2000.

42. Okahashi, Gary, and Cornish-Ward, "Japan"; Raymond, "The Joy of Empty Nesting"; and Simmons Market Research, *The New American Family: Significant and Diversified Lifestyles* (New York: Simmons Market Research Bureau, 1992).

43. Ahuja and Stinson, "Female-Headed Single Parent Families"; and Lynn Smith, "Mothers Go It Alone," *Long Beach Press-Telegram,* July 22, 1993, pp. E1, E2.

44. Richard Cimino and Don Lattin, "Choosing My Religion," *American Demographics,* April 1999, pp. 60–65.

45. See Scott Ward, "Consumer Socialization," in *Perspectives in Consumer Behavior,* Harold H. Kassarjian and Thomas S. Robertson, eds. (Glenville, IL: Scott Foresman, 1980); and George P. Moschis, "The Role of Family Communication in Consumer Socialization of Children and Adolescents," *Journal of Consumer Research* 11 (March 1985), pp. 898–913.

46. Gwen Rae Bachman, Deborah Roedder John, and Askay R. Rao, "Children's Susceptibility to Peer Group Influence: An Exploratory Investigation," in *Advances in Consumer Research,* vol. 20, Leigh McAlister and Michael L. Rothschild, eds. (Provo, UT: Association for Consumer Research, 1993), pp. 463–68; and James U. McNeal, *Kids as Customers* (New York: Lexington Books, 1992), pp. 38–61.

47. Mary T. Weismental, "The Children Cry for Bread," in *The Social Economy of Consumption,* Benjamin S. Orlove and Henry J. Rutz, eds., Monographs in Economic Anthropology No. 6. (Lanham, MD: University Press of America, 1989), pp. 101–20; and Mary T. Weismental, "Making Breakfast and Raising Babies: The Zumbagua Household as Constituted Process," in *The Household Economy: Rethinking the Domestic Mode of Production,* Richard R. Wilk, ed. (Boulder, CO: Westview Press, 1989), pp. 55–72.

48. Les Carlson and Sanford Grossbart, "Parental Style and Consumer Socialization of Children," *Journal of Consumer Research* 15 (June 1988), pp. 77–94.

49. Moschis, "The Role of Family Communication in Consumer Socialization of Children and Adolescents"; and Scott Ward and Daniel B. Wackman, *Effects of Television Advertising on Consumer Socialization* (Cambridge, MA: Marketing Science Institute, 1973).

50. Sanford Grossbart, Les Carlson, and Ann Walsh, "Consumer Socialization and Frequency of Shopping with Children," *Journal of the Academy of Marketing Science* 19 (Summer 1991), pp. 155–63.

51. U.S. Bureau of Labor Statistics, *Consumer Expenditure Survey,* 1998, Table 59, stats.bls.gov/csxhome.htm.

52. Carol Stack, *All Our Kin* (New York: Harper and Row, 1974); and Richard R. Wilk, "Decision-Making and Resource Flows within the Household: Beyond the Black Box" in *The Household Economy: Rethinking the Domestic Mode of Production,* Richard R. Wilk, ed. (Boulder, CO: Westview Press, 1989), pp. 23–54.

53. Jane Guyer, "Household and Community in African Studies," *African Studies Review* 24 (1981), pp. 87–137.

54. Okahashi, Gary, and Cornish-Ward, "Japan."

55. Ritha Fellerman and Kathleen Debevec, "Kinship Exchange Networks and Family Consumption," in *Advances in Consumer Research,* vol. 20, Leigh McAlister and Michael L. Rothschild, eds. (Provo, UT: Association for Consumer Research, 1993), pp. 458–62.

56. H. C. Phillips and R. P. Bradshaw, "How Customers Actually Shop: Customer Interaction with the Point of Sale," *Journal of the Market Research Society* 35 (1993), pp. 51–62; and Daniel Miller, Peter Jackson, Nigel Thrift, Beverley Holbrook, and Michael Rowlands, *Shopping, Place and Identity* (London and New York: Routledge, 1998).

57. In many contemporary societies, both those of the First and Third Worlds, moral frameworks are not clear-cut and groups often have to work out entitlements. Thus, some theorists argue that the household is a mere "knot of individual interests" with self-interest governing the behavior of household members.

58. Economic organizations also consider moral issues in making decisions, but these are typically a less pervasive part of purchase decisions than in the case of families. Interesting discussions of moral elements in business decision making are available in Amitai Etzioni, *The Moral Dimension: Toward a New Economics* (New York: Free Press, 1988); and Jonghee Park, Patriya Tansuhaj, Eric R. Spangenberg, and Jim McCullough, "An Emotion-Based Perspective of Family Purchase Decisions," in *Advances in Consumer Research,* vol. 22, Frank Kardes and Mita Sujan, eds. (Provo, UT: Association for Consumer Research, 1995), pp. 723–28.

59. Cohen and Kaufman, "Consumption Choice within the Black Extended Family Network"; Corfman and Lehmaan, "Models of Cooperative Group Decision-Making and Relative Influence," pp. 1–14; and Cohen and Kaufman, "The Cultural Variant Perspective in Black Family Research." For studies on African households, see Sara S. Berry, *Sons Work for Their Fathers* (Berkeley: University

of California Press, 1985); Joyce Moock, "Introduction," in *Understanding Africa's Rural Households and Farming Systems,* Joyce Moock, ed. (Boulder, CO: Westview, 1986), pp. 1–10; and Guyer, "Household and Community in African Studies." For studies on households in Belize, see Richard R. Wilk, "House, Home and Consumer Decision Making in Two Cultures," in *Advances in Consumer Research,* vol. 14, Melanie Wallendorf and Paul Anderson, eds. (Provo, UT: Association for Consumer Research, 1986), pp. 303–7; Richard R. Wilk, "The Built Environment and Consumer Decisions," paper presented at the Annual Meeting of the Society for Economic Anthropology, Champaign, IL, 1986; Richard R. Wilk, "Houses as Consumer Goods: Social Processes and Allocation Decisions," in *The Social Economy of Consumption,* Benjamin S. Orlove and Henry J. Rutz, eds. (Lanham, MD: University Press of America, 1989), pp. 297–322; and Richard R. Wilk, "Decision Making and Resources Flows within the Household: Beyond the Black Box," *The Household Economy: Rethinking the Domestic Mode of Production,* Richard R. Wilk, ed. (Boulder, CO: Westview Press, 1989), pp. 23–54.

60. Kevin Goldman (1995), "Campbell Mithun Shows Its Stuff in a Kmart Makeover Campaign," *The Wall Street Journal,* August 3, 1995, p. B3; Betsy Spethmann, "Hilton Heads toward Tie-Ins," *Brandweek,* March 8, 1993, p. 4; Betsy Spethmann, "Chrysler Rolls in the Grass Roots," *Brandweek,* March 27, 1995; and Pauline Yoshihashi, "Stars Fade as Las Vegas Bets on Families, *The Wall Street Journal,* February 5, 1993, pp. B1, B2.

61. Corfman and Lehmann, "Models of Cooperative Group Decision-Making and Relative Influence"; and Jean-Marie Choffray and Gary L. Lilien, *Market Planning for New Industrial Products* (New York: John Wiley, 1980).

62. Grant McCracken, "Lois Roget: A Curatorial Consumer," *Culture and Consumption,* 1988, pp. 44–56; and Linda L. Price, Eric J. Arnould, and Carolyn Curasi, "Older Consumer Disposition of Cherished Possession," *Journal of Consumer Research* 27 (September 2000), pp. 179–201.

63. D. J. Hempel, "Family Buying Decisions: A Cross-Cultural Perspective," *Journal of Marketing Research* 11 (August 1974), pp. 295–302; and Robert M. Press, "Kenya Manages to Slow Population Growth Rate," *Christian Science Monitor,* July 9, 1993, p. 10.

64. Robert Ferber, "Family Decision Making and Economic Behavior: A Review," in *Family Economic Behavior: Problems and Prospects,* E. Sheldon, ed. (Philadelphia: Lippincott, 1973), pp. 29–64; E. Bonfield, Carol Kaufman, and S. Hernandez, "Household Decisionmaking: Units of Analysis and Decision Processes," in *Marketing to the Changing Household,* M. Roberts and L. Wortzel, eds. (Cambridge, MA: Ballinger, 1984), pp. 231–63; and R. J. Green Leonardi, J. Chandon, I. Cunningham, B. Verhage, and A. Straieri, "Societal Development and Family Purchasing Roles: A Cross-National Study," *Journal of Consumer Research* 9 (1984), pp. 436–42.

65. David Brinberg and Nancy Schwenk, "Husband-Wife Decision Making: An Exploratory Study of the Interaction Process," in *Advances in Consumer Research,* vol. 12, Elizabeth C. Hirschman and Morris B. Holbrook, eds. (Provo, UT: Association for Consumer Research, 1985), pp. 487–91; and Irene Raj Foster and Richard W. Olshavsky, "An Exploratory Study of Family Decision Making Using a New Taxonomy of Family Role Structure," in *Advances in Consumer Research,* vol. 16, Thomas Srull, ed. (Provo, UT: Association for Consumer Research, 1989), pp. 665–70.

66. Carlson and Grossbart, "Parental Style and Consumer Socialization of Children."

67. W. Christian Buss and Charles M. Schaniger, "Recent Advances in Research on the Influence of Sex Roles on Family Decision Processes," in *Marketing to the Changing Household,* M. Roberts and L. Wortzel, eds. (Cambridge, MA: Ballinger, 1984), pp. 69–89; and Bonfield, Kaufman, and Hernandez, "Household Decisionmaking."

68. C. Whan Park, "Joint Decisions in Home Purchasing: A Muddling-through Process," *Journal of Consumer Research* 9 (1982), p. 152.

69. Foster and Olshavsky, "An Exploratory Study of Family Decision Making."

70. Eric J. Arnould, "Marketing and Social Reproduction in Zinder, Niger Republic," in *Households: Comparative and Historical Studies of the Domestic Group,* Robert M. Netting, Richard R. Wilk, and Eric J. Arnould, eds. (Berkeley: University of California Press, 1984), pp. 130–62; and Eric J. Arnould, "Toward a Broadened Theory of Preference Formation and the Diffusion of Innovations: Cases from Zinder Province, Niger Republic," *Journal of Consumer Research* 16 (September 1989), pp. 239–67.

71. Amardeep Assar and George S. Bobinski, Jr., "Financial Decision Making by Baby Boomer Couples," in *Advances in Consumer Research,* vol. 18, Rebecca H. Holman and Michael R. Solomon, eds. (Provo, UT: Association for Consumer Research, 1991), pp. 657–65; Ellen Foxman and Alvin C. Burns, "Role Load in the Household," in *Advances in Consumer Research,* vol. 14, Melanie Wallendorf and Paul Anderson, eds. (Provo, UT: Association for Consumer Research, 1987), pp. 458–62; Judith Madill and Sheri Bailey, "Household Decision Making: The Relative Influence of Husbands and Wives in the 1990s," in *European Advances in Consumer Research,* vol. 4, Bernard Dubois, L. J. Shrum, Tina Lowry, and Marc Vanhuele, eds. (Provo, UT: Association for Consumer Research, 1999), pp. 232–37; and Michael D. Reilly, "Working Wives and Convenience Consumption," *Journal of Consumer Research* 14 (September 1982), pp. 407–18.

72. Simmons Market Research, *The New American Family,* pp. 43, 48.

73. R. T. Green, B. J. Verhage, and I. C. M. Cunningham, "Household Purchasing Decisions: How Do American and Dutch Consumers Differ?" *European Journal of Marketing* 15 (1981), pp. 68–77; William J. Qualls, "Household Decision Behavior: The Impact of Husbands' and Wives' Sex Role Orientation," *Journal of Consumer Research* 14 (September 1987), pp. 264–79; Cynthia Webster, "Determinants of Marital Power on Decision Making," in *Advances in Consumer Research,* vol. 22, Frank Kardes and Mita Sujan, eds. (Provo, UT: Association for Consumer Research, 1995), pp. 717–22; Madill and Bailey, "Household Decision Making"; and Reilly, "Working Wives and Convenience Consumption."

74. P. J. O'Connor, Gary L. Sullivan, and Dana A. Pogorzelski, "Cross Cultural Family Decisions: A Literature Review," in *Advances in Consumer Research,* vol. 12, Elizabeth C. Hirschman and Morris B. Holbrook, eds. (Provo, UT: Association for Consumer Research, 1985), pp. 59–64.

75. Jonathan K. Frenzen and Harry L. Davis, "Purchasing Behavior in Embedded Markets," *Journal of Consumer Research* 17 (June 1990), pp. 1–12.

Learning Objectives

After completing this chapter, you should be able to:

- Describe the characteristics of interpersonal influence and how interpersonal influence relates to persuasion.

- Explain the importance of interpersonal influence for consumer preferences and choices.

- Recognize how particular social contexts shape consumers' preferences and choices and how the nature of interpersonal influence varies across cultures.

- Identify different types of interpersonal influence and give examples of how they are used in marketing strategies.

- Recognize commonly used influence tactics and how and why they work and give marketing examples.

- Discuss the importance of reference groups to individuals' perspectives, attitudes, and behaviors and recognize the characteristics of reference groups that help to explain different levels of influence.

- Identify how different types of product choices and other characteristics of individuals and situations affect reliance on interpersonal influence.

Chapter 15

Interpersonal Influence

Pacific Riviera: Selling Time Share Condominiums

In advance of an L.A. Marathon, Linda and Eric filled out cards for a "free drawing" at the entrance to the L.A. Convention Center. Some weeks later, Eric received a call announcing that he had been chosen to win a free prize. All he had to do to claim either a home computer, a Cadillac Seville, a $500 shopping spree at The Broadway department store, or a vacation package was listen to a two-hour presentation about the new Pacific Riviera Vacation Time Sharing Package. Eric agreed, and the following Saturday he and Linda traveled to Newport Beach to see the presentation. On arrival they left their car at a valet parking stop and entered the Pacific Riviera show room.

The walls were covered with glassed posters featuring exotic locations and a large world map that noted member vacation condos around the world. The room included mostly couples ranging in age from late 20s to late 60s. Eric filled out a short, simple form with information such as address, home ownership, and income level and then waited a few minutes before Sandy, their personal "tour guide," greeted them. Each couple was assigned their own tour guide who described that they would begin their tour of the vacation package with a short film. The small auditorium filled as show time approached. The tour guides sat with their guests. The film was introduced and the tour guides all clapped, as did almost all the guests.

The film featured Robin Leach and a young woman announcer, who claimed she was neither rich nor famous, explaining the many benefits of Pacific Riviera. The film also featured endorsements

from California family members who recommended the program and cute endorsements from a group of satisfied children. No money costs were mentioned in the film, only that PR condos were both elite and affordable. When the film was over, the tour guides again led the guests in applause.

After the film was over, Sandy led Eric and Linda to a table in another, adjoining, light-filled room, crowded with small tables around which dozens of tour guides and their guests sat. Balloons were tied to the backs of one guest chair at each table. Eric and Linda chatted for several minutes about themselves and their vacation history and preferences. At one point a balloon popped with a loud bang; the room filled with applause. Sandy explained that whenever a guest purchased a package, they popped a balloon.

Sandy then explained the benefits of the package, careful to write down notes on a sheet of paper, and tailored the examples she gave to Eric and Linda's vacation dreams and history. First she explained about the gold card package that was available only today and compared it to the standard package available everyday. The gold card package featured far more features at little additional cost. At one point, Eric asked how much this might cost, and Sandy demurred, explaining that she was not a licensed real estate broker, but she offered to have someone else explain the costs after her presentation. Sandy focused on how much their vacations were costing and how these costs would increase over the years. When summarizing the benefit package, she stopped and asked, "Which of these benefit features would you use most?" She then asked Linda and Eric if they would like to see a vacation alternative that would be less expensive and build equity at the same time. How could Eric and Linda say no? Meanwhile, balloons were popping around the room as a reminder that others were taking advantage of these deals.

After a short tour of the photo gallery in the front of the showroom and a mock-up of a condominium (not a real condo) complete with fireplace, kitchen, and in-bath Jacuzzi and imaginary window scenes, they returned to the table where Sandy called over her colleague Dan to go over costs with Linda and Eric. Dan spent a few minutes chatting, using as a focal point the notes he had been handed by Sandy. Dan then asked Eric how he liked the package so far. Dan again emphasized the benefits, noting that they were almost sold out of beachfront units and indicating how few there are in California and how much excess demand there is for them (30 to 1). He solicited Linda and Eric's agreement about the benefits of the package. Now was the crucial moment: Dan wrote down the price, around $13,000, available financing, and monthly payments. Eric explained he was not interested in this package, and Dan courteously said he understood and shook Eric's hand. Sandy stood up to take Linda and Eric to claim their gift, and Dan followed along.

To claim the gift Sandy took them through "The Avenue of Broken Dreams," featuring James Dean posters and many other prints and posters of that flavor. After a few minutes they are introduced to an entirely different kind of character with a heavy accent, a big mustache, a wild colored shirt, and a purple Pacific Riviera cap. He ushered them into a much smaller room again filled with people at small tables talking with agents. Surprise! The gold package only available today could be retained as an option, and Eric and Linda could get many of the accompanying vacation benefits for a mere $299. Again, Eric said no. Some conferring went on at a counter at the back of the room, and another woman came over to give Eric and Linda their prize. She explained a number-matching procedure and indicated that they had won a personal computer (by far the odds favor winning this and not a different gift). The personal computer retails for $649, but it lacks a monitor and is technologically out of date.

Overview

The opening vignette includes many basic influence principles documented in social research. Some of the principles illustrated are unique to Western cultures; others are shared widely across many cultures although their power may differ. We will refer back to this vignette at several points in this chapter.

We provide a description of the tools and nature of **interpersonal influence** in this chapter. By interpersonal influence we mean *altered thinking or behavior as a result of others' accidental, expressive, or rhetorical communications.*[1] By contrast with persuasion, which is a conscious intent to change thinking or behavior, influence may be conscious but may also occur accidentally. People are often totally unintentional in their effect on others. Even when people do not intend for them to, most of their actions and words stimulate some meaning in the minds of others. Sometimes just by expressing emotional enthusiasm for a movie or a book, a person can stimulate a listener, even a stranger, to decide to see the movie or read the book.[2] In this case, the effect of an expressive communication is influence.

Rhetorical communication is typified by the story that introduces this chapter. In the story, Sandy is attempting to persuade Linda and Eric to buy a vacation condominium. As compared to accidental or expressive types of communication, **rhetorical communication** is goal-directed. It assumes that the individual is trying to *achieve a goal by stimulating a specific meaning in another person's mind.* Obviously, rhetorical communication can take an expressive form. Someone may use emotions to stimulate a specific meaning in the mind of another person. For example, many service businesses emphasize certain expressions of emotions by personnel to help persuade customers of service quality. For example, Disney World coaches prospective employees on how to look like they are having fun, and McDonald's stresses the importance of displaying enthusiasm and a sense of humor.[3] Of course, in every communication, it's important to remember that the meaning stimulated may be other than the meaning intended. For example, when McDonald's opened a fast-food outlet in Moscow, management trained staff members to conform to Western norms of good service. This included smiling at customers. However, this particular norm did not exist in the former Soviet Union, and some patrons concluded that staff members were mocking them.[4]

This chapter begins with a brief discussion of where people get their beliefs about personal and social influence. Next is an overview of the social context of personal consumption behavior and a broad-based discussion of how people rely on others in purchase and acquisition decisions. Next we discuss many important tools of influence. Interpersonal influence occurs within social systems. Understanding the role of reference groups within social systems is an important aspect of understanding interpersonal influence. Throughout the chapter we integrate a discussion of marketing strategies of persuasion.

Beliefs about Personal and Social Influence

Over the years, a wide variety of beliefs about personal and social influence in many different spheres of life have accumulated. In forming personal beliefs about influence processes, people rely on many sources of information. For example, they may rely on cultural truisms that reflect their own cultural background. Stereotypes like "you cannot reason with women because they are so flighty and emotional" would be one possible cultural "truism" about influence strategies (one that we sincerely hope is changing). People also rely on observation, feedback from others about their own behavior, the moral values and standards that have been instilled in them by their family and society's institutions, their specific training or education, and of course what they see and hear in the mass media. They might also look to history, religion, literature, law, and the behavioral sciences for rich and vivid ideas about the dynamics of social and personal influence.

Three behavioral sciences that have obvious and direct relevance to influence and persuasion processes are anthropology, sociology, and psychology. An anthropologist interested in influence and persuasion would investigate various cultural and cross-cultural dimensions. For example, an anthropologist might study certain attitudes and values widely shared in a given culture that affect the willingness of members of that culture to engage in certain behaviors. A sociologist interested in influence and persuasion would focus on processes existing in society, in institutions, and within groups. For example, a sociologist might study how family, friends, classmates, and work associates shape people's beliefs, attitudes, and behaviors. Finally, a psychologist interested in influence and persuasion would focus on the individual human being. For example, a psychologist might study how various influence strategies affect an individual's feelings of esteem, control, or safety.

Paradoxically, one of the reasons people are not more attuned to others' influence is their tendency to assume a "not me" orientation, or an **illusion of personal invulnerability**.[5] A person may say of someone else, "he is swayed by opinions, but not me," or "she goes along with the group, but not me." Not only is this orientation illusory, but it is dangerous as well because it acts as a barrier to more effective personal control over the individual's responses to persuasion. It is through communication with others that people develop, cultivate, share, expand, and reshape their ideas and behaviors. Rarely does an individual develop an idea completely on his or her own.[6] We will give many dramatic illustrations in this chapter of the awesome power of others to alter one's thinking and behavior. In each of these cases it is not personal weaknesses that determine the degree of influence but rather the power of the situation.

Let's take one illustration. In a 1970 film, Allen Funt examined how adults conformed in a variety of unusual settings. In one instance, Funt arranged personal interviews with those who responded to a help-wanted advertisement. An interviewee is directed to a small office in which several other persons are already seated, apparently waiting. To the interviewee, the others appear to be fellow interviewees, but the movie viewers know they are really confederates of Funt. Responding to no apparent signal, the others abruptly rise from their seats and begin to take off their clothes. A close-up of the interviewee shows his apprehensive face as he surveys what is happening. After a few moments he, too, rises from his chair and begins to disrobe. During this process he does not ask any of the others why they are removing their clothing. As the scene ends, the interviewee is standing there, naked alongside the others, apparently waiting for some clue as to what happens next.[7]

Perhaps this interviewee in Funt's film later wished he had remained seated and clothed. After all, Americans are taught to admire those who are independent and not easily swayed by what others do or think. However, imitative behavior is likely to be adaptive in a variety of ways. When people are thrust into unfamiliar settings, their tendency to behave as others do may spring less from a desire to be similar to them than from a very rational belief that the others' information is better than theirs.[8] If everyone around you is yelling "fire" and heading for the door, it hardly makes sense to ask if they really know what's going on and wait to see the fire yourself.

Interpersonal influence touches on countless arenas of everyday life. It is one of the most potent factors affecting human behavior. Interpersonal influence has systematic, observable, and often surprising effects, but it is also often intangible and illusive. Several points from the above discussion are worth emphasizing: (1) interpersonal influence can be either intentional or accidental, verbal or nonverbal; (2) interpersonal influence is pervasive; (3) knowledge about influence processes derives from many sources, including people's own observations and experiences; (4) people are all personally vulnerable to influence processes; (5) people are influenced by others, at least in part, because to be influenced is adaptive—it makes people's lives more efficient, more comfortable, easier, and more successful.

The Social Context of Personal Consumption Behavior

To emphasize the social context of personal consumption behavior is really no different than to say that the meanings of the clothing a person wears, the food she eats, the music she listens to, her furniture, her health beliefs, the totality of her consumption universe is cultural.[9] People like to think of themselves as making their own consumption choices, but in truth, such decisions are very much shaped by the individual's particular social context. From the morning voices on the clock radio (telling the listener how to smell good, have whiter teeth, or get a better job) until going to bed at night, in a single day an individual may easily have been exposed to over a hundred influence attempts.[10] Not all of these are interpersonal influence attempts, but many of them are.

Research in the United States has consistently demonstrated that interpersonal sources have a strong impact on consumer preferences and choices.[11] For example, one study indicated that up to 40 percent of a retailer's clientele were attracted by the recommendations of friends.[12] In purchases of major durables, over 90 percent of respondents reported they would be likely to use an interpersonal source in the product purchase.[13] The study suggested that a significant percent of respondents (about 20 percent) would seek out an unknown individual (a stranger or an acquaintance of an acquaintance) for information and advice. A number of studies suggest that buyers name interpersonal sources more frequently than any other source in describing their external search efforts.[14] Consumers contemplating the purchase of services or decisions involving social and financial risks show a pronounced preference for personal sources of information.[15] Studies of nondurable consumer goods opinion seeking also reveal heavy use of interpersonal sources.[16]

The power of **word-of-mouth** communication to motivate attitudes and behaviors is well known. Estimates on the power of negative word-of-mouth communication are especially compelling, suggesting that when consumers are dissatisfied almost 60 percent tell at least one friend or acquaintance.[17] In part, word-of-mouth information has so much impact because it is salient and vivid.[18] Vivid information is easier to remember and thus has greater impact. An interesting example of the vivid quality of word-of-mouth information concerned the movie *The Crying Game*. This little-fanfare, no-big-movie-star movie was described as "the most-talked-about, least-told-about movie in memory."[19] The film steadily attracted larger and larger crowds through word-of-mouth recommendations, but the word-of-mouth itself was not very informative. Many people felt that by revealing the twists in the film some of the enjoyment would be lost. Consequently, people would enthusiastically recommend the movie but refuse to reveal what it was about.

It's not just that word-of-mouth information is vivid, but also that a recommendation from someone who knows something about you is often more useful than what experts or critics have to say. For example, John Grisham, Tom Clancy, and Danielle Steel write blockbusters; but for works by lesser-known figures, word-of-mouth can turn sleepers into hits. With a sleeper sales start slowly: A friend tells a friend, and the author, actor, or some other key figure does an interview that lots of people hear, who then recommend to their friends. The book *Divine Secrets of the Ya Ya Sisterhood* and the movie *Snow Falling on Cedars* are examples of hits that followed this sleeper route.[20]

Many times interpersonal influence is invited, but interpersonal influence also operates at more subtle levels. One study of how people select consumer nondurables such as laundry detergent confirmed that many consumers simply buy the same detergent their mother used.[21] A young woman told me a story of a coat she proudly bought and wore, until she saw the same coat on an acquaintance who she disliked. She never wore the coat again. An issue of *The Nation* reported on consumption behavior in Russia in the early to mid-90s in the following fashion:

> People are mad for American culture and its artifacts. . . . School kids in Tashkent have the look down perfectly, which this year is straight out of Gap ads; a bunch of teenagers on a bus, with their colorful canvas backpacks, strategically torn jeans, hightops and oversized jackets worn loosely like shawls, puts one in mind of Ohio or Oregon as much as Uzbekistan.[22]

In his book *Beyond Culture,* Edward T. Hall offers a perplexing and subtle description of influence. He describes years of work micro-analyzing filmed interactions. He learned that when people interact, their movements become synchronized. Sometimes this occurs in barely perceptible ways. In other cases, both bodies move as though the two were under the control of a master choreographer. Further studies suggest that syncing is pan-human and appears to be innate. However, the rhythms are culture specific. Each culture has its own characteristic manner of locomotion, sitting, standing, reclining, and gesturing.[23] In one study, for example, Hall found 15 differences in walking behavior between whites and Pueblo Indians of the American Southwest. Imagine how complicated service interactions between different cultures, with different culture-specific rhythms and rules for interaction, can become. Some experts attribute some of the difficulties between Korean store owners and black patrons in the Los Angeles, California, area to these differences in culture-specific rules for interaction.

A useful summary point in considering the social context of personal consumption is that people tend to define their social context locally rather than globally. Face-to-face interaction tends to intensify social comparison and influence. People rarely bother to seriously compare themselves to others with whom they share little in contact, interests, culture, or geography. For example, when North Americans, Asians, or Europeans are thinking about their own social standing or well-being, they do not compare themselves to Nigerians, who have an annual per capita income of about $600, because in Europe, Asia, and North America, people do not often meet Nigerians. In fact, a powerful influence tool is to isolate an individual from the usual sources of support relied on for social rewards, feedback, and identity and to provide an alternative local social context. Religious sects often employ this local social isolation as a tool of persuasion.[24]

Of course, as we have talked about in earlier chapters, local social context may have a global flavor. For example, the term *EuroKids* was coined by the pan-European advertising group Alto, which found that, increasingly, youths under 25 from Lisbon to Berlin and Stockholm to Athens have more in common with each other than with older people in their own countries.[25] They are bound not only by shared tastes in fashion, music, and food but also by lifestyle, attitudes, and values. They dance to rave music from Italy, Belgium, and Great Britain. They look for clothes from Chipie, Naf Naf, and Kookaï of France. Youth are linked globally through international style magazines and satellite television channels, primarily MTV Europe.

Although interpersonal influence has a dramatic impact on consumption choices in the United States and many other countries, there are practical limits to personal influence. For example, a study in the early 1990s of Hungarian women's purchase of personal care and cosmetic products found little evidence of interpersonal influence despite the presence of many conditions that usually foster reliance on others. Possible reasons include a lack of interpersonal trust fostered by communism and the lack of consumers with high levels of product knowledge and experience. A replication of this study in the late 1990s revealed higher levels of interpersonal influence.[26]

Tools of Influence

The tools of influence are numerous, but we can group the nature of influence into three categories: (1) normative (utilitarian), (2) value-expressive (identification), and (3) informational.[27] In practice it is very difficult to distinguish which form of influence is occurring; often more than one of these forms of influence comes into play in any given situation. The Chinese concept of guanxi, or connections, is a major component of Chinese business relationships and *connotes a form of influence that combines all three tools.*[28]

Three Forms of Influence

Normative Influence

Normative (utilitarian) influence occurs when *an individual fulfills others' expectations to gain a direct reward or to avoid a sanction.*[29] In a film entitled *Consumer Behavior and Cars,* Professor Adler interviews fraternity brothers at Pepperdine University in California who indicate that a brother might be mocked or not accepted if he drove a certain type of car. To take another example of normative influence, some of the award-winning television commercials for Federal Express humorously depict the boss's sanctions visited on a hapless employee if a vital package does not arrive on time. The solution to avoid these

normative sanctions, of course, is to use FedEx. The ad for a Wharton post-MBA program, shown above, is targeted at executives, admonishing them to "ramp up or be run over . . . join us or be left behind."

A number of marketing studies over the years have demonstrated that pressures to conform to norms affect buying decisions.[30] This is especially true when the product is conspicuous and distinct in its purchase and use, when the perceived rewards and sanctions controlled by others' are strong motivators, and when the product is viewed as relevant to obtaining rewards or avoiding sanctions. Personal care items are often promoted to help people avoid others' rejection or embarrassment.[31]

Writings on the adoption of clothing fashions assert that the diffusion of conspicuous new products like fashion goods is motivated by individuals' pursuit of social rewards through early adoption behavior.[32] The general theory states that groups in a favored social position seek out new products as a means of establishing and communicating social **differentiation.**

Others imitate these consumption patterns to affiliate themselves with the favored group and enhance their social position. As imitation threatens the integrity of the differentiating symbols, the favored group maintains their social distance by abandoning that consumption pattern and again innovating. The process of imitation and differentiation results in an ongoing cycle of change.[33] This story, in a nutshell, captures the life of 1980s "grunge" clothing, which moved from the garage bands of Seattle to clothing boutiques in LA, to the Gap, and then out by the end of the decade. In the past few decades apparel designers have invested heavily in "coolhunting." **Coolhunting** involves *heading for the street, the happening streets, collecting observations and comments from the cool people,* *and making predictions on that basis.* Jennifer, a 17-year-old high school junior, is an early adopter of what the fringe street cultures are doing, and she's an influencer among her high school friends. She explains that it's important to her reputation to "look neat"—"you have to look good when you're walking down the street, you can't look like an idiot." Normative influence, avoiding looking like an idiot, frames her sense of style.[34]

Value-Expressive Influence

Value-expressive (identification) influence occurs when *individuals use others' norms, values, and behaviors as a guide for their own attitudes, values, and behaviors.* Implicit in value-expressive influence is the *desire for psychological association or social affiliation* with others. One desired outcome may be enhanced image in the eyes of others. However, value-expressive influence operates because of an individual's desire to be like someone he or she respects and admires, even if the attitude, value, or behavior is relatively inconspicuous or even private. The effectiveness of using celebrity endorsers to promote social causes relies in part on their value-expressive influence.

Identification with a valued other enhances self-esteem and self-concept. When a five-year-old boy cries inconsolably for a pair of Michael Jordan sneakers, one might conclude that he wants to be admired and respected in the eyes of his friends; but more likely he just really wants to be like Michael Jordan, and he believes that perhaps those sneakers will do the trick. Sales of gear that features the colors, logos, and numbers of sports teams and stars (a multi-billion dollar industry) is a good example of value-expressive influence at work.

Value-expressive influence can be an important and positive motivator of personal change and can help individuals transcend the particular features of their local social context. A study of children from disadvantaged backgrounds who, as adults, substantially advanced their social and economic standing indicated that the presence of a significant role model was the biggest distinguishing difference between these children and their counterparts who remained in disadvantaged settings. Mentorship becomes a conduit for values and beliefs, as suggested by Consumer Chronicles 15.1.[35] Value-expressive influence can also be critical in the successful diffusion of a new product.[36] Some Third World consumers provide another vivid illustration.[37] Young inhabitants of some African countries associate themselves with the outside world and disassociate themselves from traditional village ways through the adoption of Western clothing. This behavior differentiates them from the norms within their village system and is symbolic of emotional allegiance to the perceived modernity and authority provided by this clothing. Consumer Chronicles 15.2 provides a similar example from the nation of Botswana in southern Africa.[38]

Of course, for value-expressive influence to operate in a positive way it's important that people choose role models well. An unfortunate illustration of a successful negative role model was the Joe Camel cigarette campaign. Research showed that even very young children recognize and respond positively to Joe Camel.[39] Another controversial

One of the first things I noticed on campus was a distinct trend in student fashion that gave the place the feel of an American theme party: sweatshirts by California Co.; multicolored gang-style kerchiefs; imitation basketball jerseys of N.B.A. teams. In some instances the cultural costumes were in comic approximation of their models in the United States. The Yankees caps were often forest green or purple. The white X on his black cap, a student replied to my feigned ignorance, stands for "*Christ*— yes, like Xmas, you know." I'd stumbled upon a clumsy game of Telephone, played by murmuring fashion fads across the Atlantic Ocean.

Source: Nicholas Weinstock, "I Was a B.M.O.C. at Botswana U.," The Nation, December 6, 1993, p. 693.

example of value-expressive influence is the endorsement of St. Ides malt liquor by Scarface and his group Geto Boys, a hard-core rap group. Critics charged that the ads attracted the attention of rap's young audience. Research released by the Philadelphia-based firm Motivational Educational Entertainment has indicated that rap is the only medium considered credible by black, urban youth. Take a look, for example, at www.hhmoteur.ctw.cc or www.ghhr.de. Many rap stars admit that at least some kids are heavily influenced by rap music (which as we have noted in other chapters has a prominent role in global youth culture), constantly mouthing their favorite songs and mimicking the style and dress of their favorite performers. Some rap performers express concern that they carry a heavy burden to promote positive values because hip-hop is so influential.[40]

Informational Social Influence

Informational social influence occurs when *an individual uses the values, norms, and behaviors of others as credible and needed evidence about reality.*[41] Marketing illustrations of informational influence abound. When it is difficult to assess product or brand characteristics by observations, when acquiring the expertise required to evaluate a product choice is difficult, or when the process of purchase or consumption is frightening, consumers rely on others as guides to their own attitudes, values, and behaviors. One consumer behavior researcher provides a compelling description of the influence of a *shopping companion,* or **purchase pal,** in the context of a tattoo service, indicating how the companion reduces purchase risk, provides social support for the decision, commiserates about the process, and acts as a social evaluator representing the opinions of others. Many other researchers have documented the frequency and extensiveness of use of a purchase pal in making consumption choices.[42] Perhaps on occasion you've been standing in the produce section of your local grocery store selecting a melon and been asked by another confused shopper how to assess the merit of the melon—do you tap it, smell it, squish it? Or perhaps your friends look to you as an expert on stereo equipment, photographic supplies, tools, cars, or how to get stains out of clothing. In all of these and many other cases, family, friends, and strangers may look to you for advice on how to manage their environment. They may not believe that you have any power to reward or sanction them, and they may not feel they want to be like you, but they see you as having knowledge and experience that will be useful to them.[43] One U.S. study reported that 46 percent of all respondents identified themselves as being an opinion leader or expert in some self-selected product category.[44]

Many marketing techniques rely on informational influence. For example, in the introductory vignette, clapping is encouraged by making sure that a salesperson sits with each customer and the salesperson claps. This offers **social proof** that clapping is the right thing to do in this situation. Social proof is used later when the balloons are popped to indicate people are buying. This lets others know that people similar to themselves recognize this offer as a good deal and have decided to make a purchase.

Relationships among Types of Influence

In many, if not most, purchase and consumption circumstances the influence of friends and acquaintances is not easily separated into normative, value-expressive, and informational forms of influence. For example, research shows a considerable amount of conformity among sorority sisters in relatively personal products such as shampoo, cosmetics, deodorants, and so forth.[45] What form of influence is operating? Well, perhaps there are social rewards and sanctions for certain brands of cosmetics and shampoo (normative influence). Anecdotal evidence from University of Colorado sorority members supports the idea that cosmetics such as Clinique, Lancôme, or Estée Lauder are more socially acceptable than Maybelline or Avon. In addition, of course, younger sisters show up on campus and hope to identify with their senior sisters who really seem to have their act together (value-expressive influence). Finally, a sorority is a wonderful environment to seek information from others about personal products. It's natural to rely on an admired and respected group for information about how to give your hair more body and what brand of lipstick really has lasting power (informational influence).

In this section we are going to outline some common tools for influencing others, talk about how these tools work, and give some marketing examples.[46]

Reciprocity

One of the most widespread practices for human interaction is the **norm of reciprocity:** that people should *try to repay what another person or group has provided them.* This differs in important ways from an economic exchange. The most crucial distinction is that it involves *unspecified* obligations. For example, if a person gives a dinner party, she can expect her guest to reciprocate, but she can hardly bargain with them about the kind of party to which they should invite her. Many social scientists report that the reciprocity norm is pervasive within human societies and it permeates exchanges of every kind.[47] Many societies' complex rules for reciprocity perpetuate constant indebtedness between members of the culture.[48] Noted paleoarcheologist Richard Leakey and anthropologist Claude Levi-Strauss have contended that the norm of reciprocity is the essence of what makes us human.[49] Relations of reciprocity can create and maintain significant social bonds. Consumer Chronicles 15.3 portrays how Mr. Dang does business in China. Interestingly, the norm of reciprocity applies not only in communications between people but between people and computers. For example, a series of experiments showed that when a computer initiates a request for information by first divulging some personal information, the subject provides more personal information than if the computer simply asks for information. This may seem strange, but it shows how important reciprocity is as a social norm for interaction.[50]

There are many studies on the impact of reciprocity on compliance. In one experiment, researchers showed that twice as many raffle tickets were sold when the request for a purchase was preceded by doing a small, unsolicited favor for the potential customer (offering someone a Coke).[51] A small bread shop based in Boulder, Colorado, illustrates an example of effective use of reciprocity. When you walk in the door, you're offered a warm slice of fresh bread with butter. There is no obligation to purchase anything, but watch the people come and go, and you will see the principle of reciprocity at work. The simple gift not only promotes the quality of the product, it also promotes the desire to reciprocate. This principle of reciprocity has been illustrated in sales techniques for centuries. There are many examples. For instance, the offering of free samples can engage the natural indebting force that requires reciprocation. Another illustration is the use of a small gift to

The Rule of Reciprocity in Mr. Dang's Factory

Mr. Dang's approach to hiring Kaiping workers is one of paternalism. He considers his offer of employment to the children of his relatives to be a way of "looking after" them *(jiu kuo)*. Both he and his wife are involved in many relations of reciprocity with local kin and friends. The depth of some of these relationships is such that Mr. Dang considers it an obligation to look after his kin through his business venture in China. In turn the employees feel obliged. Despite the unfavorable working conditions, they would not consider leaving for another factory because doing so would be a betrayal of Mr. Dang's kindness and generosity in offering them employment and taking care of them away from home. They also feel obliged to do many non-work-related chores. It is not unusual to see one of the female workers doing the laundry for Mr. Dang.

Source: Adapted from Josephine Smart and Alan Smart, "Obligation and Control: Employment of Kin in Capitalist Labour Management in China," Critique of Anthropology 13, no. 1 (1999), pp. 7–32.

accompany a request to complete a survey. The gift is often as little as 50 cents and is never intended to compensate for the respondent's efforts in completing the survey, but it is offered as a token of appreciation. The receiver is often encouraged to use the gift to brighten someone else's day. Research demonstrates that response rates are significantly increased by even this small gift.[52]

A slight variation on the reciprocity norm also plays an interesting role in many negotiation processes. This technique is commonly used in soliciting donations. The caller first asks for a rather large donation, and upon refusal, requests a much smaller amount. This technique was also used on Eric and Linda in the introductory vignette. After they declined purchasing the condominium, they were asked to make a much smaller purchase. Some writers refer to this technique as **door in the face** because it involves *following up a large request with a much smaller request.*[53] The dramatic reduction between requests is intended to create the perception that the requester is making a concession. The approach plays on the desire to reciprocate a concession.

Commitment and Consistency

The influence tools of **commitment** and **consistency** are related more generally to **attribution theory,** which suggests that people *try to explain causes to events*—people want to try to understand why things happen. **Self-perception theory,** an aspect of attribution theory, proposes that *attitudes develop as consumers look at and make judgments about their own behavior.* The influence tools of commitment and consistency relate specifically to people's desire to explain their own behavior (attribute causation) in a consistent way. It's important to note that the desire for a consistent self-image is not universally shared. For example, American businesspeople are often mystified that Indian businesspeople have very different moral codes for different parts of their lives. Many Indians live very partitioned lives, with many contradictions. They don't attempt to resolve these contradictions. Even within Western cultures the need for a consistent self-image may be much less pronounced than it used to be.[54]

Nevertheless, many societies and especially Western cultures value and support personal consistency. Inconsistency in beliefs, words, and deeds is viewed as indecisive, weak-willed, flighty, or even mentally ill. Consistency is also economical. Once a person has decided about an issue he or she doesn't have to think about it any more; once a person has learned a particular route to work, it's easiest to just automatically go that same way each day.

Influence tactics play on the desire for consistency in a variety of ways. One popular sales technique is called **foot in the door** (FITD). FITD represents a technique where *compliance with a critical request is increased if an individual first agrees to an initial small* *request.* The typical explanation offered is that people who engage in a behavior may then adopt an attitude consistent with that behavior making them more likely to engage subsequently in similar behaviors within that behavioral domain. Results studying this approach have been largely supportive, although more research is needed to identify the conditions that limit its usefulness.[55] You may have encountered this technique from an organization soliciting donations. On the first contact the organization may ask for a donation (no matter how small), hoping that you will then come to define yourself as someone who donates to that particular cause. This enhances the likelihood of continuing to get increasing donations from you. Salespeople often employ the technique of trying first to make a small sale, expecting further, much larger purchases to flow from the commitment. This technique was also employed in the opening scenario. The guests of the tour guide were encouraged to clap at the beginning and end of the film and later, at the tables, whenever a balloon went off signaling a sale. In this case clapping constituted a trivial public endorsement of the worth of the sales campaign that the tour guides hoped would prompt a larger commitment in the form of a sale.

The power of commitment as an influence tactic is substantially enhanced when the commitment is made in writing or made public.[56] The vignette at the beginning of the chapter illustrates this technique. When an individual purchased a condominium a balloon was popped and public attention was drawn to that individual. This technique was designed to make it more difficult for the individual to back out afterward. Amway Corporation has discovered that people live up to what they have written down. They are much less likely to back out of contracts if they've made a personal commitment. The effectiveness of public commitment is used in a positive way in groups such as Alcoholics Anonymous. In these groups individuals publicly acknowledge their problem and their commitment to doing something about it. The visible commitment in front of family and friends enhances the likelihood of successfully breaking addiction and other consumer pathologies (e.g., compulsive shopping).

Influencers

Many influence tactics revolve around characteristics of the influencer. Numerous source effects have been researched, including similarity, expertise, attractiveness, and likability. In many cases the celebrity endorser combines one or more of these qualities. All of these influencer characteristics are really ways of determining **communicator credibility,** or *overall believability of the source.* It's important to remember that we attend to certain types of information about the source because, in general, this strategy works very well and helps people to make good and efficient choices.

Similarity An important and often effective guide to behavior is the behavior of a similar other. For example, when consumers get recommendations for movies or CDs from people with tastes similar to their own, they are likely to feel more confident that it will be entertainment they will enjoy.[57] Commercials for first-run movies often feature recommendations from "ordinary moviegoers" similar to the target audience. Under certain circumstances consumers would prefer the advice of someone similar over someone with more expertise. In matters having to do with tastes, values, or opinions—where there is no right answer—the impact of a similar communicator is likely to be especially important.

There are other situations as well where **source similarity** may affect influence. For example, consider that you are undertaking a hike in the mountains and want to choose a route and decide what to pack. Would you prefer the advice of an expert mountain climber or someone with more experience hiking those mountains than you but with similar hiking skills? Many people might be afraid that the advice of an expert would lead them to

Collaborative filtering is simply a system that sifts through the opinions and preferences of thousands of people and systematically matches you with people who appear to have the same tastes you do and then provides you with their recommendations. A rather simple version of collaborative filtering is offered by amazon.com or by barnesandnoble.com, which recommend other books bought by people who bought books you recently purchased. However, much more sophisticated examples of collaborative filtering are available. One example is a website called Movie-Lens. After logging in to this site, you provide ratings on a series of movies and then the collaborative filtering process predicts how you will rate other popular movies, based on people like you, who rate movies similarly. After you have plugged in about 15 opinions, predictions become amazingly accurate. Try it and see. Does it accurately predict your movie preferences? Will computer-generated recommendations replace the recommendations of friends? What do you think?

Source: Malcolm Gladwell, "The Science of the Sleeper," New Yorker, October 4, 1999, pp. 48–55; and John Hagel and Marc Singer, Net Worth (Boston: Harvard Business School Press, 1999).

select a route that was too difficult and carry a pack that would not serve their particular, more novice needs. An interesting variation of this theme is illustrated by Internet services that offer collaborative filtering or individualization technology.[58] Good Practice 15.1 describes collaborative filtering and how it can be used to tailor recommendations to particular user profiles. Give it a try and see what you think.

The central idea of Leon Festinger's theory of **social comparison** is that people need to compare themselves to others in order to evaluate their own abilities and opinions.[59] Of course they don't compare themselves to just anybody; they select comparison groups on the basis of the others' similarity to them. Even though there are many pressures to use consensus to gauge reality, people's willingness to go along with a group evaluation is moderated to some extent by their judgments about the group members' similarity to them. An interesting twist on this principle is provided in some research with U.S. college students.[60] Even though previous research revealed a strong preference for a particular shade of their school color, when it was reported that students at a major rival school also preferred that shade, their preferences shifted away from that shade.

Because even small similarities can be so effective in producing a response, and because a veneer of similarity is so easy to manufacture, this tool of influence is popular in many marketing settings. One of the most familiar applications is "common man" advertising. The technique employs someone prototypical of the target segment to deliver the persuasive appeal, and it may use "testimonials" from "real consumers like yourself" advocating the product. This approach can be very successful if people believe the source is similar and believe the testimonial is heartfelt.

Expertise Another way in which people may assess the credibility of another is on **expertise.** Numerous studies have demonstrated the persuasive advantage of messages delivered by an expert.[61] When consumers rely on the expertise of their stockbrokers to guide their financial portfolio they economize on their own time and efforts.[62] People also rely on the expertise of many other professionals such as physicians and accountants. Rather than thinking through all of the arguments on a subject, consumers may seek out an expert's advice, someone who has presumably thought through those arguments. The endorsement or lack of an endorsement of a product by experts in the field can have significant consequences for the diffusion of that product. Although they are not perceived as the most influential information sources by moviegoers, film critics play a significant role in the launch of new movies. A study in France showed that moviegoers who are more knowledgeable about cinema (up to a certain point) and who show evidence of high susceptibility to social influence (informational and normative) are more affected by film critics than others.[63] Use of expertise appeals is common in personal sales and in advertising.

Expertise is a common denominator in the choice of personal influencers. **Opinion leaders** are influential with consumers as sources of information and advice because of their *involvement, expertise, and experience in a product category.*[64] Opinion leaders are highly credible sources because they are perceived as neutral, they have product expertise, and they can tailor their recommendations to the specific opinion receiver. An opinion leader in one product category is likely to be an opinion receiver in a different product category.[65] **Market mavens** are distinguishable from opinion leaders because their influence stems not from product category expertise but from general knowledge or market expertise. They *possess a wide range of information about many different types of products, retail outlets, and other aspects of markets and like to share this information with others.*[66] Similar to opinion leaders, market mavens are influential because of consumers' perception that they offer an informed (expert) opinion on many market decisions. Market mavens like to share their information—they are socially motivated and want to help consumers make good choices.[67] Finally, **innovators,** or *the earliest adopters of new products* are influential, in part because of their experience with the new product. After seeing a new trash compactor purchased by neighbors, and maybe even watching it in action, a family may decide to purchase one as well. Because of the important roles of these influencers in the diffusion of innovations, we provide a more complete description and discussion of their characteristics and how to target them in Chapter 16.

Attractiveness A number of studies have supported that physical **attractiveness** may make a source more persuasive.[68] Some particularly disturbing research suggests that attractive politicians receive more votes than unattractive candidates by a margin of more than 2 to 1, that attractive defendants are twice as likely to avoid jail as unattractive ones, and that attractive school children are viewed as better behaved and intelligent then their less attractive classmates.[69] Why good-looking people have more influence and are regarded more favorably is something of a mystery. In some cases those who are attractive may trigger value-expressive influence—people would like to appear to others as the attractive ones appear to others; thus, the attractive people are appealing to emulate. Of course, in some cases attractiveness represents a relevant cue. A beautiful model with beautiful hair certainly seems like a more credible source of information about what shampoo to use, especially if the consumers can be convinced that the model started out with the same hard-to-manage, limp, thin hair that they are working with (e.g., combining physical attractiveness with problem similarity).[70]

Liking The effects of similarity and physical attractiveness on influence may relate to a more basic element in the influence equation: **liking.** Consumers are influenced by people they like. They may seek to obtain social rewards from those they like, wanting the liked person to like them back. This is fundamental to human processes of social bonding and social exchange.[71] When people like someone, they may also want to be perceived by others the way that individual is perceived (at least in some respects), and that too makes influence possible. Finally, people are inclined to believe the liked person is trustworthy and therefore will provide useful information in helping them manage their environment. Mounting evidence suggests that trustworthiness is a crucial factor in successful strategic alliances and other partnering arrangements.[72] Many factors in addition to similarity and physical attractiveness affect whether someone likes another. For example, some research suggests that when dissimilar people are brought together in close physical contact with each other, facing common crises that require unified action, an important bonding takes place that can create lasting and strong friendships.[73] How is this relevant to marketing? This and other research suggests that salespeople's close contact and cooperation with customers can be important ways of creating commercial friendships.[74]

Scarcity A powerful and frequently employed influence tactic is summarized by the **scarcity principle**—*something in short supply is more attractive than something that is plentiful.* Use of the tactic takes many forms. For example, in the opening vignette Linda and Eric were told that the special gold package would only be available if they signed today. Several years ago the perceived scarcity of Cabbage Patch dolls may have contributed to their popularity, and more recently the scarcity of Pokémon cards and color Gameboys made them prized.

One of the powers of the scarcity principle is that North Americans hate to lose opportunities, because losing opportunities or freedoms diminishes feelings of personal control.[75] They react against this by desiring the product or object about to be withheld much more than they would otherwise.[76] *Anytime the freedom to select a product or service is impeded, consumers respond by reacting against the threat.* One-day-only sales, limited editions, and last one on the shelf all appeal to this **psychological reactance** against a loss of options and control.[77] Marketers who have discontinued or changed their product line have often faced outrage and even protests by loyal consumers.[78] This happened with Coca Cola's introduction of New Coke and with Crayola's change in their traditional crayon colors. The desire for options and control is not evenly distributed among cultures. For example, cultures with a fatalistic orientation, such as in many parts of Asia, might not react against a loss of options and control. Also, cultures in which consumers are accustomed to scarcity, such as much of central and eastern Europe and the former Soviet Union, might not experience this psychological reactance. However, even in these cultures the scarcity principle may operate, but for different reasons, as described next.

Another reason the scarcity principle works is because of a general connection, experienced over time, between demand and subsequent scarcity. Things that are in demand become scarce. In primitive societies people may observe the depletion of resources in demand, and in market-dominated societies attractive sale prices result in empty shelves. Naturally, people may infer a variant of the causality they have often experienced: Things that are scarce are in demand. Thus, scarce goods may imply popularity, also an important influencer. When a salesperson says, "They've been selling like hotcakes, I hope I have one left," the customer's interpretation is likely to be "this is a very good product since it is so popular with so many other people (consensus effect), and I may miss out if I don't buy it today." Of course, this provides an opportunity for the salesperson to take advantage of the customer. A salesperson wishing to move an especially slow item may combine a sale on the item with nearly bare shelves—just a few left, promoting the inference that this is a popular deal that won't last long. An interesting series of studies illustrates that the presence of a restriction in a promotion (i.e., purchase limit, purchase precondition, or time limit) serves to enhance value and increases sales, but not with all consumers and not all the time. Nevertheless, the public policy implications are clear. Unscrupulous marketers can use restrictions to fool some consumers into believing that a mediocre deal is a good deal.[79]

In addition, there may be a tendency to believe that things that are difficult to possess are better than those that are easy to possess. Over their lives people learn a connection between effort or investment and worth. This kicks in to explain the desire to have things that are difficult to possess. Often this feeling combines with a desire to have something that distinguishes the consumer from others—something not everyone else can have. The connection between the scarcity principle and the desire for distinction is evidenced in the limited production of many prestige goods. People in many cultures share the desire for distinction, although as discussed in Chapter 11, it is certainly less important in some cultures than in others. An unusual example of the extreme importance of distinction is described in Consumer Chronicles 15.4.[80]

Gaining Distinction in the Congo

Consumer Chronicles 15.4

An unusual example of the importance of distinction comes from the Congo and is called the *sape*. The sape is a ritual program for the transformation of ordinary unranked youth into great men. It begins and ends in Bacongo, with a phase in Paris. The youth moves to Paris and scrounges, living a life of incredible hardship, to obtain the cash and credit needed to accumulate a real haute couture wardrobe, called *la gamme*. Labels play a crucial role. Weston shoes, for example, are ranked among the highest. Copies are not acceptable. By returning with this haute couture wardrobe, the *sapeur* attempts to capture power via the accumulation of distinctive, authentic, effortful symbols of power.

Source: Jonathan Friedman, "The Political Economy of Elegance: An African Cult of Beauty," Consumption and Identity, Jonathan Friedman, ed. (Chur, Switzerland: Harwood Publishers, 1994), pp. 167–88.

Reference Groups

All people are influenced both by groups to which they belong and those to which they don't. As indicated in Chapter 14, almost all consumer behavior takes place within a group setting, and groups serve as one of the primary agents of socialization and learning. A **reference group,** or comparison group, is a group whose *presumed perspectives, attitudes, or behaviors are used by an individual as the basis for his or her perspectives, attitudes, or behaviors.* Consumer Chronicles 15.5 describes one important reference group for many Japanese youth, that is, *bosozoku* drivers. These youth use as referents media-made images of American youth as well as their vision of ancient symbols of power and courage such as Kamikaze warriors.[81]

meaning !

Types of Reference Groups

We classify groups according to membership, attraction, and degree of contact.

Membership

Formal
Informal

Some groups have formal membership, such that one is either a member or not. Other groups, such as cliques or informal collections of people, may have less formal rules for membership, and individuals may report confusion about whether or not they are

On summer nights in large Japanese cities, the busiest streets reverberate to the deafening sound of hundreds of careening motorcycles and cars, astonishing onlookers and confounding police. The teenaged *bosozoku* drivers— the "violent driving tribe"—display their elegant and bizarre costumes. Kamikaze party uniforms are combined with American punk, surfer, and rock-and-roll gear, costumes imitating what they think American teens wear.

The Japanese mass media have portrayed

bosozoku youths as juvenile delinquents, though in fact they are not major criminal offenders: the majority of those who participate in gang activities are from middle-class families, and gangs are rarely involved in illicit underworld activities. The photo above provides an image of these Kamikaze bikers.

Source: Ikuya Sato, Kamikaze Biker: Parody and Anomy in Affluent Japan *(Chicago: University of Chicago Press, 1991).*

members. For example, membership in a community may be strongly or weakly held. Many movies are built around the tension of joint membership in colliding groups that causes individuals to question their membership in one or more of the conflicting groups. Whether membership is formal or informal, strength of association with the group varies dramatically among members. For example, new initiates of a fraternity will typically feel much less secure about their membership than senior fraternity members getting ready to graduate. Similarly, a member of a group may feel only a very loose association with that group and hence participate only peripherally in its activities.

Attraction

Attraction refers to *the level and direction of affect* (or emotional response) *that the group holds for an individual.* Attraction can be either positive or negative and may be associated with either membership or nonmembership groups. Exhibit 15.1 helps summarize these four major types of reference groups. For example, a high school student may confess to being "something of a nerd" (membership group) but *feel negative attraction to the group and desire to disassociate from or disclaim membership* in it. For this student, nerds are a **disclaimant reference group.** This student may attempt to avoid consumption behaviors common to the nerd group in an attempt to disassociate from it. One study that looked at how consumers think about fashion includes an interview with a young African-American woman, Gretta, who grew up in a "project-hood." She felt stigmatized by her membership in this group at the school to which she was bused. She talked about how she never had the name-brand stuff and how it made her feel bad, "seeing everyone else have something you

Exhibit 15.1 Types of Reference Groups

can't have." For Gretta, people from the project-hood constitute a disclaimant group.[82] Alternatively, a high school cheerleader may *feel positive about her membership in that group.* In this case she is likely to adhere to the group's norms and act in ways to reinforce her membership role in that group. For her, cheerleaders constitute a **contactual reference group.** Many of her consumption behaviors may be similar to those of other members of her group, as they all use similar consumption behaviors to reinforce their membership role. The use of consumption behaviors to reinforce group membership is familiar, as evidenced by the teenaged bosozoku drivers described earlier. Certain consumption objects such Raiders caps or particular brands of sneakers have been banned in some high schools because of their strong associations with gangs. For example, a former gang member in Los Angeles reported that he can drive down the street and point out a gang member just by the way he or she dresses—the shoes, jackets, and hats are symbols, and "kids got killed over them."[83]

Some important group influence can derive from a *group the individual doesn't belong to* but has either *strong positive attraction toward*—an **aspirational reference group**—or *strong negative attraction toward*—an **avoidance reference group.** Just because an individual feels a strong positive attraction to a particular group does not necessarily mean that she or he desires membership in that group, but it may mean that the group will be very influential in certain of the individual's attitudes and behaviors.

The influence of aspirational reference groups has been demonstrated in many different studies. For example, one study asked college students at a western university in the United States about their attitudes and intentions to adopt a new "cordless headphone that could be used with any current personal or home stereo system."[84] The findings suggest that aspirational group influence affects consumer attitudes and intentions in at least three distinct ways. First, the endorsement of the product by an aspirational reference group (the U.S. ski team) enhanced students' perceptions about the social desirability of new product consumption. Second, the endorsement had a direct positive effect on the perceived visibility of early adoption behavior. Finally, the endorsement had a significant influence on perceptions of sound quality. Although members of the U.S. ski team would not necessarily have any specific expertise in judging sound quality, their endorsement led consumers to infer better sound quality. One explanation for this type of aspirational group influence is provided by the **model of meaning transfer.**[85] The focus of this model is on *the transfer of culturally relevant meanings from the endorser to the product.* In the example of the cordless headphone, meanings such as "performance" and "quality" may move from the aspirational group to the new product through the endorsement process. In this case the consumer recognizes an essential similarity between the endorser (the U.S. Ski Team) and the new product (a cordless headphone). We will have more to say about this model in Chapter 18 when we discuss consumption meanings.

What about the influence of avoidance groups? Are people influenced by nonmembership, negative-affect groups? Do consumers avoid certain clothing and behaviors out of fear that they will be mistaken for "one of them"? Certainly, in the case of gangs, the influence of avoidance groups is apparent—wearing a particular symbol could result in death. However, the influence of avoidance groups can also operate more subtly. For example, earlier we referenced a study where college students changed their color preferences to avoid sharing preferences with students from a rival school.

Degree of Contact

Degree of contact refers to *how much interpersonal contact the group members have with each other.* Groups characterized by frequent interpersonal contact are referred to as primary groups. Groups characterized by limited interpersonal contact are called secondary groups. Although, in general, we might expect primary groups to have more influence, we can think of many obvious exceptions. For example, perhaps you have a childhood friend that you don't see very often because she lives in a different part of the country. She might not influence your everyday shopping behaviors very much, but when you really need advice on something very important in your life, she may be the first person you call on. This introduces the important idea that reference groups have domains of influence. It's entirely possible to respect and be influenced by a group in one area but not in some other area.

The Degree of Reference Group Influence

A multitude of factors are likely to affect the degree of reference group influence on a particular purchase or consumption behavior. Studies have shown that some individuals are more susceptible to reference group influence than others.[86] For example, the high school girls in Shibuya and Hrajuku, Japan, will leap on any trend if the marketing is right, at least according to Sanrio's design department head. The boom-craze mentality among teens in Japan is so powerful that once 5 percent of the teen-girl market endorses a product, another 60 percent will almost certainly follow suit in less than a month.[87] A variety of studies have also shown that certain types of product and consumption choices are more likely to be influenced by reference groups than other product and consumption choices.[88] Industry Insights 15.1 illustrates some findings about influentials for the hip-hop generation. The hip-hop culture is the largest subculture of urban youth, composed of predominantly African-American teens and numbering 14 million. For members of this group peer approval is vital, and they may well be the most difficult group to reach with mainstream messages.

Exhibit 15.2 illustrates some key dimensions that are likely to influence the degree of reference group influence. Some of these factors we have already discussed. If a behavior is not visible to others or not distinctive then it is less vulnerable to reference group influence. The use of uniforms in schools is an attempt to take a highly visible behavior (which is vulnerable to group influence) and make it undistinguished. One aim is to reduce the feeling of children from poorer families that they don't belong. Of course, even within the rigid constraints of school uniforms students find ways to signal group and social class membership. A line of copy from a Lands' End catalog promotes "All uniform clothes are not created uniformly. See what sets Lands' End Kids Apart." Of course, one of the things that sets upscale catalog uniforms apart is their price.[89] By contrast, recycling programs in many cities attempt to make recycling a visible behavior. For example, in Boulder, Col-

- Messages perceived as being from outside the culture have little chance of getting in, and attempts to co-opt the culture will be resented and rejected.
- It is not an exaggeration to say that many of the hip-hop culture's members would rather risk death than subject themselves to peer group ostracism.
- Any authority figure telling them what to do is subject to immediate challenge. Messages perceived as persuasive are suspect. The cultural norm respects those who resist.
- When we asked who could speak to them about teen pregnancy or drugs, hip-hop members responded, "A single mother our age, someone who's going through it right now. Let her tell us what it's like. I'd listen to her."

Source: Dan Fost, "Reaching the Hip Hop Generation," American Demographics 15 (5, 1993), pp. 15–17.

orado, on pick-up days recycled materials are prominently displayed in the front of houses in brightly colored bins. If you don't recycle, your neighbors know it.

What constitutes distinctive behavior varies from reference group to reference group. For example, college students owning skis in Pittsburgh, Pennsylvania, may be distinctive, but in Boulder, Colorado, the vast majority of college students own skis. To be distinctive in Boulder requires this year's elite brand of skis. Of course, the effect of behavior visibility and distinctiveness also depends on the relevance of the behavior to group image, standards,

Exhibit 15.2 Consumption Situations and Degree of Reference Group Influence

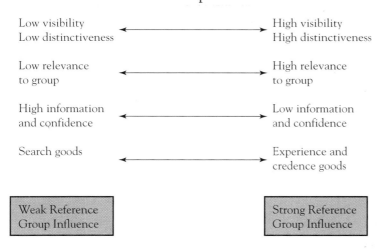

| Low visibility
Low distinctiveness | ⟷ | High visibility
High distinctiveness |

| Low relevance
to group | ⟷ | High relevance
to group |

| High information
and confidence | ⟷ | Low information
and confidence |

| Search goods | ⟷ | Experience and
credence goods |

| Weak Reference
Group Influence | | Strong Reference
Group Influence |

and norms. For example, if a neighborhood is indifferent about recycling, making recycling behavior more visible will not result in more recycling. In addition, as we discussed earlier, the opportunity to transfer meaning from the group to the object is enhanced when there is an essential similarity, that is, when the behavior seems relevant to the group image, standards, or norms. Thus, Bill Cosby is an excellent spokesperson for Jello pudding but much less effective as a spokesperson for the brokerage firm E. F. Hutton.

Finally, as we noted previously, consumers often believe that reference groups have better information than the information that they themselves have. Thus, when consumers perceive themselves to have low information as compared to a reference group and are not confident about their own attitudes or behaviors, the reference group may exert considerable influence. In unfamiliar consumption situations and complex product choices, reference groups are particularly influential. A study revealed that 25 percent of the people accompanied by a purchase pal invited that person along expressly to increase confidence in their choice.[90]

Similarly, with products and services for which consumers can't easily assess quality for themselves, reference groups may be relied on. Economist Philip Nelson talks about three types of product choices.[91] The first type is one for which *it is possible to observe the quality of the product from observation,* if the consumer has the expertise to do so. He calls products with these characteristics **search goods.** This type would include such things as fresh produce (lettuce, carrots, banana), cloth, and furniture. The second type of product choice *requires experience before it's possible to ascertain quality.* Nelson terms these products **experience goods.** For example, after seeing a movie it's easy to judge, at least for yourself, what the quality is, but it's difficult to appraise quality in advance. To decide on a movie consumers often rely on **surrogate experience,** *the reported experience of someone else,* in this case, friends or film critics. Many services are experience goods, which partially explains why interpersonal sources are so important in their selection. The third type of product choice is one for which *even after purchase and consumption it's difficult to evaluate quality.* Nelson refers to these products as **credence goods.** Checkups on people and cars are examples of credence goods. Consumers hope that if there's something wrong the physician or car mechanic found it, but they can't really be sure. In these cases people rely on information from others about the reputation of the service provider.

summary

In this chapter we described interpersonal influence. One of the reasons people are not more attuned to others' influence is because of an illusion of personal invulnerability. Interpersonal influence can be intentional or accidental; it is pervasive and to be influenced is often adaptive—it makes sense. Others can help people to make efficient and economical choices and can help them manage their environment.

Understanding personal influence begins by recognizing that one's attitudes and behaviors are very much shaped by the individual's particular social contexts. Interpersonal sources have a strong effect on consumer preferences and choices and influence others in both overt and more subtle ways. There are three important forms of influence, including normative (utilitarian), value-expressive (identification), and informational. In many, if not most, purchase and consumption situations the influence of others is not easily separated into normative, value-expressive, and informational forms of influence.

There are many familiar influence tactics that consumers encounter every day. These include reciprocity, commitment and consistency, a variety of source characteristics, and the scarcity principle. The bases for some of these influence tactics are unique to one or a few cultures (e.g., psychological reactance), whereas the bases for other influence tactics are fundamental to human exchanges (e.g., reciprocity). Finally, the bases for some influence tactics are shared by many cultures but are certainly more important in some than in others (e.g., desire for distinction).

Groups are an important aspect of interpersonal influence. Consumers compare themselves to and refer to groups in forming their own perspectives, attitudes, and behaviors. Reference groups can be identified according to membership, attraction, and degree of contact. Both membership and nonmembership groups can have significant influence on an individual within a domain of purchase and consumption behavior. Characteristics of consumption situations that contribute to strong reference group influence include visibility and distinctiveness of purchase and consumption; relevance of the consumption situation to the group; low consumer information and confidence; and certain product types (experience and credence goods).

The influence processes described in this chapter relate very closely to concepts introduced in Chapter 1. Each phase of the circle of consumption is affected by these processes. The influence processes described here also relate to many other important topics in consumer behavior. The successful diffusion of innovations relies on identifying, understanding, and managing influencers such as innovators, opinion leaders, and market mavens (Chapter 16). Persuasive advertising appeals directed at changing attitudes and behaviors also depend on many of the influence tactics we've described (Chapter 13). Source characteristics are an especially important component of many advertising campaigns, and advertisers rely heavily on endorsements by aspirational reference groups, admired celebrities, or the "common man." Discussions of group and family decision-making processes (Chapter 14), social class (Chapter 6), and lifestyle (Chapter 8) also relate to and are complemented by an understanding of interpersonal influence.

1. Exhibit 15.1 describes four common types of reference groups. Think of examples of each of these four types of reference groups in your own life.

2. Mike is getting ready to interview for a job. He would like to influence the company to give him the job rather than someone equally qualified. Of course, he plans to be well prepared, but he'd like an extra edge. Drawing on commonly used influence tactics, give Mike advice for handling the job interview.

3. Construct a promotional appeal to illustrate:
   a. Normative (utilitarian) influence
   b. Value-expressive (identification) influence
   c. Informational influence

4. A sorority is planning a theme party. Major parties are important social occasions, and party themes are typically a chapterwide decision. Based on your own knowledge of social organizations, describe how interpersonal influence might operate in planning the party.

5. Think of two recent consumption situations, one for which you think reference group influence was strong and one for which you think reference group influence was weak. Describe the characteristics of these two consumption situations. Draw on Exhibit 15.2 as appropriate.

6. Assume that you have been elected to head a group on campus to reduce student abuse of alcohol. Employing the principles from this chapter, outline a campaign to influence the decision to consume less alcohol.

7. Consider the last three movies you went to see. How did you decide to go see these movies? Did other people influence your decision to see any (all) of these movies? Explain.

8. How could findings from the research on interpersonal influence be used to develop marketing strategy for the following?

a. Hospitals	d. Photographers
b. Pizza	e. Shampoo
c. Condoms	f. Cruises

9. Build your own set of related examples to illustrate the relationship between interpersonal influence and the circle of consumption. (*Hint:* In the book we used examples related to a holiday meal.)

You Make The Call

Can Online Individualization Technology Replace Interpersonal Influence?

Sombasa is an online marketing company that empowers e-commerce through its individualized e-mail publications. When consumers visit one of Sombasa's sites they can customize their publications according to their tastes and interests. From consumers' preference information, Sombasa matches merchants' products to a specific user's profile, determining how appropriate each item is for a particular subscriber. According to Sombasa, consumers benefit because they get to hear about products and publications that are relevant to their tastes. Marketers benefit because they reach customers who most want to hear about their products. This type of mass customization was described in Chapter 2 as the leading edge in market segmentation strategy. In this chapter we also describe similar approaches such as collaborative filtering (outlined in Good Practice 15.1) designed to custom tailor recommendations to users.

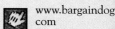
www.bargaindog.com

By tailoring messages to each subscriber's lifestyle, budget, and tastes, Sombasa is hoping to become your preferred source of information. They assume that in an age of virtually infinite choice, Internet shoppers are starved for real advice, and so far they appear to be right. The flagship for Sombasa technology is the BargainDog website, a top 100 shopping site as ranked by PC Data Online. BargainDog was launched in 1999 and features over 300 merchants, including amazon.com and pets.com. BargainDog has over a quarter of a million registered members.

www.amazon.com

1. In what ways is online, individualization technology like an interpersonal source, and in what ways is it different? How is online collaborative filtering like an interpersonal source, and how is it different?

2. Could a company like Sombasa use an understanding of interpersonal influence to improve their service delivery? Explain.

www.pets.com

1. See James C. McCroskey, Virginia P. Richmond, and Robert A. Stewart, *One on One: The Foundations of Interpersonal Communication* (Englewood Cliffs, NJ: Prentice Hall, 1986).

2. Mary Ann McGrath and Cele Otnes, "Unacquainted Influencers: When Strangers Interact in the Retail Setting," *Journal of Business Research* 32 (3, 1995), pp. 261–73.

3. David M. Johnson, "Disney World as Structure and Symbol: Re-creation of the American Experience," *Journal of Popular Culture* 15, no. 1 (1981), pp. 157–65; William B. Martin, *Quality Service: The Restaurant Manager's Bible* (Ithaca, NY: Cornell School of Hotel Administration, 1986); David Romm, " 'Restauration' Theater: Giving Direction to Service," *The Cornell Hotel and Restaurant Association Quarterly* 29 (February 1989), pp. 31–39; and Maxwell Boas and Steve Chain, *Big Mac: The Unauthorized Story of McDonald's* (New York: Dutton, 1976).

4. Blake E. Ashforth and Ronald H. Humphrey, "Emotional Labor in Service Roles: The Influence of Identity," *Academy of Management Review* 18, no. 1 (1993), p. 91.

5. See Philip G. Zimbardo, Ebbe B. Ebbesen, and Christina Maslach, *Influencing Attitudes and Changing Behavior,* 2nd ed. (Reading, MA: Addison-Wesley, 1977).

6. McCroskey et al., *One on One.*

7. This illustration comes from Allen Funt's 1970 United Artists film entitled *What Do You Say to a Naked Lady?* It is very similar in form to the classic Asch experiment. In the Asch experiment eight subjects were brought into a room and asked to determine which of a set of three unequal lines was closest to the length of a fourth line shown some distance from the other three. The subjects were to announce their judgments publicly. Seven of the subjects were working for the experimenter, and they announced incorrect matches. The order of the announcements was arranged so that the naive subject responded last. In a control situation, 37 naive subjects performed the task 18 times each without any information about others' choices. Two of the 37 subjects made a total of three mistakes. However, when another group of 50 naive subjects responded after hearing the unanimous but incorrect judgment of the other group members, 37 subjects made a total of 194 errors, all of which were in agreement with the mistake made by the group. For details on this experiment, see S. E. Asch, "Effects of Group Pressure upon the Modification and Distortion of Judgments," in *Readings in Social Psychology,* E. E. MacCoby et al., ed. (New York: Holt, Rinehart and Winston, 1958), pp.

174–83. This effect has been replicated a number of times in a variety of very different settings. For a recent example, see William O. Bearden and Randall L. Rose, "Attention to Social Comparison Information: An Individual Difference Factor Affecting Consumer Conformity," *Journal of Consumer Research* 16 (March 1990), pp. 461–72.

8. Ronald H. Frank, *Choosing the Right Pond: Human Behavior and the Quest for Status* (New York: Oxford University Press, 1985).

9. George Herbert Mead, *Mind, Self and Society* (Chicago: University of Chicago Press, 1934).

10. Richard E. Petty and John T. Caccioppo, *Attitudes and Persuasion: Classic and Contemporary Approaches* (Dubuque, IA: Wm. C. Brown, 1981).

11. Johann Arndt, "The Role of Product-Related Conversations in the Diffusion of a New Product," *Journal of Marketing Research* 4 (August 1967), pp. 291–95; and Charles W. King and John O. Summers, "Overlap of Opinion Leadership across Consumer Product Categories," *Journal of Marketing Research* 7 (February 1970), pp. 43–50.

12. A. Coskun Samli, "Interrelationships between the Market Segments and the Buyer Behavior," in *Retail Management Strategy: Selected Readings,* David J. Rachman, ed. (Englewood Cliffs, NJ: Prentice Hall, 1970), pp. 79–112.

13. Linda L. Price and Lawrence F. Feick, "The Role of Interpersonal Sources in External Search: An Informational Perspective," in *Advances in Consumer Research,* vol. 11, Thomas C. Kinnear, ed. (Ann Arbor, MI: Association for Consumer Research, 1984), pp. 250–53.

14. Geoffrey C. Kiel and Roger A. Layton, "Dimensions of Consumer Information Seeking Behavior," *Journal of Marketing Research* 18 (May 1981), pp. 233–39; J. W. Newman, "Consumer External Search: Amount and Determinants," in *Consumer and Industrial Buying Behavior,* A. G. Woodside, J. N. Sheth, and P. D. Bennett, eds. (New York: North-Holland, 1977); Hans B. Thorelli, "Concentration of Information Power among Consumers," *Journal of Marketing Research* 8 (November 1971), pp. 427–32; and J. G. Udell, "Prepurchase Behavior of Buyers of Small Electrical Appliances," *Journal of Marketing,* vol. 30 (1966), pp. 427–32.

15. Sharon E. Beatty and Scott M. Smith, "External Search Efforts: An Investigation across Several Product Categories," *Journal of Consumer Research* 14 (June 1987), pp. 83–95; Roger A. Formisano, Richard W. Olshavsky, and Shelley Tapp, "Choice Strategy in a Difficult Task Environment," *Journal of Consumer Research* 8 (March 1982), pp. 474–79; and Keith Murray, "A Test of Services Marketing Theory: Consumer Information Acquisition Activities," *Journal of Marketing* 55 (January 1991), pp. 10–16.

16. Lawrence F. Feick, Linda L. Price, and Robin A. Higie, "People Who Use People: Looking at Opinion Leadership from the Other Side," in *Advances in Consumer Research,* vol. 13, Richard J. Lutz, ed. (Provo, UT: Association for Consumer Research, 1986), pp. 409–13.

17. Marsha L. Richins, "Negative Word-of-Mouth by Dissatisfied Consumers: A Pilot Study," *Journal of Marketing* 47 (Winter 1983), pp. 68–78.

18. Paul M. Herr, Frank R. Kardes, and John Kim, "Effects of Word-of-Mouth and Product-Attribute Information on Persuasion: An Accessibility-Diagnosticity Perspective," *Journal of Consumer Research* 17 (March 1991), pp. 454–62.

19. Steve Lowery, "Secret Raves," *Press Telegram,* January 16, 1993, p. B1.

20. Malcolm Gladwell, "The Science of the Sleeper: How the Information Age Could Blow Away the Blockbuster," *The New Yorker,* October 4, 1999, pp. 48–55.

21. Wayne D. Hoyer, "An Examination of Consumer Decision Making for a Common Repeat Purchase Product," *Journal of Consumer Research* 11 (December 1984), pp. 822–29.

22. Andrew Kopkind, "From Russia with Love and Squalor," *Nation,* January 18, 1993, pp. 44–61. See also Güliz Ger, Russell W. Belk, and Dana-Nicoleta Lascu, "The Development of Consumer Desire in Marketizing and Developing Economies: The Cases of Romania and Turkey," in *Advances in Consumer Research,* vol. 20, Leigh McAlister and Michael L. Rothschild, eds. (Provo, UT: Association for Consumer Research, 1993), pp. 102–7.

23. Edward T. Hall, *Beyond Culture* (New York: Anchor, 1977); Edward T. Hall, *The Hidden Dimension* (New York: Anchor, 1990); and Edward T. Hall, *The Silent Language* (New York: Doubleday, 1959). See also, John Graham, Dong Kim Chi-Yuan Lin, and Michael Robinson, "Buyer-Seller Negotiations around the Pacific Rim: Differences in Fundamental Exchange Processes," *Journal of Consumer Research* 15 (June 1988), pp. 48–54.

24. Lawrence Wright, "Orphans of Jonestown," *The New Yorker,* November 22, 1993, pp. 66–89.

25. Jeff Kaye, "The Rave of Europe," *Los Angeles Times,* February 3, 1993, p. H1 describes the EuroKids.

26. Lawrence F. Feick, Robin A. Higie, and Linda L. Price, "Consumer Search and Decision Problems in a Transitional Economy: Hungary, 1989–1992," working paper no. 93-113, *Marketing Science Institute,* 1993; Robin Higie Coulter, Lawrence F. Feick, and Linda L. Price, "Making up Time in the 1990s in Hungary: Are the Changes Purely Cosmetic?" working paper, University of Connecticut, 2000.

27. William O. Bearden and Michael J. Etzel, "Reference Group Influence on Product and Brand Purchase Decisions," *Journal of Consumer Research* 9 (September 1982), pp. 183–94; C. Whan Park and V. Parker Lessig, "Students and Housewives: Differences in Susceptibility to Reference Group Influence," *Journal of Consumer Research* 4 (September 1977), pp. 102–10; and Paul W. Miniard and Joel B. Cohen, "Modeling Personal and Normative Influences on Behavior," *Journal of Consumer Research* 10 (September 1983), pp. 169–80.

28. John Kao, "The Worldwide Web of Chinese Business," *Harvard Business Review* 71, March–April 1993, pp. 24–33.

29. Normative influence can operate on a very subtle level. The Milgram experiments demonstrate the willingness of subjects, under the directive of a researcher, to deliver increasing levels of electrical shocks to a victim (actually a confederate in the experiment who is acting) even after the victim begged for release with "an agonized scream." See S. Milgram, *Obedience to Authority* (New York: Harper and Row, 1974). These extremely disturbing and controversial studies illustrate the inability to defy the wishes of the boss (in this case, the lab researcher) and reveal a deep-seated sense of duty to authority within all of us.

30. Paul W. Miniard and Joel B. Cohen, "Modeling Personal and Normative Influences on Behavior," *Journal of Consumer Research* 10 (September 1983), pp. 169–80; and William O. Bearden, Richard G. Netemeyer, and Jesse E. Teel, "Measurement of Consumer Susceptibility to Interpersonal Influence," *Journal of Consumer Research* 15 (March 1989), pp. 473–81.

31. Pamela E. Grimm, Jagdish Agrawal, and Paul S. Richardson, "Product Conspicuousness and Buying Motives as Determinants of Reference Group Influences," in *European Advances in Consumer Research,* vol. 4, Bernard Dubois, Tina M. Lowrey, L. J. Shrum, and Marc Vanhuele, eds. (Provo, UT: Association for Consumer Research, 1999), pp. 97–103.

32. Georg Simmel, "Fashion," *International Quarterly* 10 (1904), pp. 130–55; Eric J. Arnould, "Toward a Broadened Theory of Preference Formation and the Diffusion of Innovations: Cases from Zinder Province, Niger Republic," *Journal of Consumer Research* 16 (September 1989), pp. 239–67; and Grant McCracken, "Culture and Consumption: A Theoretical Account of the Structure and Movement of the Cultural Meaning of Consumer Goods," *Journal of Consumer Research* 13 (June 1986), pp. 71–84.

33. For lots of good examples related to fashion and style, see Craig J. Thompson and Diana L. Haytko, "Speaking of Fashion: Consumers' Uses of Fashion Discourses and the Appropriation of Countervailing Cultural Meanings," *Journal of Consumer Research* 24 (June 1997), pp. 15–42; and Robert J. Fisher and Linda L. Price, "An Investigation into the Social Context of Early Adoption Behavior," *Journal of Consumer Research* 19 (December 1992), pp. 477–86.

34. Malcolm Gladwell, "The Coolhunt," *The New Yorker,* March 17, 1997, pp. 78–87, describes DeeDee. She works for an advertising agency in Del Mar called Lambesis and puts out a quarterly tip sheet called the L Report on what the cool kids in major American cities are thinking, doing, and buying. She is a coolhunter. See also, Janine Lopiano-Misdom and Joanne De Luca, *Street Trends* (New York: HarperCollins, 1998). The example about Jennifer is taken from *Street Trends,* pp. 21–22.

35. Elizabeth Lesly and Maria Mallory, "Inside the Black Business Network," *Business Week,* November 29, 1993, p. 72.

36. Fisher and Price, "An Investigation into the Social Context of Early Adoption Behavior."

37. Melanie Wallendorf and Eric J. Arnould, " 'My Favorite Things': A Cross-Cultural Inquiry into Object Attachment, Possessiveness and Social Linkage," *Journal of Consumer Research* 14 (March 1988), pp. 531–47.

38. Nicholas Weinstock, "I Was a B.M.O.C. At Botswana U.," *The Nation,* December 6, 1993, p. 693.

39. Rick Pollay and Jean Kilbourne, *Pack of Lies* video. This film describes the strategic use of value-expressive influence by cigarette companies.

40. Charisse Jones, "Critics Fear Hip-Hop Is Eroding Kids' Morals and Touching Off Violent Episodes Like the Recent Rampage at Magic Mountain. Are These Entertainers Truly Poisoning Young Fans' Minds? Or Is That Just a Bum Rap? Rap's Bad Rep," *Los Angeles Times,* May 2, 1993, Home, p. 1; and www.move.de/amm/ECON.htm.

41. Linda L. Price and Lawrence Feick, "The Role of Interpersonal Sources in External Search. An Informational Perspective," (Chicago: American Marketing Association Winter Educator's Meetings Proceedings).

42. Clinton R. Sanders, "Tattoo Consumption: Risk and Regret in the Purchase of a Socially Marginal Service," in *Advances in Consumer Research,* vol. 12, Elizabeth C. Hirschman and Morris B. Holbrook, eds. (Provo, UT: Association for Consumer Research, 1985), p. 20; Cathy L. Hartman and Pamela L. Kiecker, "Marketplace Influencers at the Point of Purchase: The Role of Purchase Pals in Consumer Decision Making," in *AMA Educators' Proceedings,* vol. 2, Mary Gilly and Robert Dwyer, eds. (Chicago: American Marketing Association, 1991), pp. 461–69; and David F. Midgley, "Patterns of Interpersonal Information Seeking for the Purchase of a Symbolic Product," *Journal of Marketing Research* 20 (February 1983), pp. 74–83.

43. Lawrence F. Feick and Linda L. Price, "Thoughts on Search: Breaking Free of the Purchase Paradigm," in *AMA Winter Educators' Proceedings,* vol. 2, Paul Anderson and Michael Ryan, eds. (Chicago: American Marketing Association, 1984), pp. 179–83.

44. Feick, Price, and Higie, "People Who Use People."

45. Jacqueline Johnson Brown and Peter H. Reingen, "Social Ties and Word-of-Mouth Referral Behavior," *Journal of Consumer Research* 14 (December 1987), pp. 350–62; and Peter H. Reingen, Brian L. Foster, Jacqueline Johnson Brown, and Stephen B. Seidman, "Brand Congruence in Interpersonal Relations: A Social Network Analysis," *Journal of Consumer Research* 11 (December 1984), pp. 771–83.

46. These tools and others have been described in greater depth in a variety of places. One of the best and most readable treatments of influence tactics is found in Robert Cialdini, *Influence: The New Psychology of Modern Persuasion* (New York: HarperCollins, 1983).

47. A. W. Gouldner, "The Norm of Reciprocity: A Preliminary Statement," *American Sociological Review* 25 (1960), pp. 161–78; and Marcel Mauss, *The Gift,* trans. I. G. Cunnison (London: Cohen and West, 1954).

48. One famous institutionalized form of reciprocity called the Kula is described by Bronislaw Malinowski. The main principle underlying the regulation of actual exchange is that the Kula consists in the bestowing of a ceremonial gift, which has to be repaid by an equivalent countergift after a lapse of time. But it can never be exchanged from hand to hand, with the equivalence between the two objects being discussed, bargained about, and computed. The second important principle is that the equivalence of the countergift is left to the giver, and it cannot be enforced by any kind of coercion. If the article given as a countergift is not equivalent, the recipient will be disappointed and angry, but he has no direct means of redress, no means of coercing his partner. For more discussion, see Bronislaw Malinowski, *Argonauts of the Western Pacific* (London: Routledge and Kegan Paul, 1922); and Jerry W. Leach and Edmund Leach, eds. *The Kula: New Perspectives on Massim Exchange* (Cambridge: Cambridge University Press, 1983).

49. Claude Levi-Strauss, *The Elementary Structures of Relationship,* J. H. Bell, J. R. von Sturner, and R. Needham, trans. (Boston: Beacon, 1969); and R. Leakey and R. Lewin, *People of the Lake* (New York: Anchor Press/Doubleday, 1978).

50. Youngme Moon, "Intimate Exchanges Using Computers to Elicit Self-Disclosure from Consumers," *Journal of Consumer Research* 26 (March 2000), pp. 323–39.

51. D. T. Regan, "Effects of a Favor and Liking on Compliance," *Journal of Experimental Social Psychology* 7 (1971), pp. 627–39.

52. Leslie Kanuk and Conrad Berenson, "Mail Surveys and Response Rates: A Literature Review," *Journal of Marketing Research* 12 (November 1975), pp. 440–53.

53. R. B. Cialdini et al., "Reciprocal Concessions Procedure for Inducing Compliance: The Door-in-the-Face Technique," *Journal of Personality and Social Psychology* 31 (1975), pp. 206–15; and John

C. Mowen and Robert Cialdini, "On Implementing the Door-in-the-Face Compliance Strategy in a Marketing Context," *Journal of Marketing Research* 17 (May 1980), pp. 253–58.

54. Some postmodern theorists argue that increasingly consumers "don't really care whether things make sense as long as they look interesting." Consumers shift between very different and often contradictory self-images with "no such thing as an essential 'me.'" See Jack Solomon, *The Signs of Our Time: The Secret Meanings of Everyday Life* (New York: Harper and Row, 1988), p. 219. For example, an individual may have many very different styles of dressing that vary between situations and moods.

55. The initial research on FITD was conducted by J. L. Freedman and S. C. Fraser in the mid-1960s. In their research, a researcher, posing as a volunteer worker, had gone door to door in a residential California neighborhood making a preposterous request of homeowners. The homeowners were asked to allow a public service billboard to be installed on their front lawns. To get an idea of how the sign would look, they were shown a photograph depicting an attractive house, the view of which was almost completely obscured by an ugly sign reading "DRIVE CAREFULLY." Although the request was understandably refused by the great majority (83 percent) of other residents in this area, a full 76 percent of this particular group agreed to the request. Why? Two weeks earlier, they had made a small commitment to driver safety. A different volunteer worker had asked them to accept and display a small three-inch square sign that read "BE A SAFE DRIVER." See Freedman and Fraser, "Compliance without Pressure: The Foot-in-the-Door Technique," *Journal of Personality and Social Psychology* 4 (1966), pp. 195–203. For a synthesis of research results on this and related compliance techniques, see Edward Fern, Kent Monroe, and Ramon Avila, "Effectiveness of Multiple Request Strategies: A Synthesis of Research Results," *Journal of Marketing Research* 23 (May 1986), pp. 144–52.

56. M. Deutsch and H. B. Gerard, "A Study of Normative and Informational Social Influences upon Individual Judgment," *Journal of Abnormal and Social Psychology* 51 (1955), pp. 629–36.

57. Robin A. Higie and Lawrence F. Feick, "The Effects of Preference Heterogeneity and Source Characteristics on Ad Processing and Judgments about Endorsers," *Journal of Advertising* 21 (June 1992), pp. 9–25; Linda L. Price, Lawrence F. Feick, and Robin A. Higie, "Preference Heterogeneity and Coorientation as Determinants of Perceived Informational Influence," *Journal of Business Research* 19 (1989), pp. 227–42; and Stewart Bither and Peter Wright, "Preferences between Product Consultants: Choices versus Preference Functions," *Journal of Consumer Research* 4 (June 1977), pp. 39–47.

58. T. G. Brock, "Communicator-Recipient Similarity and Decision Change," *Journal of Personality and Social Psychology* 1 (June 1965), pp. 650–54.

59. Leon Festinger, "A Theory of Social Comparison Processes," *Human Relations* 7 (May 1954), pp. 117–40.

60. Bearden and Rose, "Attention to Social Comparison Information." The effect of "a much despised, in-state rival institution" preference on students' reported preferences was strongest for those students high on a scale that measures attention to social comparison information (ATSCI).

61. Arch G. Woodside and J. W. Davenport, "The Effect of Salesmen Similarity and Expertise on Consumer Purchasing Behavior," *Journal of Marketing Research* 11 (May 1974), pp. 198–202. See also, Dorothy Leonard-Barton, "Experts as Negative Opinion Leaders in the Diffusion of a Technological Innovation," *Journal of Consumer Research* 11 (March 1985), pp. 914–26.

62. Linda L. Price, Lawrence F. Feick, and Robin A. Higie, "Information Sensitive Consumers and Market Information," *Journal of Consumer Affairs* 21 (Winter 1987), pp. 328–41. See also, Michael R. Solomon, "The Missing Link: Surrogate Consumers in the Marketing Chain," *Journal of Marketing* 50 (October 1986), pp. 208–18.

63. Leonard-Barton, "Experts as Negative Opinion Leaders"; and Alain d'Astous, "A Study of Individual Factors Explaining Movie Goers' Consultation of Film Critics," in *European Advances in Consumer Research,* vol. 4, Bernard Dubois, Tina M. Lowrey, L. J. Shrum, and Marc Vanhuele, eds. (Provo, UT: Association for Consumer Research, 1999), pp. 201–8.

64. James H. Myers and Thomas S. Robertson, "Dimensions of Opinion Leadership," *Journal of Marketing Research* 9 (February 1972), pp. 41–46; Charles W. King and John O. Summers, "Overlap of Opinion Leadership across Consumer Product Categories," *Journal of Marketing Re-*

search 7 (February 1970), pp. 43–50; and Meera P. Venkatraman, "Opinion Leaders, Adopters, and Communicative Adopters: A Role Analysis," *Psychology and Marketing* 6 (Spring 1990), pp. 51–68.

65. Feick, Price, and Higie, "People Who Use People."

66. Lawrence F. Feick and Linda L. Price, "The Market Maven: A Diffuser of Marketplace Information," *Journal of Marketing* 51 (January 1987), pp. 83–97; and Robin A. Higie, Lawrence F. Feick, and Linda L. Price, "Types and Amounts of Word-of-Mouth Communications about Retailers," *Journal of Retailing* 63 (Fall 1987), pp. 260–78.

67. Linda L. Price, Lawrence F. Feick, and Audrey Guskey-Federouch, "Everyday Market Helping Behavior," *Journal of Public Policy and Marketing* 14, no. 2 (Fall 1995), pp. 255–66. For a charming description and discussion of the market maven, see Malcolm Gladwell, *The Tipping Point* (New York: Little, Brown, 2000), pp. 60–69.

68. Shelly Chaiken, "Communicator Physical Attractiveness and Persuasion," *Journal of Personality and Social Psychology* 37 (August 1979), pp. 1387–97.

69. Cialdini, *Influence.*

70. Lynn R. Kahle and Pamela M. Homer, "Physical Attractiveness of the Celebrity Endorser: A Social Adaptation Perspective," *Journal of Consumer Research* 11 (March 1985), pp. 954–61; and C. Whan Park and S. Mark Young, "Consumer Response to Television Commercials: The Impact of Involvement and Background Music on Brand Attitude Formation," *Journal of Marketing Research* 23 (February 1986), pp. 11–24.

71. See Peter M. Blau, *Exchange and Power in Social Life* (New Brunswick, NJ: Transaction Books, 1986).

72. For one example, see Gerald Zaltman and Christine Moorman, "The Importance of Personal Trust in the Use of Research," *Journal of Advertising Research* 28 (October–November 1988), pp. 16–24.

73. Eric J. Arnould and Linda L. Price, "River Magic: Extraordinary Experience and the Extended Service Encounter," *Journal of Consumer Research* 20 (June 1993), pp. 24–45. See also, Linda L. Price, Eric J. Arnould, and Patrick Tierney, "Going to Extremes: Managing Service Encounters and Assessing Provider Performance," *Journal of Marketing* 59 (April 1995), pp. 83–97.

74. Linda L. Price and Eric J. Arnould, "Commercial Friendships: Service Provider-Client Relationships in Context," *Journal of Marketing* 63 (October 1999), pp. 38–56; and Caren Siehl, David E. Bowen, and Christine M. Pearson, "Service Encounters as Rites of Integration: An Information Processing Model," *Organization Science* 3 (November 1992), pp. 537–55.

75. J. W. Brehm, *A Theory of Psychological Reactance* (New York: Academic Press, 1966).

76. S. S. Brehm, "Psychological Reactance and the Attractiveness of Unattainable Objects: Sex Differences in Children's Responses to an Elimination of Freedom," *Sex Roles* 7 (1981), pp. 937–49.

77. Mona Clee and Robert Wicklund, "Consumer Behavior and Psychological Reactance," *Journal of Consumer Research* 6 (March 1980), pp. 389–405.

78. Suein L. Hwang, "Marketing," *The Wall Street Journal,* June 14, 1991, p. B1; and Dean Starkman, "After Hue and Cry, Crayola Will Scrap Color 'Indian Red,' " *The Wall Street Journal,* March 10, 1999, p. B7.

79. J. Jeffrey Inman, Anil C. Peter, and Priya Raghubir, "Framing the Deal: The Role of Restrictions in Accentuating Deal Value," *Journal of Consumer Research* 24 (June 1997), pp. 68–79.

80. Jonathan Friedman, "The Political Economy of Elegance: An African Cult of Beauty," *Consumption and Identity,* Jonathan Friedman, ed. (Chur, Switzerland: Harwood Academic Publishers, 1994), pp. 167–88.

81. Ikuya Sato, *Kamikaze Biker: Parody and Anomy in Affluent Japan* (Chicago: University of Chicago Press, 1991), p. 1.

82. Thompson and Haytko, "Speaking of Fashion."

83. Rick Telander, "Senseless: In America's Cities, Kids Are Killing Kids over Sneakers and Other Sports Apparel Favored by Drug Dealers. Who's to Blame?" *Sports Illustrated,* May 14, 1990, pp. 36–49. The article contains an additional interview by Kristina Rebelo, "You See a Red Rag, Shoot," p. 46.

84. Fisher and Price, "An Investigation into the Social Context of Early Adoption Behavior."

85. Grant McCracken, "Who Is the Celebrity Endorser? Cultural Foundations of the Endorsement Process," *Journal of Consumer Research* 16 (December 1989), pp. 310–21.

86. Bearden, Netemeyer, and Teel, "Measurement of Consumer Susceptibility to Interpersonal Influence"; and Park and Lessig, "Students and Housewives."

87. "What's Up Pussy Cat?" www.tokyoclassified.com.

88. Bearden and Etzel, "Reference Group Influence on Product and Brand Purchase Decisions."

89. David Crockett and Melanie Wallendorf, "Sociological Perspectives on Imposed School Dress Codes: Consumption as Attempted Suppression of Class and Group Symbolism," *Journal of Macromarketing* 18 (Fall 1998), pp. 115–31.

90. Hartman and Kiecker, "Marketplace Influencers at the Point of Purchase."

91. Philip Nelson, "Information and Consumer Behavior," *Journal of Political Economy* 78 (March–April, 1970), pp. 311–29.

Learning Objectives

After completing this chapter, you should be able to:

- Distinguish characteristics of innovations that influence their rate of diffusion and help determine their market success.

- Distinguish diffusion and adoption processes.

- Describe reasons for resistance to change and for discontinuance.

- Describe strategies for changing attitudes and behavior.

- Understand how innovation and adoption processes are influenced by environmental, cultural, and social system factors.

- Identify and distinguish opinion leaders, market mavens, and innovative consumers important in the diffusion of innovations.

- Describe differences among consumers based on their time of adoption of innovations.

- Describe a common adoption decision.

Consumer Innovation

The Launch of the Toyota Prius[1]

The Japanese Launch

According to Mark Amstock, who was responsible for official launch preparations of the gas-electric hybrid Toyota Prius in North America, Toyota first demonstrated a hybrid-electric concept vehicle at the Tokyo Auto Show in 1995. "At that time it was a parallel-hybrid." he said, "We believed that hybrid-technology was a way of providing a customer benefit of high-mileage and clean operation. The motivation was to produce a car that delivered high mileage for the domestic Japanese market who are paying upwards of $3 a gallon for their gasoline. So there was a real economic motivator for the technology."

The Japanese government has also added several other powerful incentives, including sales tax exemption and tax credits worth several thousand dollars, which reduce the price of the vehicle both to corporations and individual owners. With the incentives the price for a corporate buyer drops to the equivalent of about US$15,000 and for an individual just over US$16,000.

Toyota has been criticized that it is subsidizing the Prius since analysts have estimated that it costs the company US$35–40,000 apiece to make the car. Amstock responded, "We can't be greedy and attempt to recoup that investment too quickly. We want to get the product out there. We want to understand how consumers react to it. We want to get customers comfortable with these new, maturing technologies, so we have to get it out there at a price that is affordable and can drive the market."

The North American Launch

When Toyota introduced the Prius into North America in the summer of 2000, it was significantly different then the model being sold in Japan. The most significant change was the engine, which increased from the current 1.5 liters to 1.8 liters. According to Amstock, "The car has to be more powerful, quicker, more responsive than in the domestic Japan market. Everywhere else in the world they drive at a little bit brisker pace than they do in Japan. Our U.S. roads are much more wide open than they are in the congested urban centers, so we need to deliver more performance."

Still, a recent J. D. Powers and Associates study indicates 75 percent of Americans don't know what a hybrid-electric car is much less how one operates. Hence, as part of its ongoing research and early marketing efforts, Toyota gave five American families in 12 cities the opportunity to test drive early North Americanized versions of the Prius for one month.

"The purpose is partially research and a little bit of PR (public relations) to understand how the car can adapt, how the technology can adapt to American consumer's lifestyle . . . help us understand how they react to it . . . what their likes and dislikes are not only in terms of product but also to give us a little insight on how to market and advertise the vehicle," Amstock explained.

In a clear demonstration of the power of the Internet, Toyota has accepted more than 15,000 applications to participate in the Family Demo Program through its Toyota.com website. Toyota screened applicants for their environmentalism and their acceptance of new technology. "We're looking for a mix of early adapter/techno-friendly types, environmentally friendly types, and general consumers." The online recruitment program has proven so successful that the company will not do any television advertising of the car; instead, it will initially concentrate its marketing dollars on Internet advertising.

The European Launch

The Prius launch in Europe coincided with that in North America. The European car is lighter than the U.S. model and as a result has a little better performance. "In Europe they have a significant motivation in high-priced gasoline," he remarked. "One of the questions we get from the European journalists is 'Why didn't you do it in diesel? You know that if you're really serious about fuel savings, why don't you do it in diesel?' Of course, you know their concerns are with tailpipe emissions and CO2 . . . (they are) not as concerned about particulates as we are here in the States."

Overview

As described by the economist Joseph Schumpeter, product choices (really choices between technologies) drive capitalist economies and shape them into engines of **creative destruction.** That is, capitalism encourages the creation of new markets, new technologies, and new forms of industrial organization. These innovations have the potential to increase the standard of living of the populace and are quickly adopted (within a capitalistic economic system). At the same time, however, these innovations drive out old forms of doing business. For example, the creation of the transistor makes the vacuum tube obsolete; and vacuum tube manufacturers go out of business. In time, computer chips replace the transistor. Old industries, old technologies are destroyed. New industries rise up in their place, but there is upheaval and disruption and displacement. Some companies go out of business. Workers find themselves to be ill suited for jobs in emerging industries; and they may be laid off. Consumers become dizzy with the wide array of new products and services that are introduced. Products may get more and more sophisticated over time; but consumers have less time to enjoy life, due partly to the large amount of time and energy it takes to be a consumer in the early twenty-first century.[2]

To some extent, Schumpeter's account of the triumph of technology may sound overly deterministic. In fact, it is not the technologies themselves that determine the future; rather, consumers and the individual choices they make determine how technologies are used in society. Some technologies fall by the wayside, neglected and discarded. Other technologies prosper and are adopted around the world. Nonetheless, almost all technologies evolve and adapt to the ways in which consumers use them. For instance, the radio was originally designed as a means for ships to communicate with one another and to communicate with those on land. The early pioneers of radio never imagined that they were perfecting an entertainment medium that would transform the world.

Whatever the merits of Schumpeter's arguments, this chapter focuses on innovation and change, which are at the heart of marketing. Marketers face the challenge of persuading people to change their attitudes and behaviors. Marketers ask consumers to be innovative: to buy in new places, for example. New places might include grocery stores in the developing world. Marketers ask consumers to buy in new ways. New ways might include using smart bankcards or computerized banking in the Triad countries. Marketers ask consumers to buy new products. As shown in Exhibit 16.1, most new products consist of me-too products, brand extensions, and reformulations. Sometimes marketers even ask consumers to learn a new way of life. For example, consumers in the transitional economies of the former Soviet bloc are asked to understand and decode marketing, consumer culture, and a new language of pricing and promotions.[3]

For every marketer asking the consumer to believe or do something innovative, another marketer is asking that same consumer to resist change—to be loyal to the existing product or solution. Hence, it's important to understand innovation and change and, at the same time, to understand the opposite forces: conservatism and resistance to change. The individual dynamics and social dynamics associated with change and resistance to change act together. Basic tensions between pressures for change and pressures to resist change are present at every level of society, from the individual to the nation-state.

Marketers win awards, draw public accolades, and create customer value by working with other parts of their organization to introduce successful new ideas, products, and services. Industry Insights 16.1 profiles Jim Yetter, marketing manager for Chrysler's Neon. He is an example of marketing's enhanced role in the development and introduction

Exhibit 16.1 New Product Introductions of Consumer Packaged Goods: 1980 to 1997

[Consumer packaged goods: consumable products packaged by the manufacturer for retail sale primarily through grocery and drug stores. New product: a product not previously offered for sale by a particular manufacturer including new varieties, formats, sizes, and packaging for existing products.]

Item	Food	Beverages	Health and Beauty	Household Products	Pet Products	Miscellaneous Products
Domestic and imports						
1980	1,192	256	834	331	86	197
1985	2,327	585	1,222	463	139	294
1990	3,453	630	1,531	432	164	154
1991	3,130	589	1,614	422	175	113
1992	2,987	587	1,869	417	213	127
1993	3,107	767	2,068	376	173	161
1994	3,883	807	2,655	378	161	97
1995	3,891	809	2,419	314	123	134
1996	3,889	977	3,051	369	160	148
1997, total	3,793	1,205	3,492	366	216	122
Percent						
New brands[1]	19.8	30.8	20.1	22.7	31.9	34.4
Brand extensions[2]	1.6	1.3	1.1	2.5	—	—
Line extensions[3]	78.6	67.9	78.8	74.8	68.1	65.6
Types of new product innovation (percent):[4]						
Formulation[5]	56.5	61.6	48.4	50.0	47.1	46.9
New market[6]	1.0	—	0.7	3.1	—	3.1
Packaging[7]	14.0	20.2	9.7	17.2	11.8	9.4
Positioning[8]	24.6	18.2	39.8	29.7	41.2	25.0
Technology[9]	—	—	1.4	—	—	12.5
Merchandising	3.9	—	—	—	—	3.1
Cumulative						
Domestic, except imports, 1980–97	47,796	10,093	29,520	6,447	2,575	2,965
Imports, 1980–97[10]	4,075	1,314	1,389	261	75	178
International, 1985–97[11]	18,206	5,712	15,534	3,043	2,914	985

— Represents or rounds to zero.

[1] Product introduced under completely or partly new brand name.

[2] Product introduced in a category with an existing brand name which has not been used in the category before.

[3] Introduction of a new variety, format, size, or package of an existing product/brand name.

[4] Product which offers consumers something significantly different from existing products.

[5] Added or new ingredient which offers a benefit not previously provided by existing products in its category.

[6] Special category for new products which do not compete with any existing category of products.

[7] New product packaged in a way that makes it easier to store, handle, prepare, or dispense than others in its category.

[8] New product presented for new users or uses compared to existing products in its category.

[9] New product with added consumer benefits resulting from use of a new technology.

[10] New products introduced in the United States by foreign companies.

[11] New products introduced by U.S. and foreign companies outside the United States.

Source: Marketing Intelligence Service Ltd., Naples, NY, *Product Alert Weekly;* and U.S. Census Bureau, *Statistical Abstract of the United States: 1999.*

of innovations. In addition to receiving praise, marketers' attempts to persuade people to change are also the basis for much criticism. For example, China resists the diffusion of TV satellite dishes and Singapore resists broadcasts of Star satellite TV. Both fear Western programming will erode traditional Asian values (by changing viewers' attitudes and behaviors). Marketer-driven innovations lie at the heart of many public policy debates.

In this chapter we introduce some of the theories and tools in marketing and the social sciences for understanding the topic of change. First, we present a perspective on diffusion, introducing some key concepts, such as innovation, diffusion, and adoption. In addition, we discuss the concepts of conservatism and discontinuance. The latter issues are important for understanding new-product/service failure. Then, we discuss the various contexts in which innovation, diffusion, and discontinuance take place. Our discussion of social system characteristics leads naturally to a discussion of individual adopter types. We discuss consumer adoption behavior and how adoptions lead to successful innovations from an organizational and societal perspective. In a market economy it is consumers who, in the end, determine how new inventions will be used and which technologies are successful.

Innovation

There is a vast literature on the topic of innovation, diffusion, and adoption. **Innovation** refers to *new things and ideas and new ways of behaving and interacting with things*. Innovations are defined by individuals and by social groups. What one individual or one social group perceives as novel may be old-fashioned for other individuals and other social groups. Innovations include ideas and business practices such as total quality management or the vertical auction in business-to-business marketing; products such as plastic buckets in rural Ethiopia or personal digital assistants in the most developed nations; and services such as consumer credit in Turkish banking practice. Innovation may also refer to behaviors, as when designers develop more cost-effective and resource-conserving packaging, or when individual consumers adopt any product, service, or idea that is new for them.[4] Thus, an innovation involves new ways of thinking about the world and new behaviors (e.g., buying and using a new product).

Innovation is one component of the diffusion process. Innovations come from many sources. Users are an important source of information for many innovations in both industrial and consumer markets. Government and nongovernmental organizations may also become involved, as when governmental regulators mandate the use of pollution control technologies for industry. A key challenge for business organizations is to identify and manage the production and diffusion of innovations.

As marketers strive for competitive advantage in the global marketplace they are driven to seek sales and market share through the introduction of new goods and services. Thus, as shown in Exhibit 16.1, the rate of new consumer packaged goods introductions accelerated from about 6,300 in 1990 to more than 9,100 in 1997. But fewer than 100 new products may top $1 million in sales in the first year after introduction. Eighty to 90 percent will fail in the marketplace. This flood of innovations is potentially wasteful and expensive for organizations and confusing and disruptive for consumers. Hence, finding ways to better manage innovations is critical for organizations of all kinds.[5]

Types of Innovations

Three types of innovations are discussed here: continuous, dynamically continuous, and discontinuous. These represent a continuum, with the first being relatively minor innovations and the last radically new innovations.

To improve the management of innovations, it make sense to distinguish between types in terms of the behavioral consequences for users. At one end of the continuum lie **continuous innovations.** Continuous innovations are those that *require minor changes in user behaviors.* In other words, they have a minimally disruptive effect, while still representing a change in past behavior. One industrial example is Mazda's Miller-cycle internal combustion engine, which differs from the conventional Otto-cycle engine in producing more torque by shortening the compression stroke. In the Triad countries, consumer examples include Gillette's Mach3 razor, TopsyTail ponytail inverters, Kraft fat-free mayonnaise, Diesel wide-leg jeans, and Sony cordless headphones.[6] Industry Insights 16.2 shows how high-tech tools can revive an older technology and stimulate continuous innovations.

Fads, fashions, and trends are examples of continuous innovations. They may be distinguished partly in terms of time of diffusion. **Fashions** refer to *particular combinations of desirable attributes.* For example, brightly colored and patterned Kente cloth (pictured on page 576), woven in thin strips in Ghana, has become a popular fashion among African Americans as a statement of ethnic pride. Ministers wear it on their vestments; high school and college graduates add it to their graduation gowns.

 www.kente.net

Fads are *short-lived fashions, often adopted by relatively few people, often members of a common subculture.* Fads diffuse most rapidly and disappear most quickly. For example, at the time of writing this, Japanese and Taiwanese teenagers are crazy about platform shoes. Body branding joined body piercing as a fad among the avant-garde in the United States. The 1992 film *Dracula* inspired a short-lived line of vampire fashions.

 bme.freq.com

Trends, or styles, *last longest and may define an era.* Thus, the Victorian era emanating from Great Britain in the mid-nineteenth century was associated with certain trends in

Reeves Callaway, 47, was car-crazy from an early age, souping up an Austin Healey on his own in high school and restoring an old Ferrari as his senior project in fine arts at Amherst College. After a few years on the professional racing circuit, "I decided I couldn't earn a living as a driver," remembers Callaway. So, he persuaded BMW to let him attach a turbocharger to one of the company's crisply handling but underpowered compacts. That modest project led to the creation of Callaway TurboSystems, which made a promotional splash, adding turbo-thrust to Alfa Romeo coupes, and eventually caught the eye of executives at Chevrolet. Chevrolet sold and warranted the Callaway Twin Turbo Corvette through its own dealer network. Five hundred copies of the $60,000 car were sold before Chevrolet retooled the Corvette engine in 1991.

Now, Callaway has moved on, reworking Chevrolet's mass-market Camaro into the 400-horsepower Callaway SuperNatural C-8. With money from NASA and a group of private contractors, Callaway is designing a 1.5-liter V-8 engine roughly the size of a cinder block that will generate 200 horsepower. The idea is to demonstrate the commercial potential of ultralight, ultrastrong materials—everything from titanium alumineds to a composite of iron, chromium, aluminum, and yttrium.

Callaway's relentless pursuit of speed is interesting in its own right. What makes it more interesting is that the enterprise is successful in a market cluttered with the products of huge corporations. One explanation is that advances in technology make it possible for small-scale producers like Callaway to achieve high standards at affordable cost. Off-the-shelf software permits Callaway's engine development manager to simulate engine performance the way Boeing simulates the life of a newly designed wing. Questions can now be answered on a personal computer in a matter of seconds. A pair of computer-controlled machine tools, small enough to fit in a pickup truck, gives Callaway the capacity to cut metal in an infinite variety of shapes and to tolerances of ten-thousandths of an inch. Hence, cast cylinder heads can be precision modified, and customer-designed engine parts can be duplicated with great accuracy.

architecture, dress, and interior design. Industry Insights 16.3 defines style, and Exhibit 16.2 highlights the distinction between trends and fads.[7]

Distinguishing between fads and trends at an early stage can make a business success. The first company to identify and act on a trend gains a powerful competitive advantage. The Japanese firm Sanrio, which has made a fortune licensing Hello Kitty, claims to have capitalized on "cute."[8] See the accompanying photo of the Hello Kitty vacuum cleaner on page 577, for example. Starbucks coffee capitalized on a trend in consumer desire for higher-quality coffee by franchising a standardized service idea. By correctly identifying fads, such as licensed characters (e.g., using Pokémon characters as a company spokesperson), aggressive marketers can maximize short-term sales. But they must be careful not to invest too much in a trend or fad. As the fad loses momentum, demand can collapse quickly, as with *Star Wars Episode I* action figures.[9]

When managers are considering the introduction of continuous innovations, a major challenge is demonstrating to end users that the innovation provides a differential advantage over existing products or solutions. Most new products fail because they do not offer

Platform shoes and designer jeans are an example of style innovations popular in the 1970s that reemerged in the 1990s. Style begins as a risk. Then it spreads as others seeking new ways to express themselves become aware of the style, and it ends as a cliché. Style emerges in the interplay between the deliberate inventions of designers, manufacturers, and merchandisers and the spontaneous actions of innovative consumers. Style in popular culture has replaced art as a source of aesthetic pleasure. Style depends on a process of collective selection, whereby participants in a social network agree on the value of products. Bohemian ghettos (e.g., Hamburg, Germany, the Parisian Left Bank, New York's SoHo and TriBeCa, Los Angeles' Melrose district) are a frequent source of innovations. Collective selection is a future-oriented activity that allows people to adapt to and mold the rapid pace of change in a market-driven society. Styles travel widely through popular communications vehicles such as the Bombay, Hong Kong, and Californian film industries, or via MTV and other music television networks.

Styles have an internal logic of their own, although styles are often rooted in deeper societal trends. There often is interdependence of meaning across popular cultural product categories. Styles affect the design of all sorts of products. Examples include the populux (or the "space age") streamlined designs of the 1950s when the Triad nations were infatuated with the idea of scientific progress; art deco of the 1930s, which melded a romantic sensibility to an interest in machine forms and surfaces and emerging technologies; and style of the Edwardian era, based on the mythic gentility of the British royal family of the Windsors that existed between World Wars I and II.

Source: "Advances of the Amazonesu," The Economist, July 22, 2000, pp. 61–62; and Joshua Levine, "A Lifestyle in a Label," Forbes, November 1996, p. 155.

The Ghanaian Kente cloth is in fashion among African Americans.

Exhibit 16.2 Distinguishing Trends from Fads

1. The more it fits with basic lifestyle changes, the more likely the new development will become a trend.
2. The more diverse and immediate the benefits, the more likely the new development will be a trend.
3. The more adaptable the new development is, the greater chance it has of becoming a trend.
4. If the new development is an expression of a basic theme rather than just an example of it, the more chance it has of becoming a trend.
5. New developments supported by developments in other areas are more likely to represent trends.
6. If support for a change comes from an unexpected source and key market segments, the greater chance it has of becoming a trend.

Source: Martin G. Letscher, "How to Tell Fads from Trends," *American Demographics*, December 1994, pp. 38–45.

a differential advantage. In a 1994 U.S. survey, seven out of ten new-product managers doubted their company's success rate would improve, citing products that don't deliver on their promise (35 percent) and lack of compelling or motivating positioning (33 percent) as reasons for the failure. High failure rates have driven many firms to develop innovative new-product design programs incorporating new research techniques.[10]

At the midpoint in the continuum of innovation types we identify **dynamically continuous innovations.** Dynamically continuous innovations require either *major change in an area of behavior that is relatively unimportant to the individual or a minor change in an area of behavior that is very important to the user.* Pesticide-resistant hybrid corn seed

Hello Kitty merchandise represents a fad, but who knows?

The Plastic Bucket

The plastic bucket has revolutionized the lives of Africans. You cannot survive in the tropics without water; the shortages are always acute. Water has to be carried long distances. Before the invention of the plastic bucket, water was carried in heavy vats made of clay or stone. The wheel was not a familiar aspect of African culture; everything was carried on the head, including the heavy vats of water. In the division of household labor, it was the woman's task to fetch water. The appearance of the plastic bucket was a miracle. To start with, it is relatively cheap. And, it comes in different sizes; even a small child can carry a few liters! Now, it is the child's job to fetch water. What a relief for the overworked African woman!

Source: Ryszard Kapuscinski, "Plastic Buckets and Ballpoint Pens," Granta 48 (1994).

for use in particular microclimates is an example of a dynamically continuous innovation typical of commercial agriculture in the Triad countries. Consumer examples include such things as Internet-ready cell phones, arthroscopic laser surgery, Viagra impotency medicine, and morning-after birth control pills. Digital Satellite System television that allows individual households to receive hundreds of digitally enhanced audio and visual channels is another example. A surprising example—the Ethiopian bucket—is profiled in Consumer Chronicles 16.1. Another dramatic example is provided by the rapid adoption of snowmobiles by reindeer herders in the arctic.[11]

At the other end of our innovation continuum are **discontinuous innovations.** Discontinuous innovations entail *major changes in behavior in an area of importance to the individual or group.* Free-market capitalism is a discontinuous innovation in the transitional economies. Green revolution rice in developing nations in Asia with its complement of new fertilizers, insecticides, and farming techniques is another example. Cyber auctions, MP3 music technology, and wearable computers are recent examples in the Triad nations.[12] Throughout the world the advent of inexpensive techniques of birth control has had a major effect on behavior. In the early 1950s, the frozen TV dinner revolutionized American mealtimes and may have led to more atomized North American family life. Even common consumer nondurables may be thought of as discontinuous innovations if their introduction creates dramatic changes in individual and social behavior. In Sri Lanka, for example, the introduction of Western cosmetics has fueled a crisis in the role of women and altered gender dynamics.[13]

Discussion of the microwave provides a good example of the dramatic impact discontinuous innovations can have on behavior. Microwaves became available to consumers in the 1960s, but by 1980 only 15 percent of North American households had microwaves. During the decade of the 1980s, the reentry of women into the workforce and the emergence of professional women created new time pressures. As a result, by 1989, 80 percent of North American households had microwave ovens. A *Wall Street Journal* survey found that microwaves were the respondents' favorite household product. But the widespread use of the microwave has wrought tremendous cultural changes. First, it has transformed North Americans' sense of time. The amount of time many cooks are willing to devote to meal preparation has declined from about an hour in the 1970s to a little more than 10 minutes today. Second, it has transformed the division of labor within the household. The conventional association between mothers, nurturance, and food preparation is undermined as introduction of such products as microwavable Kid's Kitchen, Kid Cuisine, and My Own Meals turns children into food preparers. These dramatic changes were facilitated by a subtle shift in North American values in the 1980s toward heightened individualism. Instant meals seem certain to remain popular as leisure time continues to shrink for many North Americans.[14]

When introducing new products, an organization is asking customers to change their behavior in some way. Implicitly, the organization is asking customers to take a risk by doing something new. As a result, success is more likely when marketers can optimize the benefits associated with the new behavior while also minimizing the risks or disadvantages. Indeed, many studies find that product characteristics are better predictors of adoption than personal characteristics of the adopters.

From the standpoint of a marketer, successful new-product introduction plays an important role in profitability. Being the *first firm to market a product successfully in an emerging market* often leads to what is called **pioneering advantage.** For example, Jeep defined in many consumers' minds what is now termed the sport-utility vehicle category. Curiously, British Leyland's Land Rover lost out on this opportunity. The fact that Jeep helped define the ideal point for this category meant that later entrants were inevitably compared with the pioneer and often suffered in such comparisons. Like the Jeep, perhaps the Prius will define the hybrid-vehicle category.[15] Can you think of examples of other products that set the standard in their categories as does Jeep for SUVs?

Extremely favorable evaluations may be formed toward the pioneer that leads. Pioneering advantage, in turn, leads to market leadership as measured by market share and return on investment. Successful new-product development is an important element in achieving long-term competitive superiority and profitability. For these reasons, identification of product characteristics that influence speed and success of diffusion and influence adoption decisions has been a focus of research not only in marketing but across the applied social sciences.[16]

Probably the most important factor to the success of an innovation is its perceived **relative advantage,** that is, the extent to which it is viewed as *providing clear benefits for the target market that are superior to those offered by competitive market offerings.* Many market failures and slow adoption rates can be traced to the absence of a relative advantage. Pen- or stylus-based computing was supposed to be the new paradigm in the late 1980s. Just one problem: The handwriting recognition software never worked, and it still does not. Hence, consumers detected no relative advantage over keyboards and voice recognition software.[17]

The nature of the relative advantage varies. In the mid-1980s, Chrysler Corporation captured a significant share of the U.S. auto market by introducing a minivan that met the transportation needs of an emerging market segment of suburban professional families. In the industrial sector, containerized freight was first used commercially in 1956. In 1968, 13 percent of North Atlantic sea freight was containerized. This figure had increased to 90 percent by 1990. The benefits to shippers in the form of ease of tracking, reuse, security, simplification of sea-land shipment, and reduced costs explain the speed with which this innovation has transformed the shipping industry. In the area of medical services, various economies (in production, contracting, and information) motivated innovative hospitals to move toward vertical integration, a managerial innovation.[18]

The examples given above illustrate functional benefits of innovative products. Symbolism is another important source of relative advantage that works to speed the diffusion of innovations. For example, many newly professional, young French couples have adopted home freezers in spite of the high retail density in urban France. Why? Freezers symbolize the link between young couples and their farm-dwelling parents. The parents provide the young couples with homemade farm foods. In turn, young couples introduce their parents to frozen foods bought in the city. To take another example, shoe and clothing styles often spread quickly between inner-city teens and suburban wannabes. Finally, in the area of medical services, it has been argued that late adopters of vertical integration in hospital administration derive legitimacy from key stakeholders through vertical integration, regardless of the economic benefits.[19]

Relative advantage must always be assessed for the target market and within the context of the consumers' current situation. Cell phones have diffused rapidly in huge central Asian countries where landlines are absent. Electric cars have been slow to catch on because of perceived disadvantages in terms of appearance, range, speed, handling, and cost, despite numerous advantages from an environmental perspective. The gas-electric hybrid Toyota Prius described in the vignette overcomes many of these disadvantages.[20]

The **compatibility** of an innovation refers to the extent to which the innovation is *consistent with present needs, motives, values, beliefs, and behaviors.* Another perspective might be that the more an innovation option tangibly resembles the traditional solution to a problem, the more likely it is to be adopted, regardless of its actual ability to perform the requisite task.[21]

Numerous examples of compatibility can be cited. Debit cards are a widely diffused payment option in the United States thanks to a well-wired communications infrastructure. Smart bankcards are more popular in Europe where electronic integration is less well developed. Wrinkle-reduction creams, sunscreens, and anti-aging formula vitamins are highly compatible with the baby boomer (those born between 1946 and 1964) segment's youthful self-image. In the African nation of The Gambia, sesame recently achieved dramatic success as a crop because it could be fit into the agricultural cycle after other major crops and because it provided a needed source of vegetable oil for the diet.[22]

Incompatibility, like relative advantage, may be based on either functional or symbolic properties, or both. For example, the diffusion of many quality improvement practices in business, including those designed to improve customer satisfaction, often involve cross-functional teamwork. Cross-functional teamwork is often incompatible with the top-down structure of traditional business organizations.[23]

In consumer goods, electric cars have been slow to achieve popularity in part because of the incompatibility between electric fueling and gas fueling options and in part because their short range conflicts with the symbolic freedom the auto provides. Again, the Toyota Prius may represent a resolution to both these problems. But notice how the vignette hints that the lack of a diesel-electric option may hinder acceptance in Europe.

Trialability, or customers' ability to *try out an innovation without incurring risk to valued resources* (financial, esteem, status, time, information), is another factor critical to successful diffusion of innovations. All sorts of strategies may be used to improve the chances of product trial. The Japanese government facilitated trial of the Prius by offering sales tax exemptions and tax credits. Celebrities may be hired to try out new consumer nondurables and report their findings to their fans. Firms may engage in sampling like E & J Gallo's online wine tastings or low-cost trials as Toyota has done in the United States with the Prius.[24]

Many products fail because of the difficulties of trial, especially products that affect the customer's body or sense of self. Thus, radial kerotomy, a Russian surgical procedure used to correct near-sightedness, has been relatively slow to catch on in the United States, at least in part because of the perceived inability to reverse the procedure in case of error.

Observability plays an important role in the diffusion of innovations. For fashion goods and other sorts of goods consumed publicly, social visibility speeds innovation. Hence, Toyota's concern to get the Prius out on the road or the use of product placement in popular films and television shows. Conversely, the nonobservability of privately consumed goods may impede diffusion. In the latter case, the evaluations of relevant opinion leaders or reference groups are less accessible to consumers.

Complexity is a factor that may impede the diffusion of innovations and hinder adoption. By **complexity** we refer to *the difficulty of understanding the benefits of the product or service and the relationship between attributes or features and those benefits.* Ignorance of what a hybrid-engine vehicle is may impede diffusion of the Prius. Almost by definition, discontinuous innovations like electric cars are complex because they ask a consumer to undertake a new way of life.

One problem for marketers is that as innovations become more complex, people may use shortcuts to evaluate them. That is, they evaluate complex innovations on the basis of a small set of familiar characteristics that may or may not be appropriate for judging the innovation.[25]

Key Concepts in the Study of Consumer Change

Diffusion

The **diffusion process** refers to *the spread of an innovation from its creative source across space and time.* The process may take a variety of forms. An S-shaped, or sigmoid, curve has been observed in a number of marketing studies of consumer durables. In such cases a few buyers are initially convinced of the merits of adoption. Then, more decide to buy. For example, 35,000 microwave ovens were sold in one Spanish town in 1987. Later, larger, more reticent groups of buyers adopt. Thus in 1995, 650,000 microwaves were sold in the same town. Later still, a smaller laggard group adopts the innovation. The snowball effect as the product diffuses gives the adoption curve its familiar S-shaped pattern. However, diffusion may also follow an exponential adoption pattern. That is, it proceeds at a constant rate. The rate may be slow in a diverse social system. The rate may be rapid if buyers face low costs of adoption, are confident of their abilities to evaluate its benefits, or are relatively uninvolved with the innovation. Sales of Viagra, the impotence medication that sold 37,000 units in the first two weeks on the market, provides an example of a rapid exponential diffusion pattern. Fads assume an inverted V shape, exponential adoption, followed by dramatic decline in adoption and sales.[26] Diffusion curve patterns are shown in Exhibit 16.3.

Diffusion and Adoption

Exhibit 16.3 Diffusion Curves

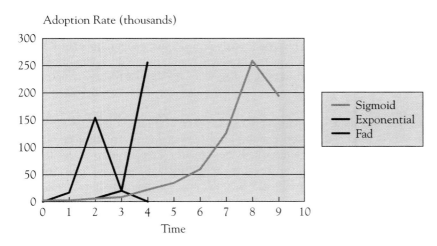

Product Life Cycle

Products, just like people, undergo a life cycle. They are born. They grow and mature. They grow old and eventually die. A generic product life cycle (PLC) takes the shape of an S-curve, because it mimics the adoption pattern discussed in the previous section. A life cycle can be constructed for a product category—such as organic food products, a category that has grown by 900 percent in the United States since the 1980s. Or it can be constructed for a specific brand: the life cycle of the Plymouth brand, for example, a brand that DaimlerChrysler is now deleting from its product line. The PLC varies by product category and across world market regions, as suggested by Consumer Chronicles 16.1. There the product (the plastic bucket) was in the growth stage; in the Triad countries it is a mature product. The speed of the PLC also varies by category and world area. The Internet seems to speed up PLCs.[27]

The first phase is labeled as introduction. At this stage, consumers have relatively little knowledge about the new product, so promotional expenses are high and consumers rely on promotion for information. Profits are expected to be negative in the initial years of introduction. Toyota is taking an initial loss on the Prius, but is mitigating its losses by relying on the Internet as its primary promotional tool rather than more expensive television or print advertising.

During the growth phase of the product life cycle, sales start to increase dramatically. Many new customers come into the market. Interpersonal influence plays a more important role in the adoption process in this phase. Attracted by this growth in sales and profits, new competitors also enter the market, and prices fall. At the maturity phase, sales begin to flatten out, and industry profits also decline. At this stage, brand loyalty is likely to be high, so it is difficult to get customers to switch to new brands. In the decline phase, industry sales begin to decline as customers lose interest in the product category, as in the U.S. chewing gum market.[28] It may be that new products are developed to satisfy the needs that were previously served by the declining industry. For instance, the microchip has replaced the integrated circuit, which previously replaced the vacuum tube. Still there are audiophiles who are highly loyal to audio products made from old vacuum tubes. The product life cycle is mentioned later in the chapter, when we discuss the five adopter categories.

Space

Diffusion takes place across geographic space. For example, a dance style may diffuse from the streets to a modern dance studio, from urban areas to rural ones, or from urban areas in one country to urban areas in another country. Product innovations that present a low financial challenge may undergo more rapid diffusion.[29] Research has found that the diffusion rate is faster for countries in which the products are introduced later than for the countries in which the product is first introduced. Hence, technologies that took a long time to diffuse in the country of origin will in certain cases diffuse more quickly when introduced into other countries. Microwave ovens have diffused rapidly in Spain since 1990, for example. An example of the rapid diffusion of commercial pop culture into Russia is provided in Consumer Chronicles 16.2.[30]

Time

Diffusion also takes place over time. Diffusion time varies with product category, product characteristics, the nature of the communications environment, and other factors, whether it involves fads or more enduring styles. For example, the **neighborhood effect** says that *people who are close to the source of information concerning an innovation will tend to adopt more quickly than potential adopters situated at a distance from the information source.*

In one Spanish market, researchers found that refrigerators and washing machines diffused slowly. Laggards (see the discussion of adopter categories below) did not consider their adoption decision until 24 years had passed from the introduction of the refrigerator and 31 years from the introduction of the washing machine. It took 11 years for the dishwasher to reach early adopters! A later study found that glass-ceramic kitchen range tops have also diffused slowly in the Spanish market. The authors point out that this adoption is related to the time when people replace their kitchen, and since this is a major purchase, the diffusion cycle will inevitably be long. Similarly, the first experimental U.S. television broadcast took place in 1933, but by 1950 only a million U.S. households owned expensive TV sets. Today, 98 percent of U.S. homes contain at least one TV set. The television market in the United States is now saturated, but television is diffusing to rural China and Africa.

Western marketers often *assume that people are predisposed to consume new and novel products, services, experiences, and the like.* We call this a **pro-innovation bias.** Prior to the consumer revolution in the West in the mid-eighteenth century, material desires for the majority of people often focused on a relatively limited set of conventionally agreed-on goods. Of course, exceptions to the rule can be found among elite groups throughout antiquity and even prehistory, but a materialist orientation is relatively recent for most people. Further, in transitional economies a history of political constraint has not produced the autonomous, innovation-prone consumer decision makers assumed by Western marketers. Traditional attitudes and resistance persist among older and lower-class consumers.[31]

Consumer conservatism and resistance is widespread in the world. By **innovation resistance,** we mean *a preference for existing, familiar products and behaviors over novel ones.* That is, resistance to change refers to any conduct that serves to maintain the status quo in the face of pressure to alter it. Bureaucratic organizations, including businesses, are notoriously allergic to changes in the status quo.

Some authors explain innovation resistance in terms of an intrinsic desire for **psychological equilibrium.** The notion of psychological equilibrium reflects *the human desire for balance, order, and consistency between beliefs and behaviors.* New ideas have the potential to disrupt existing patterns of attitude and behavior. Because changes imposed on behavior can disrupt psychological equilibrium and require psychological and behavioral adjustments, many consumers resist innovations.[32]

Some authors discuss innovation resistance in terms of **social equilibrium,** *the symmetry within social groups about the meaning of things and the meaning of one group to another.*[33] Where society is stable, innovation may be viewed as undesirable because it has the potential to disrupt the social equilibrium. Consumer Chronicles 16.3 profiles the Italian "Slow Cities" movement that represents an effort to maintain social equilibrium in the face of global marketing. Farming populations have frequently been labeled as resistant to

Conservatism, Resistance, and Discontinuance

Nearly three-dozen Italian cities and towns have banded together to form a new league of "Slow Cities," joining a burgeoning international movement to promote homestyle food, local crafts, and all-around good living. The new Slow Cities league is a project of Italy's chief municipal alliance and of Slow Food, an international movement formed in 1989 with the aim of safeguarding culinary traditions.

Born of a backlash against fast-food, the Slow Food movement boasts roughly 40,000 members in 35 countries, a slick magazine published in five languages, and a popular biennial food show.

With 33 member towns, the "Slow Cities" network aims to expand internationally while remaining exclusive, network president Paolo Saturnini says. To be eligible for membership, cities and town must introduce measures on everything from banning car alarms to the promotion of organic agriculture, including the creation of centers where visitors can sample local traditional food in a setting in harmony with nature.

Towns making the slow-food grade will benefit from a joint marketing strategy to attract tourists and investors, Saturnini says. They also will be able to proudly display the "Slow Cities" logo—a snail crawling past two buildings, one ancient and the other modern.

Source: Peter Thayer, "Italy Says 'Yes' to Slow Value," Marketing News, *August 14, 2000, p. 19.*

innovations, although their conservatism is often a response to perceived risk in the social environment. Of course, periods of social upheaval are likely to be accompanied by a breakdown of innovation resistance and an influx of new ideas, products, and services. As discussed below, perceived characteristics of innovations also affect consumer resistance.[34]

Discontinuance is another aspect of the diffusion process that is important to marketers. By discontinuance we mean that *the consumer stops purchasing or using the product.* Marketing researchers have generally not focused on this aspect of the diffusion process. Discontinuance is the other side of innovation. Changing consumer need or competition may lead to discontinuance. When VCR technologies were first introduced, several competitive technologies were offered. Although many feel it was technically superior, most users discontinued use of Betamax technology. The VHS format was perceived to have superior **product complementarity.** More video titles, that is, a fuller array of other market offerings, were available with the VHS technology. Consumers discontinued use of one product in order to adopt another, with negative consequences for sales and market share of the abandoned product or brand.

Discontinuance occurs for other reasons besides changing needs and competition. For example, the state of Vermont offered its residents a really new electricity plan. Under this plan, residents were charged different rates depending on what time of day they consumed electricity. Rates were higher during peak consumption periods and lower during off-peak periods. Adoption of this discontinuous innovation required consumers to make significant behavioral changes in order to take advantage of the differential rate structure. Households that elected to adopt the new rates without being aware of the required behavioral changes quickly became disillusioned with the new rate plan and discontinued it. Generally, behavioral changes judged too costly by consumers will fuel discontinuance.[35]

One interesting reason for discontinuance is that consumers perceive that the product or service has become too popular with other consumers or the adoption of the product by other consumers changes the benefits offered by the product. For example, people who regularly travel to Hawaii for vacations may decide it's become too commercialized and crowded and select more out-of-the-way vacation spots.

The Context of Innovation, Diffusion, and Discontinuance

The opening vignette suggests several ways in which environmental, cultural, and social factors affect the potential diffusion of the Prius. In this section we describe the environmental, cultural, and social contexts for innovation and diffusion more generally. In addition, we discuss how social groups influence innovation and adoption decisions.

The environment for change is often neglected in marketing studies of innovation, but it is crucial. In the opening vignette, note how product acceptance in Japan was linked to high gas prices and how promotional efforts in the United States relied on widespread Internet use. These are examples of how environmental factors affect diffusion. Environmental factors that affect innovation include the ecology, economic conditions, and market structures.

Ecology, including aspects such as terrain, climate and population density, has broad effects on innovation processes. The homily "necessity is the mother of invention" is not without foundation. The diffusion of many innovations is based, at least in part, on changing environmental conditions that provide incentives for adaptive responses. For example, in arid parts of the world farmers have often been quick to adopt drought- or pest-resistant crop varieties when these advantages are not outweighed by disadvantages such as increased labor requirements.[36] Good Practice 16.1 provides an example of an exciting innovation in water-harvesting technology designed to cope with arid environments.

Economic conditions and market structures also have broad influence on innovation processes. Diffusion of innovations is embedded within a particular market context. The developed world, the developing world, and transitional nations have radically different economic conditions and market structures that in turn drive different rates and types of innovative processes. True to Schumpeter's ideas, businesses in Triad economies invest heavily in innovation; this investment creates a rapid rate of introduction of new products.[37] A factor that drives receptivity to innovation on the national level is purchasing power. Greater receptivity to innovation is related to higher purchasing power. The rate of new-product introduction is also influenced by factors such as **demand density,** *the distribution and number of consumers who desire and can afford a product.*[38]

The overall rate of introduction of new products in a marketplace is an important environmental condition. In a quickly changing environment, consumers are generally aware of the need for change, the pace of technology, and the costs of choosing the wrong technology.[39] In such environments, many consumers are active participants in the change process.[40] On the other hand, in volatile and uncertain market environments such as some transitional and developing economies, consumers' reliance on informal exchange relationships for vital consumer goods may make them resistant to formal market system

The Environmental Context for Innovation

The villagers of Chungungo in northern Chile are a relatively happy bunch nowadays thanks to a Canadian-Chilean project, which could soon be providing water to thousands of desert communities around the world. In certain coastal regions, where the terrain is arid and mountainous and air rolling in from the sea very cold, a dense fog collects over the hills, forming a gloomy mass of water, which is frustratingly inaccessible to the parched communities beneath it. After years of research, scientists hit on a solution as simple as it is effective. Fine mesh nets, arranged like billboards across the mountain tops, trap the water drop by drop. As billions of droplets accumulate, they trickle down into a tube. The collected water flows down the mountain to a tank above Chungungo, where it is filtered and stored. The mesh is cheap and easily maintained. Maintenance is straightforward, and the only energy required is gravity. That is good news for isolated communities in at least 22 countries around the world. Scientists have pinpointed 47 areas on six continents, which have the right climatic conditions to implement this new system of fog-water collection.

Source: Miranda France, "Fog Harvet Makes Desert Bloom," Tampa Tribune, January 15, 1995, p. A20.

innovations.[41] Marketplace variables influence the rate of introduction of new products. Such things as channel structure and efficiency affect the rate of new-product introduction because they affect the availability both of information and products. The rate of new-product introduction is also influenced by industry competitiveness and productivity.[42]

The Cultural and Social Contexts for Innovation

The diffusion of an innovation is embedded within a particular culture and social system, although it may pass between cultures and societies.[43] Focusing on macro-level cultural and social system factors can help us understand and predict the diffusion of innovations. The cultural environment and communication system are important to the diffusion process because they determine the unique social values of a particular country and they are pervasive to all marketing activities.[44] How marketing efforts interact with a culture determine the degree of success or failure of those efforts.

Social System Values and Traditions

In Chapter 4 we emphasized that marketers must understand basic values in order to be effective in influencing specific behaviors within a culture. To understand the adoption and diffusion of new products, services, and ideas we need to consider the values related to innovation and the extent to which those values are shared across members of a culture. Important cultural values include varying degrees of pressures to engage in innovative behavior and values associated with newness, innovative behaviors, and change. Cultural attitudes toward variety, newness, and values attached to the present and ideas of the past and the future provide norms that affect individual innovative behaviors.

Historical studies suggest that some cultures have been more open to innovation than others, for example, Europe as compared with China after the eleventh century or Islam after the Arabs were expelled from Spain in the thirteenth century. These differences help to account for the economic success of Western capitalism's creative destruction relative to these systems in the nineteenth and twentieth centuries.[45]

Although comparative consumer research on relative innovativeness is scarce, some have detected national differences in innovativeness, others not. One study found that Irish women have less need to engage in innovative behaviors and that they achieve their optimum level of consumption variety at a lower level than their U.S. counterparts. Of course, behaviors considered innovative for Irish women, such as wine drinking and movie theater patronage, have no such connotations for American women.[46]

In general, the diffusion rate and maximum penetration level of an innovation depends on the *innovation's compatibility with social system values*. We've already mentioned that top-down authority structures or competitive relationships between marketing channel members in traditional business organizations are often incompatible with team-based innovations in quality management or information-sharing technologies.

One value that affects the diffusion of innovations within a culture is whether the traditions of a society are more interdependent-communitarian or more individualistic. The more interdependent-communitarian the traditions of a society, the greater is the importance of group goals and the more likely individual goals are subordinated to the larger interests of the group. In such societies, values of integration or fitting in take precedence over values of standing out or distinction. On the other hand, one author writes that so powerful is the collective boom-craze mentality in Japan, that once 5 percent of the teen-girl market endorses a product, another 60 percent will almost certainly follow suit in under a month. And if a product can reach the *kawaii* (cute) spot it can reach almost 100 percent market saturation within a week. In this cultural context, interdependence can fuel adoption of fad products. Thus, individualism may promote individual innovativeness, whereas a more interdependent orientation can speed adoption rates.[47]

Interdependence, or valuing integration over differentiation, often favors conservatism over change. For an example, look at the exaggerated conservatism of consumption in Muria located in the north-central part of Madhya Pradesh, India, described in Consumer Chronicles 16.4. The social life of the Muria is conducted as a series of large-scale eating and drinking occasions, and this establishes the standards by which Muria evaluate the world of consumer goods. Objects are desirable only if they have meaning within the context of public feasting; otherwise, they have no consumer value.

Muria Purchase Conformity

Consumer Chronicles 16.4

The Muria make purchases in order to express conformity, not originality or individuality. A concern with belonging marks all phases of Muria life. Muria consumption is bound up with the expression of collective identity and the need to assert commitment to the village and its institutions. For example, one year the girls of Manjapur all obtained new saris with identical borders for the Play of the Gods ritual. Innovative consumption items are sought because all villagers are attempting to live up to a particular collective image. Needless to say, innovations are hard to introduce into Muria life, and although modern and Western goods are easily accessible to the Muria by local bus, such goods are not attractive to them. The Muria are dedicated followers, and none of them wants to defy the restraints of collective style. The motives of the young men who are now starting to cut their hair and dress more like the local Hindus is not to "look smarter than before" but to look less conspicuous in a world that is perceived as increasingly Hindu dominated.

Source: Gell, "Newcomers to the World of Goods: Consumption Among the Muria Gonds."

As examples as diverse as the baby jogger discussed in Chapter 5 and the failure of electric cars suggest, innovations that threaten core values are subject to resistance. Promoting the use of many birth control options (male and female condoms, miscarriage-inducing drugs) is difficult for symbolic reasons related to core values. Birth control represents cultural values that make advertisers wary and some consumers resistant to their use. Another example of how core values may evoke resistance to particular innovations is provided by resistance to consumption of white bread among some Ecuadoran Indians, for whom consumption of home-prepared barley-based gruels is fundamental to values of hearth, home, women's labor, and ethnic identity. Symbolic obstacles to diffusion have no simple technical or marketing solution.[48]

Social Hierarchies

Social hierarchies within and between social systems affect diffusion; however, the effect is complex and varied. This is partly because the nature of social hierarchies and mobility of people between levels of a social hierarchy varies so much from culture to culture. Social class and other social hierarchies were discussed extensively in Chapter 6. We will have more to say about the diffusion of innovations within and between social groups in the next section. In this section, we want you to notice how hierarchical relations broadly influence these flows in the social system.

Early researchers proposed a **trickle-down theory of innovation.**[49] According to this theory, *status rivalry between social groups acts as a kind of engine or motive force for innovation.* Low-status social groups follow the principle of **imitation** and seek to establish new status claims by adopting the products, services and ideas of higher-status groups. High-status social groups follow the principle of **differentiation** and embrace new products, services, and ideas to distinguish themselves from the low-status social groups. Imitation and differentiation account for the direction, tempo, and dynamics of innovation. The **two-step flow model** is a description of communication that is closely related to the trickle-down theory.

According to the two-step flow model of communication, *new ideas flow from the mass media to influential consumers who, in turn, pass these ideas on to others who are more passive in information seeking.* The two steps imply that there is one group of influentials who are attuned to the media and quick to adopt new ideas presented there. Then, there is a second, larger group who are more passive in their media use. This second group relies on the first to learn about new developments. This two-step flow is essentially what Toyota is relying on for the diffusion of the Prius from environmentally friendly, innovative, Internet-savvy early adopters to other later adopting car buyers.

Trickle-down theory is an important theory for understanding innovation, but it makes several rigid assumptions about the hierarchical nature of social relations and social interactions. Nevertheless, in some social systems, these assumptions still hold reasonably well. Trickle-down theory has been revised to include trickle-across and trickle-up models of diffusion. These models recognize that media exposure allows simultaneous adoption of new styles at all levels of society. Often, as with American hip-hop culture that arose in the ghetto or European Afro-pop that arose in poor African nations, selective innovations of low-status groups are borrowed or imitated by high-status groups. More important, the definition of high-status and low-status groups may vary from situation to situation.[50]

Looking at the diffusion of innovations within and between social systems, we can see many illustrations of the effects of social hierarchies. For example, in countries with developed market systems, fashions tend to flow outward from larger, more complex market centers such as Paris or São Paulo to smaller, simpler market centers such as Nancy, France, or Curitiba, Brazil. Similarly, the sequence of countries adopting an innovation is dominated by a hierarchical pattern. For example, digital communication technology has diffused from the First World to the Third World over a period of several decades.[51] An example of the diffusion of commercial pop culture into Russia was provided earlier in Consumer Chronicles 16.2

The stability of the social system, including the stability of social hierarchies and the composition of membership, is another aspect of the social system that influences diffusion. The impact of opportunities for social mobility on the diffusion process can be seen in research on the adoption of technological innovations in developing nations. This research suggests that wealth and social security, and desires for social mobility, are related to innovative behaviors.[52]

Cultural Production System

A **cultural production system** (CPS) is *a set of individuals and organizations responsible for creating and marketing culturally significant products*.[53] A CPS helps determine the types of products that emerge as fashion trends. It draws on a limited pool of symbols, myths, images, and rituals to create products that are anchored in cultural context. A good example is the CPS for popular music that turns out "new" hits that regularly recycle old themes, melodies, and rhythms. Country music in the United States is a particularly highly developed example. The Dixie Chicks, a current chart-topping group, is a good example of a country music CPS product. The Chicks' tunes recycle classic country music themes, repackaged into a 1990s female delivery vehicle.

The CPS consists of three subsystems: creative, managerial, and communications. The **creative subsystem** attempts to anticipate tastes of the buying public and generate new symbols or products that express cultural values. Examples include Milanese (Italy) fashion houses or the Bombay, Hong Kong, and Hollywood entertainment industries.

The **managerial subsystem** selects and makes tangible new product ideas, produces new symbols, going so far as to create new categories of personal identity such as Euroconsumers, buppies (black urban professionals), *bon chic bon genre* French yuppies, *GQ* (magazine) warriors, and so on. The managerial subsystem serves the needs of an economic system, which depends on growth, obsolescence, and realization of profit for its existence.

Finally, the **communication subsystem** spreads the word about what's new, upcoming, and popular to various groups of adopters. The communication subsystem includes ad agencies, popularizing fashion and style magazines, fan clubs, international consumer television networks like MTV and CNN, national ones like the Home Shopping Channel, and international radio stations such as France Inter or Africa No. 1 in Gabon. Mobile sound trucks exemplify the system in rural Latin America. The communication subsystem also includes lots of tastemakers and gatekeepers such as trend researchers, agents, disk jockeys, retail buyers, magazine editors, interior designers, real estate agents, and the like. Their job is to make the new seem familiar and desirable to target markets, and, of course, their services are for hire by manufacturers. Effective elements of the communication subsystem earn enormous fees.[54]

In Chapter 1 we introduced the idea that within societies there are two opposing motivational tendencies that nonetheless are found together. We might call them the motive toward imitation, or integration and affiliation with the familiar, and the motive toward differentiation, or distinction from others. These twin motives can be thought of as social motives that underlie an individual consumer's innovation resistance and innovativeness. Consumers look both within and outside their social groups and make comparisons and judgments about taste. Comparative judgments, in turn, lead to recurring innovative (or

Social Group Influence on Innovation and Adoption

conservative) purchase and use decisions. The consumer behaviors triggered by such comparisons also reconfirm the existence of groups in society and the individuals affiliated with them as distinct, although not necessarily as superior or inferior.

Innovation and conservatism in consumer behaviors serve to integrate individuals with some groups and distinguish them from others of which they are not members. They also provide the basis for drawing distinctions within groups. Marketers are often faced with the challenge of identifying those groups and individuals to whom others turn when making social comparisons or seeking integration. Successful adoption by these opinion leaders speeds the diffusion process.

The key to understanding innovation in consumer behavior cross-culturally lies in understanding these fundamental processes of differentiation, comparison, and integration as reflected in the goods that people value. In systems undergoing qualitative economic change, such as the NICs and developing nations, consumers' motives are complex, and the search for material symbols of these processes include novel and even bizarre goods. The supertall platform shoes worn by the Japanese *amazonesu* or the taste for designer fashion among poor Congolese migrants to France mentioned earlier in the book are examples.[55]

Between- and Within-Group Communication

Exhibit 16.4 outlines a model of innovation and adoption processes. The model suggests that innovations spread through communications between groups about the meanings of goods and services. In many marketing situations inducements to innovate flow between different kinds of groups, between channel members in business-to-business contexts, from firms to consumers, or from nonprofits to stakeholder groups. The fact that the groups are different (heterophilous) may impede diffusion. This is why marketers strive to stimulate observational learning from valued role models, employ an adaptive sales force, and stimulate word-of-mouth through reference groups. These techniques shift the focus of communications from between groups to within similar (homophilous) groups.

When groups agree on the value and meanings of goods and services, consumption serves to define and defend boundaries between groups and identify members within groups. Groups are differentiated from one another, and individuals achieve group inte-

Exhibit 16.4 Innovation and Adoption Model

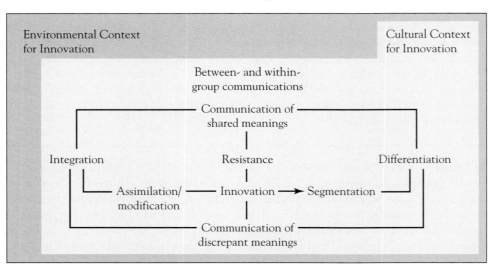

Discrepant consumption meanings fuel the snowboarding lifestyle.

gration by consuming agreed-on goods and services. For example, consumption of snow skis might serve to distinguish skiing from nonskiing groups, athletic from nonathletic groups, richer from poorer groups, residents from nonresidents of alpine environments, and so forth. Some innovations will be consistent with the overall pattern of prior beliefs and values and will, through processes of assimilation and modification, be absorbed into the common repertoire of goods and services and contribute to the status quo. Thus, skiing equipment has evolved to include novice and expert gear of various kinds, distinctions that subtly encode some of the intergroup differences.

In competitive, market-driven societies, discrepancies often arise about the meaning and value of products, services, and business practices. Discrepancies about consumption meanings create pressures for innovation. Some innovations will be dramatically new and will trigger new behavior patterns for at least some segments of the population. In some cases innovations may lead to the creation of new population segments, causing changes in the relationships among and between groups in society. To continue the skiing example, an innovative skiing device that requires dramatic changes in skill, the snowboard, developed over the last two decades. Snowboards facilitated the emergence of a new youthful market segment, snowboarders. In the early days of snowboarding, snowboarders just used their ski clothing. However, snowboarders wished to further distinguish themselves from skiers. This desire, in combination with varied needs (e.g., the need for extra padding in particular places), led to an explosion of new kinds of clothing and other paraphernalia designed specifically for snowboarders.

Through communication between and within groups, changes triggered by innovations are absorbed into society, and people agree about the nature and meaning of new products, behaviors, or market segments. Without effective communications innovations do not diffuse and are not adopted. Studies of effective diffusion emphasize the role of reinforcing communications. For example, the Prius campaign also includes an intensive training program for service personnel, a customer contact group whose expertise will be a key to the ultimate success of the Prius launch.

Between-Group Influences on Innovative, Individual Behavior

Exhibit 16.5 outlines factors related to communication between groups and high-status group influence on individual innovative behavior.[56] As illustrated in the exhibit, **high-status group influence** has an impact on innovative behavior. To constitute a high-status group for innovation, a group must be viewed as attractive and as having ties to the innovation or consumption object, including special knowledge or expertise. The more that the high-status group is viewed as attractive and having an essential similarity to the consumption object, the more influential it is likely to be in purchase and possession of that product class. Japanese *amazonesu* mentioned above are a high-status reference group for Taiwanese fashion wannabes, for example.[57]

Consistent with trickle-down theory, the endorsement of a consumption object by a high-status reference group encourages innovative behavior by increasing expectations of social approval. This explains why top management endorsement consistently helps explain the adoption of innovations within organizations.[58] Similarly, research on the diffusion of a new ethical drug among doctors in Ireland found that a highly trained and well-informed sales force strongly influenced doctors' adoption decisions. Research on quality improvement software in Norway and intranet technologies in South African companies confirms the influence of outside experts in encouraging adoption behavior. In another study, endorsement of a new cordless headphone system for a portable stereo system by U.S. ski team members had a positive influence on intentions to adopt the innovation among college students, living (and skiing) in the western United States. The endorsement by U.S. ski team members was related both to the belief that their peers would approve (adoption would have a positive effect on social approval) and that the system itself would have better sound quality (an influence on product evaluation).[59]

Another factor outlined in Exhibit 16.5 that positively influences individual innovative behavior is connections to high-status reference groups. Traditionally, this was thought of as face-to-face connections. In the case of cross-cultural diffusions we must consider connections that occur through travel, work, and social occasions. For example, family ties between Indians living in Great Britain and India is an important channel for the diffusion of

Exhibit 16.5 Group Influence on Innovative Behaviors

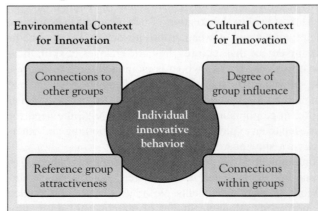

Exhibit 16.6 Multistep Media Flow Model of Communications

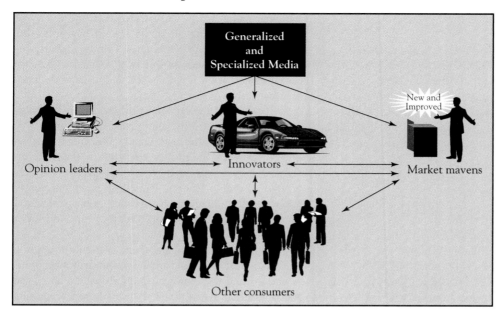

Western style and fashion into India, and travel to the West and interaction with Western-ers are associated with higher levels of innovative behavior for Hungarians. Connections may be indirect as well. In many First World countries various media offer a direct chan-nel for learning about new products via celebrity endorsement.[60]

As suggested in Exhibit 16.5, explorations of innovative behavior must also consider the spread of novel goods and meanings *within* a social system, that is, the social commu-nication networks for receiving information about an innovation. Exhibit 16.6 illustrates possible social communication networks for receiving information about an innovation. It depicts a **multistep media flow model** of communications. The figure reintroduces three important types of consumers discussed in Chapter 15 who pass along information about innovations to other consumers in their social networks: opinion leaders, innovators, and market mavens.

Opinion leaders are individuals who act as information brokers, intervening between mass media sources and the opinions and choices of the population. Industry Insights 16.4 identifies one group of opinion leaders.[61]

Early adopters desire to look like a pioneer in having purchased the new product and value the involvement and expertise that come from the actual experience with the new product. Research has indicated that early adopters like to talk about the product to confirm their assessment of it and because of the product's novelty. As with opinion leaders, re-search suggests there is no general early adopter.[62]

Market mavens are characterized by general marketplace expertise and influence. Con-sumers rely on market mavens for information, and mavens provide market information across a range of topics. An online maven can be found at the *Business Week* website.[63]

 www.maven.
businessweek.
com

Innovativeness turns on independence of judgment. Not surprisingly, opinion leaders, early adopters, and market mavens are all better connected to general and specialized media that provide them with more information than other consumers. Reliance on inter-personal information is also characteristic of opinion leaders and market mavens.[64] To take advantage of interpersonal influence networks, marketers need to locate the influential consumers for their particular product or service and find a way of getting them talking about it. Toyota has done this through their Internet campaign for Prius. Industry Insights 16.5 illustrates how Coca-Cola and Chrysler have targeted youthful and more mature opinion leaders, respectively.

Consumers are especially likely to rely on personal sources when the innovation has symbolic or communicative value and when consumers take on new roles with unfamiliar demands.[65] Industry Insights 16.6 describes a group of opinion leaders termed parenting leaders. Parenting leaders are early adopters of products and habits such as environmental conservation and recycling, and they provide other parents with advice.[66]

Where consumers are able to identify opinion leaders, a link has been found between adoption of innovations and the views of opinion leaders about the innovation. For example, in a study of the adoption by dentists of nonprecious metal alloys in the construction of crowns and bridges it was found that adopters of the nonprecious alloys cited experts whose evaluations of the innovation were favorable; nonadopters and active rejecters cited experts whose evaluations of the innovations were not favorable. Furthermore, friends of experts were likely to imitate the adoption behavior of the experts, whether positive or negative. In a different context, a study of the adoption of new Western clothing styles among the Luo people of western Kenya in the early twentieth century emphasizes the role of chiefs whose influence was based on traditional authority and migrant workers and Christian converts whose influence was based on new sources of knowledge and authority in the diffusion process.[67]

Considering how individuals are connected within a social system is important to understanding change. In the Triad nations we tend to take for granted that we will easily be able to find a friend or acquaintance who knows about stereo equipment. In many parts of the world the assumption that someone knows an opinion leader in a particular product category (much less actually seeks them out for advice) may be misguided. In transitional economies, for example, available products and services have changed so quickly that few consumers have the expertise to help other consumers with their purchase decisions.[68]

 www.mysimon.com

 www.killerapp.com

 www.botspot.com

The Effect of Other Users on the Value of Adoption

Frequently, other users influence the value of adoption to prospective users. A good example of what economists term a **positive externality** is provided by Internet price-search services. Their value is related to the number of other adopters. Their use should diffuse rapidly across the hundreds of millions of Internet consumers because the cost of using and

Targeting youthful opinion leaders

The Coca-Cola Company introduced a new soft drink, Surge, that was targeted at young teenagers. One set of TV commercials showed urban youths, full of energy, drinking Surge and performing dangerous stunts (e.g., on skateboards). Surge has a relatively large amount of caffeine, so the slogan of the brand is "Feel the rush." In 1997, the soft-drink manufacturer also attempted to stimulate a positive word-of-mouth campaign by sending free copies of a CD to leaders in the teen community. The CD contained two parts: (1) a series of songs by groups popular with the target audience (e.g., Fatboy Slim, Third Eye Blind); and (2) "an arsenal of audio samples for crafting superb mix tapes." Coca-Cola managers used a variety of methods to identify teen leaders to include on their mailing list for this CD. The mailing packet also included coupons for both Surge and Tower Records. This joint promotional effort was very effective in stimulating sales for the new soft drink by targeting opinion leaders.

Chrysler's LH cars go to market

When Chrysler introduced its LH cars—the Dodge Intrepid, Chrysler Concorde, and Eagle Vision—they worked to spur positive word-of-mouth. Chrysler dealers in several states offered LH models for a weekend to over 6,000 influential community leaders and business-people between October 1992 and January 1993. These included not only top executives but those who are frequently sought after for advice by a wide circle of people, such as barbers. A follow-up survey showed that the cars received a total of 32,000 exposures in three months, including secondary drivers and passengers. More than 98 percent of those responding said they would recommend the car to a friend, and 90 percent said their opinion of Chrysler had improved.

Source: Chip Walker, "Word of Mouth," American Demographics, July 1995, p. 44.

producing a search agent is largely a fixed cost: developing and updating the software and learning to use it. The greater the members of such services, the lower will be the cost of membership; and the greater the consumer's use of such a service, the lower will be the cost of each search to the consumer and the greater will be the incentive to use the service. Feedback processes are everywhere, benefiting innovative, wired consumers everywhere.[69]

There is a more subtle way in which the number of other adopters affects the value of the innovation. The number of other adopters can influence the *perception* of the quality of the innovation. For a dramatic example, consider the case of the transitional economies of central and eastern Europe. In much of central and eastern Europe, consumers were accustomed to a scarcity economy. Even now, as the flow of goods improves in many major cities, consumers still use lines as a cue to quality—if people are waiting in line for it, it must be good. This aspect of line psychology is illustrated in Consumer Chronicles 16.5. This bandwagon effect is found in other parts of the world too. Lines outside nightclubs and restaurants attract people who see the line as a signal of something special.

An influential group of parents seek quality over price when it comes to purchasing products, according to a study for *Parenting* magazine by Roper Starch Worldwide, Mamaroneck, N.Y. Parenting leaders, who consist of 23 percent of parents with at least one child under the age of 12, are ready and willing to buy premium products even though they are not necessarily among the most affluent consumers. Roper interviewed a random sample of 632 parents in face-to-face interviews. The margin of error was 5 percent.

The percentage of parents who were asked for advice or opinions by their peers about these issues:

	Parenting Leaders	All Other Parents
How to handle small children	59%	31%
Restaurants	51	32
Cooking/recipes	45	36
Health problems	43	21
Computers	36	9
How to handle teenagers	34	8

Most parenting leaders feel some big ticket items and package goods brands are different or better and worth paying more for:

	Parenting Leaders	All Other Parents
Toothpaste	66%	41%
Ice cream	60	42
Washing machines	59	39
Cars	58	40
Personal computers	56	37
Skincare lotion	46	35

Most parenting leaders feel ads are useful and informative.

	Parenting Leaders	All Other Parents
Newspaper ads	86%	75%
Magazine ads	76	71
Radio ads	74	68
TV ads	69	72

Source: Rickard, "'Parenting Leaders' Peddling Influence: Quality-Hungry Group Full of Consumer Advice."

Adoption

So far, we have focused almost exclusively on the dynamics of diffusion. Certainly, the diffusion of innovations is a social process, so it is appropriate to focus on cultural and group variables that influence the relative time of adoption over geographic space. However, the diffusion of innovations is also an individual process, and some individuals decide to adopt innovations before others do. In this section we turn our attention to the adoption process, that is, the decision by an individual to adopt an innovation.

The **adoption process** focuses on the *stages individual consumers or organizational buying units pass through in making a decision to accept or reject an innovation.* Marketers are very interested in the adoption process because knowing the profile of adopters, the numbers of adopters, and the timing of their adoption are critical to the success or failure of an innovation. This is equally true whether an organization is concerned with the adoption of innovations like cellular phones, high-yielding seeds or improved tillage practices, health and disease prevention behaviors, or management philosophies like relationship marketing.

When I was about 13 years old, my family took a summer trip to Leningrad, the former capital of Russia. It is the most beautiful city I have ever visited, with summer residences of Russian emperors, fountains, and museums. All of it was fascinating. But what amazed me the most was not cathedrals or monuments. What captured my attention was the grocery stores.

Different kinds of cheeses, sausages, fish, everything already cut and packaged in small packages: 150 grams, 200 grams, 300 grams each. And customers were not grabbing 20 or 30 of those little packages but just 1 or 2. There was no sight of women carrying huge bags of groceries. Why would a person kill herself by trying to drag 10 kilograms of stuff home and then store it in her refrigerator for weeks if she could come back tomorrow and buy everything fresh? There were at least three grocery stores within walking distance from any person's home in most Russian cities, so getting to the store was not the problem. Why? I, as a teenager living in Krasnoyarsk, a big industrial city thousands of miles away from the capital in the late 1980s, thought the answer was obvious.

At that time, I was used to standing in lines. It was a big part of people's lives in all 15 republics of the Soviet Union, with an exception of only two cities, Moscow and Leningrad. Residents of these cities stood in line only to buy clothing. People would learn about what was going on in the world, hear rumors about private lives of celebrities, make friends, fall in love—all while standing in lines.

If it takes someone three hours to get sausage, would that person be satisfied with just 300 grams of it, especially if there might not be any sausage in the store for a week? Only if that person is crazy. Most people weren't, so they bought enough sausage to last for about two weeks. Five or ten kilos. There always was a limit to how much one person could buy. The limit varied by store and by how much supply the store had that particular day. Sometimes, my parents would phone me and tell me to come to the store so that we could buy more. Sometimes, on the days when a rare product (e.g., coffee or bananas) was available, my parents would call all the neighbors and friends so they, too, could stand in line to buy. Other times, we would just join a long line without even knowing for certain what was for sale. For us, a long line was a signal of something special.

In today's Russia, shopping is easy. When people in my hometown go grocery shopping, they only buy 200 grams of sausage at a time, because they will simply return the next day and get fresh meat. Now, when there are at least 20 grocery stores within easy walking area, shopping is convenient. However, if a shopper wants to buy 10 kilograms, it would cost more than a monthly salary. Now that it is possible to buy coffee and bananas in every store, is life better than it was 10 years ago? I don't know. To be honest, I don't even like coffee and bananas any more. I don't know any rumors about movie stars, and I'm not as politically informed as I was 10 years ago.

Source: "Consumer Stories: Vignettes with a Message," University of Georgia, Center for Marketing Studies, Working Paper Series (2001–1) George M. Zinkhan (editor), pages 14–15.

The decision to adopt or reject an innovation takes place over time. Adoption is not just an either-or decision; rather, due to the effects of the five adoption factors mentioned earlier, it involves varying degrees of acceptance or rejection. An innovation may be purchased but not really integrated into an individual's or household's life. When personal

1. I am very attracted to rare objects.
2. I tend to be a fashion leader rather than a fashion follower.
3. I am more likely to buy a product if it is scarce.
4. I would prefer to have things custom-made than to have them ready-made.
5. I enjoy having things that others do not.
6. I rarely pass up an opportunity to order custom features on the products I buy.
7. I like to try new products and service before others do.
8. I enjoy shopping at stores that carry merchandise which is different and unusual.

Source: Michael Lynn and Judy Harris, "The Desire for Unique Consumer Products: A New Individual Difference Scale," Psychology and Marketing *14, no. 6 (1997), pp. 601–16.*

computers were first introduced, many people purchased them but then just let them sit and collect dust because they weren't sure what to do with them. This pattern persists with computer and home Internet use.[70] Similarly, many African farms are littered with unused farm equipment obtained through ill-conceived agricultural development schemes. In health care, social marketers are often very concerned about partial adoption. Consumers' erratic use of antiviral drugs is common, but it has the awful side effect of encouraging the evolution of drug-resistant viruses.

Adopter Categories

In general, those promoting innovations want to identify customers who are most likely to change their behavior or try the new products or services first. Such knowledge is helpful in targeting marketing communications to reach these people. Therefore, research has sought to classify consumers into adoption classes. Several different approaches have been used. For example, the **time-of-adoption technique** of classification defines adopter categories in terms of *purchases that occur some number of weeks, months, or years after product launch.* The **cross-sectional technique** of classification determines how many of a *prespecified list of new products a particular individual or firm has purchased.*[71]

Lead Users

Lead users play an important role in the development and spread of technological innovations. Lead users are users whose *current needs become general in a market in the future.*[72] In general, lead users develop or support the development of innovations because of an industry-based need; that is, they simply can't do what they need to without an innovation. Lead users exist because important new technologies, products, tastes, and other factors do not affect all members simultaneously. One exploration of the rate of diffusion of important industrial goods into major firms in the bituminous coal, iron and steel, brew-

Exhibit 16.7 Relationship of the Diffusion Process to the Product Life Cycle

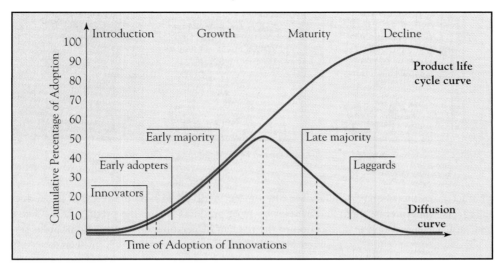

ing, and railroad industries found that in 75 percent of the cases it took over 20 years for complete diffusion of these innovations to major firms. Hence, some lead users could be found far in advance of the general market.[73]

In consumer markets, some research has identified a similar group, a small segment of consumers who exhibit a great desire for unique consumer products (DUCP). This research has also produced a scale to measure DUCP as shown in Good Practice 16.2. Care to take this test?

Exhibit 16.7 shows how the five main adopter categories map into the product life cycle. For instance, those who buy immediately after the innovation is introduced into the market are the lead users. They purchase at the early part of the introductory phase of the life cycle. Often, these lead users may have a difficult time actually finding the new product for sale, since distribution outlets are extremely limited. As such, lead users may rely on their superior marketplace and technical knowledge to ferret out sellers who carry the new product.

Innovators

According to the scheme introduced in Exhibit 16.7, innovators represent less than 3 percent of adopters of a given innovation. The kids who started wearing old Hush Puppy Dukes and Columbias they bought in N.Y. thrift shops in the early 90s and fueled a subsequent sales increase of 950 percent by the peak of the fashion in 1996 are a good example.[74]

Although researchers have identified a segment with a general desire for unique consumer products, research generally shows that no generic innovators across product or service offerings can be identified. As the Dilbert cartoon on page 600 shows, it is not always easy to identify who will be innovative for particular products nor which products will be the focus of innovation. For example, when first introduced, personal digital assistants proved incredibly popular with Japanese girls who were not the original target market.[75]

However, across studies and national markets innovative consumers share a number of characteristics. They are often venturesome, less risk averse, younger, have higher incomes, and are better educated than later adopters. Active information seeking also

characterizes their behavior. They are often more involved with media relevant to product categories that interest them and heavier users of products within the product class. Thus, researchers have found that a portion of the readers of personal computer and popular science magazines are highly involved with a range of computer and new high-tech tools and products, respectively. Innovators often have radial interpersonal networks. In other words, they are linked personally to many other people.[76]

As shown in Exhibit 16.7, the innovators purchase in the first half of the product introduction phase. These innovators play a key role in the success of the innovation by spreading the word to other consumers who might be interested in the product's benefits. When enough new users become adopters, sales start to take off, and the life cycle enters the growth phase of the life cycle.

Early Adopters

Referring again to Exhibit 16.7, early adopters typically constitute between 10 and 20 percent of adopters. They have been characterized as opinion leaders within local reference groups. This makes them important to identify since they influence others within their network.[77] They are sometimes highly involved with trends within particular product categories. When the early adopters begin to purchase, it is a sign that the innovation has entered the growth phase. Relative to the opinion-leading Japanese *yamanba* and *amazonesu* female youth tribes, the Taiwanese *hazitsu* are an example of early adopters. The hazitsu ape everything Japanese from the latest hairstyle to the cut of their trousers and, recently, what the Taiwanese call the "death shoes," tall (and dangerous) platform shoes.[78]

Research on adoption of agricultural innovations among farmers has shown how complex the early adoption profile can be. In one Mexican farming community, wealthy farmers secure in their social status and the wealthiest of poor farmers, anxious to improve their standard of living and social status, were both found to be more likely to engage in innovative behaviors than the poorest farmers and those in the middle of the social hierarchy, who are insecure in their social and financial position.[79]

Early Majority

The early majority are often characterized as deliberative decision makers. They adopt innovations sooner than most of their social group but rely more heavily on interpersonal information sources than impersonal media in making their decisions. They often have interlocking personal networks that can be mobilized to facilitate the spread of innovations. For example, the diffusion of IUD birth control devices in the Philippines was accomplished by reaching interlocking circles of middle-income housewives.[80] As shown in Exhibit 16.7, early majority consumers begin to make purchases in the later portion of the growth stage.

Late Majority

The late majority represents another third of the adopting population. They may be thought of as skeptical consumers, doubtful of the benefits of adoption. Lower prices that lower risks stimulate late majority purchases, as when the cost of PCs fell below $1,000 and nudged up the U.S. penetration rate of PCs from 40 to 60 percent.[81]

Late majority consumers may be inclined to adopt in response to social pressures rather than as a result of the perceived benefits of adoption; that is, they are vulnerable to **bandwagon effects.** They adopt because "everyone is doing it," and the failure to adopt might provoke a loss of status or self-esteem. Both individual consumers (see Dilbert cartoon below) and organizations are vulnerable to bandwagon effects. For example, most airlines have adopted frequent flier programs that reward repeat customers with reduced fares and free tickets in part because it has become expected practice. Offering such programs gives airlines legitimacy.

The bandwagon effect refers to the fact that exposure to novel information can lead to rapid shifts in mass consumption behavior, including adoption of innovations when people follow the behavior of others irrespective of what they believe or value themselves. Bandwagon effects seem to involve adoption when beliefs are not strongly held about alternatives. Bandwagon effects in politics, surgery, business, fashion, and sales of initial public stock offerings have been described. Bandwagon effects can be triggered by chance, but evidence suggests that adoption of innovations by opinion or fashion leaders can speed adoption rates.[82]

Late majority consumers often exhibit characteristics opposite those of early adopters.

Dilbert endorses the bandwagon effect.

www.dilbert.com; E-mail: SCOTTADAMS@AOL.COM; 11/21/99 © 1999 United Feature Syndicate, Inc.

Microsoft's software introduction Bob targeted the skeptical computer nonuser with what the firm hoped would be a user-friendly product.[83] Bob failed, but organizations are always looking for ways to overcome the natural skepticism of consumers, both about products and about promotional efforts.

Laggards

The final adopter segment is **laggards,** typically accounting for less that 20 percent of the adopting population. Laggards tend to be traditionalists, locally oriented in terms of networks and social horizons, and relatively dogmatic in beliefs and values. They also tend to be less educated. More older households and older consumers fall into the laggard category. Amazingly, 40 to 60 percent of customers at savings banks in New York City might be considered laggards. They still use passbook savings accounts that earn uncompetitive interest. Older consumers who recall the Depression of the 1930s, young technophobes, and recent immigrants belong to this group.[84]

Laggards may not begin to purchase until the product enters the decline phase (Exhibit 16.7). In this period, organizations may begin to minimize their promotional efforts and expenses. Competition may be reduced, as some firms choose to exit as sales and profitability levels decline. However, the firms that do remain in the decline phase may still prove to be profitable, as long as they continue to satisfy customer demand. In some instances, a declining product may be restimulated. Indeed, a good example of this phenomenon is designer jeans, revived by the trend toward casual business dress. Fashion items often display this cyclical product life cycle pattern rather than the S-curve.

It is also worth distinguishing nonadopter segments. In addition to simple rejecters of a particular innovation, one may also encounter evangelical rejectionists, like those in the Slow Cities movement, who actively and publicly oppose some marketer-driven innovations, fast-food in this case. We've mentioned Adbusters and adherents of the voluntary simplicity movement in other chapters. These examples represent rejecter movements. In Japan, some oppose the importation of foreign rice. In the United States and Europe, many oppose proposals to irradiate vegetables or to alter food plants genetically.[85]

The Adoption Process

Marketers and others interested in changing consumer behavior have devoted considerable efforts to understanding the adoption process. The nature and scope of interventions in the process should be tailored to the sequence and timing of stages adopters go through before adoption. Various models of adoption have been proposed, but the classical model of stages describes an extended high-involvement decision-making process (see Chapters 11 and 13).

Awareness

Awareness or knowledge of an innovation comes about through exposure to the innovation. Consumer inertia or lack of search may be a barrier to awareness. In media-rich environments in the Triad countries, the mass media generally promotes awareness. In the transitional economies of eastern Europe, foreign travel or contact with people who had traveled abroad was an important source of awareness of new products prior to the collapse of communist governments. In many developing countries, periodic markets or traveling peddlers have long provided rural people with a glimpse of novel products. In a recent case of diffusion of palm cooking oil to cooked food vendors in Java, Indonesia, a mobile sales force proved crucial to creating awareness. Among immigrant Mexican communities in the United States, "convenience stores on wheels," vendors selling out of trucks, provide newcomers with access to novel products.[86]

Interest

Interest followed by evaluation and persuasion is a situation that creates awareness of relative need. Once a need or want is stimulated, information search begins. Acquisition of a mentor, access to an opinion leader, or exposure to a market maven can affect the potential adopter's perceptions of available alternatives. Online search engines have revolutionized the search process for wired consumers.

At this point, a number of innovation characteristics such as **perceived risk** of adoption affect the adoption process. Perceived risk may relate to product performance or to the social, personal, or financial costs of poor product performance. Lack of knowledge and inability to appreciate the relevance of benefits of an innovation cause consumers not to seek out information related to innovative products. Marketers should take pains to address potential sources of perceived risk. Adaptive salespeople and consumer-rating services are important players in this process.

Trial

In product trial, the adopter is moved to action. Sources of innovative goods and services are evaluated and a product is chosen. Trial often involves firsthand experience, but consumers may also "try" an innovation through the experiences of trusted acquaintances or **consumer surrogates,** *specialized expert agents retained by customers to guide, direct, or transact marketplace activities.*[87]

Trial may mean trying out the product category or just a new brand. Finding ways to try and evaluate certain new products is problematic for consumers. Often innovative products possess new and complex features (e.g., hybrid-energy vehicles, DVD disks, online books, or MP3 minidisks) that do not necessarily communicate obvious benefits over existing products. Adaptive selling, guarantees, warrantees, price promotions, employment of surrogate consumers, and similar tactics facilitate trial and reduce perceived risks of trial.

Adoption

Adoption or rejection of the innovation follows trial. Although adoption is often treated as an either/or alternative, it is usually more complicated. To understand adoption, it is important to look at the ways an innovation is integrated into a consumer's lifestyle. In the case of many technologically oriented products such as home computers, the decision to purchase a technology is not as important to adoption as decisions that govern the use of the technology after adoption.[88] Does the home computer just sit in the study and collect dust, is it primarily relegated to kid's games, or is it an essential part of the household's everyday life? You may be able to think of many examples where use after purchase is important in describing adoption behavior. Perhaps you have friends who purchased exercise equipment that now sits in the garage unused or who joined a health club but now can't find time to go. In these and many other cases, consumers purchase new products or services but don't integrate them into their lifestyles. In this sense, they have not really adopted the products.

To understand adoption it is also important to consider overall adoption rates and consumption situations. For instance, studies of hospitals and retail clothing stores have found relationships between organizational adoption of innovations and overall adoption rates in competitive, urban environments. A consumer study in Taiwan showed that intentions to adopt canned Wulong tea varied, depending on the consumption situation. Specifically, the beverage was considered inappropriate for nighttime consumption because of background beliefs about the health effects of tea. A study in West Africa showed that adoption of a Western innovation, cigarette smoking, was associated with wage work in foreign, urban contexts but not farm labor in domestic, rural contexts.[89]

A final point to emphasize is that marketing tactics can influence the adoption process. For example, a penetration strategy uses low prices, extensive distribution, and extensive communications to speed innovation. The signals conveyed by these elements of the marketing mix can induce broad consumer trial without extensive search and evaluation. By contrast, a skimming strategy makes use of high prices and selective distribution and communications to induce adoption within a narrow market, thereby limiting the scope of adoption.

In this chapter we introduce several key concepts for the study of consumer change, including innovation, diffusion, and adoption. Innovation is a broad term that refers to new things, new ways of behaving and interacting with things, and new ideas, behaviors, or structures. Finding ways to improve the management of innovations is critical for organizations of all kinds. Innovations can be distinguished in terms of the behavioral consequences of the innovation for the users. Continuous innovations require only minor changes in user behaviors; discontinuous innovations require major changes. Several important characteristics of the innovation influence the adoption rate. The perceived relative advantage over existing options is the most important factor to the success of an innovation. Other important characteristics include compatibility, trialability, observability, and complexity.

Diffusion is the spread of an innovation from its creative source across space and time. Adoption refers to the stages an individual adopter goes through in making a decision to accept or reject an innovation. People in developed consumer societies may have a pro-innovation bias, but consumer conservatism and resistance are widespread. The desire for both psychological and social equilibrium contributes to innovation resistance.

Innovation and adoption processes are influenced by environmental, cultural, and social system factors. The development and diffusion of many innovations is based, at least in part, in changing environmental conditions that mandate adaptive responses. Economic conditions and market structures also have broad influence on innovation processes. The business sector of contemporary market economies invests heavily in innovation, and this investment creates a fast rate of introduction of new products.

Cultural attitudes toward newness, innovative behaviors, and change provide norms that influence individual innovative behaviors. Cultural attitudes toward integration or fitting in (versus distinction or standing out) also influence rates of adoption within a social system. In general, the diffusion rate and penetration level of an innovation will depend on the innovation's compatibility with social system values. Innovations that threaten core values are subject to resistance. Cultural production systems—consisting of creative, managerial, and communication subsystems—are responsible for creating and marketing culturally significant products. Originating in the Triad countries, these cultural production systems increasingly influence the global marketplace.

Social groups have a critical impact on the diffusion of innovations. Innovations spread through communications between groups about the meanings of goods and services. Discrepancies about consumption meanings create pressures for innovation. The twin motives of integration and differentiation are key to understanding innovation and conservatism. Consumers look both within and outside their social groups and make comparisons and judgments. Looking at the diffusion of innovations within and between social systems, we can see many illustrations of the effects of social groups. One important early theory is the trickle-down theory of diffusion. The idea that innovations flow from high-status to low-status groups is still an important theory for understanding innovation.

Influential consumers often aid the spread of innovations within a social system. We review three important types of influential consumers: opinion leaders, innovators, and market mavens. The diffusion of innovations depends heavily on the flow of information, not just from media sources but between consumers as well.

In general, marketers are interested in identifying consumers who are most likely to change their behavior or try new products and services first. This has led researchers to classify consumers by their time of adoption. Adopter categories including lead users, innovators, early adopters, early majority, late majority, and laggards. The classical adoption process typical of a high-involvement decision includes awareness, interest, trial, and adoption stages. However, a number of situational and other factors affect this general adoption process.

adoption process   596
bandwagon effects   601
communication subsystem   589
compatibility   580
complexity   581
consumer surrogates   603
continuous innovations   574
creative destruction   571
creative subsystem   589
cross-sectional technique   598
cultural production system   589
demand density   585
differentiation   588
diffusion process   581
discontinuance   584
discontinuous innovations   578
dynamically continuous innovations   577
fads   574
fashions   574
high-status group influence   592
imitation   588

innovation   573
innovation resistance   583
laggards   602
lead users   598
managerial subsystem   589
multistep media flow model   593
neighborhood effect   583
observability   580
perceived risk   603
pioneering advantage   579
positive externality   594
product complementarity   584
pro-innovation bias   583
psychological equilibrium   583
relative advantage   579
social equilibrium   583
time-of-adoption technique   598
trends   574
trialability   580
trickle-down theory of innovation   588
two-step flow model   588

1. Prepaid phone cards have been around for over a decade internationally, but the United States has been slow to adopt the new cards. How would you classify this innovation? What characteristics of the product are likely to influence the adoption and diffusion of this product?

2. Gridcore subpanels are lightweight, nontoxic, recycled alternatives to building materials such as particle board. They were invented and patented by the U.S. Department of Agriculture at the Forest Products Laboratory in Madison, Wisconsin. The engineered, molded fiber panels are produced from a variety of recycled materials. They come in several degrees of thickness without extensive use of toxic binders or resins. The manufacturing process uses no toxic chemicals, produces no toxic by-products, emits virtually no air pollution, and recycles 94 percent of the water used

to make the boards. The ultimate goal of Gridcore Systems (exclusive licensee for manufacture and sale) is to create Gridcore panels that can be used for residential building systems. Develop a strategy for the diffusion of Gridcore panels.

3. Below is a list of six products that have recently been introduced into the U.S. market. Classify each innovation, and describe the diffusion pattern that you expect each product to have. Justify your answers.
   a. Oki cellular phone
   b. Toyota Prius
   c. Celestial Seasonings Soothers herbal throat drops
   d. Rayovac renewal rechargeable batteries (reusable 25 times or more)
   e. Pokémon collectibles
   f. Remodeled Volkswagen Beetle

4. In 1999, the movie *Star Wars: The Phantom Menace* was a big success. Discuss the cultural values that contributed to the success of this film.

5. A portable color computer, with a powerful processor, weighing in at around 7 lbs. now comes with a CD-ROM and built-in videocam. Describe how the company can develop promotional, pricing, and distribution strategies targeted to the innovators for this product. Be sure to describe who you think the innovators for this product will be.

6. The growth rate of wireless communications technologies has been phenomenal. Cellular telephone service needed only nine years to attract 10 million customers. To build a customer base of that same size, the fax machine required 22 years, cable TV service took 25 years, and the traditional landline telephone needed 38 years. Describe the product factors that have contributed to the growth of cellular telephone service. How do other users affect the spread of this product?

7. Describe a new fashion popular in your area. What factors have contributed to its successful diffusion?

8. Do you know someone who is an opinion leader for you in some category of products or services? If yes, describe the characteristics of this person that help make him or her an opinion leader. Are you an opinion leader for others in some category of products or services? Explain.

9. Explain differences between innovators, opinion leaders, and market mavens. Use examples from your own experience to help.

10. Describe the diffusion process for the World Wide Web. What factors are driving this rapid diffusion process? What kinds of businesses and consumers use the Web? Who doesn't use the Web? Why? Describe those who might be resistors of the technology.

You Make the Call

Online Publishing

In a closely watched test of the Internet's potential to transform the book business, the horror writer Stephen King became the first major author to self-publish online. But demand for his new electronic book fell far short of his last, an event in March that seemed to foretell a revolution in publishing when more than 400,0000 fans jammed computers' servers trying to download it in the first two days after it appeared.

Part of the difference may be that this time King elected to publish without the support of a publisher, relying entirely on the intent and word-of-mouth to attract readers.

King added another turn of the screw that may have thrown off some readers by trying out a novel honor-system payment plan. He asked readers to pay him a dollar for each chapter they downloaded and warned that he would not post new installments unless he received payments for at least 75 percent of the downloads. Amazon.com agree to handle the payments. The company had received about 25,000 credit card payments for 40,000 downloads of the first chapter, and another 7,000 customers promised to send a check or cash. King was particularly pleased to see that the number of payments seemed to meet his 75 percent figure. Some visitors to the website objected to the installment plan. About a quarter of the visitors declined to download the chapter.

Jeff Bezos, the chief executive of Amazon.com, said he hoped that the honor-system model might inspire others to try distributing books like shareware, software circulated on the Internet with payment expected later. "If you can make it easy for people, people are going to be willing to pay," he said.

In a hint of battles to come, some other booksellers questioned King's decision to favor Amazon.com as the exclusive bill collector. "It's a shame," said Ed Morrow, owner of the Northshire bookstore in Manchester Center, Vermont, and the former president of the American Booksellers Association. He noted that King could have elected to send customers to the ABA's Booksense website or to another store, including his own.

1. Identify the innovations described in the above story.
2. Classify each innovation in terms of the three categories of innovation described in the text. Justify your answers.
3. Identify barriers to adoption for each innovation, from the five identified in the chapter.
4. What marketing steps could be taken to initiate a bandwagon effect for online publishing and payment?

This case is adapted from David D. Kirkpatrick, "King E-Novel Short of Expected Demand," New York Times, July 25, 2000, www.nytimes.com/library.tech/00/07/biztech/articles/25king.html.

1. Bill Moore, "Behind the Scenes of the Prius Launch," *EV WORLD,* www.evworld.com/interviews2/amstock2.html.
2. George M. Zinkhan and R. T. Watson, *Journal of Business Research* 37 (1996), pp. 163–71.
3. Sanford Grossbart, Lynn Samsel, and Madhavan Parthasarathy, "Diffusion, Discontinuance, and Development in Transition Economies," paper presented at the 22nd Annual Meeting of the Society for Macromarketing, Bergen, Norway, Norwegian School of Economic and Business Administration.
4. Amanda Hesser, "Man Behind the Butter Pat Now Let's You Hold the Mayo, One-Handed," *New York Times,* July 30, 2000, sect. 3, p. 5; David Midgley, "A Meta-Analysis of the Diffusion of Innovations Literature," in *Advances in Consumer Research,* vol. 14, Melanie Wallendorf and Paul Anderson, eds. (Provo, UT: Association for Consumer Research, 1987), pp. 204–7.
5. Stuart Elliot, "How New Brands Become Too Much of a New Thing," *New York Times,* June 2, 1992; "New Products: Still Rising . . . Finding a Winner . . . Hassles," *The Wall Street Journal,* November 3, 1983, p. C1; and Roger McMath, personal communication.
6. "Mazda Develops World's First Miller-Cycle Engine for Practical Use," *Japan* 21 (July 1993), pp.

12–13; Joshua Levine, "Putting a Little Tingle in Your Kisses," *Forbes,* August 26, 1996, p. 76; and Marc Maremont, "How Gillette Brought Its Mach3 to Market," *The Wall Street Journal,* April 15, 1998, p. B1.

7. "Brand New Fad Makes Its Mark," *Tampa Tribune,* December 11, 1994, p. 18; Roland Barthes, *The Fashion System* (New York: Hill and Wang, 1983); Howard S. Becker, "Art as Collective Action," *American Sociological Review* 39 (December 1973), pp. 767–76; Fred Davis, *Fashion, Culture, and Identity* (Chicago: University of Chicago Press, 1992); Dick Hebidge, *Subculture: The Meaning of Style* (London: Methuen, 1979); Thomas Hine, *Populuxe* (New York: Alfred A. Knopf, 1987); Alfred L. Kroeber and J. Richardson, *Three Centuries of Women's Dress Fashions* (Berkeley: University of California Press, 1940); Kendall Morgan, "Dracula Dress Fever," *The Sunday Camera,* November 15, 1992, pp. 1B, 9B; Michele Santos, "Kente Cloth Not a Fad, 'It's an Awakening,' Store Owner Says," *Press-Telegram,* March 13, 1994, p. J10; and Michael R. Solomon, *Consumer Behavior,* 2nd ed. (Boston: Allyn and Bacon, 1994).

8. Sam Johnson, "What's Up Pussy Cat?" *Tokyo Classified,* 202.217.215.47/tokyofeaturestories archive/272/tokyofeaturestoriesinc.htm.

9. Martin G. Letscher, "How to Tell Fads from Trends," *American Demographics,* December 1994, pp. 38–45.

10. Anonymous, "It's New, but Is It Improved?" *American Demographics,* November–December 1994, p. 20; and Robert McMath and Thom Forbes, *What Were They Thinking?* (New York: Times Books, 1998).

11. William M. Bulkeley, "Portable Phones Are Prompting Change in Business and Lifestyles," *The Wall Street Journal,* January 13, 1988, pp. 2, 27; "New Products: Still Rising"; Brad Knickerbocker, "Old Ranch Traditions Blend with New Values," *Christian Science Monitor,* October 25, 1993, pp. 9–11; Brad Knickerbocker, "Forest Managers Learn How to Grow 'Green Lumber,'" *Christian Science Monitor,* November 29, 1993, pp. 11–13; and Ryszard Kapuscinski, "Plastic Buckets and Ballpoint Pens," *Granta* 48 (1994).

12. Steven V. Brull, "Net Nightmare for the Music Biz," *Business Week,* March 2, 1998, pp. 89–90; Paul C. Judge, "Care to Slip into Something More Digital?" *Business Week,* October 20, 1997, p. 42; Julie Pitta, "Competitive Shopping," *Forbes,* February 9, 1998, p. 92; N. Rain Noe, "Let's Do Talk," *Tokyo Classified,* 202.217.215.47/tokyofeaturestoriesarchive/266/tokyofeaturestoriesinc.htm.

13. Leslie Barker, "TV Dinners: 1953 Mealtime Revolution," *Press-Telegram,* May 20, 1993, pp. F1, F6; Laurent Belsie, "Powerful Internet Should Skyrocket as Firms Go On-Line," *Christian Science Monitor,* March 16, 1994, p. 8; Kirsten A. Conover, "Rock Musicians Tackle CD-ROM with an Eye on the Future," *Christian Science Monitor,* March 14, 1994, p. 15; and Lois Therrien, "The Rage to Page Has Motorola's Mouth Watering," *Business Week,* August 30, 1993, pp. 72–73.

14. Leslie Barker, "Trend Guru Focuses on TV Dinners," *Press-Telegram,* May 20, 1993, p. F6; and Alix M. Freedman, "The Microwave Cooks up a New Way of Life," *The Wall Street Journal,* September 19, 1989, pp. B1, B2.

15. This example of pioneering advantage is taken from Gregory S. Carpenter and Kent Nakamoto, "Reflections on 'Consumer Preference Formation and Pioneering Advantage,'" *Journal of Marketing Research,* November 1994, pp. 570–73. See also, Gregory S. Carpenter and Kent Nakamoto, "Consumer Preference Formation and Pioneering Advantage," *Journal of Marketing Research* 26 (August 1989), pp. 285–98.

16. Robert D. Buzzell and Bradle T. Gale, *The PIMS Principles* (New York: Free Press, 1987); Peter N. Golder and Gerald J. Tellis, "Pioneer Advantage: Marketing Logic or Marketing Legend," *Journal of Marketing Research* 30 (May 1993), pp. 158–70; and Lyman Ostlund, "Perceived Innovation Attributes as Predictors of Innovativeness," *Journal of Consumer Research* 1 (1974), p. 23.

17. Lee Patterson, "Tanking It Five Ways: Cutting Edge Businesses Still Go Bust the Old Fashioned Way," *Forbes,* June 2, 1997, pp. 75–76.

18. Margarete Arndt and Barbara Bigelow, "Vertical Integration in Hospitals," *Medical Care Review* 49 (Spring 1992), pp. 93–115; *American Shipper,* July 1986, p. 9; Glaskowsky, Hudson, and Ivie, *Business Logistics,* 3rd ed. (New York: Harcourt, Brace, Jovanovich, 1992); James C. Johnson and Donald F. Wood, *Contemporary Logistics,* 5th ed. (New York: Macmillan, 1993), p. 117; Soyeon Sim and Antigone Kotsiopulos, "Technology Innovativeness and Adopter Categories of Apparel/Gift Retailers: From the Diffusion of Innovations Perspective," *Clothing and Textiles Research Journal*

end notes

12 (Winter 1994), pp. 46–57; and Phillip Swan, "Why TV Viewers Are Cutting the Cord," *St. Petersburg Times,* November 20, 1994, pp. 1D, 4D.

19. Arndt and Bigelow, "Vertical Integration in Hospitals"; Basil G. Englis, Michael R. Solomon, and Anna Olofsson, "Music Television as Teen Image Agent—A Preliminary Report from the United States and Sweden," in *European Advances in Consumer Research,* W. Fren van Raaij and Gary J. Bamossy, eds. (Provo, UT: Association for Consumer Research, 1993), pp. 449–50; Malcolm Gladwell, "Annals of Style: The Cool Hunt," *New Yorker,* March 17, 1997, pp. 78–87; and Anne Guillou and Pascal Guibert, "Le froid domestiqué: L'usage du congélateur," *Terrain* 12 (April 1989), pp. 7–14.

20. Reese Erlich, "Electric Car Maker Plays Down Difficulties," *Christian Science Monitor,* March 11, 1994, p. 10; and Will Nixon, "Unplugging Electric Cars," *Utne Reader,* January–February 1995, pp. 24–26.

21. Elizabeth C. Hirschman, "Adoption of an Incredibly Complex Innovation: Propositions from a Humanistic Vantage Point," in *Advances in Consumer Research,* vol. 14, Melanie Wallendorf and Paul Anderson, eds. (Provo, UT: Association for Consumer Research, 1987), pp. 57–60.

22. Asif Shaikh, Eric Arnould, Kjell Christophersen, Roy Hagen, Joseph Tabor, and Peter Warshall, *Opportunities for Sustained Development* (Washington, DC: USAID/OTR/Bureau for Africa, 1988); and Gerrit Antonides, H. Bas Amesz, and Ivo C. Hulscher, "Adoption of Payment Systems in Ten Countries—A Case Study of Diffusion of Innovations," *European Journal of Marketing* 33, nos. 11–12 (1999), pp. 1123–135.

23. Thomas J. Hoban, "Food Industry Innovation: Efficient Consumer Response," *Agribusiness* 14, no. 3 (1998), pp. 235–45.

24. Nanette Byrnes, Dean Foust, Anderson Forest, William C. Symonds, and Joseph Weber, "Brands in a Bind," *Business Week,* August 28, 2000, pp. 234–38.

25. Gregory S. Carpenter and Kent Nakamoto, "Consumer Preference Formation and Pioneering Advantage," *Journal of Marketing Research* 26 (August 1989), pp. 285–98.

26. Antonides, Amesz, and Hulscher, "Adoption of Payment Systems in Ten Countries"; and Bruce Handy, "The Viagra Craze," *Time,* May 4, 1998, p. 57.

27. Jeffrey Ball, "So Far, the PT Cruiser Isn't Igniting Enthusiasm for Other Chrysler Cars," *The Wall Street Journal,* July 20, 2000, interactive.wsj.com/archive; Elizabeth Weise, "Families Learn to Live on 'Internet Time,'" *USA Today,* Tech Report, 1999, www.usatoday.com/life/dcovwed.htm; and S. C. Gwynne, "Thriving on Health Food," *Time,* February 23, 1998, p. 53.

28. Janet Ginsburg, "Not the Flavor of the Month," *Business Week,* March, 20, 2000, p. 128.

29. Eva Martinez and Yolando Polo, "Adopter Categories in the Acceptance Process for Consumer Durables," *Journal of Product and Brand Management* 5, no. 3 (1996), pp. 34–47; and Eva Martinez, Yolando Polo, and Carlos Flavián, "The Acceptance and Diffusion of New Consumer Durables: Differences between First and Last Adopters," *Journal of Consumer Marketing* 15, no. 4 (1998), pp. 323–42.

30. Andrew Kopkind, "From Russia with Love and Squalor," *The Nation,* January 18, 1993, pp. 44–61; and Hirokazu Takada and Dipak Jain, "Cross-National Analysis of Diffusion of Consumer Durable Goods in Pacific Rim Countries," *Journal of Marketing* 55 (April 1991), pp. 48–54.

31. Jan Adam, "Transformation to a Market Economy in the Former Czechoslovakia," *Europe-Asia Studies* 45, no. 4 (1993), pp. 627–45; Stanislaw Gajewski, "Consumer Behavior in Economics of Shortage," *Journal of Business Research* 24 (1992), pp. 5–10; Brian Lofman, "Consumers in Rapid Transition: The Polish Experience," in *Advances in Consumer Research,* vol. 20, Leigh McAlister and Michael Rothschild, eds. (Provo, UT: Association for Consumer Research, 1993), pp. 18–21; and Richard Rose and Christian Haerpfer, *Europe-Asia Studies* 46, no. 1 (1994), pp. 3–28.

32. Margaret Littman, "A Dose of Reality," *Marketing News,* January 5, 1998, p. 2; and S. Ram, "A Model of Innovation Resistance," in *Advances in Consumer Research,* vol. 14, Melanie Wallendorf and Paul Anderson, eds. (Provo, UT: Association for Consumer Research, 1987), pp. 208–12.

33. Eric J. Arnould, "Toward a Broadened Theory of Preference Formation and Diffusion of Innovations: Cases from Zinder Province, Niger Republic," *Journal of Consumer Research* 16 (September 1989), pp. 239–67.

34. Arnould, "Toward a Broadened Theory of Preference Formation and the Diffusion of Innovations"; Ram, "A Model of Innovation Resistance"; and James T. Thompson, Alfred S. Waldstein, and

Karen Wiese, *Institutional Constraints on the Transfer of Agricultural and Complementary Resource-Conservation Technologies Appropriate for Semi-Arid Africa,* contract no. PDC-0000-I-00-4104-00 (Burlington, VT: Association in Rural Development/ U.S. Agency for International Development, 1987).

35. J. H. Antil, "New Product or Service Adoption: When Does It Happen?" *Journal of Consumer Marketing* 5 (Spring 1988), pp. 5–16.

36. Ester Boserup, *The Conditions of Agricultural Growth* (Chicago: Aldine Press, 1965); and Miranda France, "Fog Harvest Makes the Desert Bloom," *Tampa Tribune,* January 15, 1995, p. A20. See also Robert McC. Netting et al., *The Conditions of Agricultural Intensification in the West African Savannah* (Washington, DC: USAID-PPC, 1978); and Patricia J. Vondal, "Agricultural Extension and Innovation Diffusion: A Case Example from Indonesia," paper presented at the Annual Meetings of the American Anthropological Association, Chicago, 1987.

37. Dosi, *Microeconomic Effects of Innovation, Journal of Economic Literature* 26 (September 1988).

38. Michael Lynn and Betsy D. Gelb, "Identifying Innovative National Markets for Technical Consumer Goods," *International Marketing Review* 13, no. 6 (1996), pp. 43–57.

39. See Chris Kern, "Pulling the Reins on Computer Technology," *American Way* 18 (March 5, 1985), pp. 199; 125.

40. Consumers are often depicted as resistant or passive recipients of innovations. See, for example, Everett M. Rogers, *Diffusion of Innovations,* 3rd ed. (New York: Free Press, 1983).

41. Richard Rose, "Contradictions between Micro- and Macro-Economic Goals in Post-Communist Societies," *Europe-Asia Studies* 45, no. 3 (1993), pp. 419–44.

42. There are aspects of markets and environments that permit innovations and protect them to varying degrees against imitation. One such aspect are incentives to develop the technology. For most industries, the major mechanisms for receiving returns on innovations are lead times and learning curve advantages combined with complementary marketing efforts. For a review of the literature on business innovation, see Giovanni Dosi, "Sources, Procedures, and Microeconomic Effects of Innovation," *Journal of Economic Literature* 26 (September 1988), pp. 1120–171.

43. For a discussion of social system variables that affect diffusion, see Hubert Gatignon and Thomas S. Robertson, "A Propositional Inventory for New Diffusion Research," *Journal of Consumer Research* 11 (March 1985), pp. 849–67; and Arnould, "Toward a Broadened Theory of Preference Formation and the Diffusion of Innovations."

44. For an interesting treatment, see George Fields, *From Bonsai to Levi's* (New York: Macmillan, 1983).

45. Peter Dickson, "Understanding the Trade Winds: The Global Evolution of Production, Consumption, and the Internet," *Journal of Consumer Research* 27 (June 2000), pp. 115–22.

46. Noel M. Murray and Lalita A. Manrai, "Exploratory Consumption Behavior: A Cross-Cultural Perspective," *Journal of International Consumer Marketing* 5, no. 1 (1993), pp. 101–20.

47. John Clammer, "Aesthetics of Self: Shopping and Social Being in Contemporary Urban Japan," *Lifestyle Shopping: The Subject of Consumption* (London and New York: Routledge, 1992), pp. 195–215; Alfred Gell, "Newcomers to the World of Goods: Consumption among the Muria Gonds," in *The Social Life of Things: Commodities in Cultural Perspective,* Arjun Appadurai, ed. (Cambridge, England: Cambridge University Press, 1986), pp. 110–38; and Johnson, "What's Up Pussy Cat?" Under the communist regimes of eastern Europe, uniformity was an ideology; to be yourself, to cultivate individualism, to perceive yourself as an individual in a mass society is dangerous, it was said. For a very readable treatment of integration and differentiation in the former communist countries, see Slavenka Drakulic, *How We Survived Communism and Even Laughed* (New York: Harper Perennial, 1993).

48. Arnould, "Toward a Broadened Theory of Preference Formation and the Diffusion of Innovations"; Lisa Penaloza, "Atravasando Fronteras/Border Crossings: A Critical Ethnographic Exploration of the Consumer Acculturation of Mexican Immigrants," *Journal of Consumer Research* 21 (June 1994), pp. 32–54; and Mary J. Weismantel, "The Children Cry for Bread: Hegemony and the Transformation of Consumption," in *The Social Economy of Consumption,* Henry J. Rutz and Benjamin S. Orlove, eds. (Lanham, MD: University Press of America, 1989), pp. 85–100.

49. George Simmel, "Fashion," *International Quarterly* 10 (1904), pp. 130–55. For an excellent discussion, see Grant McCracken, *Culture and Consumption* (Bloomington: Indiana University Press, 1988).

50. Paul F. Lazarsfeld, Bernard R. Berelson, and Hazel Gaudet, *The People's Choice* (New York: Columbia University Press, 1948), p. 151: Bob White, "Soukous or Sell-Out: Congolese Popular Dance Music as Cultural Commodity," in *Commodities and Globalization,* Angelique Haugerud, M. Priscilla Stone, and Peter D. Little, eds. (Lanham, MD: Rowman and Littlefield, 2000), pp. 33–58.

51. Takada and Jain, "Cross-National Analysis of Diffusion of Consumer Durable Goods in Pacific Rim Countries."

52. Frank Cancian, "Stratification and Risk-Taking: A Theory Tested on Agricultural Innovation," *American Sociological Review* 32 (1967), pp. 912–27; Frank Cancian, *Change and Uncertainty in a Peasant Economy* (Stanford: Stanford University Press, 1972); and Billie DeWalt and Kathleen Musante DeWalt, "Stratification and Decision Making in the Use of New Agricultural Technology," in *Agricultural Decision Making,* Peggy F. Barlett, ed. (New York: Academic Press, 1980), pp. 289–317.

53. Solomon, *Consumer Behavior.*

54. Stuart Ewen and Elizabeth Ewen, *Channels of Desire: Mass Images and the Shaping of American Consciousness,* 2nd ed. (Minneapolis: University of Minneapolis Press, 1992); Richard A. Peterson, *The Production of Culture* (Beverly Hills: Sage Publications, 1976); and Cecilia Tichi, *High Lonesome: The American Culture of Country Music* (Chapel Hill: University of North Carolina Press, 1994).

55. Arnould, "Toward a Broadened Theory of Preference Formation and the Diffusion of Innovations"; and Gatignon and Robertson, "A Propositional Inventory for New Diffusion Research."

56. Linda L. Price, Lawrence F. Feick, and Robin Higie Coulter, "Adoption and Diffusion of Western Products in the 'New' Hungary," working paper, University of Nebraska, Lincoln, 1994.

57. McCracken, *Culture and Consumption.* Grant McCracken, "Who Is the Celebrity Endorser? Cultural Foundations of the Endorsement Process," *Journal of Consumer Research* 16 (December 1989), pp. 310–21.

58. Susan H. Higgins and Patrick T. Hogan, "Internal Diffusion of High-Technology Industrial Innovations: An Empirical Study," *Journal of Business and Industrial Marketing* 14, no. 1 (1999), pp. 61–75; Karen N. Kennedy, *Implementing a Customer Orientation: Viewing the Process from Multiple Perspectives,* doctoral dissertation, University of South Florida, Tampa, 1997.

59. Jam Damsgaard and Rens Scheepers, "Power, Influence and Intranet Implementation: A Safari of South African Organizations," *Information Technology & People* 12, no. 4 (1999), pp. 333–58; Robert J. Fisher and Linda L. Price, "An Investigation into the Social Context of Early Adoption Behavior," *Journal of Consumer Research* 19 (December 1992), pp. 477–86; Karlheinz Kautz and Even Åby Larsen, "Diffusion Theory and Practice: Disseminating Quality Management and Software Process Improvement Innovations," *Information Technology & People* 13, no. 1 (2000), pp. 11–26; J. F. Ryan and J. A. Murray, "The Diffusion of a Pharmaceutical Innovation in Ireland," *European Journal of Marketing* 11, no. 1 (1980), pp. 3–12.

60. Rogers, *Diffusion of Innovations.* See also Price, Feick, and Coulter, "Adoption and Diffusion of Western Products in the 'New' Hungary"; and Naseem Khan, "From Burqah to Bloggs—Changing Clothes for Changing Times," in *Chic Thrills: A Fashion Reader,* Juliet Ash and Elizabeth Wilson, eds. (Berkeley: University of California Press, 1992), pp. 61–74.

61. Lawrence F. Feick and Linda L. Price, "The Market Maven: A Diffuser of Marketplace Information," *Journal of Marketing* 51 (January 1987), pp. 83–97; David Midgley, "A Simple Mathematical Theory of Innovative Behavior," *Journal of Consumer Research* 3 (June 1976), pp. 31–41; and Marsha Richins and Teri Root-Shaffer, "The Role of Involvement and Opinion Leadership in Consumer Word-of-Mouth: An Implicit Model Made Explicit," in *Advances in Consumer Research,* vol. 15, Michael J. Houston, ed. (Provo, UT: Association for Consumer Research, 1988), pp. 32–36.

62. Feick and Price, "The Market Maven"; Steven A. Baumgarten, "The Innovative Communicator in the Diffusion Process," *Journal of Marketing Research* 12 (February 1975), pp. 12–18; and Thomas S. Robertson, *Innovative Behavior and Communication* (New York: Holt, Rinehart and Winston, 1971).

63. Feick and Price, "The Market Maven"; Linda Price, Audrey Guskey, and Lawrence Feick, "Everyday Market Helping Behavior," *Journal of Public Policy and Marketing* 14 (Fall 1995), pp. 255–66; and Mark E. Slama and Terrell G. Williams, "Generalization of the Market Maven's Information Provision Tendency across Product Categories," in *Advances in Consumer Research,* vol. 17, Thomas K. Srull, ed. (Provo, UT: Association for Consumer Research, 1990), pp. 48–52.

64. David F. Midgley and Grahame R. Dowling, "A Longitudinal Study of Product Form Innovation: The Interaction between Predispositions and Social Messages," *Journal of Consumer Research* 19 (March 1993), pp. 611–25. See also Linda L. Price, Lawrence F. Feick, and Daniel C. Smith, "A Reexamination of Communication Channel Usage by Adopter Categories," in *Advances in Consumer Research,* vol. 13, Richard J. Lutz, ed. (Provo, UT: Association for Consumer Research, 1986), pp. 409–13; and Lawrence F. Feick, Linda L. Price, and Robin A. Higie, "People Who Use People: Looking at Opinion Leadership from the Other Side," in *Advances in Consumer Research,* vol. 13, Richard J. Lutz, ed. (Provo, UT: Association for Consumer Research, 1986), pp. 301–5. See also Chip Walker, "Word of Mouth," *American Demographics,* July 1995, pp. 38–44.

65. William O. Bearden and Michael J. Etzel, "Reference Group Influence on Product and Brand Purchase Decisions," *Journal of Consumer Research* 9 (September 1982), pp. 183–94; William O. Bearden, Richard G. Netemeyer, and Jesse E. Teel, "Measurement of Consumer Susceptibility to Interpersonal Influence," *Journal of Consumer Research* 15 (March 1989), pp. 473–81; and Michael R. Solomon, "The Role of Products as Social Stimuli: A Symbolic Interactionism Perspective," *Journal of Consumer Research* 19 (December 1983), pp. 319–29.

66. Leah Rickard, " 'Parenting Leaders' Peddling Influence: Quality-Hungry Group Full of Consumer Advice," *Advertising Age,* May 8, 1995, p. 3.

67. Dorothy Leonard-Barton, "Experts as Negative Opinion Leaders in the Diffusion of a Technological Innovation," *Journal of Consumer Research* 11 (March 1985), pp. 914–26; and Margaret Jean Hays, "Western Clothing and African Identity: Changing Consumption Patterns among the Luo," paper presented at the seminar on Transformations in African Material Culture, African Studies Center, Boston University, 1989.

68. Price, Feick, and Coulter, "Adoption and Diffusion of Western Products in the 'New' Hungary."

69. Peter Dickson, "Understanding the Trade Winds: The Global Evolution of Production, Consumption, and the Internet," *Journal of Consumer Research* 27 (June 2000), p. 120.

70. Norman C. Stolzoff, Eric Chuan-Fong Shih, and Alladi Venkatesh, "The Home of the Future: An Ethnographic Study of New Information Technologies in the Home," in *Advances in Consumer Research,* vol. 28, Mary Gilly and Joan Meyers-Levy, eds. (Provo, UT: Association for Consumer Research, 2001), forthcoming; and Alladi Venkatesh, Lena Fagerström-Herluf, Josefine Höglund, and Minna Räsänen, "Project Noah Sweden: National Outlook for Automation in the Home," working paper, Center for Research on Information Technology and Organization, University of California, Irvine, 2000.

71. F. D. Midgley and R. G. Dowling, "Innovativeness: The Concept and Its Measurement," *Journal of Consumer Research* 4, no. 4 (1978), pp. 229–42; and Rogers, *Diffusion of Innovation.*

72. Eric Von Hippel, "Lead Users: A Source of Novel Product Concepts," *Management Science* 32 (July 1986), pp. 791–805.

73. Eric Von Hippel, p. 796; and Edwin Mansfield, *Industrial Research and Technological Innovation: An Econometric Analysis* (New York: W. W. Norton, 1968), pp. 134–235.

74. Malcolm Gladwell, "Annals of Style."

75. Michael Lynn and Judy Harris, "The Desire for Unique Consumer Products: A New Individual Differences Scale," *Psychology and Marketing* 14, no. 6 (1997), pp. 601–16; Andrew Plack, "Japanese Girls Enthralled with Organizers," *N.Y. Times News Service,* December 22, 1994, pp. 1–3, America Online.

76. Martinez and Polo, "Adopter Categories in the Acceptance Process for Consumer Durables"; and Martinez, Polo, and Flavián, "The Acceptance and Diffusion of New Consumer Durables."

77. Rogers, *Diffusion of Innovations.*

78. "Advances of the Amazonesu," *The Economist,* July 22, 2000, pp. 61–62.

79. Cancian, "Stratification and Risk-Taking."

80. W. T. Liu and R. W. Duff, "The Strength in Weak Ties," *Public Opinion Quarterly* 36 (Fall 1972), pp. 361–66.

81. Peter Burrows, Gary McWilliams, and Robert D. Hof, "Cheap PCs," *Business Week,* March 23, 1998, pp. 28–32.

82. Eric Abrahamson and Lori Ronsenkopf, "Institutional and Competitive Bandwagons: Using Mathematical Modeling as a Tool to Explore Innovation Diffusion," *Academy of Management Review* 18, no. 3 (1993), pp. 487–517; Sushil Bikhchandani, David Hirshleifer, and Ivo Welch, "A Theory of Fads, Fashion, Custom and Cultural Change as Informational Cascades," *Journal of Political Economy* 100, no. 5 (1992), pp. 992–1026; and David Scott Clark, "Venerable Beetle Survives and Succeeds in Mexico," *Christian Science Monitor,* March 2, 1994, p. 11.

83. J. Pfeffer and G. R. Salancik, *The External Control of Organizations* (New York: Harper & Row, 1978).

84. Lisa W. Foderaro, "Fat-Lane Banking Not for Everyone," *New York Times,* May 17, 1998, p. A25; and Wendy A. Rogers, Elizabeth E. Cabrera, Neff Walker, and Gilbert D. Kristen, "A Survey of Automatic Teller Machine Usage across the Adult Life Span," *Human Factors* 38, no. 1 (1996), pp. 156–66.

85. See the archive of negative coverage of GMOs at the Greenpeace website http://www.greenpeace.org.

86. Arjun Chaudhuri, "The Diffusion of an Innovation in Indonesia," *Journal of Product and Brand Management* 3, no. 3 (1994), pp. 19–26; Price, Feick, and Coulter, "Adoption and Diffusion of Western Products in the 'New' Hungary"; and Penaloza, "Atravesando Fronteras/Border Crossings."

87. Michael R. Solomon, "The Missing Link: Surrogate Consumers in the Marketing Chains," *Journal of Marketing* 50 (October 1987), pp. 208–18; Praveen Aggarawal, "Surrogate Buyers and the New Product Adoption Process: A Conceptualization and Managerial Framework," *Journal of Consumer Marketing* 14, no. 5 (1997), pp. 391–400.

88. Alladi Venkatesh and Nicholas Vitalari, "A Post-Adoption Analysis of Computing in the Home," *Journal of Economic Psychology* 8 (June 1987), pp. 161–80; Nicholas Vitalari and Alladi Venkatesh, "In-Home Computing and Information Services: A Twenty Year Analysis of the Technology and Its Impacts," *Telecommunications Policy* 11, no. 1 (1987), pp. 65–81; and Nancy M. Ridgway and Linda L. Price, "Exploration in Product Usage: A Model of Use Innovativeness," *Psychology and Marketing* 11 (1994), pp. 69–84.

89. Arnould, "Toward a Broadened Theory of Preference Formation and the Diffusion of Innovations"; Albert Wenben Lai, "Consumption Situation and Product Knowledge in the Adoption of a New Product," *European Journal of Marketing* 25 (1991), pp. 55–67; Alan D. Meyer and James B. Goes, "Organizational Assimilation of Innovations," *Academy of Management Journal* 31, no. 4 (1988), pp. 897–923; and Soyeon Shim and Antigone Kotsiopulos, "Technology Innovativeness and Adopter Categories of Apparel/Gift Retailers: From the Diffusion of Innovations Perspective, *Clothing and Textiles Research Journal* 12 (Winter 1994), pp. 46–57.

Learning Objectives

After completing this chapter, you should be able to:

- Describe consumer satisfaction.

- Identify basic factors that influence satisfaction.

- Discuss the relationship between needs and satisfaction.

- Explain how quality and satisfaction are related.

- Describe the expectancy disconfirmation model and its limitations.

- Identify different emotions associated with satisfaction.

- Exemplify different types of satisfaction.

- Identify the consequences of satisfaction and dissatisfaction.

Consumer Satisfaction

Bath and Body Works[1]

There are several factors that contribute to the way I feel about the company. First of all the products are not tested on animals. I feel that animal testing is inconsiderate because there are other ways you can test products without harming or even killing the animal. . . . Another important factor is customer service. This is important to me, and I feel they are a customer-oriented business because they are always friendly, not pushy, when it comes to selling their products, greet me with a pleasant smile, and assist me in finding what I am looking for. In addition, the products from Bath and Body Works give me a clean, wholesome feeling when I use them on a regular basis. They make me feel refreshed with a great smell. Most of all, the lotions and talc powder make my skin feel baby soft. I use the loofah sponge and body gel to exfoliate my skin, which also contributes to a soft, healthy look! . . . I am loyal to this company also because the prices are reasonable and each and every product is worth the price. There are always continuous sales here at Bath and Body Works. Whenever I visit Bath and Body Works and purchase accessories or toiletries, I always receive compensation such as samples of lotions and other toiletries.

I have been purchasing Bath and Body Works products for about two years . . . that's a long time being loyal to a company. Just like a friendship. If you know a person for a considerable amount of time then trust is a significant factor. I would trust my friends in many ways, such as telling them secrets, depending on them for help, and caring for them just as I would depend on Bath and Body Work products and being loyal to them as well.

Overview[2]

Individual postpurchase consumer behavior is of growing concern to marketers as they shift their focus from inducing consumers to purchase products and services to developing profitable long-term relationships with them. As suggested by the opening vignette, long-term relationships are more likely if marketers concern themselves with how best to satisfy consumers in both the short and long run and in multiple ways. This chapter describes that part of the wheel of consumption focused closely on the factors that lead to satisfaction and the outcomes of satisfaction for consumers and marketers.

All of your life people have probably been asking you questions such as, Are you satisfied? and, How satisfied are you? Understanding your satisfaction is important to your parents and family, your employer, your educational institution, and the businesses that sell you products, services, experiences, and ideas. For-profit and nonprofit organizations and even governments endeavor to deliver satisfactory outcomes to customers and other constituencies. As evidence of this concern, the American Consumer Satisfaction Index compiled at the University of Michigan comprehensively tracks customer satisfaction by industry sector and by U.S. governmental department. You can visit their website.

www.bus.umich.edu/research/nqrc

Aristotle once said that it is the nature of desire not to be satisfied, and so despite the best managerial efforts to guarantee satisfaction it's sometimes impossible to do so. It's probably easy for you to recall at least one situation in which a presumably customer-oriented company disappointed you. However, sometimes you are fulfilled—perhaps even to overflowing, and you have the kind of pleasurable response reflected in our opening vignette that is essential to the meaning of satisfaction.

The opening vignette suggests that consumption experiences evoke in participants a range of emotions from pleasure to reassurance. Emotional extremes including delight and distress also might accompany satisfaction with consumption experiences like skydiving or body piercing. By contrast, when asked about their satisfaction with a favorite brand of toothpaste, consumers may say they are satisfied and brand loyal, but most often their response doesn't include much emotion. Often, consumer satisfaction reflects a basically neutral emotional state and perhaps little cognition as well.[3] Even with a high-involvement product such as an automobile, a segment of owners report moderately high levels of satisfaction *devoid* of strong feelings. Their experience of automobiles is a more cognitive evaluation.

The vignette suggests that satisfaction in consumer contexts responds to beliefs and thoughts (cognitive appraisals) about the outcomes of purchasing, such as the consumer's beliefs abut animal testing and value for money spent. Satisfaction is also connected to the emotions that accompany purchase outcomes and related events. We will stress the hybrid emotion-cognition nature of satisfaction and the interplay between emotional and cognitive assessments.

In this chapter we will first develop a definition of satisfaction. Then, once we have outlined in basic terms what we mean by consumer satisfaction and dissatisfaction we will discuss factors that contribute to consumer satisfaction. We will then discuss different types of satisfaction of interest to marketers of different products. Finally, we will discuss some consequences of satisfaction and dissatisfaction for consumers and marketers.

Defining Satisfaction

The definition of consumer satisfaction that we will use in this chapter incorporates the emotion-cognition characteristic of this judgment. **Satisfaction** is *a judgment of a pleasurable level of consumption-related fulfillment,* including levels of **underfulfillment** or **overfulfillment.**[4] A few comments are important in explaining this definition.

First, consumers can make satisfaction judgments with respect to any or all of the aspects or stages of product and service experience. For example, in the context of a computer purchase, consumers could measure satisfaction associated with the purchase phase or any portion or all of the consumption phase (the life of the computer). In addition, they could measure satisfaction on any or all of the features of the computer (e.g., speed, software, and service) or stages and aspects of the purchase decision (salesperson, negotiations, delivery, paperwork). Because consumers make judgments about their satisfaction based on a variety of product and service aspects and events, each becomes a potential point of differentiation for a market offering.

Nevertheless, it is a mistake to assume that all these judgments sum to an overall level. Satisfaction is more complex than that. Consumer Chronicles 17.1 describes one consumer's river-rafting experience. This story reflects an array of both positive and negative emotions, and it suggests satisfaction emerges across the service or product experience.[5] And even when uncomfortable things happen, events may evolve in such a way as to make an experience satisfying (fulfilling) overall. Consumer research in service environments like banks and hotels also suggests that if bad service is followed by effective service recovery, customers may be more satisfied overall than if they had not experienced bad service in the first place. Apologies and gifts improve customer satisfaction.[6]

A second thing to observe about the definition of satisfaction is it focuses on fulfillment. Fulfillment comes in different varieties. For example, consumers may feel fulfilled or satisfied with the removal of a negative state (e.g., repair of a computer hardware problem that prevents one from running software). Or consumers may feel overfulfillment and satisfaction with a product or service experience that provides unexpected pleasure, such as expressed in the skydiving story in Consumer Chronicles 17.2. Finally, consumers can experience satisfaction when a product or service experience gives greater pleasure than anticipated in a given situation even though it does not exactly fill them up (i.e., underfulfillment). For example, a young child dreading a doctor visit may express satisfaction after the visit because "it wasn't so bad." Fulfillment also implies standards that form a basis for comparison. In this chapter we will discuss how consumers formulate standards and expectations.

A third thing to observe about this definition is that satisfaction is an **internal state.** This means *accounts of satisfaction must highlight the meanings that operate in the customers' field of awareness.*[7] This is important to emphasize. We can't say to managers that performance on a particular set of dimensions leads directly to customer satisfaction or make statements like "product quality leads to satisfaction" without examining customer experience. Judgments of satisfaction vary, and different customers make different satisfaction judgments about the same level of performance. It's partly because satisfaction is so variable that marketers tailor products and services to particular segments of consumers.

Finally, although satisfaction is an internal state, it is also social.[8] Marketers need to be savvy about how individual judgments express a broader system of cultural values, meanings, beliefs, emotions, group relationships, and conflicts. The satisfaction of household or buying group members often contributes to an individual consumer's satisfaction. An example of a social perspective on satisfaction is offered by some work on U.S. professional working mothers. These women grapple with an array of role conflicts, gender ideals, cultural values, and interpersonal demands. These conflicting influences color their consumption experiences and evaluations. For example, interviews reveal a disparity between ideals they envision and their actual everyday lives. One reflection of this is the ideal of an immaculate household.[9] In Consumer Chronicles 17.3, a working mother discusses her dissatisfaction with a maid service, illustrating how social expectations frame satisfaction.

Cross-culturally marketers should remember that the ideal of customer satisfaction is not a universal. Consumers in transitional and developing countries may not have learned to concern themselves so much with individual satisfaction as those in developed consumer cultures. Consumer satisfaction may still be considered a shameful luxury for some. Further, people in different cultural contexts may look to nonmarket-based situations—family interaction or religious devotion, for example—as sources of satisfaction in their lives. Consumer satisfaction is learned as part of socialization in consumer culture.[10]

What Is Dissatisfaction?	We can simply define **dissatisfaction** as *an unpleasant level of consumption-related fulfillment.* Although this definition makes sense, keep in mind that factors that contribute to higher levels of satisfaction may sometimes differ from those that contribute to higher levels of dissatisfaction. Let's take a simple example. Consumers at a concert are not likely to report being more satisfied because they did not have to wait in line for tickets, but they are quite likely to report being more *dissatisfied* if they had to wait in line. Although a particular product attribute or service dimension may affect both satisfaction and dissatisfaction, there are differences in what drives them.

What Causes Satisfaction?

We want to emphasize several basic points in our discussion of the causes of satisfaction. We can formulate these points as a series of questions that managers must answer in order to understand satisfaction processes. We certainly won't review all that has been written on customer satisfaction, but we will try to help you understand some factors that contribute to it.

Many managers believe that product performance or service quality paves the road to satisfaction. Mission statements, company slogans, and promotional materials often claim quality as an ideal and assert a close relationship between quality and satisfaction.[11] Using a vision of quality to guide management is evident in the mission statements of two Malcolm Baldrige Quality Award winners summarized in Good Practice 17.1, for example.

How Are Performance and Satisfaction Related?

As a result of the belief in the performance–satisfaction link, global management consultant firms from Mexico to Malaysia derive significant revenues from conducting quality and satisfaction studies for their corporate clients. Postpurchase research accounts for one-third of revenues of the largest U.S. market research firms, and strong annual growth is reported. Corporate clients in transitional economies and NICs worry that they must attend more to the performance–satisfaction relationship. Firms compete to win the J. D. Power awards for "initial quality," such as those won by the Maruti Zen and the Honda City automobiles in India in 1998, for example.[12]

Despite the fact that service or product quality is a frequent organizational goal, a single managerially useful meaning of quality and performance eludes us.[13] Good Practice 17.2 summarizes a few of the ways to think about quality. Manufacturers and consumers don't necessarily agree about product and service quality. For example, a *Fortune* survey of chief executive officers of the largest U.S. companies revealed that 60 percent of these officers believed that quality is better today, while only 13 percent believed quality was declining. A large-scale consumer survey conducted during that same period revealed that 49 percent of the respondents believed quality was declining, and 59 percent believed it would continue to decline. And in a General Electric study, appliance managers listed different components than did consumers as critical in quality perceptions.[14] These findings emphasize two points: There is no such thing as objective quality (judgments are always based on someone's perceptions), and managers interested in customer satisfaction need to find out how customers (who buy the product or service) perceive quality. Nevertheless, looking across many descriptions of quality, we can conclude that **perceived quality** involves preferences, is based on comparative standards, differs among customers and situations, and resides in the use or consumption of the product or service. Moreover, quality has both cognitive (thinking) and affective (emotional) aspects.[15]

Perceived quality *is* an important predictor of customer satisfaction.[16] Several studies support the causal chain that suggests quality $\Rightarrow$ satisfaction $\Rightarrow$ purchase intention.[17] Although not absolute, this relationship has been documented across industries and even several cultural contexts. For example, research conducted over time and across industries in Sweden revealed a significant relationship between quality (product performance) and customer satisfaction.[18]

The problem is for each organization to decide how consumers perceive quality and what features or characteristics they use in judging quality. Many lists of features have been developed. Eight general dimensions of quality have been proposed, including features, performance, reliability, conformance, durability, serviceability, aesthetics, and perceived quality.[19] Some argue for a product-category-specific approach to assessing quality. For example, research on 33 food categories revealed five quality dimensions: rich/full flavor, natural taste, fresh taste, good aroma, and appetizing looks.[20]

Researchers have not been especially successful in developing a universal set of quality criteria. For example, the SERVQUAL scale was devised to measure service quality. The scale, discussed in Chapter 9, was first published in 1988 and has undergone numerous revisions. It contains 21 perception items that are distributed through five service-quality dimensions: reliability, empathy, tangibles, responsiveness, and assurance. It also contains expectation items.[21]

I would have to say the time all of us went skydiving in January was a magical experience because there is truly no other activity in the world that is more exciting, dangerous, energetic, and still just such a mental and physical rush like there is with skydiving. All of you guys made me do it. Seriously, I heard what kind of experience it was and I just had to try it. There are just some things in this world you have to do before your time is up, and I think skydiving is definitely one of them. I had a feeling it would be amazing, but I didn't really expect that feeling to be with me for as long as it has. Every time I think back to that day I just think of how exciting it really was, and it really gives me an appreciation of what life really means to me. I believe it has also changed the way I look at my life. I try not to take things for granted as much as I once did. It was just a time that I'll never forget, and in my book that is magical.

In spite of the refinements, SERVQUAL is difficult and perhaps misleading to employ across all service industries. For example, concepts that SERVQUAL measures, such as employee responsiveness or service reliability, mean different things between service industries. That is to say they do not merely differ in importance to customers across industries. The manager of a bank, airline, HMO, or dry cleaning establishment, to name a few, needs to know exactly, behaviorally, what responsiveness and reliability mean in her industry, for her customers. For example, a UK specialty foods retailer learned that order processing (reliability) and food product quality (tangibles) were key to customer satisfaction. And Standard Life, an insurance company, discovered that its employees startled customers by answering the telephone too quickly. They were too responsive! This is a funny example of the exacting level of behavioral knowledge needed to understand service satisfaction. Companies need to deliver those elements of service relevant to their customers in their industry.[22]

In addition to between-industry variations in performance dimensions, there is a great deal of variation within and between consumer segments and cultures on what quality means. Consider a very simple example. A study of service quality in Hong Kong hotels found that Asian travelers' satisfaction was determined primarily by value, whereas Western travelers' satisfaction was influenced primarily by room quality, although other factors were also important.[23]

The basic goal for developing a performance or quality standard is to communicate clearly business performance in operational and perceptual terms. Measures need to reflect customer-defined standards but also be actionable for management. In general, to develop a performance standard that's relevant for the product or service and the customers served, a company needs to link general concepts to specific behaviors and actions managers can take to affect customer perceptions of quality.[24] Good Practice 17.3 illustrates this procedure for one aspect of one service organization.

Although we have stated that a relationship between satisfaction and purchase intention exists, we have not yet discussed it. This relationship is also complex. For some shopping and convenience goods, satisfaction and repurchase intentions may be closely related. However, if consumers do not distinguish between brands, satisfaction may not predict repurchase intention all that well. Further, sometimes consumers have especially satisfying consumption experiences with products, services, and constellations of both (such as a vacation) that they have no intention of repurchasing. This may happen for a variety of reasons, including a belief that the experience can never be repeated, a desire to retain the sacred status of the experience, or a belief that other "once in a lifetime experiences" await them. Can you think of a wonderful consumption experience that you don't intend to repeat?

Finally, dissatisfying events during a consumption episode can sometimes lead consumers to repurchase. We touched on this idea when we indicated how a global satisfaction judgment might emerge from a rafting trip on which a lot of bad things happened. We will have something more to say about the relationships between satisfaction and intention later in this chapter.

How Are Employee and Customer Satisfaction Related?

Corporate slogans and mission statements sometimes link customer satisfaction to employee satisfaction.[25] Mounting evidence suggests there is a relationship. Some research in the banking industry, for example, has demonstrated that initiatives to improve employee satisfaction also affect customer satisfaction.[26] While the effect *may* be most pronounced in service industries where satisfaction with contact employees is vital to overall customer satisfaction, there are numerous examples of how nonservice industry employees contribute to performance and customer satisfaction.[27]

Although it seems simple and obvious to say employee satisfaction is linked to customer satisfaction, translating knowledge of that link into managerial action is not so easy. An interesting study employed the critical incident technique to look at service encounters from both the customers' and the employees' perspectives. The **critical incident technique** is a *systematic procedure for recording events and behaviors observed to lead to success or failure on specific tasks.* Respondents are asked about specific events and their accounts of these events are content analyzed.[28] The authors found that at least for routine service transactions, employees and customers mostly had shared notions of the sources of customer satisfaction and dissatisfaction. Nevertheless, an examination of employee reports of episodes of customer dissatisfaction made apparent several implications for management.

One implication is that the customer is NOT always right and doesn't always behave in acceptable ways. To have happy employees who make happy customers, managers need to acknowledge this. Employees need appropriate coping and problem-solving skills to handle difficult customers, situations, and their own personal feelings.

A second implication is that contact employees generally want to provide good service and are proud of their ability to do this. Employees express frustration when for some reason they believe they cannot recover from a service failure or adjust the system to accommodate a customer need. Poorly designed systems or procedures, cumbersome bureaucracy, too many rules, and the lack of authority to do anything are often to blame.

How Are Choice and Satisfaction Related?

Although in most situations, consumers use features of product or service choice to form satisfaction judgments, in other cases the features that drive choice and satisfaction may differ, or they may differ in importance to consumers.[29] Exhibit 17.1 diagrams the distinction between product and service choice criteria and drivers of satisfaction.

Research on adventure tourism activities like river rafting illustrates differences between choice criterion and **satisfaction drivers.** Consumers choose rafting companies in terms of such things as amenities offered, rivers accessed, length of trip, and safety claims. But variation in performance on these dimensions has relatively little to do with customer satisfaction. Satisfaction is instead driven by feelings of harmony with nature, connection to a community of adventurers, and personal growth experiences, such as learning to pilot a kayak, that result from the consumption experience, not the prepurchase choice process. Similarly, some interesting research on Islamic banks in the

Jean's Maid Service

I tried a maid service and . . . I am not fastidious by any means, but I just felt like they weren't cleaning like I would clean. I don't think I am overly critical either, but I just felt like that for that amount of money you should get one heck of a shine on things. . . . I just didn't think I was getting my money's worth. And I had all these misconceptions. I thought if I had a maid service, they would come in for one day and it would stay clean for five days. I was so fussy with the kids . . . but I kept telling myself for 40 bucks I should be able to retain this for a long time.

Source: Craig J. Thompson, "Caring Consumers: Gendered Consumption Meanings and the Juggling Lifestyle," Journal of Consumer Research 22 *(March 1996), p. 399.*

Mideast suggests that adherence to Islamic banking principles (e.g., interest is not charged on loans) drives choice, but product performance drives customer satisfaction.[30]

There are a lot of possible reasons why choice criterion may differ from satisfaction drivers. One is that consumers have trouble foreseeing the possible problems and benefits of consumption. For complex, extended, or infrequently purchased services like an expensive tourist adventure, the discrepancy between choice and satisfaction drivers may be pronounced.[31] Similarly for complex, infrequently purchased high-tech products that can be used in numerous ways or to attain various goals, research has found discrepancies between choice and satisfaction drivers.[32]

A related reason for differences between choice and satisfaction drivers might be that aspects of the consumption situation that directly affect satisfaction and dissatisfaction are unpredictable and hence can't be used as choice criterion. For example, if you could predict in advance which airline and flight would experience turbulence, wouldn't that be a choice criterion? Unfortunately, as many consumers know, turbulence is unpredictable and more a function of airspace than airline. In many situations, postpurchase consumption experience with complex goods and services differs from consumers' predictions.[33]

A related issue is that consumers' satisfaction judgments focus on purchase outcomes, whereas firms emphasize differences between product or brand attributes in their marketing communications.[34] If a company can distinguish itself from competitors in terms of consumer outcomes, it may be able to more closely align choice criteria and satisfaction drivers. For example, a consumer might choose Federal Express on the belief that this choice will result in rapid, reliable package delivery. One important satisfaction driver is likely to be whether rapid, safe package delivery occurs. The close alignment between

Exhibit 17.1 Drivers of Choice and Satisfaction

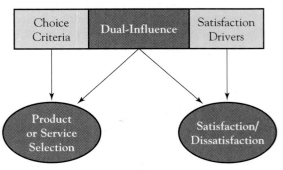

Source: Adapted from Richard L. Oliver, *Satisfaction: A Behavioral Perspective on the Consumer* (New York: McGraw-Hill, 1996), p. 42.

Cadillac

The mission of the Cadillac Motor Car Company is to engineer, produce, and market the world's finest automobiles known for uncompromised levels of distinctiveness, comfort, convenience, and refined performance. Through its people, who are its strength, Cadillac will continuously improve the quality of its products and services to meet or exceed customer expectations and succeed as a profitable business.

Motorola

It is the objective of Motorola, Inc., to produce and provide products and services of the highest quality. In its activities, Motorola will pursue goals aimed at the achievement of quality excellence. These results will be derived from the dedicated efforts of each employee in conjunction with supportive participation from management at all levels of the corporation.

Good Practice 17.1

choice criteria and satisfaction drivers is evident in FedEx advertising that emphasizes job-related outcomes from this versus other choices. Marketing communications that emphasize the outcomes of product use or nonuse can be viewed as attempts to align choice and satisfaction drivers. The ad for MCI advanced audio conference calling shown below is one illustration. Another is the United Airlines ad that positions the electronic ticket option as a solution to the problem of lost tickets.

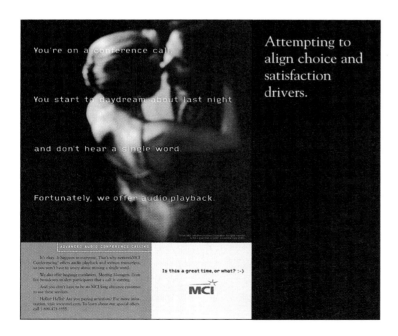

Attempting to align choice and satisfaction drivers.

1. Consumer's judgment about a product's overall excellence or superiority.
2. Totality of features and characteristics of a product or service that bear on its ability to satisfy stated and implied needs.
3. Perceived ability of a product to provide satisfaction relative to the available alternatives.
4. All attributes of a product that yield consumer satisfaction.
5. Involves the subjective response of people to objects and is therefore a highly relativistic phenomenon that differs between judges.

Source: Definitions 1 through 5 listed in the exhibit are from the following sources: (1) Valerie A. Zeithaml (1988), "Consumer Perceptions of Price, Quality, and Value: A Means-End Model and Synthesis of Evidence," Journal of Marketing 52 (July), pp. 2–22; (2) definition of the International Organization for Standardization quoted in Evert Gummesson (1992), "Quality Dimensions: What to Measure in Service Organizations," in Teresa A. Swartz, David E. Bowen, and Stephen W. Brown (eds.), Advances in Services Marketing and Management: Research and Practice, Vol. 1, JAI Press, Greenwich, CT, pp. 177–205; (3) Kent B. Monroe and R. Krishnan (1985), "The Effect of Price on Subjective Product Evaluations," in Jacob Jacoby and Jerry C. Olson (eds.), Perceived Quality (Lexington, MA: Lexington Books), pp. 209–232; (4) Alfred R. Oxenfeldt (1950), "Consumer Knowledge: Its Measurement and Extent," Review of Economics and Statistics, Vol. 32, pp. 300–316; (5) Morris B. Holbrook and Kim P. Corfman (1985), "Quality and Value in the Consumption Experience: Phaedrus Rides Again," in Jacob Jacoby and Jerry C. Olson (eds.), Perceived Quality (Lexington, MA: Lexington Books), pp. 31–57.

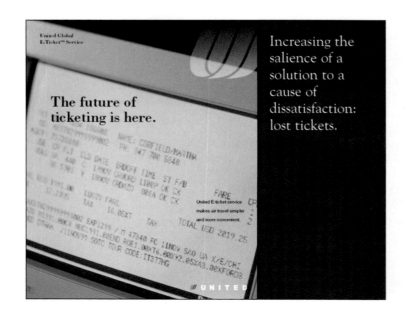

Abstract dimension	Superior service ↓
Specific dimensions	Reliability, responsiveness ↓
Consumer perceptions of reliability and responsiveness	Delivers on time Returns calls quickly ↓
Managerial actions	Delivers by Wednesday Returns calls within 2 hours

Source: Adapted from Valarie A. Zeithaml and Mary Jo Bitner, Services Marketing *(New York: McGraw-Hill, 1996), p. 219.*

How Do Consumers Judge Satisfaction?

Earlier we observed that satisfaction implies goals or standards that form a basis for comparison. How then do these standards develop, and what standards form the basis for satisfaction judgments?[35] Expectations provide one standard for later judgments of satisfaction.[36] We can define **expectations** simply as *anticipation or predictions of future events.* Expectations include predictions of future product performance and also related hopes, apprehensions, uncertainties, and probabilities. For example, the consumer in the opening vignette says that service personnel are "always friendly," there are "always continuous sales," and she always receives "compensation such as samples." These represent expectations. Consumers' basic expectation is that the products or services they purchase will fulfill their wants.

It is appropriate to outline some of the most common models for understanding the relationship between standards and satisfaction. Most research has employed some variant of the expectancy–disconfirmation model of satisfaction. However, as suggested in our discussion, there is increasing recognition that other kinds of comparative standards, such as fairness, might also affect judgments of satisfaction. We begin with a discussion of the expectancy–disconfirmation model of satisfaction and then provide a brief summary of some other comparative standards that might be used in judging satisfaction.

Expectancy– Disconfirmation Model of Satisfaction

The **expectancy–disconfirmation model of satisfaction (EDM)** states that *disconfirmation of preconsumption expectations is the key influence on consumer satisfaction.*[37] Exhibit 17.2 illustrates the expectancy–disconfirmation framework that we can use to try to understand both how these concepts are related and what this means for management strategy. Notice this model suggests that expectations and disconfirmation operate together to jointly determine satisfaction levels. When *performances exceed expectations,* **positive**

Exhibit 17.2 A Simplified Expectancy–Disconfirmation Framework

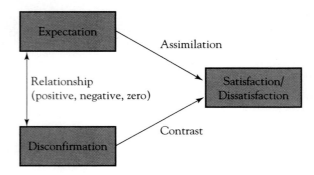

disconfirmation occurs and the likelihood of consumer satisfaction increases. When *expectations are not met,* **negative disconfirmation** occurs and the likelihood of consumer dissatisfaction increases. As was shown, for example, in a massive survey of dining in Hong Kong, positive disconfirmation leads to satisfaction and future purchase intentions. Similarly, in a large-scale study of Korean automobile purchases, negative disconfirmation negatively affected not only satisfaction but future purchase intentions as well.[38] Results such as these linking disconfirmation and satisfaction have been shown for many products and services.

Now consider what happens when performance expectations are neutrally confirmed. Not much! Meeting performance expectations is probably not the key to satisfaction. Even delivering as expected when expectations are moderate or high may evoke an emotionally neutral response. Hence, the competitor that positions itself to exceed customer's expectations will likely outperform the firm that merely meets customer expectations.

What is most important in predicting satisfaction in the EDM is the subjective disconfirmation felt by the consumer, which may differ from disconfirmation as measured by the firm. For example, perceived waiting time for fast food is a better predictor of satisfaction than the actual clock time customers wait.[39]

To more fully explicate the EDM we need to describe assimilation effects and contrast effects. These terms and related concepts have already been described in Chapter 12. Assimilation effects imply that individuals are reluctant to acknowledge discrepancies from a previously held position. Hence, individuals will explain away (rationalize) apparent discrepancies. In the context of satisfaction, this implies that repeat consumers may minimize or rationalize away discrepancies from expectations, often with a subjective report that the product is exactly as expected or even better than expected. As modeled in Exhibit 17.2, expectations function to increase satisfaction through assimilation effects. Contrast effects have been described as the tendency to exaggerate differences, making them larger than reality. In a satisfaction context, new or infrequent consumers may exaggerate more extreme differences between expectations and outcomes.[40]

Keep in mind that disconfirmation may be of two sorts—negative (worse than expected) or positive (better than expected). In both cases of disconfirmation there may be a tendency to exaggerate (contrast effects) discrepancies. As modeled in Exhibit 17.2, disconfirmation functions to exaggerate differences, thereby increasing dissatisfaction (negative disconfirmation) or delight (positive disconfirmation).

Finally, we need to mention the relationship between expectations and disconfirmation. One possible relationship that has been observed is a negative one, known as a ceiling-floor effect. In this case very high expectations (ceiling) are more likely to result in negative disconfirmation and very low expectations (floor) in positive disconfirmation. People reflect a belief in this relationship when they say, "I don't want to get my hopes too high because then I'm sure to be disappointed," or even "I'm keeping my expectations low, so I won't be disappointed." Because of these effects, firms may sometimes benefit from downplaying consumer expectations.

Many internal and external factors influence the expectations that consumers bring to their satisfaction judgments. Some important sources of expectations include memories of past experiences, influenced by such memory factors as ease and vividness of recall; word-of-mouth communications such as consumer-maintained websites (e.g., see the natwestfraud.com site, which reports claims against the unethical practices of National Westminster Bank, UK); explicit and implicit promises made by the organization through promotional and other media; product cues; and third-party information, such as from *Consumer Reports.*

Our cultural milieu is also an important source of expectations. Research on satisfaction with technological products finds it relates to American cultural myths linking technology to human perfection, intelligence, and skill. Violations of cultural expectations are an understudied source of consumers' anger, frustration, and dissatisfaction.

Exciting Postpurchase Product Attributes

When searching for a new car, one respondent found the "hill hold" feature on a Subaru to be "wonderful" and "really neat," though she had never sought out this element. Another respondent did not know his television had a sleep timer until he brought his purchase home. The sleep timer was "icing on the cake." One woman was "thrilled" when her Keds sneakers held up far beyond her expectations. One man was delighted to find the "ridiculous" heated seats in his used BMW extended the season for convertible driving and helped to sooth his chronic back troubles.

Source: Steven N. Silverman and Rajiv Grover, "Forming Perceptions of Overall Quality in Consumer Products: A Process of Quality Element Integration," Marketing Science Institute working paper, report no. 95-103, April 1995.

Consumer Chronicles 17.4

Sometimes cultural expectations will become evident in a different cultural setting (recall discussions in Chapters 1 and 5). An interesting example comes from Denmark. In Denmark many services feature queuing based on taking a number when you enter the establishment. This queuing system reflects Danish cultural values of equality and freedom. Queuing eliminates the possibility that consumers will choose the wrong line and end up having to wait longer than someone else, and it allows them the freedom to move about without fear of losing their place in line.[41]

Expectations may vary in abstractness, complexity, and accessibility. For example, before their river-rafting trips, customers often articulate abstract hopes such as "I want this trip to be something completely different than I've ever experienced" or "I'm hoping this trip will change my life." Imagine the difficulty of trying to fulfill these expectations directly. When expectations are abstract or ill-formed, thinking of satisfaction as a direct result of fulfilled expectations may not be useful. In such circumstances, satisfaction derives from the benefits that were within the range of customer expectations.[42] Several examples of product attributes that contributed to customer satisfaction but were not part of expectations are provided in Consumer Chronicles 17.4.

As just described, trying to understand and identify consumers' expectations can be challenging. As we've said, sources of expectations differ and sometimes consumers are only aware of their expectations when they are violated. Adding to the complexity, consumers often use multiple levels of expectations or standards. For example, a consumer

 www.natwest fraud.com

 www.consumer reports.org

Consumer Chronicles 17.5

Ben's Telephone Answering Machine

Ben had definite preconsumption, predictive expectations for specific features, benefits, and uses of his telephone answering machine. However, because Ben was offered a full-time position shortly after acquiring his answering machine, the calls he expected from his supervisor did not materialize. The disconfirmation of this previously significant expectation did not appear to affect his satisfaction. Ben also came to realize that he had only four friends with whom he socialized and that he saw them regularly in class. Thus, his expectation of receiving social-planning calls was also disconfirmed, and this too appeared inconsequential to his satisfaction. In fact, by the end of six months, Ben was hardly using the device to record important calls as originally intended. Instead, he was screening calls when studying, eating, or avoiding requests to work on his day off—a usage and benefit that did not figure in his predictive expectations at purchase time. In fact, because of situational changes and new realizations in his personal and social-life world, Ben derived a complete and apparently satisfying reverse of predicted product benefits—obstructing rather than facilitating communication.

taking a vacation cruise may express a goal of rest and relaxation, an expectation for good food and sunshine, and a desire for romance. It's likely the vacation will be judged satisfying even without the romance, but imagine how other goals and expectations won't matter if the consumer's hopes of a wonderful romance are realized!

In some cases the comparison object is not known at the time of purchase but is formulated during or following the consumption experience and then used in determining level of satisfaction. Consider especially trial of novel products or services. Free food samples offered in grocery stores offer a familiar example. Sometimes, consumers will try a product in a supermarket with few **active expectations** of what it will be like. That is, they haven't thought, felt, or sensed what will happen when they taste the product. That is not to say they don't have **passive expectations.** For example, consumers passively assume that they will not be poisoned and the product won't taste too bad (or stores wouldn't offer it up in a promotion). Moreover, from a variety of cues such as the response of other consumers, color, apparent texture, visible packaging, and so on, consumers may passively organize some ideas about what to expect. However, it may be that this jumble of thoughts and perceptual judgments gets organized into a comparison object only after the first taste: "Oh this tastes a little like a _____, only it is [sweeter, saltier, crunchier, and so on]." At this point a comparison object has been identified.

Marketers often attempt to identify comparison objects for consumers in a way to make their products or services seem desirable or superior. An interesting example of a product that doesn't measure up to what at first glance appears to be its competition suggests the importance of considering comparison objects as part of the broader topic of expectations. The product is the Velo-Glide bicycle. Like a previous year's Harley limited edition bicycle that sold out in four months, the Velo-Glide is built by GT Bicycles under license to Harley-Davidson. It too is a limited edition, with only 3,000 made, and can be had for a mere $1,700. At 40-plus pounds it's a big clunker that no one would really want to ride, but it offers a Harley paint job, a fake gas tank, and the signature fenders and chrome of a Harley Softail motorcycle.[43] In this case other bicycles are not relevant comparison objects, but other Harley collectibles might be.

In addition to vague or unknown expectations, multiple levels of expectations, and passive expectations, consumers' expectations change over time. With some service encounters, and probably with many product experiences as well, consumers update their expectations throughout the consumption process.[44] Although this seems intuitively obvious there is actually little understanding of how this works. In particular, it's unclear how these updated expectations are related to observed performance up to that point and how updated expectations influence satisfaction.

Consider a simple illustration. Suppose you are hoping to take your date to a nice restaurant, and on the basis of a recommendation from a friend you believe that Ambiance Unlimited is just the right place. Now suppose you walk in with your date, are seated, and given a menu. A glance at the menu and the surroundings leads you to feel disappointed, for example, it doesn't seem as fancy and exotic as you expected. At this point you may revise your expectations downward. Now suppose that although the menu doesn't seem very exotic, it turns out that many of the simple items are prepared with style and fanfare at your table and that the presentation of the food is exquisite. Included are some nice surprises such as a little appetizer or chocolate dessert. Depending on a host of other things, including the interaction between you and your date, you may leave the restaurant quite satisfied or even delighted. The question remains, is your comparison standard now that first expectation of a fancy, exotic restaurant, or is it your revised expectation following being seated at the restaurant and handed a menu? There is some preliminary work that suggests the updated expectations will be most influential in your satisfaction judgment, but more research to understand problems of this sort is needed.[45]

The preceding helps to emphasize an important point: *Satisfaction is a process extending across the entire consumption experience.* Studying consumer–product interactions following purchase is fundamental to understanding satisfaction. When researchers do this—which few have—they may find that satisfaction modeled on fulfilled expectations loses its explanatory power. An example reported in research on prolonged and repeated interactions of consumers with technology and summarized in Consumer Chronicles 17.5 suggests the inadequacies of adopting an expectations framework when considering consumption satisfaction over time.[46]

In this section we consider two other possible satisfaction standards: desires and fairness.

Other Comparative Standards for Judging Satisfaction

Desires

Individuals' goals and desires might serve as a standard against which to judge satisfaction. In a **desires model of satisfaction,** satisfaction is a function of the consumer's *assessment of the degree to which a product meets or exceeds his or her desires, the outcome being called desires congruency.* **Desires** are the *levels of products' attributes and benefits that a consumer believes will lead to, or are connected with, higher-level values,* such as the terminal values discussed in Chapter 5. Some research showed how a simple answering machine enabled one woman to fulfill her maternal desire to be available to her children and how a video camera enabled an older man to craft a legacy of stories for his children.[47]

Some advertisements emphasize a connection between product use and deeply held consumer desires, but delivering on these desires is hard. For example, ads for New Balance running shoes seem to promise fulfillment of the desire for a balanced life (a deeply held and oft-frustrated desire of many consumers). Yet, all these promises rely on significant effort from the consumer and may often result in dissatisfaction, sometimes attributed to the self rather than product failure. As we all know, obtaining a balanced life requires more than running shoes.

Most satisfaction research has assumed judgments are a rational and cognitive process of connecting product features to benefits. But consumption desires often spring from less rational and more affective processes, many below the threshold of consciousness. Much more research is needed on the desires approach to understanding satisfaction.

1. Build a collage expressing the concept of desire.

2. Imagine swimming in a sea of things (objects, experiences, people) that bring you the greatest pleasure.

3. Write a fairy tale in which someone experiences great suffering, but in the end finds great happiness.

4. List states that you regard as the opposite of desire.

5. List things that you regard as the opposite of desire, and describe your feelings about those things.

6. Describe desire and the opposite of desire as taste, smell, color, shape, texture, sound, and emotion.

7. Sketch artworks that represent desire and not desire.

8. Use examples to describe differences between wants and desires. How would someone differ in their feelings and behaviors if they desire versus want something?

9. Name an object, experience, or person (X) that you desire, and list as many words or phrases as you can that might be used in the sentence "I _____ X."

10. Describe the feelings a person might have about a desired thing before they get it, at the moment they get it, and after they get it.

Source: Adapted from Russell W. Belk, Güliz Ger, and Søren Askegaard, "Consumer Desire in Three Cultures: Results from Projective Research," in Advances in Consumer Research, vol. 24, Merrie Brucks and Deborah J. MacInnis, eds. (Provo, UT: Association for Consumer Research, 1997), pp. 24–25.

An interesting, ongoing, multicultural research project attempts to look at the nature of consumer desire using a range of projective research techniques more appropriate to tapping the irrational bases of satisfaction.[48] Such research could help us refine and extend the desires model of satisfaction. Good Practice 17.4 illustrates some of the different ways these researchers have used to attempt to understand what consumers desire. One of their techniques invites consumers to make collages to illustrate their desires.

Fairness

Perceptions of fairness affect consumers' satisfaction. The consumer in the opening vignette reports that fair prices contribute to her retail loyalty, for example.[49] When consumers feel they've been exposed to unfair or deception pricing practices, they may seek reparation by switching brands or firms.[50] Beyond seeking reparation, consumers may also seek to punish marketers for unfair treatment. When consumers perceived one bank's fees for automatic teller machine services to be unfair, they reported an intention to switch even when they gained nothing from switching, reflecting a desire to punish the firm.[51]

The **fairness** concept is built into **Homans's rule of justice,** which proclaims *parties' rewards in exchanges with others should be proportional to their investments* (or losses). (See Chapter 10 for discussion of Homans's theory of exchange.) In judging fairness, consumers compare their outcomes to their investments (or losses), but they also compare their outcomes to the perceived outcomes of other individuals or groups. Thus, senior citizen or student price discounts do not usually provoke concerns about fairness, because consumers recognize differences in relative investments between consumer groups. However, when the comparison reveals relative inequality in the distribution of gains and losses, an inequitable, or unfair, exchange exists. Perceived inequity results in feelings of distress. Because of their socialist heritage, Eastern European consumers often feel guilty if they get a better deal than someone else. More individualistic Western consumers experience anger if someone else gets a better deal than they. Consumers seem more inclined to act against firms in the latter situation.[52]

Exhibit 17.3 illustrates the relationship between three dimensions of fairness and satisfaction/dissatisfaction. Of the research in marketing focused on fairness, nearly all has considered only **distributional fairness,** or *how rewards or outcomes are partitioned among the participants in an exchange.*[53] For example, preferential seating on airlines for frequent fliers appears to be considered a fair distribution of outcomes by passengers. By contrast, some Windows customers were upset that customers of WordPerfect who switched to Microsoft Word paid the same price for a software upgrade as the Word users did. They felt their loyalty was unfairly rewarded.[54]

Research both inside and outside marketing settings suggests that two other forms of fairness are also important to satisfaction/dissatisfaction judgments. **Procedural fairness** refers to *the manner in which the outcomes are delivered.* Some research indicates that when customers both participate in and influence the outcomes of service delivery, satisfaction increases.[55]

Interactional fairness refers to *how the consumer is treated by the marketer.* Is the customer accorded respect, politeness, and dignity? Level of satisfaction and likelihood of complaint behavior depend on whether consumers perceive the outcome following a service failure to be fair, but they also depend on interactional justice. This is the degree to which the service provider, whether a Norwegian consumer service or a Singaporean shipping line, provides an explanation, shows empathy and respect, and takes steps to correct

Exhibit 17.3 The Relationship between Fairness and Satisfaction

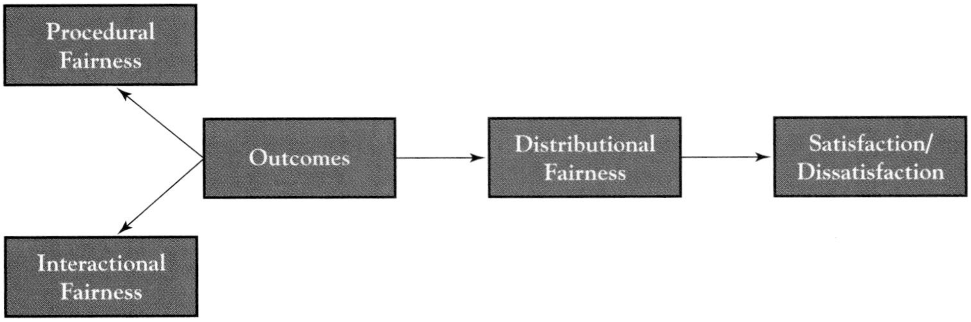

Source: Reproduced from Oliver, *Satisfaction,* p. 208.

service failures promptly. Similarly, a transatlantic study of customer call centers found that problem resolution on the first call was the most significant determinant of satisfaction.[56]

Consumer Attributions and the Satisfaction Process

When products or services fail, consumers may attempt to understand the reason why. The degree of disappointment and anger felt and also intentions to repurchase and intentions to complain are influenced by how consumers explain the failure. We have talked about consumer attributions in other chapters. Attribution theory was developed in social psychology to understand how individuals find explanations for outcomes or behaviors. Of course, the desire to understand why something happened varies between and within cultures and also between situations. Moreover, there are many situational, cultural, and individual differences in the kinds of explanations consumers give. In this chapter we focus only on the effects of consumer attributions on the emotions and judgments made by a consumer following a product or service purchase or consumption experience.

A story illustrates how such attributions work in influencing consumers' feelings and judgments. Professor Arnould, one of the co-authors of this text, had spent three weeks in the war-ravaged central African nation of Chad. He'd worked for some weeks under uncomfortable conditions with refugees out in the bush. There, a local military commander had accidentally shot himself to death at his own birthday party. And disgruntled townsfolk had approached Arnould with allegations of fraud against his employer, an international relief organization. In addition, he'd spent part of a night in the capital city, N'Djamena, under his bed avoiding stray bullets from a victory celebration. Following all this, he was anxious to catch one of the two weekly flights out of Chad. After he had waited patiently in the capital for one of the flights, sitting at the airport for three hours anticipating its arrival (a guy sitting next to him at the bar vomited on his shoes), the plane failed to land. The airline plausibly blamed a sandstorm. The local manager helped Arnould transfer his reservations to the other weekly scheduled flight on a different airline. Two days later, this plane also failed to land. The explanation offered: an African head of state had commandeered the plane. The second airline, popularly referred to as Air Tragique to reflect its service profile, offered no compensation. But the manager of the first company finally arranged to get the increasingly agitated passengers booked on a special charter flight that left the next day for a third country. There, after waiting in a "luxury hotel" all day, the passengers finally boarded a regularly scheduled flight for Paris. How upset was Professor Arnould, and at whom?

There are a variety of reasons to suspect that he was pretty dissatisfied with some aspects of his service experience, especially with Air Tragique. First of all, the consumption outcome in this case was very important to him. He'd done his job; he was tired and homesick. Second, there was nothing much that he could do; that is, he was not to blame for what happened. He did his part—he arrived in plenty of time for the flights, waited patiently, and followed directions. Third, he felt that Air Tragique management could have done things differently, especially since the other airline manager acted so proactively. Actions that are detrimental to a person and perceived by that individual as subject to the discretion of others generate anger. If the second delay had been caused by bad weather like the first, it would have been frustrating and stressful but understandable and less likely to generate anger toward the firm. Fourth, Air Tragique's behavior did not seem unusual; rather, it reflected the airline's service quality more generally. By contrast, the other firm went to extraordinary lengths to get the passengers out of Chad.[57] The story illustrates both successful and unsuccessful managerial tactics to influence consumer attributions. The relationships we have outlined between attributions and anger (dissatisfaction) toward the firm are summarized in Exhibit 17.4.

Exhibit 17.4 Consumer Attributions and Feelings of Anger
with the Firm

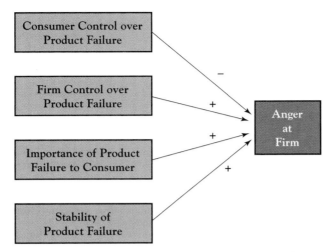

Source: Adapted from Valerie S. Folkes, Susan Koletsky, and John L. Graham, "A Field Study of Causal Inferences and Consumer Reaction: The View from the Airport," *Journal of Consumer Research* 13 (March 1987), pp. 534–39; and Valerie S. Folkes, "Consumer Reactions to Product Failure: An Attributional Approach," *Journal of Consumer Research* 10 (March 1984), pp. 398–409.

In this section we have described some of the factors that influence satisfaction. We have summarized what we currently know about the relationship between performance and satisfaction, how employee satisfaction influences customer satisfaction, differences between choice criteria and satisfaction criteria, and several different kinds of comparisons that consumers use in judging satisfaction. We have also briefly outlined how consumer explanations for failure are related to satisfaction. In the next section we examine the relationship between emotions and satisfaction.

Emotions, Ambivalence, and Satisfaction

Attention has recently shifted to the emotional content of satisfaction and especially the way in which satisfaction and emotions vary together in consumption experiences.[58] In some, emotions vary quite a bit over time. Consider white-water river-rafting again. Satisfaction with the experience sometimes has a low-arousal emotional quality (relaxing on calm water following rapids), other times a high-arousal quality (during and immediately following rapids), and other times a cognitive appraisal quality (learning a lot about oneself and others from the experience).[59] This same mixture of emotions and cognition applies to other kinds of purchase processes and consumption experiences, especially experiential (a museum tour, a roller coaster ride) and leisure (watching a movie, attending a ball game) consumption episodes, but to ongoing experiences with consumer durables as well. Five emotional response modes—contentment, pleasure, delight, relief, and ambivalence—might all be described as satisfaction.[60]

Satisfaction as Contentment

One common meaning of satisfaction is contentment. The **contentment response** is characterized by *low levels of emotional arousal and may entail disinterest.* Contentment is a passive response. This is the type of satisfaction response consumers often give when asked how satisfied they are with products or services that they don't think much about or those with which they are not very involved. What the "satisfied" consumer means is that the performance of the service or product is within expectations, and so disconfirmation is neutral. This satisfaction response could also be associated with more high-involvement products or services that have stable performance over time. For example, a consumer might express contentment over a family car that has functioned reliably over many years. While satisfaction may no longer have the emotional edge it had when the car was new, the consumer is still satisfied.

Sometimes, experiences with other products or services can lead consumers to change their evaluations from contentment to some other emotional satisfaction or dissatisfaction. For example, Consumer Chronicles 17.4 referred to experiences with a Subaru, a BMW, Keds sneakers, and a TV sleep timer that evoked pleasure for some consumers. In each case, experience with the superior product helps reframe previous product experiences, perhaps even to discontent.

Satisfaction as Pleasure

Sometimes purchase and use of a product makes the consumer happy. For example, when consumers choose a favorite piece of clothing, have a pleasing sensory experience at a restaurant, play a new CD they just purchased, or sit behind the wheel of their new automobile they may have a **pleasure response.** An ad for a Cadillac DeVille, shown on page 635, doesn't just promise "exceptional performance," it also promises a feeling of exuberance, for example. In this case, *the consumer confirms expectations and has moderate to high arousal and most likely high to moderate involvement as well.* The consumer is more actively involved in processing the performance of the product or service, in contrast with the contentment response mode.

www.landsend.com

Product and service firms that consistently deliver high-quality service are likely to evoke a pleasure response. The catalog merchandiser Lands' End prides itself on being this kind of company. Lands' End has an Internet team, serving people who use the Lands' End Live feature on the company's website. With a click of a mouse, Lands' End Live allows customers to start a live chat with a Lands' End representative or get a rep to call them at home, immediately. In many cases, sales are closed by human interaction that soothes last minute anxieties and doubts at the point of purchase and turns cognitive satisfaction into a pleasurable exchange. Perhaps, you can think of other products that evoke, for you, a pleasure response.[61]

Satisfaction as Delight

Occasionally, product or service performance evokes a combination of joy and surprise that has been termed delight. The **delight response** involves *either a positive disconfirmation of expectations or, alternatively, a positive event or outcome that the consumer did not have any expectations about.*[62] A few years ago, two of your authors stayed in a small hotel in Sweden. Right after checking in, our daughter had an accident on the bed that required changing the sheets (unpleasant even to have to ask for). An hour later when we returned to the room, not only were the sheets freshly changed but also our daughter's stuffed animals had been gently and lovingly arranged in her little toddler bed. We consumers were delighted. For many complex products and services consumers may have few expectations and, as described earlier, even articulated needs may be quite abstract. In such cases

delight may come from discovering pleasurable surprises (e.g., a useful feature after purchase).

Satisfaction as Relief

Sometimes the removal of a negative state leads to consumer satisfaction. Such a situation evokes a **relief response.** Whereas consumers seek out feelings of contentment, pleasure, and delight, most do not look for aversive stimuli that can then be eliminated.

A feeling of relief may come about as a response to unfulfilled negative expectations ("I didn't have to wait as long as I expected," "It didn't hurt as much as I expected," and so on). Relief can also result from the elimination of a negative state, as with medication, a successful legal defense, a warning instead of a ticket for speeding, and so on. The ad for Tropicana grapefruit juice, shown below, taps into satisfaction as relief, the promise of quenching your thirst.

Depending on the situation, satisfaction as relief can involve high levels of arousal and involvement. For example, a patient waiting to hear the results of a test for a serious illness would likely experience very high levels of emotional arousal (probably lots of fear and anxiety) and would be extremely involved in evaluating performance. These factors will strongly influence perceptions of waiting time, for example. When the marketer believes satisfaction as relief is a response to performance, timing service or product delivery and helping the customer manage expectations become crucial.[63]

Evoking satisfaction as relief.

Actual photo of woman in nirvana. No wonder it's America's favorite grapefruit juice.

Tropicana PURE PREMIUM

Perfect.

American Heart Association

Satisfaction as Ambivalence

Consumers in complex societies often deal with conflicting demands, social roles, and cultural values. Even self-concepts (as described in Chapter 7) involve conflicting aspects or even different selves. Hence, the **ambivalence response** is common in various purchase and consumption experiences. We can define consumer ambivalence as *the simultaneous or sequential experience of multiple emotional states associated with acquisition or consumption processes.* This may involve high levels of involvement and affective response. Many of our most memorable consumption and life experiences may be best described as evoking mixed emotions. For example, in some recent research, a bride describes the joy she got from purchasing her wedding dress. However, as the description of her purchasing process in Consumer Chronicles 17.6 shows, she also reveals anger, disappointment, and regret. Thus, as also suggested by research on the consumption of technological products, satisfaction may sometimes result from achieving balance between conflicting emotions associated with product use. When the marketer believes satisfaction as ambivalence is a response to performance, helping the customer interpret expectations and outcomes and managing assimilation and contrast effects become crucial.[64]

The Consequences of Satisfaction and Dissatisfaction

In response to satisfying or dissatisfying purchase and consumption experiences consumers may opt to exercise one or more of four behavioral responses: exit, voice, continued patronage, or "twist" (e.g., resistance).[65] Many different kinds of feelings and beliefs can be expressed in each of these behaviors, and each may be more or less active.

Exit

When a consumer has a dissatisfying purchase and consumption experience, perhaps the most common response is simply *not to purchase or use that product or service again.* That is, the consumer will **exit** as a customer of the organization. At a minimum, the dissatisfied consumer may attempt to avoid that product or service, selecting other alternatives whenever they are accessible and feasible. Of course, not all decisions to exit are based on dissatisfaction, and not all dissatisfied consumers exit. Barclays Bank in the UK found that many dissatisfied customers simply reduced their account activity to low levels, exerting a passive form of exit.[66]

We have already discussed switching behavior in Chapter 10, so we will not review the broad literature on that subject here. Sometimes consumers exit because another alternative seems superior, because they are seeking variety, or because circumstances or needs have changed and so on. Nevertheless, the average firm is estimated to lose 20 percent of its customers in a given year, mostly due to dissatisfaction.[67] Waiting until dissatisfaction expresses itself as a decision to exit can have a disastrous effect on market share and profits. Recognizing this problem, Barclays Bank developed a tracking system to detect declining account use and to intervene in an effort to restore satisfaction.

Some consumers will exit or switch, rather than complain, when markets are heterogeneous (offer lots of different alternatives) and consumers are knowledgeable about alternatives.[68] That is, when consumers perceive that they have choices and don't have to patronize a particular organization, they will switch when they are dissatisfied. We might expect that an exit strategy would often be employed with low-involvement or inexpensive products and services. Rather than make a big fuss over a little thing the consumer simply determines to do something different the next time. Of course, this invisible response to dissatisfaction can gradually erode market share unless the firm makes an effort to uncover the discontent behind this action.

Voice

Voice is highly consequential for marketers. **Voice** can take several different forms including *compliments an organization may receive when it delivers an especially satisfying outcome, complaints to the company about performance failure, negative and positive word-of-mouth with other consumers or consuming organizations, or third-party complaints or compliments.* Consumers' complaints and compliments to firms provide valuable feedback, and their interpersonal communications, both positive and negative, strongly influence other consumers' purchases. The Planned Parenthood advertisement shown on page 639 encourages the use of consumer voice to communicate to legislators.[69]

Loyal customers are most likely to engage in positive word-of-mouth. One study showed not only that loyal customers provided more recommendations than others but that the number of recommendations increased with the duration of their relationship with the firms studied, a bank and a dental office.

Consumers' interpersonal communications, both positive and negative, strongly influence others' purchases.[70] Unfortunately, customers are more apt to engage in word-of-mouth than to provide feedback.[71] The consumerama website is a clearinghouse, featuring customer complaints about dozens of U.S. firms, for example. Chapter 15 provides a fuller treatment of how word-of-mouth communications influence purchase and consumption decisions.

 www.consumer-ama.org

Management can use complaints as an important tool.[72] Dissatisfied consumers who do not complain are more likely to discontinue purchase (e.g., exit).[73] By encouraging consumers to complain and seeking to redress their problems, management can actually create more satisfied consumers who are more likely to talk favorably about the organization with other consumers. The very act of complaining can enhance ultimate satisfaction not only through initiating redress but also through the cathartic effects it provides a consumer—"getting it off my chest." On the other hand, consumers' negative word-of-mouth communications tend to reinforce or increase their levels of dissatisfaction with the firm.[74]

Management should make sure legitimate complaints are handled efficiently and effectively. For example, a study from Singapore found that the more quickly complaints were responded to, the higher the satisfaction.[75] Theoretically, management can expect market share gains and decreased costs of attracting customers through advertising if the company maximizes attempts to encourage complaints (subject to cost constraints).[76]

Voice can accompany either exit or continued patronage behavior. For example, a person dissatisfied with a particular cleaning service may continue to use that service but complain in an effort to improve performance. Alternatively, a dissatisfied consumer may stop using that service and also engage in negative word-of-mouth communications.[77]

Voice varies with culture, market infrastructure (e.g., presence of a complaint channel), the economics of complaining, and consumer psychology. In a study of the effects of culture on complaining in a banking setting, researchers found that consumers from the inegalitarian and individualistic cultures (United States and Switzerland) were more likely to complain than those from the more egalitarian, less individualistic culture (Singapore). Consumers in individualistic and inegalitarian cultures are more likely to engage in negative word-of-mouth than positive word-of-mouth, whereas those in more egalitarian, less individualistic cultures may provide more positive feedback to firms. Complaining behavior in the United States varies by ethnic group, or subculture. Mexican-American consumers are more likely to complain about problems such as delay or nondelivery than other consumers. Puerto Rican cultural norms and values lead consumers in that ethnic group to complain less than other U.S. consumers.[78] Age, income, education, attitudes, interests, and personalities have all been used as predictors of complaining behavior. Complainers tend to be younger, have higher incomes, and are less brand loyal than noncomplainers.[79]

Noncomplaining rates vary for different cultures.[80] For example, cultures with a more fatalistic worldview (belief in fate); those with totalitarian or formerly totalitarian political regimes, such as in eastern Europe; or those with a more interdependent orientation may be less likely to complain than those that emphasize individual agency.

Consumers in countries that have not developed market infrastructures to facilitate voice or where the consuming publics are relatively uninformed about their rights as consumers (hence, unsure what they can expect) may be less likely to complain. In many de-

veloping or transitional economies, consumers lack opportunity and knowledge about how to complain. In Malaysia, one of retailer Carrefour's innovations was to offer suggestion cards to facilitate feedback that are read daily by the management team.[81] Even in developed economies in Europe, people often view complaints as bad; hence, organizational mechanisms for soliciting and responding to complaints are not as well developed as in the United States. The Internet may provide increased scope for voice worldwide.[82]

There are a number of economic reasons that help explain why a consumer would or would not complain. As product or service price declines, so does complaining; it's not worth the cost of complaining. Product importance will increase complaining. The perceived costs and efforts of complaining will depress complaining behavior. Consumers will also attempt to assess the likely outcomes of complaining; a firm's reputation for addressing complaints may increase consumers' complaining behavior. But if firms institute too generous response policies to complaining, unjustified consumer complaints may be triggered.[83] The problem of **fraudulent complaining** is a legitimate concern for management, as some consumers will try to improve their outcomes through this method.

Attributions or causal inferences for product or service failure influence both complaining and complimenting firms and also positive and negative word-of-mouth. Not surprisingly, consumers are more likely to complain and compliment when they hold the seller responsible and perceive the cause of the failure or success to be stable and under the seller's control.[84]

Perceived psychological costs may hinder dissatisfied but passive consumers from complaining. For example, complaining may be viewed as confrontational, and the consumer may fear being intimidated or berated by the organization. In addition, the consumer may fear being labeled a complainer or, even worse, a chronic complainer. By contrast,

Some examples of the direct monetary value of loyal customers include:

1. $360,000 in lifetime revenues to Federal Express.
2. $4,000 in lifetime revenues to a Baltimore Pizza Hut Franchise.
3. $50,000 in 10-year revenues to a Connecticut grocery store owner.
4. $332,000 in lifetime revenues to a Texas Cadillac dealer.

Source: Gremler and Brown, "The Loyalty Ripple Effect."

---

activist consumers perceive low psychological cost from complaining, engage heavily in complaining, and are likely to complain to a third party.[85]

Continued Patronage

In this section we want to consider the relationship between customer satisfaction and continued patronage, or loyalty. Satisfaction is a relatively temporary postpurchase state that reflects how the product or service has fulfilled its purpose. We emphasized in Chapters 3 and 10 that loyalty goes beyond satisfaction.[86] **Customer loyalty** is *a deeply held commitment to rebuy or repatronize a preferred product or service consistently in the future, despite situational influences and marketing efforts having the potential to cause switching behavior.*[87] Thus, loyalty includes both readiness to act (repeat purchase) and resistance to alternatives. For firms, loyalty leads to an increase in profits, more predictable sales and profit streams, and positive word-of-mouth. In addition, high overall satisfaction protects firms from a reduction in loyalty after poor performance in a particular transaction.[88] Some calculations of the direct monetary benefits of loyalty are shown in Industry Insights 17.1.[89]

As indicated earlier in this chapter, customer satisfaction leads to loyalty and continued patronage.[90] Specifically, if a consumer is loyal and switching costs are high, decreases in satisfaction will not cause switching until some threshold of dissatisfaction is reached. Thus, people continue to fly on airlines they do not like because they need to go where the airline goes. However, defection rates among satisfied customers as high as 90 percent are reported. Product quality or switching costs alone are weak determinants of continued patronage.[91]

Companies should be quite interested in generating and maintaining consumer loyalty, but it's not easy. Although clusters of consumers claim that they find a good brand and stick with it, this doesn't seem to translate into consistent repurchase rates.[92] While 85 to 95 percent of automobile customers report they are satisfied, only 30 to 40 percent return to their previous make. A typical large study in Denmark that included 684 brands of consumer products found that only 13 percent of consumers claimed to use a specific brand 90 to 100 percent of the time. Consumers' search for variety, multibrand loyalties, and switching incentives provided by competitors and directed at changing their beliefs, attitudes, or behaviors account for weak consumer loyalties.[93]

As suggested by our opening vignette and examples given here, enduring loyalty is a long-term consequence only of some types of customer satisfaction (e.g., pleasure and delight), reinforced by ongoing positive experience and support from other members of a household or buying group or from valued reference groups. In this case, loyal consumers are quite resistant to competitive switching efforts. If product consumption is closely associated with community membership or identity, loyalty may be stronger. Loyalty to Wrangler jeans, Justin boots, Resistol hats, and Skoal smokeless tobacco among some North American cowboys, for example, or the loyalty to particular European football teams seems to reflect these identity and community-based types of loyalty.

Relational strength may lead consumers to ignore competitive alternatives. Consumers may remain loyal even when it is difficult to do so. For example, consider the case of hairstylists and consumers. Some consumers will travel long distances at considerable inconvenience to continue patronage because of their loyal feelings for the stylist. Sports and music fans also engage in this kind of behavior.[94]

With low switching costs in competitive markets, the relationship between satisfaction and continued patronage is more fluid. When people are only moderately satisfied with an automobile they may switch since there are so many brands of cars available. Satisfaction is not enough to ensure continued patronage. A firm's commitment to quality, product differentiation, and loyalty-building programs are necessary as well.

Twist[95]

Consumers may express themselves through actions other than switching, voice, or loyalty. We use the term **twist** to refer to these behaviors. Twist refers to *positive and negative ways in which consumers restructure meanings, roles, and objects in the marketplace.* The consumer reacts to consumer satisfaction/dissatisfaction with novel behaviors unanticipated by the offering organization. In one example of positive twist, loyal customers pitched in to help when the Tattered Cover Bookstore in Denver, Colorado, moved to a new location. Consumers, in effect, became partners with the firm, striving to help the organization achieve its goals.[96] In general, it seems likely that loyal consumers might be more likely to feel a sense of ownership that translates into positive, voluntary, and often novel behaviors toward the organization. Such behaviors are common for many not-for-profit organizations such as churches or public radio stations that rely on volunteers to answer phones during annual fund drives. However, for other types of organizations positive twist may be more common than most people realize. Positive twist includes little things such as picking up someone else's litter in the parking lot or rehanging a piece of clothing that some other customer knocked off the rack. To date, we know very little about positive voluntary customer behaviors or how they relate to feelings of satisfaction or loyalty. Can you think of examples of positive twist you engage in?

Alternatively, consumers may reflect their dissatisfaction with a company by engaging in negative twist: unwanted behaviors or acts of resistance against the company. Sometimes these behaviors take organized form such as picketing an establishment. Resistance may also take more subtle, unorganized forms. For example, one study identified shoplifting, covert rebundling of sales merchandise (substituting a more expensive item for a less expensive item in a bundle), switching packaging to get lower prices on more expensive products, returning merchandise under false pretenses, fraudulent coupon use, and misusing memberships (e.g., allowing nonmembers to use memberships) among a host of other practices in which disgruntled consumers engage. During the Los Angeles riots in spring 1992, establishments viewed as discriminating against certain ethnic groups in their selling practices were more likely to be broken into and looted. Lately, resistance has reached the Internet, with hackers breaking into corporate websites to inject their own commentary. An example is provided in Consumer Chronicles 17.7.[97]

Until recently, discussions of twist have been limited and focused primarily on collective (organized) actions directed at changes in marketing mix structure and composition.[98] However, as we have suggested, there are many forms of twist. We can describe these kinds of consumers along four dimensions. First, consumers can resist as individuals or collectives. Second, consumers can have goals that vary from reformist to radical. Third, tactics of resistance can vary from actions directed at altering the marketing mix (fighting for product safety features, or against ads on television), to actions directed at altering the meaning of products (using products in unintended ways). Fourth, consumers can either appropriate marketing institutions and agents as their tools of resistance or try to use nonmarketing institutions and agents, such as the courts, as instruments of change. Most instances of consumer resistance can be described using these four dimensions.[99]

One well-known example of organized consumer resistance is *Adbusters*. *Adbusters* is a quarterly magazine with the twin goals of raising consciousness of commercial excess and elevating the media awareness and skills of those in the anticonsumerist movement. *Adbusters* is a collective project with the radical goal of reducing consumerism. It uses the tools of marketing communications and employs advertising professionals to radically alter product meanings. Examples of Adbusters advertisement parodies are shown below and on page 643.

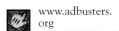 www.adbusters.org

Adbusters twists advertising conventions.

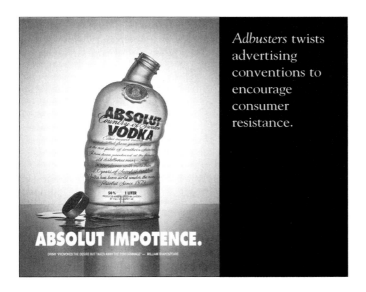

Adbusters twists advertising conventions to encourage consumer resistance.

Individual and organized resistance against marketing organizations and marketing practices may be on the increase among generation Xers, a group that tends to be less materialistic and more cynical about marketing than previous generations.[100]

Consumer Satisfaction and Profitability[101]

Exhibit 17.5 represents the direct effects on profitability of quality, satisfaction, and loyalty. As can be seen in the exhibit, quality has direct effects on both satisfaction and profitability. Quality reduces failures and operating costs and lowers the cost of recovery. Moreover, quality leads to better consumer reputations, better marketing channel member receptivity, better awareness, and lower costs of attracting new customers. Examples showing the direct quality–profit link are reported in a number of studies.

Satisfaction has direct effects on profit through its influence on retention. Satisfied consumers are easier to reach with communications, more insulated from competitive overtures, and more willing to increase volume of purchases and tolerate price increases.

Exhibit 17.5 Customer Satisfaction and Profits

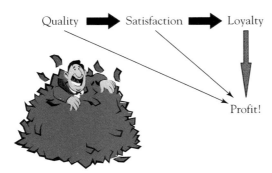

Quality ➡ Satisfaction ➡ Loyalty

Profit!

Source: Adapted from Oliver, *Satisfaction,* p. 403.

Studies that report on the value of a loyal customer are staggering. For example, Ford Motor Company has estimated the value of a one-point (percent) increase in owner loyalty to be worth $100 million in profit. In addition, loyal customers require less attention and allow firms to weather competitor attacks and budget tactical market moves.

Satisfaction is a judgment of a pleasurable level of consumption-related fulfillment, including levels of under- or overfulfillment. It involves emotional and cognitive appraisals. Satisfaction judgments can be made with respect to any or all of the aspects or stages of product and service experience. Satisfaction often reflects both positive and negative emotions. Satisfaction judgments are nested within the customer's life experience, and different customers are likely to make different satisfaction judgments about the same level of product or service performance. Individual judgments of satisfaction express a broader system of cultural values, meanings, beliefs, emotions, group relationships, and conflicts. When we look at the consumption experience over time, we realize that satisfaction with products and services shifts as current concerns and consumers' life projects shift.

Fulfillment, or the feeling of being satisfied, implies goals or standards that form a basis for comparison. Perceived quality is one important standards-based predictor of satisfaction. Expectations are another. Most satisfaction research has employed the expectancy–disconfirmation model as a way of understanding the relationship between standards and satisfaction.

The EDM model has limitations. Attributes, features, and dimensions that contribute to heightened levels of satisfaction may sometimes differ from attributes that contribute to heightened levels of dissatisfaction. Sometimes the consumer can't foresee the problems or benefits of a product before purchase. In other cases important influences on satisfaction are unpredictable. When expectations are abstract or ill formed, modeling satisfaction as a function of expectations may not be very useful.

One competing model identifies consumers' desires as a comparative standard for satisfaction. In a desires model, consumers believe that product attributes will deliver higher-level values. Fairness can also be an important comparative mechanism used in judging consumer satisfaction. Three dimensions of fairness that could influence satisfaction are procedural, interactional, and distributional.

When a product or service fails, the consumer often attempts to understand why. The degree of disappointment and anger felt and also intentions to repurchase and to complain are influenced by the attributions consumers make to explain why the product or service failed.

Satisfaction can simultaneously include a variety of positive and negative emotions. Five different response modes that might all be described as satisfaction are contentment, pleasure, delight, relief, and ambivalence.

In response to satisfying or dissatisfying purchase and consumption experiences, consumers may exercise one or more of four behavioral options. They may exit the exchange relationship. Alternatively, consumers may respond by speaking up; this is voice. The consumer may also continue to patronize the firm. We defined this loyalty as a deeply held commitment to rebuy or repatronize a preferred product or service consistently in the future. Consumers may also express their satisfaction or dissatisfaction through twist, the term we use to incorporate both positive and negative behaviors undertaken toward the firm.

The idea that higher perceived quality, higher levels of customer satisfaction, and more loyal consumers pay off has been widely supported by many different research efforts. Each firm and each industry in each country may find different levels and types of relationships among these variables.

key terms

active expectations   628
ambivalence response   636
contentment response   634
customer loyalty   640
critical incident technique   621
delight response   634
desires   629
desires model of satisfaction   629
dissatisfaction   618
distributional fairness   631
exit   637
expectancy–disconfirmation model of
   satisfaction (EDM)   625
expectations   625
fairness   631
fraudulent complaining   639

Homans's rule of justice   631
interactional fairness   631
internal state   617
negative disconfirmation   626
overfulfillment   617
passive expectations   628
perceived quality   619
pleasure response   634
positive disconfirmation   625
procedural fairness   631
relief response   635
satisfaction   617
satisfaction drivers   621
twist   641
underfulfillment   617
voice   637

review questions

1. Consider a recent purchase decision. Compare the criteria you used in making your choice with the factors that influenced your satisfaction. How were these criteria the same? How were they different?

2. Using the critical incident technique described in this chapter, interview three consumers about their most recent satisfying and dissatisfying service interactions. What factors do consumers name as causing them to feel satisfied or dissatisfied?

3. Consider your own purchase experiences. Try to think of examples where you used (a) desires and (b) fairness as your comparative standard in judging satisfaction.

4. Find examples of advertisements that seem to promise
    a. Contentment
    b. Pleasure
    c. Delight
    d. Relief

5. Choose a recent high-involvement or complex purchase decision. Describe the emotions you felt as you made this decision. Did you have mixed emotions? Explain.

6. During a business luncheon you sit at the table with a manager of a small electronics firm. He emphasizes that the key to customer loyalty is meeting customer expectations. Do you agree or disagree? What would you say? Explain your answer.

7. Interview three consumers about how they responded to a recent dissatisfying purchase experience. Categorize their responses in terms of exit, voice, continued patronage, and twist. See if you can use some of the models and discussion in this chapter to understand their responses.

8. What techniques could a company use to encourage their customers to complain?

9. Conduct an in-depth interview with a marketing professional. Ask him or her to describe
   a. How important customer satisfaction is to his or her business.
   b. How he or she works to generate customer satisfaction.
   c. What kinds of experiences he or she has had with dissatisfied consumers.

   Summarize your findings.

You Make the Call

Transformation in the Laundry Industry

Americans wash a whopping 200 billion pounds of laundry every year. In many parts of the world, laundry is still done as it has been for at least 4,000 years: people haul their baskets to the nearest river, pound the clothes clean on the rocks, and spread them in the sun to bleach and dry. But in the United States the chore of doing laundry has undergone a major transformation. Washing machines are one of the few commodities that cost less today than a generation ago. Doing laundry may be a lot easier than it used to be, but it is still a chore, and people are still looking for ways to make it less of a chore.

The United States has about 35,000 coin-operated laundries. Most are located in urban areas with large renter populations. Singles, especially those younger than 35, are much more likely to log hours at a Laundromat. The coin-laundry business is changing, however. One change is the growth of the wash/dry/fold service. People can bring in their dirty laundry and pick it up later all clean and folded. This service is moving into suburban areas and places with middle-class and upper-middle-class consumers.

Another segment of the laundry industry is beginning to offer hip, multiservice Laundromats. At Brain Wash in San Francisco customers can grab a bite or listen to live music and poetry readings while juggling loads. Stan Klein's Rock and Fold in Chicago treats customers to neon lights, movies on five screens, and gospel music. These Laundromats might be viewed as an attempt to change how consumers feel about doing laundry.

1. What type of satisfaction, if any, do you believe consumers associate with completing their laundry?

2. How are multiservice Laundromats trying to influence satisfaction?

3. What factors should Brain Wash consider in assessing satisfaction with its new multiservice Laundromat?

This case is adapted from material found at www.brainwash.com.

1. Based on an interview with a single, female social worker in her 30s living in the southeastern United States.

2. For us, Richard L. Oliver is "Dr. Satisfaction." Our understanding of the topic and its complexity has been resolutely influenced by his work. In this chapter we draw very heavily from his book *Satisfaction: A Behavioral Perspective on the Consumer* (New York: McGraw-Hill Companies, 1997).

3. Robert A. Westbrook and Richard L. Oliver, "The Dimensionality of Consumption Emotion Patterns and Consumer Satisfaction, *Journal of Consumer Research* 18 (June 1991), pp. 84–91; and Linda L. Price, Eric J. Arnould, and Sheila L. Deibler, "Service Provider Influence on Consumers' Emotional Response to Service Encounters," *International Journal of Service Industry Management* 6, no. 3 (1995), pp. 34–63.

4. Adapted from Oliver, *Satisfaction,* p. 13.

5. David T. Botterill, "Dissatisfaction with a Construction of Satisfaction," *Annals of Tourism Research* 14, no. 1 (1987), pp. 139–40; and John Deighton, "The Consumption of Performance," *Journal of Consumer Research* 19 (December 1992), pp. 362–72.

6. Chip Bell, "Turning Disappointment into Customer Delight," *Editor and Publisher,* August 6, 1994, pp. 48, 38.

7. Craig J. Thompson, William B. Locander, and Howard R. Pollio, "Putting Consumer Experience Back into Consumer Research: The Philosophy and Method of Existential Phenomenology," *Journal of Consumer Research* 16 (September 1989), pp. 133–47.

8. John E. Swan and Michael R. Bowers, "Services Quality and Satisfaction," *Journal of Services Marketing* 12, no. 1 (1998), pp. 59–72; and John F. Sherry, "Postmodern Alternatives: The Interpretive Turn in Consumer Research," in *Handbook of Consumer Behavior,* Thomas S. Robertson and Harold H. Kassarjian, eds. (Englewood Cliffs, NJ: Prentice Hall, 1991), pp. 548–91.

9. Craig J. Thompson, "Caring Consumers: Gendered Consumption Meanings and the Juggling Lifestyle," *Journal of Consumer Research* 22 (March 1996), pp. 388–407; and Susan Fournier and David Glen Mick, "Rediscovering Satisfaction," *Journal of Marketing* 63 (October 1999), pp. 5–23.

10. Slavenka Drakulić, *Café Europa: Life after Communism* (New York: Penguin Books, 1996).

11. Agnes T. Crane, "Satisfaction Guaranteed," *Business Mexico,* January 1, 1999, p. 56; Helena Ferna, "Need to Ensure That Customers Are Fully Satisfied," *Business Times,* February 8, 1999, p. 3; Richard M. Hodgetts, "Quality Lessons from America's Baldrige Winners, Malcolm Baldrige Quality Award," *Business Horizons* 37 (July 1994), pp. 74–78; and Mick James and Mary Huntington, "Customer Satisfaction: Measuring Client Satisfaction Is Anything but Straightforward," *Management Consultancy,* September 11, 1998.

12. "India: Zen Best Small Car, Says J. D. Power Asia Pacific," *Business Line,* March 24, 1999; Richard L. Oliver, "Whence Consumer Loyalty?" *Journal of Marketing* 63, Special Issue (1999), pp. 33–44.

13. For an interesting treatment of this subject, see Steven N. Silverman and Rajiv Grover, "Forming Perceptions of Overall Quality in Consumer Products: A Process of Quality Element Integration," Marketing Science Institute working paper, report no. 95-103, April 1995; and Jan-Benedict E. M. Steenkamp, "Conceptual Model of the Quality Perception Process," *Journal of Business Research* 21 (December 1990), pp. 309–33. See also C. A. Reeves and D. A. Bednar, "Defining Quality: Alternatives and Implications," *Academy of Management Review* 19, no. 3 (1994), pp. 419–46.

14. Leonard A. Morgan, "The Importance of Quality," in *Perceived Quality,* Jacob Jacoby and Jerry C. Olson, eds. (Lexington, MA: Lexington Books, 1985), pp. 209–32. See also David A. Garvin, "What Does 'Product Quality' Really Mean?" *Sloan Management Review,* Fall 1984, pp. 25–43.

15. Steenkamp, "Conceptual Model of the Quality Perception Process"; and William R. Darden and Barry J. Babin, "Exploring the Concept of Affective Quality: Expanding the Concept of Retail Personality," *Journal of Business Research* 29 (February 1994), pp. 101–9.

16. David K. Tse and Peter C. Wilton, "Models of Consumer Satisfaction Formation: An Extension," *Journal of Marketing Research* 25 (May 1988), pp. 204–12; Claes Fornell, "A National Customer Satisfaction Barometer: The Swedish Experience," *Journal of Marketing* 56 (January 1992), pp. 6–21; and Joseph J. Cronin and Steven A. Taylor, "Measuring Service Quality: A Reexamination and Extension," *Journal of Marketing* 56 (July 1992), pp. 55–67.

17. The most comprehensive of these is the structural equation modeling study performed by Cronin and Taylor, "Measuring Service Quality," which suggested that of alternative possible causal relationships between quality and satisfaction only the quality ⇒ satisfaction path was significant.

18. Fornell, "A National Customer Satisfaction Barometer."

19. David Garvin, "Competing on the Eight Dimensions of Quality," *Harvard Business Review,* November–December 1987, pp. 101–9.

20. P. Bonner and R. Nelson, "Product Attributes and Perceived Quality: Foods," in *Perceived Quality,* J. Jacoby and J. Olson, eds. (Lexington, MA: Lexington Books, 1985), pp. 64–79.

21. A. Parasuraman, Valerie A. Zeithaml, and Leonard L. Berry, "SERVQUAL: A Multiple-Item Scale for Measuring Consumer Perceptions of Service Quality," *Journal of Retailing* 64, no. 1 (Spring 1988), pp. 12–40.

22. *The Economist,* UK Edition, May 26, 1997, p. 43; Kathryn Frazer Winsted, "Service Behaviors That Lead to Satisfied Customers," *European Journal of Marketing* 34, nos. 3–4 (2000), pp. 399–417; Li-Wei Mai and Mitchell R. Ness, "Canonical Correlation Analysis of Customer Satisfaction and Future Purchase of Mail-Order Specialty Foods," *British Food Journal* 1010 no. 11 (1999) pp. 857–70; Stewart Robinson, "Measuring Service Quality: Current Thinking and Future Requirements," *Marketing Intelligence and Planning* 17, no. 1 (1999), pp. 21–32; and Syed Saad Andaleeb, "Determinants of Customer Satisfaction with Hospitals: A Managerial Model," *International Journal of Health Care Quality Assurance* 111, no. 6 (1998), pp. 181–87.

23. D. Chadee and J. Mattsson, "Customer Satisfaction in Tourist Service Encounters," *Journal of Travel and Tourism Marketing* 4 (Fall 1995), pp. 97–108; Tat Y. Choi and Raymond Chu, "Levels of Satisfaction among Asian and Western Travelers," *International Journal of Quality and Reliability Management* 17, no. 2 (2000), pp. 116–32; and D. Scott and D. Shieff, "Service Quality Components and Group Criteria in Local Government," *International Journal of Service Industry Management* 4, no. 2, (1993), pp. 18–25.

24. Valerie A. Zeithaml and Mary Jo Bitner, *Services Marketing* (New York: McGraw-Hill, 1996). See also the general discussion of customer-defined service standards, especially Chapters 5 and 8.

25. Lance A. Bettencourt and Stephen W. Brown, "Contact Employees: Relationships among Workplace Fairness, Job Satisfaction and Prosocial Service Behaviors," *Journal of Retailing* 73 (Spring 1997), pp. 39–61; and James L. Heskett, Thomas O. Jones, Gary Loveman, Earl W. Sasser, Jr., and Leonard A. Schlesinger, "Putting the Service Profit Chain to Work," *Harvard Business Review* 72 (March–April 1994), pp. 164–75.

26. Benjamin Schneider, J. J. Parkington, and V. M. Buxton, "Employee and Customer Perceptions of Service in Banks," *Administrative Science Quarterly,* June 1980, pp. 252–67; and Benjamin Schneider and David E. Bowen, "Employee and Customer Perceptions of Service in Banks: Replication and Extension," *Journal of Applied Psychology* 70 (1985), pp. 423–33.

27. Colby H. Chandler, "Quality: Beyond Customer Satisfactio—to Customer Delight," *Quality Progress,* October 1988, pp. 20–23.

28. Mary Jo Bitner, Bernard H. Booms, and Mary Stanfield Tetreault, "The Service Encounter: Diagnosing Favorable and Unfavorable Incidents," *Journal of Marketing* 54 (January 1990), pp. 71–84; and Mary Jo Bitner, Bernard H. Booms, and Lois A. Mohr, "Critical Service Encounters: The Employee's Viewpoint," *Journal of Marketing* 58 (October 1994), pp. 95–106.

29. Sarah Fisher Gardial, D. Scott Clemons, Robert B. Woodruff, David W. Schumann, and Mary Jane Burns, "Comparing Consumers' Recall of Prepurchase and Postpurchase Product Evaluation Experiences," *Journal of Consumer Research* 20 (March 1994), pp. 548–60; Arnould and Price, "River Magic"; and Lucy L. Henke, "A Longitudinal Analysis of the Ad Agency-Client Relationship: Predictors of an Agency Switch," *Journal of Advertising Research* vol. 35 (March–April 1995), pp. 24–30.

30. Arnould and Price, "River Magic"; Saad A. Metawa and Mohammed Almossawi, "Banking Behavior of Islamic Bank Customers: Perspectives and Implications," *International Journal of Bank Marketing* 16, no. 7 (1998), pp. 288–313; and Kamal Naser, Ahmad Jamal, and Khalid Al-Katib, "Islamic Banking: A Study of Customer Satisfaction and Preferences in Jordan," *International Journal of Bank Marketing* 17, no. 3, pp. 135–51.

31. See, for example, Michael D. Johnson, George Nader, and Claes Fornell, "Expectations, Per-

ceived Performance, and Customer Satisfaction for a Complex Service: The Case of Bank Loans," *Journal of Economic Psychology* 17 (1996), pp. 163–82.

32. Fournier and Mick, "Rediscovering Satisfaction."

33. For a related example (dealing with road travel), see Christy Fisher, "The Not-So-Great American Road Trip," *American Demographics,* May 1997, pp. 42–49.

34. Gardial et al., "Comparing Consumers' Recall of Prepurchase and Postpurchase Product Evaluation Experiences."

35. Richard L. Oliver, "Cognitive, Affective and Attribute Bases of the Satisfaction Response," *Journal of Consumer Research* 20 (December 1993), pp. 418–30.

36. Oliver, *Satisfaction,* pp. 66–97.

37. This section draws heavily from Oliver, *Satisfaction,* pp. 98–131. See also Eugene W. Anderson and Claes Fornell, "A Customer Satisfaction Research Prospectus," in *Service Quality: New Directions in Theory and Practice,* Roland T. Rust and Richard L. Oliver, eds. (Thousand Oaks, CA: Sage, 1994), pp. 241–68.

38. Jakia Kivela, Robet Inbakaran, and John Reece, "Consumer Research in the Restaurant Environment. Part 3: Analysis, Findings, and Conclusions," *International Journal of Contemporary Hospitality Management* 12, no. 1 (2000), pp. 13–30; and Sung-Joon Yoon and Joo-Ho Kim, "An Empirical Validation of a Loyalty Model Based on Expectation Disconfirmation," *Journal of Consumer Marketing* 17, no. 2 (2000), pp. 120–36.

39. Mark M. Davis and Janelle Heineke, "How Disconfirmation, Perception and Actual Waiting Times Impact Customer Satisfaction," *International Journal of Service Industry Management* 9, no. 1 (1998), pp. 64–73.

40. Jochen Wirtz and John E. G. Bateson, "Introducing Uncertain Performance Expectations in Satisfaction Models for Services," *International Journal of Service Industry Management* 10, no. 1 (1999), pp. 82–99.

41. For important early work on consumer mythology, see Sidney J. Levy, "Interpreting Consumer Mythology: A Structural Approach to Consumer Behavior," *Journal of Marketing* 45 (Summer 1981), pp. 49–61.

42. Richard L. Oliver, "Processing of the Satisfaction Response in Consumption: A Suggested Framework and Research Propositions," *Journal of Consumer Satisfaction, Dissatisfaction, and Complaining Behavior* 2 (1989), pp. 1–16; Westbrook and Oliver, "The Dimensionality of Consumption Emotion Patterns and Consumer Satisfaction," and Abbie Griffin and John R. Hauser, "The Voice of the Customer," *Marketing Science* 12, no. 1 (Winter 1993), pp. 1–27.

43. For a product peek, see Roy Furchgott, "Rebel without an Engine," *Business Week,* September 15, 1997, p. 8.

44. A. Parasuraman, Leonard L. Berry, and Valarie A. Zeithaml, "Understanding Customer Expectations of Service," *Sloan Management Review* 32 (Spring 1991), pp. 39–48; and David J. Ortinau and Robert P. Bush, "The Propensity of College Students to Modify Course Expectations and Its Impact on Course Performance Information," *Journal of Marketing Education* 9 (Spring 1987), pp. 42–52.

45. Rami Zwick, Rik Pieters, and Hans Baumgartner, "On the Practical Significance of Hindsight Bias: The Case of the Expectancy-Disconfirmation Model of Consumer Satisfaction," *Organizational Behavior and Human Decision Processes* 64 (October 1995), pp. 103–17.

46. David Glen Mick and Susan Fournier, "Technological Consumer Products in Everyday Life: Ownership, Meaning and Satisfaction," Marketing Science Institute, report no. 95-104, May 1995; and Fournier and Mick, "Rediscovering Satisfaction."

47. Fournier and Mick, "Rediscovering Satisfaction"; Richard W. Olshavsky and Richard A. Spreng, "A 'Desires as Standard' Model of Consumer Satisfaction," *Journal of Consumer Satisfaction/Dissatisfaction and Complaining Behavior* 2 (1989), pp. 49–54; and Richard A. Spreng and Richard W. Olshavsky, "A Desires Congruency Model of Consumer Satisfaction," *Journal of the Academy of Marketing Science* 21, no. 3 (1993), pp. 169–77. See also Gardial et al., "Comparing Consumers' Recall of Prepurchase and Postpurchase Product Evaluation Experiences." On the related idea of ideals as standards, see David K. Tse and Peter C. Wilton, "Models of Consumer Satisfaction Formulation: An Extension," *Journal of Marketing Research* 24 (August 1988), pp. 204–12.

48. Russell W. Belk, Güliz Ger, and Søren Askegaard, "Metaphors of Consumer Desire," in *Ad-*

vances in Consumer Research, vol. 23, Kim P. Corfman and John G. Lynch, eds. (Provo, UT: Association for Consumer Research, (1996), pp. 368–73; and Russell W. Belk, Güliz Ger, and Søren Askegaard, "Consumer Desire in Three Cultures: Results from Projective Research," in *Advances in Consumer Research,* vol. 24, Merrie Brucks and Deborah J. MacInnis, eds. (Provo, UT: Association for Consumer Research, 1997), pp. 24–28.

49. Two influential papers on this general topic are D. Kahneman, Jack L. Knetsch, and Richard Thaler, "Fairness as a Constraint on Profit Seeking: Entitlements in the Market," *American Economic Review* 76 (September 1986), pp. 728–41; and D. Kahneman, J. L. Knetsch, and R. H. Thaler, "Fairness and the Assumptions of Economics," *Journal of Business* 59, no. 4 (1986), pp. 285–300.

50. Susan M. Keaveney, "Customer Switching Behavior in Service Industries: An Exploratory Study," *Journal of Marketing* 59 (April 1995), pp. 71–82.

51. Thomas Madden, Peter Dickson, and Joel Urbany, "The Perceived Fairness of Automatic Teller Machine Charges: A Field Test of the Dual Entitlement Principle," working paper, Ohio State University, Columbus, 1994. See also Peter R. Dickson and Rosemary Kalapurakal, "The Use and Perceived Fairness of Price-Setting Rules in the Bulk Electricity Market," *Journal of Economic Psychology* 15, no. 3 (1994), pp. 427–48.

52. Drakulić, *Café Europa.*

53. Oliver, *Satisfaction;* and Cathy Goodwin and Ivan Ross, "Consumer Responses to Service Failures: Influence of Procedural and Interactional Fairness Perceptions," *Journal of Business Research* 25 (1992), pp. 149–63.

54. Marielza Martins and Kent B. Monroe, "Perceived Price Fairness: A New Look at an Old Construct," in *Advances in Consumer Research,* vol. 21 (Provo, UT: Association for Consumer Research, 1994), pp. 75–78.

55. Dwayne D. Gremler and Stephen W. Brown, "The Loyalty Ripple Effect: Appreciating the Full Value of Customers," *International Journal of Service Industry Management* 10, no. 3 (1999), pp. 271–93.

56. Tor Wallin Andreassen, "Antecedents to Satisfaction with Service Recovery," *European Journal of Marketing* 34, no. 1–2 (2000), pp. 156–75; Srinivas Durvasula, Steven Lysonski, and Subhas C. Mehta, "Business-to-Business Marketing Service Recovery and Customer Satisfaction Issues with Ocean Shipping Lines," *European Journal of Marketing* 34, no. 3–4 (2000), pp. 433–52; Richard A. Feinberg, Ik-Suk Kim, Leigh Hokama, Ko de Ruyter, and Cherie Keen, "Operational Determinants of Caller Satisfaction," *International Journal of Service Industry Management* 11, no. 2 (2000), pp. 131–41; and Mary Ann Hocutt, Goutam Chakraborty, and John C. Mowen, "The Impact of Perceived Justice on Customer Satisfaction and Intention to Complain in a Service Recovery," in *Advances in Consumer Research,* vol. 24, Merrie Brucks and Deborah J. MacInnis, eds. (Provo, UT: Association for Consumer Research, 1997), pp. 457–63.

57. For a related example, see Mary Jo Bitner, "Evaluating Service Encounters: The Effects of Physical Surrounding and Employee Responses," *Journal of Marketing,* April 1990, pp. 69–82.

58. See especially, Robert A. Westbrook, "Product/Consumption-Based Affective Responses and Post-purchase Processes," *Journal of Marketing Research,* August 1987, pp. 258–70; Westbrook and Oliver, "The Dimensionality of Consumption Emotion Patterns and Consumer Satisfaction"; and Haim Mano and Richard L. Oliver, "Assessing the Dimensionality and Structure of Consumption Experience: Evaluation, Feeling, and Satisfaction," *Journal of Consumer Research* 20 (December 1993), pp. 451–66.

59. See, for example, Eric J. Arnould, Linda L. Price, and Patrick Tierney, "High Water, Low Water: The Emotional Moments of River Rafting," working paper, University of South Florida, Tampa, 1997.

60. Four of these response modes are described in Oliver, *Satisfaction,* especially pages 339–42. The fifth of these, consumer ambivalence, is based on Cele Otnes, Tina M. Lowrey, and L. J. Shrum, "Toward an Understanding of Consumer Ambivalence," *Journal of Consumer Research* 24 (June 1997), pp. 80–93; and Fournier and Mick, "Rediscovering Satisfaction."

61. Malcolm Gladwell, "Annals of Retail: Clicks and Mortar," *The New Yorker,* December 6, 1999, pp. 106–15.

62. Examples of service experiences that could be termed delightful appear in Bitner, Booms, and

Tetreault, "The Service Encounter." See also, Linda L. Price, Eric J. Arnould, and Sheila L. Deibler, "Consumers' Emotional Responses to Service Encounters: The Influence of the Service Provider," *International Journal of Service Industry Management* 6, no. 3 (1998), pp. 34–63.

63. Zeithaml and Bitner, *Services Marketing.*

64. Otnes, Lowrey, and Shrum, "Toward an Understanding of Consumer Ambivalence"; and Fournier and Mick, "Rediscovering Satisfaction."

65. Albert O. Hirschman, *Exit, Voice and Loyalty: Responses to Decline in Firms, Organizations, and States* (Cambridge, MA: Harvard University Press, 1970). See also Albert O. Hirschman, "Exit, Voice, and Loyalty: Further Reflections and a Survey of Recent Contributions," *Social Science Information* 13 (February 1974), pp. 7–26. For a delightful and insightful follow-up that introduces the idea of "twist," see Veronique Aubert-Gamet, "Twisting Servicescapes: Diversion of the Physical Environment in a Re-Appropriation Process," *International Journal of Service Industry Management* 8, no. 1 (1997), pp. 26–41.

66. Kate Waterhouse and Ann Morgan, "Using Research to Help Keep Good Customers," *Marketing and Research Today,* August 1994, pp. 181–94.

67. Paul R. Timm, "Use the Profit Power of Customer Service," *Executive Excellence* 7 (June 1990), pp. 19–20.

68. Alan R. Andreasen, "Consumer Responses to Dissatisfaction in Loose Monopolies," *Journal of Consumer Research* 12 (September 1985), pp. 135–41.

69. Claes Fornell and Robert A. Westbrook, "The Vicious Circle of Consumer Complaints," *Journal of Marketing* 48 (1984), pp. 68–78.

70. Dwayne D. Gremler and Stephen W. Brown, "The Loyalty Ripple Effect: Appreciating the Full Value of Customers," *International Journal of Service Industry Management* 10, no. 3 (1999), pp. 271–93; and Linda L. Price and Lawrence F. Feick, "The Role of Interpersonal Sources in External Search: An Informational Perspective," in *Advances in Consumer Research,* vol. 11, Thomas C. Kinnear, ed. (Ann Arbor, MI: Association for Consumer Research, 1984), pp. 250–253.

71. William O. Bearden and Richard L. Oliver, "The Role of Public and Private Complaining in Satisfaction with Problem Resolution," *Journal of Consumer Affairs* 19 (Winter 1985), pp. 222–40; Mary Gilly and Betsy Gelb, "Post-purchase Consumer Processes and Complaining Consumer Behavior," *Journal of Consumer Research,* December 1982, pp. 323–28; Prashanth U. Nyer, "An Investigation into Whether Complaining Can Cause Increased Consumer Satisfaction," *Journal of Consumer Marketing* 17, no. 1 (2000), pp. 9–19; Roland T. Rust, Bala Subramanian, and Mark Wells, "Making Complaints a Management Tool," *Marketing Management* 1, no. 3 (1992), pp. 41–45; Magnus Söderland, "Customer Satisfaction and Its Consequences on Customer Behaviour Revisited," *International Journal of Service Industry Management* 9, no. 2 (1998), pp. 169–88; and Denise T. Smart and Charles L. Martin, "Manufacturer Responsiveness to Consumer Correspondence: An Empirical Investigation of Consumer Perceptions," *Journal of Consumer Affairs,* Summer 1992, pp. 104–28.

72. Mary C. Gilly and Richard W. Hansen, "Consumer Complaint Handling as a Strategic Marketing Tool," *Journal of Consumer Marketing* 2 (Fall 1985), pp. 5–16; Mary C. Gilly, "Postcomplaint Processes: From Organizational Response to Repurchase Behavior," *Journal of Consumer Affairs* 21 (Winter 1987), pp. 293–313; and Alan J. Resnick and Robert R. Harmon, "Consumer Complaints and Managerial Response: A Holistic Approach," *Journal of Marketing,* Winter 1983, pp. 86–97.

73. Claes Fornell and Nicholas M. Didow, "Economic Constraints on Consumer Complaining Behavior," in *Advances in Consumer Research,* vol. 7, Jerry Olson, ed. (Ann Arbor, MI: Association for Consumer Research, 1980), pp. 318–23.

74. Bearden and Oliver, "The Role of Public and Private Complaining in Satisfaction with Problem Resolution."

75. Chow-Hou Wee and Celine Chong, "Determinants of Consumer Satisfaction/Dissatisfaction towards Dispute Settlements in Singapore," *European Journal of Marketing* 25, no. 10 (1991), pp. 6–16.

76. Claes Fornell and Birger Wernerfelt, "Defensive Marketing Strategy by Customer Complaint Management," *Journal of Marketing Research* 24 (November 1987), pp. 337–46; and Claes Fornell and Birger Wernerfelt, "A Model for Customer Complaint Management," *Marketing Science* 7 (Summer 1988), pp. 287–98.

77. William O. Bearden and Jesse E. Teel, "An Investigation of Personal Influences on Consumer Complaining," *Journal of Retailing* 56 (Fall 1980), pp. 3–20; William O. Bearden and Jesse E. Teel, "Selected Determinants of Consumer Satisfaction and Complaint Reports," *Journal of Marketing Research* 20 (February 1983), pp. 21–28; and Rex H. Warland, Robert O. Herrmann, and Jane Willits, "Dissatisfied Consumers: Who Gets Upset and Who Takes Action," *Journal of Consumer Affairs* 9 (Winter 1975), pp. 148–63.

78. T. Bettina Cornwell, Alan David Bligh and Emin Babakus, "Complaint Behaviors of Mexican-American Consumers to a Third Party Agency," *Journal of Consumer Affairs,* Summer 1991, pp. 1–18; Sigfredo A. Hernandez, William Strahle, Hector Garcia, and Robert C. Sorenson, "A Cross-Cultural Study of Consumer Complaining Behavior: VCR Owners in the U.S. and Puerto Rico," *Journal of Consumer Policy,* June 1991, pp. 35–62; Ben Shaw-Ching Liu, Olivier Furrer, and D. Sudharshan, "Whether to Praise or to Complain Depends on Cultures: An Empirical Study in a Service Context," paper presented at the ninth annual Frontiers in Services Conference, Vanderbilt University, Nashville, 2000.

79. William O. Bearden and Barry J. Mason, "An Investigation of Influences of Consumer Complaint Reports," in *Advances in Consumer Research,* Thomas C. Kinnear, ed. (Ann Arbor, MI: Association for Consumer Research, 1984), pp. 490–95; J. B. Liefeld, F. H. Edgecombe, and Linda Wolfe, "Demographic Characteristics of Canadian Complainers," *Journal of Consumer Affairs* 9 (Summer 1975), pp. 73–80; Michelle Ann Morganosky and Hilda Mayer Buckley, "Complaint Behavior: Analysis by Demographics, Lifestyle and Consumer Values," in *Advances in Consumer Research,* Melanie Wallendorf and Paul Anderson, eds. (Ann Arbor, MI: Association for Consumer Research, 1987), pp. 223–26; and Judy Zaichkowsky and John Liefeld, "Personality Profiles of Consumer Complaint Letter Writers," in *Consumer Satisfaction, Dissatisfaction and Complaint Behavior,* Ralph L. Day, ed. (Bloomington: Indiana University, 1977), pp. 124–29.

80. Ralph L. Day, Laus Grabicke, Thomas Schaetzle, and Fritz Staubach, "The Hidden Agenda of Consumer Complaining," *Journal of Retailing* 57 (Fall 1981), pp. 86–106; Hernandez, Strahle, Garcia, and Sorensen, "A Cross-Cultural Study of Consumer Complaining Behavior"; and Angelina Villarreal-Camacho, "Consumer Complaining Behavior: A Cross-Cultural Comparison," in *American Marketing Association Educators' Proceedings,* Patrick E. Murphy et al., eds. (Chicago: American Marketing Association, 1983), pp. 68–73.

81. Güliz Ger (1996), "Problems of Marketization in Romania and Turkey," in *Consumption in Marketizing Economies,* Clifford Shultz, Russell Belk, and Güliz Ger, eds. (Greenwich, CT: JAI Press, 1996), pp. 127–56; Charlotte Klopp and John Sterrlickhi, "Customer Satisfaction Just Catching on in Europe," *Marketing News,* May 28, 1990, p. 5; Trina Thomas Raj, "Customer Satisfaction Is Carrefour's Top Priority," *New Straits Times* (Singapore), February 17, 1999, pp. 2, 18; and Harry S. Watkins and Raymond Liu, "Collectivism, Individualism and In-Group Membership: Implications for Consumer Complaining Behaviors in Multicultural Contexts," *Journal of International Consumer Marketing* 8, no. 3–4 (1996), pp. 69–96.

82. Marsha L. Richins and Bronislaw J. Verhage, "Cross-Cultural Differences in Consumer Attitudes and Their Implications for Complaint Management," *International Journal of Research in Marketing* 2 (1985), pp. 197–206.

83. Fornell and Westbrook, "The Vicious Circle of Consumer Complaints." See also, Rom Zemke and Kristin Anderson, "Customers from Hell," *Training* 27 (February 1990), pp. 25–33; and "Study Says It Pays to Settle All Complaints," *DM News,* September 1, 1984, p. 21.

84. Mary T. Curren and Valerie S. Folkes, "Attributional Influences on Consumers' Desires to Communicate about Products," *Psychology and Marketing* 4 (1987), pp. 31–45; and Marsha L. Richins, "Negative Word-of-Mouth by Dissatisfied Consumers: A Pilot Study," *Journal of Marketing* 47 (Winter 1983), pp. 68–78.

85. Jagdip Singh, "A Typology of Consumer Dissatisfaction Response Styles," *Journal of Retailing* 66 (Spring 1990), pp. 57–99; Cathy Goodwin and Susan Spiggle, "Consumer Complaining: Attributions and Identities," in *Advances in Consumer Research,* vol. 16, Thomas K. Srull, ed. (Ann Arbor, MI: Association for Consumer Research, 1989), pp. 17–22; and Jack Dart and Kim Freeman, "Dissatisfaction Response Styles among Clients of Professional Accounting Firms," *Journal of Business Research* 29 (1994), pp. 75–81.

86. Jacob Jacoby and Robert W. Chestnut, *Brand Loyalty: Measurement and Management* (New York, Wiley, 1978); and Alan S. Dick and Kunal Basu, "Customer Loyalty: Toward an Integrated Conceptual Framework," *Journal of the Academy of Marketing Science* 22 (Winter 1994), pp. 99–113.

87. Oliver, *Satisfaction,* p. 392.

88. Michael A. Jones and Jaebeom Suh, "Transaction-Specific Satisfaction and Overall Satisfaction: An Empirical Analysis," *Journal of Services Marketing* 14, no. 2 (2000).

89. Gremler and Brown, "The Loyalty Ripple Effect"; and Oliver, "Whence Consumer Loyalty?"

90. Gerard J. Tellis, "Advertising Exposure, Loyalty, and Brand Purchase: A Two-Stage Model of Choice," *Journal of Marketing Research* 25 (May 1988), pp. 134–44. This study used a 20-week interval to define the loyalty exhibited toward any one brand, which although it is still only a repeat-purchase measure increases confidence that something beyond spurious or happenstance loyalty is being measured.

91. Terence A. Oliva, Richard L. Oliver, and Ian C. Macmillan, "A Catastrophe Model for Developing Service Satisfaction Strategies," *Journal of Marketing* 56 (July 1992), pp. 83–95.

92. George B. Sproles and Elizabeth L. Kendall, "A Methodology for Profiling Consumers' Decision Making Styles," *Journal of Consumer Affairs* 20 (Winter 1986), pp. 267–79.

93. Oliver, "Whence Consumer Loyalty?"; Hugo Tranberg and Flemming Hansen, "Patterns of Brand Loyalty: Their Determinants and Their Role for Leading Brands," *European Journal of Marketing* 20, no. 3–4 (1986), pp. 81–109.

94. Robin A. Higie, Linda L. Price, and Julie Fitzmaurice, "Leaving It All Behind: Service Loyalties in Transition," in *Advances in Consumer Research,* vol. 20, Leigh McAlister and Michael L. Rothschild, eds. (Provo, UT: Association for Consumer Research, 1993), pp. 656–61; and Linda L. Price and Eric J. Arnould, "Commercial Friendships: Service Provider-Client Relationships in Context," *Journal of Marketing* 68 (October 1999), pp. 38–57.

95. The term *twist* is borrowed from Veronique Aubert-Gamet and Bernard Cove, "Exit, Voice, Loyalty and Twist: Consumer Research in Search of the Subject," Workshop on Interpretive Consumer Research, Oxford, April 10–12, 1997. Although we use the term more broadly here, our use is quite consistent with their idea of a creative consumer engaged in discreet restructuring of meanings, roles, and objects in the marketplace. See also Gamet, "Twisting Servicescapes"; and Michel de Certeau, *The Practice of Everyday Life* (Berkeley: University of California Press, 1984).

96. Leonard L. Berry, *On Great Service: A Framework for Action* (New York: Free Press, 1995).

97. "Individuals' Commission of Customer Fraud Acts: Theory Development and Managerial Insights," manuscript under review, *Journal of Marketing,* 1999.

98. Monroe Friedman, "Consumer Boycotts: A Conceptual Framework and Research Agenda," *Journal of Social Issues* 47, no. 1 (1991), pp. 149–68; and Robert O. Herrmann, "The Tactics of Consumer Resistance: Group Action and Marketplace Exit," in *Advances in Consumer Research,* vol. 20, Michael Rothschild and Leigh McAlister, eds. (Provo, UT: Association for Consumer Research, 1993), pp. 130–34.

99. Lisa Peñaloza and Linda L. Price, "Consumer Resistance: A Conceptual Overview," in *Advances in Consumer Research,* vol. 20, Leigh McAlister and Michael L. Rothschild, eds. (Provo, UT: Association for Consumer Research, 1993), pp. 123–28; and Richard Pollay and Banwari Mittal, "Here's the Beef: Factors, Determinants, and Segments in Consumer Criticism of Advertising," *Journal of Marketing* 57 (July 1993), pp. 99–115.

100. Peter Barrow, "Marketing to Generation X," *Canadian Manager,* March 1994, pp. 23–24; Judith Langer, "Twentysomethings: They're Angry, Frustrated, and They Like Their Parents," *Brandweek,* February 22, 1993, pp. 18–19; Karen Ritchie, *Marketing to Generation X* (Lexington, MA: Lexington Books, 1995); and Laurie Freeman, "Advertising's Mirror Is Cracked: Generation X Sees Ad World's Projected Image, and Isn't Buying It," *Advertising Age* 66 (February 6, 1995), p. 27.

101. This section is summarized from Oliver, *Satisfaction,* pp. 403–5.

Learning Objectives

After completing this chapter, you should be able to:

- Explain why meaning is an important issue for marketers.

- Describe the basic process of semiosis and the semiotic triangle.

- Have a working knowledge of the meaning transfer model.

- Appreciate the role of advertising and fashion in linking meanings to products.

- Describe both ordinary and ritualized processes through which consumers transfer meaning from products to themselves.

- Explain why spokespersons are important and describe the link between spokesperson selection and marketing success.

- Recognize the kinds of meanings that consumers value.

- Know why questions of meaning are important in cross-cultural contexts.

- Recognize the significance of collecting for consumers and marketers.

- Identify a variety of techniques through which consumers derive meaning and value from consumption.

Consumption Meanings[1]

Day of the Dead[2]

An interesting celebration takes place in Mexico and in many Chicano communities in North America during the first two days in November. These two days are set aside to remember the dead. November 1 is called *El dia de los santos,* or All Saints' Day, and is dedicated to the children who have died, and November 2 is called *El dia de los muertos,* All Souls' Day, and is for the mourning of adults. In the homes, families remember the children by preparing an altar, or *ofrenda,* decorated with flowers. The families that have lost a child are visited by relatives and friends who participate in the ceremony, which consists of a meal and perhaps some prayers. The meal includes a *tamal* seasoned with seeds, which symbolize happiness. The parents of the dead child place toys and foods that children like on the altar.

The ceremony for the adults who have died that follows on November 2nd is similar, except that the offerings include a special kind of sweet bread decorated with skulls and crosses called *pan de muerto.* The bakeries offer *pan de muerto* in various forms, including human beings and animals.

Since this is a grassroots celebration, the presence of death is manifested in all kinds of folkloric objects, including candies made of white sugar in the form of skulls, crosses, coffins, tombs, spirits, animals, fruits, and birds; wooden or clay toys in the form of coffins lined black; wire skeletons painted white in the form of devils, dancers, musicians, bullfighters, drunkards, salesmen, and *charros* (Mexican cowboys); funeral processions; as well as tables set with skulls, candles, food, and drink. For the

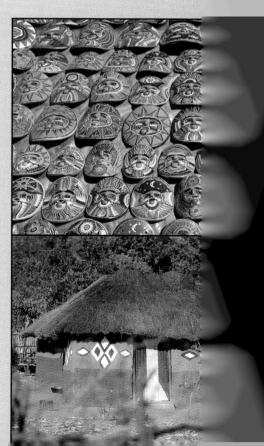

children there are white masks, skeletons, or toys in the form of a coffin from which a skeleton jumps out when a string is pulled and skeletons that dance when the little boards from which they hang are pressed.

The main activity on November 2 is a visit to the cemetery to bring offerings to the dead. This custom is kept alive in provincial towns and the countryside. The island of Janitzio on Lake Patzcuaro (state of Michoacán) is famous for its celebration. On the night of November 1, men, women, and children, holding candles in their hands, form a procession that winds slowly up the steep island streets to the hilltop where the cemetery is located. The church as well as the tombs is adorned with the yellow brilliance of the *cempasuchil* or *flor de muerto,* the flower of death. Yellow symbolizes death, and marigold petal crosses adorn many graves. Upon a framework of reeds people place fruits, squash, ears of corn, little figures of white sugar in the form of skulls, and little baskets of *pan de muerto.* The women sweep the graves and watch over the dead while the men turn the soil so the dead can "breath" and then partake of a little *charanda,* a native liquor. In the houses, an offering is prepared of those foods that the dead person liked best. The table for this offering is decorated with flowers, fruits, sweets, bread, and lighted candles.

Overview

In the preceding chapters we have been primarily concerned with addressing issues related to purchase and acquisition of products and services. In Chapter 1 we introduced the idea of the wheel of consumption, representing consumption as a moment in a cyclical process linked to disposition (discussed in Chapter 19), production, and acquisition. We focus on consumption processes in this chapter, specifically on the meanings that animate consumption behavior.

Consumer motives for purchase, consumption, and possession stem in great measure from the meaning of consumption acts and objects and the value that meaning provides. Some consumption activities seem to be primarily about the evocation of important meanings and values. The vignette on the Day of the Dead dramatically illustrates that the production, marketing, and consumption of a wide variety of toys, ornaments, food, drink, and even cleaning products help consumers to express the meanings of this old and deeply felt Mexican holiday. Tourists from other parts of Mexico may even visit the island of Janitzio to consume vicariously the traditional values expressed in the local celebration. Understanding consumers—why they buy things, why they retain some possessions and dispose of others—requires an understanding of meaning and value.

The idea that the purchase and consumption of goods is meaningful implies that goods and services are media of interpersonal communication; they are social phenomena conveying meanings that are shared by at least some others. Products can be personalized. Because people can form strong links with products and services they buy, they are important communicative devices. The Japanese wedding cake described in Consumer Chronicles

The scene is a modern Japanese wedding reception, a contemporary version of the traditional wedding feast that in prewar times often lasted three days. In the modern Shinto version of the Japanese wedding ceremony, during the *san-san-ku-do* ritual, *sake* (rice wine) is poured for the bride and groom by two young girls serving as shrine maidens, each of whom holds a vessel containing sake. Both vessels are decorated with *mizuhuki,* a decorated string made from paper, and a piece of origami representing a stylized butterfly, one male and the other female. Sake from both vessels is poured into the same cup, which is then shared by the bride and groom in succession.

One of the central objects in this ceremony is something entirely new. It is a wedding cake, of the kind one might expect to find at any American church wedding: three-tiered, frosted in white, topped with the inevitable miniature figures of a bride and groom in Western wedding dress. Behind it stand the real groom and his bride—perhaps also in Western dress or perhaps in traditional wedding kimono—the groom's hand steadying hers as she guides a be-ribboned sword into the cake. Cameras flash, and the guests applaud. As Japanese sensitivity to word play prohibits the use of the word "cut" at weddings, the emcee is forced to announce in stilted highly formal Chinese-style language: "The entering of the sword into the wedding cake has been performed." The bride and groom return to their seats and the celebrations continue, the cake forgotten. It is not divided and shared by all present, nor are pieces preserved—by freezing, as in the modern American custom—by the bridal couple as souvenirs of the event. More often than not, and as if to confirm our suspicion that it is all show and no substance, the Japanese version of the wedding cake, it turns out, is inedible.

Source: Walter Edwards, "Something Borrowed: Wedding Cakes as Symbols in Modern Japan," American Ethnologist 9 (November 1982), pp. 699–711.

18.1 is illustrative. From one perspective, the cake is just an example of consumer acculturation (see Chapter 5) and clever marketing by hotels and reception halls. Nonetheless, only a few Western consumption practices are integrated into Japanese weddings. Rice is never thrown at Japanese weddings given Japanese reverence for this product, for example. For the Japanese, the sweet (*amai*) cake provides a perfect symbolic association for children, and the "entering of the sword" makes a suitably discrete sexual reference to reproduction. A symbolic analysis thus reveals that the cake signifies reproduction and children. It marks the primary purpose of marriage in Japan, thus reinforcing other traditional symbols of union, such as the *san-san-ku-do,* or exchange of *sake.*[3]

There are many sources of meanings for the products and services that people consume. Marketing communications are only one such source, and marketed consumer products only one source of meaningful possessions.[4] Indeed, many of people's most meaningful possessions are not marketplace commodities at all, but things without much monetary value, such as heirlooms received from parents, photographs of family and friends, ex-

Nonmarket Sources of Meaning

changes of dinners and parties, gardens, and collections. A comparative study of favorite possessions in North America and West Africa identified gifts, handmade crafts, religious writings, and collections. The father of one of your authors artfully made her a bed stand from scrap lumber. The bed stand is meaningful, but these meanings could not be purchased. Meaning derives from the creative act of conception, the labor required to make it, and feelings conveyed from parent to child in the presentation of the bed stand. Over the years, memory also adds meaning to the bed stand. Recognizing the emphasis consumers in advanced consumer culture place on personal meanings, marketing managers are keen to determine meanings consumers value. Managers strive to provide consumers with value by linking apparently authentic meanings with their market offerings.[5]

Marketing Success and the Loss of Meaning	In consumer culture, marketers try to offer as many goods, services, images, ideas, and experiences as possible. This expansion happens by making more different things more widely exchangeable with each other. The concentration, expansion, and globalization of the consumer goods industries, the growth of affluent consumer segments in every nation, democratization, the loosening of class boundaries, and the greatly quickened flow of information through the commercial media contribute to market expansion and the quickened movement of consumer meaning.

The success of the global market system has some unintended consequences. One is that it tends to homogenize meaning and value. If the value of every product can be reduced to money, then there is a danger that things will come to mean little more than demonstrating that consumers have the money to obtain them. This fear seems justified since consumers often seem unable to find enduring meaning in mass-marketed goods.[6]

Both marketers and consumers face the problem of unsatisfactory meaning. Designers are strongly motivated to produce new and original products to satisfy restless consumers. Marketers strive to create differential meanings for what are often quite similar goods. To create and sustain differentiated positionings for products that are mostly similar, like soap powders and packaged foods, they must promote them heavily. Linking products to nonmarket meanings is one useful way of creating differentiation. Consumers wish to define a clear social or personal identity. Therefore, they strive to create a differentiated world of personal meanings from arrays of commercial products and through nonmarket mechanisms, such as customization, home production, and collecting. These ideas will be explained in more detail, but first we should explain *consumer meaning*.

Whose Meaning and Meaning for Whom? Semiosis

Consumers behave on the basis of the meanings that they ascribe to marketed products, services, and experiences. But what do we mean by **meaning?** When thinking about meaning and value, it's important to distinguish *the value in use to the consumer,* that is, the extent to which the consumer holds something dear, as distinct from a product's price, cost, and other measures of marketplace value. This value in use is what we call meaning.[7] A young child's irreplaceable but inexpensive favorite stuffed animal or blanket provides an example.

To understand consumer meaning, researchers draw on the science of meaning, called semiotics, which we introduced in Chapter 9. Semiotics argues that communication depends on **semiosis,** *the process of communication by any type of sign.* A **sign** is *anything* *that stands for something else.* For example, a series of Greek letters such as ΦβΚ is a sign that stands for the honorary fraternity Phi Beta Kappa. A simple marketing example of a sign would be a corporate logo, brand symbol, or brand name. Thus, the Intel logo found on many computer products stands for the Intel Corporation and its products. Similarly, Bibendum, the Michelin Man, stands for the Michelin tire company and its products. Some of the meanings of Bibendum are described in Industry Insights 18.1.[8] At a minimum, brand names and logos improve memory and product recall.[9] Brand names and logos also symbolize quality and predictability for consumers. This is true when consumers are unfamiliar with brands as in some developing and transitional economies. In Japan, brand names possess a mystique that connotes sophistication, internationalism, and taste. A novel called *Nantonaku, kirisutaru* that consisted largely of lists of brand-name goods and discussions of them sold three-quarter million copies, for example. Brands can serve as highly meaningful symbols for customers as when youth gangs members adopt branded team sports merchandise for their exclusive use. We discussed this in Chapter 15.[10]

Semiosis is a three-part process involving a sign, some object, and an interpretant, which is the meaning of the sign. This three-part system is called the **semiotic triangle.** Exhibit 18.1 illustrates the semiotic triangle and gives an example. Importantly, each semiotic triangle exists within a particular cultural context that provides consumers with the knowledge they need to interpret signs they encounter. In the advertisement for Johnny Walker Black Label Scotch Whisky, the black clarinet and sheet music are a sign of the scotch. In this context, the clarinet conveys certain meanings, a few of which are listed in Exhibit 18.1.

Exhibit 18.1 Semiotic Triangle

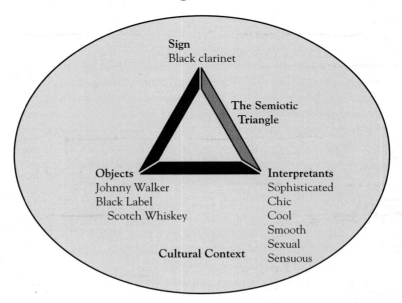

The relationships between sign, object, and interpretant are conventional. That is, meanings are relative to particular **communications communities** responding to them. Because they *share significant cultural capital* (see Chapter 6), members of a communications community agree, more or less, on these meanings. The clarinet as symbol of cool jazz requires a cultural knowledge of jazz that is not shared by everyone. Thus, meanings can vary dramatically between market segments.

We identify three different approaches to understanding the meanings of goods to consumers. First, we can examine the role of possessions in defining the self and creating

Using symbolic conventions to create brand meaning.

a sense of identity. In other words, possessions embody personal values and meanings. In the Day of the Dead vignette, offering up flowers, candles, toys, and candies to the memory of the dead is a poignant way of expressing personal values. The self is defined in part by reference to one's ancestors, and the products consumed link mourners to ancestors. As suggested in Chapter 7, narrative is one way that people make sense of their lives. Research has shown that consumers spontaneously construct life stories that involve brands. Drama ads, discussed later, encourage their use in stories. Stories may arise in brand-use situations. Brands can then become symbols of personal life stories. In these ways, they serve a referent or **indexical role.**[11]

The importance of consumer goods in providing a sense of self varies between areas of the world. As consumer societies become more complex and heterogeneous, more identity choices are available, which leads to more upheaval, ambiguity, and ambivalence. These tensions attach themselves to attributes like age, gender, physical beauty, social class, and race. As discussed in Chapter 7, people experience different and even conflicting identity choices and use consumption to reveal different aspects of themselves. Consumers in developed economies strive to create a distinctive sense of self through consumption choices and a range of **meaning transfer activities** that we will explain, including consuming, customizing, personalizing, grooming, and arranging goods.

In developing and transitional economies, in which identities of person and place remain more sharply etched in traditional roles, some consumers are also involved with consumer goods and concerned with public display. Venezuelans, for example, rank first among countries in their concern for personal beauty, and Venezuelan households spend a fifth of their income on personal care and grooming products.[12]

The meanings of possessions involve not only personal but public values as well. A second school of thinking about consumer meaning emphasizes the use of goods within a culture's social communication system. In other words, consumer goods convey public messages about identity and status. For example, Chevy trucks are "like a rock," and their performance substantiates this belief. Hence, an individual who is hardworking and who drives a Chevy truck will more than likely be perceived as being dependable and always there—like a rock.[13] Residents of the island of Janitzio mentioned in the vignette make a dramatic public statement about their traditional, regional Tarascan identity to other Mexicans through their unique way of celebrating the Day of the Dead. Neighbors communicate important social meanings by sharing food and drink and through the kind of altars they construct and the offerings they make to departed loved ones. Similarly, the wedding cake and sake consumed at Japanese weddings communicate public values.

Within particular cultural contexts and communications communities, consumers are usually able to decode the meaning of things. As we discussed in Chapter 6, consumers make inferences about social class, social status, and ethnic affiliations based on other consumers' displays of product constellations. The implication is that the meanings of consumer goods are always defined with regard to sets of recognized similarities and differences in goods. Research identifies many differences between ensembles of goods consumers within a given cultural context use to identity and differentiate groups from one another.

Across cultural contexts, people may draw mistaken inferences about the symbolic meanings of goods. For example, Danes and English consumers were shown the pair of pictures of English and Danish living rooms presented on page 662. Not only did the two groups of consumers find the taste of the other group distasteful, Danes incorrectly guessed that the English owners of this consumption set were older than they were, and the English incorrectly guessed the Danes were both younger and poorer than they were. An example such as this reinforces the importance of tailoring promotional content to the target market's cultural context in order to convey desired meanings.[14]

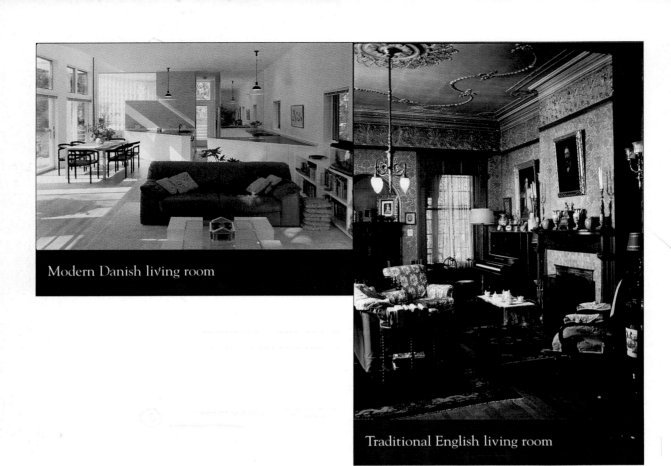

Modern Danish living room

Traditional English living room

A third approach looks for the particular meanings of goods and possessions that give them value. Referring to Consumer Chronicles 18.1, white is associated with death in traditional Japanese culture. The white of the Western-style wedding cake and dress make sense because on her wedding, the Japanese bride was traditionally felt to be lost to her birth family. The goods displayed, cleaned, consumed, and decorated on the Day of the Dead are meaningful. They convey meanings about family, tradition, religion, and the purpose of life. Another example of the conventional and context-specific meaning of goods is described in Consumer Chronicles 18.2.

Product meaning is changeable. One aspect of this is that it changes with time. For young people anything that is "bonzer" (Australian), "in," "hip," "phat," "fly," or "holic" (Japanese) changes as rapidly as youth-culture slang. The pace of change in meaning makes youth marketing especially difficult.

Second, as already illustrated by the household furnishings example, meaning is unstable across market segments. Marketers can never be certain that their images convey the meanings they wish. Consumers extract their own meanings. Idiosyncratic interpretations drawing on personal experience are common. In one study, only half the people questioned identified the most commonly given meaning for a familiar product. For example, the most frequent association with James Bond movies was "sexy girls," but only 38 percent of the subjects mentioned this meaning; the most frequent association with Breyer's ice cream was "natural," which 55 percent of subjects mentioned. Researchers have also discovered that males and females see different themes of print ads, and they even provide radically different descriptions of the advertising images themselves. This instability of meaning emphasizes the importance of carefully targeting marketing communications.

(3) A third problem is the meanings of things are contested by social groups and market segments. In 2000, the web portal Yahoo! was taken to court in France for allowing access to Nazi collectibles auctioned on eBay. French law forbids broadcast of Nazi-related materials, having determined that they are highly objectionable. However, some collectors may simply find them of historic interest. Clearly different groups contest the meanings of Nazi collectibles. The antimarketing websites mentioned in Chapter 17 also represent disagreements about the meaning of brands and firms. Firms must consider and respond when the meanings of their brand or firm is in question. An area on Procter & Gamble's website is devoted to dispelling rumors about its man-in-the-moon logo. We'll discuss the malleability of meaning further, but first we need to describe what kinds of meanings products may convey to consumers.[15]

Types of Meanings

Consumers' market choices are determined by a variety of values or meanings. Without prior research, marketers rarely know in advance which meanings are pertinent to a specific consumption behavior. Most consumption objects, services, and experiences have multiple meanings, both public and private. The meanings derive from a variety of sources.

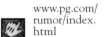 www.pg.com/rumor/index.html

Utilitarian Meanings

Traditionally, marketers viewed market choices and consumer preferences as driven by functional or utilitarian value. **Utilitarian meaning** is the *perceived usefulness of a product in terms of its ability to perform functional or physical tasks.* **Functional value** derives from *functional or physical attributes.* The attributes considered generally relate to performance, reliability, durability, number and type of product features, and price. For example, for some farmers an important functional attribute of genetically modified corn (or maize) seed is its resistance to the herbicides they also employ to control noxious weeds.

Functional meanings are important both for product category and brand-choice decisions. For instance, a consumer with no dependents will perceive little functional value in term life insurance designed to provide financial protection to survivors. This same person might see value in a long-term annuity, which contributes to financial security at retirement. Toothpaste brands are promoted on the differential presence of such functional attributes as fluoride, baking soda, antitartar substances, and breath fresheners. In business-to-business marketing situations, purchasing agents might choose suppliers on the basis of ISO 9000 quality standards, delivery times, credit terms, price, and other functional attributes.

Utilitarian or functional themes are commonly found in advertisements. In a recent study of over 400 ads from the People's Republic of China, informational cues of this type predominated. Availability was emphasized in 99 percent of ads. Performance, a functional attribute, appeared in 48 percent of ads; quality appeared in 23 percent. Price was explicitly mentioned 17 percent of the time. To the majority of low-income, highly involved consumers, utilitarian information is highly valued because most Chinese are just learning to consume. Chinese governmental policy stresses the importance of conveying utilitarian meanings in ads.

Similarly, a study of Saudi Arabian television commercials found product performance and quality were the most frequently employed cues. Again, this is appropriate in a cultural context in which consumers are unfamiliar with many consumer goods. In addition, use of advertising portrayals of emotional family relationships would be inappropriate in spite of the central place family assumes in Saudi society. Many Saudis would view this as a profane use of sacred relationships. In contrast, ads in the United States and Japan contain significantly less utilitarian content meanings. By one estimate, only 39 percent of U.S. print ads contain at least two informational cues, in contrast to 77 percent of the ads in China.[16]

Utilitarian or functional meanings are also associated with the things that people own. In a recent study of North American consumers, functional meanings including financial value accounted for almost 27 percent of responses to questions about objects' meanings. In a study of West Africans, new to the world of mass-produced consumer goods, 22 percent indicated that functional utility accounted for their favorite object preferences.

In the Triad countries, utilitarian meanings are commonly ascribed to everyday shopping experiences as well. Many see shopping as a kind of work. Some consumers also view museums and art galleries primarily as a means to acquire useful skills or ideas.[17]

Sacred and Secular Meanings

Another way to approach consumer meanings is to consider the concepts of the sacred versus the secular. Consumers sometimes express certain aspects of the sacred in their consumption behaviors. Sacred properties are summarized in Exhibit 18.2. Not all sacred things share all of these properties, but to be sacred a thing must share some of them.

Exhibit 18.2 Sacred Qualities

1. Things seem to belong to a different order of reality.
2. Things elicit strong approach as well as strong avoidance reactions.
3. Objects are contaminated with sacredness.
4. Communication with the sacred is established through sacrifice.
5. Sacred things stand apart from what is ordinary.
6. Individuals feel a focused emotional attachment to sacred things.
7. The sacred is often made concrete in a tangible representation.
8. Ritual surrounds the contact of ordinary persons with the sacred.
9. Often repeated myths document the status of sacred things.
10. Sacred things cannot be understood logically but are mysterious.
11. The spirit of *communitas* (status equality) emerges between participants in sacred experiences.
12. The sacred is capable of producing ecstatic experiences.
13. Sacred things are often inalienable; they cannot be bought and sold.

Source: Russell W. Belk, Melanie Wallendorf, and John F. Sherry, Jr., "The Sacred and Profane in Consumer Behavior: Theodicy on the Odyssey," *Journal of Consumer Research* 16 (June 1989), pp. 1–38.

Exhibit 18.3 Sacred Categories and Examples

1. **Places:** sacred sites such as Jerusalem, Lourdes, Mecca, Axum (Ethiopia), the Forbidden City (China); might also include battlefields (Verdun, Gettysburg) and locations of massacres (My Lai, Wounded Knee); dwellings, buildings (the Parthenon, the Louvre); and certain natural settings (the [Wild] West, National Parks).
2. **Times:** Sacred times include past events such as D-Day or Christian Easter; cyclically occurring events such as Islamic prayers, the secular weekend, harvest festivals; birth and naming days; episodes in certain otherwise secular consumption events, such as the playing of national anthems during sporting events.
3. **Tangible things:** Relics (both religious and secular), religious objects, things identified as sacred because of their rarity and beauty, such as certain art works; things that represent the great ideas, such as the Magna Carta or the U.S. Constitution; natural objects symbolizing life, creation, and renewal.
4. **Intangible things:** Magic formulas, dances, names, songs, fraternity and sorority rituals, recipes, and secrets.
5. **Persons or other beings:** Gods, prophets, and saints are religious examples. Military and athletic heroes, film, TV, and rock stars (Elvis, John Lennon, Madonna, Michael Jackson) and a variety of celebrities provide secular examples.
6. **Experiences:** At sacred times and places, experiences such as pilgrimages—both religious (Mecca) and secular (Graceland)—may be sacred. Certain ritual meals (Thanksgiving, Id-l-Fitr) are sacred. Participants and spectators regard certain extreme athletic activities (river rafting, high-altitude climbing) and spectator sports (World Cup, Tour de France, Super Bowl) as sacred.

Source: Russell W. Belk, Melanie Wallendorf, and John F. Sherry, Jr., "The Sacred and the Profane in Consumer Behavior: Theodicy on the Odyssey," *Journal of Consumer Research* 16 (June 1989), pp. 1–38.

The **sacred meaning** adheres in those *things that are designed or discovered to be supremely important.* Marketers may benefit by positioning products on sacred characteristics. Products that link consumers to one another and to nature and family or those offering emotional (always mysterious) benefits are positioned near the sacred pole of consumer meanings.

A variety of consumption phenomena can be experienced as sacred. These fall into six categories.[18] These categories and some examples are summarized in Exhibit 18.3. Marketers may benefit by linking consumption to sacred phenomena of the types discussed in Exhibit 18.3, such as the paraphernalia sold at religious shrines. In addition to products related to categories identified in Exhibit 18.3, a "sacred" positioning is useful for marketing health, green, and organic products.

Islamic commodities in Cairo, Egypt, provide a striking example of sacred commodities. Among ordinary people, the consumption of prayer beads, Islamic posters, banners, cards, and stickers bearing verse from the Koran become automatic triggers for devotional acts and are responded to as physical manifestations of God's presence. Similarly, in a study among some West Africans, nearly half of the male informants indicated that items with Islamic or magical connotations were among their favorite possessions. Similarly, more than 50 percent of a sample of Indians residing in Bombay cited religious items, a family shrine, a family idol, or a guru's photo as favorite possessions.[19]

We may think of the secular properties of things as the reverse of sacred ones. As an example of a product with a **secular meaning**, Static Guard spray is promoted as a technological solution designed to reduce static electric cling of some garments. Note that static cling is a potentially embarrassing but natural phenomenon. Similarly, Oil of Olay skin moisturizer is represented as a technological intervention that can overcome the natural aging process, which many in Western consumer culture see as undesirable. Oil of Olay helps the consumer fight nature. Similarly, Nuprin is a pain reliever that works "even on the worst headache pain." As such, it is a solution to an undesirable natural event, headache. From these examples, you might conclude that products most likely to benefit from positioning near the secular pole of meaning are those that can be used by consumers to counteract unwanted natural events (e.g., personal grooming products) and to conquer or dominate relevant others (e.g., sports equipment, apparel, high-performance products and services, financial products).[20]

Consumers are more likely to interpret experiences as involving the sacred than products. Some Canadian museum patrons characterize museum going as a sacred event. A sense of sanctity was associated with the wish to be surprised, humor, play, intimacy, discovery, self-knowledge and growth, and feeling "right there." The reasons for this feeling are not surprising. Similar to holy places (see Exhibit 18.3), museums enforce special codes of conduct, make formal use of space, employ dramatic and specialized architecture, dispense specialized knowledge, and set people and objects apart from everyday life (i.e., the objects in museums may not be touched). Museums also emphasize the authenticity and uniqueness of their collections. These features contribute to the sense of sacred meanings museums convey. Shopping malls have also been conceived as creating sacred space through use of the same architectural techniques as museums.[21]

| Hedonic Meanings | The value of goods, services, and experiences can also be based on hedonic or aesthetic values. Products acquire **hedonic meaning** when *associated with specific feelings or when they facilitate or perpetuate feelings.* Exhibit 18.4 shows one model that suggests the hedonic meanings of consumption can be positioned in a quadrant consisting of four emotional elements. For example, the excitement of an amusement park ride is made up of pleasure and arousal components, whereas the contentment associated with drowsing at a sunny resort beach consists in pleasure and sleepiness components. |

Music, art, and religious artifacts and the places they are consumed are associated with emotional value and hedonic meaning. These products may also symbolize past times and significant others. Products that affect self-image such as clothing, cosmetics, plastic surgery, health foods, tattoos, and other items on public display also provide hedonic value. Consumption phenomena as diverse as the explosion of popular music on cassette

Exhibit 18.4 A Model of Hedonic Meaning

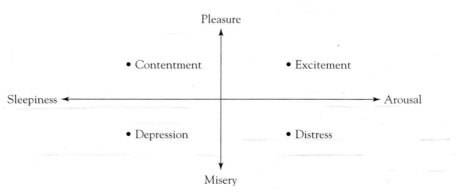

Source: Adapted from James A. Russell, "A Circumplex Model of Affect," *Journal of Personality and Social Psychology* 39, no. 6 (1980), pp. 1161–78.

tapes in developing countries, karaoke players and clubs, oldies-oriented music radio stations, and recreational and home entertainment equipment may all be explained with reference to emotions such as passion, excitement, romance, and nostalgia. Seemingly utilitarian items may also be associated with hedonic meanings. Many consumer products arouse feelings of comfort and security through their associations with pleasant childhood experiences, remembered places, and loved ones. In a recent North American study, hedonic meanings accounted for at least 22 percent of responses to questions about the meaning of objects. We discussed nostalgia and remembered consumption in Chapter 12.[22]

Familiar brands may remind people of loved ones and comfort them. Many consumers have fond associations with remedies like Vicks Vaporub or foods like Nutella used in childhood. Comfort meaning lies somewhere in the pleasure/sleepiness quadrant of Exhibit 18.4. Indeed, consumers' **brand equity** involves the accumulated history and sentiment attached to particular brands. Loyal consumers tend to purchase such brands regularly. In some cases where the emotional bond is particularly intense, brands may be imbued with sacred meanings.[23]

One of the most potent sources of hedonic meanings available to consumers are experiences. Travel, leisure, and tourist firms and recreational services are all primarily in the business of delivering hedonic meanings to consumers. These meanings often take the form of stories. Shopping too may be valued for its entertainment value and emotional worth. Street markets, themed retail spaces such as Niketown, ESPN Zone, and even Internet auction sites like eBay are noted for their hedonic meanings. One study showed that young girls found that going to the store with other children unsupervised was charged with emotion. Hanging out in commercial malls may also provide poor, inner city consumers with entertainment not available on public streets. In these experiences, perceived freedom, fantasy fulfillment, personal growth, experimentation with identity, and escapism may all be part of the meanings derived.[24]

Emotional meanings of consumption are not always positive. Research on addiction, **compulsive consumption,** and **terminal materialism** (or greed) illustrate this dark side of consumer meanings. Compulsive consumers have extremely intense material cravings that they project onto purchase or consumption without experiencing any enduring satisfaction. Some consumers engage in compulsive consumption due to feelings of inadequacy, others due to strong impulsive drives. Addicts represent an extreme case where addictive products (e.g., drugs, alcohol) or experiences (e.g., gambling) are used to create and maintain a stable, if distorted, sense of self. People afflicted with terminal materialism, a less debilitating affliction than addiction or compulsive consumption, include those who amass great collections of art, crafts, books, and so forth. They invest goods with the power to attain some sort of personal immortality.[25]

Social Meanings

As discussed in previous chapters, especially Chapter 6, social values exert a strong influence on many product and brand decisions. There is a **reflexive relationship** between social relationships and the goods individuals consume. Reflexivity means that in consumer society, *people intentionally communicate statements about who they are, what groups they identity with, and those from which they are different primarily through consumer goods. Others tend to see what people consume as expressions of who those people are.* Thus, products can be expressive of who consumers are and to whom they are connected socially (e.g., heirlooms and family photographs).

Much of social life is made up of social scripts, coherent sequences of events expected by individuals and involving them as participants or observers. People rely on the symbolic aspects of products to enact social scripts properly. For example, the U.S. Thanksgiving feast revolves around consumption of certain foods (turkey, stuffing, and cranberry sauce) as well as branded products considered central to particular family recipes. Similarly, in the Chinese Moon Festival moon cakes play a central role, and as in U.S. Thanksgiving, participants should themselves be stuffed. The Islamic Feast of Sacrifice imposes on male household heads the obligation to sacrifice, grill, and share the meat from a ram.[26]

Consumer goods can be used both to express and alter social meanings, through the conspicuous consumption discussed in Chapter 6, for example. Goods and services may acquire social value through their association with positively or negatively valued reference groups, as discussed in Chapter 15.

Some consumers organize around their interactions with brands and simultaneously create meaningful social relationships and negotiate brand meanings. They do this by using the brand to build the social group and sharing personal experiences with the brand, emphasizing some aspects of brand meaning while rejecting others. For example, a group of young Englishwomen formed around the consumption of Häagen-Dazs ice cream. Elaborating on a sexually suggestive ad campaign, consuming the brand became an occasion for getting together, and the ads became part of the group's shared fantasy life.[27]

Groups often dispute the social meanings of goods. The European powers enforced Western dress codes on school children in their former colonies as part of their "civilizing" mission. The consumption of symbolically charged goods can fuel debate, as when brand names or products associated with gang membership or the Islamic veil associated with reactionary fundamentalism are banned in public schools and uniforms are imposed. In these cases people try to control what they fear through symbolic means. Controversy about the social meanings of goods extends into fields such as law enforcement and health care, where studies show that uniforms and civilian clothing influence consumers' perceptions of the quality of service delivery differently.[28]

Movement of Meanings: Origins of Meaning[29]

From where does the meaning of goods and services come? Fundamentally, meaning is a product of consumer experience. Meanings usually develop from an initial state of vagueness to a state of refinement and stability. Once formed, meanings also may decay and disintegrate. They are formed in social interactions and respond to the definitions, denials, and affirmations given by others. People thrown into interaction, having similar ranges of experience, and sharing cultural capital develop common meanings about consumer goods and experiences. In fact, as we have said, consumption involves both the formation and expression of collective meanings. Innovative marketers, designers, artists, and everyday consumers themselves may develop new goods and services, or new arrangements of goods and services, through which meanings can take definite form. Collective taste will be an active force in an ensuing process of selection, setting limits and guiding the development of meaning. At the same time, meanings undergo refinement and organization through attachment to products, services, and experiences and to specific social groups.[30]

The meaning transfer model is shown in Exhibit 18.5. This model suggests that consumer meanings move between three locations: (1) the culturally constituted world, (2) the good (product, service, or experience), and (3) groups of consumers. Meaning moves in a trajectory between world and good, and good and consumer or consuming unit. As discussed in Chapter 5, this world is constituted by culture through categories and principles. Cultural categories segment time, space, nature, and the human community. Class, status, gender, age, and occupation (as discussed in Chapter 6) are examples of cultural categories

Exhibit 18.5 Meaning Transfer Model

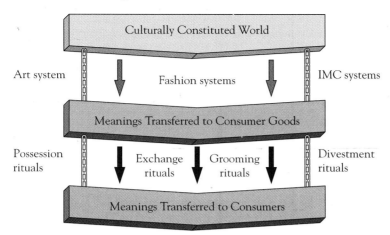

Source: Grant McCracken, "Culture and Consumption: A Theoretical Account of the Structure and Movement of the Cultural Meaning of Consumer Goods," *Journal of Consumer Research* 13 (June 1986), pp. 71–84.

that create a system of distinctions that organize the world. In addition to the cultural categories that compose the scaffolding of consumer meanings, meaning is also shaped by cultural principles. Cultural principles are the concepts, values, assumptions, and organizing ideas that allow phenomena to be distinguished, grouped into categories, ranked, and interrelated.

Acting in conformity with the cultural blueprints comprised of cultural categories and principles, members of a community or market segment constantly play out the utilitarian, personal, sacred, secular, hedonic, and social meanings of things through their purchase and consumption decisions. In an important sense, members of consumer culture are constantly engaged in the construction of the world in which they live: defining and redefining the meanings of self, community, and products and services themselves. Consumers' expression of likes and dislikes (cultural principles) not only distinguishes goods from one another but also distinguishes consumers from one another. In this way consumers are also divided into cultural categories. Thus, in Japan where people dress to meet social roles, students, businessmen, bureaucrats, intellectuals, office ladies, and youth-culture persons are all easily recognized through stereotypical clothing choices. In this context consumer likes and dislikes tend toward fine and subtle distinctions to which marketers are finely attuned.[31]

Linking Cultural Meanings and Product Meanings[32]

Marketing communications are a vehicle for connecting cultural meanings to consumption objects. As shown in Exhibit 18.5, cultural production systems discussed in Chapter 16 like the advertising, retailing, and fashion industries actively influence the meanings that are associated with goods. For example, Japanese retailers invented the cultural category of early autumn fashions to create a new product positioning.[33]

Marketing communications work to transfer meaning by bringing together the consumer good and a culturally particular representation of the world. To effect the transfer, the advertiser typically begins with the advertised product or service. Then, a communication plan is created that identifies particular meanings to be associated with the brand. The advertiser also identifies where the desired meanings to be associated with the brand are resident in the world in terms of categories of time, place, emotion, and person. He or she must choose from the alternatives established by the available network of cultural categories and principles recognized by the intended audience. Advertising formats (e.g., humor, fantasy, or slice-of-life) and treatments (e.g., drama, lecture, soap opera; one or two-sided portrayal) are selected to portray the world in a way that associates the desired meanings with the product. Verbal and visual conventions are used to provide the recipient of the advertising message with the chance to decode the intended link between the representation and the consumer good portrayed.

In the advertising model of meaning transfer depicted in Exhibit 18.6, the source of a communication includes the sponsor, author, and persona. The sponsor is the firm; its name permeates the advertisement. The author is an agency or group within a firm that collectively creates the message. The **persona** is *the spokesperson depicted or implied within the advertisement itself.* When a spokesperson is employed, the persona is explicit. When a spokesperson is not seen or heard, the persona is implicit, conveyed through other elements of the communication. The persona always is a fiction, crafted for the purposes of the advertisement even when the persona imitates real-life words spoken by a real-life person, as when Britney Spears promotes L'Oréal products. For example, popular Indian film star Ashok Kumar served as a commentator for a popular educational soap opera "Hum Log," summing up the moral lessons of each episode. In spite of the fact that he was an actor, he often received letters urging him to show more understanding of the soap opera characters. Although the persona is a symbolic phenomenon, not a part of real life, consumers may respond to them as if they were real.[34]

| Advertising Texts and Consumption Meanings | The message is the advertising text, a symbolic statement that links signs, interpretants, and meanings together. The message presumes or instructs consumers about meaningful relationships. The model in Exhibit 18.6 identifies some available message forms. Autobiography supposes a first-person account, as in a testimonial. Narrative employs the third person (he, she, it). Dramas do away with narration, allowing human or cartoon characters to act out events directly. Details about these and other message forms are shown in Ex- |

Exhibit 18.6 Advertising Model of Meaning Transfer

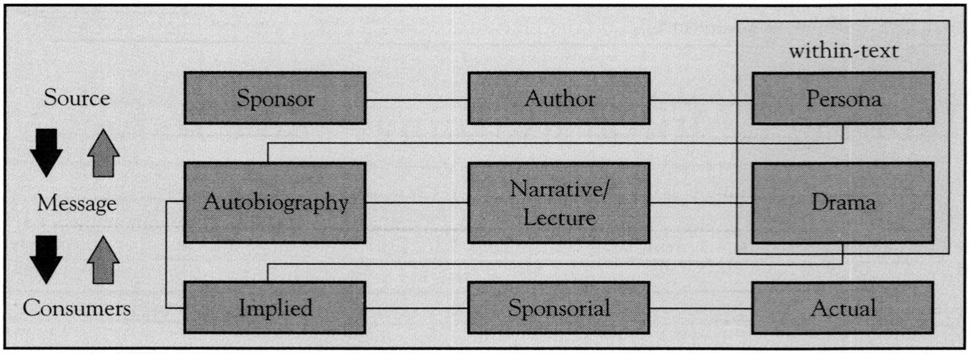

Source: Adapted from Barbara A. Stern, "A Revised Communication Model for Advertising: Multiple Dimensions of the Source, the Message, and the Recipient," *Journal of Advertising* 23 (June 1994), pp. 5–15.

hibit 18.7. Remember, the transfer of meaning supposes consumers who understand these message forms and can interpret the meanings presented within them.

Turning now to message content, it might be useful for you to imagine that advertising serves as a kind of **culture/consumption dictionary.** Its entries are *products, services, and experiences, and their definitions are cultural meanings.* Advertising typically does not draw on the entire range of meanings available in a culture but on a narrower, widely understood set in order to communicate to as many members of a target market as possible. Meanings must not be too hard for consumers/readers to understand. For example, animal characters are widely used brand symbols because most consumers understand animals' cultural meanings. Animal logos facilitate meaning transfer. However, as the technological ability to measure media preferences and customize messages increases, the constraints on symbols and meanings used in marketing communications too may loosen.[35]

The full details of meaning transfer in advertising are still being worked out. But we can discuss some figures of speech at the core of the culture/consumption dictionary employed in ads. Referring back to the semiotic triangle addressed earlier, we distinguished sign, interpretant, and object. Ads use figurative language to develop links between sign, object, and interpretant. For example, ads often use **similes,** *figures of speech that explicitly uses a comparative term such as "like" or "as."* Citizen Nobilia ads use similes to link wristwatches (the object) with animals (the sign), such as "As beautiful as a peacock." The ads aim to transfer the evocative associated meanings (the interpretant) of peacocks (the object) to their wristwatches.

Exhibit 18.7 Advertising Genres and Subgenres

1. **Lecture:** Informational content is emphasized. The message source implicitly is speaking directly to the reader. The ads use arguments to establish the validity of asserted claims; provide structured reasons in support of claims.
2. **Report:** Specific data are reported to support a claim or general principle that supports a claim. Comparative advertising for appliances and industrial equipment often adopts this mode to establish the claim of product superiority. Sometimes, these ads take the form of testimonials.
3. **Syllogism:** Claims and findings are advanced, and the reader is invited to deduce the implicit claim of product superiority. This category includes the simple announcement ad, which is common in retailing and in marketing bland industrial products.
4. **Drama:** Employs narrative, metaphor, and other literary devices to convey meaning. Dramatic ads tell a story. There is no explicit message source. For example, American Tourister asserts bellboys are gorillas when it comes to handling luggage. Merrill Lynch invokes the "herd apart" with its lone bulls. The pink bunny's (long-lasting) Energizer batteries enable it to escape King Kong.
5. **Allegory or fable:** In ads of this type, a claim is argued by deduction, but the terms employed are symbolic rather than factual. The parable of ring-around-the-collar resolved with soap powder is an example. The traveler's checks (American Express) lost or stolen in a foreign land is also an advertising fable.
6. **Myth/transformation:** Here, the object of the ad emphasizes the value or interpretation to be given to an event. The event is recounted figuratively rather than literally. In argumentation by myth, the story transforms the event's meanings. For example, Bombay Sapphire gin turns into (priceless) gemstones as it splashes out of the glass.
7. **Soap Opera:** Uses episodic, ongoing narratives, whose ostensible subject is domestic relationships in real time. These ads feature simple, unidimensional characters, and assume traditional, middle-class values and a feminine aesthetic.

Advertising copy also makes extensive use of **metaphors,** which are *like similes but with the comparative term omitted.* Examples include "Foster's is Australian for beer," "Alitalia is Italy," and the Jaguar XJ-S "is the stuff of legends." In these cases, Australia, Italy, and legend are the meaningful signs the advertisers wish to associate with the product. Visuals are typically employed to remind or instruct readers/consumers of the meaningful associations the signs are meant to evoke. See if you can find other examples of ads that use metaphors in this text.

Symbols are a powerful form of sign used in advertising. Unlike the other two figures of speech, symbols *omit any explicit expression of comparison between sign and object.* Sports team mascots are of this type, such as the Amsterdam Ajax soccer team that uses the image of an ancient Greek warrior or the Toronto Maple Leafs ice hockey team. Symbols are powerful mechanisms of meaning transfer because when readers/consumers expend the mental effort to interpret the meaning of the symbol they become actively involved and in some sense accept the associations evoked by the symbol. Of course, not all associations between sign, object, and interpretant are possible. Instead, the linkages must be plausible. Exaggeration and simplification of meanings on the basis of relatively well known cultural principles and categories help convey symbolic meaning.[36]

As diagrammed in Exhibit 18.6, the consumers or audience for an ad can be divided into three groups. The implied consumers are those presumed by the message. They are the message recipients imagined by the copywriters and other members of the author team and whom the persona addresses. For example, a StarKist advertisement featuring Charlie Tuna assumes there are consumers who believe in talking tuna fish, at least within the conventions of the ad. Implied consumers understand the symbolic relationships presented in the ad. Sponsorial consumers are outside of the advertising text; they are the sponsors of the advertisement. Actual consumers are real individuals who are the target market for the advertising. The transfer of meaning ultimately depends on the willingness of actual consumers to play along with the persona's expectations of the implied audience as conveyed by the form and content of the message.

| Pictorial Conventions and Consumption Meanings | Responses to advertising draw on a shared visual vocabulary and learned systems of pictorial conventions. The selection and combination of visual symbols to achieve persuasive effects is becoming increasingly important in marketing communications. In the United States there is a trend toward using less language in advertising, especially print media. In other countries too, the pictorial content of ads is increasing relative to the textual content.[37] |

Visuals in marketing communications are symbolic. Their significance stems from the culturally constituted world of meaning, not from any resemblance they may have to nature. Everything from the most literal portrait to the most fanciful image is equally symbolic. The visual viewpoint, focus, graphics, and layout work together in specific ways to communicate a particular meaning. Graphic elements within the pictorial field of an advertisement suggest a concept, create a fiction, or refer to other images and texts with which marketers hope the target reader is familiar.

To interpret these images, consumers/readers must recognize advertising visuals as examples of figurative communication rather than true representations. Processing pictures depends on selecting and knowledgeably combining learned pictorial conventions and then applying them to the picture at hand. Consumers engage in symbolic thought to interpret the visual message and decode its meaning. Consumers often encounter entirely fictive images like those of the (resilient) Michelin Man, (comforting, filling) Pillsbury Doughboy, (adorable, dependent) World Wildlife Federation Panda, (crafty, resilient) Asterix the Gaulois (France), (rich, royal, persuasive) Loeki the Lion (Amsterdam), or the (folkloric)

Golden Nightingale (Russia). Yet consumers do decode the metaphorical, purposeful (rhetorical) meanings of these figures as suggested by the adjectives within parentheses above. Advertisers generally do not need to resort to logical explanations. Of course, powerful associations in one culture may not apply in another, which causes problems in cross-national advertising.

Characters and Consumption Meanings

Cultural meanings are connected to the product not only through text but also through personae associated with ads. Some ads contain explicit characters such as a real or fictional spokesperson. When the persona is a real or fictional spokesperson, such as a celebrity endorser, advertising effectiveness depends on the credibility, trustworthiness, expertise, and likeability of the spokesperson, as discussed in Chapter 16. Exhibit 18.8 shows how meaning transfer works with celebrity endorsers. The celebrity endorser (media or political figure, cartoon character) develops a meaningful persona as a result of the roles she or he has assumed in the past and the social context, persons, and objects with which she or he has interacted in those roles. In this way the endorser draws meaning from the culturally constituted world. For example, the characters they portray in films and television form Harrison Ford's or Hong Kong star Jackie Chan's heroic personae and Julia Robert's or Japanese star Kaoru Kobayashi's romantic personae. Then, in the endorsement process, the meanings move from the celebrity to the product through figures of speech, contiguity (closeness), similarity, and so forth.

In one study, researchers found that the meanings attributed to previously unendorsed products—bath towels and VCRs—changed dramatically when they were linked to Madonna or to model Christie Brinkley. Interestingly, the meanings picked up from the two celebrities were similar across the products, although the meanings differed significantly between the two endorsers. Managers need to be sensitive both to the desirable and the undesirable attributes of potential endorsers since either meaning may be passed on to the products. The meaning transfer process is completed when the consumer consumes the product. The consumer has the opportunity to capture and enjoy some of the meanings associated with the endorser's persona.[38]

Advertising connects market segments and particular goods. Once having established these links, advertisers can use these symbolic relations as given, and so do consumers. For

Exhibit 18.8 Meaning Movement and the Endorsement Process

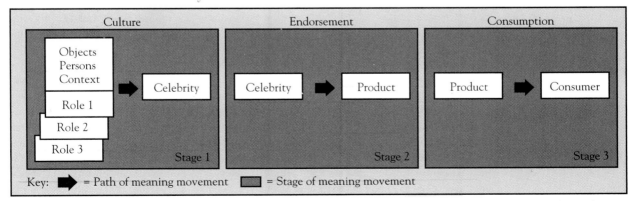

Source: Grant McCracken, "Who Is the Celebrity Endorser? Cutural Foundations of the Endorsement Process," *Journal of Consumer Research* 16 (December 1989), pp. 310–21.

Using conventional associations between color and national culture.

example, diamonds may be marketed by likening them to eternal love (a cultural category of time and emotion), creating a symbolism where the mineral (object) means something not in its own terms, as a rock, but in human terms, as a sign. Thus, a diamond comes to mean love and endurance (interpretants) for consumers. Once advertising has successfully made the connection, consumers may also begin to read meaning the other way; that is, they take the sign, the diamond, for what it signifies, enduring love. Symbolic associations like this are powerful marketing tools.[39] Silk Cut, a brand of cigarettes marketed in Great Britain and Europe, makes a symbolic reference to desirable qualities of creaminess and mildness it would like to associate with Silk Cut indirectly. Its ads do so by using a color (purple swirls) and typeface used on a Cadbury's milk chocolate bar. The famous (to European consumers) "glass and a half of full-cream dairy milk" (interpretant), which *another* advertisement has told them goes into Cadbury's chocolate, can be evoked by Silk Cut cigarettes symbolically.

The principle by which a subtly modified sign evokes a familiar set of meanings was referred to in Chapter 9. This stimulus generalization, or halo effect, can be seen underlying the principle of product line packaging and in brand extensions of all types. For example, the distinctive red and yellow colors and design elements on Ortega Mexican food products are those that have already been established through previous media portrayals as those associated with Mexican cuisine and culture. Of course, this symbolic association is purely conventional; there is nothing intrinsically red or yellow about Mexican culture![40]

Linking Product Meanings and Consumption Meanings

Neither advertising nor other cultural production systems simply bestow meanings on objects or consumers. Consumers play an active role in linking product and consumption meanings.[41] The success of many marketing campaigns depends on actively engaged consumers. This is true of markets in the Triad nations as well as in the emerging markets of the NICs and transitional economies. In fact, as shown in Exhibit 18.5, consumers are actively involved in meaning transfer. In some senses, they create product meanings. They take meanings from products. They allow themselves to be created in the image of products and services. They even create themselves both in interpreting marketing communications and through consumption of the goods and services promoted.

Consumers provide products or their advertising images with meaning through their recognition of what they stand for, what they symbolize, at least within the space of an ad. Thus, consumers give the clarinet in the Johnny Walker ad mentioned earlier its meaning for use in the ad. By presenting the instrument and the scotch together, marketers invite consumers to transfer meaning from the culturally constituted world of meanings associated with clarinets to the product, the Johnny Walker. Similarly, in a series of television ads for Grey Poupon mustard, Rolls Royce automobiles are prominently featured. Again, no explicit claim is made about the luxuriousness, quality, good taste, and timeliness of either the automobile or the mustard. Consumers draw on their already constituted fund of cultural knowledge to decode the meaning of the automobile and link it to the mustard. Thus, in the sense just indicated, advertisers are correct when they claim that they cannot create meaning; consumers create the meaning of the ad through their interpretations.[42]

Second, people take meanings from ads and products. By using particular products, with particular associated meanings and not others, consumers differentiate themselves from other people who consume different products with presumably different meanings. The woman who wears Chanel No. 5, advertised by French actress Catherine Deneuve, differs from the woman who wears Babe, advertised by American actress Margaux Hemingway. By consuming one and not the other of these products people partake of the meanings associated with the products and the characters that serve as signs for the products. Consumers may use products to create meaningful new distinctions between groups. This has been discussed more thoroughly in Chapter 8 on lifestyles.

Third, there is a sense in which consumers allow themselves to be created by ads and products. People sometimes buy not just to become a part of the group that the product represents but because they *already* feel that they *naturally* belong to that group and therefore will buy the product on offer. In some cases a consumer does not so much choose products from an array, nor in response to an advertisement, but more powerfully, by recognizing oneself as the kind of person who will use a specific product or brand. Some successful ads and acts of consumption create their own consumers. They tell the consumer what he or she is like.

It is easy to think of ads for products that hail consumers directly. This technique of *direct hailing* is a rhetorical device termed **apostrophe.** A Kirin Light Beer can label in Japan reads, "I'm off. I'll gladly work off 12 ozs. to savor a good beer." Similarly an outdoor ad for Bang & Olufsen music systems reads, "I want, I want, a life less ordinary" (see advertising banner below), and a print ad for a French discount store reads, "Tati, it's me." Using first- and second-person pronouns in ads suggests that the consumer is already a person desirous of savoring a good beer in the first case and of possessing the features of

Using the rhetorical device termed apostrophe.

extraordinariness in the second. Advertisements of the Bang & Olufsen and Tati variety invite the consumers to read their individual qualities into the product, implying they had them in the first place. In other words, having been attributed with the qualities connected with a product, viewers are projected as buyers. Given that they embody the beliefs implied in the ad, they will act in accordance and buy products that symbolize those beliefs.

Direct hailing is consistent with the ideas of marketing communication held by many copywriters. Copywriters argue that they create effective advertisements when they develop an empathic emotional connection between some product meaning and the desires of an imagined consumer. That is, they seek to make ads so that consumers recognize the product is hailing them directly.[43]

Finally, consumers derive meaning from both ads and consumption by actually creating themselves via particular products. An ad for Saab asks consumers to "Peel off your inhibitions. Find your own road." Here the implication is that the Saab automobile is literally and figuratively the vehicle for this realization of a new self.

An ad for a plastic surgeon in Beverly Hills, California, provides an extreme case of this sort of ad. It states simply "a new you," showing a drawing of a woman's face with lines drawn between her features and phrases such as "new eyes," "a new nose," "a new mouth," and so on. The ad suggests that you, the consumer, can literally recreate yourself through the services of the surgeon. The individual consumer can create her own individuality through the different kinds of surgical options available. Such ads invite the consumer to see him- or, more commonly, herself as a purchasable object. Research on consumers of plastic surgery confirms that the procedures are often viewed as mechanisms for self-completion, self re-creation, and experimentation with identity.[44]

Modes and Rituals of Meaning Transfer

The final step in meaning transfer involves more than just interpretation of marketing communications; it involves temporary or permanent acquisition of goods and services. Various forms of symbolic action transfer meaning from goods to consumers. Among these forms of symbolic action we can distinguish ordinary behaviors that consumers engage in on a regular basis and behaviors that have a ritual character.

Exhibit 18.9 identifies four main categories of ordinary consumption modes and provides some examples. The exhibit distinguishes hedonic and instrumental activities. Experience and playing are hedonic meaning transfer activities, whereas integrating and classifying are utilitarian ones. This division is consistent with the distinction made earlier between utilitarian and hedonic meanings.

As described in Exhibit 18.9, playing and classifying are more social activities, whereas experiencing and integrating are more individual activities. The former types of meaning transfer activities help consumers to establish social identity. For instance, dressing in team colors to symbolize fandom is a form of classification through objects commonly seen among world soccer fans. The latter types (experiencing and integrating) help consumers establish individual identity. Contrasting features of different brands of major appliances provides a form of utilitarian meanings—evaluation—to a consumer, for example. Or taking a solo hiking trip through Germany's Black Forest might provide a form of hedonic meanings—appreciation—to a consumer.

In addition to the ordinary modes of meaning transfer, we can also identify a number of special behaviors. Among the special behaviors consumers employ to transfer meaning from objects to themselves are possession rituals, grooming rituals, exchange rituals, and divest-

Exhibit 18.9 Modes of Meaning Transfer

Modes	Definitions	Examples
Experiencing		
Accounting	Typifying actions and objects, assigning them specific meanings and values, then contextualizing the account to enrich it.	Doing play-by-play of a live or televised sports event or dance recital.
Evaluating	Making comparisons to norms, history, and conventions.	Citing historical games or players to characterize recent ones; comparing pizzas in terms of crust, toppings, cheese, delivery speed, price.
Appreciating	Applying aesthetic and emotional frameworks to actions and to objects.	A graceful play in sports is much discussed; a hot dog is said to taste special at the ballpark.
Playing		
Communing	Sharing consumption experiences with others so that consumption becomes a mutual experience.	The temporary community that develops among participants in sporting events, tours, adventure recreations, religious pageants, community festivals, and so on.
Socializing	Consumers use their personal (past or present) consumption experiences to entertain one another.	Consumption-related storytelling of all kinds; acting as a market maven.
Integrating		
Assimilating	Methods by which consumers become competent participants (see Experiencing above).	Joining "the wave"; following one's preferred football team to away games; adopting the jargon of the consumption context; creating personalized, traditional holiday celebrations.
Producing	Methods by which consumers act to enhance their perception that they are significantly involved in production of the object or action.	The variety of celebrity-worship activities that enable people to feel bonded with those celebrities; contributing comments or suggestions; predicting the outcome of sports events.
Personalizing	Practices through which consumers add extrainstitutional elements to consumption to assert the individuality of their relationship to the object or action.	Developing innovative uses for products; modifying holiday celebrations significantly; customizing dress, cars, houses, bodies, and other products.
Classifying		
Through objects	Using shared meanings of consumption objects to classify oneself or others.	Using documentary markers like souvenirs, T-shirts, bumper stickers, matched clothing, jewelry, cycles, or cars.
Through actions	Using the manner in which one experiences a consumption object or event to classify oneself or others; mentoring novice consumers.	Engaging in novice/expert behaviors; expressions of connoisseurship in sports, crafts, or the arts.

Source: Douglas B. Holt, "How Consumers Consume: A Typology of Consumption Practices," *Journal of Consumer Research* 22 (June 1995), pp. 1–16.

ment rituals. The first two types are mechanisms by which people invest personal, idiosyncratic meanings in goods. The latter two, discussed in Chapters 10 and 19, respectively, involve the further movement of goods and the meanings they hold to other consumers.[45]

Possession rituals allow consumers to assume ownership of product meanings. Customizing, decorating, personalizing, cleaning, discussing, displaying, and photographing are some of the activities consumers engage in to assert possession and draw from the object the qualities that advertising, the fashion system, or retailing generally have invested in them. At the simplest level, consumers may remove tags, packaging, pins, labels, and other markers of the retail origins of goods. To assert possession of paperbound books sold in Great Britain or bedding and cushions sold in North America, consumers tear off covers and tags, respectively, which prohibit commercial resale. One study found that inner-city children left the tags on their clothing to display to their peers. The tag provided evidence that the item was purchased at a prestigious retail outlet and became a potent personal statement.[46]

Customizing is a far more elaborate procedure for asserting ownership. Customization allows for the encoding of personal meanings into products. For example, tailoring and monogramming of new clothing are devices that allow consumers to assert unique claims to ownership. Custom building of homes enables consumers to express more elaborate personal meanings. In one study, the authors found that custom-made homes in North America express the idea of the home as a process that starts with the anticipation of building and extends into the living experience. The custom-built home is an expression of lifestyle. Thus, a colonial-style home symbolizes traditional values to one consumer. The construction of a solar home symbolizes a harmonious, natural lifestyle to another.[47]

Evidence of repeated interaction with possessions seems to be one way in which meaning and value are asserted. Many kinds of collections are cleaned, arranged, and displayed for public view. Postage-stamp collectors, for example, compete for prizes at international competitions on the basis of quality and creativity of the arrangements and displays they make of the stamps. These displays may include stories (called postal history) about the stamps and their use. Unique, personal arrangements may dramatically increase the value of the stamps. Note that in these collections, canceled stamps without instrumental value are generally more valuable than unused stamps.

Various institutions, including governments, engage in possession rituals to assert ownership of public property. Examples include the crown jewels in Great Britain; the tombs of Chinese emperors; originals of the Constitution and Bill of Rights in the United States; and Belweder, the Polish presidential palace. All are possessions enshrined behind bricks, glass, and security systems. Ordinary citizens' access to them is regulated. These goods have been definitively removed from the marketplace; they are priceless, perhaps even sacred. Similarly, historical preservation commissions lobby to apply the label "historical" to landmarks, buildings, and even neighborhoods. This device asserts special ownership qualities and may even protect these items from resale or redevelopment.

Grooming rituals are repeated actions necessary to draw perishable meanings from goods. Human grooming behavior is a form of body language communicating specific messages about an individual's social status, maturity, aspirations conformity, and morality. The meaning of certain items of clothing, hairstyles, makeup, and even certain "looks" are coaxed out through the performance of a sequence of special behaviors. Ritual paraphernalia like shampoo, lotions, henna, paint, hair curlers, hair dryers, and false hair are valued for their transformational properties. Sometimes modern consumer products are invested with the same sort of energizing magical power that indigenous peoples may ascribe to herbal concoctions devised by local shamans. The aim of many grooming rituals is to enable the consumer to take on the powers of confidence, beauty, defense, glamour, and so forth, perceived to be resident in certain brands. Events ranging from "voguing" to Carnival are further examples of events related to extended grooming rituals.

In Japan, packaging may convey more meaning than the product it contains.

Often, it is not the consumer but the good that needs to be groomed in order to maintain meaning. In North America culture, automobiles and homes are highly likely to be subject to such attention. In Japan, wrapping and packaging are important art forms, and most retail stores will wrap or package even the most conventional purchase with great care. Packaging conveys more meaning than the gift itself. An example of traditional Japanese packaging appears above. The Chinese or Indian family altar is also subject to such special care. Collections are typically subject to grooming rituals. Cleaning, rearranging, sorting, and labeling these objects are symbolic behaviors that allow consumers to freshen the meanings they draw from them.[48]

Malleability and Movement of Meanings

The meanings of products and services are highly malleable. There is considerable variation in the extent to which consumers share meanings. This malleability can be examined either at the product level or at the social level. For marketers, the choice depends on whether one is more interested in the development of product strategy or segmentation and targeting strategies. Both approaches provide insight into consumer behavior.

It may be useful to think about product meaning as a multilevel construct. Meaningful associations attached to product concept might be arranged into four types: (1) tangible attributes, (2) cultural associations, (3) subcultural associations, (those relevant to a particular group), and (4) unique, personal associations. These four categories of meaning are a continuum, ranging from commonly shared judgments about the tangible qualities of products to unique, intangible personal meanings. Another way of phrasing this is that people are more likely to agree about the physical attributes of products than about their personal meanings.[49]

Products may be viewed as displaying varying proportions of common cultural, subcultural, and unique, personal associations, depending on varying points of view. This conception of meaning entails a number of implications. For example, the meaning of individual products may range from the highly idiosyncratic to the commonplace. The elective quality of personal meaning in advanced consumer cultures means that consumers often proclaim self-definition by appropriating the meaningful properties of consumer goods.

Self-proclaiming is carried out in a variety of ways, from the wearing of T-shirts to the adoption of sets of consumption paraphernalia that proclaims a particular identity. T-shirts are vehicle for proclaiming personal meaning. Emblazoned with words and pictures, they are used to indicate occupation of a cultural category such as sports fan (Texas Longhorn), affiliate of a university or corporation, member of a family (Smith family reunion, Provo, Utah, 1995) or other group (I am a UFO); to indicate passage through a social status change (U2 Unforgettable Fire, 1985 Tour; I survived Woodstock 94); or as a trophy of some personal accomplishment (Beautiful British Columbia) or group success (Run for Cancer). Savvy marketers use consumers' chameleon-like behavior to advantage by providing them with promotional T-shirts and other identity-bestowing giveaways.[50] **Special possessions,** those regarded as *extensions of the self* (see Chapter 7)—pets, collections, memory-laden objects and symbols of core cultural values, for example—often proclaim idiosyncratic meanings.[51]

By contrast with idiosyncratic meanings, heavily advertised, branded consumer goods probably carry a widely shared set of meanings, even if these are taken for granted by consumers. Individuals, groups, and firms might exploit differences in widely shared product meanings. Thus, Harley-Davidson motorcycles carry a general set of meanings recognized by North American consumers, other subcultural sets of meanings recognized by members of HOG (Harley Owners Group) and outlaw motorcycle groups, and still other sets of meanings recognized by individual Harley owners contemplating a customized bike. Please note, however, that all goods are invested with varying proportions of meaning types. It makes no sense to speak of goods without cultural meaning since meaning, however idiosyncratic or general, is a cultural phenomenon.

Intermediate between culturally common and idiosyncratic meanings are subcultural associations. Rastafarian consumer behaviors and products provide a great example of subcultural meanings. Rastafarianism is a cultural, religious movement that began in Jamaica in the 1930s. Goods and behaviors loaded with sacred meanings are consumed by Rastafarians through an ideology that combines biblical scripture with Ethiopian history. Rastafarianism influences subcultural consumption through the use of what's called an ital diet (avoiding meat, salt, processed foods, tobacco, and alcohol) and Iyaric language (purged of negative associations), symbolic hairstyle ("dreadlocks"), clothing (woven tams), colors (red, yellow, green, and black), and adornment. For some members of this subculture, Rastafarianism is a religious belief system, regulating daily life and conduct; for others it is a fashion style used to manipulate social status. For an international segment of people, primarily of lower socioeconomic status, and who have experienced social and economic upheaval, consumption of the music and paraphernalia of Rastafarianism has become an important source of meaning and personal identity. The key point is that Rastafarianism represents a consumption subculture with values distinct from those of the surrounding cultures.[52]

Marketers commonly work to change meanings at each of the four levels cited above in order to align their products with the desires of target markets. Consider tangible attributes. The North American beef industry has worked hard to promote beef as a low-fat food in response to concern about the fat content of red meats. It has done so in part by re-engineering beef cattle so that they are leaner than they were 30 years ago. In this way, the beef industry has changed the tangible attributes of beef to reflect consumers' beliefs about the link between fat and health. You can explore these industry marketing efforts at the industry website.

Marketers seek to exploit the unique, personal meanings that develop between people and products. IBM's ad campaign for its Powerbook computers was called "What's on Your Powerbook?" It showed unique semicelebrity spokespersons with their Powerbooks

www.beef.org

Consumer Chronicles 18.3

- Movie memorabilia is especially rewarding to collectors. A pair of ruby slippers worn in the *Wizard of Oz* fetched $1,650,000. Someone purchased a uniform worn by Elvis Presley in *G.I. Blues* for $12,000. A large poster of the movie *Casablanca* sells for $17,500.

- The founder of the G.I. Joe Club of America, himself an avid collector of more than 500 of the action figures, desires to build a national monument to the character. Early model versions of the toy now sell for more than $2,000.

- A teddy bear was recently sold at Sotheby's for a record $85,000. The auction house also sold 152 cookie jars owned by Andy Warhol for $247,830 and three Campbell's soup can banks for $7,150.

- Among the rapidly appreciating speculative investments some experts view as a hedge against inflation are Elvis memorabilia, presidential autographs, rare books, toy figurines, and American muscle cars (1950–1960s).

- Collecting behavior radiates to increasingly novel niches. In Japan, prepaid magnetic cards intended to render service encounters more automatic and convenient have spawned a market of more than 200,000 collectors. In France, several magazines specialize in displaying automatic telephone credit cards on which advertising appears for avid collectors. Even junk mail has become a collectible for some consumers.

Source: Russell W. Belk, Melanie Wallendorf, John F. Sherry, Jr., and Morris B. Holbrook, "Collecting in a Consumer Culture," Highways and Buyways: Naturalistic Research from the Consumer Behavior Odyssey, *Russell W. Belk, ed., (Provo, UT: Association for Consumer Research, 1991), pp. 185–86.*

and lists of the idiosyncratic but meaningful items stored on their computers. Photographs, creative works, personal phone numbers, and other personalized items figure prominently in these lists, suggesting that the Powerbook is a vehicle for the expression of customers' unique qualities.

Marketers also work to change subcultural associations between products and meanings. Forty years ago Honda successfully enlarged the market for motorcycles with its, "You Meet the Nicest People on a Honda" campaign, showing that motorcycles were not just for outlaws. Today, Harley-Davidson works hard to differentiate the Harley market into a variety of groups for whom particular types of motorcycles are appropriate. Keeping product meanings in flux between segments is part of the current marketing strategy of the Harley-Davidson Company.

Collecting and Museums

Collecting is *the selective, active, and longitudinal acquisition, possession, and disposition of an interrelated set of differentiated objects (material things, ideas, beings, or experiences) that contribute to and derive extraordinary meaning from the set itself.* Collecting

Andrew Foster, then five years old, had been attending his new school, a private progressive day school in Rochester, New York, no more than a few weeks when he came home with two trading cards and a plastic sheet into which to insert them. He had received these cards from one of the oldest and most popular boys in his school, a boy whose collection of cards was perhaps the largest and most extensive. As it happened, there was a box of baseball cards in the attic, and Andrew added some of these to his sheet. The next day, Andrew returned from school with no baseball cards; but he did have an assortment of other cards, including football cards, a GI Joe card, and a Batman card. Andrew had been recruited into a social network of card traders.

Soon, Andrew would sit with two of his newcomer friends on the edge of a circle of older boys who were examining and trading their cards. The young ones would say nothing but watch and listen avidly as the older boys discussed the relative merits of the cards and negotiated trades. Later, Andrew became a participant in this sort of trading. He acquired a binder and many more plastic display pages. He developed a repertory of phrases he had heard from the older boys and learned how to talk about cards, to evaluate trades, and to articulate trading rules. While Andrew managed to enlarge his collection through trading the baseball cards, he also asked his parents to buy packs of certain super hero cards, Marvel Masterpieces Series 2 and Skybox's Marvel Universe Series 4, that were extremely popular at school.

Source: Nancy Foster and Robert J. Foster, "Learning Fetishism? Boys Consumption Work with Marvel Super Heroes Trading Cards," paper presented at the 93rd annual meeting of the American Anthropological Association, Atlanta, November 30, 1994.

provides consumers with important benefits. These include opportunities to experience hedonic and sacred meanings and to engage in possession and exchange rituals. Once items enter a collection they stop serving their utilitarian functions as, for instance, advertisements, shells on a beach, postage stamps, or dolls for ordinary play. For collectors, the meaning of even those objects that retain their original uses, like antique furniture or recordings, is more than utilitarian. Through collecting, objects are imbued with a personal significance. Products leave the marketplace and become **singularized** through *possession and grooming rituals (accounting, evaluating, appreciating, and assimilating).* Consumer Chronicles 18.3 provides some evidence of the monetary value and importance of collecting to consumers.[53]

Items are added to collections according to some systematic pattern, although the cultural principles that provide a blueprint for the collection and meanings that consumers derive from them may be highly personal. Consumer Chronicles 18.4 concerns boys who trade superhero cards. In this case, aesthetic and textual meanings and market value are the guiding criterion for collecting. Older boys focus more on market value and **textual meanings,** that is, the character's role in comics, television shows, video games, and so forth. Younger boys focus more on aesthetic meaning, the way the cards look and feel. They prize holographic and specially coated cards. Boys value trading for itself, as an extended

Above the sink in the kitchen of Marilyn and Ivan Karp's 150-year-old farmhouse in upstate New York hang rows of food choppers, beaters, and graters. The walls in one bathroom are covered with boldly graphic tin signs hawking products of a century ago. Other parts of the house contain collections of painted country furniture, quilts, maps, and old photographs. And hidden away in drawers are root beer mugs and old medicine bottles.

The Karps—he is 69, she is 56—are an unusual couple among collectors because both of them collect, though she admits that she is the more obsessive of the two. "I can't remember a time when I was not collecting something," said Mrs. Karp, a professor of art at New York University. Mr. Karp, a Manhattan art dealer, has collected on and off since childhood.

One of Mrs. Karp's earliest memories was watching her mother save the wires that held on the tops of Borden's milk bottles. Her mother saved them in order to use them again, but Mrs. Karp had no interest in recycling. She collected the cardboard stoppers from those bottles that were imprinted with Borden's name and an image of Elsie the cow. "Even then, I needed to collect things that signified a time—the present—as evidence of being there," she said. As a child, she also collected dolls, campaign buttons, comic books, bubble gum cards, Dixie cup lids, and syrup bottles. Later she branched out into nineteenth-century objects: kitchen utensils, enameled tin signs, and blue-and-white sponge ware.

While Mrs. Karp has gone from collecting one kind of object to another, her attitude about the process has remained the same. "All I ever needed was one full set—of everything," she said. "And I never parted willingly with any object, unless it was a duplicate." She considers herself a caretaker, she said, giving objects safe haven before they move on to "whom or where they are going next."

Her husband takes a Freudian view in explaining why he collects. "Collecting is an act of replacing something ineffable lost in childhood," Mr. Karp said. "It doesn't mean that you have a serious psychological problem. You can stop any day of the week. . . . Collecting does not make us better people. It is something we need." His holdings range from washboards to elaborately detailed paper cigar-box covers, to metal and stone ornaments salvaged from buildings in New York City. Mr. Karp says, for him, collecting is a matter of aesthetics: "You look at objects in the world, and some have an incredible vitality. And you have to acquire them. The visual appetite is a rampant condition—and it is not destructive."

Source: Rita Reif (1995), "Two Collectors Bound By Marriage But Not by Tastes," The New York Times, July 9, 1995, p. A33.

game (hedonic meaning) that builds social networks among the boys. Older boys also calculate both current and future market values in building their collections.[54]

Collecting is a behavior characteristic both of individuals and institutions. Individual collectors come in so many guises so it is difficult to generalize about the profile of serious collectors. Consumer Chronicles 18.5 offers a profile of two U.S. collectors, but if you are familiar with the British or American television series "Antiques Roadshow" you've

www.exhibitions
online.org/
artbrief/corpart1.
htm

probably encountered all sorts of collectors. Religious institutions have long been reposi-tories of collections of art and other relics. The Catholic Church holds enormous stocks of art and relics. The political and economic strength of corporations and nations is judged in part by the size and diversity of their collections.[55] The British Museum (Great Britain), the Hermitage (Russia), the Imperial Library (China), the Louvre (France), the Rijksmu-seum (Netherlands), the Smithsonian Institution (United States), and the National Museum of Anthropology (Mexico) are just a few among the great collections held by nations.

What do collections mean to consumers? Among the important overlapping meanings collections appear to hold are control; magical power; evocation of other times, people, and places; legitimization for materialism; an expanded sense of self; and of course he-donic pleasure. Evidence for magical meanings of collections can be seen in the setting apart of collections from the ordinary, the reverent care given them, the treasure tales that surround collecting arenas, and their ability to evoke other times and places.

Some collections allow collectors to enter into fantasy worlds represented by their dolls, baseball cards, stamps, and so forth. One of the authors of this text knew a young man whose passion for the Victorian Age led not only to furnishing his home in Victoriana but to wearing Victorian clothing, using no electricity or electric appliances, driving a turn-of-the-century vehicle, and earning his living as a vintage player-piano restorer. By sur-rounding himself with Victoriana, this man sought to create a more comfortable, pre-dictable, controllable world for himself than the world inhabited by the rest of us. Many antique dealers have strong attachments to the persons, eras, and places that their collec-tions represent. As suggested in Consumer Chronicles 18.5, a kind of curatorial passion seems to motivate some collectors. Themes of completion and closure are also evident in the comments of the collectors described in Consumer Chronicles 18.5.

Collecting is big business. The modern collecting industry consists of a cultural pro-duction system that, like the advertising system discussed above, serves to transfer mean-ing from the culturally constituted world to collectibles as well as to distribute them among the collectors. Auction houses such as Sotheby's and Christie's are widely known. Muse-ums and retail galleries display collections of various kinds and place the stamp of con-noisseurship on them. Media vehicles for every type of collectible exist. The "Antiques Roadshow" has brought collecting to a mass audience, and cable shopping networks fea-ture collectibles programming as well.

Also of interest to consumer researchers and marketers are those institutions whose mission is the mass merchandising of pre-singularized collectibles to consumers who de-sire special objects. Firms such as the Wintherthur Museum, the Bradford Exchange, or the Franklin Mint advertise in mass circulation magazines and offer just such portfolios to their clients. Similarly, firms such as Hummel, Lladro, and Waterford encourage collect-ing by producing items whose principle value or point-of-difference resides in their col-lectibility. These commercial firms reinforce the social and economic significance of col-lecting behavior by pre-packing the experience for consumers and providing the comforting assurance of authenticity. These firms have commercialized a social activity, co-opting it and reinforcing collecting behavior.[56]

Museum shops and catalogs are an important part of the growing collecting industry. Although museums vary in their attitudes toward consumer marketing, purchasing sou-venirs of museum attendance is an important mechanism of meaning transfer for many at-tendees. The Louvre in Paris has extensive gift shops, whereas gift shops at Dutch muse-ums have limited product selections and do not display a consumer-friendly orientation. The Smithsonian Institute's shops and catalogs had combined sales of about $60 million in 1993. The Metropolitan Museum of Art in New York mails about 20 million mail-order catalogs each year.[57]

Cross-Cultural Perspectives on the Meanings of Possessions

We suggested in Chapters 4 and 5 that possessions and their meanings vary cross-culturally. There we mentioned a number of key differences between consumption priorities in different regions of the world. Any attempt to document differences in the dictionaries of consumer meaning cross-culturally is doomed. Either we'd end up cataloguing great long lists of differences and mountains of examples to illustrate them, or we'd be reduced to making such general characterizations of differences in key meanings that they would provide little guidance to marketers or to students of cultural differences.[58]

Since we have emphasized the malleability and dynamism of consumption meanings in this chapter, we can mention a number of dimensions along which consumer researchers can expect to find differences in meaning between cultural areas. One obvious dimension is the underlying meaning of consumer goods. The vignette that opens the chapter illustrates the differences in consumption meanings attached to goods cross-culturally.

We can go on in this vein to contrast the meanings of goods in different cultural contexts. Contrast the meaning of a house in the United States, where customization and self-expression are often prized, to its meaning in Great Britain, where conformity, solidity of construction, and longevity are favored. The meaning of the house among the Suku of Zaire, Africa, is different still. Over its 10-year life a thatch house becomes successively a dwelling, a kitchen, and, finally, a lowly chicken coop. Or contrast the meanings of personal property expressed in the Anglo-American belief that "a man's home is his castle" with the Swedish view that the countryside is public space open to everyone, even parts immediately adjacent to the country homes that dot the Swedish countryside. On a darker note, many critics have pointed out that loss of meaning occurs when arts and crafts made by indigenous peoples for utilitarian, sacred, or artistic (hedonic) purposes, are reused in Western interior decorating or placed behind museum glass.

Another dimension along which consumer meaning varies cross-culturally is the identity of goods that are the focus of consumption meanings. For North Americans, the home, including the lawn, and the car are extremely meaningful consumer goods. Interesting homes and cars are important sources of meaning to women and men, respectively, on the island of Trinidad as well. The home but not the car is also critically important in Sweden, Great Britain, Belize, and many other nations. By contrast, the apartment is a focus of attention for many Japanese. The family altar concerns some Chinese. As mentioned elsewhere in the text, some young Congolese focus intense interest on French designer fashions.[59]

A third dimension is the quantity of meaningful possessions in circulation. Consumers in the more economically and socially differentiated societies of the Triad nations invest meanings in many types of objects. T-shirts and bumper stickers reading "The person that dies with the most toys wins" are playful examples of the value of quantity in U.S. consumer culture. By contrast, consumers in less developed economies may attach meaning to a smaller number of goods. With the globalization of markets this is changing rapidly.

In the newly industrialized countries of Asia, for example, what some herald as a new stage in consumer demand may also be seen in the emergence of young people with ever-expanding consumer wants. The emergence of individual consumers who are increasingly concerned both with quantity as well as quality in consumer goods in the NICs and developing economies is likely to continue with the expansion of the global market system.[60]

A fourth dimension of interest cross-culturally is the stability of consumer meanings. The development of a global market economy creates a situation in which consumers'

Sanse, dressing up or dressing well, is highly valued among women in the cities of Senegal and The Gambia, West Africa. The elegant style of Senegalese women—the well-starched copious folds of their colorful garments, accompanied by matching headdresses and abundant qualities of gold jewelry—draws praise when well executed from men and women alike. Achieving such a style is expensive and appears to reflect the dominance of Western consumerist values in which foreign commodities are valued symbols of cosmopolitanism. *Sanse* forges a link between having and being, displaying both wealth and social identity. But *sanse* is an indexical communicative act [that is, it is indicative of true social status]; it derives its meaning from its context of use, pointing to a larger social hierarchy within which the actor is situated and can only be understood in this context.

Sanse and the practices that surround it reflect accents of identity and difference (heteroglossia) on a number of different levels: tradition and modernity, Western and African style, religious devotion and heterodoxy, women's autonomy and dependence. Thus, urban tailors create a rapidly changing array of styles often incorporating design elements of apparent Western origin such as flounces, lace, and fitted, zippered bodices drawn from Western fashion magazines. On the important public occasions at which *sanse* is performed, the preferred costume is the *mbubb,* a voluminous unfitted garment that is less tailored and more African. In addition, two types of cloth figure among the most highly prized in the execution of *sanse.* One is the imported machine-made, polished [cotton] damask. Sometimes a less expensive, locally manufactured version that is never confused with the luxury fabric it imitates is worn. It signals social difference, reinforcing the distance between women of greater and those of lesser means. But its display also reinforces a sense of identity, through exclusion, among lower-class women. The other type of fabric used in the *mbubb* is luxurious, hand-woven strip cloth with its brightly colored designs that originated in the cloth currency produced by slaves as early as the mid-1500s. This hand-loomed cloth provides an alternative to factory made textiles and partial autonomy from the circuits of mass-produced commodities. Thus, both tradition and modernity, African

demand for meaningful goods becomes nearly insatiable, as the money economy reduces the intrinsic differences in value between them. Global growth in marketing communications may be expected to continue for the foreseeable future, especially in the NICs and the transitional economies. With its growth may come the generalization of certain characteristics of consumer culture found in the West. Cultural categories and principles become less and less fixed. Consumption meaning moves ever more quickly, becoming more differentiated, more compartmentalized, more transitory.

At the same time, we may expect that ad effectiveness will continue to rely on the elicitation of shared meanings from a dictionary common to members of particular target markets. Cross-national studies of advertising themes and executions do not reveal a tendency toward convergence on a set of global conventions but toward the recycling of national and

and Western meanings fluctuate within the overall practice of *sanse*.

In addition to these contending meanings, *sanse* also reflects the social organization of women's independence in urban Senegal. Many women amass the cloth necessary to execute *sanse* through complex networks of gift giving and exchange. Women exchange cloth at baptisms and weddings, for example. More commonly, a prospective groom, a husband, or suitor offers cloth to a woman on the occasion of a life-cycle ceremony. Such gifts make a public statement about what the women's suitor or husband has and who he is. In this way, *sanse* serves as a public display of someone else's generosity and is viewed as a service, a communicative act for someone else's behalf. A woman also may be expected to carry out a display of *sanse* to display her husband's wealth. In this case, he is then considered her master. However, in Senegalese culture, the possession and display of material goods through *sanse* is tied to the notion of generosity and hospitality. Related to this is the notion that wealth is an aspect of honor and respectability. Thus, wearing cloth and clothing contributed by her husband, a woman conveys a message designed to enhance the latter's reputation for honor. Paradoxically, by communicating that her male kin are men of means, a woman may also be communicating the possibility that she too is a person of means, capable of displaying generosity toward others. In this way, she may be making a statement about her independence rather than dependence. Thus, the meaning of *sanse* is always ambiguous, always moving, always slightly in dispute.

In contrast to these complex symbolic statements in fashion, true antifashions may be found in urban Senegal as well. Adepts of the Baay Fal Muslim sect use scraps of brightly colored locally manufactured wax print cloth to fashion voluminous patchwork pantaloons. Along with other behaviors, such as the rejection of imported tea or Nescafé, their patchwork costumes exemplify their rejection of Western consumerism and what some of them characterize as worldly materialism in general.

Source: Deborah Heath, "Fashion, Anti-Fashion and Heteroglossia in Urban Senegal," American Ethnologist 19 (February 1992), pp. 19–33.

regional conventions. Thus, national or regional markets are likely to continue to differ in the symbols and meanings they find compelling. Managing meaning transfer processes will remain central to successful global marketing.[61]

Consumer Chronicles 18.6 illustrates each of these aspects of consumer meaning cross-culturally. The meaning of fashion in Senegal clearly varies from its meaning in Western and Eastern cultures. *Sanse* is also a focus for consumer meaning particular to Senegal. It also concentrates a great many personal, social, and hedonic meanings in one product category. Notice too that Senegalese consumers contest the meaning of *sanse*. Finally, the system is open to outside influences, as Western fashion elements are eagerly incorporated into the Senegalese fashion system. Given the *sanse* system of meaning transfer, how would you market wax print cloth in Senegal?

Consumption meanings are at the core of demand for products (goods, services, experiences, and ideals). Central to understanding consumer demand is the idea of semiosis, or the nature of meaning. Semiosis is a meaning-making process linking objects, meanings, and symbols of various kinds. Consumer meaning is a set of cultually particular and fundamentally arbitrary associations consumers connect with commercial products such as those linked to blue jeans, street fashions, or diamond rings. Meaning attaches to objects as signs, symbols, or indexes. In consumption, people extract both individual and social meanings from products and services. Five general kinds of consumption meanings may be derived from products: utilitarian, sacred, secular, hedonic, and social. Often these overlap in a single product, yet specific meanings associated with a product may vary between market segments and individuals.

The origin and movement of consumption meanings can be understood through the meaning transfer model. Meaning develops in the culturally constituted world as a natural part of human experience and our interpretations of sensory stimuli. Cultural principles and categories help us to organize novel experiences into meaningful ones. Next, in consumer culture available meanings are linked to products through the advertising and fashion systems. Marketing communications professionals and other tastemakers link products to cultural categories of time, place, emotion, and person. Advertising formats and treatments portray the world in ways designed to associate desired meaning with products. Verbal conventions such as metaphors and similes, and visual ones like familiar celebrities whose persona are well-known, are used to provide the recipients of advertising messages the clues to decode the intended links between product and meanings.

Consumers play active roles in interpreting and assimilating advertising meanings. They interpret the meanings in marketing communications; they sometimes seek to take on the meanings of products as portrayed in marketing communications. In other cases, they allow themselves to be identified as a participant in the meanings linked to a particular brand through consumption of the brands. Sometimes consumers use products to physically or mentally transform themselves. We identify a set of ordinary activities that consumers may use to assimilate meanings from goods such as personalizing and categorizing, and also discuss the possession and grooming rituals that they employ. The meanings of consumer goods are malleable and dynamic. Meanings fluctuate both within and between market segments.

Collecting is a peculiar and economically significant vehicle for the consumption of meaning. It provides consumers with opportunities to experience hedonic and sacred meanings and to engage in possession and exchange rituals. Both individual and institutional collecting takes place; institutional collecting of art and antiques enables corporations and governments to appropriate sacred meanings for their secular purposes. Providing collectibles to individual consumers is big business.

Consumption meanings vary cross-culturally. Cataloguing all possible consumption meanings is impossible, given the fluid quality of demand in a global economy. The underlying meaning of products varies as does the particular goods valued in different cultural contexts. Cultures also vary both in the terms of the quantity of possessions that are meaningful to them and the stability of the meanings valued within a particular culture. Seeking to manage the apparently universal human propensity to invest products with meaning requires that marketers pay attention to the ever-shifting play of cultural meanings.

1. Choose a number of your favorite consumer goods for which you can find print ads or commercials. Describe a semiotic triangle for each of them.

2. Choose a number of products for which you are brand loyal. Can you explain the meaning of these products for you? Explain why alternative brands just wouldn't mean the same to you.

3. Make a list of your favorite possessions. Can you list the kinds of meanings your favorite possessions have for you?

4. Clip a number of print advertisements. Can you identify the main consumption meanings contained in the ads?

5. Using this same set of ads, identify the kind of advertising format (lecture, drama, fairy tale, allegory, soap opera) and some rhetorical elements (metaphor, simile, symbol) employed.

6. Choose an advertisement without an obvious spokesperson or persona. Describe the implied persona by interpreting the format and text of the ad.

7. Take as an example a common consumption event such as a visit to a fast-food restaurant or attendance at a sports or musical event, a birthday party, a garage sale, or any similar event. Can you identify examples of the many modes of consumer meaning transfer described in the chapter?

8. Some morning as you prepare for the day, make a list of your grooming rituals. What are they? How many? What do they mean to you? Identify any that you consider essential, that is, you wouldn't leave the house without performing it. What products are involved with these rituals?

9. Are you a collector? Try to take stock of your possessions and see. If so, try to make an objective appraisal of the meanings you derive from collecting in terms of the modes and rituals of meaning transfer described in the text.

10. The chapter discussed cases of dispute over the meaning of products between and within consumer segments. Can you think of examples of products for which you have been involved in some such dispute? (*Hint:* Perhaps you and some family members have quarreled about consumption at some point.)

You Make the Call
Kola Nut Shortage in Niger

"Give me a kola nut!" "It'll cost you more than that!"
Source: http://www.txdirect.net/~jmayer/kakaki/blues/

Get it? Probably you don't unless you are familiar with kola nuts and West African markets and celebrations. But this You Make the Call describes a very real crisis in meaning.

In Chapter 1 of Nigerian author Chinua Achebe's novel *Things Fall Apart,* Okoye says to Unoka, "He who brings kola brings life," referring to the kola nut and showing people of the Ibo culture's reverence of this native nut. The kola nut is actually the seed of a large African tree with the Latin name *Cola acuminata.* The nut is reddish gray in color, about an inch in size, and grows in long pods containing from five to twelve seeds each. The shape is irregular, with one side being flat and round, and the other side irregularly scooped or unfolded. Kola has the consistency of an unripe apple and is bitter in taste. Chewing kola is an acquired taste. According to fans throughout West Africa, kola nut makes ideas clearer, thoughts flow more easily and clearly, and fatigue and drowsiness decrease. Laborers use it to increase physical endurance, and people use it to treat a variety of illnesses.

As to the kola's spiritual nature, it's not hard to see why the Ibo and many other West African peoples hold it in such high esteem. It makes them feel good, and in this respect they use it at the beginning of important functions to heighten their senses both physically and mentally. In Chapter 3 of *Things Fall Apart,* Okonkwo presents kola nut and alligator pepper to a wealthy clansmen, and typical of its use in ceremony, the kola nut is passed around for "all to see," then returned to Okonkwo to be broken and distributed among the men present. Okonkwo, affirming the group's desire for a long and happy life with children and good harvests, says a small prayer. Achebe goes into detail here to show the importance of kola in the Ibo culture and the ceremony surrounding it.

This same use of kola can be found in Niger and indeed throughout West Africa, where the collection and redistribution of kola nut accompanies all important celebrations. Family members contribute to the kola fund, and at the ceremony, the host breaks and distributes the kola to the participants. Kola is essential for weddings and baptisms, during which the nuts are distributed to all the guests. It is also common to offer kola nuts in a variety of social situations, and, with its heavy concentration of caffeine, it is virtually the only stimulant allowed by Islam.

Nigeriens have been suffering a serious kola nut shortage for several weeks. This is due in part to a poor harvest in the kola-producing countries of Nigeria and Ghana, and the crisis has been exacerbated by a recent transport workers strike. In the capital Niamey's Katako Market, the price for a single kola nut has risen from a range of 15–50 CFA francs to 100–250 CFA francs (US$0.15–0.35), if one can even find it. As for the 100-kilogram sack, its price has risen from a range of 40,000–70,000 CFA to as much as 300,000 CFA (US$414), or the equivalent of three metric tons of millet, the staple food grain.

Because of its importance in social life, the current shortage is a real crisis for many Nigeriens. To cope with the crisis, hosts have been offering their guests dates at various types of ceremonies, and state-controlled media has urged people not to be offended if given dates instead of kola.

1. What do you think are some of the types of meanings Nigeriens attach to kola nuts?
2. Can you explain the meanings Nigeriens attach to kola nuts using the meaning transfer model described in this chapter?
3. What factors will determine whether dates make an effective substitute for kola nuts?
4. If you were a Nigerien kola marketer, how might you respond to this crisis in meaning?

This case is adapted from Kakaki: News of Niger, *users.idworld.net/jmayer/kakaki.*

1. This chapter draws heavily on the work of a small number of researchers, especially Grant McCracken, *Culture and Consumption* (Bloomington: Indiana University Press, 1986).
2. Center for Chicano Studies and Coleccion Tloque Nahuaque University Library, *Dia de Los Muertos: An Illustrated Essay and Bibliography* (Santa Barbara: University of California Press, 1983); Juanita Garciagodoy, *Digging the Days of the Dead: A Reading of Mexico's Dias de Muertos* (Niwot, CO: University Press of Colorado, 1998); Maria Garza-Lubeck and Ana Maria Salinas, *Mexican Celebrations* (Austin: University of Texas, Institute of Latin American Studies, 1986); and Judith Winningham, "Beyond Halloween," *Texas Monthly,* October 1986, pp. 140–47.
3. Elizabeth C. Hirschman, "Comprehending Symbolic Consumption: Three Theoretical Issues, " in *Symbolic Consumer Behavior,* Elizabeth C. Hirschman and Morris Holbrook, eds. (Ann Arbor, MI: Association for Consumer Research, 1981), pp. 4–6: and Marsha L. Richins, "Valuing Things: The Public and Private Meanings of Possessions," *Journal of Consumer Research* 21 (December 1994), pp. 504–21.
4. Kent Grayson and David Shulman, "Indexicality and the Verification Function of Irreplaceable Possessions: A Semiotic Analysis," *Journal of Consumer Research* 27 (June 2000), pp. 17–30.
5. U. Beck, *Risk Society: Towards a New Modernity,* M. Ritter, trans. (London: Sage Publications, 1992); Mike Featherstone, *Consumer Culture and Postmodernism* (London: Sage Publications, 1991); S. Lash and J. Urry, *Economies of Signs and Space* (London: Sage Publications, 1994); Melanie Wallendorf and Eric J. Arnould, " 'My Favorite Things': A Cross-Cultural Inquiry into

Object Attachment Possessiveness and Social Linkage," *Journal of Consumer Research* 14 (March 1988), pp. 531–47.

6. Colin Campbell, *The Romantic Ethic and the Spirit of Modern Consumerism* (Oxford: Basil Blackwell, 1987); Fred Davis, *Fashion, Culture, and Identity* (Chicago: University of Chicago Press, 1992); Ed Housewright, "Do Church Ads Work or Compromise Gospel?" *Marketing News,* March 13, 1995, p. 21; Robert H. Frank, *Luxury Fever* (New York: Free Press, 1999); and Lewis Hyde, *The Gift: Imagination and the Erotic Life of Property* (New York: Vintage Books, 1983).

7. Hirschman, "Comprehending Symbolic Consumption"; and Richins, "Valuing Things."

8. Brad Herzog, "They're Great!" *Attache,* August 1999, pp. 54–59.

9. Deborah J. MacInnis, Stewart Shapiro, and Gayathri Mani, "Enhancing Brand Awareness through Brand Symbols," in *Advances in Consumer Research,* vol. 26, Eric Arnould and Linda Scott, eds. (Provo, UT: Association for Consumer Research, 1999), pp. 601–9.

10. John Clammer, "Aesthetics of the Self: Shopping and Social Being in Contemporary Urban Japan," in *Lifestyle Shopping: The Subject of Consumption,* Ron Shields, ed. (London: Routledge, 1992), p. 210; and David Crockett and Melanie Wallendorf, "Sociological Perspectives on Imported School Dress Codes: Consumption as Attempted Suppression of Class and Group Symbolism," *Journal of Macromarketing* 18 (Fall 1998), pp. 115–32.

11. Jennifer Edson Escalas and James M. Bettman, "Using Narratives to Discern Self-Identity Related Consumer Goals and Motivations," in *The Why of Consumption,* S. Ratneshwar, David Glen Mick, and Cynthia Huffman, eds. (London and New York: Routledge, 2000), pp. 237–58; and Grayson and Shulman, "Indexicality and the Verification Function of Irreplaceable Possessions."

12. Davis, *Fashion, Culture, and Identity;* Hyde, *The Gift;* Igor Kopytoff, "The Cultural Biography of Things: Commoditization as Process," in *The Social Life of Things,* Arjun Appadurai, ed. (Cambridge: Cambridge University Press, 1989), pp. 64–94; Barbara Olsen, "Exploring Women's Brand Relationships and Enduring Themes at Mid-Life," in *Advances in Consumer Research,* vol. 26, Eric Arnould and Linda Scott, eds. (Provo, UT: Association for Consumer Research, 1999), pp. 615–20; and Larry Rohter, "Who Is Vainest of All? Venezuela," *New York Times,* August 13, 2000, p. A4.

13. Mark Ligas and June Cotte, "The Process of Negotiating Brand Meaning: A Symbolic Interactionist Perspective," in *Advances in Consumer Research,* vol. 26, Eric Arnould and Linda Scott, eds. (Provo, UT: Association for Consumer Research, 1999), pp. 609–14.

14. Pierre Bourdieu, *Distinction: A Social Critique of the Judgment of Taste* (Cambridge: Harvard University Press, 1984); Davis, *Fashion, Culture, and Identity;* Dick Hebidge, *Subculture: The Meaning of Style* (London: Methuen, 1976); Johanna L. Holland and James W. Gentry, "The Impact of Cultural Symbols on Advertising Effectiveness: A Theory of Intercultural Accommodation," in *Advances in Consumer Research,* vol. 24, Merrie Brucks and Deborah L. MacInnis, eds. (Provo, UT: Association for Consumer Research, 1997), pp. 483–89; John W. Schouten and James M. McAlexander, "Subcultures of Consumption: An Ethnography of the New Bikers," *Journal of Consumer Research* 22 (June 1995), pp. 43–61; and Malene Djursaa and Simon Ulrik Kragh, "Syntax and Creolization in Cross-Cultural Readings of Rooms," in *European Advances in Consumer Research,* vol. 4, Bernard Dubois, Tina M. Lowery, L. J. Shrum, and Marc Vanhuele, eds. (Provo, UT: Association for Consumer Research, 1999), pp. 293–303.

15. Elizabeth C. Hirschman, "Commonality and Idiosyncracy in Popular Culture: An Empirical Examination of the 'Layers of Meaning' Concept," in *Symbolic Consumer Behavior,* Elizabeth C. Hirschman and Morris Holbrook, eds. (Ann Arbor, MI: Association for Consumer Research, 1981), pp. 29–34; David Glen Mick, "Consumer Research and Semiotics: Exploring the Morphology of Signs, Symbols, and Significance," *Journal of Consumer Research* 13 (September 1986), pp. 196–213; David Glen Mick and Laura G. Politi, "Consumers' Interpretations of Advertising Images: A Visit to the Hell of Connotation," in *Interpretive Consumer Research,* Elizabeth C. Hirschman, ed. (Provo, UT: Association for Consumer Research, 1989), pp. 85–96; and Richins, "Valuing Things."

16. Nabil Razzouk and Jamal Al-Khatib, "The Nature of Television Advertising in Saudi Arabia: Content Analysis and Marketing Implications," *Journal of International Consumer Marketing* 6, no. 2 (1993), pp. 65–90; Richins, "Valuing Things"; Jagdish N. Sheth, Bruce I. Newman, and Barbara L. Gross, *Consumption Values and Market Choices: Theory and Applications* (Cincinnati: South-Western, 1991), pp. 18–19; and Wallendorf and Arnould, "My Favorite Things."

17. Russell W. Belk and Nan Zhou, "Learning to Want Things," in *Advances in Consumer Research,* vol. 14, Melanie Wallendorf and Paul Anderson, eds. (Provo, UT: Association for Consumer Research, 1987), pp. 478–81; Barry J. Babin, William R. Darden, and Mitch Griffin, "Work and/or Fun: Measuring Hedonic and Utilitarian Shopping Value," *Journal of Consumer Research* 20 (March 1994), pp. 644–56; Jean-Marie Floch, "The Contribution of Structural Semiotics to the Design of a Hypermarket," *International Journal of Research in Marketing* 4 (1988), pp. 233–52; Marshall D. Rice and Zaiming Lu, "A Content Analysis of Chinese Magazine Advertisements," *Journal of Advertising* 17, no. 4 (1988), pp. 43–48; Jean Umiker-Sebeok, "Meaning Construction in a Cultural Gallery: A Sociosemiotic Study of Consumption Experiences in a Museum," in *Advances in Consumer Research,* vol. 19, John F. Sherry, Jr., and Brian Sternthal, eds. (Provo, UT: Association for Consumer Research, 1992), pp. 46–55.

18. Russell W. Belk, Melanie Wallendorf, and John F. Sherry, Jr., "The Sacred and Profane in Consumer Behavior: Theodicy on the Odyssey," *Journal of Consumer Research* 16 (June 1989), pp. 1–38; and Annette Weiner, *Inalienable Possessions* (Berkeley: University of California Press, 1989).

19. Raj Mehta and Russell W. Belk, "Artifacts, Identity, and Transition: Favorite Possessions of Indians and Indian Immigrants to the United States," *Journal of Consumer Research* 17 (March 1991), pp. 398–411; Wallendorf and Arnould, "My Favorite Things"; and Gregory Starrett, "The Political Economy of Religious Commodities in Cairo," *American Anthropologist* 97 (March 1995), pp. 51–68.

20. Elizabeth C. Hirschman, "Point of View: Sacred, Secular, and Mediating Consumption Imagery in Television Commercials," *Journal of Advertising Research* 36 (December–January 1991), pp. 38–43.

21. Janeen Arnold Costa and Gary J. Bamossy, "Culture and the Marketing of Culture: The Museum Retail Context," in *Marketing in a Multi-Cultural World,* Janeen Arnold Costa and Gary J. Bamossy, eds. (Thousand Oaks, CA: Sage Publications, 1995), pp. 299–328; Carole Duhaime, Annamma Joy, and Christopher Ross, "Learning to 'See': A Folk Phenomenology of Contemporary Canadian Art," in *Contemporary Marketing and Consumer Behavior: An Anthropological Sourcebook,* John F. Sherry, Jr., ed. (Thousand Oaks, CA: Sage Publications, 1995), pp. 399–432; and Ira G. Zepp, Jr., *The New Religious Image of Urban America: The Shopping Mall as Ceremonial Center* (Westminster, MD: Christian Classic, Inc., 1986).

22. David A. Aaker, *Managing Brand Equity* (New York: Free Press, 1991); Eric J. Arnould and Linda L. Price, "River Magic: Extraordinary Experience and the Extended Service Encounter," *Journal of Consumer Research* 20 (June 1993), pp. 24–45; Morris B. Holbrook, and Elizabeth C. Hirschman, "The Experiential Aspects of Consumption: Consumer Fantasies, Feelings, and Fun," *Journal of Consumer Research* 9 (September 1982), pp. 132–40; Morris B. Holbrook "Nostalgia and Consumption Preferences: Some Emerging Patterns of Consumer Tastes," *Journal of Consumer Research* 20 (September 1993), pp. 245–56; Barbara Olsen, "Brand Loyalty and Consumption Patterns: The Lineage Factor," in *Contemporary Marketing and Consumer Behavior: An Anthropological Sourcebook,* John F. Sherry, Jr. (Thousand Oaks, CA: Sage Publications, 1995), pp. 245–81; John W. Schouten, "Selves in Transition: Symbolic Consumption in Personal Rites of Passage and Identity Reconstruction," *Journal of Consumer Research* 17 (March 1991), pp. 412–25; Richins, "Valuing Things"; and Sheth, Newman, and Gross, *Consumption Values and Market Choices,* pp. 20–21.

23. Olsen, "Exploring Women's Brand Relationships and Enduring Themes at Mid-Life."

24. Arnould and Price, "River Magic"; Babin, Dardin, and Griffin, "Work and/or Fun"; Richard L. Celsi, Randall L. Rose, and Thomas W. Leigh, "An Exploration of High-Risk Leisure Consumption through Skydiving," *Journal of Consumer Research* 20 (June 1993), pp. 1–23; Elizabeth Chin, "Bullfighters in the China Shop: Children, Consumption, and Social Process," paper presented at the annual meetings of the American Anthropological Association, Chicago, 1991; Pauline McLaran and Lorna Stephens, "Romancing the Utopian Marketplace: Dallying with Bakhtin in the Powerscourt Townhouse Center," in *Romancing the Market,* Stephen Brown, Anne Marie Doherty, and Bill Clarke, eds. (London and New York: Routledge, 1998), pp. 172–86; John F. Sherry, Jr., "The Soul of the Company Store: Niketown Chicago and the Emplaced Brandscape," in *Servicescapes,* John F. Sherry, Jr., ed. (Chicago: NTC, 1998), pp. 109–46; and Peter Varley and Geoff Crowther, "Performance and the Service Encounter: An Exploration of Narrative Expectations and Relationship

Management in the Outdoor Leisure Market," *Market Intelligence and Planning* 16, no. 5 (1998), pp. 311–17.

25. Elizabeth C. Hirschman, "Secular Immortality and the American Ideology of Affluence," Journal of Consumer Research 17 (June 1990), pp. 31–42; Elizabeth C. Hirschman, "The Consciousness of Addiction: Toward a Generalized Theory of Compulsive Consumption," *Journal of Consumer Research* 19 (September 1992), pp. 155–79; Thomas C. O'Guinn and Ronald J. Faber, "Compulsive Buying: A Phenomenological Exploration," *Journal of Consumer Research* 16 (September 1989), pp. 147–57; and Rob Shields, ed., *Lifestyle Shopping: The Subject of Consumption* (New York: Routledge, 1992).

26. William D. Well and Qimei Chen, "Melodies and Counterpoints: American Thanksgiving and the Chinese Moon Festival," in *Advances in Consumer Research,* vol. 26, Eric Arnould and Linda Scott, eds. (Provo, UT: Association for Consumer Research, 1999), pp. 555–61.

27. Albert M. Muniz, Jr., "Brand Community and the Negotiation of Brand Meaning," in *Advances in Consumer Research,* vol. 24, Merrie Brucks and Deborah J. MacInnis, eds. (Provo, UT: Association for Consumer Research, 1997), pp. 308–9; and Richard Elliott and Mark Ritson, "Practicing Existential Consumption: The Lived Meaning of Sexuality in Advertising," in *Advances in Consumer Research,* vol. 22, Frank Kardes and Mita Sujan, eds. (Provo, UT: Association for Consumer Research, 1995), pp. 740–45.

28. Crockett and Wallendorf, "Sociological Perspectives on Imported School Dress Codes."

29. The following sections were inspired by and rely heavily on material presented in Grant McCracken, "Culture and Consumption: A Theoretical Account of the Structure and Movement of the Cultural Meaning of Consumer Goods," *Journal of Consumer Research* 13 (June 1986), pp. 71–84.

30. This paragraph paraphrases Herbert Blumer, "Fashion," in *International Encyclopedia of the Social Sciences* (New York: Macmillan, 1968), pp. 341–45; see also Ligas and Cotte, "The Process of Negotiating Brand Meaning."

31. Clammer, "Aesthetics of the Self"; and Dorinne Kondo, "The Aesthetics and Politics of Japanese Identity in the Fashion Industry," in *Re-Made in Japan,* Joseph J. Tobin, ed. (New Haven: Yale University Press, 1993), pp. 176–203.

32. This section of the chapter relies heavily on the work of Barbara Stern and Linda Scott. Specific references are cited in the text.

33. Clammer, "Aesthetics of the Self."

34. Veena Das, "On Soap Opera: What Kind of Anthropological Object Is It?" in *Worlds Apart,* Daniel Miller, ed. (London: Routledge, 1995), pp. 169–89.

35. Anthony Lewis, "Boom Box," *New York Times Magazine,* August 11, 2000, pp. 36–41, 51, 65–67; and Barbara J. Phillips, "Advertising and the Cultural Meaning of Animals," in *Advances in Consumer Research,* vol. 23, Kim P. Corfman and John G. Lynch, eds. (Provo, UT: Association for Consumer Research, 1996), pp. 354–60.

36. Barbara B. Stern, "How Does an Ad Mean? Language in Services Advertising," *Journal of Advertising* 17, no. 2 (1988), pp. 3–14.

37. William Leiss, Stephen Kline, and Sut Jahly, *Social Communication in Advertising: Persons, Products, and Images of Well-Being* (Toronto: Methuen, 1986).

38. C. Anthony Di Benedetto, Mariko Tamate, and Rajan Chandran, "Developing Creative Advertising Strategy for the Japanese Marketplace," *Journal of Advertising Research* 32 (January–February 1992), pp. 39–48; Grant McCracken, "Who Is the Celebrity Endorser? Cultural Foundations of the Endorsement Process," *Journal of Consumer Research* 16 (December 1989), pp. 310–21; and Mary Walker, Lynn Langmeyer, and Daniel Langmeyer, "Celebrity Endorsers: Do You Get What You Pay For?" *Journal of Consumer Marketing* 9 (Spring 1992), pp. 69–76.

39. Lance State, "The Cultural Meaning of Beer Commercials," in *Advances in Consumer Research,* vol. 18, Rebecca H. Holman and Michael R. Solomon, eds. (Provo, UT: Association for Consumer Research, 1991), pp. 115–19.

40. Judith Williamson, *Decoding Advertisements: Ideology and Meaning in Advertising* (New York: Marion Boyars, 1993), pp. 7, 12; and Coleman, Lipuma, Segal & Morrill, Inc., *Package Design and Brand Identity* (Rockport, MA: Rockport Publishers, 1994).

end notes

41. Stephanie O'Donohue and Caroline Tynan, "Beyond the Semiotic Strait-Jacket: Everyday Experiences of Advertising Involvement," in *Consumer Research: Postcards from the Edge,* Stephan Brown and Darach Turley, eds. (London: Routledge, 1997), pp. 220–48; and Mark Ritson and Richard Elliott, "The Social Uses of Advertising: An Ethnographic Study of Adolescent Advertising Audiences," *Journal of Consumer Research* 26 (December 1999), pp. 260–77.

42. Arthur J. Kover, "Copywriters' Implicit Theories of Communication: An Exploration," *Journal of Consumer Research* 21 (March 1994), p. 603; and Williamson, *Decoding Advertisements,* pp. 40–44.

43. Kover, "Copywriters' Implicit Theories of Communication"; and Williamson, *Decoding Advertisements.*

44. John W. Schouten, "Selves in Transition: Symbolic Consumption in Personal Rites of Passage and Identity Reconstruction," *Journal of Consumer Research* 17 (March 1991), pp. 412–25.

45. Kopytoff, "The Cultural Biography of Things."

46. Elizabeth Chin, "Fettered Desire: Consumption and Social Experience Among Minority Children in New Haven, Connecticut," unpublished Ph.D. dissertation (New York: Graduate School of the City University of New York, 1996).

47. C. B. Claiborne and Julie L. Ozanne, "The Meaning of Custom-Made Homes: Home as a Metaphor for Living," in *Advances in Consumer Research,* vol. 17, Marvin Goldberg, Gerald Gorn, and Richard Pollay, eds. (Provo, UT: Association for Consumer Research, 1990), pp. 367–74.

48. Clammer, "Aesthetics of the Self"; Patrick Geary, "Sacred Commodities: The Circulation of Medieval Relics," in *The Social Life of Things,* Arjun Appadurai, ed. (Cambridge: Cambridge University Press, 1986), pp. 169–91; Martin J. Gannon and Associates, *Understanding Global Cultures* (Thousand Oaks, CA, Sage Publications, 1994); Joy Hendry, *Wrapping Culture: Politeness, Presentation and Power in Japan and Other Societies* (Oxford: Clarendon Press, 1995); and Hideyuki Oka, *How to Wrap Five More Eggs* (New York: Weatherhill, 1975).

49. Hirschman, "Comprehending Symbolic Consumption."

50. T. Bettina Cornwell, "T-Shirts as Wearable Diary: An Examination of Artifact Consumption and Garnering Related to Life Events," in *Advances in Consumer Research,* vol. 17, Marvin E. Goldberg, Gerald Gorn, and Richard W. Pollay, eds. (Provo, UT: Association for Consumer Research, 1990), pp. 375–79.

51. Marsha L. Richins, "Special Possessions and the Expression of Material Values," *Journal of Consumer Research* 20 (December 1994), pp. 522–33.

52. Barbara Olsen, "Consuming Rastafari: Ethnographic Research in Context and Meaning," in *Advances in Consumer Research,* vol. 22, Frank R. Kardes and Mita Sujan, eds. (Provo, UT: Association for Consumer Research, 1994), pp. 481–85; and Neil J. Savishinsky, "Rastafari in the Promised Land: The Spread of a Jamaican Socioreligious Movement among the Youth of West Africa," *African Studies Review* 37 (December 1994), pp. 19–50.

53. Russell W. Belk, Melanie Wallendorf, John F. Sherry, Jr., and Morris B. Holbrook, "Collecting in a Consumer Culture," in *Highways and Buyways: Naturalistic Research from the Consumer Behavior Odyssey,* Russell W. Belk, ed. (Provo, UT: Association for Consumer Research, 1991), pp. 185–86.

54. Nancy Foster and Robert J. Foster, "Learning Fetishism? Boys Consumption Work with Marvel Super Heroes Trading Cards," paper presented at the 93rd annual meeting of the American Anthropological Association, Atlanta, November 30, 1994.

55. S. R. Howarth, "Corporate Art: An Integral Part of the Company Image," manuscript, The Humanities Exchange/International Art Alliance, Largo, FL.

56. Belk, Wallendorf, Sherry, Jr., and Holbrook, "Collecting in a Consumer Culture," pp. 178–215.

57. Costa and Bamossy, "Culture and the Marketing of Culture"; Duhaime, Joy, and Ross, "Learning to 'See'"; and Jan Larson, "The Museum Is Open," *American Demographics,* November 1994, pp. 32–38.

58. Di Benedetto, Tamate, and Chandran, "Developing Creative Strategy for the Japanese Marketplace"; Geert Hofstede, *Culture's Consequences: International Differences in Work-Related Values* (Thousand Oaks, CA: Sage Publications, 1984); Carolyn A. Lin, "Cultural Differences in Message Strategies: A Comparison between American and Japanese TV Commercials," *Journal of Advertis-*

ing Research 33 (July–August 1993), pp. 40–47; Barbara Mueller, "Standardization vs. Specialization: An Examination of Westernization in Japanese Advertising," *Journal of Advertising Research* 32 (January–February 1992), pp. 15–24; Richard Tansey, Michael R. Hyman, and George M. Zinkhan, "Cultural Themes in Brazilian and U.S. Auto Ads: A Cross-Cultural Comparison," *Journal of Advertising* 19, no. 2 (1990), pp. 30–39; Ludmilla Gricenko Wells, "Western Concepts, Russian Perspectives: Meanings of Advertising in the Former Soviet Union," *Journal of Advertising* 23 (March 1994), pp. 83–93; and Fred Zandpour, Cypress Chang, and Joelle Catalano, "Stories, Symbols, and Straight Talk," *Journal of Advertising Research* 32 (January–February 1992), pp. 25–38.

59. Gannon and Associates, *Understanding Global Cultures;* Igor Kopytoff, "Leisure, Boredom, Luxury Consumerism: The Lineage Mode of Consumption in a Central African Society," in *Consumption and Identity,* Jonathan Friedman, ed. (Chur, Switzerland: Harwood Academic Publishers, 1994), pp. 207–32; Witold Rybczysnski, *Home* (New York: Viking Press, 1986); Valene L. Smith, ed., *Hosts and Guests,* 2nd ed. (Philadelphia: University of Pennsylvania Press, 1989); and Polly Weissner, "Reconsidering the Behavioral Basis for Style: A Case Study among the Kalahari San," *Journal of Anthropological Archaeology* 3 (1984), pp. 190–234.

60. Nancy Rosenberger, "Images of the West: House Style in Japanese Magazines," *Re-Made in Japan,* Joseph J. Tobin, ed. (New Haven: Yale University Press, 1992), pp. 106–25.

61. Marieke de Mooij, *Global Marketing and Advertising: Understanding Cultural Paradoxes* (Thousand Oaks, CA: Sage Publications, 1998).

Learning Objectives

After completing this chapter, you should be able to:

- Understand that disposition is a growth industry that provides many marketing opportunities.

- Recognize that product disposition is an increasingly important area for public policy.

- Discuss some of the practical implications that disposition has for managers.

- Explain the differences between voluntary and involuntary disposition.

- Describe the social, individual, and situational factors that affect disposition choices.

- Realize how understanding disposition provides key insights into consumption behavior.

Disposal, Recycling, and Reuse

The Gods Must Be Crazy!

The Gods Must Be Crazy is a zany film with a twisted plot that really must be broken down into sections. First, it is a story of the quest of Xi (N'gao), a Juntwasi tribesman from the African Kalahari Desert. Xi's family lives deep in the Kalahari. They have never seen a white person and have rarely had contact with anyone else. They live a peaceful life, sharing everything and hunting and gathering for their livelihood. One day, a pilot carelessly drops a Coca-Cola bottle out of his plane. Landing near the camp of Xi's group, it changes their lives drastically. Since there was only one bottle, everyone wanted to use it. For the first time ever, the members of the group grew jealous of one other. The discord mounts until Xi decides that it would be best to give the bottle back to the gods. Not everyone agrees, but eventually the group decides that this is what must be done. On his way to find the end of the world, there to dispose of the bottle, Xi meets Afrikaners Andrew and Kate, the film's second set of protagonists. He thought at first they might be gods, but as their Land Rover is stuck in the top of a tree, they are unable to help him. So, he goes on.

The film's second plot is a comic love story. Andrew Stein (Marius Weyers), a biologist working in the Kalahari, agrees to pick up the new school teacher for the Reverend (Jamie Uys). Kate Thompson (Sandra Prinsloo), a big-city reporter, is trying to escape the pressures of the city by taking a job as a teacher in Botswana. Stein and Thompson have an exhilarating and hilarious two-day ride from the bus stop to the village. Stein and Xi cross paths again when Xi is arrested for shooting a goat. Mbudi

(Michael Thys), Stein's mechanic, is called on to interpret for Xi's trial. Stein agrees to hire Xi as an "environmental expert," thus getting him out of prison.

The third subplot is a tale of a bungled revolution. Sam Boga's (Louw Verwey) anti-apartheid forces flub an assassination attempt. The government forces follow them to their hideaway and attack. Boga and his henchmen then flee toward the Kalahari Desert, where they hope to escape. Boga takes Miss Thompson hostage in an attempt to escape from the government troops. Stein and Xi eventually capture Boga, and in the end, Stein wins Miss Thompson's heart. And finally, Xi's search for the end of the world is completed when he reaches spectacular Victoria Falls. Naturally, he reasons that this must be the end of the world, since the land, indeed, comes to an end. From the cliffs, he hurls the Coke bottle into the mist and, at last, returns to his people.

Overview

Disposition and the Wheel of Consumption

What do consumers or organizations do with products that have outlived their value? This question provides a basis for developing the main ideas in this chapter. Disposal encompasses all those behaviors that consuming units undertake to divest themselves of undesired goods and services. Disposition is an inevitable part of the wheel of consumption, and there are a variety of markets and professions devoted to managing disposition, including auction houses, demolition specialists, flea markets, and mortuaries.

Why be interested in the general question of consumer disposition? There are several reasons. Foremost, disposition is a growth industry providing many marketing opportunities in areas ranging from "green" product design, to solid-waste management, to developing secondary markets for previously owned or leased goods. Green products are hot in many significant global markets.[1] In *The Gods Must Be Crazy*, Xi's first encounter with Western consumer goods immediately poses a disposition problem, and he becomes an unwitting solid-waste engineer for his small band of Kalahari Desert nomads.

Second, product disposition is an important area for policy activity. Even Xi's group was faced with a public policy dilemma: what to do with the envy-producing Coke bottle? In the Triad, both the European Community and the United States have important environmental watchdog agencies that monitor and pinpoint sources of pollution. In addition, industrial and consumer product emissions, both during manufacture and use, are subject to government regulation in the developed world. For example, six European nations in the Rhine River basin recently signed a convention banning boats from dumping any waste into the Rhine and requiring them to pay a tax on fuel in return for free access to waste-disposal stations established along the river. International Standards Organization (ISO) 14000 environmental quality standards focus attention on the environmental effects of a product's life cycle. Like the ISO 9000 quality standards, these environmental standards are likely to become an important mechanism for encouraging industry self-regulation.

Enormous public policy problems surface over such questions as, What qualifies as organic food? Who bears responsibility for radioactive wastes? and What should be done about hazardous wastes? For example, an ongoing dispute rages over the Black Triangle region on the common borders between Poland, Germany, and the Czech Republic where power-plant waste seriously polluted the environment. The only area of agreement is that most people do not want the waste products deposited anywhere close to where they live. Similar disputes have flared between some Native American tribes and their off-reservation neighbors. Some tribes want to establish solid-waste dumps on their impoverished reservations as a way to bring in desperately needed revenues. At the same time, they face strong opposition from their neighbors.[2]

A third reason to be interested in disposition is that it has practical implications for managers. Disposition is linked to acquisition and consumption. As a result, many opportunities for resolving consumer needs can be found at the intersection of these different phases of the wheel of consumption. Interest in environmentally responsible consumption is growing both among individual and institutional consumers. Good Practice 19.1 features stories about successful marketing for reused and recycled products. Business opportunities for **backward channel members,** that is, *those who link consumers back to producers,* show signs of continued development. Some channel members serve as materials brokers for discarded products; others provide centralized processing facilities.[3] See for yourself. Try searching the Internet, using the key word *recycle.*

A fourth reason to be interested in disposition is that it provides insight into consumption behaviors. For example, while it might be unpleasant to analyze the contents of people's garbage, such an analysis can furnish valuable information about product preferences, repeat purchase behavior, and brand loyalty. Garbage can tell us about products purchased and discarded but not consumed and about actual, as opposed to claimed, recycling behaviors.[4]

Three possible disposition tactics are prominent: storing or keeping the product; disposing of it temporarily; or disposing of it permanently.[5] We have discussed the idea of keeping products in Chapter 18, which is devoted to the issue of consumption meanings. Hoarding, saving, and collecting are all meaningful activities that fall under the general heading of storing. In this chapter we focus primarily on the other disposition behaviors (e.g., disposing, recycling).

A fourth general tactic, which we can credit to the modern environmental movement, might be added to this list. The green approach seeks to minimize the problem of disposition. Planned reuse and recycling of materials reduces discarded waste. Good Practice 19.1 provides examples of how the dynamic recycling industry reuses materials. Another green approach for minimizing the waste generated by consumption is through **deconsumption,** that is, *consuming less.* One pioneering study found that consumers in Los Angeles were willing to pay more for a gasoline that was advertised as producing dramatically less air pollution. They preferred it, even in the face of a price war initiated by competing companies. A U.S. catalog company called Real Goods offers a portfolio of long-lasting, energy-efficient light bulbs that decrease consumption both of energy and bulbs. In some instances consumers may decide voluntarily to deconsume without a lot of stimulation. The ULS (Use Less Stuff) newsletter found at the Cygnus Group website provides advice about deconsumption.[6]

www.realgoods.com

www.cygnus-group.com/ULS/About_ULS.html

In a recent example of waste-minimizing practice, Volvo, the Swedish automaker (now part of Ford), decided to use water-based paints as an alternative to prepainting its products with chemical solvents. These solvents emitted volatile organic compounds (VOCs) into the environment. Deconsumption occurred as a side effect of the new process. It eliminated the need for expensive air-pollution control equipment. Volvo could then market its products as greener than those of its competitors.[7] As shown in Good Practice

Mail-order recyclables

Dennis Lashier, an employee at Art's Tire Service in Greenfield, Massachusetts, has been making neckties from old car tires for five years. These ties are touted as "the ultimate gift for the fashion-conscious environmentalist," and Lashier has sold more than 5,000 "Rubber Necker" ties in 32 countries. His outlet is the One Song Enterprises catalog, a mail-order service offering, among other things, natural baby diapers, beeswax candles, and ecological light bulbs. Walden's, a mail-order company in Oxnard, California, offers pitchers and goblets made from recycled glass and bronze sculptures crafted from telephone cables. The number of such green catalogs has increased in recent years. In the words of Deborah Zizmor, spokeswoman for the Direct Marketing Association in New York, "Catalogs tend to follow the trends of consumers."

Reclaiming wood for maximum value

Wood recycling programs tend to focus on grinding as a primary means of recovering fiber. Big City Forest, a for-profit spin-off of the nonprofit Bronx 2000 in New York City, focuses on reuse of lumber for furniture, fixtures, flooring, and refurbished pallets. Big City Forest recycled 3,600 tons of used pallets in the 12-month period ending September 1995. Currently, about 75 percent of the recovered lumber is used in refurbished pallets and 25 percent in furniture and flooring. "We're shifting that ratio as much as possible to furniture and flooring, because that's where the biggest job creation potential is," explained a spokesperson. Currently, Big City Forest's 20 employees were building butcher-block counters for Ben & Jerry's ice cream shops, a table for a resort lodge in Maine, furniture to be sold at two New York environmental stores, and flooring for affordable housing rehabilitation projects.

Land application looks easy in Madison, Wisconsin

At first glance, the achievements of the Madison, Wisconsin, Metropolitan Sewerage District (MMSD) during the past 16 years seems to have fallen into place naturally. In that time, approximately 200,000 tons of dry solids have been applied to nearby farmland, saving millions of dollars in fertilizer costs and garnering international attention. Over 30,000 acres of farmland have been approved for bio-solids land application, although MMSD produces only enough for 3,000 to 4,000 acres per year. From the start, MMSD has made marketing a basic component of the Metrogro program. Even before the sludge was rechristened *bio-solids,* MMSD realized that there are potential public relations problems associated with the term, *sewage sludge.* In Madison, therefore, the preferred term is simply *Metrogro.* Public outreach (public relations) efforts include informational brochures and videos, an open ear to the public, attention to management and operations, and voluntary testing of water quality in rural wells. Unrelated field demonstrations in rural Washington indicate that the application of bio-solids provides corn yields equal to or better than the yields from commercial fertilizer.

Source: Leslie Albrecht Popiel, "Mail-Order Firms Go Green, Even Selling Rubber Neckties," Biocycle, February 1993, p. 8; "Reclaiming Wood for Maximum Value," Biocycle, January 1995, p. 38; Julia Barrett, "Why Land Applications Looks Easy in Madison, Wisconsin," Biocycle, January 1996, pp. 63–64; and Jeffrey G. Faust and Rhonda L. Oberst, "Economic Value of Biosolids to Farmers," Biocycle, January 1996, pp. 67–69.

Marketers strive to save on packaging materials and gain some "green" cachet. Pepperidge Farm Inc. puts garlic bread in an all-plastic bag that can go into an oven or microwave but is 24 percent lighter than regular foil-and-paper bags. To hold refills of its liquid cleaners, L&F Products in New Jersey switched from plastic bottles to plastic-saving pouches that feature screw-on caps. Meanwhile, can makers at Anheuser-Busch and American National Can Co. work at shrinking tops of beverage cans to save on aluminum.

Consumer products are being wrapped in more environment- and user-friendly packaging in other countries too, finds Euromonitor, a marketing research firm. Euromonitor says less packaging is being used, and it's being made of fewer raw materials. Today's packaging also tends to be recyclable or biodegradable.

The company also finds that consumers around the world are demanding and receiving packages that are resealable and reusable, as well as tamper-resistant and childproof where necessary.

Source: Loundes Lee Valeriano, *"Business Bulletin,"* The Wall Street Journal, *April 29, 1993, p. A1.*

19.2, this deconsumption trend also affects the global packaging industry. The BP Amoco ad shown on page 704 states the company is committed to solving the paradox of a world that wants mobility and a cleaner environment.

Disposition is not so much an event as a process. This is an important distinction for a number of reasons. For groups and individuals alike, physical and emotional disposition processes often take place in stages. As Xi found, it is not always easy to get rid of something. For disposition to lead to new production, as in recycling, marketers and governments are often faced with the problem of creating and managing what we can call a **backward channel of distribution.** Such channels *move goods in the opposite direction from traditional channels that move goods from producers to consumers.* An elaborate backward channel that recycles urban solid waste exists in Ho Chi Minh City, Vietnam, for example. It employs hundreds of people. But the creation of backward channels is not necessarily a simple matter, as would-be recyclers often discover. The DuPont ad shown on page 705 focuses on the successful backward channel the company created through a reclamation program.[8]

Disposition issues have been around since human beings began settling in villages, towns, and cities. From prehistoric times to as late as the periods of classical civilization in both the new and old worlds, garbage was often left where it lay in human dwellings with layers of new flooring occasionally laid over the waste. Or it was simply dumped out of doors and windows to settle where it might. Many parts of the Middle East from Syria, through Iraq, Israel, and Iran are dotted with rounded hills that are, in fact, the remains of ancient towns built up in successive levels over their garbage. In ancient Greece and Rome, garbage was thrown into the streets as well into the rivers flowing through the towns. The

Historical and Cross-Cultural Perspectives on Disposition

BP Amoco repositions itself as champion of deconsumption.

What on earth does it mean for an energy company to go beyond?

It means solving the paradox of a world that wants mobility and a clean environment.

It means investing in alternative fuels, processes and ideas.

It means delivering total energy solutions, including electricity.

It means starting a journey that will take the world's expectations of energy beyond what anyone can see today.

bp

beyond petroleum

bp.com

Maya of ancient Central America used household refuse as fill in the construction of major civil and religious buildings like their picturesque temples.

Historically and cross-culturally, there are many examples of disposition-related behaviors. The archaeological record is crowded with artifacts that display the results of recycling behavior. In ancient times, pottery was the equivalent of modern containers made of glass or plastic. It was extensively recycled. Broken pottery, in the form of shards, was frequently ground and used as temper in the manufacture of new batches of pottery. Around the world, masonry structures are often found to harbor stone that had once been used for another purpose, such as the grinding of meal. Much of medieval Rome, to cite one famous instance, was constructed of marble and stone scavenged from buildings erected during the times of the Roman Empire. In this way, the Roman Coliseum served for centuries as a quarry.

Disposition has been a particular problem in the world's cities. In the late Middle Ages in Europe, the failure to deal with urban solid-waste disposal led to the Black Plague that killed a quarter of the population. In the cities of the industrial age, livestock, especially swine, often roamed the streets feeding on garbage that accumulated there. Spas and summer resorts got their start in part because the wealthy wanted to escape the urban stench and fear of disease provoked by inadequate garbage recovery. Although Ben Franklin was the first U.S. sage to call for solid-waste disposal ordinances, it wasn't until the nineteenth century that organized waste disposal became routine in the United States.

Scavenging and recycling regimes in many Third World countries differ little, save for the matter of scale, from those employed in the past. As many do in Ho Chi Minh City, Cairo, or Manila, some 17,000 garbage-pickers, or *pepenadores,* in Mexico City make their living from the city's refuse. They systematically pick through the garbage delivered to the capital's sprawling dumps, looking to reclaim cans, bottles, cardboard, scrap metal, broken appliances, paper, plastic sheeting, and meat bones (these last destined for the manufacturer of bouillon cubes and glue). The pepenadores are tightly organized by a network of *caciques,* or headmen, who are politically powerful. The pepenadore system is driven by money and increments of marginal advantage. This is apparent in the pepenadores' pyramidal pecking order, which reserves to certain classes of garbage worker the scavenging rights to Mexico City's wealthier neighborhoods.

This type of economy was a reality for large number of people in the United States as recently as the turn of the century. Boston's elegant Back Bay neighborhood, once a tidal marsh, owes its existence not only to ample loads of gravel and other kinds of fill but also to the copious amounts of garbage that Bostonians dumped into the site. An etching done by Winslow Homer in 1859 shows scavengers—"chiffoniers," he delicately called them, "pickers up of unconsidered trifles"—combing furiously among the Back Bay garbage dumps. The trade in rags was particularly important, with a class of material known as "thirds and blues"—rags that were thirdhand and blue or lighter in color—being a staple of papermaking and of reprocessed, "shoddy" clothes.[9]

The Disposition Process

Disposition really consists of two interrelated components. First, there is a physical or spatial detachment from a possession object. Second, there is detachment from the meanings and emotions associated with objects. People may have nostalgic longings for lost, destroyed, stolen, or abandoned possessions, indicating their lack of detachment from the emotions and meanings associated with the absent thing. Think for a minute about the stockpiles of possessions kept in attics, cellars, relatives' closets, and public storage facilities. Notice that there are many possessions that you don't want around all the time but can't quite part from because of emotional and meaningful associations. A recent New York auction of Jackie Kennedy Onassis's belongings shows how physical detachment of the things from Ms. Kennedy is not at all the same as the detachment of the meanings. Many people bought items at the auction in order to obtain meanings associated with the American "Camelot" presidency of the early 1960s. In this way, disposition may be triggered by affective, hedonic, or situational concerns.[10]

A Model of Disposition

At the household or firm level, we can diagram the physical disposition process. See Exhibit 19.1 for a schematic drawing of the **model of disposition.** The physical disposition cycle starts when raw materials enter the manufacture process and then are distributed to households (or firms) X and Y that acquire, use, and dispose of them. After usage, some used-up products or their residuals are returned to the environment directly in the form of litter or waste. Alternatively, they may be returned indirectly after collection as garbage and landfill or treatment (e.g., adding rubber-tire cinder to road bedding). As suggested in the exhibit, households can also dispose of products in ways that result in reuse of various kinds.

Simple Reuse

Simple reuse occurs when a product is reused by the consumer for its original purpose or for a different purpose. Empty jars are used for storage. Newspapers line litter pans and shelves or else are used to light fires. Leftovers are fed to pets. Antique furniture may be recovered or refinished. Simple reuse is shown in the exhibit as arrows from usage to usage (1a) and production to production (1b).

Secondhand Reuse

Secondhand reuse of products takes place when a product is given away—as a gift or through inheritance to friends, family, or even strangers—or sold to another household or traded for another product. This kind of transaction is called **lateral recycling.** Most people are probably familiar with boot sales and swap meets, supermarket bulletin boards, Internet auction sites, and newspaper classified sections. In Senegal, colored comics pages from newspapers are sold and used to line luggage made of hammered tin cans; and the poor in many countries scavenge newspapers to use to line shacks and shanties. Interhousehold networks for hand-me-down baby clothing provide an interesting example of secondhand reuse. Inheritance networks generally provide another example of secondhand reuse. In industrial markets, some firms enter into agreements with producers to have them remanufacture the firms' used machine tools for resale back to the firm. These networks are shown in Exhibit 19.1 as an arrow (2) from household X to household (firm) Y.

Exhibit 19.1 Model of Disposition

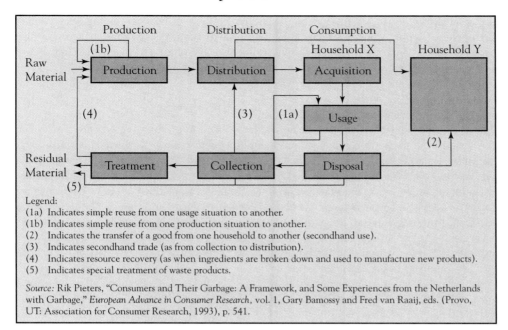

Legend:
(1a) Indicates simple reuse from one usage situation to another.
(1b) Indicates simple reuse from one production situation to another.
(2) Indicates the transfer of a good from one household to another (secondhand use).
(3) Indicates secondhand trade (as from collection to distribution).
(4) Indicates resource recovery (as when ingredients are broken down and used to manufacture new products).
(5) Indicates special treatment of waste products.

Source: Rik Pieters, "Consumers and Their Garbage: A Framework, and Some Experiences from the Netherlands with Garbage," *European Advance in Consumer Research*, vol. 1, Gary Bamossy and Fred van Raaij, eds. (Provo, UT: Association for Consumer Research, 1993), p. 541.

Secondhand Trade

Secondhand trade takes place when the ownership for the used products is first transferred to an intermediary before distribution to new users. Such trade is depicted in the exhibit as an arrow from collection to distribution (3). The secondhand clothes trade in the less affluent world is an important growth industry as a result of trade liberalization and persistent poverty.[11] Many charitable organizations also conduct drives to collect household goods for redistribution to the needy. Notice in this disposition process that no sale links the charitable organization to the donor. A firm called Hannah Anderson, which manufactures children's clothing, offers to buy the clothing back for redistribution to needy children. In 16 years, the firm donated 16 million garments. A U.S. organization called Second Harvest collects leftover food from restaurants for redistribution to over 200 food banks. Used auto parts firms are another example of secondhand trade. Auction houses, including the fashionable Christy's and Sotheby's, also fall into the category of firms that cater to the secondhand market.

www.hannah-anderson.com

www.second-harvest.org

In each of these first three disposition chains, products usually retain their original form and function. Thus, deposit return bottles may be refilled with similar liquid contents for resale after cleaning. The 1930s and 1940s were the heyday of the returnable soft-drink bottle in the United States. Both retailers and consumers began to reject this system because of the inconvenience of returning bottles, and the practice declined in the United States, except in a few states (e.g., New York, Michigan) where it is required by law.

Please notice that some products may acquire additional meanings or value by virtue of their **product biography,** *the history of their movement in and out of markets and from one consumer to another.* Women often receive jewelry, china, silver plate, linens, or other consumer goods from their female ancestors. The sentimental value acquired often singularizes the objects, rendering them irreplaceable in their owners' minds. Similar meanings are attached to the *kula* shell valuables that circulate among islanders in the New Guinea archipelago. Art objects and archaeological specimens acquire a pedigree made up of previous collectors and museums. This property is called the objects' provenience. In the case of classical Chinese art, the red stamps visible on many scrolls represent the "chops" of previous owners and indicate provenience.[12]

Resource Recovery

In a fourth disposition chain, **resource recovery** (4), the product ingredients are broken down and used to manufacture new products. Resource recovery, what many think of as **recycling,** takes place when the product or its parts are used as a secondary resource in the production of new products. Glass bottles or aluminum cans may be melted down and remanufactured. Newspapers may be ground, cleaned, and added to new papermaking processes. Gypsum board can be ground up for use in agriculture. Plastic bottles may be melted down and spun into fiber for clothing. In many cities, nonhazardous waste such as yard clippings and sweepings are composted and reused in gardens, farms, or yards. More examples are provided in Good Practice 19.1. In the recycling business, governments have become involved in creating markets. For instance, some U.S. state governments work to link woody materials generators, processors, and end users together to create new markets for construction materials, animal bedding, and landscaping materials. The UK set a target of 40 percent waste content in newsprint for the year 2000, for example, and helped set up a new plant to recycle newsprint and established a vigorous public relations campaign to encourage recycling.[13]

Composting: special treatment to recover resources.

Special Treatment

Special treatment of waste products is depicted in Exhibit 19.1 as an arrow from treatment to residual materials (5). Metrogro, discussed in Good Practice 19.1, requires some special treatment before application to farm fields. Special treatment of hazardous waste is often required, for example, by incinerating it under controlled conditions and using the cinder for landfill. Household composting is a simple example of a home treatment process that has become a significant activity in both the developed and developing worlds. Spain reports composting over 10 percent of its municipal waste; Denmark composts over 8 percent. The United States, Canada, and Mexico are not as ambitious; like Germany and the Czech Republic they compost less than 4 percent of their municipal waste.[14] Composted waste is a useful input into household gardening. Marketing easy-to-use household composting technologies is a growing business derived from the demand for household waste treatment supplies. An ad from *Biocycle* magazine for the Earth Machine, shown on page 708, illustrates this trend.

In the disposition process, supply and demand are reversed. Consumers produce various kinds of waste products, and producers consume these secondary resources. One might say that the top half of Exhibit 19.1 illustrates the demand for secondary resources, while the bottom half represents the supply side.[15]

Voluntary and Involuntary Disposition

There is an important distinction between voluntary and involuntary disposition behaviors. We describe both methods and give examples of voluntary and involuntary disposition behaviors in Exhibits 19.2 and 19.3.

Exhibit 19.2 presents a typology of voluntary disposition behaviors. The entries in the exhibit imply that people make considered decisions about disposition much in the way the theories of consumer decision making discussed in Chapter 10 describe acquisition behaviors. Thus, when the value derived from a good begins to lag behind the costs of having it around, consumers dispose of it in one way or another.[16] Of course, the disposition process does not always have to be so rational and considered. Feelings and emotions play a strong role in disposal. Just as there are impulse purchases, there are also impulse disposals (see Consumer Chronicles 19.1).

In contrast to the highly deliberative forms of disposition discussed in the North American context where it is a means to achieve other ends, voluntary disposition is part of the taken-for-granted terminal value systems in some cultures. From the Buddhist perspective, for example, a value system that influences people throughout south Asia and in the Far East, it is said that the extent of one's problems are equal to the size of one's possessions. In Buddhist psychology, the need to possess is posited to be a major cause of psychopathology and suffering. The Buddhist middle path allows for the enjoyment of possessions without attachment to them, without a need for possession. In Islam, acts of

Exhibit 19.2 A Taxonomy of Voluntary Disposition Behaviors

Methods	Personal Focus	Interpersonal Focus	Societal Focus
Sell—Convert objects to money	As a current example, consumers may go to the eBay website (www.ebay.com) to sell goods that they no longer want or need	Businesses of all sorts; sell personal collections and constructions; sell one's body, blood, body parts, art, crafts, or ideas; auctions; garage and yard sales; flea markets	Sell resources, waste, radio spectrum, used capital goods and weapons
Trade—Exchanging resources in kind	Trading off work, sleep, leisure, or quality time; a skin graft	Countertrades; cooperative labor exchanges, including day care; stock swaps; trading in consumer durables; exchanging ideas; trading sports players	Countertrades
Give away— Transferring objects and sometimes meanings	Possible feelings of altruism; affiliation motive	Donate body organs; charitable donations; pass baby clothes to siblings and friends; living inheritances; giving advice to others	Redistribution of land, labor, commodities, services, time from less to more needy persons
Recycle—Convert it to something else	Making a quilt from scraps, picture frames from old barn board; composting	Recycling animal waste, newspapers, aluminum, yard trimmings, tires, waste pulp and paper	Recycling buildings, neighborhoods, waste water, mining or industrial facilities, ruins
Throw away—Discard in a societally approved manner	Use of trash cans, garbage disposals, sewage systems, land fills; diet; give up an unhealthy lifestyle	Neighborhood, park, or beach cleanup; divorce, separate from, or disown a person; diet plans	Dump garbage in space or the oceans; stockpile nuclear and chemical waste
Abandon—Discard in a societally unacceptable manner	Strew property about in public places	Abandon family members and pets; eschew accepted codes of conduct; violate a trust	Abandon social groups (poor, homeless, mentally ill; minorities); abandon political allies; abandon environmental responsibilities
Use up—Physical consumption	Eat; use nonrenewable energy sources; wear out tools or clothing	Use employees' time; use family, friends', or neighbors' resources	Use nonrenewable resources: fossil fuels, ecosystems; use citizens in war
Destroy—Intentionally damage	Suicide; burn down one's house; shred old pictures or love letters	Arson; euthanasia; infanticide; murder; terrorist bombing; redline a neighborhood	Conduct war, genocide, revolution; executions and regicides

Source: Melissa Martin Young and Melanie Wallendorf, "Ashes to Ashes, Dust to Dust: Conceptualizing Consumer Disposition of Possessions," *Proceedings,* Educators' Conference, American Marketing Association, 1989, pp. 32–37.

charitable giving are one of the five pillars that must be practiced by every devout person. These forms of voluntary disposition, then, are not rational in the narrow economic sense, but they do influence consumers' attitudes and beliefs, probably lowering generalized materialism and acquisitiveness and promoting the giving away of possessions.[17]

Exhibit 19.3 A Taxonomy of Involuntary Disposition Behaviors

Methods	Personal Focus	Interpersonal Focus	Societal Focus
Use up	Accidentally or unintentionally use up possessions, food, time	Loss of time at mandatory meetings; friend or family member uses up gas, tennis balls, aspirin	Ozone layer; ocean fish; fresh air and water
Legal transfer		Patent or copyright revoked or ended; lose property or children in divorce; house or car repossessed; treasured possessions dispersed after death	Eminent domain; war crimes retribution; boundary redemarcation
Illegal transfer		Burglary, theft, extortion, bribery; patent or copyright infringement; gray markets	Artwork or historical artifacts stolen; lose land or population in war; black markets
Loss	Misplace objects; forget information; lose track of time; abandon in a geographic move	Death of a loved one; losing track of people; loss of other's possessions and resources, time	Historical buildings, archives, records, heroes, values, history neglected
Destruction	Own death; breakage	Be vandalized, burgled, murdered; reputation ruined by gossip or media; gamble away an inheritance	Overpopulation or pollution destroys natural resources, or biodiversity; war or disease wipes out a population; chemical waste depresses sperm counts

Source: Melissa Martin Young and Melanie Wallendorf, "Ashes to Ashes, Dust to Dust: Conceptualizing Consumer Disposition of Possessions," *Proceedings,* Educators' Conference, American Marketing Association, 1989, pp. 32–37.

Most likely you can think of involuntary acquisition behaviors, such as inappropriate birthday or wedding gifts you have received. Similarly, you can imagine involuntary disposition behaviors. Losing a wedding ring down the drain; getting burgled; being compelled by poverty or illness to sell favored possessions; or giving up household goods in a divorce are all examples. Of course, death is the ultimate source of involuntary disposition since "you can't take it with you." Exhibit 19.3 presents a typology of involuntary disposition behaviors, a few of which we discuss below.

Involuntary loss of possessions is relatively common. Divorce touches almost half of all marriages in the United States and is frequent in most European and African countries as well. Loss of property is commonplace for both parties to a divorce, but women suffer the most loss of property.[18]

A study of 16 countries found that over 4 percent of the citizenry became victims of one form of theft, burglary, or attempted burglary. Reactions to the loss of property accompanying burglary are relatively strong. The most intense and long-lasting reactions to burglary are found among women, the elderly, singles, and the poor. Interestingly, children's reactions to theft become increasingly harsh with age, as possession becomes progressively more a part of self-concept and perceived self-efficacy. Two characteristics of the experience may account for the special severity of adult emotional responses to burglary. The whole of the personal possessions of the victims has been attacked. Thus, consistent with the notion of the extended self, discussed in Chapter 7, meanings of intense personal importance congealed in one's possessions are attacked and compromised in a burglary. Burglary and other forms of theft attack the boundaries of the self and the family. Feelings of alienation from the home, intrusion, loss of perceived personal control, and contamination are common. Not surprisingly, almost three-quarters of consumers in Western countries are insured against some financial consequences of residential burglary. Victims appreciate services that provide informational and emotional support, but such services are not always available. Perhaps you can identify additional marketing opportunities here.[19]

Profiles of Disposition Behaviors

In this section we provide more detail about the behaviors mentioned in the model of disposition shown in Exhibit 19.1. Specifically, we discuss discarding, selling, donating, gift giving, storing, and recycling.

Discard It

When people think about disposition, probably the first possibility that comes to mind is simply throwing something away. The United States has been accused of being a **waste-making society,** *one in which people's first thought is to discard rather than reuse or recycle unwanted possessions.* Indeed, Americans throw away a lot of trash, almost two kilograms a day. There are patterns to this waste making. For example, American families discard approximately 15 percent of the food they buy and approximately 1 percent of their garbage is composed of hazardous waste, or about 12 ounces a year. But, as we have already suggested, not everything gets tossed.

In the United States, consumers discard about 12 billion tons of material each year, of which about 209 million metric tons is the solid waste that comes from households, institutions, small businesses, towns, and municipalities. The average per capita amount of waste produced by Americans has not changed much in the past 100 years, 1.5 to 1.9 pounds per day.[20]

The Japanese discard only approximately 1.1 kilograms per day, but Japan too is a throw-away culture, in part because of a high value placed on newness and a distaste for used items. In Tokyo, weekly collections of large throwaways attract tons of discarded consumer products, many in mint condition. Students and the poor enjoy attractive scavenging and reuse options.[21]

The more diversity and novelty there is in consumption patterns, the more people throw away as waste. Richer countries discard more than poorer ones. Consider the thousands of new consumer products that are introduced each year in North America, most of which fail in the marketplace. Thus, marketers who thrive on providing consumers with novel and diverse product offerings contribute to the discard phenomenon.

Sell It

Flea markets, swap meets, garage, barn, and jumble sales (UK), antique dealerships, and acres of secondhand car lots are as characteristic of contemporary consumer society as the shopping mall. Together, they represent a major type of household disposition behavior, **selling.** At **swap meets,** consumers get together in informal markets to buy or trade their used goods. Such selling is a key way people get rid of unwanted possessions. For example, a study in Tucson, Arizona, found that 34 percent of household appliances that had recently been replaced had been sold to stores or strangers. Selling is often occasioned by changes in family life-cycle stage, geographic movements, and role transitions, such as divorces. Flea markets, garage, and yard sales are a primary vehicle for secondhand reuse or lateral recycling from household to household, as discussed above. In lateral recycling, the use and form of used merchandise remains constant while the user changes. Under traditional recycling, form, use, and users all change.

North American garage sales provide a dramatic example of lateral recycling. Garage sales probably began in California in the early 1960s and spread across the continent from there. Between six and nine million North American garage sales now generate between one and two billion dollars in sales every year. Most participants are of middle- and working-class backgrounds, in their twenties and thirties.[22]

 eBay.com

Internet auction sites, such as eBay, can be viewed as **electronic flea markets** that facilitate lateral recycling. Consumers come to these sites to sell goods that are no longer of use to them. The procedure is a bit different from a traditional flea market in that rival bids are posted over a period of time. Individuals, not corporations, use eBay to buy and sell items in more than 4,300 categories, including automobiles, collectibles, antiques, sports memorabilia, computers, toys, Beanie Babies, dolls, figures, coins, stamps, books, magazines, music, pottery, glass, photography, electronics, jewelry, and gemstones. Every day, four million new auctions are offered in counties such as Australia, Canada, Germany, Japan, the United Kingdom, and the United States. Just like a traditional marketplace, electronic marketplaces strive to serve community needs such as social interaction and meeting with other users who share similar interests.

Disposition, just like acquisition, provides a means of expressing important values. One U.S. study identified four themes or motives for garage sales. The first is reclaiming control of one's work, which recognizes that garage sales create a sense of empowerment that middle- and working-class consumers may not have in daily life. The second is creating a sense of social justice, as reflected in the common tendency to lower prices for the deserving. A third theme or motive is beating the system, which refers to buyers' satisfaction with their reduced dependence on traditional retail outlets and their ability to acquire goods inexpensively. Fourth is feeling part of a nurturing community, which reflects the communal aspects of lateral recycling as goods pass from consumers who no longer need them to those who do.[23]

For some consumers, swap meets and flea markets represent personal freedom and are viewed as a bastion of free enterprise. The festive, carnival-like atmosphere of the flea market may represent a release from the rule-governed world of normal life. Distinctions of wealth and status tend to be relaxed, expressing the North American value of equality. Some participants consider garage sales as an appropriate venue for family entertainment and an expression of togetherness.[24]

Both garage sales and the items sold in them reflect norms and values associated with gender. Gender-typed items tend to attract shoppers of the appropriate gender, and sellers may even direct men and women to the expected grouping of objects. The quintessential men's sale involves a jumble of items, focused on tools, recreation gear, and some computer equipment, for example. Prices are usually negotiated, and some men delight in drumming up enthusiasm among shoppers through a display of expertise about the items on offer.[25]

Disposition involves both physical and emotional separation from possessions. Selling household goods is one way consumers separate personal meanings from goods, or separate that part of themselves associated with objects that have been part of their lives. Sales of household goods can be a way of getting rid of the past, of an unattractive prior self, a divorced spouse, or a deceased family member. Since sales are direct, face-to-face transactions, sellers are able to maintain some control over who receives their former possessions. Because the transformation of possessions into commodities for sale may be a

The big blue-and-white trucks roll up and disgorge their cargo: A tobacco-colored vinyl lounger, a rickety croquet set, pink hair rollers, a copy of *Atlas Shrugged,* a 45-rpm Shaun Cassidy record. It's a typical day at Goodwill central out on San Fernando Road, a few miles north of downtown. Mauricio Hernandez patrols the loading dock. It's his job to see that the day's bounty—the discards of an average of 200 households—are sorted, priced, and sent on their way to some of the 26 Goodwill thrift stores throughout the county. "The show starts here," he says, as the trucks' treasures are dumped into big metal bins and wheeled to sorting tables. Clothing (8,000–10,000 items today) goes onto one conveyor belt, "hard goods"—lamps, hair dryers, pots and pans—onto another. On the fourth floor of the cavernous building, in the denim wing, recycled Guess jeans are tagged $10. Nearby, a man is "hanging" clothing and a trio of workers sift through a huge pile of shoes, seeking mates. One floor below, sofa beds are stripped and reupholstered. Goodwill of Southern California depends on the kindness of strangers. Sale of donated items raises $12 million of its $15-million annual budget.

Source: Beverly Beyette, "Around Town," Los Angeles Times, *July 22, 1993, pp. E1, E2.*

meaningful emotional event, sellers of household goods often engage in divestment rituals, such as cleaning, sorting, folding, arranging, and tagging them. These rituals serve to empty goods of meaning before they are passed on to others.[26]

Donate It

Giving things away is a third form of disposition. Attitudes toward the **donation** of goods and services to others vary widely around the world. Charity is enshrined in both Catholic and Islamic religious doctrine, and charitable giving is common in many Protestant denominations as well. Millions of people donate blood to the member organizations of the International Red Cross. As such, donations are the lifeblood of thousands of charitable organizations around the world, including Second Harvest discussed above. Consumer Chronicles 19.2 provides a glimpse of how one charity that relies on donations operates. In many countries, people are encouraged to donate their body parts and to designate their eyes or other organs for reuse. Even human reproductive matter, sperm and eggs, may be donated to help redress the problem of human infertility.

The donation decision process is unique among disposition decisions. Unlike the typical marketing exchange, the donation process is often a reaction to a serious or even desperate human condition. Thus, this process may tap into feelings of joy, improved self-esteem (altruism), guilt, or denial. Donation also differs from gift giving discussed in Chapter 10 in that reciprocation and relationship maintenance are secondary considerations. Donation involves giving something tangible with little provision of any return. Moreover, rewards received are usually intangible or delayed.[27]

<hr>

Gift It

Gift giving has been discussed in Chapter 10 as a form of consumer acquisition. Of course, gift giving can also be a mode of disposition. One form of gift disposition, **inheritance,** provides numerous business opportunities and is an important household consumer behavior. Family inheritance decisions involve gifts from older generations of family members to younger ones and from the departed to the living. Important distinctions are made in some societies between the way immovable property (land and buildings), movable property (other tangible property, including consumer goods), and even intangible assets (such as specialized knowledge of various kinds) are inherited. In the urban West, social norms promote relatively egalitarian inheritance decisions, especially in the United States.[28] There is evidence of convergence toward this pattern in Japan as well.[29]

Between 1995 and 2000, nearly $1 trillion was passed on to baby boomers in the form of bequests. This event represents "the largest intergenerational transfer of wealth in American history."[30] As in previous generations, aging confronts consumers with decisions about how to distribute their wealth. If populations in the Triad countries become top heavy with older citizens as expected, inheritance issues will come increasingly to the forefront, providing new entrepreneurial opportunities for visionary consumer marketers.

In south Asia and Africa, dowry and bride wealth constitute two contrasting forms of what we might call **preinheritance,** *living bequests of household resources.* In dowry, the wife's family provides important stocks of consumer goods and money to the husband's family. The custom of bride wealth works in the reverse way. The size and composition of these forms of preinheritance are often hotly debated because size and composition contribute to social status. In addition, the size and composition of dowry and bride wealth strongly affect the standard of living of the newly wed household. Both forms of preinheritance have become important systems for the diffusion of innovative consumer goods into south Asian and African societies, as they are often part of the dowry and bride wealth. Thus, these customary transfers become the vehicle for new forms of conspicuous consumption of consumer goods. Since women often contribute to and benefit from these transfers, the size and composition of dowry and bride wealth may influence the comfort and control wives exert in their new homes as well.[31]

<hr>

Store It

Storage is a basic consumer necessity. Of course, some of this function is performed by retail stores and other channel members. Nonetheless, consumers make provisions for the storage of food, valuables, and sacred objects. Even Australian Aborigines, people with limited material wealth, maintain sacred sites where they store elaborately carved and painted boards called *alcheringa* that serve as permanent records of important myths and stories.

In the contemporary urban West, some trace of traditional storage behaviors can be seen in the frequent use of food cellars. Consistent with these traditions, many French people place modern electric freezers in their cellars. A study conducted in Tucson, Arizona, found that in 30 percent of cases in which a household appliance had recently been replaced, the old one was kept around the house somewhere. Both individual and institutional consumers store objects in corporate, historical, and other museum collections.[32]

In most places around the world, the home has become people's most important storehouse of consumer goods.[33] Homes are used to store goods that act as objects of temporal

The Re-Source

Looking for a T-shirt made entirely from a plastic soda bottle? You can buy them by the caseload, thanks to environmental distributors like Mary Jarret. Jarret's Amazing Recycled Products in Denver gives retailers one-stop access to 250 unique environmental products of all shapes and sizes. A briefcase made of recycled factory wastes (from wetsuits) is a hot item; so are pens made from recycled cardboard. And Jarret sells "lumber" made from recycled milk containers for building park benches and picnic tables. "I don't have to sell the idea of using recycled products anymore," says the 45-year-old entrepreneur, who started her company seven years ago. "I'm getting 40 to 50 calls a day."

Source: Entrepreneur, September 1993, p. 14.

stability in people's lives. **Time-marked goods** (e.g., trophies, souvenirs, awards, religious artifacts, wedding gifts, photos) *remind people who they once were, invite comparison with who they are now, and highlight how they have changed.* In addition, many of the items people keep around them may be thought of as stimuli for an evolving network of associated memories. Not only do such memories provide an anchor to the sense of self, they may also provide people with cues for internal search behaviors when considering future consumption choices.[34]

In homes in the West, an attic or a cellar may become a repository for special possessions. Upper-class households may contain heirloom collections that provide symbols of family continuity. That is, the things people store in attics and cellars may convey social affiliation meanings. At the same time, the things hidden away in attics and basements may also play a role in differentiation and self-definition. The existence of these objects—heirloom linens, school yearbooks, yellowing photos, old dolls—are physical markers of the special beings who inhabit the house. In addition, people say they also store things because they never know when they may need them again. Hence, these stored items allow people to anticipate future needs. Finally, attics and cellars may symbolize the consumption of time. Stored objects allow people to remember themselves as they were when old possessions were new. Attics and cellars also allow people to remember themselves and the events and persons associated with stored objects when they periodically sort through these spaces. Stored objects allow people to recall former times and former selves.[35]

In contemporary consumer society, storing material possessions has assumed dramatic proportions and spawned numerous marketing activities devoted to providing companies and individuals with storage options. For example, there are firms that specialize in storage of legal documents and closet remodeling. There's a retail company called Hold Everything that specializes in storage containers and facilities. Shopping suggestions are a staple of travel guides, and souvenirs are preserved as mementos of the tourist experience. In Salt Lake City, Utah, a firm called Summum has even revived the ancient Egyptian practice of preserving bodies for posterity through mummification. For a minimum of $32,000, Summum will turn you into a museum-quality corpse! And this is just one of the many new options on offer from the trillion dollar global funeral business.[36]

Recycle It

Recycling has always been around. In the last 30 years it has become enshrined in consumer behavior and business practices as a result of a series of resource crises that hit the First World, beginning with the oil price shock in 1973. Threats of a shortage of landfill space began in the mid-1980s. This threat is being felt throughout the developed and developing worlds and has also helped fuel consumer and business recycling activities. Aggressive environmental education in schools, science museums—even specialized "garbage museums"—and some places in the media has also increased consumer concern and some recycling behaviors. Consumer activists have turned the spotlight on consumer product companies whose packaging is difficult to recycle. In the European Community and North America, recycling is written into national regulatory law. One EC proposal mandates that early this century 90 percent of all packaging waste by weight must be recovered. The innovative Netherlands National Environmental Policy Plan II calls for integrated life-cycle management that will make producers responsible for whatever remains of their products after the users are through with them. The idea is that producers are more likely to design products and packaging that can be reused or recycled if they are responsible for disposal costs. As a result, some international firms, including Body Shop International PLC, Nestlé, Texas Instruments, VeryFine Products, Inc., Volvo, and BMW, have moved aggressively to recycle or to encourage employees to recycle. Of course, numerous entrepreneurs have emerged to meet the demand for recycled goods as shown in Industry Insights 19.1 and 19.2.[37]

Curiously, the recycling industry is in flux. Recycling is probably the most well known and publicized environmental service. Technological advances constantly extend the list of materials that can be recycled, breaking new ground for recycling companies. Demand for recycled and recyclable products is strong, but consumer recycling rates have stagnated.

Nevertheless, interest in **close-loop manufacturing,** where *simplified recycling is built into products from the design phase on,* is developing in Scandinavia, Germany, and to a lesser extent Japan. In Germany, for example, the so-called dual system allows for the collection of all recyclable packaging materials for sorting and recycling. This effort is supported by a financing system, the Green Point, run by a former Nestlé CEO. In Europe, government regulations will tax people on their cars until they can show that they have been disposed of cleanly at an accredited disassembly plant. BMW, VW, the PSA group, which markets Peugeot and Citroën, are actively involved in the effort. The VW Golf is designed to be recycled, and BMW has a disassembly plant in Wackersdorf, Bavaria. Detroit automakers are also involved in closed-loop recycling, experimenting with recyclable plastic body parts, brake pads, and taillights.[38]

Giving Old Notes New Currency

Best known for its deluxe stationery, Crane & Co., the Massachusetts paper manufacturer, has come up with a new line of recycled stationery made primarily from shredded U.S. currency. Befitting the source, the paper is green and is called Old Money and includes thank-you notes, boxed stationery, and pads adorned with dollar signs. According to Timothy Crane, a sixth-generation descendent of the company's founder, Old Money was a response to a Federal Reserve Board request for inventive ways to get rid of the 15 million pounds of worn paper bills it deems unfit for circulation each year.

Source: "Econotes," Los Angeles Times, August 16, 1993, p. E1.

Industry Insights 19.2

Situational and Individual Factors Affecting Disposal Choices

What factors influence the disposition choices of consumers, firms, and organizations? Here, we suggest a number of factors and group them into the following categories.[39]

Factors Intrinsic to the Product

Materials, purchase price, and replacement cost influence disposition decisions. For example, the materials from which products are made influence recycling significantly. Aluminum is the easiest to recycle thanks to high prices for aluminum and aluminum ore. Paper recycling is increasing, as is recycling of plastics. Organic materials like yard sweepings and tree trimmings are recyclable through composting, fueling a global municipal composting industry as represented in the Lubo Starscreen™ ad shown above. By contrast, rubber, especially vulcanized rubber used in tires, is one of the more difficult products to recycle, and markets for recycled rubber have been slow to develop.

Both consumers and organizations consider purchase price and replacement costs in making disposition decisions. Higher costs result in delays in disposition, and when disposition occurs, selling is a common strategy. Higher-priced goods thus tend to enter secondary markets. Higher-priced consumer goods that have been personalized in some way are often laterally recycled through inheritance.

Competitive Pressures

In businesses, competitive pressures play an important role in disposition. For example, new capacity for recycling fibers in the United States in 1994 created a supply shortage that drove prices for corrugated containers to $140 per short ton.[40] Competition for supply will call forth new sources of recyclable materials.

Competitive pressures also influence firms to undertake deconsumption measures or engage in special handling of waste. As shown below in the ad for Saturn, companies can then employ credible green appeals in product differentiation and market positioning strategies. Similarly, Shell Oil claims that they have reduced their net greenhouse gas emissions at a rate that puts the company ahead of the schedule in the Kyoto (Japan) agreement on the environment.[41]

www.shell.com/biodiversity

Sometimes, competitive pressures are formalized as self-imposed industry norms for materials handling and life-cycle management. The new **ISO 14000** standards for environmental management are an example. The International Organization for Standardization set out to develop ISO 14000 standards that organizations can use to improve their environmental performance over time. ISO 14000 consists of five families of standards, including environmental management system (EMS), environmental auditing, environmental

Employing a green appeal for product differentiation.

Elderly people, facing retirement and death, encounter special disposition problems. Decisions related to the disposition of possessions often are fraught with tension. The decision process is complicated by the fact that family members may avoid any discussion related to the disposition of the older persons' possessions.

Older consumers' possessions represent who they are and the life they have led. Possessions represent emotional connections to individuals who mean the most to them. An older person's possessions may take on value based on the length of time the person has owned them and the circumstances surrounding acquisition of that belonging. In addition, possessions help owners reminisce about significant time periods and events in their lives. The disposition of objects, possessions, and experiences that are infused with personal meanings through inheritance is often painful.[49] Deciding what will become of those possessions, to leave a legacy that validates one's life and affirms relationships with important survivors, becomes an important responsibility for older consumers.

The tensions felt by aging consumers are different from ordinary consumer disposition decisions in three important ways. First, the relationship between older consumers and their possessions is unique because of the retrospective dimension inherent in possessions that have been held for extended periods of time. Second, as people age, they witness many changes. Special possessions may be among the most stable things in the lives of older consumers. Third, there is an inevitability in the disposition of possessions that is much more strongly felt by older consumers than their younger counterparts (see Consumer Chronicles 19.1). Whether individuals have a disease or physical condition that will lead to death in a predictable period of time or simply have an awareness of their passage through the life cycle, older consumers become increasingly concerned about the ongoing biography their possessions will have after their own life passage comes to an end.

Disposition of older consumers' cherished possessions presents an array of mostly untapped marketing opportunities. Products and services could be devised to record and store special possession meanings and stories. Counseling and consulting services could help families confront and process the disposition needs of older consumers and help charities and other beneficiaries respond to older consumers' desires to leave a legacy. Finally, channels could be devised to more easily facilitate lateral recycling of older consumers' special possessions.[50]

Serious life-threatening illness and death may be viewed as a complex array of dispossession events. Life-threatening illness and or impending death may stimulate a chain of voluntary, and ultimately involuntary, dispossession behaviors. For the ill, dispossession may be experienced as a loss of control or a diminution of the self. Alternatively, illness may so change the sense of self that dispossession of some possessions linked to the previous sense of self may be relatively easy. Knowledge of the impending end of life sometimes stimulates a belief that material possessions are less important than other aspects of life, such as relationships with others. In turn, the relationships may be strengthened by dispossession. After death, possessions can become important symbols by which individuals wish to be remembered.[51]

Disposition: Segmentation and Psychographic Factors

Traditionally, marketers strive to create marketing plans so as to achieve, simultaneously, two objectives. First, following the marketing concept, they attempt to satisfy customer needs. Second, they attempt to achieve organizational goals (e.g., in terms of shareholder wealth, market share, sales levels). In his pioneering book *Sustainable Marketing,* Donald

Fuller argues that a third criterion needs to be added to this set. Specifically, **sustainable marketing** means that *marketing plans should be constructed so that they are compatible with ecosystems.* With an emphasis on sustainable marketing, organizations can find ways to reduce costs and serve the long-term well-being of society. In this section, we review a group of segmentation strategies and issues that are congruent with Fuller's notion of sustainable marketing.[52]

Markets can be segmented on the basis of consumers' green orientation. Specifically, **green segments** are *consumers whose acquisition behavior is affected by proenvironmental attitudes and behaviors.* A green orientation is a variable one.[53] That is, a particular consumer may be green with respect to purchasing products with organic or recycled content but, at the same time, resist acts related to deconsumption. Examples of a number of green segmentation profiles are summarized in Exhibit 19.4.

These segmentation profiles assume that there is a relationship between the propensity to reuse, recycle, and consider the environmental impacts of waste disposal and a green psychographic profile (see Chapter 8 for a discussion of psychographics). At the other end of the continuum, it is probable that "brown" consumers, through disinterest, lower incomes, less education and environmental knowledge, or diminished sense of self-efficacy, are likely to be concerned less about the environmental consequences of manufacturing, packaging, and solid-waste disposal.

Exhibit 19.5 summarizes four types of segments for environmentally responsible buying (ERB). Socially responsible purchasing includes such judgments as considering what the product is made of (e.g., office paper from recycled postconsumer waste versus virgin materials), from where it comes (e.g., wood from sustainably managed forests versus unmanaged forests), or from whom it comes (e.g., companies whose other products are unobjectionable versus companies that also make objectionable products). Politically savvy policy entrepreneurs play a key role in initiating environmentally responsible buying in the organization buying center. Successful initiation of comprehensive ERB programs involves the emergence of a group of volunteers in the organization. If organizations are to pursue ERB objectives, it is important that extrinsic rewards (i.e., monetary and career advancing) for purchasing agents be created to foster such actions.[54]

Segmentation

At the individual level, the decision maker's psychological characteristics play a role in determining disposition decisions. As with other consumption decisions, differences in motivation, knowledge, affect, experience, and involvement play a role in explaining disposition behaviors.

Green consumers tend to be younger and more highly educated and, to some extent, have higher incomes than other consumers. Gender, political affiliation, and social class are not strongly related to green consumer behaviors. Green consumers are conscious of the implicit costs of consumption and try to minimize them. Such awareness is at the root of the movement toward voluntary simplicity or to the idea of eating farther down the food chain (e.g., minimizing the processing of food products). Green consumers are motivated by a concern for social well-being. They tend to exhibit a relatively strong sense of personal efficacy; that is, they think that their daily behaviors can have a positive environmental impact.[55]

Personal values such as altruism and the **biospheric orientation,** or earth-first orientation, of committed ecologists relate to *positive beliefs and attitudes toward recycling and waste reduction behaviors.* But the link is relatively weak. One study conducted in

Demographic and Psychographic Factors

Exhibit 19.4 Green Consumer Segments

Company	Segment	Characteristics
Cambridge Reports	Green consumer (12%)	Strongly identify with the term *environmentalist* and support environmental organizations.
FIND/SVP	Dedicated (1.4%)	Bring environmental concerns to bear on most or all purchase decisions.
	Selective (12%)	Engage in environmentally aware shopping on a selective basis, isolating specific products and companies for scrutiny.
	Impulsive (20%)	Engage in green shopping in response to situational stimuli (behavioral learning).
J. Walter Thompson	Greener than green (23%)	Make many sacrifices for the environment.
	Green (59%)	Concerned about environment but make only some sacrifices.
	Light green (15%)	Concerned but not willing to make any personal sacrifices.
	Un-green (3%)	Plain don't care about the environment.
Roper/S. C. Johnson	True-blue greens (11%)	Actual behavior is consistent with strong concerns about the environment.
	Greenback greens (11%)	Commitment to the environment mainly manifested by willingness to pay substantially higher prices for green products.
	Sprouts (26%)	Show middling levels of concern about the environment and equally middling levels of behavioral response.
	Grousers (24%)	Consistently rationalize their lack of proenvironmental behavior by offering all kinds of excuses and criticizing the poor performance of others.
	Basic browns (28%)	Do not believe individuals can make a difference in solving environmental problems, and do not want to make a difference.
Green MarketAlert	Visionary greens (5–15%)	Have embraced the paradigm shift. Green is a way of life for this group, not a shopping style. Passionately committed to environmental change.
	Maybe-greens (55–80%)	Express high degree of environmental concern but act on those concerns only irregularly.
	Hard-core browns (15–30%)	Indifferent or implacably antienvironmentalist. Tend to have lower incomes and educational levels.
Simmons Market Research Bureau	Premium green (22%)	Sophisticates, totally committed, in word and deed, to protecting planet Earth. Willing to spend more, do more, vote more.
	Red, white, and green (20%)	Traditionalists, equally committed to the environment, but think more in terms of their own turf and their beloved outdoors.
	No-costs ecologists (28%)	Sound like dedicated ecologists, but less likely to commit actions and money, unless it's the government's.
	Convenient greens (11%)	Environmental attitudes strong, but actions are motivated by convenience in lifestyle.
	Unconcerneds (19%)	The name says it all.

Source: The Bridge Group, *Green MarketAlert* (Bethlehem, CT: The Bridge Group, 1991).

Germany suggests a reason. The authors argue that different proenvironmental disposition behaviors such as reuse, waste reduction, garbage sorting, or recycling might be linked to different values and motives. Hence, to stimulate different proenvironmental disposition behaviors, marketers may have to appeal to different values.[56]

Exhibit 19.5 Overview of Organizational Segments for Environmentally Responsible Buying (ERB)

Primary Motivation/ Firm Characteristics	Type I— Founder's Ideals	Type II—Corporate Symbolism	Type III— Opportune	Type IV— Restraint
Organization type	Consumer products	Industrial products/services; business/consumer services	Consumer services; consumer/business services	Industrial products; consumer services
Policy entrepreneur	Founder or middle management	Often external relations manager	Not present	Middle manager, often in operations
Basis of demand	Founder's principles	Perceived long-term advantage	Bottom-line benefits	Consumer derived; public relations
Common focal purchase type	Product essentials	Consumption supplies	Support essentials	Product essentials
Extrinsic rewards for ERB	Yes	Yes	No	No
Attempt comprehensive approach to ERB	Yes	Yes	No	Sometimes
Meaning of environmental responsibility	What, where, who	What	What	What, frequently where, and who

The "simple life," or deconsumption, may be a way to relieve stress on the environment. Consumers embracing this philosophy opt for a lifestyle that requires fewer material resources to support them. Such consumers can be regarded as a psychographic market segment with specific needs to be addressed. For example, such a segment can be labeled as true-blue greens (see Exhibit 19.4). This segment engages in the following behaviors: willing to pay more for green products, cuts down on car use, uses biodegradable soaps, writes to politicians about environmental issues, and seeks alternatives to automobile transport. Thus, a portion of the population has decided that happiness in life does not necessarily come from owning more things. Rather, it comes from seeking simple, practical, sustainable solutions to life's problems.[57] Advertisers can attract this segment with appeals such as "slow your life down and smell the roses" or "enjoy people more and material goods less." A spokesperson for Patagonia, Inc., a well-known seller of environmental sportswear, adds a twist: "The idea is to buy less, but buy our stuff." Patagonia appeals successfully to the true-blue greens by simplifying its products lines and by placing a heavy emphasis on the longevity and ruggedness of its products.[58]

Governments are beginning to experiment with consensual, or voluntary, environmental policies; that is, instead of passing laws to mandate environmental policies, governments negotiate with organizations or consumer groups to make them partners or collaborators. As one example, Mattel, the world's largest toy maker, recently announced an initiative to make its plastic toys out of organically based materials derived from edible oils and plant starches. Beginning in 2001, these toys will be widely marketed.[59] Traditionally, the U.S. government takes a role in regulating the safety of children's toys. In this instance, Mattel is pursuing its own initiative, without responding to some particular law or regulatory effort. To cite a similar initiative, McDonald's runs a model restaurant in Bensenville, Illinois, where new energy-reducing technologies are tested before being introduced elsewhere. The Bensenville restaurant saves energy through high-efficiency air-conditioning units, automatic lights, and skylights that cut the need for indoor lighting. Initiatives such as these are consistent with the notion of sustainable marketing.[60]

Disposition as a Product Choice Criterion

Disposition considerations can drive product choice. At the same time, the marketing of green products can benefit from a thorough understanding of disposition attitudes and behaviors.

Disposition and Product Choice

Consumers make product choices to satisfy their desires. A clean, habitable ecosystem is a legitimate need without which consumers literally cannot survive. But in many choice situations, this need is not particularly associated with the exchange process. Rather, the environmental benefits remain an underlying or latent factor. For this reason, ecological needs are unlikely to serve as the primary trigger for many consumer decisions. One challenge for marketing managers is to find ways to make ecological needs and concerns more salient.[61]

As discussed above, there are segments of green consumers who recognize that the production, marketing, and disposition of products lead to social and environmental costs (e.g., pollution). They evaluate these costs negatively and try to minimize them through purchase decisions.[62] In surveys conducted over the past 25 years, a broad majority of consumers in the Triad countries say their purchase decisions are influenced by companies' environmental reputation. In the abstract, approximately two-thirds of consumers express willingness to pay more for products that are environmentally friendly. For many consumers, however, environmental concerns often remain in the background when they make decisions in the marketplace.

In the 1970s, researchers found that consumers became more willing to purchase phosphate-free detergents when they learned of the negative effects of phosphate pollution on water quality. In 1991 the University of Illinois found that, assuming price parity, 64.3 percent of respondents would choose paper towels labeled recycled paper over paper towels without the label. For a plastic shampoo bottle marketed as recycled, the figure was virtually identical—63.1 percent. Similar percentages of consumers reported they would choose a glass peanut butter jar labeled recyclable over one without the label and opt for a plastic shampoo bottle marked recyclable.

A study conducted in Denmark focused on the purchase of organically produced foods, which have fewer environmental costs. A wide variety of food products with labels identifying them as organic can be found in any Danish grocery store. Over half of the consumers surveyed agreed that organic foods are better than conventional foods, and 84 percent distrusted food-processing technologies. Thus, in Denmark, there is a potentially large segment of consumers whose purchase decisions might be influenced by disposition criteria. In general, Danish consumers have positive attitudes toward environmental problems, and they accept recycling as a fact of life. Nonetheless, few Danish consumers have specific understandings about the connection between specific environmental problems and the consumer behaviors they could undertake to alleviate them.[63]

Government-mandated schemes to introduce disposition criteria into consumer behaviors may result in negative feelings against the activity the regulation is meant to encourage. This is an example of psychological reactance. Examples of regulations might include bans on ozone-depleting chemicals in aerosol sprays or air-conditioning units, deposit fees on liquid containers, or programs requiring home garbage separation for recycling. The Philippine government tried unsuccessfully to regulate recyclers in a context where a vibrant informal recycling economy operated. Reactance is common where monetary effects are felt or the regulations are perceived to be unequal. Reactance may be higher in cultures with strong traditions of individual freedom, such as the United States,[64] and lower in nations with a stronger collectivist orientation (e.g., some Scandinavian nations). Denmark's bottle deposit program is successful, for example, although Danes complain about it, whereas deposit bottles have not been very successful in the United States.

Some people fear being labeled a "sucker" if they participate in green programs while others do not. Achieving environmental goals (e.g., reducing solid waste) depends on the participation of many consumers. But individual consumers cannot be sure that most others will cooperate. For example, people may believe that disposal fees applied to waste lubricants replaced by commercial garages will lead to illicit dumping and noncompliance by some, thereby aggravating existing disposition problems. Belief that others may not comply reduces compliance levels overall. This is an example of the classic **prisoner's dilemma** problem in psychology: *Everyone benefits if all comply; but if one person doesn't comply, his or her immediate benefits may outweigh the general good.* Hence, mistrust of others may reduce the likelihood of green behaviors. Marketing communications must address issues such as reactance and concerns about prisoner's dilemma if firms hope to increase the responsiveness of green marketing campaigns.

Finally, a related but separate problem has to do with the extent to which individual consumers apply private, personal cost-benefit calculations to their consumption decisions without regard for broader impacts. When many consumers are inclined to base their consumption decisions primarily on private cost-benefit calculations, as those in developed countries, it seems likely that private economic incentives (e.g., price breaks on environmentally friendly products) are necessary to encourage cooperation.[65]

Recycled and Green Products

Recycled and green products represent product categories in the introduction and growth phase of the product life cycle discussed in Chapter 16. For example, in 1989 Lever Brothers launched a $20 million campaign to reduce adverse environmental effects of its products. Canada's largest grocer, Loblaw's, also introduced a line of **green products** in 1989. Similarly, Procter & Gamble has introduced a host of green improvements to its products and production processes. Take a look at P&G's website for details. From 1985 to 1990, green product introductions increased at an annual rate of more than 100 percent. Sales of green products were estimated to total $8.8 billion in 1995. Elsewhere we have mentioned the skyrocketing sales of the organic foods in an industry with otherwise flat sales. Some other examples of green products are shown in Industry Insights 19.3. Faced with a history of price disincentives for green consumption, green marketers have been working hard to dispel the idea that recycled and organic products cost more than conventional commercial goods.[66]

www.pg.com/docInfo/enviro/qualinit.htm

Many people in the retail apparel industry who are concerned with the environment see promise in two areas: organic cotton and fiber made by recycling soda-pop bottles. In all areas, "low-impact" is the in adjective. Here are a few samples:

- Esprit's Ecollection offers a line of "socially and environmentally sensitive clothing," which debuted in the spring of 1992. The clothing is made from organically grown cotton; transitional cotton (cotton grown in accordance with organic standards, but on land that is under a three-year mandatory chemical-free period); and Tencel, a low-impact cellulosic fiber similar to rayon. Clothes in the collection are produced using low-impact dyes, natural enzyme washes (to soften, smooth, and prevent pilling), nonelectroplated hardware (zippers, rivets), and tangua nut buttons. This fall, Ecollection will add wool jackets made from 100 percent recycled wool.

- Patagonia is introducing PCR (postconsumer recycled) Synchilla; outerwear that is made from polyester extracted from plastic soda bottles. Patagonia spokesman Mike Harrelson says people often perceive natural fibers as more environmentally friendly, but as more life-cycle analysis is done researchers are finding that's not necessarily true. Patagonia prides itself on its environmental assessments of various fabrics. Wellman Inc. and Dyersburg Fabrics make the fleece for Patagonia out of Fortrel Ecospun, a fiber created from 100 percent recycled plastic beverage bottles.

Source: Kristen A. Conover, "The Environment's New Clothes," Christian Science Monitor, August 19, 1993, pp. 10–11.

Disposition is closely linked to other aspects of consumer behavior. By learning more about disposition trends and patterns, we can increase our knowledge about consumer behavior in general.

We present an overview of the disposition process by outlining a model of disposition. Objects may take different paths after acquisition, following various forms of reuse and recycling. The examples show how reuse is a frequent alternative to the acquisition of new goods. Consumers often sidestep the market in their disposition behaviors. From a marketing perspective, managing disposition can be viewed as a backward channel of distribution problem.

There are several types of voluntary and involuntary disposition behaviors that consumers experience. These include discard behavior, donations, inheritance, giving, storage, and recycling. A variety of the situational and individual factors affect disposal choices. Factors intrinsic to the product affect disposition, as does the influence of competitive pressures both on firms and individual consumers. Self-imposed industry norms, such as the ISO 14000 principles, may well encourage organizations to pursue some green business strategies over the next decade. In addition, situational factors and consumers' life cycles affect disposition. Disposition should be thought of as a recurring social and psychological process.

Green consumers are those who take disposition issues into account either in their acquisition behaviors (e.g., buying recycled goods) or in their disposition behaviors (e.g., engaging in composting or waste reduction). In general, there are relatively weak relationships between consumers' demographic profiles, values, attitudes, knowledge, beliefs, and disposition behaviors. A variety of psychological and social psychological factors affect people's propensity to engage in particular disposition behaviors. For example, the desire for voluntary simplicity is an individual factor. Changing fashions is an example from the social world.

Product disposition may enter into consumers' product choice criteria, and there are a variety of marketing considerations related to recyclable or recycled objects. Some firms and some consumers are beginning to include disposition attributes of products when making acquisition decisions. For example, some firms are making an effort to close the loop between disposition and production by making things from recycled materials; that is, by pursuing a strategy of sustainable marketing, organizations can find ways to compete effectively in the marketplace and simultaneously pursue the goal of sustaining ecosystems.

backward channel members   701
backward channel of distribution   703
biospheric orientation   723
close-loop manufacturing   717
deconsumption   701
donation   714
electronic flea markets   713
green products   727
green segments   723
inheritance   715
ISO 14000   719
lateral recycling   706
model of disposition   706
preinheritance   715

prisoner's dilemma   727
product biography   707
psychological reactance   721
recycling   708
resource recovery   708
secondhand reuse   706
secondhand trade   707
selling   712
simple reuse   706
storage   715
sustainable marketing   723
swap meets   712
time-marked goods   716
waste-making society   712

1. Identify situations for different product categories in which items are no longer fit for consumer reuse and instead are discarded or recycled.

2. Think about the various paths (e.g., 1a, 1b, 2, 3) shown in Exhibit 19.1. For each path, give a specific example for firms or households. Be certain to provide examples that are different from those presented in the text.

3. Consider your household furnishings. How much of it and what types of things were obtained new? Describe the items that were obtained used. What was scavenged?

4. Identify personal possessions that you have disposed of voluntarily and involuntarily. What methods were used in the disposition process?

5. Take a look at Exhibit 19.4. What sort of green consumer segment do you fall into? Try to identify individual and situational reasons for your green and brown consumption behaviors.

6. Marketers are a long way from exploring the full range of opportunities available in the realm of disposition. Identify some untapped marketing opportunities connected with consumers' disposition behaviors.

7. Think about disposition processes at your place of business, or a place of business with which you are familiar. Identify different categories of products that are disposed of in different ways. For example, paper clips are probably reused; surplus restaurant food may be donated to charity; waste paper may be recycled. Identify some links in a backward channel of distribution that, if put in place, would change the firm's disposition behavior.

8. Do you attend swap meets, garage sales, flea markets, or other mechanisms for lateral recycling? Why or why not? What do you like or dislike about them? What do you think motivates participants apart from the obvious reasons of getting a deal or getting rid of things?

9. Speculate as to why some individuals have attachments to possessions so strong that they can throw nothing away (pack rats), whereas others regularly purge their homes of items with assumed sentimental value.

You Make the Call
Cash for Trash

Back in July 1978, some concerned citizens of the city of Manila, the Philippines, presented the Cash for Trash Program to the minister of Human Settlements. The plan was to implement a solid-waste separation and resource recovery program. The original plan envisioned the use of the existing informal system of resource recovery as the cornerstone of the proposed plan. The government released a budget of P5,600,000 (approximately US$200,000) to fund the program.

Later in 1983, the Women's Balikatan Movement of the Philippines started organizing existing junk shop dealers in San Juan, Metro Manila, to buy recycled items as part of their aim to protect the environment. There are over 1,000 junk dealers in Metro Manila. The Balikatan campaigned for waste separation at the household level, and started to organize the junk shops in a Metro Manila municipality and link them with residential communities to make the collection of recyclable more efficient. It acted as guarantor on behalf of the junk shops so lending institutions would provide them with credit for working capital. It also popularized the term "eco-aide" to refer to scavengers and pushcart collectors, thereby highlighting their role in ecological care.

At the start of the project, Balikatan got the cooperation of the municipal government of San Juan. Upon instructions from the mayor, community assemblies convened in each of the 21 *barangays* (local districts) of San Juan to explain the concept of solid-waste separation and its benefits. Discussions were held on how to increase solid-waste recovery. Permission was obtained from the government water utility company for the use of one of its vacant lots as a junkyard or collection center.

Now, Balikatan operates in other municipalities in Metro Manila. The group has started to organize junk shops into cooperatives to avail themselves of government subsidies and credit and enable them to get better deals with bigger junk shops and recyclers.

Through the intercession of Balikatan and other groups, new government resources are becoming available. The Department of Trade and Industry is in the process of approving a P250,000 (US$9,000) soft loan package for eco-aides to be used as working capital in their daily chores of buying recyclables from households. The Department of Social Welfare and Development released P100,000 to provide seed capital for funding income-generating projects.

Other nongovernmental organizations (NGOs) have joined the movement. The Ayala Foundation, Inc., wants to campaign to change the name of junk dealers to "waste managers." Waste separation at the source is becoming a popular campaign of other NGOs, such as the Recycling Movement of the Philippines. Business and civic organizations, like the Rotary Club, are willing donors to community-based waste management drives.

Back in 1978, under pressure from certain interest groups, the original Cash for Trash Program was modified from its initial conception. The office of Human Settlement tried to create a parallel system of ecocenters to compete with the informal system of junk collecting, with the eco-aides serving as collectors. After two years the program failed because of resistance from the informal system of junk dealers. Now, new pressures may emerge to encourage the government to compete with the local initiatives or to allow large waste management companies to take over the recycling business in Metro Manila. Many new players are getting into the act.

1. At present, what is the best way for the government to organize environmental programs?

2. As more players get involved, what is the reaction of the informal-sector junk dealers likely to be?

3. What factors are likely to promote or depress the level of popular participation in the Cash for Trash and other recycling programs in Metro Manila?

This case is adapted from Danilo G. Lapid, "Supporting and Strengthening Junk Dealers and Recyclers," paper presented at the 20th Water, Engineering and Development Centre (WEDC) Conference, Colombo, Sri Lanka, 1994.

1. "Report from Tokyo: Net, Leisure, Green Products Hot in Japan," *Marketing News,* May 25, 1998, pp. 2, 21.

2. "Survey Finds Litter More Troubling than Global Warming," *Green Business Letter,* July 1996, p. 3; "6 Nations Agree to Cut Pollution in Rhine Basin," *International Herald Tribune,* September 10, 1996, p. 5; Joanna Lamparska, "Curse of the Black Triangle," *The Warsaw Voice,* June 4, 1995, pp. G2, G4; Dan McGovern, *The Campo Indian Landfill War* (Norman, OK: University of Oklahoma Press, 1995); and Marlise Simons, "EU's Environmental Agency Is Discovering It's Pretty Messy out There," *International Herald Tribune,* September 10, 1996, p. 5.

3. Minette E. Drumwright, "Socially Responsible Organizational Buying: Environmental Concern as a Noneconomic Buying Criteria," *Journal of Marketing* 58 (July 1994), pp. 1–19; Linda R. Stanley and Karen M. Lasonde, "The Relationship between Environmental Issue Involvement and Environmentally-Conscious Behavior," in *Advances in Consumer Research,* vol. 23, Kim P. Corfman and John G. Lynch, eds. (Provo, UT: Association for Consumer Research, 1996), pp. 183–88.

4. William Rathje and Cullen Murphy, *Rubbish: The Archaeology of Garbage* (New York: Harper College, 1992).

5. Jacob Jacoby, Carol K. Berning, and Thomas F. Dietvorst, "What about Disposition?" *Journal of Marketing,* April 1977, pp. 22–28.

6. Harold H. Kassarjian, "Incorporating Ecology into Marketing Strategy," *Journal of Marketing* 35 (July 1971), pp. 61–65.

7. Joyce Miller and Francisco Szekely, "What Is 'Green'?" *Environmental Impact Assessment Review* 15 (1995), pp. 401–20.

8. Rekha Mehra, "Women in Waste Collection and Recycling in Ho Chi Minh City," *Population and Environment* 18, no. 2 (1996), pp. 187–99; and William G. Zikmund and William J. Stanton, "Recycling Solid Wastes: A Channels-of-Distribution Problem," *Journal of Marketing* 35 (July 1971), pp. 34–39.

9. Rathje and Murphy, *Rubbish,* pp. 191–94.

10. Calvin Trillin, "One More Lot," *The Nation* 262 (May 20, 1996), p. 6.

11. Simone Field, Hazel Barrett, Angela Brown, and Roy May, "The Second-Hand Clothes Trade in the Gambia," *Geography* 81, no. 4 (1996), pp. 371–74.

12. Igor Kopytoff, "The Cultural Biography of Things: Commoditization as Process," in *The Social Life of Things,* Arjun Appadurai, ed. (Cambridge: Cambridge University Press, 1986), pp. 64–94; and Grant McCracken, " 'Ever Dearer in Our Thoughts': Patina and the Representation of Status before and after the Eighteenth Century," and "Lois Roget: Curatorial Consumer in a Modern World," in *Culture and Consumption* (Bloomington: Indiana University Press, 1988), pp. 31–43, 44–56.

13. "Environment," *The Futurist,* May–June 1997, p. 7; David A. Munn and James Carr, "Cropland Utilization of Ground Drywall," *Biocycle* 37 (July 1996), p. 57; and David Riggle and Gaye Wiekierak, "The Big and Small of Woody Materials Recycling," *Biocycle* 37 (July 1996), pp. 53–56.

14. OECD, *OECD Environmental Data* (Paris: Organization for Economic Cooperation and Development, 1995).

15. Text of this section adapted from Rik Pieters, "Consumers and Their Garbage; A Framework, and Some Experiences from the Netherlands with Garbage," in *European Advances in Consumer Research,* vol. 1, Gary Bamossy and Fred Van Raaij, eds. (Provo, UT: Association for Consumer Research, 1993), pp. 541–46.

16. Jacoby, Berning, and Dietvorst, "What about Disposition?"

17. Eric J. Arnould, "Toward a Broadened Theory of Preference Formation and the Diffusion of Innovations: Cases from Zinder Province, Niger Republic," *Journal of Consumer Research* 16 (September 1989), pp. 239–67; and Stuart A. Ross, "Freedom from Possession: A Tibetan Buddhist View," *Journal of Social Behavior and Psychology* 6, no. 6 (1991), pp. 415–26.

18. Scott Dawson and Gary Bamossy, "If 'We Are What We Have,' What Are We When We Don't Have?: An Exploratory Study of Materialism among Expatriate Americans," *Journal of Social Behavior and Personality* 6, no. 6 (1991), pp. 363–84.

19. Adrian Furnham and Steven Jones, "Children's Views Regarding Possessions and Their Theft," *Journal of Morad Education* 16 (January 1987), pp. 18–25; and Joop Vand den Bogaard and Oene Wiegman, "Property Crime Victimization: The Effectiveness of Police Services for Victims of Residential Burglary," *Journal of Social Behavior and Personality* 6, no. 6 (1991), pp. 329–62.

20. Paul Hawken, "Resource Waste," *Mother Jones,* March–April 1997, pp. 44–46.

21. John Clammer, "Aesthetics of the Self: Shopping and Social Being in Contemporary Urban Japan," in *Lifestyle Shopping: The Subject of Consumption,* Ron Shields, ed. (London and New York: Routledge, 1992), pp. 195–215.

22. Elizabeth Razzi, "A Profitable Way to Ditch Your Junque," *Kiplinger's Personal Finance Magazine* 50, no. 6 (1996), pp. 100–2.

23. Stephen M. Soiffer and Gretchen M. Hermann, "Visions of Power: Ideology and Practice in the American Garage Sale," *Sociological Review* 35, no. 1 (1987), pp. 48–83.

24. Russell W. Belk, John F. Sherry, Jr., and Melanie Wallendorf, "A Naturalistic Inquiry into Buyer and Seller Behavior at a Swap Meet," *Journal of Consumer Research* 14 (March 1988), pp. 449–70; Gretchen M. Hermann and Stephen M. Soiffer, "For Fun and Profit: An Analysis of the American Garage Sale," *Urban Life* 12, no. 4 (1984), pp. 397–421; Lynn O'Reilly, Margaret Rucker, Rhonda Hughes, Marge Gorang, and Susan Hand, "The Relationship of Psychological and Situational Variables to Usage of Second-Order Marketing System," *Academy of Marketing Science* 12, no. 3 (1984), pp. 53–76; Glen Reichen, Ugur Yavas, and Charles Battle, "Pre-owned Merchandise Buying:

A Neglected Retailing Phenomenon," *Developments in Marketing Science* 2 (1979), pp. 58–61; Michael B. Schiffer, Theodore E. Downing, and Michael McCarthy, "Waste Not, Want Not: An Ethnoarchaeological Study of Refuse in Tucson, Arizona," in *Modern Material Culture: The Archaeology of Us,* Michael Gould and Michael B. Schiffer, eds. (New York: Academic Press, 1981), pp. 67–86; and John F. Sherry, Jr., "A Sociocultural Analysis of a Midwestern American Flea Market," *Journal of Consumer Research* 17 (June 1990), pp. 13–30.

25. Gretchen M. Hermann, "His and Hers: Gender and Garage Sales," *Journal of Popular Culture* 29, no. 1 (Summer 1995), pp. 127–45.

26. Grant McCracken, "Culture and Consumption: A Theoretical Account of the Structure and Movement of the Cultural Meaning of Consumer Goods," *Journal of Consumer Research* 13 (June 1986), pp. 71–84; and Linda L. Price, Eric J. Arnould, and Carolyn Curasi, "Older Consumers' Disposition of Valued Possessions," *Journal of Consumer Research* 27 (September 2000), pp. 179–201.

27. John J. Burnett and Van R. Wood, "A Proposed Model of the Donation Decision Process," in *Research in Consumer Behavior,* Elizabeth Hirschman and Jagdish Sheth, eds. (Greenwich, CT: JAI Press, 1988), pp. 1–47; and Mitch Griffin, Barry J. Babin, Jill S. Attaway, and William R. Darden, "Hey You, Can Ya Spare Some Change? The Case of Empathy and Personal Distress as Reactions to Charitable Appeals," in *Advances in Consumer Research,* vol. 20, Leigh McAlister and Michael L. Rothschild, eds. (Provo, UT: Association for Consumer Research, 1993), pp. 508–14.

28. Debra S. Judge and Sarah Blaffer Hardy, "Allocation of Accumulated Resources among Close Kin: Inheritance in Sacramento, California, 1890–1984," *Ethnology and Sociobiology* 13 (1992), pp. 495–522.

29. B. Douglas Bernheim, Andrei Shleifer, and Lawrence H. Summers, "The Strategic Bequest Motive," *Journal of Political Economy* 93 (1985), pp. 1045–76.

30. "Baby-Boomers Slated to Inherit Nearly $10.4 Trillion," *Trusts & Estates,* September 1994, pp. 6–10; and "Baby Boomers Slated for Inheritance Windfall," *Journal of Accountancy,* July 1994, pp. 17–21.

31. Arnould, "Toward a Broadened Theory of Preference Formation and the Diffusion of Innovations," Robert M. Netting, Richard R. Wilk, and Eric J. Arnould, eds., *Households: Comparative and Historical Studies of the Domestic Group* (Berkeley: University of California Press, 1983); and Tamar Rapoport, Edna Lomski-Feder, and Mohammed Masaha, "Female Subordination in the Arab-Israeli-Community: The Adolescent Perspective of 'Social Veil,' " *Sex Roles* 20, no. 5–6 (1989), pp. 255–69.

32. T.G.H. Strethlow, *Aranda Traditions* (Melbourne: Melbourne University Press, 1977); and A. Guillou and P. Guibert, "Le froid domestiqué: l'usage du congélateur," *Terrain* 12 (1989), pp. 7–14.

33. Peter Menzel, *Material World: A Global Family Portrait* (San Francisco: Sierra Club Books, 1994).

34. Russell W. Belk, "The Role of Possessions in Constructing and Maintaining a Sense of Past," in *Advances in Consumer Research,* vol. 17, Marvin E. Goldberg, Gerald Gorn, and Richard W. Pollay, eds. (Provo, UT: Association for Consumer Research, 1990), pp. 669–76; and Kent Grayson and David Shulman, "Indexicality and the Verification Function of Irreplaceable Possessions: A Semiotic Analysis," *Journal of Consumer Research* 27 (June 2000), pp. 17–30.

35. N. Haumont and H. Raymond, "Habitat et pratique de l'espace: etude des relations entre l'Intérieur et l'extérieur du logement," working paper, Institut de Sociologie Urbain, Paris, 1975; Perla Korosec-Serfaty, "The Home from Attic to Cellar," *Journal of Environmental Psychology* 4 (1984), pp. 303–21; and Kay M. Tooley, "The Remembrance of Things Past: On the Collection and Recollection of Ingredients Useful in the Treatment of Disorders Resulting from Unhappiness, Rootlessness, and the Fear of Things to Come," *American Journal of Orthopsychiatry* 48 (1978), pp. 174–82.

36. "The Death Business: Staying Alive," *Economist,* August 5, 2000, p. 61; Roy Rivenburg, "Return of the Mummy," *Los Angeles Times,* January 27, 1993, pp. E1, E27; and Thomas Lynch, "Socko Finish," *New York Times Magazine,* July 12, 1998, pp. 34–36.

37. Laurent Belsie, "EPA Incentives Put PCS on a Diet," *Christian Science Monitor,* December 30, 1993, p. 2; Jonathan Gaw, "Dump Profit Gets Trashed," *Los Angeles Times,* July 22, 1993, pp. D1, D4; Mary Beth Jannakos, "Wastemaker Awards Go to Food Products with Lots of Wrapping," *Daily Camera,* October 21, 1992, p. 22: Zofia Jozwiak, "Dump Space Running Out," *The Warsaw Voice,* May 28, 1995, p. 8; Peter Nye, "Clean Drinking Water Becomes a National Problem," *Public*

Citizen no. 13, 4 (July–August 1993), pp. 10–13; Elizabeth Ross, "Garbage Museum Aims to Change Wasteful Ways," *Christian Science Monitor,* September 21, 1993, p. 12; David Shenk, "Buy a Hat, Save the Earth," *Hemispheres,* May 1993, pp. 25–27; FTC, *The Application of Section 5 of the Federal Trade Commission Act to Environmental Advertising and Marketing Practices* (Washington, DC: Federal Trade Commission, 1992); "The Netherlands' Radical, Practical Green Plan," *Whole Earth Review,* Fall 1995, pp. 94–99; Catherine Vial, "Why EC Environmental Policy Will Affect American Business," *Business America,* March 8, 1993, pp. 24–27; and *Wall Street Journal,* April 27, 1993, p. A1.

38. Jeff Bailey, "Two Major Garbage Rivals Find Their Profits Trashed," *The Wall Street Journal,* March 1993, p. B1; Paul A. Eisenstein, "Your Used New Car Is Here," *World Traveler,* October 1995, pp. 20–22; "Seeing Green," *Entrepreneur,* April 1993, p. 214; Naomi Freundlich, "The White House Versus the Greenhouse," *Business Week,* August 19, 1996, p. 75; Paul Hawken, "A Declaration of Sustainability," *Utne Reader,* September–October 1993, p. 54–60; Kenneth Howe, "Wanna Make Cash? Get Rid of 28 Million Tires Annually," *Press Telegram,* January 3, 1993, p. B6; Helmet Maucher, "Industry and the Environment: The Views of an Industrialist," *Columbia Journal of World Business,* Summer 1993, pp. 6–10; John McPhee, "Duty of Care," *New Yorker,* June 28, 1993, pp. 72–80; Ken Ohlson, "Seeing Green: Eco Entrepreneurs Clean Up," *Entrepreneur,* February 1993, pp. 114–18; and David Taylor, "Auto Motives," *Profiles* 6 (January 1994), pp. 51–57.

39. Jacoby, Berning, and Dietvorst, "What About Disposition?"

40. Raymond Communications, *News: How Do Countries Stack Up on Recycling Rates?* (Riverdale, MD: Raymond Communications, 1995).

41. Shell International Petroleum Company, *How Do We Stand? People, Planets and Profits, The Shell Report 2000* (London: Shell International Petroleum Company, 2000).

42. Mary Litsikas, "U.S. Perspectives Varies on ISO 14000," *Quality* 36 (December 1997), pp. 28–33; and William R. Smith and Raymond J. Patchak, "So Long! Command and Control . . . Hello! ISO 14000," manuscript, Environmental Management Systems, New York City, 1996.

43. Richard R. Wilk, "Learning Not to Want Things," working paper, presented at the annual meetings of the Association for Consumer Research, Tuscon, AZ, October 1996, pp. 10–13.

44. "Curbing Pollution an Urgent Task," *Beijing Review* 39, no. 32 (1996), p. 4; Joseph Weber, "3M's Big Cleanup," *Business Week,* June 5, 2000, pp. 96–98; and Shell International Petroleum Company, *How Do We Stand?*

45. Suzanne C. Gruenert, "Everybody Seems Concerned about the Environment, but Is This Concern Reflected in (Danish) Consumers' Food Choices?" working paper, First European Association for Consumer Research Conference, Amsterdam, 1991.

46. Schiffer, Downing, and McCarthy, "Waste Not, Want Not."

47. Russell W. Belk, "Moving Possessions: An Analysis Based on Personal Documents from the 1847–1869 Mormon Migration," *Journal of Consumer Research* 19 (December 1992), pp. 339–61.

48. Robin A. Higie, Linda L. Price, and Julie Fitzmaurice, "Leaving It All Behind: Service Loyalties in Transition," in *Advances in Consumer Research,* vol. 20, Leigh McAlister and Michael L. Rothschild, eds. (Provo, UT: Association for Consumer Research, 1993), pp. 656–61; James H. McAlexander, "Divorce, the Disposition of the Relationship, and Everything," in *Advances in Consumer Research,* vol. 18, Michael Solomon and Rebecca Holman, eds. (Provo, UT: Association for Consumer Research, 1991), pp. 43–48; Scott D. Roberts, "Consumption Responses in Involuntary Job Loss," in *Advances in Consumer Research,* vol. 18, Michael Solomon and Rebecca Holman, eds. (Provo, UT: Association for Consumer Research, 1991), pp. 40–42; Melissa Martin Young, "Disposition of Possessions during Role Transitions," in *Advances in Consumer Research,* vol. 18, Michael Solomon and Rebecca Holman, eds. (Provo, UT: Association for Consumer Research, 1991), pp. 33–39.

49. Higie, Price, and Fitzmaurice, "Leaving It All Behind."

50. Belk, Sherry, and Wallendorf, "A Naturalistic Inquiry into Buyer and Seller Behavior at a Swap Meet," Mihaly Csikszentmihalyi and Eugene Rochberg-Halton, *The Meaning of Things: Domestic Symbols and the Self* (New York: Cambridge University Press, 1981); and John W. Schouten, "Selves in Transition: Favorite Possessions of Indians and Indian Immigrants to the United States," *Journal of Consumer Research* 17, no. 4 (1991), pp. 412–25.

51. Mara Adelman, "Rituals of Adversity and Remembering: The Role of Possessions for Persons

and Community Living with Aids," in *Advances in Consumer Research,* vol. 19, Brian Sternthal and John F. Sherry, Jr., eds. (Provo, UT: Association for Consumer Research, 1992), pp. 401–3; and Teresa Pavia, "Dispossession and Perceptions of Self in Late Stage HIV Infection," in *Advances in Consumer Research,* vol. 20, Leigh McAlister and Michael L. Rothschild, eds. (Provo, UT: Association for Consumer Research, 1993), pp. 425–28.

52. Donald A. Fuller, *Sustainable Marketing* (Thousand Oaks, CA: Sage Publications, 1999), p. 4.

53. Roper Organization, *Environmental Behavior: North America, Canada, Mexico, United States* (New York City: Roper Organization, 1992); Prem Shamdasani, Gloria Ong Chon-Lin, and Daleen Richard, "Exploring Green Consumers in an Oriental Culture: Role of Personal and Marketing Mix Factors," in *Advances in Consumer Research,* vol. 20, Leigh McAlister and Michael Rothschild, eds. (Provo, UT: Association for Consumer Research, 1993), pp. 488–93.

54. Minette E. Drumright, "Socially Responsible Organizational Buying: Environmental Concern as a Noneconomic Buying Criterion," *Journal of Marketing* 58 (July 1994), pp. 1–19.

55. Dorothy Leonard-Barton, "Voluntary Simplicity Lifestyles and Energy Conservation," *Journal of Consumer Research* 8 (December 1981), pp. 243–52; Pam Scholder Ellen, Joshua Lyle Wiener, and Cathy Cobb-Walgren, "The Role of Perceived Consumer Effectiveness in Motivating Environmentally Conscious Behavior," *Journal of Public Policy and Marketing* 10 (Fall 1991), pp. 101–17; and Kent Van Liere and Riley E. Dunlap, "The Social Bases of Environmental Concern: A Review of Hypotheses, Explanations, and Empirical Evidence," *Public Opinion Quarterly* 44, no. 2 (1980), pp. 181–97.

56. Ingo Balderjahn, "Personality Variables and Environmental Attitudes as Predictors of Ecologically Responsible Consumption Patterns," *Journal of Business Research* 17 (1988), pp. 51–56; John A. McCarty and L. J. Shrum, "A Structural Equation Analysis of the Relationships of Personal Values, Attitudes and Beliefs about Recycling and the Recycling of Solid Waste Products," in *Advances in Consumer Research,* vol. 20, Leigh McAlister and Michael Rothschild, eds. (Provo, UT: Association for Consumer Research, 1993), pp. 641–46; and Paul C. Stern and Thomas Dietz, "The Value Basis of Environmental Concern," *Journal of Social Issues* 50, no. 3 (1994), pp. 65–84.

57. Henry David Thoreau, *Walden* (New York: Random House, 1937).

58. Fuller, *Sustainable Marketing,* pp. 338–41 and George M. Zinkhan and Les Carlson, "Green Advertising and the Reluctant Consumer," *Journal of Advertising* 24, no. 2 (1995), pp. 1–6.

59. "Mattel Announces Decisions to Eliminate PVC," *Greenpeace Magazine,* Spring 2000, p. 4.

60. Cathy L. Hartman, P. S. Hofman, and E. R. Stafford, "Partnerships: A Path to Sustainability," in *Business Strategy and the Environment,* John Wiley, (1999), pp. 255–67; *The Green Business Letter,* "A Look Ahead," January 2000, www.GreenBiz.com.

61. Fuller, *Sustainable Marketing,* p. 322.

62. Suzanne C. Grunert, "Green Consumerism in Denmark: Some Evidence from the KO Foods Project," *Der Markt* 126, no. 3 (1993), pp. 140–51.

63. Grunert, "Green Consumerism in Denmark."

64. Robert N. Bellah, Richard Madsen, William M. Sullivan, Ann Swidler, and Steven M. Tipton, *Habits of the Heart* (Berkeley: University of California Press, 1985).

65. Suzanne C. Grunert and John Thogersen, "Waste Handling Systems as Perceived by Citizens of Two Danish Municipalities," in *The Natural Environment: Interdisciplinary Views,* Proceedings of the First Interdisciplinary Conference on the Environment, K. L. Hickey and D. Kantarelis, eds. (Worcester, MA: Assumption College, 1994), pp. 87–100.

66. Drumright, "Socially Responsible Organizational Buying"; "Shattering a Myth: Organic Packaged Food *Can* Be the Cheapest Buy," *The Green Guide,* April 4, 1995; Michel Laroche, Roy Toffoli, and Chankom Kim, "The Influence of Culture on Pro-Environmental Knowledge, Attitudes, and Behavior: A Canadian Perspective," in *Advances in Consumer Research,* vol. 23, Kim P. Corfman and John G. Lynch, eds. (Provo, UT: Association for Consumer Research, 1996), pp. 196–202; Secretary James M. Seif, "Testimony before the Pennsylvania Senate Environmental Resources and Energy Committee," Pennsylvania Department of Environmental Protection, Philadelphia, 1996; and Smart Business Supersite, "The Selling O' the Green," 1996, www.smartbiz.com.

Company/brand index

Subject index